Tuttle

Compact Indonesian Dictionary

Indonesian-English
English-Indonesian

Katherine Davidsen

TUTTLE Publishing

Tokyo | Rutland, Vermont | Singapore

The Tuttle Story: "Books to Span the East and West"

Many people are surprised to learn that the world's leading publisher of books on Asia had humble beginnings in the tiny American state of Vermont. The company's founder, Charles E. Tuttle, belonged to a New England family steeped in publishing.

Immediately after WWII, Tuttle served in Tokyo under General Douglas MacArthur and was tasked with reviving the Japanese publishing industry. He later founded the Charles E. Tuttle Publishing Company, which thrives today as one of the world's leading independent publishers.

Though a westerner, Tuttle was hugely instrumental in bringing a knowledge of Japan and Asia to a world hungry for information about the East. By the time of his death in 1993, Tuttle had published over 6,000 books on Asian culture, history and art—a legacy honored by the Japanese emperor with the "Order of the Sacred Treasure," the highest tribute Japan can bestow upon a non-Japanese.

With a backlist of 1,500 titles, Tuttle Publishing is more active today than at any time in its past—still inspired by Charles Tuttle's core mission to publish fine books to span the East and West and provide a greater understanding of each.

Published by Tuttle Publishing, an imprint of Periplus Editions (HK) Ltd.

www.tutlepublishing.com

Cataloged with the Library of Congress with the previous ISBN 978-0-8048-3740-8
LCCN 2008942321

ISBN 978-0-8048-4517-5

19 18 17 16 15
6 5 4 3 2 1   1506CM

Printed in China

TUTTLE PUBLISHING® is a registered trademark of Tuttle Publishing, a division of Periplus Editions (HK) Ltd.

Distributed by

Indonesia
PT Java Books Indonesia
Jl. Rawa Gelam IV No. 9,
Kawasan Industri Pulogadung,
Jakarta 13930
Tel: (62) 21 4682-1088
Fax: (62) 21 461-0206
crm@periplus.co.id
www.periplus.com

Asia Pacific
Berkeley Books Pte. Ltd.
61 Tai Seng Avenue, #02-12,
Singapore 534167
Tel: (65) 6280 1330
Fax: (65) 6280 6290
inquiries@periplus.com.sg
www.periplus.com

North America, Latin America & Europe
Tuttle Publishing
364 Innovation Drive, North Clarendon,
VT 05759-9436 USA.
Tel: 1(802) 773 8930
Fax: 1(802) 773 6993
info@tuttlepublishing.com
www.tuttlepublishing.com

untuk
Kang Joni, Adi & Dani,
yang selalu sabar menanti

and also for my two grandmothers,
both thoughtful users of dictionaries and the written word

Contents

Introduction

A brief introduction to Indonesian

Indonesia is the world's fourth-largest nation with a population of over 200 million people. The national language is Indonesian, which in 1990 was spoken by an estimated 67% of people, and was the mother tongue for approximately 27 million. Indonesian acts as a unifying force among speakers of around 750 regional dialects across the archipelago. Indonesian is also understood in Singapore and Malaysia, as it is mutually intelligible with Malay, thus making it one of the major languages of Southeast Asia. Indonesian belongs to the Malayo-Polynesian subgroup of Austronesian languages, and is therefore distantly related to languages as diverse as Malagasy, Cham, Tagalog, Maori and Fijian. It is a modern language deliberately cultivated from the Riau variety of Malay by the Indonesian nationalist movement, as preparation for its role as the official language of the new Indonesian state in 1945. Its ability to absorb new influences yet repackage them in a typically Indonesian way makes it highly dynamic in its interaction with other languages, but also susceptible to regional variation and inclined to inconsistency in spellings of borrowed words. Regional languages such as Sundanese and Javanese, being the mother tongue of an even larger number of Indonesians, constantly influence Indonesian not only in terms of vocabulary borrowings, but also collocations, sentence structure and idioms. The similarity in structure and vocabulary of Indonesian and the regional languages enables both parties to exert influence on each other, adding a local flavor, or additional tone or register.

Indonesian is considered a relatively easy language to learn. It is almost completely free of irregularities. Adjectives follow the noun, as in French. Word order is flexible but generally follows a SVO (subject-verb-object) pattern. Indonesian is rich in verbs, with single words which translate into a complicated phrase in English (e.g. *mengupil* = to pick your nose, *berjinjit-jinjit* = to walk on tiptoe). Words may also be left out if the context is clear, making the language succinct and snappy.

Pronunciation in Indonesian is similar to Spanish or Italian. Accents vary, but the standard pronunciation below is a guide.

Vowels:	a	as in *father*
	e	Most commonly as in *loosen* (swallowed 'shwa' sound); Occasionally as in *egg*. In older texts this is written as é
	i	as in *marine*
	o	as in *open*
	u	as in *blue*

Diphthongs:	ai	as in *aisle*
	au	as in *sauerkraut*

Consonants:		as in English, except for:
	c	like **ch** in *child*
	g	always hard, as in *gum*, never soft as in *gem*
	kh	throaty sound as in *loch*
	ng	as in *thing*
	ngg	as in *finger* (ng+g)
	r	rolled, as in Spanish

Dictionaries of Indonesian

Indonesian dictionaries for English-speakers and those learning English are numerous, but differ in terms of quality and date of publication. The most widely-used publication for both target groups would still have to be Echols and Shadily's *Kamus Indonesia Inggris* and *Kamus Inggris Indonesia*, with their extensive entries, many of which are still used today. However, despite revisions, these volumes date from the 1960s and 1970s so they do not cover Indonesian's development since the onset of political reform in 1998, nor the wide-ranging influence of globalization and the internet. Locally-published dictionaries often include new entries and words, but lack accuracy and authenticity in their English translations. On the other hand, foreign publications tend to use rather archaic Indonesian terms. This **Tuttle Compact Indonesian Dictionary** hopes to be a quality bilingual dictionary for language professionals in Indonesia and abroad, particularly students, educators, translators, interpreters and employees in a bilingual working environment. While reflecting usage, it also has a prescriptive role, promoting authentic local alternatives to lazy foreign borrowings.

This dictionary focuses on the inclusion of new terminology, accuracy and authenticity, commonly-used collocations and phrases, and specific cultural terms which enhance the users understanding of the target language. Unlike most large-scale quality Indonesian dictionaries, this edition does not presume prior knowledge of Indonesian word structure. For example, the word *melihat* is not just listed under its base *lihat*, but is also given directly under *melihat*. This feature from *Tuttle's Concise* and *Pocket* editions of Indonesian-English dictionaries has been retained due to its popularity with users.

Selection of entries

No dictionary is ever 'complete', ie. contains every single word of a language. This dictionary attempts to reflect general, everyday usage that will be understood throughout Indonesia and the three main Anglophone countries (the United States, the United Kingdom and Australia), as well as a range of terminology found in the mass media, popular culture and on the street. It includes words that are important to tertiary students and language learners. English entries use American spelling, with any British variant listed subsequently. There is naturally some reflection of the editor's own linguistic background, as an Australian having lived 10 years in Java interacting with speakers of Jakarta dialect, Javanese and Sundanese, in themselves Indonesia's two major regional languages.

There are differences between spoken (colloquial) and written forms in all languages, and Indonesian and English are no exceptions. Informal Indonesian as heard on the street tends to drop verb prefixes and suffixes, and does not repeat words if the context is clear. American English slang, in turn, has been popularized by Hollywood. A knowledge of what is slang (sub-standard, oral) or colloquial (everyday), and which words appear in written form, is essential for mastering a deeper knowledge of language and culture. This dictionary, while primarily aiming at foreigners learning Indonesian, also hopes to be of use to Indonesian students of English, and to explode the many myths, false friends and incorrect usage that abounds in the current atmosphere, where competence in English is a high priority at university, in the workplace and especially among middle- to upper socioeconomic groups.

Guide to using this dictionary

The dictionary is divided into two sections, Indonesian-English and English-Indonesian. (There is a quick reference covering numbers, dates and time, and colors on pages xii-xiv.) Entries are listed alphabetically, in the following order:

menghalau	entry (in bold, blue type)
halau: menghalau	first word is not found (or commonly used) alone. Sub-entries (derived words) follow after semi-colons. Subsequent sub-entries are in the same bold font, but black.
n	word type (see list of dictionary symbols). This is not always given if there is no single word form in the other language: eg. **cas** charge (could be *n*, *v*)
v	verb (can be both transitive and intransitive, ie. may or may not take an object)
vi	intransitive verb (no object)
vt	transitive verb (has an object)
child *n* **children**	irregular plurals are given after the noun symbol *n*
put *v* **put put**	irregular past tense forms (simple past and past perfect) are given after the verb symbol *v*
[nait]	Indonesian phonetic pronunciation of an irregularly-spelled word (see spelling guides)
malam	meaning (in plain type)
session, meeting; hearing	Similar meanings are divided by commas, while different meanings are separated with a semi-colon
~ *tiri* stepmother; *anak* ~ mother and child	The preceding entry or sub-entry is indicated by ~ in common phrases, collocations or idioms (in italics). In the example on the left, ~ represents *ibu*.

out-of-date (of a joke)	Round brackets either contain additional information;
to (be able to) speak or	Or they may contain a possible additional meaning.
baik ... maupun ... both ... and ...	... represents any word, in a set phrase
bersih, membersihkan,	All entries are grouped, where possible,
pembersihan	with sub-entries, generally in alphabetical order.
nutty ← nut	Related entries which do not follow
	alphabetically have a left-pointing arrow indicating that they come from a base word.
abis → habis	A right-pointing arrow shows an entry for further information or reference;
went → go	or the base of an irregular past tense verb form.

Acknowledgments

It has been a very rewarding experience to compile this dictionary. The editor would like to thank everyone involved in the project. In particular, thanks to Eric M. Oey of Periplus for his enthusiasm and support; Associate Professor Stuart O. Robson of Monash University for his thoughtful suggestions, proof-reading and constant encouragement; Nancy Goh of Periplus for her endless patience, tight editing and checking plus helpful suggestions; Tony Mansanulu for his patient and thorough editing and explanations; Judo Suwidji and Kiki at Java Books in Jakarta.

I would also like to thank the following friends and family who have both asked and answered questions related to the compilation of this dictionary: Elizabeth and Rudy R. Alwi, Andrew Denney, Robert Greaves, Chiyako Hatano, *Paklik* Kamaluddin and *Bulik* Tati, Ian Peirson, Nanik and Lastri, Yeon Soo Ok, Rainier Revireino, Angela Rogers and Iding Handiman, Dini Soraya and Sulistio, Achmad Sumidjan, Ibu Sunarti (Zuster), Kristina Sutiyono, Jane Sweed and family, and Adrian Thirkell. Special thanks go to Jonathan Roche and Sarah Bagus Musdiantoko for their enthusiasm, unwavering support and valuable feedback on many aspects of the dictionary.

Lastly, I am deeply grateful to *keluarga besar* Sumirat and *keluarga besar* Moch. Yunus, my family here in Indonesia; as I am to the household of Fauzi Bowo; my own family in Melbourne, always supportive, interested and curious; and my students over the years, who show me how they learn language. The biggest *terima kasih* of all goes to my husband Johansjah Sugianto, always my first and last port of call for checks on usage, language and other inside information, and my son Suriadi Wulandaru Johansjah, for being understanding and patient with his busy mother.

References

Abdul Kadir Usman (2002). *Kamus Umum Bahasa Minangkabau Indonesia.* Anggrek Media, Padang.

Abdul Rahman bin Yusop (1975). *Collins Gem Malay Dictionary: Malay-English English-Malay.* HarperCollins.

Echols, John M. & Hassan Shadily (1994). *Kamus Indonesia-Inggris: an Indonesian-English Dictionary.* Direvisi & diedit oleh John U. Wolff & James T. Collins. PT Gramedia Pustaka Utama, Jakarta.

Echols, John M. & Hassan Shadily (1975). *Kamus Inggris-Indonesia: an English-Indonesian Dictionary.* PT Gramedia, Jakarta.

Hajek, John & Tilman, Alexandre Vital (2001). *East Timor Phrasebook.* Lonely Planet, Melbourne.

Hardjadibrata, R.R. (2003). *Sundanese English Dictionary.* Pustaka Jaya, Jakarta.

Hawkins, Joyce M. (1990). *The New Oxford School Dictionary.* Oxford University Press, Oxford.

Hornby, A.S. (1995). *Oxford Advanced Learner's Dictionary of Current English.* Editor: Jonathan Crowther. Fifth edition. Oxford University Press, Oxford.

Maman S. Mahayana, Nuradji & Totok Suhardiyanto (1997). *Kamus Ungkapan Bahasa Indonesia.* PT Grasindo/Gramedia Widiasarana Indonesia, Jakarta.

McGlynn, John H. (ed). (1998). *Language and Literature.* Indonesian Heritage Series, vol. 10. Archipelago Press, Singapore.

Menayang, Jan F. (2004). *Kamus Melayu Manado – Indonesia Indonesia – Melayu Manado.* IPCOS, Jakarta.

Panitia Kamus Lembaga Basa & Sastra Sunda (1994). *Kamus Umum Basa Sunda.* Penerbit Tarate Bandung.

Pusat Bahasa, Departemen Pendidikan Nasional (2002). *Kamus Besar Bahasa Indonesia.* Edisi Ketiga. Balai Pustaka, Jakarta.

Robson, Stuart (2004). *Welcome to Indonesian: a Beginner's Survey of the Language*. Tuttle, Singapore.

Robson, S. & Singgih Wibisono (2002). *Javanese English Dictionary*. Periplus, Hong Kong.

R.R. Hardjadibrata (2003). *Sundanese-English Dictionary*. Pustaka Jaya, Jakarta.

S. Prawiroatmodjo (1995). *Bausastra Jawa – Indonesia: Jilid I Abjad A–Ny*. Edisi ke-2. PT Toko Gunung Agung, Jakarta.

S. Prawiroatmodjo (1981). *Bausastra Jawa – Indonesia: Jilid II Abjad Ny–Z*. Edisi ke-2. Gunung Agung, Jakarta.

S. Wojowasito (2000). *Kamus Umum Belanda Indonesia*. IBVT/PT Ichtiar Baru van Hoeve, Jakarta.

Sahanaya, Wendy & Tan, Albert (2001). *Oxford Study Indonesian Dictionary*. Oxford University Press, Melbourne.

Simbolon, Parakitri T. (1999). *Pesona: Bahasa Nusantara Menjelang Abad ke-21*. Kepustakaan Populer Gramedia, Jakarta.

Simorangkir, J.C.T., Rudy T. Erwin & J.T. Prasetyo (1995). *Kamus Hukum*. Bumi Aksara, Jakarta.

Sinclair, John (editor-in-chief) (1995). *Collins Cobuild English Dictionary*. Harper-Collins Publishers, London.

Stevens, Alan M. & A. Ed. Schmidgall-Tellings (2004). *A Comprehensive Indonesian-English Dictionary*. Ohio University Press, Athens USA.

Susi Moeimam & Steinhauer, Hein (2005). *Kamus Belanda-Indonesia*. PT Gramedia Pustaka Utama, Jakarta.

Taniguchi, Goro (1995). *Kamus Standar Bahasa Jepang – Indonesia*. Edisi revisi. Dian Rakyat, Jakarta Timur.

Dictionary symbols

abbrev	abbreviation	*lit*	literally; literary
adj	adjective	*m*	male
adv	adverb	*Mak*	Macassarese
Amb	Ambonese	*Mal*	Malay
arch	archaic	*mil*	military
art	article	*Min*	Minangkabau
Aus	Australian usage	*n*	noun
aux	auxiliary (helping) verb	*neg*	negative (meaning)
Bal	Balinese	*obj*	object
Bat	Batak	*pf*	past form
Bet	Betawi	*pl*	plural
Budd	Buddhist	*pol*	polite
Cath	Catholic	*poss*	possessive
Ch	Chinese	*pref*	prefix
child	children's language	*prep*	preposition
Chr	Christian	*pron*	pronoun
coll	colloquial	*resp*	respectful
conj	conjunction	*s, sing*	singular
derog	derogatory, rude	*sl*	slang
eg	for example	*subj*	subject
E Ind	Eastern Indonesia	*suf*	suffix
ejac	ejaculation	*Sum*	Sumatran usage
esp	especially	*Sund*	Sundanese
etc	et cetera, and so on	*tit*	title
euph	euphemism	*tsl*	teen slang
excl	exclamation	*UK*	British usage
f	female	*US*	American usage
fin	financial	usu	usually
form	formal	*v*	verb (both intransitive and transitive)
gr	greeting		
Hind	Hindu	*vi*	intransitive verb (no object)
inf	informal	*vt*	transitive verb (with object)
interrog	interrogative, question word	*vulg*	vulgar
interj	interjection	~	(base word +)
Isl	Islamic, Muslim	←	comes from the base word
Jav	Javanese	→	see following entries
Jkt	Jakarta usage		

Quick Reference Guide

Days of the week (Nama Hari)
Monday: *hari Senin*
Wednesday: *hari Rabu*
Friday: *hari Jumat*
Sunday: *hari Minggu*

Tuesday: *hari Selasa*
Thursday: *hari Kamis*
Saturday: *hari Sabtu*

Months of the year (Nama Bulan)
January: *bulan Januari*
March: *bulan Maret*
May: *bulan Mei*
July: *bulan Juli*
September: *bulan September*
November: *bulan November*

February: *bulan Februari*
April: *bulan April*
June: *bulan Juni*
August: *bulan Agustus*
October: *bulan Oktober*
December: *bulan Desember*

Colors (Nama Warna)
blue: *biru*
dark blue: *biru tua*
green: *hijau*
yellow: *kuning*
pink: *merah muda, merah jambu*
orange: *oranye, jingga*

light blue: *biru muda*
brown: *cokelat*
black: *hitam*
red: *merah*
white: *putih*
purple: *ungu*

Cardinal numbers (Bilangan Pokok)
one: *satu*
three: tiga
five: *lima*
seven: *tujuh*
nine: *sembilan*
eleven: *sebelas*
thirteen: *tiga belas*
fifteen: *lima belas*
twenty-one: *dua puluh satu*
forty: empat *puluh*
one hundred: *seratus*
one thousand: *seribu*

two: *dua*
four: *empat*
six: *enam*
eight: *delapan*
ten: *sepuluh*
twelve: *dua belas*
fourteen: *empat belas*
twenty: *dua puluh*
thirty: *tiga puluh*
fifty: *lima puluh*
two hundred: *dua ratus*
two thousand and six: *dua ribu enam*

five thousand: *lima ribu*
twenty thousand: *dua puluh ribu*
one hundred thousand: *seratus ribu*

ten thousand: *sepuluh ribu*
fifty thousand: *lima puluh ribu*
one million: *sejuta*

Times of the day (Pembagian Waktu)

morning (12 midnight to 12 noon) ⎱ *malam (jam 12–jam 4),*
⎰ *pagi (jam 4–10.30)*
afternoon (12 noon to 6 p.m.) *siang (jam 10.30–jam 3),*
sore (jam 3–jam 6)
evening (6 p.m. to 12 midnight) *malam (jam 6–jam 12)*

What time is it? (Jam berapa sekarang?)

one o'clock: *jam satu*
two o'clock: *jam dua*
five (minutes) past two (o'clock): *jam dua lewat lima (menit)*
a quarter past two: *jam dua (lewat) seperempat*
half past two: *jam setengah tiga*
a quarter to three: *jam tiga kurang seperempat*
three o'clock: *jam tiga*
three forty: *jam tiga empat puluh*
four a.m., four o'clock in the morning: *jam empat pagi*
four p.m., four o'clock in the afternoon: *jam empat sore*
midday, noon: *jam dua belas siang*
midnight: *jam dua belas malam*
nine p.m.: *jam 21.00 (dua puluh satu)*
half an hour: *setengah jam*
five minutes: *lima menit*

Fractions and decimals (Pecahan dan angka desimal)

half: *setengah*
one third: *sepertiga*
two thirds: *dua pertiga*
one quarter: *seperempat*
one point six (1.6): *satu koma enam (1,6)*

Ordinal numbers (Bilangan Urutan)

first: *pertama*

second: *kedua*

third: *ketiga*

fourth: *keempat*

fifth: *kelima*

sixth: *keenam*

seventh: *ketujuh*

eighth: *kedelapan*

ninth: *kesembilan*

tenth: *kesepuluh*

eleventh: *kesebelas*

twelfth: *kedua belas*

fifteenth: *kelima belas*

nineteenth: *kesembilan belas*

twentieth: *kedua puluh*

twenty-first: *kedua puluh satu*

twenty-second: *kedua puluh dua*

twenty-third: *kedua puluh tiga*

thirtieth: *ketiga puluh*

thirty-first: *ketiga puluh satu*

fortieth: *keempat puluh*

fiftieth: *kelima puluh*

one hundredth: *keseratus*

Personal pronouns (Kata ganti)

I—*saya; aku* (familiar); *gue, gua* (Jakarta slang)

you—*anda* (neutral, formal); *saudara* (neutral); *kamu* (familiar, to younger
people); *engkau, kau* (less common) [name of person]

he (male), she (female), it (object)—*dia; beliau* (very respectful)

we—*kita* (including person addressed); *kami* (excluding person addressed)

you—*kalian; anda sekalian* (formal)

they—*mereka*

INDONESIAN–ENGLISH

A

a *a*, first letter of the alphabet

aba: mengaba *vt* to conduct; **pengaba** *n* conductor

aba-aba *n* order, command (in army or at school)

abad *n* century; age, era; ~ *keemasan* golden age; ~ *Pertengahan* the Middle Ages; **berabad-abad** *adv* for centuries

abadi *adj* eternal, everlasting; *cinta* ~ endless love; **mengabadikan** *vt* to immortalize; *nama sang pelukis akan diabadikan dalam patung* the artist will be immortalized in stone

abai *adj* neglectful; **mengabaikan** *vt* to neglect, disregard, ignore; **terabaikan** *adj* neglected, ignored

abang, bang (esp in Malay areas) *n, m, pron* elder brother; term of address for male person (slightly) older than yourself, or worker in service industry; ~ *None* Mr and Miss Jakarta

abang: abangan *n* Javanese Muslim who follows local traditions rather than Islam (*cf.* **santri**)

abaté *n* insecticide used against mosquito larvae

abdi *n* servant, (in past) slave; ~ *dalem* court servant at a Javanese palace; **mengabdi** *vi* to serve; *Sunarti telah lama ~ di kediaman itu* Sunarti has served that household for a long time; **pengabdian** *n* service, servitude, devotion

ABG *abbrev anak baru gedé n* teenager, youth

abis *adv, sl* completely, totally; *keren* ~ so cool; *adj, coll* → **habis**

abjad *n* alphabet; *menurut* ~ in alphabetical order, alphabetically

abon *n* shredded dry meat, eaten as a side-dish

abonemén *n* subscription, billing; **karcis abonemen** commuter ticket, monthly ticket

Aborijin *adj bahasa* ~ Aboriginal language; *orang* ~ Aboriginal person, indigenous Australian

aborsi, abortus *n* abortion; *melakukan aborsi* to have an abortion; **mengaborsi** *vt* to abort (a fetus)

abrek: seabrek *adj* lots, many, a large number, numerous; *Lies punya* ~ *kegiatan di dunia musik* Lies is involved in a large number of activities in the world of music

ABRI *abbrev Angkatan Bersenjata Republik Indonesia* Indonesian Armed Forces

absah *adj* legal, legitimate, valid; **keabsahan** *n* legality, legitimacy, validity; **mengabsahkan** *vt* to legalize, legitimize, validate

absén *adj* not present; *vi* report for duty; **mengabsén** *vi* to call the roll

abses *n* abscess

abstrak *adj, n* abstract

abu *n* ash; dust; ~ *gergaji* sawdust; ~ *rokok* cigarette ash; **abu-abu** *adj* gray; **mengabukan, memperabukan** *vt* to cremate; **perabuan** *n* urn (for ashes)

AC *abbrev* [a sé] air-conditioner, air-conditioning

acak random, mixed; **acak-acakan** *adj* messed up, untidy; **mengacak** *vt* to scramble, encode; **mengacak-acak** *vt* to mess up

acap ~ *(kali)* often

acar *n* finely-cut pickled cucumber, shallot, carrot and chilli, eaten with fried rice, satay etc; **mengacar** *vt* to pickle

acara *n* agenda, program, event; ~ *hari ini* today's program; **pengacara** *n* lawyer, solicitor

acc *adj* [asésé] approved, agreed

aci *n* starch; flour

aco: mengaco, ngaco *vi, sl* to shoot off your mouth, talk without thinking; to misbehave

acu: acuan *n* reference; ~ *silang* cross-reference; **mengacu** *v* ~ *(pada)* to refer to, to use as a point of reference; to aim; ~ *pada hukum negara* following Indonesian law; **mengacukan** *vt* to point, refer to; to threaten with; ~ *arah* to indicate direction; ~ *senapan* to wave a weapon

acuh (don't) care; *(tidak/tak)* ~ indifferent, not care; ~ *tak* ~ to ignore, take no notice of; **mengacuhkan** *vt* to care about; *Yuni sering* ~ *adik iparnya* Yuni pays little attention to her sister-in-law

acung *vt* raise; **acungan** *n* ~ *jempol* thumbs-up; **mengacungkan** *vt* to raise, hold up; ~ *tangan* raise your hand

AD *abbrev Angkatan Darat* Army

ada *vi* to be (present); to have, exist; ~ *Firman?* is Firman here?; ~ *apa?* what's up? what's wrong?; *tidak* ~ there isn't, there aren't, not here; **ketidakadaan** *n* absence, lack of; **ada-ada** ~ *saja* well, I never! Words fail me!; **adakah** whether; ~ *kesempatan nanti?* will there be an opportunity later?; **adakala, adakalanya** *adv* sometimes; **adalah** *vi* is, are (followed by a noun); *Rina* ~ *sepupu Dian* Rina is Dian's cousin; *yang menang* ~ *orang Madura* it was the Madurese who won; **adanya** *n* the existence of; *apa* ~ as it is, without any pretensions; **adapun** *conj* there is (also); now (it so happens); ~ *seorang putri datang kemari* it happened that a princess came here; **berada** *vi* to be somewhere; to exist; *Ibu Menteri* ~ *di Padang* the Minister is in Padang; *adj* well-to-do, well-off; **keberadaan** *n* presence; **keadaan** *n* situation, condition; ~ *darurat* emergency; **mengada-ada** *vi* to invent, make up; *sungguh* ~ to push your luck; **mengadakan** *vt* to do, run, hold, create, organize, make available; ~ *angket* to do a survey; ~ *kampanye* to run a campaign; ~ *riset* to do research; **pengadaan** *n* supply, provision; **seadanya** *adj* what's there; *makan* ~ eat what's there

adab *n* culture, good manners, courtesy; **beradab** *adj* civilized, polite; *vt* to

have a civilization; **peradaban** *n* culture, civilization; ~ *Mesir kuno* ancient Egyptian civilization

adakah whether; ~ *kesempatan nanti?* will there be an opportunity later?

adakala, adakalanya *adv* sometimes ← **ada**

adalah *vi* is, are (followed by a noun); *Rina* ~ *sepupu Dian* Rina is Dian's cousin; *yang menang* ~ *orang Madura* it was the Madurese who won ← **ada**

adanya *n* the existence of; *apa* ~ as it is, without any pretensions ← **ada**

adaptasi *v* adaptation; **beradaptasi** *vi* to adapt

adaptor *n* adaptor

adapun *conj* there is (also); now (it so happens); ~ *seorang putri datang kemari* it happened that a princess came here

adas *n* fennel

adat *n* tradition, custom, customary law, esp of an ethnic group; ~ *istiadat* customs and traditions; ~ *Sunda* Sundanese tradition; *upacara* ~ traditional ceremony

adé, adék *pron, coll* little one (used for the youngest or only child) ← **adik**

adegan *n* act, scene; ~ *panas* steamy scene

adem *adj* cool, calm; ~ *ayem* quiet, calm; **mengademkan** *vt* to cool something down

adem pauze *n* break, breather

adéndum *n* appendix, additional section

adhésif adhesive

adi- *pref* higher; **adiboga** *n* cuisine, haute cuisine; **adibusana** *n* haute couture; **adidaya, adikuasa** *adj* *(negara)* ~ superpower; **adikarya** *n* masterpiece; **adipura** *n* tidy town, cleanest town

adik *n* younger brother or sister; ~ *ipar* (younger) brother- or sister-in-law; ~ *laki-laki* (younger) brother; ~ *kandung* (younger, blood) brother or sister; ~ *sepupu* cousin (of lower status); ~ *tiri* (younger) stepbrother or stepsister; *kakak-ber*~ (to have) siblings

adikarya *n* masterpiece

adikuasa *adj (negara)* ~ superpower

adil *adj* just, righteous; *Ratu* ~ the Just Ruler, who is believed will save Indonesia (Java) one day; **diadili** *v* to be tried, taken to court; **ketidakadilan** *n* injustice; **keadilan** *n* justice; ~ *sosial* social justice; **mengadili** *vt* to try someone, put someone on trial; **peng-adilan** *n* court of justice or law, trial; ~ *militer* court-martial; ~ *negeri* district court; ~ *tinggi* high court; **seadil-adilnya** *adv* as fairly or justly as possible

adimarga *n* boulevard; superhighway

adinda *pron* form of address to younger sibling or wife (in letters); ~ *tersayang* my dear sister

adipati *n, arch* colonial title for head of a *kadipatén*

adipura *n* tidy town, cleanest town

adjéktiva, adjéktif *n* adjective

administrasi *n* administration, manage-ment; ~ *negara* public administration; **administratif, administratip** *adj* ad-ministrative; *kota* ~ *(kotip)* administra-tive city, municipality; **administrator, administratur** *n* administrator, manager

adon: adonan *n* batter, dough, mixture; **mengadon** *vt* to knead

adopsi *n* adoption; **mengadopsi** *vt* to adopt (a child)

adu hit; ~ *jotos* fistfight; **beradu** *vi* to hit (accidentally); to fight; **mengadu** *vi* to complain, report; ~ *domba* to play two parties against each other; **mengadukan** *vt* to report someone/ something, to make a complaint about; ~ *seseorang ke pengadilan* to sue, take to court; **pengaduan** *n* com-plaint; *surat* ~ letter of complaint

aduh *ejac* ouch! ow! (expression of pain); *excl* oh! (expression of sorrow); wow!; ~ *sakit!* ow, that hurts!; ~ *berat sekali* oh, how difficult!; ~ *cantiknya!* isn't she beautiful?

aduhai *ejac, lit* oh! *adj* amazing, outstanding; ~ *negeriku* oh, my be-loved country; *pemain yang* ~ a fan-tastic player

aduk *campur* ~ (all) mixed up; **meng-aduk** *vt* to stir, mix; ~ *semen* to mix cement

Advén, Advént Advent; *gereja* ~ (Seventh-Day) Adventist Church; *masa* ~ advent, time leading up to Christmas

advérba *n* adverb

advértorial *n* informative advertisement, advertisement disguised as information

advokat *n* lawyer

adzan → **azan**

aéronautika *n* aeronautics

afdol, afdal *adj* right, good; complete; *lebih* ~ better

afdruk *n* (photo) negative; **mengafdruk** *vt* ~ *foto* to develop photos, to get photos developed

Afganistan, Afghanistan *n* Afghanistan; *orang* ~ Afghan

afiat *sehat wal*~ in good health

afiks *n* affix

afiliasi *n* affiliation; **diafiliasi, terafilia-si** *adj* affiliated; ~ *dengan Universitas Atma Jaya* affiliated with Atma Jaya University

afinitas *n* affinity

Afrika *n* Africa; *orang* ~ African; ~ *Selatan (Afsel)* South Africa

Aga *orang Bali* ~ the original (pre-Hindu) inhabitants of Bali

agak *adv* rather, somewhat; ~ *gemuk* rather fat; **agaknya** *adv* apparently, it seems; I wonder

agama *n* religion; ~ *Budha* Buddhism; ~ *Hindu* Hinduism; ~ *Islam* Islam; ~ *Katolik* Catholicism, the Catholic church; ~ *Kong Hu Cu* Confucianism; ~ *Kristen* Christianity; Protestant church; ~ *Yahudi* Judaism; *Departemen* ~ Department of Religious Affairs; *Menteri* ~ Minister for Religious Affairs; **beragama** *vt* to have a religion; *adj* religious; *Daniel* ~ *Kristen* Daniel is Christian; *Siti* ~ *Islam* Siti is Muslim; **keagamaan** *adj* religious affairs; **agamais, agamis** *adj* religious, God-fearing

agar *conj* in order that/to; ~ *maklum* let it be known; ~ *supaya* in order that;

dia belajar keras ~ lulus ujian he studied hard in order to pass the exam

agar, agar-agar *n* a kind of seaweed; a kind of jelly made from this seaweed; a crystallizing agent extracted from this seaweed

agén *n* agent, agency, distributor; ~ *kargo* cargo agent, shipping agent; ~ *koran* news agency; ~ *perjalanan* travel agent; ~ *rahasia* secret agent; ~ *tunggal* sole distributor

agénda *n* agenda; appointment diary; **mengagéndakan** *vt* to put on the agenda

agraria *n* agrarian affairs

agrési *n* aggression; *arch* police action (under the Dutch); **agrésif** *adj* aggressive; **agrésor** *n* aggressor, aggressive party

agrowisata *n* agricultural tourism

agun, agunan *n* security, collateral; **mengagunkan** *vt* to use (something) as collateral; *Nuh ~ mobilnya ke bank* Nuh used his car as collateral when dealing with the bank

agung *adj* great, high, supreme; *Jaksa ~* Attorney-General; **keagungan** *n* greatness, majesty; **mengagungkan** *vt* to glorify; **mengagung-agungkan** *vt* to glorify, place on a pedestal

Agustus *bulan ~* August; **agustusan** *coll* (to hold a) celebration on Independence Day (17 August)

ah *excl* oh (showing mild annoyance); *ke sana aja ~!* oh, let's just go there! (and stop wasting time)

Ahad *n, Isl hari ~* Sunday → **Minggu**

ahimsa *n* non-violence

ahli *n* authority, expert, specialist; member; ~ *bahasa* linguist; ~ *bedah* surgeon; ~ *gigi* dentist; dental practitioner; ~ *gizi* nutritionist; ~ *hukum* legal adviser; ~ *kitab* Peoples of the Book (Jews and Christians); ~ *nujum* astrologer; ~ *purbakala* archeologist; ~ *waris* heir; *tenaga ~* specialist (staff); **keahlian** *n* expertise

aib *adj* shameful; *n* shame, disgrace; flaw; **keaiban** *n* shame, disgrace, humiliation

air *n* water; juice; fluid, liquid; ~ *aki* distilled water (for car batteries); ~ *api* spirit, volatile liquid; ~ *bah* flood; ~ *hujan* rainwater; ~ *jeruk* orange juice; ~ *kelapa* coconut milk; ~ *keras* acid; ~ *ketuban* amniotic fluid; ~ *ketuban sudah pecah* the waters have broken; ~ *laut* seawater; ~ *ledeng* reticulated water; ~ *limbah* effluent, polluted water; ~ *liur*, ~ *ludah* saliva; ~ *mani* sperm; ~ *mata* tears; ~ *minum*, ~ *putih* drinking water; ~ *muka* facial expression; ~ *pasang* high tide, incoming tide; ~ *raksa* mercury; ~ *seni* urine; ~ *soda*, ~ *Belanda* soda water; ~ *suci* holy water; ~ *sumur* well water; ~ *surut* low tide, outgoing tide; ~ *susu*, ~ *susu ibu (ASI)* mother's milk; ~ *tanah* ground water; ~ *tape*, ~ *tapai* fermented rice wine; ~ *tawar* fresh water; ~ *tebu* sugar-cane juice; ~ *terjun* waterfall; ~ *wudu Isl* water for ablutions before praying; ~ *zamzam Isl* holy water from Mecca; *buang ~* to go to the toilet; *buang ~ (kecil)* urinate; *buang ~ besar* to empty your bowels, defecate, poo; *cacar ~* chicken pox; *mata ~* spring; *pintu ~* sluice, floodgates, lock; *tahan ~* waterproof; *tanah ~ Indonesia*, native country, homeland; ~ *tenang menghanyutkan* still waters run deep; **berair** *vi* juicy, containing water; **mengairi** *vt* to irrigate; **pengairan** *n* irrigation; **perairan** *n* territorial waters; waterworks

ajaib *adj* miraculous, strange; *aneh bin ~* wonder of wonders; **keajaiban** *n* wonder, miracle; *Tujuh ~ Dunia* the Seven Wonders of the World; **mengajaibkan** *adj* amazing, astonishing, astounding

ajak, mengajak *vt* to invite, ask out; to urge; ~ *jalan-jalan* to ask out; ~ *kawin*, ~ *nikah* to ask someone to marry you; **ajakan** *n, inf* invitation

ajal *n* moment of death; *menemui ~nya, sampai ~nya* to die

ajang *n* arena; venue; ~ *pertandingan* match venue

ajar guide; *kurang ~* rude, badly brought-up; **ajaran** *n* teaching; ~

agama religious doctrine; *tahun* ~ academic year, school year; **belajar** *v* to learn, study; ~ *bahasa Jepang* to learn Japanese; ~ *pada* to learn from; ~ *jarak jauh* (to study via) distance learning; ~ *ke luar negeri* to study abroad; *Yuni masih* ~ Yuni's still learning; **belajar-mengajar** *kegiatan* ~ teaching and learning; **pembelajaran** *n* learning (process); **mengajar** *v* **ngajar** *sl* to teach; **mengajari** *vt* **ngajarin** *sl* to teach someone; **mengajarkan** *vt* to teach something; **pelajar** *n* pupil, (school) student; schoolboy, schoolgirl; **mempelajari** *vt* to study something in depth; **pelajaran** *n* lesson; *mata* ~ (school) subject; **terpelajar** *adj* educated; **pengajar** *n* teacher; **pengajaran** *n* teaching, tuition

aji *n* charm

ajinomoto *n* MSG (monosodium glutamate), flavor enhancer

ajojing *n* modern, Western-style dancing; **berajojing** *vi* to dance (Western-style)

aju: **mengajukan** *vt* to forward, propose; to submit; ~ *pertanyaan* to ask a question

ajudan *n* adjutant

Akabri *abbrev Akademi Angkatan Bersenjata Republik* Indonesia Armed Forces Academy

akad *n* contract, agreement; ~ *nikah Isl* Muslim marriage contract, Muslim wedding ceremony

akadémi *n* academy, institute of higher education; ~ *Angkatan Bersenjata (Akabri)* Armed Forces Academy; ~ *Pemerintahan Dalam Negeri (APDN)* Academy of Public Administration, civil service academy; **akademik** *adj* academic

akal *n* mind, intellect; logic; way, means; ~ *budi*, ~ *sehat* intellect, common sense; ~ *bulus* trickery, deceit; *mencari* ~ find a way; *kehilangan* ~ to be at one's wits' end; *masuk* ~ make sense; **berakal** *adj* to be intelligent; *vi* to have a mind; **mengakali** *vt* to find a way; to deceive, play a trick on; *kita* ~ *saja* we'll find a way

akan *v, aux* will, going to (marks future time); *prep* about, concerning, regarding; ~ *tetapi* however; *sudah lupa* ~ has forgotten about; *minggu yang* ~ *datang* next week; **seakan-akan** *adv* as if, as though

akar *n* root; *kata* ~ base word, root; ~ *kuadrat* square root; *tingkat* ~ *rumput* grassroot level; **berakar** *adj* rooted; **mengakar** *v* to take root

akasia *n* acacia

akbar *adj* big, great; *Allahu* ~ Allah is great; *tablig* ~ big Islamic meeting

akékah → akikah

akhir *n* end; ~*nya* finally; ~~ *ini* recently; ~ *kata* finally, in conclusion; ~ *minggu*, ~ *pekan* weekend; *sampai* ~ *hayat* until the end of your life; **akhiran** *n* ending, suffix; **berakhir** *vi* to end; **mengakhiri** *vt* to end, finish something; **terakhir** *adj* last, final, latest

akhirat *n* the hereafter

akhlak *n* morals, ethics

aki *n* vehicle battery; *air* ~ distilled water (for car batteries); *mengisi* ~ to charge a car battery

aki *n, pron* Grandpa; grandfather; ~~ elderly, like a grandfather; ~ *nini* grandparents; very old

akibat *n* result, consequence; *conj* due to, consequently; ~*nya* as a result; **berakibat** *vi* to have consequences, implications; **mengakibatkan** *vt* to result in

akidah *n* belief, faith

akik *batu* ~ agate

akikah, akékah, kékah *coll, Isl* thanksgiving held after the birth of a child, usu through cutting the child's hair and slaughtering a goat

akil ~ *balig* of age, ready to take on religious obligations, etc

aklamasi *secara* ~ unanimously, without voting

akomodasi *n* accommodation

akrab *adj* close, intimate, friendly; **keakraban** *n* closeness, intimacy

akréditasi *n* accreditation; **terakreditasi** *adj* accredited (of higher education)

akrobat *n* acrobat; **berakrobat** *vi* to do acrobatics

akronim *n* acronym

aksara *n* letter, character, alphabet; ~ *Cina* Chinese characters; ~ *fonetis* phonetic alphabet; ~ *Jawa* Javanese script; ~ *Jawi* Arabic script used for writing Malay; ~ *Latin* the Latin alphabet; *buta* ~ illiterate

aksélerasi *n* acceleration; **aksélerator** *n* accelerator, gas

aksén *n* accent; **beraksén** *adj* -style; *vi* to have a touch of; *rumah* ~ *Jawa* a house with Javanese-inspired decor → **logat**

akséptor *n* participant in the national family planning program (KB)

aksés access; *jalan* ~ access road; **mengaksés** *vt* to access

aksésori *n* accessory; ~ *mobil* car accessory

aksi *n* action, demonstration; behavior; ~ *militer* military action by the Dutch, 1945–50; ~ *sepihak* unilateral action; **beraksi** *vi* to take action, do something; to perform

akta, akte *n* official document, certificate; ~ *lahir*, ~ *kelahiran* birth certificate; ~ *mengajar* teaching certificate; ~ *nikah*, ~ *pernikahan* marriage certificate

aktif *adj* activated, active, on, working; ~ *di kampus* involved in many university activities; *HP saya masih belum* ~*!* my mobile phone still isn't working!; **mengaktifkan** *vt* to activate, switch on; **aktivitas** *n* activity; **beraktivitas** *vi* to do something, keep busy

akting *adj* acting, temporary (of a position at work)

aktiva *n* assets; ~ *beku* frozen assets; ~ *bergerak* movable assets; ~ *tetap* fixed assets

aktivis *n* activist; ~ *HAM,* ~ *hak azasi manusia* human rights activist

aktivitas *n* activity; **beraktivitas** *vi* to do something, work, keep busy

aktor *n, m* actor; ~ *intelektual* the brains behind something; **aktris** *n, f* actress

aktual *adj* latest, up-to-date; *berita* ~ current affairs

aku *pron* I, me; **mengaku** *vi* to admit, confess, acknowledge; to claim; ~ *salah* to admit guilt; **mengakui** *vt* to admit something; to acknowledge, recognize; **diakui** *adj* recognized (of university programs); *hak-hak TKW harus diakui* the rights of migrant workers must be recognized; **pengakuan** *n* confession, acknowledgment; ~ *dosa* confession (Catholic)

akuarium *n* aquarium

akumulasi *n* accumulation; **terakumulasi** *adj* accumulated

akun *n* account; **akuntan** *n* accountant; **akuntansi** *n* accounting; ~ *keuangan* financial accounting

akur *vi* agree, agreed, get along; *keluarga itu sangat* ~ that family gets along very well

akustik *adj* acoustic; *n* acoustics

akut *adj* acute

AL *abbrev Angkatan Laut* Navy

a.l. *abbrev antara lain* among others

ala *adj* in the style of, à la; ~ *kadarnya* what's on offer, what's available

alah *ejac* (expression of exasperation) ~*! Lampunya rusak* damn, the light's broken!

alah beaten, defeated, conquered; **kealahan** *n* defeat, loss; **mengalah** *vi* to lose, be defeated; **mengalahkan** *vt* to defeat, conquer; **pengalahan** *n* process of losing, defeat; **peralahan** *n* loss, defeat, conquest → **kalah**

alaikum *(wa)* ~ *salam* (and) upon you be peace (used when responding to *salam alaikum*)

alam *adj* natural; *n* nature, world; ~ *baka* the hereafter; ~ *bebas,* ~ *terbuka* open air; ~ *semesta* the whole natural world; *dua* ~ two habitats; *ilmu pengetahuan* ~ *(IPA)* science; *sumber daya* ~ natural resources; **alami, alamiah** *adj* natural

alam: mengalami *vt* to experience, undergo; **pengalaman** *n* experience; **berpengalaman** *adj* experienced, skilled; *vi* to have experience

alamat *n* address; sign, omen; ~ *imel* email address; *salah* ~ wrong address or person; **beralamat** *adj* addressed; *vi* to have an address; **mengalamatkan**

vt to address to; to indicate

alami, alamiah *adj* natural ← **alam**

alan-alan *n* clown, jester

alang → **halang**

alang-alang *n* tall, coarse grass

alangkah *adv* how ...! what a ...!; ~ *bagusnya!* how beautiful!

alap-alap *n* kind of hawk or kestrel; thief

alas *n* foundation, basis, base; ~ *kaki* footwear; ~ *meja* tablecloth; **alasan** *n* cause, reason, motive; ~ *yang dicari-cari* pretext; **beralasan** *adj* with reason, reasonable; *vi* to have reason; *tidak* ~ ungrounded, unfounded, without reason; **beralaskan** *vi* based upon

alat *n* tool, instrument, means; organ; ~ *kelamin* genitals; ~ *kontrasepsi,* ~ *KB* form of contraception, contraceptive device; ~ *masak* kitchen utensil; ~ *musik gesek,* ~ *musik petik* string instrument; ~ *musik tiup* woodwind instrument; ~ *musik pukul* percussion instrument; ~ *pembayaran yang sah* legal tender; ~ *peraga* (teaching) aid; ~ *tulis* stationery; ~ *vital* genitals; ~~ *sekolah* school supplies; ~ *bantu dengar* hearing aid; **memperalat** *vt* to use or take advantage of someone; *Tina diperalat oleh kawannya* Tina was used by her friend; **peralatan** *n* equipment

alat: peralatan *n* feast, celebration

Albania *n* Albania; *orang* ~, *bahasa* ~ Albanian

album *n* album; ~ *foto* photo album; *mengeluarkan* ~ *baru* to release a new album

alérgi allergy, allergic; **beralérgi** *vi* to have an allergy; ~ *terhadap mangga* allergic to mangoes

Al-Fatihah *n, Isl* first chapter of the Koran; common prayer

algojo *n* hangman, executioner; *sl* butcher, murderer

algoritme *n* algorithm

alhamdulillah *ejac, Isl* thanks be to God; bless you! (when sneezing)

alhasil *conj* in the end, consequently

aliansi *n* alliance; **beraliansi** *vi* to be allied with

alias also known as, alias; in other words

alif ba ta (the first three letters of) the Arabic alphabet

alih *v* to shift, change position; ~ *profesi* change of career; ~ *teknologi* to upgrade technology; ~ *bahasa* translation, interpreting; **mengalihbahasakan** *vt* to translate or interpret something; **alih-alih** *conj* instead of; **beralih** *vi* to move, change, shift; **mengalih, mengalihkan** *vt* to shift something; ~ *perhatian* to shift attention, change the subject; **peralihan** *n* transition, change; *masa* ~ transition period

alim *adj, Isl* pious, religious

alinéa *n* paragraph

aling *tedeng* ~~ shield, cover, concealment

alir flow; **aliran** *n* stream, current; ideology, school, sect; ~ *kepercayaan* unofficial religious movement; ~ *listrik* electric current; **beraliran** *vi* to have an ideology; ~ *kiri* leftist; **mengalir** *vi* to flow; **mengalirkan** *vt* to channel; **pengaliran** *n* flow (esp of money)

alis *n* eyebrow; *mengangkat* ~ to raise your eyebrows

aliyah *n, Isl* senior high school (level)

aljabar *n* algebra

Aljazair *n* Algeria; *orang* ~ Algerian

alkisah the story goes; once upon a time

Alkitab *n* the Bible

alkohol *n* alcohol; **beralkohol** *adj* alcoholic; *v* to contain alcohol; *minuman* ~ alcoholic drink

Allah *n* God, *Isl* Allah; ~*u Akbar* God is great; *demi* ~ by God, for God's sake; *firman* ~ the word of God; ~ *sub-hanahu wa taala (SWT)* Allah the Most High

alm. *adj, Isl* **almarhum** *m* **almarhumah** *f* the late

almanak *n* calendar; almanac → **kalénder**

almarhum *adj, m, Isl* the late; **al-marhumah** *adj, f, Isl* the late; ~ *Ibu* my late mother

almari → **lemari**

Almasih *n* the Messiah; *Kenaikan Isa* ~ Assumption

alokasi *n* allocation; **mengalokasikan** *vt* to allocate

alot *adj* tough (of meat); heavy-going; *rapat berjalan ~* the meeting went very slowly

alpa *adj* forgetful, neglectful; **kealpaan** *n* forgetfulness, neglect

alpukat, apokat, avokat *n* avocado; *jus ~* avocado drink

Alqur'an, Al-quran, Alquran *n* the Koran; *Tempat Pendidikan ~ (TPA)* Islamic Study Center

AL(RI) *abbrev Angkatan Laut (Republik Indonesia)* (Indonesian) Navy

alternatif *n* alternative

altiméter *n* altimeter

alu *n* pestle; *~ lumpang* mortar and pestle

aluminium *n* aluminium; *atap ~* aluminium roof

alumni *n* graduate of a school, college or university

alun: alunan *n* swell; *~ suara* chorus; **beralun** *vi* to pitch, heave; **mengalunkan** *vt* to put something in motion, sing something

alun-alun *n* town square

alur *n* groove, channel; *~ cerita* plot; *~ sungai* river bed; **aluran** *n* channel

am *adj* general, common

ama *conj, sl* with; and; *Sastri ~ Tio* Sastri and Tio ← **sama**

amal *n* charity; *~ ibadah* service to God; *badan ~* charitable institution; *konser ~* charity concert; **beramal** *adj* charitable; *vi* to give to charity; **mengamalkan** *vt* to do something for charity; to carry out

aman *adj* safe, in peace; **keamanan** *n* safety, security; *Dewan ~ (PBB)* (UN) Security Council; **mengamankan** *vt* to make safe, restore order; place in custody; **pengaman** *n* safety device; **pengamanan** *n* securing, pacification

amanah, amanat *n* message, instruction, mandate; *Partai Amanat Nasional (PAN)* National Mandate Party; *Amanat Penderitaan Rakyat (Ampera)* Message of the People's Suffering (Sukarnoist slogan); **mengamanatkan** *vt* to entrust

amandel *n* tonsil

amar *n* injunction; *~ putusan* legal verdict

amarah → **marah**

amat *adv* very, extremely; *kasihan ~!* poor thing!; **teramat** *~ sangat* terribly, extremely

amat: mengamati *vt* to watch closely, keep an eye on; **pengamat** *n* observer; *~ politik* political observer; **pengamatan** *n* observation, monitoring

amatir *n* amateur

ambang *n* threshold, doorstep, verge; *~ batas* threshold, limit; *~ jendela* window sill; *~ kebangkrutan* verge of bankruptcy; *~ nyeri* pain threshold; *~ pintu* doorstep, verge

ambang, mengambang *vi* to float, be suspended in water; *kurs mengambang* floating exchange rate

ambar *n* ambergris; *batu ~* amber → **damar**

ambéien *n* hemorrhoid; piles

ambek, mengambek *v* to get angry

ambil *vt* to take; to subtract; to bring; *~ saja* help yourself; *~ bagian* to participate, take part in; *~ foto* to take a photo; *~ keputusan* to make a decision; *~ kesimpulan* to conclude, make the conclusion (that); *~ pusing* to worry (over); *tiga ~ dua sama dengan satu* three minus two is one; *tolong ~ air* please bring some water; **mengambil** *vt* to take, get, fetch; *~ alih* to take over; *~ sumpah* to swear, take an oath; **mengambilkan** *vt* to get something for someone; **pengambilan** *n* act of taking, removal; *~ gambar* photo shoot; *~ sumpah* taking an oath

ambin *n* strap, sling; **berambin** *vi ~ lutut* to sit hugging your knees; **mengambin** *vt* to carry in a sling on the shoulder or back

ambing *n* udder

ambisi *n* ambition; **berambisi** *adj* ambitious; *vi* to have an ambition, have ambitions; **ambisius** *adj* ambitious

amblas *coll* disappear, vanish

ambruk *vi* to collapse, break, crash; *jembatan ~* broken bridge

ambulans *n* ambulance

ambung bounce, soar; **mengambung-kan** *vt* to toss or throw something up; **terambung-ambung** *adj* to float or bob about

amdal *abbrev* environmental impact study ← **analisis mengenai dampak lingkungan**

amén: (me)ngamén *vi* to sing in the street for money, busk; **pengamén** *n* street singer, busker

améndemen, amandemen *n* amendment

Amérika *n* America; ~ *Serikat (AS)* United States of America (USA); ~ *Latin* Latin America

amfibi *adj* amphibious; *n* amphibian

amin *ejac* amen; **mengamini** *vt* to agree to, approve of

amis *adj* putrid, smelling fishy; *bau* ~ fishy smell

amit-amit *ejac* God forbid, no way

amnésti *n* amnesty

amoy, amoi *n* (ethnic) Chinese girl

ampas *n* dregs, grounds; ~ *kopi* coffee grounds

ampela, empela *n* gizzard; *ati* ~ liver and gizzards

Ampéra *n* Message of the People's Suffering (Sukarnoist slogan) ← **Amanat Penderitaan Rakyat**

amplop *n* envelope; *coll* bribe; *kasih* ~ hand over a bribe

ampuh *adj* powerful, potent; *obat yang* ~ powerful medicine

ampun *n* mercy, forgiveness, pardon; *ejac* Mercy! (expression of astonishment or disapproval); *minta* ~ beg for mercy; ~ *deh, macetnya!* I've never seen traffic like it!; **ampunan** *n* forgiveness; **mengampuni** *vt* to forgive; **pengampun** *n Tuhan Maha* ~ God is all-forgiving; **pengampunan** *n* pardon, reprieve, amnesty

Amrik *n, sl* America ← **Amerika**

amsal *n* proverb, saying; **Amsal** *n, Chr* the Book of Proverbs

amuk *adj* amok; **mengamuk** *vi* to run amok, go berserk

amunisi, munisi *n* ammunition, munitions; ~ *kosong* blanks

anak *n* child; young (of an animal); member of a group; small part of a whole; ~ *angkat* adopted child; ~ *anjing* puppy; ~ *ayam* chick; ~ *bawang* someone insignificant; ~ *buah* assistant, staff; ~ *buah kapal (ABK)* able seaman; ~ *bungsu* youngest child; ~ *campuran* child of mixed descent; ~ *cucu* descendants; ~ *dara* young girl, virgin; ~ *didik* pupil, student; ~ *emas* favorite; ~ *gedongan* rich kid; ~ *genta, ~ lonceng* clapper (of bell); ~ *haram, ~ jadah* illegitimate child, bastard; ~ *ingusan* toddler; still a child, inexperienced; ~ *itik* duckling; ~ *jalanan* street kid; ~ *kalimat* sub-clause; ~ *kambing* kid; ~ *kapal* crew, sailor; ~ *kembar* twins; ~ *kesayangan* favorite, pet; ~ *kolong, ~ tentara* soldier's child; ~ *kos* boarder; ~ *kucing* kitten; ~ *kuda* foal; ~ *kunci* key; ~ *laki-laki* son; ~ *mata* pupil; ~ *Medan* native of Medan; ~ *muda* young person, youth; ~ *panah* arrow; ~ *perempuan* daughter; ~ *perusahaan* subsidiary company; ~ *pinak* descendants, children and grandchildren; ~ *pungut* adopted child; ~ *rambut* small hairs at hairline, baby hairs; ~ *sapi* calf; ~ *singa* (lion) cub; ~ *semata wayang, ~ tunggal* only child; ~ *sulung* eldest child; ~ *sungai* tributary, creek; ~ *tangga* rung of a ladder; ~ *yatim* orphan; ~ *tiri* stepchild; **menganaktirikan** *vt* to treat as a second-class citizen; **anak-anak** *n, pl* children; **beranak** *vi* to have a child; (of animals) to give birth to, have offspring; *Ibu Tuti* ~ *lima* Tuti has five children; ~ *pinak vi* to have descendants; **peranakan** *n* uterus; *adj* of mixed Chinese and Indonesian blood, Straits Chinese; *masakan* ~ locally-influenced Chinese food → **kanak**

analisa, analisis *n* analysis; *analisis mengenai dampak lingkungan (amdal)* environmental impact study; **menganalisa, menganalisir, menganalisis** *vt* to analyze

anasir *n* element

ancam *v* to make a threat or threats; to

threaten; **ancaman** *n* threat; **mengancam** *vi* to make a threat; *vt* to threaten, intimidate; **terancam** *adj* threatened; *harimau Jawa* ~ *punah* the Javan tiger is threatened with extinction

anda, Anda *pron* you (neutral, without status, capitalized when used as reference); *untuk kenyamanan* ~ for your comfort

andai, andaikan, andaikata, andainya, seandainya *conj* if, supposing that; **berandai-andai** *vi* to speak hypothetically, imagine; **mengandaikan** *vt* to suppose, assume

andal *adj* reliable; **andalan** *n* mainstay, security; **mengandalkan** *vt* to rely on, trust

Andalas *n* Sumatra

andil *n* share, contribution

andong *n* four-wheeled horse-drawn carriage in Jogja and Solo

anéh *adj* strange, peculiar; *~nya* the strange thing is...; ~ *bin ajaib* wonder of wonders; **keanéhan** *n* peculiarity, oddity

anéka *adj* all kinds of, various; ~ *jenis* all sorts; ~ *macam,* ~ *ragam* varied; ~ *warna* various colors, multicolored; **beranéka** ~ *ragam* various; **keanékaragaman** *n* diversity; ~ *hayati* biological diversity

angan-angan *n* idea, thought, fantasy; **berangan-angan** *vi* to daydream, build castles in the air, fantasize

angdés *n* public minibus in rural areas ← **angkutan désa**

anggap, menganggap *vt* to consider, regard; ~ *enteng* to take lightly; *sudah dianggap saudara* to be considered part of the family; **anggapan** *n* point of view, opinion; **beranggapan** *vi* to be of the opinion

anggar *n* fencing (sport)

anggar: anggaran *n* budget, estimate; ~ *rumah tangga (ART)* by-laws, budgeted funds; ~ *Pendapatan dan Belanja Negara (APBN)* National (Revenues and Expenditures) Budget; **menganggarkan** *vt* to budget

anggota *n* member; ~ *badan* limb; ~ *DPR* Member of Parliament (MP); ~ *kehormatan* honorary member; ~ *keluarga* family member; **beranggota** *vi* to have members; **beranggotakan** *vi* to have a membership, have as members; *PKI dulu* ~ *jutaan orang* the PKI once had millions of members; **keanggotaan** *n* membership; *kartu* ~ membership card

anggrék *n* orchid

angguk, mengangguk *v* to nod; **menganggukkan** *vt* ~ *kepala* to nod your head

anggun *adj* elegant, stylish, graceful; **keanggunan** *n* grace, style

anggur *n* wine, grapes; ~ *merah* red grapes; red wine; ~ *putih* white wine; *buah* ~ grapes

anggur: menganggur *vi* to be unemployed, idle; **pengangguran** *n* unemployment, unemployed person; ~ *tersembunyi* hidden unemployment

angin *n* wind, breeze; ~ *mati* dead calm, doldrums; ~ *puyuh* whirlwind; ~ *ribut,* ~ *topan* cyclone, typhoon; ~ *semilir* zephyr; ~ *sepoi-sepoi* breeze, zephyr; *buang* ~ to pass wind; *coll* fart; *masuk* ~ to catch a cold, feel unwell; *mata* ~ point of the compass; *tambah* ~ to pump up a tire; ~ *puting beliung* whirlwind, willy-willy; *~nya sedang baik* *coll* to be in a good mood; *berada di atas* ~ to prosper, thrive; **menganginkan** *vt* to air (clothes, crackers)

angka *n* figure, numeral, digit; score, mark; ~ *ganjil* odd number; ~ *genap* even number; ~ *kelahiran* birth rate; ~ *kematian* death rate; ~ *Romawi* Roman numeral; ~ *sial* unlucky number

angkasa *n* space, sky; ~ *luar* outer space; *ruang* ~ space; **angkasawan** *n, m* **angkasawati** *n, f* astronaut

angkat *vt* to lift; ~ *berat,* ~ *besi* weightlifting; ~ *kaki* leave, go; ~ *koper* pack your bags, leave; ~ *tangan* give up; raise your hand; ~ *telepon* pick up, answer the phone; *orang tua* ~ adoptive parents; **angkatan** *n* generation, year level (at school or university); force; ~ *darat (AD)* army; ~ *laut (AL)* navy; ~ *udara (AU)* air force; **be-rangkat** *vi* to depart, leave; **keber-angkatan** *n* departure; *pintu* ~ departure gate; **memberangkatkan** *vt* to dispatch (a group); *rombongan ke Medan sudah diberangkatkan* the party to Medan has departed; **mengangkat** *vt* to lift or pick up, raise; appoint; to remove, amputate; *diangkat menjadi menteri* to be made a minister; ~ *alis* to raise your eyebrows; ~ *bahu* to shrug your shoulders; ~ *payudara* to remove a breast; **pengangkatan** *n* appointment (to a position)

angkat: perangkat *n* equipment, tool; **seperangkat** *n* set, suite

angker *adj* spooky, eerie, creepy

angkét *n* survey (form); *melakukan ~, mengadakan ~ vt* to do a survey

angklung *n* bamboo instrument, played in an orchestra

angkot *n, coll* public minibus ←
angkutan kota

angkuh *adj* arrogant, proud, conceited; **keangkuhan** *n* arrogance, rudeness

angkut *vt* to carry, lift, transport; **angkutan** *n* transport, transportation; ~ *darat* land transportation; ~ *kota (angkot)* city transportation; ~ *umum* public transport; **mengangkut** *vt* to transport; **pengangkut** *n* carrier; *kapal* ~ *minyak* oil tanker; **pengangkutan** *n* transporting, transportation; **terangkut** *adj* transported

anglo *n* small brazier

Angola *n* Angola; *orang* ~ Angolese

angpao, angpau *n* a red envelope containing money, given at Chinese New Year

angsa *n* goose

angsana *n* (Burmese) rosewood

angsur, mengangsur *vt* to pay in instalments; **angsuran** *n* instalment; **berangsur(-angsur)** *adv* gradually, little by little; *vi* to do little by little

angus → **hangus**

ani-ani *n* small knife for cutting rice stalks

aniaya: menganiaya *vt* to mistreat, oppress; **penganiayaan** *n* oppression, mistreatment; **teraniaya** *adj* oppressed, tyrannized

animis *adj* animist; **animisme** *n* animism

animo *n* interest, energy

anis *n* aniseed

anjak, beranjak *vi* to move, shift; ~ *dewasa vi* to become a young adult

anjing *n* dog (also insult); ~ *betina* bitch; ~ *galak* vicious dog; ~ *herder* German shepherd; ~ *pelacak* sniffer dog; ~ *pudel* poodle; ~ *ras, ~ trah* pure-breed (dog)

anjlok *vi* to derail, come off its rails; to collapse (of bridges, buildings); to fall drastically; *kereta api* ~ derailed train

anjung: anjungan *n* gallery, upper level (of a split-level house); ship's bridge; ~ *tunai mandiri (ATM)* automated teller machine (ATM)

anjur: anjuran *n* suggestion; **meng-anjurkan** *vt* to suggest, propose

anoa *n* dwarf buffalo of Sulawesi

anonim *adj* anonymous

antagonis *adj* antagonistic; *n* antagonist; *peran* ~ anti-hero, *sl* bad guy, baddie

antak: berantakan *adj* messy, in a mess

antah: berantah-antah *negeri* ~ never-never land

antan *n* (rice) pestle

antar *vt* **anter** *coll* take, escort; ~ *jemput* pick up and take home, door-to-door; ~ *pesan* delivery; **antaran** *n* things taken or carried; **mengantar** *vt* to take, escort, accompany; **mengantarkan** *vt* to take someone or something; **peng-antar** *kata* ~ preface, foreword

antar- *pref* between; **antarbagian** *adj* inter-departmental; **antarbangsa** *adj* international; **antarbenua** *adj* inter-continental; **antarbudaya** *adj* cross-cultural; **antarcabang** *adj* inter-branch, between branches; **antargo-longan** *adj* inter-group, between (ethnic) groups; **antarnegara** *adj* international; **antarpropinsi** *adj* inter-provincial

antara *conj* between; ~ *lain* among others; *di ~nya* among them; **perantara** *n* broker, intermediary, go-between

antarbagian *adj* inter-departmental
antarbangsa *adj* international
antarbenua *adj* inter-continental
antarbudaya *adj* cross-cultural
antarcabang *adj* inter-branch, between branches
antargolongan *adj* inter-group, between (ethnic) groups
antarnegara *adj* international
antarpropinsi *adj* inter-provincial
Antartika *n* Antarctica
antem: berantem *vi* to fight, scuffle ← **hantam**
anténa *n* antenna, aerial
anténg *adj, Jav* calm, quiet (of child)
antéro *n* whole, entire; **seantéro ~ dunia** across the entire world
anti-, anti *pref, adj* against, resistant to; **~ Barat** anti-Western; **~biotik** *adj, n* antibiotic; **~ peluru** bullet-proof; **~ perang** anti-war
antik *adj* quaint; *n* antique
anting *n* earring
antré, antri queue; **antréan** *n* queue; **mengantri** *vi* to queue; **pengantri** *n* person who queues
antologi *n* anthology
antonim *n* antonym
antropolog *n* anthropologist; **antropologi** *n* anthropology
antuk: mengantuk, terantuk-antuk *adj* sleepy; *vi* to be sleepy → **kantuk**
antusias *adj* enthusiastic; **antusiasme** *n* enthusiasm
anu um, er; *n* so-and-so, what's-its-name; *si Anu* So-and-So; *~nya sl* genitals
anugerah *n* gift, grace, blessing; **menganugerahi** *vt* to confer upon; **menganugerahkan** *vt* to confer something upon; **penganugerahan** *n* presentation of an award
anumerta *adj* posthumous
anut, menganut *vt* to follow; **penganut** *n* follower, believer; **~ agama Katolik** a Catholic
anyam, menganyam *vt* to weave, plait, braid; **anyaman** *n* plait, braid; *kursi ~* wicker chair
anyar *adj, Jav, Sd* new

anyelir *n* carnation
anyir *adj* fishy-smelling, rancid
apa *interrog, n* what; *conj, coll* or; *~nya* what part; *~ adanya* as it is, without any pretensions; *~ daya* what can you do?; *~ kabar?* how are you?; *~ lagi* what else; *~ namanya* whatsitsname, what's it called?; *~ saja* anything; *~ siapa* what and who; *~ boleh buat* it can't be helped; *macam ~?* what sort?; *hijau ~ biru?* green or blue?; *~ hendak dikata, ~ mau dikata* what can you say?; **apa-apa** *n* something; *bukan ~* nothing; *tidak ~* it doesn't matter; **apabila** *conj* if, when; **berapa** *interrog* how many? what number?; *adj, coll* several ← **beberapa**; *~ banyak?* how much? how many?; *~ harganya?* how much is it?; *umur ~?* how old?; *nomor telepon Adi ~?* what's Adi's phone number?; **beberapa** *adj* several, a number of; **keberapa** *interrog, coll* which number? which one?; **seberapa** *tidak ~* not many; *~ jauh* as far as; **mengapa** *interrog* why; *tak ~* it doesn't matter; **ngapain** *sl* why, do what; **siapa** *interrog, n* who; *~ saja* whoever; **siapa-siapa** *n* anybody; *bukan ~* nobody
apakah, apa (question marker); *~ Bapak ada di rumah?* is your master in? ← **apa**
apal → **hafal**
apalagi *adv, conj* especially, moreover
aparat *n* government official
apatis *adj* apathetic, indifferent
apartemén *n* apartment, flat
APBN *abbrev Anggaran Pendapatan dan Belanja Negara* National (Revenues and Expenditures) Budget
APDN *abbrev Akademi Pemerintahan Dalam Negeri* Academy of Public Administration, civil service academy
apek *adj* smelling musty, moldy
apel *n* apple; *~ Malang* Malang apples
apél call; assembly; *~ besar* rally; *~ nama* roll call; *vi, coll* to visit your girlfriend's house
api *n* fire, flame; *~ unggun* (camp) fire; *air ~* spirit, volatile liquid; *gunung ~* volcano; *kapal ~* steamship; *kembang ~* fireworks; *kereta ~* train, railway;

korek ~ match; **berapi** *vi* to produce fire; *gunung* ~ volcano; **berapi-api** *adj* fiery, fervent, spirited; **perapian** *n* fireplace, oven

apik *adj* neat, tidy

apit, mengapit *vt* to pinch, press, squeeze; to flank

apkiran *adj, coll* rejected, discarded

aplikasi *n* application

apokat → **alpukat**

apostrof *n* apostrophe

apoték, apotik *n* pharmacy, chemist (shop), dispensary; **apotéker** *n* pharmacist

aprésiasi *n* appreciation

April *bulan* ~ April

apung float; *batu* ~ pumice; **mengapung** *vi* to float, be suspended; **pengapung** *n* buoy, float; **terapung** *adj* drifting, floating

ara *n* fig tree

Arab *bahasa* ~ Arabic; *huruf* ~, *tulisan* ~ Arabic script; *Laut* ~ the Arabian Sea; *negeri* ~ Arabia; *orang* ~ an Arab; **kearab-araban** *adj* like an Arab

arah *n* direction; ~ *jarum jam* clockwise; ~ *kiri* to the left; *berbelok* ~ to change direction; *satu* ~ one way; same direction; **mengarah** *vi* to aim something towards; **mengarahkan** *vt* to direct; **pengarah** *n* director; **pengarahan** *n* direction, guidance, briefing; **searah** *adj* the same direction; **terarah** *adj* directed

arak *n* rice wine

arak: arak-arakan *n* procession

aral *bila tidak ada* ~ *melintang* if all goes well

arang *n* charcoal

arbéi *n, arch* strawberry

arca *n* statue

are *n* 100 square meters

aréal *n* area, acreage; ~ *parkir* car park, parking lot

arék *n, Jav* child, kid, son; ~ *Suroboyo* a Surabayan

arén *n* areca palm; *gula* ~ palm sugar

Argéntina *n* Argentina; *orang* ~ Argentinian; *daging sapi* ~ Argentine or Argentinian beef

arisan *n* (monthly) social gathering involving a lottery

argo, argométer *n* taxi meter; ~ *kuda* taxi meter showing an inflated tariff

arguméntasi *n* reasoning, argument; **berarguméntasi** *vi* to argue, reason

ari *kulit* ~ epidermis

ari-ari *n* placenta; *tali* ~ umbilical cord

arif *adj* wise, learned; **kearifan** *n* wisdom, learning

arit *n* sickle; *palu* ~ hammer and sickle

arkéolog *n* archeologist; **arkéologi** *n* archeology

arloji *n, arch* watch; fob watch, watch and chain

Arménia *n* Armenia; *bahasa* ~, *orang* ~ Armenian

arnal *n* hairpin

arogan *adj* arrogant; **arogansi** *n* arrogance

aroma *n* aroma, smell

arsip *n* archive, file; *gedung* ~ archives (building); **kearsipan** archives, archival

arsiték *n* architect; ~ *lanskap* landscape architect; **arsitéktur** *n* architecture

artéri *n* artery; *jalan* ~ arterial road

arti *n* meaning; ~*nya* it means, that is to say; *dalam* ~ in the sense; **berarti** *vi* to mean; *adj* meaningful; *tidak* ~ meaningless; **mengartikan** *vt* to define, interpret as; **pengartian** *n* understanding, interpretation → **erti**

artikel *n* article (in print media)

artis *n* celebrity; actor, actress or singer

arung ~ *jeram* white water rafting; **mengarungi** *vi* to cross water, wade, ford

arus *n* stream, current, flow; ~ *balik* flow back, feedback (esp of people returning back from their villages after Idul Fitri); ~ *bolak-balik* alternating current; ~ *listrik* electric current; ~ *mudik* flow of people going back to the village (usu at Idul Fitri); ~ *searah* direct current; *melawan* ~ *v* to go against the flow or tide

arwah *n* soul (of a dead person); *misa* ~ Requiem Mass

arwana *ikan* ~ kind of decorative fish

AS *abbrev Amerika Serikat* the United States

as *n* ace (in cards)

as *n* axle; axis

asa *n* hope; *putus* ~ lose hope, despair

asah sharpen; ~ *otak* brain sharpener, brainteaser; **mengasah** *vt* to sharpen, whet; **pengasah** ~ *agah pensil* pencil sharpener

asal *n* origin; ~*-muasal* root; ~*-usul* origins; **berasal** *vi* to come from

asal, asalkan *conj* as long as, providing that

asal-asalan *adv* carelessly, in any old way

asalkan *conj* as long as, providing that ← **asal**

asam, asem sour, tamarind; acid; ~ *belerang* sulfuric acid; ~ *cuka* acetic acid; ~ *garam* hydrochloric acid; ~ *jawa* tamarind; ~ *manis* sweet and sour; ~ *sendawa* nitric acid; *kurang* ~ rude, impolite; *muka* ~ sour look; **sayur asem** *n* sour vegetable soup

asap *n* smoke, exhaust, pollution; vapor; ~ *kabut (asbut)* smog; ~ *rokok* cigarette smoke; *daging* ~ smoked meat (usu beef); **berasap** *adj* smoky

asar *n, Isl* the afternoon prayer

asas, azas *n* foundation, principle, base; **berasas, berasaskan** *adj* based on; *vi* to have as a base; ~ *Pancasila* based on Pancasila; **asasi, asazi** *adj* basic; *hak* ~ *manusia (HAM)* human rights

asbak *n* ashtray

asbés *n* asbestos

asbun *adj* love to hear the sound of one's own voice ← **asal bunyi**

asbut *n* smog ← **asap kabut**

asésé, acc approved, agreed

asét *n* asset

ASI *abbrev air susu ibu* breast milk

Asia *n* Asia; *bahasa-bahasa* ~ Asian languages; *orang* ~ Asian; ~ *Tenggara* Southeast Asia

asin *adj* salty, salted; *ikan* ~ salted fish; **asinan** *n* sour vegetable and fruit dish; **mengasinkan** *vt* to salt, pickle

asing *adj* strange, alien, foreign; *orang* ~ stranger; foreigner; *bahasa* ~ foreign language; **mengasingkan** *vt* to

exile; **pengasingan** *n* exile; *tempat* ~ internment camp, exile

asistén *n* assistant; ~ *pribadi (aspri)* personal assistant, PA

Askés *n* (government) health insurance (scheme) ← **asuransi keséhatan**

asli *adj* original, indigenous; authentic, genuine; *orang* ~, *penduduk* ~ indigenous person, native; ~ *tapi palsu (aspal)* good imitation; ~*nya dari mana?* where do you come from?; **keaslian** *n* authenticity

asma *n* asthma

asma *n, Isl* ~*ul husna* the 99 names of God

asmara *n* romantic love, passion

aso, mengaso *vi* to take a rest, break

asoi, asoy *adj* hot, passionate; super, great fun

asong: asongan *n* street vendor; goods sold on the street (cigarettes, magazine, drinking water etc); *pedagang* ~ street vendor; **mengasong** *vt* to sell on the street

asosiasi *n* association

aspal *n* asphalt; *Pulau* ~ Buton; **beraspal** *adj* asphalted; *vi* to have a layer of asphalt; *jalan* ~ made or macadamized road; **mengaspal** *vt* to asphalt; **pengaspalan** *n* asphalting

aspal *coll* (good) imitation, fake ← **asli tapi palsu**

asparagus, aspersé *n* asparagus

aspék *n* aspect, point of view

aspirasi *n* aspiration

aspri *n* personal assistant, PA ← **asistén pribadi**

asrama *n* boarding house, dormitory; *mil* barracks

asri *adj* beautiful, scenic (of a view); **keasrian** *n* (natural) beauty

assalamualaikum, assalamu alaikum, salam alaikum *gr, Isl* peace be upon you (responded to with *wa alaikum salam*); ~ *warahmatullahi wabarakatuh (Wr Wb)* peace be upon you and may God bestow His mercy and blessing (in formal situations)

astaga, astaganaga *ejac* gosh, golly, gee whiz!

astagfirullah *ejac, Isl* God forbid
astronom *n* astronomer; **astronomi** *n* astronomy
asuh care; *orang tua* ~ foster parents; **asuhan** *n* upbringing; column in print media; **mengasuh** *vt* to care for; **pengasuh** *n* carer; ~ *anak* nursemaid, babysitter
asumsi *n* assumption
asuransi *n* insurance; ~ *jiwa* life insurance; ~ *kesehatan (Askes)* health insurance; **mengasuransikan** *vt* to insure
asusila *adj* amoral
asut → **hasut**
asyik *adj* fun; *adv* absorbed, engrossed; eager; ~ *membaca* busy reading; **keasyikan** *n* absorption; **mengasyikkan** *adj* fascinating, engrossing
atap *n* roof; ~ *genteng* tiled roof; **beratap** *adj* -roofed; *vi* to have a roof; ~ *rumbia* to have a thatched roof
atas *adj* upper, higher; *prep* up; *n* upper part; ~ *permintaan* on request; ~ *usul* on the suggestion of; *di* ~ on (top of), upon, above, over; upstairs; *di* ~ *jam 10* after 10 o'clock; ~ *nama* on behalf of; **mengatasnamakan** *vt* to do in the name of; *terdiri* ~ to consist of; **atasan** *n* superior, boss; **mengatasi** *vt* to overcome; **teratasi** *adj* able to be overcome
atasé *n* attaché; ~ *kebudayaan* cultural attaché
atau *conj* or
atéis *adj* atheist; **atéisme** *n* atheism
ati ampela *n* liver and gizzards
atlét, atlit *n* athlete; **atlétik** *cabang* ~ athletics
atmosfér *n* atmosphere (around Earth)
atol *n* atoll
atom *n* atom; *bom* ~ atomic bomb, atom bomb
atraksi *n* attraction, event
atribut *n* paraphernalia, decoration; attribute
atur arrange; **aturan** *n* rule, regulation; ~ *main* rules of the game; **mengatur** *v* to arrange, organize, regulate; **pengatur** *n* regulator; **peraturan** *n* rule, regulation; **teratur** *adj* organized, (at)

regular (intervals); **keteraturan** *n* order, regularity
AU, AURI *abbrev Angkatan Udara (Republik Indonesia)* (Indonesian) Air Force
audisi *n* audition
aula *n* hall (at school), auditorium
aum roar; **mengaum** *vi* to roar, growl (of tigers)
aur *n* kind of bamboo
aurat *n, Isl* part of body that should be covered (esp during prayer)
AURI *abbrev Angkatan Udara (Republik Indonesia)* (Indonesian) Air Force
aus *adj* eroded, worn
Australia *n* Australia; ~ *Barat* Western Australia; ~ *Selatan* South Australia; ~ *Utara* Northern Territory; *orang* ~ Australian
Austria *n* Austria; *orang* ~ Austrian
autis *adj* autistic; **autisme** *n* autism
autopsi → **otopsi**
avokad → **alpukat**
awak *n* person; ~ *kabin*, ~ *pesawat* cabin crew; ~ *kapal* (ship's) crew; **perawakan** *n* stature, build, figure; **berperawakan** *v* to have a build, stature
awal beginning, early; **awalan** *n* prefix; **berawal** *vi* to begin with; **mengawali** *vt* to start; to precede
awam *adj* common, lay; *orang* ~ layman
awan *n* cloud; **berawan** *adj* cloudy, overcast
awang-awang *n* heavens, atmosphere
awas *ejac* be careful, beware; ~ *ada anjing* beware of the dog; **mengawasi** *vi* to supervise; **pengawas** *badan* ~ supervisory board, trustees; **pengawasan** *n* supervision, control
awét *adj* durable, long-lasting; ~ *muda* youthful; **mengawétkan** *vt* to preserve (food); **pengawétan** *n* preservation
awur → **ngawur**
ayah, Ayah *n, pron* father; ~ *bunda* parents; **ayahanda** *pron, lit* Father (in letters)
ayak, mengayak *vt* to sieve, sift; **ayakan** *n* sieve
ayal *tak* ~ without a doubt; without delay
ayam *n* chicken, hen; ~ *betina hen;* ~ *bakar* baked chicken; ~ *berkokok*

rooster's crow; ~ *goreng* (traditional) fried chicken; ~ *jago,* ~ *jantan* rooster, cock; ~ *kampung* free-range chicken; ~ *mutiara* guinea-fowl; ~ *negeri* battery hen; ~ *panggang* barbecued chicken; ~ *pop* chicken dish from Padang; ~ *sabung* fighting cock; *anak* ~ chick; *dada* ~ chicken breast; *paha* ~ chicken leg; ~ *panggang* roast chicken

ayan *n* epilepsy

ayat *n* verse (of a religious text)

ayo come on, let's go; goodbye (esp on telephone)

ayom: mengayomi *vt* to protect, care for, look after; **pengayom** *n* protector, carer; **pengayoman** *n* protection

ayu *adj* beautiful; *pagar* ~ girl attendants at a wedding reception

ayun sway; **ayunan** *n* swings; *main* ~ play on the swings; **berayun** *vi* to sway, rock; **mengayun** *vt* to rock, swing, sway; **mengayunkan** *v* to rock

azab *n* torture

azan, adzan *n* call to prayer

azas → **asas**

Azerbaijan *n* Azerbaijan; *orang* ~ Azerbaijani; Azeri

B

b [bé] second letter of the alphabet

ba *excl* boo!; *ci luk* ~ peekaboo!; *tanpa ~-bi-bu* without saying anything, without a word

bab *n* chapter

babad *n* chronicle; ~ *Tanah Jawa* the Chronicles of Java

babak *n* round (in sport); half (in football); phase, stage; ~ *final* final (match); ~ *pertama* first half

babak ~ *belur* (beaten) black-and-blue

babar: membabarkan *vt* to lay out; to explain; *Pak Ditya* ~ *rencana jangka panjang perusahaan* Ditya explained the company's long-term plans; **terbabar** *adj* spread out; explained

babat *n* a kind of meat (from the stomach); *soto* ~ a soup using this meat

babat *wingko* ~ small coconut slice, a specialty of Semarang

babat: membabat *vt* to cut or chop down, clear away; **pembabatan** *n* felling, chopping; ~ *hutan* (unregulated) deforestation

babé *n, sl* boss, Big Daddy

Babel *abbrev Bangka-Belitung* a group of islands in Riau province

babi *n* pig, boar; *derog* swine; ~ *hutan* wild boar; *daging* ~ pork; **membabi** ~ *buta vi* to act blindly and rashly; *anak* ~ piglet

baca *v* to read; **bacaan** *n* reading material; **membaca** *v* to read; ~ *bibir* to lip-read; ~ *cepat* to skim; ~ *dalam hati* to read silently to yourself; ~ *doa* to say a prayer; ~ *dengan suara keras* to read out loud; **membacakan** *vt* to read something to someone; *sebaiknya orang tua* ~ *buku kepada anaknya* parents should read books to their children; **pembaca** *n* reader; **pembacaan** *n* (act of) reading aloud; *tidak ada yang bicara selama* ~ *doa* nobody spoke when the prayers were being said; **terbaca** *adj* legible, able to be read

bacang *n* Chinese delicacy made from sticky rice and meat

bacem *adj* soaked, marinated; *tempe* ~ sweet tempe

bacok, membacok *vt* to hack, chop, slash (with something hard); *korban pembunuhan diikat lalu dibacok* the murder victim had been tied up and then hacked to death

badai *n* hurricane, cyclone; storm; ~ *topan* typhoon; ~ *tropis* tropical cyclone

badak *n* rhino, rhinoceros; ~ *air* hippo, hippopotamus; ~ *bercula satu* one-horned rhino; *berkulit* ~ thick-skinned

badan *n* body, agency; board, committee; ~ *amal* charitable institution; ~ *pengawas* supervisory board, trustees; *gerak* ~ physical exercise; ~ *Intelijen Negara (BIN)* State Intelligence Agency; ~ *Keamanan Rakyat (BKR)* People's Security Agency (after independence; later became Indonesian

Army); ~ *Resérse Kriminal (Bareskrim)* Criminal Investigation Agency, crime squad; ~ *Urusan Logistik (Bulog)* Logistics Management Board; ~ *Koordinasi Survéi dan Pemetaan Nasional (Bakosurtanal)* National Co-ordinating Agency for Surveying and Mapping; ~ *Pengkajian dan Penerapan Teknologi (BPPT)* Agency for the Research and Application of Technology; ~ *Penyehatan Perbankan Nasional (BPPN) arch* Indonesian Bank Restructuring Agency (IBRA): ~ *Perencanaan Pembangunan Daerah (Bappeda)* Regional Development Planning Agency; ~ *Perencanaan Pembangunan Nasional (Bappenas)* National Development Planning Agency; ~ *Réhabilitasi dan Rékonstruksi Nanggroe Aceh Darussalam (BRR)* Aceh Rehabilitation and Reconstruction Agency (post-tsunami); ~ *Tenaga Atom Nasional (Batan)* National Atomic Energy Agency; ~ *Usaha Milik Negara (BUMN)* state-owned corporation; **berbadan** *vi* to have a body; ~ *dua* to be pregnant

badik *n* small dagger

badkip *n, coll* bathtub

Badui, Baduy *orang* ~ a Sundanese sub-ethnic group

badut *n* clown; *pesta Safira lengkap dengan kue tar dan* ~ there was both cake and a clown at Safira's party

bagai *conj* like, as; ~ *bumi dan langit* as different as night is from day; **berbagai** *adj* various, several; **sebagai** *conj* like, as; *dan ~nya* and so on; **bagaikan** *conj* as (if), though; **bagaimana** *interrog, conj* how, in what way; **sebagaimana** *conj* in such a way that, in that way

bagan *n* blueprint, chart; *nama Made tidak masuk* ~ *organisasi* Made's name was not on the organizational chart

bagan *n* fishing platform

bagasi *n* baggage; boot (of vehicle); hold (of ship or aircraft); ~ *kabin* cabin luggage

bagi *v* divide; **bagian** *n* part, share, section; *mengambil* ~ to take part,

participate; **berbagi** *vi* to share; ~ *hasil adj* profit-sharing; *v* to share profits; **kebagian** *v* to get a share; **membagi** *vt* to divide, distribute; ~ *rapot* to hand out (school) reports; ~ *rata vt* to divide evenly; **membagi-bagi** *vt* to split up; **pembagian** *n* distribution, division; **sebagian** *n* some, a section of

bagi *prep* for; ~ *saya* as for me

baginda *pron, m* His Majesty; *f* Her Majesty

bagus *adj* good, fine, excellent (external qualities of concrete objects); *pagar* ~ boy attendants at a wedding reception; *buku ini* ~ *sekali* this is a very good book; ~*nya!* isn't it lovely?

bah *n* flood; *air* ~ flood

bahagia *adj* happy, joyous; **berbahagia** *vi* to be happy; *Selamat* ~ Congratulations (at a wedding); **kebahagiaan** *n* happiness; **membahagiakan** *vt* to make happy; *suami-isteri harus saling* ~ couples must work to make each other happy

bahak: berbahak-bahak *vi* to roar with laughter; *Kun tertawa* ~ *melihat kelakuan anjing itu* Kun laughed her head off, watching the dog's antics

bahan *n* material, ingredients; cloth, fabric; ~ *bakar* fuel; ~ *bangunan* building materials; ~ *diskusi* topic for discussion; ~ *kimia* chemical; ~ *mentah* raw material; ~ *peledak* explosive; ~ *pelekat* adhesive; ~ *pengajaran* teaching/study materials; ~ *bakar minyak (BBM)* fuel oil; *aku mau cari* ~ *untuk seragam sekolah* I want to get some material for a school uniform

bahari *adj* maritime; *Musium* ~ Maritime Museum

bahas *vi* to discuss; **bahasan** *n* discussion, review; **membahas** *vt* to discuss, debate; **pembahasan** *n* discussion, debate; ~ *undang-undang baru berlanjut sampai larut malam* the discussion of the new laws went late into the night

bahasa *n* language; ~ *asing* foreign language; ~ *baku* standard language; ~ *Mandarin, coll* ~ *Cina* Chinese;

Mandarin; ~ *daerah* regional language; ~ *gado-gado* mixture of Indonesian and another language; ~ *halus* refined language; speech level in some regional languages; ~ *ibu* mother tongue; *Bahasa Indonesia* Indonesian; ~ *Inggris* English; ~ *isyarat* sign language; ~ *Kamboja* Khmer; ~ *Kawi* Old Javanese; ~ *Pali* ancient language of Buddhist scriptures; ~ *pengantar* medium (of instruction); ~ *percakapan, ~ sehari-hari* colloquial or everyday language; ~ *prokem* Jakarta teen slang; ~ *Sansekerta, ~ Sanskerta* Sanskrit; ~ *serumpun* language related to Indonesian (such as Malay and Tagalog); ~ *tarzan* gestures; ~ *tubuh* body language; ~ *Yahudi* Yiddish; *ilmu* ~ linguistics; *juru* ~ interpreter (oral), translator (written); *tata* ~ grammar; **berbahasa** *vi* to (be able to) speak or use a language; *Nenek hanya ~ Jawa* Grandma only speaks Javanese; **kebahasaan** *adj* language, linguistic; **peribahasa** *n* proverb, idiom

bahasan *n* discussion, review ← **bahas**

bahaya *n* danger; *tanda* ~ warning signal, siren; *waspadai ~ narkoba* beware of the dangers of drugs; **berbahaya** *vi* to be dangerous; *adj* dangerous; **membahayakan** *vt* to endanger, jeopardize; *adj* dangerous; *tindakan Ridwan menculik anak-anak itu sangat ~ nyawa mereka* Ridwan put those children's lives in great danger when he kidnapped them

bahénol *adj* shapely; *banyak penyanyi dangdut yang ~ tapi tidak bisa bernyanyi* lots of *dangdut* singers are sexy, but can't sing

bahkan *conj* moreover; on the contrary; indeed, even; *Nanda tidak bisa telepon, ~ dia tidak sanggup berbicara saat itu* Nanda couldn't even speak, let alone ring at that time

bahtera *n* ark

bahu *n* shoulder; ~ *jalan* hard shoulder; **bahu-membahu** *adv* shoulder to shoulder; *vi* to help each other; **sebahu** *adj* shoulder-length

bahwa *conj* **bahwasanya** *lit* that; *Saya tahu ~ itu tidak benar* I know that it's not true

baik *adj* good, fine, well, OK (ie. internal qualities of abstract objects); **baik-baik** *adj* fine; respectable; ~ *hati* kind; *Apa kabar?/~ saja* How are you?/Fine; ~ ... *maupun* ..., ~ ... ~ ... (spoken) both ... and ...; **kebaikan** *n* goodness, kindness; **membaik** *vi* to improve; **memperbaiki** *vt* to repair, fix; **perbaikan** *n* repair, improvement; **sebaiknya** *adv* preferably, it's best if; **terbaik** *adj* the best

bait *n* couplet; *Amir membaca beberapa ~ dari syairnya* Amir read several lines from his poem

baja *n* steel

bajaj *n* [bajai] three-wheeled motorized form of transport in Jakarta

bajak *n* plow; **membajak** *vt* to plow

bajak *laut* pirate; **membajak** *vt* to hijack; to copy illegally; ~ *pesawat* to hijack a plane; **bajakan** *adj* pirated; *CD* ~ pirated CD; **pembajakan** *n* hijacking; piracy

bajigur *n* warm night drink containing coffee and coconut milk

bajing *n* squirrel; **bajingan** *n, sl, derog* bastard!

baju *n, inf* clothes; clothing for the upper body; ~ *bodo* women's tunic in South Sulawesi; ~ *dalam* singlet; underwear; ~ *gamis* long Arab-style shirt; ~ *hamil* maternity wear; ~ *ketat* tight clothes; ~ *kurung* women's long tunic worn in Malay areas; ~ *loreng* camouflage gear; *sl* cammo; ~ *Muslim* Islamic dress; ~ *pelampung* lifejacket; ~ *pengantin* wedding dress or costume; ~ *polos* plain shirt; ~ *renang* swimming costume, swimsuit; ~ *salin* change of clothes; ~ *selam* diving suit; ~ *senam* leotard; **berbaju** *vi* to put on, wear clothes

bak *n* tub, basin, box, container; ~ *mandi* large tank in the bathroom from which water is taken; ~ *pasir* sand box; ~ *sampah* rubbish bin, garbage can, trash can; dumpster

bak *conj, lit* like, as; *~ seorang putri raja* like a princess

baka *adj* eternal, everlasting; *alam ~* the hereafter

bakal *adj* future, potential; will; *apa yang ~ terjadi?* what's going to happen?

bakar burn; *kayu ~* firewood; *luka ~* burn; **kebakaran** *n* fire; *~ hutan* forest fire, bushfire; *~ jenggot* to lose your head, be unable to cope; *ada ~!* fire!; **membakar** *vt* to burn; **pembakaran** *n* burning, combustion; **terbakar** *adj* burnt; *kulit Bapak ~ oleh sinar matahari* Father was sunburnt

bakat *n* talent, gift; *~ nyanyi* a talent for singing; **berbakat** *adj* talented, gifted; *vi* to have a talent

bakau *n* mangrove

baki *n* tray (for food)

bakiak *n* wooden sandals

bakmi, bami *n* Chinese noodles

Bakosurtanal *abbrev* National Co-ordinating Agency for Surveying and Mapping ← **Badan Koordinasi Survéi dan Pemetaan Nasional**

bakpao *n* steamed white bread with filling of nuts or chicken

bakpia *n* sweet cake from Jogja with nutty filling

bakso, baso *n* meatball; meatball soup; *~ tahu* meatballs and tofu (specialty of Bandung)

baktéri *n* bacteria

bakti *n* service, devotion; *kerja ~* volunteer work; **berbakti** *vi* to serve, devote oneself to; **kebaktian** *n* (Protestant) service

baku *adj* standard; *harga ~* standard price; **membakukan** *vt* to standardize, make standard

baku *pron* each (other); *~ hantam* hit each other, come to blows

bakul *n* basket hung on a pole for selling goods; *f* vendor

bakwan *n* corn fritter, a specialty of Malang

bala *n, arch* army; *~ Keselamatan* Salvation Army; *~tentara* army

balai *n* house, building, office; *~ desa* village hall, village administrative building; *~ kota* town hall; *~ Sidang (Jakarta)* Jakarta Convention Centre (JCC); *~ lelang* auction hall; **balai-balai** *n* traditional sofa, bamboo bed

balairung *n* (royal) reception room, where the king meets his people

balak: pembalakan *n* logging; *~ liar* illegal logging

balap race; **balapan** *n* race; *~ mobil* car race; **membalap** *vi* to race

balas reply; *~ dendam* take revenge; **balasan** reply, answer; **berbalas** *vi* **membalas** *vt* to reply, respond

bale-bale *n* traditional sofa, bamboo bed → **balai**

balét *n* ballet; **pebalét** *n* ballet dancer, *f* ballerina

Bali *n pulau ~* Bali; *bahasa ~, orang ~* Balinese

balig, baligh *akil ~* of age, ready to take on religious obligations, etc

baliho *n* billboard, huge advertisement

balik *v* to return, reverse, retreat; *~ nama* transfer of ownership; *n* back, flipside; return; *bolak-~ adv* back and forth, to and fro, there and back; *di ~* behind; **berbalik** *vi* to turn around, return; **membalik** *vt* to return, reverse, turn over; **membalikkan** *vt* to turn something over; **sebaliknya** *conj* on the contrary; **terbalik** *adj* overturned, upside-down, opposite

baling-baling *n* propeller

balita *n, coll (anak) ~* toddler ← **bawah lima tahun**

balkon *n* balcony, gallery

balok *n* beam, crossbeam (of a building); *~ not* (musical) staff, note

balon *n* balloon

balur smear with oil; massage; **membalur** *vt* to smear or massage with oil

balut *n* bandage; **membalut** *vt* to bandage; **pembalut** *n* (sanitary) pad

bambu *n* bamboo; *~ runcing* bamboo spear

ban *n* tire; *~ cubles* tubeless tire; *~ gundul* bald tire; *~ kempes* flat tire; *~ serep* spare tire; *coll* replacement person

banci *n* transvestite, cross-dressing male, often a prostitute; eunuch; *derog* male homosexual

balon *n* proposed candidate (for an election) ← **bakal calon**

bandang *banjir* ~ flash flood

bandar *n* (sea)port; ~ *udara* → **bandara**

bandar *n* dealer (often in drugs), croupier

bandara *n* airport ← **bandar udara**

bandel *adj* naughty, disobedient (usually of children); **membandel** *vi* to do something naughty, be disobedient

bandeng *ikan* ~ milkfish, a specialty of the north coast of Java

banding *tiada* ~, *tidak ada* ~ unequalled, incomparable; **dibandingkan** *v* to be compared with; **membandingkan** *vt* to compare something; **perbandingan** *n* comparison, ratio; **sebanding** *adj* comparable, proportionate, balanced

banding *naik* ~ to appeal against a court decision

bando *n* ribbon, scarf or Alice band worn in the hair by girls, from ear to ear

bandrék *n* ginger drink

bandul *n* pendulum

bang *pron* older brother (in Jakarta or Malay areas) → **abang**

bang → **bank**

bangau *n* heron

banget *adj, sl* very, excessively; **kebangetan** *adj, coll* too much, excessive (of behavior or a situation)

bangga *adj* proud; **berbangga** *vi* to be proud; **kebanggaan** *n* pride; something of which you are proud; **membanggakan** *vt* to make proud, please

bangjo *n, Jav (lampu)* ~ traffic light, red light ← **abang ijo**

bangkai *n* carcass (usually of animals); *bunga* ~ the Rafflesia flower

bangkang: membangkang *vi* to defy, resist, disobey; **pembangkang** *n* someone who defies; **pembangkangan** *n* act of defiance

bangkit, berbangkit *vi* to rise, get up; **kebangkitan** *n* rise, awakening; *Partai* ~ *Bangsa (PKB)* Party of National Awakening; **membangkit** *vt* to arouse, stimulate; **membangkitkan** *vt* to resurrect; **pembangkit** ~ *listrik* power station; ~ *listrik tenaga air (PLTA)* hydroelectric power station; ~ *Listrik*

Tenaga Nuklir (PLTN) nuclear power station

bangkrut *adj* bankrupt; **kebangkrutan** *n* bankruptcy

bangku *n* bench (for sitting); stool; desk; ~ *kelas* school bench

bangsa *n* people, nation, race; ~ *Indonesia* the Indonesian people; *Perserikatan* ~~ *(PBB)* the United Nations (UN); *sl* category; **berbangsa** *vi* to have a nationality; **kebangsaan** *adj* national; *lagu* ~ national anthem; **bangsawan** *n* aristocrat, member of royalty

bangsal *n* ward (in hospital), dormitory; shed

bangsat *n* flea; (term of abuse) scoundrel

bangsawan *n* aristocrat, member of royalty

bangun *vi* get up, wake up; **membangunkan** *vt* to (intentionally) wake someone up; **terbangun** *adj* woken up (of your own accord)

bangun: bangunan *n* building; ~ *bersejarah*, ~ *kuno* historic building; **membangun** *vt* to build or create; **pembangunan** *n* development

banjir *n* flood; ~ *bandang* flash flood; **kebanjiran** *adj* flooded, inundated; **membanjiri** *vt* to flood, inundate

bank *n* bank; ~ *Dunia* (the) World Bank; ~ *negara* state-owned bank; ~ *Central Asia (BCA)* Asian Central Bank; ~ *Negara Indonesia (BNI)* Indonesian State Bank; ~ *Rakyat Indonesia (BRI)* Indonesian People's Bank; ~ *Tabungan Negara (BTN)* State Savings Bank; **perbankan** *adj* banking; *dunia* ~ the banking world; **bankir** *n* banker

bantah, membantah *vt* to deny, dispute

bantai, membantai *vt* to slaughter, kill viciously; **pembantaian** *n* slaughter, mass killings

bantal *n* cushion; pillow; ~ *guling* bolster, Dutch wife (long cushion to hold when sleeping); *salah* ~ have a sore neck from an uncomfortable sleeping position

bantar: bantaran *n* levee

banténg *n* (Javan) ox

banting throw down, slam; ~ *harga* cut

prices; ~ *stir* change direction; **membanting** *vt* to throw down (with a bang); ~ *pintu* to slam the door; ~ *tulang* to toil, work yourself to the bone

bantu *v* to help; **bantuan** *n* assistance, help, aid; ~ *dana* financial assistance; **membantu** *vt* to help (someone); **pembantu** *n* servant, maid; assistant; ~ *dekan* assistant dean; ~ *rektor* assistant vice-chancellor; *kantor* ~ (larger) branch office; ~ *rumah tangga (PRT)* domestic help, household servant

banyak *adj* many, much; *orang* ~ the public; **kebanyakan** *n, adj* too much; most; ~ *orang tidak setuju* most people don't agree; **memperbanyak** *vt* to increase, multiply; **terbanyak** *adj* most; *suara* ~ majority

banyol *adj* funny, silly; **banyolan** *n* joke, joking; **membanyol** *vi* to joke

Bapa *pron* Father (title for own father or respected older man), also *Bapak*; *Chr* God, Father, Lord; ~ *Suci* Holy Father

bapa *n* father; ~ *permandian* godfather

Bapak *pron* Father (title for own father or respected older man); ~ *Pembangunan* Father of Development (used by Soeharto)

bapak *n* father; ~ *angkat* adopted father; ~ *permandian* godfather; ~ *tiri* stepfather; *ibu* ~ parents; **kebapakan** *adj* fatherly; **bapakisme** *n* paternalism

Bappeda *abbrev Badan Perencanaan Pembangunan Daerah* Regional Development Planning Agency

Bappenas *abbrev Badan Perencanaan Pembangunan Nasional* National Development Planning Agency

baptis *adj* baptist; **membaptis** *vt* to baptize, christen

bara *n* embers; *batu* ~ coal; **membara** *vi* to glow with heat

barak *n* barracks

barang *n* goods, things; ~ *bergerak* moveable property; ~ *berharga* valuable items; ~ *bukti* evidence, exhibit; ~ *cetak* printed material; ~ *gelap* contraband, illegal goods; ~ *jadi* finished product, ready-made goods; ~ *mewah* luxury items or goods; ~ *sitaan* confiscated goods; *daftar* ~ inventory

barang *adj* some (indicating uncertainty); **barangkali** *conj* perhaps, maybe; **barangsiapa** *pron* whoever, whosoever; **sembarang** *adj* any, whichever; **sembarangan** *adv* arbitrarily, at random

Barat *n* the West; **barat** *adj* west; ~ *daya* southwest; ~ *laut* northwest; *dunia* ~ the western world; **kebarat-baratan** *adj* Westernized

Barélang *Batam, Rempang, Galang* group of islands in Riau Archipelago province

bareng *conj, sl* with; *v* to go together; *dia* ~ *sama Dini* she's coming with Dini; **berbarengan** *adj* together, at the same time; **membarengi** *vt* to accompany (someone)

baréskrim Criminal Investigation Agency, crime squad ← **Badan Resérse Kriminal**

barét *n* beret; ~ *Merah* the Red Berets (nickname for Kopassus troops)

barikade *n* barricade

baring: berbaring *vi* to lie down; **membaringkan** *vt* to lay something down in rows; **terbaring** *adj* stretched out, lying down

baris *n* line, row, rank; **barisan** *n* line; forces; ~ *depan* frontline; *Bukit* ~ mountain range in Sumatra; **berbaris** *vi* to line up

barongsai *n* Chinese dragon for dance performances

barter *n, v* barter, trade

baru *adj* new, recent; modern; just, only; ~ *saja* just now; ~~ *ini* just the other day; *orang* ~ newcomer; **memperbarui** *vt* to renew, make new; **pembaruan** *n* renewal; **terbaru** *adj* latest, newest; **barusan** *adv, sl* just now

basa *n* alkali, base

basa: basa-basi *n* good manners, politeness; platitudes

basah *adj* wet, moist, soaked; ~ *kuyup* soaking wet; *tisu* ~ wet towel, wipe; **membasahi** *vt* to moisten, wet

basi *adj* off, rotten, inedible (of food);

sudah ~ *sl* outdated, not funny any more

baskét *bola* ~ basketball

baskom *n* washbasin; large bowl for washing dishes, vegetables etc

basmi destroy; **membasmi** *vt* to exterminate, destroy, wipe out; **pembasmi** ~ *rayap* termite exterminator; **pembasmian** *n* extermination, destruction, eradication

basuh, membasuh *vt* to wash with water; ~ *wajah* to wash the face

bata *batu* ~ brick

bata-bata: terbata-bata *adv* in a broken fashion, not fluently

batagor *n* fried tofu and meatballs, a specialty of Bandung ← **bakso tahu goréng**

Batak *adj* ethnic group of North Sumatra; *bahasa* ~, *orang* ~ Batak

batako *n* concrete brick

batal *adj* cancelled; *vi* not take place; break (a fast); **membatalkan** *vt* to cancel, repeal; ~ *puasa* to break your fast (esp intentionally); **pembatalan** *n* cancellation, annulment

batalyon, batalion *n* battalion

Batan *abbrev Badan Tenaga Atom Nasional* National Atomic Energy Agency

batang *n* trunk, stem, stick (of a tree); shaft; handle; penis; counter for long cylindrical objects; ~ *pohon* tree trunk; ~ *sungai* tributary; *sebatang* ~ *kara* alone in the world; *minta rokok tiga* ~ I'd like three cigarettes

batas *n* limit, border; ~ *kesabaran* limit of your patience; ~ *kota* city limits; **berbatas** *vi* to have a boundary; *tak* ~ limitless; **berbatasan** *vi* to be adjacent to; **membatasi** *vt* to limit, restrict, curb something; **pembatas** *n* divider; ~ *buku* bookmark; **pembatasan** *n* restriction; **perbatasan** *n* border, frontier; **terbatas** *adj* limited; *perseroan* ~ *(PT)* proprietary limited; **keterbatasan** *n* limitation

baterai *n* battery

bathin → **batin**

batik *n* application of wax onto fabric

to create a pattern after dyeing; fabric or clothes with designs produced in this manner; fabric or clothes resembling batik but with printed designs; ~ *cap* stamped batik; ~ *modern* batik produced with chemicals instead of wax; ~ *pesisir* batik from the north coast of Java; ~ *tulis* handmade batik; ~ *Yogya* Jogja-style batik; **membatik** *v* to apply wax onto fabric

batin, bathin *adj, n* inner, spiritual; soul, spirit; *(mohon) maaf lahir* ~ to ask forgiveness for all sins (at Idul Fitri); **kebatinan** *n* mysticism; **membatin** *vi* to say to yourself

batok *n* shell, skull; ~ *kelapa* coconut shell; ~ *kepala* skull

batu *n* stone; ~ *ambar* amber; ~ *apung* pumice; ~ *arang* charcoal; ~ *bara* coal; ~ *bata* brick; ~ *empedu* gallstones; ~ *gamping*, ~ *kapur* limestone; ~ *ginjal* kidney stone; ~ *giok* jade; ~ *karang* coral reef; ~ *kecubung* ruby; ~ *loncatan* stepping-stone, springboard; ~ *mulia* precious stone, gem; ~ *pasir* sandstone; ~ *pualam* marble; ~ *safir* sapphire; ~ *sandungan* stumbling block; ~ *tulis* slate; inscription; *gula* ~ lump of sugar; *kepala* ~ obstinate, stubborn; **berbatu** *adj* rocky, stony; **membatu** *vi* to freeze, become petrified, fossilized

batuk *vi* cough; ~ *berdahak* chesty cough; ~ *darah* to cough up blood; ~ *rejan* whooping cough

bau *n, vi, adj* smell, smelly; ~ *amis* fishy smell; ~ *badan (BB)* body odor (BO); ~ *busuk* bad smell; ~ *gosong* burnt smell; ~ *kencur* still young; ~ *pesing* stink of urine; **berbau** *vi* to smell, have connotations of

baur *campur* ~ mixed up; **berbaur, membaur** *vi* to integrate, mix with society; **pembauran** *n* integration, mixing of different ethnic groups

baut *n* bolt

bawa *vi* to take, bring, carry; to conduct; ~ *diri* to conduct yourself; **bawaan** *adj* carried or inherited; *penyakit* ~ hereditary disease; **membawa** *vt* to take, bring, carry; to conduct; ~ *diri* to conduct yourself; **membawakan** *vt* to bring or carry for someone; to sing; *dia ~ lagu-lagu keroncong* she performed *keroncong* songs; **pembawa** *n* bearer, carrier; *~ acara* host, MC; **pembawaan** *n* temperament, nature; **terbawa** *adj* (accidentally) taken away; *~ arus* swept away in the current

bawah *prep* below; *~ angin* leeward; *~ sadar* subconscious; *di ~* below, under; *di ~ tangan* underhand, privately; *di ~ umur* underage; *yang bertanda tangan di ~ ini* the undersigned; **bawahan** *n* inferior, assistant; **membawahi** *vt* to head a section (with staff under you)

bawal *ikan ~* pomfret

bawang *n* onion; *~ bombai* (brown) onion; *~ merah* red onion, shallot; *~ putih* garlic; *anak ~* a nobody; *daun ~* spring onion; leek

bawel *adj, coll* fault-finding, complaining

baya *n* age; *setengah ~* middle-aged; **sebaya** *adj* the same age

bayam, bayem *n* spinach

bayang *n* shadow, image; **bayangan** *n* shadow; **membayangi** *vt* to overshadow; **terbayang** *adj* imagined, conceivable

bayar *v* to pay; **bayaran** *adj* paid, hired; *pembunuh ~* hired assassin; **membayar** *vt* to pay (for); *~ di muka* to pay in advance; **pembayaran** *n* payment; *tanda ~ yang sah* legal currency

bayi *n* baby; *~ tabung* test-tube baby; *toko ~* shop selling baby needs

bayonét *n* bayonet; **membayonét** *vt* to stab someone with a bayonet

bayu *n, lit* wind; *tenaga ~* wind power

bazar *n* bazaar

BB *abbrev bau badan* body odor (BO)

BBM *abbrev bahan bakar minyak* fuel oil

BCA *abbrev Bank Central Asia* Asian Central Bank

bé b, second letter of the alphabet

béa *n* tax, duty, excise; *~ cukai* customs; *~ masuk* import duty; **béasiswa** *n* scholarship, bursary

beban *n* burden, load; responsibility; **membebani** *vt* to burden someone

with something; **membebankan** *vt* to charge something to someone

bébas *adj* free; *~ banjir* safe from floods; **kebébasan** *n* freedom; **membébaskan** *vt* to exempt, liberate, free someone; **pembébasan** *n* liberation, release, exemption

bébék *n* duck; **membébék** *v* to quack; to follow blindly

bébér: membébérkan *vt* to reveal, explain; to unfold

beberapa *adj* several, a number of ← **apa, berapa**

bebuyutan *adj* ancestral; arch enemy; *musuh ~* arch enemy ← **buyut**

bécak *n* pedicab, rickshaw tricycle; *tukang ~* pedicab driver

bécék *adj* muddy, wet

becus *tak ~* incapable, incompetent

béda *adj* different; *~nya ...* the difference is, ...; **berbéda** *adj* different; **membédakan** *vt* to discriminate, differentiate between, consider different; **pembédaan** *n* discrimination, differential treatment; **perbédaan** *n* difference

bedah *n* surgery; *~ buku* book discussion; *~ mayat* autopsy; *~ plastik* plastic or cosmetic surgery; *ahli ~* surgeon; **membedah** *vt* to operate on; **pembedahan** *n* operation

bedak *n* powder

bedil *n* rifle

bedong *n* bunny rug (for babies)

bedug, beduk *n* big drum, especially in a mosque; *menunggu ~* to wait for the drum indicating the end of fasting at sunset

begadang *vi* to stay up all night; to sleep late

begawan *n* expert, guru

begini *adv* like this, in this manner ← **ini**

begitu *adv* like that, in that manner; *adv* so; *conj* as soon as; *~lah* that's how it is ← **itu**

bégo *excl, adj, sl* idiot; stupid

béha *n* bra; *tali ~* bra strap

bejana *n* vessel, container

bejat *adj* depraved, filthy; *perbuatan ~* sexual crime

bekal *n* provisions; supply, stock; something for future use; **berbekal** *vi* to carry provisions (consisting of); **membekali** *vt* to supply someone with provisions; **pembekalan** *n* supply

bekantan *n* proboscis monkey

bekas *adj* used, old, former; ~ *cacar* pock-mark; ~ *luka* scar; ~ *pacar* ex-boyfriend or ex-girlfriend; ~ *pakai* used; *barang* ~ second-hand goods; **berbekas** *vi* to show; *kekecewaannya tidak ~ pada sikapnya* his disappointment did not show in his attitude; **membekas** *vi* to leave an impression; *nasihat itu sangat ~ di hatinya* the advice left a deep impression on him

békel *n* (game of) jacks

bekén *adj, sl* famous, well-known

bekerja *vi* to work; ~ *sama* to co-operate, work together ← **kerja**

bekicot *n* type of edible snail

bekléding *n* upholstery (usu of seats in vehicles)

beku *adj* frozen; **membeku** *vi* to freeze; **membekukan** *vt* to freeze something; **pembekuan** *n* freezing; ~ *aset* freezing of assets

bekuk, membekuk *vt* to arrest; **pembekukan** *n* arrest

bél *n* bell; **mengebél** *vt, coll* to ring, telephone

béla *vt* defend; ~ *diri* self-defense; **membéla** *vt* to defend; **pembéla** *n* defender; ~ *Tanah Air* defender of the homeland; **pembélaan** *n* defense

belacan *n* shrimp paste

belah *n* crack, fissure; *vi* crack, split, divide, splinter; ~ *ketupat* rhombus; ~ *pecah* crockery, breakable household goods; *seperti pinang di~ dua* like two peas in a pod; **belahan** *n* half, side; ~ *jiwa* other half (of a couple); ~ *bumi selatan* Southern Hemisphere; **membelah** *vt* to split in two; **sebelah** ~ *kiri* on the left (side); ~ *mana* which side, where; *rumah* ~ next door; **bersebelahan** *vi* to be next to

belai, membelai *vt* to stroke, caress; **belaian** *n* stroke, caress

belajar *v* to learn, study; ~ *pada* to

learn from; ~ *bahasa Jepang* to learn Japanese; ~ *jarak jauh* (to study via) distance learning; *Yuni masih* ~ Yuni is still learning; ~ *ke luar negeri* to study abroad; **belajar-mengajar** *kegiatan* ~ teaching and learning ← **ajar**

belaka *adj, neg* only, mere, pure

belakang *prep, n* behind; back, rear; *lampu* ~ tail-light; *tulang* ~ spine, backbone; **belakangan** *adv* later (on), afterwards; after others; finally, at last; ~ *(ini)* recently; **membelakangi** *vt* to turn your back on someone; **terbelakang, terkebelakang** *adj* backward, neglected; **keterbelakangan** *n* backwardness, neglect

belalai *n* trunk (of an elephant)

belalak: membelalak *vi* to stare; **membelalakkan** ~ *mata* to stare, open your eyes wide

belalang *n* grasshopper, locust; ~ *sembah* praying mantis

Belanda *n* the Netherlands, Holland; ~ *Depok* local descendants of Dutch since the eighteenth century; *air* ~ soda water; *bahasa* ~ Dutch (language); *orang* ~ Dutch (people); *terong* ~ tree tomato, tamarillo

belang *adj* striped; *lelaki hidung* ~ womanizer

belanja *vi* to go shopping; **belanjaan** *n* shopping, purchases; **berbelanja** *vi* to go shopping; **membelanjakan** *vt* to spend money; **pembelanjaan** *n* expenditure, spending, financing; **perbelanjaan** *n* expenditure; *pusat* ~ shopping center, mall

belantara *adj hutan* ~ forest, wilderness

belantika, blantika *n* world; *Ari sudah beberapa tahun berkiprah di* ~ *musik* for some years Ari has been involved in the world of music

belas: belas kasihan *n* pity, compassion; **berbelas-kasihan** *vi* to pity, feel compassion; **memelas** *adj* pitiful, pathetic

belas *n* number between 10-20, -teen; *lima* ~ fifteen; **belasan** *n* dozens; **sebelas** *n, adj* eleven; **kesebelasan** *n* team of eleven, soccer team

bélasungkawa *n* condolences; *Pak RT melayat ke rumah untuk menyampaikan* ~ the neighborhood leader went to the house to express his condolences

belatung *n* maggot

beledru, beludru *n* velvet

belenggu *n* handcuffs, shackles; **membelenggu** *v* to shackle, handcuff; **terbelenggu** *adj* in shackles, irons

belépotan *adj* smeared, stained; spotty ← **lépot**

belérang *n* sulfur; *asam* ~ sulfuric acid

Bélgia *n* Belgium; *orang* ~ Belgian

beli *vt* to buy; *jual* ~ buying and selling, business, trade; **membeli** *vt* to buy, purchase; **membelikan** *vt* to buy something for someone; *Sinta* ~ *anak itu boneka* Sinta bought the child a doll; **pembeli** *n* buyer, purchaser; **pembelian** *n* purchase; purchasing

belia *adj* young

beliak: membeliakkan *v* ~ *mata* to open your eyes wide

beliau *pron* he, she; him, her (respectful form of **dia**); *Bisa bertemu dengan Bapak?/Maaf,* ~ *tidak boleh diganggu* may I see your master?/sorry, but he mustn't be disturbed

belikat *tulang* ~ shoulder blade

belimbing, blimbing *n* starfruit

beling *n* fragment, shard, splinter

belit *n* coil, bend; **berbelit** *vi* to wind, twist in and out; **berbelit-belit** *vi* to wind around; to ramble; **membelit** *vt* to twist; **terbelit** *adj* twisted, involved; ~ *hutang* debt-ridden

bélok bend, turn; ~ *kiri* turn left; **berbélok** *vi* to turn; ~ *arah vi* to change direction; ~-*belok* windy, lots of bends and turns; **bélokan** *n* bend, turn in the road; **membélok** *v* to bend, turn; **membélokkan** *vt* to turn, divert something

belon *sl* not yet ← **belum**

bélot: membélot *vi* to defect, desert

beludak, bludak: membeludak *vi* to burst out, spread everywhere, explode

beludru → **beledru**

belukar *semak* ~ bushland, scrub

belulang *tulang* ~ skin and bones

belum *adv* **belon** *sl* not yet; no (not until now); ~ *pernah* until now, never (but possibly in the future); **sebelum** *adj* before; **sebelumnya** *adv* previously, before, beforehand

belut *n* eel

bémo *n* motorized three-wheeled vehicle still operating in a few parts of Jakarta ← **bécak bermotor**

bémper *n* bumper bar

benah: berbenah, berbenah-benah *vi* to clean or tidy up, sort out; **membenahi** *vt* to get to the bottom of, clear up, fix, straighten out

benak *n* brains, mind; *tidak terbayang di* ~ *saya* I couldn't imagine

benalu *n* epiphyte, (tree) parasite

benam: terbenam *adj* set, sunken; *matahari* ~ sunset

benang *n* thread; ~ *emas* gold thread; ~ *gigi* dental floss; ~ *merah* connecting thread (of a story or series of happenings)

benar, bener *adj* true, correct, right; **benar-benar** *adv* truly, really; **kebenaran** *n* truth; *Komisi* ~ *dan Rekonsiliasi* Truth and Reconciliation Commission; **membenarkan** *vt* to confirm, verify; to justify; **pembenaran** *n* correction; confirmation; justification; **sebenarnya** *adv* in fact, actually → **betul**

bencana *n* disaster, catastrophe; ~ *alam* natural disaster, act of God

benci *v* to hate; ~ *tapi rindu* love-hate relationship; **kebencian** *n* hatred; **membenci** *vt* to hate

béncong *n, sl* transvestite; *m* homosexual

benda *n* thing, object; goods, valuables; ~ *asing* foreign object; ~ *bergerak* moveable goods; ~ *cair* liquid; ~ *padat* solid; ~ *pos* postal items (postcards, stamps etc); *harta* ~ worldly goods; *kata* ~ noun

bendahara *n* treasurer; bishop (in chess); **perbendaharaan** *n* treasury; ~ *kata* vocabulary

bendéra *n* flag

benderang *terang* ~ bright, dazzling

béndi *n* two-wheeled horse-carriage

bendung: bendungan *n* dam; **membendung, membendungi** *vt* to dam, stop a flow; **terbendung** *tak* ~ unstoppable

bener → **benar**

bengék *n* tetek-~ trivialities, unimportant details

bengis *adj* cruel, heartless; **kebengisan** *n* cruelty, harshness

bengkak *adj* swollen; **membengkak** *vt* to swell up; **pembengkakan** *n* swelling, expanding

bengkalai, terbengkalai *adj* neglected, unfinished

béngkél *n* garage; workshop; ~ *las* welding workshop; ~ *seni* artist's workshop, atelier, studio

béngkok *adj* bent, crooked; **membéngkokkan** *vt* to bend something

bengkuang, bengkoang *n* kind of small fruit with brown skin and white flesh, used in salads and cosmetics

bengong *adj, coll* stunned, dazed; vacant, lost in thought; not knowing what to do

benih *n* seed, germ, sperm; **pembenihan** ~ *buatan* artificial insemination

bening *adj* clear, transparent, clean (of glass, water etc)

bénjol, bénjolan *n* mole, lump, tumor

bénsin *n* petrol, gasoline

bentak shout; **bentakan** *n* shout; **membentak** *vt* to shout, scold, snap (at)

bentang: membentang *vi* to spread out, extend; **membentangi** *vt* to spread something over; **membentangkan** *vt* to spread something out

bentar → **sebentar**

bénténg *n* fort, fortress; castle or rook (in chess)

bentrok *vi* to clash head-on; **bentrokan** *n* clash, conflict

bentuk *n* shape, form; **berbentuk** *adj* shaped, with the shape of; *vi* to have a shape; **membentuk** *vt* to form, set up something (eg. committee); **pembentukan** *n* formation, act of forming; **terbentuk** *adj* formed, shaped, created

bentur *vi* to collide, bump; **membentur** *vt* to hit, collide with; **terbentur** *adj* accidentally bumped; *kepalanya* ~ *di atap* he banged his head on the roof

benua *n* continent; ~ *Asia* Asia; *antar* ~ intercontinental

béo *burung* ~ mynah (bird); **membéo** *vt* to parrot, imitate (superiors etc)

bepergian *vi* to travel, be away ← **pergi**

berabad-abad *adv* for centuries ← **abad**

berabé *adj, sl* annoying; complicated

beracun *adj* poisonous; *vi* to contain poison; *gas* ~ poison gas ← **racun**

berada *vi* to be somewhere; *Ibu Menteri* ~ *di Padang* the Minister is in Padang ← **ada**; *adj* well-to-do, well-off

beradab *adj* civilized, polite; *vt* to have a civilization ← **adab**

beradu *vi* to hit (accidentally); to fight ← **adu**

beragam *adj* various ← **ragam**

beragama *adj* religious; *vi* to have a religion; *Daniel* ~ *Kristen* Daniel is Christian; *Siti* ~ *Islam* Siti is Muslim ← **agama**

berahi, birahi *n* lust, desire; heat (of animals); ~ *tinggi* (*BT* or *bété*) sexually excited, horny; bad-tempered

berai *cerai*-~ scattered, disordered

berair *vi* to be juicy, containing water ← **air**

berajojing *vi* to dance (Western-style) ← **ajojing**

bérak *vi* poo, defecate; *n* poo, feces

berakal *adj* to be intelligent; *vi* to have a mind ← **akal**

berakar *adj* rooted; *vi* to have a root ← **akar**

berakhir *vi* to end ← **akhir**

berakibat *vi* to have consequences, implications ← **akibat**

berakit *vi* to (travel by) raft; **berakit-rakit** *vi* ~ *ke hulu, berenang-renang ke tepian, bersakit-sakit dahulu, bersenang-senang kemudian* after trouble, success will come (*lit.* raft upstream, swim to the bank; suffer a little first then enjoy the fruits of your labors) ← **rakit**

beraksén *adj* -style; *vi* to have a touch of; *rumah* ~ *Jawa* a house with

Javanese-inspired decor ← **aksén**

beraktivitas *vi* to do something, to keep busy ← **aktivitas**

beralamat *adj* addressed; *vi* to have an address ← **alamat**

beralasan *adj* with reason, reasonable; *vi* to have reason; *tidak* ~ ungrounded, unfounded, without reason; **beralaskan** *vi* based upon ← **alasan, alas**

beralérgi *vi* to have an allergy; ~ *terhadap mangga* allergic to mangoes ← **alérgi**

beraliansi *vi* to be allied with ← **aliansi**

beralih *vi* to move, change ← **alih**

beraliran *vi* to have an ideology; ~ *kiri* leftist ← **aliran, alir**

beralkohol *adj* alcoholic; *vi* to contain alcohol; *minuman* ~ alcoholic drink ← **alkohol**

beramal *adj* charitable; *vi* to give to charity ← **amal**

berambin *v* ~ *lutut* to sit hugging your knees ← **ambin**

berambisi *adj* ambitious; *vi* to have an ambition, have ambitions ← **ambisi**

berambut *adj* hairy; *vi* to have hair; ~ *coklat* dark-haired, *f* brunette; ~ *pirang*, *m* blond, *f* blonde ← **rambut**

beranak *vi* to have a child; (of animals) to give birth to, have offspring; ~ *pinak* to have descendants; *Ibu Tuti* ~ *lima* Tuti has five children ← **anak**

beranda *n* veranda, balcony

berandai-andai *vi* to speak hypothetically, imagine ← **andai**

beranéka ~ *ragam* various ← **anéka**

bérang *adj* furious, enraged

berangan-angan *vi* to daydream, build castles in the air, fantasize ← **angan-angan**

berang-berang *n* otter

beranggapan *vi* to be of the opinion ← **anggapan, anggap**

beranggota *vi* to have members; **beranggotakan** *vi* to have a membership, have as members; *PKI dulu* ~ *jutaan orang* the PKI once had millions of members ← **anggota**

berangkat *vi* to depart, leave; **keberangkatan** *n* departure; **diberangkatkan** *vt* to depart; *rombongan ke Medan sudah* ~ the party to Medan has departed; **pemberangkatan** *n* departure, sending off ← **angkat**

berangsur, berangsur-angsur *adv* gradually, little by little; *vi* to do little by little ← **angsur**

berangus *n* muzzle; **memberangus** *vt* to muzzle, bridle; ~ *pers* to curb press freedom

berani *adj* brave, courageous, bold; **berani-berani** *v* to dare, have the nerve to; **keberanian** *n* bravery, courage; **memberanikan** *vt* ~ *diri* to dare, get up the courage; **pemberani** *n* brave or courageous person, hero

beranjak *vi* to move, shift; ~ *dewasa* to become a young adult ← **anjak**

berantai *vi* to have a chain; *adj* in a chain or sequence; *pembunuh* ~ serial killer, mass murderer; *reaksi* ~ chain reaction ← **rantai**

berantak: berantakan *adj* messy, in a mess; **memberantakkan** *vt* to mess up ← **antak**

berantas, memberantas *vt* to wipe out, fight against; ~ *korupsi* to wipe out corruption; **pemberantasan** *n* destruction, fight against; *Komisi* ~ *Korupsi (KPK)* Corruption Eradication Commission

berantem *vi* to fight, scuffle ← **antem, hantam**

berapa *interrog* how many? what number?; *adj, coll* several ← **beberapa**; ~ *banyak?* how much? how many?; ~ *harganya?* how much is it?; *umur* ~ how old; *nomor telepon Adi* ~? what's Adi's phone number? **beberapa** *adj* several, a number of; **keberapa** *coll, interrog* which number?; **seberapa** *tidak* ~ not many; ~ *jauh* as far as ← **apa**

berapi *adj* burning, fire-producing (of volcanoes); **berapi-api** *adj* fiery, fervent ← **api**

berarguméntasi *vi* to argue, reason ← **arguméntasi**

berarti *vi* to mean; *adj* meaningful; *tidak* ~ meaningless ← **arti**

beras *n* rice (husked and uncooked, as

sold in shops); ~ *kencur* traditional Javanese drink; ~ *merah* uncooked brown rice

berasa *vi* to feel (a physical sensation); *tanganku ~ sakit* my hand hurts ← **rasa**

berasal *vi* to come from ← **asal**

berasap *adj* smoky ← **asap**

berasas, berasaskan *adj* based on; *vi* to have as a base; ~ *Pancasila* based on Pancasila ← **asas**

beraspal *adj* asphalted; *vi* to have a layer of asphalt; *jalan ~* made or macadamized road ← **aspal**

berat heavy, severe, difficult; weight; ~ *badan* body weight; ~ *bersih* net weight; ~ *hati* unwilling, reluctant; ~ *mata* sleepy; ~ *sebelah* unbalanced, tending to favor one side; *gaya ~* gravity; **keberatan** *n* objection; *v* to object; **berkeberatan** *v* to object; **memberatkan** *vt* to burden, make heavy; *adj* incriminating; *kesaksian yang ~* incriminating evidence; **pemberat** *n* weight

beratap *vi* to have a roof; ~ *rumbia* to have a thatched roof ← **atap**

beratus-ratus *adj* hundreds of ← **ratus**

berawal *vi* to begin with ← **awal**

berawan *adj* cloudy, overcast ← **awan**

berbagai *adj* various, several ← **bagai**

berbagi *vi* to share; ~ *hasil adj* profit-sharing; *vi* to share profits ← **bagi**

berbahagia *vi* to be happy; *selamat ~* congratulations (at a wedding) ← **bahagia**

berbahak-bahak *vi* to roar with laughter ← **bahak-bahak**

berbahasa *vi* to (be able to) speak or use a language; *Nenek hanya ~ Jawa* Grandma only speaks Javanese ← **bahasa**

berbahaya *vi* to be dangerous; *adj* dangerous ← **bahaya**

berbaju *vi* to put on, wear clothes ← **baju**

berbakat *adj* talented, gifted; *vi* to have a talent ← **bakat**

berbakti *vi* to serve, devote oneself to ← **bakti**

berbalas *vi* to reply, respond ← **balas**

berbalik *vi* to turn around, return ← **balik**

berbangga *vi* to be proud ← **bangga**

berbangkit *vi* to rise, get up ← **bangkit**

berbangsa *vi* to have a nationality ← **bangsa**

berbarengan *adj* together, at the same time ← **bareng**

berbaring *vi* to lie down ← **baring**

berbaris *vi* to line up ← **baris**

berbatas *vi* to have a boundary; *tak ~* limitless; **berbatasan** *vi* to be adjacent to ← **batas**

berbatu *adj* rocky, stony ← **batu**

berbau *vi* to smell, have connotations of ← **bau**

berbaur *vi* to integrate, mix with others (of people) ← **baur**

berbéda *adj* different ← **béda**

berbekal *vi* to carry provisions (consisting of) ← **bekal**

berbekas *vi* to show; *kekecewaannya tidak ~ pada sikapnya* his disappointment did not show in his attitude ← **bekas**

berbelanja *vi* to go shopping, shop ← **belanja**

berbelas-kasihan *vi* to pity, feel compassion ← **belas kasih**

berbelit *vi* to wind, twist in and out; **berbelit-belit** *vi* to wind around ← **belit**

berbelok *vi* to turn; ~ *arah* to change direction ← **belok**

berbenah, berbenah-benah *vi* to clean or tidy up, sort out ← **benah**

berbentuk *adj* shaped, with the shape of; *vi* to have a shape ← **bentuk**

berbesar hati *adj* big-hearted, accepting ← **besar**

berbicara *vi* to speak; ~ *dalam bahasa Sunda* to speak in Sundanese ← **bicara**

berbinar-binar *adv* shining, gleaming ← **binar**

berbincang, berbincang-bincang *vi* to chat, discuss ← **bincang**

berbingkai *vi* to have a frame; *adj* framed ← **bingkai**

berbintang *vi* to have a star (sign); *jenderal ~ tiga* three-star general; *Dini*

~ *Aries* Dini's star sign is Aries ← **bintang**

berbintik-bintik *adj* spotty, spotted; *vi* to have spots or freckles ← **bintik**

berbisa *adj* poisonous; *ular* ~ poisonous snake ← **bisa**

berbisik *adj* whispering; *vi* to whisper ← **bisik**

berbisnis *vi* to do business ← **bisnis**

berbobot *adj* heavy, weighty; *bukunya* ~ his book was heavy reading ← **bobot**

berbohong *vi* to lie ← **bohong**

berbolong-bolong *adj* full of holes ← **bolong**

berbondong-bondong *adv* in droves ← **bondong**

berbuah *vi* to bear fruit, produce ← **buah**

berbuat *vi* to do; ~ *salah* to do wrong ← **buat**

berbudaya *vi* to have a culture ← **budaya**

berbuih *adj* frothy, foaming ← **buih**

berbuka *vi* ~ *puasa* to break the fast ← **buka**

berbukit *adj* hilly ← **bukit**

berbulan ~ *madu vi* to (have a) honeymoon

berbulu *adj* hairy; *vi* to have fur or feathers ← **bulu**

berbunga *vi* to flower, blossom; to gain interest; *bunga* ~ compound interest ← **bunga**

berbuntut *vi* to go further, end; *ceritanya* ~ *sedih* the tale had a sad ending ← **buntut**

berbunyi *vi* to sound, make a noise ← **bunyi**

berburu *vi* to go hunting ← **buru**

berbusa *adj* foamy; *vi* to have a layer of foam ← **busa**

berbusana *vi* to wear ← **busana**

bercabang *vi* to have a branch; *adj* split, branched ← **cabang**

bercahaya *vi* to glow, shine ← **cahaya**

bercak *n* spot, blemish, pock (on body)

bercakap *vi* to speak; **bercakap-cakap** *vi* to chat ← **cakap**

bercambang *adj* whiskered, bearded; *vi* to have whiskers or a beard ← **cambang**

bercampur *adj* mixed with; *vi* to mix with ← **campur**

bercanda *vi* to joke; ~ *kok* just kidding ← **canda**

bercas-cis-cus *vi* to speak a European language ← **cas-cis-cus**

bercawat *vi* to wear a loincloth ← **cawat**

bercécéran *adj* scattered, dispersed ← **cécér**

bercékcok *vi* to quarrel, have a fight ← **cékcok**

bercelana *vi* to wear trousers, trousered ← **celana**

bercelotéh *vi* to babble, gurgle ← **celotéh**

bercengkrama *vi* to chat, hold a discussion ← **cengkrama**

bercerai *vi* to be divorced ← **cerai**

berceramah *vi* to give a lecture or talk ← **ceramah**

bercerita *vi* to tell (a story) ← **cerita**

bercermin *vi* to look in the mirror; to take as an example ← **cermin**

bercinta *vi* to make love; to be in love ← **cinta**

bercita-cita, bercita-citakan *vi* to dream of ← **cita-cita**

berciuman *vi* to kiss each other ← **cium**

berciut-ciut *vi* to squeak ← **ciut**

bercocok *v* ~ *tanam* to work or till the soil ← **cocok**

bercorak *vi* to have a design ← **corak**

bercucuran *vi* to trickle down, drip, flow ← **cucur**

bercula *vi* to have a horn; *badak* ~ *satu* one-horned rhino ← **cula**

bercumbu *vi* to flirt, flatter ← **cumbu**

berdada *vi* to have a chest ← **dada**

berdagang *vi* to trade, do business ← **dagang**

berdahaga *adj* thirsty ← **dahaga**

berdahak *adj* containing phlegm or mucus; *batuk* ~ chesty cough ← **dahak**

berdalih *vi* to pretend, give a pretext ← **dalih**

berdalil *adj* based on, grounded in; *vi* to have a base ← **dalil**

berdamai *vi* to make peace ← **damai**

berdampak *vi* to have a (negative) effect ← **dampak**

berdampingan *adj* side by side ←
damping

berdandan *vi* to dress, put on make-up
← **dandan**

berdansa *vi* to dance (Western-style)
← **dansa**

berdarah *vi* to bleed ← **darah**

berdasar *adj* based; **berdasarkan** *adj*
based on; in accordance with, pursuant
to ← **dasar**

berdasi *vi* to wear a tie; *kaum* ~ white-
collar workers ← **dasi**

berdatangan *vi* to come (of many) ←
datang

berdaulat *adj* sovereign, independent;
vi to have sovereignty; *negara yang* ~
sovereign state ← **daulat**

berdaya *vi* to have power; ~ *guna* efficient; *tak* ~ powerless; **pemberdayaan**
n empowerment; *Kementerian* ~
Perempuan Ministry for the
Empowerment of Women ← **daya**

berdayung *vi* to go by boat or bicycle
← **dayung**

berdebar *vi* to beat quickly; *hati* ~ a
racing heart ← **debar**

berdebat *vi* to have a debate or discussion ← **debat**

berdebu *adj* dusty ← **debu**

berdeham *vi* to clear the throat, cough
← **deham**

berdekap-dekapan, berdekapan *vi* to
embrace each other ← **dekap**

berdekatan *adj* close (of two or more
things) ← **dekat**

berdelapan *adj* a group of eight ←
delapan

berdémo *vi* to hold a protest ← **démo**

berdémpét *adj* stuck together ← **démpét**

berdendam *vi* to be resentful, full of
revenge ← **dendam**

berdéndang *vi* to sing, chant ← **déndang**

berdengung *vi* to drone, hum, shake
with sound ← **dengung**

berdentang *vi* to clang, jangle ←
dentang

berdentaman *vi* to crackle or pound (of
gunfire) ← **dentam**

berdenyut *vi* to throb, to beat ← **denyut**

berderap *vi* to click-clack (of shoes),
trot along ← **derap**

berdérét-dérét *vi* to line up ← **dérét**

berdering *vi* to ring, tinkle ← **dering**

berdesah *vi* to sigh, make a swishing
noise ← **desah**

berdesakan *vi* to push each other ←
desak

berdesir *vi* to hiss, rustle ← **desir**

berdialog *vi* to converse, have a dialog
← **dialog**

berdiam *vi* to reside; ~ *diri* to keep silent ← **diam**

berdiét *vi* to diet, go on a diet ← **diét**

berdikari *adj* self-reliant ← **berdiri di
atas kaki sendiri**

berdikir *vi, Isl* to say additional prayers
← **dikir, zikir**

berdingin-dingin *vi* to enjoy cold
weather ← **dingin**

berdisiplin *adj* disciplined; *vi* to have
discipline ← **disiplin**

berdiskusi *vi* to have a discussion ←
diskusi

berdoa *vi* to pray, say a prayer; ~
menurut keyakinan masing-masing to
pray according to one's own religion
← **doa**

berdomisili *vi* to be domiciled, reside
← **domisili**

berdosa *vi* to sin, commit a sin ←
dosa

berdua *adj* together, in pairs ← **dua**

berduit *adj* well-off; *vi* to have money
← **duit**

berduka *vi* ~ *(cita)* to grieve, be in
mourning ← **duka**

berdurasi *vi* to last, have a duration of
← **durasi**

berduri *adj* thorny; with fish bones;
kawat ~ barbed wire ← **duri**

berdusta *vi* to lie ← **dusta**

beréaksi *vi* to react ← **réaksi**

berebut *vi* to fight for; **berebutan** *vi* to
fight each other for ← **rebut**

berédar *vi* to circulate ← **édar**

beregu *vi* to be in a team; *adj* in teams
← **regu**

berékor *vi* to have a tail; *bintang* ~
comet; *tulang* ~ coccyx ← **ékor**

berembuk *vi* to confer, discuss ← **rembuk**

berembun *adj* moist, dewy ← **embun**

berembus *vi* to blow ← **embus**

berémosi *adj* emotional ← **émosi**

berempat *adj* in a group of four ← **empat**

berenam *adj* in a group of six ← **enam**

berenang *vi* to swim ← **renang**

berencana *vi* to plan; *Keluarga ~ (KB)* family planning ← **rencana**

berénda *adj* lacy, lace ← **rénda**

berendam *vi* to soak ← **rendam**

berénérgi *adj* energetic; *vi* to have energy ← **énérgi**

bérés finished, ready; *~, bos!* done, boss!; **memberéskan** *vt* to clear up, make ready

beréstafét *adj* in stages ← **éstafét**

berétika *adj* ethical; to behave; *~ baik* to behave well ← **étika**

berfaédah *adj* useful, worthwhile; *vi* to have a use; *tidak ~* useless ← **faédah**

berfasilitas *adj* with facilities; *vi* to have facilities ← **fasilitas**

berféderasi *vi* to be federated ← **féderasi**

berfilsafat *vi* to have a philosophy ← **filsafat**

berfirman *vi* to utter, say; *Allah ~* God said ← **firman**

berfokus *adj* focused; *vi* to have a focus ← **fokus**

berfoya-foya *vi* to waste money, live frivolously ← **foya-foya**

berfungsi *vi* to work, go; to act as ← **fungsi**

bergabung *vi* to join together ← **gabung**

bergadang ← **begadang**

bergagap-gagap *vi* to stammer, stutter ← **gagap**

bergairah *adj* lusty, passionate; enthusiastic; *vi* to have lust or passion ← **gairah**

bergambar *adj* illustrated ← **gambar**

bergamit *vi* to touch, nudge; **bergamitan** *vi* to touch each other ← **gamit**

bergandéng *vi* to join or do together; **bergandéngan** *vi* *~ tangan* to link arms or hands ← **gandéng**

berganti *vi* to change; **berganti-ganti,**

bergantian *adv* in turns, repeatedly; *vi* to take turns ← **ganti**

bergantung *vi* *~ pada* to depend on ← **gantung**

bergaransi *adj* guaranteed; *vi* to have a guarantee ← **garansi**

bergaris *adj* lined; *vi* to have lines ← **garis**

bergaul *vi* to mix or associate with ← **gaul**

bergaung *vi* to echo ← **gaung**

bergaya *adj* stylish, with style; *vi* to have style ← **gaya**

bergegas-gegas *vi* to hurry ← **gegas**

bergejolak *vi* to flare up, burst out ← **gejolak**

bergelantungan *vi* to hang from (of several things) ← **gelantung**

bergelar *adj* titled; *vi* to have a title ← **gelar**

bergelimang *adj* smeared; *~ lumpur* muddy, mud-stained ← **gelimang**

bergelimpang *adj* sprawled; **bergelimpangan** *adj* sprawled all around; *mayat ~* dead bodies lay everywhere

bergelinding *vi* to roll; **bergelindingan** *vi* to roll (of many objects) ← **gelinding**

bergelombang *adj* wavy ← **gelombang**

bergelung *adj* coiled; *vi* to have a coil ← **gelung**

bergelut *vi* to wrestle; to romp ← **gelut**

bergema *vi* to echo, reverberate ← **gema**

bergembira *vi* to be happy, joyous ← **gembira**

bergeming *tak ~ vi* not bat an eyelid, make not the slightest reaction ← **geming**

bergenang *adj* flooded; *vi* to flood, be wet ← **genang**

bergéngsi *adj* prestigious; *vi* to have prestige ← **géngsi**

bergerak *vi* to move; *aset ~* movable assets ← **gerak**

bergerigi *adj* serrated, jagged; *vi* to have serrated edges or points ← **gerigi**

bergerilya *vi* to wage guerrilla warfare ← **gerilya**

bergerombol *vi* to gather in a group, amass ← **gerombol**

bergetar *vi* to vibrate, tremble ← **getar**

bergidik *vi* to shudder, shiver ← **gidik**

bergigi *vi* to have teeth; *tidak* ~ toothless; powerless ← **gigi**

bergilir, bergiliran *adj* in turns ← **gilir, giliran**

bergizi *adj* nutritious ← **gizi**

bergoncang *vi* to rock, sway ← **goncang**

bergosip *vi* to gossip ← **gosip**

bergoyang *vi* to shake, sway; to dance ← **goyang**

bergulat *vi* to wrestle, fight ← **gulat**

bergumam *vi* to mumble ← **gumam**

bergumpal *vi* to clot ← **gumpal**

bergumul *vi* to wrestle ← **gumul**

berguna *adj* useful, worthwhile; *vi* to have a use; *tidak* ~ useless ← **guna**

berguncang *vi* to rock, sway ← **guncang**

bergundah *vi* ~ *hati* sad ← **gundah**

bergunjing *vi* to gossip ← **gunjing**

berguru *vi* ~ *kepada* to study under, learn from, have as a teacher ← **guru**

berhadapan *vi* face to face; ~ *muka* face to face ← **hadap**

berhadiah *adj* with prizes; *vi* to have a prize ← **hadiah**

berhak *vi* to have a right to, be entitled to ← **hak**

berhala *n* idol

berhalangan *vi* to be prevented, unable ← **halangan, halang**

berhaluan *vi* to have a direction; ~ *kiri* leftist ← **haluan, halu**

berhamburan *adj* scattered about ← **hambur**

berharap *vi* to hope ← **harap**

berharga *adj* precious, valuable; *vi* to be of value ← **harga**

berhari-hari *adv* for days ← **hari**

berhasil *vi* to succeed ← **hasil**

berhati *vi* to have a heart; ~ *besar* openhearted; ~ *emas* to have a heart of gold

berhati-hati *vi* to be careful ← **hati-hati**

berhawa *vi* to have a climate; ~ *sejuk* to have a cool climate ← **hawa**

berhémat *vi* to be economical ← **hémat**

berhenti *vi* to stop, cease; **pemberhentian** *n* stop; dismissal, discharge; stoppage ← **henti**

berhias *vi* to dress up, put on make-up ← **hias**

berhimpit *adv* very close together; **berhimpitan** *vi* to be close to each other ← **himpit**

berhimpun *vi* to meet, assemble ← **himpun**

berhitung *vi* to count ← **hitung**

berhobi *vi* to have as a hobby ← **hobi**

berhubung *conj* in connection to, related with; ~ *dengan* in connection with; **berhubungan** *vi, pl* to have a link or connection ← **hubung**

berhulu *vi* to rise, have a source; *Sungai Mekong* ~ *di Cina* the source of the Mekong is in China ← **hulu**

beri *vt* to give; ~ *semangat* give a cheer; ~ *tahu* inform, let know → **beritahu; memberi** *vt* to give; **memberikan** *vt* to give someone (as an act of kindness); to give something (for someone); **pemberi** *n* giver, donor; **pemberian** *n* present, gift, something given to someone

beriak *vi* to ripple ← **riak**

beribadah *vi* to worship, serve; *orang* ~ religious person ← **ibadah**

beribu *v* ~ *bapak* to have parents ← **ibu**

beribu, beribu-ribu *adj* thousands of ← **ribu**

berijazah *adj* certified, qualified; *vi* to have a certificate or qualification ← **ijazah**

beriklim *vi* to have a climate; ~ *dingin* to have a cool climate ← **iklim**

berikrar *vi* to promise, pledge ← **ikrar**

berikut *adj* following; ~ *itu* after that; *yang* ~, ~*nya* the next ← **ikut**

berilmu *adj* learned ← **ilmu**

beriman *adj* religious ← **iman**

berimbang *adj* balanced, proportional; *vi* to have (a) balance ← **imbang**

berimplikasi *vi* to have implications ← **implikasi**

beringas *adj* hot-tempered, furious; wild-eyed

beringin *n* banyan; *(pohon)* ~ *banyan* tree; *Partai* ~ Golkar

beringsut *vi* to shift slowly ← **ingsut**

berinisiatif *vi* to take the initiative ← **inisiatif**

berinteraksi *vi* to interact ← **interaksi**

berintrospéksi *vi* to be introspective ← **introspéksi**

berirama *adj* rhythmical; *adv* with a rhythm; *vi* to have a rhythm ← **irama**

beriring-iringan *adv* in succession ← **iring**

berisi *vi* to contain; *adj* full, filled out ← **isi**

berisik *adj* noisy, loud; to rustle ← **risik**

berisiko *vi* to be risky ← **risiko**

beristeri, beristri *adj, m* married; *vi* to have a wife; *pria* ~ married man ← **isteri, istri**

beristirahat *vi* to rest, take a break ← **istirahat**

beristri → **beristeri**

berita *n* news, information; ~ *acara* minutes; ~ *aktual* current affairs; ~ *duka* death notice, obituary; ~ *hangat* latest news; ~ *malam* evening news; ~ *miring* negative story; **memberitakan** *vt* to report

beritahu, beri tahu *vt* to inform, let know; **memberitahu** *vt* to inform, tell; **pemberitahuan** *n* announcement, notice

berjabat, berjabatan *vi* ~ *tangan* to shake hands ← **jabat**

berjaga *vi* to stand guard ← **jaga**

berjajar *adj* in a row; *vi* to be in a row ← **jajar**

berjalan *vi* to walk, move; ~ *dengan baik* go well ← **jalan**

berjam-jam *adj* for hours and hours ← **jam**

berjamaah *adv, Isl* together, as a congregation ← **jamaah**

berjambul *vi* to have a quiff or crest ← **jambul**

berjamur *adj* moldy; **berjamuran** *vi* to pop up everywhere ← **jamur**

berjangka *adj* for a term; *deposito* ~ term deposit ← **jangka**

berjangkit *vi* to spread, be infectious or contagious ← **jangkit**

berjanji *vi* to promise ← **janji**

berjarak *adj* -distance; *vi* to be a certain distance away; ~ *jauh* long-distance; *pohon-pohon* ~ *10 meter* the trees were spaced 10 meters apart ← **jarak**

berjasa *adj* meritorious, deserving of reward; *vi* to perform a service ← **jasa**

berjatuhan *vi, pl* to fall (in numbers) ← **jatuh**

berjaya *adj* victorious, winning; prosperous ← **jaya**

berjejalan, berjejal-jejal *adv* crowded, jammed ← **jejal**

berjéjér, berjéjéran *adv* in a row, in a line; *vi* to stand in a row ← **jéjér**

berjemur *vi* to sunbathe, sun yourself ← **jemur**

berjénggot *adj* bearded; *vi* to have a beard ← **jénggot**

berjenis-jenis *adj* all kinds of, various ← **jenis**

berjerawat *adj* pimply; *vi* to have pimples ← **jerawat**

berjeruji *adj* fitted with bars ← **jeruji**

berjibun *vi* to pile up, teem (with) ← **jibun**

berjihad *vi* to conduct a war or crusade; to strive toward a noble goal ← **jihad**

berjilbab *adj* in a (full) veil, veiled; *vi* to wear the veil ← **jilbab**

berjilid *adj* in volumes ← **jilid**

berjingkrak, berjingkrak-jingkrak *vi* to jump for joy ← **jingkrak**

berjinjit-jinjit *vi* to walk on tiptoe ← **jinjit**

berjiwa *adj* alive; *vi* to have a soul; ~ *muda* young at heart ← **jiwa**

berjogét *vi* to dance ← **jogét**

berjongkok *vi* to squat ← **jongkok**

berjual *vi* to trade, sell ← **jual**

berjuang *vi* to fight, struggle ← **juang**

berjubah *vi* to wear a robe ← **jubah**

berjubel-jubel *vi* to crowd around; *adj* chock-full, chock-a-block ← **jubel**

berjudi *vi* to gamble ← **judi**

berjudul *adj* titled; *vi* to have a title

berjumlah *vi* to number ← **jumlah**

berjumpa *vi* to meet ← **jumpa**

berjuntai *vi* to dangle ← **juntai**

berjuta *vi* to have millions of ← **juta**

berkabung *vi* to mourn; *hari* ~ *nasional* day of national mourning ← **kabung**

berkabut *adj* cloudy ← **kabut**

berkaca-kaca *vi* to fill with tears (of eyes) ← **kaca**

berkacamata *vi* to wear glasses; ~ *min(us)* to be short-sighted ← **kaca mata**

berkain *vi* ~ *kebaya* to wear the female national dress ← **kain kebaya**

berkaitan *vi* to be related to ← **kaitan, kait**

berkaki *vi* to have feet; ~ *telanjang* barefoot; ~ *tiga* three-legged ← **kaki**

berkala *adj* regular; *secara* ~ periodically ← **kala**

berkali-kali *adv* repeatedly, again and again ← **kali**

berkalung *vi* to wear a necklace; *adj* wearing a necklace ← **kalung**

berkampanye *vi* to (hold a) campaign; to join a parade for a candidate ← **kampanye**

berkamuflase *vi* to use camouflage ← **kamuflase**

berkantong *vi* to have a pocket; ~ *tebal* wealthy ← **kantong**

berkantor *vi* to have an office ← **kantor**

berkapasitas *vi* with a capacity of ← **kapasitas**

berkarat *adj* rusty; *vi* to be rusty ← **karat**

berkas *n* bundle; file, dossier, brief

berkat *n* blessing; *conj* thanks to; ~ *doamu, aku sudah sembuh* thanks to your prayers, I am well again; **memberkati** *vt* to bless; *Chr Tuhan* ~ God bless; **pemberkatan** *n* consecration, blessing

berkata *vi* to say, speak ← **kata**

berkawan *vi* to have or be friends with ← **kawan**

berkayuh *vi* to paddle, row; pedal ← **kayuh**

berkeberatan *vi* to object ← **keberatan, berat**

berkecambah *vi* to sprout ← **kecambah**

berkecamuk *vi* to rage ← **kecamuk**

berkecil *vi* ~ *hati* to be disappointed or offended; timid ← **kecil hati**

berkecukupan *vi* to have enough, get by ← **kecukupan, cukup**

berkedip *vi* to blink (two eyes) or wink (one eye); **berkedip-kedip** *adj* blinking ← **kedip**

berkedok *vi* to hide behind a mask, pretend; *banyak SMS yang* ~ *berasal dari bank* many text messages pretending to be from a bank ← **kedok**

berkehendak *vi* to have the intent ← **kehendak, hendak**

berkeinginan *vi* to have a desire or wish ← **keinginan, ingin**

berkejang *vi* to have a cramp ← **kejang**

berkekurangan *vi* to lack, be lacking or needy ← **kekurangan, kurang**

berkelahi *vi* to quarrel, fight, fall out ← **kelahi**

berkelakar *vi* to joke ← **kelakar**

berkelakuan *vi* to behave, act ← **kelakuan, laku**

berkelana *vi* to roam, wander ← **kelana**

berkelas *adj* classy; *vi* to have class ← **kelas**

berkeliaran *vi* to swarm or wander about ← **keliar**

berkeliling *vi* to go around ← **keliling**

berkelip *vi* to twinkle, flicker ← **kelip**

berkelit *vi* to get out of, avoid ← **kelit**

berkelompok *adj* in groups, group ← **kelompok**

berkeluarga *vi* to have a family, be married ← **keluarga**

berkeluh *vi* to complain ← **keluh**

berkeluyuran *vi* to hang around; *banyak preman* ~ *dekat setasiun* lots of thugs hang around the station ← **keluyur, luyur**

berkémah *vi* to camp, go camping ← **kémah**

berkemas-kemas *vi* to tidy up, pack ← **kemas**

berkembang *vi* to develop, expand; ~ *biak* to breed, grow; *negara* ~ developing nation ← **kembang**

berkenaan ~ *dengan* in connection with, regarding ← **kena**

berkencan *vi* to go on a date ← **kencan**

berkendaraan *vi* to go by means of (a vehicle, usu car); ~ *motor* to go by motorcycle ← **kendaraan, kendara**

berkepala *vi* to have a head ← **kepala**

berkepanjangan *adj* continuous, protracted ← **kepanjangan, panjang**

berkepentingan *vi* to have an interest in; *yang* ~ concerned party ← **kepentingan, penting**

berperikemanusiaan *adj* humane ← **perikemanusiaan, kemanusiaan, manusia**

berkepul *vi* to smoke, billow ← **kepul**

berkeramas *vi* to wash your hair ← **keramas**

berkeringat *vi* to sweat ← **keringat**

berkeriput *adj* wrinkly, lined; *vi* to have wrinkles ← **keriput**

berkerudung *adj* veiled; *vi* to wear a veil ← **kerudung**

berkerumun *vi* to swarm, crowd ← **kerumun**

berkerut *vi* to frown ← **kerut**

berkesan *adj* impressive; *vi* to give an impression ← **kesan**

berkesempatan *vi* to have an opportunity ← **kesempatan, sempat**

berkesimpulan *vi* to make the conclusion ← **kesimpulan, simpul**

berkesinambungan *adj* sustained, continuous; *perkembangan yang* ~ sustained development ← **kesinambungan, sambung**

berkesudahan *tidak* ~ endless, infinite ← **sudah**

berketombé *rambut* ~ dry scalp, dandruff ← **ketombé**

berkewarganegaraan *vi* to have citizenship or be a citizen of ← **kewarganegaraan, warga negara**

berkeyakinan *vi* to be convinced ← **keyakinan, yakin**

berkhasiat *adj* beneficial, therapeutic; to have a benefit ← **khasiat**

berkhayal *vi* to dream, imagine ← **khayal**

berkhianat *vi* to betray ← **khianat**

berkibar *vi* to wave, flutter ← **kibar**

berkiblat *vi* to be oriented toward; ~ *pada Amerika* to look to America ← **kiblat**

berkicau *vi* to warble, twitter; to babble ← **kicau**

berkilap *vi* to shine, gleam ← **kilap**

berkilat *vi* to shine, sparkle ← **kilat**

berkilau *adj* glittering, sparkling; *vi* to glitter, sparkle ← **kilau**

berkiprah *vi* to move, dance, be active in ← **kiprah**

berkisah *vi* to tell a story ← **kisah**

berkisar *vi* to revolve, rotate, turn ← **kisar**

berkoalisi *vi* to be in a coalition ← **koalisi**

berkobar *vi* to blaze, burn ← **kobar**

berkokok *vi* to crow; *ayam* ~ rooster's crow ← **kokok**

berkolaborasi *vi* to collaborate, work together ← **kolaborasi**

berkolésterol *vi* ~ *tinggi* to be high (in) cholesterol; to have high cholesterol; *adj* having high-cholesterol ← **kolésterol**

berkomat-kamit *vi* to move your lips silently (as if praying) ← **komat-kamit**

berkoméntar *vi* to (make a) comment ← **koméntar**

berkompromi *vi* to compromise, reach a compromise ← **kompromi**

berkorban *vi* to make sacrifices, do without ← **korban**

berkoték *vi* to cackle (of a hen) ← **koték**

berkotéka *adj* wearing a penis sheath; *vi* to wear a penis sheath ← **kotéka**

berkréasi *vi* to be creative ← **kréasi**

berkuah *adj* with a soup or sauce; *vi* to have a soup or sauce ← **kuah**

berkuala *vi* to have a mouth or confluence ← **kuala**

berkualitas *adj* quality; *vi* to be of quality ← **kualitas**

berkuasa *adj* powerful, mighty; *vi* to have power ← **kuasa**

berkubah *adj* domed; *vi* to have a dome ← **kubah**

berkubang *vi* to wallow (in mud) ← **kubang**

berkuda *vi* to ride a horse, go (horse-) riding ← **kuda**

berkuku *adj* having nails or claws; clawed; *vi* to have nails or claws ← **kuku**

berkulit *vi* to have skin, skinned; ~ *badak* thick-skinned ← **kulit**

berkuman *adj* full of germs, bacteria ← **kuman**

berkumandang *vi* to echo ← **kumandang**

berkumpul *vi* to assemble, meet ← **kumpul**

berkumur, berkumur-kumur *vi* to gargle ← **kumur**

berkunjung *vi* to visit, pay a visit to; *besok kelas I ~ ke Musium Fatahillah* tomorrow the first graders will visit the Fatahillah Museum ← **kunjung**

berkurang *vi* to decrease, diminish, subside; *~nya* the fall in ← **kurang**

berkurban *vi* to make a sacrifice, have a sacrifice slaughtered ← **kurban**

berkutat *vi* to be busy or concerned with ← **kutat**

berkutik *vi* to move slightly, budge ← **kutik**

berkutu *vi* to have fleas or lice ← **kutu**

berlabuh *vi* to anchor ← **labuh**

berladang *vi* to cultivate the land ← **ladang**

berlagak *vi* to act, pretend ← **lagak**

berlainan *adj* differing, different ← **lain**

berlaku *adj* effective, valid; *vocer ini sudah tidak ~* this voucher is no longer valid; *vi* to behave ← **laku**

berlalu *vi* to pass; *badai pasti ~* the storm will pass ← **lalu**

berlama-lama *vi* to draw out, take a long time ← **lama**

berlambang *vi* to have a symbol ← **lambang**

berlandaskan *adj* based on; *vi* to be based on ← **landas**

berlangganan *vi* to subscribe to ← **langganan, langgan**

berlangsung *vi* to take place ← **langsung**

berlanjut *vi* to continue ← **lanjut**

berlantai *vi* to have floors, stories ← **lantai**

berlapis *adj* layered; *vi* to have a layer; **berlapiskan** *vi* to have a layer of ← **lapis**

berlari *vi* to run ← **lari**

berlatarkan *vi* to have as a background, be based on ← **latar**

berlawanan *vi* to be opposed ← **lawan**

berlayar *vi* to sail ← **layar**

berlebaran *vi* to celebrate Idul Fitri ← **Lebaran**

berlebihan *adj* excessive ← **lebih**

berléha-léha *vi* to relax, be idle ← **léha**

berlendir *adj* mucous, slimy ← **lendir**

berlépotan → **belépotan**

berlian *n* diamond

berlibur *vi* to go or be on holiday ← **libur**

berliku-liku *adj* twisted, complicated; *vi* to have twists and turns ← **liku-liku, liku**

berlima *adj* the five of them, as a group of five ← **lima**

berlimpah-limpah *adj* overflowing, abundant; *vi* to overflow, be in abundance ← **limpah**

berlinang *vi* to trickle, drip; *air mata ~* eyes filled with tears ← **linang**

berlindung *vi* to (take) shelter ← **lindung**

berlipat *~ ganda* many times over ← **lipat**

berliur *vi* to drool, salivate ← **liur**

berlogat *vi ~ Jawa* to have a Javanese accent ← **logat**

berlokasi *adj* located; *vi* to be located ← **lokasi**

berlomba *vi* to compete, race ← **lomba**

berlubang *vi* to have a hole ← **lubang**

berlumpur *adj* muddy; *vi* to be muddy ← **lumpur**

berlumuran *adj* smeared, stained ← **lumur**

berlutut *vi* to kneel (down) ← **lutut**

bermaaf-maafan *vi, Isl* to beg forgiveness of each other (at Idul Fitri) ← **maaf**

bermacam-macam *adj* various ← **macam**

bermain *vi* to play; *~ api* to play with fire; *~ sulap* to do magic ← **main**

bermakna *adj* meaningful; *vi* to have meaning; *itu bukan perbuatan yang ~* that (action) doesn't mean anything ← **makna**

bermaksud *vi* to intend ← **maksud**

bermalam *vi* to spend or stay the night ← **malam**

bermalas-malas, bermalas-malasan *vi* to lie or laze around, be lazy ← **malas**

bermandi *vi* to bathe; *~ keringat* to be soaked in sweat; **bermandikan** *adj* bathed in; *vi* to bathe in; *~ darah* to be soaked in blood ← **mandi**

bermanfaat *adj* useful, of benefit; *vi* to have a use or benefit ← **manfaat**

bermartabat *adj* dignified; *vi* to have dignity ← **martabat**

bermasalah *adj* problematic, troublesome ← **masalah**

bermérek *vi* to have a label; *adj* branded ← **mérek**

bermigrasi *vi* to migrate ← **migrasi**

bermimpi *vi* to dream ← **mimpi**

berminat *vi* to have an interest, be interested ← **minat**

berminggu-minggu *adv* for weeks ← **minggu**

berminyak *adj* oily, greasy ← **minyak**

bermodal *vi* to have capital; ~ *dengkul* with only hard work ← **modal**

bermotif *vi* to have a design ← **motif**

bermotivasikan *vi* to be motivated by ← **motivasi**

bermuara *vi* to have a mouth, empty into ← **muara**

bermuatan *vi* to be laden with ← **muatan, muat**

bermuka *vi* to have a face; ~ *dua* two-faced ← **muka**

bermukim *vi* to reside, stay ← **mukim**

bermula *vi* to start, begin ← **mula**

bermunculan *vi* to show up (in large numbers) ← **muncul**

bermusuhan *vi* to be enemies ← **musuh**

bermusyawarah *vi* to deliberate, discuss ← **musyawarah**

bermutu *adj* quality; ~ *rendah* low quality ← **mutu**

bernada *vi* to have a tone or edge; ~ *sinis* mockingly, sarcastically ← **nada**

bernafaskan, bernapaskan *vi* with a breath of ← **nafas**

bernafsu *adj* passionate, lusty ← **nafsu**

bernama *adj* named; *vi* to have a name ← **nama**

bernanah *vi* to fester ← **nanah**

bernaung *vi* to (take) shelter ← **naung**

berniat *vi* to intend ← **niat**

bernostalgia *vi* to reminisce, be nostalgic ← **nostalgia**

bernuansa *adj* with a touch of; *vi* to have a touch of ← **nuansa**

bernyala *vi* to burn, blaze ← **nyala**

bernyali *adj* brave; *vi* to have guts, courage ← **nyali**

bernyanyi *vi* to sing ← **nyanyi**

bernyawa *adj* alive; *vi* to live, be alive ← **nyawa**

berobat *vi* to go to the doctor, seek medical advice; ~ *jalan* to be treated as an outpatient ← **obat**

berobsési *vi* to have an obsession, be obsessed with; *Tony ~ merenovasi rumah* Tony is obsessed with renovating his house ← **obsési**

beroda *adj* wheeled; *vi* to have wheels ← **roda**

berolahraga *vi* to do or play sport ← **olahraga**

berombak *adj* wavy; *rambut* ~ wavy hair ← **ombak**

beronani *vi* to masturbate ← **onani**

berontak, memberontak *vi* to rebel, revolt; **pemberontak** *n* rebel; **pemberontakan** *n* rebellion, revolt, mutiny

beroperasi *vi* to operate, work, function ← **operasi**

beroriéntasikan *vi* to be oriented towards; *PKI semakin ~ RRC* the PKI became increasingly oriented towards the PRC ← **oriéntasi**

berotak *vi* to have a brain; ~ *tajam* to be sharp-witted ← **otak**

berotot *adj* muscular; *vi* to have muscles ← **otot**

berpagar *vi* to have a fence; *adj* fenced ← **pagar**

berpahala *adj* meritorious ← **pahala**

berpakaian *adj* dressed in; *vi* to be dressed in ← **pakaian, pakai**

berpaling *vi* to turn away or from ← **paling**

berpamit *vi* to take leave ← **pamit**

berpancar *vi* to shine out ← **pancar**

berpandangan *vi* to look at each other; to have a certain view ← **pandangan, pandang**

berpangkal *adj* based; *vi* to have a base ← **pangkal**

berpangkat *vi* to have the rank of ← **pangkat**

berpantang *vi* to not be allowed, abstain

from; *makan* ~ to be on a diet, not eat certain foods ← **pantang**

berpantulan *vi* to reflect (of many things) ← **pantul**

berpantun *vi* to recite or write a traditional poem ← **pantun**

berpapasan *vi* to pass each other (very closely); *banyak mobil* ~ *di gang sempit ini* lots of cars pass close by in this narrow lane ← **papas**

berparas *vi* to have a face or appearance ← **paras**

berpasang-pasangan *adv* in pairs ← **pasang**

berpautan *vi* to be related; *adj* related; *saling* ~ interconnected ← **paut**

berpedoman *vi* to be guided by, based on ← **pedoman**

berpegang *vi* to hold onto; ~ *teguh* to hold fast to ← **pegang**

berpeluang *vi* to have an opportunity, a chance; *Susi masih* ~ *menjadi juara* Susi still has a chance to win the tournament ← **peluang, luang**

berpeluh *vi* to sweat, perspire ← **peluh**

berpelukan *vi* to hug each other ← **peluk**

berpencaran *vi* to disperse (of many things) ← **pencar**

berpendapat *vi* to have an opinion, believe ← **pendapat, dapat**

berpendidikan *adj* educated; *vi* to have an education; ~ *SD* have a primary school education ← **pendidikan, didik**

berpendirian *vi* to hold, be of an opinion ← **pendirian, diri**

berpengalaman *adj* experienced, skilled; *vi* to have experience, be experienced ← **pengalaman, alam**

berpengaruh *adj* influential; *vi* to have influence ← **pengaruh**

berpengetahuan *adj* knowledgeable ← **pengetahuan, tahu**

berperan *vi* to play a role or part ← **peran**

berperang *vi* to wage war, go to war ← **perang**

berperawakan *vi* to have a build, stature; ~ *tinggi* tall ← **perawakan, awak**

berperilaku *vi* to behave, act ← **perilaku**

berpesan *vi* to leave a message ← **pesan**

berpésta *vi* to (have a) party; ~ *pora* to have a big, lavish party ← **pésta**

berpidato *vi* to make a speech, give an address ← **pidato**

berpihak *vi* to take sides ← **pihak**

berpijak *vi* to stand on ← **pijak**

berpikir *vi* to think; ~ *panjang* to think hard; ~ *positif* to think positive; **berpikiran** *vi* to have a thought; ~ *sempit* narrow-minded ← **pikir, pikiran**

berpiknik *vi* to have a picnic ← **piknik**

berpindah *vi* to move ← **pindah**

berpinggul *vi* to have (a certain type of) hips; *adj* -hipped; ~ *besar* wide-hipped, big-hipped ← **pinggul**

berpisah *vi* to part, separate ← **pisah**

berpola *vi* to have a pattern; *adj* patterned ← **pola**

berpolémik *vi* to debate, argue over ← **polémik**

berpolitik *vi* to play politics ← **politik**

berponi *vi* to have a fringe or bangs ← **poni**

berpori *adj* porous; *vi* to have pores; *kulit* ~ *besar* skin with large pores ← **pori**

berpose *vi* to pose for a photograph ← **pose**

berposisi *vi* to hold a position, be positioned ← **posisi**

berpoténsi *vi* to have potential → **kemampuan**

berpotongan *adj* of a certain style or cut ← **potongan, potong**

berprasangka *vi* to be prejudiced ← **prasangka, sangka**

berprédikat *adj* with the title of; *vi* to have the title of ← **prédikat**

berpréstasi *adj* prestigious; successful ← **préstasi**

berprét, énsi *vi* to be pretentious, give the impression of ← **préténsi**

berprinsip *vi* to have principles; *adj* principled ← **prinsip**

berproduksi *vi* to be in production ← **produksi**

berprofési *vi* to have a profession, work as ← **profési**

berpuasa *vi* to fast ← **puasa**

berpukul-pukulan *vi* to hit each other ← **pukul**

berpulang *vi* to pass away, die ← **pulang**

berpura-pura *vi* to pretend, fake ← **pura-pura**

berpusar *vi* to revolve, whirl ← **pusar**

berpusat *vi* ~ *pada* to focus or center on ← **pusat**

berputar *vi* to rotate, turn ← **putar**

bersabar *vi* to be patient ← **sabar**

bersabda *vi* to say or speak; *Sri Sultan* ~ the Sultan expressed ← **sabda**

bersabun *adj* soapy ← **sabun**

bersahabat *adj* to be friends ← **sahabat**

bersahaja *adj* simple, natural ← **sahaja**

bersaing *vi* to compete; *harga* ~ competitive price; **bersaingan** *vi* to compete with each other; *perusahaan layanan HP sekarang saling ~ untuk mendapat konsumen* mobile phone providers are now competing against each other to get customers ← **saing**

bersaksi *vi* to testify ← **saksi**

bersalah *adj* guilty; *vi* to be guilty ← **salah**

bersalam-salaman *vi, pl* to shake hands with others ← **salam**

bersalin *vi* to give birth; *rumah sakit* ~ maternity hospital ← **salin**

bersalju *adj* snowy, snow-covered ← **salju**

bersalto *vi* to (do a) somersault ← **salto**

bersama *adv* together; jointly; *kepentingan* ~ common interest; **bersamaan** *vi* to coincide, be equal; *adv* at the same time ← **sama**

bersambung *adj* in parts; to be continued; *cerita* ~ *(cerber)* serial ← **sambung**

bersambut *vi gayung* ~ receive a response ← **sambut**

bersampingan *adj* next to each other ← **samping**

bersampul *adj* in an envelope or folder ← **sampul**

bersandar *vi* to lean ← **sandar**

bersanding *vi* to stand or sit next to; **bersandingan** *v* to stand or sit next to each other ← **sanding**

bersandiwara *vi* to pretend ← **sandiwara**

bersanggama *vi* to have sex ← **sanggama**

bersanggul *vi* to wear a bun ← **sanggul**

bersangka *vi* to suspect or think; ~ *buruk* to think the worst ← **sangka**

bersangkut *vi* to be concerned; ~ *paut* to have a connection or link; **bersangkutan** *adj* concerned, involved; *yang* ~ *(ybs)* person concerned or involved ← **sangkut**

bersantai *vi* to relax, take it easy ← **santai**

bersantan *adj* containing coconut milk; *vi* to contain coconut milk ← **santan**

bersantap *vi, pol* to eat, partake of; ~ *pagi* breakfast ← **santap**

bersarang *vi* to (make a) nest ← **sarang**

bersarung *adj* in a sarung; with a cover ← **sarung**

bersatu *vi* to unite; ~ *padu* to unite, integrate ← **satu**

bersaudara *vi* to be related; to have brothers and sisters; ~ *enam* to be one of six (children) ← **saudara**

bersayap *adj* winged; *vi* to have wings ← **sayap**

bersebelahan *conj* next to ← **sebelah, belah**

berseberangan *adj* opposing, in disagreement ← **seberang**

bersedekah *vi* to make a donation ← **sedekah**

bersedekap *vi* to put your hands on your stomach (as during the daily prayers in Islam) ← **sedekap, dekap**

bersedia *vi* to be prepared or willing ← **sedia**

bersedih *vi* to be or feel sad ← **sedih**

bersejarah *adj* historic, historical ← **sejarah**

bersekolah *vi* to go to school ← **sekolah**

bersekongkol *vi* to plot, conspire against ← **sekongkol, kongkol**

bersekutu *vi* to be allies ← **sekutu**

berselancar *vi* to surf, go surfing; ~ *angin* to go windsurfing, sailboarding ← **selancar, lancar**

berselang *adj* with an interval of; ~*seling* alternating, staggered ← **selang**

berseléra *vi* to have a taste or appetite for; *adj* tasteful, classy ← **seléra**

berselimutkan *vi* to have a blanket of ← **selimut**

berselingkuh *vi* to have an affair ← **selingkuh**

berselisih *vi* to differ in opinion, have a different opinion, quarrel ← **selisih**

berseliweran *vi* to move around, come and go ← **seliweran, seliwer**

berselonjor *adj* with outstretched legs ← **selonjor**

berseloroh *vi* to joke ← **seloroh**

berselubung *adj* veiled ← **selubung**

bersemangat *adj* spirited, enthusiastic ← **semangat**

bersembahyang *vi* to pray, perform a prayer ← **sembahyang**

bersemboyan *adj* with the motto ← **semboyan**

bersembunyi *vi* to hide (yourself) ← **sembunyi**

bersemedi *vi* to meditate ← **semedi**

bersemi *vi* to sprout buds ← **semi**

bersenandung *vi* to hum, sing ← **senandung**

bersenang-senang *vi* to enjoy yourself, have fun ← **senang**

bersenda *vi* ~ *gurau* to joke around ← **senda**

bersendawa *vi* to burp, belch ← **sendawa**

bersénggolan *vi, pl* to bump into each other ← **sénggol**

bersenjata *adj* armed ← **senjata**

bersentuh *vi* to touch; **bersentuhan** *adv* touching each other ← **sentuh**

bersenyawa *vi* to become a chemical compound ← **senyawa**

bersepakat *vi* to agree, to have an agreement ← **sepakat, pakat**

bersepatu *adj* in shoes ← **sepatu**

bersepéda *vi* to ride a bicycle ← **sepéda**

bersérakan *adj* scattered everywhere ← **sérak**

berserat *makanan* ~ high-fiber food ← **serat**

berseri *adj* beaming, glowing ← **seri**

bersértifikat *adj* with papers (of a house) ← **sértifikat**

berseru *vi* to call, cry; ~ *kepada* to call on, appeal ← **seru**

berseteru *vi* to be hostile, at odds with ← **seteru**

bersetubuh *vi* to have sex ← **setubuh, tubuh**

bersetuju *vi* to agree ← **setuju, tuju**

bersiaga *vi* to be on the alert, on guard ← **siaga**

bersiap *vi* to get ready; **bersiap-siap** *vi* to make preparations ← **siap**

bersidang *vi* to convene, be in session ← **sidang**

bersifat *vi* to have the quality of ← **sifat**

bersih *adj* clean, neat; net; *berat* ~ net weight; **kebersihan** *n* cleanliness, hygiene; **membersihkan** *vt* to clean; wipe out (eg. disease); **pembersih** *n* cleaning agent; **pembersihan** *n* cleaning, purification; purge

bersikap *vi* to display an attitude ← **sikap**

bersikeras *vi* to maintain, stick to, be obstinate ← **keras**

bersikukuh *vi* to hold fast to ← **kukuh**

bersila *duduk* ~ to sit cross-legged ← **sila**

bersilang *adj* crossed ← **silang**

bersilaturahmi *vi* to maintain good relations, visit or meet friends ← **silaturahmi**

bersimbah *vi* to be spattered or wet with ← **simbah**

bersimbol *vi* to have a symbol, be symbolized by ← **simbol**; → **berlambang**

bersimpang *vi* to branch ← **simpang**

bersimpati *adj* sympathetic ← **simpati**

bersimpuh *vi* to sit kneeling with feet to one side

bersin *vi* to sneeze

bersinambung *adj* continuous ← **sambung**

bersinar *vi* to shine, gleam ← **sinar**

bersisik *adj* scaly, rough; *vi* to have scales ← **sisik**

bersitegang *vi* to stand fast, persevere ← **tegang**

bersiul *vi* to whistle ← **siul**

berskala *vi* to be on a scale; ~ *besar* large-scale ← **skala**

berski *vi* to ski, go skiing ← **ski**

bersobat *vi* to be friends with ← **sobat**

bersoda *adj* carbonated; *minuman* ~ carbonated drink ← **soda**

bersolék *vi* to put on make-up, dress up ← **solék**

bersorak *vi* to cheer, shout ← **sorak**

bersosok *vi* to have a figure; ~ *tinggi* tall ← **sosok**

berspékulasi *vi* to speculate ← **spékulasi**

bersua *vi* to meet ← **sua**

bersuami *adj, f* married; *vi* to have a husband; **bersuamikan** *vi* to be married to ← **suami**

bersuap-suapan *vi* to feed each other (in marriage rituals) ← **suap**

bersuara *vi* to sound, have a voice ← **suara**

bersuasana *vi* to have an atmosphere; *Bali masih* ~ *santai* Bali still has a relaxed atmosphere ← **suasana**

bersuhu *vi* to have a temperature ← **suhu**

bersuit *vi* to whistle using your fingers ← **suit**

bersujud *vi* to prostrate yourself ← **sujud**

bersulang *vi* to toast, drink to ← **sulang**

bersumpah *vi* to swear ← **sumpah**

bersungguh-sungguh *vi* to do your best ← **sungguh**

bersusah ~ *payah* to work hard ← **susah**

bersusila *vi* to have good morals ← **susila**

bersyarat *adj* conditional; *vi* to have conditions ← **syarat**

bersyukur *adj* grateful ← **syukur**

bertabiat *vi* to be of a character, be of a temperament ← **tabiat**

bertabrakan *vi* to run into each other, collide ← **tabrak**

bertaburan *adj* scattered over ← **tabur**

bertahan *vi* to hold out ← **tahan**

bertahap *adj* in stages ← **tahap**

bertahun-tahun *adv* for years and years ← **tahun**

bertajuk *vi* to have a topic ← **tajuk**

bertakhta *vi* to reign ← **takhta**

bertakwa *vi* pious ← **takwa**

bertamasya *vi* to travel (for pleasure), go sightseeing ← **tamasya**

bertambah *vi* to increase ← **tambah**

bertambal *adj* patched; *vi* to have a patch ← **tambal**

bertambat *vi* to moor ← **tambat**

bertaméng *vi* to hide behind, use as a shield or pretext ← **taméng**

bertanda *adj* marked; *vi* to have a mark ← **tanda**

bertandang *vi* to (pay a) visit ← **tandang**

bertanding *vi* to compete, play ← **tanding**

bertangan *adj* -handed; *vi* to have a hand; ~ *hampa* empty-handed ← **tangan**

bertanggal *vi* to have a date; *tak* ~ undated ← **tanggal**

bertanggung jawab *adj* responsible; *vi* to be responsible, have responsibility ← **tanggung jawab**

bertani *vi* to farm, till the soil ← **tani**

bertanya *vi* to ask; **bertanya-tanya** *vi* to wonder, ask yourself ← **tanya**

bertapa *vi* to live as an ascetic or hermit, seclude oneself ← **tapa**

bertaraf *adj* of a certain standard ← **taraf**

bertaruh *vi* to bet ← **taruh**

bertatapan *vi* to look at each other, be face-to-face ← **tatap**

bertato *adj* tattooed; *vi* to have a tattoo ← **tato**

bertébaran *adj* scattered ← **tébar**

berteduh *vi* to take shelter ← **teduh**

bertékad *vi* to be determined ← **tékad**

bertekuk *vi* to bend your knees ~ *lutut* to surrender, go down on your knees ← **tekuk**

bertekun *vi* to work hard, be diligent ← **tekun**

bertelanjang *vi* to be bare; ~ *dada* bare-chested ← **telanjang**

bertélé-télé *adj* long-winded ← **télé**

bertelinga *vi* to have ears; ~ *tebal* thick-skinned, impervious to criticism ← **telinga**

bertelur *vi* to lay an egg ← **telur**

bertéma *vi* to have as a theme ← **téma**

berteman *vi* to be friends ← **teman**

bertempat *vi* to take place or happen; ~ *tinggal* to live or reside ← **tempat**

bertempur *vi* to fight ← **tempur**

bertemu *vi* to meet; *sampai* ~ *lagi* see you later, so long ← **temu**

berténggér *vi* to perch, land ← **ténggér**

bertengkar *vi* to quarrel ← **tengkar**

bertentangan *adj* contradictory, contrary, opposing ← **tentang**

bertenun *vi* to weave ← **tenun**

bertepatan *adj* coinciding with, at the same time as ← **tepat**

bertepuk tangan *vi* to applaud, clap ← **tepuk tangan**

berteriak *vi* to scream or shout ← **teriak**

berterima kasih *vi* to be grateful or thankful ← **terima kasih**

bertetangga *vi* to have neighbors ← **tetangga**

bertiga *adj* in a three ← **tiga**

bertikai *vi* to quarrel or disagree ← **tikai**

bertimbun-timbun *adv* in heaps, piled up ← **timbun**

bertindak *vi* to act, take action ← **tindak**

bertingkah *vi* to act, behave ← **tingkah**

bertingkat *vi* to have different levels; *rumah* ~ two-storied house ← **tingkat**

bertinju *vi* to box ← **tinju**

bertitel *vi* to have the title ← **titel**

bertiup *vi* to blow ← **tiup**

bertobat *vi* to repent ← **tobat**

bertolak *vi* form to depart, leave ← **tolak**

bertongkat *adj* with a stick ← **tongkat**

bertransaksi *vi* to make a transaction ← **transaksi**

bertuah *adj* lucky; *vi* to have magical powers ← **tuah**

bertualang *vi* to have an adventure ← **tualang**

bertubi-tubi *adv* repeatedly, without stopping, unceasing ← **tubi**

bertubuh *vi* to have a body; ~ *gemuk* fat; **bersetubuh** *vi* to have sex ← **tubuh**

bertuhan *vi* to believe in God; *tidak* ~ atheist ← **tuhan**

bertujuan *adj* with a purpose of; *vi* to have a purpose ← **tujuan, tuju**

bertukar *vi* to change ← **tukar**

bertumpang *vi* ~ *tindih* to overlap ← **tumpang**

bertumpu *vi* to rest on ← **tumpu**

bertumpuk *vi* to be in piles; **bertumpuk-tumpuk** *adv* in piles ← **tumpuk**

berturut-turut *adj* consecutive, successive ← **turut**

bertutur *vi* to speak or talk ← **tutur**

beruang *n* bear; ~ *kutub,* ~ *putih* polar bear

berubah *vi* to change ← **ubah**

beruban *vi* to have gray hairs ← **uban**

berudara *vi* to have air (of a certain quality); ~ *panas* hot ← **udara**

berujar *vi* to speak or say ← **ujar**

berujung *vi* to (have an) end ← **ujung**

berukuran *vi* to have a size, -sized ← **ukuran, ukur**

berulah *vi* to behave ← **ulah**

berulang *vi* to happen again, recur; **berulang-ulang** *adv* again and again, repeatedly ← **ulang**

berumah tangga *adj* married; *vi* to have your own family ← **rumah tangga**

berumbai *vi* to have tassels; *adj* tasseled ← **rumbai, umbai**

berumur *adj* aged ← **umur**

berunding *vi* to discuss ← **runding**

berunjuk *vi* ~ *rasa* to demonstrate, hold a demonstration ← **unjuk**

beruntun *adj* in a chain; *tabrakan* ~ pile-up ← **runtun**

beruntung *adj* lucky, fortunate; *vi* to have luck, good fortune ← **untung**

berupa *adj* in the shape or form of; *vi* to have a shape or form ← **rupa**

berupaya *vi* to make an effort, try ← **upaya**

berurai *vi* to hang down or loose ← **urai**

berurusan *vi* to have dealings with, deal with ← **urusan, urus**

berurutan, berurut-urutan *adj* successive, consecutive, sequential ← **urutan, urut**

berusaha *vi* to try, make an effort ← **usaha**

berusia *adj* (to be) aged ← **usia**

berutang *vi* to owe; ~ *budi* to have a debt of gratitude ← **utang**

bervibrasi *vi* to vibrate ← **vibrasi**

berwajah *vi* to have a face; ~ *muram* sour-faced ← **wajah**

berwajib *adj* responsible, competent ← **wajib**

berwarna *adj* colored; *vi* to have a color ← **warna**

berwatak *vi* to have a certain nature; ~ *keras* strict, stern, unyielding ← **watak**

berwawasan *vi* to have an outlook; ~ *luas* broad or open mind ← **wawasan**

berwenang *adj* competent, in charge ← **wenang**

berwibawa *adj* esteemed, respected, of good standing ← **wibawa**

berwisata *vi* to travel or holiday ← **wisata**

berwudu *vi* to wash before praying ← **wudu**

berwujud *vi* in the form or shape of ← **wujud**

beryodium *vi garam* ~ iodized salt ← **yodium**

berziarah *vi* to make a pilgrimage, visit a holy place ← **ziarah**

berzikir *vi, Isl* to say additional prayers ← **zikir**

berzina *vi* to commit adultery ← **zina**

bésan *n* relationship between two couples whose children have married; ~*nya orang tentara* his daughter's father-in-law is in the army

besar *adj* big, large, great; ~ *kepala* big-headed, arrogant; *hari* ~ (religious) holiday; **besar-besaran** *adj* large-scale; **berbesar** ~ *hati adj* big-hearted, accepting; **kebesaran** *n* greatness; *adj* too big; *Celana ini* ~*!* these pants are too big!; **membesar** *vi* to get bigger, grow; **membesarkan** *vt* to bring up, raise (children); **memperbesar** *vt* to enlarge something; **pembesar** *n* big-shot, official; **pembesaran** *n* enlargement, expansion; **terbesar** *adj* largest, biggest

beserta *conj* along with, and ← **serta**

besi *n* iron; ~ *tempa* wrought iron; ~ *tua* scrap metal; ~ *tuang* cast iron; *tukang* ~ blacksmith

bésok *adv* tomorrow; *coll* in the future; ~ *lusa* tomorrow ← **ésok**

besuk *v* to visit someone in hospital; *jam* ~ visiting hours; **membesuk** *vt* to visit someone in hospital

béta *lit, arch* I, me

betah *v* settle in, feel at home

betapa *adv* how (very); ~ *cantiknya!* how pretty she is!; *conj* ~*pun* however → **alangkah**

Betawi original inhabitants of Jakarta (since 1527); *orang* ~ the Betawi people

bété, BT *adj, sl* moody, bad-tempered ← **berahi tinggi**

beterbangan *vi, pl* to fly about ← **terbang**

betina *adj* female (of animals); *anjing* ~ bitch

betis *n* calf, lower part of leg

beton *n* concrete

betul *adj* true, correct, right; real; *adv* really, truly; *besar* ~ it's really big; **betul-betul** *adv* truly, completely; **kebetulan** *adv* by chance, accidentally; *n* coincidence; **membetulkan** *vt* to correct, repair; **pembetulan** *n* correction, repair; **sebetulnya** *adv* in fact, actually

bhinneka ~ *Tunggal Ika* Unity in Diversity

BI *abbrev Bank Indonesia* Bank Indonesia, the central reserve bank

bi *pron* Aunt; term of address for older housemaid ← **bibi**

biadab *adj* uncivilized, savage; **kebiadaban** *n* savagery

biak *berkembang* ~ *vi* to multiply, breed; **membiakkan** *vt* to breed, cultivate; **pembiakan** *n* breeding, cultivation

biang *n* cause; ~ *keladi* source of the problem, mastermind, ringleader; ~ *kerok* agitator, troublemaker; ~ *keringat* prickly heat

bianglala *n* rainbow

biar let, no matter if; *conj* so that; ~*lah!* never mind!; ~*pun* even if, although; **membiarkan** *vt* to let, allow, permit; *biarkan!* let it be!; **biarin** *sl* who cares?

biara *n* abbey, monastery, convent; *kepala* ~ *m* abbot, *f* abbess; **biarawan** *n* monk; **biarawati** *n* nun

bias *n* ray; refraction

biasa *adj* normal, usual, common, ordinary; ~*nya* usually; *luar* ~ extraordinary; **kebiasaan** *n* habit, custom; **membiasakan** *vt* ~ *diri* to accustom yourself; **terbiasa** *adj* used to, accustomed

biawak *n* type of iguana, monitor lizard

biaya *n* cost, expense (for a service); ~ *hidup* cost of living; ~ *pengiriman* dispatch cost; ~ *perawatan* cost of treatment, cost of upkeep; **membiayai** *vt* to finance someone or something; **pembiayaan** *n* financing

bibi *n, pron* aunt, sister of parent; mother's female cousin

bibir *n* lip; edge, mouth; ~ *atas* upper lip; ~ *sumbing* harelip, cleft palate

bibit *n* seedling; **pembibitan** *n* sowing, planting of seeds, cultivation

bicara *v* speak; **berbicara** *vi* to speak; ~ *dalam bahasa Sunda* to speak in Sundanese; **membicarakan** *vt* to discuss; **pembicara** *n* speaker; **pembicaraan** *n* discussion

bidadari *n* fairy

bidak *n* pawn (in chess)

bidan *n* midwife; **kebidanan** *n* midwifery

bidang *adj* spacious, wide; *n* area, field; *Sumitro adalah ahli dalam* ~ *ekonomi* Sumitro is an expert in the field of economics; *se~ tanah* piece of land

bidik aim; **membidik** *vi* to take aim

biduan *n* vocalist; **biduanita** *n, f* vocalist, diva

bihalal *halal* ~ social gathering (especially after Idul Fitri)

bihun *n* vermicelli noodles

bijak *adj* wise; **kebijakan** *n* policy; **bijaksana** *adj* wise, prudent; **kebijaksanaan** *n* caution, prudence; policy

biji *n* seed, grain; counter for very small objects; *sl* counter; ~ *mata* eyeball; ~ *melinjo* seed used for making *emping* chips; *biji* ~ a kind of sweet porridge made to break the fast; *Mau beli kancing berapa* ~*?* how many buttons do you want to buy?; **biji-bijian** *n* seeds, grains

bijih *n* ore

bika ambon *n* yellow cake like a crumpet, a specialty of Medan

bikin *vi, coll* to make; ~ *marah* make angry; **bikinan** *n* product; ~ *Australia* product of Australia; **dibikin** *v* to be made → **buat**

biksu *n* Buddhist monk; **biksuni** *n* Buddhist nun

bila, bilamana *conj* if; when (usually in written form); ~ *kuingat* if I remember

bilah *n* chip; counter for long, narrow objects; *se~ tombak* one spear, a spear

bilang *v, sl* say; *Jangan* ~*!* don't tell anyone; **dibilang** *v* to be said

bilang: bilangan *n* number, figure, sum; **terbilang** *adj* counted; *tidak* ~ countless; *Esa hilang, dua* ~ one lost, two scored (epigraph at military cemeteries)

bilas *v* **membilas** *vt* to rinse; *Gosokkan pada rambut, lalu* ~ rub into the hair, then rinse

biliar, bilyar *n* billiards

bilik *n* small room, chamber

biliun, bilyun *n* billion (1,000,000,000); **biliunér** *n* billionaire

bimasakti *n* the Milky Way

bimbang *adj* nervous, doubtful; *hati yang* ~ an uncertain heart

bimbing *vt* to lead, guide; **bimbingan** *n* guidance; ~ *belajar* (bimbel) extracurricular course to prepare for exams; **membimbing** *vt* to lead, guide, coach; **pembimbing** *n* guide, coach, leader

BIN *abbrev Badan Intelijen Negara* State Intelligence Agency

bin *n, Isl* son of (father's name); **binti** *n, Isl* daughter of (father's name)

bin *aneh* ~ *ajaib* very strange

bina *vi* build up; ~ *Graha* Presidential office during New Order; ~ *Marga* roads board; ~ *raga* body-building; **binaragawan** *n, m* body-builder; **membina** *vt* to build up, found; **pembina** *n* founder, patron; coach; **pembinaan** *n* development

binar: berbinar-binar *adj* shining, gleaming

binasa *adj* destroyed, ruined; **membinasakan** *vt* to destroy, ruin

binatang *n* animal; ~ *buas* wild animal; ~ *melata* reptile; ~ *menyusui* mammal; ~ *mengerat*, ~ *pengerat* rodent

binatu *n* (commercial) laundry

bincang: berbincang, berbincangbincang *vi* to chat, discuss; **perbincangan** *n* discussion

bindeng *adj, Jav* nasal (due to a cold)

bingkai *n* frame; ~ *kacamata* glasses frames; **berbingkai** *vi* to have a frame; *adj* framed; **membingkai** *vt* to frame

bingkis: bingkisan *n* wrapped or free gift

bingung *adj* confused; **kebingungan** *n* confusion; **membingungkan** *adj* confusing; *vt* to confuse

bini *sl* wife

binokular *n* binoculars

bintang *n* star; asterisk (*); ~ *berekor* comet; ~ *film* film star; ~ *ibukota* star from the capital; ~ *iklan* advertising model; ~ *jatuh* shooting star; ~ *kejora* morning star (symbol of Papuan independence movement), Venus; ~ *laut* starfish; ~ *pari* the Southern Cross; ~ *tamu* guest star; ~ *timur* morning star; hotel ~ *tiga* three-star hotel; **berbintang** *vi* to have a star (sign); *jenderal* ~ *tiga* three-star general; *Dini* ~ Aries Dini's star sign is Aries; **membintangi** *vt* to star (in); *Dian Sastro* ~ *film 'Pasir Berbisik'* Dian Sastro starred in *Pasir Berbisik*

bintara *n* low military rank, equivalent to sergeant

binti *n, Isl* daughter of (father's name) ← **bin**

bintik *n* spot, stain, freckle; **berbintik-bintik** *adj* spotty, spotted; *vi* to have spots or freckles

bintit, bintitan, bintil *n* stye (swollen eyelid)

binturung *n* bearcat

biodata *n* personal profile (name, address, date of birth, hobbies etc)

biografi *n* biography

biola *n* violin; fiddle; *pemain* ~ violinist, violin player; fiddler

biologi *n ilmu* ~ biology; **biologis** *adj* biological

bioskop *n* cinema, movie theater

bir *n* beer; ~ *niralkohol* non-alcoholic beer

biri-biri *n* sheep, goat

birit: terbirit-birit *adv* hurriedly, helterskelter

biro *n* office, center; ~ *iklan* advertising agency; ~ *perjalanan*, ~ *wisata* travel agency; ~ *Pusat Statistik (BPS)* Central Statistics Office

birokrasi *n* bureaucracy; red tape; **birokrat** *n* bureaucrat; **birokratis** *adj* bureaucratic

biru *adj* blue; ~ *langit* sky blue; ~ *laut* aquamarine; ~ *lebam* black and blue; ~ *tua* dark blue; **kebiru-biruan** *adj* bluish; **membiru** *vi* to turn blue; *karena lama tenggelam, badannya sudah mulai* ~ since he had been underwater for some time, his body was already turning blue

bis ~ *surat* letter box, mailbox (for posting)

bis, bus *n* bus; ~ *carteran* chartered or rented bus or coach; ~ *kota* city bus; ~ *pariwisata* tourist bus; ~ *patas (penumpang terbatas)* bus with a passenger limit; ~ *tingkat* double-decker bus; *halte* ~ bus stop

bisa *v, aux* can, be able; ~ *jadi coll* possible, it could be; **bisa-bisa** *conj* it could happen that; ~ *kamu dipecat* you could get fired; **sebisanya, sebisabisanya** *adv* as well as you can, to the best of your ability

bisa *n* poison (of animals), venom; **berbisa** *adj* poisonous; *ular* ~ venomous snake

bisbol *n* baseball; *pemain* ~ baseball player

bisik *n* whisper; **bisikan** *n* whisper; ~ *hati* conscience; **berbisik** *adj* whispering; *vi* to whisper; **membisik** *vt* to whisper; **pembisik** *n* whisperer

bising *adj* noisy; *n* static; **kebisingan** *n* noise, buzz

biskuit *n* biscuit, cracker

bismillah *ejac, Isl* in the name of God

bisnis *n* business, trade; **berbisnis** *vi* to do business; **pebisnis** *n* businessman, businesswoman

bistik *n* steak; ~ *ayam* cut of barbecued chicken

bissu *n* transvestite priest of South Sulawesi

bisu *adj* mute, dumb; ~ *tuli* deaf-mute; **kebisuan** *n* silence, lack of speech; **membisu** *vi* to be silent, say nothing

bisul *n* abscess, boil, ulcer

bius *n* drug; *obat* ~ anesthetic; **membius** *vt* to drug, anesthetize; **pembiusan** *n* anesthesia

BKR *abbrev Badan Keamanan Rakyat* People's Security Agency (after independence; later became Indonesian Army)

blak-blakan *adv* outspoken; *Adam selalu bicara secara* ~ Adam always speaks his mind

blangko *n* form

blangkon *n* traditional Javanese men's headwear

blantika → **belantika**

blasteran *adj* mixed, hybrid; *Sari* ~ *Sunda-Jerman* Sari is half-Sundanese, half-German

bléncong *n* oil lamp used during a *wayang* performance

blénder *n* blender; **memblénder** *vt* to puree or juice something

bléwah *n* kind of melon

blits *n* flash (of camera)

blok *n* block (in addresses); ~ *Timur* Eastern bloc

blokir, memblokir *vt* to block; ~ *jalan* to block the road; *Begitu kecopetan, dia langsung* ~ *kartu kredit* after being robbed, he blocked his credit card

bloknot *n* writing pad

blong *adj, coll* loose, not taut; *remnya* ~ the brakes failed

bloon *adj, coll* silly, naive, impressionable; *Mr Bean* ~ *tapi pinter* Mr Bean is naive but cunning

bludak → **beludak**

blus *n* blouse

BNI *abbrev Bank Negara Indonesia* Indonesian State Bank

bo *tsl* man; *dia seksi,* ~ he's sexy, man

bobo, bobok *vi, sl* to sleep (children's language)

bobol *vi* to collapse; **membobol** *vt* to break into; *mesin ATM dibobol maling* thieves broke into the ATM machine; **pembobolan** *n* breaking into, breach

bobot *n* weight; **berbobot** *adj* heavy, weighty; *bukunya* ~ his book was substantial reading

bobrok *adj* dilapidated, rotten

bocah *n* young child

bocor *vi* to leak; *rahasia itu sudah* ~ *ke mana-mana* the secret has leaked out everywhere; **kebocoran** *n* leak; **membocorkan** *vt* to leak something; **pembocoran** *n* leakage, divulging (of secrets)

bodoh *adj* bodo *coll* stupid; **kebodohan** *n* stupidity, ignorance; **membodohi** *vt* to make someone stupid; **membodohkan** *vt* to make stupid; **pembodohan** *n* tricking, duping; ~ *rakyat* fooling the people

boga *n* food, catering; *jasa* ~ catering

bogem ~ *mentah n* (blow with the) fist, hit; *v* hit

bohlam *n* light bulb

bohong lie; **berbohong, membohong** *vi* to lie; **kebohongan** *n* lie, deceit; **membohongi** *vt* to lie to someone; **pembohong** *n* liar; **pembohongan** *n* deception, lying

boikot *n* boycott; **memboikot** *vt* to boycott something; **pemboikotan** *n* boycotting

bokap *n, tsl* father ← **bapak**

bokék *adj, sl* broke, penniless

bokong *n* buttocks, bottom

bokor *n* metal bowl (often for ceremonial use)

boks *n* playpen, bassinet; *mobil* ~ (closed) truck

bola *n* ball; football, soccer; ~ *basket* basketball; ~ *bumi* globe; ~ *lampu* light bulb; ~ *mata* eyeball; ~ *tenis* tennis ball; ~ *voli* volleyball; ~ *voli pantai* beach volleyball; *main* ~ to play football; *menjemput* ~ to be proactive

bolak-balik *adv* back and forth, to and fro, there and back; *vi* to go back and forth; **membolak-balik** *vt* to turn over and over

boléh may, can; allowed, permitted; okay; ~ *jadi* possible, it could be; ~~~ *saja* sure you can; **kebaléhan** *n* ability, what you can do; **memperboléhkan** *vt* to allow, permit

boling *n* ten-pin bowling; *main* ~ to go bowling; **peboling** *n* bowler

bolong *adj* holey, perforated; *batu* ~ coastal rock form with a hole in it; **berbolong-bolong** *adj* full of holes; **membolongi** *vt* to pierce

bolong *siang* ~ broad daylight

bolos, membolos *vi* to skip, be absent, play truant, wag, skive; ~ *sekolah* to skip school; **pembolos** *n* truant, absentee; **pembolosan** *n* absenteeism, truancy

bolpoin *n* ballpoint pen, biro

bom *n* bomb; ~ *atom* atomic bomb; ~ *nuklir* nuclear bomb; **mengebom** *vt* to bomb something; **pengeboman** *n* bombing

bombai *bawang* ~ large onion

bon *n* bill, check, receipt; *minta* ~ to ask for the bill; *pakai* ~ to make out a receipt before paying (at another counter)

boncéng, memboncéng *vt* to ride with someone else on a two-wheeled vehicle, dink; to sponge or cadge a lift; **boncéngan** *n* passenger

bondong: berbondong-bondong *adv* in droves

bonék *n* football fan or hooligan from Surabaya ← **bondo nékat**

bonéka *n* doll (like a person); soft toy (animal); puppet; *pemerintah* ~ puppet government

bonggol *n* lump, growth

bongkah *n* counter for lumps; *se~ tanah* a clod of earth

bongkar, membongkar *vt* to pull apart, dismantle; unpack; to unearth; ~ *sauh* *vi* to weigh anchor; **bongkaran** *n* component parts, unpacked goods; **pembongkaran** *n* dismantling; exposure; ~ *usaha judi sudah lama dilakukan* there have long been efforts to expose gambling joints

bontot *n* youngest child in a family ← **buntut**

boong → **bohong**

boorwater, borwater *n* boric acid (as an eye salve)

bopéng *adj* pock-marked

bopong, membopong *vt* to carry someone (bodily, or on the shoulders)

bor *n* drill; *mata* ~ drill bit; **mengebor** *vt* to drill, bore; **pengeboran** *n* drilling

bordil *n* brothel, bordello; *rumah* ~ brothel

bordir *n* embroidery; **bordiran** *n* embroidery, lace edging; **membordir** *vt* to embroider

borgol *n* handcuffs; **memborgol** *vt* to handcuff

borjuis *adj* bourgeois

boro-boro *conj* what's the point of ...? it's not even worth ...; ~ *datang, telepon saja dia tidak mau* he won't even telephone, let alone come

borong memborong *vt* to buy up, buy in bulk; **borongan** *n* goods bought in bulk; *taksi* ~ un-metered taxi; **pemborong** *n* developer, contractor

boros *adj* wasteful; **memboroskan** *vt* to waste something; **pemboros** *n* spendthrift; **pemborosan** *n* wastage

borwater ← **boorwater**

bos *pron, sl* boss, sir; *n* boss

bosan *adj* **bosen** *coll* bored, fed up with, tired of; **membosankan** *adj* boring, tiresome

Bosnia *n* Bosnia; *bahasa* ~ Bosnian; *orang* ~ Bosnian, Bosniak

bot *sepatu* ~ boots

botak *adj* bald; **kebotakan** *n* baldness, hair loss; **membotak** *vi* to go bald; **membotaki** *vt* to shave, make bald

botok, bothok *n* Javanese side-dish of shredded coconut and fresh vegetables

botol *n* bottle; *teh* ~ bottled tea

Bouraq, borak *n* mythical winged creature with a woman's head and unicorn's body

boyong, memboyong *vt* to take (someone) away; *isteri barunya diboyong ke Padang* he took his new bride with him to Padang

BPKB *abbrev Buku Pemilik Kendaraan Bermotor* vehicle registration papers

BPPN *abbrev Badan Penyehatan Perbankan Nasional* Indonesian Bank Restructuring Agency (IBRA)

BPPT *abbrev Badan Pengkajian dan Penerapan Teknologi* Agency for the Research and Application of Technology

BPS *abbrev Biro Pusat Statistik* Central Statistics Bureau

brahmana, brahmin, brahma *n* highest Hindu caste in Bali

BRAj *Bendoro Raden Ajeng* Javanese title for unmarried female aristocracy

brankas, brangkas *n* safe

Brasil *n* Brazil; *orang ~* Brazilian

BRAy *Bendoro Raden Ayu* Javanese title for married female aristocracy

brédel, membrédel *vt* to muzzle, bridle, ban; *majalah Tempo dibredel pada tahun 1994 Tempo* magazine was closed down in 1994; **pembrédelan** *n* muzzling, being closed down

bréndi *n* brandy

bréngsék *excl* blast! damn!; *n* bastard!; *adj* damn, bloody; *~ lu!* You bastard!

brem *n* a soft white biscuit made from fermented rice; alcoholic drink

bréwok, beréwok *n* beard, whiskers, sideburns; **bréwokan** *adj* whiskered, bearded

BRI *abbrev Bank Rakyat Indonesia* Indonesian People's Bank

brigadir *n* brigadier; *~-Jenderal (Brigjen)* Brigadier-General

Britania Raya *n* Great Britain

brokat *n* brocade

brokoli *n* broccoli

bromocorah *n* recidivist, repeat offender

bros n brooch

brosur *n* brochure; *~ wisata* travel brochure

BRR *abbrev Badan Réhabilitasi dan Rékonstruksi Nanggroe Aceh Darussalam* Aceh Rehabilitation and Reconstruction Agency (post-tsunami)

bruder *n* Christian brother (Catholic); **bruderan** *n* Christian Brothers seminary

brutal *adj* brutal, violent; **kebrutalan** *n* brutality, violence

bruto *adj* gross; *pendapatan ~* gross income

BTN *abbrev Bank Tabungan Negara* State Savings Bank

bu *pron* Mother (to respected older women); Mum(my), Mom(my); *~ Dé, Budé pron, Jav* aunt (older than one's parents); *~ Haji* title for a woman who has completed the pilgrimage to Mecca; *~ Lik pron, Jav* aunt (younger than one's parents)

buah *n* fruit, result; piece, general counter for objects; *~ anggur* grapes; *~ dada* breast; *~ delima* pomegranate; *~ hati* darling (child); *~ kedondong* kind of fruit; *~ kelengkeng, ~ lengkeng* small lychee; *~ kesemak* persimmon, soft fruit with sweet orange flesh; *~ kiwi* kiwifruit; *~ melinjo* fruit used for making *emping* chips; *~ nangka* jackfruit; *~ pala* nutmeg; *~ pelir* testicles; *~ salak* fruit with a hard brown skin like a snake, snakefruit; *~ simalakama* a mythical fruit, which if eaten, will cause one parent to die, but if not eaten, will cause the other parent to die; dilemma, Catch-22 situation; *~ sukun* breadfruit; *~ tangan* souvenir, gift brought home; *~ zakar* testicles; **buah-buahan** *n* fruit(s); **berbuah** *vi* to bear fruit, produce; **membuahkan** *vt* to result in; **membuahi** *vt* to impregnate, fertilize; **sebuah** *adj* a, one (generic counter); *~ kursi* a chair

buai: membuai *vt* to swing, rock, sway something

bual, membual *vi* to foam; to froth at the mouth, talk rubbish; **bualan** *n* foaming; nonsense

buana *n* universe

buang *vt* to throw (away); *~ air* to go to the toilet; *~ air (kecil)* to urinate; *~ air besar* to empty your bowels, defecate, poo; *~ hajat* to defecate; *~ sampah* to throw rubbish away; *~ sauh* to cast anchor; **buangan** *adj orang ~* exile; **membuang** *vt* to throw out; waste; exile; *~ ingus* to blow your nose; *~*

kesempatan to waste an opportunity; ~ *muka* to look the other way; **terbuang** *adj* thrown out, wasted

buas *adj* fierce, wild; *binatang* ~ wild animal; **kebuasan** *n* ferocity

buat *prep* for; ~ *kamu* for you; *vt* to do, make; *apa boleh* ~ never mind, it can't be helped; **buatan** *n* made in, product of; ~ *lokal* made locally; **berbuat** *vi* to do; ~ *salah* to do wrong; **membuat** *vt* to make; ~ *marah* to make angry; **membuat-buat** *vt* to pretend; **pembuat** *n* producer, maker; **pembuatan** *n* production, manufacture; **perbuatan** *n* act, deed; **terbuat** *adj* made

buaya *n* crocodile, alligator; ~ *darat* conman

bubar *vi* to disperse, break up, spread out; **membubarkan** *vt* to break something up; *demo itu dibubarkan polisi* the demo was broken up by the police; **pembubaran** *n* dissolution, breaking up

bubuh: membubuhkan *vt* to attach something; ~ *tanda tangan* to attach your signature

bubuk *n* powder, dust; ~ *kopi* coffee grounds; *kayu sudah menjadi* ~ the wood has rotted

bubung: membubung *vi* to peak, go upward

bubur *n* porridge; pulp; ~ *ayam* chicken porridge; ~ *kayu* wood pulp; ~ *kertas* paper pulp; ~ *sumsum* porridge made from rice flour; ~ *ketan hitam* black sticky rice porridge; *nasi telah menjadi* ~ it's too late now; no use crying over spilt milk (*lit.* the rice has become porridge)

bubut *n* lathe; *mesin* ~ lathe; *tukang* ~ worker who operates a lathe; **membubut** *vt* to use a lathe

budak *n* slave; **perbudakan** *n* slavery

budaya *n* culture; **berbudaya** *vi* to have a culture; **kebudayaan** *n* culture, civilization; **membudaya** *vi* to spread, become entrenched; *korupsi sudah* ~ corruption is part of the culture; **budayawan** *n* cultural figure

Budé, Bu Dé *pron, Jav* aunt (older than one's parents)

budeg, budek *coll, Jav* deaf

Budha *agama* ~ Buddhism; *orang* ~ Buddhist

budi *n* goodness; intellect; ~ *pekerti* good conduct, ethics; **budiman** *adj* wise, sensible

budidaya *n* cultivation; **membudidayakan** *vt* to cultivate, grow; **pembudidayaan** *n* cultivation

bufét *n* buffet meal; sideboard, buffet

bugar *adj* fit; *segar* ~ fit and healthy; **kebugaran** *n* health; *pusat* ~ gym, fitness centre

bugénvil, bogénvil *n* bougainvillea

bugil *adj* naked, nude

Bugis ethnic group from South Sulawesi; *orang* ~, *bahasa* ~ Buginese

bui *n* jail, prison

buih *n* foam, froth; **berbuih** *adj* frothy, foaming; *vi* to have froth

bujang *adj* single, unmarried (man); **bujangan** *n* bachelor; **membujang** *vi* to remain unmarried

bujuk, membujuk *vt* to coax; ~ *rayu* to flatter; **bujukan** *n* enticement

bujur *n* longitude; vertical line down a sphere; crack in buttocks; ~ *sangkar* square, rectangle; ~ *timur* east longitude

buk → **buking**

buka open; ~ *keran* turn on the tap; **berbuka** *vi* ~ *puasa* to break the fast; **membuka** *vt* to open; ~ *baju* to take off clothes; ~ *rahasia* to reveal a secret; ~ *jendela hati* to open your heart; ~ *lembar baru* to turn over a new leaf; **membukakan** *vt* to open (for someone); **pembuka** *adj* opening; *kata* ~ preface; *makanan* ~ starters, appetizers; **pembukaan** *n* opening; **terbuka** *adj* open; *sidang* ~ public session; **keterbukaan** *n* openness

bukan no, not (of things, nouns); ~ *apa-apa* nothing; ~ *main* extraordinary, no kidding!; ~*nya* isn't it ...?; ~ *siapa-siapa* nobody; *ini* ~ ? this one, isn't it?; *Fitri* ~ *adik saya* Fitri's not my sister; **bukan-bukan** *adj* undesirable, not right

bukét *n* bouquet

buking, booking *n* booking; **mem-buking, mengebuk** *vt* to book; **pembukingan** *n* bookings

bukit *n* hill; ~ *Barisan* mountain range in Sumatra; **berbukit** *adj* hilly; **perbukitan** *n* (range of) hills

bukti *n* proof, evidence; *barang* ~ evidence, exhibit; **membuktikan** *vt* to prove; **terbukti** *adj* proven

buku *n* book; ~ *alamat* address book; ~ *bacaan* reader; ~ *catatan* notebook; ~ *harian* journal, diary; ~ *panduan* guide(book); ~ *pelajaran* textbook; ~ *peta* atlas; ~ *peta jalan* road atlas, street directory; ~ *petunjuk* manual, guide; ~ *petunjuk telepon* telephone directory, *coll* phone book; ~ *pintar* reference book; ~ *tulis* notebook, exercise book; ~ *Pemilik Kendaraan Bermotor (BPKB)* vehicle registration papers; **membukukan** *vt* to enter into the accounts, books; **pembukuan** *n* book-keeping

buku *n* joint; ~ *jari* knuckle

bulak-balik → **bolak-balik**

bulan *n* moon, month; ~ *Februari* February; ~ *madu* honeymoon; *ber~ madu* to (have a) honeymoon; ~ *puasa* fasting month, Ramadan; ~ *purnama* full moon; ~ *sabit* crescent moon; *datang* ~ menstruate, have your period; **bulan-bulanan** *n* laughing-stock, object of derision

bulat *adj* round; fat; ~ *panjang* cylindrical; *telanjang* ~ stark naked; *dengan suara* ~ unanimously; **bulatan** *n* circle; **membulatkan** *vt* to round off; **pembulatan** *n* rounding-off

bulé *adj* white(-skinned), Caucasian, Western; albino; *orang* ~ Westerner; *n, derog* white person, whitey, paleface

Bulik, Bu lik *pron, Jav* aunt (younger than one's parents)

Bulog *abbrev Badan Urusan Logistik* Logistics Management Board

bulu *n* feather; fur; body hair; ~ *ayam* feather; ~ *domba* wool; ~ *kuduk* hairs on the back of your neck; ~ *mata* eyelashes; ~ *roma* body hair; ~ *tangkis* badminton; *tidak pandang* ~ to be objective, not discriminate; **berbulu** *adj* hairy; *vi* to have fur or feathers

buluh *n* bamboo; **pembuluh** *n* ~ *darah* blood vessel, artery

bulus *n* turtle; *akal* ~ trickery, deceit

bum boom!

bumbu *n* spice; **membumbui** *vt* to season

bumerang *n* boomerang; *itu sudah menjadi* ~ *bagi Hari* it's come back to haunt Hari

bumi *n* earth, ground; *ilmu* ~ geography; *minyak* ~ *petroleum* crude oil; *bagai* ~ *dan langit* (as different as) night and day; ~ *hangus* scorched earth; **membumihanguskan** *vt* to scorch the earth, apply a scorched earth policy; **bumiputera, pribumi** *n* native inhabitant, son of the soil

BUMN *abbrev Badan Usaha Milik Negara* state-owned corporation

buncis *n* string bean

buncit *adj* pot-bellied, fat; *sl* pregnant; *perut* ~ pot belly; pregnant

bunda *pron, pol, lit* Mother ← **ibunda**

bundar *adj* bunder *coll* round; *meja bundar* round table; **bundaran** *n* roundabout

Bung *pron* brother; ~ *Karno* President Sukarno; *ayo ~!* come on, mate!

bunga *n* flower, blossom; interest; ~ *bangkai* Rafflesia flower; ~ *berbunga* compound interest; ~ *desa* village beauty; ~ *hidup* cut flowers; ~ *kamboja* frangipani; ~ *matahari* sunflower; ~ *mawar*, ~ *ros* rose; ~ *pala* mace; ~ *seroja* kind of lotus; ~ *rampai* bouquet, bunch of flowers; *karangan* ~ wreath, bouquet; *musim* ~ spring; ~ *hanya 3%* only 3% interest; **berbunga** *vi* to flower, blossom; to gain interest; *bunga* ~ compound interest

bungalo *n* bungalow, cottage, one-story house

bungkam *adj* quiet, silent; **membungkam** *vi* to keep silent

bungker, bunker *n* (underground) bunker, hiding place

bungkuk, bongkok *adj* crooked, bent; **membungkuk** *vi* to bow, be hunched; **membungkukkan** *vt* ~ *badan* to bow

bungkus *n* takeaway, pack; *nasi* ~ a takeaway rice meal; **membungkus** *vt* to wrap; ~ *kado* wrap a gift; **pembungkus** *n* wrapping, packing; **pembungkusan** *n* packaging

bunglon *n* chameleon

bungsu *n* youngest child in a family; *anak ~, si ~* youngest child

buntel *n* knapsack

bunting *adj* pregnant (of animals)

buntu *adj* one-way, useless; *jalan ~* dead-end; cul-de-sac, court, no through road

buntung *adj* amputated; unlucky; *ingin untung malah ~* wanting good luck, but being unlucky instead

buntut *n* tail; *~nya* the consequence; *sop ~* oxtail soup; **berbuntut** *vi* to go further, end; *ceritanya ~ sedih* the tale had a sad ending; **membuntuti** *vt* to follow someone

bunuh, membunuh *vt* to kill; ~ *diri* to kill yourself, commit suicide; **pembunuh** *n* murderer, killer; ~ *bayaran* hitman, hired killer; **pembunuhan** *n* murder, killing; **terbunuh** *adj* killed

bunyi *n* sound, noise; **berbunyi** *vi* to sound, make a noise; **membunyikan** *vt* to sound, ring something

bupati *n* regent; **kabupatén** *n* regency

buram *adj* cloudy, frosted, dull

Burkina Faso *n* Burkina Faso; *orang ~* Burkinabé

buron *n* fugitive

bursa *n* exchange; ~ *efek* stock exchange; ~ *kerja* job market; ~ *komputer* computer market

buru, memburu *vt* to hunt, chase; **buruan, buron** *n* the hunted; **berburu** *vi* to go hunting; **keburu** *sl* in time; too early; had already; ~ *habis* already run out; **pemburu** *n* hunter; **pemburuan** *n* hunt, chase; **terburu, terburu-buru** *adj* in a hurry

buruh *n* laborer; ~ *bangunan* construction worker; *Hari ~* Labor Day; *Partai ~* Labor Party; **perburuhan** *n* concerning labor

buruk *adj* bad (of a situation, weather); ugly; *kabar ~* bad news; **memburuk** *vi* to worsen; **memperburuk** *vt* to make even worse

burung *n* bird; ~ *béo* parrot; ~ *camar* seagull; ~ *dara* pigeon, dove; ~ *elang* eagle, hawk, falcon, bird of prey; ~ *gagak* crow, raven; ~ *gereja* sparrow; ~ *hantu* owl; ~ *jalak* starling; ~ *kakatua* cockatoo; ~ *kasuari* cassowary; ~ *kenari* canary; ~ *kutilang* thrush; ~ *manyar* weaverbird; ~ *murai* magpie; ~ *nasar* vulture; ~ *nuri* parrot; ~ *parkit* parakeet; ~ *pelikan* pelican; ~ *perkici* rainbow lorikeet; ~ *perkutut* turtle-dove; ~ *punai* kind of green pigeon; ~ *puyuh* quail; ~ *unta* ostrich; ~ *walet* swift; *kabar ~* rumor, gossip

busa *n* foam, lather; **berbusa** *adj* foamy; *vi* to have a layer of foam

busana *n* clothing, wear; ~ *kantor* office wear; ~ *pengantin* wedding dress or costume; **berbusana** *vi* to wear

busét *ejac* hell! damn!

busi *n* spark plug

busuk *adj* rotten; *bau ~* bad smell; *hati ~* evil, depraved; **membusuk** *vi* to rot; **pembusukan** *n* (process of) decay

busung *adj* swollen, distended; ~ *lapar* disease caused by starvation; **membusung** *vi* to puff up, be bloated

busur *n* bow

buta *adj* blind; ~ *akan* blind to; ~ *aksara, ~ huruf* illiterate; ~ *warna* color-blind; *pagi ~* in the early hours of the morning, before sunrise

butek *adj* turbid, muddy

butik *n* boutique

butir *n* grain, counter for small oval objects; *se~ nasi* a grain of rice; *tiga ~ telur* three eggs

butuh *vt* need; **kebutuhan** *n* need, necessity; **membutuhkan** *vt* to need something

buyar *vi* to run, bleed (of ink); to break down; **membuyarkan** *vt* to scatter, disperse; to interrupt

buyung *n* boy, lad; ~ *upik* boy and girl, son and daughter

buyut *n* ancestor from your great-grandparents' generation; *nenek ~* great-grandmother; *musuh be~an* arch enemy

byarpet, byar pet *adv* on and off; *lampu masih* ~ the lights still go out sometimes

byur splash, sound of an object falling into water

C

C Celsius

c [cé] c, third letter of the alphabet

ca → cah

cabai ← cabé

cabang *n* branch; ~ *atlet* athletics; ~ *olahraga* a type of sport; ~ *pembantu (capem)* branch office; ~ *pohon* tree branch; *kantor* ~ branch (office); **bercabang** *vi* to have a branch; *adj* split, branched

cabé, cabai *n* chilli; ~ *rawit* small, hot red chilli; small but fiery (of a person)

cabik shred; **mencabik** *vt* to tear; **tercabik-cabik** *adj* torn, to shreds

cabo *n* whore

cabul *adj* obscene, indecent, rude; *film* ~ pornographic film; **mencabuli** *vt* to rape, assault someone

cabut *vt* to pull out, remove; *sl* to leave; **mencabut** *vt* to pull out, remove; to take back; ~ *gigi* to extract a tooth; **pencabutan** *n* withdrawal, removal; **tercabut** *adj* removed

cacah minced, chopped; *daging* ~ mincemeat; **mencacah** *vt* to mince, chop up

cacah tattoo; **mencacah** *vt* to vaccinate

cacah ~ *jiwa* population figure

cacar *n* pock, pox; ~ *air* chicken pox; *bekas* ~ pock; *penyakit* ~ smallpox; **cacaran** *vi* to have chicken pox

cacat *n* fault, defect, flaw; *adj* disabled, handicapped; flawed; ~ *lahir* birth defect; *orang* ~, *penyandang* ~ disabled or handicapped person

caci ~ *maki* insults; **mencaci** *v* ~ *maki* to insult, abuse

cacing *n* worm; ~ *pita* tapeworm; ~ *tanah* earthworm; *obat* ~ worming tablets; **cacingan** *vi* to have (intestinal) worms

cadang *suku* ~ spare part; **cadangan** *adj* spare, reserve; stocks; ~ *devisa* exchange reserves; ~ *minyak* oil reserves; **mencadangkan** *vt* to reserve, set aside; to suggest something

cadar *n* veil

cadel, cedal *adj* to have a speech impediment

cagar *n* preserve; ~ *alam* nature reserve; ~ *budaya* cultural heritage area

cagub *n* candidate for governor; gubernatorial candidate ← **calon gubernur**

cah, ca *n* sauce in Chinese cooking; *daging sapi* ~ *cabai* beef in spicy sauce

cahar: pencahar *n* laxative

cahaya *n* light, shine, glow; ~ *bulan* moonlight; *titik* ~ point of light; **bercahaya** *vi* to glow, shine; **pencahayaan** n lighting

cair flow; melt; **cairan** *n* liquid; **mencair** *vi* to melt, turn into liquid; **mencairkan** *vt* to melt something; to make (funds) available

caisim *n* mustard greens

cakalang *n (ikan)* ~ skipjack tuna

cakalélé *n (tari)* ~ war-dance in Minahasa and Maluku

cakap, cakep *adj* handsome, good-looking; *sl* pretty; able, capable; **kecakapan** *n* ability

cakap: bercakap *vi* to speak; **bercakap-cakap** *vi* to chat; **percakapan** *n* conversation

cakar *n* claw; ~ *ayam* chicken feet; scrawl, very bad handwriting; **cakaran** *n* scratch; **mencakar** *vt* to scratch; *dicakar kucing* scratched by a cat; *pencakar* ~ *langit* skyscraper

cakra *n* mythical weapon (in shadow-puppet plays)

cakram *n* disc; discus; *lempar* ~ discus (throw); *rem* ~ disc brakes

cakrawala *n* horizon; sky

cakup: cakupan *n* scope; **mencakupi** *vt* to include, cover; **pencakupan** *n* coverage

cakwé *n* snack consisting of fried strips of dough

calég *calon anggota legislatif* electoral candidate (for Parliament)

calo *n* ticket scalper, profiteer; *percaloan praktek* ~ profiteering

calon *adj* future; *n* candidate, -to-be; *sl, m* fiancé, *f* fianceé; ~ *gubernur (cagub)* gubernatorial candidate; ~ *perwira* cadet; ~ *presiden (capres)* presidential candidate; ~ *suami* husband-to-be; ~ *anggota legislatif (caleg)* electoral candidate (for Parliament); ~ *wakil presiden (cawapres)* vice-presidential candidate; ~ *Pegawai Negeri Sipil (CPNS)* public or civil servant applicant; **mencalonkan** *vt* to nominate someone; **pencalonan** *n* nomination, candidacy

cam: mencamkan *vt* to note carefully

camar *burung* ~ seagull

camat *n* sub-district head; **kecamatan** *n* sub-district

cambang *n* whiskers, beard; **bercambang** *adj* whiskered, bearded; *vi* to have whiskers or a beard

cambuk *n* whip; **mencambuk** *vt* to whip; **mencambuki** *vt* to whip repeatedly

camil, camilan → **cemil**

campak *n* measles; ~ *Jerman* German measles; *penyakit* ~ measles

campak: mencampakkan *vt* to throw (something) down

campur mix; ~ *baur* mix with society; ~ *mulut* argue; ~*sari* a blend of traditional and modern Javanese music; ~ *tangan* get involved, interfere; *nasi* ~ rice with various side-dishes; ~ *aduk* (all) mixed up; **mencampuradukkan** *vt* to mix up, confuse; **campuran** *n* mix, mixture; *anak* ~ child of mixed descent; **bercampur** *adj* mixed with; *vi* to mix with; **mencampur** *vt* to mix, blend; **mencampuri** *vt* to mix into; to meddle; to have sex with; **mencampurkan** *vt* to mix something to; **pencampuran** *n* mixing; **percampuran** *n* mixing, association

canai *roti* ~ kind of pancake

canang *n* cymbal, small gong; **mencanangkan** *vt* to proclaim, announce

canda *n* joke; ~ *gurau* joking, jokes; **bercanda** *vi* to joke; ~ *kok* just kidding

candi *n* temple, ancient Hindu or Buddhist temple or monument; ~ *Borobudur* Borobudur; ~ *induk* main temple

candu *n* opium, drug; ~ *asmara* intoxicating love; **kecanduan** *n* addiction; *adj* addicted to; ~ *obat* drug addiction; **pecandu** *n* addict

canggih *adj* sophisticated; *teknologi* ~ hi-tech; **kecanggihan** *n* sophistication

canggung *adj* awkward, clumsy; **kecanggungan** *n* clumsiness, awkwardness

cangkir *n* cup, mug; ~ *teh* teacup; *se*~ *kopi* a cup of coffee

cangkok graft, transplant; ~ *ginjal* liver transplant; **cangkokan** *n* graft; **mencangkokkan** *vt* to graft (of plants), transplant (of organs); **pencangkokan** *n* transplant operation, grafting

cangkul *n* hoe; **cangkulan** *n* card game; **mencangkul** *vt* to hoe

cantik *adj* beautiful, pretty; *nomor* ~ lucky (mobile phone) number; **kecantikan** *n* beauty; *ratu* ~ beauty queen; **mempercantik** *vt* ~ *diri* to make yourself beautiful

canting *n* tool to apply wax in making batik

cantol: kecantol *coll* to be or get hooked; **mencantol** *vt* to hook onto

cantrik *n* student or disciple of a religious teacher; **nyantrik** *vi, coll* to be a religious student or disciple

cantum: mencantumkan *vt* to attach; **tercantum** *adj* attached, included, inserted

cap *n* seal; brand, mark; stigma; ~ *dagang* trademark; ~ *jempol* thumbprint; ~ *pos* postmark; *batik* ~ stamped batik; **mengecap** *vi* to brand; to stigmatize

cap *Ch* ten; ~ *go ceng* (Rp) 15 000; ~ *go meh* 15th day after Chinese New Year

capai, mencapai *vt* to reach, attain; **tercapai** *adj* achieved; *cita-cita tak* ~ unfulfilled dreams

capcay, cap cai *n* chop suey, Chinese vegetables in sauce

capék, capai *adj* tired; ~ *sekali* exhausted; **kecapékan** *adj* tired out; *n* exhaustion

capem *n* branch office ← **cabang pembantu**

caping *n* conical hat

caprés *n* presidential candidate ← **calon présidén**

capung *n* dragonfly

cara *n* way, style, means, method; ~ *jitu* great way; **secara** *adv* in a way; used to form adverbs; ~ *besar-besaran* on a large scale

cari *v* to look for, search for, seek; ~ *duit*, ~ *uang* to earn a living; **mencari** *vt* to look or search for, seek; ~ *angin* to take a break; ~ *jalan* to find a way; ~ *muka* get on; ~ *makan, ~ nafkah* to earn a living; ~ *penyakit* to look for trouble; ~ *salah* to find fault; ~ *tahu* to try to find out; **mencari-cari** *v* to search repeatedly, everywhere; **mencarikan** *vt* to look for something for someone; **pencarian** *n* search, hunt

carik: carikan *n* scrap; **mencarik** *vt* to rip or tear up

carter charter; **carteran** *adj* chartered; *bis* ~ chartered or rented bus; **mencarter** *vt* to hire, charter

cas charge; **mengecas** *vt* to charge (electrical equipment)

cas-cis-cus European language (especially English); **bercas-cis-cus** *vi* to speak a European language

cat *n* cét *coll* paint; ~ *air* watercolors; ~ *basah* wet paint; ~ *kuku* nail polish; ~ *oven* vehicle paint applied through heat; **mengecat** *vt* to paint, dye; ~ *rambut* to dye, color your hair; **pengecatan** *n* painting, dyeing

catat, mencatat *v* to note; **catatan** *n* notes; ~ *kaki* footnotes; *buku* ~ notebook; *dengan* ~ on the condition or proviso; *kantor* ~ *sipil* civil registry office; **pencatat** *n* registrar; **pencatatan** *n* registration; **tercatat** *adj* registered; noted; *surat* ~ registered mail

catur *n* chess; *buah* ~ chess piece; **pecatur** *n* chess player

caturwulan *n* **cawu** *abbrev* quarter, term (one of three in a year); ~ *ketiga* third term

catut *n* (carpenter's) pincers; *tukang* ~ ticket scalper, profiteer; **mencatut** *vt* ~ *nama* to use someone else's name illegally

cawan *n* cup with no handle; small bowl

cawaprés *n* vice-presidential candidate ← **calon wakil présidén**

cawat *n* loincloth; **bercawat** *vi* to wear a loincloth

cawu *n* term ← **caturwulan**

cc cubic centiliter, milliliter

CD compact disk

cébok *vi* to wash your bottom after using the toilet; **cébokan** *n* pail of water to wash your bottom

cébol *n* dwarf, midget; *si* ~ *hendak mencapai bulan* to seek the impossible

cébong → **kecébong**

cebur fall into water; **kecebur** *adj, coll* **tercebur** *adj* fallen into water; **menceburkan** *vt* to push into water

cecak → **cicak**

cecar: mencecar *vt* to assault, attack; to interrogate

cécér: bercécéran *adj* scattered, dispersed; **mencécérkan** *vt* to scatter, disperse

cedera, cidera injured, injury; ~ *lutut* knee injury; **mencederai** *vt* to damage, injure

cédok ← **ciduk**

cegah, mencegah *vt* to prevent, fight against; **pencegahan** *n* prevention; ~ *AIDS* prevention of AIDS

cegat, mencegat *vt* to hold up, bar; **pencegatan** *n* barring

ceguk, cekuk: cegukan *n* hiccups; *vi* to have the hiccups

cék *n* cheque, check; ~ *kosong* blank cheque

cék, mengecék *vt* to check, confirm; **pengecékan** *n* checking

cekal *kena* ~ not allowed to go abroad; **mencekal** *vt* to prevent from leaving the country; **pencekalan** *n* ban on foreign travel ← **cegah dan tangkal**

cekam, cengkam: mencekam *adj* frightening, ominous; *situasi sudah* ~

things looked black

cekat: cekatan *adj* clever, good, adept

cékcok, bercékcok *vi* to quarrel, have a fight; **percékcokan** *n* quarrel, dispute

cékér *n, sl* claw; ~ *ayam* chicken feet (dim sum)

cekik, mencekik *vt* to strangle; **tercekik** *adj* strangled

cekikik: cekikikan *vi* to giggle

ceking *adj* thin, gaunt, skin and bones; *si* ~ skinny

ceklék, ceklik click, sound of camera

Céko *n* the Czech Republic; *bahasa* ~, *orang* ~ Czech; ~*slowakia* Czechoslovakia

cekung *adj* concave, sunken; *mata* ~ sunken eyes; **cekungan** *n* basin, cavity, groove

cela *n* fault; **mencela** *vt* to find fault with, criticize; **tercela** *adj* wrong; *perbuatan yang* ~ misdeed, wrong

celah *n* gap, crack, crevice; ~ *gigi* gap between teeth

celaka accident, bad luck, misfortune; **kecelakaan** *n* accident, disaster; ~ *pesawat* plane crash; **mencelakakan** *vt* to bring misfortune on

celana *n* trousers; ~ *berenang* swimming trunks; ~ *cutbrai* bell-bottom trousers; ~ *dalam* underpants; ~ *kolor* (boxer) shorts; ~ *panjang* (long) trousers, slacks; ~ *pendek* shorts; **bercelana** *vi* to wear trousers, trousered

celemék *n* apron

céléng, céléngan *n* piggy bank, savings box

celetuk, menyeletuk *vi* **nyeletuk** *sl* to interrupt, call out, say suddenly

Célsius, sélsius Celsius; *35 derajat* ~ 35 degrees Celsius

celotéh *n* babble; **bercelotéh** *vi* to babble, gurgle

celup, mencelup *vt* to dye, dip; **celupan** *n* dip; **pencelupan** *n* dyeing process

celurit, clurit *n* crescent-shaped knife, sickle (traditionally carried by Madurese men)

cemar: mencemari *vt* to dirty, pollute; **pencemar** *n* polluter; **pencemaran** *n* pollution; ~ *udara* air pollution;

tercemar *adj* polluted

cemara *n* casuarina (tree)

cemas *adj* worried, anxious; **kecemasan** *n* anxiety, concern; **mencemaskan** *adj* worrying, sobering; *vt* to cause worry

cemberut *adj* bad-tempered, in a bad mood

cembung *adj* convex

cemburu *adj* jealous; ~ *buta* blind jealousy; **kecemburuan** *n* jealousy; **pencemburu** *n* jealous person

cemerlang *adj* glittering, sparkling, brilliant; *ide* ~ brainwave; **kecemerlangan** *n* genius, brilliance

cemeti *n* whip

cemil, camil *v* to snack; **cemilan** *n* snack food

cemooh *n* mockery, scorn; **mencemoohkan** *vt* to mock, ridicule

cempaka *n* a white kind of gardenia or magnolia

cempedak *n* fruit which is cut into slices and fried

cemplung plunge into water; **mencemplungkan** *vt* to plunge something into water; **kecemplung** *adj, sl*; **tercemplung** *adj* fallen into water

cenayang *n* psychic, medium

cendana *kayu* ~ sandalwood; *Keluarga* ~ the Suharto family (resident at Jl Cendana in Jakarta); *Pulau* ~ Timor

cendawan *n* fungi, toadstool, mushroom

cendekia: cendekiawan *n* intellectual; *Ikatan* ~ *Muslim seIndonesia (ICMI)* Indonesian Association of Muslim Intellectuals

cenderung *vi* to tend; **kecenderungan** *n* tendency, trend

céndol *n* sweet drink of green rice flour, molasses and coconut milk

cenderawasih, cendrawasih *n* bird of paradise

cenderamata, cendramata, cinderamata *n* souvenir, keepsake

cendrawasih, cenderawasih *n* bird of paradise

céng *Ch* one hundred; *ce*~ one hundred; *go*~ five hundred

cengang: tercengang *adj* surprised, astonished

cengéng *adj* whiny, complaining

cengir *cengar-~* grimace, grin sheepishly

cengkam → **cekam**

cengkéh *n* cloves

cengkeram *vt* to grip; **cengkeraman** *n* grip, squeeze; **mencengkeram** *vt* to grip, squeeze

cengkrama, cengkerama: bercengkrama *vi* to chat, hold a discussion

centil *adj* attention-seeking, coquettish

céntong *~ nasi* spoon for serving rice

cepak *adj* shaven-headed; *rambut ~* crew cut

cepat *adj* **cepet** *coll* fast, quick; *yang ~, dapat* first come, first served; *~ marah* quick-tempered, hot-headed; *~ sembuh* get well soon; *kereta api ~* express train; **cepat-cepat** *adv* quickly; **cepatan** *excl* hurry up!; **kecepatan** *n* speed; **mempercepat** *vt* to speed up, accelerate; **secepat** *conj* as fast as; *~ mungkin,* **secepatnya, secepat-cepatnya** *adv* as fast as possible; **tercepat** *adj* fastest

cepék *n* Rp.100 (coin)

ceplas-ceplos *adv* forthright, blunt, straight from the heart (of speech or behavior); **keceplosan** *n* directness, speaking without thinking

ceplok *telur ~* fried egg

ceprét → **jeprét**

cerah *adj* clear, sunny; *di Banjarmasin ~, 33 derajat* clear in Banjarmasin, 33 degrees; *wajah ~* happy face; **mencerahkan** *vt* to enlighten, clear matters up; **pencerahan** *n* enlightenment, guidance; *Abad ~* the Enlightenment

cerai divorce; *~ mati* widowed; *~-berai adj* torn apart, dispersed; **menceraiberaikan** *vt* to tear apart, separate; **bercerai** *vi* to be divorced; **mencerai, menceraikan** *vt* to divorce someone; **perceraian** *n* divorce

ceramah *n* lecture, talk; *~ agama* sermon; **berceramah** *vi* to give a lecture or talk; **penceramah** *n* speaker

cerat *n* spout

cerber *n* short story ← **cerita bersambung**

cerca: cercaan *n* verbal attack; disdain; **mencerca** *vt* to reprimand, deride

cerdas *adj* intelligent, bright; **kecerdasan** *n* intelligence; **mencerdaskan** *vt* to educate, sharpen your mind

cerdik *adj* clever, smart; cunning; **kecerdikan** *n* intelligence; shrewdness

cérék, cérét *n* watering can; kettle

ceret, crét *ceret berét* diarrhea; **mencrét** *vi* to have diarrhea

ceréwét *adj* fussy, finicky, hard to please; talkative; **keceréwétan** *n* fussiness

céri *buah ~* cherry

ceria *adj* happy, in a good mood; **keceriaan** *n* happiness, good mood; **menceriakan** *vt* to liven up, make happy

cerita, ceritera story, tale; tell; *~ bersambung (cerber)* serial; *~ jorok* dirty story; *~ pendek (cerpen)* short story; *~ rakyat* folk tale; *habis ~* and that was it; *~nya panjang* it's a long story; **bercerita** *vi* to tell (a story); **menceritakan** *vt* to describe, relate

ceriwis *adj* talkative; fussy

cermai, cermé *n* small, sour plum

cermat *adj* thorough, careful, accurate; **kecermatan** *n* precision, accuracy; **mencermati** *vt* to observe closely

cermin mirror; **bercermin** *vi* to look in the mirror; to take as an example; **mencerminkan** *vt* to reflect; **tercermin** *adj* reflected

cerna, mencerna *vt* to digest; **pencernaan** *n* digestion; *gangguan ~* digestive complaint

ceroboh *adj* careless; **kecerobohan** *n* carelessness

cerobong *n* chimney; *~ asap* smokestack

cerocos, mencerocos *vi* **nyerocos** *coll* to talk too much, blather, chatter or rattle on

cerpelai *n* mongoose

cerpén *n* short story; **cerpénis** *n* short story writer ← **cerita péndék**

cerucut → **kerucut**

cerutu *n* cigar

cespleng *adj* very effective

cét → **cat**

cétak print; ~ *biru* blueprint; ~ *ulang* reprint; *barang* ~ printed material; *media* ~ print media; **cétakan** *n* mold; impression, printing; ~ *kedua* second edition; **mencétak** *vt* to print; ~ *gol* to score a goal; **pencétak** *n* printer; ~ *gol* goal-scorer; **percétakan** *n* printers, printing office; press

cetus: mencetus *vt* to scrape; *vi* to burst out, say something unexpected; **mencetuskan** *vt* to spark off, provoke; **pencetus** *n* initiator, someone who creates ideas

céwék *n, f, coll* girl, gal, young woman; *adj* female; ~ *matré* material girl; *anaknya cowok atau* ~? is the baby a boy or girl?

CGI Consultative Group on Indonesia

ciamik *adj, Ch* fine, good-looking

cibir: mencibir *vi* to sneer, curl your lips

cicak, cecak *n* gecko, house lizard

cicil pay in instalments; **cicilan** *n* (payment by) instalments; **mencicil** *vt* to pay by instalments

cicip taste; **mencicipi** *vt* to try, taste something

cicit *n* great-grandchild

cidera → **cedera**

cidomo *n* horse-drawn cart in Lombok ← **cikar dokar mobil**

ciduk, cédok *n* dipper; **menciduk** *vt* to scoop with a dipper

ciduk: menciduk *vt, coll* to arrest

cihuy *ejac* whoopee! hooray! great!

Cik *pron* you, Sister (for Chinese women)

cikal ~ *bakal* origins

Cilé *n* Chile; *orang* ~ Chilean

cilik *adj* small, little; *penyanyi* ~ child singer

cilukba, ci luk ba *excl* peekaboo!

ciméng *n, tsl* marijuana

Cina *n, coll* China; *derog* Chinese person; *bahasa* ~ Chinese; Mandarin; *orang* ~ Chinese; ~ *totok* 100% or overseas Chinese; **Pecinan** *n* Chinatown

cincang minced; *daging* ~ mincemeat; **mencincang** *vt* to mince, chop up

cincau *n* jelly made from cinchona leaves, used in drinks; ~ *hijau* green cinchona jelly

cincin *n* ring; ~ *kawin* wedding ring, wedding band

cindai *n* printed (silk) fabric

cinderamata, cenderamata, cendramata *n* souvenir, keepsake

cingur *rujak* ~ spicy food made from fruit and ox-snout

cinlok *n, sl* a temporary love affair in a certain place ← **cinta lokasi**

cinta love, like; ~ *monyet* puppy love; ~ *damai* peace-loving; ~ *lokasi (cinlok)* a temporary love affair in a certain place; ~ *segi tiga* love triangle; ~ *pada pandangan pertama* love at first sight; **bercinta** *vi* to make love; to be in love; **kecintaan** *n* love (for something); **mencinta** *vt* to love; **mencintai** *vt* to love someone; **pencinta, pecinta** *n* lover (of something), fan; **tercinta** *adj* dear, beloved; *Hari yang* ~ Dear Hari

ciprat splash; **kecipratan** *adj* be splashed, sprayed accidentally

cipta idea, creativity; *daya* ~ creativity; **ciptaan** *n* creation; **mencipta** *v* to create; to compose; **menciptakan** *vt* to create, make; **pencipta** *n* creator; ~ *lagu* song-writer; **tercipta** *adj* created

ciput *n* head-covering worn under veil or scarf

ciri *n* characteristic, identifying mark; ~ *khas* special feature

cita ~ *rasa* taste; *duka* ~ sorrow, grief; **cita-cita** *n* ideal, dream, ambition; **bercita-cita, bercita-citakan** *vi* to dream of

cita *n* cloth, fabric

citra *n* image; **mencitrakan** *vt* to depict

cium kiss; smell; ~ *pipi* peck, kiss on the cheek; ~ *tangan* kiss someone's hand (as a sign of respect); **ciuman** *n* kiss; sniff; **berciuman** *vi* to kiss each other; **mencium** *v* to smell, to sniff; to kiss; **penciuman** *n* sense of smell; **tercium** *adj* smelt; found out

ciut: berciut-ciut, menciut-ciut *vi* to squeak

ciut, menciut *vi* to shrivel; **menciutkan** *vt* to reduce

clurit → **celurit**

cm centimeter

coba *v, aux* try; please; *uji* ~ experiment; **mengujicobakan** *vt* to test something; **cobaan** *n* trial, ordeal; **mencoba** *vt* to try, attempt; **percobaan** *n* experiment, test

cobék, coék *n* pestle for grinding chillies

coblos vote; pierce; ~ *moncong putih!* vote for the white snout! (symbol of PDIP); **mencoblos** *vt* to vote, pierce

cocok: bercocok *vi* ~ *tanam* to work or till the soil

cocok fit, match, suitable; **kecocokan** *n* suitability, compatibility; **mencocokkan** *vt* to match

cocol *vt* dip into a liquid; *sambal* ~ chilli sauce dip; **mencocol** *vt* to dip into a liquid

coék → **cobék**

cokelat, coklat chocolate; *(warna)* ~ brown; *pohon* ~ cacao tree; *rasa* ~ chocolate-flavored; *sebatang* ~ chocolate bar; **kecoklatan** *adj* brownish

colék pinch; *sabun* ~ cream soap for hand-washing clothes

colok: colokan *n* power point; **mencolok, menyolok** *adj* glaring, standing out; *vi* to glare, stand out

colong, mencolong *vt* to steal, nick, filch; **kecolongan** *adj* robbed; lost unjustly

combéran *n* ditch, sewer

comblang *mak* ~ matchmaker

comél: mencomél *vi* to grouse, grumble

compang-camping *adj* ragged, in tatters

comro, combro *n* fried snack containing *oncom* ← **oncom di jero**

condong *vi* lean, incline; *matahari* ~ *ke barat* the sun shifts to the west

Conéfo *abbrev, arch Conference of the New Emerging Forces* Sukarnoist alternative to the United Nations

congak: mencongak *vi* to do mental arithmetic

congkél, mencongkél *vt* to prise open

congklak *n* traditional game played with shells in a long wooden box

conték, menconték *v* to copy, cheat; **contékan** *n* cram notes

contoh *n* example, model, sample; ~ *baik* a good example; ~*nya* for example; **mencontoh** *vt* to copy, imitate; **mencontohi** *vt* to give as an example; **percontohan** *adj* experimental; model

copét *n* pickpocket; **kecopétan** *adj* to be pickpocketed, robbed; *n* pickpocketing; **mencopét** *vt* to pick someone's pocket; **pencopét** *n* pickpocket

copot *vi* to come off (accidentally); *excl* gracious! (when something falls); **mencopot** *vt* to pull (off); *coll* to sack, fire; **pencopotan** *n* removal

cor: mengecor *vt* to cast, pour (concrete)

corak *n* design, pattern, motif, style; ~ *Madura* Madurese style; **bercorak** *vi* to have a design

coréng-moréng *adj* streaked, smeared all over

corét scratch; **corét-corét** doodle, graffiti; **corétan** *n* scratch; **mencorét** *vt* to scratch, cross out

corong *n* funnel, spout; ~ *radio* mike; *berbentuk* ~ funnel-shaped

coto *n* clear meat soup, specialty of Makassar

cowok *n, m, sl* boy, guy; boyfriend

CPNS *abbrev Calon Pegawai Negeri Sipil* public or civil servant applicant

cs [sé és] *cum suis* and associates; and friends

CSIS Centre for Strategic and International Studies

cuaca *n* weather; ~ *baik* fine weather; ~ *buruk* foul weather, bad weather; *dinas* ~ meteorological or weather service; *ramalan* ~ weather forecast

cubit pinch; **mencubit** *vt* to pinch; **secubit** *n* pinch; ~ *garam* a pinch of salt

cucuk rawa *n* a kind of bird, straw-headed bulbul

cuci *vt* to wash; ~ *darah* kidney dialysis; ~ *gudang* stocktake sale; ~ *mata* window-shopping; ~ *mulut* dessert; ~ *otak* brainwash; ~ *tangan* wash your hands; **cucian** *n* laundry; **mencuci** *v* to wash, clean; ~ *cetak* to develop photos (negatives and prints); ~ *piring* to wash the dishes; **pencucian** *n* ~ *uang* money laundering

cucu *n* grandchild; *anak* ~ descendants

cucur flow, trickle; **cucuran** *n* flow; ~ *air mata* flow of tears; **bercucuran** *vi* to trickle down, drip, flow

cuék *adj* uncaring, unfeeling, ignoring; independent; ~ *aja* who cares?

cuil *n* bit, speck; **secuil** *n* tiny bit; ~ *pun tidak* not one bit

cuka *n* vinegar

cukai *n* duty; *bea* ~ customs

cukil, cungkil *n* pick

cukong *n* wealthy businessman

cukup *adj* enough, sufficient; *adv* quite; ~ *sudah* enough; **berkecukupan** *vi* to have enough, get by; **mencukupi** *vt* to satisfy, fulfill; **secukupnya** *adv* sufficient, adequate

cukur shave; *pisau* ~ razor; *tukang* ~ barber; **mencukur** *vt* to shave

cula *n* horn; **bercula** *vi* to have a horn; *badak* ~ *satu* one-horned rhino

culas *adj* lazy, cheating

culik, menculik *vt* to kidnap; **penculik** *n* kidnapper; **penculikan** *n* kidnapping

cum laude [kum laude] *adj* with honors

cum suis [kum suis], *cs* [sé és] and associates; and friends

cuma *adv* **cuman** *coll* but, only; **cuma-cuma** free, at no cost; **percuma** *adv* in vain; *secara* ~ free (of charge)

cumbu flattery; ~ *rayu* flirt; **bercumbu** *vi* to flirt, flatter

cumi, cumi-cumi *n* squid

cundang: memecundangi *vt* to swindle or trick; to beat or defeat; **pecundang** *n* loser

cungkil, cukil *n* pick

cupang *n* love-bite, hickey

cuping *n* lobe; ~ *telinga* ear lobe

cuplik: cuplikan *n* quote; **mencuplik** *vt* to cite, quote from

curah fall, pour; ~ *hati (curhat) coll* to pour out your heart; ~ *hujan* rainfall; **mencurahkan** *vt* to pour out; ~ *tenaga* to spend energy

curam *adj* steep, sloping, precipitous

curang *adj* dishonest, cheating; **kecurangan** *n* cheating, dishonesty

curanmor *n* theft of motor vehicles ← **pencurian kendaraan bermotor**

curhat *vi, coll* to pour out your heart ← **curah hati**

curi *v* steal; **curi-curi** surreptitious, secret; **kecurian** *adj* to be robbed, burgled; **mencuri** *vt* to steal; ~ *pandang* to steal a look; **pencuri** *n* thief, burglar; **pencurian** *n* theft, burglary; ~ *kendaraan bermotor (curanmor)* theft of motor vehicles

curiga *adj* suspicious; **kecurigaan** *n* suspicion; **mencurigai** *vt* to suspect someone; **mencurigakan** *adj* suspicious, suspect; *vt* to cause suspicion

cutbrai, cutbray *celana* ~ bell-bottom trousers

cuti *n* leave (rest from work, activity); ~ *hamil* maternity leave; ~ *panjang* long service leave; ~ *tahunan* annual leave

CV *abbrev* curriculum vitae

D

d [dé] d, fourth letter of the alphabet

D1 *Diploma Satu* 1-year diploma course

D2 *Diploma Dua* 2-year diploma course

D3 *Diploma Tiga* 3-year diploma course

da, dag, dah *gr* bye; **da-da** *gr* (children) bye-bye

d/a *dengan alamat* care of, c/-

dabus, debus *n* mystical cultural performance in Banten, involving displays of invulnerability

dada *n* breast, chest, bosom; *buah* ~ *f* breast; *telanjang* ~ bare-chested; **berdada** *vi* to have a chest

dadak: dadakan *adj* sudden; **mendadak** *adj* sudden; ~ *sontak* all of a sudden; *secara* ~ suddenly

dadar ~ *gulung* small green cylindrical cake; *telur* ~ omelet

dadu *n* dice; *main* ~ to play games requiring dice

daéng, Dg *tit* Buginese title

daérah *n* region, territory, area; provinces, country(side); ~ *banjir* area prone to flooding; ~ *elit* elite residential area; *bahasa* ~ regional language; *otonomi* ~ *(otda)* regional autonomy; ~ *aliran sungai (DAS)* watershed, catchment area; ~ *Istimewa Yogyakarta (DIY)* Special Region of Jogjakarta; ~ *Khusus Ibukota (DKI)* Special Capital City Region; ~ *Operasi Militer (DOM)* region of military operations

daftar list, register, roll; ~ *barang* inventory, catalog; ~ *harga* price list; ~ *hadir* roll; ~ *hitam* blacklist; ~ *isi* contents, index; ~ *istilah* glossary; ~ *makanan* menu; ~ *pustaka* bibliography; **mendaftar** *vi* to register; **mendaftarkan** *vt* to register something; **pendaftar** *n* applicant; **pendaftaran** *n* enrolment, registration; **terdaftar** *adj* registered, enrolled

dag → **da**

dagang trade; **dagangan** *vi* to sell goods informally; *n* merchandise; **berdagang** *vi* to trade, do business; **memperdagangkan** *vt* to deal in; **pedagang** *n* merchant; ~ *keliling* seller who circulates through an area; ~ *kaki lima (PKL)* itinerant food vendor; **perdagangan** *n* commerce, trade; ~ *bebas* free trade; ~ *perempuan* trade in women

dag dig dug thump, thump, thump (of heartbeat)

daging *n* meat, flesh; ~ *asap* smoked meat (usu beef); ~ *babi* pork; ~ *cincang*, ~ *giling* mincemeat; ~ *kambing* goat; mutton, lamb; ~ *sapi* beef; *tukang* ~ butcher; *mendarah-*~ to become second nature

dagu *n* chin

dah → **da**

dah → **sudah**

dahaga *n* thirst; **berdahaga** *adj* thirsty

dahak *n* phlegm, mucus; **berdahak** *adj* containing phlegm or mucus; *batuk* ~ chesty cough

dahan *n* branch

dahi *n* forehead

dahlia *n* dahlia

dahsyat *adj* terrible, dreadful, awesome; **kedahsyatan** *n* power

dahulu *adj* before, former(ly); first (more formal than *dulu*); ~ *kala* ancient times, the old days; *lebih* ~ first(ly); **mendahului** *vi* to precede, overtake; **mendahulukan** *vt* to put before, give precedence to; **pendahulu** *n* predecessor; **pendahuluan** *n* introduction; *kata* ~ preface → **dulu**

da'i, dai *n* Islamic preacher

daif *adj* weak, feeble

Dairi ethnic sub-group of the Batak people

dak *n* (outer) roof

daki: mendaki *vt* to climb, ascend; ~ *gunung* (to go) mountaineering, bushwalking; **pendaki** *n* ~ *gunung* mountaineer, bushwalker, hiker

daki *n* dirt, grime (of the skin)

daksa *n* body; *tuna*~ disabled, handicapped

daku *pron, lit* me; *jangan tinggalkan* ~ don't leave me ← **aku**

dakwa: dakwaan *n* charge, accusation; **pendakwa** *n* plaintiff; **terdakwa** *n* the accused

dakwah *n, Isl* mission, religious proselytizing; **pendakwah** *n* preacher, missionary

dalam *pron* in, inside, into; *adj* deep, profound; inner; *n* inside; ~ *negeri (DN)* national, domestic, internal; ~ *rangka* in connection with, under the auspices of; *celana* ~ underpants; *di* ~ in, inside; *ke* ~ into; *Menteri* ~ *Negeri (Mendagri)* Minister of the Interior (or Home Affairs), home secretary; **kedalaman** *n* depth; **mendalam** *adj* deep; *duka cita yang* ~ deepest sympathy; **mendalami** *vt* to delve into; **memperdalam** *vt* to deepen; to study in detail, broaden your knowledge; **pedalaman** *n* inland, hinterland

dalang *n* puppeteer (in shadow puppet plays); mastermind; **mendalangi** *vt* to orchestrate (events)

dalih *n* excuse, pretext; reason; *dia mundur, dengan* ~ *terlalu sibuk* he resigned, on the pretext that he was too busy; **berdalih** *vi* to pretend, give a pretext

dalil *n* thesis, proposition, theorem; **berdalil** *adj* based on, grounded in; *vi* to have a base

daluwarsa, kedaluwarsa, kadaluwarsa *n* expired, overdue; *tanggal ~* expiry date, use-by date (food)

damai peace; *~ hati* inner peace; **berdamai** *vi* to make peace; **kedamaian** *n* peace; **mendamaikan** *vt* to reconcile, pacify; **perdamaian** *n* peace, reconciliation

damar *n* resin

damba *v* to long, yearn, wish for; **dambaan** *n* idol, dream; *cowok ~* dream guy; **mendambakan** *vt* to long or wish for; *~ gadis mandiri, lulusan S1* seeking an independent woman, university graduate

dampak *n* ill-effect; **berdampak** *vi* to have a (negative) effect

dampar: mendamparkan *vt* to wash ashore, beach; **terdampar** *adj* beached, grounded, washed ashore; *ada ikan paus ~ di pantai* a whale was beached on the sands

damping next to, close; **berdampingan** *adj* side by side; **mendampingi** *vt* to accompany, flank; **pendamping** *n* companion; *~ hidup* spouse; **pendampingan** *n* assistance

damprat curse, scold; **mendamprat** *vt* to curse, scold

dan *conj* and; *~ lain-lain (dll)* et cetera (etc); *~ sebagainya (dsb)* and so on, and the like

dana *n* funds, money, grant; *~ pensiun* superannuation, pension fund; *~ Moneter Internasional* International Monetary Fund (IMF); **mendanai** *vt* to fund something; **pendanaan** *n* funding

danau *n* lake

dandan *vi* to dress up, put on make-up; **dandanan** *n* dress, make-up; *~nya norak* her clothes are really tacky; **berdandan** *vi* to dress, put on make-up; **mendandani** *vt* to decorate, dress, adorn

dangdut *n* popular Indian-inspired music; *penyanyi ~ dangdut* singer; **dangdutan** *vi, coll* to go to a *dangdut* show; to dance to *dangdut* music

dangkal *adj* shallow, superficial; **kedangkalan** *n* shallows, (low) depth; *~ laut* sea depth; **pendangkalan** *n* silting-up, process of becoming shallower

dansa *n* Western-style dance; *~-dansi n* Western-style dancing; **berdansa** *vi* to dance

dapat *v, aux* be able to, can; *vt* find, get, obtain; *~ kesulitan* to have difficulties; **kedapatan** *adj* to be caught in the act; **mendapat** *vt* to obtain, receive; *~ kabar* to receive news; **mendapati** *vt* to experience; **mendapatkan** *vt* to obtain, get; discover; **pendapat** *n* opinion, point of view; *menurut ~ saya* in my opinion; **berpendapat** *vi* to have an opinion, believe; **pendapatan** *n* income, revenue; *~ bruto, ~ kotor* gross income; **sedapatnya** *adv* what you can get

dapur *n* kitchen; *~ bersih* room where prepared food is kept; *~ rekaman* recording studio; *~ umum* soup kitchen; *perkakas ~* kitchen utensils

dara *n* (young) girl; *anak ~* young girl; *selaput ~* hymen

dara *burung ~* pigeon, dove

darah *n* blood; *~ rendah* low blood pressure; *~ tinggi* high blood pressure; *golongan ~* blood group, type; *peredaran ~* blood circulation; *pertumpahan ~* spilling of blood, casualties; *~ daging* flesh and blood; **mendarah daging** *vi* to become second nature; **berdarah** *vi* to bleed; **pendarahan** *n* bleeding

darat *n* land, shore; *angkatan ~* army; *di, ke ~* ashore; **daratan** *n* mainland; **mendarat** *vi* to land; **mendarati** *vt* to land on; **pendaratan** *n* landing (of vessel); *~ darurat* emergency landing

dari *prep* from, (out) of; *conj* from the time; *~ mana* from where; who's calling?; *~ segi* from the point of view of; *selain ~* except for; *~ enam orang, hanya satu yang datang* out of six people, only one came; **sedari** *conj* since, from the time when; **daripada** *conj* than

darma, dharma: darmawisata *n* excursion

darurat *adj* emergency, pressing; *keadaan* ~ emergency; *Unit Gawat* ~ *(UGD)* emergency room, casualty ward

Darusalam, Darussalam *n* nation of peace, nation of Islam; *Brunei* ~ Brunei

DAS *daérah aliran sungai n* watershed, catchment area

dasa *adj* ten; *~lomba* decathlon; *~sila* the Ten Commandments; **dasawarsa** *n* decade

dasar *n* base, basis, foundation; *pada ~nya* in principle; *Undang-Undang* ~ *(UUD)* constitution; **berdasar** *adj* based; *vi* to have a base; **berdasarkan** *adj* based on; *vi* to have a base of; in accordance with, pursuant to; **mendasar** *adj* basic; **mendasarkan** *vi* to base on something

dasar *coll* all because, that's; indeed; ~ *maling!* that's thieves for you!

dasawarsa *n* decade

dasbor *n* dashboard

dasi *n* necktie; **berdasi** *vi* to wear a tie; *kaum* ~ white-collar workers

daster *n* house-coat, nightgown, nightie

data *n* data, information; ~ *pribadi* personal information; **mendatakan** *vt* to record, document, collect data on; **pendataan** *n* documentation

datang *vi* to come, arrive; ~ *bulan* menstruate, have your period; *yang akan* ~ *(yad)* future; *minggu yang akan* ~ next week; **berdatangan** *vi* to come (of many); **kedatangan** *n* arrival; **mendatang** *adj* coming, next; **mendatangkan** *vt* to bring, import; **pendatang** *n* immigrant, migrant; newcomer

datar *adj* level, flat, horizontal; **dataran** *n* plain; ~ *tinggi* plateau; **mendatarkan** *vt* to make flat, level

DATI *abbrev Daerah Tingkat* administrative level; ~ *I* province or former residency; ~ *II* city or regency

datuk *pron* (male) head of family; title in Malay areas

daulat *adj* sovereign, majesty; **berdaulat** *adj* sovereign, independent; *vi* to have sovereignty; *negara yang* ~ sovereign state; **kedaulatan** *n* sovereignty; *Partai* ~ *Rakyat (PKR)* People's Sovereignty Party

daun *n* leaf; ~ *bawang* spring onion; leek; ~ *bunga* petal; ~ *jendela* window pane; ~ *ketumbar* (fresh) coriander; ~ *lontar* palm leaf once used as writing material; ~ *muda* young girl or woman; ~ *pandan* pandanus leaf, used for green coloring in food; ~ *salam* bay leaf; ~ *singkong* cassava leaves; ~ *telinga* ear; *hijau* ~ leaf green; **dedaunan** *n* leaves, foliage

daur *n* cycle; ~ *haid* menstrual cycle; ~ *ulang* recycling; **didaur ulang** *v* to be recycled

dawai *n* string (of musical instrument); ~ *biola* violin string

dawet *n* sweet Javanese drink of green rice flour, pink syrup and coconut milk

daya *n* power, energy; ~ *beli* purchasing power; ~ *cipta* creativity; ~ *ingat* memory; ~ *kuda (DK)* horsepower; ~ *serap* absorbency; ~ *upaya* efforts, means, resources; *barat* ~ southwest; **berdaya** *vi* to have power; ~ *guna* efficient; *tak* ~ powerless; **memberdayakan** *vt* to empower; **pemberdayaan** *n* empowerment; *Kementerian* ~ *Perempuan* Ministry for the Empowerment of Women

daya *tipu* ~ deceit, trick; **memperdaya** *vt* to deceive, use, trick

Dayak generic name for indigenous (non-Malay) inhabitants of Kalimantan and Borneo; *orang* ~ Dayak; ~ *Iban* a Dayak of the Iban sub-group

dayang *n, f* young palace attendant

dayung *n* oar; **berdayung** *vi* to go by boat or bicycle; **mendayung** *vt* to stroke (an oar), row; to pedal; **pedayung** *n* professional rower; **pendayung** *n* rower, oarsman, sculler

dé d, fourth letter of the alphabet

dé, dék *pron* little one (nickname for babies or youngest child in the family) ← **adé, adik**

debar pulse, beat; ~ *jantung* heart beat; **berdebar** *vi* to beat quickly; *hati* ~ a racing heart; **mendebarkan** *adj* pulsating, throbbing; *vt* to make the heart beat quickly

debat *n* debate; **berdebat** *vi* to have a debate or discussion; **mendebat** *vt* to argue against, debate; **perdebatan** *n* debate, discussion

débet, débit *n* debit; **kedébet** *sl* to be wrongly debited (of a bank card); **mendébet** *vt* to debit

débit ~ *air* rate of water flow

debu *n* dust; **berdebu** *adj* dusty

debus, dabus *n* mystical cultural performance in Banten, involving displays of invulnerability

dedaunan *n* leaves, foliage ← **daun**

dédikasi *n* dedication

défénsif *adj* defensive

définisi *n* definition; **mendéfinisikan** *vt* to define

deg: deg-degan *adj* anxious, worried

dégradasi *n* relegation (from a football league)

déh OK then, well; *ayo, ~ !* come on, then!; *saya nasi goreng ~* I'll have fried rice then ← **sudah**

deham, dehem, berdeham, mendeham *vi* to clear the throat, cough

déhidrasi *n* dehydration

dék *pron* [dé] little one (nickname for babies or youngest child in the family) ← **adé, adik**

dék *n* deck

dékan *n* (university) dean

dekam: mendekam *vi* to crouch, be cooped up

dekap: dekapan *n* embrace; **berdekap-dekapan, berdekapan** *vi* to embrace each other; **bersedekap** *vi* to put your hands on your stomach (as during the daily prayers in Islam); **mendekap** *vt* to hug, embrace

dékar: pendékar *n* (in martial arts) master, champion, leader

dekat *prep* close, near; *dalam waktu ~* soon; **berdekatan** *adj* close to each other (of two or more things); **kedekatan** *n* close relationship, close-

ness, proximity; **mendekati** *vt* to approach; **mendekatkan** *vt* to bring close; **pendekatan** *n* approach; getting to know; **terdekat** *adj* closest, nearest

dekil *adj* grimy, caked with dirt, filthy

déklamasi *n* declamation, reading poetry aloud; **mendéklamasikan** *vt* to declaim

déklarasi *n* declaration; **mendéklarasikan** *vt* to declare

dékor *n* decor

delapan *adj* eight; ~ *belas* eighteen; ~ *puluh* eighty; *segi* ~ octagon; **berdelapan** *adj* a group of eight; **kedelapan** *adj* eighth

délégasi *n* delegation

délik *n* offense, misdemeanor

delima *n* pomegranate; *(buah)* ~ pomegranate

délman *n* two-wheeled horse-drawn carriage

demam *n* fever; *vt, coll* mad about; ~ *berdarah* dengue fever; ~ *panggung* stage fright

demen, deman *vt, coll* to like

demi *conj* for (the sake of); ~ *keadilan, tolong mengatakan yang benar* for the sake of justice, please tell the truth

demi *conj* by, in the name of; per; ~ *Allah* I swear to God; *seorang ~ seorang* one by one

demikian *adv* such, so, in this way, thus; *se~ rupa sehingga* in such a way that

démo, démonstrasi *n* demo, demonstration, protest; **berdémo** *vi* to hold a protest; **mendémo** *vt* to protest against

démokrasi *n* democracy; ~ *terpimpin* Guided Democracy (under Sukarno); *pesta ~* 'celebration of democracy' (general election); **démokrat** *n* democrat; *Partai ~* Democrat Party; **démokratis** *adj* democratic

démonstrasi *n* demo, demonstration, protest

démpét: berdémpét *adj* stuck (together)

dempul *n* putty

dénah *n* plan, map, diagram; ~ *rumah* house plan

denda fine; *kena* ~ be fined; **mendenda** *vt* to fine

dendam revenge; grudge; ~ *kesumat* revenge; **berdendam** *vi* to be resentful, full of revenge

déndang *n* (happy) song, chant; **berdéndang** *vi* to sing, chant

déndéng *n* dried meat, jerky; ~ *rusa* dried venison meat

dengan *conj* with; *adv* -ly; ~ *hormat* Dear Sir or Madam (in letter); ~ *alamat (d/a)* care of (c/o); ~ *nama* in the name of; ~ *sendirinya* by itself; ~ *syarat* on condition, conditionally; *sampai* ~ until, to, up to the point of, as far as; *sesuai* ~ in accordance with

dengar *v* to hear; **dengar-dengar** *conj, coll* I heard...; **kedengaran, terdengar** *adj* audible; **mendengar** *vt* to hear; **mendengarkan** *vt* to listen to; ~ *lagu* to listen to music; **memperdengarkan** *vt* to play, broadcast; **pendengar** *n* listener; **pendengaran** *n* hearing; *indera* ~ sense of hearing

dengki spite, jealousy; **kedengkian** *n* spite

dengkul *n* knee; *modal* ~ hard work

dengkur snore; **mendengkur** *vt* to snore; to purr (of a cat)

dengung *n* hum, buzz; **berdengung, mendengung** *vi* to drone, hum, shake with sound

dentang clang; **berdentang** *vi* to clang, jangle

dentam boom, bang; **berdentaman** *vi* to crackle or pound (of gunfire)

denyut pulse; throb; ~ *jantung* heartbeat; ~ *nadi* pulse; **berdenyut** *vi* to throb, to beat

déodoran *n* deodorant

Dep. *abbrev Departemen* (government) department, ministry

depa *n* fathom

Depag *abbrev Departemen Agama* Department of Religion

depak kick; **mendepak** *vt* to kick something, kick out; *Haris didepak dari tim* Haris was kicked out of the team

depan *prep, n* front; *adj* next; *di* ~ front, in front of; *ke* ~ forward, to the front; *tahun* ~ next year; **mengedepankan** *vt* to put forward, propose

departemén *n* department, ministry; ~ *Agama (Depag)* Department of Religious Affairs; ~ *Kehakiman (Depkeh)* Department of Justice; ~ *Luar Negeri (Deplu)* Department of Foreign Affairs; ~ *Tenaga Kerja (Depnaker)* Department of Manpower; ~ *Perikanan dan Kelautan* Department of Fisheries and Marine Affairs; **Dépdagri** *Departemen Dalam Negeri* Department of Home Affairs, State Department, Ministry of the Interior; **Dépdiknas** *Departemen Pendidikan Nasional* Department of National Education; **Déperindag, Dépperindag** *Departemen Perindustrian dan Perdagangan* Department of Industry and Trade; **Depkumham** *Departemen Kehukuman dan Hak Azasi Manusia* Department of Justice and Human Rights; **Dépkés** *Departemen Kesehatan* Department of Health; **Dépkéu** *Departemen Keuangan* Department of Finance; **Déplu** *Departemen Luar Negeri* Department of Foreign Affairs; **Dépnaker** *Departemen Tenaga Kerja* Department of Manpower

dépo, dépot *n* depot

déposito *n* (bank) deposit

dépot → **dépo**

Déperindag, Dépperindag *abbrev Departemen Perindustrian dan Perdagangan* Department of Industry and Trade

déprési *n* depression

Dépsos *abbrev Departemen Sosial* Department of Social Affairs

déra: mendera *vt* to whip, flog

derajat *n* degree, rank; *Balikpapan, hujan, tiga puluh* ~ Balikpapan, rain, thirty degrees; *Tommy berubah pikiran 180* ~ Tommy did a 180-degree about-turn

derap *n* stamp, clack; clap, hitting sound; **berderap** *vi* to click-clack (of shoes), trot along

deras *adj* swift; heavy; *hujan* ~ heavy

rain; *mengalir* ~ to flow swiftly

dérék tow (a vehicle); *mobil* ~ tow truck; **mendérék** *vt* to tow; **pendérékan** *n* towing

dérét *n* row, line; **dérétan** *n* row; **berdérét-dérét** *vi* to line up

dering ring, chime; **berdering, mendering** *vi* to ring, tinkle

derita *n* suffering; **menderita** *v* to suffer, endure; **penderita** *n* sufferer; **penderitaan** *n* suffering

derma, darma *n* charity, donation; **dermawan** *n* donor, philanthropist; *adj* charitable

dermaga *n* pier, jetty

dermawan *n* donor, philanthropist; *adj* charitable ← **derma**

deru roar; **menderu** *vi* to roar

désa *n* village; hometown; *gadis* ~ village girl; **pedésaan** *n* country(side), rural areas; *angkutan* ~ country minibus

desah *n* sigh, hiss, swish; **berdesah, mendesah** *vi* to sigh, make a swishing noise

désain, disain *n* design; ~ *industri* industrial design; *jurusan* ~ design major; **mendésain** *vt* to design; **désainer** *n* designer

desak push; **desakan** *n* pressure, push; **berdesakan** *vi* to push each other; **mendesak** *adj* pressing, urgent; *vt* to press, urge, push

desas-desus *n* rumor

Désémber *bulan* ~ December

désérsi *n* desertion (from the military); **désértir** *n* deserter

désinféktan, disinféktan *n* disinfectant

desir hiss, rustle; **desiran** *n* hiss, rustle, swish; **berdesir, mendesir** *vi* to hiss, rustle

desis hiss; **mendesis** *vi* to hiss

déskripsi *n* description

destar *n, m* head cloth

desus: desas-desus *n* rumor

detak *n* tick, beat; ~ *jantung* heartbeat

détéksi *n* detection; **mendétéksi** *vt* to detect

déterjén *n* detergent

detik *n* second

dévisa *n* foreign currency, foreign exchange; *cadangan* ~ exchange reserves

déwa *n, m* god; ~ *asmara* god of love; **mendéwakan** *vt* to worship, idolize, put on a pedestal; **déwa-déwi, déwata** *n, pl, m & f* gods; *Pulau Dewata* Island of the Gods (Bali); **déwi** *n* goddess; ~ *Sri* Goddess of Rice

déwan *n* council, board; ~ *hakim* judicial board; ~ *juri* panel of judges, jury; ~ *Keamanan (PBB)* (UN) Security Council; ~ *komisaris* commission; ~ *Pertimbangan Agung (DPA)* Supreme Advisory Council; ~ *Perwakilan Rakyat (DPR)* Parliament, People's Representative Council

déwasa adult; *orang* ~ adult, grown-up; *untuk* ~ adults only; **kedéwasaan** *n* maturity

déwasa ~ *ini* nowadays, recently

déwata *n, pl, m & f* gods; *Pulau* ~ Island of the Gods (Bali) → **déwa**

déwi *n, f* goddess; ~ *fortuna* goddess of luck; *dewa-*~ gods → **déwa**

Dg *(Daéng) tit* Buginese title

dh *dahulu* formerly

dharma ~ *Wanita* association of wives of civil servants → **darma**

DI *abbrev, arch Darul Islam* 1950s separatist movement

di *prep* at; on; in; ~ *atas* above, on top of; ~ *dalam* inside; ~ *mana* where; ~ *mana saja* wherever; ~ *samping* beside; *Saman tinggal* ~ *Cirebon* Saman lives in Cirebon; *makanan ada* ~ *meja* the food is on the table; ~ *Amerika orang tidak begitu* people aren't like that in America

dia *pron* he, she, it; him, her (often replaced by *–nya* for possessive)

diabétés *n* **diabét** *coll* diabetes; *penyakit* ~ diabetes

diadili *v* to be tried, taken to court ← **mengadili, adil**

diagnosa *n* diagnosis; **mendiagnosa** *vt* to diagnose

diakui *adj* recognized (of university programs) ← **aku**

dialék *n* dialect; ~ *Surabaya* Surabayan dialect

dialog *n* dialog; **berdialog** *vi* to converse, have a dialog

diam silent, not moving; **diam-diam** *adv* secretly; **berdiam** *vi* ~ *diri* to keep silent; **pendiam** *n* quiet, shy person; **terdiam** *vi* to fall silent

diam: berdiam *vi* to reside; **kediaman** *n* residence

diaméter *n* diameter

dian *n* (kerosene) lamp

diaré *n* diarrhea

dibandingkan *v* to be compared with ← **banding**

diberangkatkan *v* to depart, be sent off; *rombongan ke Medan sudah* ~ the party to Medan has departed ← **berangkat, angkat**

dibikin *v, coll* to be made ← **bikin**

dibilang *v* to be said ← **bilang**

didaur ulang *v* to be recycled ← **daur ulang**

didih: mendidih *adj* boiling; *vi* to boil; **mendidihkan** *vt* to boil water

didik educate; *anak* ~ pupil (of a teacher); **mendidik** *vt* to educate, bring up, teach; **pendidik** *n* educator; **pendidikan** *n* education; *ilmu* ~ pedagogy; **berpendidikan** *adj* educated; *vi* to have an education; ~ *SD* to have a primary school education

diét *n* diet; **berdiét** *vi* to diet, go on a diet

difaks *v* to be faxed ← **faks**

difotokopi *v* to be photocopied ← **fotokopi**

digdaya *adj* powerful, invulnerable; **kedigdayaan** *n* power, invulnerability

digips *v* be in or have a plaster cast ← **gips**

dihipnotis *v* to be hypnotized ← **hipnotis**

diinfus *v* to be put on a drip ← **infus**

dijus *v* to be made into juice, juiced ← **jus**

dik *pron* you (used to a child, or young employee) ← **adik**

dikapling *v* to be divided up into blocks for development ← **kapling**

dikarenakan *v* caused by ← **karena**

dikau *pron, lit* you, thou

dikerjain *v, sl* to be tricked, taken for a ride ← **kerja**

dikir, dzikir, zikir *Isl* (recite) additional prayers; **berdikir** *vi, Isl* to say additional prayers → **zikir**

dikit *coll, adj* a little, a few, a bit ← **sedikit**

diklakson *v* to be tooted at ← **klakson**

diklat *n* education and training for employees ← **pendidikan dan latihan**

dikliring *v* to be cleared (in a bank) ← **kliring**

dikontrakkan *adj* for rent, lease ← **kontrak**

diktat *n* photocopied lecture notes or textbook

diktator *n* dictator

dikté *n* dictation; **mendikté** *vt* to dictate (terms)

dilarang *v* to be prohibited; ~ *masuk* no entry, no admittance; ~ *merokok* no smoking ← **larang**

dilélang *adj* for auction, tender ← **lélang**

dilém *v* to be glued ← **lém**

dimaksud, dimaksudkan *v* to be meant or intended ← **maksud**

dimaling *v* to be robbed ← **maling**

dimengerti *v* to be understood ← **mengerti, erti, arti**

dimensi *n* dimension

dimutasi *v* to have your status changed ← **mutasi**

dinamika *n* dynamic, dynamics

dinamis *adj* dynamic

dinamit *n* dynamite

dinas (to work at a) government office; ~ *kesehatan* health service; ~ *pertamanan* parks service; ~ *rahasia* secret service; ~ *Ketenteraman dan Ketertiban (Tramtib)* city public order agency; *mobil* ~ office car, work car

dinding *n* (inner) wall; ~ *pembuluh darah* blood vessel wall

ding *coll* no, I mean (as correction); *Dia datang Sabtu. Eh, enggak* ~*, Jumat* He's coming on Saturday. No, I mean, Friday

dingin *n* cold, cool, chilly; **berdingin-dingin** *vi* to enjoy cold weather;

kedinginan *n* cold; feeling cold; **mendinginkan** *vt* to chill, cool; **pendingin** *n* ~ *ruangan* air conditioning, cooling

dingklik *n* low stool for sitting on (when washing clothes, grinding spices, etc)

dini *adj* very early, premature; ~ *hari* dawn, daybreak; *kelahiran* ~ premature birth; **sedini** ~ *mungkin* as early as possible

dinosaurus *n* dinosaur

diopname *v* to be admitted to hospital, be hospitalized; *kalau kena tifus, tidak selalu harus* ~ if you get typhoid, you don't always need to stay in hospital ← **opname**

diorama *n* diorama

diotopsi *v* to have an autopsy performed ← **otopsi**

dipéhakakan *v* to lose your job, be fired ← **pé ha ka, PHK**

dipél *v* to be mopped, cleaned ← **pél**

diperban *v* to be bandaged ← **perban**

dipercaya *v* to be believed, trusted ← **percaya**

dipermak *v* to be altered, shortened ← **permak**

dipernis *v* to be varnished ← **pernis**

dipéstakan *v* to be celebrated with a party ← **pésta**

dipikir *v* to be thought ← **pikir**

dipingit *v* to be secluded, kept at home

dipingpong *v* to be sent here and there, messed about ← **pingpong**

diplomasi *n* diplomacy; diplomat *n* diplomat

diplonco *v* to undergo an initiation at school or university ← **plonco**

diportal *v* to be blocked by a barrier, have a barrier lowered ← **portal**

diprétéli *v* to be dismantled, taken apart or off ← **prétél**

diréksi *n* management, managing board; **diréktorat** *n* directorate; ~ *Jenderal Minyak dan Gas Bumi (Ditjen Migas)* Directorate-General of Oil and Gas; **diréktur** *n* director, manager; ~ *Jenderal (Dirjen)* Director-General; **diréktorat** *n* directorate; ~*Jenderal (Ditjen)* Directorate-General

dirgahayu *ejac* long live!

dirgantara *n* sky, air; aerospace

diri *n* self; ~*nya* he, she, it; himself, herself, itself; ~ *saya* me, myself; *membunuh* ~ to commit suicide, kill yourself; *seorang* ~ alone, by yourself, single-handed; *lupa* ~ to forget yourself; *tahu* ~ humble, to know your place

diri: berdiri *vi* to stand, get up; **mendirikan** *vt* to build, establish, erect; **pendiri** *n* founder; **pendirian** *n* foundation; opinion, point of view; **berpendirian** *vi* to hold, be of an opinion; **sendiri** *adv* alone; *pron* self; *salah* ~ it's your own fault; *dengan* ~*nya* automatic, by itself; **sendiri-sendiri** *adv, pl* alone, individually; **sendirian** *adv* alone, single-handedly; **kesendirian** *n* solitude; **menyendiri** *vi* to go off by yourself; **penyendiri** *n* loner; **tersendiri** *adj* its own; apart, separate; **terdiri** *vi* ~ *atas*, ~ *dari* to consist of, be based or founded on

dirigén *n* (music) conductor

dirjén *n* director-general ← **diréktor jénderal**

dironsen *v* to be x-rayed ← **ronsen**

diruilslag [dirélslag] *v* to be swapped, exchanged ← **ruilslag**

dirundung *v* ~ *malang* to be cursed with or suffer bad luck ← **rundung**

dirut *n* (chief) director, director ← **diréktur utama**

disahkan *v* to be legalized ← **sah**

disain ← **désain**

disanggul *v* to have your hair put into a bun ← **sanggul**

disantét *v* to have spells cast on you, be a victim of black magic ← **santét**

disaté *v* to be made into satay ← **saté**

disayangkan *adj* regrettable, unfortunate ← **sayang**

disebut-sebut *v* to be frequently mentioned ← **sebut**

disegani *v* to be respected ← **segan**

diselot *v* to be bolted ← **selot**

disemayamkan *v* to be laid out (of a dead body) ← **semayam**

disengaja *v* to be done deliberately, intentionally or on purpose ← **sengaja**

diserut *v* to be sharpened ← **serut**

disérvis *v* to be serviced ← **sérvis**

disésar *v* to have a Cesarian ← **sésar**

disetrap *v* to be punished (at school) ← **setrap**

disholatkan *v* to be prayed for, have a prayer performed for you (after death) ← **sholat**

disinar *v* to have radiotherapy or chemotherapy ← **sinar**

disinféktan, désinféktan *n* disinfectant

disiplin discipline, disciplined; **berdisiplin** *adj* disciplined; *vi* to have discipline

diskét *n* diskette, disket

diskon *n* discount

diskors *v* to be suspended (from school, work etc) ← **skors**

diskoték *n* disco, nightclub

diskriminasi *n* discrimination; ~ *rasial* racial discrimination; **mendiskriminasi, mendiskriminasikan** *vt* to discriminate against

diskusi *n* discussion; *bahan* ~ topic for discussion; **berdiskusi** *vi* to have a discussion

disomasi *v* to be summoned ← **somasi**

disoto *v* to be made into clear soup ← **soto**

dispénsasi *n* permission, leave, dispensation

distémpel *v* to be stamped ← **stémpel**

distribusi *n* distribution; **mendistribusikan** *vt* to distribute

distrik *n* district

disun *v* to be kissed on the cheek ← **sun**

disunat *v* to be circumcised ← **sunat**

dités *vi* to be tested ← **tés**

ditilang *v* to be fined ← **tilang**

ditim *v* to be steamed ← **tim**

ditipéks *v* to be whited-out, corrected ← **tipéks**

Ditjén *n* Directorate-General ← **Diréktorat Jénderal**

ditrap *v* to be layered (of hair) ← **trap**

ditumbuhi *adj* overgrown with ← **tumbuh**

divaksinasi, divaksin *v* to be vaccinated ← **vaksinasi, vaksin**

divakum *v* to be vacuumed; assisted delivery ← **vakum**

divalidasi *v* to be validated ← **validasi**

divérifikasi *v* to be verified ← **vérifikasi**

divisi *n* division (of a company)

divonis *v* to be sentenced ← **vonis**

DIY *abbrev Daerah Istimewa Yogyakarta* Special Region of Yogyakarta

DK *abbrev daya kuda* horsepower

DKI *abbrev Daerah Khusus Ibukota* Special Capital City Region

dkk *abbrev dan kawan-kawan* and friends

dll *abbrev dan lain-lain* et cetera (etc)

doa *n* prayer; ~ *restu* blessing; *membaca* ~ to pray, say a prayer; **berdoa** *vi* to pray, say a prayer; ~ *menurut keyakinan masing-masing* to pray according to your own religion; **mendoakan** *vt* to pray for

doang *adv, coll* only, just; *nasi* ~ just rice (no side-dishes)

dobel *adj* double, twice as much

dobrak, mendobrak *vt* to break open, smash; ~ *pintu* to break down the door

dodol *n* soft, chewy sweet made from brown sugar or fruit; ~ *durian* durian sweet

dodor: kedodoran *adj* scruffy; ill-fitting

doeloe [dulu] *tempo* ~ the olden days, times past; colonial times (old spelling of **témpo dulu**)

doi *pron, tsl* he, she, boyfriend or girlfriend; *si* ~ your guy/girl ← **dia**

dok *pron* Doc, Doctor (used when addressing a doctor) ← **dokter**

dokar *n* (two-wheeled horse-drawn) buggy

dokter, dr *n* doctor, surgeon; ~ *ahli* specialist; ~ *anak* pediatrician; ~ *gigi (drg)* dentist; ~ *hewan (drh)* vet; ~ *jaga* doctor on duty; ~ *mata* oculist, optometrist; ~ *saraf* neurologist; ~ *umum* general practitioner (GP); **kedokteran** *adj* medical; *Fakultas* ~ *(FK)* School of Medicine

Doktor, Dr *pron* title for holder of a Ph.D.

Doktoranda, Dra *pron, f* graduate (Bachelor's degree); **Doktorandus,**

Drs *pron, m* graduate (Bachelor's degree)

dokumén *n* document; **dokuméntasi** *n* documentation; **mendokuméntasi** *vt* to document, file

dolar n dollar; ~ *Amerika* US dollar; *tukar* ~ to exchange dollars

DOM *abbrev Daerah Operasi Militer* region of military operations

domba *n* sheep; *adu* ~ play off against each other; **mengadudombakan** *vt* to play people off against each other

doméstik *adj* domestic, internal, national; *penerbangan* ~ domestic flights

dominan *adj* dominant

dominé *n, Chr* pastor; minister

domisili *n* domicile; **berdomisili** *vi* to be domiciled, reside

dompét *n* purse, wallet; fund; ~ *saya hilang!* I've lost my wallet!

donat *n* donut, doughnut

donatur *n* donor

Donau *(sungai)* ~ the Danube

dong, donk *sl* you should know that; *jangan begitu* ~ please don't do that

dongéng *n* (fairy) tale, story, fable; *cerita* ~ tale; **mendongéng** *vi* to tell a story

dongkol *adj* annoyed, resentful; **kedongkolan** *n* annoyance, resentment

dongkrak *n* (car) jack, lever; **mendongkrak** *vt* to jack, lever, raise; ~ *popularitas* to boost popularity

dop *n* hubcap (metal cover/disc for center of a wheel)

dor bang! (sound of gun, burst balloon, etc)

dorang *ikan* ~ kind of fish, pomfret

dorong *vt* to push; **dorongan** *n* push, urge; ~ *hati* impulse; **mendorong** *vt* to push, encourage; **terdorong** *adj* pushed, shoved

dosa *n* sin; ~ *asal Cath* original sin; *pengakuan* ~ *Cath* confession; **berdosa** *vi* to sin, commit a sin

dosén *n* (university) lecturer

dosin → **lusin**

dosis *n* dose, dosage

dot *n* dummy; **mengedot** *vt* to suck

doyan *vt* to like, enjoy; ~ *kambing* enjoy eating goat or lamb

DPA *abbrev Dewan Pertimbangan Agung* Supreme Advisory Council

DPR *abbrev Dewan Perwakilan Rakyat* People's Representative Council

DPRD *abbrev Dewan Perwakilan Rakyat Daerah* Regional People's Representative Council

Dr *Doktor* holder of a Ph.D.

dr *dokter* doctor

dra *doktoranda* female holder of a Bachelor's degree

draf *n* draft

drainase *n* drainage

drakula *n, coll* vampire

drastis *adj* drastic; *turun* ~ to fall drastically

drg *dokter gigi* dentist

drh *dokter hewan* vet(erinary surgeon)

drs *doktorandus* male holder of a Bachelor's degree

dsb *dan sebagainya* and so on

dua *adj* two; ~ *belas* twelve; ~ *kali* twice; ~ *puluh* twenty; ~ *sejoli* a couple; *tiada* ~*nya* incomparable; **dua-duanya** *adj* both, the two of them; **berdua** *adj* together, in pairs; **kedua** *adj* second; **keduanya, kedua-duanya** *adj* both; **menduakan** *vt* to be loyal to more than one; ~ *Tuhan* to worship more than one god

dubes *n* ambassador; ~ *Australia* the Australian ambassador ← **duta besar**

dubur *n* anus; *liang* ~ anus

duda *n* widower; divorced man; ~ *cerai* divorced man; **menduda** *vi* to become or live as a widower

duduk *vi* to sit, be placed; ~ *bersila* to sit cross-legged; ~ *bersimpuh* to sit with legs folded back to one side; ~ *perkara* facts of the case; *silahkan* ~ please sit down, please be seated; **menduduki** *vt* to sit on something; to occupy; *Indonesia pernah diduduki Jepang* Indonesia was once occupied by Japan; **penduduk** *n* inhabitant, citizen, resident; ~ *tetap* permanent resident; **pendudukan** *n* occupation

duga, menduga *vt* to suppose, suspect; **dugaan** *n* suspicion; **terduga** *tidak ~* unexpected

dugem *n, sl* jetset, nightlife; underworld ← **dunia gemerlap**

duh → **aduh**

duit *n, sl* money, cash, dirt, dosh; *cari ~* earn a living, earn a crust; *mata ~an* materialist, money-minded; **berduit** *adj* well-off; *vi* to have money

duka *n* sorrow; *~ cita* grief, sorrow; *~ cita yang mendalam* deepest sympathy; *suka ~* good and bad times, ups and downs, happiness and sadness; **berduka** *vi ~ (cita)* to grieve, be in mourning; **kedukaan** *n* grief, sorrow

duku *n* small sweet fruit with light brown skin, clear flesh and large dark seed

dukuh *n* hamlet

dukun *n* traditional or spiritual healer, shaman; *~ bayi, ~ beranak* traditional midwife; *~ santet* witchdoctor, sorcerer

dukung, mendukung *vt* to support; **dukungan** *n* support; *~ moral* moral support; **pendukung** *n* supporter

dulang *n* serving tray; pan; **mendulang** *vt* to pan (for gold); **pendulang** *n* prospector; **pendulangan** *n* panning, prospecting

dulu *adv* first, former, before; *kemarin ~* the day before yesterday; *makan ~* have something to eat (said when eating first before others); **duluan** *adv, coll* first, before others ← **dahulu**

dungu *adj* stupid, slow; *orang ~* idiot

dunia *n* world; *~ akhirat* the hereafter; *~ barat* the Western world; *~ fana* on Earth; *~ gemerlap (dugem) n, sl* jetset, nightlife; underworld; *~ ketiga* Third World; *~ luar* outside world; *~ maya* cyberspace; *~ usaha* business world; *juara ~* world champion; *keliling ~* go around the world; **duniawi** *adj* earthly, secular; **mendunia** *vi* to become global, known around the world; **sedunia** *adj* all around the world, global

dupa *n* incense; **pedupaan** *n* stand for burning incense

durasi *n* duration; **berdurasi** *vi* to last, have a duration of

durén → **durian**

durhaka *adj* treacherous, rebellious; *anak ~* treacherous child

duri *n* thorn; (fish) bone; **berduri** *adj* thorny; with fish bones; *vi* to have thorns; *kawat ~* barbed wire; **durian** *n* durian, spiky yellow-skinned fruit with a strong smell

dus *conj, coll* so, then

dus, dos *n* cardboard box ← **kardus**

dusta *n* lie, fib; **berdusta** *vi* to lie; **pendusta** *n* liar

dusun *n* hamlet, village

duta *n* envoy, messenger, representative; *~ bangsa* representative of the nation; *~ besar (dubes)* ambassador; *~ keliling* roving ambassador; *kedutaan ~ (besar)* embassy

duyung *n* seacow; *putri ~* mermaid

dwi- *pref* two; *~bahasa* bilingual; *~fungsi* dual function (of army); *Dwikora (Dwikomando Rakyat)* People's Dual Mandate, Sukarnoist army slogan; *~mingguan adj* fortnightly; *~tunggal* partnership, usu to refer to Sukarno and Hatta; *~warna n* the red-and-white (Indonesian flag); *adj* two-tone, two-colored

E

e [é] e, fifth letter of the alphabet

é *ejac* hey (showing recognition, disagreement)

é, éh *ejac* I mean; *datang besok, ~, maksudnya lusa* come tomorrow, no, I mean the day after

ébi *n* (dried) shrimp

écéng *~ gondok* water hyacinth

écér: écéran *adj* retail; *harga ~* retail price; **mengécér** *vt* to retail, sell retail; **pengécér** *n* retailer

éco *adj, Jav* delicious, tasty

édan *adj, Jav* crazy, mad

édar: édaran *n* circular; *surat ~* memo; **berédar** *vi* to circulate; **mengédarkan** *vt* to circulate something; **pengédar** *n* dealer; **pengédaran** n circulation; ~ udara air circulation

édisi n edition; édit, **mengédit** vt to edit; **éditor** n editor

é-é n, child poo-poo

éf f, sixth letter of the alphabet

éfék n effect; ~ samping side-effect; **éféktif** adj effective; **éféktivitas** n effectiveness, effect

éfék n stock, share, security; bursa ~ stock exchange

éfisién adj efficient; secara ~ efficiently; **éfisiénsi** n efficiency

égalitér adj egalitarian

égois adj egoist, egotistical

égrang n stilts

éh ejac I mean; datang besok, ~, maksudnya lusa come tomorrow, no, I mean the day after

éja: éjaan n spelling; ~ Yang Disempurnakan (EYD) Reformed Spelling of 1972; **mengéja** vt to spell; **pengéjaan** n spelling

éjakulasi n ejaculation (of semen)

ejan: mengejan vi to strain, push the abdominal muscles (when defecating, giving birth)

éjék, mengéjék vt to tease, mock, ridicule; **éjékan** n mockery, insult

ék pohon ~ oak (tree)

éka pref one, mono- (in compounds)

ékologi n ecology

ékonom n economist; **ékonomi** n economy; ~ pasar market economy; ilmu ~ economics; kereta ~ economy-class train; **perékonomian** n economic affairs; **ékonomis** adj economical, cheap

ékor n tail; counter for animals; ~ kuda pony tail; tulang ~ coccyx; tiga ~ kucing three cats; **berékor** vi to have a tail; bintang ~ comet

ékosistém n ecosystem

ékowisata n eco-tourism

éks x, 24th letter of the alphabet

éks pref ex-, former → **mantan**

éksakta ilmu ~ exact sciences (mathematics, physics etc)

éksékusi n execution; **mengéksékusi** vt to execute, carry out the death penalty; to carry out a legal decision

éksékutif executive; ~ muda young executive; kereta ~ executive-class train

éksémplar n copy (of a publication)

éksis → **ada**

éksklusif adj exclusive

ékskul n extra-curricular activities, classes outside school; ~ matematika extra maths lessons ← **ékstra kurikulér**

éksotik, éksotis adj exotic

ékspatriat orang ~ expatriate (esp Caucasian)

ékspédisi n forwarding agent, freight service

éksploitasi n exploitation; **mengéksploitasi** vt to exploit; to get benefit from

éksplorasi n exploration (for mineral resources)

ékspor export; **mengékspor** vt to export; **pengékspor** n exporter; ~ beras exporter of rice

éksprés, éksprés adj express; kereta api ~ express train

ékstra adj, adv extra; pron extra- (in compounds)

ékstradisi n extradition; **mengékstradisi** vt to extradite (someone)

ékstrém, ékstrim adj extreme

él l, 12th letter of the alphabet

élak v **mengélakkan** vt to avoid, dodge, evade; **terélakkan** tidak ~ unavoidable, inevitable

élan n fighting spirit

elang n (burung) ~ eagle, hawk, falcon, bird of prey

élastis adj elastic

éléktro teknik ~ electrical engineering; **éléktronik** adj electronic; media ~ electronic media; **éléktronika** n electronics

élemén n element

éliminasi n elimination; **teréliminasi** adj eliminated → **singkir**

élit, élite [élit] n elite; ~ politik political elite; daerah ~ elite residential area

élok adj beautiful; **keélokan** n beauty

élpiji n liquid petroleum gas, LPG

ELS abbrev Europese Lagere School European Lower School, elementary school in colonial times

elu: mengelu-elukan *vt* to welcome
elu → **lu**
elus stroke, caress; **elusan** *n* stroke, caress; **mengelus** *vt* to caress, stroke or pat (an animal)
ém m, 13th letter of the alphabet
émail *n* (tooth) enamel
emak, mak *n* mother
émang → **mémang**
emas, mas *n* gold; ~ *kawin* dowry; ~ *kertas*, ~ *prada* gold leaf; *kalung* ~ gold necklace; *kesempatan* ~ golden opportunity; *tukang* ~ goldsmith
emban: mengemban *vt* to carry out, perform; **pengemban** *n* guardian, executor; ~ *tugas* worker responsible for performing a duty
embara: mengembara *vi* to wander, roam; **pengembara** *n* wanderer, rover; **pengembaraan** *n* roaming, wandering
embék, embik bleat *coll* sheep or goat; **mengembék** *vi* to bleat
émbél-émbél *n* details; extra decorations
émbér *n* bucket, pail
embun *n* dew; **berembun** *adj* moist, dewy; **mengembun** *vi* to condense, fog up; **pengembunan** *n* condensation
embus, hembus blow; **embusan** *n* blow; bellows; **berembus, mengembus** *vi* to blow
émirat *n* emirate
emis: mengemis *vi* to beg; **pengemis** *n* beggar
émisi *n* emission; ~ *kendaraan* vehicle emissions
emong: mengemong *v* to bring up or care for
émosi, berémosi, émosional *adj* emotional
empal *n* slice of beef
empang *n* dam, fish pond
empas → **hempas**
empat *adj* four; ~ *belas* fourteen; ~ *puluh* forty; ~ *mata* face-to-face; ~ *persegi* square; ~ *persegi panjang* rectangle; *persegi* ~ square; *segi* ~ square; **berempat** *adj* in a group of four; **keempat** *adj* fourth; **keempat-nya, keempat-empatnya** *n* all four of

them; **perempat** *n* quarter; ~ *final* quarter-final; *tiga* ~ three-quarters, ³/₄; **perempatan, prapatan** *n* crossroads, intersection; **seperempat** *n* one quarter, ¹/₄
empedu *n* gall, bile; *kandung* ~ gall bladder
empék-empék → **pémpék**
empela → **ampela**
émpér, émpéran *n* awning; stall, booth
emping *n* chips made from the *melinjo* bean
empu *n* creese-maker
empuk *adj* soft, tender; *kursi* ~ armchair
empunya *yang* ~, *si* ~ the owner → **punya**
émsi *n* MC, emcee; **ngémsi** *vi, coll* to be or work as an MC
emut, kemut, mengemut *vt* to suck on (sweets etc)
én n, 14th letter of the alphabet
én *conj, sl* and
énak *adj* nice, tasty, delicious; pleasant; ~*nya* the good thing is; ~ *saja*, ... ~ *aja* (sarcastically) that's nice! how dare they!; *tidak* ~ *badan* not feeling well; **énakan** *adj, sl* better, nicer, tastier; **keénakan** *adj* too enjoyable or good; **seénaknya** *adv, neg* just how you like, at will
enam *adj* six; ~ *belas* sixteen; ~ *puluh* sixty; *segi* ~ hexagon; **berenam** *adj* in a group of six; **keenam** *adj* sixth; *indera* ~ sixth sense; **keenamnya, keenam-enamnya** *n* all six of them; **seperenam** *n* one-sixth
enas: mengenaskan *adj* pitiful, saddening
enau *n* (*pohon*) ~ sugar palm
éncér *adj* liquid, runny, watery; **mengéncér** *vi* to melt, become liquid; **mengéncérkan** *vt* to melt, liquefy; **pengéncéran** *n* liquefaction, melting
éncik, cik *pron* form of address to Chinese woman
encim *kebaya* ~ Chinese-style traditional blouse
éncok *n* rheumatism, arthritis
endap: endapan *n* precipitate, sediment;

mengendap *vi* to sink, silt up; **peng-endapan** *n* siltation

éndémis *adj* endemic

endus: mengendus *vt* to sniff, get wind of, smell a rat

enek *adj* nauseous, sick, ill

énérgi *n* energy; **berénérgi** *adj* energetic; *vi* to have energy; **énérgik** *adj* energetic → **tenaga**

enga, engah: terengah-engah *adj* gasping, puffing

enggak *coll* no, not ← **tidak**

enggan *adj* reluctant, unwilling; ~ *bicara* unwilling to speak; **keengganan** *n* reluctance

enggang *n* hornbill

engkau, kau, dikau *pron* you; **Engkau** *pron* You (when referring to God); ~ *yang punya langit dan bumi* both Earth and Heaven are Yours

engkol *n* crank

engku *pron* title used for men in Malay areas

éngsél *n* hinge; joint

énsiklopédi, énsiklopédia *n* encyclopedia

entah who knows; ~ *ke mana* who knows where

entak: mengentak *vt* to stamp on something; **mengentakkan** *vt* to stamp something; ~ *kaki* to stamp your foot

entar soon ← **sebentar**

entas: mengentaskan *vt* to take out, remove; ~ *kemiskinan* to wipe out poverty

énténg *adj* light; flippant; *menjawab* ~ to give a light, flippant answer

éntot, mengéntot *vt, vulg* to fuck, screw, root

éntri *n* entry (in a dictionary)

enyah *ejac* go away, get out, get lost, beat it

énzim *n* enzyme

épiséntrum *n* epicenter

ér r, 18th letter of the alphabet

eram: mengeram *vi* to sit on eggs, brood, hatch; **pengeraman** *n* brooding, hatching

erang groan; **erangan** *n* groan, moan; **mengerang** *vi* to groan, moan

erat *adj* close, solid, strong; *hubungan* ~ close relations; **mempererat** *vt* to strengthen, make closer

Éritréa *n* Eritrea (a North African state); *orang* ~ Eritrean

Éropa, Éropah *n* Europe; *orang* ~ European; *kebudayaan* ~ European civilization; *Uni* ~ European Union (EU)

érosi *n* erosion

érotis *adj* erotic; *penari* ~ erotic dancer

erti → **arti, mengerti**

eru *pohon* ~ casuarina (tree)

és s, 19th letter of the alphabet

és *n* ice; ~ *batu* ice cube; ~ *balok* slab of ice; ~ *doger* kind of dessert; ~ *kopyor* sweet drink made from soft coconut flesh; ~ *krim* ice cream; ~ *lilin* icypole, iced lolly, popsicle; ~ *puter* home-made ice cream; ~ *serut* shaved ice; ~ *teler* sweet dessert with ice; *hujan* ~ hail; *lemari* ~ refrigerator

esa, ésa *n, lit* one, only; *Yang Maha* ~ *(YME)* the one and only (God); **keesa-an** *n* oneness; ~ *Tuhan* the oneness of God

ésai, éséi *n* essay; *lomba* ~ essay competition

éskalator *n* escalator

éstétika *n* aesthetics

Éslandia *n* Iceland; *bahasa* ~ Icelandic; *orang* ~ Icelander

ésok *adv* ~ *hari* tomorrow; **keésokan** ~ *harinya* the next day → **bésok**

ésprés → **éksprés**

éstafét *n* relay; *lari* ~ relay race; **beréstafét** *adj* in stages

étalase *n* shop window

étape *n* stage (of a cycling race)

éternit *n* plasterboard

étika *n* ethics, good manners; **berétika** *adj* ethical; *vi* to behave; ~ *baik* to behave well; **étis** *adj* ethical

étnik, étnis *n* ethnic group; ~ *Madura* the Madurese (ethnic group); *adj* ethnic, non-Western

étos *n* ethic; ~ *kerja* work ethic

étsa *n* etch; **mengétsa** *v* etch

évakuasi *n* evacuation → **ungsi**

évaluasi *n* evaluation; **mengévaluasi** *vt* to evaluate

EYD *abbrev Ejaan Yang Disempurnakan* Reformed Spelling, implemented in 1972

éyél: mengéyél *vi* to be stubborn, obstinate

F

f [éf] f, sixth letter of the alphabet

faédah *n* (insurance) benefit, use; **berfaédah** *adj* useful, worthwhile; *vi* to have a use; *tidak ~* useless

faham → **paham**

fajar *n* dawn, daybreak; *~ menyingsing* crack of dawn

fakir *~ miskin* poor person

faks, faksimili *n* fax, facsimile; *lewat ~* by fax; *mesin ~* fax machine; **difaks** *v* to be faxed

fakta *n* fact, the facts; **faktual** *adj* factual

faktor *n* factor

faktur *n* invoice, bill

fakultas *n* faculty, school; *~ Ekonomi (FE)* Faculty of Economics; *~ Hukum (FH)* Faculty of Law; *~ Kedokteran (FK)* Faculty of Medicine; *~ Kedokteran Gigi (FKG)* Faculty of Dentistry; *~ Kedokteran Hewan (FKH)* Faculty of Veterinary Science; *~ Keguruan* Faculty of Education; *~ Pertanian* School of Agriculture; *~ Sastra (FS)* Faculty of Letters, Arts Faculty; *~ Teknik* Faculty of Engineering; *~ Ilmu Sosial dan Ilmu Politik (FISIP)* School of Social and Political Sciences

fakultatif *adj* not fixed; optional; *kereta ~* train operated only at certain times; *hari libur ~* optional holiday

falak *ilmu ~* astronomy

fals *adj* off-key, false (of music)

falsafah → **filsafat**

fam *n, coll* family name

famili *adj* related, distant family

familiér *adj* intimate, friendly

fana *adj* transitory, earthly; *dunia ~* on Earth

fanatik *n* fan; fanatic; *Kristen tapi tidak ~* Christian but not fanatical

fans: ngefans *vi, sl* to be a fan of; *~ berat* to be a great fan of

fantasi *n* fantasy, imagination; *Dunia ~ (Dufan)* Fantasy World, an amusement park in Jakarta; **fantastis** *adj* fantastic

farsi → **Parsi**

fase *n* phase; *~ perangsangan* foreplay

fasih *adj* fluent, eloquent; *~ berbahasa Indonesia* to speak Indonesian fluently; **kefasihan** *n* ease, eloquence

fasilitas *n* facilities; *~ sosial (fasos)* social facilities (eg. orphanage); *~ umum (fasum)* public facilities (eg. reception hall, toilets); **berfasilitas** *adj* with facilities; *vi* to have facilities

fasis *adj* fascist; **fasisme** *n* fascism

fasos *n* social facilities (eg. orphanage) ← **fasilitas sosial**

fasum *n* public facilities (eg. reception hall, toilets) ← **fasilitas umum**

fatal *adj* very bad; fatal

fatamorgana *n* mirage

Fatihah → **Al-Fatihah**

fatwa *n* fatwa, religious ruling

favorit *adj* favorite; *sekolah ~* top school

FE *abbrev Fakultas Ekonomi* Faculty of Economics

Fébruari *bulan ~* February

féderal *adj* federal; **féderasi** *n* federation; *Piala ~* Federation Cup; **berféderasi** *vi* to be federated

félbét, vélbét *n* camp bed, cot

féminin *adj* feminine

féng sui, hong sui *n* feng shui; *menurut ~* according to feng shui

fénoména *n* phenomenon

féodal, féodalis *adj* feudal, feudalistic; **féodalisme** *n* feudalism

féri *n* ferry

férméntasi *n* fermentation

féstival *n* festival

FH *abbrev Fakultas Hukum* Faculty of Law

figuran *peran ~* cameo role; minor role

fikir → **pikir**

fiksi *n* fiction; **fiktif** *adj* fictitious, fictional

filatéli *n* philatelic sales; philately

Filipina *n* the Philippines; *orang ~* Filipino, *f* Filipina

film *n* film; *~ biru* blue film, pornographic film; *~ cabul, ~ jorok, ~ porno* porn(ographic) film; *~ dokumenter* documentary; *~ horor* horror film; *~ kartun* cartoon; *~ laga* action film; *~ seri* serial, series; *bintang ~* film star

filsafat, falsafah *n* philosophy; **berfilsafat** *vi* to have a philosophy

final *adj* final; *babak ~* final (match); *semi-~* semi-final; **finalis** *n* finalist

Finlandia *n* Finland; *bahasa ~* Finnish; *orang ~* Finn

firasat *n* presentiment, foreboding, bad feeling; *~ buruk* bad feeling

Firaun *n* Pharaoh

firdaus *n* paradise

firman *n* word of God; **berfirman** *vi* to utter, say; *Allah ~* God said

fisik *adj* physical; *bentrokan ~* physical clash

fisika *n* physics; *ilmu ~* physics; **fisikawan** *n* physicist

fisioterapi *n* physiotherapy

FISIP *abbrev Fakultas Ilmu Sosial dan Politik* Faculty of Social Science and Politics

fiskal *n* departure payment (for residents)

fitnah *n* slander (spoken), libel (written); attack on someone; **memfitnah** *vt* to slander

fitrah *zakat ~* contribution to the poor at Idul Fitri

fitri *adj* pure; *Idul ~* feast after the fasting month of Ramadan

FK *abbrev Fakultas Kedokteran* Faculty of Medicine

FKG *abbrev Fakultas Kedokteran Gigi* Faculty of Dentistry

FKH *abbrev Fakultas Kedokteran Hewan* Faculty of Veterinary Science

flamboyan *pohon ~* flame tree

flék *n* blemish, spot (on face)

flu *n* flu, influenza; *~ burung* bird flu; *~ berat* bad or severe flu

fokus *n* focus; *~ pada* focus on; **berfokus** *adj* focused; *vi* to have a focus; **memfokuskan** *vt* to focus something; *~ diri* to focus yourself

fondasi *n* foundation (of a building)

formal, formil *adj* formal

formasi *n* formation

formulir *n* (blank) form

fosil *n* fossil

foto *n* photo, photograph; *~ bugil* nude photograph; *~ model* (professional) model; *~ udara* aerial photo; **berfoto** *vi* to take, pose for a photo; **fotokopi** *n* photocopy; **difotokopi** to be photocopied

foya: foya-foya, berfoya-foya *vi* to waste money, live frivolously

fraksi *n* faction; *~ Golkar* Golkar faction

frambosen, frambozen *adj, arch* raspberry-flavored

frasa, frase *n* phrase

frustrasi *adj* frustrated

FS *abbrev Fakultas Sastra* Faculty of Letters, Arts Faculty

fulus *n* money, cash, lucre

fumigasi *n* fumigation

fungsi *n* function; *dwi~* dual function (of the army); **berfungsi** *vi* to work, go; to act as; **fungsionaris** *n* party functionary, official

fusi *n* fusion

futsal *n* indoor soccer or football

fuyung hai, puyung hai *n* sweet-and-sour omelet

G

G. *Gunung* Mt (name of mountain)

g [gé] g, seventh letter of the alphabet

G30S (alleged) *Gerakan Tiga Puluh September* 30th September Movement

GA Garuda (Indonesia Airways)

gabah *n* unhusked rice

gabung connect, join; **gabungan** *adj* joint; *tim ~* team (comprising various elements); **bergabung** *vi* to join together; **menggabungkan** *vt* to connect, combine, fuse

Gabon *n* Gabon; *orang ~* Gabonese

gabus *n* cork

gadai *surat ~* pawn ticket; **menggadai**

vt to accept something as a pawn; **menggadaikan** *vt* to pawn something; **pegadaian** *n* pawnshop

gadang *rumah* ~ traditional Minangkabau house

gadang: begadang *vi* to stay up all night; to sleep late

gading tusk, ivory (colored); *Pantai* ~ Ivory Coast; *tak ada* ~ *yang tak retak* nobody's perfect (*lit.* there is no ivory that isn't cracked)

gadis *n* girl, maiden, virgin, unmarried woman; ~ *sampul* cover girl; *sekolah* ~ girls' school; **kegadisan** *n* virginity

gado: menggado *vi* to eat side-dishes without rice

gado-gado *n* cooked salad with peanut sauce; *adj* mixed; *bahasa* ~ mixture of Indonesian and another language

gaduh *adj* noisy; **kegaduhan** *n* noise, uproar

gadungan *adj* fake, false

gaék *adj* old, veteran; *wartawan* ~ veteran reporter

gaét, gait, kait: menggaét *vt* to get (on board), snatch, hook → **gait, kait**

gagah *adj* strong; ~ *perkasa* heroic; handsome; **menggagahi** *vt* to overpower, violate, rape

gagak *burung* ~ crow, raven

gagal *vi* to fail; ~ *ginjal* kidney failure; **kegagalan** *n* failure; **menggagalkan** *vt* to frustrate, make something fail

gagang *n* handle; ~ *telepon* handset, telephone cradle

gagap stammer, stutter; ~ *teknologi* (*gaptek*) technophobe; **bergagap-gagap, menggagap** *vi* to stammer, stutter

gagas: gagasan *n* idea, concept; **penggagas** *n* initiator, inventor

gagu *adj* mute; *si* ~ deaf-mute

gaharu *kayu* ~ aloe wood, eaglewood

gaib *adj* mysterious, invisible; *kekuatan* ~ unseen power, magic

gairah *n* passion, lust; enthusiasm; **bergairah** *adj* lusty, passionate; enthusiastic; *vi* to have lust or passion; **menggairahkan** *adj* exciting, stimulating; *vt* to excite, stimulate

gait: menggait *vt* to pull, hook → **gaét, kait**

gajah *n* elephant; bishop (in chess); ~ *oleng* a batik design

gaji *n* (monthly) salary, pay; ~ *bersih* net salary, take-home pay; ~ *buta* pay for no work; ~ *kotor* gross salary; ~ *pokok* base salary; *kenaikan* ~ pay rise; *makan* ~ *buta* to have an easy job; **menggaji** *vt* to pay, remunerate, employ

gak *sl* no, not → **enggak, tidak**

galah *n* long pole, spear; *lompat* ~ pole vault

galak *adj* fierce, wild, vicious; *anjing* ~ vicious dog; *guru yang* ~ strict teacher

galang *n* girder, prop; **galangan** *n* ~ (*perahu*) dry dock; **menggalang** *vt* to support, consolidate

galau *adj* noisy, in uproar

galeri *n* gallery → **paméran**

gali *v* to dig; **galian** *n* excavations, diggings; **menggali** *vt* to dig; **penggalian** *n* digging

galon *n* gallon

Galungan *n* Balinese festival

GAM *abbrev Gerakan Aceh Merdeka* Free Aceh Movement

gamang *adj* nervous, dizzy; ~ *tinggi* scared of heights

gambang *n* a kind of xylophone

gambar picture, drawing, illustration; **gambaran** *n* sketch, idea; **bergambar** *adj* illustrated; **menggambar** *v* to draw, depict; **menggambarkan** *vt* to describe, illustrate; **penggambaran** *n* depiction

gambir *n* gambier, spice used in chewing betel nut

gamblang *adj* clear, obvious, plain

gamelan *n* traditional orchestra

gamis *baju* ~ long Arab-style shirt

gamit: bergamit *vi* to touch, nudge; **bergamitan** *vi* to touch each other; **menggamitkan, menggamit-gamitkan** *vt* to touch or nudge something

gampang *adj, coll* easy; ~~ *susah* not as easy as it looks → **mudah**

gamping *n* limestone**

ganas *adj* fierce, wild, ferocious; uncontrolled; *tumor* ~ malignant growth or lump; **keganasan** *n* ferocity

gancang *adj* quick, agile

ganda double; -fold; over; ~ *campuran* mixed doubles; ~ *putra* men's doubles; *berlipat* ~ many times; **menggandakan** *vt* to duplicate, multiply; **penggandaan** *n* duplication

gandapura *n* tree with medicinal properties

gandéng link, join; *truk* ~ semi-trailer; **bergandéng** *vi* to join or do together; **bergandéngan** *vi* ~ *tangan* to link arms or hands; **menggandéng** *vt* to include, involve, link with

gandol → **gandul**

gandrung: kegandrungan *adj, sl* to be absorbed or swept up in, madly in love; **menggandrungi** *vt* to love, be swept up in

gandul *n* pendulum, clapper

gandum *n* wheat; *roti* ~ whole wheat bread

Ganésa, Ganésha, Ganéça *n* Hindu elephant god of wisdom

gang *n* alley, lane

Gangga *sungai* ~ the Ganges River

ganggang *n* pond weed, algae; ~ *laut* seaweed

ganggu, mengganggu *vt* to bother, disturb; ~ *gugat* to contest, challenge, sue; **gangguan** *n* disturbance, interference; problem; ~ *jiwa* mental illness; ~ *pendengaran* hearing problem; **terganggu** *adj* bothered, disrupted, disturbed

ganja *n* marijuana; *mengisap* ~ to smoke marijuana

ganjal *v* to wedge; to fill a gap; *makan bakso yuk, buat* ~ let's have some meatball soup, to fill us up; **mengganjal** *vt* to wedge

ganjar: ganjaran *n* reward

ganjil *adj* uneven, odd; *angka* ~ odd number; **keganjilan** *n* oddity, peculiarity

ganjing → **gonjang**

ganteng *adj, coll* handsome

ganti change, substitute; ~ *baju,* ~ *pakaian* change your clothes; ~ *nama* change name; ~ *oli* drain sump oil; ~ *rugi* compensation; *gonta-*~ change frequently; **gantian** *v, sl* to change over; **berganti** *vi* to change; *silih* ~, **berganti-ganti, bergantian** *vi* in turns; *adv* repeatedly; **mengganti** *vt* to change, substitute, replace; **menggantikan** *vt* to substitute or replace someone/something; **pengganti** *n* replacement, substitute, successor; **penggantian** *n* substitution; **pergantian** *n* change; ~ *tahun* new year

gantolé *n* hang-glider, hang-gliding; *main* ~ to go hang-gliding

gantung hang; ~ *diri* hang yourself; *jembatan* ~ suspension bridge; **gantungan** *n* hanger; ~ *baju* clothes hanger; **bergantung** *vi* ~ *pada* to depend on; **menggantung** *vt* to hang, suspend; **menggantungkan** *vt* to hang something; ~ *jam pada dinding* to hang a clock on the wall; **tergantung** *adj* depending (on), it depends; **ketergantungan** *n* dependency; ~ *obat* drug dependency

ganyang *v* to crush, wipe out; ~ *Malaysia!* crush Malaysia! (1960s political slogan); **mengganyang** *vt* to crush, wipe out; to eat raw

gapai: menggapai *vt* to strive for, reach; ~ *cita-cita* to chase your dreams

gaplé *n* dominoes

gapték *n* technophobe ← **gagap téknologi**

gapura *n* (ornamental) gateway, entrance

gara-gara *adv, sl* all because of; *n* forest scene in shadow puppet play; fuss → **goro-goro**

garam *n* salt; *sudah makan* ~ experienced, an old salt

garang *adj* fierce, savage, cruel

garansi *n* guarantee (on a product); **bergaransi** *adj* guaranteed; *vi* to have a guarantee

garap: garapan *adj* produced by, product; **menggarap** *vt* to work on, produce; ~ *tanah* to till the land; **penggarapan** *n* production; ~ *film* film or movie production

garasi *n* carport, garage

gardan *n* differential gear → **kardan**

gardu *n* post, station; ~ *listrik* transmission station

garebeg, garebek *n* one of the big Islamic festivals; ~ *Besar,* ~ *Haji* Idul Adha Feast of the Sacrifice; ~ *Maulud* Birthday of the Prophet; ~ *Puasa* Idul Fitri, post-fasting celebrations

Garéng *n* shadow puppet character

garing *adj* dry, crisp; *sudah* ~ *sl* stale, out-of-date (of a joke)

garis line, scratch; ~ *akhir* finish line; ~ *alas* baseline; ~ *edar* orbit; ~ *pantai* coast(line); ~ *peperangan* front, front line; ~ *tengah* diameter; ~ *tegak lurus* perpendicular (line); **bergaris** *adj* lined; *vi* to have lines; **menggaris** *vt* to draw a line; **menggarisbawahi** *vt* to underline, emphasize; **penggaris** *n* ruler

garmén *pabrik* ~ garment factory

garong *n* robber; **menggarong** *vt* to rob, loot

garpu *n* fork; ~ *tala* tuning fork; *sendok* ~ spoon and fork

garuda *n* mythical bird of prey, national symbol of Indonesia

garuk, menggaruk *vt* to scratch, scrape; ~ *kepala* to scratch your head; **menggaruk-garuk** *vt* to scratch repeatedly

gas *n* gas; ~ *alam,* ~ *bumi* natural gas; ~ *lebam,* ~ *lembam,* ~ *mulia* inert or noble gas; ~ *racun* poisonous gas; ~ *saraf* nerve gas; *menancap* ~ to step on the gas; ~ *air mata* tear gas

gasing *n* (spinning) top; *main* ~ to spin a top

gatal *adj* itchy; *sl* lustful; **gatal-gatal** *vi* to have a rash

Gatotkaca, Gatutkaca *n* flying warrior in shadow puppet plays, son of Bima

gatra *n* phrase; aspect

gaul *v* to mix, associate; *adj, sl* trendy; *kafé* ~ trendy café; **bergaul** *vi* to mix or associate; **menggauli** *vt* to have sexual intercourse with; **pergaulan** *n* mixing, social intercourse; association; ~ *bebas* promiscuity, permissiveness

gaun *n* (evening) gown; ~ *malam* evening gown

gaung *n* echo; **bergaung** *vi* to echo

gawang *n* goal (in field sports); hurdle; *lari* ~ hurdles; *penjaga* ~ goalkeeper

gawat *adj* serious, very bad; *Instalasi* ~ *Darurat (IGD), Unit* ~ *Darurat (UGD)* emergency room, casualty ward

gaya *n* style, stroke (in swimming); ~ *dada* breast stroke; ~ *kodok* frogkick; *penuh* ~ stylish; **bergaya** *adj* stylish, with style; *vi* to have style

gaya *n* energy, strength, force; ~ *berat,* ~ *bobot* gravity

Gayo Acehnese sub-ethnic group

gayung *n* water dipper; stick; ~ *bersambut* to respond

Gd. *abbrev gedung* building

gé *n* g, seventh letter of the alphabet

gedebak: gedebak-gedebuk sound of objects falling

gebrak blow, bang, hit; **gebrakan** *n* bang, slam, blow; **menggebrak** *vt* to hit or slam; ~ *meja* to hit the table

gebu: menggebu *vi* to rage, bubble, froth over

gebuk hit, bash; **menggebuk** *vt* to batter, bash

gebyar sparkle, glitter

gedé *adj, coll* big, large; ~ *banget* enormous, very big; ~ *rasa (GR)* stuck-up, full of yourself; **gedéan** *adj, sl* larger or bigger than

gedék *n* panel of woven bamboo, for huts or buildings

gedong *n* brick or concrete house; **gedongan** *anak* ~ rich kid, child who lives in a brick house

gedor: menggedor *vt* to bang on repeatedly; ~ *pintu* to bang on the door

gedung *n* building, public hall; ~ *Arsip* State Archives; ~ *Putih* the White House; ~ *serba guna* all-purpose building, wedding hall

géér, gé ér, GR *adj, coll* stuck-up, full of yourself ← **gedé rasa**

gegabah *adj* reckless, hasty

gegap ~ *gempita* noisy, thunderous

gegar shake, quiver; ~ *budaya* culture shock; ~ *otak* concussion

gegas: bergegas-gegas *vi* to hurry

gégér noise, clamor

geguyon *n* joke ← **guyon**

gejala *n* symptom, sign

gejolak *n* uprising, outburst, riot; **bergejolak** *vi* to flare up, burst out

geladah → **geledah**

geladak *n* deck of a ship

geladi → **gladi**

gelagap: gelagapan confused; stammer, stutter

gelagat *n* mark, sign, omen

gelak laugh; ~ *tawa* burst or gale of laughter

gelambir *n* wattle (on a bird), dewlap, fold of skin

gelandang *n* half-back

gelandang: gelandangan *n* tramp, homeless person

gelang *n* bracelet; **pergelangan** ~ *kaki* ankle; ~ *tangan* wrist

gelanggang *n* arena, stadium; ~ *dunia* world stage; ~ *olah raga (GOR, gelora)* sports complex

gelantung hang, suspend; **gelantungan** *adj* hanging from; **bergelantungan** *vi* to hang from (of several things)

gelap *adj* dark; illicit; ~ *gulita* pitch black; *barang* ~ contraband, illegal goods; *imigran* ~ illegal immigrant; *pasar* ~ black market; **kegelapan** *n* darkness; **menggelapkan** *vt* to embezzle, misappropriate; **penggelapan** *n* embezzlement

gelar *n* title; **bergelar** *adj* titled; *vi* to have a title

gelar: menggelar, menggelarkan *vt* to hold (an event)

gelas *n* (drinking) glass, tumbler

gelatik *n burung* ~ Java sparrow, Java finch

gélatin *n* gelatine

gelatuk → **geletuk**

gelédah, geladah, menggelédah *vt* to search; to ransack; **penggelédahan** *n* search, raid, operation

gelédék *n* lightning

gelegar *n* rumbling, thunder

gelembung *n* bubble

géléng: menggéléng, menggélengkan *vt* ~ *kepala* to shake your head

gelétak *vi* to shudder; **tergelétak** *adj* sprawled

geletuk, gelatuk: menggeletuk *vi* to chatter (of teeth)

geli ticklish; uncomfortable; *merasa* ~ to feel uncomfortable; **menggelikan** *adj* funny, comic; off-putting

geliat ~ *geliut* wriggle, writhe; **menggeliat** *vi* to stretch, twist

gelimang: bergelimang *adj* smeared; ~ *lumpur* muddy, mud-stained

gelimpang: bergelimpang, tergelimpang *adj* sprawled; **bergelimpangan** *adj* sprawled all around; *mayat* ~ dead bodies lay everywhere

gelincir: menggelincir *vi* to slip, slide; **tergelincir** *adj* skidded, slipped; *pesawat itu* ~ the plane skidded

gelinding *n* wheel; **bergelinding** *vi* to roll; **bergelindingan** *vi* to roll (of many objects); **menggelinding** *vi* to roll; **menggelindingkan** *vt* to roll something

gelintir: segelintir *n* a small number

gelisah *adj* nervous, restless; **kegelisahan** *n* anxiety, nerves; **menggelisahkan** *vt* to make nervous

gelitik, menggelitik *vt* to tickle; **tergelitik** *adj* tickled

geliut *geliat* ~ wriggle, writhe

gelombang *n* wave; (radio) frequency; **bergelombang** *adj* wavy

gelora *n* storm, surge, passion; ~ *asmara* passion; **menggelora** *vi* to rage, storm, surge

gelora *n* sports complex ← **gelanggang olah raga**

geluduk *n* thunder

gelung *n* coil; **bergelung** *adj* coiled; *vi* to have a coil; **menggelungkan** *vt* to coil something

gelut: bergelut *vi* to wrestle; to romp; **menggeluti** *vt* to be involved, deal with

gema *n* echo, reverberation; **bergema** *vi* to echo, reverberate

gemar like, enjoy; **kegemaran** *n* hobby; **menggemari** *vt* to like, enjoy; **penggemar** *n* fan, enthusiast

gemas, gemes *coll* cute, sweet (often said to children); annoyed; **menggemaskan** *adj* annoying; *vt* to annoy gembala, penggembala *n* shepherd; **menggembala** *vt* to herd

gembar: gembar-gembor make a big deal, shout; **menggembar-gemborkan** *vt* make a big deal of, shout about

gembira *adj* cheerful, happy, joyous; **bergembira** *vi* to be happy, joyous; **kegembiraan** *n* joy, happiness; **menggembirakan** *adj* exciting, happy; *vt* to make happy, excite; *berita yang ~* good news

gembok *n* padlock; **menggembok** *vt* to padlock

gémbong *n* brains, leader

gembos flat, deflated; **menggembos** *vt* to deflate

gembrot *adj* fat, flabby, out of shape

gembul *adj* greedy; fat

gembung, kembung *adj* filled with air, inflated; bloated; *perut ~* bloated belly → **kembung**

gemercik splash, spray, spatter

gemerencing, gemerincing sound of jingling (coins etc)

gemerlap shine, sparkle; **gemerlapan** *pl* shine, sparkle

gemes → **gemas**

gemetar shiver, tremble; **gemetaran** *adj* shivering, trembling

gemilang glitter, shine; brilliant; *gilang ~* glittering, brilliant

geming: bergeming *vi tak ~* not bat an eyelid, make not the slightest reaction

gempa *n* quake, shudder; *~ bumi* earthquake; *~ tektonik* earthquake, tectonic movement; **menggempakan** *vt* to jolt, stir

gempar clamor, noise, uproar; **menggemparkan** *vt* to cause a stir

gempita *gegap ~* noisy, thunderous

gempur: menggempur *vt* to attack, destroy

gemuk *adj* fat, plump, obese; *n* grease; *jalur ~* busy route; **kegemukan** *n* fatness; *adj* overweight

gemulai *adj* supple, swaying

gemuruh *n* thunder → **guruh**

gén *n* gene; **génétik** *adj* genetic; **génétika** *n* genetics; *rekayasa ~* genetic engineering

genang: genangan *n* puddle, flood; **bergenang** *adj* flooded; *vi* to flood, be wet; **menggenangi** *vt* to flood something

genap *adj* even, complete, exact; *angka ~* even number; **segenap** *adj* each, all

gencar *adj* incessant, non-stop

gencat: gencatan *~ senjata* ceasefire, truce, armistice

gendang *n* (kettle) drum; *~ telinga* eardrum

genderang *n* kind of drum

genderuwo, gendruwo *n* malevolent spirit

géndong, menggéndong *vt* to carry on the hip

gendruwo → **genderuwo**

gendut *adj* fat, pot-bellied

génerasi *n* generation

génétik *adj* genetic; **génétika** *n* genetics; *rekayasa ~* genetic engineering ← **gén**

géng, génk *n* gang

genggam fist; **genggaman** *n* grip, grasp; **menggenggam** *vt* to grip, grasp; **segenggam** *n* handful

géngsi *n* prestige, face; *~ dong* mustn't lose face!; **bergéngsi** *adj* prestigious; *vi* to have prestige

genit *adj* flirtatious

genjot, menggenjot *vt* to push, pedal; *~ sepeda* to pedal a bike

génsét *n* generator

genta *n* (church) bell

gentar shiver, tremble; *tak ~* unafraid

gentayangan *vi* to wander, roam

genténg, genting *n* roof tile

genting *adj* critical; narrow; *tanah ~* isthmus; **gentingan** *n* isthmus; *~ Kra* Isthmus of Kra

gentong *n* water pitcher

géografi *n* geography (school subject) → **ilmu bumi**

géolog *n* geologist; **géologi** *n* geology

Georgia [Jorjia] *n* Georgia; *bahasa ~, orang ~* Georgian

gépéng *adj* flat, concave, sunken

gepok: segepok *n* a bundle, bunch, wad

ger ha ha ha, sound of mass laughter

gerabah *n* earthenware pot

gerah *adj* sultry, muggy

geraham *gigi* ~ molar

gerai *n* counter, kiosk, (retail) outlet

gerak move; ~ *badan* (physical) exercises; ~ *gerik* movements, body language; ~ *jalan* long march; demonstration; **gerakan** *n* movement; ~ *Aceh Merdeka (GAM)* Free Aceh Movement; ~ *Séptémber Tiga Puluh (Gestapu)* (alleged) 30th September Movement (in 1965); **bergerak** *vi* to move; *aset* ~ movable assets; **menggerakkan** *vt* to move, shift something

geram *adj* very angry, furious; **menggeram** *vi* to become very angry; to growl, roar

gerangan can it be?

gerayang: menggerayangi *vt* to grope

gerbang *n* gate, gateway, door; ~ *tol* toll gate; *pintu* ~ main gate

gerbong *n* carriage; ~ *kereta* (train) carriage, car; ~ *restorasi* restaurant car

gerebek, gerebeg: menggerebek *vt* to raid, search; **penggerebekan** *n* raid, search

gereget: geregetan *adj* filled with pent-up emotion

geréja *n* church; ~ *Advent* (Seventh-Day) Adventist Church; ~ *Anglikan* Anglican Church; ~ *Katolik* Catholic Church; ~ *Kristen* Protestant Church; ~ *Ortodoks* Orthodox Church; ~ *Pantekosta* Pentecostal Church; *burung* ~ sparrow

gergaji *n* saw; *abu* ~ sawdust; **menggergaji** *vt* to saw

gerhana *n* eclipse; ~ *bulan* lunar eclipse; ~ *matahari* solar eclipse

gerigi *n, pl* teeth, points; **bergerigi** *adj* serrated, jagged; *vi* to have serrated edges or points

gerilya *adj* guerrilla; *perang* ~ guerrilla war; **bergerilya** *vi* to wage guerrilla warfare; **gerilyawan** *n* guerrilla

gerimis drizzle; *(hujan)* ~ drizzle

gerinda *n* grindstone; **menggerinda** *vt* to grind, sharpen

gerip *n, arch* (slate) pencil

gerobak *n* cart; ~ *kaki lima* itinerant food vendor; ~ *sampah* rubbish cart

gerogot: menggerogoti *vt* to eat into, erode, gnaw on; *digerogoti rayap* to be eaten by termites

gerombol: gerombolan *n* group, mass; **bergerombol, menggerombol** *vi* to gather in a group, amass

gersang *adj* arid

gertak snarl, snap; ~ *sambal* empty threat; **menggertak** *vt* to snarl or snap at; to intimidate, threaten

gerutu: menggerutu *vi* to grumble, complain, gripe

gesa: tergesa-gesa *adj* in a hurry or rush

gését rub; **gésékan** *n* stroke, scrape; friction; **menggését** *vt* to rub, scrape; ~ *biola* to play the violin; ~ *kartu* to swipe a card; **pergésékan** *n* friction

gésér, menggésér *v* to move aside or over; **pergéséran** *n* movement, shift

gesit *adj* nimble, adept, adroit; **kegesitan** *n* agility, adroitness

géspér *n* (belt) clasp, buckle

Gestapu *n* (alleged) 30th September Movement (in 1965) ← **Gerakan Séptémber Tiga Puluh**

getah *n* sap, latex, gum; ~ *perca gutta(-percha)* (used in silk painting)

getah ~ *bening* lymph gland

getar shake, tremor; **getaran** *n* vibration, shake, tremor; **bergetar** *vi* to vibrate, tremble

géték *n, Jkt* small raft to cross a river

getol *adj, coll* hard-working, diligent

getuk *n, Jav* snack made from cassava

Gg gang lane, alley

Ghana *n* Ghana; *orang* ~ Ghanaian

GIA Garuda Indonesia Airways

giat *adj* active, busy; **kegiatan** *n* activity; **pegiat** *n* activist

gidik: bergidik *vi* to shudder, shiver

gigi *n* tooth; cog, *coll* gear; ~ *dua* second gear; ~ *geraham* molar; ~ *mundur* reverse gear; ~ *palsu* false teeth; ~ *rontok* tooth that has fallen out; ~ *susu* milk tooth; ~ *taring* fang, incisor, canine tooth; *ahli* ~ dental practitioner, dentist; *dokter* ~ dentist; **menggosok** ~ to brush your teeth; *pasta* ~ toothpaste; *sakit* ~ toothache; *sikat* ~ toothbrush; *tusuk* ~ toothpick; **bergigi** *vi* to have teeth; *tidak* ~ toothless; power-less

gigih *adj* persevering, tenacious; **kegigihan** *n* perseverance, tenacity

gigil: menggigil *vi* to shiver

gigit ~ *jari* be disappointed or frustrated; **gigitan** *n* bite; **menggigit** *vt* to bite

gila *adj* crazy, mad, insane; *orang* ~ lunatic; tramp; **kegilaan** *n* craze; **ter-gila-gila** ~ *dengan* crazy about

gilang ~ *gemilang* brilliant, glittering

gilas, menggilas *vt* to crush, pulverize; flatten; **penggilas** *n* crusher; rolling pin; ~ *jalan* steamroller

giling *daging* ~ mincemeat; **gilingan** *n* mill, grinder; rolling pin; **menggiling** *vt* to grind, mill; to roll out (pastry); **penggilingan** *n* mill

gilir: giliran *n* turn; **bergilir, bergiliran** *adj* in turns

gimana *coll* how; ~ *sih?* what about that? → **bagaimana**

gincu *n, arch* lipstick, lip gloss

ginékolog *n* gynecologist; **ginékologi** *n* gynecology → **kandungan**

gini *adv, coll* like this, in this way → **begini**

ginjal *n* kidney; *sakit* ~ kidney disease

giok *n batu* ~ jade

gips *n* plaster, plaster cast; **digips** *v* to be in or have a plaster cast

gipsi *n* gypsy

gir *n* gear

girang *adj* pleased, glad, happy; *tante* ~ flirtatious older woman; **kegirangan** *n* gladness, happiness

giring, menggiring *vt* to herd, drive (cattle); **penggiring** *n* herder

giro *n* transfer, clearing (money); ~ *pos* postal transfer; *rekening* ~ check account

gita *n* hymn, song

gitar *n* guitar; **gitaris** *n* guitarist, guitar player

gitu *adv, coll* like that, in that way; ~ *lho* like that, you know → **begitu**

giur: menggiurkan *adj* tempting, mouth-watering; **tergiur** *adj* tempted

giwang *n* earring, stud

gizi *n* nutrient; *ahli* ~ nutritionist;

penyakit kurang ~ malnutrition; **bergizi** *adj* nutritious

gk *gaya kuda* horsepower

gladi, geladi ~ *resik,* ~ *bersih* dress-rehearsal

gladiol *n* gladiolus

glasir, glazur *n* (tile) glazing; **meng-glasir** *vt* to glaze (tiles)

glétser *n* glacier

global *adj* global, worldwide; *secara* ~ overall; **globalisasi** *n* globalization

glukosa *n* glucose

go *Ch, sl* five (usu re money); ~ *ban* fifty thousand; ~ *cap* fifty; ~ *ceng* five thousand; ~ *pek* five hundred

goa, gua *n* cave, tunnel; ~ *Jepang* Japanese-built tunnel from World War II

goblok *derog* stupid, moron

gocéng *adj, sl* five thousand (rupiah) ← **go**

goda tempt; **godaan** *n* temptation; **meng-goda** *vt* to tempt; **menggodai** *vt* to tempt someone; **tergoda** *adj* tempted

godok boil; **menggodok** *vt* to boil

gokar *n* go-kart

gol *n* goal; ~ *bunuh diri* own goal; **mengegolkan** *vt* to promote, campaign for someone

golak: pergolakan *n* disturbance, upheaval

golék *wayang* ~ (performance using) three-dimensional wooden puppets from West Java

golf *n* golf; *lapangan* ~, *padang* ~ golf course; **pegolf** *n* golfer

Golkar *n, arch* Functional Group (Soehartoist party, until 1998); *Partai* ~ Golkar Party ← **Golongan Karya**

golok *n* machete, chopping knife; **menggolok** *vt* to cut with a machete

golong: golongan *n* group, category; rank; ~ *darah* blood group or type; *IV A* Rank IV A (in civil service); ~ *Karya (Golkar) arch* Functional Group; ~ *putih (golput)* 'white' group (abstainers in elections); **menggolongkan** *vt* to group, classify; **penggolongan** *n* classification; **tergolong** *adj* to include, be part of or considered

gombal *adj* worthless; *n* old, worthless piece of cloth; *rayuan* ~ sweet talk

goncang, guncang rock, sway; **goncangan** *n* shock wave, quake; **bergoncang** *vi* to rock, sway; **menggoncangkan** *vt* to rock or make something move

gondok *n* goitre

gondok *adj* (silently) angry

gondong: gondongan *vi* have the mumps

gondrong (excessively) long hair

gong *n* gong

gonggong woof, sound of dog barking; **menggonggong** *vi* to bark; *anjing* ~ a dog barking

goni *n* jute; *karung* ~ gunny sack

gonjang ~-*ganjing* shake, tremble, rock

gono-gini *n* shared goods and chattels during a marriage, split up during divorce

gonta-ganti *vt* to change constantly or frequently; ~ *pacar* to have had lots of boyfriends/girlfriends → **ganti**

gopék *n* five hundred (rupiah) ← **go**

gopoh: tergopoh-gopoh *adv* hurriedly, in a rush

GOR *abbrev Gelanggang Olah Raga* stadium, sports complex

gordén, hordén *n* curtain(s)

goréng fry; *mi* ~ fried noodles; *nasi* ~ fried rice; **goréngan** *n* fried snacks (such as tofu, tempe); **menggoréng** *vt* to fry; **penggoréngan** *n* wok, frying pan; process of frying

gorés line, scratch; **gorésan** *n* scratch, stroke; **menggorés** *vt* to scratch, make a stroke; **tergorés** *adj* scratched

goro-goro *n* scene in shadow puppet play → **gara-gara**

gorong-gorong *n* underground sewer or drain

gosip gossip; *raja* ~ (*ragos*) *m*, *ratu* ~ *f* gossip (queen); **bergosip** *vi* to gossip; **menggosipkan** *vt* to gossip about something or someone

gosok rub; *minyak* ~ massage oil; **menggosok** *vt* to rub, polish; *coll* to iron; ~ *gigi* to clean your teeth; ~ *sepatu* to polish, shine (shoes)

gosong *adj* burnt, singed, scorched; *bau* ~ burnt smell

got *n* roadside drain or ditch; *masuk* ~ to fall in the drain; *tikus* ~ sewer rat

gotong carry; ~ *royong* mutual assistance; **menggotong** *vt* to carry together

goyah *adj* unstable, wobbly; **tergoyahkan** *tak* ~ unshakable

goyang shake, wobble, unsteady; **bergoyang** *vi* to shake, sway; to dance; **menggoyang** *vt* to shake, rock; ~ *pinggul* to sway your hips; **menggoyangkan** *vt* to shake or rock something

GR, gé ér *adj* stuck-up, full of yourself ← **gedé rasa**

grafik *n* graph; diagram; **grafis** *adj* graphic; *seni* ~ graphic design

graha, grha *n* building, house; *Bina* ~ presidential office

gram *n* gram

granat *n* grenade

grasi *n* pardon (from the President), clemency; *memberi* ~ to pardon someone (for a crime)

gratis *adj* free (of charge), gratis

greget, gereget: gregetan *adj* filled with pent-up emotion

gréndel *n* latch, bolt; **menggréndel** *vt* to bolt

grés *adj* newest, latest; *paling* ~ most up-to-date

gringsing, geringsing *n* double-*ikat* cloth from Bali

griya *n* house

grogi *adj* nervous, groggy

grosir *n* wholesaler; **grosiran** *adj* wholesale

grup *n* group (esp business)

gua → **goa**

gua → **gué**

Guam *n* Guam; *orang* ~ Guamanian

gubah, menggubah *vt* to arrange, compose

gubernur *n* governor; *calon* ~ gubernatorial candidate

gubris: menggubris *vt* to pay heed or attention to; *tidak digubris* ignored

gubuk *n* hut; ~ *derita* my humble abode

guci *n* (earthenware) jar or pot

gudang *n* warehouse, shed, store; *cuci ~* stocktake sale

gudeg *n* sweet dish of cooked jackfruit, a specialty of Jogjakarta

gué, gua *pron, sl* me, I; *gue lu* on very close terms; *gue gue lu lu* you mind your business, I'll mind mine

gugat sue; *ganggu ~, menggangu ~* contest, challenge, sue; **gugatan** *n* lawsuit, accusation; **menggugat** *vt* to sue, accuse; **penggugat** *n* plaintiff

gugup *adj* nervous; **kegugupan** *n* nervousness, panic

gugur *vi* to fall, be killed (in action) or eliminated; *musim ~* autumn, fall; **keguguran** *n* miscarriage; **menggugurkan** *vt* to abort; **pengguguran** *n* abortion

gugus cluster; *~ bintang* constellation; **gugusan** *n* bunch, group, cluster; *~ pulau* chain of islands

gula *n* sugar; *~ aren* palm sugar; *~ batu* sugar lump; *~ Jawa* palm sugar; *~ merah* brown sugar; palm sugar; *~ pasir* (white) sugar; *kembang ~* fairy floss; *ada ~ ada semut* if you have money, people will come; **gula-gula** *n* candy, sweets; mistress

gulai, gulé *n* curry; *~ kambing* goat curry

gulat wrestling; **bergulat** *vi* to wrestle, fight; **pergulatan** *n* wrestling, struggle, fight; **pegulat** *n* wrestler

gulden *n, arch* (Dutch) guilder

guling *(bantal) ~* bolster, Dutch wife; *babi ~* suckling pig; **mengguling** *vi* to roll; **menggulingkan** *vt* to topple, roll something over

gulita *gelap ~* pitch-black

gulung *~ tikar* close down, close shop; go bankrupt; **gulungan** *n* roll, spool; **menggulung** *vt* to roll up

gumam, bergumam *vi* to mumble; **menggumamkan** *vt* to mumble or mutter something

gumpal *n* clot, lump; **gumpalan** *n* clot, lump; *~ darah* clot of blood; **bergumpal** *vi* to clot

gumul, bergumul *vi* to wrestle

guna use, benefit; for; *tepat ~* effective; appropriate; *tidak ada ~nya* there's no use; **berguna** *adj* useful, worthwhile; *vi* to have a use; *tidak ~* useless; **kegunaan** *n* usefulness, use; **menggunakan** *vt* to use; **pengguna** *n* user; **pengunaan** *n* usage, use

guna-guna *n* black magic

guncang, goncang rock, sway; **guncangan** *n* shock wave, quake; **berguncang** *vi* to rock, sway; **mengguncangkan** *vt* to rock or make something move

gundah *adj* depressed; **bergundah** *vi ~ hati* sad

gundik *n* mistress, concubine

gundul *adj* bald; **menggunduli** *vt* to shave, denude, make bald; *bukit itu sudah digunduli* the hill has been deforested

gunjing: gunjingan *n* gossip, slander; **bergunjing** *vi* to gossip; **menggunjing** *vt* to talk about someone behind their back

gunting scissors, cut; *~ kuku* nail clippers; *~ rambut* trim; **guntingan** *n* cutout; *~ koran* newspaper clipping; **menggunting** *vt* to cut (out)

guntur *n* thunder

gunung *n Gg abbrev* mountain, mount; remote area; *~ api, ~ berapi* volcano; *~ Bromo* Mount Bromo; *mendaki ~* mountain-climbing, bushwalking; **gunungan** *n* symbolic mountain used in shadow-puppet plays; **pegunungan** *n* mountain range; *~ Jayawijaya* the Jayawijaya range

gurah *n* rinsing, as an alternative medical treatment

guramé, guraméh, gurami *ikan ~* large freshwater fish

gurat: guratan *n* scratch

gurau joke, jest; *bersenda ~* to joke around

gurem *adj* tiny, insignificant; *partai ~* minor party (with very small vote)

gurih *adj* tasty, delicious, mouth-watering

gurindam *n* couplet, verse

gurita *ikan ~* octopus

gurita *n* cloth used by mothers after giving birth, to bind their stomach

guru *n* teacher; *~ besar* professor; *~*

kepala headmaster; ~ *les* private teacher; ~ *ngaji* Arabic teacher; ~ *kencing berdiri, murid kencing berlari* teachers are always examples to their students; **berguru** *vi* ~ *kepada* to study under, learn from, have as a teacher; **menggurui** *vt* to lecture; to talk condescendingly to someone; **perguruan** ~ *tinggi* university, institute of higher learning

guruh *n* thunder

gurun *n* desert; ~ *Sahara* the Sahara Desert

Gus, Bagus *title, m, Isl* East Javanese title; ~ *Dur* common name for Abdurrahman Wahid

gusar *adj* angry, vexed; **kegusaran** *n* annoyance, anger

gusi *n* gums

gusti *n, pron, arch* lord; ~ *Allah* the Lord God; *kawula* ~ Javanese servant-patron relationship

gusur: menggusur *vt* to evict, sweep aside, forcibly remove; **penggusuran** *n* eviction, forcible removal

guyon joke; **guyonan, geguyon** *n* joke

guyur: mengguyur *vi* to soak, drench; *diguyur hujan* drenched by the rain; **terguyur** *adj* soaked, drenched

H

H *hijriah* Islamic calendar

H. *Haji* title for man who has performed the major pilgrimage to Mecca

h, ha [ha] h, eighth letter of the alphabet

ha *ejac* ha!; sound showing happiness

habis *adj* finished, over; empty; *adv* entirely; *sl* well; prep, *coll* after; ~ *terjual* sold out; ~ *perkara* end of story; that was it; *stok sudah* ~ out of stock; ~ *mandi dia pergi* after washing, he went out; ~ *manis, sepah dibuang* use something then abandon it; **habisnya** *coll, adv* well, in any case; **habishabisan** *adv* completely, all out; **kehabisan** *v* to run out of (water; food; stock); ~ *air* to be out of water; **meng-**

habisi *vt* to finish (off), kill; **menghabiskan** *vt* to finish, use up, spend; ~ *uang jutaan rupiah* to spend millions of rupiah; **penghabisan** *n* end; *ujian* ~ final examination; **sehabis** *conj* after

habitat *n* habitat

hablur *n* crystal

hacih, haciu a-choo! (sound of sneezing)

hadap face; ~ *kiri* face left; **hadapan** *n* front; facing; *di* ~ in front of; **berhadapan** *vi* to face (each other); *adv* ~ *(muka)* face to face; **menghadap** *vt* to face, appear before; **menghadapi** *vt* to face someone or something; **menghadapkan** *vt* to aim or point something; to confront, put in front of; *penjahat itu dihadapkan dengan kepala polisi* the criminal was brought before the chief of police; **terhadap** *conj* regarding; against; with respect to

hadiah *n* present, gift; prize; ~ *Nobel* Nobel Prize; ~ *pertama* first prize; **berhadiah** *adj* with prizes; *vi* to have a prize; **menghadiahkan** *vt* to give as a present or prize; **menghadiahi** *vt* to give someone a present or prize

hadir present; available; *tidak* ~ absent; **hadirin** *n* audience; **kehadiran** *n* presence; attendance; **menghadiri** *vt* to attend; **menghadirkan** *vt* to present; to bring forward; ~ *saksi baru* bring forward a new witness

hadis, hadith *n, Isl* traditions of the Prophet Muhammad

hafal, hapal know by heart; **hapalan** *n* memorization; **menghafalkan** *vt* to learn by heart

hai *sl* hi

haid *n* menstruation; *nyeri* ~ menstrual pain; *siklus* ~, *daur* ~ menstrual cycle

Haiti *n* Haiti; *orang* ~ Haitian

Haj, hajj → **haji**

hajah → **hajjah**

hajar, menghajar *vt* to thrash; to beat up

hajat *n* want, need, wish; *buang* ~ to defecate; *punya* ~ to hold a feast

haji *n, Isl* person who has made the pilgrimage to Mecca; ~ *kecil* minor pilgrimage → **umroh**; *Lebaran* ~ Idul

Adha, Feast of the Sacrifice (performed during the annual pilgrimage); *naik* ~ go on the annual pilgrimage to Mecca; *Pak* ~ title for a man who has made the pilgrimage to Mecca; *ongkos naik* ~ *(ONH)* cost of making the pilgrimage; **hajjah, hajah** *Isl, f* title for a woman who has made the pilgrimage to Mecca

hak *n* right; ~ *cipta* copyright; ~ *milik* ownership; ~ *pengarang* copyright; ~ *perempuan* women's rights; ~ *pilih* right to vote; suffrage; ~ *siar* telecast or broadcast rights; ~ *azasi manusia (HAM)* human rights; ~ *guna bangunan (HGB)* building rights; ~ *kekayaan intelektual (HAKI)* intellectual property rights; **berhak** *vi* to have a right to, be entitled to

hak *n* heel; *sepatu* ~ *tinggi* high heels

HAKI *abbrev Hak Kekayaan Intelektual* Intellectual Property Rights

hakikat, hakékat *n* nature, essence; *pada ~nya* basically, essentially; **hakiki** *adj* true, real

hakim *n* judge; *dewan* ~ judicial board; **kehakiman** *Departemen* ~ Department of Justice; **menghakimi** *vt* to judge; to pass sentence on, convict

hal *n* matter, case; ~-*ihwal* related matters; circumstances; ~ *ini* this; ~ *sepele* trifle, small matter; *dalam* ~ *itu* in that case

halal *adj, Isl* permitted (to eat); killed according to Islamic practice; *pekerjaan yang* ~ a decent job; **menghalalkan** *vt* to permit, allow

halal bihalal *n, Isl* social gathering, usu after fasting month

halaman *n* yard, open area, page; ~ *rumah* yard; *lihat* ~ *sebelah (lhs)* please turn over (PTO)

halang: halangan *n* obstacle; hindrance; *kalau tidak ada* ~ if there are no problems; **berhalangan** *vi* to be prevented; unable; *lagi* ~ have your period (said about a woman not fasting); **menghalangi** *vt* to hinder, prevent; **terhalang** *adj* blocked; prevented

halau: menghalau *vt* to chase away

haléluya *ejac, Chr* hallelujah

halia *n* ginger

hal-ihwal *n* related matters; circumstances ← **hal**

halilintar *n* lightning bolt, thunderclap

halimun *n* mist

halo *gr* hello (also when answering telephone)

halte *n* stop; ~ *bis* bus stop

haluan *n* bow (of a ship); prow, course, direction; **berhaluan** *vi* to have a direction; ~ *kiri* leftist

halus *adj* fine; soft; refined; *bahasa* ~ refined language; speech level in some regional languages; *makhluk* ~ spirit; **kehalusan** *n* delicacy; grace; **menghaluskan** *vt* to refine; grind

HAM *abbrev Hak Asasi Manusia* Human Rights

hama *n* pest; plague; *suci* ~ sterile

hamba *n, pron, arch* slave; me; your servant; ~ *Allah* mankind; anonymous (*lit.* servant of God)

hambar *adj* flavorless; bland

hambat, menghambat *vt* to obstruct, impede, hamper; **hambatan** *n* obstacle

hambur: berhamburan *adj* scattered about; **menghamburkan** *vt* to scatter; throw about

hamil *adj* pregnant; ~ *muda* first trimester; ~ *tua* heavily pregnant; **kehamilan** *n* pregnancy; **menghamili** *vt* to make someone pregnant

hampa *adj* empty; ~ *udara* vacuum

hampar: hamparan ~ *sungai* flood plain; **menghampar** *vt* to spread out

hampir *adv* nearly, almost; **hampir-hampir** *adv* very nearly; **menghampiri** *vt* to approach

hanacaraka *n* Sundanese alphabet; [hanacaraka] Javanese alphabet → **honocoroko**

hancur smashed, crushed; ~ *lebur* completely crushed, pulverized; **kehancuran** *n* destruction, ruin; **menghancurkan** *vt* to smash, crush, destroy

handai *n* friend, companion; ~ *tolan,* ~ *taulan* friends

handal *adj* reliable; **kehandalan** *n* reliability ← **andal**

handphone → **hénpon, HP, hapé, télépon**

handuk *n* towel

Hang *pron, m, lit* title in old tales; ~ *Tuah dan* ~ *Jebat adalah pahlawan masa lalu Hang* Tuah and Hang Jebat were heroes long ago

hangat *adj* warm, hot; *berita* ~ latest news; ~~ *tahi ayam* as hot as chicken shit, a fleeting enthusiasm; **kehangatan** *n* warmth, friendliness; **menghangatkan** *vt* to warm something (up); **penghangat** heater

hanggar *n* (aircraft) hangar

hangus *adj* burnt, scorched; expired; *karcis itu sudah* ~ that ticket has expired; *bumi* ~ scorched earth; completely burnt down; **membumihanguskan** *vt* to conduct a scorched-earth policy; **menghanguskan** *vt* to burn down

Hanoman *n* white monkey from the Ramayana epic

hansip *n* local security guard; civil defense ← **pertahanan sipil**

hantam strike, blow; ~ *kromo* punch, attack, finish off (blindly); *baku* ~ hit each other, come to blows; **menghantam** *vt* to strike

hantar *vt* carry, take; **menghantarkan** *vt* to conduct (electricity or heat); **penghantar** *n* ~ *listrik* electrical conductor

hantu *n* ghost; ~ *pocong* ghost in a white sheet; *burung* ~ owl; *rumah* ~ haunted house; **menghantui** *vt* to haunt

hanya *adv* only

hanyut drift, float; **terhanyut** *adj* drifting, floating; washed away

hapé, HP *n, sl* mobile phone, cell phone ← **hénpon**

hapermot → **havermut**

hapus, menghapus *vt* to delete, erase, wipe; **menghapuskan** *vt* to wipe out, eliminate; **penghapus** *n* eraser; duster; **terhapus** *adj* disappeared; accidentally deleted

hara *huru-*~ riot, uproar; *polisi (anti) huru-*~ riot police

haram *adj, Isl* forbidden, not permitted; *anak* ~ illegitimate (child), bastard; *daging babi itu* ~ pork is forbidden; **mengharamkan** *vt* to forbid; to avoid, abstain from

harap hope; please; ~ *maklum* please understand; **harapan** *n* hope, expectation; ~ *tipis* little hope; **berharap** *vi* to hope; **mengharapkan** *vt* to expect

hardik shout; scold; **menghardik** *vt* to shout at; scold

harfiah *adj* literal

harga *n* price; value; ~ *beli* buying price; ~ *diri* dignity; self-worth, self-respect; ~ *eceran* retail price; ~ *jual* selling price; ~ *mati*, ~ *pas* fixed price; last offer; not negotiable; ~ *miring* cheap price; *banting* ~ price cut; **berharga** *adj* precious; valuable; *vi* to be of value; **menghargai** *vt* to appreciate; **penghargaan** *n* appreciation; award; **seharga** *adj* of equal value; the same price

hari *n* day; ~ *Ahad Isl* Sunday; ~ *baik* lucky day, fortuitous day; ~ *besar* (religious) holiday; ~ *Buruh* Labor Day; ~ *Ibu* Mother's Day (22 December); ~ *ini* today; ~ *jadi*, ~ *ulang tahun (HUT)* birthday, anniversary; ~ *Jumat*, ~ *Jum'at* Friday; ~ *Kamis*, ~ *Kemis coll* Thursday; ~ *Kartini* Kartini Day (21 April); ~ *kerja* weekday, working day; ~ *kiamat* day of judgment; ~ *kelahiran* birthday, anniversary; ~ *libur* holiday, day off; ~ *Minggu* Sunday; ~ *Pahlawan* Heroes' Day (10 November); ~ *Rabu coll* ~ *Rebo* Wednesday; ~ *raya* holiday, feast day; ~ *Raya*, ~ *Lebaran* Idul Fitri, Eid(-ul-Fitr); ~ *Raya Haji* Idul Adha, Feast of the Sacrifice; ~ *Selasa* Tuesday; ~ *Senin*, ~ *Senen coll* Monday; ~ *tua* old age; *malam* ~ nighttime; *sepanjang* ~ all day long; *siang* ~ daytime; *Angkatan Bersenjata*, ~ *ABRI* Armed Forces Day (5 October); ~ *Kasih Sayang* Valentine's Day; *di kemudian* ~ in the future; *keesokan* ~*(nya)* the day after, the following day; **harian** *adj* daily; *buku* ~ diary; **berhari-hari** *adv* for days; **sehari-hari** *adv* every day, daily; **seharian** *adv, coll* all day

haribaan *n* lap → **riba**

harimau *n* tiger

haring, héring *n* herring

harkat *n* level; dignity

harmonika *n* harmonica

harmonis *adj* harmonious

harpa *n* harp; **harpis** *n* harpist

hart *n* hearts (in cards)

harta *n* wealth, belongings; ~ *benda* property; goods and chattels; ~ *karun* hidden treasure; **hartawan** *n* wealthy person

haru emotion; touched; **mengharukan** *adj* moved, touched (emotionally); **terharu** *adj* moved, touched

haru: haru-biru *n* commotion, uproar

harum *adj* fragrant; perfumed; ~ *namanya* well-known; **keharuman** *n* fragrance

harus *v, aux* must, ought to, have to; **keharusan** *n* obligation, necessity, requirement; **mengharuskan** *vt* to require; **seharusnya** should

hasil *n* product; result; ~ *panen* harvest; **berhasil** *v* to succeed; **keberhasilan** *n* success; **menghasilkan** *vt* to produce; **penghasil** *n* producer; **penghasilan** *n* production; income

hasrat *n* desire; lust

hasut, menghasut *vt* to incite, agitate; **penghasut** *n* agitator, provocateur, trouble-maker; **penghasutan** *n* agitation, provocation

hati *n* heart; ~ *kecil* conscience; ~ *kecut* afraid; ~ *nurani* inner self, conscience; ~ *sanubari* innermost heart; *buah* ~ darling; *jantung* ~ sweetheart; *kecil* ~ timid; offended; disappointed; *keras* ~ never give up; *makan* ~ brood, dwell on; be upset; *sakit* ~ offended, hurt; upset; *(di) dalam* ~ in your heart; to yourself; *membaca dalam* ~ to read silently, to yourself; *(dari)* ~ *ke* ~ heart-to-heart; **berhati** *vi* to have a heart; ~ *baja* to never give up; ~ *besar* open-hearted; ~ *emas* to have a heart

of gold; **memerhatikan** *vt* to notice, pay attention to; **pemerhati** *n* observer; **perhatian** *n* attention; **sehati** *adj* of one mind

hati *n* **ati** *coll* liver; ~ *ayam* chicken liver

hati-hati take care; **berhati-hati** *vi* to be careful

haul *n* annual commemoration of someone's death

haus *adj* thirsty; ~ *akan* longing for, needing; ~ *perhatian* longing for attention; **kehausan** *adj* to be thirsty; *n* thirst

havermut, hapermot *n* oatmeal porridge

Hawa *n, Chr* Eve; *Siti* ~ *Isl* Eve

hawa *n* air, atmosphere, weather, climate; ~ *nafsu* passion; lust; **berhawa** *vi* to have a climate; ~ *sejuk* to have a cool climate

hayat *n* life; *sampai akhir* ~ until the end of your life; **hayati** *adj* biological; **menghayati** *vt* to inspire, instill, vivify

HBS *abbrev Hogere Burger School* a high school in colonial times

hé *ejac* hey!

hébat *adj* great; violent; terrific; **kehébatan** *n* force

héboh sensational; **kehébohan** *n* sensation, phenomenon; **menghébohkan** *vt* to cause an uproar; *adj* sensational

Héiho *n* local Japanese-trained militia during World War II

héjo → **hijau**

héktar *n* hectare

héla pull; *kuda* ~ draught horse; **menghéla** *vt* to draw; drag, pull; ~ *nafas* to sigh; to draw a breath

helai *n* (counter) sheet; counter for thin fine objects; *sehelai* ~ *kertas* a piece of paper; *beberapa* ~ *rambut tertinggal di atas bantal* several strands of hair were left on the pillow

hélat: perhélatan *n* celebration, feast

héli *n, coll* helicopter ← **hélikopter**

hélicak *n, arch* motorized rickshaw with passenger seat in front → **hélikopter** + **bécak**

hélikopter *n* **héli** *coll* helicopter

hélm *n* helmet

hém *n* (office) shirt

hémat *adj* economical, thrifty; ~ *air* save water; **berhémat** *vi* to be economical; **menghémat** *vt* to save on or economize

hémat *n* judgment; opinion; *menurut* ~ saya, *pada* ~ *saya* in my opinion

hembus, embus blow, puff; **meng-hembus** *vt* to blow

hémoroid *n* hemorrhoid

hempas, empas *vt* to throw down; **menghempaskan** *vt* ~ *diri* to throw yourself down; **terhempas** *adj* thrown down

hendak *v, aux* to will, wish, intend; ~*nya* should; **kehendak** *n* will; ~ *rakyat* will of the people; **berkehendak** *vi* to have the intent; **menghendaki** *vt* to want

hénfon → **hénpon**

héngkang *vi* to flee, leave

hening clear; quiet; ~ *cipta* observe a moment's silence; **menciptakan** ~ *vt* to have a moment's silence; **keheningan** *n* peace, quiet; clarity; **menghening-kan** *vt* ~ *cipta* to observe a moment's silence

hénpon, hénfon (HP) *n* mobile phone, cell phone → **télépon**

henti stop; **berhenti** *vi* to stop, cease; **menghentikan** *vt* to stop something; **memberhentikan** *vt* to stop (a vehicle); to dismiss; *Oto diberhentikan* Oto was sacked; **pemberhentian** *n* stop; dismissal, discharge; stoppage; **perhentian** *n* stop, stopping place

hépatitis *n* hepatitis

hér resit a test or exam; *ujian* ~ make-up test or exam

héran *adj* astonished, amazed; **héran-héran** *adj* (greatly) amazed; **kehéran-an** *n* astonishment; amazement; wonder; **menghérankan** *adj* astonishing, astounding; *vt* to astonish, astound

hérbisida *n* herbicide

hérder *anjing* ~ German shepherd (dog)

héring, haring *n* herring

héwan *n* animal, beast; ~ *piaraan*, ~ *peliharaan* pet; ~ *primata* primate; *dokter* ~ vet, veterinarian; ~ *bertulang belakang* vertebrate

hias decorative; *ikan* ~ ornamental fish; **hiasan** *n* decoration; **berhias** *vi* to dress up, put on make-up; **menghiasi** *vt* to adorn; to decorate something; **perhiasan** *n* jewelry

hibah *n* donation, bequest, gift; **meng-hibahkan** *vt* to donate, bequeath

hibrida *n* hybrid

hibur: hiburan *n* entertainment; **menghibur** *vt* to entertain; to comfort, console; **penghibur** *n wanita* ~ escort, prostitute

hidang: hidangan *n* dish, food served; **menghidangkan** *vt* to serve up, offer

hidayah, hidayat *n* guidance; *taufik dan* ~ divine guidance, God's guidance

hidrogén *n* hydrogen

hidung *n* nose; ~ *belang* womanizer; ~ *mampet*, ~ *tersumbat* blocked nose; ~ *mancung* straight nose; ~ *pesek* flat nose

hidup live; alive; lively; ~ *Indonesia!* long live Indonesia!; ~ *melarat* live in poverty; ~ *rukun* live in harmony; ~ *sederhana* live simply; *bunga* ~ cut flowers; *riwayat* ~ biography; curriculum vitae; *sepanjang* ~ lifelong, all your life; **kehidupan** *n* life, existence; **menghidupi** *vt* to provide for; **menghidupkan** *vt* to bring to life; to start or turn on (a device); ~ *kembali* to revive; ~ *mesin* to turn on the engine

higénis, higinis *adj* hygienic

hijau *adj* **hijo, héjo** *coll* green; ~ *daun* leaf green; chlorophyll; ~ *lumut* moss green, bright green; ~ *muda* light green; ~ *toska* turquoise green; ~ *tua* dark green; *jalur* ~ nature strip, median strip; **kehijau-hijauan** *adj* greenish; **menghijau** *vi* to become green; **menghijaukan** *vt* to make green; **penghijauan** *n* greening (of an area)

hijrah evacuate, pack up and leave; move somewhere unexpected for a long time; **hijriah, H** *adj tahun* ~ the Islamic calendar; *tahun 1415 H* 1997 AD (1415 in the Islamic calendar)

hikayat *n* tale, story; ~ *Hang Tuah* the tale of Hang Tuah

hikmah *n* wisdom, insight, moral; *ada ~nya* there's some good of it

hilang disappear; lost, missing; *~ muka* lose face; *orang ~* missing person; **kehilangan** *n* (feeling of) loss; *~ selera makan* to lose your appetite; **menghilang** *vi* to disappear, vanish; **menghilangkan** *vt* to remove

hilir, ilir downstream; *~ mudik* back and forth, up and down; *Sungai Mahakam ~* the Lower Mahakam (River); **menghilir** *vi* to go downstream

himbau → **imbau**

himne *n* hymn, song of praise

himpit, impit: berhimpit *adv* very close together; **berhimpitan** *vi* to be close to each other; **menghimpit** *vt* to squeeze or press; **menghimpitkan** *vt* to squeeze against

himpun: himpunan *n* association, gathering; **berhimpun** *vi* to meet, assemble; **menghimpunkan** *vt* to bring together, gather; **penghimpun** *n ~ listrik* accumulator, storage cell, battery; **perhimpunan** *n* union, association, club; *~ Mahasiswa Jambi* Jambi Students Assocation

hina low, insulting; humble; **hinaan** *n* insult; **menghinakan** *vt* to humiliate, insult; **penghinaan** *n* insult, libel (written), slander (spoken); *~ terhadap Presiden* insulting the President

hindar: menghindar *vt* to steer clear, avoid; **menghindari** *vt* to avoid something

Hindia *n* the Indies; *~ Barat* the West Indies; *~ Belanda* the Dutch East Indies; *Samudera ~* the Indian Ocean

Hindu *agama ~* Hinduism; *orang ~* Hindu

hingar *~bingar adj* noisy, clamorous

hingga until; *~ sekarang* up to now; **sehingga** *conj* to the point that, as far as, until, so that; **terhingga** *tidak ~* unlimited, boundless

hinggap *vi* to land, perch (of a bird)

hio *n, Ch* joss stick

hiperténsi *n* high blood pressure, hypertension

hipnotis: dihipnotis *v* to be hypnotized

hipoték *n* mortgage

hirau: menghiraukan *vt* to take heed, to listen to advice; *tidak dihiraukan* ignored

hiruk *~-pikuk, ~-piruk* clamor, confusion

hirup inhale; suck; *obat ~* lozenge; **menghirup** *vt* to breathe in; *~ udara bebas* to breathe the air of freedom (be out of prison)

HIS *abbrev Hollands Inlandse School* Dutch lower school for natives in colonial times

hisit *n* shark's fin; *sup ~* shark's fin soup

histéris *adj* hysterical

hitam *adj* black; *~ legam, ~ pekat* pitch black, jet black; *~ manis* dark and pretty; *~ putih* black and white; *daftar ~* blacklist; *orang ~* black person, Negro; *~ di atas putih* in black and white; **kehitam-hitaman** *adj* blackish; **menghitamkan** *vt* to blacken, make black

hitung count; *ilmu ~* arithmetic; **hitungan** *n* calculation, sum; **berhitung** *vi* to count; **memperhitungkan** *vt* to calculate; to take into account; **menghitung** *vi* to count; *vt* to calculate, reckon; **menghitungkan** *vt* to count or calculate something; **perhitungan** *n* calculation; **penghitungan** *n* counting; **terhitung** *adj* counted, included

hiu, yu *ikan ~* shark

Hj. *Hajjah, Hajah* title for woman who has performed the major pilgrimage to Mecca

HKBP *abbrev Huria Kristen Batak Protestan* Batak Protestant church

HMI *abbrev Himpunan Mahasiswa Islam* Muslim Students Association

hobi *n* hobby; **berhobi** *vi* to have as a hobby

hoek, huk *n* [huk] street corner; *rumahnya di ~* her house is on the corner

hoki *n* good luck or fortune

homo *m, sl orang ~* homosexual, gay

homogén *adj* homogeneous

honai *n* round hut in Papua (Irian Jaya)

Hongaria *n* Hungary; *bahasa ~, orang ~* Hungarian

hong sui, féng sui *n* feng shui; *menurut ~* according to feng shui

honocoroko, hanacaraka *n* Javanese alphabet → **hanacaraka**

honor, honorarium *n* fee (for a guest or part-time employee); **honorér** *adj* honorary

horas *ejac, Bat* greetings; long live!

hordén, gordén *n* curtain(s); *tukang ~* itinerant curtain-rod seller

horé *ejac* hooray!

horisontal *adj* horizontal; at one level; *konflik ~* conflict within a group or level of society

hormat respect, honor; *~ saya* yours faithfully; *kurang ~* disrespectful; *memberi ~* to salute, pay respect; **kehormatan** *n* respect; *anggota ~* honorary member; **menghormat, menghormati** *vt* to honor or respect; **penghormatan** *n* display of honor, sign of respect; **terhormat** *adj* respected; *yang ~ (yth)* to; dear

hormon *n* hormone

horor *n* horror; *film ~* horror film

horoskop *n* horoscope

hostés *n* hostess, bargirl

hot *adj, sl* sexy

hotél *n* hotel; *~ melati* cheap hotel; *~ (ber)bintang lima* five-star hotel; *~ prodeo* prison, jail; **perhotélan** *n* hotel studies; hospitality

hotmiks, hotmix *n* asphalt; *jalan sudah dihotmiks* the road has been macadamized

HP *abbrev* **hénpon, hénfon** *n* [hapé] mobile phone, cell phone ← **handphone, hénpon**

HPH *abbrev* Hak Penebangan Hutan Forest Concession Rights

HT, handy-talky walkie-talkie

hubaya: hubaya-hubaya make sure that, watch out, be warned

hubung: hubungan *n* link, connection, relationship; *~ diplomatik* diplomatic relations, diplomatic links; *~ intim, ~ seks* sexual relations, sexual intercourse; *~ masyarakat (humas)* public relations (PR); *~ saudara* family (relationship); *~ timsuis, ~ intim suami isteri* conjugal relations, sex; **berhubung** *conj* in connection with,

relating to; *~ dengan* in connection with; **berhubungan** *vi, pl* to have a link or connection; **menghubungi** *vt* to contact someone; **menghubungkan** *vt* to connect, join, link different parts; **penghubung** *n* switch, connector; *kata ~* conjunction, connector, connective; **perhubungan** *n* communications, connection; *~ udara* air route; *Menteri ~ (Menhub)* Minister of Communications

hujan rain; *~ angin* wind and rain; *~ asam* acid rain; *~ batu, ~ es* hail; *~ deras, ~ lebat* heavy rain, downpour; *~ lokal* local showers; *~ rintik-rintik* drizzle; *curah ~* rainfall; *musim ~* rainy season, monsoon; **kehujanan** *adj* caught in the rain; **menghujani** *vt* to pelt, rain down upon; **penghujan** *musim ~* rainy season; monsoon

hujat: hujatan *n* insult, blasphemy; **menghujat** *vt* to swear, blaspheme

hujung: penghujung *n* end; *~ musim hujan* end of the rainy season → **ujung**

huk, hoek *n* street corner; *rumahnya di ~* her house is on the corner

hukum law; punish; *~ fisika* laws of physics; *~ perdata* civil code; *~ pidana* criminal code; *~ syariah* Islamic law; **hukuman** *n* punishment; *~ mati* capital punishment, death penalty; *~ penjara* imprisonment; **menghukum** *vt* to punish, sentence, condemn

hulu *n* source, beginning; *~ sungai* source, headwaters; **berhulu** *vi* to rise, have a source; *Sungai Mekong ~ di Cina* the source of the Mekong is in China

huma *n* field, earth

humaniora *n* humanities

humas *n* PR, public relations ← **hubungan masyarakat**

humor *n* humor; *selera ~* sense of humor

huni: menghuni *vt* to live in, occupy; **penghuni** *n* occupant, resident; **penghunian** *n* occupancy; *tingkat ~* rate of occupancy, occupancy rate

hunjam, menghunjam *vt* to plunge, dive; **menghunjamkan** *vt* to thrust in; **terhunjam** *adj* stuck, inserted

hunus: menghunus *vt* to unsheathe, take out; ~ *pedang* to pull out a sword

huru ~*-hara* riot, uproar; *polisi (anti)* ~*hara* riot police

huruf *n* letter, character; ~ *besar* capital letters, upper case; ~ *bersambung, sambung* cursive; ~ *cetak* block letters, printing; ~ *Cina* Chinese characters; ~ *hidup*, ~ *vokal* vowel; ~ *kecil* small letters, lower case; ~ *mati* consonant; ~ *miring* italics; ~ *Romawi* Roman letters, Latin alphabet; ~ *timbul* raised print; *buta* ~ illiterate; *melek* ~ literate

hus *ejac* hush, ssh

HUT *abbrev hari ulang tahun* birthday, anniversary

hutan *n* forest, jungle, wood; ~ *belantara* forest, wilderness; ~ *kota* urban forest; ~ *lindung* protected forest; ~ *rimba* jungle; **kehutanan** *n* forestry

hutang → **utang**

I

i *n* i, ninth letter of the alphabet

ia *lit* he, she, it ← **dia**

ia, iya yes (emphatic); **ialah** yes, indeed; **seia** ~ *sekata* in complete agreement, unanimous

IAIN *abbrev, arch Institut Agama Islam Negeri State* Institute for Islamic Studies

ialah yes, indeed ← **ia**

iba pity, compassion; *merasa* ~ to feel sorry for

ibadah *n* worship, religious devotion; **beribadah** *vi* to worship, serve

ibarat *conj* like, as, example; ~ *air dan api* like fire and water, like chalk and cheese; **mengibaratkan** *vt* to use figuratively, as an example

iblis *n* devil, Satan

Ibrahim *n* Abraham

Ibrani *bahasa* ~, *orang* ~ Hebrew

ibtidaiyah *adj, Isl* elementary, primary, basic (school)

ibu *n, pron, f* mother; ~ *angkat* adopted mother; ~ *bapak* parents; ~ *jari* thumb; ~ *kandung* birth mother, biological mother; ~ *kos* concierge, house-mother; ~ *kota* capital (city); ~ *mertua* mother-in-law; ~ *mutiara* mother-of-pearl; ~ *Negara* First Lady; ~ *peri* fairy godmother; ~ *pertiwi* motherland; ~ *RT* (wife of) local neighborhood leader; ~ *semang* house-mother, landlady; ~ *suri* mother of the king or queen; ~ *susu* wet-nurse; ~ *tiri* stepmother; *bahasa* ~ mother tongue; ~ *rumah tangga* housewife, homemaker; **ibu-ibu** *n, pl* ladies; *adj* of an age to be a mother; middle-aged; **beribu** ~ *bapak vi* to have parents; ~ *kota vi* to have as a capital city; **keibuan, keibuibuan** *adj* motherly; **seibu** *adj* having the same mother; **ibunda, bunda** *pron, pol, lit* Mother

ICMI *abbrev Ikatan Cendekiawan Muslim se-Indonesia* Indonesian Islamic Intellectuals Association

Id → **Idul, Ied**

Ida *tit, Bal* title given to Balinese nobility; ~ *Ayu f* title given to Balinese females from the Brahman caste; ~ *Bagus m* title given to Balinese males from the Brahman caste

idam craving, longing; **idaman** *adj* dream, ideal; *rumah* ~ dream home; **mengidam** *vt* **ngidam** *coll* to crave (esp of pregnant woman)

idap: mengidap *vt* to suffer from; ~ *penyakit* to suffer from or have a disease; **pengidap** *n* sufferer; ~ *AIDS* AIDS sufferer

idé, ide *n* idea; ~ *cemerlang*, ~ *gemilang* brainwave, great idea; **idéal** *adj* ideal, perfect

idem ditto, same as previous

idéntifikasi *n* identification; **mengidéntifikasi** *vt* to identify (someone)

idéntik *adj* identical, same; ~ *dengan* just like, the same as

idéntitas *n* (proof of) identity; ~ *palsu* fake ID; *kartu* ~ ID card → **jati diri**

idéologi *n* ideology

IDI *abbrev Ikatan Dokter Indonesia* Indonesian Doctors' Association

idih *excl* yuck! (expressing disgust or revulsion); ~-~ ooh, that's disgusting

idiot *adj* simple, mentally handicapped; *n* simpleton, mentally handicapped person

idola *n* idol, star; **mengidolakan** *vt* to worship, idolize

Idul, Ied ul *Isl* ~ *Adha* Feast of the Sacrifice; ~ *Fitri* end of fasting celebrations; *sholat Ied* mass prayer on the mornings of these holidays

iga *n* rib; ~ *bakar* barbecued ribs

igau: mengigau *vi* to talk in one's sleep, be delirious

IGD *abbrev Instalasi Gawat Darurat* emergency room, casualty ward

iglo *n* igloo

ih *excl* exclamation of shock or disgust, ugh!

IHSG *abbrev, n Indeks Harga Saham Gabungan* Jakarta Joint Stock Exchange Index

ihwal *hal-*~ related matters

ijab ~ *kabul Isl* marriage contract

ijazah *n* certificate, qualification; **berijazah** *adj* certified, qualified; *vi* to have a certificate or qualification

ijin, izin permission; *minta* ~ to ask permission; *surat* ~ *mengemudi (SIM)* driver's license; **mengijinkan** *vt* to permit, allow

ijuk *n* black sugar palm-fiber, used in brushes and brooms

ikal *adj* curly; *rambut* ~ curly hair, wavy hair

ikan *n* fish; *coll* meat (as a side-dish); ~ *arwana* kind of decorative fish; ~ *asin* salty fish; ~ *bakar* baked fish, barbecued fish; ~ *bandeng* milkfish, a specialty of the north coast of Java; ~ *bawal* pomfret; ~ *buntal* puffer fish; ~ *cakalang* skipjack tuna; ~ *dorang* kind of fish, pomfret; ~ *emas* goldfish; ~ *haring*, ~ *hering* herring; ~ *hias* ornamental fish; ~ *hiu* shark; ~ *kakap* large fish, giant perch; *coll* big fish, important person; ~ *kaleng* tinned fish, canned fish; ~ *kerapu* groper; ~ *koi* Japanese carp; ~ *koki* kind of decorative fish; ~ *laut* ocean fish; ~ *lele*

catfish; ~ *lindung* eel; ~ *nila* a kind of freshwater fish; ~ *nus* a kind of squid; ~ *pari* ray; ~ *paus* whale; ~ *ricarica* spicy Menadonese-style fish; ~ *salmon* salmon; ~ *sarden* sardines; ~ *sepat* a kind of freshwater fish; ~ *sotong* cuttlefish, squid; ~ *tenggiri* mackerel; ~ *teri* anchovy, small fry; ~ *tongkol* tuna (fish); *pepes* ~ fish steamed in a banana leaf; ~ *air tawar* freshwater fish; *lain* ~, *lain lubuk* (different pond, different fish) each to their own; ~ *di laut, asam di gunung, bertemu di belanga* (fish in the sea, salt on the mountain, meet in the cooking pot) said of a couple from different backgrounds, who were destined to meet; **perikanan** *n* fisheries

ikat tie, knot; bunch; weaving, ikat; ~ *kepala* headband; ~ *Lombok* Lombok weaving; ~ *pinggang* belt; **ikatan** *n* alliance, union; ~ *Dokter Indonesia (IDI)* Indonesian Doctors' Association; ~ *Cendekiawan Muslim seIndonesia (ICMI)* Indonesian Association of Muslim Intellectuals; **mengikat** *adj* binding; *vt* to tie, fasten; ~ *janji* to take vows, get married; *perjanjian yang* ~ binding agreement; **terikat** *adj* bound; **keterikatan** *n* bind, bond, commitment

ikhlas *adj* sincere; accepting; **keikhlasan** *n* sincerity

ikhtiar *n* initiative; decision

ikhtisar *n* summary

IKIP *abbrev, arch Institut Keguruan Ilmu Pendidikan* (former) teacher training college

ikke, ik *pron, coll* I, me

iklan *n* advertisement; ~ *baris*, ~ *mini* classified (advertisement); *bintang* ~ advertising model; *biro* ~ advertising bureau; **mengiklankan** *vt* to advertise; **periklanan** *n* advertising

iklim *n* climate; ~ *tropis* tropical climate; **beriklim** *vi* to have a climate; ~ *dingin* to have a cool climate

ikrar *n* promise, pledge, oath, commitment; **berikrar** *vi* to promise, pledge

ikut *vi* join in, go along with; ~ *Ibu* go

with Mother; ~ *prihatin* feel concerned; ~ *serta* take part, participate; **keikutsertaan** *n* participation; **ikutan** *vi, sl* to join in, go along with; **berikut** *adj* following; *yang* ~, ~*nya* the next; **mengikut** *vt* to follow, accompany; **mengikuti** *vt* to follow, join, participate in; ~ *kursus* to do a course; **pengikut** *n* participant; follower

ilahi *Isl* divine, godly

ilalang, lalang → **alang-alang**

ilanun → **lanun**

ilégal *adj* illegal

iler drool, slobber; **mengiler** *vi* to drool, slobber

ilham *n* (divine) inspiration; **mengilhami** *vt* to inspire, be a source of inspiration

ilir → **hilir**

ilmiah *adj* scientific; **ilmu** *n* science, study; ~ *bahasa* linguistics; ~ *biologi* biology; ~ *bumi* geography; ~ *ekonomi* economics; ~ *eksakta* the exact sciences (mathematics, physics etc); ~ *falak* astronomy; ~ *filsafat* philosophy; ~ *fisika* physics; ~ *hitam* black magic; ~ *hitung* arithmetic; ~ *jiwa* psychology; ~ *kedokteran* medicine; ~ *kimia* chemistry; ~ *padi* humility; ~ *pasti* the physical sciences, esp mathematics; ~ *pendidikan* pedagogy; ~ *pengetahuan* science; knowledge; ~ *Pengetahuan Alam (IPA)* natural sciences; ~ *Pengetahuan Sosial (IPS)* social sciences, humanities; ~ *sejarah* history; ~ *sihir* black magic; **berilmu** *adj* learned; *vi* to have knowledge; **keilmuan, ilmiah** *adj* scientific; **ilmuwan** *n* scientist

ilusi *n* illusion

ilustrasi *n* illustration

imajinasi *n* imagination; **imajinér** *adj* imaginary

imam *n, Isl, m* prayer leader in the mosque

iman *n* faith, belief; *beda* ~ of a different religion; **beriman** *adj* religious; *vi* to have a faith or religion

IMB *abbrev izin mendirikan bangunan* construction permit

imbal: imbalan *n* compensation, reward, repayment

imbang balanced; **berimbang** *adj* balanced, proportional; *vi* to have (a) balance; **mengimbangi** *vt* to balance, offset; **perimbangan** *n* proportion; **seimbang** *adj* balanced, well-proportioned; **keseimbangan** *n* balance

imbas *n* impact, effect; current

imbau: imbauan *n* call, appeal; **mengimbau** *vt* to call, summon, appeal

imbuh extra, supplement; **imbuhan** *n* affix

imél *n* email; *alamat* ~ email address

imigran *n* immigrant; ~ *gelap* illegal immigrant; **imigrasi** *n* immigration

iming: mengiming-iming, mengimingimingkan *vt* to tantalize, tempt

imitasi *n* fake

imla *n* dictation

Imlék *n* Chinese New Year; *(Tahun Baru)* ~ Chinese New Year

impas *n* impasse, balance

impérialis *n* imperialist; **impérialisme** *n* imperialism

impi: impian *n* dream; **mengimpikan** *vt* to dream of → **mimpi**

impit → **himpit**

implikasi *n* implication; **berimplikasi** *vi* to have implications; **mengimplikasikan** *vt* to implicate; **terimplikasi** *adj* to be implicated

impor import; ~ *ekspor* import-export; **mengimpor** *vt* to import; **pengimpor, importir** *n* importer

impotén *n* impotent; **impoténsi** *n* impotence

imsak *n* time ten minutes before dawn, when those intending to fast should stop eating (around 5 a.m.)

imun *adj* immune; **imunisasi** *n* immunization

inai *n* henna

inang *n* wet nurse

inap stay the night; *rawat* ~ stay in hospital, be hospitalized; **menginap** *vi* to stay the night, stay over; **penginapan** *n* accommodation, hotel

incar: incaran *n* target, something aimed for, aim; **mengincar** *vt* to set your sights on, target, aim

inci *n* inch

indah *adj* beautiful; *hari yang* ~ a lovely day; **keindahan** *n* beauty; **memperindah** *vt* to beautify; **terindah** *adj* the most beautiful

indah: mengindahkan *vt* to take heed, pay attention to

indehoi, indehoy *n* heavy petting, making out, making love

indekos → **kos**

indéks *n* index; ~ *Harga Saham Gabungan (IHSG)* Jakarta Joint Stock Exchange Index; ~ *prestasi (IP)* grade point average (GPA)

indera, indra *n* sense; ~ *keenam* sixth sense; ~ *pencium* sense of smell; ~ *pendengar* sense of hearing; ~ *penglihat* sense of sight; ~ *peraba* sense of touch; ~ *perasa* sense of taste

India *n* India; *orang* ~ Indian

Indian *orang* ~ Native American, (South) American Indian

indikator *n* indicator

individu *n* individual

Indo *orang* ~ person of mixed Western and Indonesian descent

Indonésia Indonesia; ~ *Raya* the national anthem; *Bahasa* ~, *orang* ~ Indonesian; **keindonésiaan** *n* sense of being Indonesian; **mengindonésiakan** *vt* to translate into Indonesian, to make Indonesian; **seIndonésia** *adj* all-Indonesia, across Indonesia

induk mother (animal); ~ *ayam* mother hen; ~ *semang* house-mother, landlady; *kalimat* ~ main clause; *kapal* ~ mother ship; aircraft carrier

induksi *n* induction

indung mother (of animals); home; ~ *telur* ovary; *anak kucing dan* ~*nya* a kitten and its mother

industri *n* industry; ~ *berat* heavy industry; ~ *jasa* service industry; *desain* ~ industrial design; **perindustrian** *n* industry, industrial affairs; *Departemen* ~ *dan Perdagangan (Depperindag)* Department of Industry and Trade

inféksi *n* infection; **terinféksi** *adj* infected

inflasi *n* inflation

info, informasi *n* information, info; **menginformasikan** *vt* to inform

informatika *n* information technology (IT)

inframérah *adj* infra-red

infus *n* (saline) drip; **diinfus** *v* to be put on a drip

inga: teringa-inga *adj* dazed and confused

ingat remember; *daya* ~ memory; **ingatan** *n* memory; **mengingat** *vt* to remember, bear in mind; **mengingatkan** *vt* to remind someone about something; **memperingati** *vt* to commemorate; **memperingatkan** *vt* to warn; **peringatan** *n* warning; commemoration, remembrance; **teringat** *vi* to be reminded, come to mind

Inggris Britain; England, English; ~ *Raya* Great Britain; *bahasa* ~ English; *Kerajaan* ~ the United Kingdom; *orang* ~ English; British; *Sally orang* ~ Sally's British; **keinggris-inggrisan** *adj* affecting a use of English or anglicisms; anglicized

ingin *vt* to wish, desire; ~ *tahu* curious; to want to know; **keingintahuan** *n* curiosity; hunger for knowledge; **keinginan** *n* desire, wish; **berkeinginan** *vi* to have a desire or wish; **menginginkan** *vt* to wish for, desire

ingkar *vt* to break (a vow etc); ~ *janji* to break a promise; **mengingkari** *vt* to renege or go back on

ingsut: beringsut *vi* to shift slowly ← **ingsut**

ingus *n* nasal mucus; *membuang* ~ *vt* to blow your nose; **ingusan** *anak* ~ toddler; still a child, inexperienced

ini *pron* this, these; here; now; ~ *nih* this one; ~ *pena* this is a pen; *pena* ~ this pen; *hari* ~ today; *sekarang* ~, *belakangan* ~ recently; **begini** *adv* like this, in this manner; **segini** *adj, coll* like this, as far as this, to this degree

inisial initial, first letter of name

inisiasi ~ *dini* early attachment, breastfeeding straight after birth

inisiatif, inisiatip *n* initiative, enterprise; **berinisiatif** *vi* to take the initiative → **prakarsa**

injak *v* to tread, pedal; **menginjak** *vt* to

step, tread, or stamp on; ~ *gas* to accelerate, step on the gas; **menginjak-injak** *vt* to trample on; **menginjakkan** *vt* to set down; ~ *kaki* to step upon, set (foot) upon; **terinjak** *adj* stepped upon; downtrodden

injéksi *n* injection, shot

injil *n, Chr* gospel; *Kitab* ~ gospel, holy book; **penginjil** *n* preacher, evangelist

inkaso *n* cashing in a check; payment of a bill

inna lillahi wa inna ilahi rojiun *excl, Isl* we are truly God's, and to Him we must return (said on hearing of someone's death); ashes to ashes, dust to dust

inovasi *n* innovation; **inovatif** *adj* innovative

Inprés *n* Presidential Decree; *SD* ~ primary school built under a presidential instruction ← **Instruksi Présidén**

insaf, insyaf aware, conscious; realize; **menginsafkan** *vt* to make conscious, raise awareness

insan *n* human, person; *setiap* ~ everyone; **insani** *adj* human

insang *n* gill

inséminasi *n* insemination; ~ *buatan* artificial insemination

inséntif *n* incentive

insidén *n* incident → **peristiwa**

insinyur, Ir *n* engineer; holder of a degree in a technical science (architecture etc); *tit* B.Eng; ~ *pertanian* agricultural engineer

inspéksi *n* inspection; ~ *mendadak* (*sidak*) spot inspection; **inspéktorat** *n* inspectorate; **inspéktur** *n* inspector; ~ *jenderal* inspector-general

inspirasi *n* inspiration; **menginspirasikan** *vt* to inspire; **terinspirasi** *adj* inspired (by)

instalasi *n* installation, unit; ~ *Gawat Darurat (IGD)* emergency room, casualty ward

instan *adj* instant; *mi* ~ instant noodles, packet noodles

instansi *n* agency, authority (esp state); ~ *terkait* related agencies

insting *n* instinct; *bos kita punya* ~ *bisnis yang kuat* our boss has a strong business instinct

instruksi *n* instruction; ~ *Presiden (Inpres)* presidential decree → **petunjuk**; **instruktur** *n* instructor

insya Allah *Isl* God willing

intai: **mengintai** *vt* to spy on or watch, conduct surveillance; **pengintai** *pesawat* ~ reconnaissance plane

intan *n* diamond

intégrasi *n* integration; **mengintégrasi** *vt* to integrate; *Timor Timur diintegrasi dengan Indonesia sejak 1975 sampai dengan 1999* East Timor was integrated with Indonesia from 1975 to 1999

intél *n* secret agent, spy; **intélijén** *n* secret intelligence; *Badan* ~ *Negara (BIN)* State Intelligence Agency

intélék *n* brains, intellect; **intéléktual** *n* intellectual → **cendekiawan**

inténsif *adj* intensive

interaksi *n* interaction; **berinteraksi** *vi* to interact

interlokal *adj* long-distance (dialing); *telepon* ~ long-distance call

interméso *n* break, interlude

intérn, internal *adj* internal

internasional *adj* international

internat *n* dormitory

internir: **menginternir** *vt* to intern (someone)

intérnis *n* specialist (doctor)

intérogasi *n* interrogation; **mengintérogasi** *vt* to interrogate

interpelasi *n* interpellation (in parliament)

interupsi *n* interruption (in parliament)

interviu, interpiu *n* interview; **menginterviu** *vt* to interview → **wawancara**

inti *n* core, kernel, nucleus; ~*nya* basically; ~ *bumi* the Earth's core; ~ *sari* essence

intim *adj* intimate, close; *hubungan* ~ sexual relations

intimidasi *n* intimidation; **mengintimidasi** *vt* to intimidate ← **intimidasi**

intip, mengintip *vt* to peep at, spy on

intisari *n* essence, extract

intonasi *n* intonation

intrik *n* intrigue, gossip

introspéksi *n* introspection, self-evaluation; **berintrospéksi** *vi* to be introspective

invéntaris *n* inventory

invértébrata *n* invertebrate (animal)

invéstasi *n* investment; **menginvéstasikan** *vt* to invest something

IP *abbrev indeks prestasi* grade point average

IPA *abbrev ilmu pengetahuan alam* natural sciences

ipar in-law; *adik* ~ (younger) brother- or sister-in-law

IPB *abbrev Institut Pertanian Bogor* Bogor Agricultural University

IPS *abbrev ilmu pengetahuan sosial* social sciences

Ir *insinyur* title for holder of a degree in a technical science (engineering, architecture etc); B.Eng

Irak *n* Iraq; *orang* ~ Iraqi

irama *n* rhythm; ~ *cepat* fast-paced, with a fast rhythm; **berirama** *adj* rhythmical; *adv* with a rhythm; *v* to have a rhythm

Iramasuka *abbrev Irian Jaya, Maluku, Sulawesi, Kalimantan* eastern Indonesia

Iran *n* Iran; *orang* ~ Iranian

iri envy; ~ *(hati)* envious

Irian *n, arch* (West) Papua, Irian; ~ *Jaya (Irja)* Indonesian province between 1963 & 2000; *orang* ~ Irianese, Papuan

irigasi *n* irrigation; **mengirigasi** *vt* to irrigate

iring: iring-iringan *n* parade, convoy; **beriring-iringan** *adv* in succession; **mengiringi** *vt* to accompany, escort; **pengiring** *n* escort, companion; **seiring** ~ *dengan* along with, together

iris *vt* slice thinly; **irisan** *n* slice; **mengiris** *vt* to slice

irit economical; save money; *lebih* ~ cheaper, more economical; **mengirit** *vt* to economize

iritasi *n* irritation

Irja *n* Irian Jaya, Papua ← **Irian Jaya**

Irlandia *n* Ireland; ~ *Utara* Northern Ireland; *bahasa* ~ Irish (Gaelic); *orang* ~ Irish

ironi *n* irony

Isa *n* Jesus; ~ *Almasih* Christ the Savior; *Nabi* ~ Jesus

isak sob; ~ *tangis* crying; **mengisak, mengisak-isak** *vi* to sob; **terisak, terisak-isak** *adj* sobbing

isap *v* to suck on; to smoke; **isapan** ~ *jempol* lie, untruth; **mengisap** *vt* to suck; to smoke; ~ *cerutu* to smoke a cigar; ~ *ganja* to smoke marijuana); **pengisap** ~ *darah* vampire; *mesin* ~ *debu* vacuum cleaner

iseng for fun, not serious; waste or kill time; ~ *aja* just for fun

isi contents, volume, full; *sl* pregnant; ~ *rumah* household, people in a house; *sudah* ~ *belum?* are you pregnant yet?; **berisi** *vi* to contain; *adj* full, filled out; **mengisi** *vt* to fill, load; ~ *aki* to charge a (car) battery; ~ *bensin* to fill up with petrol; ~ *waktu* to fill in time; **pengisi** *n* filler; ~ *suara* dubber; **seisi** ~ *rumah* the whole family, everyone at home

islah *Isl* reconciliation; *mengadakan* ~ to come to a settlement

Islam Islam; ~ *telu wektu* kind of Islam practiced in Lombok; *agama* ~ Islam; *masuk* ~ to become Muslim, convert to Islam; *orang* ~ Muslim; **meng-islamkan** *vt* to Islamize, make Islamic; **islami** *adj* Islamic, Muslim

isolasi *n* isolation, insulation; adhesive tape; **terisolasi, terisolir** *adj* isolated → **terpencil**

Isra Miraj *n, Isl* holiday commemorating Muhammad's ascent to Heaven

Israél Israel; *orang* ~ Israeli

istal *n* stable

istana *n* palace; ~ *Olahraga (Istora)* Sports Palace, stadium; ~ *presiden* presidential palace

isteri, istri *n* wife; ~ *gelap* mistress; second (secret) wife; ~ *kedua* second wife; ~ *muda* new or second wife; **beristeri, beristri** *adj, m* married; *vi* to have a wife; *pria* ~ married man

istiadat *adat* ~ customs and traditions

istilah *n* term, word; *~nya* in other words, you could say; **mengistilahkan** *vt* to define something

istiméwa *adj* special; **keistiméwaan** *n* special quality; **mengistiméwakan** *vt* to treat as special

istiqlal *n* freedom; *Mesjid ~* biggest mosque in Jakarta (& Southeast Asia)

istirahat rest, break; recreation; **beristirahat** *vi* to rest, take a break; **mengistirahatkan** *vt* to rest (someone); **peristirahatan** *n* place for rest or recreation; *~ terakhir* final resting place, grave

Istora *abbrev Istana Olahraga* Sports Palace; *~ Senayan* smaller stadium at Senayan, Jakarta

istri, isteri *n* wife; *~ kedua* second wife; *~ muda* new or second wife; **beristeri, beristri** *adj, m* married; *vi* to have a wife; *pria ~* married man

isu *n* issue, controversy

isya night prayer (during the hours of darkness)

isyarat *n* signal, sign, gesture; *bahasa ~* sign language; *memberi ~* to give a signal; **mengisyaratkan** *vt* to give a sign, signal

Itali, Italia *n* Italy; *bahasa ~, orang ~* Italian

ITB *abbrev Institut Teknologi Bandung* Bandung Institute of Technology

itik *n* duck; *anak ~* duckling

itikad *n* faith, conviction; *dengan ~ baik* in good faith

itu *pron* that, those; there; then; *~ dia!* that's the problem!; **begitu** *adv* like that, in that manner; so; as soon as; *~lah* that's how it is; **segitu** *adv, coll* like that, as far as that, to that degree

IUD intra-uterine device, form of contraception

iuran *n* contribution, regular payment; *~ keanggotaan* membership fee

iya *coll* yes (emphatic); *~ ya* it is, isn't it?; **mengiyakan** *vt* to agree or assent to

izin, ijin permission; *~ praktek* license to practice; *~ terbit* publishing permit; *~ usaha* business permit; *minta ~ to* ask permission; *surat ~ mengemudi (SIM)* driver's license; **mengizinkan** *vt* to permit, allow; **seizin** *adv* with the permission of

J

j [jé] j, tenth letter of the alphabet

Jababeka *abbrev Jawa Barat Bekasi* area of development east of Jakarta

jabang *~ bayi* unborn child, fetus, embryo

Jabar *n* West Java → **Jawa Barat**

jabar: jabaran *n* explanation, analysis; **menjabarkan** *vt* to clarify, spell out

jabat: jabatan *n* position, work; **berjabat, berjabatan** *~ tangan* to shake hands; **menjabat** *vt* to hold; to work as; *~ Menteri Keuangan* to be Minister of Finance; **pejabat** *n* (government) official; *~ sementara (Pjs)* acting official; *~ tinggi* high-ranking official; **penjabat** *n* official (esp temporary or acting)

jablay, jablai *adj, sl* untouched, discarded (of a lover) ← **jarang dibelai**

Jabotabék *n* Greater Jakarta ← **Jakarta Bogor Tangerang Bekasi**

jadah *anak ~* illegitimate child, bastard

jadi *v* to become, happen; *conj* so; *~nya* outcome; *~ orang* to succeed, make something of yourself; *~ tidak?* Is it going ahead or not?; *bisa ~ coll* possible, it could be; *tidak ~* it didn't happen, it fell through; **jadi-jadian** *adj* pretend, fake, imitation; **kejadian** *n* event, happening; creation; **menjadi** *vi* to be or become; *~ marah* to get angry; **menjadi-jadi** *vi* to get worse; **menjadikan** *vt* to create, make; **terjadi** *vi* to happen, become, occur

jadul *adj, sl* old-fashioned, out of date ← **jaman dulu**

jadwal *n* timetable, schedule; *~ acara* program of events; *~ penerbangan* flight schedule; **menjadwal, menjadwalkan** *vt* to timetable

jaga guard, nightwatchman; look after; *~ diri* look after yourself, take care;

berjaga *vi* to stand guard; **menjaga** *vi* to guard, keep watch; ~ *anak* to look after children, babysit; ~ *jarak* to keep a distance; **penjaga** *n* guard; ~ *gawang* goalkeeper; **terjaga** *adj* alert, on guard

jagad, jagat *n* world; ~ *raya* universe, cosmos; **sejagat** *adj* worldwide; *ratu* ~ Miss Universe

jagal *tukang* ~ butcher; **pejagalan** *n* abattoir

jago *n* champion; cock, rooster; ~ *kandang* home ground specialist; *ayam* ~ rooster; ~ *bulu tangkis* good at badminton; *si* ~ *merah* fire; **jagoan** *n, sl* good at; **menjagokan** *vt* to support

Jagorawi *jalan tol* ~ Jakarta-Bogor-Ciawi toll road ← **Jakarta Bogor Ciawi**

jagung *n* corn, maize; ~ *bakar* roasted sweet corn

jahanam *n, Isl* hell

jahat *adj* bad, wicked, evil; **kejahatan** *n* crime; **penjahat** *n* criminal; ~ *perang* war criminal

jahé *n* ginger

jahil *adj* ignorant; **jahiliyah, jahiliah** *adj, Isl masa* ~ pre-Islamic times, time of ignorance

jahit *v* to sew; *mesin* ~ sewing machine; *tukang* ~ tailor; **jahitan** *n* stitches; sewing; **menjahit** *v* to sew; *tangan Pepi harus dijahit* Pepi's hand had to have stitches; **penjahit** *n* tailor

jail *adj* mischievous, naughty; **menjaili** *vt* to annoy, play a trick on

jaipong *tari* ~ modern Sundanese dance; **jaipongan** *n* traditional dance; *vi, coll* to dance the *jaipong*

jaja: **menjajakan** *vt* to hawk, peddle; ~ *permen* to sell sweets, candy; **penjaja** *n* hawker, pedlar

jajah: **jajahan** *n* colony, territory; **menjajah, menjajahi** *vt* to colonize, rule another country; **penjajah** *n* colonizer, ruler, colonial power; **penjajahan** *n* colonization

jajak: **menjajaki** *vt* to probe, sound out

jajan buy cheap goods; buy sweets; *sl* to play around, use prostitutes (of men); *uang* ~ pocket money; **jajanan** *n* cheap snacks; ~ *pasar* traditional snacks

jajar row, line, file; **jajaran** *n* level; **berjajar** *adj* in a row; *vi* to be in a row; **sejajar** *adj* parallel

Jakbar *n* West Jakarta ← **Jakarta Barat**

jakét *n* jacket; ~ *kulit* leather jacket

Jakpus *n* Central Jakarta ← **Jakarta Pusat**

jaksa *n* judge; ~ *Agung* Attorney-General; ~ *umum* public prosecutor; **kejaksaan** *n* district attorney's office; ~ *Tinggi (Kejati)* regional Attorney-General's office

Jaksél *n* South Jakarta ← **Jakarta Selatan**

Jaktim *n* East Jakarta ← **Jakarta Timur**

jakun *n* Adam's apple

Jakut *n* North Jakarta ← **Jakarta Utara**

jala *n* fishing net; *roti* ~ kind of Malay pancake; **menjala** *vt* to catch fish by casting a net

jalak *n* starling, mynah

jalan *n* street, road, way, path; *vi* walk; operate, go; ~ *akses* access road; ~ *besar* main road; ~ *buntu* dead-end, cul-de-sac, court, no through road; ~ *darat* overland; ~ *keluar* exit, way out; ~ *lingkar* ring road; ~ *masuk* entrance; ~ *pintas* short cut; ~ *protokol* main street (passed by official visitors); ~ *raya* highway; ~ *terbaik* the best way; ~ *tikus* back street; ~ *tol* toll road; *bahu* ~ hard shoulder; *rawat* ~ outpatient; ~ *bebas hambatan* freeway; **jalan-jalan** *vi* to go for a walk; to go out (for fun); **jalanan** *n* streets, on the road; **berjalan** *vi* to walk, move; ~ *dengan baik* to go well; **menjalani** *vt* to undergo, do; ~ *hukuman penjara 3 tahun* to serve three years in jail; **menjalankan** *vt* to operate, run, set in motion; ~ *perintah* to carry out orders; **pejalan** *n* ~ *kaki* pedestrian; **perjalanan** *n* journey, trip; *biro* ~, *agen* ~ travel agency; **sejalan** *adv* in line, in the same direction; ~ *dengan kebijakan partai* in line with party policy

jalang *adj* wild, untamed; *perempuan* ~ street walker

jalar *adj* creeping; *ubi* ~ sweet potato; **menjalar** *vi* to creep, climb; *tanaman* ~ climbing plant

jalin: jalinan *n* net, network; **menjalin** *vt* to forge links, network; **terjalin** *adj* forged, involved

jalu *n* cock's spur

jalur lane, track; ~ *cepat* fast track, express lane; ~ *gemuk* busy route; ~ *hijau* median strip, nature strip; ~ *khusus* fast track; ~ *lambat* slow lane; ~ *sepeda* bicycle lane

jalusi *n* louvre, Venetian blinds

jam *n* hour; clock; ~ *berapa?* what time is it?; ~ *besuk* visiting hours; ~ *bicara* consultation hours; ~ *buka* opening hours; ~ *dinding* (wall) clock; ~ *karet* rubber time, unpunctuality; ~ *kerja* working hours; ~ *lima* five o'clock; ~ *malam* curfew; ~ *pasir* hourglass, eggtimer; ~ *praktek* consulting hours; ~ *tangan* (wrist)watch; ~ *weker* alarm clock; *lima* ~ five hours; *setengah* ~ half an hour; ~ *setengah sepuluh* half past nine, 9.30; **jam-jaman** *adj* hourly; **berjam-jam** *adj* for hours and hours

jamaah *n, Isl* congregation; **berjamaah** *adv* together, as a congregation

jamah: menjamah, menjamahi *vt* to touch; to have sex with

Jamaika *n* Jamaica; *orang* ~ Jamaican

jamak *adj* plural, more than one; *bentuk* ~ plural form

jaman, zaman *n* age, era, time, period; ~ *dahulu*, ~ *dulu* in the old days, times past; *(jadul)* old-fashioned, out of date; ~ *Belanda* the Dutch era; ~ *meleset* the Great Depression; ~ *purbakala* prehistoric times; ~ *Revolusi* the Indonesian Revolution, 1945-49; ~ *saya* in my day; *ketinggalan* ~ outdated

jambak *n* tuft; **menjambak** *vt* to pull someone's hair

jamban *n* toilet, latrine

jambang, jambangan *n* vase, urn, pot

jamblang *nasi* ~ rice dish, specialty of the Cirebon area

jamboré *n* jamboree

jambrét snatch; **menjambrét** *vt* to snatch;

penjambrét *n* thief, bag-snatcher; penjambrétan *n* theft, snatching

jambu *n* kind of fruit; ~ *air* rose-apple; ~ *batu*, ~ *biji* guava; ~ *monyet*, ~ *mede* cashew; *buah* ~ guava, rose-apple; *merah* ~ pink

jambul *n* quiff, cowlick; crest; **berjambul** *vi* to have a quiff or crest

jami *mesjid* ~ (principal or large) mosque

jamin, menjamin *vt* to guarantee, promise; **jaminan** *n* guarantee; *surat* ~ (letter of) guarantee; ~ *hari tua* (old-age) pension; **penjamin** *n* guarantor; **terjamin** *adj* guaranteed

jampi *n* magic formula or spell

jamrud, zamrud *n* emerald

Jamsosték *n* state social security system ← **Jaminan Sosial Tenaga Kerja**

jamu *n* traditional herbal medicine; ~ *kuat* aphrodisiac; tonic

jamu: jamuan *n* dinner, something served to guests; **menjamu** *vt* to entertain guests, host an event, hold a feast; **perjamuan** *n* feast, party; entertainment; ~ *kudus Chr* holy communion; ~ *Suci* the Last Supper

jamur *n* mushroom, mold, fungus; ~ *kaki* athlete's foot; ~ *kuping* kind of mushroom, tree ear; *pakai* ~ with mushrooms; **berjamur** *adj* moldy; **menjamur** *vi* to spring up; **berjamuran** *vi* to pop up everywhere

janda *n* widow; ~ *cerai* divorced woman, divorcée; ~ *muda* young (attractive) widow; **menjanda** *vi* to be widowed, live as a widow

jangan *neg* don't, do not; ~ *begitu* don't do (or say) that; ~ *kuatir* don't worry; ~ *malu* don't be shy; ~ *sampai* don't (let it happen that), avoid; ~ *sekali-kali* never (do this); **jangan-jangan** *adv, neg* or else, otherwise, maybe even; **jangankan** *conj* let alone, not to mention

janggal *adj* odd, strange; **kejanggalan** *n* oddity, anomaly

janggut, jénggot *n* beard, goatee; **berjénggot** *adj* bearded; *vi* to have a beard

jangka *n* distance, term; compass; ~

panjang long term; ~ *pendek* short term; **berjangka** *adj* for a term; *deposito* ~ term deposit

jangkar *n* anchor

jangkau: jangkauan *n* reach, grasp, range; **menjangkau** *vt* to reach; **terjangkau** *adj* affordable; within reach or range

jangkit: berjangkit, menjangkit *vi* to spread, be infectious or contagious; **menjangkiti** *vt* to infect; **terjangkit** *adj* infected

jangkrik, jéngkerik *n* cicada, cricket

jangkung *adj, sl* tall, lanky

janin *n* fetus, embryo (more than two months after fertilization)

janji promise; *ingkar* ~ to break a promise; *menepati* ~ to keep a promise; *mengikat* ~ to get married, exchange vows; **janjian** *vi, sl* to make a date, promise; **berjanji** *vi* to promise; **menjanjikan** *vt* to promise something; **perjanjian** *n* agreement, contract

jantan male (animal), manly; *ayam* ~ cock, rooster; **kejantanan** *n* masculinity; **pejantan** *n* stud

jantung *n* heart, core; ~ *hati* sweetheart; ~ *kota* city center, heart of the city; *serangan* ~ heart attack; **jantungan** *vi, sl* to have a heart attack; to be very scared

Januari *bulan* ~ January

janur *n* decoration woven from coconut leaves, used at weddings; ~ *kuning* wedding decoration; *memasang* ~ to put up a *janur* decoration to indicate the wedding location

jarah: jarahan *n* stolen or looted goods; **menjarah** *vt* to loot; **penjarah** *n* looter; **penjarahan** *n* looting

jarak *n* distance, space; ~ *dekat* short distance, up close; ~ *jauh* long distance; ~ *pendek* short distance; *jaga* ~ keep a distance; *sambungan langsung* ~ *jauh (SLJJ)* long-distance direct dialing; **berjarak** *adj* -distance; *vi* to be a certain distance away; *pohon-pohon* ~ *10 meter* the trees were spaced 10 meters apart

jarak *minyak* ~ castor oil

jarang *adj, adv* seldom, rare, rarely, hardly ever; ~ *dibelai (jablai) adj, sl* untouched, discarded (of a lover)

jari *n* finger; ~ *jemari* fingers; ~ *kaki* toe; ~ *kelingking* little or baby finger; ~ *manis* ring finger; ~ *telunjuk* forefinger, index finger; ~ *tengah* middle finger; *ibu* ~ thumb; *sidik* ~ fingerprint; **jari-jari** *n, pl* spokes

jaring net, shoal; **jaringan** *n* network; **menjaring** *vt* to fish with a net; to filter or sift; **terjaring** *adj* netted, caught

jarum *n* needle; hand; ~ *jam* hand (of a clock or watch); *arah* ~ *jam* clockwise; ~ *suntik* (injection) needle; ~ *pentul* pin; *tusuk* ~ acupuncture

jas *n* coat; ~ *hujan* raincoat; *pakai* ~ *coll* wear a suit and tie

jasa *n* service, merit; ~ *boga* catering service; ~ *kurir* courier service; ~ *Marga* Indonesia Highways Corporation; **berjasa** *adj* meritorious, deserving of reward; *vi* to perform a service

jasad *n* corpse, dead body

jasmani *adj* physical; *hubungan* ~ sexual relations

jatah *n* ration, serve; **menjatahkan** *vt* to deal out, allocate

Jateng *n* Central Java ← **Jawa Tengah**

jati *kayu* ~ teak

jati ~ *diri* identity; **sejati** *adj* genuine, original, real

Jatim *n* East Java ← **Jawa Timur**

jatuh *vi* fall; ~ *bangun* fall down and get up; ~ *cinta,* ~ *hati* fall in love; ~ *pingsan* to faint (away); ~ *sakit* fall ill; ~ *tempo* to mature, be due; *bintang* ~ shooting star; **berjatuhan** *vi, pl* to fall (in numbers); **kejatuhan** *n* fall; *adj* be struck by something falling; **menjatuhi** *vt* to impose; to fall on top of; **menjatuhkan** *vt* to fell, let drop; ~ *hukuman* to sentence, condemn; **terjatuh** *adj* (accidentally) fallen

jauh *adj* far; *jarak* ~ long-distance; ~~~ *hari* well in advance; ~ *di mata, dekat di hati* absence makes the heart grow fonder; **kejauhan** *adj* too far; **menjauh** *v* to move away; **menjauhi** *vt* to avoid; **sejauh** *conj* how far; ~ *mana* to what point; **sejauh-jauhnya** *adv* as far away as possible

Jawa Java; ~ *Barat (Jabar)* West Java; *aksara* ~ Javanese script; *bahasa ~, orang* ~ Javanese; *gula* ~ palm sugar; *pulau* ~ Java

jawab answer, reply; *tanya* ~ question and answer; *tanggung* ~ responsibility; **bertanggung jawab** *adj* responsible; *vi* to be responsible, have responsibility; **jawaban** *n* answer, reply, response; **menjawab** *vt* to answer, reply; **terjawab** *adj* answered

jawat: jawatan *n* office, division → **jabat**

jawi *adj* Malay or Indonesian; *aksara* ~ Arabic script for writing Malay

jaya *adj* great, prosperous; victorious; **berjaya** *adj* victorious, winning; prosperous; **kejayaan** *n* victory, glory

jayus *adj, sl* not funny, stupid, pathetic

jé *n* j, tenth letter of the alphabet

jebak trap; **jebakan** *n* trap; **menjebak, menjebakkan** *vt* to trap; **terjebak** *adj* trapped, caught; ~ *macet* caught in traffic

jeblos *vi* to push or stick through

jebol *vi* to collapse, fall apart, break through; **jebolan** *n* graduate

jeda *n* pause, break, ceasefire

jégal: menjégal *vt* to stop (from winning), prevent, hamper, foil

jejak *n* footprint, track; ~ *kaki, ~ langkah* footprint; **menjejaki** *vt* to step on, trail, trace

jejaka *n* bachelor, young single man

jejal: berjejalan, berjejal-jejal *adv* crowded, jammed; **menjejalkan** *vt* to crowd, fill, jam

jejamu → **jamu**

jéjér row, line; **berjéjér, berjéjéran** *adv* in a row or line; *vi* to stand in a row or line; **menjéjérkan** *vt* to place in rows

jelajah: menjelajahi *vt* to travel through or explore a place; **penjelajah** *n* explorer

jelang: menjelang *vt* to approach (usu time)

jelangkung *n* effigy used as spirit medium in seances

jelantah *n* cooking oil to be reused

jelas *adj* clear, obvious; **kejelasan** *n* clarity; **menjelaskan** *vt* to explain, clarify; **penjelasan** *n* explanation

jelata *rakyat* ~ common people, masses

jelatang *n* nettle

jelék *adj* bad, ugly; ~*nya* the bad side is; **kejelékan** *n* badness, ugliness; **menjelékkan** *vt* to criticize, say bad things about

jeli *adj* careful, cautious

jelimet: menjelimet *vi* to be meticulous, nit-picking

jelita *adj, f* beautiful, charming

jelma: menjelma *vi* to be incarnated, turn into, materialize; **menjelmakan** *vt* to create or realize something; **penjelmaan** *n* incarnation

jemaah *n, Isl* followers, (Muslim) community → **jamaah**; **jemaat** *n, Chr* congregation, followers

jemari *n* finger; *jari* ~ fingers → **jari**

jembatan *n* bridge; ~ *ambruk* broken bridge; ~ *besi* iron bridge; ~ *gantung* suspension bridge; ~ *penyeberangan* pedestrian overpass, footbridge; ~ *timbang* weighbridge; **menjembatani** *vt* to bridge (two things)

jempol *n* thumb; *acungan* ~ thumbs-up sign; *cap* ~ thumb print

jemput *vi* pick up; *antar* ~ pick up and bring home, door to door; **jemputan** *n* vehicle which picks you up; **menjemput** *vt* to pick up; ~ *bola* be proactive; **penjemputan** *n* act of picking up

jemu *adj* sick or tired of, bored; **menjemukan** *adj* tedious, boring

jemur dry (in the sun); **jemuran** *n* clothes or food drying in the sun; **berjemur** *vi* to sunbathe, sun yourself; **menjemur** *vt* to air, dry in the sun; ~ *krupuk* to air crackers before frying; ~ *baju cucian* to hang out the washing

jenak: sejenak *adv* briefly, a moment

jenaka *adj* funny, amusing, cute

jenang *n* kind of fruit jelly; ~ *apel* apple-flavored jelly

jenazah *n* dead body, corpse; *mobil* ~ hearse

jendéla *n* window; *membuka* ~ *hati* to open your heart

jénder *n* gender; *soal* ~ gender issue

jénderal *n* general; ~ *Besar* (Field) Marshal, General of the Army (awarded to Nasution and Suharto in 1997, and posthumously to Sudirman); ~ *bintang empat* four-star general; ~ *polisi* police general; *Brigadir-~ (Brigjen)* Brigadier-General; *Letnan-~ (Letjen)* Lieutenant-General; *Mayor-~ (Mayjen)* Major-General; ~ *(Polisi)* Police General

jénéwer *n* gin, genever

jengah *adj* embarrassed, ill at ease

jénggot, janggut *n* beard; *kebakaran jenggot* to lose your head, be unable to cope; **berjénggot** *adj* bearded; *vi* to have a beard

jengkal: sejengkal *adj* handspan (between thumb and little finger)

jéngkél *adj* annoyed; **kejéngkélan** *n* annoyance, bad mood; **menjéngkélkan** *adj* annoying

jéngkol *n* pungent vegetable

jenguk, menjenguk *vt* to visit (in hospital), pay a call on

jenis *n* kind, sort, type; species; ~ *kelamin* sex, gender; *lawan* ~ opposite sex; **berjenis-jenis** *adj* all kinds of, various; **sejenis** *adj* same type or species; *pasangan* ~ same-sex couple

jenjang *n* rank, stage, hierarchy; ~ *pendidikan* stage of education

jentik ~ *nyamuk* mosquito larvae

jenuh *adj* fed up, bored; saturated; *lemak* ~ saturated fats; **kejenuhan** *n* saturation; boredom

Jepang *n* Japan; *bahasa* ~, *orang* ~ Japanese

jepit *n* tweezers; **jepitan** *n* clip; tweezers; ~ *rambut* hair clip; **menjepit** *vt* to pinch, squeeze; **penjepit** *n* clip; **terjepit** *adj* pinched, caught in an uncomfortable situation

jeprét snap, click (like a camera); **jeprétan, penjeprét** *n* stapler; **menjeprét** *vt* to snap, staple; ~ *foto* to take a photo

Jepun → **Jepang**

jera *adj* wary, deterred

jeram *n* rapids; *arung* ~ white water rafting

jerami *n* straw; *beratap* ~ thatched roof

jerapah *n* giraffe

jerat snare, trap, noose; **menjerat** *vt* to snare, trap; **terjerat** *adj* snared, trapped, caught

jerawat *n* pimple; **jerawatan** *adj* pimply; **berjerawat** *adj* pimply; *vi* to have pimples

jerembab: menjerembabkan *vt* to upset, push over; **terjerembab** *adj* to fall over, fall forward

jéréng *mata* ~ one eye looking outwards

jeri *adj* afraid

jérigén *n* jerrycan

jerih *adj* exhausted, tired; ~ *payah* toil, hard work

jerit scream, shriek; **jeritan** *n* scream, shriek; **menjerit** *v* to scream, shriek

Jérman *n* Germany; *bahasa* ~, *orang* ~ German; *campak* ~ rubella, German measles

jernih *adj* clear, transparent, pure; *air* ~ clear water; **menjernihkan** *vt* to purify (water); **penjernihan** *n* purification

jero: jeroan *n* innards

jeruji *n* trellis, iron bars; *di balik* ~ behind bars; **berjeruji** *adj* fitted with bars

jeruk ~ *Bali* pink grapefruit, pomelo; ~ *Garut*, ~ *keprok* kind of tangerine; ~ *lemon* lemon; ~ *limau* lime; ~ *nipis* lemon, lime; ~ *peras* orange; *air* ~ orange juice; *buah* ~ orange, mandarin; *rasa* ~ orange(-flavored)

jerumus: menjerumuskan *vt* to let drop, send down; **terjerumus** *adj* plunged into

jéwér: jéwéran *n* pinch, reprimand; **menjéwér** *vt* to pinch someone's ear, scold

jibun: berjibun *vi* to pile up, teem (with)

Jibuti *n* Djibouti; *orang* ~ Djiboutian

jidat *n* forehead

jihad *n, Isl* crusade (often in terms of personal behavior); holy war; **berjihad** *vi* to conduct a war or crusade; to strive towards a noble goal

jijik *adj* disgusting, revolting, filthy; *rasa* ~ disgust; **menjijikkan** *adj* disgusting, revolting, foul jika, jikalau *conj* if, should

jilat lick; **jilatan** *n* lick; ~ *api* flames; **menjilat** *vt* to lick; *sl* to suck up, flatter; **menjilati** *vt* to lick something; to fawn, suck up; **penjilat** *n* crawler, flatterer, lickspittle

jilbab *n, Isl* (full) veil; **berjilbab** *adj* in a (full) veil, veiled; *vi* to wear the veil

jilid *n* volume; **jilidan** *n* binding; **berjilid** *adj* in volumes; **menjilid** *vt* to bind; **penjilid** *n* binder; **penjilidan** *n* binding (process)

jimat *n* lucky charm, talisman

jin *n* spirit; *dunia* ~ spirit world

jinak *adj* tame, domesticated, friendly; ~~ *merpati* coy, pretending to be shy; **menjinakkan** *vt* to tame

jingga *adj* orange (color)

jingkrak: **berjingkrak, berjingkrak-jingkrak** *vi* to jump for joy

jinjing *komputer* ~ laptop (computer); *tas* ~ carrybag; **jinjingan** *n* something carried by hand; **menjinjing** *vt* to carry by hand

jinjit: **berjinjit-jinjit** *vi* walk on tiptoe

jintan *n* cumin

jip *mobil* ~ jeep

jiplak: **jiplakan** *n* copy, plagiarism; **menjiplak** *vt* to copy, plagiarize; **penjiplak** *n* cheat; **penjiplakan** *n* plagiarism, cheating

jiran *n* neighbor; *negeri* ~ neighboring country, usu Malaysia

jitu *adj* exact, accurate; *cara* ~ exact method; *penembak* ~ sniper

jiwa *n* life, soul; ~ *melayang* to die; ~ *raga* body and soul; *asuransi* ~ life insurance; *ilmu* ~ psychology; *rumah sakit* ~ *(RSJ)* mental hospital; **berjiwa** *adj* alive; *vi* to have a soul; ~ *muda* to be young at heart; **kejiwaan** *adj* mental; **menjiwai** *vt* to bring to life, inspire; **penjiwaan** *n* inspiration

JJS *abbrev, sl* jalan-jalan sore going out in the afternoon

Jl, Jln *Jalan* street, road

jo, juncto *n* [yo] leg in connection with

jodoh *n* life partner, match; *m* Mr Right; **menjodohkan** *vt* to set up, match; **perjodohan** *n* marriage, match

jogét, jogéd (spontaneous) dance; **berjogét** *vi* to dance

joging *n* (early morning) walk or jog for exercise

joglo *rumah* ~ traditional Javanese house

jok *n* seat (in vehicle); ~ *belakang* back seat

joki *n* jockey; paid passenger (to avoid traffic restrictions)

joli: sejoli *dua* ~ a couple

jompo *adj* elderly; *panti* ~, *rumah* ~ old persons' home, senior citizens' home

jongkok, berjongkok *vi* to squat

joran *n* fishing rod

jorok *adj* obscene, disgusting; sloppy; *cerita* ~ dirty story; *film* ~ pornographic film

jorok: menjorok *vi* to stick out, protrude; **menjorokkan** *vt* to poke something out

jotos fist; *adu* ~ fistfight

jréng *adj, sl* bright, lively

jua only; also, too; *tidak sedikit* ~ not a bit

jual *vt* to sell; ~ *beli* business, buying and selling; ~ *diri* to sell yourself, prostitute yourself; ~ *mahal* to have a high asking price; ~ *muka,* ~ *tampang* to succeed on looks alone; to show off; *harga* ~ selling price; **jualan** *v* to sell informally; **berjual** *vi* to trade, sell; **menjual** *vt* to sell; **penjual** *n* seller, dealer; **penjualan** *n* sale, sales; **terjual** *adj* sold; *habis* ~ sold out

juang: berjuang *vi* to fight, struggle; **memperjuangkan** *vt* to fight for; **pejuang** *n* fighter; **perjuangan** *n* battle, fight, struggle; *Partai Demokrasi Indonesia-~ (PDIP)* Indonesian Democratic Party of Struggle

juara *n* champion; ~ *dunia* world champion; ~ *satu* first place; **kejuaraan** *n* championship; **menjuarai** *vt* to win (a competition)

jubah *n* gown, robe; **berjubah** *vi* to wear a robe

jubel: berjubel-jubel *vi* to crowd around; *adj* chock-full, chock-a-block

jubir *n* spokesperson ← **juru bicara**

judes *adj* mean, cruel, bitchy

judi *vi* to gamble; *main* ~ to gamble;

berjudi *vi* to gamble; **penjudi** *n* gambler; **perjudian** *n* gambling

judo *n* judo; **pejudo, judoka** *n* judo athlete

judul *n* title; **berjudul** *adj* titled; *vi* to have a title

juga too, also; *hari itu* ~ that very day

jujur *adj* honest; **kejujuran** *n* honesty

julang: menjulang *vi* to soar; ~ *tinggi* to rise high

Juli *bulan* ~ July

juling *adj* cross-eyed (one eye looking inwards); *mata* ~ squint

juluk: julukan *n* nickname, alias; **menjuluki** *vt* to give a nickname to

Jumat, Jum'at ~ *Agung* Good Friday; *hari* ~ Friday; *malam* ~ Thursday night (when some believe ghosts are out); *sholat* ~ Friday prayers

jumlah *n* amount, total, sum, number; ~ *korban* total casualties; **berjumlah** *vi* to (have the) number; **menjumlahkan** *vt* to add (up); **penjumlahan** *n* addition, tallying; **sejumlah** *adj* a number of, some

jumpa meet; ~ *pers* press conference; *sampai* ~ see you later; **berjumpa** *vi* to meet; **menjumpai** *vt* to meet someone

jumpalit *n* somersault

juncto, jo *n* [yungto] leg in connection with

jung *n* (Chinese) junk

jungkir ~ *balik* somersault

Juni *bulan* ~ June

junior, yunior *n* junior; student in a younger year level; co-worker of a lower rank

junjung: menjunjung ~ *tinggi* to honor

juntai: berjuntai, menjuntai *vi* to dangle

junub *adj, Isl* state of impurity after having sex; *mandi* ~ to wash or shower after sex

Jupiter *n* (the planet) Jupiter

juragan *n* boss, master

jurang *n* ravine, gorge

juri *n* jury

jurnal *n* journal; **jurnalis** *n* journalist, reporter → **wartawan**

juru expert, skilled; ~ *bahasa* interpreter (spoken); translator (written); ~ *bicara* (*jubir*) spokesperson; ~ *kamera* (*jurkam*) cameraman; ~ *ketik* typist; ~ *kunci* gatekeeper; ~ *lelang* auctioneer; ~ *masak* cook; ~ *mudi* helmsman; ~ *rawat* nurse; ~ *rias* make-up artist; ~ *selamat* savior; ~ *sita* bailiff, process-server; ~ *tulis* clerk; **kejuruan** *adj* technical; *sekolah* ~ technical or trade school

juru: penjuru *n* corner

jurus *n* moment

jurus *n* step; **jurusan** *n* direction; major (at university); ~ *desain* design major; *bis* ~ *Palangkaraya* bus to Palangkaraya; ~ *sastra* arts major; **menjurus** *vi* to lead to

jus *n* juice; ~ *alpukat* avocado juice; ~ *sirsak* soursop juice; **dijus** *v* to be made into juice, juiced

justru *adv* precisely, exactly

juta *n* million; *sepuluh* ~ ten million; **jutaan** *adj* millions; **berjuta** *vi* to have millions of; **jutawan** *n* millionaire

juték *adj, sl* bad-tempered, unfriendly

K

K. *kali* creek, stream, river

k [ka], **ka** k, eleventh letter of the alphabet

KA *abbrev kereta api* train

Ka *Kepala* head of section

Kaabah, ka'abah *n* the black-covered shrine in the Great Mosque of Mecca

Kab. *Kabupaten* regency

kabag *n* head of section ← **kepala bagian**

kabar *n* news; ~*nya* people say; ~ *angin*, ~ *burung* rumor; ~ *baik* good news; I'm well; ~ *buruk* bad news; *apa* ~? how are you?; *surat* ~ newspaper; **mengabari** *vt* to tell or inform someone; **mengabarkan** *vt* to announce, report

kabé, ka bé, KB *n, coll* state family planning program → **keluarga berencana**

kabel *n* cable; ~ *listrik* electrical cable; ~ *tanam* underground cable or wires

kabin *n* cabin (of a ship or aeroplane); *awak* ~ cabin crew; *bagasi* ~ cabin luggage

kabinét *n* cabinet; *rapat* ~ cabinet meeting; ~ *Indonesia Bersatu* the United Indonesia cabinet

kabisat *tahun* ~ leap year

kabul: mengabulkan *vt* to grant, approve, consent to; *semoga doanya dikabulkan* may your prayers be answered; **terkabul** *adj* granted

kabung: berkabung *vi* to mourn; *hari* ~ *nasional* day of national mourning; **perkabungan** *n* mourning

kabupatén *n* regency; ~ *Bandung* Regency of Bandung ← **bupati**

kabur *adj* blurry, hazy; *mata sudah* ~ blurred vision; *vi* to disappear, vanish

kabut *n* fog, mist; **berkabut** *adj* cloudy

kaca *n* glass; ~ *depan* windscreen, windshield; ~ *patri* stained glass; ~ *pembesar* magnifying glass; ~ *spion* rear-view mirror; *tukang* ~ glazier; ~ *mata* glasses, spectacles; ~ *mata baca* reading glasses; ~ *mata hitam* sunglasses, dark glasses; **berkacamata** *vi* to wear glasses; ~ *min(us)* to be shortsighted; ~ *plus* to be long-sighted; **berkaca-kaca** *vi* to fill with tears (of eyes)

kacang *n* bean, legume; ~ *atom* nuts fried in batter; ~ *hijau* mung bean; ~ *kapri* snow pea; ~ *kedelai* soybean, soya bean; ~ *mede* cashew (nut); ~ *merah* kidney bean; ~ *panjang* kind of long bean; ~ *polong* (green) pea; ~ *rebus* boiled peanuts; ~ *tanah* peanut; *selai* ~ peanut butter; ~ *lupa kulit* forget your origins; **kacangan** *adj, sl* cheap, petty

kacapiring *n* gardenia

kacau *adj* disordered, confused, chaotic; ~ *balau* complete disorder; **kekacauan** *n* chaos; **mengacaukan** *vt* to mix or mess up; **pengacau** *n* provocateur; **pengacauan** *n* disturbance

kadal *n* lizard

kadaluwarsa, kedaluwarsa *adj* expired; *tanggal* ~ expiry date, use-by date (food) ← **daluwarsa**

kadang, kadang-kadang, terkadang *adv* sometimes, occasionally

kadar *n* level, degree; *ala* ~*nya* the best you can; **sekadar** *adj* just; ~*nya* as necessary

kade *n* quay, dock

kader *n* cadre, party member

kadét *n* cadet

kadi *n, Isl* judge in religious court

Kadin *n* Chamber of Commerce ← **Kamar Dagang dan Industri**

kadipatén *n, arch* area ruled by an *adipati* in colonial times ← **adipati**

kadung *adv, Jav* too, excessive

kafan *kain* ~ shroud, white cloth for wrapping a dead body

kafé *n* café, bar, pub, nightspot; ~ *gaul* popular café; **kafétaria** *n* cafetaria, canteen

kaféin *n* caffeine

kafilah *n* caravan

kafir *n, Isl* infidel, pagan

kagak *sl* no, not ← **tidak**

kagét *n* startled, surprised; *pasar* ~ temporary street market; *rasa* ~ surprise; **mengagétkan** *vt* to surprise, startle

kagok *adj* stuck (in an awkward position)

kagum *adj* admiring; **kekaguman** *n* admiration; **mengagumi** *vt* to admire; **pengagum** *n* admirer; **terkagum-kagum** *adj* amazed, astonished, very surprised

-kah (suffix to make a question) *bisa*~? Can?; *tidak*~ isn't?

kaidah *n* law, rule; ~ *fisika* laws of physics

kail *n* fishing rod; **mengail** *v* to fish

kailan *n* Chinese broccoli, kailan

kain *n* cloth; ~ *kafan* shroud; ~ *kasa* gauze, muslin; ~ *katun* cotton fabric or cloth; ~ *kebaya* national dress for women; ~ *lurik* striped Javanese cloth; ~ *mori* white cotton for making batik; ~ *panjang* long piece of unsewn batik worn with *kebaya*; ~ *pel* rag for mopping the floor; ~ *sarung* batik or woven cloth sewn into a sarong; ~ *songket* woven cloth, often with gold thread; ~ *tenun* woven cloth; **berkain** *vi* ~ *kebaya* to wear female national dress

kais, mengais *vt* to scratch; ~ *rejeki* to scratch a living

kaisar *n, pron* emperor; **kekaisaran** *n* empire; ~ *Romawi* the Roman Empire

kait hook; **kaitan** *n* relationship, link; *tidak ada* ~*nya* unrelated; **berkaitan** *vi* to be related to; **mengaitkan** *vt* to link, connect, join; **pengait** *n* catch ← **gaét, gait**

kaji: kajian *n* studies; ~ *Indonesia* Indonesian studies; **mengkaji** *vt* to study, investigate; **pengkajian** *n* study, studying

kaji: mengaji, ngaji *vi* to recite or read the Koran; **pengajian** *n* Koranic recitation

kak *pron* term for older sibling or slightly older person; **kakak** *n* pron elder brother or sister; ~~*beradik* *vi* (to have) siblings; ~ *kelas* someone in a class higher than you; ~ *laki-laki* elder brother; ~ *tiri* (older) stepbrother or stepsister; **kakanda** *pron, lit* form of address to older brother or sister; ~ *yang tersayang* dear (older) sister/brother

kakao *n* cacao, cocoa

kakap *ikan* ~ large fish; *penjahat kelas* ~ big-time criminal

kakas: perkakas *n* tool, implement; ~ *dapur* kitchen utensils

kakatua *n burung* ~ cockatoo

kakék *n, pron* grandfather; old man; **kakék-kakék** *adj, m* old and ailing

kaki *n* foot, leg; ~ *keseleo* sprained foot; *(pedagang)* ~ *lima* itinerant food vendor; ~ *langit* horizon; ~ *tangan* henchman, stooge; *jari* ~ toe; *pergelangan* ~, *mata* ~ ankle; *semata* ~ to the ankle; *telapak* ~ footprint, sole; **berkaki** *vi* to have feet; ~ *telanjang* barefoot; ~ *tiga* three-legged

kaktus *n* cactus

kaku *adj* stiff, frozen

kakus *n* toilet, outhouse

kala *n* time; *conj* when; *ada* ~*nya* sometimes; *dahulu* ~ the old days; **berkala** *adj* regular; *secara* ~ periodically

kalah lose, be defeated; less than; ~ *cepat* miss out, too slow; **kekalahan** *n* defeat, loss; **mengalah** *vi* to give in, accept defeat; **mengalahkan** *vt* to conquer, defeat

kalajengking *n* scorpion

kalam *lit, Isl* pen, stylus

kalang ~ *kabut* confused, mixed up

kalang: kalangan *n* circle, group; *untuk* ~ *sendiri* for believers or members only

kalau *conj* if; as for; ~ *tidak salah* if I'm not mistaken; ~ *saya, tidak masalah* as for me, it's not a problem; **kalau-kalau** *conj* in case; **kalaupun** *conj* even if

Kalbar *n* West Kalimantan ← **Kalimantan Barat**

kalbu, kaldéra *n* heart

kaldéra *n* caldera, crater

kaldu *n* broth; ~ *sapi* beef stew

kalem *adj* calm, steady

kaléndar, kalénder *n* calendar ~ *Masehi* Christian calendar

kaléng *n* tin, can; *ikan* ~ tinned fish; *surat* ~ anonymous letter; **mengaléngkan** *vt* to can, tin

kali time, times; ~ *lipat* times (over), multiple; *satu* ~, *se*~ once; *dua* ~ twice; *enam* ~ six times; *dua* ~ *lipat* double, twice over; *lima* ~ *delapan* five times eight; **berkali-kali** *adv* repeatedly, again and again; **mengalikan** *vt* to multiply; **sekali** *adv* once; very; *besar* ~ very large; **sekali-sekali, sesekali** *adv* every now and then, occasionally; **sekali-kali** *jangan* ~ never (do this); **sekalian** *adv* all together, all at once; *anda se*~ all of you; *coll* at the same time; **sekaligus** *adv* all at once; **sekalipun** *conj* even though

kali *n* creek, stream, river; ~ *Brantas* the River Brantas

kali *coll* maybe, perhaps ← **barangkali**

kalian *pron, pl* you

kaligrafi *n, Isl* Arabic calligraphy

Kalimantan *n* Kalimantan, Borneo; ~ *Timur (Kaltim)* East Kalimantan; ~ *Utara* Malaysian Borneo, North Borneo

kalimat *n* sentence; ~ *induk* main clause; *pokok* ~ subject (of a sentence); *menyusun* ~ to make a sentence

kalium *n* potassium

kalk *n* limestone, chalk

kalkulator *n* calculator

kalkun *n* turkey

kalo *sl* → **kalau**

kalori *n* calorie; ~ *rendah* low-calorie

Kalpataru *n* award presented for services to the environment

Kalsél *n* South Kalimantan ← **Kalimantan Selatan**

Kalteng *n* Central Kalimantan ← **Kalimantan Tengah**

Kaltim *n* East Kalimantan ← **Kalimantan Timur**

kalung *n* necklace; **berkalung** *vi* to wear a necklace; *adj* wearing a necklace; **mengalungkan** *vt* to drape around someone's neck

kalut → **karut**

kamar *n* room; *sl* bedroom; ~ *belajar* study; ~ *dagang (dan industri, Kadin)* chamber of commerce; ~ *ganti* changing room, dressing room; ~ *jenazah,* ~ *mayat* morgue; ~ *kecil* toilet, lavatory; ~ *makan* dining room; ~ *mandi* bathroom; ~ *pas* fitting room; ~ *pengantin* bridal chamber; ~ *rias* dressing room; ~ *tamu* room for receiving guests, front room; living room; spare room; ~ *tidur* bedroom; ~ *tunggu* waiting room

kambing *n* goat, sheep; *daging* ~ goat; mutton, lamb; *kelas* ~ cheapest class (on transport); *potong* ~ sacrifice a goat; ~ *hitam* scapegoat; **mengambing-hitamkan** *vt* to make a scapegoat of someone

kamboja *bunga* ~ frangipani

Kamboja *n* Cambodia; *bahasa* ~ Khmer; *orang* ~ Cambodian

kambuh relapse, chronic attack; *asmanya* ~ having an asthma attack

kaméra *n* camera; **kamérawan** *n, m* cameraman

kamerad *n* comrade

kamérawan *n, m* cameraman ← **kaméra**

kami *pron* we, us, our (excluding the listener); (very polite) I; ~ *punya* our, ours; *surat* ~ my letter, our letter

Kamis *hari* ~ Thursday; ~ *Putih* Maundy Thursday

kamisol *n* camisole, strapless top

kampak → **kapak**

kampanye *n* campaign; **berkampanye** *vi* to (hold a) campaign; to join a parade for a candidate

kamper *n* camphor, mothballs

kamprét *n* small bat

kampung, kampong *n* village, hometown; ~ *halaman* hometown; ~ *Melayu* Malay quarter; *pulang* ~ to go home to the village; **kampungan** *adj* uneducated, backward, provincial; **perkampungan** *n* settlement, cluster of villages

kampus *n* university, campus

kamsia *Ch* thank you

kamu *pron, sing* you (to children and familiars); ~ *punya* yours

kamuflase *n* camouflage; smokescreen; **berkamuflase** *vi* to use camouflage

kamus *n* dictionary; ~ *dwibahasa* bilingual dictionary; ~ *Indonesia-Inggris* Indonesian-English dictionary; ~ *istilah* specialist dictionary (on a subject); ~ *saku* pocket dictionary

kan, 'kan you know; isn't it? ← **bukan**

Kanada *n* Canada; *orang* ~ Canadian

kanak-kanak *taman* ~ *(TK)* kindergarten; **kekanak-kanakan** *adj* childish, infantile

kanal *n* canal

kanan *adj* right; ~ *kapal* starboard; *ke* ~ to the right; *sebelah* ~ on the right; *stir* ~ right-hand drive; *tangan* ~ right hand

kancil *n* mouse-deer; smart car used as a taxi ← **kendaraan angkutan niaga cilik irit dan lincah**

kancing *n* button, stud; ~ *pencet* press-stud; *lubang* ~ buttonhole; **mengancing** *vt* to button

kancut *n* underpants, loincloth

kandang *n* stable, pen; *coll* home ground; ~ *anjing* kennel, doghouse; ~ *ayam* chicken coop; ~ *kuda* stable; ~ *lawan* opponent's home ground

kandas *adj* stranded, aground; *vi* to fail; **mengandaskan** *vt* to strand, beach; to frustrate, foil

kandidat *n* candidate → **calon**

kandung *n* uterus; bladder; ~ *empedu* gall bladder; ~ *kemih* bladder; *ibu* ~ birth mother, biological mother; **kandungan** *n* fetus, unborn child; contents; ~ *merkuri* mercury content;

mengandung *vt* to contain, carry; *adj* to be pregnant

kangen *adj* long for, miss; *rasa* ~ longing

kangguru, kanguru *n* kangaroo; *negeri* ~ Australia

kangkang: mengangkang *vi* to sit with legs wide apart; *vt* to straddle

kangkung *n* water spinach; ~ *tumis* stir-fried water spinach

kanibal *n* cannibal

kanji *n* starch; Japanese (non-alphabetic) characters

kanker *n* cancer; ~ *darah* leukaemia; ~ *paru-paru* lung cancer; ~ *payudara* breast cancer; ~ *rahim* cervical cancer; ~ *indung telur* ovarian cancer; ~ *usus besar* cancer of the colon

kano *n* canoe

kans *n, coll* chance

kansel, kénsel, mengansel *vt, coll* to cancel → **batal**

kanselir *n* chancellor, German or Austrian prime minister; embassy first secretary; ~ *Jerman yang baru adalah Angela Merkel* Angela Merkel is the new German Chancellor

kantin *n* canteen

kantong, kantung *n* pocket, pouch; **berkantong** *vi* to have a pocket; ~ *tebal* wealthy; ~ *teh* tea-bag; **mengantongi** *vt* to pocket; *Iwan* ~ *banyak tip dari tamu* Iwan pocketed lots of tips from guests

kantor *n* office; ~ *cabang*, ~ *perwakilan* branch office; ~ *pajak* tax office; ~ *pembantu* (larger) branch office; ~ *polisi* police station; ~ *pos* post office; ~ *pusat* head office; ~ *wilayah (kanwil)* regional office; ~ *catatan sipil* civil registry office; ~ *Urusan Agama (KUA) Isl* Religious Affairs Office; *orang* ~ someone from work; *pergi ke* ~ go to work; **kantoran** *adj, coll* office; *orang* ~ white-collar workers; **berkantor** *vi* to have an office; **ngantor** *coll, vi* to go to work; **perkantoran** *n* office block

kantuk *rasa* ~ sleepiness; **mengantuk, ngantuk, terkantuk-kantuk** *adj* sleepy

kantung → **kantong**

kanwil *n* regional office ← **kantor wilayah**

kaos → **kaus**

kapak, kampak *n* ax, axe; ~ *merah* the Red Axes, a gang in Jakarta

kapal *n* ship, vessel; ~ *api*, ~ *uap* steamer; ~ *induk* mother ship; aircraft carrier; ~ *keruk* dredger; ~ *laut* ship; ~ *penumpang* passenger ship; ~ *perang* warship; ~ *pesiar* cruise ship, pleasure craft; ~ *pinisi*, ~ *phinisi* Buginese cargo boat; ~ *selam* submarine; ~ *tempur* fighter; ~ *terbang* aeroplane, airplane; ~ *wisata* tourist boat, pleasure craft; *awak* ~ crew; ~ *penyapu ranjau* minesweeper; *anak buah* ~ *(ABK)* able seaman; **perkapalan** *n* shipping

kapal: kapalan *vi* to have corns, callouses

kapan *interrog* when; ~ *saja* whenever, any time; **kapan-kapan** *adv* one day, some time in the future

kapan → **kafan**

kapar: terkapar *adj* fallen, strewn

kapas *n* cotton, cotton wool; *seputih* ~ as white as snow

kapasitas *n* capacity; **berkapasitas** *vi* with a capacity of

kapitalis capitalist; **kapitalisme** *n* capitalism

kapitan, kapitén *n* captain; ~ *Cina* leader of local Chinese in past times

kapling, kavling, kaveling, kav *n* block (in addresses); **dikapling** *v* to be divided up into blocks for development

kapok *vi, coll* to learn a lesson (and not do again); *Lastri* ~ *sesudah tersesat di taman* Lastri learned her lesson after getting lost in the park

Kapolda *n* Regional Chief of Police (rank below *Kapolri*) ← **Kepala Polisi Daérah**

Kapolrés *n* Local Chief of Police (rank below *Kapolwil*) ← **Kepala Polisi Résort**

Kapolri *n* National Chief of Police ← **Kepala Polisi Republik Indonésia**

Kapolsék *n* Section Chief of Police ← **Kepala Polisi Séktor** (below *Kapolrés*)

Kapolwil *n* District Chief of Police (rank below *Kapolda*) ← **Kepala Polisi Wilayah**

kaporit *n* chlorine (especially for swimming pools)

kapri *kacang* ~ snow pea

kapster *n, arch* female hairdresser

kapstok *n* stand for clothes or hats

kapsul *n* capsule; *Kijang* ~ rounded model of Kijang car (post 1996)

kapuk, kapok *n* kapok

kapulaga *n* cardamom

kapur *n* lime(stone), chalk; ~ *barus* mothball; *tanah* ~ limestone country; **mengapur** *vt* to whitewash; **pengapuran** *n* calcification; **sekapur** ~ *sirih* foreword, opening words

kara *sebatang* ~ alone in the world

karam *adj* shipwrecked; *vi* to sink

karamba *n* large basket for catching fish

karambola, karambol *n* children's game

karamél *n* caramel pudding; *rasa* ~ caramel-flavored

karang *n* coral reef; *batu* ~ coral reef; *pulau* ~ coral island, atoll

karang: karangan *n* essay; ~ *bunga* bouquet, wreath; **mengarang** *vt* to write, compose; *lomba* ~ essay competition; **ngarang** *vt, coll* to make something up (off the top of your head); **pengarang** *n* author, writer, composer; *hak* ~ copyright

karang: pekarangan *n* yard; ~ *sekolah* schoolyard

karantina *n* quarantine

karapan ~ *sapi* Madurese bull races

karat *n* rust; **karatan, berkarat** *adj* rusty; *vi* to be rusty

karat *n* carat; *emas delapan belas* ~ eighteen-carat gold

karawang → **kerawang**

karawitan *n* art of the *gamelan* (Indonesian traditional orchestra)

karbohidrat *n* carbohydrate

karbol *n* carbolic acid, floor cleaner

karbon *n* carbon; ~ *dioksida* carbon dioxide (CO_2); ~ *monoksida* carbon monoxide (CO)

karburétor, karburator *n* carburettor

karcis *n* ticket (of small value); ~ *abonemen* commuter ticket, monthly ticket; ~ *bis* bus ticket; ~ *masuk* entrance ticket; ~ *peron* platform ticket; *loket* ~ ticket office; *penjual* ~ ticket seller; ~ *kereta api* local train ticket

kardan, gardan *n* differential gear

kardinal *n, Cath* cardinal

kardus *n* cardboard (box)

karé → **kari**

karédok *n* Sundanese fresh salad with peanut sauce

karena *conj* because, since; **dikarenakan** *v* caused by

karéséh-péséh *vi* to chatter in a European language

karésidénan *n, arch* Residency, administrative unit in Dutch times headed by a Resident ← **résidén**

karét *n* rubber; rubber band; ~ *gelang* rubber band; *jam* ~ lack of punctuality; *kebun* ~ rubber plantation; *permen* ~ chewing gum, bubble gum

kargo *n* cargo, hold

kari, karé *n* curry; ~ *ayam* chicken curry

karib *adj* close, intimate

karikatur *n* caricature

karir *n* career; *wanita* ~ career woman

karisma *n* charisma; **karismatik** *adj* charismatic

karma *n* karma

karnaval *n* carnival

Karo sub-ethnic group of the Batak people, living around Brastagi in North Sumatra

karoseri *n* carosserie, body (of vehicle)

karpét *n* carpet

kartika *n, lit* star

karton *n* cardboard

kartu *n* card; ~ *anggota* membership card; ~ *ATM* ATM card; ~ *debit* debit card; ~ *identitas* identity card; ~ *keluarga (KK)* family identity card; ~ *kredit* credit card; ~ *kuning* yellow card (in soccer); ~ *merah* red card (in soccer); ~ *nama* name card; ~ *Natal* Christmas card; ~ *pelajar* student card; ~ *pengenal* identity card, ID; ~ *pos* postcard; ~ *pelajar* student card; ~ *remi* playing cards; ~ *SIM* SIM card (for mobile phone); ~ *télepon* phone card; ~ *truf* trump card, trumps; ~ *ucapan* greeting card; *main* ~ to play cards; ~ *Tanda Penduduk (KTP)* identity card

kartun *n* cartoon, anime; **kartunis** *n* cartoonist

karuan, keruan *tidak* ~ very badly, in chaos

karun *harta* ~ hidden treasure

karung *n* sack; ~ *beras* sack of rice; ~ *goni* gunny sack

karunia *n* blessing, grace; ~ *Allah* gift from God; **mengaruniai** *vt* to bless; **mengaruniakan** *vt* to bless someone with

karut, kalut *adj* confused, chaotic; ~ *marut* completely confused, mixed up

karya *n* works; *loka*~ workshop, seminar; **karyawan** *n* (salaried) employee; **karyawati** *n, f* (salaried) employee

kasa *kain* ~ gauze, muslin

Kasad *n* Army Chief of Staff ← **Kepala Staf Angkatan Darat**

kasar *adj* rough, rude, vulgar; *bahasa Jawa* ~ low Javanese; *sikap* ~ rudeness; **kekasaran** *n* coarseness, roughness

kasasi *n* leg appeal (to Supreme Court)

kasatmata *adj* clear, with the naked eye

kasét *n* cassette

kasidah *n, Isl* religious chant or poem

kasih, kasi *vt, coll* give; ~ *amplop* hand over a bribe; ~ *lihat* show; ~ *makan* feed, give food; ~ *pinjam* lend; ~ *tahu* inform, tell; **mengasih** *vt* to give

kasih *n* affection, love; ~ *ibu* mother's love; ~ *sayang* love; *terima* ~ thank you; **kasihan** pity, feel sorry for; ~ *amat!* poor thing!; ~ *dia* poor thing; **mengasihani** *vt* to pity, feel sorry for; **kekasih** *n* darling, sweetheart, beloved; ~ *gelap* secret lover

kasino *n* casino

kasir, kassa *n* cashier

kasmaran *adj* in love, smitten ← **asmara**

kassa → **kasir**

kasta *n* caste; ~ *sudra* lowest caste

kasti *n* a game like rounders

kastroli *n* castor oil

kasuari *burung* ~ cassowary

kasur *n* mattress; ~ *pegas, ~ per* spring bed

kasus *n* case

kasut *n* sandal, slipper

kata *n* word; ~*nya, ~ orang* people say; ~ *benda* noun; ~ *dasar* base or root of a word; ~ *depan* preposition; ~ *ganti* pronoun; ~ *hati* conscience; ~ *kerja* verb; ~ *keterangan* adverb; ~ *kunci* key word; password; ~ *lawan* antonym, opposite; ~ *majemuk* compound (word); ~ *pendahuluan, ~ pengantar* preface; ~ *penghubung, ~ sambung* conjunction, connector, connective; ~ *pinjaman* borrowing, loanword; ~ *sambutan* words of welcome, welcome address; ~ *sandang* article; ~ *sandi* code, password; ~ *seru* exclamation; ~ *sifat* adjective; *akar* ~ base word, root; *lawan* ~ antonym; *pendek* ~ in short, in a word; *singkat* ~ in brief, briefly; *dengan* ~ *lain* in other words; **berkata** *v* to say, speak; **mengatakan** *v* to say; **perkataan** *n* phrase, words; **prakata** *n* foreword, preface

katabélece *n* note asking for a favor

katai *n* pygmy, midget, dwarf

katak *n* frog, toad; *seperti* ~ *di bawah tempurung* narrow-minded (*lit.* like a frog under half a coconut shell)

katalog *n* catalog

katarak *n* cataract (eye disease)

katédral *n* cathedral; ~ *Santa Maria* St Mary's Cathedral

kategori *n* category; **mengategorikan** *vt* to categorize

katimumul *n* corn (on foot)

Katolik Catholic; *agama* ~ Catholicism, the Catholic church; *gereja* ~ Catholic church; *orang* ~ Catholic

katrol *n* pulley

katulistiwa, khatulistiwa *n* the Equator

katun *n* cotton; *kain* ~ cotton fabric or cloth

katup *n* valve

kau *pron, s* you (to equals or inferiors) ← **engkau**

kaum *n* people, community; ~ *berdasi* white-collar workers; ~ *buruh* laborers; ~ *intelektual* intellectuals; ~ *kolot* conservatives; ~ *papa* the destitute, the poor; ~ *wanita* women

kaus, kaos *n* stocking, sock; garment; ~ *kaki* sock; stocking; ~ *oblong* T-shirt; ~ *tangan* glove, mitten

kav, kavling, kaveling → **kapling**

kawah *n* crater

kawakan *adj* veteran, experienced; *wartawan* ~ veteran journalist

kawal guard; **kawalan** *n* escort, guard; **mengawal** *vt* to guard, escort; **pengawal** *n* (body)guard, sentry

kawan *n* friend; ~ *baik* good friend; *setia* ~ loyal friend; **kesetiakawanan** *n* loyalty; **kawanan** *n* flock, swarm; **berkawan** *vi* to have or be friends with; ~ *dengan tetangga* to be friends with your neighbor; **sekawan** *tiga* ~ a trio (of friends)

kawanua *n* fellow Menadonese

kawas: kawasan *n* area, region; ~ *Asia-Pasifik* Asia-Pacific region

kawat *n* wire; ~ *berduri* barbed wire; ~ *listrik* electrical wire

kawi *bahasa* ~ Old Javanese

kawin *v* marry; have sex, mate; ~ *gantung* to marry but still live in separate houses, unconsummated (usu of children); ~ *kontrak* (of foreign workers) to marry a local woman for their period of employment in Indonesia; ~ *lari* elope; ~ *masal* mass wedding; ~ *muda* marry young; ~ *silang* cross-breed; ~ *siri* marry in secret; ~ *suntik* artificial insemination; *belum* ~ single, unmarried; *emas* ~, *mas* ~ dowry; *musim* ~ on heat; *sudah* ~ married; *tidak* ~ unmarried (for life); ~ *dengan teman lama* marry an old friend; *sudah* ~ *belum nikah* have sex before marriage; **kawinan** *n, coll* wedding ceremony or reception; **mengawini** *vt* to marry someone; **mengawinkan** *vt* to marry someone off; ~ *anak* to marry off a son or daughter; **perkawinan** *n* marriage, wedding; ~ *campuran* mixed marriage

kawula ~ *muda* youth, young people

kaya *adj* rich; ~ *raya* very rich; *orang* ~ *baru* new money, nouveau riche; **kekayaan** *n* wealth, riches; *pajak* ~ property tax; **pengayaan** *n* enrichment; ~ *uranium* uranium enrichment

kayak, kaya *conj, coll* like, as; **kayaknya** it seems, apparently

kayau: mengayau *vt* to hunt heads; **pengayau** *n* head-hunter

kayu *n* wood; ~ *bakar* firewood; ~ *cendana* sandalwood; ~ *gaharu* aloe wood, eaglewood; ~ *gelondongan* log; ~ *jati* teak; ~ *mahoni* mahogany; ~ *manis* cinnamon; ~ *meranti* kind of reddish wood, morantee; ~ *putih* eucalyptus; ~ *ulin* very hard wood; *kulit* ~ bark; *mata* ~ knot; *tukang* ~ carpenter

kayuh, berkayuh *vi* paddle, row; pedal; **mengayuh** *vt* to paddle or pedal something; ~ *sepeda* to ride a bicycle

Kazakhstan *n* Kazakhstan; *bahasa* ~, *orang* ~ Kazakh

KB *abbrev kelompok bermain* playgroup

KB *abbrev Keluarga Berencana* Family Planning; *alat* ~ contraceptive device

KBK *abbrev Kurikulum Berdasarkan Kompetensi* competency-based curriculum

KBRI *abbrev Kedutaan Besar Republik Indonesia* Embassy of the Republic of Indonesia

KDRT *abbrev Kekerasan Dalam Rumah Tangga* domestic violence

ke *prep* to, towards; ~ *atas* up, upwards; ~ *dalam* into; ~ *luar* out; ~ *mana* where; ~ *muka* to the front or top; forward; ~ *sana* in that direction; over there; ~ *sini* in this direction; over here; ~ *tengah* to the middle; ~ *mana saja* wherever; ~ *sana kemari* here and there; ~ *depan* to the front, forward; **mengedepankan** *vt* to put forward, propose; ~ *ke samping* to the side; **mengesampingkan** *vt* to put to one side

keabsahan *n* legality, legitimacy, validity ← **absah**

keadaan *n* situation, condition; ~ *darurat* emergency situation ← **ada**

keadilan *n* justice; ~ *sosial* social justice ← **adil**

keagamaan *adj* religious affairs ← **agama**

keagungan *n* greatness, majesty ← **agung**

keahlian *n* expertise ← **ahli**

keaiban *n* shame, disgrace, humiliation ← **aib**

keajaiban *n* wonder, miracle; *Tujuh ~ Dunia* the Seven Wonders of the World ← **ajaib**

kealahan *n* defeat, loss ← **alah**

keakraban *n* closeness, intimacy ← **akrab**

keamanan *n* safety, security; *Dewan ~* (UN) Security Council ← **aman**

keanéhan *n* peculiarity, oddity ← **anéh**

keanékaragaman *n* diversity; *~ hayati* biological diversity ← **anéka ragam**

keanggotaan *n* membership; *kartu ~* membership card ← **anggota**

keanggunan *n* grace, style ← **anggun**

keangkuhan *n* arrogance, rudeness ← **angkuh**

kearifan *n* wisdom, learning ← **arif**

kearsipan archives, archival ← **arsip**

keaslian *n* authenticity ← **asli**

keasrian *n* (natural) beauty ← **asri**

kebagian *v* to get a share ← **bagi**

kebahagiaan *n* happiness ← **bahagia**

kebahasaan *adj* language, linguistic ← **bahasa**

kebaikan *n* goodness, kindness ← **baik**

kebakaran *n* fire; *~ hutan* forest fire, bushfire; *~ jenggot* to lose your head, be unable to cope; *ada ~!* fire! ← **bakar**

kebaktian *n* (Protestant) service ← **bakti**

kebal *adj* resistant, immune; *~ hukum* legal immunity; **kekebalan** *n* immunity; *~ diplomatik* diplomatic immunity

kebangetan *adj, coll* too much, excessive (of behavior or a situation) ← **banget**

kebanggaan *n* pride; something of which you are proud ← **bangga**

kebangkitan *n* rise, awakening; *Partai ~ Bangsa (PKB)* Party of National Awakening ← **bangkit**

kebangkrutan *n* bankruptcy ← **bangkrut**

kebangsaan *adj* national; *lagu ~* national anthem ← **bangsa**

kebanjiran *adj* flooded, inundated ← **banjir**

kebanyakan *n, adj* too much; most; *~ orang tidak setuju* most people don't agree ← **banyak**

kebapakan *adj* fatherly ← **bapak**

kebarat-baratan *adj* Westernized ← **barat**

kebas *adj* numb; without feeling, pins and needles (of a limb); *kakinya sudah ~ setelah duduk lama* his legs had gone numb after sitting so long

kebatinan *n* mysticism ← **batin**

kebaya *n, f* women's blouse worn as national costume; *~ encim* Chinese-style traditional blouse; *~ Kartini* in the style as worn by female emancipist Kartini; *kain ~* national dress for women

kebébasan *n* freedom ← **bébas**

kebelet *adj, coll* busting, desperate to go to the toilet ← **belet**

kebenaran *n* truth; *Komisi ~ dan Rekonsiliasi* Truth and Reconciliation Commission ← **benar**

kebencian *n* hatred ← **benci**

kebengisan *n* cruelty, harshness ← **bengis**

keberadaan *n* presence ← **berada, ada**

keberangkatan *n* departure; *pintu ~* departure gate ← **berangkat, angkat**

keberanian *n* bravery, courage ← **berani**

keberapa *interrog, coll* which number? which one? ← **berapa, apa**

keberatan *n* objection; *v* to object ← **berat**

keberhasilan *n* success ← **berhasil, hasil**

kebersamaan *n* sense of togetherness, solidarity ← **bersama, sama**

kebersihan *n* cleanliness, hygiene ← **bersih**

keberuntungan *n* good fortune or luck ← **beruntung, untung**

kebesaran *adj* greatness; *adj* too big; *celana ini ~!* these pants are too big! ← **besar**

kebetulan *adv* by chance, accidentally; *n* coincidence ← **betul**

kebiadaban *n* savagery ← **biadab**

kebiasaan *n* habit, custom ← **biasa**

kebidanan *n* midwifery ← **bidan**

kebijakan *n* policy ← **bijak**

kebijaksanaan *n* caution, prudence; policy ← **bijaksana**

kebingungan *n* confusion ← **bingung**

kebiri *adj* castrated, neutered; *kuda* ~ gelding; **mengebiri** *vt* to castrate, neuter

kebiru-biruan *adj* bluish ← **biru**

kebisingan *n* noise, buzz ← **bising**

kebisuan *n* silence, lack of speech ← **bisu**

kebo *kumpul* ~ to live together without being married

kebocoran *n* leak ← **bocor**

kebodohan *n* stupidity, ignorance ← **bodoh**

kebohongan *n* lie, deceit ← **bohong**

keboléhan *n* ability, what you can do ← **boléh**

kebotakan *n* baldness, hair loss ← **botak**

kebrutalan *n* brutality, violence ← **brutal**

kebuasan *n* ferocity ← **buas**

kebudayaan *n* culture, civilization ← **budaya**

kebugaran *n* health; *pusat* ~ gym, fitness center ← **bugar**

kebuli *nasi* ~ lamb and rice dish of Middle Eastern origin

kebun, kebon *n* garden, plantation; ~ *apel* orchard; ~ *binatang* zoo; ~ *karet* rubber plantation; ~ *kopi* coffee plantation; ~ *raya* botanical garden; *tukang* ~ gardener; **berkebun** *vi* to garden, do gardening; **perkebunan** *n* plantation, estate; ~ *teh* tea plantation

keburu *adj, adv, coll* in time; too early; had already; ~ *habis* already run out ← **buru**

kebut *tukang* ~ speed merchant, speedster; **kebut-kebutan** *n* drag-racing; **mengebut** *vi* **ngebut** *coll* to speed; **pengebut** *n* speedster

kebutuhan *n* need, necessity ← **butuh**

Kec., kecamatan *n* sub-district ← **camat**

kécak *tari* ~ a Balinese dance, monkey dance

kecakapan *n* ability ← **cakap**

kecam: mengecam *vt* to criticize; **kecaman** *n* criticism

kecamatan, Kec. *n* sub-district ←

camat

kecambah *n* shoot, sprout; **berkecambah** *vi* to sprout

kecamuk *n* rage, frenzy; **berkecamuk** *vi* to rage

kecanduan *n* addiction; *adj* addicted to; ~ *obat* drug addiction ← **candu**

kecanggihan *n* sophistication ← **canggih**

kecanggungan *n* clumsiness, awkwardness ← **canggung**

kecantikan *n* beauty; *ratu* ~ beauty queen ← **cantik**

kecantol *coll* to be or get hooked ← **cantol**

kecap sound of smacking lips; **mengecap** *vt* to taste

kécap *n* soy sauce; ~ *asin* soy sauce; ~ *manis* sweet soy sauce

kecapékan *adj* tired out; *n* exhaustion ← **capék**

kecapi *n* Sundanese zither; ~ *suling* flute and zither, instruments in traditional Sundanese music

kécé *adj, coll* good-looking; *banyak cewek* ~ *yang mejeng di mal* lots of pretty girls hang out at the mall

kecébong *n* tadpole

kecebur *adj, coll* fallen into water ← **cebur**

kecelakaan *n* accident, disaster; ~ *pesawat* plane crash ← **celaka**

kecemasan *n* anxiety, concern ← **cemas**

kecemburuan *n* jealousy ← **cemburu**

kecemerlangan *n* genius, brilliance ← **cemerlang**

kecemplung *adj, sl* fallen into water ← **cemplung**

kecenderungan *n* tendency, trend ← **cenderung**

kécéng: ngécéng *vi* to have your eye on someone; *Rizka sudah lama* ~ *dia* Rizka had had her eye on him for some time

kecepatan *n* speed ← **cepat**

keceplosan *n* directness ← **ceplos**

kecerdasan *n* intelligence ← **cerdas**

kecerdikan *n* intelligence; shrewdness ← **cerdik**

keceréwétan *n* fussiness ← **ceréwét**

keceriaan *n* happiness, good mood ← ceria

kecermatan *n* precision, accuracy ← cermat

kecerobohan *n* carelessness ← ceroboh

kecéwa *adj* disappointed; ~ berat bitterly disappointed; kekecéwaan *n* disappointment; mengecéwakan *vt* to disappoint; *adj* disappointing

kecil *adj* small, little; young; ~ hati disappointed; timid; offended; ~ molek delicate; dari ~, sejak ~ since youth; nama ~ everyday name; orang ~ the little people, the poor; berkecil ~ hati *vi* to be disappointed; kekecilan *adj* too small; memperkecil *vt* to reduce something, make even smaller; foto diperkecil supaya bisa dibingkai the photo was reduced so it could be framed; mengecil *vi* to shrink, become smaller; mengecilkan *vt* to make smaller, decrease; sekecil *adj* as small as; masa hal ~ itu menjadi masalah! how come such a small thing is such a big problem?

kecintaan *n* love (for something) ← cinta

kecipratan *adj* be splashed, sprayed accidentally ← ciprat

kecoa *n* cockroach

kecocokan *n* suitability, compatibility ← cocok

kecoklatan *adj* brownish ← coklat

kecolongan *adj* to be robbed; to lose unjustly ← colong

kecopétan *adj* to be pickpocketed, robbed; *n* pickpocketing ← copét

kecrék, kecrékan *n* bottle-top rattle shaken by beggars

kecuali *conj* except; kekecualian, pengecualian *n* exception; mengecualikan *vt* to except; terkecuali tidak ~, tanpa ~ without exception

kecubung batu ~ ruby

kecup sound of a kiss; kecupan *n* peck; mengecup *vt* to kiss lightly, peck

kecurangan *n* cheating, dishonesty ← curang

kecurian *adj* to be robbed, burgled ← curi

kecurigaan *n* suspicion ← curiga

kecut *adj* sour, acidic

kecut *adj* shrivelled; hati ~ afraid; pengecut *n* coward

kedahsyatan *n* power ← dahsyat

kedai *n* stall, kiosk; ~ kopi small coffee shop

kedalaman *n* depth ← dalam

kedaluwarsa, kadaluwarsa *adj* expired; tanggal ~ expiry date, use-by date (food) ← daluwarsa

kedamaian *n* peace → damai

kedangkalan *n* shallows, (low) depth; ~ laut sea depth ← dangkal

kedap *adj* free from; ~ air waterproof; ~ cahaya light-proof; ~ suara soundproof; ~ udara air-tight

kedapatan *adj* to be caught in the act ← dapat

kedatangan *n* arrival ← datang

kedaulatan *n* sovereignty; Partai ~ Rakyat (PKR) People's Sovereignty Party ← daulat

kedaung *n* large tree with round seeds

kedébet *sl* to be wrongly debited (of a bank card) ← débet

kedekatan *n* close relationship ← dekat

kedelai, kedelé soy; kacang ~ soya bean, soybean; susu (kacang) ~ soya milk, soymilk

kedelapan *adj* eighth ← delapan

keden: ngeden *vi, coll* to push, strain (when giving birth or passing feces)

kedengaran *adj* audible ← dengar

kedengkian *n* spite ← dengki

kéder *adj, coll* scared; confused; ~ sih kalau lewat kuburan pada malam hari I'm scared to go past the cemetery at night

kedéwasaan *n* maturity ← déwasa

kediaman *n* residence ← diam

kedigdayaan *n* power, invulnerability ← digdaya

kedinginan cold; feeling cold ← dingin

kedip blink; wink; berkedip *vi* to blink (two eyes) or wink (one eye); berkedip-kedip *adj* blinking; mengedipkan *vt* ~ mata to blink

kedodoran *n* scruffy; too big, ill-fitting ← dodor

kedok *n* mask; guise; **berkedok** *vi* to hide behind a mask, to pretend; *banyak SMS yang ~ berasal dari bank* many text messages pretending to be from a bank

kedokteran *adj* medical; *fakultas ~* School of Medicine ← **dokter**

kedondong *buah ~* kind of fruit

kedongkolan *n* annoyance, resentment ← **dongkol**

kedua *adj* second; **keduanya, kedua-duanya** *adj* both ← **dua**

kedubes *n* embassy; *~ Amerika* the American embassy ← **kedutaan besar**

kedudukan *n* position ← **duduk**

kedukaan *n* grief, sorrow ← **duka**

kedutaan *n ~ (besar)* embassy ← **duta**

keélokan *n* beauty ← **élok**

keempat *adj* fourth; **keempatnya, keempat-empatnya** *adj, n* all four of them ← **empat**

keénakan *adj* too enjoyable or good ← **énak**

keenam *adj* sixth; *indera ~* sixth sense; **keenamnya, keenam-enamnya** *adj, n* all six of them ← **enam**

keengganan *n* reluctance ← **enggan**

keesaan *n* oneness; *~ Tuhan* the oneness of God ← **esa**

keésokan *~ harinya* the next day ← **ésok, bésok**

kefasihan *n* ease, eloquence ← **fasih**

kegadisan *n* virginity ← **gadis**

kegaduhan *n* noise, uproar ← **gaduh**

kegagalan *n* failure ← **gagal**

keganasan *n* ferocity ← **ganas**

kegandrungan *adj, sl* to be absorbed or swept up in, madly in love ← **gandrung**

keganjilan *n* oddity, peculiarity ← **ganjil**

kegelapan *n* darkness ← **gelap**

kegelisahan *n* anxiety, nerves ← **gelisah**

kegemaran *n* hobby ← **gemar**

kegembiraan *n* joy, happiness ← **gembira**

kegemukan *n* fatness; *adj* overweight ← **gemuk**

kegesitan *n* agility, adroitness ← **gesit**

kegiatan *n* activity ← **giat**

kegigihan *n* perseverance, tenacity ← **gigih**

kegilaan *n* craze ← **gila**

kegirangan *n* gladness, happiness ← **girang**

kegugupan *n* nervousness, panic ← **gugup**

keguguran *vi* to miscarry; *n* miscarriage ← **gugur**

kegunaan *n* usefulness, use ← **guna**

kegusaran *n* annoyance, anger ← **gusar**

kehabisan *v* to run out of (water, food, stock) ← **habis**

kehadiran *n* presence, attendance ← **hadir**

kehakiman *Departemen ~ (Depkeh)* Department of Justice ← **hakim**

kehalusan *n* delicacy, grace ← **halus**

kehamilan *n* pregnancy ← **hamil**

kehancuran *n* destruction, ruin ← **hancur**

kehandalan *n* reliability ← **handal, andal**

kehangatan *n* warmth, friendliness ← **hangat**

keharuman *n* fragrance ← **harum**

keharusan *n* obligation, necessity, requirement ← **harus**

kehausan to be thirsty; thirst ← **haus**

kehébatan *n* force ← **hébat**

kehébohan *n* sensation, phenomenon ← **héboh**

kehendak *n* will, wish; *~ rakyat* will of the people; **berkehendak** *vi* to have the intent; **mengehendaki** *vt* to wish, want ← **hendak**

keheningan *n* peace, quiet; clarity ← **hening**

kehéranan *n* astonishment, amazement, wonder ← **héran**

kehidupan *n* life, existence ← **hidup**

kehijau-hijauan *adj* greenish ← **hijau**

kehilangan (feeling of) loss; *~ 20 juta rupiah* to lose 20 million rupiah ← **hilang**

kehitam-hitaman *adj* blackish ← **hitam**

kehormatan *n* respect; *anggota ~* honorary member ← **hormat**

kehujanan *adj* caught in the rain ← **hujan**

kehutanan *n* forestry ← **hutan**

keibuan, keibu-ibuan *adj* motherly ← **ibu**

keikhlasan *n* sincerity ← **ikhlas**

keikutsertaan *n* participation ← **ikut serta**

keilmuan *adj* scientific ← **ilmu**

keindahan *n* beauty ← **indah**

keindonésiaan *n* sense of being Indonesian ← **Indonésia**

keinggris-inggrisan *adj* affecting a use of English or anglicisms; anglicized ← **Inggris**

keinginan *n* desire, wish; **berkeinginan** *vi* to have a desire or wish ← **ingin**

keingintahuan *n* curiosity; hunger for knowledge ← **ingin tahu**

keistiméwaan *n* special quality ← **istiméwa**

kejadian *n* event, happening; creation ← **jadi**

kejahatan *n* crime ← **jahat**

kejaksaan *n* district attorney's office ← **jaksa**

kejam *adj* cruel, merciless; **kekejaman** *n* cruelty

kejam: mengejamkan *vt* ~ *mata* to close your eyes

kejang *adj* stiff; **berkejang** *vi* to have a cramp; **mengejang** *vi* to cramp, seize up

kejanggalan *n* oddity, anomaly ← **janggal**

kejantanan *n* masculinity ← **jantan**

kejap: mengejapkan *vt* ~ *mata* to blink your eyes; **sekejap** *n* moment, flash, blink; *dalam* ~ *mata* in a moment, in the twinkling of an eye

kejar *vt* chase; ~ *tayang* continuous shooting (of a TV series); **kejar-kejaran** *vt* chase each other; **mengejar** *vt* to chase; ~ *waktu* to race against the clock

Kejati *abbrev Kejaksaan Tinggi* regional Attorney-General's office

kejatuhan *n* fall; *adj* be struck by something falling ← **jatuh**

kejauhan *adj* too far ← **jauh**

kejawén *n* Javanese traditional mysticism

kejayaan *n* victory, glory ← **jaya**

kejeduk *vi, coll* to bump your head

kejelasan *n* clarity ← **jelas**

kejelékan *n* badness, ugliness ← **jelék**

kejéngkélan *n* annoyance, bad mood ← **jéngkél**

kejenuhan *n* saturation; boredom ← **jenuh**

keji *adj* low, mean, despicable; **kekejian** *n* meanness

kejiwaan *adj* mental ← **jiwa**

kejora *bintang* ~ morning star (symbol of West Papuan independence movement), Venus

kéju *n* cheese

kejuaraan *n* championship ← **juara**

kejujuran *n* honesty ← **jujur**

kejurnas *n* national championship → **kejuaraan nasional**

kejuruan *adj* technical; *sekolah* ~ technical or trade school ← **juru**

kejut *adj* surprised, startled; **kejutan** *n* surprise; *bikin* ~ to (make a) surprise; **mengejutkan** *adj* surprising, startling; *vt* to surprise or startle; **terkejut** *adj* surprised

kék *pron, sl* Pa, Pop, Granddad ← **kakék**

kék whether it's this, or that; *sate* ~, *soto* ~, *saya mau* whether it's satay or soup, I'll have some

kekacauan *n* chaos ← **kacau**

kekaguman *n* admiration ← **kagum**

kékah *coll, Isl* thanksgiving held after the birth of a child, usu through cutting the child's hair and slaughtering a goat ← **akikah, akékah**

kekaisaran *n* empire; ~ *Roma* the Roman Empire ← **kaisar**

kekal *adj* everlasting, eternal; **kekekalan** *n* eternity

kekalahan *n* defeat, loss ← **kalah**

kekanak-kanakan *adj* childish, infantile ← **kanak-kanak**

kekang *n* bridle; *tali* ~ rein; **mengekang** *vt* to bridle, pull in the reins, curb; *pemerintah sering* ~ *kebebasan aktivis* governments often limit the freedom of activists; **terkekang** *adj* held in, curbed, not free

kekar *adj* solid, strong

kekasaran *n* coarseness, roughness ← **kasar**

kekasih *n* sweetheart, beloved, darling; ~ *gelap* secret love ← **kasih**

kekayaan *n* wealth, riches; *pajak ~* property tax ← **kaya**

kekecéwaan *n* disappointment ← **kecéwa**

kekecilan *adj* too small ← **kecil**

kekecualian *n* exception ← **kecuali**

kékéh: terkékéh-kékéh *vt* to laugh

kekejaman *n* cruelty ← **kejam**

kekejian *n* meanness ← **keji**

kekekalan *n* eternity ← **kekal**

kekeliruan *n* mistake, error ← **keliru**

kekeluargaan *adj* family, relating to family matters ← **keluarga**

kekentalan *n* thickness, viscosity ← **kental**

kekenyalan *n* elasticity ← **kenyal**

kekenyangan *adj* having eaten too much ← **kenyang**

kéker *n* binoculars, field glasses

kekerabatan *n* kinship ← **kerabat**

kekerasan *n* violence; *~ dalam rumah tangga (KDRT)*, *~ domestik* domestic violence; *~ terhadap perempuan* violence against women ← **keras**

kekeringan *n* dryness, aridity ← **kering**

kekesalan *n* annoyance, bad mood ← **kesal**

kekhasan *n* special feature ← **khas**

kekisruhan *n* confusion, chaos ← **kisruh**

kekompakan *n* solidarity ← **kompak**

kekosongan *n* emptiness ← **kosong**

kekuasaan *n* power; authority ← **kuasa**

kekuatan *n* strength, power ← **kuat**

kekuatiran *n* worry, fear ← **kuatir**

kekurangan *n* shortcoming (of a person), lack; flaw, mistake, defect ← **kurang**

kekurusan *adj* too thin ← **kurus**

Kel., kelurahan *n* administrative unit, village ← **lurah**

kel. *keluarga* family

kelab, klab *n* club; *~ malam* nightclub

kelabakan *vi* to be at a loss, flounder ← **labak**

kelabu *adj* gray, cloudy; **mengelabui** *vt* to trick, pull the wool over someone's eyes ← **abu**

keladi *biang ~* cause, ringleader, mastermind; *tua-tua ~* the older, the more

kelahi: berkelahi *vi* to quarrel, fight, fall out; **perkelahian** *n* fight, scuffle

kelahiran *n* birth; *adj* born; anniversary; *~ pradini* premature birth; *~ Semarang* born in Semarang; *hari ~* birthday ← **lahir**

kelainan *n* abnormality ← **lain**

kelak later, in the future

kelakar *n* joke; **berkelakar** *vi* to joke

kelakuan *n* act, behavior ← **laku**

kelalaian *n* forgetfulness, negligence ← **lalai**

kelalawar → **kelelawar**

kelam *adj* dark, dull

kelamaan *adj* too long (a time) ← **lama**

kelambanan *n* lack of action, inertia ← **lamban**

kelambu *n* mosquito net

kelamin *alat ~* sex organs, genitalia; *jenis ~* gender, sex; *penyakit ~* venereal disease, sexually transmitted disease (STD)

kelana: berkelana *vi* to roam, wander

kelancangan *n* impudence, presumptiousness ← **lancang**

kelancaran *n* smoothness, good progress, fluency ← **lancar**

kelanggengan *n* eternity ← **langgeng**

kelanjutan *n* continuation, result ← **lanjut**

kelapa *n* coconut; *~ muda* young coconut; *~ sawit* oil-palm; *air ~* coconut milk; *minyak ~* coconut oil; *pohon ~* coconut palm; *sabut ~* coconut fiber

kelaparan *n* hunger, famine, starvation; *adj* very hungry ← **lapar**

kelar *adj, coll* finished, ready

kelas *n* class; classroom; *~ kakap* bigtime; *~ kambing* cheapest class of seat; *~ menengah* middle-class; *~ satu SD* grade 1 at primary or elementary school; **berkelas** *adj* classy; *vi* to have class

kelasi *n* sailor

kelautan *adj* maritime; *Departemen Perikanan dan ~* Department of Fisheries and Marine Affairs ← **laut**

kelayakan *n* suitability; *studi ~* feasibility study ← **layak**

kelebihan *n* extra, excess ← **lebih**

keledai *n* donkey

kelelahan *n* fatigue, weariness ← **lelah**

kelelap *adj* submerged, sunken into water

kelelawar, kelalawar *n* bat

kelelep *adj, coll* sunk, submerged ← **lelep**

keleluasaan *n* freedom (of choice) ← **leluasa**

kelemahan *n* weakness ← **lemah**

kelembaban *n* humidity ← **lembab**

kelembaman *n* inertia ← **lembam**

kelembutan *n* softness ← **lembut**

kelénéng *n* (sound of) bell

kelengahan *n* carelessness ← **lengah**

keléngkéng *n buah* ~ small lychee ← **léngkéng**

kelenjar *n* gland; ~ *getah bening* lymph gland; ~ *gondok* thyroid gland; ~ *prostat* prostate

kelénténg, klénténg *n* Chinese or Confucian temple, pagoda

kelentit *n* clitoris

kelép → **klép**

keléréng *n* marble; *main* ~ to play marbles

kelestarian *n* preservation, conservation ← **lestari**

keléwat *adv, sl* too, unacceptably; **kelewatan** *n* too much ← **léwat**

kelezatan *n* delicious taste ← **lezat**

keliar: berkeliaran *vi* to swarm or wander about

kelicikan *n* trickery, cunning ← **licik**

kelihaian *n* shrewdness, cunning ← **lihai**

kelihatan *adj* visible; ~*nya* apparently, it seems ← **lihat**

keliling around; edge, perimeter, circumference; ~ *dunia* go around the world; *duta* ~ roving ambassador; **berkeliling** *vi* to go around; **mengelilingi** *vt* to circle, go around; **sekeliling** *adj* around, surrounding

kelim *n* seam, hem

kelima *adj* fifth ← **lima**

kelimpahan *n* abundance, wealth ← **limpah**

kelincahan *n* agility ← **lincah**

kelinci *n* rabbit; ~ *percobaan* guinea-pig; *sate* ~ rabbit satay

Keling *n, derog (orang)* ~ southern Indian

kelingking *n* little or baby finger

kelip: berkelip *vi* to twinkle, flicker

kelipatan *n* multiple ← **lipat**

keliru *adj* wrong, mistaken; **kekeliruan** *n* mistake, error

kelit: berkelit *vi* to get out of, avoid

kélok *n* bend, curve; ~ *empat puluh empat* forty-four bends (on the descent to Lake Maninjau)

kelola: mengelola *vt* to manage, run; **pengelola** *n* manager; **pengelolaan** *n* management

kelom, klompen *n* clogs; *kelom geulis* clogs made near Tasikmalaya, West Java

kelompok *n* group, category; ~ *bermain (KB)* playgroup; ~ *kerja* working group; **berkelompok** *adj* in groups, group; **mengelompokkan** *vt* to group

kelon *Jav minta* ~ to ask an adult to lie down with you (of a small child); **mengeloni** *vt* to lie down with (a small child)

kelonggaran *n* facility, dispensation ← **longgar**

kelontong *barang* ~ odds and ends, small wares; *pedagang* ~ pedlar, hawker; *toko* ~ shop selling cheap goods

kelop → **klop**

kelopak *n* lid, sheath; ~ *mata* eyelid

kelu *adj* speechless, dumb

keluak, keluwak, kluwek *n* kind of tree, the seed of which is used for making *rawon* soup

keluar *vi* go out; be issued; *prep* out, outside; *n* exit; **keluaran** *n* issue, edition, version; *majalah ini* ~ *Singapura* this magazine is a Singapore edition; **Keluaran** *n, Chr* Exodus; **mengeluarkan** *vt* to issue, send out, release, publish; *Hendro dikeluarkan dari lapangan setelah pelanggarannya* Hendro was sent off the field after his misdemeanor; **pengeluaran** *n* expenditure ← **ke luar**

keluarga *n* family; ~ *berencana (KB)* state family planning program; ~ *besar* community, extended family; ~ *inti* nuclear family; *anggota* ~ family members; *kartu* ~ *(KK)* family ID card;

kepala ~ head of the family; *tunjangan* ~ family allowance; **berkeluarga** *vi* to have a family, be married; **kekeluargaan** *adj* family, relating to family matters; **sekeluarga** *adj* and family; *Anton* ~ Anton and family

kelucuan *n* cuteness ← **lucu**

keluh sigh; ~ *kesah* complaint; **keluhan** *n* complaint; **berkeluh, mengeluh** *v* to complain

kelugasan *n* simplicity; directness; objectivity ← **lugas**

keluguan *n* naivety, simplicity ← **lugu**

kelumit: sekelumit *adj* a very small amount, a bit, a little

kelupaan *n* something forgotten ← **lupa**

kelupas, mengelupas *vt* to peel, come off (of a skin)

kelurahan, Kel. *n* administrative unit, village ← **lurah**

keluwesan *n* attractiveness, style ← **luwes**

keluyur: berkeluyuran *vi* to hang around; *banyak preman* ~ *dekat setasiun* lots of thugs hang around the station

kemacetan *n* jam; ~ *lalu lintas* traffic jam ← **macet**

kémah *n* tent; **berkémah** *vi* to camp, go camping; **perkémahan** *n* camping, camp; *tempat* ~ camping ground, campsite

kemahalan *adj* too expensive ← **mahal**

kemahiran *n* skill ← **mahir**

kemajuan *n* progress, advance ← **maju**

kemakmuran *n* prosperity ← **makmur**

kemaksiatan *n* immorality, vice ← **maksiat**

kemalaman *adv* too late (at night); after dark ← **malam**

kemalangan *n* bad luck, misfortune ← **malang**

kemalasan *n* laziness ← **malas**

kemalingan *v* to be robbed ← **maling**

kemaluan *n* genital, sex organ ← **malu**

kemampuan *n* ability, capability ← **mampu**

kemandulan *n* infertility ← **mandul**

kemangi *n* Indonesian mint

kemanisan *adj* too sweet ← **manis**

kemantapan *n* stability ← **mantap**

kemanusiaan *n* humanity; **perikemanusiaan** *adj* humanitarian ← **manusia**

kemarahan *n* anger ← **marah**

kemarau *musim* ~ dry season

kemari here, in this direction; *ke sana* ~ here and there

kemarin *adv* yesterday; the other day; last; ~ *dulu* the day before yesterday; *minggu* ~ last week

kemas *peti* ~ freight container; **kemasan** *n* packaging; **berkemas-kemas** *vi* to tidy up, pack; **mengemaskan** *vt* to package

kemasukan *adj* possessed; accidentally got in ← **masuk**

kemasyarakatan *adj* social ← **masyarakat**

kematangan *n* maturity ← **matang**

kematian *n* death, passing ← **mati**

kemauan *n* want, will, desire ← **mau**

kemayu *adj* girlish, effeminate (of boys)

kembali back, return; again; ~ *ke Sang Pencipta, Isl* ~ *ke rahmatullah* pass away; *(terima kasih)* ~ you're welcome; *meninjau* ~ to review; *uang* ~ change; **kembalian** *n* small change; **kembalinya** *n* the return; **mengembalikan** *vt* to give or send back, return; *pihak bank masih belum* ~ *uang saya* the bank still hasn't returned my money; **pengembalian** *n* return, act of returning

kemban *n* cloth wrapped around a woman's chest

kembang *n* flower; ~ *api* fireworks, sparkler; ~ *desa* village beauty; ~ *gula* fairy floss, candy floss; ~ *kol* cauliflower; ~ *sepatu* hibiscus; ~ *tahu* sweet snack of soft tofu in syrup; **berkembang** *vi* to develop, expand; ~ *biak* to breed, grow; *negara* ~ developing nation; **mengembang** *vi* to rise; *tanpa soda, kue tidak bisa* ~ cakes won't rise without baking powder; **mengembangkan** *vt* to develop something; *misi Pusat Bahasa adalah* ~ *Bahasa Indonesia* the mission of the

Language Centre is to develop Indonesian; **mengembang-biakkan** *vt* to propagate, breed; **pengembang** *n* developer; **pengembang-biakan** *n* propagation, breeding; **perkembangan** *n* development

kembar *n* twin; ~ *lima* quintuplets; ~ *tiga* triplets; *saudara* ~ twin; **kembaran** *adj* dressed alike

kembara → **embara**

kembaran *adj* twin, matching ← **kembar**

kembung, gembung *adj* filled with air, inflated; bloated; *perut* ~ bloated belly

kemegahan *n* glory, luxury ← **megah**

keméja *n* Western-style shirt (with collar); ~ *tangan panjang* long-sleeved shirt

kemelaratan *n* poverty ← **melarat**

kemelék-hurufan *n* literacy ← **melék**

kemelut *n* crisis

kemenakan → **keponakan**

kemenangan *n* victory ← **menang**

kementerian *n* ministry, department, office ← **menteri**

kemenyan *n* incense

kemérah-mérahan *adj* reddish ← **mérah**

kemerdékaan *n* freedom, independence, liberty ← **merdéka**

kemerosotan *n* descent, deterioration ← **merosot, rosot**

kemesraan *n* intimacy ← **mesra**

keméwahan *n* luxury ← **méwah**

kemih *kandung* ~ bladder; *saluran* ~ urinary tract

kemilau shiny, sheen

kemiri *n* candle nut

kemiringan *n* slope ← **miring**

Kemis → **Kamis**

kemis, emis: mengemis *v* to beg; **pengemis** *n* beggar

kemiskinan *n* poverty ← **miskin**

kemitraan *n* partnership ← **mitra**

kemocéng, kemucing *n* feather duster

kemolékan *n* beauty ← **molék**

kemontokan *n* plumpness ← **montok**

kémotérapi *n* chemotherapy

kempés, kempis *adj* deflated, flat; hollow; *ban* ~ flat tire; **mengempiskan** *vt* to deflate

Kémpétai *n* Japanese military police (during the occupation)

kémpo *n* (Japanese) martial art

kemudahan *n* ease, facility ← **mudah**

kemudi *n* rudder, steering wheel; **mengemudikan** *vt* to drive, steer; ~ *mobil* to drive a car; **pengemudi** *n* driver

kemudian *conj* then; ~ *hari* in the future, later on

kemuka: mengemukakan *vt* to put forward, advance, nominate; **terkemuka** *adj* prominent ← **ke muka**

kemuliaan *n* honor, glory; ~ *Tuhan* the glory of God ← **mulia**

kemunafikan *n* hypocrisy ← **munafik**

kemunduran *n* deterioration, decline, setback ← **mundur**

kemungkinan *n* possibility; ~ *tipis* slim chance ← **mungkin**

kemuning *n* kind of tree, myrtle

kemurahan *n* cheapness ← **murah**

kemuraman *n* gloom ← **muram**

kemurkaan *n* anger, fury ← **murka**

kemurnian *n* purity ← **murni**

kemut, emut, mengemut *vt* to suck on, chew

kena touch; affected (by); hit; subject to; ~ *batunya* get into trouble; ~ *cekal* be prohibited from leaving the country; ~ *denda* be fined; ~ *musibah* suffer a misfortune, disaster; ~ *rayap* eaten by termites; ~ *semprot coll* be shouted at or told off; ~ *tifus*, ~ *tipus* catch or have typhoid (fever); **berkenaan** *vi* ~ *dengan* in connection with, regarding; **mengena** *vi* to hit the spot, be on target; **mengenai** *conj* about, concerning; **mengenakan** *vt* to put on; ~ *pakaian* to put on clothes, dress

kenaikan *n* rise, raise; ~ *gaji* pay rise; ~ *kelas* promotion to the next grade (at school); end of academic year; ~ *Isa Almasih* Assumption ← **naik**

kenakalan *n* naughtiness ← **nakal**

kenal *vt* to know, be acquainted with; *tak* ~ *lelah* untiring; **kenalan** *n* acquaintance; **mengenal** *vt* to know, be acquainted with, recognize; **mengenali** *vi* to identify; **memperkenal-**

kan *vi* to introduce; **pengenal** *tanda* ~ identity card; **pengenalan** *n* introduction; **perkenalan** *n* introduction; **terkenal** *adj* well-known

kenamaan *adj* famous, well-known ← **nama**

kenan: memperkenankan *vt* to approve, grant, allow; *~ saya mengucapkan terima kasih* allow me to express my gratitude (in formal letters etc)

kenang recall; **kenangan** *n* memories; **kenang-kenangan** *n* souvenir, keepsake; **mengenang** *vt* to commemorate, remember; *100 tahun ~ Bung Karno* 100 years of remembering Sukarno

kenanga *n* kind of flower, ylang-ylang

kenang-kenangan *n* souvenir, keepsake ← **kenang**

kenapa *interrog, coll* why, how come; what did you say?

kenari *burung* ~ canary

kenari *pohon* ~ kind of tree

kencan *n* date; *~ buta* blind date; *teman ~* date; **berkencan** *vi* to go on a date

kencana *adj, lit* gold; *kereta ~* golden chariot

kencang tight, taut; **mengencangkan** *vt* to tighten

kencing urine; urinate; *~ manis* diabetes; *saluran ~* urinary tract; *guru ~ berdiri, murid ~ berlari* students follow their teacher's example to extremes

kencur *bau ~* still young; *beras ~* traditional Javanese drink

kendala *n* obstacle, problem, hindrance

kendali *n* reins; *lepas ~* out of control; *peluru ~ (rudal)* guided missile; **mengendalikan** *vt* to control; **pengendalian** *n* control; *~ mutu* quality control; **terkendali** *adj* controlled

kendang *n* small drum → **gendang**

kendara: kendaraan *n* vehicle; *~ bermotor* motor vehicle; *~ umum* public transport; *~ roda dua* two-wheeled vehicle; **berkendaraan** *vi* to go by (a vehicle, usu car); *~ motor* to go by motorcycle; **mengendarai** *vt* to ride or drive (a vehicle); **pengendara** *n* rider; driver

kendati, kendatipun *conj* although, however

kendi *n* earthen water flask

kéndo *n* Japanese fencing with swords or bamboo sticks

kendur, kendor *adj* slack, loose; **mengendurkan** *vt* to loosen, slacken

kenduri *n* feast, celebration

kenés *adj* showing off, flirtatious

kenegaraan *adj* state (affairs) ← **negara**

kenék, kernét *n* assistant on a bus or truck

kenékatan *n* determination, resolve, recklessness ← **nékat**

kenikmatan *n* pleasure, enjoyment ← **nikmat**

kening *n* forehead, brow; *mengerutkan ~ vt* to frown

kenop *n* knob, button → **tombol**

kénsel → **kansel**

kental *adj* thick, sticky, congealed; *logat ~* thick accent; *susu ~* condensed milk; **kekentalan** *n* thickness, viscosity; **mengental** *vi* to congeal, thicken

kentang *n* potato; *coll* french fries; *~ bakar* baked potato; *~ goreng* (hot) potato chips, french fries; *~ puré* mashed potato; *~ rendang* baby potatoes

kentara *adj* clear, evident, visible

kentut fart, break wind; *gas ~* methane

kenyal *adj* elastic, rubbery; tough (of meat); **kekenyalan** *n* elasticity

kenyam: mengenyam *vt* to taste, experience; *Sungkono hanya sempat ~ pendidikan SD* Sungkono only had an elementary school education

kenyamanan *n* comfort ← **nyaman**

kenyang *adj* full, not hungry; *~ pengalaman* have plenty of experience; **kekenyangan** *adj* having eaten too much

kenyataan *n* fact ← **nyata**

keolahragaan *adj* sports, sporting (affairs) ← **olahraga**

keonaran *n* commotion, disturbance, sensation ← **onar**

kéong *n* snail

Kep. *kepulauan* archipelago, chain of islands; *~ Seribu* the Thousand Islands

kepada *prep* to, for (someone); *~ yang*

tercinta (kpd ytc) dearest; ~ *yang terhormat (kpd yth)* to, for (in letters); to (in addresses)

kepadatan *n* density; ~ *penduduk* population density ← **padat**

kepagian *adj* too early ← **pagi**

kepahitan *n* bitterness ← **pahit**

kepahlawanan *n* heroism ← **pahlawan**

kepailitan *n* bankruptcy ← **pailit**

kepak: **mengepakkan** *vt* ~ *sayap* to flutter wings

kepal fist; **kepalan** *n* fist; **mengepal** *vi* to form a fist; **sekepal** *adj* fistful, handful

kepala *n* head, chief; ~ *bagian (kabag)* head of section; ~ *batu*, *keras* ~ obstinate; ~ *berita* headline; ~ *daerah* regional leader; ~ *desa* village chief, village head; ~ *dingin* cool-headed, calm; ~ *kantor* boss; ~ *keluarga (KK)* head of the family; ~ *negara* head of state; ~ *sekolah* principal, head; ~ *setasiun* stationmaster; ~ *staf* chief of staff; ~ *Staf Angkatan Darat (Kasad)* Army Chief of Staff; ~ *suku* tribal chief; ~ *susu* cream; *sakit* ~, ~ *pusing* headache; **berkepala** *vi* to have a head; **mengepalai** *vt* to be head of

kepandaian *n* ability, intelligence ← **pandai**

kepanduan *n* scouting, Scouts; *n, f* guiding, Guides ← **pandu**

képang plait, weave

kepanjangan *adj* too long ← **panjang**

kepapaan *n* destitution, poverty ← **papa**

keparat *ejac, vulg* damn

kepariwisataan *n* tourist industry ← **pariwisata, wisata**

kepasrahan *n* submission ← **pasrah**

kepastian *n* certainty ← **pasti**

kepatihan *n, arch* area presided over by *patih* ← **patih**

kepatuhan *n* obedience ← **patuh**

kepedasan *adj* too hot or spicy ← **pedas**

kepedihan *n* stinging ← **pedih**

kepedulian *n* concern ← **peduli**

kepegawaian *adj* staff, personnel ← **pegawai**

kepekaan *n* sensitivity ← **peka**

kepekatan *n* thickness, viscosity ← **pekat**

kepelését *adj, coll* slipped, skidded ← **pelését, lését**

kepemilikan *n* ownership → **pemilik, milik**

kepemimpinan *n* leadership (qualities) ← **pemimpin, pimpin**

kepencét *adj, coll* accidentally pressed ← **pencét**

kependékan *n* abbreviation ← **péndék**

képéng *n, arch* round coin with a square hole in it, worth less than a cent

kepéngén, kepingin *v, aux, coll* really want to ← **péngén**

kepengurusan *n* management ← **pengurus, urus**

kepentingan *n* importance, interest; ~ *bersama* common interest; ~ *umum* public or common interest ← **penting**

kepenuhan *adj* too full, overloaded ← **penuh**

kepépét *adj, sl* in a fix, trapped; no time, rushed ← **pépét**

keperawanan *n* virginity ← **perawan**

kepercayaan *n* belief, faith; *menurut* ~ *masing-masing* each according to his/her own religion ← **percaya**

kepergian *n* departure ← **pergi**

kepergok *adj, coll* caught in the act, caught red-handed ← **pergok**

keperluan *n* needs, requirements; ~ *hidup* necessities of life ← **perlu**

kepiawaian *n* skill, expertise ← **piawai**

kepik *n* small bug, pest; ladybug, ladybird

kepikiran *adj* considered, thought of, sprang to mind ← **pikir**

kepincut *adj, coll* enchanted, taken with; attracted or drawn to ← **pincut**

keping *n* piece (counter for flat objects); splinter; ~ *kayu* woodchip; *album itu sudah terjual satu juta* ~ the album has already sold one million copies; **kepingan** *n* fragment, shard

kepingin → **kepéngén**

kepintaran *n* cleverness ← **pintar**

kepiting *n* crab

képlését *adj, coll* slipped, tripped, fell ← **plését**

kepodang, kepudang *burung* ~ oriole

kepolosan *n* simplicity, straight-forwardness, lack of pretension ← **polos**

kepompong *n* cocoon, chrysalis

keponakan, kemenakan *n* niece or nephew; cousin; ~ *laki-laki* nephew; ~ *perempuan* niece; ~ *satu buyut* second cousin

kepongahan *n* arrogance ← **pongah**

Keppres *n* Presidential Decree ← **keputusan Présidén**

kepraktisan *n* practicality ← **praktis**

kepramukaan *adj* scouting ← **pramuka**

keprésidénan *adj* presidential ← **présidén**

Kepri *Kepulauan Riau* Riau Archipelago, a province in Sumatra

kepribadian *n* personality ← **pribadi**

keprihatinan *n* concern ← **prihatin**

keprok *jeruk* ~ mandarin (orange)

kepuasan *n* satisfaction ← **puas**

kepul, kepulan *n* wisp, puff; **berkepul, mengepul** *vi* to smoke, billow

kepulauan *n* archipelago, chain; ~ *Maladewa* the Maldives; ~ *Seribu* the Thousand Islands; **Kepulauan Solomon** *n* the Solomon Islands; *orang dari* ~ Solomon Islander ← **pulau**

kepunahan *n* extinction ← **punah**

kepung, mengepung *vt* to surround, encircle, besiege; **kepungan** *n* encirclement, surrounded area

kepunyaan *n* possession, belonging ← **punya**

kepustakaan *n* bibliography, list of references; literature ← **pustaka**

keputihan *n* thrush, vaginal itching (white discharge) ← **putih**

keputusan *n* decision, decree ← **putus**

kera *n* ape

kerabat *n* relative, family; ~ *kerja* (production) team, crew; **kekerabatan** *n* kinship

keracunan *adj* poisoned; ~ *makanan* food poisoning ← **racun**

keragaman *n* variety ← **ragam**

keraguan, keragu-raguan *n* doubt, uncertainty ← **ragu**

kerah *n* collar; ~ *Cina* Chinese-style collar

kerah: mengerahkan *vt* to mobilize

kerahasiaan *n* secrecy ← **rahasia**

kerajaan *n* kingdom, monarchy; ~ *Inggris* the United Kingdom ← **raja**

kerajinan *n* crafts; ~ *tangan* handicrafts ← **rajin**

kerak *n* crust; ~ *bumi* the Earth's crust; ~ *telor* Betawi snack

kerakusan *n* greed ← **rakus**

kerakyatan *adj* populist; democratic ← **rakyat**

keram cramp

keramahan *n* friendliness ← **ramah**

keramaian *n* noise, din; lively atmosphere ← **ramai**

keramas, berkeramas *vi* to wash your hair

keramat *adj* holy, sacred; *tempat* ~ place sacred to locals; **mengeramatkan** *vt* to consider or make sacred

keramik ceramic, earthenware

keran *n* tap, faucet; *buka* ~ turn on the tap

kerancuan *n* confusion ← **rancu**

keranda *n* structure for carrying a coffin

kerang *n* shell; mollusc; cockle; *kulit* ~ seashell; **kerang-kerangan** *n, pl* shellfish, various types of mollusc

kerangka *n* skeleton, framework

kerangkéng *n* cage, enclosure

kerang-kerangan *n, pl* shellfish, various types of mollusc ← **kerang**

keranjang *n* basket; ~ *sampah* rubbish or garbage bin, trash can; *mata* ~ have a wandering eye

keranjingan *adj* addicted to, fanatic ← **ranjing**

kerap *adv* often; ~ *kali* often, frequently

kerapian *n* neatness, tidiness ← **rapi**

kerapu *n* kind of fish, grouper

kerapuhan *n* fragility, brittle state ← **rapuh**

keras *adj* hard, strong; severe, strict, violent; loud; ~ *kepala* stubborn; *minuman* ~ liquor, alcohol; *membaca dengan suara* ~ to read out loud; **bersikeras** *vi* to maintain, stick to, be obstinate; **kekerasan** *n* violence; ~ *terhadap perempuan* violence against women; ~ *dalam rumah tangga (KDRT)*, ~ *domestik* domestic violence; **mengeras** *vi* to get louder, harder;

mengeraskan *vt* to make something harder, louder; **pengeras** ~ *suara* loudspeaker; **pengerasan** *n* hardening

kerasan *coll* settled, comfortable, feel at home ← **rasa**

kerasukan *adj* possessed ← **rasuk**

kerat: mengerat *vt* to gnaw, nibble, eat away; *binatang* ~ rodent; **pengerat** *binatang* ~ rodent

keraton, kraton *n* Javanese palace; *lingkungan* ~ palace circles

kerawang, karawang *n* filigree embroidery, esp from Menado

kerbau *n* **kebo** *coll* buffalo

kerdil *n* dwarf

kéré *adj, coll* very poor, destitute; *n* beggar, tramp

kérék *n* pulley; **mengérék** *vt* to hoist, pull; ~ *bendera* to raise the flag

kerélaan *n* willingness, readiness ← **réla**

kerén *adj, coll* great, cool; trendy

kerendahan *n* lowness; ~ *hati* humility ← **rendah**

kerenggangan *n* rift, gulf, distance ← **renggang**

kerenyahan *n* crispness, crispiness ← **renyah**

keresahan *n* restlessness, nervous energy ← **resah**

keresak, keresek rustle, sound of rustling leaves

keréta *n* train; carriage; ~ *anak* baby carriage; stroller, pusher; ~ *angin arch* bicycle; ~ *api* train; ~ *(api) barang* ~ goods train; ~ *(api) ekonomi* economy-class train; ~ *(api) ekspres* express train; ~ *gantung* cable car; ~ *kencana* royal (horse-drawn) carriage~ *kuda* horse and carriage; ~ *makan* restaurant car; *gerbong* ~ (train) carriage, car; *naik* ~ go by train

keretakan *n* crack, fissure ← **retak**

keréték, kréték *n (rokok)* ~ clove cigarette

keréwélan *n* fussiness, choosiness ← **réwél**

keributan *n* disturbance; loud noise ← **ribut**

kericuhan *n* chaos ← **ricuh**

kerikil *n* gravel, pebble; small but an-noying problem; *ada* ~ *di sepatu* there's a stone in my shoe

kerikuhan *n* feeling of awkwardness ← **rikuh**

kerimbunan *n* thickness (of foliage) ← **rimbun**

kerincing *n* sound of a small bell or coins, jingling; triangle

kerinduan *n* longing, craving ← **rindu**

kering *adj* dry; ~ *kerontang* bone-dry; **kekeringan** *n* dryness, aridity; **me-ngering** *vi* to become dry; **mengeri-ngkan** *vt* to dry something; ~ *rambut* to dry your hair; **pengering** ~ *rambut* hair dryer

keringanan *n* ease, assistance, relief ← **ringan**

keringat *n* sweat, perspiration; ~ *dingin* cold sweat; *mandi* ~ soaked in sweat; **keringatan** *adj* sweaty, sweating; **berkeringat** *vi* to sweat

keripik, kripik *n* small chip or crisp; ~ *kentang* potato chips; ~ *singkong* cas-sava chips

keriput *n* wrinkle, line; **keriputan, ber-keriput** *adj* wrinkly, lined; *vi* to have wrinkles

keris, kris *n* traditional dagger, creese; *pembuat* ~ creese-maker

kerisauan *n* worry, anxiety ← **risau**

keriting curl, curly; clubs (in cards); **mengeriting** *vt* ~ *rambut* to perm your hair

keriuhan *n* din, clamor ← **riuh**

kerja work; job, occupation; ~ *bakti* community work; ~ *paksa*, ~ *rodi* forced labor; ~ *sama* co-operation; ~ *sambilan*, ~ *sampingan* job on the side, additional job; *kelompok* ~ *(pokja)* working group; *lapangan* ~ employment opportunity; *mencari* ~ to look for work; ~ *paruh waktu* work part-time; **kerjaan** *n* work, job, things to do; **kinerja** *n* performance; **bekerja** *vi* to work; ~ *sama* to co-operate, work together; **mempekerjakan** *vt* to put to work, employ; *perusahaan itu* ~ *1000 karyawan* that company employs 1,000 workers; **mengerjakan** *vt* to do, carry out; ~ *PR* to do your homework; **kerjain** *vt, sl* to trick, take for a ride;

dikerjain *vt, sl* to be tricked, taken for a ride; **pekerja** *n* worker, laborer; **pekerjaan** *n* work, profession; ~ *rumah (PR)* homework

kerling: mengerling *vi* to (steal a) glance, glance sideways

kernét, kenék *n* assistant on a bus or truck

kernyit: mengernyit *vt* ~ *dahi*, ~ *kening* to frown

kerobohan *n* collapse ← **roboh**

kerok traditional treatment for minor illnesses by rubbing the back with a coin; *biang* ~ troublemaker, agitator; **kerokan** *v* to be massaged in this way; **mengerok** *vt* to rub someone's back with a coin

keroncong, kroncong *n* traditional songs and music of Portuguese origin

kerongkongan *n* throat ← **rongkong**

kerontang *kering-*~ bone-dry

kerontokan *n* shedding; ~ *rambut* hair loss ← **rontok**

keropos *adj* eroded, eaten away; ~ *tulang* osteoporosis; **mengeropos** *vi* to be eaten away, eroded; **pengeroposan** *n* (process of) erosion; ~ *tulang* osteoporosis

keroyok, mengeroyok *vt* to beat savagely in a mob; *dikeroyok massa* beaten up by a mob

kérsen *n* cherry

kertas *n* paper; ~ *ampelas*, ~ *pasir* sandpaper; ~ *coret* paper for scribbling on; ~ *kado* wrapping paper; ~ *perak* aluminium foil; ~ *tebal* cardboard; ~ *tulis* writing paper, stationery; *uang* ~ banknotes

keruan, karuan *tidak* ~ very badly, unthinkably

kerubung: mengerubungi *vt* to encircle; *Gubernur dikerubungi para pendemo* the Governor was surrounded by demonstrators

kerucut, cerucut *n* cone

kerudung, kudungan *n, Isl* veil; **berkerudung** *adj* veiled; *vi* to wear a veil; **mengerudungi** *vt* to (cover with a) veil

kerugian *n* loss; damage ← **rugi**

keruh *adj* turbid, cloudy; **mengeruh** *vi* to become cloudy; **mengeruhkan** *vt* to muddy, make cloudy

keruk dredge; *kapal* ~ dredger; **mengeruk** *vt* to dredge, scrape out

kerumitan *n* complication; complexity ← **rumit**

kerumun: berkerumun *vi* to swarm, crowd; **mengerumuni** *vt* to mob, surround, crowd around someone

keruntuhan *n* collapse, fall ← **runtuh**

kerupuk, krupuk *n* large cracker, crisp, chip; ~ *ikan* fish-flavored cracker; ~ *kulit* cracker made from buffalo hide; ~ *udang* prawn cracker

kerusakan *n* damage ← **rusak**

kerusuhan *n* riot, disturbance ← **rusuh**

kerut *n* wrinkle; **berkerut** *vi* to frown; **mengerut** *vi* to shrink, shrivel, contract; **mengerutkan** *vt* ~ *kening* to frown

keruwetan *n* complexity ← **ruwet**

kés *n, coll* cash

kesabaran *n* patience; *batas* ~ limit of your patience ← **sabar**

kesadaran *n* consciousness, awareness ← **sadar**

kesahajaan *n* simplicity ← **sahaja**

kesakitan *adj* in pain ← **sakit**

kesakralan *n* holy or sacred state ← **sakral**

kesaksian *n* evidence, testimony; *memberi* ~ to give evidence, bear witness; *surat* ~ testimonial, recommendation ← **saksi**

kesaktian *n* magic power ← **sakti**

kesal *adj* **kesel** *coll* annoyed, in a bad mood; **kekesalan** *n* annoyance, bad mood

kesalahan *n* mistake ← **salah**

kesampaian *adj* achieved, reached, realized ← **sampai**

kesamping: mengesampingkan *vt* to put to one side, put aside, sideline ← **ke samping**

kesan *n* impression; *memberi* ~ *vt* to give an impression; **berkesan, mengesankan** *adj* impressive; *vi* to give an impression; **terkesan** *adj* impressed; seemed

kesana → **ke sana**

kesandung *adj, coll* to stumble on, trip (up) on ← **sandung**

kesanggupan *n* ability ← **sanggup**

kesasar *coll* to lose your way, (get) lost ← **sasar**

kesatria → **ksatria**

kesatu *adj, sl* first; **kesatuan** *n* unity; ~ *dan persatuan* national unity and integration ← **satu**

kesayangan *adj* favorite; *anak* ~ favorite, pet ← **sayang**

kesebelasan *n* team of eleven, soccer team ← **sebelas, belas**

kesederhanaan *n* simplicity, modesty ← **sederhana**

kesediaan *n* readiness, willingness ← **sedia**

kesedihan *n* sadness, sorrow ← **sedih**

keseganan *n* reluctance, unwillingness ← **segan**

kesegaran *n* freshness ← **segar**

keséhatan *n* health; *dinas* ~ health service ← **séhat**

keseimbangan *n* balance ← **seimbang, imbang**

kesejahteraan *n* welfare ← **sejahtera**

kesejukan *n* coolness ← **sejuk**

kesekian *adj* umpteenth, nth; *untuk* ~ *kali dia tidak hadir* for the umpteenth time, he hasn't shown up ← **sekian, kian**

keseksamaan *n* thoroughness, care ← **seksama**

kesel *coll* **kesal** *adj* annoyed, cheesed off

keselak *vi, coll* to choke ← **selak**

keselamatan *n* safety; salvation; *Bala* ~ Salvation Army ← **selamat**

keselarasan *n* harmony ← **selaras, laras**

keselek, keselak *adj* choking (due to food or drink) ← **selak**

keseléo sprain; sprained; ~ *lidah* (make) a slip of the tongue; *kaki* ~ sprained foot

keseluruhan *secara* ~ totally, completely ← **seluruh**

kesemak, kesemek *n buah* ~ persimmon, soft fruit with sweet orange flesh

kesembuhan *n* recovery ← **sembuh**

kesempatan *n* opportunity; ~ *emas* golden opportunity; ~ *dalam kesempitan* take an opportunity in difficult circumstances ← **sempat**

kesempitan *n* narrowness ← **sempit**

kesempurnaan *n* perfection ← **sempurna**

kesemrawutan *n* chaos → **semrawut**

kesemutan *vi* to have pins and needles ← **semut**

kesenangan *n* amusement, hobby ← **senang**

kesendirian *n* solitude ← **sendiri, diri**

kesengajaan *n* deliberate or intentional act ← **sengaja**

kesengsaraan *n* torture, misery, suffering → **sengsara**

kesengsem *adj, coll* engrossed in, absorbed with ← **sengsem**

kesenian *n* art (form); ~ *tradisional* traditional art form ← **seni**

kesenjangan *n* gap, divide; ~ *sosial* social imbalance, social divide ← **senjang**

kesenyapan *n* silence ← **senyap**

kesepakatan *n* agreement ← **sepakat, pakat**

kesepian *n* loneliness, solitude ← **sepi**

keserakahan *n* greed, avarice ← **serakah**

keserasian *n* compatibility, suitability ← **serasi, rasi**

keseringan *n* frequency; *adv* too often ← **sering**

kesériusan *n* solemnity, seriousness ← **sérius**

kését *n* door mat

kesetiaan *n* allegiance, faithfulness ← **setia**

kesetiakawanan *n* solidarity ← **setia kawan**

kesetrum *vi, coll* to receive an electric shock ← **setrum**

kesiagaan *n* readiness, preparedness ← **siaga**

kesiangan *adj* late, too late in the day ← **siang**

kesiapan *n* readiness, willingness ← **siap**

kesibukan *n* activity, fuss, bustle, business ← **sibuk**

kesigapan *n* efficiency, readiness ← **sigap**

kesilapan *n* mistake, error ← **silap**

kesima: terkesima *adj* amazed, astonished; *vi* to be amazed or astonished

kesimpulan *n* conclusion ← **simpul**

kesinambungan *n* continuity ← **sambung**

kesini → **ke sini**

kesohor *adj, coll* famous ← **sohor**

kesoléhan *n* piety ← **soléh**

kesombongan *n* arrogance, pride ← **sombong**

kesopanan *n* manners, politeness ← **sopan**

kesopan-santunan *n* manners, etiquette ← **sopan santun**

kesoréan *adv* too late ← **soré**

kesturi *n* musk

kesuburan *n* fertility ← **subur**

kesucian *n* purity; virginity ← **suci**

kesudahan → **berkesudahan**

kesudian *n* readiness, willingness ← **sudi**

kesukaan *n* hobby; enjoyment ← **suka**

kesukaran *n* difficulty ← **sukar**

kesukuan *adj* ethnic, tribal ← **suku**

kesulitan *n* difficulty, trouble ← **sulit**

kesultanan *n* sultanate ← **sultan**

kesuma → **kusuma**

kesumat *dendam* ~ revenge

kesungguhan *n* earnestness, sincerity, truth ← **sungguh**

kesungkanan *n* reluctance; aversion ← **sungkan**

kesunyian *n* quiet, still ← **sunyi**

kesuraman *n* gloom, darkness ← **suram**

kesurupan *vi* to be possessed by a spirit or ghost ← **surup**

kesusahan *n* trouble, difficulty ← **susah**

kesusasteraan, kesusastraan *n* literature ← **sastra**

kesusilaan *n* modesty, decency, ethics ← **susila**

ketaatan *n* obedience ← **taat**

ketabahan *n* strength of character ← **tabah**

ketabrak *adj, coll* to be hit; ~ *mobil* to be hit by a car ← **tabrak**

ketagihan *adj* addicted to ← **tagih**

ketahanan *n* endurance ← **tahan**

ketahuan to be found out ← **tahu**

ketajaman *n* sharpness ← **tajam**

ketakutan *adj* frightened, terrified, scared ← **takut**

ketamakan *n* greed ← **tamak**

ketampanan *n* good looks ← **tampan**

ketan *n* sticky rice; ~ *bakar* grilled slabs of sticky rice; *bubur* ~ *hitam* black sticky rice porridge

ketangkap *adj, coll* to be caught, arrested ← **tangkap**

ketangkasan *n* agility, dexterity; *menguji* ~ to test your skill ← **tangkas**

ketapang *n* kind of almond tree

ketapél *n* catapult

ketar ~-*ketir* tremble, shake with nerves

ketat *adj* tight, strict; *baju* ~ tight clothes; *keamanan* ~ high security; **memperketat** *vt* to tighten (up)

ketawa *vi, coll* to laugh; ~ *ketiwi* giggle; **mengetawakan** *vt* to laugh at ← **ketawa, tawa**

ketebalan *n* thickness ← **tebal**

keteduhan *n* calm, stillness ← **teduh**

ketegangan *n* tension ← **tegang**

ketegaran *n* determination ← **tegar**

ketegasan *n* resolve, determination ← **tegas**

keték → **kétiak**

ketekunan *n* diligence, dedication ← **tekun**

kétél *n* boiler, kettle

ketéla *n* yam

ketelantaran *n* neglect ← **telantar**

ketelatan *n* lateness ← **telat**

ketelaténan *n* patience, perseverance ← **telatén**

ketelédoran *n* carelessness ← **telédor**

ketelitian *n* accuracy, care ← **teliti**

ketemu *vt, coll* to meet ← **temu**

ketenangan *n* calm, peace ← **tenang**

ketenaran *n* popularity ← **tenar**

ketenteraman *n* peace ← **tenteram**

ketentuan *n* condition, stipulation ← **tentu**

ketepatan *n* precision, accuracy ← **tepat**

keterangan *n* explanation; *kata* ~ adverb ← **terang**

keterbatasan *n* limitation ← **terbatas, batas**

keterikatan *n* bind, bond, commitment ← **terikat, ikat**

keterlaluan *n* excess, too much ← **terlalu, lalu**

keterlambatan *n* delay; *mengalami ~ vt* to be delayed ← **terlambat, lambat**

keterlibatan *n* involvement, association ← **terlibat, libat**

keterpaduan *n* integration ← **terpadu, padu**

keterpaksaan *n* compulsion ← **terpaksa, paksa**

keterpurukan *n* depression, abyss ← **terpuruk, puruk**

ketersediaan *n* availability; readiness ← **tersedia, sedia**

ketertarikan *n* interest, attraction ← **tertarik, tarik**

ketertiban *n* discipline, order; *~ lalu lintas* traffic discipline, highway code; *Dinas Ketenteraman dan ~ (Tramtib)* city public order agency ← **tertib**

ketetapan *n* regulation; stipulation ← **tetap**

ketiadaan *n* absence, lack ← **tiada, tidak ada**

kétiak, kéték *n* armpit

ketiban *vi, coll* hit by, struck by; *~ rezeki nomplok* enjoy a windfall, get lucky

ketidakadaan *n* absence, lack of ← **tidak ada**

ketidakadilan *n* injustice ← **tidak adil**

ketiduran *v* to fall asleep ← **tidur**

ketiga *adj* the third; **ketiganya, ketiga-tiganya** *n, adj* all three ← **tiga**

ketik *v* type; *juru ~* typist; *mesin ~* typewriter; **ketikan** *n* typing; **mengetik** *vt* to type; **pengetikan** *n* typing ← **ketik, tik**

ketika *conj* when (in past); *~ itu* at that time; **seketika** *n* a second, a moment; *dalam ~, pencopet sudah menghilang* in an instant, the pickpocket had disappeared

ketilang → **kutilang**

ketimbang *conj, coll* than; instead of ← **timbang**

ketimpangan *n* inequality, imbalance; *~*

sosial social inequality ← **timpang**

ketimun → **mentimun**

ketimuran *adj* Eastern, Oriental ← **timur**

ketimus *n* kind of cake

ketinggalan *adj* left behind; *~ jaman, ~ zaman* outdated; *~ kereta api* miss the train ← **tinggal**

ketinggian *n* altitude, height ← **tinggi**

ketinting *n* water taxi used on the rivers of Kalimantan

ketir *ketar-~* tremble, shake with nerves

ketok *v* to knock; panel-beat; *~ magic* 'magic' panel-beating

ketololan *n* stupidity ← **tolol**

ketolongan *adj* **ketulungan** *coll tidak ~* beyond help ← **tolong**

ketombé *n* dandruff; *sampo anti ~* anti-dandruff shampoo; **ketombéan** *vi, coll* to have dandruff; **berketombé** *rambut ~* dry scalp, dandruff

ketoprak *n* Betawi dish of vegetables in peanut sauce

ketoprak *n* folk play

ketrampilan *n* skill ← **trampil**

kéts *sepatu ~* sports shoes, running shoes, sneakers

ketua *n* chief, chair, president, elder; *~ RT* neighborhood leader; *wakil ~* deputy chair; **mengetuai** *vt* to preside over

ketuban *air ~* amniotic fluid; *air ~ sudah pecah* the waters have broken

ketuhanan *n* divinity, deity; belief in God ← **tuhan**

ketuk, ketok knock; **mengetuk** *vt* to knock; *~ hati* to prick your conscience; *~ pintu* knock on the door; **terketuk** *~ hati* to have it in your heart

ketularan *adj* infected, caught something ← **tular**

ketulusan *~ hati* sincerity ← **tulus**

ketumbar *n* (ground) coriander; *daun ~* (fresh) coriander

ketupat *n* coconut fronds woven into a diamond-shape for cooking rice, traditionally used at Idul Fitri; decorations in this shape; *belah ~* rhombus

keturunan *n* descendant; *~ WNI* Indonesian of Chinese descent ← **turun**

ketus *adj* sharp (of words)

keuangan *n* finance; *Menteri ~ (Menkeu)* Minister of Finance, *UK* Chancellor of the Exchequer ← **uang**

keulungan *n* superiority ← **ulung**

keunggulan *n* superiority ← **unggul**

keunikan *n* unique thing, uniqueness ← **unik**

keuntungan *n* advantage, profit ← **untung**

keuskupan *n* diocese ← **uskup**

keutuhan *n* entirety, whole state ← **utuh**

kewajaran *n* sense, logic ← **wajar**

kewajiban *n* obligation, duty ← **wajib**

kewalahan *adj* unable to cope, overcome

kewarasan *n* sanity, mental health ← **waras**

kewarganegaraan *n* citizenship; **berkewarganegaraan** *vi* to have citizenship or be a citizen of ← **warga negara**

kewaspadaan *n* caution ← **waspada**

kewenangan *n* authority ← **wenang**

keyakinan *n* belief, conviction, faith ← **yakin**

kg kilogram

KH *abbrev Kiai Haji Isl, m* title for religious leader who has completed the pilgrimage to Mecca

khabar → **kabar**

khalayak *n* public

khalik *n (Sang) ~* the Creator, God

khas *adj* special, specific; *~ Ambon* Ambonese; *ciri ~* characteristic; **kekhasan** *n* special feature

khasiat *n* benefit, special effect; **berkhasiat** *adj* beneficial, therapeutic; *vi* to have a benefit

khatam finish reading or reciting the Koran

khatib, khotib *n, Isl* preacher

khatulistiwa, katulistiwa *n* the Equator

khawatir, kuatir *v* to worry, fear; *jangan ~* don't worry; **kekuatiran** *n* worry, fear; **menguatirkan** *vt* to worry about something

khayal *n* imagination; **khayalan** *n* dream, hallucination; **berkhayal** *vi* to dream, imagine

khazanah *n* treasure

khianat *n* treachery, betrayal; disloyalty; **berkhianat** *vi* to betray; **mengkhianati** *vt* to betray someone; **pengkhianat** *n* traitor; **pengkhianatan** *n* treason, treachery, betrayal

khidmat *n* respect; *dengan ~* respectfully, solemnly

khilaf *vi* to be wrong, make a mistake

khitan *n* circumcision; **khitanan** *n* feast held in honor of a circumcision; **mengkhitan, mengkhitankan** *vt* to circumcise; *~ anak* to have a child circumcised

khotib, khatib *n, Isl* preacher

khotbah *n* sermon; **pengkhotbah** *n* preacher

khusus *adj* special, particular; *~nya* in particular, especially; **mengkhususkan** *vt* to give special treatment

khusyuk *adj* devout, religious, pious

ki q, 17th letter of the alphabet

ki, kiai, kyai *n, pron, Isl, m* religious leader; *~ Haji (KH)* title for leader who has completed the pilgrimage to Mecca

kiamat *hari ~* day of judgment

kian *adv* such; increasingly, more and more; **sekian** *adv* so much, this much; *~ banyak* so many, so much; *~ dulu* that's all for now (used in speeches and letters); **kesekian** *adj* umpteenth, nth; *untuk ~ kali dia tidak hadir* for the umpteenth time, he hasn't shown up

kias *n* comparison, analogy, allusion; **kiasan** *n* figure of speech, metaphor

kiat *n* means, way, method

kibar: berkibar, berkibar-kibar *vi* to wave, flutter; **mengibarkan** *vt* to wave, unfurl; *~ bendera* to fly a flag

kibas: mengibaskan *vt* to wag (a tail)

kiblat, qiblat *n* direction of Mecca; **berkiblat** *vi* to be oriented toward; *~ pada Amerika* to look to America

kibor *n* keyboard; *pemain ~* keyboardist

kibul *n, coll* bottom, bum; **mengibuli** *vt* to fool someone

kicau *n* chirp, warble, twitter; **berkicau** *vi* to warble, twitter; to babble

kidal *adj* left-handed

kidung *n* song, hymn

kijang *n* barking deer, kind of antelope; **Kijang** *n* large car produced by Toyota

kikil *n* animal foot (in food)

kikir *n* file

kikir *adj* stingy, tight, miserly

kikis *adj* scraped; **kikisan** *n* scrapings, erosion; **mengikis** *vt* to erode, eat away; **pengikisan** *n* scraping; erosion; **terkikis** *adj* eaten away, eroded

kikuk *adj* clumsy, awkward

kilang *n* refinery, mill; ~ *minyak* oil refinery; **perkilangan** *n* refinery

kilap shine; **berkilap, mengkilap** *vt* to shine, gleam

kilas ~ *balik* flashback; **sekilas** *n* flash, glance

kilat *n* lightning; *kursus* ~ crash course; *penangkal* ~ lightning rod; **berkilat** *vi* to shine, sparkle

kilau: berkilau *adj* glittering, sparkling; *vi* to glitter, sparkle

kiler *n, coll* mean teacher

kilir twist; **terkilir** *adj* twisted, sprained

kilo *n* kilo, kilogram; kilometer; *se~ pisang* a kilo of bananas; *60* ~ *per jam* 60 kilometers per hour; **kiloan** *adv* by the kilogram, in kilograms; **kilogram** *n* kilogram; **kilometer** *n* kilometer

kimia *n* chemistry; *bahan* ~ chemical; *ilmu* ~ chemistry; **kimiawi** *adj* chemical

kimono *n* kimono; dressing gown

KIM(S) *abbrev Kartu Izin Menetap (Sementara)* (temporary) residence permit for foreigners

kina *n* quinine; *pohon* ~ cinchona tree

kincir *n* wheel; ~ *air* waterwheel; ~ *angin* windmill; *negeri* ~ *angin* the Netherlands

kinerja *n* performance ← **kerja**

kini *adv* now, nowadays (often when comparing with past); **terkini** *adj* the latest

kios *n* stall, kiosk; **kiostél, kiospon** *n* small phone agency, phone kiosk ← **kios télépon**

kipas *n* fan; ~ *angin,* ~ *listrik* (electric) fan; **mengipasi** *vt* to fan someone or something

kiper *n* (goal)keeper

kiprah *n* pace, progress; **berkiprah** *vi* to move, dance, be active in

kir *n* inspection (for vehicles)

kira *v* to think, guess, estimate; **kira-kira** *adv* approximately, around, about;

kiranya *adv* hopefully; **memperkira-kan** *vt* to estimate, calculate; **mengira** *vt* to assume, think; **mengira-ngira** *vi* to roughly estimate, guess; **perkiraan** *n* estimate, guess; **prakiraan** *n* forecast; ~ *cuaca* weather forecast; **sekira-nya** *adv* if perhaps; **terkira** *tak* ~ unsuspected, not thought of

kirab *n* (traditional or bridal) procession, parade

kiri *adj* left; ~ *kanan* left and right; ~ *kapal* port, portside; *belok* ~ turn left; *sayap* ~ left-wing; *di sebelah* ~ on the left

kirim *n* send; ~ *salam* to send your best wishes; **kiriman** *n* parcel; **mengirim** *vt* to send; **pengirim** *n* sender; **pengirim-an** *n* dispatch, forwarding; ~ *barang* goods dispatch; **terkirim** *adj* sent; *pesan* ~ message sent

Kirgistan *n* Kyrgyzstan; *bahasa* ~, *orang* ~ Kyrgyz

kirmizi *adj* scarlet, crimson

kisah *n* tale, story; ~ *sejati* true story; **berkisah** *vi* to tell a story; **mengisah-kan** *vt* to tell the story of

kisar: kisaran *n* rotation, revolution; **berkisar** *vi* to revolve, rotate, turn

kisi, kisi-kisi *n* grate, grating, grill; lattice, mesh; spokes (of a wheel)

kismis *n* sultana, currant; *roti* ~ sultana bread

kisruh *adj* chaotic; **kekisruhan** *n* confusion, chaos

kista *n* cyst

kita *pron* we, us, our (inclusive); ~ *punya* our

kitab *n* holy book; ~ *Baru* the New Testament; ~ *kuning* books containing interpretations of Islamic law, thought and traditions; ~ *Lama* the Old Testament; ~ *suci* holy book; the Koran; *ahli* ~ Peoples of the Book (Jews and Christians); ~ *Undang-Undang Hukum Acara Pidana (KUHAP)* criminal law statutes; ~ *Undang-Undang Hukum Perdata (KUHP)* civil code

KITAP *abbrev Kartu Izin Tinggal Tetap* permanent residence permit for foreigners

kitar: mengitari *vt* to orbit; *bumi ~ matahari* the Earth orbits the Sun; **sekitar** *adv* around; near; *prep* around; **sekitarnya** *di ~* around (a place); *dan ~* and environs

KITAS *abbrev Kartu Izin Tinggal Sementara* temporary residence permit for foreigners

kitorang *pron, coll* we; us (in Eastern Indonesia) ← **kita orang**

kiu *n* (billiards) cue

kiwi *(buah)* ~ kiwifruit; *burung ~* kiwi kiwi

KK *abbrev kepala keluarga* head of family, household

KKN *abbrev korupsi, kolusi, nepotisme* corruption (collusion and nepotism)

KKN *abbrev kuliah kerja nyata* practical work experience for graduating university students

KKO *abbrev, arch Korps Komando Marinir* Marine Corps, Marines

klaim *n* claim; *~ asuransi* insurance claim; **mengklaim** *vt* [mengklém] to claim (a fact); *para penghuni ~ belum dibayar kompensasi* the residents claim they haven't been paid compensation

klakson *n* horn; **diklakson** *v* to be tooted at; **mengklakson** *vi* to toot or beep; *vt* to toot or beep (at someone)

klarifikasi *n* clarification; **mengklarifikasi** *vt* to clarify

klarinét *n* clarinet

klasifikasi *n* classification; **mengklasifikasi** *vt* to classify

klasik *adj* classic, classical; *musik ~* classical music

klém *n* clamp

klenik *n* black magic or belief, negative in connotation

klénténg, kelénténg *n* Chinese or Confucian temple, pagoda

klép, kelép *n* valve, catch

klepon *n* steamed rice cake with sugar inside

klién *n* client

klimaks *n* climax

klimis *adj* slick, oily, smooth, shiny (of hair)

klinik *n* clinic

kliping *n* news clipping

kliring: dikliring *v* to be cleared (in a bank)

klisé *n* (photo) negative

klisé *n* cliché

klitoris *n* clitoris

Kliwon *n* fifth and final day of the Javanese week

klompen *n, pl* (Dutch) clogs

klon *n* clone; **mengklon** *vt* to clone; **pengklonan** *n* cloning; **kloning** *n, coll* cloning

klop → **kelop** *adj* suitable, comfortable

klorin *n* chlorine (Cl)

klosét *n* cistern (of toilet)

kloter *n* departure group for the pilgrimage to Mecca ← **kelompok terbang**

klub *n* (sports) club; *~ tenis* tennis club

KM *abbrev Kapal Motor* ship

km *kamar* room (in a hotel); kilometer

knalpot *n* exhaust pipe, muffler

KNIL *abbrev Koninklijk Nederlandsch-Indisch Leger* Royal Dutch-Indies Army, in colonial times

knop → **kenop**

koalisi *n* coalition; **berkoalisi** *vi* to be in a coalition

ko-as, koasistén *n* (medical) intern, internship

kobar: kobaran *~ api* flame; **berkobar** *vi* to blaze, burn; **mengobarkan** *vt* to fan, fuel

koboi *n* cowboy

kobokan *n* bowl for washing fingers before eating

kobra *n (ular)* ~ cobra

kocak *adj* funny, amusing, entertaining

kocék *n, sl* pocket (in clothes)

kocok *mie ~* kind of noodles; **mengocok** *vt* to shake, shuffle; *~ dadu* to roll the dice; *~ kartu* to shuffle cards

Kodam *n* Regional Military Komando ← **Komando Daérah Militér**

kode *n* code; *~ etik* code of ethics; *~ Morse* Morse code; *~ pos* postcode; *~ telepon* dialling code, telephone code

kodi *n* score, twenty; *kiriman 50 ~ kain dari India telah sampai* the shipment of 50 scores of fabric from India has arrived

kodok *n* frog; *gaya* ~ frogkick; *mobil* ~ Volkswagen, VW Beetle

kodrat *n* nature; ~ *wanita* female nature

Kodya *n* municipality, city ← **kotamadya**

koi *ikan* ~ Japanese carp

koin *n* coin

kok you know (emphasizing contrary argument); *tidak apa-apa* ~ really, it's OK; *interrog* how come, why; ~ *sakit?* how come you're sick?

kok *n* shuttlecock

kokain *n* cocaine

koki *n* cook

koko *baju* ~ Islamic-style shirt for men, worn to the mosque, usu with a *péci*

kokoh, kukuh *adj* strong, robust

kokok *n* crowing; **berkokok** *vi* to crow; *ayam* ~ rooster's crow

kokpit *n* cockpit

koktil *n* cocktail

Kol. *kolonel* colonel

kol *n* cabbage; ~ *putih* cabbage; *kembang* ~ cauliflower

kolaborator *n* collaborator; **kolaborasi** *n* collaboration; **berkolaborasi** *vi* to collaborate, work together

kolak *n* sweet fruit stew; ~ *pisang* banana *kolak*

kolam *n* pond; ~ *ikan* fish pond; ~ *renang* swimming pool

kolang-kaléng, kolang-kaling *n* sugar-palm fruit used in desserts and *kolak*

kolase *n* collage

koléga *n* colleague

koléksi *n* collection

koléra *n* cholera

kolésterol *n* cholesterol; **berkolésterol** *vi* ~ *tinggi* to be high (in) cholesterol; to have high cholesterol; *adj* high-cholesterol

koli *n* package; counter for baggage; *Rp 3.000 per* ~ Rp. 3,000 per piece

kolintang *n* large wooden xylophone from Minahasa

kolokan *adj* spoilt, mollycoddled

kolom *n* column

Kolombia *n* Colombia; *orang* ~ Colombian

kolonél *n, pron* colonel; *letnan-*~ *(letkol)* lieutenant-colonel

kolong *n* space under a large object; ~ *meja* under the table; *anak* ~ army kid, child of a soldier; ~ *tempat tidur* under the bed

kolonial *adj* colonial; **kolonisasi** *n* colonization → **jajah**

kolor *n* drawstring shorts; *celana* ~ (boxer) shorts

kolot *n* old-fashioned, out of date; conservative; *kaum* ~ conservatives

kolumnis *n* columnist

kolusi *n* collusion; *korupsi,* ~ *dan nepotisme (KKN)* corruption

koma *n* comma; *titik* ~ semicolon

koma *n* coma

komandan *n* commander

komando *n* command; ~ *Strategis Angkatan Darat (Kostrad)* Army Strategic Command

komat-kamit, berkomat-kamit *vi* to move your lips silently (as if praying)

kombinasi *n* combination

Komdak *abbrev Komando Daerah Kepolisian* Regional Military Command, large police complex in south Jakarta

komédi *n* comedy

koméntar *n* comment; **berkoméntar** *vi* to (make a) comment; **mengoméntari** *vt* to comment on; **koméntator** *n* (sports) commentator

komérsial *adj* commercial

komét *n* comet

komidi ~ *putar* merry-go-round

komik *buku* ~ comic (book); **komikus** *n* comic book author or artist

komisaris *n* commissioner; ~ *polisi* superintendent of police; *dewan* ~ commission

komisi *n* committee, commission; ~ *Pemberantasan Korupsi (KPK)* Corruption Eradication Commission; ~ *Pemilihan Umum (KPU)* Electoral Commission; ~ *Nasional Hak-Hak Asasi Manusia (Komnasham)* Human Rights Commission

komisi *n* commission, fee

komité *n* committee; ~ *Olahraga Nasional Indonesia (KONI)* Indonesian National Sports Commission → **panitia**

Komnasham *abbrev Komisi Nasional Hak-Hak Asasi Manusia* Human Rights Commission

komoditas *n* commodity

komodo *n* komodo (dragon), giant lizard found only around the island of Komodo between Sumbawa and Flores

kompak *adj* close-knit, solid; **ke-kompakan** *n* solidarity

kompas *n* compass → **pedoman**

Kompéni *n* the Dutch East Indies Company (VOC); colonial government

kompénsasi *n* compensation; **mengkompénsasi** *vt* to compensate

kompetén *adj* competent, appropriate, rightful; **kompeténsi** *n* competence, competency; *kurikulum berdasarkan* ~ competency-based curriculum

kompi *n, mil* company

kompilasi *n* compilation

komplék, kompléks, kompléx *n* housing complex, compound

komplét → **komplit**

komplikasi *n* complication

komplit, komplét *adj* complete; *nasi* ~ rice with various side-dishes → **lengkap**

komplot: komplotan *n* plot against; **berkomplot** *vi* to plot

komponén *n* component

komponis *n* composer

kompor *n* stove, cooker; ~ *gas* gas cooker

kompos *n* compost; **mengomposkan** *vt* to compost; **pengomposan** *n* (process of) composting

komposisi *n* composition

komprés *n* compress, pack; ~ *dingin* ice pack

komprésor *n* compressor

kompromi *n* compromise; **berkompromi** *vi* to compromise, reach a compromise

komputer *n* computer; ~ *jinjing* laptop; **komputerisasi** *n* computerization

komunikasi *n* communication; **komunikatif** *adj* communicative

komunis *adj, n* communist; *arch Partai* ~ *Indonesia (PKI)* Indonesian Communist Party; **komunisme** *n* communism

komunitas *n* community (usu in urban context) → **masyarakat**

konblok *n* paver, paving block

konci → **kunci**

konco *n, neg* buddy, mate; crony

kondang *adj* famous, well-known

kondangan *v* be invited to an event

kondé *n, f* small bun worn with national costume; *tusuk* ~ hair pin

kondéktur *n* conductor, guard (on a train or city bus)

kondénsasi *n* condensation

kondisi *n* condition; ~ *cuaca* weather conditions → **keadaan**

kondom *n* condom

kondusif *adj* conducive, allowing

konéksi *n* connections, contacts (at an institution)

konféksi *n* garment; *pabrik* ~ garment factory

konferénsi, konperénsi *n* conference; ~ *pers* press conference; ~ *Asia-Afrika* the Asian-African conference; ~ *Tingkat Tinggi (KTT)* (international) high-level conference

konfirmasi *n* confirmation; *v* confirm

konflik *n* conflict; ~ *horisontal* conflict within a group or level of society; ~ *kepentingan sendiri* conflict of interest

konfrontasi *n* confrontation; Indonesian aggression towards Malaysia in the 1960s

Kong Hu Cu Confucius, Confucian; *agama* ~ Confucianism

kongkalikong *n* intrigue, conspiracy; **berkongkalikong** *vi* to conspire

kongkol: sekongkol, bersekongkol *vi* to plot, work against; **persekongkolan** *n* plot, intrigue

konglomerat *n* wealthy financier

Kongo *n* (the) Congo; *orang* ~ Congolese; *Republik* ~ Congo; *Republik Demokratik* ~ Democratic Republic of the Congo (formerly Zaire)

kongrés *n* congress, convention

kongsi *n* commercial partnership

KONI *abbrev Komite Olahraga Nasional Indonesia* Indonesian National Sports Commission

konjén *n* consulate-general; consul-general ← **konsulat jénderal; konsul jénderal**

konkrét *adj* concrete, clear, evident

konon it is said, allegedly

konotasi *n* connotation

konperénsi → **konferénsi**

konsékuén *adj* consistent, logical

konséling *n* counselling; **konsélor** n counsellor

konsén, konséntrasi *adj* focused, concentrating

konsép *n* concept, draft; **konséptor** *n* creator, initiator

konsér *n* concert; ~ *amal* charity concert; *menonton* ~ to go to a concert

konsérvasi *n* conservation

konsérvatif *adj* conservative

konsési *n* concession → **hak guna**

konsistén *adj* consistent

konsolidasi *n* consolidation

konspirasi *n* conspiracy

konstélasi *n* constellation, configuration, alignment

konstitusi *n* constitution; **konstitusional** *adj* constitutional → **UUD, Undang-Undang Dasar**

konstruksi *n* construction, building → **bangunan**

konsul *n* consul; ~ *jenderal (konjén)* consul-general; **konsulat** *n* consulate; ~ *jenderal (konjén)* consulate-general

konsultan *n* adviser, consultant; **konsultasi** *n* consultation

konsumén *n* consumer

konsumsi *n* refreshments; *Joni dan teman-temannya yang mengurus bagian* ~ Joni and his friends organized the refreshments

kontak contact; *stop* ~ power point; **mengontak** *vt* to contact someone → **hubung**

kontaminasi *n* contamination; **ter-kontaminasi** *adj* contaminated

kontan *uang* ~ cash

kontémporér *adj* contemporary; *tarian* ~ contemporary dance

kontés *n* contest; ~ *kecantikan*, ~ *mismisan coll* beauty pageant

kontingén *n* contingent, group (of sportspeople, pilgrims etc from a certain place); ~ *Indonesia dulu meraih banyak medali di SEA Games* the Indonesian contingent used to win lots of medals at the SEA Games

kontol *n, derog* dick, cock

kontra *adj* against, opposing, anti

kontradiksi *n* contradiction

kontrak *n* contract; ~ *kerja* employment contract; **kontrakan** *n* rented (house); **mengontrakkan** *vt* to lease or rent out a house; **dikontrakkan** *adj* for rent, lease

kontraktor *n* (building) contractor

kontras *n* contrast

Kontras *n* Victims of Violence, a human-rights NGO ← **Korban Tindakan Kekerasan**

kontrasépsi *alat* ~ form of contraception, contraceptive device

kontribusi *n* (financial) contribution

kontrol *n* control; *lepas* ~ out of control; **kontrolir** *n* supervisor, controller → **kendali**

kontrovérsi *n* controversy; **kontrovérsial** *adj* controversial

konvénsi *n* convention; ~ *Jenewa* the Geneva Convention

konvoi *n* convoy

konyol *adj* silly, foolish

konyong: sekonyong-konyong *adv* suddenly

koor *n* choir → **paduan suara**

koordinasi *n* co-ordination; **koordinator** *n* co-ordinator

kop *n* head; ~ *surat* letterhead

Kopaja *n* medium-sized green and white bus in Jakarta ← **Kopérasi Angkutan Jakarta**

koper, kopor *n* suitcase, baggage

koperasi *n* co-operative, co-op; ~ *Unit Desa (KUD)* village co-operative; ~ *simpan pinjam* savings and loan co-operative

kopi *n* coffee; ~ *bubuk*, ~ *instan* instant coffee; ~ *luak* coffee made from beans excreted by a civet cat; ~ *pahit* black coffee without sugar; ~ *susu* white or milk coffee, latte; ~ *tubruk* ground coffee; **ngopi** *vi, sl* to drink or have a coffee

kopi *n* copy; ~ *darat* meet face-to-face → **fotokopi**

kopiah *n, Isl* flat-topped cap, worn to the mosque; national headwear for men → **péci**

kopling *n* clutch

kopyor *n* very soft coconut flesh; *es ~* sweet drink made from this coconut

Koramil *abbrev Komando Rayon Militér* Military District Command

koran *n* newspaper; *~ dinding* newspaper posted up on a wall for public reading; *loper ~* paper boy

korban *n* victim; *~ jiwa* fatality; *~ luka* injured; **berkorban** *vi* to make sacrifices, do without; **mengorbankan** *vt* to sacrifice; **pengorbanan** *n* (act of) sacrifice

Koréa *n* Korea; *~ Selatan (Korsel)* South Korea; *~ Utara (Korut)* North Korea; *bahasa ~, orang ~* Korean

korék *~ api* matches; *~ kuping* cotton bud; **mengorék** *vt* to scrape, scratch

koréksi *n* correction; **mengoréksi** *vt* to correct

korélasi *n* correlation

Korém *abbrev Komando Resort Militer* Military Area Command

koréografer *n* choreographer; **koréografi** *n* choreography

koréspondén *n* correspondent; **koréspondénsi** *n* correspondence, letter-writing

kori *n, m* **koriah** *f* reciter of the Koran ← **qari, qariah**

koridor *n* corridor, passage; route; *tahun depan akan dibuka beberapa ~ busway yang baru* next year several new busway routes will be opened

korma, kurma *n* date; *pohon ~* date palm

kornét, kornéd *n* (tinned) corned beef

korosi *n* corrosion

Korpri *n* civil servant corps powerful during the New Order era ← **Korps Pegawai Negeri**

korps *n* [korp, korep] corps; *~ diplomatik* diplomatic corps; *~ Marinir* Marine Corps

Korsél *n* South Korea ← **Koréa Selatan**

korsél *n* carousel, merry-go-round

korsi → **kursi**

korsléting, kortsléting *n* short-circuit

korup *adj* corrupt; **korupsi** *n* corruption; *adj* corrupt; *~ kolusi dan nepotisme (KKN)* corruption; **mengorupsi** *vt* to be corrupt; to corrupt; **koruptor** *n* corrupt person

Korut *n* North Korea ← **Koréa Utara**

kos board, lodging; *~ putri* female boarding-house; *anak ~* boarder; *terima ~* boarder wanted; *uang ~* board **kos-kosan** *n* boarding-houses, rooms for board

kosa → **perkosa**

kosa *~ kata* vocabulary

kosén → **kusén**

kos-kosan *n* boarding-houses, rooms for board ← **kos**

kosmétik *adj* cosmetic; *n* cosmetics

kosong *adj* empty, blank; hollow; zero; *~ melompong* completely empty; *mata ~* unseeing; *skornya dua ~* it's two nil; **kekosongan** *n* emptiness; **mengosongkan** *vt* to empty

Kosovo *n* Kosovo; *orang ~* Kosovar

Kostrad *n* Army Regional Strategic Command ← **Komando Stratégis Angkatan Darat**

kota *n* town, city; *~ Administratif, ~ Administratip (Kotip)* administrative city, municipality; *~ Batik* Pekalongan, town of batik; *~ Hujan* Bogor, the Rainy City; *~ Gudeg* Jogjakarta, the city of *gudeg* (a traditional food); *~ hantu, ~ mati* ghost town; *~ Kembang* Bandung, the Flower City; *~ Pahlawan* Surabaya, the City of Heroes; *~ satelit* satellite, dormitory town; *~ Udang* Cirebon, City of Prawns; *~ Vatikan* (the) Vatican City; *angkutan ~* city transport; *balai ~* town hall, city hall; *ibu ~* capital (city); *pusat ~* downtown, city center; *wali ~* mayor; **perkotaan** *n* metropolitan area; **kotamadya** *n* municipality

kotak *n* box; square; *~ pos* (public) letterbox, mailbox; *~ suara* ballot box; *surat* letter box, mailbox (at home); *nasi ~* box meal of rice and side-dishes; **kotak-kotak** *adj* check; *baju ~* check shirt; **mengotak-ngotakkan** *vt* to categorize, box, put in boxes

kotamadya *n* municipality ← **kota**

koték *n* cackle; **berkoték** *vi* to cackle (of a hen)

kotéka *n* penis sheath, worn in Papua; **berkotéka** *adj* wearing a penis sheath; *vi* to wear a penis sheath

Kotip, Kotif *n* administrative city, municipality ← **kota administratif**

kotor *adj* dirty, filthy; gross; *gaji ~* gross salary; *penyakit ~* venereal disease; *pikiran ~* dirty thought, dirty mind; **kotoran** *n* excrement; dirt; **mengotori** *vt* to (make) dirty, defile

kotrék *n* corkscrew

koyak *adj* torn; **terkoyak** *adj* torn

Kp. *kampung* village; densely-inhabited area in city

kpd *abbrev, pron* to, for (in letters); to (in addresses); *~ ytc.* dearest ← **kepada yang tercinta**; *~ yth* dear; the respected ← **kepada yang terhormat**; *~ yts. abbrev* dearest, beloved ← **kepada yang tersayang**

KPK *Komisi Pemberantasan Korupsi* Corruption Eradication Commission

KPU *abbrev Komisi Pemilihan Umum* Electoral Commission

kram *n, coll* cramp; *vi* to have cramp; *kaki saya ~* I've got cramp in my legs

kran → **keran**

kraton, keraton *n* Javanese palace; *lingkungan ~* palace circles

krayon *n* crayon

kréasi *n* creation; **berkréasi** *vi* to be creative; **kréativitas** *n* creativity

krédit *n* credit; *~ macet* non-performing loan; *~ ringan* easy credit; *~ rumah* home loan; *kartu ~* credit card

kréi *n* blind(s)

krém *adj* cream(-colored); *dulu ruangan ini dicat warna ~* this room used to be painted a cream color

krémasi *n* cremation; **krématorium** *n* crematorium

kréték, keréték *n (rokok) ~* clove cigarette

KRI *abbrev Kapal Republik Indonesia* Indonesian warship

kribo *rambut ~* Afro

krida *n* physical activity; sport

krim *n* cream, creme; *~ wajah* face cream

krimer *n* creamer (for tea or coffee)

kriminal *adj* criminal; **kriminolog** *n* criminologist → **jahat**

kring *adj* active (of telephones); sound of telephone ringing

kripik, keripik *n* small chip or crisp; *~ kentang* potato chips, *~ singkong* cassava chips

krisan *n (bunga) ~* chrysanthemum

krisis *n* crisis; *~ moneter*, **krismon** *n* financial crisis of 1997-98

kristal crystal

Kristen *adj* Christian, Protestant; *agama ~* Christianity, Protestant church; *gereja ~* Protestant church; *Gereja ~ Indonesia (GKI)* Indonesian Protestant Church; *orang ~* Christian, Protestant; **mengkristenkan** *vt* to convert someone to Christianity, Christianize; **kristenisasi** *n* Christianization

kristik *n* cross-stitch

Kristus *Yesus ~* Jesus Christ

kritéria *n* criteria → **syarat**

kritik *n* criticism, critique; **mengkritik** *vt* to criticize

kritis *adj* critical → **genting**

kriya *n* skill, craft

Kroasia *n* Croatia; *bahasa ~, orang ~* Croat

krokét *n* croquette

kroncong → **keroncong**

kru *n* (production) crew, team

kruk *n* crutches

krupuk → **kerupuk**

ksatria, kesatria *n* knight, warrior; *adj* chivalrous; *kaum ~* warrior class

KTP *abbrev Kartu Tanda Penduduk* national identity card

KTT *abbrev Konferensi Tingkat Tinggi* (international) high-level conference

ku, -ku *pron* I, my, mine; *akan ~cari* I'll look for it; *rumah~* my home

KUA *abbrev, Isl Kantor Urusan Agama* Religious Affairs Office

kuaci *n* (sunflower, watermelon, pumpkin etc) seed

kuadrat *n* square; *tiga ~ dua sama dengan sembilan* three to the power of two is nine ($3^2 = 9$)

kuah *n* soup, sauce, gravy (accompanying a food); **berkuah** *adj* with a soup or sauce; *vi* to have a soup or sauce

kuak: terkuak *adj* to part, open; be revealed, exposed

kuala *n* mouth, confluence; **berkuala** *vi* to have a mouth or confluence

kualat *adj* cursed; disastrous

kuali *n* wok, cooking pot

kualifikasi *n* qualification

kualitas, kwalitas *n* quality; **berkualitas** *adj* quality; *vi* to be of quality → **mutu**

kuantitas, kwantitas *n* quantity; **kuantitatif** *adj* quantitative → **banyak**

kuap: menguap *vi* to yawn

kuartal *n* quarter (of a year)

kuas *n* brush (for art or cosmetics); paintbrush

kuasa *n* power; ~ *hukum* legal counsel; *negara adi~* superpower; *surat* ~ proxy letter, letter of authorization; power of attorney; **berkuasa** *adj* powerful, mighty; *vi* to have power; **kekuasaan** *n* power; authority; **menguasai** *vt* to control, have power over; ~ *bahasa asing* to be able to speak a foreign language; **penguasa** *n* (person in) authority, power, administration

kuat *adj* strong; *tidak* ~ *berdiri* unable to stand up; **kekuatan** *n* strength, power; **menguatkan** *vt* to strengthen; **memperkuat** *vt* to reinforce, make stronger; **sekuat** *adj* as strong as; **sekuat-kuatnya** *adv* as strong or hard as possible; *dia berusaha* ~ *untuk menang* she strove her best to win; **terkuat** *adj* the strongest

kuatir, khawatir *vi* to worry, fear; *jangan* ~ don't worry; **kekuatiran** *n* worry, fear; **menguatirkan** *vt* to worry about something; *adj* worrying

Kuba *n* Cuba; *orang* ~ Cuban

kubah *n* dome; **berkubah** *adj* domed; *vi* to have a dome

kubang: berkubang *vi* to wallow (in mud)

kubik *adj* cubic; *liter* ~ cubic liter

kubis *n* cabbage

kubu *n* block, faction; ~ *PKB* the PKB faction

kubur *n* grave, tomb; **kuburan** *n* cemetery, graveyard; ~ *Cina* Chinese cemetery; **menguburkan** *vt* to bury; **terkubur** *adj* buried in an accident

kubus *n* cube; *berbentuk* ~ cube-shaped

kucai *n* leek

kucek, ucek *vt* rub; **mengucek** *vt* ~ *mata* to rub your eyes; ~ *pakaian* to rub clothes together when washing

kucil: mengucilkan *vt* to ostracize, shun

kucing *n* cat; ~ *angora* Persian cat; ~ *belang* tabby cat; ~ *kampung* alley cat; ~ *Siam* Siamese cat; *kumis* ~ kind of plant; *malu-malu* ~ feign disinterest; *tahi* ~ cat poo; bullshit!; *membeli* ~ *dalam karung* to buy a pig in a poke, buy something without knowing exactly what it is; **kucing-kucingan** *vi* to play tag

kucur: kucuran *n* flow, torrent; ~ *dana* flow of funds; **mengucurkan** *vt* to gush, pour

KUD *abbrev Koperasi Unit Desa* village co-operative

kuda *n* horse; knight (in chess); ~ *belang*, ~ *loreng* zebra; ~ *hela* draught horse; ~ *hitam* dark horse; ~ *kebiri* gelding; ~ *laut* seahorse; ~ *lumping* flat woven horse; Javanese performance using these toy horses; ~ *nil* hippo, hippopotamus; ~ *troya* Trojan horse; **kuda-kuda** *n* sawhorse; easel; roof beam; **kuda-kudaan** *n* hobby horse, rocking-horse; **berkuda** *vi* to ride a horse, go (horse-)riding

kudap: kudapan *n* snack

kudéta *n* coup, coup d'etat; ~ *militer* military coup

kudis *n* scab; scabies

kuduk *bulu* ~ hairs on the back of your neck

kudung, kerudung *n* loose veil; **berkudung** *vi* to wear a loose veil

kudus *adj, Chr* holy; *Roh* ~ the Holy Ghost

kué *n* cake, pastry; ~ *kering* biscuit; ~ *basah* moist boiled or steamed cakes; ~ *bolu* small steamed sponge cakes; ~ *bugis* small cakes made from sticky rice flour; ~ *bulan* moon cakes (at

Chinese New Year); ~ *cubit* small cakes made in a pinched shape, sold on the street; ~ *kering* cookies, biscuits; ~ *lapis* layer cake; ~ *lapis legit* kind of layer cake; ~ *lupis* small round cakes made from palm sugar, pandan and desiccated coconut; ~ *mangkok* cupcake, patty-cake; ~ *nagasari* kind of small banana cakes; ~ *pasar* traditional cakes; ~ *pengantin* wedding cake; ~ *putu* steamed pandan cakes eaten with coconut and palm sugar; ~ *semprong* cylindrical wafers which resemble brandy snaps; ~ *sus* small sweet buns containing rum-flavored cream; ~ *tar*, ~ *tart* (birthday) cake; *bahan pembuat* ~ cake ingredients

KUHAP *abbrev Kitab Undang-Undang Hukum Acara Pidana* criminal law statutes

KUHP *abbrev Kitab Undang-Undang Hukum Perdata* civil code

kuil *n, Ch, Hind* temple

kuis *n* quiz

kuitansi → **kwitansi**

kujur: sekujur ~ *badan* whole body; ~ *badan Iskandar penuh dengan gigitan serangga* Iskandar's whole body was covered in insect bites

kuku *n* nail (of people), claw (of animals); *cat* ~ nail polish; *gunting* ~ nail clippers; *penyakit* ~ *mulut* foot and mouth disease; **berkuku** *adj* having nails or claws; clawed; *vi* to have nails or claws

kukuh, kokoh *adj* strong, robust; **bersikukuh** *vi* to hold fast; **mengukuhkan** *vt* to strengthen; to ratify; **pengukuhan** *n* strengthening, reinforcement; ratification

kukuruyuk cock-a-doodle-doo

kukus steam; **mengukus** *vt* to steam (food)

kulai: terkulai *adj* sprawled, splayed, fallen

kulak *v* to buy in bulk; **kulakan** *adj* wholesale; *v* to buy in bulk

kuli *n* laborer, coolie; ~ *bangunan* builder's laborer; ~ *sindang* (general) laborer; ~ *tinta* journalist

kuliah *n* lecture; *vi, coll* to study at university or college; *mata* ~ (university) subject; ~ *kerja nyata (KKN)* practical work experience for graduating university students

kulit *n* skin, hide (of animals); leather; peel, rind (of fruit); ~ *ari* epidermis; ~ *asli* real or genuine leather; ~ *badak* thick-skinned; ~ *bumi* the Earth's crust; ~ *imitasi*, ~ *tiruan* imitation leather; ~ *jeruk* orange rind; ~ *kayu* bark; ~ *kepala* scalp; ~ *kerang* seashell; ~ *muka* front cover (of a magazine); ~ *mutiara* mother-of-pearl; ~ *telur* eggshell; *krupuk* ~ crackers made from cow hide; *kacang lupa* ~ forget your origins; *orang* ~ *putih* white person, Caucasian; **berkulit** *vi* to have skin, -skinned; ~ *badak* thick-skinned

kulkas *n* refrigerator, fridge

kultum *n, Isl* short TV sermon ← **kuliah tujuh menit**

kultus *n* cult; ~ *pribadi* personality cult

kulum: mengulum *vt* to suck in the mouth

kumal *adj* dishevelled, dingy, grubby

kuman *n* germ, bacteria; *pembasmi* ~ kills germs; **berkuman** *adj* full of germs, bacteria

kumandang echo; **berkumandang** *vi* to echo; **mengumandangkan** *vt* to sing; to sound, reverberate

kumat, komat relapse

kumbang *n* beetle; bumblebee

kumis *n* mustache; ~ *kucing* kind of plant

kumpul *vi* to get together, gather; ~ *kebo* to live together without marrying; **kumpulan** *n* collection; group; ~ *puisi*, ~ *cerita pendek* anthology; **berkumpul** *vi* to assemble, meet; **mengumpulkan** *vt* to collect, gather; ~ *perangko* to collect stamps; **pengumpul** *n* collector; **pengumpulan** *n* collection, act of collecting; **perkumpulan** *n* association, club; assembly

kumuh *adj* dirty, slummy; *daerah* ~ slum

kumur *obat* ~ mouthwash; **berkumur, berkumur-kumur** *vi* to gargle

kunang-kunang *n* firefly

kunci key; lock; fastener; solution, answer; ~ *inggris* wrench; ~ *kombinasi* combination lock; ~ *kontak* ignition key; ~ *maling* skeleton key; ~ *mobil* car lock; ~ *soal* answer key; ~ *slot* bolt; *anak* ~ key; *juru* ~ gatekeeper; *saksi* ~ key witness; **mengunci** *vt* to lock (up)

kuncup *n* bud; ~ *bunga* flower bud

kungkung *n* fetters, shackles; **kungkungan** *n* hold, lock; domination; **mengungkung** *vt* to shackle

kuning *adj* yellow; *coll* light brown; *n* saffron, turmeric; ~ *langsat* creamy yellow skin; ~ *telur* yolk; *kucing* ~ ginger cat; *sakit* ~ jaundice; **kuningan** *n* brass; **menguning** *vi* to turn or become yellow; **kuningisasi** *n* support for Golkar, in the form of the color yellow

kunir → **kunyit**

kunjung *tak* ~ never

kunjung: kunjungan *n* visit, excursion; ~ *kenegaraan* state visit; ~ *resmi* official visit; ~ *sekolah* school trip; **berkunjung** *vi* to visit, pay a visit to; *besok kelas I* ~ *ke Musium Fatahillah* tomorrow the first graders will visit the Fatahillah Museum; **mengunjungi** *vt* to visit a place

kuno *adj* ancient, historic; out-of-date, old-fashioned, conservative; *barang* ~ antique; *bangunan* ~ colonial building; *mobil* ~ classic or vintage car

kuntilanak *n* ghost that preys on pregnant women

kuntum *n* ripening bud

kunyah: mengunyah *v* to chew

kunyit, kunir, kuning *n* saffron; turmeric

kunyuk *n, sl, Jkt* monkey; idiot

kuota *n* quota

kupang *n* edible shellfish

kupas peel; **kupasan** *n* peeling; analysis; **mengupas** *vt* to peel; to analyze

kuper *adj, sl* sheltered, inexperienced ← **kurang pergaulan**

kuping *n* ear; **menguping** *vt* **nguping** *coll* to eavesdrop, listen in

kupnat *n* dart (in sewing)

kupon *n* coupon

kupu: kupu-kupu *n* butterfly; ~ *malam* lady of the night, prostitute

kura: kura-kura *n* tortoise

kurang *adj, adv* less, lacking; *vt* minus; ~ *ajar* rude, badly brought up; ~ *darah* anemia, anemic; ~ *lebih* more or less, about; ~ *makan* under-nourished; ~ *mampu* poor, not well-off; ~ *percaya diri*, ~ *pede*, ~ *PD* lack self-confidence; ~ *pergaulan (kuper) sl* sheltered, inexperienced; ~ *suka* to not really like; ~ *tahu* don't really know; *masih* ~ still not enough; *sepuluh* ~ *enam sama dengan empat* ten minus six is four (10–6 = 4); **berkurang** *vi* to decrease, diminish, subside; **kekurangan** *n* shortcoming (of a person), lack; flaw, mistake, defect; **berkekurangan** *vi* to lack, be lacking or needy; **mengurangi** *vt* to take from, subtract, minus; *enam dikurangi dua sama dengan empat* six minus two is four; **mengurangkan** *vt* to reduce, make smaller; **sekurangnya, sekurang-kurangnya** *adv* at least

kurap *n* ringworm

kuras, menguras *vt* to clean out, drain; ~ *tenaga* to use up energy; **terkuras** *adj* drained

kurban, qurban *n, Isl* sacrifice, usu goats or cattle; **berkurban** *vi* to make such a sacrifice, have a sacrifice slaughtered

kurcaci *n* gnome, dwarf; *Putri Salju dan Tujuh* ~ Snow White and the Seven Dwarfs

kurét *n* curette; **menguret** *vt* to scrape out, perform a curette

kurikulum *n* curriculum; ~ *baru* new curriculum; ~ *berdasarkan kompetensi (KBK)* competency-based curriculum

kurir *n* courier; *jasa* ~ courier service

kurma, korma *n* date; *pohon* ~ date palm

kurs *n* exchange rate; ~ *mengambang* floating exchange rate; **mengurskan** *vt* to convert (currency); *satu dolar AS kalau dikurskan sekarang kira-kira Rp 10.000* one US dollar is worth about Rp 10,000 right now

kursi *n* chair, seat; position; ~ *anyaman,* ~ *rotan* wicker chair; ~ *ayunan,* ~ *goyang* rocking chair; ~ *empuk* armchair; ~ *malas* easy chair; ~ *panjang* sofa; ~ *roda* wheelchair

kursus course; ~ *kilat* crash course; ~ *pengembangan diri* self-development course; **mengursuskan** *vt* to send someone on a course

kurun time; ~ *waktu* period, length of time

kurung cage; brackets; *dalam* ~ in brackets (); **kurungan** *n* cage; *hukuman* ~ imprisonment; **mengurung** *vt* to cage, put in a cage, lock up; **terkurung** *adj* locked up

kurus *adj* thin, skinny; ~ *kering,* ~ *kerempeng* as thin as a rake; **kekurusan** *adj* too thin

kusam *adj* dull

kusén, kosén *n* frame (of door or window)

kusir *n* coachman, driver

kuskus *n* cuscus

kusta *penyakit* ~ leprosy; *orang yang sakit* ~ leper

kusuma, kesuma *n, lit* flower

kusut *adj* tangled, tousled, unkempt; complicated; **mengusutkan** *vt* to complicate, confuse

kutak, utak: mengutak-ngatikkan *vt* to work on or tinker with

kutang *n* bra, bodice

kutat: berkutat *vi* to be busy or concerned with

kuték, kutéks *n, coll* nail polish

kutik: berkutik *vi* to move slightly, budge; **mengutik** *vt* to tinker with; to touch on

kutil *n* wart; **kutilan** *adj* to have warts

kutilang, ketilang *burung* ~ thrush

kutip, mengutip *vt* to quote, cite an extract; *mahasiswa itu sering* ~ *pidato Bung Karno* the student often quoted from Sukarno's speeches; **kutipan** *n* extract, quotation

kutu *n* louse, flea; ~ *air* athlete's foot; ~ *buku* bookworm; ~ *busuk* bedbug; **berkutu** *vi* to have fleas or lice

kutub *n* pole; ~ *selatan* the South Pole;

~ *utara* the North Pole; *beruang* ~ polar bear

kutuk curse; **kutukan** *n* curse; **mengutuk** *vt* to curse; **terkutuk** *adj* cursed, accursed

Kuwait *n* Kuwait; *orang* ~ Kuwaiti

kuyup *basah* ~ soaking wet

kwaci → **kuaci**

kwalitas → **kualitas**

kwantitas → **kuantitas**

kwétiau, kwétiauw *n* large Chinese egg noodles; ~ *siram* boiled noodles

kwitansi, kuitansi *n* bill, receipt

kyai → **ki, kiai**

L

L *abbrev liter* liter, l

l [él] l, twelfth letter of the alphabet

la → **lha**

laba *n* profit, gain; ~ *bersih* net profit; ~ *kotor* gross profit; *nir*~ non-profit

laba: laba-laba, labah-labah *n* spider; *rumah* ~, *sarang* ~ cobweb

labak: kelabakan *vi* to be at a loss, flounder

labil *adj* unstable, unreliable; *tanah* ~ shaky ground, unstable ground

lab, laboratorium *n* laboratory

labrak, melabrak *vt* to beat (up), attack, lay into

labu *n* gourd, pumpkin, squash

labuh: pelabuhan port, harbor; ~ *udara (pelud) arch* airport; **berlabuh** *vi* to anchor

labuhan *n* traditional ceremony held on the beach

lacak: melacak *vt* to trace; **pelacak** *anjing* ~ sniffer dog

laci *n* drawer; chest of drawers, dresser

lacur immoral; **melacurkan** *vt* ~ *diri* to sell your body, prostitute yourself; **pelacur** *n* prostitute; **pelacuran** *n* prostitution; *tempat* ~ red-light district

lacur *apa* ~ what can you do?

lada *n* pepper

ladam *n* horseshoe

ladang *n* field; area of opportunity; ~

minyak oilfield; ~ *padi* dry ricefield; ~ *tebu* cane fields; **berladang** *vi* to cultivate the land

laden: meladéni *vt* to serve someone

lafal *n* pronunciation; **melafalkan** *vt* to pronounce; **pelafalan** *n* pronunciation

laga *n* fight; *film* ~ action film

lagak *n* manner, fashion, way; ~ *bahasa* way of speaking, accent; **berlagak** *vi* to act, pretend

lagi *adv* again; more; still; as well as; *apa*~ especially; *dia* ~ him again; *se-minggu* ~ in a week; *siapa minta* ~ who else; ~ *sedikit lagi* may I have a little more?; **lagipula** *n* furthermore, moreover; **selagi** *prep* during, as

lagi *sl* in the act of; ~ *makan* eating; ~ *pergi* out, not here → **sedang**

lagipula *n* furthermore, moreover ← **lagi pula**

lagu *n* song, music; ~ *anak-anak* children's song; ~ *daerah* song or music from a certain region; ~ *kebangsaan* national anthem; ~ *lama* old song; *neg* familiar refrain; ~ *Latin* Spanish-language song; ~ *Natal* Christmas carol; ~ *rohani* religious song; *Chr* gospel; ~ *wajib* song that must be learnted at school; *pencipta* ~ songwriter

laguna *n* lagoon

-lah added after a word to soften the message; *baik*~ OK then; *mari*~ let us go

lahan *n* ground, land, terrain; ~ *basah* area of financial opportunity; ~ *kosong* waste land

lahap gluttonous; **melahap** *vt* to devor, gorge yourself on

lahar *n* lava; ~ *dingin* mud flow

lahir born; external; ~*nya* the birth of; *(mohon) maaf* ~ *batin* to ask forgiveness for all sins (at Idul Fitri); **kelahiran** *n* birth; *adj* born; *hari* ~ birthday, anniversary; ~ *Semarang* born in Semarang; **melahirkan** *vt* to give birth to; to create; *Duwi* ~ *anak laki-laki* Duwi gave birth to a baby boy; **terlahir** *adj* born

laik → **layak**

lain *adj* other, different; ~ *ibu* from a different mother (of siblings); ~ *lagi* different again; ~ *ikan* ~ *lubuk* each to their own; *dan* ~~ *(dll)* etc, et cetera; **berlainan** *adj* differing, different; **kelainan** *n* abnormality; **melainkan** *conj* rather, instead; **selain** except, apart from

lajang *adj* single, unmarried; *masih* ~ single; **melajang** *vi* to live as a single; *adik saya masih* ~ my brother is still unmarried

laju fast, rapid, quick; rate; ~ *inflasi* inflation rate; ~ *perkembangan* rate of growth; **melaju** *vi* to proceed quickly; *mobil Mercedes itu* ~ *cepat ke arah Bogor* the Mercedes sped off towards Bogor; **pelaju** *n* commuter

lajur *n* lane (one of many); column; ~ *kiri* left lane → **jalur**

lak *n* lacquer, shellac, varnish; wax

lakban *n* adhesive tape

laki *adj, sl* male; *n, sl* husband; ~ *bini* man and wife; **lelaki** *adj, n* male; **laki-laki** *adj, n* male; *adik* ~, *kakak* ~, *saudara* ~ brother; *anak* ~ son; ~ *hidung belang* womanizer

laklakan *n, coll* gullet, throat

laknat *n* curse; **melaknat** *vt* to curse; *Hari dilaknat penyihir tetapi tetap bertahan hidup* Hari was cursed by the sorcerer but managed to survive

lakon *n* play; act

laksa *n* Malay dish of vermicelli noodles with chicken in coconut sauce

laksa: selaksa *adj, lit* ten thousand

laksamana *n* admiral; ~ *madya*, ~ *muda*, ~ *pertama* vice-admiral

laksana *conj* like, as; **melaksanakan** *vt* to realize, execute, carry out; **pelaksana** *n* manager, producer, administrator; ~ *harian* acting manager; **pelaksanaan** *n* realization, execution

laktosa *n* lactose

laku *adj* popular, in vogue; saleable; valid; ~ *keras* selling like hot cakes; *tingkah* ~ behavior, conduct; **berlaku** *adj* effective, valid; *vocer ini sudah tidak* ~ this voucher is no longer valid; *vi* to behave; **kelakuan** *n* act, behavior; **berkelakuan** *vi* to behave, act;

melakukan *vt* to do, perform, carry out; *komplotan itu sudah beberapa kali ~ pembunuhan* that gang has committed many murders; **memperlakukan** *vt* to treat; **pelaku** *n* agent, one who does something; culprit, perpetrator; **perlakuan** *n* treatment; act; **selaku** *adj* (acting) as, in the capacity of

lalai *adj* careless, negligent; **kelalaian** *n* forgetfulness, negligence

lalap, lalapan *n* raw vegetables, eaten as a side-dish

lalat, laler *n* fly

lalim → **zalim**

lalu *conj* then; *adj* last, past; *~ lalang* to and fro; *~ lintas* traffic; *bulan (yang) ~* last month; *sambil ~* in passing; *sepintas ~* at a glance; **berlalu** *vi* to pass; *badai pasti ~* the storm will pass; **melalui** *vt* to pass through; *conj* through, via; *ada bis Transjakarta ~ Jalan Sudirman* there is a busway along Sudirman; **selalu** *adv* always; **terlalu** *adv* too; **keterlaluan** *adj* too much, overly, unacceptable

lama *adj* long; old, former; *~~kelamaan* gradually, in the end; *teman ~* old friend; **lama-lama** *adj* too long; *jangan ~* don't be too long; **berlama-lama** *vi* to draw out, take a long time; **kelamaan** *adj* too long (a time); **melama-lamakan** *vt* to make longer, draw something out; **selama** *conj* for, during, as long as; **selamanya** *adv* always, forever; **selama-lamanya** *adv* forever and ever

lamar, melamar *vi* to apply; **lamaran** *n* application; proposal; *surat ~* application letter; *upacara ~* proposal ceremony; **pelamar** *n* applicant; one making a proposal

lambai: melambaikan *vt* to wave something; *~ tangan* to wave (goodbye); *orang yang selamat di pulau itu ~ handuk putih* the castaways were waving a white towel

lamban *adj* slow; **kelambanan** *n* lack of action, inertia

lambang *n* symbol; *~ kebangsaan, ~ negara* national symbol; **berlambang**
vi to have a symbol; **melambangkan** *vt* to symbolize, represent; **perlambang** *n* sign, omen

lambat *adj* slow, late; *~ laun* gradually; **melambatkan** *vt* to slow something down; **memperlambat** *vt* to slow something down (even further); **selambat-lambatnya** *adv* at the latest; **terlambat** *adj* (too) late, delayed; **keterlambatan** *n* delay; *mengalami ~* to be delayed

lambung *n* stomach; *~ kapal* hull

lambung: melambung *v* to bounce; **melambungkan** *vt* to bounce something

lamin: pelaminan *n* bridal sofa where the couple greet guests; *naik ke ~* get married

laminasi *n* laminating *coll* laminating; **melaminasi** *vt* to laminate

lampau past; *masa ~* the past; **melampaui** *vt* to surpass, outdo, overtake; *Taufik sudah ~ keberhasilan pelatihnya* Taufik has already become more successful than his coach; **terlampau** *adj* too, extremely

lampias: melampiaskan *vt* to release, indulge in; *~ hawa nafsu* to release your sexual urges; **pelampiasan** *n* act of releasing, indulgence

lampiau *n* monkey (in West Kalimantan)

lampion *n* paper lantern

lampin *n* diaper, nappy; pot-holder

lampir: lampiran *n* attachment, appendix; **melampirkan** *vt* to attach, enclose; **terlampir** *adj* attached, enclosed

lampit *n* rattan mat

lamtoro *n* a kind of tree

lampu *n* light, lamp; *~ belakang* tail-light; *~ depan* headlight; *~ inframerah* infra-red light; *~ jalanan* street light; *~ lalu lintas, ~ merah* traffic light; *~ petromaks* kerosene lantern; *~ pijar* light bulb; *~ rem* brake light; *~ sen* indicator; *~ senter* flashlight; *~ sorot* searchlight

lampung: pelampung *n* floater; flotation device; *baju ~* lifejacket

lamun: melamun *vi* to day-dream, fantasize; **ngelamun** *coll* to day-dream, fantasize

LAN *abbrev* Lembaga Administrasi

Negara National Institute of (Public) Administration

lancang *adj* impudent, impolite, shameless; **kelancangan** *n* impudence, presumptuousness

lancar *adj* smooth, fluent; ~ *berbahasa* Indonesia speak Indonesian fluently; **kelancaran** *n* smoothness, good progress, fluency; **memperlancar** *vt* to ease, make easier; *makan buah* ~ *pencernaan* eating fruit improves your digestion; **selancar** *papan* ~ surfboard; **berselancar** *vi* to surf, go surfing; ~ *angin* to go windsurfing, sailboarding; **peselancar** *n* surfer

lancip *adj* pointed, pointy

lancong: melancong *vi* to go traveling, sightseeing; ~ *ke Malaysia* to visit Malaysia; **pelancong** *n* tourist

landa: melanda *vt* to engulf, attack, hit; *dilanda kelaparan* to be hit by starvation

landai *adj* sloping

landak *n* porcupine, echidna

landas *n* base, ground; *lepas* ~ take-off; **landasan** *n* base; anvil; ~ *pacu* runway; **berlandaskan** *adj* based on; *vi* to be based on; **melandasi** *vt* to base something on

langgam *n* model, style

langgan: langganan *n* subscription; regular customer; *uang* ~ subscription; **berlangganan** *vi* to subscribe to; **pelanggan** *n* subscriber, customer

langgar *n, Isl* small prayer house

langgar: melanggar *vt* to disobey, offend; ~ *hukum* to break the law; **pelanggaran** *n* violation

langgeng *adj* everlasting, eternal; **kelanggengan** *n* eternity

langit *n* sky; *bagai bumi dan* ~ as different as night is to day; **langit-langit** *n* palate, roof of your mouth; ceiling; **selangit** *adj* very high, sky-high

langka *adj* rare

langkah *n* step; ~ *tepat* the right move; ~ *demi* ~ step by step; **melangkah** *vi* to step; **melangkahi** *vt* to step across; to marry before an older sibling

langlang: melanglang *vt* ~ *buana* to see the world, travel great distances

langsam *adj, coll* slow

langsat *pohon* ~ tree with yellow fruit; *kuning* ~ creamy yellow skin

langseng *n* steamer, traditional rice cooker

langsing *adj* slim, slender; **melangsingkan** *vt* ~ *badan* to (go on a) diet

langsir: melangsir *vt* to shunt

langsung *adj* direct, straight; *tayangan* ~ live telecast; **berlangsung** *vi* to take place; **melangsungkan** *vt* to continue; to carry out

lanjur: terlanjur *adv* too late, already; ~ *berangkat* already left

lanjut *adj* advanced, further; ~ *usia adj* old, elderly; *usia* ~ *n* old age; *manusia usia* ~ *(manula)* senior citizen; *stadium* ~ advanced stage (of illness); **lanjutan** *n* continuation; *sekolah* ~ secondary school; **berlanjut** *vi* to continue; **kelanjutan** *n* continuation, result; **melanjutkan** *vt* to continue something; **selanjutnya** *adv* then, after that

lansekap, lanskap *n* landscape

lansia *adj* elderly → **lanjut usia**

lanskap → **lansekap**

lantai, lt *n* floor (of building), story (of house); ~ *bawah* ground floor; **berlantai** *vi* to have floors, stories

lantang *adj* loud, clear; piercing, shrill

lantar: lantaran *conj* because, the reason being

lantar: terlantar, telantar *adj* neglected, abandoned; **ketelantaran** *n* neglect

lantas *adv* then, next

lantik, melantik *vt* to install, inaugurate; **pelantikan** *n* inauguration

lanting *rumah* ~ traditional house in Kalimantan

lantun: melantunkan *vt* ~ *lagu* to sing (a song)

lanud *n* airfield ← **lapangan udara**

lanun, ilanun *n* pirate

Laos *n* Laos; *bahasa* ~ Lao, *orang* ~ Lao, Laotian

laos *n* galingale → **lengkuas**

lap *n* rag, cloth; ~ *piring* tea-towel, dishcloth; **mengelap** *vt* to wipe, mop

lapang *adj* wide, spacious; ~ *dada* openly, without reservation; **lapangan** *n* field; ~ *(bola) basket* basketball court; ~ *(sepak) bola* soccer field, football pitch; ~ *golf* golf course; ~ *kerja* job vacancy; ~ *tenis* tennis court; ~ *terbang, ~ udara (lanud)* airfield, airport

lapar *adj* hungry; *busung* ~ disease caused by starvation; **kelaparan** *n* hunger, famine, starvation; *adj* very hungry

lapis layer, fold, lining; *kue* ~ layer cake; ~ *legit* kind of layer cake; **lapisan** *n* coat, layer; ~ *ozon* the ozone layer; **berlapis** *adj* layered; *vi* to have a layer; **berlapiskan** *vi* to have a layer of; **melapis** *vt* to layer, overlay; **melapisi** *vt* to add a layer to; *tukang perak* ~ *cincin dengan lapisan pelindung* the silversmith put a protective layer over the ring

lapor, melapor *vi* to report; **laporan** *n* report; ~ *tahunan* annual report; **melaporkan** *vt* to report, inform

laptop *n* laptop computer, notebook

lapuk rotten, decayed; **melapuk** *vi* to rot, decay

larang: melarang *vt* to ban, prohibit, forbid; **dilarang** *adj* prohibited; ~ *masuk* no entry, no admittance; ~ *merokok* no smoking; **larangan** *n* ban, prohibition; **terlarang** *adj* forbidden, banned; *buku* ~ banned book

lara *adj, lit* sad, sorrowful; ill, sick at heart

laras *n* barrel; counter for rifles; *se~ bedil* a rifle

laras *n* pitch, key, scale; **selaras** *adj* harmonious; **keselarasan** *n* harmony

larat: melarat *adj* miserable, poor; poverty-stricken; *hidup* ~ live in poverty; **kemelaratan** *n* poverty

lari *vi* run; ~ *cepat* sprint; ~ *estafet* relay (race); ~ *gawang* hurdles; *kawin* ~ elope; *lomba* ~ (foot or running) race; ~ *maraton* marathon; ~ *pagi* jogging; ~ *rintangan* obstacle race; **berlari** *vi* to run; **melarikan** *vt* to run off with, abduct, kidnap; ~ *diri* to run away, flee, escape; **pelari** *n* runner; **pelarian** *n* escape, solace; abduction, kidnapping

laris *adj* popular, in great demand; ~ *manis* very popular

laron *n* flying white ant

lars *sepatu* ~ boot

larut dissolve; **larutan** *n* solution; **melarutkan** *vt* to dissolve; **pelarut** *n* solute

larut *adj* late; ~ *malam* late at night

las weld; ~ *karbit* oxy welding; ~ *listrik* electric welding; *bengkel* ~ workshop; *tukang* ~ welder; **mengelas** *vt* to weld

laskar *n* army, troops; ~ *Jihad* volunteer Muslim soldiers; ~ *pemuda* youth army; ~ *rakyat* people's army

laso *n* lasso

lata: melata *vi* to crawl, creep; *binatang* ~ reptile

latah *vi* to (unconsciously) imitate; to talk non-stop

latar *n* base; ~ *belakang* background; **berlatarkan** *vi* to have as a background, be based on

latéks *n* latex

latih, melatih *vt* to train; **latihan** *n* training, practice, exercise; ~ *jasmani* physical exercise; **pelatih** *n* coach, trainer; **pelatihan** *n* training; *mengadakan* ~ to run a course; **terlatih** *adj* trained

Latin *Amerika* ~ Latin America; *bahasa* ~ Latin; *lagu* ~ Spanish-language song

lauk *n* side-dish; ~ *pauk* side-dish

laun *lambat* ~ slowly, gradually

laut *n* sea; ~ *Jawa* the Java Sea; ~ *Karang* the Coral Sea; ~ *Kidul* the Indian Ocean; ~ *lepas* the open sea; ~ *Merah* the Red Sea; ~ *Tengah* the Mediterranean; *air* ~ sea water; *bajak* ~ pirate; *barat* ~ northwest; *kapal* ~ ship; *orang* ~ sea nomad; *timur* ~ northeast; ~ *Cina Selatan* the South China Sea; **lautan** *n* ocean; ~ *api* sea of flames; ~ *Hindia* the Indian Ocean; ~ *Teduh, ~ Pasifik* the Pacific Ocean; **kelautan** *adj* maritime; *Departemen Perikanan dan* ~ Department of Fisheries and Marine Affairs; **melaut** *vi* to go to sea; **pelaut** *n* sailor, seaman

lawak joke; **lawakan** *n* joke, jest; **melawak** *vi* to joke, jest; **pelawak** *n* comedian, comic, clown

lawan *n* opponent, adversary; opposite; *conj* against; ~ *bicara* interlocutor, person one is talking to; ~ *jenis* opposite sex; ~ *kata* opposite, antonym; ~

main opposite (role); **berlawanan** *vi* to be opposed; **melawan** *vt* to oppose, resist; ~ *arus* against the flow; **perlawanan** *n* opposition, resistance

lawas *adj* old; *mobil* ~ classic car

lawat: lawatan, perlawatan *n* trip, visit; **melawat** *vi* to visit, make a trip; *Presiden sedang* ~ *ke Thailand* the President is on a visit to Thailand

layak, laik *adj* proper, suitable; ~ *jalan* roadworthy; **kelayakan** *n* suitability; *studi* ~ feasibility study; **selayaknya** *adv* properly, should

layan: layanan *n* service; **melayani** *vt* to serve; **pelayan** *n* waiter, *m* waitress *f* attendant; **pelayanan** *n* service ~ *masyarakat* public services

layang: layang-layang kite; **melayang** *vi* to float (in the air); *jiwa* ~ to die; **selayang** ~ *pandang* overview

layar sail; ~ *lebar* silver screen; ~ *perak* small screen, television; ~ *tancap* open-air makeshift cinema; **berlayar** *vi* to sail; **pelayaran** *n* voyage; *perusahaan* ~ shipping company

layat: melayat *vt* to visit a house in mourning, pay your respects; *saya* ~ *ke rumah duka malam-malam* I went to the house late at night to pay my respects; **pelayat** *n* person who pays their respects

layu wither, wilt

layuh paralysis; *lumpuh* ~ polio

lazim *adj* usual; *tidak* ~ unusual

LBH *abbrev Lembaga Bantuan Hukum* Legal Aid Agency

lebah *n* bee; *sarang* ~ beehive

lebam, lembam *biru* ~ black-and-blue; *gas* ~ inert or noble gas

lébar *adj* wide, broad; *layar* ~ silver screen; *panjang* ~ detailed, extensive; **lébarnya** *n* width; **melébarkan** *vt* to widen; **pelébaran** *n* widening; ~ *jalan* widening the road, roadworks

lebar: Lebaran *n* Idul Fitri, first two days after the Ramadan fast; ~ *Haji* Idul Adha, Feast of the Sacrifice (performed during the annual pilgrimage); **berlebaran** *vi* to celebrate Idul Fitri

lébarnya *n* width ← **lébar**

lebat *adj* thick, dense; *hujan* ~ heavy rain, downpour

lebay *adj, sl* over-the-top (OTT), excessive

lebih *adv* more, -er; ~ *baik*, ~ *bagus* better; ~ *buruk*, ~ *jelek* worse; ~ *dahulu* first, firstly; ~ *gemuk* fatter; *kurang* ~ about; **berlebihan** *adj* excessive; **kelebihan** *n* extra, excess; ~ *bagasi* excess luggage; **melebihi** *vt* to exceed, surpass; **selebihnya** *n* the rest or remainder; **terlebih** *adj* especially; ~ *dahulu* first, firstly

lebur: melebur *vi* to merge, fuse; **peleburan** *n* melting; merger

lécéh: melécéhkan *vt* to insult; **pelécéhan** *n* contempt; ~ *seksual* sexual harassment

lécét sore, blister; *luka* ~ blister

léci *n* lychee

ledak: ledakan *n* explosion; **meledak** *vi* to explode; *bom* ~ *pada jam 12 malam* the bomb exploded at midnight; **meledakkan** *vt* to explode or detonate something; **peledak** *bahan* ~ explosive; **peledakan** *n* bombing

lédék, melédék *vt* to tease, provoke

lédéng, léding *air* ~ plumbing, water pipes; *tukang* ~ plumber

lédré, lédri *pisang* ~ thinly sliced banana chips, a specialty of Malang

lega *adj* relieved; **melegakan** *adj* reassuring, consoling

légal *adj* legal; **légalisasi** *n* legalization; **melégalisasi, melégalisir** *vt* to legalize

legam *hitam* ~ pitch-black, jet black

légénda *n* legend, myth; **légéndaris** *adj* legendary

Legi *n* first day of the Javanese week

legit *lapis* ~ kind of layer cake

légiun *n* legion

légo *v, coll* to sell cheaply, get rid of, let go

légong *tari* ~ Balinese trance dance performed by young girls

léha: berléha-léha *vi* to relax, be idle

léhér *n* neck; ~ *rahim* cervix

lejit: melejit *vi* to shoot up, skyrocket; *namanya* ~ she suddenly became famous

lekas *adj* fast, quick, speedy; *(semoga)* ~ *sembuh* get well soon

lekat *adj* close; sticky, adhesive; **melekat** *vi* to stick; *pelekat bahan* ~ adhesive

Lékra *abbrev, n* Institute of People's Culture, left-wing artists association under Sukarno ← **Lembaga Kebudayaan Rakyat**

léktor *n* lecturer

lekuk *n* hollow, cavity; concave; ~ *mata* eye socket

léla → **rajaléla**

lelah *adj* tired, weary; *melepas* ~ to take a rest; **kelelahan** *n* fatigue, weariness; **melelahkan** *adj* tiring

lelaki, laki-laki *adj* male; *n* man, male; ~ *hidung belang* womanizer

lélang *n* auction; *juru* ~ auctioneer; **dilélang** *adj* for auction, tender; **melélangkan** *vt* to auction (off)

lelap *adj* sound, fast, completely; *tidur* ~ sound asleep

lélé *ikan* ~ catfish; *pecel* ~ catfish with rice and peanut sauce

léléh melt, run; **léléhan** *n* trickle; **meléléh** *vi* to drip, run; **meléléhkan** *vt* to melt something

lelep: kelelep *adj, coll* sunk, submerged

leluasa *adj* free, unrestricted; *dengan* ~ freely; **keleluasaan** *n* freedom (of choice) ← **luasa**

lelucon *n* joke ← **lucu**

leluhur *n* ancestor; *tanah* ~ ancestral home → **luhur**

lém *n* glue; ~ *tikus* sticky paper to catch rats; **dilém** *v* to be glued

lemah *adj* weak; ~ *lembut* gentle, tender; ~ *syahwat* impotent; **kelemahan** *n* weakness; **melemah** *vi* to weaken, become weak

lemak *n* fat; grease; ~ *jenuh* saturated fats; ~ *nabati* vegetable fat; *menimbun* ~ to store fat

lemak *adj* delicious; *nasi* ~ a Malay rice specialty

lemari, almari *n* cupboard, closet, shelf; ~ *arsip* filing cabinet; ~ *baju*, ~ *pakaian* wardrobe; ~ *besi* safe; ~ *buku* bookcase; ~ *es* refrigerator, fridge; ~ *kaca* display case; dresser

lemas, lemes *adj* weak, drained; *mati* ~ suffocated, drowned

lembab, lembap *adj* humid, damp, moist; *cuaca* ~ humid weather; **kelembaban** *n* humidity; **pelembab, pelembap** *n* moisturizer

lembaga *n* institute, foundation, board, agency; ~ *Pemasyarakatan (LP)* jail, prison; ~ *Administrasi Negara (LAN)* ~ National Institute of (Public) Administration; ~ *Bantuan Hukum (LBH)* Legal Aid Agency; *Kebudayaan Rakyat (Lékra)* Institute of People's Culture, left-wing artists association under Sukarno; ~ *Pertahanan Nasional (Lemhanas)* National Defense Agency; ~ *swadaya masyarakat (LSM)* non-government organization (NGO); ~ *Ilmu Pengetahuan Indonesia (LIPI)* Indonesian Institute of Sciences; ~ *Minyak dan Gas Bumi (Lemigas)* Institute for Oil and Natural Gas; **melembagakan** *vt* to make into an institution

lembah *n* valley

lembam, lebam *adj* slow, inert; *gas* ~ inert or noble gas; **kelembaman** *n* inertia

lembap → **lembab**

lembar *n* sheet (of paper), page; *membuka* ~ *baru* to turn over a new leaf; **lembaran** *n* page, sheet; issue; ~ *Negara* State Gazette

lembayung *adj* crimson

lembék *adj* soft, weak, flimsy

lembing *n* javelin, spear; *lempar* ~ javelin (throw)

lembu *n* cow

lembur *n* overtime; *vi* to work overtime, stay late

lembut *adj* soft, gentle; *lemah* ~ gentle, tender; **kelembutan** *n* softness; **melembut** *vi* to soften, become soft; **melembutkan** *vt* to soften; **pelembut** *n* softener

lemes → **lemas**

Lémhanas *n* National Defense Agency ← **Lembaga Pertahanan Nasional**

Lemigas *abbrev, n* Institute for Oil and Natural Gas ← **Lembaga Minyak dan**

Gas Bumi

lémpar ~ *cakram* discus (throw); ~ *lembing* javelin (throw); **lémparan** *n* throw; **melémpar** *vt* to throw; **melémpari** *vt* to pelt, throw something at; ~ *kereta api dengan batu* to throw rocks at a train; **melémparkan** *vt* to throw something; **pelémpar** *n* bowler, pitcher, thrower; something to throw with; **pelémparan** *n* (act of) throwing; **terlémpar** *adj* thrown, flung

lempeng *adj, coll* straight (ahead)

lémpéng *n* large slightly curved shell; ~ *bumi*, ~ *tektonik* tectonic plate

lemper *n* sweet cake of sticky rice with a meat filling

léna: terléna *adj* off-guard

lencana *n* emblem, badge

léncéng: meléncéng *vi* to deviate, go out of your way

lendir *n* mucus; **berlendir** *adj* mucous, slimy

léngah *adj* off-guard, careless; **kelengahan** *n* carelessness

lengan *n* arm, sleeve; *baju* ~ *panjang* long-sleeved shirt

lengang *adj* deserted, quiet, empty

lenggang *adj* rest, pause; *waktu* ~ spare time

lénggang *adj* swaying; **melénggangkan** *vt* ~ *tangan* to swing your arms while walking

lengkap *adj* complete; *adat* ~ full ceremony; **melengkapi** *vt* to furnish, supply; **pelengkap** *n* accessory; **perlengkapan** *n* outfit, equipment

léngkéng, keléngkéng *n buah* ~ small lychee

léngkét *adj* sticky, close

lengking: melengking *vi* to trill, soar (of a voice)

lengkuas *n* a kind of spice, galingale → **laos**

lengkung *adj* bent, convex; **lengkungan** *n* curve, bend; arch; **melengkung** *vt* to arch

léngsér *vi* to abdicate, descend from power

lénong *n Betawi* folk play; ~ *bocah* children's *lenong*

lénsa *n* lens; ~ *bifokal* bifocal lenses; ~ *cekung* concave lens; ~ *cembung* convex lens; ~ *kontak* contact lenses; ~ *progresif* progressive lenses

lénso *tari* ~ dance with a handkerchief

lentéra *n* lantern

lentur *adj* elastic, pliable

lenyap *adj* disappeared, gone, vanished

lepas loose, free; (come) off; escape; *adj* freely; ~ *kendali* out of control; ~ *landas* take-off; ~ *pantai* offshore; *penerjemah* ~ freelance translator; ~ *dari itu* apart from that; **melepaskan** *vt* to release, let free; ~ *lelah* to take a rest; ~ *tembakan* to fire a shot; **pelepasan** *n* departure, farewell; *acara* ~ goodbye (party); **selepas** *prep, conj* after

lepéh, melepéh *vt, coll* to spit out

lépot → **belépotan**

lépra *n* leprosy

lepuh *n* blister; **melepuh** *vi* to blister

lerai *adj* separated

léréng *n* slope; ~ *gunung* foothills

lés (to attend) a private class or course; ~ *bahasa* language class; ~ *piano* piano lesson; *guru* ~ private teacher

lesat: melesat *vi* to fly along, take off

lésbi lesbian

lését: melését *vi* to slip, skid; to miss the target; *jaman* ~ the Great Depression; **memelésétkan** *vt* to parody; to up-end, send off-course; **pelésétan** *n* parody; **terpelését** *adj* slipped

lestari *adj* eternal, everlasting; **kelestarian** *n* preservation, conservation; **melestarikan** *vt* to preserve, maintain; ~ *hutan* to protect the forest; **pelestarian** *n* protection, preservation

lesu *adj* tired, weary; *letih* ~ dead tired, exhausted

lesung *n* dimple, hollow; mortar; ~ *pipit* dimple

letak place, location; **letaknya** *n* the location, position; **meletakkan** *vt* to put in place, set down; ~ *jabatan* to resign; ~ *senjata* to lay down arms; **terletak** *adj* situated, located

letih *adj* ~ *lesu* dead tired, exhausted

létjén *n* lieutenant-general; **létkol** *n*

lieutenant-colonel; **létnan** *n* lieutenant; **léttu** *n* first lieutenant ← **létnan satu**

letup: meletup *vi* to pop, explode

letus: letusan *n* eruption; **meletus** *vi* to erupt; *Gunung Merapi sedang ~* Mount Merapi is erupting

léukémia *n* leukemia, leukaemia → **kanker darah**

léver *n* liver → **hati**

léwat *prep* past; via; *~ faks* by fax; *~ pos* by mail, by post; *jam empat ~ lima* five past four; **keléwat** *adj, sl* too, unacceptable; **keléwatan** *n* too much; **meléwati** *vt* to pass or go through; **meléwatkan** *vt* to miss something; *jangan lewatkan tawaran ini!* don't miss this offer!

lezat *adj* delicious, tasty; **kelezatan** *n* delicious taste

lha well (expression of mild surprise)

lho you know (used to emphasize a statement, often denying something); *ejac* well!; *gitu ~* like that, you know

lhs *abbrev lihat halaman sebelah* please turn over (PTO)

liang n hole, passage; *~ dubur* anus; *~ kubur* grave

liar *adj* wild, untamed; unregulated; *kucing ~* wild cat; *pungutan ~ (pungli)* unofficial charge

liat *adj* tough; *tanah ~* clay

Libanon *n* Lebanon; *orang ~* Lebanese

libat: melibatkan *vt* to involve, include; **terlibat** *adj* involved, implicated; **keterlibatan** *n* involvement, association

liberal *adj* liberal, open-minded

libur be free, on holiday (from school or work); *~ panjang* long holiday; *hari ~* holiday; **liburan** *n* holiday; *~ sekolah* school holidays; **berlibur** *vi* to go or be on holiday; **meliburkan** *vt* to give a holiday to; *perusahaan mau ~ semua karyawan besok* the company will give all employees the day off tomorrow

lichtdruk *n, arch* duplicate, phototype

licik *adj* cunning, tricky; **kelicikan** *n* trickery, cunning

licin *adj* smooth; slippery; *kertas ~* glossy paper

lidah *n* tongue; *~ api* flame; *~ buaya* aloe vera; *~ kucing* a kind of plant

lidi *n* palm-leaf rib; *sapu ~* small broom

lift *n* elevator, lift; *~ barang* goods lift

lifter *n* weightlifter

liga *n* (football) league; *~ Arab* the Arab League; *~ Inggris* FA, English league

lihai *adj, neg* tricky, shrewd, cunning; **kelihaian** *n* shrewdness, cunning

lihat *vt* to see; *~ halaman sebelah (lhs)* please turn over (PTO); **lihat-lihat** *~ saja* just looking; **kelihatan** *adj* visible; *~nya* apparently, it seems; **melihat** *vt* to see, look; **melihat-lihat** *v* to look around, have a look; **memperlihatkan** *vt* to show, display; **penglihatan** *n* vision, sight

liku *n* turn, bend; **berliku-liku** *adj* twisted, complicated; *vi* to have twists and turns

likuidasi *n* liquidation

likuiditas *n, fin* liquidity

lilin *n* candle; wax; *es ~* icypole, iced lolly, popsicle

liliput *adj* very small, mini

lilit turn, twist; **lilitan** *n* turn, twist; **melilit** *vt* to wind, twist; **terlilit** *adj* caught up, twisted

lima *adj* five; *~ belas* fifteen; *~ puluh* fifty; *(sholat) ~ waktu* (pray) five times a day; *kembar ~* quintuplets; *simpang ~* five-way intersection; *~ rukun Islam* the five pillars of Islam; **berlima** *adj* the five of them, (as) a group of five; **kelima** *adj* fifth; **seperlima** *n* one-fifth

limau *jeruk ~* lime

limbah *n* waste; *~ nuklir* nuclear waste; *air ~* effluent, polluted water; *pengolahan ~* waste processing

limosin, limusin *n* limo *coll* limousine, limo

limpa *n* spleen

limpah *adj* abundant, plenty; **berlimpah-limpah, melimpah** *adj* overflowing, abundant; *vi ~ (ruah)* to overflow, be in abundance; **kelimpahan** *n* abundance, wealth; **melimpahkan** *vt* to shower upon

limun *n (jeruk) ~* lemon

limusin → **limosin**

linang: berlinang *vi* to trickle, drip; *air mata* ~ eyes filled with tears

lincah *adj* nimble, deft, agile; **kelincahan** *n* agility

lindas: melindas *vt* to run over, squash; **terlindas** *adj* run over

lindung *n* eel

lindung: berlindung *vi* to (take) shelter; **melindungi** *vt* to protect, shelter; **pelindung** *n* protective device; **perlindungan** *n* protection; **terlindung** *adj* protected, guarded

lingga *n* obelisk, traditional male symbol; ~ *yoni* obelisk in a square hole, traditional symbol of male and female sexuality

linggis *n* crowbar

lingkar *n* ring, circle, circumference; *jalan* ~ ring road; **lingkaran** *n* circle; ~ *setan* vicious circle; **melingkar** *vi* to go around, coil; **melingkari** *vt* to circle or surround

lingkung: lingkungan *n* environment, surroundings, circle(s); *aktivis* ~ environmental activist

lingkup *n* scope, reach; **melingkupi** *vt* to encompass, embrace

linglung *adj* dazed, confused

lingsang, linsang *n* otter

linguistik *adj* linguistic; *n pl* linguistics; ~ *terapan* applied linguistics

lini *n* line (in sport, war)

linsang, lingsang *n* otter

lintah *n* leech; ~ *darat* loan shark

lintang across, latitude; ~ *selatan* southern latitude; **melintang** *adj* horizontal, across; *vi* to cross, go across; *bila tidak ada aral* ~ if all goes well

lintas ~ *budaya* cross-cultural; *lalu* ~ traffic; **lintasan** *n* path, route; **melintas** *vi* to pass by

linting *rokok* ~ (hand-)rolled cigarette; *rokok* ~ *dhewe (rokok tingwe)* (hand-)rolled cigarette; **lintingan** *n* rolled; **melinting** *vt* to roll

linu *pegal* ~ aches and pains, sore

liontin *n* pendant

lipan *n* centipede

lipat fold; ~ *paha* groin; *dua kali* ~ double, twice; **lipatan** *n* fold; **berlipat** *vi* ~ *ganda* many times over; **kelipatan** *n* multiple; **melipat** *vt* to fold

LIPI *abbrev Lembaga Ilmu Pengetahuan Indonesia* Indonesian Institute of Sciences

lipstik *n* lipstick

lipur: pelipur ~ *hati* consolation

liput: liputan *n* coverage, reporting; **meliput** *vt* to cover, report on; **meliputi** *vt* to include, cover

lirih *adj* low-pitched, soft

lirik ~ *lagu* (song) lyrics

lirik: melirik *vt* to steal a glance

lis *n* trim (especially between wall and ceiling), cornice

Lisabon *n* Lisbon

lisan *adj* oral, verbal; *secara* ~ orally; *ujian* ~ oral examination

lisénsi *n* license, licence

listrik electric, electricity; *arus* ~ electric current; *pembangkit tenaga* ~ power station

litani *n, Cath* litany

litbang *n* research and development (R & D) ← **penelitian dan pengembangan**

liter *n* liter, litre; ~ *kubik* cubic liter

litsus *n* special investigation ← **penelitian khusus**

liur *air* ~ saliva, spit; **berliur** *vi* to drool, salivate

liwet *nasi* ~ rice cooked in coconut milk, a specialty of Solo; a rice dish in West Java

LN *abbrev luar negeri* overseas, foreign

lo → **lho**

lo → **lo mie**

loak second-hand; *pasar* ~ flea market; *toko* ~ second-hand shop, opportunity shop; *tukang* ~ ragman

loba *adj* greedy

lobak *n* radish

lobang → **lubang**

lobi *n* lobby (of hotel or building)

lobi lobby; **melobi** *vt* to lobby

lobi-lobi *buah* ~ kind of red fruit

lodéh *sayur* ~ vegetables in coconut milk

loe → **lu**

logam *n* metal; ~ *mulia* precious metal; *uang* ~ coin, small change

logat *n* accent; *~ Batak* a Batak accent; *~ kental* thick accent; **berlogat** *vi ~ Jawa* to have a Javanese accent

logika *n* logic; **logis** *adj* logical

logistik *n* logistics

logo *n* logo

loh → **lho**

lohor *Isl* the midday prayer

lok *n, coll* locomotive, engine ← **lokomotif**

lokakarya *n* seminar, workshop

lokal *adj* local; *hujan ~* local showers; **lokalisasi** *n* red-light district

lokasi *n* location; *~ syuting* on location; *cinta ~ (cinlok)* a temporary love affair in a certain place; **berlokasi** *adj* located; *vi* to be located

lokét *n* counter, desk, ticket window or office; *~ karcis* ticket office; *~ retour* counter for return tickets

lokio *n* chives

lokomotif, lok *n* locomotive

lolong howl; **melolong** *vi* to howl (of dogs)

lolos *vi* to escape; succeed, progress; *~ seleksi* to be selected

lomba race, competition, contest; *~ lari* (foot or running) race; *~ mengarang* essay competition; **berlomba** *vi* to compete, race; **perlombaan** *n* competition

lombok *n* chilli

lo mie *n* kind of Chinese noodles

lompat jump, leap; *~ galah* pole vault; *~ jauh* long jump; *~ tali* jump rope, skipping (rope); *~ tinggi* high jump; **lompatan** *n* jump; **melompat** *vi* to jump, leapfrog; **melompati** *vt* to jump over

lompong: melompong *kosong ~* completely empty

loncat jump (over something); *~ indah* diving; *papan ~* springboard; **loncatan** *n* jump; *batu ~* stepping-stone, springboard; **meloncat** *vi* to spring, jump; **meloncati** *vt* to jump over

loncéng *n* bell

londo *n, coll* white person; *orang ~* white person ← **Belanda**

longdrés *n, coll* gown, evening dress

longgar *adj* loose, wide; **kelonggaran** *n* facility, dispensation; **melonggarkan** *vt* to loosen (restrictions)

longo: melongo *vi* to gape or stare

longsor slip; *tanah ~* landslide

lonjak: lonjakan *n* surge, sudden rise; **melonjak** vi to increase sharply, peak

lonjong *adj* oval; *bulat ~* oval

lontar *daun ~* palm leaf once used as writing material

lontar throw; *~ martil* hammer throw; **lontaran** *n* throw; **melontarkan** *vt* to throw; *~ pertanyaan* to ask or pose a question

lontong *n* cooked, solid slab of rice

loper *n* delivery boy; *~ koran* newspaper delivery boy

lopor → **pelopor**

loréng *adj* striped; *baju ~* camouflage gear, *sl* cammo

lorong *n* path; lane, alley

Lorosae *Timor ~* East Timor

lorot: melorot *vi* to fall, drop, plummet; *celananya ~* his pants fell down

los *n* stall; *~~ pasar* market stalls

losin → **lusin**

losmén *n* guest house, accommodation, cheap hotel

loték *n* a dish of fresh vegetables with peanut sauce

loténg *n* attic, loft

loteré, lotré *n* lottery

lotong → **lutung**

lotot: melotot *vi* to stare or gape with bulging eyes; **memelototi** *vt* to stare at someone; **melototkan** *vt ~ mata* eyes bulging

lotré → **loteré**

lowong *adj* vacant; **lowongan** *adj* wanted, vacancy; *~ kerja* work opportunities

loyang *n* cake tin, tray, mould

loyo *adj* very tired, exhausted

LP *abbrev lembaga pemasyarakatan* jail, prison

LSM *abbrev lembaga swadaya masyarakat* non-government organization, NGO

Lt. *lantai* floor, level

lu *sl* you; *gue ~* on very close terms; *derog* you (bastard); *pergi ~* get lost

luak *n* civet cat; *kopi ~* coffee made

from beans excreted by a civet cat

luang *adj* free, empty; *waktu* ~ spare time; **meluangkan** *vt* ~ *waktu* to set aside time for; **peluang** *n* chance, opportunity; **berpeluang** *vi* to have an opportunity, a chance

luap: luapan *n* wave, wash; **meluap** *vi* to overflow, swell, wash

luar out, external; ~ *biasa* outstanding, extraordinary; ~ *dalam* inside and out; ~ *kepala* by heart; ~ *kota* out of town; ~ *negeri* overseas, abroad; *dunia* ~ outside world; *ke* ~ go out, outside; *orang* ~ outsider, stranger; foreigner; **keluar** go out; be issued; *prep* out, outside; **keluaran** *n* edition, version, issue; **mengeluarkan** *vt* to issue, publish, send out, release

luas wide, broad; space; **luasnya** *n* width; area; **memperluas** *vt* to widen, expand, enlarge

luasa *arch* → **leluasa**

lubang, lobang *n* hole, passage; ~ *angin* air vent; ~ *dubur* anus; ~ *gigi* cavity; ~ *hidung* nostril; ~ *jarum* eye (of a needle); ~ *kancing* buttonhole; ~ *di jalan* pothole; **berlubang** *vi* to have a hole; **melubangi** *vt* to pierce, put a hole in

lubér *vi* leak, expand, seep out

lubuk *n* deep pool; ~ *hati* depth of your heart; *lain* ~ *lain ikan* everyone is different

lucu *adj* cute, sweet; funny; odd; **kelucuan** *n* cuteness; **lelucon** *n* joke; **melucu** *vi* to make jokes, be funny

lucut: melucuti *vt* to strip or pull off; ~ *senjata* to disarm; **perlucutan** ~ *senjata* disarmament

ludah *n* saliva, spit; *air* ~ saliva; **meludah** *vi* to spit; **meludahi** *vt* to spit at, on

ludes *adj* wiped out, finished off; ~ *dilahap api* completely gutted

ludruk *n* East Javanese folk play

lugas *adj* straightforward, to the point, direct; **kelugasan** *n* simplicity; directness; objectivity

lugu *adj* naive, gullible; **keluguan** *n* naivety, simplicity

luhur *adj* lofty, noble, esteemed; **leluhur** *n* ancestor; *tanah* ~ ancestral home

luka wound; injured; ~ *bakar* burn; ~ *lecet* blister; ~ *parah* badly wounded or injured; ~ *ringan* mild injury, slight wound; ~ *tikam* stab wound; **melukai, melukakan** *vt* to hurt or wound; **terluka** *adj* wounded, hurt, injured

lukis *v* to paint, draw; *seni* ~ (visual) art; **lukisan** *n* painting, picture, portrait (of a person); **melukis** *vt* to paint, draw; **pelukis** *n* painter, artist; **terlukis** *adj* painted; engraved

luks *adj* luxury

Luksémburg *n* Luxembourg; *orang* ~ Luxembourger

lulu → **melulu**

luluh ~ *lantak* crushed, pulverized

lulur *mandi* ~ traditional massage with body scrub; **luluran** *vi, coll* to have such a traditional massage

lulus *vi* to pass; ~ *ujian* pass an exam; *tidak* ~ fail; **lulusan** *n* graduate; **meluluskan** *vt* to pass someone (in an exam or test)

lumas: pelumas *n* lubricant

lumayan *adv, adj* quite, not bad, fairly

lumba-lumba *n* dolphin, porpoise

lumbung ~ *padi* rice silo or barn

lumér *vi* leak, expand, seep out

lumpang *n* pestle, rice pounder; *alu* ~ mortar and pestle

lumpat → **lompat**

lumpia *n* spring rolls; ~ *basah* spring rolls eaten cold

lumping *kuda* ~ flat woven toy horse; East Javanese performance using a toy horse

lumpuh *adj* paralysed, lame; ~ *layuh* polio; **melumpuhkan** *vt* to knock out, paralyse

lumpur *n* mud; **berlumpur** *adj* muddy; *vi* to be muddy

lumrah *adj* usual, accepted, common

lumur smear; **berlumuran** *adj* smeared, stained; **melumuri** *vt* to smear, cover with; **melumurkan** *vt* to smear something onto; *anak itu* ~ *selai pada kursi* the child smeared jam onto the chair

lumut *n* moss; *hijau* ~ moss green, bright green

lunak *adj* soft; *piranti* ~ software; **melunak** *vi* to soften, become soft; **melunakkan** *vt* to soften something, make soft, tenderize

lunas *adj* paid off, in full; **melunasi** *vt* to pay off; ~ *hutang* to repay, pay off a debt

luncur: meluncurkan *vt* to launch, set in motion; **peluncuran** *n* launch

lunglai *adj* weak, powerless

lungsur: lungsuran *n* hand-me-down (clothing); **melungsurkan** *vt* to hand down, pass on

luntur fade, lose color, run

lupa *v* to forget; ~ *daratan* to lose your head; ~ *diri* to forget yourself; ~ *akan keluarga* to forget about your family; ~~ *ingat* to vaguely remember; **kelupaan** *n* something forgotten; **melupakan** *vt* to forget something; **pelupa** *n* forgetful person; **terlupakan** *tak* ~ unforgettable

lupis *kue* ~ small round cakes made from palm sugar, pandan and desiccated coconut

lupus *penyakit* ~ a skin disease, lupus

luput *vi* to escape, slip away; ~ *dari perhatian* to escape attention

lurah *n* head of a *kelurahan*, village chief; **kelurahan** *n* administrative unit, village

lurik *kain* ~ striped Javanese cloth

luruh moult, fall out (of hair or fur)

lurus *adj* straight; *jalan yang* ~ the right path; **meluruskan** *vt* to straighten; **pelurusan** *n* straightening

lusa *adv* the day after tomorrow; *besok* ~ tomorrow or the day after

lusin, losin, dosin *n* dozen, twelve; **selusin** *n* a dozen; *teh botol* ~ a dozen bottles of tea

lusuh *adj* old, faded (of clothes)

lutung, lotong *n* black monkey

lutut *n* knee; *tempurung* ~ kneecap; *bertekuk* ~ to surrender; *menekuk* ~ to go down on your knees; **berlutut** *vi* to kneel (down)

luwes *adj* attractive, well-presented;

keluwesan *n* attractiveness, style

luyur: berkeluyuran *vi* to hang around; *banyak preman* ~ *dekat setasiun* lots of thugs hang around the station → **keluyur**

M

M *Masehi* Christian calendar

m [ém] m, 13th letter of the alphabet

m meter

maaf sorry; *minta* ~ to apologize, say you're sorry; *seribu* ~ a thousand apologies; *tidak ada* ~ no excuse, unforgivable; *mohon* ~ *lahir (dan) batin* ask forgiveness for all sins (at Idul Fitri); **bermaaf-maafan** *vi, Isl* to beg forgiveness of each other (at Idul Fitri); **memaafkan** *vt* to forgive, pardon; **pemaaf** *adj* forgiving

maag, mag *n, coll* stomach (disorder); *obat* ~ antacid; *sakit* ~ weak stomach, gastric pain

Mabad *n* Army Headquarters ← **Markas Besar Angkatan Darat**

mabes *n* headquarters; ~ *Polri* National Police Headquarters ← **markas besar**

mabrur *Isl haji* ~ pilgrim accepted by God

mabuk *adj* drunk; ill; motion sickness; ~ *asmara*, ~ *cinta*, ~ *kepayang* head over heels in love; ~ *jalan* carsick; ~ *laut* seasick; *orang* ~ drunk, drunkard; **memabukkan** *adj* alcoholic; intoxicating

macam *n* kind, sort, model; ~ *apa?* what sort?; *aneka* ~ all kinds, variety; **macam-macam** *adj, neg* all sorts; **bermacam-macam** *adj* various; **semacam** *adj* a kind or type of; ~ *itu* like that, of that type

macan *n* large spotted cat; *n, coll* tiger; ~ *kumbang* leopard, panther; ~ *tutul* cheetah

macet, macét jammed, blocked; traffic jam; ~ *total* gridlock; *kredit* ~ nonperforming loans; **kemacetan** *n* jam; ~ *lalu lintas* traffic jam

Madagaskar *n* Madagascar, the Malagasy Republic; *bahasa* ~, *orang* ~ Malagasy

madani *adj* civil; *masyarakat* ~ civil society

madat *n* opium; *vi, coll* to do drugs; **pe-madat** *n* (opium) addict

Madinah *n* Medina (in Saudi Arabia)

madrasah *n, Isl* school, college

madu *n* honey; co-spouse; *bulan* ~ honeymoon; *berbulan* ~ to (have a) honeymoon; **memadu** *vt* to cheat on

madya *adj* medium, middle; *bahasa Jawa* ~ middle level of Javanese; *kota~* municipality

maem → **mam**

mafhum *v* to understand, know

mag → **maag**

magang (do) work experience, apprentice

maghrib → **magrib**

magis *adj* magical

magister *n* Master's degree; ~ *hukum* Master of Law

magnét → **maknit**

magrib, maghrib *n* sunset; sunset prayer

mah *coll* way of adding stress to phrases (often contrasting); *Tina tidak mau, tapi saya* ~ *oke saja* Tina doesn't want to, but as for me, that's fine

maha- *adj* great; *~bharata* Mahabharata, shadow puppet epic; *~siswa* university student; *Tuhan Yang* ~ *kuasa* Almighty God

mahal *adj* expensive, dear; *jual* ~ to have a high asking price; **kemahalan** *adj* too expensive; **memahalkan** *vt* to raise the price, make more expensive

mahar *n, Isl* dowry, bride price

mahasiswa *n* (university or college) student; **mahasiswi** *n, f* (female) student; ~ *abadi derog* professional student; ~ *pascasarjana* post-graduate student

mahir *adj* expert, skilled; **kemahiran** *n* skill

mahkamah *n* court of law; ~ *Agung (MA)* High Court; ~ *Militer Luar Biasa (Mahmilub)* extraordinary court-martial

mahkota *n* crown, crest; *putra* ~ crown prince

mahligai *n* palace; ~ *perkawinan* institution of marriage

Mahmilub *n* extraordinary court-martial → **Mahkamah Militer Luar Biasa**

mahoni *n* mahogany

main *v* to play, do (a sport), to go ...ing; ~ *api* to play with fire; ~ *ayunan* to play on the swings; ~ *bola* to play football or soccer; ~ *gila* to have an affair, play around; ~ *golf* to play golf; ~ *judi* to gamble; ~ *kartu* to play cards; ~ *kasar* to play rough or dirty; ~ *mata* to flirt, keep looking at (someone); ~ *perempuan* to fool around with women; ~ *piano* to play the piano; ~ *pukul* to hit, be violent; ~ *serobot* to push in, jump the queue; ~ *serong* to commit adultery, have an affair; ~ *sinetron* to appear in a local TV comedy or drama; *bukan* ~ wow, extraordinary; ~ *hakim sendiri* to take the law into your own hands; *bioskop* ~ *jam 8* the film starts at 8; **main-main** *vi* to joke around, not be serious; **mainan** *n* toy; **bermain** *vi* to play; ~ *api* to play with fire; ~ *sulap* to do magic; **memainkan** *vt* to play something; ~ *biola* to play the violin; *Hadi* ~ *peranan Gatotkaca* Hadi played the part of Gatotkaca; **mempermainkan** *vt* to ridicule, make a fool of; **pemain** *n* player, actor; ~ *film* actor; ~ *bola* basketball; ~ *film* actor; ~ *harpa* harpist; ~ *kibor* keyboardist; ~ *sofbol* softballer, softball player; ~ *terompet* trumpet player, trumpeter; ~ *voli* volleyballer, volleyball player; **permain-an** *n* game, match; **sepermainan** *teman* ~ friend you play or hang out with (from childhood)

maizéna *n* corn; *tepung* ~ cornflour

majal *adj* blunt

majalah *n* magazine; ~ *bulanan* monthly (magazine)

majelis *n* assembly, council; ~ *Per-musyawaratan Rakyat (MPR)* People's Consultative Assembly (Parliament); ~ *Syuro Muslimin Indonesia (Masyumi)* n Consultative Council of Indonesian Muslims, an Islamic association before 1960

majemuk *adj* compound, complex; *kata*

~ compound (word)

majikan *n* employer

maju *vi* go forward, advance, progress, improve; *adj* advanced, progressive; ~ *mundur* back and forth; *negara* ~ developed country; ~ *tak gentar* ever onward; **kemajuan** *n* progress, advance; **memajukan** *vt* to bring forward, propose

mak *pron* mother; ~ *cik* aunt; ~ *comblang* matchmaker

maka *conj* therefore, so, then; **makanya** *conj* that's why, so

makalah *n* paper, essay

makam *n* grave; *Taman* ~ *Pahlawan (TMP)* heroes' cemetery; **memakamkan** *vt* to bury (someone); **pemakaman** *n* funeral, burial; ~ *negara* state funeral

makan eat; ~ *dulu* said when eating first before others; ~ *hati* brood, dwell on; be upset; ~ *korban* claim victims; ~ *malam* (eat or have) dinner; ~ *obat* to take medicine (in solid form); ~ *pagi* breakfast; ~ *siang* lunch, dinner; ~ *sirih* chew betel; ~ *tempat* to take up space; ~ *waktu* take (time); *kasih* ~ to feed, give food; *kereta* ~ restaurant car; *kurang* ~ undernourished; *mencari* ~ to earn a living; *nafsu* ~ appetite; *rumah* ~ restaurant; *sudah* ~? have you eaten?; ~ *gaji buta* to have an easy job; ~ *makan garam* experienced, an old salt, an old hand; **makanan** *n* food; ~ *berserat* high-fiber food; **memakan** *v* to eat, consume, take; ~ *obat* to take a pill or capsule; *dimakan rayap* to be eaten by termites; **pemakan** *n* eater; ~ *daging* carnivore; **termakan** *adj* eaten, consumed (by accident)

makanya *conj* that's why, so ← **maka**

makar *vi* to betray the government, be subversive

makaroni *n* macaroni; ~ *skotel* kind of macaroni loaf

Makasar, Makassar *n* Macassar (formerly Ujung Pandang); *bahasa* ~, *orang* ~ Macassarese

makasi, makasih *coll* thanks → **terima kasih**

Makau *n* Macau; *orang* ~ Macanese

makcik *n* aunt

Makédonia *n* Macedonia; former Yugoslav Republic of Macedonia (FYROM); *bahasa* ~, *orang* ~ Macedonian

makelar *n* broker

makét *n* model

makhluk, mahluk *n* creature; ~ *halus* spirit

maki *caci* ~ insult, abuse; **mencaci-maki** *vt* to insult, abuse; **memaki, memaki-maki** *vt* to insult, heap abuse on

makin *adv* increasingly; ~ *lama*, ~ *besar* the longer, the bigger; **semakin** *adv* even more

maklum *vi* to know, be aware of; *agar* ~ let it be known; **memaklumi** *vt* to be aware of, accept; **maklumat** *n* announcement, proclamation, notice

makmur *adj* prosperous; **kemakmuran** *n* prosperity; **memakmurkan** *vt* to make prosperous, develop; **Persemakmuran** *n* (British) Commonwealth

makna *n* meaning; **bermakna** *adj* meaningful; *vi* to have meaning; *itu bukan perbuatan yang* ~ that (action) doesn't mean anything

maknit, magnét *n* magnet

makruh *adj, Isl* not sinful, but discouraged; *makan di depan orang yang sedang berpuasa itu* ~ it's not the right thing to eat in front of someone who's fasting

maksiat *n* immoral; *tempat* ~ brothel; **kemaksiatan** *n* immorality, vice

maksimal maximal(ly); **semaksimal** ~ *mungkin* to the maximum; **memaksimalkan** *vt* to maximize; **maksimum** *n* maximum

maksud *n* purpose, intention, meaning; ~ *saya* I mean; **bermaksud** *vi* to intend; **dimaksud, dimaksudkan** *v* to be meant or intended; **memaksudkan** *vt* to intend

mal, mol *n* shopping center, mall

Maladéwa *(Kepulauan)* ~ the Maldives

malagizi *n* malnutrition

malah, malahan instead, rather, on the other hand

malaikat *n* angel; ~ *Jibril* the Archangel Gabriel; ~ *(ul)maut* angel of death

Malaka, Melaka *n* Malacca; *Selat* ~ Straits of Malacca

malam *n* night, evening; ~ *Jumat* Thursday night (when some believe ghosts are out); *Jumat* ~ Friday night; ~ *hari* at night; ~ *Kudus* Holy Night (Christmas Eve); ~ *minggu* Saturday night; ~ *mingguan* go out on Saturday night; ~ *Natal* Christmas Eve; ~ *perta-ma* wedding night; ~ *takbiran* eve of Idul Fitri; *larut* ~ late at night; *selamat* ~ good evening; *siang* ~ day and night; *tadi* ~ last night; *tengah* ~ midnight; ~ *Tahun Baru* New Year's Eve; **malam-malam** *adv* late at night; **bermalam** *vi* to spend or stay the night; **kemalaman** *adv* too late (at night); after dark; **se-malam** *adv* last night; ~ *suntuk* all night long; **semalaman** *adv* all night long

malam *n* wax (for making batik)

malang *adj* unlucky; ~ *melintang* lie across; **kemalangan** *n* bad luck, misfortune

malapetaka *n* disaster, calamity; ~ *Lima Belas Januari (Malari)* riots in Jakarta on January 15, 1974

malaprakték *n* (medical) malpractice

Malari *n* riots in Jakarta on January 15, 1974 ← **Malapetaka Lima Belas Januari**

malaria *n* malaria

malas *adj* lazy, can't be bothered; ~ *makan* not feel like eating; **bermalas-malas(an)** *vi* to lie or laze around, be lazy; **kemalasan** *n* laziness; **pemalas** *n* lazy person, lazybones

Malaysia *n* Malaysia; *bahasa* ~, *orang* ~ Malaysian

maléo *burung* ~ a kind of bird

maling *n* thief; **dimaling, kemalingan** *v* to be robbed

Malta *n* Malta; *bahasa* ~, *orang* ~ Maltese

malu *adj* shy, ashamed, embarrassed; *jangan* ~ don't be shy; **malu-malu** *adj* shy; ~ *kucing* feign disinterest; **ke-maluan** *n* genitals, sex organs; **memalukan** *adj* embarrassing;

mempermalukan *vt* to embarrass, shame; **pemalu** shy (person)

Maluku *n* Maluku, the Moluccas; ~ *Utara (Malut)* North Maluku

mam, mam-mam *v, child* eat

Mama *pron, f* Mama, Mom, Mum

mamah, memamah *v* to chew, ruminate

mamalia *n* mammal

Mami, Mi *pron, coll* Mum, Mummy (in Westernized circles); madam (of a brothel)

mampet *adj* stuck, blocked, jammed; *hidung* ~ blocked nose

mampir *vi* to drop in, call on

mampu *vi, aux* able, capable; *adj* well-off; *kurang* ~ poor, not well-off; **ke-mampuan** *n* ability, capability; **se-mampunya** *adv* as well as you can, to the best of your ability

mampus *sl* die, croak; *coll* in big trouble

mana *pron* where, which; ~ *bisa* how is it possible?; ~ *mungkin* how could it be?; ~ *saja* whichever; *dari* ~ from where; *di* ~ where; *di* ~ *saja* wherever; *ke* ~ where; *ke* ~ *saja* wherever; **mana-mana** *di* ~, *ke* ~ everywhere

manajemén *n* management → **penge-lolaan**; **manajer** *n* manager → **penge-lola**

manakala *conj* when, if

mana-mana *di* ~, *ke* ~ everywhere ← **mana**

manasik ~ *haji* preparations for the pilgrimage to Mecca

manca- *adj* many; ~*negara* internation-al, overseas

mancing → **pancing**

mancung *adj* straight (of noses)

mancur *air* ~ fountain ← **pancur**

mandala *n* zone, circle

Mandar ethnic group in South Sulawesi; *bahasa* ~, *orang* ~ Mandarese

mandat *n* mandate

mandau *n* knife used in Kalimantan

mandek, mandeg *vi* stop, cease, get stuck, stagnate

mandi *vi* bathe, take or have a bath, wash (the body); swim; ~ *junub Isl* to wash or shower after sex; ~ *kucing* wash only part of your body; ~ *lulur* traditional body scrub; ~ *matahari* sunbathe; ~ *rendam* soak in a bathtub; ~ *uap* take or have a steam bath; **bermandi** *vi* to bathe; ~ *keringat* to be soaked in sweat; **bermandikan** *adj* bathed in; *vi* to bathe in; ~ *darah* to be soaked in blood; **memandikan** *vt* to wash someone; **mempermandikan** *vt* to christen, baptize; **permandian** *n* bathing pool; christening, baptism; *bapak* ~ godfather

mandor *n* supervisor, overseer

mandul *adj* infertile, sterile, childless; **kemandulan** *n* infertility

manekin *n* dummy, mannequin

manfaat *n* benefit, use; **bermanfaat** *adj* useful, of benefit; *vi* to have a use or benefit; **memanfaatkan** *vt* to take advantage of, (draw) benefit from

mangga *n* mango

manggan *n* manganese

manggis *n* mangosteen

manggung *vi, coll* to perform ← **panggung**

mangkal *vi, coll* to use as a base, wait for work; ; *banyak tukang becak ~ di perapatan* lots of pedicab drivers wait for work at the crossroads ← **pangkal**

mangkat *vi, pol* to pass away

mangkir *vi* to not attend, be absent

mangkok, mangkuk *n* bowl

mangsa *n* prey

mangu: termangu-mangu *adj* confused, dazed; speechless

mani *air ~* sperm

mania *n* mania

manifés *n* passenger list (on an aircraft); cargo list

manifésto *n* manifesto; ~ *Politik (Manipol)* political manifesto announced by President Sukarno on 17 August, 1959

manik: manik-manik *n* beads

manikam *n* precious stone

manikur *n* manicure

Manipol *n* political manifesto announced by President Sukarno on 17 August, 1959 ← **Manifésto Politik**

manipulasi *n* manipulation; ~ *politik* political manipulation; **memanipulasikan** *vt* to manipulate

manis *adj* sweet; pretty; nice; ~*nya* the sweetness; *jari* ~ ring finger; *kayu* ~ cinnamon; *mulut* ~ sweet talk; *duduk yang* ~ sit nicely, sit properly; *habis* ~, *sepah dibuang* use something then abandon it; **manisan** *n* sweets, candy; sugared snacks; **kemanisan** *adj* too sweet; **pemanis** *n* sweetener; ~ *buatan* artificial sweetener

manja spoilt; *anak* ~ spoilt child; **memanjakan** *vt* to spoil someone

manjur *adj* potent, effective; *obat yang* ~ strong medicine

mansét *n* cufflinks

mantan *adj* former (of people); ~ *Presiden* former President; ~ *suami* ex-husband

mantap *adj* stable, steady; **kemantapan** *n* stability; **memantapkan** *vt* to stabilize or steady something

mantel *n* (long) coat, raincoat

mantera, mantra *n* mantra, chant

mantri *n* (low-ranking) assistant

mantu *n* son- or daughter-in-law; *vi* to marry off a son or daughter → **menantu**

manual *n* guidebook, manual → **buku panduan**

manual *adj* manual, by hand

manula *n* old person, senior citizen → **manusia lanjut usia**

manunggal *adj* integrated, becoming one

manusia *n* human (being); humanity; ~ *lanjut usia (manula)* senior citizen; ~ *salju* snowman; **kemanusiaan** *n* humanity; **perikemanusiaan** *adj* humanitarian; **manusiawi** *adj* humanitarian

manuver *n* maneuver

manyar *burung* ~ weaverbird

map *n* folder; ~ *gantung* file (in filing cabinet)

mapan *adj* settled, comfortable

marabahaya *n* great danger

marah *adj* angry; *cepat* ~, *gampang* ~ short-tempered, quick-tempered, hot-headed; **marah-marah** frequently angry; in a bad mood; **kemarahan** *n* anger; **memarahi** *vt* to scold, be angry with; **pemarah** *adj* bad-tempered

Marah *pron, m, Min* Minangkabau title

marak, semarak shine, glow, bright; glittering, exciting; **memarakkan** *vt* to light up, brighten; *acara Tahun Baru dimarakkan bintang-bintang ibukota* New Year's festivities with glittering stars from Jakarta

maraton *n* marathon

Maret *bulan* ~ March; *Surat Perintah Sebelas* ~ *(Supersemar)* Eleventh of March Instruction (enabling Suharto to take over power in 1966)

marga *n, lit* road; *Jasa* ~ Indonesia Highways Corporation; *Sapta* ~ the Seven Paths (military motto)

marga *n* (Batak) family name

margarin *n* margarine

margasatwa *n* wild animals, fauna

marhaban *Isl* welcome, hello; ~ *ya Ramadhan* happy fasting month

marhaén *arch kaum* ~ proletariat

mari let's go, come on; please (said when someone begs leave); ~*lah* let us

marinir *n* Marines; *Korps* ~ Marine Corps

markas *n* office, headquarters; ~ *besar (mabes)* headquarters; ~ *Besar Polri (Mabes Polri)* National Police Headquarters; ~ *Besar Angkatan Darat (Mabad)* Army Headquarters

markisa *n* kind of passionfruit; *sirop* ~ passionfruit cordial or syrup

marmer *n* marble

marmot, marmut *n* guinea pig, marmot

Maroko, Marokko *n* Morocco; *orang* ~ Moroccan

Mars *n* (the planet) Mars

mars *n* march; *lagu* ~ march

marsekal *n* marshal

martabak *n* large fried snack with filling; ~ *keju* kind of cheese pancake; ~ *manis* kind of sweet pancake; ~ *telur* kind of omelet

martabat *n* dignity, rank; **bermartabat** *adj* dignified; *vi* to have dignity

martil *n* hammer; *lontar* ~ hammer throw

martir *n* martyr

Maryam *n, Isl* Mary

mas, emas *n* gold; ~ *kawin* dowry; ~ *putih* platinum, white gold; *anak* ~ fa-vorite, pet; *toko* ~ jewelers; *tukang* ~ goldsmith

Mas *pron, m* address for elder brother, male person slightly older than yourself, or worker in service industry

masa *n* time, period; *conj* when; ~ *advent* advent, time leading up to Christmas; ~ *depan*, ~ *mendatang* future; ~ *kecil* childhood, youth; ~ *lalu*, ~ *lampau* the past; ~ *paceklik* drought, time of hardship before the harvest; ~ *peralihan* transition period; ~ *perangsangan* foreplay; ~ *puber* puberty; ~ *remaja* youth; puberty; ~ *subur* fertile period; ~ *sulit* hard times; ~ *tenggang* (period of) grace; ~ *transisi* transition (period); ~ *saya di Bandung* when I lived in Bandung; *sepanjang* ~ forever; **semasa** *conj* when, during, throughout ← **masa**

masa, masak no! I can't believe it! it's not possible (expression of disbelief); ~ *bodoh* not care, I don't care

masak cook; cooked; *juru* ~ cook, chef; **masakan** *n* food, cooking, dish; ~ *Cina* Chinese food, Chinese cuisine; **memasak** *vt* to cook, make

masalah *n* problem; ~*nya* the problem is; *tidak* ~ no problem; **bermasalah** *adj* problem, troublesome; **mempermasalahkan** *vt* to make a problem out of

masam, masem *adj* sour; acid; *bermuka* ~ sour-faced

Maséhi *adj* Christian; *tahun* ~ Christian calendar

masih *adv* still, yet

masin *adj* salty, brackish (of water)

masing: masing-masing *pron* each, respectively

masinis *n* train driver, engineer

masjid, mesjid *n* mosque

maskapai *n, arch* company; ~ *penerbangan*, airline

maskara *n* mascara, eyeshadow

maskawin → **mas**

masker *n* surgical mask

maskot *n* mascot

maslahat *n* benefit, advantage, profit; use

massa *n* the masses, the public; *dikeroyok* ~ beaten up by a mob; **massal** *adj* mass; *perkawinan* ~ mass wedding
masturbasi *n* masturbation
masuk *vi* to come in, enter; to be part of, be present, attend; ~ *akal* make sense, logical; ~ *angin* have or catch a cold; ~ *hitungan* included, considered; ~ *Islam* to become Muslim, convert to Islam; ~ *kantor*, ~ *kerja* to go to work; ~ *sekolah* to go to school; **kemasukan** *adj* possessed; **memasuki** *vt* to enter (illicitly); **memasukkan** *vt* to put in, insert, import, enter; **termasuk** *adj* including
masya Allah it is God's will, heavens above!
masyarakat *n* society; ~ *madani* civil society; ~ *Ekonomi ASEAN* ASEAN Economic Community; **kemasyarakatan** *adj* social; **pemasyarakatan** *lembaga* ~ correctional center, prison
masygul *adj* sad, troubled, down-hearted
masyhur *adj* famous, celebrated; **termasyhur** *adj* most famous
Masyumi *n* Consultative Council of Indonesian Muslims, an Islamic association before 1960 ← **Majelis Syuro Muslimin Indonesia**
mata *n* eye, center, point; ~ *air* spring, well; ~ *angin* direction, compass point; ~ *bor* drill bit; ~ *duitan* money-hungry; ~ *hari* sun; ~ *juling* squint; ~ *kaki* ankle; ~ *kayu* knot (in wood); ~ *keranjang* wandering eye; ~ *kuliah* (university) subject; ~ *panah* arrowhead; ~ *pelajaran* (school) subject; ~ *rantai* link (in a chain); ~ *sipit* slanted eyes (esp of East Asians); ~ *telanjang* the naked eye; ~ *uang* currency; *air* ~ tears; *memasang* ~ to keep your eyes open, watch for; *bermain* ~ *vi* to flirt, ogle; *cindera* ~ souvenir; *telur* ~ *sapi* fried egg, sunny side up; **mata-mata** *n* spy; **memata-matai** *vt* to spy on; **semata** ~ *kaki* to the ankle; *anak* ~ wayang only child; **semata-mata** *adv* only, entirely, solely
matahari *n* sun; *bunga* ~ sunflower; ~ *terbenam* sunset; ~ *terbit* sunrise

mata-mata *n* spy ← **mata**
matang *adj* ripe, cooked, mature; *setengah* ~ medium, half-cooked; **kematangan** *n* maturity
matématika *n* mathematics, maths; **matématikus** *n* mathematician
matéri *n* material; **matérial** *adj* material; **matérialis** *adj* materialist; **matérialisme** *n* materialism
mati die; go out, be extinguished; off; ~ *konyol* die for nothing; ~ *lampu* blackout; ~ *lemas* suffocate, drown; ~ *rasa* numb, without feeling; ~ *suri* coma; ~ *syahid Isl* martyr; *harga* ~ not negotiable; **mati-matian** *adv* as hard as possible, to the death; **kematian** *n* death, passing; **mematikan** *adj* deadly; *vt* to kill, extinguish, put out; ~ *lampu* to turn off the light
matra *n* dimension
matras *n* mat (in gymnastics or martial arts)
matré *cewek* ~ material girl ← **matéri**
matriks *n* matrix
matoa *n* small fruit from Papua, similar to the lychee or rambutan
mau *vi* to want, will; ~*nya* would like (but); ~ *tidak* ~ whether you want to or not, there's no avoiding it; **kemauan** *n* want, will, desire; *semau* ~ *gue* as I please; **semaunya** *adv* at will, as you like
Maulid, Maulud, Mulud *n, Isl* birthday (esp of the Prophet Muhammad)
maung *n, Sund* tiger
Mauritius *n* Mauritius; *orang* ~ Mauritian
maut *n* death; *malaikat* ~, *malaikatul* ~ angel of death
mawar *bunga* ~ rose
mawas ~ *diri* self-correction, introspection
maya *dunia* ~ cyberspace
mayang *n* palm blossom
mayat, mayit *n* corpse; *membuang* ~ to dispose of a body
mayjén *n* major-general; **mayor** *n* major; ~*-Jenderal (Mayjen)* Major-General
mayonés *n* mayonnaise
mayoritas *n* majority

mazhab *n, Isl* school of thought

Mbah *pron, Jav* term used to address grandparents or Javanese of your grandparents' generation

Mbak *pron, f* address for elder sister, female person slightly older than yourself, or worker in service industry

mbeling *adj* naughty, disobedient; anti-establishment; *kiai* ~ Islamic scholars speaking out against the government

mbok *coll* perhaps (softens message)

Mbok *pron, f* mother; address for female servants

MCK *abbrev mandi cuci kakus* toilet and bathing facilities

MEA *Masyarakat Ekonomi ASEAN* ASEAN Economic Community

mébel, meubel *n* furniture; *toko* ~ furniture store

medali, médali *n* medal; ~ *emas* gold medal; ~ *perak* silver medal; ~ *perunggu* bronze medal

médan *n* field, plain, square; ~ *perang* battlefield

médé, ménté, mété *kacang* ~ cashew (nut)

média *n* media; ~ *cetak* print media; ~ *elektronik* electronic media; ~ *massa* mass media; ~ *sosial (médsos)* social media

médio *adj* mid-

médis *adj* medical

méditasi *n* meditation

medok *adj* very thick (of an accent, esp Javanese)

médsos *n, sl* social media ← **média sosial**

MEE *abbrev, arch Masyarakat Ekonomi Eropa* European Economic Community (EEC)

méga *n* cloud; ~ *mendung* storm cloud

megah *adj* glorious, luxurious, grand; **kemegahan** *n* glory, luxury

Méi *bulan* ~ May

méja *n* table; ~ *bilyar* billiards table, pool table; ~ *bundar* round table; ~ *hijau* court (of law); ~ *makan* dining table; ~ *rias* dressing table; ~ *perundingan* discussion table; ~ *tulis* desk

méjéng *v, sl* to hang out, be on display

Mekah, Mekkah *n* Mecca; *Serambi* ~ Aceh, the Gateway to Mecca

mékanik, mékanika, mékanis *adj* mechanical

mekar *vi* to blossom; **pemekaran** *n* expansion, development

Méksiko *n* Mexico; *orang* ~ Mexican

melabrak *vt* to beat (up), attack, lay into ← **labrak**

melacak *vt* to trace ← **lacak**

melacurkan *vt* ~ *diri* to sell your body, prostitute yourself ← **lacur**

meladéni *vt* to serve someone ← **ladén**

melafalkan *vt* to pronounce ← **lafal**

melahap *vt* to devour, gorge yourself on

melahirkan *vt* to give birth to; to create; *Duwi* ~ *anak laki-laki* Duwi gave birth to a baby boy ← **lahir**

melainkan *conj* rather, instead

melajang *vi* to be single; *adik saya masih* ~ my brother is still unmarried ← **lajang**

melaju *vi* to proceed quickly; *mobil Mercedes itu* ~ *cepat ke arah* Bogor the Mercedes sped off towards Bogor ← **laju**

Melaka, Malaka *n* Malacca; *Selat* ~ Straits of Malacca

melaknat *vt* to curse; *Hari dilaknat penyihir tetapi tetap bertahan hidup* Hari was cursed by the sorcerer but managed to survive ← **laknat**

melaksanakan *vt* to realize, execute, carry out ← **laksana**

melakukan *vt* to do, perform, carry out; ~ *angket* to do a survey; *komplotan itu sudah beberapa kali* ~ *pembunuhan* that gang has committed many murders ← **laku**

melalui *vt* to pass through; *conj* through, via; *ada bis Transjakarta* ~ *Jalan Sudirman* there is a busway along Sudirman ← **lalu**

melama-lamakan *vt* to take a long time, draw something out ← **lama**

melamar *v* to apply ← **lamar**

melambaikan *vt* to wave something; ~ *tangan* to wave goodbye; *orang yang selamat di pulau itu* ~ *handuk putih* the castaways were waving a white towel ← **lambai**

melambangkan *vt* to symbolize, represent ← **lambang**

melambatkan *vt* to slow something down ← **lambat**

melambung *vi* to bounce; **melambungkan** *vt* to bounce something ← **lambung**

melaminasi *vt* to laminate ← **laminasi**

melampaui *vt* to surpass, outdo, overtake; *Taufik sudah ~ keberhasilan pelatihnya* Taufik has already become more successful than his coach ← **lampau**

melampiaskan *vt* to release, indulge in; *~ hawa nafsu* to release your sexual urges ← **lampias**

melampirkan *vt* to attach, enclose

melamun *vi* to day-dream, fantasize ← **lamun**

melancong *vi* to go traveling, sightseeing; *~ ke Malaysia* to visit Malaysia ← **lancong**

melanda *vt* to engulf, attack, hit; *dilanda kelaparan* to be hit by starvation ← **landa**

melandasi *vt* to base something on ← **landas**

melanggar *vt* to disobey, offend; *~ hukum* to break the law ← **langgar**

melangkah *vi* to step; **melangkahi** *vt* to step across; to marry before an older sibling ← **langkah**

melanglang *vt ~ buana* to see the world, travel great distances ← **langlang**

melangsingkan *vt ~ badan* to (go on a) diet ← **langsing**

melangsungkan *vt* to continue; to carry out ← **langsung**

melangsir *vt* to shunt ← **langsir**

melanjutkan *v* to continue something ← **lanjut**

mélankolis *adj* melancholic

melantik *vt* to install, inaugurate ← **lantik**

melantunkan *vt ~ lagu* to sing (a song) ← **lantun**

melapis *vt* to layer, overlay; **melapisi** *vt* to add a layer to; *tukang perak ~ cincin dengan lapisan pelindung* the silver-smith put a protective layer over the ring ← **lapis**

melapor *vi* to report; **melaporkan** *vt* to report, inform ← **lapor**

melapuk *vi* to rot, decay ← **lapuk**

melar *vi* stretch, expand

melarang *vt* to ban, prohibit, forbid ← **larang**

melarat *adj* miserable, poor, poverty-stricken; *hidup ~* live in poverty; **kemelaratan** *n* poverty

melarikan *vt* to run off with, abduct, kidnap; *~ diri* to run away, flee, escape ← **lari**

melarutkan *vt* to dissolve ← **larut**

melas: memelas *adj* pathetic, pitiful

melata *vi* to crawl, creep; *binatang ~* reptile ← **lata**

melati *n* jasmine

melatih *vt* to train ← **latih**

melaut *vi* to go to sea ← **laut**

melawak *vi* to joke, jest ← **lawak**

melawan *vt* to oppose, resist; *~ arus* against the flow ← **lawan**

melawat *vi* to visit, make a trip; *Presiden sedang ~ ke Thailand* the President is on a visit to Thailand ← **lawat**

melayang *vi* to float (in the air); *jiwa ~* to die ← **layang**

melayani *vt* to serve ← **layan**

melayat *vi* to visit a house in mourning, pay your respects; *saya ~ ke rumah duka malam-malam* I went to the house late at night to pay my respects ← **layat**

Melayu *adj* Malay; Indonesian; *coll* local, non-Caucasian; second-rate; *bahasa ~*, *orang ~* Malay; *Semenanjung ~ Malaya*, the Malay Peninsula; *spion ~* local (ineffective) spy

mélébarkan *vt* to widen ← **lébar**

melebihi *vt* to exceed, surpass ← **lebih**

melebur *vi* to merge, fuse ← **lebur**

melécéhkan *vt* to insult ← **lécéh**

meledak *vi* to explode; *bom ~ pada jam 12 malam* the bomb exploded at midnight; **meledakkan** *vt* to explode or detonate something ← **ledak**

melédék *vt* to tease, provoke ← **lédék**

melegakan *adj* reassuring, consoling ← **lega**

melégalisasi, melégalisir *vt* to legalize ← **légalisasi**

melejit *vi* to shoot up, skyrocket; *namanya* ~ she suddenly became famous ← **lejit**

melék awake, eyes open; ~ *huruf* literate; **kemelék-hurufan** *n* literacy

melekat *vi* to stick ← **lekat**

melelahkan *adj* tiring ← **lelah**

melélangkan *vt* to auction (off) ← **lélang**

meléléh *vi* to drip, run; **meléléhkan** *vt* to melt something ← **léléh**

melemah *vi* to weaken, become weak ← **lemah**

melembagakan *vt* to make into an institution ← **lembaga**

melembut *vi* to soften, become soft; **melembutkan** *vt* to soften ← **lembut**

melémpar *vt* to throw; **melémpari** *vt* to pelt, throw something at; ~ *kereta api dengan batu* to throw rocks at a train; **melémparkan** *vt* to throw something ← **lémpar**

meléncéng *vi* to deviate, go out of your way ← **léncéng**

melénggangkan *vt* ~ *tangan* to swing your arms while walking ← **lénggang**

melengkapi *vt* to furnish, supply ← **lengkap**

melengking *vi* to trill, soar (of a voice) ← **lengking**

melengkung *vi* to arch ← **lengkung**

melepaskan *vt* to release, let free; ~ *tembakan* to fire a shot ← **lepas**

melepuh *vi* to blister ← **lepuh**

mélér *vi* to run (of a nose)

melesat *vi* to fly along, take off ← **lesat**

melését *vi* to slip, skid; to miss the target; *jaman* ~ The Great Depression; **pelésétan, plésétan** *n* parody ← **lését**

melestarikan *vt* to preserve, maintain; ~ *hutan* to protect the forest ← **lestari**

meletakkan *vt* to put in place, set down; ~ *jabatan* to resign; ~ *senjata* to lay down arms ← **letak**

meletup *vi* to pop, explode ← **letup**

meletus *vi* to erupt; *Gunung Merapi sedang* ~ Mount Merapi is erupting ← **letus**

meléwati *vt* to pass or go through; **meléwatkan** *vt* to miss something; *jangan lewatkan tawaran ini!* don't miss this offer! ← **léwat**

melibatkan *vt* to involve, include ← **libat**

meliburkan *vt* to give a holiday to; *perusahaan mau* ~ *semua karyawan besok* the company will give all employees the day off tomorrow ← **libur**

melihat *v* to see, look; **melihat-lihat** *v* to look around, have a look; **memperlihatkan** *vt* to show, display ← **lihat**

melilit *vt* to wind, twist ← **lilit**

melimpah *adj* overflowing, abundant; *vi* ~ *(ruah)* to overflow, be in abundance; **melimpahkan** *vt* to shower upon ← **limpah**

melindas *vt* to run over, squash ← **lindas**

melindungi *vt* to protect, shelter ← **lindung**

melingkar *vi* to go around, coil; **melingkari** *vt* to circle or surround ← **lingkar**

melingkupi *vt* to encompass, embrace ← **lingkup**

melinjo *n buah* ~, *biji* ~ seeds and nuts which are used for making *emping* chips

melintang *adj* horizontal, across; *vi* to cross, go across; *bila tidak ada aral* ~ if all goes well ← **lintang**

melintas *vi* to pass by ← **lintas**

melinting *vt* to roll ← **linting**

melipat *vt* to fold ← **lipat**

meliput *vt* to cover, report on; **meliputi** *vt* to include, cover ← **liput**

melirik *vt* to steal a glance ← **lirik**

melobi *vt* to lobby ← **lobi**

mélodi *n* melody

melolong *vi* to howl (of dogs) ← **lolong**

melompat *vi* to jump, leapfrog; **melompati** *vt* to jump over ← **lompat**

melompong *kosong* ~ completely empty ← **lompong**

mélon *n* rockmelon, cantaloupe

meloncat *vi* to spring, jump (over something); **meloncati** *vt* to jump over ← **loncat**

melonggarkan *vt* to loosen (restrictions) ← **longgar**

melongo *vi* to gape or stare at ← **longo**

melonjak *vi* to increase sharply, peak ← **lonjak**

melontar, melontarkan *vt* to throw; ~ *pertanyaan* to ask or pose a question ← **lontar**

melorot *vi* to fall, drop, plummet; *celananya* ~ his pants fell off ← **lorot**

melotot *vi* to stare or gape, with bulging eyes; **melototkan** *vt* ~ *mata* eyes bulging ← **lotot**

meluangkan *vt* ~ *waktu* to set aside time for ← **luang**

meluap *vi* to overflow, swell, wash ← **luap**

melubangi *vt* to pierce, put a hole in ← **lubang**

melucu *vi* to make jokes, be funny ← **lucu**

melucuti *vt* to strip or pull off; ~ *senjata* to disarm ← **lucut**

meludah *vi* to spit; **meludahi** *vt* to spit at, on ← **ludah**

melukai, melukakan *vt* to hurt or wound ← **luka**

melukis *v* to paint, draw ← **lukis**

melulu *adv* always, all the time, continuously

meluluskan *vt* to pass someone (in an exam or test) ← **lulus**

melumpuhkan *vt* to knock out, paralyze ← **lumpuh**

melumuri *vt* to smear, cover with; **melumurkan** *vt* to smear something onto; *anak itu* ~ *selai pada kursi* the child smeared jam onto the chair ← **lumur**

melunak *vi* to soften, become soft; **melunakkan** *vt* to soften something, make soft, tenderize ← **lunak**

melunasi *vt* to pay off; ~ *hutang* to repay, pay off a debt ← **lunas**

meluncurkan *vt* to launch, set in motion ← **luncur**

melungsurkan *vt* to hand down, pass on ← **lungsur**

melupakan *vt* to forget something ← **lupa**

meluruskan *vt* to straighten ← **lurus**

memaafkan *vt* to forgive, pardon ← **maaf**

memabukkan *adj* alcoholic, intoxicating ← **maaf**

memacari *vt* to date, go out with someone ← **pacar**

memacu *vt* to spur on ← **pacu**

memacul *vt* to hoe ← **pacul**

memadai *adj* enough, sufficient; *vi* to be enough or sufficient ← **pada**

memadamkan *vt* to put out, extinguish ← **padam**

memadati *vt* to fill (with), make full ← **padat**

memadu *vt* to cheat on ← **madu**

memadu *vt* to unite, fuse; ~ *kasih* to (be in) love, have a relationship; **memadukan** *vt* to combine, unite ← **padu**

memaés *vt* to make up (someone) in traditional style ← **paés**

memagari *vt* to fence (off) ← **pagar**

memagut *vt* to bite (of a snake) ← **pagut**

memahalkan *vt* to raise the price, make more expensive ← **mahal**

memahami *vt* to understand, comprehend ← **paham**

memahat *vt* to sculpt, chisel ← **pahat**

memainkan *vt* to play something; ~ *biola* to play the violin; *Hadi* ~ *peranan Gatotkaca* Hadi played the part of Gatotkaca ← **main**

memajang *vt* to display ← **pajang**

memajukan *vt* to bring forward, propose ← **maju**

memakai *vt* to wear; to use; ~ *kacamata* to wear glasses ← **pakai**

memakamkan *vt* to bury (someone) ← **makam**

memakan *vt* to eat, consume, take; ~ *obat* to take a pill or capsule; *dimakan rayap* to be eaten by termites ← **makan**

memaki, memaki-maki *vt* to insult, heap abuse on ← **maki**

memaklumi *vt* to be aware of, accept ← **maklum**

memakmurkan *vt* to make prosperous, develop ← **makmur**

memaksa *vt* to force ← **paksa**

memaksimalkan *vt* to maximize ← **maksimal**

memaksudkan *vt* to mean, intend ← **maksud**

memaku *vt* to nail ← **paku**

memalak *vt* to force (usu to pay money) ← **palak**

memalsukan *vt* to falsify, forge ← **palsu**

memalu *vt* to hammer, strike ← **palu**

memalukan *adj* embarrassing ← **malu**

memamah *vi* to chew, ruminate ← **mamah**

memamérkan *vt* to display, exhibit ← **pamér**

memampangkan *vt* to spread out; to explain ← **pampang**

memanah *vt* to shoot (with a bow) ← **panah**

memanas *vi* to get hot, heat up; **memanaskan** *vt* to heat (up) ← **panas**

memancang *vt* to stake or drive in ← **pancang**

memancarkan *vt* to broadcast ← **pancar**

memancing *v* to fish (with hook and line) ← **pancing**

memancung *vt* to cut off, mutilate; ~ *kepala* to behead or decapitate ← **pancung**

memancur *vi* to pour, gush, flow out ← **pancur**

memandang *vt* to view, consider; ~ *rendah* to underestimate, disregard ← **pandang**

memandikan *vt* to wash someone ← **mandi**

memandu *vt* to guide ← **pandu**

memanén *vt* to harvest ← **panén**

memanfaatkan *vt* to take advantage of, (draw) benefit from ← **manfaat**

mémang *conj*, émang *coll* indeed; ~*nya neg* do you think ...?

memanggang *vt* to roast, bake, toast ← **panggang**

memanggil *vt* to call ← **panggil**

memanggul *vt* to carry on your hip ← **panggul**

memangkas *vt* to cut, shear, trim ← **pangkas**

memangku *vt* to take on (your lap); ~ *jabatan* to occupy a post ← **pangku**

memanipulasikan *vt* to manipulate ← **manipulasi**

memanjakan *vt* to spoil someone ← **manja**

memanjang *vi* to become long, lengthen; **memperpanjang** *vt* to extend, make longer ← **panjang**

memanjat *vt* to climb; **memanjatkan** *vt* to send up; ~ *doa* to offer prayers → **panjat**

memantapkan *vt* to stabilize or steady something → **mantap**

memantau *vt* to observe, watch ← **pantau**

memantul *vi* to rebound; **memantulkan** *vt* to reflect something ← **pantul**

memapah *vt* to support, prop up ← **papah**

memaparkan *vt* to explain ← **papar**

memar *adj* bruised

memaraf *vt* to initial, sign ← **paraf**

memarahi *vt* to scold, be angry with ← **marah**

memarakkan *vt* to light up, brighten; *acara Tahun Baru dimarakkan bintang-bintang ibukota* New Year's festivities with glittering stars from Jakarta ← **marak**

memarkir *vt* to park ← **parkir**

memarut *vt* to grate ← **parut**

memasak *vt* to cook, make ← **masak**

memasak *vt* to peg ← **pasak**

memasang *vt* to put up, attach, fix; ~ *bendera* to hoist a flag; ~ *iklan* to advertise; ~ *lampu* to switch on a light; ~ *mata* to keep your eyes open, watch for; ~ *telinga* to listen carefully; ~ *weker* to set the alarm (clock) ← **pasang**

memasarkan *vt* to market ← **pasar**

memasok *vt* to supply ← **pasok**

memastikan *vt* to confirm, make sure, ascertain ← **pasti**

memasuki *vt* to enter (illicitly); **memasukkan** *vt* to put in, insert, import, enter ← **masuk**

memasung *vt* to put in the stocks ← **pasung**

mematahkan *vt* to break ← **patah**

memata-matai *vt* to spy on ← **mata-mata**

mematikan *adj* deadly; *vt* to kill, extinguish, put out; *~ lampu* to turn off the light ← **mati**

mematok *vt* to fix, set; *~ harga* to set a price ← **patok**

mematri *vt* to solder ← **patri**

mematuhi *vt* to obey ← **patuh**

mematuk *vt* to peck, bite ← **patuk**

mematung *vi* to freeze, not move, be as still as a statue ← **patung**

memayungi *vt* to hold an umbrella over someone ← **payung**

membabarkan *vt* to lay out; to explain; **terbabar** *adj* spread out; explained ← **babar**

membabat *vt* to cut or chop down, clear away ← **babat**

membabi *vi* ~ *buta* to act blindly and rashly ← **babi**

membaca *v* to read; *~ bibir* to lip-read; *~ cepat* to skim; *~ doa* to say a prayer; *~ dalam hati* to read silently, to yourself; *~ dengan suara keras* to read out loud; **membacakan** *vt* to read something to someone ← **baca**

membacok *vt* to hack, chop, slash (with something hard) ← **bacok**

membagi *vt* to divide, distribute; **membagi-bagi** *vt* to split up ← **bagi**

membahagiakan *vt* to make happy ← **bahagia**

membahas *vt* to discuss, debate ← **bahas**

membahayakan *vt* to endanger, jeopardize; *adj* dangerous ← **bahaya**

membaik *vi* to improve ← **baik**

membajak *vt* to hijack; to copy illegally; *~ pesawat* to hijack a plane ← **bajak**

membajak *vt* to plough ← **bajak**

membakar *vt* to burn ← **bakar**

membakukan *vt* to standardize, make standard ← **baku**

membalap *vi* to race ← **balap**

membalas *vt* to reply, respond ← **balas**

membalik *vt* to return, reverse, turn over; **membalikkan** *vt* to turn something over ← **balik**

membalur *vt* to smear or massage with oil ← **balur**

membalut *vt* to bandage ← **balut**

membandel *vi* to do something naughty, be disobedient ← **bandel**

membandingkan *vt* to compare something ← **banding**

membanggakan *vt* to make proud, please ← **bangga**

membangkang *vi* to defy, resist, disobey ← **bangkang**

membangkit *vt* to arouse, stimulate ← **bangkit**

membangun *vt* to build or create

membangunkan *vt* to wake someone up ← **bangun**

membanjiri *vt* to flood, inundate ← **banjir**

membantah *vt* to deny, dispute ← **bantah**

membantai *vt* to slaughter, kill viciously ← **bantai**

membanting *vt* to throw down (with a bang); *~ pintu* to slam the door; *~ tulang* to toil, work yourself to the bone ← **banting**

membantu *vt* to help (someone) ← **bantu**

membanyol *vi* to joke ← **banyol**

membaptis *vt* to baptize, christen ← **baptis**

membara *vi* to glow with heat ← **bara**

membarengi *vt* to accompany (someone) ← **bareng**

membaringkan *vt* to lay something down in rows ← **baring**

membasahi *vt* to moisten, wet ← **basah**

membasmi *vt* to exterminate, destroy, wipe out ← **basmi**

membasuh *vt* to wash with water; *~ wajah* to wash the face ← **basuh**

membatalkan *vt* to cancel, repeal; *~ puasa vi* to break your fast (esp intentionally) ← **batal**

membatasi *vt* to limit, restrict, curb something ← **batas**

membatik *vi* to apply wax onto fabric ← **batik**

membatin *vi* to say to yourself ← **batin**

membatu *vi* to freeze, become petrified, fossilized ← **batu**

membaur *vi* to integrate, mix with society ← **baur**

membawa *vt* to take, bring, carry; conduct; ~ *diri* to conduct yourself; **membawakan** *vt* to bring or carry for someone; to sing; *dia ~ lagu-lagu keroncong* she performed *keroncong* songs ← **bawa**

membawahi *vt* to head a section (with staff under you) ← **bawah**

membayangi *vt* to overshadow ← **bayang**

membayar *vt* to pay (for); ~ *dimuka* to pay in advance ← **bayar**

membayonét *vt* to stab someone with a bayonet ← **bayonét**

membebani *vt* to burden someone with something; **membebankan** *vt* to charge something to someone ← **beban**

membébaskan *vt* to exempt, liberate, free someone ← **bébas**

membébék *vi* to quack; follow blindly ← **bébék**

membébérkan *vt* to reveal, explain; to unfold ← **bébér**

membedah *vt* to operate on ← **bedah**

membédakan *vt* to discriminate, differentiate between, consider as different ← **béda**

membekali *vt* to supply someone with provisions ← **bekal**

membekas *vi* to leave an impression; *nasihat itu sangat ~ di hatinya* the advice left a deep impression on him ← **bekas**

membeku *vi* to freeze; **membekukan** *vt* to freeze something ← **beku**

membekuk *vt* to arrest ← **bekuk**

membéla *vt* to defend ← **béla**

membelah *vt* to split in two ← **belah**

membelakangi *vt* to turn your back on someone ← **belakang**

membelalak *vi* to stare; **membelalakkan** *vt* ~ *mata* to stare, open your eyes wide ← **belalak**

membelanjakan *vt* to spend money ← **belanja**

membelenggu *vt* to shackle, handcuff ← **belenggu**

membeli *vt* to buy, purchase; **membelikan** *vt* to buy something for someone; *Sinta ~ anak itu boneka* Sinta bought the child a doll ← **beli**

membeliakkan *vt* ~ *mata* to open your eyes wide ← **beliak**

membélok *vi* to bend, turn; **membélokkan** *vt* to turn, divert something ← **bélok**

membeludak *vi* to burst out, spread everywhere, explode ← **beludak**

membenahi *vt* to get to the bottom of, clear up, fix, straighten out

membenarkan *vt* to confirm, verify; justify ← **benar**

membenci *vt* to hate ← **benci**

membendung, membendungi *vt* to dam, stop a flow ← **bendung**

membengkak *vi* to swell up ← **bengkak**

membéngkokkan *vt* to bend something ← **béngkok**

membentak *vt* to shout, scold, snap (at) ← **bentak**

membentang *vi* to spread out, extend; **membentangi** *vt* to spread something over; **membentangkan** *vt* to spread something out ← **bentang**

membentuk *vt* to form, set up something (eg. committee) ← **bentuk**

membentur *vt* to hit, collide with ← **bentur**

membéo *vi* to parrot, imitate (superiors etc) ← **béo**

memberangus *vt* to muzzle, bridle; ~ *pers* to curb press freedom ← **berangus**

memberanikan *vt* ~ *diri* to dare, get up the courage ← **berani**

memberantakkan *vt* to mess up ← **berantak, antak**

memberantas *vt* to wipe out, fight against; ~ *korupsi* to wipe out corruption ← **berantas**

memberatkan *vt* to burden, make heavy; *adj* incriminating; *kesaksian yang ~* incriminating evidence ← **berat**

memberdayakan *vt* to empower ← **berdaya, daya**

memberéskan *vt* to clear up, make ready ← **bérés**

memberhentikan *vt* to stop (a vehicle); dismiss ← **berhenti, henti**

memberi *vt* to give; ~ *grasi* to pardon someone (for a crime); ~ *hormat* to salute, pay respect; ~ *isyarat* to give a signal; ~ *kesaksian* to give evidence, bear witness; ~ *kesan* to give an impression; ~ *suara* to (cast a) vote; ~ *sun* to kiss on the cheek; **memberikan** *vt* to give someone (as an act of kindness); to give something (for someone) ← **beri**

memberitahu *vt* to advise, inform, tell ← **beri tahu**

memberitakan *vt* to report ← **berita**

memberkati *vt* to bless; *Tuhan* ~ God bless ← **berkat**

memberontak *vi* to rebel, revolt ← **berontak**

membersihkan *vt* to clean; wipe out (eg disease) ← **bersih**

membesar *vi* to get bigger, grow; **membesarkan** *vt* to bring up, raise (children) ← **besar**

membesuk *vt* to visit someone in hospital ← **besuk**

membetulkan *vt* to correct, repair ← **betul**

membiakkan *vt* to breed, cultivate ← **biak**

membiarkan *vt* to let, allow, permit; *biarkan!* let it be! ← **biar**

membiasakan *vt* ~ *diri* to accustom yourself ← **biasa**

membiayai *vt* to finance someone or something ← **biaya**

membicarakan *vt* to discuss ← **bicara**

membidik *vt* to take aim ← **bidik**

membilas *vt* to rinse; *gosokkan pada rambut, lalu* ~ rub into the hair, then rinse ← **bilas**

membimbing *vt* to lead, guide, coach ← **bimbing**

membina *vt* to build up, found ← **bina**

membinasakan *vt* to destroy, ruin ← **binasa**

membingkai *vt* to frame ← **bingkai**

membingungkan *adj* confusing; *vt* to confuse → **bingung**

membintangi *vt* to star in; *Dian Sastro* ~ *film 'Pasir Berbisik'* Dian Sastro starred in *Pasir Berbisik* ← **bintang**

membiru *vi* to turn blue; *karena lama tenggelam, badannya sudah mulai* ~ since he had been underwater for some time, his body was already turning blue ← **biru**

membisik *vt* to whisper ← **bisik**

membisu *vi* to be silent, say nothing ← **bisu**

membius *vt* to drug, anesthetize ← **bius**

mémblé *vi* pout; *adj* stupid, silly

memblénder *vt* to puree or juice something ← **blender**

memblokir *vt* to block; ~ *jalan* to block the road; *begitu kecopetan, dia langsung* ~ *kartu kreditnya* after being robbed, he blocked his credit card ← **blokir**

membobol *vt* to break into; *mesin ATM dibobol maling* thieves broke into the ATM machine ← **bobol**

membocorkan *vt* to leak something ← **bocor**

membodohi *vt* to make someone stupid; **membodohkan** *vt* to make stupid ← **bodoh**

membohong *vi* to lie; **membohongi** *vt* to lie to someone ← **bohong**

memboikot *vt* to boycott something ← **boikot**

membolak-balik *vt* to turn over and over ← **bolak-balik**

membolongi *vt* to pierce ← **bolong**

membolos *v* skip, be absent, play truant, wag, skive; ~ *sekolah* to skip school ← **bolos**

memboncéng *vt* to ride with someone else on a two-wheeled vehicle, dink; to sponge or cadge a lift ← **boncéng**

membongkar *vt* to pull apart, dismantle; to unpack; to unearth; ~ *sauh* to weigh anchor ← **bongkar**

membopong *vt* to carry someone (bodily, or on the shoulders) ← **bopong**

membordir *vt* to embroider ← **bordir**

memborgol *vt* to handcuff ← **borgol**

memborong *vt* to buy up, buy in bulk → **borong**

memboroskan *vt* to waste something → **boros**

membosankan *adj* boring, tiresome ← **bosan**

membotak *vi* to go bald; **membotaki** *vt* to shave, make bald ← **botak**

memboyong *vt* to take (someone) away; *isteri barunya diboyong ke Padang* he took his new bride with him to Padang ← **boyong**

membrédel *vt* to muzzle, bridle, ban; *majalah Tempo dibredel pada tahun 1994 Tempo* magazine was closed down in 1994 ← **brédel**

membuahkan *vt* to result in; **membuahi** *vt* to impregnate, fertilize ← **buah**

membuai *vt* to swing, rock, sway something ← **buai**

membual *vi* to foam; to froth at the mouth, talk rubbish ← **bual**

membuang *vt* to throw out; to waste; to exile; ~ *ingus* to blow your nose; ~ *muka* to look away (from someone); ~ *kesempatan* waste an opportunity; ~ *sauh* vi to cast anchor; ~ *waktu* to waste time ← **buang**

membuat *vt* to make; ~ *marah* to make angry; ~ *SIM* to get your driver's license; **membuat-buat** *vt* to pretend ← **buat**

membubarkan *vt* to break something up; *demo itu dibubarkan polisi* the demo was broken up by the police ← **bubar**

membubuhkan *vt* to attach something; ~ *tanda tangan* to attach your signature ← **bubuh**

membubung *vi* to peak, go upward ← **bubung**

membubut *vt* to use a lathe ← **bubut**

membudaya *vi* to spread, become entrenched; *korupsi sudah* ~ corruption is part of the culture ← **budaya**

membudidayakan *vt* to cultivate, grow ← **budidaya**

membujang *vi* to remain unmarried ← **bujang**

membujuk *vt* to coax ← **bujuk**

membuka *vt* to open; ~ *rahasia* to reveal a secret; ~ *jendela hati* to open your heart; ~ *lembar baru* to turn over a new leaf; **membukakan** *vt* to open (for someone) ← **buka**

membuking *vt* to book ← **buking**

membuktikan *vt* to prove ← **bukti**

membukukan *vt* to enter into the accounts books ← **buku**

membulatkan *vt* to round off ← **bulat**

membumbui *vt* to season ← **bumbu**

membumihanguskan *vt* to scorch the earth, apply a scorched earth policy; to completely burn down ← **bumi hangus**

membungkam *vi* to keep silent ← **bungkam**

membungkuk *vi* to bow, be hunched; **membungkukkan** *vt* ~ *badan* to bow ← **bungkuk**

membungkus *vt* to wrap; ~ *kado* wrap a gift ← **bungkus**

membuntuti *vt* to follow someone ← **buntut**

membunuh *vt* to kill; ~ *diri* to kill yourself, commit suicide ← **bunuh**

membunyikan *vt* to sound, ring something ← **bunyi**

memburu *vt* to hunt, chase ← **buru**

memburuk *vi* to worsen ← **buruk**

membusuk *vi* to rot ← **busuk**

membutuhkan *vt* to need something ← **butuh**

memecah *vt* ~ *belah* to break into fragments, cause divisions; **memecahkan** *vt* to break; to solve; ~ *soal* to solve a problem ← **pecah**

memecat *vt* to fire, dismiss ← **pecat**

memecundangi *vt* to swindle or trick; to beat or defeat ← **pecundang, cundang**

memedulikan *vt* to care or be bothered about ← **peduli**

memegang *vt* to hold, grasp ← **pegang**

memejamkan *vt* ~ *mata* to close your eyes ← **pejam**

memekakkan *adj* deafening, loud ← **pekak**

memekik *vt* to scream or shriek ← **pekik**

memelankan *vt* to slow something down ← **pelan**

memelantingkan *vt* to throw everywhere ← **pelanting**

memelas *adj* pitiful, pathetic ← **belas**

memelésétkan *vt* to parody; to up-end, send off-course ← **pelését**

memelihara *vt* to take care of, look after, cultivate ← **pelihara**

memelintir, memelintirkan *vt* to twist ← **pelintir**

memelitur *vt* to polish, varnish ← **pelitur**

memelopori *vt* to pioneer, lead ← **pelopor**

memelotot *vi* to stare, have bulging eyes; **memelototi** *vt* to stare at someone; **memelototkan** *vt* ~ *mata* to stare ← **pelotot, lotot**

memeluk *vt* to hug or embrace; ~ *agama* to follow a religion ← **peluk**

memenangi *vi* to defeat; **memenangkan** *vt* to win (a prize or contest) ← **menang**

memencét *vt* to press (a button, key) ← **pencét**

memendamkan *vt* to hide (away), conceal, bury ← **pendam**

meméndékkan *vt* to shorten ← **péndék**

memengaruhi *vt* to influence, affect ← **pengaruh**

memenggal *vt* to cut off, amputate; ~ *kepala* to behead ← **penggal**

memenjara, memenjarakan *vt* to put in prison, imprison ← **penjara**

meménsiunkan *vt* to pension off ← **pénsiun**

mementaskan *vt* to stage, present ← **pentas**

mementingkan *vt* to make important, emphasize ← **penting**

memenuhi *vt* to fulfill, meet requirements ← **penuh**

memeragakan *vt* to display, show ← **peraga**

memérah *vi* to blush ← **mérah**

memerah *vt* to milk or squeeze ← **perah**

memerangi *vt* to fight against ← **perang**

memerankan *vt* to portray, play the role of ← **peran**

memeras *vt* to squeeze, press; to blackmail, extort ← **peras**

memerawani *vt* to take someone's virginity, deflower ← **perawan**

memerban *vt* to bandage ← **perban**

memercayai *vt* to trust someone; **memercayakan** *vt* to entrust with ← **percaya**

memerciki *vt* to spatter something; **memercikkan** *vt* to splash with something ← **percik**

memergoki *vt* to catch sight of ← **pergok**

memerhatikan *vt* to notice, pay attention to ← **hati**

memeriahkan *vt* to liven up, enliven ← **meriah**

memeriksa *vt* to examine or investigate; ~ *ulang* to review ← **periksa**

memerintah *vt* to rule, govern, reign; **memerintahkan** *vt* to order or command something ← **perintah**

memerkosa *vt* to rape ← **perkosa**

memerlahankan *vt* to slow something → **perlahan**

memerlukan *vt* to need, require ← **perlu**

memerosokkan *vt* to push something into ← **perosok**

memesan *vt* to order ← **pesan**

memesona, memesonakan *adj* enthralling, enchanting ← **pesona**

memetakan *vt* to map ← **peta**

memetiéskan *vt* to put on hold, put on the back burner ← **peti és**

memetik *vt* to pick; to strum; ~ *gitar* to play or strum the guitar ← **petik**

memfitnah *vt* to slander ← **fitnah**

memfokuskan *vt* to focus something; ~ *diri* to focus yourself ← **fokus**

memicu *vt* to trigger, set off ← **picu**

memigura *vt* to frame ← **pigura**

memihak *vi* to take sides ← **pihak**

memijak *vt* to tread or step on ← **pijak**

memijat *vt* to massage ← **pijat**

memikat *adj* attractive, enticing ← **pikat**

memikirkan *vt* to think about ← **pikir**

memikul *vt* to bear, carry on the shoulder ← **pikul**

memilah *vt* to sort; *sampah basah harus dipilah dari sampah kering* you have to sort the rubbish between organic and non-organic ← **pilah**

memilih *vt* to choose or select; to elect or vote (for) ← **pilih**

memiliki *vt* to own, possess ← **milik**

memilukan *adj* moving, touching ← **pilu**

memimpikan *vt* to dream of ← **mimpi**

memimpin *vt* to lead ← **pimpin**

meminang *vt* to propose, ask for a girl's hand in marriage ← **pinang**

memindah *coll* **memindahkan** *vt* to move, transfer ← **pindah**

meminggir *vi* to move to the side, pull over; **meminggirkan** *vt* to move to one side, cast aside ← **pinggir**

memingit *vt* to seclude, keep at home ← **pingit**

meminjam *vt* to borrow; **meminjami** *vt* to lend someone; **meminjamkan** *vt* to lend something ← **pinjam**

meminta *vt* to ask for, request; **meminta-minta** *vi* to beg, ask for money; **memintakan** *vt* to ask for something for someone else ← **minta, pinta**

memintal *vt* to spin (thread) ← **pintal**

memiringkan *vt* to slant, tilt ← **miring**

memisah *vt* to separate; **memisahkan** *vt* to separate something ← **pisah**

mémoar *n* memoirs

memodérnkan *vt* to modernize ← **modérn**

memodifikasi *vt* to modify ← **modifikasi**

memojokkan *vt* to force into a corner ← **pojok**

memolés *vt* to polish ← **polés**

memompa *vt* to pump ← **pompa**

memonitor *vt* to monitor ← **monitor**

memonopoli *vt* to monopolize ← **monopoli**

memopulérkan *vt* to popularize, make popular ← **populér**

memorak-porandakan *vt* to cause chaos, turn upside-down ← **porak-poranda**

mémori *n* (electronic) memory

mémori *n* legal brief; ~ *banding* brief attached to an appeal at the District Court level; ~ *kasasi* brief attached to an appeal at the High Court level

memosisikan *vt* to position (something); *dia ~ diri sebagai pemimpin daerah* he maneuvred himself into the position as a regional leader ← **posisi**

memotivasi *vt* to motivate ← **motivasi**

memotong *vt* to cut, deduct; to slaughter, amputate; to interrupt ← **potong**

memotori *vt* to be the driving force behind, to power ← **motor**

memotrét *vt* to photograph ← **potrét**

mempan *adj* effective

mempekerjakan *vt* to put to work, employ; *perusahaan itu ~ 1000 karyawan* that company employs 1,000 workers ← **pekerja, kerja**

mempelai *kedua* ~ bridal couple; ~ *pria* groom; ~ *wanita* bride

mempelajari *vt* to study something in depth ← **ajar**

memperabukan, mengabukan *vt* to cremate ← **abu**

memperalat *vt* to use or take advantage of someone; *Tina diperalat oleh kawannya* Tina was used by her friend ← **alat**

memperbaiki *vt* to repair, fix → **baik**

memperbanyak *vt* to increase, multiply ← **banyak**

memperbarui *vt* to renew, make new ← **baru**

memperbesar *vt* to enlarge something ← **besar**

memperboléhkan *vt* to allow, permit ← **boléh**

memperburuk *vt* to make even worse ← **buruk**

mempercantik *vt* ~ *diri* to make yourself beautiful ← **cantik**

mempercepat *vt* to speed up, accelerate ← **cepat**

memperdagangkan *vt* to deal in ← **dagang**

memperdalam *vt* to deepen; to study in detail, broaden your knowledge ← **dalam**

memperdaya *vt* to deceive, use, trick ← **daya**

memperdengarkan *vt* to play, broadcast ← **dengar**

memperebutkan *vt* to seize, take by force ← **rebut**

mempererat *vt* to strengthen, make closer ← **erat**

memperindah *vt* to beautify ← **indah**

memperingati *vt* to commemorate; **memperingatkan** *vt* to warn ← **ingat**

memperjuangkan *vt* to fight for ← **juang**

memperkecil *vt* to reduce something, make even smaller; *foto diperkecil supaya bisa dibingkai* the photo was reduced so it could be framed ← **kecil**

memperkenalkan *vt* to introduce ← **kenal**

memperkenankan *vt* to approve, grant, allow; *~ saya mengucapkan terima kasih* allow me to express my gratitude (in formal letters etc) ← **kenan**

memperkirakan *vt* to estimate, calculate ← **kira**

memperkuat *vt* to reinforce, make stronger ← **kuat**

memperlakukan *vt* to treat ← **laku**

memperlambat *vt* to slow something down (even further) ← **lambat**

memperlancar *vt* to ease, make easier; *makan buah ~ pencernaan* eating fruit improves your digestion ← **lancar**

memperluas *vt* to widen, expand, enlarge ← **luas**

mempermainkan *vt* to ridicule, make a fool of ← **main**

mempermalukan *vt* to embarrass, shame ← **malu**

mempermandikan *vt* to christen, baptize ← **mandi**

mempermasalahkan *vt* to make a problem out of ← **masalah**

mempermudah *vt* to make easier ← **mudah**

memperoléh *vt* to obtain, get ← **oléh**

memperolok *vt* to tease, taunt ← **olok**

memperparah *vt* to make worse, aggravate ← **parah**

memperpéndék *vt* to shorten, make even shorter ← **péndék**

mempersalahkan *vt* to blame ← **salah**

mempersandingkan *vt* to place next to each other (of the bride and groom at a wedding) ← **sanding**

mempersatukan *vt* to unite various things ← **satu**

mempersembahkan *vt* to offer (up), present ← **sembah**

mempersenjatai *vt* to arm someone ← **senjata**

mempersiapkan *vt* to prepare something, get something ready ← **siap**

mempersilakan *vt* to invite someone to do something ← **sila**

mempersingkat *vt* to shorten ← **singkat**

mempersoalkan *vt* to question, discuss ← **soal**

mempersulit *vt* to make harder, further complicate ← **sulit**

mempersunting *vt* to marry (a woman) ← **sunting**

mempertahankan *vt* to defend or maintain ← **tahan**

mempertajam *vt* to sharpen, exacerbate ← **tajam**

mempertanggungjawabkan *vt* to account for ← **tanggung jawab**

mempertanyakan *vt* to query ← **tanya**

mempertaruhkan *vt* to stake, risk, bet; *~ nyawa* to risk your life ← **taruh**

mempertegas *vt* to further clarify, reiterate ← **tegas**

mempertemukan *vt* to bring together (with a view to marriage) ← **temu**

mempertimbangkan *vt* to consider ← **timbang**

mempertunjukkan *vt* to display or perform ← **tunjuk**

memperuntukkan *vt* to allocate or assign ← **untuk**

mempesona, mempesonakan *adj* enthralling, enchanting ← **pesona;** → **memesona**

mempopulérkan *vt* to popularize, make popular ← **populér**

memposkan *vt* to post (on the internet) ← **pos**

memprakarsai *vt* to take the initiative ← **prakarsa**

mempraktékkan *vt* to put into practice ← **prakték**

memprihatinkan *adj* worrying ← **prihatin**

memprioritaskan *vt* to prioritize ← **prioritas**

memproduksi *vt* to produce ← **produksi**

memproklamasikan *vt* to proclaim (independence) ← **proklamasi**

mempromosikan *vt* to promote ← **promosi**

memprosés *vt* to process ← **prosés**

memprotés *vt* to (make a) protest ← **protés**

memproyéksikan *vt* to project ← **proyéksi**

mempunyai *vt* to have, own, possess ← **punya**

memuai *vi* to expand, swell ← **muai**

memuakkan *adj* revolting, disgusting ← **muak**

memuaskan *adj* satisfactory ← **puas**

memuat *vt* to contain ← **muat**

memudar *vi* to fade ← **pudar**

memugar *vt* to restore, renovate ← **pugar**

memuja *vt* to worship ← **puja**

memuji *vt* to praise; **memuji-muji** *vt* to praise excessively ← **puji**

memukau *vt* to fascinate; to drug ← **pukau**

memukul *vt* to hit, beat, strike; **pukul-memukul** *vt* to hit each other; **memukuli** *vt* to hit repeatedly, batter ← **pukul**

memulai *vt* to start or begin something ← **mula, mulai**

memulakan *vt* to start something; to cause ← **mula**

memulangkan *vt* to give back; to send back, repatriate ← **pulang**

memuliakan *vt* to honor, glorify ← **mulia**

memulihkan *vt* to restore ← **pulih**

memulung *vt* to scavenge ← **pulung**

memuluskan *vt* to ease the way, help ← **mulus**

memuncak *vi* to culminate, reach a peak ← **puncak**

memunculkan *vt* to bring forward ← **muncul**

memundurkan *vt* to retract, bring back ← **mundur**

memunggungi *vt* to turn your back on ← **punggung**

memungkari *vt* to deny; to betray ← **mungkar**

memungkinkan *adj* conducive; *vt* to enable, make possible ← **mungkin**

memungkiri *vt* to deny ← **mungkir**

memungut *vt* to pick up, collect ← **pungut**

memuntahkan *vt* to vomit or bring up ← **muntah**

memupuskan *vt* to wipe out, destroy ← **pupus**

memusatkan *vt* to focus; ~ *perhatian* to concentrate ← **pusat**

memusingkan *vt* ~ *kepala* puzzling ← **pusing**

memusnahkan *vt* to destroy; **pemusnahan** *n* act of destruction ← **musnah**

memusuhi *vt* to fight against, antagonize, make an enemy of ← **musuh**

memutar *vt* to wind; to rotate; ~ *balik* to turn around, do a U-turn; **memutarbalikkan** *vt* to reverse, distort; **memutari** *vt* to go around, orbit; **perputaran** *n* rotation ← **putar**

memutasi *vt* to change someone's status ← **mutasi**

memutih *vi* to fade, become white; **memutihkan** *vt* to whiten, bleach ← **putih**

memutus *vt* to break; ~ *hubungan* to break off or sever contact; **memutuskan** *vt* to terminate or break; to decide ← **putus**

memvaksinasi *vt* to vaccinate ← **vaksinasi**

memvakum *vt* to vacuum ← **vakum**

memvalidasi *vt* to validate ← **validasi**

memvérifikasi *vt* to verify ← **vérifikasi**

memvonis *vt* to sentence ← **vonis**

mena: semena-mena *(tidak)* ~ arbitrary, without reason, unjust

menaati *vt* to obey or follow something ← **taat**

menabrak *vt* to collide with; **menabrakkan** *vt* to ram something into; *Tri ~ mobil ayahnya pada tembok rumah* Tri drove his father's car into their fence ← **tabrak**

menabuh *vt* to beat (a drum) ← **tabuh**

menabung *vt* to save or deposit money ← **tabung**

menabur *vt* to scatter or sprinkle ← **tabur**

menafikan *vt* to deny ← **nafi**

menafsirkan *vt* to interpret something ← **tafsir**

Ménag *n* Minister of Religious Affairs → **Menteri Agama**

menagih *vt* to ask for payment, bill ← **tagih**

menahan *vt* to bear, endure; to detain; ~ *diri* to hold yourself back, restrain yourself; ~ *nafas* to hold your breath ← **tahan**

menahbiskan *vt* to consecrate, ordain ← **tahbis**

menahun *adj* chronic; *penyakit* ~ chronic illness ← **tahun**

menaik *vi* to be on the increase; **menaiki** *vt* to ride, mount, get on; **menaikkan** *vt* to raise, hoist ← **naik**

menakar *vt* to measure ← **takar**

menakdirkan *vt* to determine, to pre-destine ← **takdir**

menakjubkan *adj* astonishing, amazing ← **takjub**

menaklukkan *vt* to defeat, conquer, subdue ← **takluk**

menaksir *vt* to estimate, appraise, value; to like, find someone or something attractive ← **taksir**

menakuti *vt* to scare someone; **menakut-nakuti** *vt* to frighten or intimidate (re-peatedly); **menakutkan** *vt, adv* fright-ening; to frighten or scare ← **takut**

menala *vt* to tune ← **tala**

menamakan *vt* to call, name ← **nama**

menamatkan *vt* to end, finish, conclude ← **tamat**

menambah *vt* to add to or increase; **menambahi** *vt* to increase something; **menambahkan** *vt* to add something to ← **tambah**

menambak *vt* to dam (up) ← **tambak**

menambal *vt* to mend, patch, darn; ~ *gigi* to fill a tooth, have a filling; ~ *jalan* to fill in a pothole ← **tambal**

menambang *vt* to mine, dig for ← **tambang**

menambat, menambatkan *vt* to fasten, tie up ← **tambat**

menampakkan *vt* to show, make appear ← **tampak**

menampar *vt* to slap ← **tampar**

menampi *vt* to winnow ← **tampi**

menampias *v* to splash ← **tampias**

menampik *vt* to reject, refuse ← **tampik**

menampilkan *vt* to present ← **tampil**

menampung *vt* to collect, hold ← **tampung**

menanak *vt* ~ *nasi* to cook rice ← **tanak**

menanam *vt* to plant or grow; to invest; ~ *modal* to invest (capital); **menanam-kan** *vt* to plant or invest something ← **tanam**

menancap *vt* to step on; ~ *gas* to step on the gas, accelerate ← **tancap**

menandai *vt* to mark ← **tanda**

menandaskan *vt* to use up ← **tandas**

menandatangani *vt* to sign something ← **tanda tangan**

menandu *vt* to carry in a litter ← **tandu**

menanduk *vt* to butt ← **tanduk**

menang *v* to win; ~ *telak* to thrash, beat outright; ~ *tipis* narrowly defeat; **ke-menangan** *n* victory; **memenangi** *vi* to defeat; **memenangkan** *vt* to win (a prize or contest); **pemenang** *n* winner, victor

menangani *vt* to handle ← **tangan**

menanggalkan *vt* to take off or remove; ~ *pakaian* to undress ← **tanggal**

menanggapi *vt* to respond, reply ← **tanggap**

menangguhkan *vt* to delay, postpone, put something off ← **tangguh**

menanggulangi *vt* to deal or cope with ← **tanggulang**

menanggung *vt* to guarantee, be re-sponsible; ~ *beban* to bear ← **tanggung**

menangis *vi* to cry; **menangisi** *vt* to cry over, mourn ← **tangis**

menangkal *vt* to ward off, repel ← **tangkal**

menangkap *vt* to catch, capture ← **tangkap**

menangkis *vt* to defend yourself, fend off, parry ← **tangkis**

menanjak *adj* rising, climbing, steep; *vi* to rise, climb ← **tanjak**

menantang *vt* to challenge; *adj* chal-lenging ← **tantang**

menanti *vt* to wait; **menanti-nanti** *vt* to wait for a long time; **menantikan** *v* to wait for ← **nanti**

menantu *n* son- or daughter-in-law ←
  mantu

menanya *vt* to ask; **menanyai** *vt* to
  question someone; **menanyakan** *vt* to
  ask about ← **tanya**

menapak *vt* ~ *tilas* to retrace your steps,
  make a journey again ← **tapak**

menapis *vt* to filter ← **tapis**

menara *n* tower; minaret (of a mosque)

menargétkan *vt* to aim for ← **targét**

menari *vi* to dance, perform a traditional dance; **menari-nari** *vi* to dance
  about ← **tari**

menarik *vt* to pull or draw; *adj* interesting, attractive; ~ *kesimpulan* to conclude, draw a conclusion; ~ *napas* to
  inhale ← **tarik**

menaruh *vt* to put (away); ~ *dendam* to
  bear a grudge ← **taruh**

menasihati *vt* to advise → **nasihat**

menata *vt* to arrange, lay out, organize
  ← **tata**

menatap *vt* to gaze at ← **tatap**

menawan *vt* to detain, take someone
  prisoner, intern; *adj* attractive,
  appealing ← **tawan**

menawar *tawar-*~ bargaining; **menawar-**
  kan *vt* to offer or bid ← **tawar**

menayangkan *vt* to telecast, show on TV
  ← **tayang**

mencabik *vt* to tear ← **cabik**

mencabuli *vt* to rape, assault someone
  ← **cabul**

mencabut *vt* to pull out, remove; to take
  back; ~ *gigi* extract a tooth ← **cabut**

mencacah *vt* to mince, chop up ←
  cacah

mencacah *vt* to vaccinate ← **cacah**

mencaci *vt* ~ *maki* to insult, abuse ←
  caci

mencadangkan *vt* to reserve, set aside;
  suggest something ← **cadang**

mencair *vi* to melt, turn into liquid;
  mencairkan *vt* to melt something; to
  make (funds) available ← **cair**

mencakar *vt* to scratch; *dicakar kucing*
  scratched by a cat ← **cakar**

mencakupi *vt* to include, cover ← **cakup**

mencalonkan *vt* to nominate someone
  ← **calon**

mencambuk *vt* to whip; **mencambuki**
  vt to whip repeatedly ← **cambuk**

mencamkan *vt* to note carefully ← **cam**

mencampakkan *vt* to throw (something) down ← **campak**

mencampur *vt* to mix, blend; ~ *baur vi*
  to mix with society; ~ *tangan* to get
  involved, interfere; **mencampur-**
  adukkan *vt* to mix up, confuse; **men-**
  campuri *vt* to mix into; to meddle; to
  have sex with; **mencampurkan** *vt* to
  mix something to ← **campur**

mencanangkan *vt* to proclaim, announce ← **canang**

mencangkokkan *vt* to graft (of plants),
  transplant (of organs) ← **cangkok**

mencantol *vt* to hook onto ← **cantol**

mencantumkan *vt* to attach ← **cantum**

mencapai *vt* to reach, attain ← **capai**

mencari *vt* look or search for, seek; ~
  kerja to look for work; ~ *makan* to
  earn a living; ~ *suaka* to seek asylum;
  mencari-cari *vt* to search repeatedly,
  everywhere; **mencarikan** *vt* to look
  for something for someone ← **cari**

mencarik *vt* to rip or tear up ← **carik**

mencarter *vt* to hire, charter ← **carter**

mencatat *vt* to note (down) ← **catat**

mencatut *vt* ~ *nama* to use someone
  else's name illegally ← **catut**

menceburkan *vt* to push into water ←
  cebur

mencecar *vt* to assault, attack; to interrogate ← **cecar**

mencécérkan *vt* to scatter, disperse ←
  cécér

mencederai *vt* to damage, injure ←
  cedera

mencegah *vt* to prevent, fight against
  ← **cegah**

mencegat *vt* to hold up, bar ← **cegat**

mencekal *vt* to prevent from leaving
  the country ← **cekal, cegah dan**
  tangkal

mencekam *adj* frightening, ominous;
  situasi sudah ~ things looked black ←
  cekam

mencekik *vt* to strangle ← **cekik**

mencela *vt* to find fault with, criticize
  ← **cela**

mencelakakan *vt* to bring misfortune on ← **celaka**

mencelup *vt* to dye, dip ← **celup**

mencemari *vt* to dirty, pollute ← **cemar**

mencemaskan *adj* worrying, sobering ← **cemas**

mencemoohkan *vt* to mock, ridicule ← **cemooh**

mencemplungkan *vt* to plunge something into water ← **cemplung**

mencengkeram *vt* to grip, squeeze ← **cengkeram**

mencerahkan *vt* to enlighten, clear up matters ← **cerah**

mencerai, menceraikan *vt* to divorce someone; **mencerai-beraikan** *vt* to tear apart, separate ← **cerai**

mencerca *vt* to reprimand, deride ← **cerca**

mencerdaskan *vt* to educate, sharpen your mind ← **cerdas**

menceriakan *vt* to liven up, make happy ← **ceria**

menceritakan *vt* to describe, relate ← **cerita**

mencermati *vt* to observe closely ← **cermat**

mencerminkan *vt* to reflect ← **cermin**

mencerna *vt* to digest ← **cerna**

mencerocos *vi* **nyerocos** *coll* to talk too much, blather, chatter or rattle on

mencétak *vt* to print; ~ *gol* to score a goal ← **cétak**

mencetus *vt* to scrape; *vi* to burst out, say something unexpected; **mencetuskan** *vt* to spark off, provoke ← **cetus**

mencibir *vi* to sneer, curl your lips ← **cibir**

mencicil *vt* to pay by instalments ← **cicil**

mencicipi *vt* to try, taste something ← **cicip**

menciduk *vt* to scoop with a dipper ← **ciduk**

menciduk *vt, coll* to arrest ← **ciduk**

mencincang *vt* to mince, chop up ← **cincang**

mencinta *vt* to love; **mencintai** *vt* to love someone ← **cinta**

mencipta *vt* to create; to compose; **menciptakan** *vt* to create, make; ~ *hening vt* to have a moment's silence ← **cipta**

mencitrakan *vt* to depict ← **citra**

mencium *vt* to smell, to sniff; to kiss ← **cium**

menciut *vi* to shrivel ← **ciut**

menciut-ciut *vi* to squeak ← **ciut**

menciutkan *vt* to reduce ← **ciut**

mencoba *vt* to try, attempt ← **coba**

mencoblos *vt* to vote, pierce ← **coblos**

mencocokkan *vt* to match ← **cocok**

mencocol *vt* to dip into a liquid ← **cocol**

mencolok *adj* glaring, standing out ← **colok**

mencolong *vt* to steal, nick, filch ← **colong**

mencomél *vi* to grouse, grumble ← **comél**

méncong *adj* bent, skewed, not straight

mencongak *v* to do mental arithmetic ← **congak**

mencongkél *vt* to prise open ← **congkél**

menconték *v* to copy, cheat ← **conték, sonték**

mencontoh *vt* to copy, imitate; **mencontohi** *vt* to give as an example ← **contoh**

mencopét *vt* to pick someone's pocket ← **copét**

mencopot *vt* to pull off; *coll* to sack, fire ← **copot**

mencorét *vt* to scratch, cross out ← **corét**

méncrét *vi* to have diarrhea

mencubit *vt* to pinch ← **cubit**

mencuci *vt* to wash, clean; ~ *piring* to wash dishes ← **cuci**

mencukupi *vt* to satisfy, fulfill ← **cukup**

mencukur *vt* to shave ← **cukur**

menculik *vt* to kidnap ← **culik**

mencuplik *vt* to cite, quote from ← **cuplik**

mencurahkan *vt* to pour out; ~ *tenaga* to spend energy ← **curah**

mencuri *vt* to steal ← **curi**

mencurigai *vt* to suspect someone; **mencurigakan** *adj* suspicious, suspect; *vt* to cause suspicion ← **curiga**

mendadak *adj* sudden; ~ *sontak* suddenly; *secara* ~ suddenly ← **dadak**

mendaftar *vt* to register; **mendaftarkan** *vt* to register something ← **daftar**

Méndagri *n* Minister of the Interior, Minister of Home Affairs ← **Menteri Dalam Negeri**

mendahului *vt* to precede, overtake; **mendahulukan** *vt* to put before, give precedence to ← **dahulu**

mendaki *vt* to climb, ascend; ~ *gunung* (to go) mountaineering, bushwalking ← **daki**

mendalam *adj* deep; *duka cita yang* ~ my deepest sympathy; **mendalami** *vt* to delve into ← **dalam**

mendalangi *vt* to orchestrate (events) ← **dalang**

mendamaikan *vt* to reconcile, pacify ← **damai**

mendambakan *vt* to long or wish for; ~ *gadis mandiri, lulusan S1* seeking an independent woman, university graduate ← **damba**

mendamparkan *vt* to wash ashore, beach ← **dampar**

mendampingi *vt* to accompany, flank ← **damping**

mendamprat *vt* to curse, scold ← **damprat**

mendanai *vt* to fund something ← **dana**

mendandani *vt* to decorate, dress, adorn ← **dandan**

mendapat *vt* to obtain, receive; ~ *kabar* to receive news; **mendapati** *vt* to experience; **mendapatkan** *vt* to obtain, get; discover ← **dapat**

mendarah-daging *vi* to become second nature ← **darah**

mendarat *vi* to land; **mendarati** *vt* to land on ← **darat**

mendasar *adj* basic; **mendasarkan** *vt* to base on something ← **dasar**

mendatakan *vt* to record, document, collect data on ← **data**

mendatang *adj* coming, next; **mendatangkan** *vt* to bring, import ← **datang**

mendatarkan *vt* to make flat, level ← **datar**

mendayung *v* to stroke (an oar), row; to pedal ← **dayung**

méndé ← **médé**

mendebarkan *adj* pulsating, throbbing; *vt* to make the heart beat quickly ← **debar**

mendebat *vt* to argue against, debate ← **debat**

mendébet *vt* to debit ← **débet**

mendéfinisikan *vt* to define ← **définisi**

mendeham *vi* to clear the throat, cough ← **deham**

mendekam *vi* to crouch, be cooped up ← **dekam**

mendekap *vt* to hug, embrace ← **dekap**

mendekati *vt* to approach; **mendekatkan** *vt* to bring close ← **dekat**

mendéklamasikan *vt* to declaim ← **déklamasi**

mendéklarasikan *vt* to declare ← **déklarasi**

mendémo *vt* to protest against ← **démo**

mendenda *vt* to fine ← **denda**

mendengar *vt* to hear; **mendengarkan** *vt* to listen to; ~ *lagu* to listen to music ← **dengar**

mendengkur *vi* to snore; to purr (of a cat) ← **dengkur**

mendengung *vi* to drone, hum, shake with sound ← **dengung**

mendepak *vt* to kick something, kick out; *Haris didepak dari tim* Haris was kicked off the team ← **depak**

mendera *vt* to whip, flog ← **dera**

mendérék *vt* to tow ← **dérék**

mendering *vi* to ring, tinkle ← **dering**

menderita *vt* to suffer, endure ← **derita**

menderu *vi* to roar ← **deru**

mendesah *vi* to sigh, make a swishing noise ← **desah**

mendésain *vt* to design ← **désain**

mendesak *adj* pressing, urgent; *vt* to press, urge, push ← **desak**

mendesir *vi* to hiss, rustle ← **desir**

mendesis *vi* to hiss ← **desis**

mendétéksi *vt* to detect ← **détéksi**

mendéwakan *vt* to worship, idolize, put on a pedestal ← **déwa**

mendiagnosa *vt* to diagnose ← **diagnosa**

mendiang *adj* the late

mendidih *adj* boiling; *vi* to boil; **mendidihkan** *vt* to boil water ← **didih**

mendidik *vt* to educate, bring up, teach ← **didik**

Méndiknas *n* Minister of National Education ← **Menteri Pendidikan Nasional**

mendikté *vt* to dictate (terms) ← **dikté**

mending, mendingan *adj, coll* better, better off

mendinginkan *vt* to chill, cool ← **dingin**

mendirikan *vt* to build, establish, erect ← **diri**

mendiskriminasi, mendiskriminasikan *vt* to discriminate against ← **diskriminasi**

mendistribusikan *vt* to distribute ← **distribusi**

mendoakan *vt* to pray for ← **doa**

mendobrak *vt* to break open, smash; ~ *pintu* to break down the door ← **dobrak**

mendokuméntasi *vt* to document, file ← **dokuméntasi**

mendongéng *vi* to tell a story ← **dongéng**

mendongkrak *vt* to jack, lever, raise; ~ *popularitas* to boost popularity ← **dongkrak**

mendorong *vt* to push, encourage ← **dorong**

menduakan *vt* to be loyal to more than one; ~ *Tuhan* to worship more than one god ← **dua**

menduda *vi* to become or live as a widower ← **duda**

menduduki *vt* to sit on something; to occupy; *Indonesia pernah diduduki Jepang* Indonesia was once occupied by Japan ← **duduk**

mendukung *vt* to support ← **dukung**

mendulang *vt* to pan (for gold) ← **dulang**

mendung *adj* cloudy, overcast

mendunia *vi* to become global, known around the world ← **dunia**

menebak *vt* to guess ← **tebak**

menebang *vt* to fell, cut down ← **tebang**

menébarkan *vt* to scatter; to cast (a net) ← **tébar**

menebas *vt* to cut down, clear ← **tebas**

menebus *vt* to pay a ransom; ~ *dosa* to atone for a sin ← **tebus**

menegakkan *vt* to erect; to uphold or maintain; ~ *hukum* to uphold the law ← **tegak**

menegangkan *adj* tense, stressful ← **tegang**

menegaskan *vt* to clarify, point out, affirm ← **tegas**

meneguk *vt* to gulp or guzzle ← **teguk**

menegur *vt* to speak to, address; to warn, rebuke, tell off ← **tegur**

menekan *vt* to press; **menekankan** *vt* to stress, emphasize ← **tekan**

menéken *vt* to sign, initial ← **téken**

menekuni *vt* to apply yourself to; *Anto* ~ *ilmu hukum* Anto is studying law ← **tekun**

menelaah *vt* to analyze ← **telaah**

menelan *vt* to swallow something ← **telan**

menelanjangi *vt* to strip or denude ← **telanjang**

menélépon *vt* to ring (up), call, (tele)phone ← **télépon**

meneliti *vt* to investigate or research ← **teliti**

menelusuri *vt* to follow, go along, trace ← **telusur**

menemani *vt* to accompany ← **teman**

menémbak *vt* to shoot; **menémbaki** *vt* to shell ← **témbak**

menembangkan *vt* to sing something ← **tembang**

menémbok *vt* to wall up; to cover an area with wax (when making batik); **menémboki** *vt* to wall something up ← **témbok**

menembus *vt* to pierce, stab ← **tembus**

menempa *vt* to forge ← **tempa**

menempati *vt* to occupy, take a place; **menempatkan** *vt* to place ← **tempat**

menémpél *vt* to stick or adhere to; **menémpélkan** *vt* to stick, paste or glue something ← **témpél**

menempuh *vt* to endure, go through; to take on, take up; ~ *jalan* to go a certain way; ~ *ujian* to do an exam ← **tempuh**

menemui *vt* to meet up with, arrange to meet; ~ *ajal* to die; **menemukan** *vt* to discover ← **temu**

menenangkan *vt* to calm someone (down) ← **tenang**

menendang *vt* to kick ← **tendang**

menengadahi *vt* to look up at ← **tengadah**

menengah *adj* intermediate; *kelas* ~ middle class; *sekolah* ~ high school, secondary school ← **tengah**

menenggelamkan *vt* to sink or drown something ← **tenggelam**

menéngok *vt* to look or see; to look in on someone ← **téngok**

menentang *vt* to oppose, resist ← **tentang**

menénténg *vt* to carry dangling from the hand ← **ténténg**

menentu *tidak* ~ not fixed, vague; **menentukan** *vt* to decide, determine, stipulate ← **tentu**

menenun *vt* to weave ← **tenun**

menepak *vt* to slap, clap (someone's shoulder) ← **tepak**

menepati *vt* to fulfill; ~ *janji* to keep a promise ← **tepat**

menepi *vi* to move to the side, move over ← **tepi**

menepis *vt* ward off, deflect ← **tepis**

menepuk *vt* to pat, slap ← **tepuk**

menerangi *vt* to illuminate; **menerangkan** *vt* to explain ← **terang**

menerapkan *vt* to apply something ← **terap**

menerawang *vi* to appear (through something translucent) ← **terawang**

menerbangkan *vt* to fly something ← **terbang**

menerbitkan *vt* to publish, issue ← **terbit**

meneriaki *vt* to shout at someone; **meneriakkan** *vt* to shout something ← **teriak**

menerima *vt* to receive, accept ← **terima**

menerjang *vt* to kick, attack, charge ← **terjang**

menerjemahkan *vt* to translate (writing); to interpret (speaking) ← **terjemah**

menerjunkan *vt* to drop something ← **terjun**

menerka *vt* to guess ← **terka**

menerkam *vt* to pounce, attack ← **terkam**

menernakkan *vt* to breed ← **ternak**

menerobos *vt* to break through ← **terobos**

menéror *vt* to terrorize ← **téror**

menerpa *vt* to attack ← **terpa**

menertawakan *vt* to laugh at ← **tawa**

menertibkan *vt* to keep order, discipline ← **tertib**

meneruskan *vt* to continue, keep doing something ← **terus**

menetap *vi* to stay; **menetapkan** *vt* to appoint, fix, stipulate ← **tetap**

menetas *vi* to hatch ← **tetas**

menéték *vi* to suck, feed from the breast ← **téték**

menétés *vi* to drip; **menétéskan** *vt* to drip something, release something in drips ← **tétés**

menétralkan *vt* to neutralize ← **nétral**

menéwaskan *vt* to kill someone ← **téwas**

mengaba *vt* to conduct ← **aba**

mengabadikan *vt* to immortalize ← **abadi**

mengabaikan *vt* to neglect, disregard, ignore ← **abai**

mengabari *vt* to tell or inform someone; **mengabarkan** *vt* to announce, report ← **kabar**

mengabdi *vi* to serve ← **abdi**

mengaborsi *vt* to abort (a fetus) ← **aborsi**

mengabsahkan *vt* to legalize, legitimize, validate ← **absah**

mengabsén *vi* to call the roll ← **absén**

mengabukan, memperabukan *vt* to cremate ← **abu**

mengabulkan *vt* to grant, approve, consent to; *semoga doanya dikabulkan* may your prayers be answered ← **kabul**

mengacak *vt* to scramble, encode; **mengacak-acak** *v* to mess up ← **acak**

mengacar *vt* to pickle ← **acar**

mengacaukan *vt* to mix or mess up ← **kacau**

mengaco *vi* **ngaco** *vi, sl* to shoot one's mouth off, talk without thinking; misbehave ← **aco**

mengacu *vt* ~ (*pada*) to refer to, to use as a point of reference; ~ *pada hukum negara* following Indonesian law; **mengacukan** *vt* to point, refer to; ~ *arah* indicate direction ← **acu**

mengacuhkan *vt* to ignore, not care about ← **acuh**

mengacungkan *vt* to raise, hold up; ~ *tangan* to raise your hand ← **acung**

mengadakan *vt* to do, run, hold, create, organize, make available; ~ *angket* to do a survey; ~ *kampanye* to run a campaign; ~ *riset* to do research ← **ada**

mengademkan *vt* to cool something down ← **adem**

mengada-ada *vi* to invent, make up; *sungguh* ~ to push your luck; **mengadakan** *vt* to create, organize, make available; ~ *kampanye* to run a campaign ← **ada**

mengadili *vt* to try someone, put someone on trial; to punish ← **adil**

mengadu *vi* to complain, report; **mengadukan** *vt* to report someone/something, to make a complaint about; ~ *ke pengadilan* to sue, take to court; **mengadudombakan** *vt* to play people off against each other ← **adu**

mengaduk *vt* to stir, mix; ~ *semen* to mix cement ← **aduk**

mengagétkan *vt* to surprise, startle ← **kagét**

mengagumi *vt* to admire ← **kagum**

mengagunkan *vt* to use (something) as collateral ← **agun**

mengagungkan *vt* to glorify; **mengagung-agungkan** *vt* to glorify, place on a pedestal ← **agung**

mengail *vi* to fish ← **kail**

mengairi *vt* to irrigate ← **air**

mengais *vt* to scratch; ~ *rejeki* to scratch a living ← **kais**

mengaitkan *vt* to link, connect, join ← **kait**

mengajaibkan *adj* amazing, astonishing, astounding ← **ajaib**

mengajak *vt* to invite, ask out; to urge; ~ *jalan-jalan* to ask out; ~ *kawin*, ~ *nikah* to ask someone to marry you ← **ajak**

mengajar *v* **ngajar** *sl* to teach; **mengajari** *vt* **ngajarin** *sl* to teach someone; **mengajarkan** *vt* to teach something ← **ajar**

mengaji *vi* to recite or read the Koran ← **kaji**

mengajukan *vt* to forward, propose; to submit; ~ *pertanyaan* to ask a question ← **aju**

mengakali *vt* to find a way; to deceive, play a trick on; *kita* ~ *saja* we'll find a way ← **akal**

mengakar *vi* to take root ← **akar**

mengakhiri *vt* to end, finish something ← **akhir**

mengakibatkan *vt* to result in ← **akibat**

mengaksés *vt* to access ← **aksés**

mengaktifkan *vt* to activate, switch on ← **aktif**

mengaku *vt* to admit, confess, acknowledge; to claim; ~ *salah* to admit guilt; **mengakui** *vt* to admit something; to acknowledge, recognize; **diakui** *adj* recognized (of university programs); *hak-hak TKW harus diakui* the rights of migrant workers must be recognized ← **aku**

mengalah *vi* to give in, accept defeat; **mengalahkan** *vt* to conquer, defeat ← **kalah, alah**

mengalamatkan *vt* to address to; to indicate ← **alamat**

mengalami *vt* to experience; ~ *keterlambatan* to experience delays, be delayed ← **alam**

mengaléngkan *vt* to tin, can ← **kaléng**

mengalih, mengalihkan *vt* to shift something; ~ *perhatian* to shift attention, change the subject ← **alih**

mengalihbahasakan *vt* to translate or interpret something ← **alih bahasa**

mengalikan *vt* to multiply ← **kali**

mengalir *vi* to flow ← **alir**

mengalungkan *vt* to drape around someone's neck ← **kalung**

mengalunkan *vt* to put something in motion, sing something ← **alun**

mengamalkan *vt* to do something for charity; to carry out ← **amal**

mengamanatkan *vt* to entrust ← **amanat**

mengamankan *vt* to make safe, restore order; to place in custody ← **aman**

mengamati *vt* to watch closely, keep an eye on ← **amat**

mengambang *vi* to float, be suspended in water ← **ambang**

mengambek *vi* **ngambek** *coll* to get angry ← **ambek**

mengambil *vt* to take, get, fetch; ~ *alih* to take over; ~ *bagian* to take part, participate; ~ *inisiatif* *vi* to take the initiative; ~ *keputusan* to make a decision; ~ *tindakan* to act, take action or measures; ~ *wudu* *v* to wash before praying; **mengambilkan** *vt* to get something for someone ← **ambil**

mengambin *vt* to carry in a sling on the shoulder or back ← **ambin**

mengambing-hitamkan *vt* to make a scapegoat of someone ← **kambing hitam**

mengambungkan *vt* to toss or throw something up ← **ambung**

mengamén *vi* **ngamén** *coll* to sing in the street for money, busk ← **amén**

mengamini *vt* to agree to, approve of ← **amin**

mengampuni *vt* to forgive ← **ampun**

mengamuk *vi* to run amok, go berserk ← **amuk**

menganalisa, menganalisir, menganalisis *vt* to analyze ← **analisa, analisis**

mengancam *vi* to make a threat; *vt* to threaten, intimidate ← **ancam**

mengancing *vt* to button ← **kancing**

mengandaikan *vt* to suppose, assume ← **andai**

mengandalkan *vt* to rely on, trust ← **andal**

mengandaskan *vt* to strand, beach; to frustrate, foil ← **kandas**

mengandung *vt* to contain, carry; *adj* to be pregnant ← **kandung**

menganga *vi* to gape, be open(-mouthed) ← **nganga**

menganggap *vt* to consider, regard; ~ *enteng* to take lightly; *sudah dianggap saudara* to be considered part of the family ← **anggap**

menganggarkan *vt* to budget ← **anggar**

mengangguk *vi* to nod; **menganggukkan** *vt* ~ *kepala* to nod your head ← **angguk**

menganggur *vi* to be unemployed, idle ← **anggur**

menganginkan *vt* to air (clothes, crackers) ← **angin**

mengangkang *vi* to sit with legs wide apart; *vt* to straddle ← **kangkang**

mengangkat *vt* to lift or pick up, raise; to appoint; to remove, amputate; ~ *alis* to raise your eyebrows; ~ *payudara* to remove a breast; *diangkat menjadi menteri* to be made a minister ← **angkat**

mengangkut *vt* to transport ← **angkut**

mengangsur *vt* to pay in instalments ← **angsur**

menganiaya *vt* to mistreat, oppress ← **aniaya**

menganjurkan *vt* to suggest, propose ← **anjur**

mengansel *vt* to cancel ← **kansel**

mengantar *vt* to take, escort, accompany; **mengantarkan** *vt* to take someone or something ← **antar**

mengantongi *vt* to pocket ← **kantong**

mengantri *vi* to queue ← **antri, antré**

mengantuk *adj* sleepy; *vi* to be sleepy ← **kantuk**

menganugerahi *vt* to confer upon ← **anugerah**

menganut *vt* to follow ← **anut**

menganyam *vt* to weave, plait, braid ← **anyam**

mengapa why; *tak* ~ it doesn't matter ← **apa**

mengapit *vt* to pinch, press, squeeze; to flank ← **apit**

mengapung *vi* to float, be suspended ← **apung**

mengapur *vt* to whitewash ← **kapur**

mengarah *vi* to aim something towards; **mengarahkan** *vt* to direct ← **arah**

mengarang *v* to write, compose; *lomba* ~ essay competition ← **karang**

mengartikan *vt* to define, interpret as ← **arti**

mengarungi *vt* to cross water, wade, ford ← **arung**

mengaruniai *vt* to bless ← **karunia**

mengasah *vt* to sharpen, whet ← **asah**

mengasih *vt* to give ← **kasih**

mengasihani *vt* to pity, feel sorry for ← **kasihan**

mengasingkan *vt* to exile ← **asing**

mengasinkan *vt* to salt, pickle ← **asin**

mengasong *vt* to sell in the street ← **asong**

mengaspal *vt* to asphalt ← **aspal**

mengasuh *vt* to care for ← **asuh**

mengasuransikan *vt* to insure ← **asuransi**

mengasyikkan *adj* fascinating, engrossing ← **asyik**

mengatakan *vt* to say ← **kata**

mengatasi *vt* to overcome ← **atas**

mengategorikan *vt* to categorize ← **kategori**

mengatur *vt* to arrange, organize, regulate ← **atur**

mengaum *vi* to roar, growl (of tigers) ← **aum**

mengawal *vt* to guard, escort ← **kawal**

mengawali *vt* to start; to precede ← **awal**

mengawasi *vt* to supervise ← **awas**

mengawétkan *vt* to preserve (food) ← **awét**

mengawini *vt* to marry someone; **mengawinkan** *vt* to marry someone off; ~ *anak* to marry off a son or daughter ← **kawin**

mengayak *vt* to sieve, sift ← **ayak**

mengayau *vi* to hunt heads ← **kayau**

mengayomi *vt* to protect, care for, look after ← **ayom**

mengayuh *vt* to paddle or pedal something; ~ *sepeda* to ride a bicycle ← **kayuh**

mengayun *vt* to rock, swing, sway; **mengayunkan** *vt* to rock ← **ayun**

mengebél *vt, coll* to ring, telephone ← **bél**

mengebom *vt* to bomb something ← **bom**

mengebor *vt* to drill, bore ← **bor**

mengebuk *vt, coll* to book ← **buk**

mengecap *vt* to brand ← **cap**

mengecas *vt* to charge (electrical equipment) ← **cas, charge**

mengecat *vt* to paint, dye; ~ *rambut* to dye, color your hair ← **cat**

mengecék *vt* to check, confirm ← **cék**

mengécér *vt* to retail, sell retail ← **écér**

mengecéwakan *vt* to disappoint; *adj* disappointing ← **kecéwa**

mengecil *vi* to shrink, become smaller; **mengecilkan** *vt* to make smaller, decrease ← **kecil**

mengecor *vt* to cast, pour (concrete) ← **cor**

mengecualikan *vt* to except, make an exception ← **kecuali**

mengecup *vt* to kiss lightly, peck ← **kecup**

mengédarkan *vt* to circulate something ← **édar**

mengedepankan *vt* to put forward, propose ← **ke depan**

mengedipkan *vt* ~ *mata* to blink ← **kedip**

mengédit *vt* to edit ← **édit**

mengedot *vt* to suck ← **dot**

mengegolkan *vt* to promote, campaign for someone ← **gol**

mengéja *vt* to spell ← **éja**

mengejamkan *vt* ~ *mata* to close your eyes ← **kejam**

mengejan *vi* to strain, push the abdominal muscles (when defecating, giving birth) ← **ejan**

mengejang *vi* to cramp, seize up ← **kejang**

mengejapkan *vt* ~ *mata* to blink your eyes ← **kejap**

mengejar *vt* to chase; ~ *waktu* to race against the clock ← **kejar**

mengéjék *vt* to tease, mock, ridicule ← **éjék**

mengejutkan *adj* surprising, startling; *vt* to surprise or startle ← **kejut**

mengekang *vt* to bridle, pull in the reins, curb; *pemerintah sering ~ kebebasan aktivis* governments often limit the freedom of activists ← **kekang**

mengéksékusi *vt* to execute (carry out the death penalty) ← **éksékusi**

mengéksploitasi *vt* to exploit; to get benefit from ← **éksploitasi**

mengékspor *vt* to export ← **ékspor**

mengékstradisi *vt* to extradite (someone) ← **ékstradisi**

mengelabui *vt* to trick, pull the wool over someone's eyes ← **kelabu, abu**

mengélakkan *vt* to avoid, dodge, evade ← **élak**

mengelap *vt* to wipe, mop ← **lap**

mengelas *vt* to weld ← **las**

mengelilingi *vt* to circle, go around ← **keliling**

mengelola *vt* to manage, run ← **kelola**

mengelompokkan *vt* to group ← **kelompok**

mengeloni *vt* to lie down with (a small child) ← **kelon**

mengeluarkan *vt* to issue, send out, release; *Hendro dikeluarkan dari lapangan setelah pelanggarannya* Hendro was sent off the field after his misdemeanor ← **keluar**

mengelu-elukan *vt* to welcome ← **elu**

mengeluh *v* to complain → **keluh**

mengelupas *vt* to peel, come off (of a skin) ← **kelupas**

mengelus *vt* to caress, stroke or pat (an animal ← **elus**

mengemaskan *vt* to package ← **kemas**

mengembalikan *vt* to give or send back, return; *pihak bank masih belum ~ uang saya* the bank still hasn't returned my money ← **kembali**

mengemban *vt* to carry out, perform ← **emban**

mengembang *vi* to rise; *tanpa soda, kue tidak bisa ~* cakes won't rise without baking powder; **mengembangkan** *vt* to develop something; *misi Pusat Bahasa adalah ~ Bahasa Indonesia* the mission of the Language Centre is to develop Indonesian; **mengembangbiakkan** *vt* to propagate, breed ← **kembang**

mengembara *vi* to wander, roam ← **embara**

mengembék, mengembik *vi* to bleat ← **embék**

mengembun *vi* to condense, fog up ← **embun**

mengembus *vt* to blow ← **embun**

mengemis *vi* to beg ← **emis, kemis**

mengemong *vt* to bring up or care for ← **emong**

mengempiskan *vt* to deflate ← **kempis**

mengemudikan *vt* to drive, steer; *~ mobil* to drive a car ← **kemudi**

mengemukakan *vt* to put forward, advance, nominate ← **ke muka**

mengemut *vt* to suck on (sweets etc ← **emut, kemut**

mengena *vi* to hit the spot, be on target; **mengenai** *conj* about, over, on, concerning; **mengenakan** *vt* to put on; *~ pakaian* to put on clothes, dress ← **kena**

mengenal *vt* to know, be acquainted with, recognize; **mengenali** *vt* to identify; **memperkenalkan** *vt* to introduce ← **kenal**

mengenaskan *adj* pitiful, saddening ← **enas**

mengenang *vt* to commemorate, remember; *100 tahun ~ Bung Karno* 100 years of remembering Sukarno ← **kenang**

mengencangkan *vt* to tighten ← **kencang**

mengéncér *vi* to melt, become liquid; **mengéncérkan** *vt* to melt, liquefy ← **éncér**

mengendalikan *vt* to control ← **kendali**

mengendap *vi* to sink, silt up ← **endap**

mengendarai *vt* to ride or drive (a vehicle) ← **kendara, kendor**

mengendurkan, mengendorkan *vt* to loosen, give slack to ← **kendur, kendor**

mengendus *vt* to sniff, get wind of, smell a rat ← **endus**

mengentak *vt* to stamp on something; **mengentakkan** *vt* to stamp something; *~ kaki* to stamp your foot ← **entak**

mengental *vi* to congeal, thicken ← **kental**

mengentaskan *vt* to take out, remove; *~ kemiskinan* to wipe out poverty ← **entas**

mengéntot *vt, vulg* to fuck, screw, root ← **éntot**

mengenyam *vt* to taste, experience; *Sungkono hanya sempat ~ pendidikan SD* Sungkono only had an elementary school education ← **kenyam**

mengepak *vt* to pack ← **pak**

mengepakkan *vt ~ sayap* to flutter wings ← **kepak**

mengepal *vi* to form a fist ← **kepal**

mengepalai *vt* to be head of ← **kepala**

mengepél *vt* to mop (up) ← **pél**

mengeposkan *vt* to post (an item through the post) ← **pos**

mengepul *vi* to smoke, billow ← **kepul**

mengepung *vt* to surround, encircle, besiege ← **kepung**

mengerahkan *vt* to mobilize ← **kerah**

mengeram *vi* to sit on eggs, brood, hatch ← **eram**

mengeramatkan *vt* to consider or make sacred ← **keramat**

mengerang *vi* to groan, moan ← **erang**

mengeras *vi* to get louder, harder; **mengeraskan** *vt* to make something harder, louder ← **keras**

mengerat *vt* to gnaw, nibble, eat away; *binatang ~* rodent ← **kerat**

mengérék *vt* to hoist, pull; *~ bendera* to raise the flag ← **kérék**

mengerém *vt* to brake ← **rém**

mengerikan *adj* terrifying, horrifying ← **ngeri**

mengering *vi* to become dry; **mengeringkan** *vt* to dry something; *~ rambut* to dry your hair ← **kering**

mengeriting *vt ~ rambut* to perm your hair ← **keriting**

mengerjakan *vt* to do, carry out; *~ PR* to do your homework ← **kerja**

mengerling *vi* to (steal a) glance, glance sideways ← **kerling**

mengernyit *vt ~ dahi, ~ kening* to frown ← **kernyit**

mengerok *vt* to rub someone's back with a coin ← **kerok**

mengeropos *vi* to be eaten away, eroded ← **keropos**

mengeroyok *vt* to beat savagely in a mob; *dikeroyok massa* to be beaten up by a mob ← **keroyok**

mengerti *vi* to understand; **dimengerti** *v* to be understood; **pengertian** *n* understanding ← **erti, arti**

mengerubungi *vt* to encircle; *Gubernur dikerubungi para pendemo* the Governor was surrounded by demonstrators ← **kerubung**

mengerudungi *vt* to (cover with a) veil ← **kerudung**

mengeruh *vi* to become cloudy; **mengeruhkan** *vt* to muddy, make cloudy ← **keruh**

mengeruk *vt* to dredge, scrape out ← **keruk**

mengerumuni *vt* to mob, surround, crowd around someone ← **kerumun**

mengerut *vi* to shrink, shrivel, contract; **mengerutkan** *vt ~ kening* to frown ← **kerut**

mengesahkan *vt* to validate, ratify, legitimize, legalize ← **sah**

mengesampingkan *vt* to put to one side, to put aside, sideline ← **ke samping**

mengesankan *adj* impressive; *vt* to give an impression ← **kesan**

mengetahui *vt* to know something, have knowledge of ← **tahu**

mengetawakan *vt* to laugh at ← **tawa**

mengetés *vt* to test ← **tés**

mengetik *vt* to type ← **ketik**

mengétsa *vt* etch ← **étsa**

mengetuai *vt* to preside over ← **ketua, tua**

mengetuk *vt* to knock; *~ hati* to prick your conscience; *~ pintu* to knock on the door ← **ketuk**

mengévaluasi *vt* to evaluate ← **évaluasi**

mengéyél *vi* to be stubborn, obstinate ← **éyél**

menggabungkan *vt* to connect, combine, fuse ← **gabung**

menggadaikan *vt* to pawn something ← **gadai**

menggado *vi* to eat side-dishes without rice ← **gado**

menggaét *vt* to get (on board), snatch, hook ← **gaét, gait, kait**

menggagahi *vt* to overpower, violate, rape ← **gagah**

menggagalkan *vt* to frustrate, make something fail ← **gagal**

menggagap *vi* to stammer, stutter ← **gagap**

menggairahkan *adj* exciting, stimulating; *vt* to excite, stimulate, enthuse ← **gairah**

menggait *vt* to pull, hook ← **gait, gaét, kait**

menggaji *vt* to pay, remunerate, employ ← **gaji**

menggalang *vt* to support, consolidate ← **galang**

menggali *vt* to dig ← **gali**

menggambar *v* to draw, depict; **menggambarkan** *vt* to describe, illustrate ← **gambar**

menggamitkan, menggamit-gamitkan *vt* to touch or nudge something ← **gamit**

menggandakan *vt* to duplicate, multiply ← **ganda**

menggandéng *vt* to include, involve, link with ← **gandéng**

menggandrungi *vt* to love, be swept up in ← **gandrung**

mengganggu *vt* to bother, disturb; ~ *gugat* to contest, challenge, sue ← **ganggu**

mengganjal *vt* to wedge ← **ganjal**

mengganti *vt* to change, substitute, replace; **menggantikan** *vt* to substitute or replace someone/something ← **ganti**

menggantung *vt* to hang, suspend; **menggantungkan** *vt* to hang something; ~ *jam pada dinding* to hang a clock on the wall ← **gantung**

mengganyang *vt* to crush, wipe out; to eat raw ← **ganyang**

menggarap *vt* to work on, produce; ~ *tanah* to till the land → **garap**

menggaris *vt* to draw a line; **menggaris-bawahi** *vt* to underline, emphasize ← **garis**

menggarong *vt* to rob, loot ← **garong**

menggaruk *vt* to scratch, scrape; ~ *kepala* to scratch your head; **meng-**

garuk-garuk *vt* to scratch repeatedly ← **garuk**

menggauli *vt* to have sexual intercourse with ← **gaul**

menggebrak *vt* to hit or slam; ~ *meja* to hit the table → **gebrak**

menggebu *vi* to rage, bubble, froth over ← **gebu**

menggebuk *vt* to batter, bash ← **gebuk**

menggedor *vt* to bang on repeatedly; ~ *pintu* to bang on the door → **gedor**

menggelapkan *vt* to embezzle, misappropriate ← **gelap**

menggelar, menggelarkan *vt* to hold (an event) ← **gelar**

menggelatuk → **menggeletuk**

menggelédah *vt* to search; to ransack ← **gelédah**

menggéléng, menggéléngkan *vt* ~ *kepala* to shake your head ← **géléng**

menggeletuk, menggelatuk *vi* to chatter (of teeth) ← **geletuk**

menggeliat *vi* to stretch, twist ← **geliat**

menggelikan *adj* funny, comic, off-putting ← **geli**

menggelincir *vi* to slip, slide ← **gelincir**

menggelinding *vi* to roll; **menggelindingkan** *vt* to roll something ← **gelinding**

menggelitik *vt* to tickle ← **gelitik**

menggelisahkan *vt* to make nervous ← **gelisah**

menggelora *vi* to rage, storm, surge ← **gelora**

menggelungkan *vt* to coil something ← **gelung**

menggeluti *vt* to be involved, deal with ← **gelut**

menggemari *vt* to like, enjoy ← **gemar**

menggemaskan *adj* annoying; *vt* to annoy ← **gemas**

menggembala *vt* to herd ← **gembala**

menggembar-gemborkan *vt* make a big deal of, shout about ← **gembar-gembor**

menggembirakan *adj* exciting, happy; *vt* to make happy, excite; *berita yang* ~ good news ← **gembira**

menggembok *vt* to padlock ← **gembok**

menggembos *vi* to deflate, go flat ← **gembos**

menggempakan *vt* to jolt, stir ← **gempa**

menggemparkan *vt* to cause a stir ← **gempar**

menggempur *vt* to attack, destroy ← **gempur**

menggenangi *vt* to flood something ← **genang**

menggéndong *vt* to carry on the hip ← **géndong**

menggenggam *vt* to grip, grasp ← **genggam**

menggenjot *vt* to push, pedal; ~ *sepeda* to pedal a bike ← **genjot**

menggerakkan *vt* to move, shift something ← **gerak**

menggeram *vi* to become angry; to growl, roar ← **geram**

menggerayangi *vt* to grope ← **gerayang**

menggerebek *vt* to raid, search ← **gerebek**

menggergaji *vt* to saw ← **gergaji**

menggerinda *vi* to grind, sharpen ← **gerinda**

menggerogoti *vt* to eat into, erode, gnaw on; *digerogoti rayap* to be eaten by termites ← **gerogot**

menggerombol *vi* to gather in a group, amass ← **gerombol**

menggertak *vi* to snarl or snap at; to intimidate, threaten ← **gertak**

menggerutu *vi* to grumble, complain, gripe ← **gerutu**

menggésék *vt* to rub, scrape; ~ *biola* to play the violin; ~ *kartu* to swipe a card ← **gésék**

menggésér *vt* to move aside or over ← **gésér**

menggigil *vi* to shiver ← **gigil**

menggigit *vt* to bite ← **gigit**

menggilas *vt* to crush, pulverize ← **gilas**

menggiling *vt* to grind, mill; to roll out (pastry) ← **giling**

menggiring *vt* to herd, drive (cattle) ← **giring**

menggiurkan *adj* tempting, mouth-watering ← **giur**

mengglasir *vt* to glaze (tiles) ← **glasir**

menggoda *vt* to tempt; **menggodai** *vt* to tempt someone ← **goda**

menggodok *vt* to boil ← **godok**

menggolok *vt* to cut with a machete ← **golok**

menggolongkan *vt* to group, classify ← **golong**

menggoncangkan *vt* to rock or make something move ← **goncang**

menggonggong *vi* to bark ← **gonggong**

menggoréng *vt* to fry ← **goréng**

menggorés *vt* to scratch, make a stroke ← **gorés**

menggosipkan *vt* to gossip about something or someone ← **gosip**

menggosok *vt* to rub, polish; *coll* to iron; ~ *sepatu* to polish, shine (shoes) ← **gosok**

menggotong *vt* to carry together ← **gotong**

menggoyang *vt* to shake, rock; ~ *pinggul* to sway your hips; **menggoyangkan** *vt* to shake or rock something ← **goyang**

menggréndel *vt* to bolt ← **gréndel**

menggubah *vt* to arrange, compose ← **gubah**

menggubris *vt* to pay heed or attention to; *tidak digubris* ignored ← **gubris**

menggugat *vt* to sue, accuse ← **gugat**

menggugurkan *vt* to abort ← **gugur**

mengguling *vt* to roll; **menggulingkan** *vt* to topple, roll over ← **guling**

menggulung *vt* to roll up ← **gulung**

menggumamkan *vt* to mumble or mutter something ← **gumam**

menggunakan *vt* to use ← **guna**

mengguncangkan *vt* to rock or make something move ← **guncang**

menggunduli *vt* to shave, denude, make bald; *bukit itu sudah digunduli* the hill has been deforested ← **gundul**

menggunjing *vt* to gossip about, talk about someone behind their back ← **gunjing**

menggunting *vt* to cut (out) ← **gunting**

menggurui *vt* to lecture or talk ← **guru**

menggusur *vt* to evict, sweep aside, forcibly remove ← **gusur**

mengguyur *vt* to soak, drench; *diguyur hujan* drenched by the rain ← **guyur**

menghabisi *vt* to finish (off), kill; **menghabiskan** *vt* to finish, use up, spend; *~ uang jutaan rupiah* to spend millions of rupiah ← **habis**

menghadap *vt* to face, appear before; **menghadapi** *vt* to face someone or something; **menghadapkan** *vt* to aim or point something; to confront, put in front of; *penjahat itu dihadapkan dengan kepala polisi* the criminal was brought before the chief of police ← **hadap**

menghadiahkan *vt* to give as a present or prize; **menghadiahi** *vt* to give someone a present or prize ← **hadiah**

menghadiri *vt* to attend; **menghadirkan** *vt* to present, bring forward; *~ saksi baru* bring forward a new witness ← **hadir**

menghafalkan *vt* to learn by heart ← **hafal**

menghajar *vt* to thrash; to beat up ← **hajar**

menghakimi *vt* to judge; to pass sentence on, convict ← **hakim**

menghalalkan *vt* to permit, allow ← **halal**

menghalau *vt* to chase away ← **halau**

menghaluskan *vt* to refine, grind ← **halus**

menghambat *vt* to obstruct, impede, hamper ← **hambat**

menghamburkan *vt* to scatter, throw about ← **hambur**

menghamili *vt* to make someone pregnant ← **hamil**

menghampar *vt* to spread out ← **hampar**

menghampiri *vt* to approach ← **hampir**

menghancurkan *vt* to smash, crush, destroy ← **hancur**

menghangatkan *vt* to warm something (up) ← **hangat**

menghanguskan *vt* to burn down ← **hangus**

menghantam *vt* to strike ← **hantam**

menghantarkan *vt* to conduct (electricity or heat) ← **hantar**

menghantui *vt* to haunt ← **hantu**

menghapus *vt* to delete, erase, wipe; **menghapuskan** *vt* to wipe out, eliminate ← **hapus**

mengharamkan *vt* to forbid; to avoid, abstain from ← **haram**

mengharapkan *vt* to expect ← **harap**

menghardik *vt* to shout at, scold ← **hardik**

menghargai *vt* to appreciate ← **harga**

mengharukan *adj* moved, touched (emotionally); *vt* to move, touch emotionally ← **haru**

mengharuskan *vt* to require ← **harus**

menghasilkan *vt* to produce ← **hasil**

menghasut *vt* to incite, agitate ← **hasut**

menghayati *vt* to inspire, instill, vivify ← **hayat**

menghébohkan *vt* to cause an uproar; *adj* sensational ← **héboh**

menghéla *vt* to draw, drag, pull; *~ nafas* to sigh, draw a breath ← **héla**

menghémat *vt* to save on or economize ← **hémat**

menghembus *vt* to blow ← **hembus**

menghempas *vt* to throw down; **mengempaskan** *vt ~ diri* to throw yourself down ← **empas**

menghendaki *vt* to want ← **hendak**

mengheningkan *vt ~ cipta* to observe a moment's silence ← **hening**

menghentikan *vt* to stop something ← **henti**

menghérankan *adj* astonishing, astounding ← **héran**

menghiasi *vt* to adorn, decorate something ← **hias**

menghibahkan *vt* to donate, bequeath ← **hibah**

menghibur *vt* to entertain; to comfort, console ← **hibur**

menghidangkan *vt* to serve up, offer ← **hidang**

menghidupi *vt* to provide for; **menghidupkan** *vt* to bring to life, start or turn on (a device); *~ kembali* to revive; *~ mesin* to turn on the engine ← **hidup**

menghijau *vi* to become green; **menghijaukan** *vt* to make green ← **hijau**

menghilang *vi* to disappear, vanish; **menghilangkan** *vt* to remove ← hilang

menghilir *vi* to go downstream ← **hilir**

menghimbau ← **mengimbau**

menghimpit *vt* to squeeze or press; **menghimpitkan** *vt* to squeeze against ← himpit

menghimpunkan *vt* to bring together, gather ← **himpun**

menghinakan *vt* to humiliate, insult ← hina

menghindar *vi* to steer clear, avoid; **menghindari** *vt* to avoid something ← hindar

menghiraukan *vt* to take heed, listen to advice; *tidak dihiraukan* ignored ← hirau

menghirup *vt* to breathe in ← **hirup**

menghitam *vi* to become black; **menghitamkan** *vt* to blacken, make black ← hitam

menghitung *vi* to count; *vt* to calculate, reckon; **menghitungkan** *vt* to count or calculate something ← hitung

menghormat, menghormati *vt* to honor or respect

menghubungi *vt* to contact someone; **menghubungkan** *vt* to connect, join, link different parts ← hubung

menghujani *vt* to pelt, rain down upon ← hujan

menghujat *vt* to swear, blaspheme ← hujat

menghukum *vt* to punish, sentence, condemn ← hukum

menghuni *vt* to live in, occupy ← huni

menghunjam *vi* to plunge, dive; **menghunjamkan** *vt* to thrust in ← hunjam

menghunus *vt* to unsheathe, take out; ~ *pedang* to pull out a sword ← hunus

mengibaratkan *vt* to use figuratively, as an example ← ibarat

mengibarkan *vt* to wave, unfurl; ~ *bendera* to fly a flag ← kibar

mengibaskan *vt* to wag (a tail) ← kibas

mengibuli *vt* to fool someone ← kibul

mengidam *vi* to crave (esp of pregnant woman) ← idam

mengidap *vt* to suffer from; ~ *penyakit* to suffer from or have a disease ← idap

mengidéntifikasi *vt* to identify (someone) ← idéntifikasi

mengidolakan *vt* to worship, idolize ← idola

mengigau *vi* to talk in one's sleep, be delirious ← igau

mengijinkan *vt* to permit, allow ← ijin, izin

mengikat *adj* binding; *vt* to tie, fasten; ~ *janji* to take vows, get married; *perjanjian yang* ~ binding agreement ← ikat

mengikis *vt* to erode, eat away ← kikis

mengiklankan *vt* to advertise ← iklan

mengikut *vt* to follow, accompany; **mengikuti** *vt* to follow, join, participate in; ~ *kursus* to do a course ← ikut

mengiler *vi* to drool, slobber ← iler

mengilhami *vt* to inspire, be a source of inspiration ← ilham

mengimbangi *vt* to balance, offset ← imbang

mengimbau *vt* to call, summon, appeal ← imbau

mengiming, mengiming-iming, mengimingkan, mengiming-imingkan *vt* to tantalize, tempt ← iming

mengimpikan *vt* to dream of ← impi

mengimplikasikan *vt* to implicate ← implikasi

mengimpor *vt* to import ← impor

menginap *vi* to stay the night, stay over ← inap

mengincar *vt* to set your sights on, target, aim ← incar

mengindahkan *vt* to take heed, pay attention to ← indah

mengindonésiakan *vt* to translate or make into Indonesian ← Indonésia

menginformasikan *vt* to inform ← informasi

mengingat *vt* to remember, bear in mind; **mengingatkan** *vt* to remind someone about something ← ingat

menginginkan *vt* to wish for, desire ← ingin

mengingkari *vt* to renege or go back on ← **ingkar**

menginjak *vt* to step, tread, or stamp on; ~ *gas* to accelerate, step on the gas; **menginjak-injak** *vt* to trample on; **menginjakkan** *vt* to set down; ~ *kaki* to step upon, set (foot) upon ← **injak**

menginsafkan *vt* to make conscious, raise awareness ← **insaf**

menginspirasikan *vt* to inspire ← **inspirasi**

mengintai *vt* to spy on or watch, conduct surveillance ← **intai**

mengintégrasi *vt* to integrate; *Timor Timur diintegrasi dengan Indonesia sejak 1975 sampai dengan 1999* East Timor was integrated with Indonesia from 1975 to 1999 ← **intégrasi**

menginternir *vt* to intern (someone) ← **internir**

mengintérogasi *vt* to interrogate ← **intérogasi**

menginterviu *vt* to interview ← **interviu**

mengintimidasi *vt* to intimidate ← **intimidasi**

mengintip *v* to peep at, spy on ← **intip**

menginvéstasikan *vt* to invest something ← **invéstasi**

mengipasi *vt* to fan someone or something ← **kipas**

mengira *vt* to assume, think; **mengira-ngira** *vi* to roughly estimate, guess ← **kira**

mengirigasi *vt* to irrigate ← **irigasi**

mengirim *vt* to send ← **kirim**

mengiringi *vt* to accompany, escort ← **iring**

mengiris *vt* to slice ← **iris**

mengirit *vt* to economize ← **irit**

mengisahkan *vt* to tell the story of ← **kisah**

mengisak, mengisak-isak *vi* to sob ← **isak**

mengisap *vt* to suck; to smoke; ~ *cerutu* to smoke a cigar; ~ *ganja* to smoke marijuana ← **isap**

mengisi *vt* to fill, load; ~ *aki* to charge a car battery; ~ *bensin* to fill up with petrol; ~ *waktu* to fill in time ← **isi**

mengislamkan *vt* to Islamize, make Islamic ← **Islam**

mengistilahkan *vt* to define something ← **istilah**

mengistiméwakan *vt* to treat as special ← **istiméwa**

mengistirahatkan *vt* to rest (someone) ← **istirahat**

mengisyaratkan *vt* to give a sign, signal ← **isyarat**

mengitari *vt* to orbit; *bumi ~ matahari* the Earth orbits the Sun ← **kitar**

mengiyakan *vt* to agree or assent to ← **iya**

mengizinkan *vt* to permit, allow ← **izin, ijin**

mengkaji *vt* to study, investigate ← **kaji**

mengkhianati *vt* to betray someone ← **khianat**

mengkhitan, mengkhitankan *vt* to circumcise; ~ *anak* to have a child circumcised ← **khitan**

mengkhususkan *vt* to give special treatment ← **khusus**

mengkilap *vi* to shine, gleam ← **kilap**

mengklaim *vt* to claim (a fact); *para penghuni ~ belum dibayar kompensasi* the residents claim they haven't been paid compensation ← **klaim**

mengklakson *v* to toot or beep (at someone) ← **klakson**

mengklarifikasi *vt* to clarify ← **klarifikasi**

mengklasifikasi *vt* to classify ← **klasifikasi**

mengklon *vt* to clone ← **klon**

mengobarkan *vt* to fan, fuel ← **kobar**

mengkompénsasi *vt* to compensate ← **kompénsasi**

mengkristenkan *vt* to convert someone to Christianity, Christianize ← **Kristen**

mengkritik *vt* to criticize ← **kritik**

mengkudu *n* kind of root, used as a spice

mengobati *vt* to treat, cure ← **obat**

mengobrak-abrik *vt* to upset, turn upside-down ← **obrak-abrik**

mengobral *vt* to put on sale ← **obral**

mengobras *vt* to overlock ← **obras**

mengobrol *vi* to chat ← **obrol**

mengobservasi *vt* to observe, keep watch on ← **obsérvasi**

mengobyék *vi* to have a job on the side, moonlight ← **obyék**

mengocéh *vi* to babble, talk nonsense ← **océh**

mengocok *vt* to shake, shuffle; ~ *dadu* to roll the dice; ~ *kartu* to shuffle cards ← **kocok**

mengojék *vi* to take passengers around on your motorbike ← **ojék**

mengolah *vt* to process, treat ← **olah**

mengolés *vt* to grease, spread, lubricate; **mengolési** *vt* to grease something; **mengoléskan** *vt* to smear with something ← **olés**

mengomél *vi* to complain, grumble, whinge, whine ← **omél**

mengoméntari *vt* to comment on ← **koméntar**

mengompol *vi* to wet your pants, the bed ← **ompol**

mengomposkan *vt* to compost ← **kompos**

mengontak *vt* to contact someone ← **kontak**

mengontrakkan *vt* to lease or rent out a house ← **kontrak**

mengoper *vt* to transfer, hand over; ~ *bola* to pass the ball; **mengoperkan** *vt* to pass (on) ← **oper**

mengoperasi *vt* to operate on; *Tiwi dioperasi kemarin* Tiwi had surgery yesterday; **mengoperasikan** *vt* to operate something; *tukang yang ~ alat derek sedang dalam bahaya* the workman operating the crane is in danger ← **operasi**

mengoplos *vt* to mix in another liquid illegally ← **oplos**

mengoptimalkan *vt* to optimize, get the most out of ← **optimal**

mengorbankan *vt* to sacrifice → **korban**

mengorbitkan *vt* to launch, put into orbit; *penyanyi itu semula diorbitkan suaminya* that singer's career was launched by her husband ← **orbit**

mengorék *vt* to scrape, scratch

mengoréksi *vt* to correct ← **koréksi**

mengorupsi *vt* to be corrupt; to corrupt ← **korupsi**

mengosongkan *vt* to empty ← **kosong**

mengotak-ngotakkan *vt* to categorize, box, put in boxes ← **kotak**

mengotori *vt* to (make) dirty, defile ← **kotor**

menguap *vi* to yawn ← **kuap**

menguap *vi* to evaporate or steam ← **uap**

menguasai *vt* to control, have power over; ~ *bahasa asing* to be able to speak a foreign language ← **kuasa**

menguatirkan *vt* to worry about something ← **kuatir**

menguatkan *vt* to strengthen; **memperkuat** *vt* to reinforce, make stronger ← **kuat**

mengubah *vt* to change or alter ← **ubah**

menguber *vt, coll* to chase, go after ← **uber**

menguburkan *vt* to bury ← **kubur**

mengucap, mengucapkan *vt* to say or express something; ~ *terima kasih* to say thank you; to thank ← **ucap**

mengucek *vt* ~ *mata* to rub your eyes; ~ *pakaian* to rub clothes together when washing ← **kucek, ucek**

mengucilkan *vt* to ostracize, shun ← **kucil**

mengucurkan *vt* to gush, pour ← **kucur**

mengudarakan *vt* to broadcast or air ← **udara**

menguji *vt* to examine or test; ~ *ketangkasan* to test your skill ← **uji**

mengujicobakan *vt* to test something ← **uji coba**

mengukir *vt* to carve or engrave ← **ukir**

mengukuhkan *vt* to strengthen; to ratify ← **kukuh**

mengukur *vt* to measure ← **ukur**

mengukus *vt* to steam (food) → **kukus**

mengulang *vt* to repeat, do again; **mengulangi** *v* to repeat something ← **ulang**

mengulas *vt* to comment, review, critique ← **ulas**

mengulek *vi* to make fresh chilli sauce ← **ulek**

mengultimatum *vt* to give (someone) an ultimatum ← **ultimatum**

mengulum *vt* to suck in the mouth ← **kulum**

mengulur-ulur *vt* to spin out, take a long time; **mengulurkan** *vt* to extend something ← **ulur**

mengumandangkan *vt* to sing; to sound, reverberate ← **kumandang**

mengumpat *v* to curse, swear ← **umpat**

mengumpet *vi* to hide or conceal yourself; **mengumpetkan** *vt* to hide something ← **umpet**

mengumpulkan *vt* to collect, gather; ~ *perangko* to collect stamps ← **kumpul**

mengumumkan *vt* to announce or declare ← **umum**

mengunci *vt* to lock (up) ← **kunci**

mengundang *vt* to invite (formally) ← **undang**

mengundi *vt* to conduct a draw or lottery ← **undi**

mengundurkan *vt* to postpone ← **undur**

mengungguli *vt* to surpass, outdo; **mengunggulkan** *vt* to consider superior, seed (in tennis) ← **unggul**

mengungkap *vt* to uncover; **mengungkapkan** *vt* to express ← **ungkap**

mengungkit *vt* to lever; to pry; **mengungkit-ungkit** *vt* to drag something up (from the past) ← **ungkit**

mengungkung *vt* to shackle ← **kungkung**

mengungsi *vi* to evacuate or flee; **mengungsikan** *vt* to evacuate someone ← **ungsi**

menguning *vi* to turn or become yellow ← **kuning**

mengunjukkan *vt* to show something ← **unjuk**

mengunjungi *vt* to visit a place ← **kunjung**

menguntai *vt* to string, tie together ← **untai**

menguntungkan *vt* to benefit (someone); *adj* profitable ← **untung**

mengunyah *v* to chew ← **kunyah**

mengupah *vt* to employ, hire, pay someone (to do work) ← **upah**

mengupas *vt* to peel; to analyze ← **kupas**

mengupayakan *vi* to try, to enable ← **upaya**

mengupil *vt* to pick your nose ← **upil**

menguping *v* to eavesdrop, listen in ← **kuping**

menguraikan *vt* to explain; to untangle ← **urai**

mengurangi *vt* to take from, subtract, minus; *enam dikurangi dua sama dengan empat* six minus two is four; **mengurangkan** *vt* to reduce, make smaller ← **kurang**

menguras *vt* to clean out, drain; ~ *tenaga* to use up energy ← **kuras**

mengurét *vt* to scrape out, perform a curette ← **kurét**

mengurskan *vt* to convert (currency); *satu dolar AS kalau dikurskan sekarang kira-kira Rp 10.000* one US dollar is worth about Rp 10,000 right now ← **kurs**

mengursuskan *vt* to send someone on a course ← **kursus**

menguruk *vt* to fill (with earth) ← **uruk**

mengurung *vt* to cage, put in a cage, lock up ← **kurung**

mengurungkan *vt* to abandon ← **urung**

mengurus *vt* to arrange, organize, manage; **mengurusi** *vt* to take care of, look after ← **urus**

mengurut *vt* to massage ← **urut**

mengurut *vt* to put in order or sequence ← **urut**

mengusahakan *vt* to try, endeavor to ← **usaha**

mengusap *vt* to wipe; to stroke or fondle ← **usap**

mengusik *vt* to tease, make fun of ← **usik**

mengusir *vt* to drive away or out, chase away, expel ← **usir**

mengusulkan *vt* to propose or suggest ← **usul**

mengusung *vt* to carry on the shoulders ← **usung**

mengusut *vt* to investigate, sort out ← **usut**

mengusutkan *vt* to complicate, confuse ← **kusut**

mengutak-atik, mengutak-ngatikkan *vt* to work on or tinker with ← **kutak, utak-atik**

mengutamakan *vt* to give preference or priority to ← **utama**

mengutarakan *vt* to put forward ← **utara**

mengutik *vt* to tinker with; to touch on → **kutik, utik**

mengutip *vt* to quote, cite an extract; *mahasiswa itu sering ~ pidato Bung Karno* the student often quoted from Sukarno's speeches ← **kutip**

mengutuk *vt* to curse ← **kutuk**

mengutus *vt* to send or delegate ← **utus**

Ménhub *n* Minister of Transportation ← **Menteri Perhubungan**

meniadakan *vt* to undo or cancel ← **tiada, tidak ada**

meniduri *vt* to sleep with someone, have sex with someone; **menidurkan** *vt* to put to sleep ← **tidur**

menikah *vi* to marry, get married; **menikahi** *vt* to marry someone; **menikahkan** *vt* to marry off (a child) ← **nikah**

menikam *vt* to stab → **tikam**

menikmati *vt* to enjoy → **nikmat**

menikung *vi* to bend, curve → **tikung**

menilai *vt* to evaluate, appraise ← **nilai**

menilang *vt* to fine ← **tilang**

menimang-nimang *vt* to rock (a child) ← **timang**

menimba *vt* to bail out, remove water from ← **timba**

menimbang *vt* to weigh (up) ← **timbang**

menimbulkan *vt* to give rise, bring to the surface ← **timbul**

menimbun *vt* to pile up, accumulate; to hoard, stockpile; *~ makanan* to hoard food ← **timbun**

menimpa *vt* to fall upon, befall → **timpa**

meninabobokan *vt* to sing to sleep ← **nina bobo, ninabobo**

menindaklanjuti *vt* to follow up ← **tindak lanjut**

menindas *vt* to oppress ← **tindas**

menindik *vt* to pierce (ears) ← **tindik**

meninggal *vi* ~ *(dunia)* to die; **meninggalkan** *vt* to leave (behind), abandon ← **tinggal**

meninggikan *vt* to raise, elevate ← **tinggi**

meningkat *vi* to rise, increase, improve; **meningkatkan** *vt* to increase or raise the level of something ← **tingkat**

meninjau *vt* to observe, view; *~ kembali* to review → **tinjau**

menipis *vi* to become thin ← **tipis**

menipu *vt* to trick, deceive ← **tipu**

meniru *vt* to copy or imitate ← **tiru**

menit *n* minute

menitikberatkan *vt* to emphasize ← **titik berat**

menitip *vt* to leave in someone's care, entrust ← **titip**

meniup *vt* to blow; *~ lilin* to blow out a candle ← **tiup**

menjabat *vt* to hold; to work as; *~ Menteri Keuangan* to be Minister of Finance ← **jabat**

menjabarkan *vt* to clarify, spell out ← **jabar**

menjadi *v* to be or become; *~ marah* to get angry; **menjadi-jadi** *vi* to get worse; **menjadikan** *vt* to create, make ← **jadi**

menjadwal, menjadwalkan *vt* to timetable ← **jadwal**

menjaga *vt* to guard, keep watch ← **jaga**

menjagokan *vt* to support ← **jago**

menjahit *vt* to sew ← **jahit**

menjaili *vt* to annoy, play a trick on ← **jail**

menjajah, menjajahi *vt* to colonize, rule another country ← **jajah**

menjajakan *vt* to hawk, peddle; *~ permen* to sell sweets, candy ← **jaja**

menjajaki *vt* to probe, sound out ← **jajak**

menjala *vt* to catch by casting a net ← **jala**

menjalani *vt* to undergo, do; *~ hukuman penjara 3 tahun* to serve three years in jail; **menjalankan** *vt* to operate, run, set in motion; *~ perintah* to carry out orders ← **jalan**

menjalar *vi* to creep, climb; *tanaman ~* climbing plant ← **jalar**

menjalin *vt* to forge links, network ← **jalin**

menjamah, menjamahi *vt* to touch; to have sex with ← **jamah**

menjambak *vt* to pull someone's hair ← **jambak**

menjambrét *vt* to snatch ← **jambrét**

menjamin *vt* to guarantee, promise ← **jamin**

menjamu *vt* to entertain guests, host an event, hold a feast ← **jamu**

menjamur *vi* to spring up ← **jamur**

menjanda *vi* to be widowed, live as a widow ← **janda**

menjangan *n* deer

menjangkau *vt* to reach ← **jangkau**

menjangkit *vt* to spread, be infectious or contagious; **menjangkiti** *vt* to infect ← **jangkit**

menjanjikan *vt* to promise something ← **janji**

menjarah *vt* to loot ← **jarah**

menjaring *vt* to fish with a net; to filter or sift ← **jaring**

menjatahkan *vt* to deal out, allocate ← **jatah**

menjatuhkan *vt* to fell, let drop; ~ *hukuman* to sentence, condemn ← **jatuh**

menjauh *vi* to move away; **menjauhi** *vt* to avoid ← **jauh**

menjawab *vi* to answer, reply ← **jawab**

menjebak, menjebakkan *vt* to trap ← **jebak**

menjeblos *vt* to break or fall through ← **jeblos**

menjégal *vt* to stop (from winning), prevent, hamper, foil ← **jégal**

menjejaki *vt* to step on, trail, trace ← **jejak**

menjejalkan *vt* to crowd, fill, jam ← **jejal**

menjéjérkan *vt* to place in rows ← **jéjér**

menjelajahi *vt* to travel through or explore a place ← **jelajah**

menjelang *vt* to approach (usu time) ← **jelang**

menjelaskan *vt* to explain, clarify ← **jelas**

menjelékkan *vt* to criticize, say bad things about ← **jelék**

menjelimet *vi* to be meticulous, nitpicking ← **jelimet**

menjelma *vi* to be incarnated, turn into, materialize; **menjelmakan** *vt* to create or realize something ← **jelma**

menjembatani *vt* to bridge (two things) ← **jembatan**

menjemput *vt* to pick up; ~ *bola* to be proactive ← **jemput**

menjemukan *adj* tedious, boring ← **jemu**

menjemur *vt* to air, dry in the sun; ~ *krupuk* to air crackers before frying; ~ *baju cucian* to hang out the washing ← **jemur**

menjéngkélkan *adj* annoying ← **jéngkél**

menjenguk *vt* to visit (in hospital), pay a call on ← **jenguk**

menjepit *vt* to pinch, squeeze ← **jepit**

menjeprét *vt* to snap, staple; ~ *foto* to take a photo ← **jeprét**

menjerat *vt* to snare, trap ← **jerat**

menjerembabkan *vt* to upset, push over ← **jerembab**

menjerit *vi* to scream, shriek ← **jerit**

menjernihkan *vt* to purify (water) ← **jernih**

menjerumuskan *vt* to let drop, send down ← **jerumus**

menjéwér *vt* to pinch someone's ear, scold ← **jéwér**

menjijikkan *adj* disgusting, revolting, foul ← **jijik**

menjilat *vt* to lick; *sl* to suck up, flatter; **menjilati** *vt* to lick something; to fawn, suck up ← **jilat**

menjilid *vt* to bind ← **jilid**

menjinakkan *vt* to tame ← **jinak**

menjinjing *vt* to carry by hand ← **jinjing**

menjiplak *vt* to copy, plagiarize ← **jiplak**

menjiwai *vt* to bring to life, inspire ← **jiwa**

menjodohkan *vt* to set up, match ← **jodoh**

menjorok *vi* to stick out, protrude; **menjorokkan** *vt* to poke something out ← **jorok**

menjual *vt* to sell ← **jual**

menjuarai *vt* to win (a competition) ← **juara**

menjulang *vi* to soar; ~ *tinggi* to rise high ← **julang**

menjuluki *vt* to give a nickname to ← **juluk**

menjumlahkan *vt* to add (up) ← **jumlah**

menjumpai *vt* to meet someone ← **jumpa**

menjunjung *vt* ~ *tinggi* to honor ← **junjung**

menjuntai *vi* to dangle ← **juntai**

menjurus *vi* to lead to ← **jurus**

Ménkés *n* Minister of Health ← **Menteri Keséhatan**

Ménkéu *n* Minister of Finance ← **Menteri Keuangan**

Ménko *n* Co-ordinating Minister; ~ *Kesra (Menteri Koordinasi Kesejahteraan Rakyat)* Co-ordinating Minister for Public Welfare → **Menteri Koordinasi**

Ménlu *n* Foreign Minister ← **Menteri Luar Negeri**

menobatkan *vt* to install, crown ← **nobat**

menodai *vt* to stain; to defile, rape, deflower (a girl) ← **noda**

menodong *vt* to threaten or hold up at knifepoint ← **todong**

menolak *vt* to refuse, reject ← **tolak**

menoléh *vi* to look in a different direction, turn your head ← **toléh**

menolong *vt* to help or assist ← **tolong**

menomorsatukan *vt* to put first, give priority ← **nomor satu**

menonaktifkan *vt* to release from active service, non-activate ← **nonaktif**

menonjok *vt* to punch, hit ← **tonjok**

menonjol *vi* to stick out, protrude; *adj* prominent; **menonjolkan** *vt* to show; to make something stick out ← **tonjol**

menonton *vi* to go to the cinema; *vt* to watch, look on; ~ *konser* to go to a concert ← **tonton**

menopang *vt* to prop up, support ← **topang**

ménor *adj* gaudy, garish, trashy, tacky (of dress)

menoréh *vt* to scratch, etch ← **toréh**

menormalkan *vt* to normalize, return to normal ← **normal**

menorpédo *vt* to torpedo ← **torpédo**

Ménpora *n* Minister of Youth and Sports ← **Menteri Pemuda dan Olahraga**

Ménristék *n* Minister of Research and Technology ← **Menteri Risét dan Téknologi**

méns *coll* period; *lagi* ~ have your period; *sakit* ~ menstrual pain ← **ménstruasi**

mensablon *vt* **menyablon** *coll* to screen-print ← **sablon**

mensabotase *vt* to sabotage ← **sabotase**

mensangsikan *vt* **menyangsikan** *coll* to doubt ← **sangsi**

mensejahterakan → **menyejahterakan**

mensénsor *vt* to censor, cut out ← **sénsor**

Ménsésnég, Ménséknég *n* Secretary of State ← **Menteri Sékretaris Negara**

mensiasati → **menyiasati**

mensinyalir *vt* to signal, make a sign, point out ← **sinyalir**

mensortir *vt* to sort, organize ← **sortir**

Ménsos *n* Minister of Social Affairs ← **Menteri Sosial**

mensosialisasikan *vt* to introduce to the public, disseminate ← **sosialisasi**

mensponsori *vt* to sponsor ← **sponsor**

menstérilkan *vt* to sterilize; to neuter or spay (an animal) ← **stéril**

ménstruasi *n* **méns** *coll* menstruation

mensubsidi *vt* to subsidize ← **subsidi**

mensukséskan *vt* to make something succeed ← **suksés**

menswastakan *vt* to privatize ← **swasta**

mensyukuri *vt* to be thankful for or appreciate ← **syukur**

mentabulasi *vt* to tabulate, put into a table format ← **tabulasi**

mentah *adj* raw, uncooked, not ripe; ~*nya coll* cash; *bahan* ~ raw material

mental *vi* to bounce off, deflect

méntal, méntalitas *n* way of thinking, mentality

Méntan *n* Minister of Agriculture → **Menteri Pertanian**

mentang: mentang-mentang just because

mentari *n* sun

ménté → **médé**

mentéga *n* butter

mentéréng *adj* dressed up, fancy

menteri *n* minister; bishop (in chess); ~ *Keuangan (Menkeu)* Minister of Finance, *UK* Chancellor of the Exchequer; ~ *Penerangan* Minister for Information; ~ *Perhubungan* Minister for Defense; ~ *Sosial (Mensos)* Minister of Social Affairs; *Perdana* ~ Prime Minister; ~ *Dalam Negeri (Mendagri)* Minister of Home Affairs; ~ *Luar Negeri (Menlu)* Foreign Minister; ~ *Sekretaris Negara (Mensesneg)* Secretary of State; ~ *Kehakiman dan Hak Azasi Manusia (Menkeh HAM)* Minister of Justice and Human Rights; **kementerian** *n* ministry, department, office

mentimun, timun *n* cucumber

mentolérir *vt* to tolerate ← **tolérir**

mentraktir *vt* to invite out, shout, treat, pay for another ← **traktir**

mentransfer *vt* to transfer or send (money) ← **transfer**

ménu *n* menu

menuang, menuangkan *vt* to pour something ← **tuang**

menuding *vt* to accuse, point the finger ← **tuding**

menuduh *vt* to accuse ← **tuduh**

menugasi *vt* to assign someone; **menugaskan** *vt* to give a task ← **tugas**

menuju *vt* to approach, go towards ← **tuju**

menukar *vt* to change; **menukarkan** *vt* to change something ← **tukar**

menukas *vi* to counter, retort ← **tukas**

menukik *vi* to dive, freefall ← **tukik**

menular *vi* to infect; *adj* contagious, infectious; *penyakit* ~ contagious or infectious disease ← **tular**

menulis *vt* to write ← **tulis**

menumbangkan *vt* to fall, cause something or someone to fall ← **tumbang**

menumbuhkan *vt* to nurture, cultivate ← **tumbuh**

menumbuk *vt* to pound (rice), crush, grind ← **tumbuk**

menumpahkan *vt* to spill something; ~ *darah* to shed blood ← **tumpah**

menumpang *vi* **numpang** *coll* to make use of someone else's facilities; to get a lift or ride ← **tumpang**

menumpuk *vi* to pile up ← **tumpuk**

menunaikan *vt* to pay cash; to fulfill; ~ *ibadah puasa* to perform the Ramadan fast ← **tunai**

menunda *vt* to delay, put off, postpone; **menundakan** *vt* to delay or postpone something ← **tunda**

menunduk *vi* to bow your head; **menundukkan** *vt* to bow or lower something; to defeat ← **tunduk**

menung: termenung *adj* lost in thought

menunggak *vi* to owe money ← **tunggak**

menunggang *vt* to ride; ~ *kuda* to ride a horse ← **tunggang**

menungging *adv* tail up, with bottom sticking out ← **tungging**

menunggu *v* to wait for something; **menunggu-nunggu** *vt* to wait a long time for; **menunggui** *vt* to wait for someone ← **tunggu**

menunjuk *vt* to indicate, point out, refer to; **menunjukkan** *vt* to show, point out; ~ *jalan* to give directions ← **tunjuk**

menuntaskan *vt* to finish off, be done with, do thoroughly ← **tuntas**

menuntun *vt* to guide, prop up ← **tuntun**

menuntut *vt* to claim or demand ← **tuntut**

menurap *vt* to coat, line, seal, plaster; to dam ← **turap**

menurun *vi* to fall, drop, decline; **menurunkan** *vt* to lower or reduce ← **turun**

menurut *conj* according to; ~ *pendapat saya* in my opinion; **menuruti** *vt* to follow, obey ← **turut**

menusuk *vt* to stab, prick, pierce ← **tusuk**

menutup *vt* to close or shut; **menutupi** *vt* to cover (up) ← **tutup**

menuturkan *vt* to tell ← **tutur**

Ménwa student regiment ← **Résimén Mahasiswa**

menyabet *vt* to snatch or grab; to whip ← **sabet**

menyabit *vt* to cut with a sickle ← **sabit**

menyablon → **mensablon**

menyabuni *vt* to soap or lather ← **sabun**

menyadap *vt* to tap (rubber, telephones) ← **sadap**

menyadari *vt* to realize, be aware of; *dia tidak ~ bahayanya* he did not realize the danger; **menyadarkan** *vt* to make someone realize, raise someone's awareness; *guru berusaha ~ murid akan pentingnya belajar* teachers try to make students aware of the importance of studying ← **sadar**

menyadur *vt* to gild; to rewrite, adapt ← **sadur**

menyahut *vt* to answer, reply, respond ← **sahut**

menyaingi *vt* to compete with ← **saing**

menyajikan *vt* to serve, present, offer ← **saji**

menyakiti *vt* to hurt, treat badly; **menyakitkan** *adj* painful ← **sakit**

menyaksikan *vt* to witness ← **saksi**

menyala *vi* to burn, blaze; **menyalakan** *vt* to light, set fire to; *~ lilin* to light a candle ← **nyala**

menyalahi *vt* to blame someone; **menyalahkan** *vt* to blame ← **salah**

menyalami *vt* to greet ← **salam**

menyalib *vt* to crucify ← **salib**

menyalin *vt* to copy ← **salin**

menyalip *vt* overtake, slip past ← **salip**

menyalurkan *vt* to channel ← **salur**

menyamai *vt* to resemble, be like; to equal; **menyamakan** *vt* to equate, consider the same ← **sama**

menyamar *vi* to be in disguise; **menyamarkan** *vt* ~ *diri* to disguise yourself ← **samar**

menyamaratakan *vt* to treat equally ← **sama rata**

menyambar *vt* to pounce on, strike; *disambar petir* to be struck by lightning ← **sambar**

menyambung *vi* to join, continue; **menyambungkan** *vt* to connect to (something else) ← **sambung**

menyambut *vt* to welcome or receive ← **sambut**

menyampaikan *vt* to deliver, hand over, pass on ← **sampai**

menyamper *vt, sl* to greet, acknowledge, say hello ← **samper**

menyampingi *vt* to escort, accompany, flank ← **samping**

menyamun *vt* to rob, plunder ← **samun**

menyandang *vt* to bear or have; *Mario sudah ~ gelar sarjana kedokteran* Mario already has a medical degree ← **sandang**

menyandar *vi* to lean; **menyandarkan** *vt* to tilt back ← **sandar**

menyandera *vt* to take hostage ← **sandera**

menyangga *vt* to hold up, support ← **sangga**

menyanggah *vt* to object to, oppose, protest ← **sanggah**

menyanggupi *vt* to be capable of, prepared to; to promise ← **sanggup**

menyangka *vt* to suspect, suppose, presume; *tidak ~* never thought ← **sangka**

menyangkal *vt* to deny ← **sangkal**

menyangkut *vt* to involve, concern; *coll* to get caught, snagged; *conj* about

menyangrai *vt, Sund* to fry without oil ← **sangrai**

menyangsikan ← **mensangsikan**

menyanjung *vt* to flatter ← **sanjung**

menyantét *vt* to cast spells on someone ← **santét**

menyanyi *v* to sing; **menyanyikan** *vt* to sing something ← **nyanyi**

menyapa *vt* to greet ← **sapa**

menyapih *vt* to wean ← **sapih**

menyapu *vt* to sweep or wipe; *~ bersih* to clean thoroughly; to wipe out, annihilate; *tim Indonesia ~ bersih lawannya dalam Piala Thomas* the Indonesian team wiped out its opponents in the Thomas Cup ← **sapu**

menyaput *vt* to cover, veil, shroud ← **saput**

menyarankan *vt* to suggest ← **saran**

menyarap *v* to eat breakfast ← **sarap**

menyaring *vt* to filter (through), screen, select ← **saring**

menyasak *vt* ~ *rambut* to tease hair into a stiff position ← **sasak**

menyasar *vi* to lose your way, get lost ← **sasar**

menyatakan *vt* to declare, state, certify ← **nyata**

menyatroni *vt* to break into (with intent to rob) ← **satron**

menyatu *vi* to become one; **menyatukan** *vt* to unite various things ← **satu**

menyayangi *vt* to love; **menyayangkan** *vt* to regret ← **sayang**

menyayat *vt* to slice or cut off ← **sayat**

menyebabkan *vt* to cause ← **sebab**

menyebalkan *adj* annoying, tiresome ← **sebal**

menyebar *vi* to spread; **menyebarkan** *vt* to spread something ← **sebar**

menyebarluaskan *vt* to disseminate, spread something ← **sebar luas**

menyeberang *vt* to cross; **menyeberangi** *vt* to cross something ← **seberang**

menyebut *vt* to mention, name, say; **menyebut-nyebut** *vt* to frequently mention ← **sebut**

menyedekahkan *vt* to donate something to the poor → **sedekah**

menyederhanakan *vt* to simplify ← **sederhana**

menyediakan *vt* to prepare, get ready ← **sedia**

menyedihkan *adj* depressing, sad ← **sedih**

menyedot *vt* to suck (up) ← **sedot**

menyeduh *vt* to add hot water (when making a drink) ← **seduh**

menyegani *vt* to respect ← **segan**

menyegarkan *adj* refreshing ← **segar**

menyégel *vt* to seal (off), close up (a building) ← **ségel**

menyéhatkan *adj* healthy, with curing powers ← **séhat**

menyejahterakan *vt* to make prosperous, enrich ← **sejahtera**

menyejukkan *adj* cooling, refreshing ← **sejuk**

menyéka *vt* to wipe or rub off ← **séka**

menyekap *vt* to lock up, detain ← **sekap**

menyekat *vt* to partition, block off ← **sekat**

menyekolahkan *vt* to send to school ← **sekolah**

menyela *vt* to interrupt ← **sela**

menyelam *vi* to dive; *sambil ~ minum air* to kill two birds with one stone; **menyelami** *vt* to dive into; to study in depth ← **selam**

menyelamatkan *vt* to save, rescue ← **selamat**

menyelangi *vt* to interrupt ← **selang**

menyelenggarakan *vt* to run, hold, organize ← **selenggara**

menyelesaikan *vt* to finish, end, settle; *~ masalah* to overcome a problem ← **selesai**

menyeletuk *vi* to interrupt, call out, say suddenly ← **celetuk**

menyeléwéng *vi* to deviate; to have an affair ← **seléwéng**

menyelidiki *vt* to investigate ← **selidik**

menyelimuti *vt* to (cover with a) blanket ← **selimut**

menyelinap *vi* to sneak, move quietly ← **selinap**

menyelingi *vt* to go between, intervene ← **seling**

menyelip *vt* to slip; **menyelipkan** *vt* to slip an object (into something) ← **selip**

menyelonong *vi* to appear suddenly, turn up (often by accident) ← **selonong**

menyelubungi *vt* to veil or cover ← **selubung**

menyelundup *vi* to sneak in illegally, infiltrate; **menyelundupkan** *vt* to smuggle (in) ← **selundup**

menyeluruh *vi* to spread, cover completely; *adj* comprehensive ← **seluruh**

menyelusup *vi* to penetrate, infiltrate ← **susup**

menyelusur *vi* to slide; **menyelusuri** *vt* to follow something, go along ← **selusur**

menyemai, menyemaikan *vt* to grow seedlings, propagate ← **semai**

menyemangati *vt* to enthuse, inspire, give spirit to ← **semangat**

menyemarakkan *vt* to brighten ← **semarak**

menyematkan *vt* to pin, fasten with pins ← **semat**

menyembah *vt* to pay homage to, worship ← **sembah**

menyembelih *vt* to slaughter, butcher ← **sembelih**

menyembuhkan *vt* to cure, heal ← **sembuh**

menyembunyikan *vt* to hide or conceal something ← **sembunyi**

menyembur *vt* to spurt out; **menyemburkan** *vt* to spit or spray something out ← **sembur**

menyemir *vt* to polish; ~ *rambut* to touch up gray roots, dye to cover gray hairs ← **semir**

menyempatkan *vt* ~ *diri* to make time to ← **sempat**

menyempit *vi* to (become) narrow ← **sempit**

menyemprit *vt* to blow a whistle ← **semprit**

menyemprot *vt* to spray; **menyemprotkan** *vt* to spray with something ← **semprot**

menyempurnakan *vt* to perfect, complete; *Ejaan Yang Disempurnakan (EYD)* standardized spelling reform of 1972 ← **sempurna**

menyenangi *vt* to like, enjoy; **menyenangkan** *adj* pleasing, agreeable ← **senang**

menyendiri *vi* to go off by yourself ← **sendiri, diri**

menyengat *vt* to sting ← **sengat**

menyénggol *vt* to bump, brush, tweak ← **sénggol**

menyengir *vi* to smile nervously, grimace ← **sengir**

menyengsarakan *vt* to torture, cause suffering ← **sengsara**

menyentak *vt* to pull, jerk ← **sentak**

menyentil *vt* to flick with your finger (often to rebuke a child) ← **sentil**

menyentuh *vt* to touch ← **sentuh**

menyépak *vt* to kick (out) ← **sépak**

menyepakati *vt* to agree to ← **sepakat, pakat**

menyepélékan *vt* to make light of, treat lightly ← **sepélé**

menyepi *vi* to go away by yourself ← **sepi**

menyepuh *vt* to plate or gild ← **sepuh**

menyerah *vi* to surrender, give in, give up; **menyerahkan** *vt* to hand over ← **serah**

menyeramkan *adj* creepy, frightening ← **seram**

menyerang *vt* to attack ← **serang**

menyerap *vt* to absorb, soak up ← **serap**

menyerbu *vt* to attack (as a group), charge on, invade ← **serbu**

menyerémpét *vt* to scrape, scratch against ← **serémpét**

menyérét *vt* to drag ← **sérét**

menyergap *vt* to apprehend, ambush, catch ← **sergap**

menyeringai *vi* to grimace ← **seringai**

menyerobot *vi* to push in front ← **serobot**

menyertai *vt* to accompany; **menyertakan** *vt* to enclose, send with; enter ← **serta**

menyeru *vi* to call out; **menyerukan** *vt* to call out something ← **seru**

menyeruduk *vt* to butt, headbutt ← **seruduk**

menyerupai *vt* to resemble, be similar to, look like ← **rupa**

menyesal *vi* to regret; **menyesalkan** *vt* to feel bad about, regret (another's action) ← **sesal**

menyesatkan *adj* misleading, confusing ← **sesat**

menyesuaikan *vt* to adapt, bring into line; ~ *diri* to adapt ← **sesuai**

menyeték *vt* to make a graft or cutting; to grow from a cutting ← **seték**

menyetél *vt* to tune, set, adjust; ~ *mesin mobil* to tune an engine ← **setél**

menyetém *vt* to tune (a piano) ← **setém**

menyetir *vt* to drive ← **setir**

menyetop *vt* to stop (a vehicle) ← **setop**

menyetor *vt* to pay in, deposit ← **setor**

menyetrika *v* to iron ← **setrika**

menyetubuhi *vt* to have sex with ← **tubuh, setubuh**

menyetujui *vt* to agree to, approve, ratify ← **tuju: tujuan**

menyéwa *vt* to rent, hire; **menyéwakan** *vt* to let (a house), hire out, lease ← **séwa**

menyia-nyiakan *vt* to waste ← **sia-sia**

menyiapkan *vt* to prepare something, get something ready ← **siap**

menyiarkan *vt* to telecast, broadcast, disseminate ← **siar**

menyiasati *vt* to delve or pry into something, as a tactic ← **siasat**

menyibak *vt* to part; to reveal ← **sibak**

menyibukkan *vt* ~ *diri* to keep yourself busy, spend your time ← **sibuk**

menyidangkan *vt* to hold a session, convene; to put on trial ← **sidang**

menyidik *vt* to investigate ← **sidik, selidik**

menyihir *vt* to perform magic ← **sihir**

menyikat *vt* to brush ← **sikat**

menyiksa *vt* to torture ← **siksa**

menyilang *silang-~ vi* to cross (over, of two lines), criss-cross ← **silang**

menyilét *vt* to cut with a knife, slit ← **silét**

menyimak *vt* to hear, monitor; *latihan* ~ listening practice ← **simak**

menyimpan *vt* to keep, save up, store ← **simpan**

menyimpang *vi* to deviate ← **simpang**

menyimpulkan *vt* to conclude or summarize ← **simpul**

menyindir *vt* to insinuate, allude ← **sindir**

menyinggahi *vt* to stop over in ← **singgah**

menyinggung *vt* to touch on; ~ *perasaan* to offend someone, hurt someone's feelings ← **singgung**

menyingkap *vt* to open slightly, reveal; ~ *rahasia* to reveal a secret; **menyingkapkan** *vt* to open something slightly ← **singkap**

menyingkatkan *vt* to abbreviate, shorten ← **singkat**

menyingkir *vi* to step or move aside; **menyingkirkan** *vt* to remove, brush aside ← **singkir**

menyingsing *vt* to lift, rise; ~ *lengan baju* to roll up your shirt sleeves, get to work; *fajar* ~ daybreak ← **singsing**

menyiram *vt* to pour, water (plants); **menyirami** *vt* to pour onto; **menyiramkan** *vt* to pour something ← **siram**

menyisakan *vt* to leave behind ← **sisa**

menyisihkan *vt* to set aside ← **sisih**

menyisipkan *vt* to insert ← **sisip**

menyisir *vt* to comb, check thoroughly ← **sisir**

menyita *vt* to confiscate ← **sita**

menyobék *vt* to tear off; **menyobék-nyobék** *vt* to rip up ← **sobék**

menyodét *vt* to make an incision, cut a connecting channel ← **sodét**

menyodok *vt* to poke ← **sodok**

menyodomi *vt* to sodomize ← **sodomi**

menyodori *vt* to hand to, offer; **menyodorkan** *vt* to offer up, put forward ← **sodor**

menyogok *vt* to bribe ← **sogok**

menyokong *vt* to support, bolster ← **sokong**

menyoldér *vt* to solder ← **soldér**

menyolok *adj* glaring, standing out; *vi* to glare, stand out ← **colok**

menyombongkan *vt* ~ *diri* to show off, blow your own trumpet ← **sombong**

menyongsong *vt* to welcome, greet ← **songsong**

menyonték *v* to copy, cheat ← **conték, sonték**

menyorong *vt* to push, propose ← **sorong**

menyoroti *vt* to light up, illuminate, focus on ← **sorot**

menyoto *vt* to make into clear soup ← **soto**

menyuap *vt* to feed by hand; to bribe; **menyuapi** *vt* to feed someone by hand; **menyuapkan** *vt* to feed something by hand, to someone ← **suap**

menyuarakan *vt* to voice ← **suara**

menyuburkan *vt* to fertilize ← **subur**

menyucikan *vt* to purify, cleanse ← **suci**

menyudahi *vt* to end ← **sudah**

menyudutkan *vt* to push into a corner, deflect ← **sudut**

menyuguhi *vt* to offer (food), present (a performance) ← **suguh**

menyukai *vt* to like ← **suka**

menyulam *v* to embroider ← **sulam**

menyulap *vt* to conjure up; to make something vanish or change ← **sulap**

menyulih-suarakan *vt* to dub ← **sulih**

menyuling *vt* to distill ← **suling**

menyulitkan *vt* to make difficult, complicate, cause problems ← **sulit**

menyuluh *vt* to illuminate; to inform ← **suluh**

menyumbang *vi* to contribute, make a donation; **menyumbangkan** *vt* to contribute or donate something ← **sumbang**

menyumbat *vt* to plug, stop ← **sumbat**

menyumpahi *vt* to swear at or curse someone ← **sumpah**

menyumpit *vt* to shoot at with a blowpipe ← **sumpit**

menyunatkan *vt* to have someone circumcised ← **sunat**

menyundul *vt* ~ *bola* to head the ball (in soccer) ← **sundul**

menyungkem *vt* to request an elder's blessing by kneeling down and placing one's forehead on an elder's lap ← **sungkem**

menyuntik *vt* to inject or vaccinate; **menyuntikkan** *vt* to inject something ← **suntik**

menyunting *vt* to edit ← **sunting**

menyupir *vi* to drive ← **supir**

menyurat *surat-~ vi* to correspond with someone; **menyurati** *vt* to write a letter to ← **surat**

menyuruh *vt* to command, order ← **suruh**

menyurut *vi* to fall, subside ← **surut**

menyusahkan *vt* to bother, make difficult ← **susah**

menyusu *vi* to feed, suckle; **menyusui** *vt* to feed; *binatang* ~ mammal ← **susu**

menyusul *vi* to follow, go after ← **susul**

menyusun *vt* to heap or pile; to arrange, organize, compile; ~ *kalimat* to make a sentence ← **susun**

menyusup *vi* to penetrate, infiltrate; **menyusupkan** *vt* to slip something in, infiltrate ← **susup**

menyusur *vt* to skirt; **menyusuri** *vt* to skirt or move along, follow ← **susur**

menyusut *vi* to shrink, become smaller; **menyusutkan** *vt* to reduce ← **susut**

menyutradarai *vt* to direct ← **sutradara**

menzalimi *vt* to oppress, be cruel to ← **zalim**

méong meow; *coll* puss, cat

mépét *adj* tight, squeezed

meraba *vt* to feel or grope something; **meraba-raba** *vi* to feel around or grope (in the dark) ← **raba**

meracik *vt* to create a mix of; ~ *obat* to mix up medicine ← **racik**

meracuni *vt* to poison ← **racun**

meradang *vi* to become inflamed; to become angry ← **radang**

meragukan *vt* to doubt something ← **ragu**

mérah *adj* red; ~ *jambu* pink; ~ *putih* red and white; *Sang* ~ *Putih* the Red and White (Indonesian flag); ~ *tua* dark red, maroon; *lampu* ~ traffic light, red light; *Palang* ~ Red Cross; **kemérah-mérah** *adj* reddish; **memérah** *vi* to blush; **pemérah** ~ *pipi* rouge

merahasiakan *vt* to keep secret ← **rahasia**

meraih *vt* to reach for; to achieve ← **raih**

merajah *vt* to tattoo ← **rajah**

merajaléla *vi* to be out of control, act violently ← **rajaléla**

merajam *vt* to stone to death ← **rajam**

merajut *vt* to knit; to crochet ← **rajut**

merak *n* peacock

merakit *vt* to assemble ← **rakit**

merakyat *vi* to become popular ← **rakyat**

meralat *vt* to correct a mistake ← **ralat**

meramaikan *vt* to liven up, enliven ← **ramai**

meramal *vt* to tell fortunes; **meramalkan** *vt* to predict, foretell ← **ramal**

merambah *vt* ~ *hutan* to clear away the forest, clear the land ← **rambah**

merambat *vi* to spread; *tanaman* ~ vine, climbing plant ← **rambat**

merampas *vt* to take by force, rob, plunder ← **rampas**

merampingkan *vt* to make slender or slim; *Diah cepat ~ badan setelah melahirkan* Diah slimmed down quickly after giving birth ← **ramping**

merampok *vt* to rob, hold up; ~ *bank* to rob or hold up a bank ← **rampok**

meramu *vt* to gather, collect ← **ramu**

merana *vi* to suffer, waste away; to live miserably, in poverty

merancang *vt* to plan, design ← **rancang**

merancap *vi* to masturbate ← **rancap**

merang *n* rice-straw

merangkai *vt* to bind together, combine ← **rangkai**

merangkak *vi* to crawl; *pada umur 8 bulan, Lastri sudah bisa* ~ Lastri could crawl at 8 months ← **rangkak**

merangkap *vt* to hold another position (temporarily) ← **rangkap**

merangkul *vt* to hug, embrace; to get someone involved ← **rangkul**

merangkum *vt* to carry in your arms ← **rangkum**

merangkup *vi* to cup hands together; *vt* to cover, embrace ← **rangkup**

merangsang *vt* to stimulate, excite ← **rangsang**

merantai *vt* to chain up ← **rantai**

merantau *vi* to sail away, seek your fortune, settle overseas ← **rantau**

meranti *kayu* ~ kind of reddish wood, morantee

merapat *vi* to move closer; *perahu mulai* ~ *pada jeti* the boat began to approach the jetty; **merapatkan** *vt* to bring close to ← **rapat**

merapikan *vt* to clean or tidy up, neaten; ~ *kamar* vt to clean up a room ← **rapi**

merasa *vt* to think, feel; ~ *iba* to feel sorry for; **merasakan** *vt* to feel something ← **rasa**

merasuk *vt* to enter into, possess ← **rasuk**

merata *vi* to level out, become evenly distributed; **meratakan** *vt* to level, flatten ← **rata**

meratap *vi* to lament, wail ← **ratap**

meraun-raun *vi, coll* to go out, around ← **raun**

meraung *vi* to roar ← **raung**

meraup *vt* to scoop up in your hands ← **raup**

meraut *vt* to shape; to sharpen; ~ *pensil* to sharpen a pencil ← **raut**

merawat *vt* to nurse, care for; to maintain, look after ← **rawat**

merayakan *vt* to celebrate ← **raya**

merayap *vi* to crawl, creep ← **rayap**

merayu *vt* to tempt, flatter, seduce ← **rayu**

mercon *n* fireworks

mercu *n* top, summit; ~ *suar* lighthouse

Mércy *n, coll* Merc, Mercedes-Benz car ← **Mercédes-Benz**

merdéka *adj* free, independent; **kemerdékaan** *n* freedom, independence, liberty

merdu *adj* sweet, melodious, honeyed

merebah *vi* to fall down, collapse ← **rebah**

meréboisasi *vt* to reforest, replant trees ← **réboisasi**

merebus *vt* to boil (in) water ← **rebus**

merebut *vt* to snatch, capture; ~ *kembali* to recapture; **merebutkan** *vt* to snatch something ← **rebut**

mereda *vi* to subside, abate; **meredakan** *vt* to soothe; to calm something down ← **reda**

meredamkan *vt* to muffle or stifle ← **redam**

meregang *vi* to become tight or taut; **meregangkan** *vt* to tighten, make taut ← **regang**

mereguk *vt* to gulp down, take a shot ← **reguk**

mérek, mérk *n* brand, make (vehicle), label (clothes); **bermérek** *vi* to have a label; *adj* branded

meréka *pron, pl* they, them, their; ~ *punya* theirs

merekam *vt* to record ← **rekam**

merékayasa *vt* to engineer ← **rékayasa**

merékoméndasikan *vt* to recommend ← **rékoméndasi**

merékonstruksi *vt* to reconstruct ← **rékonstruksi**

merékrut *vt* to recruit ← **rékrut**

merélakan *vt* to approve, agree to ← **réla**

merem be asleep, eyes shut

meremajakan *vt* to revitalize, refurbish, update ← **remaja**

meremas *vt* to press, squeeze, knead ← **remas**

merembes *vi* to seep in, leak, ooze ← **rembes**

meréméhkan *vt* to belittle, treat as unimportant ← **réméh**

meremukkan *vt* to crush, smash into pieces ← remuk

merencanakan *vt* to plan ← rencana

merénda *vi* to crochet ← rénda

merendah *vi* to be humble; *sikap ~* humility; merendahkan *vt* to lower; to humiliate ← rendah

merendam *vt* to soak something ← rendam

meréngék *vi* to whimper, whine ← réngék

merenggangkan *vt* to keep or pull apart, split ← renggang

merenggut *vt* to snatch, tug; *~ nyawa* to take a life, kill ← renggut

merengut *vi* to grumble ← rengut

merénovasi *vt* to renovate ← rénovasi

merentang *vt* to span, stretch over; merentangkan *vt* to extend, stretch out ← rentang

merenung *vi* to daydream; merenungi, merenungkan *vt* to think about, reflect on, muse ← renung

meréparasi *vt* to repair ← réparasi

merépotkan *vt* to make someone busy or go to some trouble ← répot

meresahkan *adj* disturbing, worrying ← resah

meresap *vi* to be absorbed, penetrate, seep into ← resap

merésépkan *vt* to write a prescription for a drug ← resép

meresmikan *vt* to formalize, make official ← resmi

meréstorasi *vt* to restore ← réstorasi

merestui *vt* to agree to, give your blessing to ← restu

meretak *vi* to crack ← retak

meretas *vi* to break or split open (of stitches) ← retas

merévisi *vt* to revise, rewrite ← révisi

meriah *adj* merry, lively; memeriahkan *vt* to liven up, enliven

meriak *vi* to ripple ← riak

meriam *n* cannon

meriang feel unwell, sick ← riang

merias *vt* to make up ← rias

meributkan *vt* to make a fuss about ← ribut

merica *n* pepper

merilis *vt* to release, put out ← rilis

merinci *vt* to specify, detail ← rinci

merinding *vi* to have goose-bumps or an eerie feeling, be spooked ← rinding

merindu *vi* to feel longing; merindukan *vt* to miss, long for ← rindu

meringankan *vt* to ease, relieve, make easier ← ringan

meringis *vi* to grimace ← ringis

meringkaskan *vt* to summarize ← ringkas

meringkik *vi* to whinny (of horses) ← ringkik

meringkus *vt* to catch (esp by the arm or leg), take into custody ← ringkus

merintih *vi* to moan or groan ← rintih

merintis *vt* to trace; to pioneer ← rintis

merisaukan *vt* to worry about ← risau

merisihkan *vt* to disturb, make you feel uncomfortable ← risih

mérk ← mérek

Mérkurius *n* (the planet) Mercury

merobék *vt* to tear up, shred ← robék

merobohkan *vt* to knock down, demolish ← roboh

merogoh *vt* to grope around in, search for inside ← rogoh

merokét *vi* to soar to prominence; *namanya ~ sejak dia pindah dari Surabaya* she became very famous after she left Surabaya ← rokét

merokok *v* to smoke; *dilarang ~* no smoking ← rokok

merombak *vt* to pull down, demolish; to reorganize ← rombak

merompak *vt* to commit piracy ← rompak

meronda *vi* to do the rounds, keep guard ← ronda

merongrong *vt* to gnaw at, undermine ← rongrong

meronta, meronta-ronta *vi* to struggle, squirm to get loose ← ronta

merosot *vi* fall down, descend, plummet; *celananya ~* his pants fell down; kemerosotan *n* descent, deterioration ← rosot

merpati *n* pigeon, dove

merta *serta-~* automatically, immediately

mertua *n* parents-in-law; *ibu ~* mother-in-law

merubah → **mengubah**

merugi *vi* to make a loss, lose out; **merugikan** *vt* to hurt, harm, injure ← **rugi**

merujuk *vi* to refer, use as a source ← **rujuk**

merumahkan *vt* to be laid off (from work) ← **rumah**

merumitkan *vt* to complicate or make difficult ← **rumit**

merumuskan *vt* to formulate ← **rumus**

meruncing *vi* to become critical or sharp ← **runcing**

merundingkan *vt* to discuss something, deliberate over ← **runding**

merungut *vi* to grumble, complain ← **rungut**

meruntai *vi* to hang loosely ← **untai**

meruntuhkan *vt* to overthrow, destroy ← **runtuh**

merupakan *vt* to be, form, constitute ← **rupa**

merupiahkan *vt* to convert into rupiah; *kalau dirupiahkan, kira-kira satu milyar* if you convert it to rupiah, it's about one billion ← **rupiah**

merusak *vt* to spoil, damage; **merusakkan** *vt* to destroy, break ← **rusak**

meruwat *vt* to purify or cleanse someone (through a special ritual) ← **ruwat**

més *n* company accommodation or housing, boarding house; *~ perwira* housing for highly-ranked military officers

mésem smile

méses *n* chocolate sprinkles

mesin *n* machine, engine; *~ faks* fax machine; *~ jahit* sewing machine; *~ ketik* typewriter; *teknik ~* mechanical engineering; *~ penyedot debu* vacuum cleaner

Mesir *n* Egypt; *~ kuno* ancient Egypt; *orang ~* Egyptian

mesjid, masjid *n* mosque; *~ agung*, *~ raya* great mosque

meski, meskipun *conj* although, even though

mesra *adj* intimate, close; **kemesraan** *n* intimacy

mesti, musti *v, aux* should; *~nya* should; **semestinya** should have (been)

mesum *adj* dirty, immoral, sleazy; *tempat ~* seedy place, red-light district

méter *n* meter; metre; **méteran** *n* tape measure

meterai, méterai *n* seal; *~ tempel* adhesive seal

méteran *n* tape measure ← **méter**

métode *n* method

Métromini *n* medium-sized orange and blue bus in Jakarta

métropolitan *adj* metropolitan; *kota ~* metropolitan city, metropolis

mewabah *vi* to spread (uncontrollably) ← **wabah**

méwah *adj* luxurious; **keméwahan** *n* luxury

mewahyukan *vt* to reveal something (in a vision) ← **wahyu**

mewajibkan *vt* to enforce or make obligatory ← **wajib**

mewakafkan *vt* to donate or bequeath land or other items to the local Muslim community ← **wakaf**

mewakili *vt* to represent; **mewakilkan** *vt* to delegate, send a proxy; *Bapak ~ deputinya untuk menghadiri rapat di Surabaya* the boss sent his representative to attend the meeting in Surabaya ← **wakil**

mewanti-wanti *vi* to warn ← **wanti**

mewarisi *vt* to inherit; **mewariskan** *vt* to bequeath or leave something ← **waris**

mewarnai *vt* to color (in) ← **warna**

mewaspadai *vt* to watch out for, guard against ← **waspada**

mewawancarai *vt* to interview ← **wawancara**

méwék *vi* to start crying

mewujudkan *vt* to make something real, realize something ← **wujud**

meyakini *vt* to believe (in), be convinced; **meyakinkan** *adj* convincing, believable; *vt* to convince someone ← **yakin**

Mi, Mami *pron, coll* Mum, Mummy (in Westernized circles)

mi, mie *n* noodles; *~ ayam* chicken noodles; *~ bakso* noodles with meatballs; *~ goreng* fried noodles; *~ instan* instant noodles, packet noodles; *~ kocok* kind of noodles; *~ pangsit* noodles with dumplings; ~ *rebus* boiled noodles (in soup); ~ *tek-tek* wandering noodle sellers who tap on their carts; noodles bought from such vendors

miang *n* fine plant hairs

midi *rok* ~ medium-length skirt or dress

midodaréni *n, Jav (malam)* ~ ceremony for the bride-to-be the night before her wedding

migas *n* oil and natural gas ← **minyak dan gas bumi**

migrasi *n* migration; **bermigrasi** *vi* to migrate; **migran** *n* migrant

migrén *n* migraine; *sakit kepala* ~ migraine

mik, mikrofon *n* microphone, mike

mikrolét *n* small minibus converted for transport in Jakarta → **mikro oplét**

Mikronésia *n* Micronesia; *orang* ~ Micronesian

mikroskop *n* microscope

mil *n* mile; ~ *laut* nautical mile

milénium *n* millenium

mili, milimétér *n* millimeter, millimetre

miliar, milyar *n* billion → **milyar**

milik *n* property, possession; ~ *negara* state-owned; *hak* ~ proprietary rights, ownership; **memiliki** *vt* to own, possess; **pemilik** *n* owner; ~ *lama* previous owner; **kepemilikan** *n* ownership

milis *n* mail list

milisi *n* militia

militan *adj* militant; **militér** *n* military; *wajib* ~ *(wamil)* military service

milyar, miliar *n* billion; **milyarder** *n* billionaire

mimbar *n* pulpit, platform, forum

mimi, mimik *v, coll, child* to eat

mimisan nose bleed, blood nose

mimpi dream; ~ *buruk* nightmare, bad dream; ~ *indah* sweet dreams; **bermimpi** *vi* to dream; **memimpikan** *vt* to dream of → **impi**

min → **minus**

minal aidin (wal faidzin) greeting at Idul Fitri

Minang, Minangkabau ethnic group of West Sumatra; *bahasa* ~, *orang* ~ Minang, Minangkabau; *ranah Minang* the Minangkabau lands

minat *n* interest, attention; **berminat** *vi* to have an interest, be interested; **peminat** *n* interested party

minder *coll* to lack confidence, low self-esteem; to feel inferior

minggir *vi, coll* move to one side, pull over (on the road) ← **pinggir**

minggu *n* week; Sunday; ~ *depan* next week; ~ *ini* this week; ~ *yang lalu*, ~ *kemarin* last week; *hari* ~ Sunday; *malam* ~ Saturday night; **berminggu-minggu** *adv* for weeks; **mingguan** *n* weekly (publication); **seminggu** *adj* a week; *tiga kali* ~ three times a week

miniatur *adj* miniature

minim, minimal, minimum minimum, minimal(ly)

minoritas *n* minority

minta *v* to ask, beg, request; to apply for; ~ *ampun* to beg for mercy; ~ *bon* to ask for the bill; ~ *diri* to beg leave, excuse yourself; ~ *doa restu* to ask for prayers and blessings; ~ *izin* to ask permission; ~ *maaf* to apologize, say you're sorry; ~ *tolong* to ask for help; please help me; ~ *uang* to ask or beg for money; **minta-minta** *vi* to beg (alms); **meminta** *vt* to ask for, request; **memintakan** *vt* to ask for something for someone else; **permintaan** *n* request; *atas* ~ on request

minum drink; ~ *obat* to take (liquid) medicine; *air* ~ drinking water; *sambil menyelam* ~ *air* to kill two birds with one stone (*lit.* to drink while diving); **minum-minum** *vi* to go out drinking, drink (alcohol); **minuman** *n* drink; ~ *bersoda* carbonated drink; ~ *hangat* hot drink, beverage; ~ *keras*, ~ *beralkohol* alcoholic drink, liquor; ~ *penyegar* tonic, energy drink; ~ *ringan* soft drink; **peminum** *n* drinker

minus, min *adj* minus; *berkacamata* ~ to be short-sighted

minyak *n* oil; ~ *bumi* petroleum, crude oil; ~ *goreng* cooking oil; ~ *ikan* cod-liver oil; ~ *jarak* castor oil; ~ *kayu putih* a kind of eucalyptus oil; ~ *kelapa* coconut palm oil; ~ *mentah* crude oil; ~ *rambut* hair tonic or oil; ~ *solar* diesel fuel; ~ *tanah* kerosene; ~ *tawon* oil used for insect bites; ~ *telon* oil used for babies and sprains; ~ *wangi* perfume; ~ *zaitun* olive oil; *ladang* ~ oil field; *raja* ~ oil baron, sheik; ~ *dan gas (migas)* oil and natural gas; *Perusahaan Pertambangan ~ dan Gas Bumi Negara (Pertamina)* Pertamina, the state-owned oil company; **berminyak** *adj* oily, greasy; **perminyakan** *n* oil and gas

miring *adj* sloping, slanting; not straight; *berita* ~ negative story; *tulisan* ~ italics; **kemiringan** *n* slope; **memiringkan** *vt* to slant, tilt

mis. *abbrev* **misalnya** eg., e.g. (for example)

misa *n, Cath* mass; ~ *agung* high mass

misai *n* mustache

misal *n* example; **misalnya, misalkan** for example, for instance

Mises *pron, coll, f* term of address for Western woman

misi *n* mission; *visi dan* ~ mission statement; **misionaris** *n* missionary

miskin *adj* poor, lacking in; *orang* ~ pauper; *pl* the poor; ~ *sumber daya alam* lacking natural resources; **kemiskinan** *n* poverty

mistar *n* crossbar of goal; ruler

Mister *pron, coll* term of address for Westerner (esp male)

mistéri *n* mystery; **mistérius** *adj* mysterious

mistik, mistis *adj* mystical

mitoni *n, Jav, Sund* ceremony held for a woman who is 7 months' pregnant

mitos *n* myth

mitra *n* partner, friend; ~ *usaha* business partner; **kemitraan** *n* partnership

mitraliur, mitralyur *n* machine-gun

mobil *n* car; ~ *baja* armored car, tank; ~ *bekas* second-hand car, used car; ~ *boks* (closed) truck; ~ *butut* old car, bomb; ~ *derek* tow truck; ~ *dinas,* ~ *kantor* office car, work car; ~ *jenazah* hearse; ~ *jip* jeep; ~ *kodok* Volkswagen, (VW) Beetle; ~ *kuno* classic or vintage car; ~ *mewah* luxury car; ~ *pengantin* bridal car; ~ *sedan* sedan, saloon

modal *n* capital, fund; *menanam* ~ to

invest (capital); **bermodal** *vi* to have or use capital; ~ *dengkul* hard work; **bermodalkan** *vi* to use as capital or will

mode *n* fashion, trend; **modiste** *n* dressmaker

modél *n* model; *foto~* model → **raga**

modérn *adj* modern; **memodérnkan** *vt* to modernize

modifikasi *n* modification; **memodifikasi** *vt* to modify

modis *adj* fashionable; **modiste** *n* dressmaker

moga: moga-moga, semoga may, hopefully; ~ *sukses* good luck, every success

mogok strike; break down; ~ *kerja* strike; ~ *makan* hunger strike; *mobil* ~ broken-down car; **pemogok** *n* striker; **pemogokan** *n* strike, act of going on strike

mohon *vt* to request, ask, beg; please; ~ *diri* to take leave; ~ *perhatian* attention please; ~ *maaf lahir batin* to ask forgiveness for all sins (at Idul Fitri); **pemohon** *n* applicant; **permohonan** *n* request, application → **pohon**

mol → **mal**

molék *adj* pretty, charming; *kecil* ~ delicate; **kemolékan** *n* beauty

molor *vi* stretch, become longer

momok *n* ghost, phantom

momong *vt* take care of a baby; **momongan** *n* baby, child

Monako *n* Monaco; *orang* ~ Monegasque

Monas *n* National Monument in Central Jakarta ← **Monumén Nasional**

moncong *n* muzzle, nose; ~ *putih* the white nose (symbol of PDIP)

mondar-mandir *vi* to go back and forth, to and fro

mondok *vi, coll* to board, stay; *uang* ~ board ← **pondok**

monetér *adj* monetary; *krisis* ~ *(krismon)* financial crisis of 1997–98

Mongolia *n* Mongolia; *bahasa* ~ Mongolian; *orang* ~ Mongol, Mongolian

monitor *n* (computer) monitor, screen; **memonitor** *vt* to monitor

monoksida *n* monoxide; *karbon ~* carbon monoxide (CO)

monolog *n* monologue

monopoli *n* monopoly; **memonopoli** *vt* to monopolize

monorél *n* monorail

monoton *adj* monotonous

Montenégro *n* Montenegro; *bahasa ~, orang ~* Montenegrin

montir *n* mechanic

montok *adj* plump, rounded, well filled-out; **kemontokan** *n* plumpness

monumén *n* monument; *~ Nasional (Monas)* National Monument

monyét *n* monkey; *derog* term of abuse; *baju ~* baby's suit; *rumah ~* sentry-box

monyong *adj* sticking out, protruding (of teeth), like a dog's muzzle

moral, moril moral; *dukungan ~* moral support

moréng *coreng-~* streaked, smeared all over

morfin *n* morphine

mori *kain ~* white cloth for batik-making

mortir *n* mortar, shell

mosaik, mozaik *n* mosaic

mosi *n* motion; *~ tidak percaya* vote of no confidence

Moskwa *n* Moscow; *orang ~* Muscovite

moster *n* mustard

motif *n* design, pattern, motif; **bermotif** *vi* to have a design

motif *n* motive; **motivasi** *n* motivation; **bermotivasikan** *vi* to be motivated by; **memotivasi** *vt* to motivate

moto *n* MSG, monosodium glutamate ← **Ajinomoto**; motto, chant, slogan

motor *n* motorcycle, (motor)bike; *sepeda ~* motorbike; **memotori** *vt* to be the driving force behind, to power

moyang *nenek ~* ancestors

Mozambik *n* Mozambique; *orang ~* Mozambican

mpok *pron, f, Jak* term of address for slightly older female, big sister

MPP *abbrev Masa Persiapan Pensiun* retirement preparation period

MPR *abbrev Majelis Permusyarawatan Rakyat* People's Consultative Council

mr *abbrev, arch* title for a law graduate ← **meester in de rechten**

MTQ *abbrev Musabaqah Tilawatil Qu'ran* Koranic recitation competition

MU *abbrev Majelis Ulama* Council of Islamic Scholars

MU *abbrev Muktamar Umum* General Congress

-mu *pron, poss, s* your; *buku~* your book → **kamu**

mua *n* eel

muai: memuai *vi* to expand, swell; **pemuaian** *n* expansion

muak loathe; disgusted, fed up; **memuakkan** *adj* revolting, disgusting

mual *adj* nauseous, queasy, sick

mualaf *n, Isl* recent convert

Muang Thai *n, arch* Thailand

muara *n* mouth (of a river); **bermuara** *vi* to have a mouth, empty into

muasal *asal ~* root, origin ← **asal**

muat contain; *tidak ~* it won't fit; **muatan** *n* load, cargo; **bermuatan** *vi* to be laden with; **memuat** *vt* to contain

mubazir *adj* wasted, not used

mucikari, muncikari *n* pimp, procurer; *f* madam

muda *adj* young; *~ belia* very young; **muda-mudi** *n, pl* young people; *hijau ~* light green; *isteri ~* new (younger) wife; *merah ~* pink; *Laksamana ~* Vice-Admiral; *tulang ~* cartilage; **pemuda** *n* youth; young man; **pemudi** *n* young woman

mudah *adj* easy; *~ marah* easily angry, quick-tempered; *~ tersinggung* touchy, over-sensitive; **kemudahan** *n* ease, facility; **mempermudah** *vt* to make easier

mudah: mudah-mudahan *adv* hopefully, maybe

mudi *juru ~* helmsman

mudik *vi* to go upstream, back to the village; *~ Lebaran* to return to your hometown at Idul Fitri; *arus ~* flow of people going back to the village (usu at Idul Fitri); *hilir ~* to go up and down the river, back and forth ← **udik**

mufakat *n* agreement, consensus; **permufakatan** *n* discussion, deliberation

Muhammadiyah *n* Islamic community association founded by KH Achmad Dahlan, strong in Central Java

Muharam, Muharram *n* Islamic New Year; first month of the Islamic calendar

MUI *abbrev Majelis Ulama Indonesia* Indonesian Council of Islamic Scholars

mujair *n* a kind of freshwater fish

mujarab *adj* effective (esp of medicine)

mujur straight on; lucky

muka *n* face, front, surface; ~ *asam* sour look; ~ *badak*, ~ *tebal* shameless, thick-skinned; ~ *bumi* the Earth's surface; *air* ~, *raut* ~ look, expression; *di* ~ in front of; ahead, in advance; *ke* ~ to the front, forward; *kulit* ~ front cover (of a magazine); *membuang* ~ to look away (from someone); **mengemukakan** *vt* to put forward, advance, nominate; **terkemuka** *adj* prominent; **bermuka** *vi* to have a face; ~ *dua* two-faced; **permukaan** *n* surface; ~ *air* water level; *di atas* ~ *laut* above sea level

mukenah *Isl* white prayer shawls

mukim: bermukim *vi* to reside, stay; **permukiman** *n* housing, residential area

mukjizat *n* miracle

muktamar *Isl* congress, conference

mula beginning, start; **mula-mula** *adv* in the beginning, at first; **bermula** *vi* to start, begin; **memulai** *vt* to start or begin something; **memulakan** *vt* to start something; to cause; **pemula** *n* beginner; **permulaan** *n* beginning; **semula** *adj* original; *adv* originally

mulai *vi* to begin, start; ~ *tanggal 23 Desember* from December 23; **memulai** *vt* to start or begin something ← **mula**

mula-mula *adv* in the beginning, at first ← **mula**

mulas, mules *n* (abdominal) cramp

mulia *adj* honorable, noble; *batu* ~ precious stone, gem; *logam* ~ precious metal; *Paduka Yang* ~ His/Her/Your Excellency; **kemuliaan** *n* honor, glory; ~ *Tuhan* the glory of God; **memuliakan** *vt* to honor, glorify

Mulo *n* secondary school in Dutch times ← **Meer Uitgebreid Lager Onderwijs**

Mulud → **Maulid, Maulud**

muluk *adj* lofty, pompous, high-sounding; *janji* ~ an ambitious promise

mulus *adj* smooth, flawless; **memuluskan** *vt* to ease the way, help

mulut *n* mouth; ~ *kotor* filthy mouth; ~ *manis* sweet talk; *tutup* ~ to hold your tongue, keep silent

mumi *n* mummy

mumpung *vi* to make the most of, capitalize on

munafik *adj* hypocrite; **kemunafikan** *n* hypocrisy

munas *n* national convention ← **musyawarah nasional**

muncikari → **mucikari**

muncrat *vi* to spurt, spray

muncul *vi* to appear, turn up; **bermunculan** *vi* to show up (in large numbers); **memunculkan** *vt* to bring forward

mundur *vi* to go backwards, reverse, retreat; to resign; *gigi* ~ reverse gear; **kemunduran** *n* deterioration, decline, setback; **memundurkan** *vt* to retract, bring back → **undur**

mungil *adj* small, tiny, delicate; *rumah* ~ small house

mungkar: memungkari *vt* to deny; to betray

mungkin *conj* maybe, possibly; *tidak* ~ impossible; **kemungkinan** *n* possibility; ~ *tipis* slim chance; **memungkinkan** *adj* conducive; *vt* to enable, make possible

mungkir, memungkiri *vt* to deny

munisi → **amunisi**

munsyi *n* language teacher, linguist

muntabér *n* diarrhea and vomiting ← **muntah bérak**

muntah *v* to vomit, throw up; **memuntahkan** *vt* to vomit or bring up

mur *n* nut; *baut dan* ~ nut and bolt

murah *adj* cheap; ~ *hati* generous; ~ *senyum* always smiling; **murahan** *adj* cheap, inexpensive; **kemurahan** *n* cheapness; **termurah** *adj* the cheapest

murai *burung* ~ magpie

muram *adj* gloomy, somber, mournful; **kemuraman** *n* gloom

murba *adj* common, lowly, ordinary, plain, proletarian

murbai, murbéi *n* mulberry

murid *n* pupil, student

murka *adj* furious, wrathful; **kemurkaan** *n* anger, fury

murni *adj* pure; only; **kemurnian** *n* purity

murtad convert from Islam, apostate

murung *adj* gloomy, despondent

Musa *Nabi* ~ Moses

musafir *n, Isl* traveler

musang *n* civet cat

muséum → **musium**

mushola, musholla, mushala, mushal-la, musola, musala *n, Isl* small prayer-house

musibah *n* disaster, calamity; *kena* ~ suffer a misfortune, disaster

musik *n* music; **pemusik, musikus, musisi** *n* musician

musim *n* season; ~ *bunga*, ~ *semi* spring; ~ *dingin* winter; ~ *gugur*, ~ *rontok* autumn, fall; ~ *hujan*, ~ *penghujan* rainy season, monsoon; ~ *kawin* in heat; ~ *kemarau* dry season; ~ *panas* summer; ~ *pancaroba* transition between seasons; ~ *salju* snow season; *sedang* ~ in fashion; **musiman** *adj* seasonal

musium, muséum *n* museum; ~ *Bahari* Maritime Museum; ~ *Gajah* National Museum

muslihat *n* trick; *tipu* ~ (dirty) trick, deceit

Muslim *adj, Isl* Muslim; *baju* ~ Islamic dress; *orang* ~ Muslim; **Muslimah** *adj, Isl, f* Muslim (woman) → **Islam**

musnah *adj* destroyed; **memusnahkan** *vt* to destroy; **pemusnahan** *n* act of destruction

mustahil *adj* impossible

musti → **mesti**

musuh *n* enemy; ~ *bebuyutan* archenemy; ~ *dalam selimut* a wolf in sheep's clothing (*lit.* an enemy in the blanket); **bermusuhan** *vi* to be enemies; **memusuhi** *vt* to fight against, antagonize, make an enemy of; **permusuhan** *n* enmity, animosity, hostility

musyawarah *n* meeting, discussion (to reach an agreement); ~ *nasional (munas)* national convention; **bermusyawarah** *vi* to reach an agreement

mutakhir *adj* modern, latest

mutasi *n* change (in status), mutation; **dimutasi** *v* to have your status changed

mutiara *n* pearl; *ibu* ~ mother-of-pearl

mutih *vi, coll* to only eat white rice, as a form of fasting ← **putih**

mutlak *adj* absolute, unconditional

mutu *n* quality; **bermutu** *adj* quality; ~ *rendah* low quality

Myanmar *n* Myanmar, Burma; *bahasa* ~, *orang* ~ Burmese

N

n [én] n, 14th letter of the alphabet

naas, nahas *adj* unfortunate, unlucky

nabati *adj* vegetable, plant; *lemak* ~ vegetable fat

nabi *n, Isl, Chr* prophet; ~ *Isa Isl* Jesus; ~ *Nuh* Noah; ~ *Yunus* Jonas

nada *n* note, tone, sound; ~*sela* call waiting; ~ *dering* ringtone; *tangga* ~ scale; **bernada** *vi* to have a tone or edge; ~ *sibuk* busy tone; ~ *sinis* mockingly, sarcastically

nadi *n* pulse; *denyut* ~ pulse, heartbeat; *pembuluh* ~ artery

nafas, napas breath, breathe; *menarik* ~ to take a breath; *sesak* ~ hard to breathe, asthmatic; **bernafas** *vi* to breathe; **bernafaskan** *vi* with a breath of; **pernafasan** *n* breathing, respiration; ~ *buatan* artificial respiration; *sistem* ~ respiratory system

nafi: menafikan *vt* to deny

nafkah *n* means of livelihood; **menafkahi** *vt* to pay for someone's daily needs

nafsu *n* desire; ~ *makan* appetite; *hawa* ~ passion, lust; **bernafsu** *adj* passionate, lusty

naga *n* dragon; *Tahun* ~ Year of the Dragon

nagasari *kue* ~ small coconut cake wrapped in a banana leaf

nah, na well, well then; look! ~ *lu* well then, how about that?

nahas → **naas**

Nahdlatul Ulama (NU) *n* Islamic social organization; **nahdlatin** *n, pl* members of NU

naif *adj* **naif** → **lugu**

naik go up, climb, rise, ascend; go by; ~ *banding* appeal against a court decision; ~ *darah* get angry; ~ *daun* become popular or famous; ~ *gunung* climb a mountain; ~ *haji* go on the pilgrimage to Mecca; ~ *mobil* go by car; ~ *pangkat* be promoted; ~ *pesawat* board, boarding; fly; ~ *pitam* get angry; ~ *sepeda* ride a bicycle; go by bicycle; ~ *takhta* ascend to the throne; **kenaikan** *n* rise, raise; promotion; ~ *gaji* pay rise; ~ *kelas* promotion to the next grade (at school); end of academic year; ~ *Isa Almasih* Assumption; **menaik** *vi* to be on the increase; **menaiki** *vt* to ride, mount, get on; **menaikkan** *vt* to raise, hoist

najis *n* dirt, filth; excrement

nak *pron* child, son, lass ← **anak**

nakal *adj* naughty; **kenakalan** *n* naughtiness

naker *n, abbrev* manpower, workforce ← **tenaga kerja**

nakhoda *n* captain (of a ship)

naksir *vt, coll* to like, find someone or something attractive ← **taksir**

nalar *n* reason, common sense

naluri *n* instinct; **naluriah** *adj* instinctive

nama *n* name; ~ *dagang* trade name; ~ *depan* first name; ~ *jelas* printed name (as opposed to signature); ~ *kecil*, ~ *panggilan* everyday name, nickname; ~ *keluarga* family name, surname; ~ *pena* assumed name of an author, nom-de-plume; ~ *samaran* pseudonym, alias; *atas* ~ for; **namanya** *n* the name, it's called; ~ *Yusuf* his name is Yusuf; *apa* ~ whatsitsname, what's it called; ~ *juga copet* that's pickpockets for you!; **bernama** *adj* named; *vi* to

have a name; **kenamaan, ternama** *adj* famous, well-known; **menamakan** *vt* to call, name

Namibia *n* Namibia; *orang* ~ Namibian

nampak → **tampak**

nampan *n* tray

namun *conj* however, yet

nan *conj, lit* who, which

nanah *n* pus; **bernanah** *vi* to fester

nanar *adj* confused, dazed

nanas, nenas *n* pineapple

nangka *n* jackfruit

nangkring *vi, coll* to sit somewhere high up, perch → **tangkring**

nanti *adv* later; ~ *malam* tonight; ~ *sore* this afternoon

nanti *vi* to wait; ~ *dulu* not now, later on; **menanti** *vt* to wait; **menanti-nanti** *vt* to wait for a long time; **menantikan** *vt* to wait for; **penantian** *n* wait, process of waiting

napas, nafas breath, breathe; *menarik* ~ take a breath, inhale; *sesak* ~ hard to breathe, asthmatic; **bernapas** *vi* to breathe; **bernapaskan** *vi* with a breath of; **pernapasan** *n* breathing, respiration; ~ *buatan* artificial respiration; *sistem* ~ respiratory system

napi *n* prisoner, inmate, criminal → **narapidana**

napsu → **nafsu**

Napza *abbrev narkotika, alkohol, psikotropika dan zat adiktif lainnya* narcotics, alcohol and other addictive drugs

nara: narapidana *n* prisoner, inmate, criminal; **narasumber** *n* source (person)

narasi *n* narration

narik *vt, coll* to work as a driver of public transport; *Asep masih* ~ *angkot* Asep is still driving a minibus (for a living) ← **tarik**

narkoba *n* (illegal) drugs, narcotics and other banned substances ← **narkotika, psikotropika dan obat terlarang**

narkotika *n* narcotics; ~ , *alkohol, psikotropika dan zat adiktif lainnya (Napza)* narcotics, alcohol and other addictive drugs

nasabah *n* (bank) customer

Nasakom *n* nationalism, religion and communism, policy under Sukarno around 1959-65 ← **nasionalisme, agama, komunisme**

naséhat → **nasihat**

nasi *n* (cooked) rice; ~ *biryani* a Middle Eastern-style dish with goat or lamb; ~ *bungkus* a takeaway rice meal; ~ *goreng* fried rice; ~ *jamblang* rice dish, specialty of the Cirebon area; ~ *kapau* Minangkabau rice dish; ~ *kebuli* lamb and rice dish of Middle Eastern origin; ~ *komplit* rice with various side-dishes; ~ *kotak* box meal of rice and side-dishes; ~ *kucing* small portions of rice; ~ *kuning* yellow rice cooked for a special occasion; ~ *lemak* a Malay rice specialty; ~ *lengko* rice with vegetables, a specialty of the north coast of Central Java; ~ *liwet* rice cooked in coconut milk, a specialty of Solo; a rice dish from West Java; ~ *rames* rice with side-dishes; ~ *pecel* rice and salad with peanut sauce; ~ *pulen* delicious, well-cooked rice; ~ *tim* steamed rice; ~ *timbel* rice cooked and served in a rolled banana leaf; ~ *uduk* coconut rice with chicken, a specialty of Jakarta; ~ *telah menjadi bubur* it's too late now, no use crying over spilt milk (*lit.* the rice has become porridge)

nasib *n* fate, lot, destiny; **senasib** *adj* fellow sufferer

nasihat, naséhat *n* advice; **menasihati** *vt* to advise; **penasihat** *n* adviser

nasional *n* national; *Partai* ~ *Indonesia (PNI)* Indonesian National Party; **nasionalis** *n* nationalist; **nasionalisme** *n* nationalism

naskah *n* manuscript, original (text); *penulis* ~ script writer

Nasrani *adj* Christian

Natal *Hari* ~ Christmas Day; *Malam* ~ Christmas Eve; **natalan** *vi, coll* to celebrate Christmas

natrium *n* sodium (Na)

naung: naungan *n* shade, shelter; protection; *di bawah* ~ under the auspices of; **bernaung** *vi* to (take) shelter

Nauru *n* Nauru; *bahasa* ~, *orang* ~ Nauruan

navigator *n* navigator

nb *abbrev nota bene* note (well)

ndableg, ndablek *adj, coll, Jav* stubborn, unhearing; thick-skinned

ndak, nggak, enggak *coll* no, not ← **tidak**

ndoro *pron, m, Jav* master, respectful term of address; ~ *putri* mistress

nduk *pron, f, Jav* term used for a little girl ← **genduk**

nébéng *vi, sl* to sponge, get a lift, use something without paying ← **tébéng**

nécis *adj* well-dressed

negara *n* state, country; ~ *asal* country of origin; ~ *barat* Western country, the West; ~ *berkembang* developing nation; ~ *boneka* puppet state; ~ *kerajaan* monarchy; ~ *maju* developed nation; ~ *tetangga* neighbor; *antar* ~ international; *Ibu* ~ First Lady; *lambang* ~ national symbol; *milik* ~ state-owned; *warga*~ citizen; ~ *Kesatuan Republik Indonesia (NKRI)* the unitary state of the Republic of Indonesia; **kewarganegaraan** citizenship; **kenegaraan** *adj* state (affairs); **negarawan** *n* statesman

négatif *adj* negative

négro *n (orang)* ~ black person, African, Negro

negeri *adj* state, government; *n* country, land, state; ~ *berantah-antah* never-never land; ~ *jiran* neighbor, Malaysia; ~ *kangguru* Australia; ~ *Sakura* Japan; ~ *seberang* overseas, foreign country (usu neighboring); ~ *singa* Singapore; *ayam* ~ battery hen; *dalam* ~ national, domestic, internal; *luar* ~ overseas, abroad; *pegawai* ~ *(sipil, PNS)* civil servant, government employee; ~ *kincir angin* the Netherlands; ~ *tirai bambu* China

Nék *pron* term of address for a grandmother or elderly woman → **nénék**

nékad, nékat reckless; stubborn; *bondo* ~ *(bonek)* Surabaya soccer hooligans; **kenékatan** *n* determination, resolve, recklessness

Nékolim *arch* neo-colonialist; neo-colonialism, colonialism and imperialism, Sukarnoist slogan of the early 1960s ← **néokolonialisme, kolonialisme, impérialisme**

nelangsa *adj* miserable, wretched (due to sadness)

nelayan *n* fisherman

nenas → **nanas**

nénék *n, pron, f* grandmother; great-aunt; female relative of grandmother's generation; ~ *buyut* great-grandmother; ~ *moyang* ancestors → **Nék; nénénda** *pron, f* Grandmother (term of address in letters)

nénén *vi, coll* to nurse, breastfeed; *bayi itu masih* ~ the baby is still being breastfed

Néng *pron* term of address for girl or young woman in western Java

néng-nong sound of bell, railway crossing signal etc

néngok → **téngok**

néon *n* neon; *lampu* ~ neon light

Népal *n* Nepal; *bahasa* ~ Nepali; *orang* ~ Nepalese

népotisme *n* nepotism; *korupsi, kolusi,* ~ *(KKN)* corruption (collusion and nepotism)

Néptunus *n* (the planet) Neptune

neraca *n* scales, balance; ~ *dapur* kitchen scales

neraka *n* hell; *api* ~ flames of hell

nerocos, nyerocos *vi* to talk too much, blather, chatter or rattle on ← **cerocos**

nestapa *adj* miserable, sorrowful, grieving

nét *n* net (in sports)

néto *adj* nett

nétral *adj* neutral; **menétralkan** *vt* to neutralize

neurolog *n* neurologist → **dokter saraf**

ngabén Balinese funeral ceremony

ngabuburit *vi, sl* to fill in time waiting for the end of the fast at sunset

ngaco *vi, sl* to shoot off your mouth, talk without thinking; misbehave ← **aco**

ngadat *vi* to break down, *jam; laptopku selalu* ~ *kalau membuka gambar* my laptop always hangs when I open click onto a picture file

ngajar *v, sl* to teach; **ngajarin** *vt, sl* to teach someone ← **ajar, mengajar**

ngaji *vi, coll* to recite or read the Koran; *guru* ~ Arabic teacher ← **kaji**

ngambek *vi, coll* to get angry → **ambek**

ngamén *vi, coll* to sing in the street for money, busk; *tukang* ~ street singer, busker → **amén, mengamén**

nganga: menganga *vi* to gape, be open(-mouthed); **ternganga** *adj* gaping, flabbergasted, wide open

ngantor *vi, coll* to go to work ← **kantor**

ngantuk *adj, coll* sleepy ← **antuk**

ngarai *n, Sum* gorge, ravine, steep valley

ngarang *vi, coll* to make something up (off the top of your head) ← **karang**

ngawur *vi, coll* to do something without reason; to talk nonsense

ngebet *v* to want very much to, long for

ngebut *vi, coll* to speed ← **kebut**

ngecéng *vi* to show off; to hang out

ngeden *vi, coll* to push, strain (when giving birth or passing feces) ← **keden**

ngefans *vi, sl* to be a fan of; ~ *berat vi* to be a great fan of ← **fans**

ngémsi *vi, coll* to be or work as an MC ← **émsi**

ngengat *n* moth

ngeri *adj* terrified; **mengerikan** *adj* terrifying, horrifying

ngerumpi *vi, sl* to (get together for a) chat or gossip ← **rumpi**

ngetém *vi, coll* to wait for passengers (of public transport) ← **tém**

ngetop *vi, sl* to be on top ← **top**

ngetrén, ngetrénd *adj, coll* trendy, fashionable; *vi* to be trendy, fashionable ← **trénd**

nggak, enggak, ndak *coll* no, not → **tidak**

ngilu *adj* painful (of teeth), smarting; *rasa* ~ pain

ngobrol *v, coll* to chat ← **obrol**

ngocéh *vi, coll* to babble (of babies) ← **océh**

ngoko *n* lowest Javanese speech level, used with family and close acquaintances

ngomél *vi, coll* to complain, grumble, whinge, whine ← **omél**

ngomong *v, coll* to speak, talk; **ngomong-ngomong** *adv* by the way

ngompol *vi, coll* to wet your pants or the bed ← **ompol**

ngopi *vi, sl* to drink or have a coffee ← **kopi**

ngorok *vi, coll* to snore; to sleep

ngos: ngos-ngosan *vi* to puff, pant, gasp

ngotot *vi, coll* to be stubborn, refuse to back down → **otot**

ngoyo *vi, coll* to exert yourself, tire yourself out

nguping *vi, coll* to eavesdrop, listen in ← **kuping**

Ni *pron, f* term of address for Balinese woman

niaga *n* commerce; **perniagaan** *n* commerce, trade, business

nian *adv* very, greatly

niat *n* intention; **berniat** *vi* to intend

NICA *abbrev* Netherlands Indies Civil Administration

nifas *n* childbirth; *masa ~ Isl* 40-day confinement after childbirth

Nigéria *n* Nigeria; *orang ~* Nigerian

nih *pron, sl* this, these; here; *ini ~* this one → **ini**

nihil *adj* nothing, nil

nikah *pol* marry; *~ tamasya* to marry abroad (without a celebration); *akad ~ Isl* marriage contract; **menikah** *vi* to marry, get married; **menikahi** *vt* to marry someone; **menikahkan** *vt* to marry off (a child); **pernikahan** *n* wedding; *pesta ~* wedding reception

nikel *n* nickel

nikmat *adj* enjoyable, delicious; *~nya* how enjoyable! isn't it good?; **ke-nikmatan** *n* pleasure, enjoyment; **menikmati** *vt* to enjoy; **penikmat** *n* fan, connoisseur, someone who enjoys something

nikotin *n* nicotine

Nil *sungai ~* the (River) Nile

nil *kuda ~* hippo(potamus)

nila *n* indigo; *ikan ~* a kind of freshwater fish

nilai *n* value, worth; mark, grade (at school); *~ jual* selling price; *~ plus* added bonus; *~ seni* artistic value; *~ tambah* added value; **menilai** *vt* to evaluate, appraise; **penilaian** *n* evaluation; **ternilai** *tidak ~* priceless, invaluable

NIM *abbrev Nomor Induk Mahasiswa* (university) student number

nimbrung *vi, coll* to join in someone else's conversation, butt in

nina bobo, ninabobo, ninabobok lullaby; sing to sleep; **meninabobok-an** *vt* to sing to sleep

ningrat *adj* aristocratic

NIP *abbrev Nomor Induk Pegawai* civil servant number

nipah *pohon ~* kind of palm

nipis *jeruk ~* lemon, lime

nir- *pref* without; **nirlaba** *adj* non-profit, not for profit; **nirmala** *adj* clean, pure; **nirmana** *n* interior design; **Nirwana** *n* Nirvana

nira *n* sap or juice of the sugar palm

nisan *n* headstone, gravestone

niscaya *adv* surely, certainly, undoubtedly

NISP *Bank ~* Bank NISP ← **Nilai Inti Sari Penyimpan**; *arch* **Nederlandsch-Indische Spaar en Deposito Bank**

nista *n* insult, abuse; stigma

Niugini → **Nugini**

NKRI *abbrev Negara Kesatuan Republik Indonesia* the unitary state of the Republic of Indonesia

Nn. *abbrev Nona* Miss, title for unmarried woman, especially a non-Indonesian

nobat: menobatkan *vt* to install, crown

noda *n* stain; *~ bandel* hard-to-remove stain; **menodai** *vt* to stain; to defile, rape, deflower (a girl); *banyak gadis etnis Cina yang dinodai saat kerusuhan* many ethnic Chinese girls were raped during the riots

noktah *n* point, dot

nol *adj* zero, nil

nomad, nomaden *n* nomad, gypsy

nomina *n* noun → **kata benda**

nominasi *n* nomination; *masuk* ~ to be nominated → **calon**

nomor, nomer (nr) *n* number; event, match; issue; ~ *cantik* lucky mobile phone number; ~ *depan* next issue; ~ *ganjil* odd number; ~ *genap* even number; ~ *induk* serial number; ~ *Induk Mahasiswa (NIM)* student number; ~ *Induk Pegawai (NIP)* Civil Servant Number; ~ *penerbangan* flight number; ~ *polisi (nopol)* vehicle registration number; ~ *sandi* (secret) code; ~ *satu* number one, first; ~ *urut* queue number; ~ *wahid* number one, best; ~ *Pokok Wajib Pajak (NPWP)* tax file number; **menomorsatukan** *vt* to put first, give priority

nomplok *adj, coll* abundant, in large quantities; *rejeki* ~ windfall

non- *pref* not; non-; **nonaktif** *adj* not in active service; **menonaktifkan** *vt* to release from active service, non-activate; **nonblok** *adj* Third World, neither Western nor Communist; **nonformal** *adj* irregular, informal; **nonpri, nonpribumi** *adj* ethnic Chinese, non-indigenous

Nona *pron* **Non** *coll* (**Nn**) Miss, title for unmarried woman

nonaktif *adj* not in active service

nonblok *adj* Third World, neither Western nor Communist

Noné *Abang* ~ Mr and Miss Jakarta contest

nonformal *adj* irregular, informal

nongkrong → **tongkrong**

nongol *vi* to stick out

nonpri, nonpribumi *adj* ethnic Chinese, non-indigenous ← **pribumi**

nonton *vi, coll* to go to the cinema; *vt* to watch, look on; ~ *bola* to watch a football or soccer game ← **tonton**

Nopémber → **November**

nopol *n* vehicle registration number ← **nomor polisi**

norak *adj, coll* tasteless, vulgar, tacky

norit *n* diarrhea tablets, made from black carbon

norma *n* norm; ~ *sosial* social norms

normal *adj* normal; **menormalkan** *vt* to normalize, return to normal; **normalisasi** *n* normalization

Norwégia *n* Norway; *bahasa* ~, *orang* ~ Norwegian

nostalgia, nostalgi *n* nostalgia; **bernostalgia** *vi* to reminisce, be nostalgic

not *n* note (music); ~ *balok* (musical) note

nota *n* note, memo; bill, account

notaris *n* notary

notasi *n* notation

notés *n* notepad, jotter

notulen *n* minutes (of a meeting)

novél *n* novel

Novémber, Nopémber *bulan* ~ November

NPWP *abbrev Nomor Pokok Wajib Pajak* tax file number

nr *abbrev nomor* number

ntar, entar *sl* just a minute, wait; ~ *malam* tonight ← **sebentar**

NTB *abbrev Nusa Tenggara Barat* West Nusa Tenggara (the lesser Sunda islands)

NTT *abbrev Nusa Tenggara Timur* East Nusa Tenggara (the lesser Sunda islands)

NU *abbrev Nahdlatul Ulama* Islamic organization based in East Java

nuansa *n* touch, nuance; **bernuansa** *adj* with a touch of; *vi* to have a touch of

Nugini, Niugini *Papua* ~ Papua New Guinea (PNG)

Nuh *Nabi* ~ Noah

nujum *ahli* ~ astrologer

nuklir *adj* nuclear; *bom* ~ nuclear bomb; *limbah* ~ nuclear waste; *tenaga* ~ nuclear power; *pembangkit listrik tenaga* ~ *(PLTN)* nuclear power station

numpang → **menumpang**

nun *lit* yonder, far away

nungging *adv, coll* tail up, with bottom sticking out → **tungging**

nurani *adj* inner; *hati* ~ inner self, conscience

nuri *burung* ~ parrot

nus *ikan* ~ a kind of squid

nusa *n* island; ~ *Tenggara* the Lesser Sunda Islands; ~ *Tenggara Barat (NTB)* West Nusa Tenggara (the lesser Sunda

islands); ~ *Tenggara Timur (NTT)* East
Nusa Tenggara (the lesser Sunda
islands); ~ *dan bangsa* Indonesia and
its people; **Nusakambangan** *n* prison
island off the coast of Cilacap, Central
Java; **Nusantara** *n* Indonesia
nutrisi *n* nutrition
Nuzulul Quran *n* commemoration of
the first revelation of the Koran to the
Prophet Muhammad, on the 17th day
of Ramadan
NV *abbrev Naamloze Vennootschap* Pty
Ltd
Ny. *abbrev Nyonya* Madam, title for
married woman, especially a non-
Indonesian
-nya *suf, poss* added to words to indicate possession; the; *itu ibu~* that's her
mother; *saya mau beli baju, tapi toko~
sudah tutup* I want to buy a shirt, but
the shop's closed
nyahur *vi, sl* to eat before dawn during
fasting month ← **sahur**
nyai *pron* mistress (in colonial times)
nyala flame, blaze, burn; **bernyala,
menyala** *vi* to burn, blaze; **menyalakan** *vt* to light, set fire to; ~ *lilin* to
light a candle
nyalé annual fishing ceremony in
southern Lombok; sea-worm
nyali *n* guts, bravery; **bernyali** *adj*
brave; *vi* to have guts, courage
nyaman *adj* comfortable, pleasant;
kenyamanan *n* comfort
nyamuk *n* mosquito; *obat* ~ mosquito
repellent
nyana: menyana *vt* to think, conceive,
contemplate; *sungguh tidak dinyana*
completely unthought of
nyangkut *vt, coll* to get caught, snagged
← **sangkut**
nyantri, nyantrik *vi, coll* to be a religious
student or disciple
nyanyi *v* sing; **nyanyian** *n* song;
bernyanyi, menyanyi *vi* to sing;
menyanyikan *vt* to sing something;
penyanyi *n* singer, vocalist; ~ *latar*
backing vocalist
nyaring *adj* clear, loud, shrill
nyaris *adv, neg* nearly, almost

nyata *adj* clear, obvious, plain; **kenyataan** *n* fact; **menyatakan** *vt* to
declare, state, certify; **pernyataan** *n*
statement, declaration; **ternyata** *conj*
apparently, as it turned out
nyawa *n* soul, life; *tiga puluh* ~ thirty
lives; **bernyawa** *adj* alive; *vi* to live,
be alive; **senyawa** *n* (chemical)
compound
nyekar *vi, coll* to strew flower petals on
a grave; to visit a grave → **sekar**
nyeletuk *vi, sl* to interrupt, call out, say
suddenly ← **celetuk**
nyelonong *vi, coll* to appear suddenly,
turn up (often by accident) ← **selonong**
nyéntrik *adj, coll* eccentric, unusual
nyenyak *adj* sound asleep
Nyepi *n* Balinese Day of Seclusion
nyeri *n* pain; ~ *haid* menstrual pain or
cramp; ~ *otot* cramp
nyerocos *vi, coll* to talk too much,
blather, chatter or rattle on ← **cerocos**
nyiru *n* winnow
nyiur *n* coconut palm
nyokap *n, tsl* Mum, Ma
nyong *n, m, Amb* young man; *pron*
term of address for a young man
nyonték → **conték**
nyonya *pron, f* term of address for a
married woman, Madam; Mrs; ~
rumah the lady (mistress) of the
house; *untuk* ~ for Madam; ~ *Iskandar*
Mrs Iskandar
nyut throbbing pain

O

o o, 15th letter of the alphabet
o *excl* oh; ~ *ya* oh yes, by the way
oase, oasis n oasis
obah → **ubah**
obat *n* medicine, drug; chemical; ~
batuk cough medicine; ~ *bebas* over-
the-counter medicine; ~ *bius* anesthetic; ~ *cacing* worming tablet; ~ *generik*
generic drug; ~ *gosok* salve, lotion,
liniment; ~ *hirup* lozenge; ~ *kuat* aphrodisiac; ~ *kumur* mouthwash; ~

luar medicine for external use; ~ *maag*, ~ *mag* antacid; ~ *merah* mercurochrome; ~ *nyamuk* mosquito repellent; ~ *pel* floor disinfectant; ~ *penenang* tranquilizer, anti-depressant; ~ *psikotropika* drugs, medicine (esp when abused); ~ *tidur* sleeping tablet; *makan* ~ take a pill or capsule; *minum* ~ take liquid medicine; *narkotik, psikotropika dan* ~ *terlarang (narkoba)* (illegal) drugs; **berobat** *vi* to go to the doctor, seek medical advice; ~ *jalan* to be treated as an outpatient; **mengobati** *vt* to treat, cure; **pengobatan** *n* treatment; **terobati** *adj* soothed, comforted; treated, cured

obéng *n* screwdriver; ~ *kembang* Phillips-head screwdriver

obésitas *n* obesity

obituari *n* obituary

objék → **obyék**

objéktif → **obyéktif**

obligasi *n* bond

oblong *kaos* ~, *kaus* ~ T-shirt

obo *n* oboe

obor *n* torch

obrak-abrik → **ubrak-abrik**

obral *n* sale; **mengobral** *vt* to put on sale

obras *n* overlocking, machine hemming; **mengobras** *vt* to overlock

obrol: mengobrol *vi* **ngobrol** *coll* to chat; **obrolan** *n* chat

obsérvasi *n* observation; **mengobsérvasi** *vt* to observe, keep watch on

obsési *n* obsession; **berobsési** *vi* to have an obsession, be obsessed with; *Tony* ~ *merenovasi rumah* Tony is obsessed with renovating his house

obyék: ngobyék *vi, coll* to have a job on the side, moonlight

obyék *n* object; ~ *wisata* tourist destination, sight; **obyéktif** *adj* objective

océh: océhan *n* babble; **mengocéh** *vi* **ngocéh** *coll* babble, talk nonsense

OD *abbrev* overdose

ODHA *abbrev orang dengan HIV-AIDS* person infected with the HIV virus or AIDS

oditur *n* military prosecutor

odol *n, arch* toothpaste

odométer *n* odometer, instrument for calculating distance traveled (on a vehicle)

ogah *adj, sl* unwilling, reluctant; *Pak* ~ man who directs traffic for payment

oh → **o**

oi *excl* hey! oy! (to get attention)

ojék, ojég *n* motorcycle taxi; *pangkalan* ~ place where motorcycle taxis wait; *tukang* ~ motorcycle taxi driver; **mengojék** *vi* to take passengers around on your motorbike; **pengojék** *n* motorcycle taxi driver

oké *sl* okay, OK

oker *adj* ochre(-colored); *n* ochre

oknum *n, neg* individual (causing trouble in a group or company)

oksida *n* oxide; **oksidasi** *n* oxidation; **oksigén** *n* oxygen

oktaf *n* octave

oktagon → **segi delapan**

oktan *n* octane; ~ *tinggi* high-octane; **oktana** *n* (chemical group of) octanes

Oktober *bulan* ~ October

oktroi *n* patent

olah manner, process; ~ *nafas* breathing exercises; ~*raga* sport; **olahan** *adj* processed; **mengolah** *vt* to process, treat; **pengolahan** *n* processing; **seolah-olah** *adv, conj* as if

olahraga *n* sport; *gelanggang* ~ *(GOR)* stadium; *lapangan* ~ sports ground, athletic field; ~ *bela diri* self-defense; **berolahraga** *vi* to do or play sport; **olahragawan** *n, m* sportsman; **olahragawati** *n, f* sportswoman; **keolahragaan** *adj* sports, sporting (affairs)

oléh *conj* by, through; ~ *karena*, ~ *sebab* because of, due to; **memperoléh** *vt* to obtain, get; **pemeroléhan** *n* acquisition, process of acquiring; **peroléhan** *n* acquisition; ~ *suara* vote, (number of) votes

oléh-oléh *n* souvenir

oléng *adj* on a lean, leaning to one side; *gajah* ~ a batik design

olés: olésan *n* smear; **mengolés** *vt* to grease, spread, lubricate; **mengolési** *vt* to grease something; **mengoléskan** *vt* to smear with something

oli, olie *n* (engine) oil; *ganti* ~ drain sump oil

Olimpiade *n* the Olympics, the Olympic Games

olok: olok-olok tease, teasing; **memperolok** *vt* to tease, taunt

om *Hind* ~ *swasiastu* greetings, peace be upon you; ~ *santi santi* ~ words said to close a speech

Om, Oom *pron* Uncle; term of address to extended family, parents' friends, friends' parents etc

Oma *pron* Grandma

ombak *n* wave; **berombak** *adj* wavy; *rambut* ~ wavy hair

ombang-ambing: terombang-ambing *vi* to bob (up and down), float; to fluctuate

omél: mengomél *vi* to complain, grumble, whinge, whine ← **omél**

omnivora *n* omnivore

omong *vi* chat, talk, speak; ~ *Sunda* (speak) Sundanese; ~ *kosong* nonsense; **omongan** *n* chat; gossip; **ngomong** *vi, coll* to speak, talk; **ngomong-ngomong** *conj* by the way

ompol: mengompol *vi* to wet the bed, wet your pants

ompong *adj* toothless

ompréng: ompréngan *n* truck converted into a passenger vehicle, unofficial taxi

omzét, omsét *n* turnover

onak *n* thorn

onani *n* masturbation; *melakukan* ~ to masturbate; **beronani** *vi* to masturbate

onar *n* stir, commotion; *membuat* ~ to make a scene; **keonaran** *n* commotion, disturbance, sensation

oncom *n* fermented soybean cake, esp popular in West Java

ondé: ondé-ondé *n* small round cakes made of green peanuts, covered in sesame seeds

ondél: ondél-ondél *n* giant figures used in Betawi celebrations

onderdil *n* (automotive) spare part

onderok *n* petticoat, slip

ongkos *n* cost (for a service), expense, charge; ~ *hidup* cost of living, living expenses; ~ *pengiriman* cost of freight or postage; ~ *naik haji (ONH)* cost of the package covering the pilgrimage to Mecca

ONH *abbrev ongkos naik haji* cost of the package covering the major pilgrimage to Mecca; ~ *Plus* cost of a package covering the pilgrimage to Mecca plus extras

oniks *n* onyx

ons, on *n* ounce

onta → **unta**

ontél, onthél *n* crank(shaft); *sepeda* ~ old-fashioned bicycle

oom → **om**

Opa *pron* Grandpa

opak *n* crisp or chip made from rice or cassava

opal *n (batu)* ~ opal → **kalimaya**

opas *n* nightwatchman, attendant

openkap *n* convertible, open-hood vehicle

oper, mengoper *vt* to transfer, hand over; ~ *bola* to pass the ball; **mengoperkan** *vt* to pass (on)

opelét → **oplét**

opera *n* opera; ~ *sabun* soap opera

operasi *n* operation; ~ *khusus (opsus)* special military operation; **beroperasi** *vi* to operate, work, function; **mengoperasi** *vt* to operate on; *Tiwi dioperasi kemarin* Tiwi was operated on yesterday; **mengoperasikan** *vt* to operate something; *tukang yang* ~ *alat derek itu sedang dalam bahaya* the workman operating the crane is in danger

operator *n* operator; switchboard attendant

opini *n* opinion → **pendapat**

oplah *n* circulation; print run

oplét *n, arch* old-fashioned minibus used in the 1960s, similar to the *bemo*

oplos: oplosan *adj* adulterated, mixed; **mengoplos** *vt* to mix in another liquid illegally; **pengoplosan** *n* illegally adding another liquid

OPM *abbrev Organisasi Papua Merdeka* Free Papua Organisation, secessionist movement

opname go into hospital, hospitalization; **diopname** v to be admitted to hospital, be hospitalized; *kalau kena tifus, tidak selalu harus* ~ if you get typhoid, you don't always need to stay in hospital

opor ~ *ayam* chicken in coconut sauce, traditionally eaten at Idul Fitri

oposan n opponent; **oposisi** n opposition

opsét adj off-side

opsi n option (in a referendum)

opsir n, mil, coll officer

Opsus n special military operation ← **Operasi Khusus**

optik optician; optical

optimal adj optimal, best; **meng-optimalkan** vt to optimize, get the most out of; **seoptimal** ~ *mungkin* to the utmost, as well as possible

optimis adj optimistic; n optimist

opung tit, Bat, m Grandfather, title used for elderly Batak men

orak: orak-arik n scrambled egg with beans

oral adj oral; *(seks)* ~ oral sex

oralit n powder mixed with water for rehydration after diarrhea

orang adj someone else's; n person, human; counter for people; ~*nya* he/she, him/her, the person; that kind of person; ~ *Asia* Asian; ~ *asing* foreigner, stranger; ~ *asli* indigenous people;~ *awam* layman, public; ~ *banyak* public, people; ~ *Barat* Westerner; ~ *baru* newcomer; ~ *besar* person in power or authority, VIP; ~ *biasa* ordinary person; ~ *buangan* exile; ~ *bule* albino; *derog* white person, whitey, paleface; ~ *cacat* disabled or handicapped person; ~ *Cina*, ~ *Tionghoa* (ethnic) Chinese; ~ *dalam* insider; ~ *dewasa* adult, grown-up; ~ *Eropa* European; ~ *gila* tramp; mentally-ill person, lunatic; ~ *hilang* missing person; ~ *hitam* black person, Negro; ~ *hutan* forest dweller; orangutang; *Indo* person of mixed European and Indonesian descent; ~ *Indonesia* Indonesian; ~ *Irian arch* Irianese,

Papuan; ~ *Islam* Muslim; ~ *jahat* criminal; ~ *Kamboja* Cambodian; Khmer; ~ *kaya baru* new money, nouveau riche; ~ *kecil* the little people, the poor; ~ *kepercayaan* confidant; ~ *ketiga* third party (usu in love affair); third person; ~ *kulit putih* white person; ~ *Kristen*, ~ *Nasrani* Christian; ~ *lama* old-timer; ~ *laut* sea nomad, sea gypsy; ~ *luar* outsider, stranger; foreigner; ~ *mabuk* drunk, drunkard; ~ *Melayu* Malay; ~ *minta-minta* beggar; ~ *miskin* pauper; *pl* the poor; ~ *perahu* (Vietnamese) boat people, refugee; ~ *pintar* paranormal, soothsayer; ~ *ramai* the public; ~ *sebelah* neighbor; ~ *tua* parents; ~ *tua angkat* adoptive parents; ~ *tua asuh* foster parents; ~ *tua kandung* biological parents; ~ *tua tunggal* single parent, sole parent; ~ *utan* orangutang; ~ *Yahudi* Jewish (person); *kata* ~ people say; *kucing* ~ someone else's cat; ~ *dengan HIV-AIDS (ODHA)* person infected with the HIV virus or AIDS; *tiga* ~ *Surabaya* three Surabayans, three people from Surabaya; *Dani itu* ~ *rajin* Dani is a very industrious type; **orang-orangan** n doll, dummy; **perorangan** adj personal, individual; **seorang** a (person); counter for people; ~ *Arab* an Arab; ~ *diri* alone, single-handedly; **perseorangan** adj individual; **seseorang** n a certain person, somebody

orang conj, coll because; expression of surprise or defensiveness; ~ *saya baru pulang jam 12 malam* I only got home at midnight (so how would I know?)

orang-aring → **urang-aring**

oranye adj orange → **jingga**

orasi n oratory, speech; **orator** n orator, demagogue, public speaker; *Soekarno terkenal sebagai* ~ Sukarno was famous for his oratory skills

Orba n New Order, Suharto's rule ← **Orde Baru**

orbit n orbit; **mengorbitkan** vt to launch, put into orbit; *penyanyi itu semula diorbitkan suaminya* that singer's career was launched by her husband

orde *n* order; ~ *Baru (Orba)* New Order; ~ *Lama (Orla)* Old Order

ordo *n, Cath* order

org *abbrev orang* person

organ, orgel *n* organ

organ *n* organ, part of the body

organik *adj* organic; *makanan* ~ organic food

organisasi *n* organization; ~ *masyarakat (ormas)* social or people's organization; ~ *Pembebasan Palestina* Palestinian Liberation Front (PLO); *aktif dalam* ~ active in a movement or group; ~ *Siswa Intrasekolah (OSIS)* high school students' organization, Student Council

orgasme *n* orgasm

orgel → **organ**

oriéntal *adj* Oriental, Eastern; Chinese; *gadis berwajah* ~ a girl of Chinese appearance

oriéntasi *n* orientation; ~ *seksual* sexual orientation; ~ *studi dan pengenalan kampus (ospek)* O-week, (school) orientation; **beroriéntasikan** *vi* to be oriented towards; *dulu PKI semakin* ~ *RRC* at one stage, the PKI became increasingly oriented towards the PRC

orisinal, orisinil *adj* original → **asli**

orkés *n* orchestra; ~ *Melayu* Malay orchestra, traditional music group

Orla *n* Old Order, Sukarno's rule ← **Orde Lama**

ormas *n* social or people's organization ← **organisasi masyarakat**

orok *n* (newborn) baby

ortodoks *adj* orthodox; *gereja Kristen* ~ the Orthodox Church

ortu *n, sl* parents, oldies → **orang tua**

oséng: oséng-oséng *n* stir-fried vegetables

Osing → **Using**

OSIS *abbrev Organisasi Siswa Intrasekolah* high school students' organization, Student Council

ospék *n* O-week, (school) orientation ← **oriéntasi studi dan pengenalan kampus**

ostéoporosis *n* osteoporosis → **keropos tulang**

otak *n* brain; ~ *encer* sharp-witted, clever; ~ *udang derog* idiot; *gegar* ~ concussion; **berotak** *vi* to have a brain; ~ *tajam* to be sharp-witted

otak: otak-atik → **utak-atik**

otak: otak-otak *n* steamed fish cakes, baked in banana leaves

otda *n* regional autonomy ← **otonomi daérah**

otobiografi *n* autobiography

otodidak *n* a self-educated person; *secara* ~ self-educated

otomat *n* automated machine; automatic dialling

otomatis *adj* automatic; *secara* ~ automatically

otomotif *adj* automotive

otonomi *n* autonomy; ~ *daerah (otda)* regional autonomy

otopét *n* scooter

otopsi *n* autopsy; **diotopsi** *v* to have an autopsy performed

otorita *n* authority (esp in administrative sense); ~ *Batam* Batam Authority; **otoritas** *n* authority; ~ *Palestina* the Palestinian Authority

otoritér *adj* authoritarian

otot *n* muscle; *nyeri* ~ cramp; **berotot** *adj* muscular; *vi* to have muscles; **ngotot** *vi, coll* to be stubborn, refuse to back down

oval *adj* oval → **lonjong**

oven *n* oven, kiln; *cat* ~ vehicle paint applied through heat

overdosis, OD overdose

ovulasi *n* ovulation

oya, o ya oh yes, by the way

ozon *n* ozone; *lapisan* ~ the ozone layer

P

P. *abbrev Pulau* Island

P. *abbrev Pangeran* Prince; *P. Diponegoro* Prince Diponegoro

p [pé] p, sixteenth letter of the alphabet

P3, PPP *abbrev Partai Persatuan Pembangunan* United Development Party, a Muslim party

pabéan *n* customs (house) → **béa**

pabrik factory; ~ *garmen* garment factory; ~ *kertas* paper mill; **pabrikan** *n* manufacturer

pacar *n* boyfriend, girlfriend; **pacaran** *vi, coll* **berpacaran** *vi* to be going out, go out, date; **memacari** *vt* to date, go out with someone

pacar *n* henna, used to decorate the nails

pacé *n* kind of tree and its root, used as a spice → **mengkudu**

paceklik *n* famine, drought; *masa* ~ hard times before the harvest

pacu *n* spur; *alat* ~ *jantung* pacemaker; **pacuan** ~ *kuda* racecourse; **memacu** *vt* to spur on

pacul *n* hoe; **memacul** *vt* to hoe

pada *prep* in, at, on (expressing time); to; ~ *waktunya* in due time, at the right time; *tergantung* ~ depending on; ~ *hari itu* on that day

pada *coll, pl* pluralizing word; *sudah* ~ *pulang* everybody's going home

pada: memadai *adj* enough, sufficient; *vi* to be enough or sufficient

padahal *conj* whereas, however

padam put out, extinguish; **memadamkan** *vt* to put out, extinguish; **pemadam** *n* extinguisher; ~ *api* fire extinguisher; *pasukan* ~ *kebakaran* fire brigade

padan: padanan *n* synonym; comparison, something that matches or fits; **sepadan** *adj* in keeping or proportion with

padang *n* field, plain; ~ *golf* golf course; ~ *pasir* desert, sand dune

padat *adj* dense, full, crammed; **kepadatan** *n* density; ~ *penduduk* population density; **memadati** *vt* to fill (with), make full

padépokan *n* dormitory

paderi, padri *n, Cath* priest

padi *n* (unhusked) rice; *lumbung* ~ rice-producing area

padma *n* lotus

padri, paderi *n, Cath* priest

padu fused; *bersatu* ~ united; **paduan** *n* combination, fusion; ~ *suara* choir; **memadu** *vt* to unite, fuse; ~ *kasih* to (be in) love, have a relationship;

memadukan *vt* to combine, unite; **perpaduan** *n* blend, synthesis; **terpadu** *adj* integrated; **keterpaduan** *n* integration

paduka *pron* title for rulers; ~ *Yang Mulia* His Excellency

paés *n, Jav* make-up (esp bridal); **memaés** *vt* to make up (someone) in traditional style

pagar *n* fence; hedge; ~ *ayu* girl attendants at a wedding reception; ~ *bagus* boy attendants at a wedding reception; ~ *betis* (volunteer) guard; ~ *hidup* hedge; ~ *kawat berduri* barb-wire fence; **berpagar** *vi* to have a fence; *adj* fenced; **memagari** *vt* to fence (off); **pemagaran** *n* fencing (off)

pagi *n* morning; *adj* early; ~ *buta* in the early hours of the morning, before sunrise; *kain* ~ *sore* reversible sarong worn during the war; *makan* ~ breakfast; *selamat* ~ good morning; *senam* ~ morning exercise; **pagi-pagi** *adv* (very) early; **kepagian** *adj* too early; **sepagi** ~ *mungkin* as early as possible

pagoda *n, Budd* temple, pagoda

pagupon *n* nesting box for pigeons (including pole)

pagut peck, bite; **memagut** *vt* to bite (of a snake)

paguyuban *n* group, association

paha *n* thigh; ~ *ayam* chicken leg; *lipat* ~ groin; *pangkal* ~ hip

pahala *n* reward, merit; **berpahala** *adj* meritorious

paham, faham *v* to understand, know; *n* understanding, belief; ~ *komunis* communism; *salah* ~ misunderstanding; **memahami** *vt* to understand, comprehend; **pemahaman** *n* comprehension, understanding; **sepaham** *adj* of the same opinion or belief

pahat chisel; *seni* ~ sculpture; **pahatan** *n* sculpture; **memahat** *vt* to sculpt, chisel; **pemahat** *n* sculptor

Pahing *n* second day of the Javanese week

pahit *adj* bitter; *kopi* ~ black coffee without sugar; **kepahitan** *n* bitterness

pahlawan *n* hero; *Taman Makam* ~

heroes' cemetery; **kepahlawanan** *n* heroism

pai *n* pie

pailit *adj* bankrupt; **kepailitan** *n* bankruptcy

Pajajaran *n* ancient Sundanese kingdom

pajak tax; ~ *kekayaan* property tax; ~ *pendapatan*, ~ *penghasilan* income tax; ~ *penjualan (PPn)* sales tax at restaurants and hotels; ~ *Bumi Bangunan (PBB)* land tax, household rates; **pemajakan** *n* taxation

pajang: pajangan *n* display; **memajang** *vt* to display

pak: mengepak *vt* to pack

Pak, Bapak *pron* Father; term of address to older, respected men; ~ *Dé*, ~*dé pron, Jav* uncle (older than one's parents); ~ *Lik pron, Jav* uncle (younger than one's parents); ~ *Ogah* man who directs traffic for payment; ~ *Pos* the postman; ~ *RT* neighborhood leader

pakai, paké wear; use; ~ *bon* make out a receipt before paying (at another counter); *bekas* ~ used; *siap* ~ ready to use (or wear); **pakaian** *n* clothes, dress; ~ *adat* traditional dress; ~ *dalam* underwear; ~ *dinas* (work) uniform; ~ *resmi* formal dress; ~ *santai* casual dress; **berpakaian** *adj* dressed in; *vi* to be dressed in; **memakai** *vt* to wear; to use; ~ *kacamata* to wear glasses; **pemakai** *n* user; **pemakaian** *n* use, usage; **terpakai** *adj* used, in use

pakan *n* feed; ~ *ikan* fish food

pakansi → **vakansi**

pakar *n* expert, authority

pakat: sepakat *v* to agree; **bersepakat** *vi* to agree, to have an agreement; **kesepakatan** *n* agreement; **menyepakati** *vt* to agree to

paké → **pakai**

pakem *n* mold, norm

pakét *n* packet, package, promotion; ~ *hemat (pahe)* cheap package; ~ *perdana* starter kit; ~ *wisata* tourist package

pakis *n* fern

Pakistan *n* Pakistan; *orang* ~ Pakistani

Pak Lik *pron, Jav* uncle (younger than one's parents)

paksa force; *kerja* ~ forced labor; **paksaan** *n* force, compulsion; **memaksa** *vt* to force; **pemaksaan** *n* force, pressure; **terpaksa** *adj* forced; *karena* ~ had or was forced to do it; **keterpaksaan** *n* compulsion

pakta *n* pact

paku *n* nail; **memaku** *vt* to nail

paku *n* fern

pal *n, arch* milestone, post

pala *buah* ~ nutmeg; *bunga* ~ mace

palak: memalak *vt* to force (usu to pay money); **pemalak** *n* extortionist, someone who demands payment

palang *n* barrier, bar, cross; ~ *Merah* Red Cross; ~ *jalan kereta api* boomgates (at a railway crossing)

Palapa *n* Indonesia's communications satellite

palawija *n* secondary crop, planted in dry season

palem *n* palm

Palestina *n* Palestine; *orang* ~ Palestinian; *Otoritas* ~ the Palestinian Authority; *Organisasi Pembebasan* ~ the Palestinian Liberation Front (PLO)

Pali *bahasa* ~ ancient language of Buddhist scriptures

paling *adv* most; at the most; ~ *baik* the best; ~ *jelek* the worst

paling: berpaling *vi* to turn away or from

palka *n* hold (of a ship)

palsu *adj* false, forged; *identitas* ~ fake ID; *rambut* ~ wig; *sumpah* ~ perjury; *uang* ~ counterfeit money; **memalsukan** *vt* to falsify, forge; **pemalsuan** *n* forgery

palu *n* hammer, gavel (in court); ~ *arit* hammer and sickle; **memalu** *vt* to hammer, strike

palung *n* trough, riverbed; ~ *hati* the bottom of your heart; **palungan** *n* eating or drinking trough for animals; manger

PAM *abbrev Perusahaan Air Minum* company providing reticulated water, water board

pamali *n* taboo

paman *n* uncle, male relative of parents' generation; ~ *Sam* Uncle Sam (America)

paméo, peméo *n* saying, proverb

pamér show off; **paméran** *n* exhibition; **memamérkan** *vt* to display, exhibit

pamit, pamitan, berpamit *vi* to take leave

pamong ~ *praja* civil service

pamor *n* prestige, lustre, glow

pampang: memampangkan *vt* to spread out; to explain

pamper, pampers *n, coll* disposable diapers or nappies

pamrih *n* reward; *tanpa* ~ altruistic, without expecting anything in return

pamungkas *adj* final, last

PAN *abbrev Partai Amanat Nasional* People's Mandate Party

pana: terpana *adj* struck, stunned

panah *n* bow; *anak* ~ arrow; **panahan** *n* archery; **memanah** *vt* to shoot (with a bow); **pemanah** *n* archer

Panama *n* Panama; *orang* ~ Panamanian

panas *adj* hot, warm; ~ *badan* body temperature; *coll* high temperature; ~ *dingin* hot and cold; ~ *hati* angry; ~ *terik* hot and dry, dry heat; ~ *suam-suam kuku* lukewarm; **kepanasan** *n* heat; *adj* too hot; **memanas** *v* to get hot, heat up; **memanaskan** *v* to heat (up); **pemanas** *n alat* ~ heater; **pemanasan** *n* heating, warming; warm-up; ~ *bumi* global warming; **terpanas** *adj* the hottest

panau → **panu**

panca *adj* five; **pancaindera** *n* the five senses; **pancalomba** *n* pentathlon; **Pancasila** *n* Indonesian state philosophy of five principles

pancang *n* pole, stake; **memancang** *vt* to stake or drive in; **pemancangan** *n* planting, insertion

pancar: pancaran *n* emission; **berpancar** *vi* to shine out; **memancarkan** *vt* to broadcast; **pemancar** *n* transmitter; **terpancar** *adj* emitted, sent, broadcast

pancaroba *n* change of season; *musim* ~ transition between seasons

Pancasila *n* Indonesian state philosophy of five principles

panci *n* saucepan, pan

pancing *n* fishing rod or hook; **memancing** *vi* to fish (with hook and line); **terpancing** *adj* hooked, caught up; involved

pancung: memancung *vt* to cut off, mutilate; ~ *kepala* to behead or decapitate

pancur: pancuran, pancoran *n* fountain; shower; **memancur** *vi* to pour, gush, flow out; **mancur** *air* ~ fountain

pandai *adj* clever; ~ *emas* goldsmith; **kepandaian** *n* ability, intelligence

pandai ~ *besi* smith

pandan *daun* ~ pandanus leaf, used for green coloring in food

pandang see, gaze; *tak* ~ *bulu* not discriminate; **pandangan** *n* view, sight; **berpandangan** *vi* to look at each other; to have a certain view; **memandang** *vt* to view, consider; ~ *rendah* to underestimate, disregard; **pemandangan** *n* view

pandu guide, scout, pilot; **panduan** *n buku* ~ manual, guidebook; **kepanduan** *n* scouting, Scouts; *n, f* guiding, Guides; **memandu** *vt* to guide

panekuk *n* pancake

panén *n* harvest, windfall; **memanén** *vt* to harvest

Pangab *n* Commander-in-Chief of the Armed Forces ← **Panglima Angkatan Bersenjata**

pangan *n* food; *sandang* ~ food and clothing

Pangdam *n* Regional Commander ← **Panglima Daérah Militér**

pangéran *n* prince

panggang *adj* roast, baked, barbecued; *v* roast, bake, toast, barbecue; *ayam* ~ barbecued chicken; *roti* ~ toast; **memanggang** *vt* to roast, bake, toast, barbecue; **pemanggang** ~ *roti* toaster; **pemanggangan** *n* spit, barbecue

panggil *vi* call; **panggilan** *n* call, summons; *wanita* ~ callgirl; **memanggil** *vt* to call; **pemanggilan** *n* summons; ~ *kembali* recall; **terpanggil** *adj* called, summoned; *dia merasa* ~ *untuk* *mengabdikan diri di daerah terpencil* he feels called upon to serve in a remote area

panggul *n* hip; **memanggul** *vt* to carry on your hip

panggung *n* stage; *demam ~* stage fright; **manggung** *vi, coll* to perform

pangkal *n* base; **pangkalan** *n* terminal, base; *~ ojek* place where motorcycle taxis wait; *~ udara (lanud)* air base; **berpangkal** *adj* based; *vi* to have a base; **mangkal** *vi, coll* to use as a base, wait for work; *banyak tukang becak ~ di perapatan* lots of pedicab drivers wait for work at the crossroads

pangkas cut; *~ rambut* barber; **memangkas** *vt* to cut, shear, trim

pangkat *n* rank, class; to the power of; *naik ~* be promoted, get a promotion; **berpangkat** *vi* to have the rank of

pangkat (maths) to the power of; *~ dua* squared; *~ tiga* cubed

pangku lap; **pangkuan** *n* lap; **memangku** *vi* to take on (your lap); *~ jabatan* to occupy a post; **pemangku** *n* functionary

panglima *n* commander; *~ besar* general for life; *~ tertinggi* commander-in-chief

pangling not recognize, unrecognizable

pangsa *n* segment; *~ jeruk* segment of orange; *~ pasar* market share

pangsit *n* wonton, dumpling

panik panic

paniki *n* dish made from bat meat, a specialty of Minahasa

panili → **vanili**

panitera *n* clerk, secretary; *~ pengadilan* registrar, clerk (of the court)

panitia *n* committee, board; *~ penyelenggara* organizing committee

panjang *adj* long; *~nya* length; *bulat ~* cylindrical; *~ ingatan* a long or good memory; *~ lebar* detailed, extensive; *(empat) persegi ~* rectangle; *~ tangan* light-fingered, a thief; *~ umur* long life; *rumah ~* longhouse; **kepanjangan** *adj* too long; **berkepanjangan** *adj* continuous, protracted; **memanjang** *vi* to become long, lengthen; **memperpanjang** *vt* to extend, make longer;

perpanjangan *n* extension; **sepanjang** *conj, adj* as long as; *~ hari* all day long; *~ hidup* lifelong, all your life; *~ jalan* the whole way; **terpanjang** *adj* the longest

panjat climb; *~ pinang* climbing a greased areca-nut palm, an Independence Day competition; *~ tebing* abseiling; **memanjat** *vt* to climb; **memanjatkan** *vt* to send up; *~ doa* to offer prayers

panser *n* tank, armored car

pansus *n* special committee (in Parliament) ← **panitia khusus**

pantai *n* beach, coast; *~ batu* pebble beach; *~ Gading* Ivory Coast; *garis ~* coast(line); *(bola) voli ~* beach volleyball

pantang forbidden, prohibited; *~ menyerah* never give up, never say die; *~ mundur* never look back; ever onward; **berpantang** *vi* to not be allowed, abstain from; *~ makan* to be on a diet, not eat certain foods

pantas, pantes *adj* proper, decent, right; **pantasan, pantesan** *sl* no wonder; **sepantasnya** *adv* proper, rightly

pantat *n* bottom, backside

pantau: pantauan *n* observation; **memantau** *vt* to observe, watch; **pemantau** *n* observer, monitor; **pemantauan** *n* monitoring

Pantékosta *n* Pentecost, Whitsun; *Gereja ~* Pentecostal Church

pantes *sl* no wonder ← **pantas**

panti *n* building; *~ asuhan* orphanage; *~ jompo, ~ wreda* old people's home; *~ pijat* massage parlor

panting: pontang-panting helter skelter

pantul: pantulan *n* reflection; **berpantulan** *vi* to reflect (of many things); **memantul** *vi* to rebound; **memantulkan** *vt* to reflect something; **terpantul** *adj* reflected

pantun *n* traditional poem (of four lines); **berpantun** *vi* to recite or write a traditional poem

panu, panau *n* white spots caused by skin fungus; **panuan** *vi, coll* to suffer from white spots

panut: panutan *n* leader, good example → **anut**

Papa *pron, m* Papa, Dad, Daddy

papa *adj* destitute, poor; *kaum* ~ the destitute, the poor; **kepapaan** *n* destitution, poverty

papah: memapah *vt* to support, prop up

papan *n* plank, board, bench; ~ *catur* chessboard; ~ *loncat* springboard; ~ *nama* name plate; ~ *selancar* surf-board; ~ *tulis* blackboard, whiteboard; ~ *tuts* keyboard

papar: memaparkan *vt* to explain; **pemaparan** *n* explanation

papas: berpapasan *vi* to pass each other (very closely); *banyak mobil* ~ *di gang sempit ini* lots of cars pass close by in this narrow lane

papaya → **pepaya**

Papi, Pi *pron* Papa, Daddy (in Westernized circles)

paprika *n* red or green pepper, paprika

Papua *n* Papua, Irian Jaya; *arch* West Irian; ~ *Nugini n* Papua New Guinea, PNG; *orang* ~ Papuan

para pluralizes the following word; ~ *pembaca* readers; ~ *pemirsa* viewers; ~ *pendengar* listeners; ~ *penonton* audience; ladies and gentlemen

parabola *n* satellite dish; parabola; *TV* ~ satellite TV

parade *n* parade

paradigma *n* paradigm

paradoks *n* paradox

paraf *n* initials; **memaraf** *vt* to initial, sign

paragraf *n* paragraph → **alinéa**

parah *adj* grave, serious, bad; *luka* ~ badly wounded; *sakit* ~ gravely ill; **memperparah** *vt* to make worse, aggravate

paralél *adj* parallel; *n* (phone) exten-sion; *parkir* ~ right-angle parking

parang *n* chopper, machete

paranormal *n* clairvoyant

paras *n* face, countenance; **berparas** *vi* to have a face or appearance

parasit *n* parasite

parasut *n* parachute → **payung**

parau *adj* hoarse

paré, paria, peria *n* kind of bitter gourd or squash

parfum *n* perfume → **wangi**

pari *bintang* ~ Southern Cross; *ikan* ~ ray

paria → **paré**

paripurna *adj* complete; *sidang* ~ plenary session

parit *n* (roadside) ditch

pariwara *n* advertisement

pariwisata *n* tourism; *bis* ~ tourist bus; **kepariwisataan** *n* tourist industry

parkét *n* parquet

parkir park (a vehicle); ~ *gratis* free parking; ~ *paralel* right-angle parking; ~ *serong* angle parking; *tempat* ~ car park, parking lot; *tukang* ~ parking attendant; **parkiran** *n, sl* car park; **memarkir** *vt* to park

parkit *burung* ~ parakeet

parlemén *n* parliament

paro → **paruh**

parodi *n* parody

paroki *n, Cath* parish

parpol *n* (political) party ← **partai politik**

Parsi, Farsi *bahasa* ~ Farsi; *orang* ~ Persian, Iranian

partai *n* party; ~ *Demokrat* Democratic Party, Democrats; ~ *gurem* minor party (with very small votes); ~ *politik (parpol)* political party; ~ *tunggal* one party; *politik* ~ party politics; ~ *Amanat Nasional (PAN)* National Mandate Party; ~ *Demokrasi Indonesia–Perjuangan (PDIP)* Indonesian Democratic Party of Struggle; ~ *Kebangkitan Bangsa (PKB)* Party of National Awakening; ~ *Komunis Indonesia (PKI) arch* Indonesian Communist Party; ~ *Nasional Indonesia (PNI)* Indonesian National Party; ~ *Persatuan Pembangunan (PPP, P3)* United Development Party

partai *n* event; *Indonesia sudah meme-nangkan* ~ *ganda* Indonesia has won the doubles event

paru, paru-paru *n* lung; *radang* ~ pneumonia

paruh, paro *n* half, part; *kerja ~ waktu* work part-time; **separuh** *n* half; **separuh-separuh** *adj* half and half

paruh *n* bill, beak

parut grater; **memarut** *vt* to grate

pas exact, just (as); just enough; fit; *kamar ~* fitting room; *~ dia buka pintu* just as he opened the door; **pas-pasan** *adv* just enough; *hidup ~* to live from day to day

pasak *n* peg, wooden nail; **memasak** *vt* to peg

pasal *n, leg* paragraph, section; *conj* regarding, concerning

pasang *n* pair, couple; **pasangan** *n* pair; **berpasangan** *adv* in pairs; **sepasang** *n* a pair of

pasang, memasang *vt* to put up, attach, fix; *~ bendera* to hoist a flag; *~ iklan* to advertise; *~ lampu* to switch on a light, light a lamp; *~ mata* to keep your eyes open, watch for; *~ weker* to set the alarm (clock); **pemasangan** *n* installation

pasang *air ~* rising tide; *~ surut* rise and fall, ebb and flow

pasar *n* market, bazaar; *~ bebas* free market; *~ dunia* global market; *~ gelap* black market; *~ induk* large wholesale market; *~ kaget* temporary street market; *~ loak* flea market; *~ malam* fair, carnival; *~ modal* capital market; *~ raya, pasaraya* supermarket; *~ senggol* crowded market; *~ uang* money market; *~ tenaga kerja* job market; **pasaran** *n* market (in abstract sense); **memasarkan** *vt* to market; **pemasaran** *n* marketing

pasasi *n* department dealing with fares and travel (of a company)

pasca [pasca, paska] *pref* after, post-; *~ krismon* after the financial crisis; *~ perang* post-war; *layanan ~jual* after-sales service; **pascasarjana** *adj* postgraduate

paséban *n, Jav* audience hall

pasfoto *n* passport(-sized) photo

pasi *adj* pale; *pucat ~* deathly pale

pasién *n* patient

pasif *adj* passive; *~ bahasa Inggris* passive English, can understand English

Pasifik *Lautan ~, Lautan Teduh* the Pacific (Ocean); *Kawasan Asia ~* (Asia-)Pacific region

pasir *n* sand; *gula ~* (white) sugar; *jam ~* hourglass, eggtimer; *kertas ~* sandpaper; *padang ~* desert, sand dune

Paskah *n* Easter; *Hari ~* Easter Sunday

Paskibraka, Pasibraka *n* select group of high-school students who unfurl and raise the flag on Independence Day ← **Pasukan Pengibar Bendéra Pusaka**

pasok: pasokan *n* supply; **memasok** *vt* to supply; **pemasok** *n* supplier; **pemasokan** *n* supply, supplying

Paspamprés *n* Presidential guards ← **pasukan pengamanan Présidén**

paspor *n* passport

pasrah *adj* accepting, fatalistic; **kepasrahan** *n* submission

pasta *n* paste; pasta, spaghetti; *~ gigi* toothpaste

pastél *n* samosa, small pasty containing vegetables, egg and vermicelli noodles

pasti sure, certain, definite; *ilmu ~* the physical sciences, mathematics; **kepastian** *n* certainty; **memastikan** *vt* to confirm, make sure, ascertain

pastor *n, Chr* priest

pasuk: pasukan *n* troops; *~ berkuda* cavalry; *~ gegana* bomb squad; *~ infantri, ~ jalan* infantry; *~ khusus* elite troops, special troops; *~ pemadam kebakaran* fire brigade

Pasundan *n, Sund* the Sundanese lands, West Java

pasung, pasungan *n* stocks; **memasung** *vt* to put in the stocks

patah break, fracture (of bones); *~ hati* broken-hearted; *~ semangat* lose heart; *~ tulang* break or fracture a bone; **patahan** *n* fault, crack; **mematahkan** *vt* to break; **pepatah** *n* proverb, saying; **sepatah** *~ kata* a single word; **terpatah-patah** *adj* broken; *bahasa Inggrisnya masih ~* her English is still halting

patas *bis ~* bus with a passenger limit ← **penumpang terbatas**

patén *n* patent → **hak cipta**

patérnalis *adj* paternalistic

pat gulipat *n* children's game; hanky-panky, shady deals

pati *n* starch, essence

patih *n, arch* high-ranking official, vice-governor; **kepatihan** *n* area presided over by *patih*

patina *n* sheen, patina (of polished metal)

patok: patokan *n* standard, peg; **mematok** *vt* to fix, set; ~ *harga* to set a price

patri solder; *kaca* ~ stained glass; **mematri** *vt* to solder

patroli *n* patrol

patron *n* (dressmaker's) pattern

patuh *adj* loyal, obedient; **kepatuhan** *n* obedience; **mematuhi** *vt* to obey

patuk: mematuk *vt* to peck, bite

patung *n* statue, figurine; **mematung** *vi* to freeze, not move, be as still as a statue; **pematung** *n* sculptor

patung: patungan *vi* to pay together; to work together; *perusahaan* ~ joint venture

patut *adj* decent, proper, deserving; **sepatutnya** *adv* rightly, properly

pauk *lauk* ~ side dishes served with rice

paus *ikan* ~ whale

Paus *Sri* ~ the Pope, Holy Father; ~ *Benedictus XVI* Pope Benedict XVI; ~ *Johannes Paulus II* Pope John Paul II

pause, pauze *n* break, half-time (in sport); *adem* ~ break, breather

paut *sangkut* ~ to be connected with; **berpautan** *vi* to be related; *adj* related; *saling* ~ interconnected; **terpaut** *adj* fastened, bound; separated

paviliun *n* smaller house attached to a larger one, guest quarters in colonial times

pawai *n* procession, parade

pawang *n* tamer, animal trainer; ~ *gajah* elephant trainer

paya *n* swamp, marsh

payah *adj* difficult, serious; tired; *bersusah* ~ to work hard

payau *adj* brackish, briny (of water)

payét *n* sequin

payudara *n, f* breast; *kanker* ~ breast cancer

payung *n* umbrella; parachute; *terjun* ~ parachuting; *menyediakan* ~ *sebelum hujan* to prepare for the worst; **memayungi** *vt* to hold an umbrella over someone

PBB *abbrev Persatuan Bangsa-Bangsa* United Nations, UN

PBB *abbrev Pajak Bumi dan Bangunan* Land and Building Tax

PD *abbrev Partai Demokrat* Democrat Party

PD I *abbrev Perang Dunia Pertama* First World War

PD II *abbrev Perang Dunia Kedua* Second World War

PDAM *abbrev Perusahaan Daerah Air Minum* regional water board

PDI *abbrev Partai Demokrasi Indonesia* Indonesian Democratic Party

PDIP *abbrev Partai Demokrasi Indonesia Perjuangan* Indonesian Democratic Party of Struggle

Pdt. *abbrev Pendeta* (Protestant) minister, clergyman

pebalét *n* ballet dancer, *f* ballerina ← **balét**

pebisnis *n* businessman, businesswoman ← **bisnis**

peboling *n* bowler ← **boling**

Pébruari → **Fébruari**

pecah break, smash; curdled (of milk); *(barang)* ~ *belah* earthenware; ~*nya perang* outbreak of war; **pecahan** *n* piece, fragment; fraction; denomination; ~ *Rp.50.000* Rp.50,000 notes; **memecah** ~ *belah vi* to break into fragments, cause divisions; **memecahkan** *vt* to break; to solve; ~ *soal* to solve a problem; **pemecahan** *n* solution

pecandu *n* addict ← **candu**

pecat fired, sacked, dismissed; **memecat** *vt* to fire, dismiss; **pemecatan** *n* sacking, dismissal

pecatur *n* chess player ← **catur**

pecel ~ *lele* catfish with rice and side-dishes; *nasi* ~ rice and salad with peanut sauce

péci, pici *n* black, flat-topped cap worn by men, also with national dress

Pecinan *n* Chinatown ← **Cina**

pecinta, pencinta *n* lover (of something), fan ← **cinta**

pecundang loser; **memecundangi** *vt* to swindle or trick; to beat or defeat ← **cundang**

pedagang *n* merchant; ~ *kaki lima (PKL)* itinerant food vendor ← **dagang**

pédal *n* pedal

pedanda *n* Balinese priest

pedang *n* sword; **pedang-pedangan** *n* toy sword

pedas *adj* **pedes** *coll* spicy, hot; **kepedasan** *adj* too hot or spicy

pedati *n* cart drawn by horse or ox

pedayung *n* professional rower, oarsman ← **dayung**

pédé, PD *sl* self-confidence; *kurang* ~ lack self-confidence ← **percaya diri**

pedes → **pedas**

pedésaan *n* country(side), rural areas; *angkutan* ~ country minibus ← **désa**

pedih, perih smart, sting; *sampo anti* ~ shampoo that won't sting your eyes; **kepedihan** *n* stinging

pédikur *n* pedicure

pédofil *n* pedophile; **pédofilia** *n* pedophilia

pedoman *n* compass; guide; manual; **berpedoman** *vi* to be guided by, based on

peduli *v* **perduli** *coll* to care, bother; *tidak* ~ not care; **kepedulian** *n* concern; **memedulikan** *vt* to care or be bothered about

pedupaan *n* stand for burning incense ← **dupa**

Peg. *abbrev Pegunungan* (mountain) range

pegadaian *n* pawnshop ← **gadai**

pegal *adj* sore, cramped, stiff; ~ *linu* aches and pains

pégang, pegang hold, grip, grasp; **pegangan** *n* handle, grip; belief, principle; **berpegang** *vi* to hold onto; ~ *teguh* to hold fast to; **memegang** *vt* to hold, grasp; **pemegang** *n* keeper, holder

pegas *n* spring; *kasur* ~ spring bed

pegawai *n* official, employee; ~ *negeri (sipil, PNS)* public or civil servant; **kepegawaian** *adj* staff, personnel

pegel → **pegal**

pegiat *n* activist ← **giat**

pegolf *n* golfer ← **golf**

pégon *n* modified Arabic script used to write Indonesian languages

pegulat *n* wrestler ← **gulat**

pegunungan *n* mountain range; ~ *Jayawijaya* the Jayawijaya range ← **gunung**

péhaka, PHK to lose your job, be unemployed; **dipéhakakan** *v* to lose your job, be fired; **mempehakakan, memPHKkan** *vt* to fire someone ← **putus hubungan kerja**

pejabat *n* (government) official; ~ *tinggi* high-ranking official ← **jabat**

pejagalan *n* abattoir ← **jagal**

pejalan *n* ~ *kaki* pedestrian ← **jalan**

pejam: memejamkan *vt* ~ *mata* to close your eyes; **terpejam** *adj* closed

pejantan *n* stud ← **jantan**

pejuang *n* fighter ← **juang**

pejudo *n* judo athlete ← **judo**

pék *sl, Ch* hundred; *go* ~ five hundred, Rp. 500 coin

peka *adj* sensitive; **kepekaan** *n* sensitivity

pekak *adj* deaf; **memekakkan** *adj* deafening, loud

pekan *n* week; market; *akhir* ~ weekend; ~ *Olahraga Nasional (PON)* National Sports Week, national championships; ~ *Raya Jakarta (PRJ)* Jakarta Fair; **sepekan** *n* a week

pekarangan *n* yard; ~ *sekolah* schoolyard ← **karang**

pekat *adj* thick, strong, concentrated; *hitam* ~ pitch black; **kepekatan** *n* thickness, viscosity

pekerja *n* worker, laborer; **pekerjaan** *n* work, profession; ~ *rumah (PR)* homework; *lapangan* ~ employment opportunity; **mempekerjakan** *vt* to put to work, employ; *perusahaan itu* ~ *1.000 karyawan* that company employs 1,000 workers ← **kerja**

pekerti *n* character, nature; *budi* ~ good conduct, ethics

pekik scream, yell; **pekikan** *n* scream, yell; **memekik** *vi* to scream or shriek

pél *kain* ~ rag for mopping the floor; *obat* ~ floor disinfectant; **mengepél** *vt* to mop (up); **dipél** *v* to be mopped, cleaned

pelabuhan port, harbor ← **labuh**

pelacak *anjing* ~ sniffer dog ← **lacak**

pelacur *n* prostitute; **pelacuran** *n* prostitution; *tempat* ~ red-light district ← **lacur**

pelafalan *n* pronunciation ← **lafal**

pelajar *n* pupil, (school) student; schoolboy, schoolgirl; **pelajaran** *n* lesson; *mata* ~ (school) subject; **mempelajari** *vt* to study something in depth ← **ajar**

pelaju *n* commuter ← **laju**

pelaksana *n* manager, producer, administrator; ~ *harian* acting manager; **pelaksanaan** *n* realization, execution ← **laksana**

pélak *tak* ~ no mistake, for sure, undeniable

pelaku *n* agent, one who does something; culprit, perpetrator ← **laku**

pelamar *n* applicant; one making a proposal ← **lamar**

pelaminan *n* bridal sofa where the couple greet guests; *naik ke* ~ get married ← **lamin**

pelampiasan *n* act of releasing, indulgence ← **lampias**

pelampung *n* floater, flotation device; *baju* ~ lifejacket ← **lampung**

pelan, perlahan: pelan-pelan, perlahan-lahan *adv* slowly, softly; **memelankan** *vt* to slow something down

pelana *n* saddle

pelancong *n* tourist ← **lancong**

pelanggan *n* subscriber, customer ← **langgan**

pelanggaran *n* violation ← **langgar**

pelangi *n* rainbow; *warna* ~ all the colors of the rainbow

pelan-pelan *adv* slowly, softly ← **pelan**

pelantikan *n* inauguration ← **lantik**

pelanting: memelantingkan *vt* to throw everywhere; **terpelanting** *v* to fall heavily

pelari *n* runner; **pelarian** *n* escape, solace; abduction, kidnapping ← **lari**

pelarut *n* solute ← **larut**

pelat *n* plate; ~ *hitam* ordinary number plate; ~ *kuning* yellow number plate (for public transport & taxis); ~ *merah* government number plate; ~ *polisi* (vehicle) number plate, license plate

pelatih *n* coach, trainer; **pelatihan** *n* training; *mengadakan* ~ to run a course ← **latih**

Pelatnas *n* national training squad ← **pelatihan nasional**

pelatuk *n* trigger (of a gun); woodpecker

pelaut *n* sailor, seaman ← **laut**

pelawak *n* comedian, comic, clown ← **lawak**

pelayan *n* waiter *m*, waitress *f*, attendant; **pelayanan** *n* service; ~ *masyarakat* public services ← **layan**

pelayaran *n* voyage; *perusahaan* ~ shipping company ← **layar**

pelayat *n* person who visits a house in mourning, pays his respects ← **layat**

pelbagai, berbagai *adj* all kinds or sorts of, various ← **bagai**

pélbét, vélbéd *n* camp-bed

pelébaran *n* widening; ~ *jalan* widening the road, roadworks ← **lébar**

peleburan *n* melting; merger ← **lebur**

pelécéhan *n* contempt; ~ *seksual* sexual harassment ← **lécéh**

peledak *bahan* ~ explosive; **peledakan** *n* bombing ← **ledak**

pélek *n* rim of wheel ← **vélg**

pelekat *bahan* ~ adhesive ← **lekat**

pelembab, pelembap *n* moisturizer ← **lembab**

pelembut *n* softener ← **lembut**

pelémpar *n* bowler, pitcher, thrower; something to throw with; **pelémparan** *n* (act of) throwing ← **lémpar**

pelengkap *n* accessory; **perlengkapan** *n* outfit, equipment ← **lengkap**

pelepasan *n* departure, farewell; *acara* ~ goodbye (party) ← **lepas**

pelését: kepelését *adj, coll* terpelését *adj* slipped, skidded; tripped; **memelésétkan** *vt* to parody; to up-end; to send off-course; **pelésétan, plésétan** *n* parody ← **lését**

pelesir: pelesiran *adj, arch* recreation,

pleasure, amusement; *tempat* ~ place for recreation

pelestarian *n* protection, preservation ← **lestari**

pélét *n* magic or spell to make someone fall in love

pélét *n* pellet, capsule

peleton *n* platoon

pelihara take care of; **peliharaan** *hewan* ~ pet; **memelihara** *vt* to take care of, look after; to cultivate; **pemeliharaan** *n* care, maintenance, cultivation; **terpelihara** *adj* well cared-for, well-maintained ← **piara**

pelik *adj* complicated

pélikan *burung* ~ pelican

pelindung *n* protective device ← **lindung**

pelintat: pelintat-pelintut → **plintat-plintut**

pelintir: memelintir, memelintirkan *vt* to twist; **terpelintir** *adj* twisted

pelipis *n* temple (on head)

pelipur ~ *hati* consolation ← **lipur**

pelir *n* penis; *buah* ~ testicles

pelita *n, lit* (oil) lamp; light

Pelita *n* Five-Year Development; **Repelita** *n* Five-Year Plan ← **Pembangunan Lima Tahun**

pelitur polish; **memelitur** *vt* to polish, varnish

Pélni *n* National Shipping Line, state passenger shipping service ← **Pelayaran Nasional Indonésia**

pélog *n, Jav* seven-tone scale for *gamelan* orchestras

pelonco ← **plonco**

pelopor *n* pioneer, leader, forerunner; **memelopori** *vt* to pioneer, lead

pelor → **peluru**

pelosok *n* remote place

pelotot: melotot, memelotot *vi* to stare, have bulging eyes; **memelototi** *vt* to stare at someone; **memelototkan** *vt* ~ *mata* to stare ← **lotot**

peluang *n* opportunity; ~ *kerja* job opportunity; **berpeluang** *vi* to have an opportunity, a chance; *Susi masih* ~ *menjadi juara* Susi still has a chance to win the tournament ← **luang**

pelud *n, arch* airport ← **pelabuhan udara**

peluh *n* sweat, perspiration; **berpeluh** *vi* to sweat, perspire

peluit, pluit *n* whistle; ~ *kereta api* train whistle

peluk hug; ~ *cium* hugs and kisses; **pelukan** *n* embrace; **berpelukan** *vi* to hug each other; **memeluk** *vt* to hug or embrace; ~ *agama* to follow a religion; **pemeluk** *n* follower, adherent

pelukis *n* painter, artist ← **lukis**

pelumas *n* lubricant ← **lumas**

peluncuran *n* launch ← **luncur**

peluntur *n* laxative ← **luntur**

pelupa *n* forgetful person ← **lupa**

peluru *n* bullet; ~ *kosong* blank (cartridge); ~ *kendali (rudal)* guided missile

pelurusan *n* straightening ← **lurus**

pemaaf *adj* forgiving ← **maaf**

pemadam *n* extinguisher; ~ *api* fire extinguisher; *pasukan* ~ *kebakaran* fire brigade ← **padam**

pemadat *n* (opium) addict ← **madat**

pemagaran *n* fencing (off) ← **pagar**

pemahaman *n* comprehension, understanding ← **paham**

pemahat *n* sculptor ← **pahat**

pemain *n* player, actor; ~ *biola* violinist, violin player; fiddler; ~ *bisbol* baseballer, baseball player; ~ *bola* basket basketballer; ~ *film* actor; ~ *harpa* harpist; ~ *kibor* keyboardist; ~ *sofbol* softballer, softball player; ~ *terompet* trumpet player, trumpeter; ~ *voli* volleyballer, volleyball player ← **main**

pemajakan *n* taxation ← **pajak**

pemakai *n* user; **pemakaian** *n* use, usage ← **pakai**

pemakaman *n* funeral, burial; ~ *negara* state funeral ← **makam**

pemakan *n* eater; ~ *daging* carnivore ← **makan**

pemaksaan *n* force, pressure ← **paksa**

pemalak *n* extortionist, someone who demands payment ← **palak**

pemalas *n* lazy person, lazybones ← **malas**

pemalsuan *n* forgery ← **palsu**

pemalu shy (person) ← **malu**

pemanah *n* archer ← **panah**

pemanas *n alat* ~ heater; **pemanasan** *n* heating, warming; warm-up; ~ *bumi* global warming ← **panas**

pemancangan *n* planting, insertion ← **pancang**

pemancar *n* transmitter ← **pancar**

pemandangan *n* view ← **pandang**

pemanggang ~ *roti* toaster; **pemanggangan** *n* spit ← **panggang**

pemanggilan *n* summons; ~ *kembali* recall ← **panggil**

pemangku *n* functionary ← **pangku**

pemanis *n* sweetener; ~ *buatan* artificial sweetener ← **manis**

pemantau *n* observer, monitor; **pemantauan** *n* monitoring ← **pantau**

pemaparan *n* explanation ← **papar**

pemarah *adj* bad-tempered ← **marah**

pemasangan *n* installation ← **pasang**

pemasaran *n* marketing ← **pasar**

pemasok *n* supplier; **pemasokan** *n* supply, supplying ← **pasok**

pemasyarakatan *lembaga* ~ correctional centre, prison ← **masyarakat**

pematang *n* small dike (in a rice field)

pematung *n* sculptor ← **patung**

pembabatan *n* felling, chopping; ~ *hutan* (unregulated) deforestation ← **babat**

pembaca *n* reader; **pembacaan** *n* (act of) reading aloud ← **baca**

pembagian *n* distribution, division ← **bagi**

pembahasan *n* discussion, debate ← **bahas**

pembajakan *n* hijacking; piracy ← **bajak**

pembakaran *n* burning, combustion ← **bakar**

pembalakan *n* logging; ~ *liar* illegal logging ← **balak**

pembalut *n* sanitary pad ← **balut**

pembangkang *n* someone who defies; **pembangkangan** *n* act of defiance ← **bangkang**

pembangkit *n* ~ *listrik* power station; ~ *listrik tenaga air* hydroelectric power stationi; ~ *Listrik Tenaga Nuklir (PLTN)* nuclear power station ← **bangkit**

pembangunan *n* development ← **bangun**

pembantaian *n* slaughter, mass killings ← **bantai**

pembantu *n* servant, maid; assistant; ~ *dekan* assistant dean; ~ *rektor* assistant vice-chancellor; *kantor* ~ (larger) branch office; ~ *rumah tangga (PRT)* domestic help, household servant ← **bantu**

pembaruan *n* renewal ← **baru**

pembasmi ~ *rayap* termite exterminator; **pembasmian** *n* extermination, destruction, eradication ← **basmi**

pembatalan *n* cancellation, annulment ← **batal**

pembatas *n* divider; ~ *buku* bookmark; **pembatasan** *n* restriction ← **batas**

pembauran *n* integration, mixing of different ethnic groups ← **baur**

pembawa *n* bearer, carrier; ~ *acara* host, MC; **pembawaan** *n* temperament, nature ← **bawa**

pembayaran *n* payment; *tanda* ~ *yang sah* legal currency ← **bayar**

pembébasan *n* liberation, release, exemption ← **bébas**

pembédaan *n* discrimination, differential treatment ← **béda**

pembedahan *n* operation ← **bedah**

pembekalan *n* supply ← **bekal**

pembekuan *n* freezing; ~ *aset* freezing of assets ← **beku**

pembekukan *n* arrest ← **bekuk**

pembéla *n* defender; ~ *Tanah Air (Peta)* defender of the homeland; **pembélaan** *n* defense ← **béla**

pembelajaran *n* learning process ← **belajar, ajar**

pembelanjaan *n* expenditure, financing ← **belanja**

pembeli *n* buyer, purchaser; **pembelian** *n* purchase; purchasing ← **beli**

pembenaran *n* correction; confirmation; justification ← **benar**

pembengkakan *n* swelling, expanding ← **bengkak**

pembenihan ~ *buatan* artificial insemination ← **benih**

pembentukan *n* formation, act of forming ← **bentuk**

pemberangkatan *n* departure, sending off ← **berangkat, angkat**

pemberani *n* brave or courageous

person, hero → **berani**

pemberantasan *n* destruction, fight against ← **berantas**; *Komisi ~ Korupsi (KPK)* Corruption Eradication Commission

pemberat *n* weight ← **berat**

pemberdayaan *n* empowerment; *Kementerian ~ Perempuan* Ministry for the Empowerment of Women ← **berdaya, daya**

pemberhentian *n* stop; dismissal, discharge; stoppage ← **berhenti, henti**

pemberi *n* giver, donor; **pemberian** *n* present, gift, something given to someone ← **beri**

pemberitahuan *n* announcement, notice ← **beri tahu**

pemberkatan *n* consecration, blessing ← **berkat**

pemberontak *n* rebel; **pemberontakan** *n* rebellion, revolt, mutiny ← **berontak**

pembersih *n* cleaning agent; **pembersihan** *n* cleaning, purification; purge ← **bersih**

pembesar *n* big-shot, official; **pembesaran** *n* enlargement, expansion ← **besar**

pembetulan *n* correction, repair ← **betul**

pembiakan *n* breeding, cultivation ← **biak**

pembiayaan *n* financing ← **biaya**

pembibitan *n* sowing, planting of seeds, cultivation ← **bibit**

pembicara *n* speaker; **pembicaraan** *n* discussion ← **bicara**

pembimbing *n* guide, coach, leader ← **bimbing**

pembina *n* founder, patron; coach; **pembinaan** *n* development ← **bina**

pembisik *n* whisperer ← **bisik**

pembiusan *n* anesthesia ← **bius**

pembobolan *n* breaking into, breach ← **bobol**

pembocoran *n* leakage, divulging (of secrets) ← **bocor**

pembodohan *n* tricking, duping; making stupid; *~ rakyat* fooling the people ← **bodoh**

pembohong *n* liar; **pembohongan** *n*

deception, lying ← **bohong**

pemboikotan *n* boycotting ← **boikot**

pembolos *n* truant, absentee; **pembolosan** *n* absenteeism, truancy ← **bolos**

pembongkaran *n* dismantling; exposure; *~ usaha judi sudah lama dilakukan* there have long been efforts to expose gambling joints ← **bongkar**

pemborong *n* developer, contractor ← **borong**

pemboros *n* spendthrift; **pemborosan** *n* wastage ← **boros**

pembrédelan *n* muzzling, being closed down ← **brédel**

pembuat *n* producer, maker; **pembuatan** *n* production, manufacture ← **buat**

pembubaran *n* dissolution, breaking up ← **bubar**

pembudidayaan *n* cultivation ← **budidaya**

pembuka *adj* opening; *kata ~* preface; **pembukaan** *n* opening ← **buka**

pembukingan *n* bookings ← **buking**

pembukuan *n* book-keeping ← **buku**

pembulatan *n* rounding-off ← **bulat**

pembuluh *~ darah* blood vessel, artery ← **buluh**

pembungkus *n* wrapping, packing; **pembungkusan** *n* packaging ← **bungkus**

pembunuh *n* murderer, killer; *~ bayaran* hitman, hired killer; *~ berantai* serial killer, mass murderer; **pembunuhan** *n* murder, killing ← **bunuh**

pemburu *n* hunter; **pemburuan** *n* hunt, chase ← **buru**

pembusukan *n* (process of) decay ← **busuk**

Pémda *n* Regional Government → **Pemerintah Daérah**

pemecahan *n* solution ← **pecah**

pemecatan *n* sacking, dismissal ← **pecat**

pemegang *n* keeper, holder ← **pegang**

pemekaran *n* expansion, development ← **mekar**

pemeliharaan *n* care, maintenance, cultivation ← **pelihara**

pemeluk *n* follower, adherent ← **peluk**

pemenang *n* winner, victor ← **menang**

pementasan *n* staging, production ← **pentas**

peméo ← **paméo**

pemérah ~ *pipi* rouge ← **mérah**

pemeran *n* actor, actress ← **peran**

pemerasan *n* blackmail, extortion ← **peras**

pemerataan *n* levelling out, equal distribution ← **merata, rata**

pemerhati *n* observer → **hati**

pemeriksa *n* examiner; **pemeriksaan** *n* examination, investigation ← **periksa**

pemerintah *n* government; ~ *Daerah (Pemda)* regional government, provincial government; ~ *pusat* central government, national government; **pemerintahan** *n* administration, government ← **perintah**

pemerkosa *n* rapist; **pemerkosaan** *n* act of raping, rape ← **perkosa**

pemeroléhan *n* acquisition, process of acquiring ← **oléh**

pemerosotan *n* decline ← **merosot, rosot**

pemersatu *n* unifying agent, unifier ← **satu**

pemesanan *n* order, request ← **pesan**

pemetaan *n* mapping ← **peta**

pemetik *n* picker; ~ *daun teh* tea-picker ← **petik**

pemicu *n* trigger ← **picu**

pemikir *n* thinker; **pemikiran** *n* thinking, consideration ← **pikir**

pemilahan *n* sorting ← **pilah**

pemilih *n* voter; **pemilihan** *n* election; ~ *umum (pemilu)* general election ← **pilih**

pemilik *n* owner; ~ *lama* previous owner; **kepemilikan** *n* ownership ← **milik**

pemilu *n* general election ← **pemilihan umum**

pemimpin *n* leader ← **pimpin**

peminat *n* interested party ← **minat**

pemindahan *n* transfer, shifting, removal → **pindah**

pemindai *n* scanner; **pemindaian** *n* scanning ← **pindai**

peminjam *n* borrower; *kartu* ~ borrowing card; **peminjaman** *n* lending, borrowing ← **pinjam**

pemintal *n* spinning wheel; spinner ← **pintal**

peminum *n* drinker ← **minum**

pemipaan *n* piping, system of pipes ← **pipa**

pemirsa *n* television audience, viewer ← **pirsa**

pemisahan *n* separation ← **pisah**

pemogok *n* striker; **pemogokan** *n* strike, act of going on strike ← **mogok**

pemohon *n* applicant ← **mohon**

pemompaan *n* pumping ← **pompa**

pemotongan *n* act of cutting; slaughter ← **potong**

pemotrétan *n* photo session ← **potrét**

pémpék, mpék mpék *n* fried fish-cakes, a specialty of Palembang; ~ *kapal selam* large fish-cake containing an egg

pémprop, pemprov *n* provincial government ← **pemerintah propinsi**

pemrosésan *n* processing ← **prosés**

pemrakarsa *n* someone who takes the initiative, innovator ← **prakarsa**

pemuaian *n* expansion ← **muai**

pemuda, pemudi *n* youth; young man; **pemudi** *n, f* young woman ← **muda**

pemugaran *n* restoration, renovation ← **pugar**

pemuja *n* worshipper, fan ← **puja**

pemukul *n* beater, something used for hitting ← **pukul**

pemula *n* beginner ← **mula**

pemulangan *n* return, repatriation ← **pulang**

pemulihan *n* recovery, restoration; ~ *nama baik* rehabilitation ← **pulih**

pemulung *n* scavenger ← **pulung**

pemungut *n* collector; **pemungutan** *n* collection; ~ *suara* vote ← **pungut**

pemusatan *n* focus, concentration ← **pusat**

pemusik *n* musician ← **musik**

pemusnahan *n* act of destruction ← **musnah**

pemutaran *n* screening; ~ *perdana* premiere, opening night (of a film) ← **putar**

pemutih *n* bleach ← **putih**

pemutusan *n* termination, breaking-off;

~ *hubungan kerja (PHK)* to lose your job ← **putus**

pén *n* pin; *jam tanganku hampir jatuh karena ~ talinya copot* my watch almost came off because the pin in the strap came out

péna *n* (fountain) pen, quill; *nama ~* assumed name of an author, nom-de-plume; *sahabat ~* penfriend, penpal

penabung *n* depositor ← **tabung**

penabur *n* sower ← **tabur**

penafsiran *n* interpretation ← **tafsir**

penahanan *n* detention, arrest ← **tahan**

penaklukan *n* surrender, submission ← **takluk**

penaksiran *n* evaluation ← **taksir**

penakut *n* coward ← **takut**

penala *n* tuning fork; **penalaan** *n* tuning ← **tala**

pénalti *n* penalty (esp in sport)

penambang *n* miner ← **tambang**

penampakan *n* apparition; visitation ← **tampak**

penampi *n* winnow ← **tampi**

penampilan *n* performance ← **tampil**

penampung *n* container; **penampungan** *n* reception, place that receives something ← **tampung**

penanaman *~ modal* investment ← **tanam**

penanda *~ tangan* signatory ← **tanda**

penanganan *n* handling ← **tangan**

penanggalan *n* calendar, dating ← **tanggal**

penangguhan *n* delay, postponement ← **tangguh**

penanggulangan *n* tackling, fight against ← **tanggulang**

penangkal *~ petir* lightning rod; **penangkalan** *n* preventative measure ← **tangkal**

penangkapan *n* capture, arrest ← **tangkap**

penantian *n* wait, process of waiting ← **nanti**

penanya *n* person who asks a question ← **tanya**

penapis *n* filter ← **tapis**

penari *n* dancer ← **tari**

penasaran *adj* curious, inquisitive, impatient

penasihat *n* adviser ← **nasihat**

penat *adj* tired

penata *n ~ rambut* hair stylist; *~ rias* make-up artist; **penataan** *n* structuring, system ← **tata**

penawar *n* antidote ← **tawar**

penawaran *n* offer, bid ← **tawar**

pencabutan *n* withdrawal, removal ← **cabut**

pencahar *n* laxative ← **cahar**

pencahayaan *n* lighting ← **cahaya**

pencak *~ silat* traditional self-defense

pencakar *~ langit* skyscraper ← **cakar**

pencakupan *n* coverage ← **cakup**

pencalonan *n* nomination, candidacy ← **calon**

pencampuran *n* mixing ← **campur**

pencangkokan *n* transplant operation, grafting ← **cangkok**

pencar: berpencaran *vi* to disperse (of many things); **terpencar** *adj* dispersed

pencari *n* seeker, searcher; *~ suaka* asylum-seeker; **pencarian** *n* search, hunt ← **cari**

pencatat *n* registrar; **pencatatan** *n* registration ← **catat**

pencegahan *n* prevention; *~ AIDS* prevention of AIDS ← **cegah**

pencegatan *n* barring ← **cegat**

pencekalan *n* ban on foreign travel ← **cekal, cegah tangkal**

pencelupan *n* dyeing process ← **celup**

pencemar *n* polluter; **pencemaran** *n* pollution; *~ udara air* pollution ← **cemar**

pencemburu *n* jealous person ← **cemburu**

pencerahan *n* enlightenment, guidance ← **cerah**

penceramah *n* speaker ← **ceramah**

pencernaan *n* digestion; *gangguan ~* digestive complaint ← **cerna**

pencét press; *kancing ~* press-stud; **memencét** *vt* to press (a button, key); **terpencét** *adj* **kepencét** *adj, coll* accidentally pressed

pencétak *n* printer; *~ gol* goal-scorer ← **cétak**

pencetus *n* initiator, someone who creates ideas ← **cetus**

pencil: terpencil *adj* isolated, remote

pencinta, pecinta *n* lover (of something), fan ← **cinta**

pencipta *n* creator; ~ *lagu* song-writer ← **cipta**

penciuman *n* sense of smell ← **cium**

pencopét *n* pickpocket ← **copét**

pencopotan *n* removal → **copot**

pencucian *n* ~ *uang* money laundering ← **cuci**

penculik *n* kidnapper; **penculikan** *n* kidnapping ← **culik**

pencuri *n* thief, burglar; **pencurian** *n* theft, burglary ← **curi**

pendaftar *n* applicant; **pendaftaran** *n* enrollment, registration ← **daftar**

pendahulu *n* predecessor; **pendahuluan** *n* introduction; *kata* ~ preface ← **dahulu**

pendaki ~ *gunung* mountaineer, bushwalker, hiker ← **daki**

pendakwa *n* plaintiff ← **dakwa**

pendakwah *n, Isl* preacher, missionary ← **dakwah**

pendam: memendamkan *vt* to hide (away), conceal, bury; **terpendam** *adj* hidden, concealed

pendamping *n* companion; ~ *hidup* spouse; **pendampingan** *n* assistance ← **damping**

pendanaan *n* funding ← **dana**

pendangkalan *n* silting-up, process of becoming shallower ← **dangkal**

pendapa ← **pendopo**

pendapat *n* opinion, point of view; *menurut* ~ *saya* in my opinion; **pendapatan** *n* income, revenue; ~ *bruto*, ~ *kotor* gross income ← **dapat**

pendarahan *n* bleeding ← **darah**

pendaratan *n* landing (of vessel); ~ *darurat* emergency landing ← **darat**

pendataan *n* documentation ← **data**

pendatang *n* immigrant, migrant; newcomer; ~ *gelap* illegal immigrant (especially to Indonesia or Malaysia) ← **datang**

pendayung *n* rower, oarsman, sculler ← **dayung**

péndék *adj* short; ~*nya* in a word; ~ *kata* in short; *celana* ~ shorts; *cerita* ~ *(cerpen)* short story; **kepéndékan** *n* abbreviation; **meméndékkan** *vt* to shorten; **memperpéndék** *vt* to shorten, make even shorter; **terpéndék** *adj* the shortest

pendékar *n* (in martial arts) master, champion, leader ← **dékar**

pendekatan *n* approach; getting to know ← **dekat**

pendengar *n* listener; **pendengaran** *n* hearing; *alat* ~ sense of hearing; *indera* ~ sense of hearing ← **dengar**

pendérékan *n* towing ← **dérék**

penderita *n* sufferer; **penderitaan** *n* suffering ← **derita**

pendéta *n, Chr* minister, clergyman, vicar; *Hind* priest

pendiam *n* quiet, shy person ← **diam**

pendidik *n* educator; **pendidikan** *n* education; *ilmu* ~ pedagogy; ~ *dan latihan (diklat)* education and training for employees; **berpendidikan** *adj* educated; *vi* to have an education; ~ *SD* to have a primary school education ← **didik**

pendingin ~ *ruangan* air conditioning, cooling ← **dingin**

pendiri *n* founder; **pendirian** *n* foundation; opinion, point of view ← **diri**

pendopo, pendapa *n* traditional large roofed verandah in front of an official residence

penduduk *n* inhabitant, citizen, resident; **pendudukan** *n* occupation; ~ *tetap* permanent resident ← **duduk**

pendukung *n* supporter ← **dukung**

pendulang *n* prospector; **pendulangan** *n* panning, prospecting ← **dulang**

pendusta *n* liar ← **dusta**

penebang *n* logger, woodcutter; **penebangan** *n* logging; ~ *liar* illegal logging ← **tebang**

penébaran *n* spread, spreading ← **tébar**

penebus *n* redeemer; ransom; **penebusan** *n* redemption ← **tebus**

penegakan *n* upholding or maintenance; ~ *hukum* upholding the law ← **tegak**

penegasan *n* affirmation, reiteration ← **tegas**

peneliti *n* researcher; **penelitian** *n* research; ~ *khusus (litsus)* special investigation; ~ *dan pengembangan (litbang)* research and development (R & D)

penémbak *n* marksman, gunman; ~ *jitu* sniper ← **témbak**

penemu *n* inventor, discoverer; **penemuan** *n* invention, discovery ← **temu**

penentang *n* opponent ← **tentang**

penentu *faktor* ~ deciding factor; **penentuan** *n* setting, fixing, determining ← **tentu**

penerangan *n* information; lighting, enlightenment ← **terang**

penerapan *n* application ← **terap**

penerbang *n* pilot, aviator; **penerbangan** *n* flight; aviation; *perusahaan* ~ airline ← **terbang**

penerbit *n* publisher ← **terbit**

penerima *n* recipient; addressee; **penerimaan** *n* receipt; revenue; acceptance ← **terima**

penerjangan *n* attack, charge ← **terjang**

penerjemah *n* translator; ~ *lepas* freelance translator; ~ *tersumpah* sworn translator; **penerjemahan** *n* translation ← **terjemah**

penerjun *n* ~ *(payung)* parachutist, sky diver ← **terjun**

penertiban *n* reorganization, putting in order, crackdown; ~ *kios-kios penjual bunga berdampak besar pada ekonomi lokal* the reorganization of the flower stalls will affect the local economy greatly ← **tertib**

penerus *n* successor; someone who continues another's work ← **terus**

penetapan *n* appointment ← **tetap**

pénétrasi *n* penetration

pengaba *n* conductor ← **aba**

pengabdian *n* service, servitude, devotion ← **abdi**

pengacara *n* lawyer, solicitor ← **acara**

pengacau *n* provocateur; **pengacauan** *n* disturbance ← **kacau**

pengadaan *n* supply, provision ← **ada**

pengadilan *n* court of justice or law; trial; ~ *negeri* district court ← **adil**

pengaduan *n* complaint; *surat* ~ letter of complaint ← **adu**

pengagum *n* admirer ← **kagum**

pengairan *n* irrigation ← **air**

pengait *n* catch ← **gait, gaét**

pengajar *n* teacher; **pengajaran** *n* teaching, tuition ← **ajar**

pengakuan *n* confession, acknowledgment; ~ *dosa* confession (Catholic) ← **aku**

pengalaman *n* experience ← **alam**

pengaliran *n* flow (esp of money) ← **alir**

pengaman *n* safety device; **pengamanan** *n* securing, pacification; *satuan* ~ *(satpam)* security guard ← **aman**

pengamat *n* observer; ~ *politik* political observer; **pengamatan** *n* observation, monitoring ← **amat**

pengambilan *n* act of taking, removal; ~ *gambar* photo shoot; ~ *sumpah* taking an oath ← **ambil**

pengamén *n* street singer, busker ← **amén**

pengampun *n Tuhan Maha* ~ God is all-forgiving; **pengampunan** *n* pardon, reprieve, amnesty ← **ampun**

penganan *n* snack, food

pengangguran *n* unemployment, unemployed person; ~ *tersembunyi* hidden unemployment ← **anggur**

pengangkatan *n* appointment (to a position) ← **angkat**

pengangkut *n* carrier; *kapal* ~ *minyak* oil tanker; **pengangkutan** *n* transporting, transportation ← **angkut**

penganiayaan *n* oppression, mistreatment ← **aniaya**

pengantar *kata* ~ preface, foreword ← **antar**

pengantin, pengantén *n* marrying couple; *f* bride; *n, m* (bride)groom; ~ *baru* newlyweds; *baju* ~, *busana* ~ wedding dress or costume; *kue* ~ wedding cake; *mobil* ~ bridal car; ~ *pria* (bride)groom; ~ *wanita* bride

pengantri *n* person who queues ← **antré, antri**

penganugerahan *n* presentation of an award ← **anugerah**

penganut *n* follower, believer; ~ *agama Katolik* Catholic ← **anut**

pengap *adj* stuffy; stale, musty

pengapung *n* buoy, float ← **apung**

pengapuran *n* calcification ← **kapur**

pengarah *n* director; **pengarahan** *n* direction, guidance, briefing ← **arah**

pengarang *n* author, writer, composer; *hak* ~ copyright ← **karang**

pengartian *n* understanding, interpretation ← **arti**

pengaruh *n* influence; ~ *obat* effect of medicine or drugs; **berpengaruh** *adj* influential; *vi* to have influence; **memengaruhi** *vt* to influence, affect; **terpengaruh** *adj* affected or influenced

pengasah ~ *pensil* pencil sharpener ← **asah**

pengasingan *n* exile; *tempat* ~ internment camp, exile ← **asing**

pengaspalan *n* asphalting (pouring asphalt to lay the roads) ← **aspal**

pengasuh *n* carer; ~ *anak* nursemaid, babysitter ← **asuh**

pengatur *n* regulator ← **atur**

pengawal *n* (body)guard, sentry ← **kawal**

pengawas *badan* ~ supervisory board, trustees; **pengawasan** *n* supervision, control ← **awas**

pengawétan *n* preservation ← **awét**

pengayaan *n* enrichment; ~ *uranium* uranium enrichment ← **kaya**

pengayau *n* head-hunter ← **kayau**

pengayom *n* protector, carer ← **ayom**

pengeboman *n* bombing ← **bom**

pengeboran *n* drilling ← **bor**

pengebut *n* speedster ← **kebut**

pengecatan *n* painting, dyeing, coloring ← **cat**

pengecékan *n* checking ← **cék**

pengécér *n* retailer ← **écér**

pengecualian *n* exception ← **kecuali**

pengecut *n* coward ← **kecut**

pengédar *n* dealer; **pengédaran** *n* circulation; ~ *udara* air circulation ← **édar**

pengéjaan *n* spelling ← **éja**

pengékspor *n* exporter; ~ *beras* exporter of rice ← **pengékspor**

pengelola *n* manager; **pengelolaan** *n* management ← **kelola**

pengeluaran *n* expenditure ← **ke luar**

pengembalian *n* return, act of returning ← **kembali**

pengemban *n* guardian, executor; ~ *tugas* worker responsible for performing a duty ← **emban**

pengembang *n* developer; **pengembang-biakan** *n* propagation, breeding ← **kembang**

pengembara *n* wanderer, rover; **pengembaraan** *n* roaming, wandering ← **embara**

pengembunan *n* condensation ← **embun**

pengemis *n* beggar ← **emis, kemis**

pengemudi *n* driver ← **kemudi**

péngén, pingin, kepéngén, kepingin *v, aux, coll* to really want to

pengenal *tanda* ~ identity card; **pengenalan** *n* introduction ← **kenal**

pengéncéran *n* liquefaction, melting ← **éncér**

pengendalian *n* control; ~ *mutu* quality control ← **kendali**

pengendapan *n* siltation ← **endap**

pengendara *n* rider; driver ← **kendara**

pengeraman *n* brooding, hatching ← **eram**

pengeras ~ *suara* loudspeaker; **pengerasan** *n* hardening ← **keras**

pengerat *binatang* ~ rodent ← **kerat**

pengeréman *n* braking ← **rém**

pengering ~ *rambut* hair dryer ← **kering**

pengeroposan *n* (process of) erosion; ~ *tulang* osteoporosis ← **keropos**

pengertian *n* understanding → **erti, arti**

pengesahan *n* validation, legalization ← **sah**

pengetahuan *n* knowledge; *ilmu* ~ *alam* (IPA) science; **sepengetahuan** *adj* with knowledge; ~ *saya* to my knowledge ← **tahu**

pengetésan *n* testing ← **tés**

pengetikan *n* typing ← **ketik, tik**

penggagas *n* initiator, inventor ← **gagas**

penggal: memenggal *vt* to cut off, amputate; ~ *kepala* to behead

penggalian *n* digging ← **gali**

penggambaran *n* depiction ← **gambar**

penggandaan *n* duplication ← **ganda**

pengganti *n* replacement, substitute,

successor; **penggantian** *n* substitution
← **ganti**

penggarapan *n* production; ~ *film* film
or movie production ← **garap**

penggaris *n* ruler ← **garis**

penggelapan *n* embezzlement ← **gelap**

penggelédahan *n* search, raid, operation
← **gelédah**

penggemar *n* fan, enthusiast ← **gemar**

penggembala *n* shepherd ← **gembala**

penggerebekan *n* raid, search ←
gerebek

penggilas *n* crusher; rolling pin; ~ *jalan*
steamroller ← **gilas**

penggiring *n* herder ← **giring**

penggolongan *n* classification ←
golong

penggoréngan *n* wok, frying pan;
process of frying ← **goréng**

penggugat *n* plaintiff ← **gugat**

pengguguran *n* abortion ← **gugur**

pengguna *n* user; **pengunaan** *n* usage,
use ← **guna**

penggusuran *n* eviction, forcible
removal ← **gusur**

penghabisan *n* end; *ujian* ~ final
examination ← **habis**

penghangat *n* heater ← **hangat**

penghantar ~ *listrik* electrical conductor
← **hantar**

penghapus *n* eraser; duster ← **hapus**

penghargaan *n* appreciation, award ←
harga

penghasil *n* producer; **penghasilan** *n*
production; income ← **hasil**

penghasut *n* agitator, provocateur, trouble-maker; **penghasutan** *n* agitation,
provocation ← **hasut**

penghibur *wanita* ~ escort, prostitute ←
hibur

penghijauan *n* greening (of an area) ←
hijau

penghimpun ~ *listrik* accumulator,
storage cell, battery ← **himpun**

penghinaan *n* insult, libel (written),
slander (spoken); ~ *terhadap Presiden*
insulting the President ← **hina**

penghitungan *n* counting ← **hitung**

penghormatan *n* display of honor, sign
of respect ← **hormat**

penghubung *n* switch, connector; *kata*
~ conjunction, connector, connective
← **hubung**

penghujan *musim* ~ rainy season,
monsoon ← **hujan**

penghulu *n, Isl* local chief who performs
marriage ceremonies

penghuni *n* occupant, resident;
penghunian *n* occupancy; *tingkat* ~ rate
of occupancy, occupancy rate ← **huni**

pengidap *n* sufferer; ~ *narkoba* drug
addict → **idap**

pengikisan *n* scraping; erosion ← **kikis**

pengikut *n* participant; follower ← **ikut**

pengimpor *n* importer ← **impor**

penginapan *n* accommodation, hotel
← **inap**

penginjil *n, Chr* preacher, evangelist
← **injil**

pengintai *pesawat* ~ reconnaissance
plane ← **intai**

pengirim *n* sender; **pengiriman** *n* dispatch, forwarding; ~ *barang* goods
dispatch ← **kirim**

pengiring *n* escort, companion ← **iring**

pengisap ~ *darah* vampire; ~ *debu*
vacuum cleaner ← **isap**

pengisi *n* filler; ~ *suara* dubber ← **isi**

pengkhianat *n* traitor; **pengkhianatan** *n*
treason, treachery, betrayal ← **khianat**

pengkhotbah *n* preacher ← **khotbah**

pengklonan *n* cloning ← **klon**; →
kloning

penglihatan *n* vision, sight ← **lihat**

pengobatan *n* treatment ← **obat**

pengojék *n* motorcycle taxi driver ←
ojék

pengolahan *n* processing ← **olah**

pengomposan *n* (process of) composting ← **kompos**

pengoplosan *n* illegally adding another
liquid ← **oplos**

pengorbanan *n* (act of) sacrifice ←
korban

pengrajin *n* craftsman, artisan; ~ *perak*
silversmith ← **rajin**

penguapan *n* evaporation ← **uap**

penguasa *n* (person in) authority,
power, administration ← **kuasa**

pengucapan *n* expression ← **ucap**

penguji *n* examiner ← **uji**

pengujung *n* end; ~ *musim hujan* end of the rainy season ← **ujung**

pengukuhan *n* strengthening, reinforcement; ratification ← **kukuh**

pengukur *n* measuring device; person who measures; **pengukuran** *n* measuring, measurement ← **ukur**

pengumpul *n* collector; **pengumpulan** *n* collection, act of collecting ← **kumpul**

pengumpan *n* feeder, someone who passes (in soccer or football); someone who sets a bait ← **umpan**

pengumuman *n* notice, announcement ← **umur**

pengunduran *n* postponement, delay ← **undur**

pengungkapan *n* expression, revelation ← **ungkap**

pengungkit *n* lever ← **ungkit**

pengungsi *n* refugee, evacuee; **pengungsian** *n* evacuation ← **ungsi**

pengurukan *n* filling; ~ *laut* land reclamation ← **uruk**

pengurus *n* manager, organizer; ~ *besar* board of directors, executive ← **urus**

pengusaha *n, m* businessman; *f* businesswoman ← **usaha**

peniadaan *n* cancellation, abolition ← **tiada, tidak ada**

penikmat *n* fan, connoisseur, someone who enjoys something ← **nikmat**

penimbun *n* hoarder; **penimbunan** *n* stockpiling, hoarding ← **timbun**

penindakan *n* upholding, taking of measures, action ← **tindak**

penindasan *n* oppression ← **tindas**

pening *adj* dizzy; ~ *kepala* dizzy, light-headed

peninggalan *n* remains, remnants ← **tinggal**

peningkatan *n* rise, increase ← **tingkat**

peninjau *n* observer; **peninjauan** *n* observation; ~ *kembali* review ← **tinjau**

penipu *n* con man, trickster; **penipuan** *n* deception ← **tipu**

peniru *n* imitator ← **tiru**

pénis *n* penis

peniti *n* safety-pin; brooch

penitipan *n* care; deposit; *tempat* ~ *anak* child-minding center, creche ← **titip**

penjabat *n* official (esp temporary or acting) ← **jabat**

penjaga *n* guard; ~ *gawang* goalkeeper ← **jaga**

penjahat *n* criminal ~ *perang* war criminal ← **jahat**

penjahit *n* tailor ← **jahit**

penjaja *n* hawker, pedlar ← **jaja**

penjajah *n* colonizer, ruler, colonial power; **penjajahan** *n* colonization ← **jajah**

penjambrét *n* thief, bag-snatcher; **penjambrétan** *n* theft, snatching ← **jambrét**

penjamin *n* guarantor ← **jamin**

penjara *n* prison, jail; *hukuman* ~ imprisonment; **memenjara, memenjarakan** *vt* to put in prison, imprison

penjarah *n* looter; **penjarahan** *n* looting ← **jarah**

penjelajah *n* explorer ← **jelajah**

penjelasan *n* explanation ← **jelas**

penjelmaan *n* incarnation ← **jelma**

penjemputan *n* act of picking up ← **jemput**

penjepit *n* clip ← **jepit**

penjeprét *n* stapler ← **jeprét**

penjernihan *n* purification ← **jernih**

penjilat *n* crawler, flatterer, lickspittle ← **jilat**

penjilid *n* binder; **penjilidan** *n* binding (process) ← **jilid**

penjiplak *n* cheat; **penjiplakan** *n* plagiarism, cheating ← **jiplak**

penjiwaan *n* inspiration ← **jiwa**

penjual *n* seller, dealer; ~ *karcis* ticket seller; **penjualan** *n* sale, sales ← **jual**

penjudi *n* gambler ← **judi**

penjumlahan *n* addition, tallying ← **jumlah**

penjuru *n* corner; *seluruh* ~ *dunia* all parts of the world

penodong *n* attacker; **penodongan** *n* knife attack ← **todong**

penolakan *n* refusal, rejection ← **tolak**

penonton *n* spectator, audience; *para* ~ audience; ladies and gentlemen ← **tonton** penopang *n* prop, support ← **topang**

pénsil *n* pencil; *rautan* ~ (pencil) sharpener

pénsiun pension, retired; ~ *dini* early pension; **pénsiunan** *n* pensioner; **meménsiunkan** *vt* to pension off

pentahbisan *n* consecration, ordination ← **tahbis**

pental: terpental *adj* flung, thrown down

pentas stage; **mementaskan** *vt* to stage, present; **pementasan** *n* staging, production

péntil *n* valve; ~ *ban* tire valve

penting *adj* important; ~*nya* the importance of; *urusan* ~ urgent business; **kepentingan** *n* importance, interest; ~ *bersama* common interest; **berkepentingan** *vi* to have an interest in; *yang* ~ concerned party; **mementingkan** *vt* to make important, emphasize

pentol: pentolan *n* boss, big shot

penuaan *n* ageing (process) ← **tua**

penugasan *n* assignment ← **tugas**

penuh *adj* full; ~ *sesak* crowded, chock-full; *sehari* ~ a full or whole day; **kepenuhan** *adj* too full, overloaded; **memenuhi** *vt* to fulfill, meet requirements; **sepenuh** ~ *hati* with all of one's heart; **sepenuhnya** *adv* fully, completely; **terpenuhi** *adj* satisfied, fulfilled

penulis *n* author, writer; ~ *naskah* script writer; ~ *novel* novelist ← **tulis**

penumpang *n* passenger ← **tumpang**

penunjuk *n* guide, indicator; **penunjukan** *n* appointment ← **tunjuk**

penuntut *n* claimant, plaintiff, prosecuting party ← **tuntut**

penurunan *n* lowering ← **turun**

penurut *adj* obedient, meek ← **turut**

penutup *n* stopper, lid; end; **penutupan** *n* closing ← **tutup**

penutur *n* speaker; ~ *asli* native speaker ← **tutur**

penyabot *n* saboteur ← **sabot**

penyadap *n* tapper; **penyadapan** *n* tapping ← **sadap**

penyaing *n* competitor (in nature) ← **saing**

penyair *n* poet ← **syair**

penyajian *n* presentation ← **saji**

penyakit *n* disease, illness, complaint; ~ *cacar* smallpox; ~ *campak* measles; ~ *gula* diabetes; ~ *jiwa* mental problem; ~ *kelamin*, ~ *menular seksual (PMS)* sexually transmitted disease (STD), venereal disease; ~ *kusta* leprosy; ~ *menahun* chronic illness; ~ *menular* infectious or contagious disease; ~ *saraf* nervous disorder; ~ *anjing gila* rabies; ~ *kuku mulut* foot and mouth disease ← **sakit**

penyaliban *n* crucifixion ← **salib**

penyaluran *n* channelling ← **salur**

penyamaran *n* disguise ← **samar**

penyambung ~ *lidah* mouthpiece, spokesperson; *Bung Karno dikenal sebagai* ~ *lidah rakyat Indonesia* Sukarno was known as the mouthpiece of the Indonesian people ← **sambung**

penyambut *n* person with task of welcoming; **penyambutan** *n* welcoming, welcome ceremony ← **sambut**

penyampaian *n* handing over, presentation ← **sampai**

penyamun *n* robber, bandit ← **samun**

penyandang *n* bearer; ~ *cacat* disabled person ← **sandang**

penyandera *n* hostage-taker; **penyanderaan** *n* taking of hostages ← **sandera**

penyangkalan *n* denial ← **sangkal**

penyanyi *n* singer, vocalist; ~ *latar* backing vocalist ← **nyanyi**

penyapuan *n* sweeping ← **sapu**

penyaringan *n* filtration, screening ← **saring**

penyayang *adj* merciful ← **sayang**

penyebab *n* cause ← **sebab**

penyebar *n* carrier, infectious person; **penyebaran** *n* distribution ← **sebar**

penyeberangan *n* crossing ← **seberang**

penyedap *n* ~ *rasa* flavoring agent, commercial spice powder, usu MSG ← **sedap**

penyedot *mesin* ~ *debu* vacuum cleaner ← **sedot**

penyegar *minuman* ~ tonic, energy drink ← **segar**

penyégelan *n* sealing (off), closure ← **ségel**

penyejuk *n* cooler, cooling agent, coolant; *minuman* ~ cooling drink ← **sejuk**

penyekapan *n* detention ← **sekap**

penyelam *n* diver ← **selam**

penyelamatan *n* rescue (operation) ← **selamat**

penyelenggara *n* organizer; *panitia* ~ organizing committee; **penyelenggaraan** *n* organization ← **selenggara**

penyelesaian *n* solution, settlement ← **selesai**

penyeléwéngan *n* affair, deviation ← **seléwéng**

penyelidik *n* investigator, detective; **penyelidikan** *n* investigation ← **selidik**

penyelundup *n* smuggler ← **selundup**

penyemaian *n* process of growing seedlings ← **semai**

penyemat *n* pin ← **semat**

penyembelih *n* butcher, slaughterer; **penyembelihan** *n* slaughter ← **sembelih**

penyembuhan *n* cure, healing ← **sembuh**

penyempitan *n* narrowing ← **sempit**

penyendiri *n* loner ← **diri**

penyengat *n* something which stings, stinging insect ← **sengat**

penyerahan *n* handing over, handover ← **serah**

penyerang *n* attacker; **penyerangan** *n* attack, aggression ← **serang**

penyerapan *n* absorption ← **serap**

penyerbuan *n* attack, charge, invasion ← **serbu**

penyergapan *n* ambush, capture ← **sergap**

penyesalan *n* repentance, remorse ← **sesal**

pényét *adj* flattened; *tempe* ~ thin, fried slices of tempe

penyetélan *n* tuning ← **setél**

penyetor *n* depositor ← **setor**

penyiar *n* announcer; **penyiaran** *n* broadcasting ← **siar**

penyidik *n* investigator, detective; **penyidikan** *n* investigation ← **sidik, selidik**

penyihir *n* wizard, witch, sorcerer ← **sihir**

penyiksaan *n* torturing, (process of) torture ← **siksa**

penyimpanan *n* storage ← **simpan**

penyimpangan *n* aberration, deviation ← **simpang**

penyinaran *n* radiation ← **sinar**

penyingkiran *n* exclusion, elimination ← **singkir**

penyisihan *n* elimination; *babak* ~ elimination round, qualifying round ← **sisih**

penyisiran *n* combing, checking ← **sisir**

penyitaan *n* confiscation, seizure ← **sita**

pényok, péyot, péot *adj* dented

penyu *n* turtle; *rumah* ~ (tortoise) shell

penyulap *n* magician, conjurer ← **sulap**

penyulingan *n* distillation ← **suling**

penyulih ~ *suara* dubber; **penyulihan** ~ *suara* dubbing ← **sulih**

penyuluh *n* scout; education worker; **penyuluhan** *n* education ← **suluh**

penyumbatan *n* blockage ← **sumbat**

penyunting *n* editor; **penyuntingan** *n* editing ← **sunting**

penyusun *n* compiler, author ← **susun**

penyusupan *n* infiltration ← **susup**

penyusuran *n* tracing ← **susur**

penyusutan *n* reduction; *fin* depreciation ← **susut**

péot → **péyot**

pepatah *n* proverb, saying ← **patah**

pepaya, papaya *n* paw-paw, papaya

peperangan *n* battle ← **perang**

pépés method of cooking by steaming or roasting in banana leaves; ~ *tahu* tofu steamed in banana leaves; *ikan* ~ steamed fish; **pépésan** *n* food cooked in this way; ~ *kosong* lie

pepet *n* shwa, unemphasized 'e' in Indonesian

pépét: mépét *sl* tight; *waktunya sudah* ~ time's running out; **kepépét** *adj, sl* in a fix, trapped; no time, rushed

Per. *abbrev Perusahaan* company

pér *n* spring

perabot *n* tools; ~ *dapur* kitchen utensils; ~ *rumah* furniture; **perabotan** *n* furnishings

peraba *alat* ~ (sense of) touch; feeler; *indera* ~ sense of touch perabuan *n* urn (for ashes) ← **abu**

peracunan *n* (deliberate) poisoning ← **racun**

perada → **prada**

peradaban *n* culture, civilization; ~ *Mesir kuno* ancient Egyptian civilization ← **adab**

peraga *n* visual aid; **memeragakan** *vt* to display, show; **peragawan** *n, m* male model; **peragawati** *n, f* model

perah *sapi* ~ dairy cow; something valuable to milk dry; endless source; **memerah** *vt* to milk or squeeze

perahu *n* (sail)boat; ~ *layar* sailing boat; *naik* ~ go on board; travel by boat

perairan *n* territorial waters; waterworks ← **air**

perai → **préi**

peraih *n* winner; one who achieves or receives something; ~ *medali perak langsung naik ke atas podium* the silver medalist stepped straight up onto the podium ← **raih**

perajin *n* craftsman, artisan; ~ *perak* silversmith ← **rajin**

pérak *n* silver; silver coin; *layar* ~ small screen; *medali* ~ silver medal; *perajin* ~ silversmith; *seratus* ~ *coll* one hundred rupiah

perakitan *n* assembly ← **rakit**

peralatan *n* equipment ← **alat**

peralihan *n* transition, change; *masa* ~ transition period ← **alih**

peramal *n* fortune-teller, clairvoyant ← **ramal**

perampasan *n* hold-up, robbery ← **rampas**

perampok *n* robber; **perampokan** *n* robbery ← **rampok**

peran *n* part, role; **berperan** *vi* to play a role or part; **memerankan** *vt* to portray, play the role of; **pemeran** *n* actor, actress

peranakan *n* uterus; *adj* of mixed Chinese and Indonesian blood, Straits Chinese; *masakan* ~ locally-influenced Chinese food ← **anak**

perancang *n* designer, planner; ~ *busana* fashion designer; **perancangan** *n* design, planning ← **rancang**

Perancis, Prancis *n* France; *bahasa* ~, *orang* ~ French; *(negeri)* ~ France

perang *n* war, warfare; ~ *Dingin* the Cold War; ~ *lidah*, ~ *mulut* war of words; ~ *gerilya* guerrilla war; ~ *Salib* the Crusades; ~ *saraf* war of nerves; ~ *saudara* civil war; ~ *Dunia Kedua* World War II; **perang-perangan** *n* war games; paintball; **berperang** *vi* to wage war, go to war; **memerangi** *vt* to fight against; **peperangan** *n* battle

pérang → **pirang**

perangah: **terperangah** *adj* open-mouthed, astonished

perangai *n* character, nature

perangkap *n* trap; **memerangkap** *vt* to trap, catch; **terperangkap** *adj* trapped, caught

perangkat *n* equipment, tool ← **angkat**

perangko, prangko *n* (postage) stamp; *mengumpulkan* ~ to collect stamps

perang-perangan *n* war games; paintball ← **perang**

perangsang *adj, n* stimulant; *obat* ~ aphrodisiac; **perangsangan** *n* stimulation; *fase* ~, *masa* ~ foreplay ← **rangsang**

peranjat: **terperanjat** *adj* startled, surprised

perantara *n* broker, intermediary, go-between ← **antara**

perantau *n* settler (in a foreign place); **perantauan** *n* abroad, in another place ← **rantau**

peranti, piranti *n* apparatus, equipment; ~ *lunak* software

perapatan → **prapatan**

perapian *n* fireplace, oven ← **api**

peras *jeruk* ~ orange (for juicing); **memeras** *vt* to squeeze, press; to blackmail, extort; **pemerasan** *n* blackmail, extortion

perasa *n* sensitive person; *alat* ~, *indera* ~ sense of taste; **perasaan** *n* feeling ← **rasa**

peraturan *n* rule, regulation ← **atur**

perawakan *n* stature, build, figure ← **awak**

perawan *n* virgin; **keperawanan** *n* virginity; **memerawani** *vt* to take someone's virginity, deflower

perawat *n* nurse, sister; **perawatan** treatment; maintenance, upkeep; *biaya* ~ cost of treatment, cost of upkeep ← **rawat**

perayaan *n* celebration ← **raya**

perbaikan *n* repair, improvement ← **baik**

perban *n* bandage, dressing; **diperban** *v* to be bandaged; **memerban** *vt* to bandage

Perbanas *n* private banking college in Jakarta ← **Perhimpunan Bank-Bank Nasional Swasta**

perbandingan *n* comparison, ratio ← **banding**

perbankan *adj* banking; *dunia* ~ the banking world ← **bank**

perbatasan *n* border, frontier ← **batas**

perbédaan *n* difference ← **béda**

perbelanjaan *n* expenditure, spending; *pusat* ~ shopping center, mall ← **belanja**

perbendaharaan *n* treasury; ~ *kata* vocabulary ← **bendahara**

perbincangan *n* discussion ← **bincang**

perboden, perboten → **verboten**

perbuatan *n* act, deed ← **buat**

perbudakan *n* slavery ← **budak**

perbukitan *n* (range of) hills ← **bukit**

perburuhan *n* concerning labor ← **buruh**

perca *n* rag, scrap; *getah* ~ gutta-percha

percakapan *n* conversation ← **cakap**

percaloan *praktek* ~ profiteering ← **calo**

percampuran *n* mixing, association ← **campur**

percaya trust, believe; ~ *akan* believe in; ~ *diri (PD)* self-confidence; **keper-cayaan** *n* belief, faith; *menurut* ~ *masing-masing* each according to their own religion; **dipercaya** *v* to be believed, trusted; **memercayai** *vt* to trust someone; **memercayakan** *vt* to entrust with; **terpercaya** *adj* trusted, reliable

percékcokan *n* quarrel, dispute ← **cékcok**

perceraian *n* divorce ← **cerai**

percétakan *n* printers, printing office; press ← **cétak**

percik *n* spot; **memerciki** *vt* to spatter something; **memercikkan** *vt* to splash with something

percobaan *n* experiment, test ← **coba**

percontohan *adj* experimental; model ← **contoh**

percuma in vain ← **cuma**

perdagangan *n* commerce, trade; ~ *bebas* free trade; ~ *perempuan* trade in women ← **dagang**

perdamaian *n* peace, reconciliation ← **damai**

perdana *adj* first, starter; ~ *Menteri* Prime Minister; *paket* ~ starter kit; *penerbangan* ~ inaugural flight

perdata *hukum* ~ civil law

perdebatan *n* debate, discussion ← **debat**

perdu *tanaman* ~ shrub, bush

perduli → **peduli**

peredam *n* device to muffle or reduce noise ← **redam**

peré → **préi**

perebutan *n* fight, struggle, grab ← **rebut**

peregangan *n* tightening, straining ← **regang**

perék *n, sl* slut ← **perempuan ékspérimén**

perekam *alat* ~ recording device ← **rekam**

perekat *n* glue, adhesive → **rekat**

perékonomian *n* economic affairs ← **ékonomi**

peréli *n* rally driver ← **réli**

peremajaan *n* renewal, revitalization ← **remaja**

perempat *n* quarter; *tiga* ~ three-quarters; **seperempat** *n* one quarter, 1/4; **perempatan** *n* **perapatan, prapatan** *coll* crossroads, intersection ← **empat**

perempuan *n* woman, female; ~ *jalan*, ~ *jalanan* street-walker; ~ *jalang* street walker; *anak* ~ daughter; *hak* ~ women's rights

perenang *n* swimmer ← **renang**

perencana *n* planner; **perencanaan** *n* planning ← **rencana**

peresmian *n* formal ceremony, inauguration ← **resmi**

peretas *n* tool used to break or split open ← **retas**

perétél → **prétél**

pérforasi *n* perforation, hole; **pérforator** *n* hole-punch

pergantian *n* change; ~ *tahun* new year ← **ganti**

pergaulan *n* mixing, social intercourse; association; ~ *bebas* promiscuity, permissiveness ← **gaul**

pergelangan ~ *kaki* ankle; ~ *tangan* wrist ← **gelang**

pergésékan *n* friction ← **gésék**

pergéséran *n* movement, shift ← **gésér**

pergi *vi* go (out), leave; ~ *jauh* travel far; ~ *lu* get lost; *pulang* ~ there and back, both ways; *sedang* ~, *lagi* ~ out, not here; ~ *ke kantor* go to work; **bepergian** *vi* to travel, be away; **kepergian** *n* departure

pergok: kepergok *adj, coll* **tepergok** *adj* caught in the act, caught red-handed; **memergoki** *vt* to catch sight of

pergolakan *n* disturbance, upheaval ← **golak**

pergulatan *n* wrestling, struggle, fight ← **gulat**

perguruan ~ *tinggi* university, institute of higher learning ← **guru**

perhatian *n* attention ← **hati**

perhélatan *n* celebration, feast ← **hélat**

perhentian *n* stop, stopping place ← **henti**

perhiasan *n* jewelery ← **hias**

perhimpunan *n* union, association, club; ~ *Mahasiswa Jambi* Jambi Students Assocation ← **himpun**

perhitungan *n* calculation ← **hitung**

perhotélan *n* hotel studies, hospitality ← **hotél**

perhubungan *n* communications, connection; ~ *udara* air route; *Menteri* ~ *(Menhub)* Minister of Communications ← **hubung**

peri- *pref* concerning; **perihal** *n* subject; *conj* about, concerning; **perikemanusiaan** *n* humanitarianism; **berperikemanusiaan** *adj* humane

peri *n* fairy; *ibu* ~ fairy godmother

peria → **paré**

periang *n* cheerful person ← **riang**

perias *n* make-up artist ← **rias**

peribahasa *n* proverb, idiom

perigi *n* well, spring

perih, pedih smart, sting

perihal *n* subject; *conj* about, concerning

perikanan *n* fisheries ← **ikan**

perikemanusiaan *adj* humanitarianism ← **kemanusiaan, manusia**

periklanan *n* advertising ← **iklan**

periksa investigate, check; *ruang* ~ consultation room; **memeriksa** *vt* to examine or investigate; ~ *ulang* to review; **pemeriksa** *n* examiner; **pemeriksaan** *n* examination, investigation

perilaku *n* behavior; **berperilaku** *vi* to behave, act

perimbangan *n* proportion ← **imbang**

perincian *n* details, detailed explanation ← **rinci**

perindustrian *n* industry, industrial affairs; *Departemen* ~ *dan Perdagangan (Depperindag)* Department of Industry and Trade ← **industri**

perintah order, command; *memberi* ~ to (give an) order or command; *menjalankan* ~ to carry out orders; **memerintah** *vt* to rule, govern, reign; **memerintahkan** *vt* to order or command something; **pemerintah** *n* government; **pemerintahan** *n* administration, government

perintis *n* pioneer ← **rintis**

période *n* period, time

perisai *n* shield

périskop *n* periscope

peristirahatan *n* place for rest or recreation; ~ *terakhir* final resting place, grave ← **istirahat**

peristiwa *n* incident, occurrence, happening

periuk *n* cooking pot

perjaka *n* bachelor, young single man

perjalanan *n* journey, trip; *biro* ~, *agen* ~ travel agency ← **jalan**

perjamuan *n* feast, party; entertainment; ~ *kudus Chr* holy communion; ~ *Suci* the Last Supper ← **jamu**

perjanjian *n* agreement, contract ← **janji**

perjodohan *n* marriage, match ← **jodoh**

perjuangan *n* battle, fight, struggle; *Partai Demokrasi Indonesia-~ (PDIP)* Indonesian Democratic Party of Struggle ← **juang**

perjudian *n* gambling ← **judi**

perkakas *n* tool, instrument; *~ dapur* kitchen utensils

perkampungan *n* settlement, cluster of villages ← **kampung**

perkantoran *n* office block ← **kantor**

perkapalan *n* shipping ← **kapal**

perkara *n* matter, case, affair; *habis ~* and that was the end of it, matter closed

perkasa *adj* powerful; manly, virile; *gagah ~* brave, strong

perkataan *n* phrase, words ← **kata**

perkawinan *n* marriage, wedding; *~ campuran* mixed marriage ← **kawin**

perkedél *n* (potato) patty, croquette; *~ jagung* corn patty

perkelahian *n* fight, scuffle ← **kelahi**

perkémahan *n* camping, camp; *tempat ~* camping ground, campsite ← **kémah**

perkembangan *n* development ← **kembang**

perkenalan *n* introduction ← **kenal**

perkici *burung ~* rainbow lorikeet

perkilangan *n* refinery ← **kilang**

perkiraan *n* estimate, guess ← **kira**

perkolator *n* (coffee) percolator

perkosa: memerkosa *vt* to rape, violate; **pemerkosa** *n* rapist; **pemerkosaan** *n* rape, raping; **perkosaan** *n* rape

perkotaan *n* metropolitan area ← **kota**

perkumpulan *n* association, club; assembly ← **kumpul**

perkusi *n* percussion

perkutut *burung ~* turtledove

perlahan, pelan, perlahan-lahan, pelan-pelan *adv* slowly, softly; **memerlahankan** *vt* to slow something down

perlak *adj* varnished; *n* varnish

perlakuan *n* treatment; act ← **laku**

perlambang *n* sign, omen ← **lambang**

perlawanan *n* opposition, resistance ← **lawan**

perlawatan *n* trip, visit ← **lawat**

perlengkapan *n* outfit, equipment ← **lengkap**

perlénté *adj* smartly dressed; *n* dandy

perlindungan *n* protection ← **lindung**

perlombaan *n* competition ← **lomba**

perlu need, necessary; **keperluan** *n* needs, requirements; *~ hidup* necessities of life; **memerlukan** *vt* to need, require; **seperlunya** *adv* as (much as) necessary

perlucutan *~ senjata* disarmament ← **lucut**

permadani *n* carpet

permai *adj* beautiful, lovely

permainan *n* game, match; **sepermainan** *teman ~* friend you play or hang out with (from childhood) ← **main**

permaisyuri, permaisuri *n* queen

permak, vermak alteration to clothes; **dipermak** *adj* altered, shortened

permandian *n* bathing pool; christening, baptism; *bapak ~* godfather ← **mandi**

permanén *adj* permanent

permata *n* jewel; *~ hijau* emerald

permén *n* sweet, lolly, candy; *~ karet* chewing gum, bubble gum

Permésta *n* 1950s secessionist movement in North Sumatra and Sulawesi ← **Perjuangan Seméstra**

permintaan *n* request; *atas ~* by request ← **minta**

perminyakan *n* oil and gas ← **minyak**

permisi excuse me; *~ dulu* excuse me, excuse yourself

permohonan *n* request, application ← **mohon**

permufakatan *n* discussion, deliberation ← **mufakat**

permukaan *n* surface; *~ air* water level; *di atas ~ laut* above sea level ← **muka**

permukiman *n* housing, residential area ← **mukim**

permulaan *n* beginning ← **mula**

permusuhan *n* enmity, animosity, hostility ← **musuh**

pernafasan, pernapasan *n* breathing, respiration; *~ buatan* artificial respiration; *sistem ~* respiratory system ← **nafas**

pernah *adv* ever; once; have + past perfect form of verb; *saya ~ ke Bali* I've been to Bali; *~ makan bebek?* Have you ever eaten duck?; *Tidak ~* Never

pernak: pernak-pernik *n* little things; small beads and trinkets

perniagaan *n* commerce, trade, business ← **niaga**

pernikahan *n* wedding; *pesta ~* wedding reception ← **nikah**

penilaian *n* evaluation ← **nilai**

pernis *n* varnish; **dipernis** *v* to be varnished

pernyataan *n* statement, declaration ← **nyata**

peroléhan *n* acquisition; *~ suara* (number of) votes ← **oléh**

perombakan *n* reorganization ← **rombak**

perompak *n* pirate; **perompakan** *n* piracy ← **rompak**

péron *n* platform; *karcis ~* platform ticket

perona *~ mata* eyeshadow; *~ pipi* rouge ← **rona**

perosok: memerosokkan *vt* to push something into; **terperosok** *adj* fallen, sunk, plunged

perosotan *n* (children's) slide ← **rosot**

perpaduan *n* blend, synthesis ← **padu**

perpeloncoan *n* practice of initiation ← **pelonco**

perpisahan *n* parting, farewell; *acara ~, pesta ~* farewell (party) ← **pisah**

Perprés *n* Presidential Regulation ← **Peraturan Présidén**

perpustakaan *n* library ← **pustaka**

pérs *n* press, media; *jumpa ~, konperensi ~* press conference

persada *n* group (of nations), center; platform

persahabatan *n* friendship; *pertandingan ~* friendly (match) ← **sahabat**

persaingan *n* competition; *~ ketat* intense competition ← **saing**

persalinan *n* childbirth ← **salin**

persamaan *n* similarity, likeness, resemblance; equation ← **sama**

persatuan *n* union, association ← **satu**

persaudaraan *n* brotherhood, fraternity; sisterhood; family ties ← **saudara**

persediaan *n* stock, supply ← **sedia**

persegi *adj* square; sided; *~ empat adj* square; *(empat) ~ panjang n* rectangle; *empat ~ n* square ← **segi**

persekolahan *n* schooling; *~ di rumah* home schooling ← **sekolah**

persekongkolan *n* plot, intrigue, conspiracy ← **sekongkol, kongkol**

persekot *n* downpayment

persekutuan *n* alliance, partnership ← **sekutu**

perselingkuhan *n* affair ← **selingkuh**

perselisihan *n* dispute, difference of opinion ← **selisih**

persemaian *n* nursery, bed ← **semai**

Persemakmuran *n* (British) Commonwealth ← **semakmur, makmur**

persembahan *n* offering; product or service ← **sembah**

persembunyian *n* hiding place, hideout; *dalam ~* in hiding ← **sembunyi**

persén *n* percent; *seratus ~* one hundred percent; **persénan** *n* tip; **perséntase, proséntase** *n* percentage

persendian *n* joints ← **sendi**

persengkétaan *n* dispute ← **sengkéta**

persenyawaan *n* chemical compound ← **senyawa**

perseorangan *adj* individual ← **seorang, orang**

persépsi *n* perception

perserikatan *n* federation; *~ Bangsa-Bangsa (PBB)* the United Nations (UN) ← **serikat**

perséro *adj* proprietary limited (Pty Ltd); **perséroan** *n* company; *~ terbatas* proprietary limited ← **séro**

persétan *ejac* go to hell! ← **sétan**

perseteruan *n* feud ← **seteru**

persetubuhan *n* sexual intercourse ← **setubuh, tubuh**

persetujuan *n* agreement, approval ← **setuju, tuju**

persiapan *n* preparations ← **siap**

persidangan *n* meeting, assembly; (extended) court session ← **sidang**

persik *(buah) ~* peach

persil *n* plot, block (of land)

persilangan *n* crossing ← **silang**

persimpangan *n* intersection ← **simpan**

persinggahan *n* stopover ← **singgah**

persis *adv* exactly; *~ ibunya* just like his mother

persnéling *n* gear(box); *~ tiga* third gear

persoalan *n* problem, issue, matter ← **soal**

personalia, personél *adj* personnel, staff

perspéktif *n* perspective

persyaratan *n* (set of) conditions ← **syarat**

pertahanan *n* defense; *~ sipil (hansip)* local security guard; civil defense; *Menteri ~* Minister for Defense ← **tahan**

pertalian *n* connection, relationship ← **tali**

pertama *adj* first; *hadiah ~* first prize; **pertama-tama** *adv* first of all

pertamanan *adj* parks and gardens; *dinas ~* parks service ← **taman**

pertambahan *n* increase ← **tambah**

pertambangan *n* mining; *Perusahaan ~ Minyak dan Gas Bumi Negara (Pertamina)* Pertamina, the former state-owned oil company ← **tambang**

Pertamina *n* state-run national oil and gas company ← **Perusahaan Pertambangan Minyak dan Gas Bumi Negara**

pertanda *n* sign, omen, indication ← **tanda**

pertandingan *n* contest, competition, match; *~ persahabatan* friendly (match) ← **tanding**

pertanggungan *n* insurance, responsibility ← **tanggung**

pertanian *n* agriculture; *sekolah ~* agricultural college ← **tani**

pertanyaan *n* question; *mengajukan ~* to ask a question ← **tanya**

pertapa *n* ascetic, hermit, recluse; **pertapaan** *n* hermitage, retreat ← **tapa**

pertemanan *n* friendship ← **teman**

pertempuran *n* battle ← **tempur**

pertemuan *n* meeting ← **temu**

pertengahan *n* middle; *Abad ~* the Middle Ages ← **tengah**

pertengkaran *n* quarrel ← **tengkar**

pertentangan *n* conflict ← **tentang**

pertiga *dua ~* two-thirds; **pertigaan** *n* T-junction ← **tiga**

pertikaian *n* quarrel, disagreement ← **tikai**

pertimbangan *n* consideration ← **timbang**

pertiwi *n* earth; *ibu ~* motherland, native country

pertokoan *n* shopping center or complex, mall ← **toko**

pertolongan *n* help, assistance, aid; *~ pertama* first aid ← **tolong**

pertukangan *n* repairs ← **tukang**

pertukaran *n* exchange; *~ pikiran* exchange of ideas or views ← **tukar**

pertumbuhan *n* growth, development ← **tumbuh**

pertunangan *n* engagement ← **tunang**

pertunjukan *n* show, performance ← **tunjuk**

Péru *n* Peru; *orang ~* Peruvian

perubahan *n* change, alteration ← **ubah**

perujukan *n* cross-reference ← **rujuk**

perumahan *n* housing (complex) ← **rumah**

perumahtanggaan *n* household affairs ← **rumah tangga**

Perumnas National Housing ← **Perumahan Nasional**

perumpamaan *n* parable, metaphor ← **umpama**

Perumtél *n, arch* telephone company (now Telkom) ← **Perusahaan Umum Télékomunikasi**

perumusan *n* formulation ← **rumus**

perundang-undangan *n* legislation ← **undang-undang, undang**

perundingan *n* discussion; *meja ~* discussion table ← **runding**

perunggu *n* bronze; *medali ~* bronze medal

peruntukan *n* allocation ← **untuk**

peruntungan *n* (good) fortune or luck ← **untung**

perupa *n* sculptor ← **rupa**

perusahaan *n* company; *~ patungan* joint venture; *~ penerbangan* airline ← **usaha**

perut *n* stomach, belly; ~ *bumi* bowels of the earth, deep underground; ~ *buncit* fat belly; pregnant; ~ *kembung*, ~ *gembung* bloated (belly); ~ *kapal* hold; *sakit* ~ stomach ache, upset stomach

perutusan *n* delegation ← **utus**

perwakilan *n* representation, delegation; *Dewan* ~ *Rakyat (DPR)* parliament, legislative assembly ← **wakil**

perwalian *n* guardianship, representation ← **wali**

perwira *n* officer; ~ *tinggi* general

pés *penyakit* ~ plague ← **sampar**

pesaing *n* competitor; *sekarang di pasar ponsel ada begitu banyak* ~ there are so many competitors in the mobile phone market nowadays ← **saing**

pesakitan *n* accused or convicted party, prisoner ← **sakit**

pesan message, instruction, order; ~ *terkirim* message sent; **pesanan** *n* order; *antar* ~ delivery; **berpesan** *vi* to leave a message; **memesan** *vt* to order; **pemesanan** *n* order, request

pesanggrahan *n* resting-place ← **sanggrah**

pesangon *n* severance pay ← **sangon**

pesantrén *n* Islamic boarding school → **santri**

pesat *adj* fast, rapid

pesawat *n* machine; extension; *coll* plane; ~ *amfibi* amphibious vehicle; ~ *baling-baling* propeller plane, turboprop; ~ *radio* radio; ~ *siluman* spy plane; ~ *telepon* telephone; ~ *televisi* television (set); ~ *tempur* fighter (plane); ~ *terbang*, ~ *udara* aeroplane, airplane; ~ *ulang-alik* shuttle; *nomornya 32676* ~ *108* her phone number is 32676, extension 108

pésék *adj* flat-nosed

peselancar *n* surfer ← **selancar, lancar**

pésér *n, arch* half-cent; **sepésér** *tidak ada* ~ *pun* to have not even a cent

peséro → **perséro**

peserta *n* participant ← **serta**

pesiar *n* trip, cruise; *kapal* ~ cruise ship, pleasure craft ← **siar**

pésimis *adj* pessimistic

pesindén *n, f* singer accompanying a *gamelan* orchestra ← **sindén**

pesinétron *n* actor or actress in a local TV comedy or drama ← **sinétron**

pesing *bau* ~ stink of urine

pesisir *n* coast; *batik* ~ batik from the north coast of Java

pesohor *n* famous person, celebrity ← **sohor**

pesona *n* magic; **memesona, memesonakan** *adj* enthralling, enchanting; **terpesona** *adj* enthralled, enchanted

pésta *n* party, celebration; ~ *perkawinan*, ~ *pernikahan* wedding reception; ~ *perpisahan* farewell party; ~ *pora* big, lavish party; **berpésta** *vi* to (have a) party; ~ *pora* to have a big, lavish party; **dipéstakan** *v* to be celebrated with a party

péstisida *n* pesticide

pesuling *n* flautist, flutist ← **suling**

pesuruh *n* messenger, errand boy; ~ *kantor* office boy ← **suruh**

pesut *n ikan* ~ freshwater dolphin, porpoise

pét *topi* ~ cap

peta *n* map, chart; ~ *buta* blank map (to be labelled); ~ *dunia* world map; *buku* ~ atlas; *buku* ~ *jalan* road atlas, street directory; **memetakan** *vt* to map; **pemetaan** *n* mapping

Péta *n* local paramilitary under the Japanese occupation ← **Pembéla Tanah Air**

petai → **peté**

petak *n* compartment, division; *rumah* ~ tenement, communal house

petang *adj, form* late afternoon to evening (from around 2.30 to sunset); *berita* ~ evening news

petani *n* farmer; ~ *cengkeh* clove farmer; ~ *plasma (pengembangan lahan dan sumber daya alam)* farmer who supplies a commodity to a factory ← **tani**

petas: petasan *n* firecracker, fireworks

peté, petai *n* stinkbean; *nasi goreng* ~ fried rice with stinkbeans

petémbak *n* (target) shooter (as athlete) ← **témbak**

peténis *n* tennis player ← **ténis**

peterjun ~ *payung* parachutist, sky diver ← **terjun**

peternak *n* (cattle) farmer; **peternakan** *n* cattle farm, ranch ← **ternak**

péterséli *n* parsley

peti *n* chest, case, box; ~ *jenazah*, ~ *mati*, ~ *mayat* coffin, casket; ~ *kemas* packing case, freight container; ~ *es* ice-box; **memetiéskan** *vt* to put on hold, put on the back burner

petik pluck; **petikan** *n* extract, quotation; **memetik** *vt* to pick; to strum; ~ *gitar* to play or strum the guitar; **pemetik** *n* picker; ~ *daun teh* tea-picker

petinggi n high-ranking official ← **tinggi**

petinju *n* boxer ← **tinju**

petir *n* thunder, lightning; *disambar* ~ to be struck by lightning

petis *n* sauce made from fermented fish; *tahu* ~ fried tofu in this spicy sauce

petisi *n* petition; ~ *Lima Puluh n* protest petition in the late 1970s against Suharto's rule

pétrokimia *adj* petrochemical

pétromaks *lampu* ~ kerosene lantern

Pétruk *n* clown figure in shadow-puppet plays

pétrus *n* mysterious killer (in the 1980s) ← **penémbak mistérius**

petuah *n* advice

petualang *n* adventurer; **petualangan** *n* adventure ← **tualang**

petunjuk *n* instruction, direction; *buku* ~ manual; *buku* ~ *jalan* street directory; *buku* ~ *telepon* telephone book ← **tunjuk**

pewaktu *n* timer ← **waktu**

pewangi *n* perfume (in washing detergent) ← **wangi**

pewarna *n* dye, stain; **pewarnaan** *n* dyeing, coloring ← **warna**

pewawancara *n* interviewer ← **wawancara**

pewayangan *n* the world of *wayang* ← **wayang**

péyék *n, sl* peanut crisp ← **rempéyék**

péyot, péot, pényok *adj* dented

peziarah *n* pilgrim ← **ziarah**

PGRI *abbrev Persatuan Guru Republik Indonesia* Indonesian Teachers' Association

phinisi → **pinisi**

PHK *abbrev, euph pemutusan hubungan kerja* unemployment

Pi → **Papi**

piagam *n* charter

piala *n* trophy, cup; ~ *bergilir* perpetual trophy; ~ *Sudirman* Sudirman Cup (badminton)

pialang *n* broker, intermediary

pianika *n* small keyboard operated by blowing into a tube

pianis *n* pianist; **piano** *n* piano

piara, pelihara: piaraan *hewan* ~ pet

piatu *n* motherless child; *rumah* ~ orphanage; *yatim* ~ orphan

piawai *adj* expert, skilled; **kepiawaian** *n* skill, expertise

pici → **péci**

picik *adj* narrow; berpikiran ~ *vi* to be narrow-minded

picis: picisan *adj* cheap; *novel* ~, *roman* ~ dime novel, cheap novel

picu *n* trigger; **memicu** *vt* to trigger, set off; **pemicu** *n* trigger

pidana *hukum* ~ criminal law; **terpidana** *n* the condemned

pidato *n* speech, address; ~ *pembukaan* opening speech; ~ *kenegaraan* state-of-the-nation speech; **berpidato** *vi* to make a speech, give an address

pigi → **pergi**

pigméntasi *n* pigmentation

pigura *n* picture frame; **memigura** *vt* to frame

pihak *n* party; side; ~ *ayah* paternal line, father's side; ~ *lawan* opponent; *di satu* ~ on the one side; *di lain* ~ on the other hand; **berpihak, memihak** *vi* to take sides; **sepihak** *adj* unilateral

pijak: pijakan *n* foothold, something to stand on; ~ *kaki* pedal; **berpijak** *vi* to stand on; **memijak** *vt* to tread or step on

pijar *lampu* ~ light bulb

pijat, pijit massage; *panti* ~ massage parlor; *tukang* ~ masseur, masseuse; **pijatan** *n* massage; **memijat** *vt* to massage pikap *n* pick-up, utility

pikat: memikat *adj* attractive, enticing; terpikat *adj* attracted, enchanted

pikét report for duty or be on stand-by outside work hours

pikir, fikir *v* to think; pikiran *n* thought, idea; ~ *kotor* dirty thought, dirty mind; berpikir *vi* to think; ~ *panjang* to think hard; ~ *positif* to think positive; berpikiran *vi* to have a thought; ~ *sempit* narrow-minded; dipikir *v* to be thought; kepikiran *v* considered, thought of, sprang to mind; memikirkan *vt* to think about; pemikir *n* thinker; pemikiran *n* thinking, consideration

piknik *n* picnic; berpiknik *vi* to have a picnic

pikolo *n* piccolo

pikuk *hiruk-~ n* clamor, confusion → hiruk

pikul *n, arch* old measurement of weight; memikul *vt* to bear, carry on the shoulder

pikun *adj* senile, dotty

pil *n* (contraceptive) pill, tablet

PIL *n, abbrev* lover, another man ← pria idaman lain

pilah: memilah *vt* to sort; *sampah basah harus dipilah dari sampah kering* you have to sort out the rubbish between organic and non-organic; pemilahan *n* sorting

pilar *n* pillar

pilek sniffle, have a cold or runny nose

pilem → film

pilih choose; ~ *kasih* take sides; *hak* ~ right to vote; *salah* ~ make the wrong choice; pilihan *n* choice, selection; *adj* select; memilih *vt* to choose or select; to elect or vote (for); pemilih *n* voter; pemilihan *n* election; ~ *umum (pemilu)* general election; terpilih *adj* elected; *n* elected party, winner of an election

Pilipina → Filipina

pilkada *n* local or regional election ← pemilihan kepala daérah

pilot *n* pilot

pilu moved; memilukan *adj* moving, touching

pimpin: pimpinan *n* leadership, guidance; administration; ~ *puncak* top-level management; memimpin *vt* to lead; pemimpin *n* leader; kepemimpinan *n* leadership (qualities); terpimpin *adj* led, guided; *Demokrasi* ~ Guided Democracy (under Sukarno)

pinak *anak* ~ descendants, children and grandchildren; beranak-pinak *vi* to have (many) descendants

pinang *n* areca nut; s*eperti* ~ *dibelah dua* like two peas in a pod; meminang *vt* to propose, ask for a girl's hand in marriage

pinatua *n, Chr* church elders

pincang *adj* crippled, lame; *kaki* ~ bad or gammy leg

pincut: kepincut *adj* enchanted, taken with; attracted or drawn to

pindah *v* move; change; ~ *agama* change religions; ~ *rumah* move (house); ~ *kewarganegaraan* change your nationality; pindahan *n* furniture etc to be moved; berpindah *vi* to move; memindahkan *vt* to move, transfer; pemindahan *n* transfer, shifting, removal

pindai: pemindai *n* scanner; pemindaian *n* scanning

pindakas *n* peanut butter → selai kacang

pindang *adj* salted, preserved; *ikan* ~ fish preserved by salting

pinggan *n* bowl, plate

pinggang *n* waist; *ikat* ~ belt

pinggir *n* edge, border; pinggiran *n* edges, outskirts; ~ *kota* city outskirts or limits; meminggir *vi* minggir *coll* to move to the side, pull over; meminggirkan *vt* to move to one side, cast aside; terpinggirkan *adj* cast aside, marginalized

pinggul *n* hip; berpinggul *vi* to have (a certain type of) hips; *adj* -hipped; ~ *besar* wide-hipped, big-hipped

pingit: pingitan *n* seclusion; dipingit *v* to be secluded, kept at home; memingit *vt* to seclude, keep at home

pingpong *n* table tennis, pingpong; dipingpong *v* to be sent here and there, messed about ← ténis méja

pingsan faint, collapse; unconscious; *jatuh* ~ faint (away)

pinguin *n* penguin

pinisepuh *n, Jav* elders, older family members

pinisi, phinisi *kapal* ~ Buginese cargo boat

pinjam borrow; **pinjaman** *n* loan; *kata* ~ borrowing, loanword; **meminjam** *vt* to borrow; **meminjami** *vt* to lend someone; **meminjamkan** *vt* to lend something; **peminjam** *n* borrower; *kartu* ~ borrowing card; **peminjaman** *n* lending, borrowing

pinsét *n* tweezers

pinta *n, arch* request; **minta, meminta** *v* to request, ask for; **minta-minta, meminta-minta** *vi* to beg, ask for money; **permintaan** *n* request; *atas* ~ by request

pintal: memintal *vt* to spin (thread); **pemintal** *n* spinning wheel; spinner

pintar *adj* **pinter** *coll* clever; **kepintaran** *n* cleverness

pintas *jalan* ~ short cut; **sepintas** ~ *lalu* at first glance

pinter → **pintar**

pintu *n* door, gate; ~ *air* sluice, floodgates, lock; ~ *belakang* back door, back entrance; ~ *darurat* emergency exit; ~ *depan* front door, front entrance; ~ *gerbang* main gate; ~ *geser* sliding door; ~ *keberangkatan* departure gate; ~ *keluar* exit; ~ *masuk* entrance; ~ *pagar* front gate; ~ *tol* tollbooth, tollgate; ~ *utama* main gate, main entrance; *mengetok* ~ *vi* to knock at/on the door

pinus *pohon* ~ (European) pine (tree)

pion *n* pawn (in chess)

pionir *n* pioneer

pipa *n* pipe, tube; ~ *karet* rubber tube; ~ *saluran* pipeline; **pemipaan** *n* piping, system of pipes; **pipanisasi** *n* replacement of tanker delivery by pipelines (in the oil industry)

pipi *n* cheek; *cium* ~ kiss on the cheek

pipih *adj* flat

pipis *v, child* wee, pee, go to the toilet

pipit *burung* ~ various types of small bird

piramida *n* pyramid; *berbentuk* ~ *vi* pyramid-shaped

pirang, pérang *adj, m* blond, *f* blonde, fair-haired

piranti, peranti *n* apparatus, equipment; ~ *lunak* software

piring *n* plate, dish; ~ *terbang* flying saucer; *mencuci* ~ *vi* to wash the dishes; *sabun cuci* ~ dishwashing liquid; *tari* ~ dance from West Sumatra performed with plates; **piringan** *n* plate-shaped object; ~ *hitam* record, LP

pirsa: pemirsa *n* television audience, viewer

piruk *hiruk-~ n* clamor, confusion → **hiruk**

pirus *n* turquoise

pisah *vi* separate, split; ~ *ranjang* separate (of a couple); **berpisah** *vi* to part, separate; **memisah** *vi* to separate; **memisahkan** *vt* to separate something; **pemisahan** *n* separation; **perpisahan** *n* parting, farewell; *acara* ~, *pesta* ~ farewell (party); **terpisah** *adj* separated

pisang *n* banana; ~ *ambon* large, green banana; ~ *batu* banana with seeds, used for *rujak*; ~ *goreng (pisgor)* fried banana; ~ *ledre* thinly sliced banana chips, a specialty of Malang; ~ *molen* kind of cake containing fried banana, a specialty of Bandung; ~ *raja* large, sweet banana; ~ *sale* dried banana chips

pisau *n* knife; ~ *bedah* scalpel; ~ *belati* dagger; ~ *cukur*, ~ *silet* razor; ~ *kertas* letter-opener

pisgor *n, sl* fried banana, banana fritter ← **pisang goréng**

pispot *n* chamber pot, potty

pistol *n* pistol

piston *n* piston

pita *n* ribbon; ~ *suara* vocal cords; *cacing* ~ tapeworm

pitam *n* fit; *naik* ~ get angry

pités *n* psychotest, psychological test, IQ test

piton *n (ular)* ~ python

piutang *n* credit ← **utang**

piyama *n* pyjamas, pajamas

Pjs. *abbrev Pejabat Sementara* acting official

PK *abbrev paardekracht* horsepower

PK *abbrev permanganat kalium* potassium permanganate (used for washing wounds)

PKB *abbrev Partai Kebangkitan Bangsa* Party of National Awakening

PKI *abbrev Partai Komunis Indonesia* Indonesian Communist Party

PKK *abbrev Pendidikan Kesejahteraan Keluarga* Family Welfare Education

PKL *pedagang kaki lima* itinerant food vendor

PKS *abbrev Partai Keadilan Sejahtera* Prosperous Justice Party

plafon *n* ceiling

plagiat *n* plagiarism; **plagiator** *n* someone who copies or commits plagiarism

plak *n* plaque (on teeth)

plakat *n* placard, poster

planét *n* planet

plang *n* board, signpost; plank; barrier

planolog *n* town planner; **planologi** *n* town planning

plasénta *n* placenta → **tembuni, ari-ari**

plasma *n* plasma; *TV* ~ plasma TV

plasma *petani* ~ farmer who supplies a commodity to a factory ← **pengembangan lahan dan sumber daya alam**

plastik *adj* plastic; *n* plastic bag, carrier bag

plat → **pelat**

platina *n* platinum

plaza *n* mall, (indoor) shopping center

plédoi, pléidoi *n* (legal) defense

pléno *adj* plenary; *sidang* ~ plenary session, full session

pléster *n* sticking plaster, bandaid

pléster *n* plaster, stucco

plin-plan, plintat-plintut *adj* swaying this way and that, bend with the wind

PLN *abbrev Perusahaan Listrik Negara* State Electricity Corporation

plonco, pelonco *n* new student or freshman awaiting initiation; **diplonco** *v* to undergo an initiation at school or university; **perpeloncoan** *n* practice of initiation

plong *adj* relieved

plontos *adj* (completely) bald, shaven-headed

PLTA *abbrev Pembangkit Listrik Tenaga Air* hydro-electric power station

PLTPB *abbrev Pembangkit Listrik Tenaga Panas Bumi* geothermal power station

PLTN *abbrev Pembangkit Listrik Tenaga Nuklir* nuclear power station

PLTU *abbrev Pembangkit Listrik Tenaga Uap* steam power station

pluit → **peluit**

pluralis *adj* pluralist; **pluralisme** *n* pluralism, plurality

plus *adj* plus, added; *berkacamata* ~ *vi* to be long-sighted; *nilai* ~ added bonus

Pluto *n* Pluto

PM *abbrev Perdana Menteri* Prime Minister

PMA *abbrev Penanaman Modal Asing* foreign investment

PMI *abbrev Palang Merah Indonesia* Indonesian Red Cross

PMS *abbrev penyakit menular seksual* STD, sexually transmitted disease

PN *abbrev Perusahaan Negara* state corporation

PNG *abbrev Papua Nugini* Papua New Guinea

PNI *abbrev Partai Nasional Indonesia* Indonesian National Party

PNS *abbrev Pegawai Negeri Sipil* civil servant

poci *n* teapot; *teh* ~ tea made in an earthenware pot, a specialty of the Tegal area

poco: poco-poco *n* line dance from North Sulawesi

pocong *n* ghost (wrapped in a shroud); *sumpah* ~ oath taken while wrapped in a shroud

poco-poco *n* line dance from North Sulawesi

podéng *es* ~ a kind of ice-cream snack ← **puding**

pohon *n* tree; ~ *beringin* banyan (tree); *coll* Golkar; ~ *cendana* sandalwood tree; ~ *cemara*, ~ *eru* casuarina (tree); ~ *enau* sugar palm; ~ *flamboyan* flame tree; ~ *jati* teak; ~ *kalpataru* Tree of

Life; ~ *kelapa* coconut palm; ~ *kina*
cinchona tree; ~ *kurma* date palm; ~
langsat tree with yellow fruit; ~ *natal*,
~ *Terang* Christmas tree; ~ *nipah* kind
of palm; ~ *pinus* (European) pine
(tree); ~ *waru* kind of hibiscus tree
pohon → **mohon**
poin *n* point, mark
pojok *n* corner; **pojokan** *n, sl* corner;
memojokkan *vt* to force into a corner;
terpojok, terpojokkan *adj* forced into
a corner
pokok main; ~*nya* basically, the main
thing is; ~ *kalimat* subject of a sentence;
~ *pembicaraan* discussion topic; *gaji* ~
base salary
pokrol *n* lawyer
pol *adj, coll* full; *bis ke Semarang sudah*
~ the bus to Semarang is already full
pola *n* pattern; ~ *baju* sewing pattern;
berpola *vi* to have a pattern; *adj* patterned
polan *si* ~ so-and-so, whatshisname,
whatshername
Polandia *n* Poland; *bahasa* ~ Polish;
orang ~ Pole *pl* Polish
polantas *n* traffic police ← **polisi lalu
lintas**
polarisasi *n* polarization
polaritas *n* polarity
Polda *n* Regional Police; ~ *Metro Jaya*
Jakarta Metropolitan Police station ←
Polisi Daérah
polémik *n* debate, polemic; **berpolémik**
vi to debate, argue over
polés polish; **memolés** *vt* to polish
poligami *n* polygamy
poliklinik *n* **poli** *coll* polyclinic, doctor's
surgery; ~ *gigi* dentist's surgery; ~
umum GP's surgery, doctor's surgery
Polinésia *n* Polynesia; *orang* ~ Polynesian; ~ *Perancis* French Polynesia
polip *n* polyp
polis *n* (insurance) policy
polisi *n* police; ~ *Daérah (Polda)*
Regional Police; ~ *militer* military police; ~ *pariwisata* tourist police (esp in
Bali); ~ *sektor (polsek)* local police
station; ~ *tidur* speed hump; ~ *wanita
(polwan)* policewoman; *kantor* ~ police

station; ~ *lalu lintas (polantas)* traffic
police; ~ *Republik Indonesia (Polri)*
Indonesian police force
politik *n* politics; ~ *dagang sapi* horse-
trading, wheeling and dealing; **berpolitik** *vi* to play politics; **politikus** *n*
politisi politician; **politis** *adj* political
polo *n* polo; ~ *air* water polo
polong *kacang* ~ (green) pea
polos *adj* plain, unpretentious; smooth;
baju ~ plain shirt; **kepolosan** *n* simplicity, straight-forwardness, lack of
pretension
Polri *n* Indonesian police force; *Mabes*
~ Indonesian federal police headquarters ← **Polisi Republik Indonésia**
polsék *n* local police station ← **polisi
séktor**
polusi *n* pollution; ~ *udara* air pollution;
polutan *n* pollutant
polwan *n* policewoman ← **polisi wanita**
pom ~ *bensin* petrol station, gasoline
pump, service station → **pompa**
pompa pump; ~ *angin* air pump; ~
bensin petrol station, gasoline pump,
service station; *rumah* ~ pumping
house; **memompa** *vt* to pump; **pemompaan** *n* pumping
PON *n* National Sports Week, national
championships ← **Pekan Olahraga
Nasional**
Pon *n* third day of the Javanese week
pon *n* pound; ~ *sterling* pound sterling
ponakan *n, sl* nephew, niece
ponco *n* poncho, cloak
pondok *n* hut, cottage; ~ *pesantren
(ponpes)* Islamic boarding school;
mondok *vi, coll* to board, lodge, stay
pong *tahu* ~ tofu eaten with spicy sauce
pongah *adj* arrogant; **kepongahan** *n*
arrogance
poni *n* fringe, bangs; **berponi** *vi* to have
a fringe or bangs
ponok → **punuk**
ponpés *n* Islamic boarding school ←
pondok pesantrén
ponsél *n* mobile phone ← **télépon
sélulér**
pontang: pontang-panting *adv* helter-
skelter

ponten *n, arch* points, marks

pop *n* pop (music); ~ *Bali* Balinese pop (music)

popok *n* napkin, diaper; **mengganti** ~ to change a nappy; *ruam* ~ nappy rash

popularitas *n* popularity; **populér** *adj* popular; **memopulérkan, mempopulérkan** *vt* to popularize, make popular

porak-poranda *n* in a mess; **memorak-porandakan** *vt* to cause chaos, turn upside-down

pori *n* pore; **berpori** *adj* porous; *vi* to have pores; *kulit* ~ *besar* skin with large pores

porno *adj* pornographic; *film* ~ porn(ographic) film; **pornoaksi** *n* pornographic actions; **pornografi** *n* pornography

poros *n* axis; ~ *bumi* the Earth's axis; ~ *Setan* the Axis of Evil; ~ *Tengah* coalition of Muslim parties in late 1990s

porselén *n* porcelain

porsi *n* serve, portion; ~ *besar* large serve

portal *n* iron gateway into a building complex; barrier blocking access into a complex; **diportal** *v* to be blocked by a barrier, have a barrier lowered

porto *n* cost of freight or postage; *bebas* ~ freepost

Portugal, Portugis *n* Portugal; *bahasa* ~, *orang* ~ Portuguese

pos *n* post, checkpoint; ~ *koordinasi (posko)* post (for a political party or fund-raising effort); ~ *penjagaan*, ~ *satpam* security post; ~ *polisi* police post; ~ *keamanan lingkungan (poskamling)* neighborhood security post; ~ *pelayanan terpadu (posyandu)* all-in-one government administrative office

pos *n* post; ~ *kilat* express mail; ~ *restan* post to be kept at a post office for collection by the addressee, *poste réstante*; ~ *udara* airmail; ~ *wesel* postal money order; *cap* ~ postmark; *kantor* ~ post office; *Pak* ~, *tukang* ~ postman; **memposkan** *vt* to post (on

the internet); **mengeposkan** *vt* to post (an item through the post)

pose *n* pose (for a photograph); **berpose** *vi* to pose for a photograph

posisi *n* position; **berposisi** *vi* to hold a position, be positioned; **memosisikan** *vt* to position (something); *dia* ~ *diri sebagai pemimpin daerah* he maneuvered himself into the position as a regional leader

positif *adj* positive; *berpikir* ~ *vi* to think positive

poskamling *n* neighborhood security post ← **pos keamanan lingkungan**

posko *n* post (for a political party or fund-raising effort) ← **pos koordinasi**

poswésél *n* (postal) money order

posyandu *n* all-in-one government administrative office ← **pos pelayanan terpadu**

pot *n* pot, vase; ~ *bunga* vase (indoors), flowerpot (outdoors)

potéhi *n* Chinese puppets, similar to *wayang golek*

poténsi *n* potential; **berpoténsi** *vi* to have potential → **kemampuan**

potong piece, cut; ~ *kambing* slaughter a goat; ~ *kuku* cut your nails; ~ *rambut* cut your hair, get your hair cut; hairdresser, barber (for men); **potongan** *n* discount, reduction; cut (of clothes); **berpotongan** *adj* of a certain style or cut; **memotong** *vt* to cut, deduct; to slaughter, amputate; to interrupt; **pemotongan** *n* act of cutting; slaughter; **terpotong** *adj* cut (off)

potrét *n* portrait; photograph of a person; *tukang* ~ photographer; **memotrét** *vt* to photograph; **pemotrétan** *n* photo session

PP *abbrev pulang pergi* there and back, shown on public transport, to indicate that the vehicle also returns from its destination

PPLH *abbrev Pembinaan dan Pelestarian Lingkungan Hidup* Cultivation and Preservation of the Environment

PPn *abbrev Pajak Penjualan* sales tax at restaurants and hotels

PPP (P3) *abbrev Partai Persatuan*

Pembangunan United Development Party, a Muslim party

PR *abbrev pekerjaan rumah* homework

pra- *pref* pre-, before; **pradini** *adj* premature; **praduga** *n* presumption; ~ *tidak bersalah* presumption of innocence; **prakarsa** *n* initiative; *mengambil* ~, **memprakarsai** *vt* to take the initiative; **pemrakarsa** *n* someone who takes the initiative, innovator; **prakarya** *n* handicraft, vocational subject; **prakata** *n* foreword, preface; **prakiraan** *n* forecast; ~ *cuaca* weather forecast; **pranikah** *adj* premarital; *perjanjian* ~ premarital agreement; **praperadilan** *adj* pre-trial; **prasangka** *n* prejudice; **berprasangka** *vi* to be prejudiced; **prasarana** *n* infrastructure; **prasasti** *n* inscription, memorial plaque; **prasejahtera** *adj* underprivileged; **prasejarah** *adj* prehistoric; *n* ancient history

prada, perada *n* coating, leaf; ~ *emas* gold-leaf

pradini *adj* premature; *kelahiran* ~ premature birth

praduga *n* presumption; ~ *tidak bersalah* presumption of innocence

Praha *n* Prague

prahoto *n* truck, lorry

praja *n* student of Academy of Public Administration (APDN); *pamong* ~ civil service; ~ *Muda Karana (Pramuka)* Scouts

prajurit *n* soldier

prakarsa *n* initiative; *mengambil* ~, **memprakarsai** *vt* to take the initiative; **pemrakarsa** *n* someone who takes the initiative, innovator

prakarya *n* handicraft, vocational subject

prakata *n* foreword, preface ← **kata**

prakiraan *n* forecast; ~ *cuaca* weather forecast ← **kira**

prakték, praktik *n* practice; practical; ~ *umum* general practitioner's; **mempraktékkan** *vt* to put into practice

praktikum *n* practical work

praktis *adj* practical; *~nya* in practice; **kepraktisan** *n* practicality; **praktisi** *n* practitioner

pramu- *pref* used in compounds denoting service providers; **pramugara** *n, m* steward; cabin crew; **pramugari** *n, f* stewardess, air hostess; cabin crew; **pramuniaga** *n* salesperson, sales clerk; **pramuria** *n* hostess, host; **pramuwisata** *n* tourist guide

Pramuka *n* Scouts; **kepramukaan** *adj* scouting → **Praja Muda Karana**

pramuniaga *n* salesperson, sales clerk

pramuria *n* hostess, host

pramuwisata *n* tourist guide

prana *n* life force

Prancis → **Perancis**

prangko → **perangko**

pranikah *adj* premarital; *perjanjian* ~ premarital agreement

prapatan, perapatan *n, coll* crossroads, intersection ← **perempatan**

praperadilan *adj* pre-trial

prasangka *n* prejudice; **berprasangka** *vi* to be prejudiced ← **sangka**

prasarana *n* infrastructure ← **sarana**

prasasti *n* inscription, memorial plaque

prasejahtera *adj* underprivileged

prasejarah *adj* prehistoric; *n* ancient history ← **sejarah**

prasmanan *adj* buffet-style

PRD *abbrev Partai Rakyat Demokratik* Democratic People's Party

prédikat *dengan* ~ with the title or designation; **berprédikat** *adj* with the title of; *vi* to have the title of

préféktur *n* prefecture (in Japan)

préi, peréi, perai *coll* free, holiday, off work

préman *n* thug

prématur *adj* premature

prémi *n* (insurance) premium

présdir *n* president-director ← **présidén diréktur**

présedén *n* precedent; ~ *buruk* (bad) precedent

préséntasi *n* (oral) presentation

présiden *n* president; ~ *direktur* (presdir) president-director; *wakil* ~ *(wapres)* vice-president; **keprésidénan** *adj* presidential

préstasi *n* performance, achievement; **berpréstasi** *adj* prestigious; successful prétél: diprétéli *v* to be dismantled, taken apart or off

préténsi *n* pretense; **berpréténsi** *vi* to be pretentious, give the impression of

pri → **pribumi**

pria *n* male, man; ~ *beristeri* married man; *pengantin* ~ (bride)groom; ~ *idaman lain (PIL)* lover, another man

pribadi *n* self, individual, personality; *saya* ~ personally; *secara* ~ privately; **kepribadian** *n* personality

pribahasa → **peribahasa**

pribumi *n* **pri** *coll* native inhabitant, indigenous Indonesian; **non-pri** *coll* ethnic Chinese

prihatin concerned, worried; **keprihatinan** *n* concern; **memprihatinkan** *adj* worrying

prima *adj* outstanding, first-rate

primadona *n* primadonna

primata *hewan* ~ primate

primbon *n* kind of Javanese almanac or handbook

primitif *adj* primitive

prinsip *n* principle; **berprinsip** *vi* to have principles; *adj* principled

prioritas *n* priority; ~ *tinggi* high priority; **memprioritaskan** *vt* to prioritize

prisma *n* prism

prit sound of a whistle

privat *les* ~ private tutoring or lesson

priyayi *n* upper class, esp in colonial era

pro- *pref* pro-; *kubu* ~-*Soeharto akhirnya menyerah pada tahun 1998* the Suharto supporters finally gave up in 1998

problém, problim *n* problem

prodéo *n* without paying court costs, free

produk *n* product → **buatan; produksi** *n* production; *rumah* ~ production house; **berproduksi** *vi* to be in production; **memproduksi** *vt* to produce; **produsén** *n* producer

profési *n* profession; **berprofési** *vi* to have a profession, work as; **profésional** *adj* professional

profésor *n* professor → **guru besar**

profil *n* profile, outline

program *n* program, programme; ~

komputer computer program; ~ *studi* study program, course of study

prokém *bahasa* ~ Jakarta teen slang

proklamasi *n* proclamation (of independence); **memproklamasikan** *vt* to proclaim (independence); **proklamator** *n* proclaimer (of independence)

prolog *n* prolog, prologue

promosi *n* promotion; **mempromosikan** *vt* to promote

propaganda *n* propaganda

properti *n* property, real estate

propinsi *n* **Prop.** *abbrev* province; ~ *Sumatera Selatan* Province of South Sumatra; *antar* ~ interprovincial

proporsi *n* proportion; **proporsional** *adj* proportional, reasonable

prosa *n* prose

prosédur *n* procedure; **prosédural** *adj* procedural

proséntase → **persén, perséntase**

prosés *n* process; court case; **memprosés** *vt* to process; **pemrosésan** *n* processing

prospék *n* prospect, chance

prostat *n (kelenjar)* ~ prostate (gland)

protés protest; **memprotés** *vt* to (make a) protest

Protéstan *n* Protestant → **Kristen**

protokol *jalan* ~ main street (passed through by official visitors)

provinsi → **propinsi**

provokasi *n* provocation; **provokator** *n* trouble-maker, provocateur

provost *n* military police

proyék *n* project, scheme

proyéksi *n* projection; **memproyéksikan** *vt* to project

PRRI/Permesta *abbrev Pemerintah Revolusioner Republik Indonesia/ Perjuangan Semesta* Revolutionary Government of the Republic of Indonesia/Total Struggle, a secessionist movement in Sumatra and Sulawesi in the 1950s

PRT *abbrev pembantu rumah tangga* household servant

Ps. *abbrev pasar* market

psikiater [sikiater] *n* psychiatrist → **jiwa**

psikis *adj* [sikis] psychological

psikolog [sikolog] *n* psychologist;
psikologi *n* psychology → **jiwa**
psikotés [sikotés], **pités** *n* psychotest,
psychological test, IQ test
psikotropika [sikotropika] *obat* ~ drugs,
medicine (esp when abused)
Pt. *abbrev, tit, Chr Pendeta* Rev., minister, clergyman, vicar
PT *abbrev Perseroan Terbatas* Pty Ltd
PT KAI *abbrev PT Kereta Api Indonesia*
Indonesian Railways Pty Ltd, formerly
known as *Perumka (Perusahaan
Umum Kereta Api)*
PTM *abbrev Pola Transportasi Makro*
Mass Transportation Plan
PU *abbrev Pekerjaan Umum* Public Works
pualam *n* marble; *batu* ~ marble
puas *adj* satisfied, content; **kepuasan** *n*
satisfaction; **memuaskan** *adj* satisfactory; **sepuasnya** *adv* to your heart's
content
puasa fast; ~ *lohor,* ~ *setengah hari*
fast until the midday prayer; ~ *nasi*
give up eating rice; *buka* ~ break the
fast, breaking of the fast; *bulan* ~ fasting month, Ramadan; *membatalkan* ~
vt to break your fast (intentionally); ~
Senin Kamis fast on Mondays and
Thursdays; **berpuasa** *vi* to fast
puber *n* puberty; *masa* ~ puberty
pucat *adj* pale; *adj, coll* scared; ~ *pasi*
deathly pale
pucuk *n* shoot, sprout; counter for guns
and letters; **sepucuk** ~ *surat* a letter
pudar faded, washed-out; **memudar** *vi*
to fade
pudel *anjing* ~ poodle
puder *n* powder
puding *n* pudding, dessert
Puerto Rico *n* Puerto Rico; *orang* ~
Puerto Rican
pugar: memugar *vt* to restore, renovate;
pemugaran *n* restoration, renovation
puing *n* ruins; rubble; *terima* ~ *bangunan*
we take building rubble
puisi *n* poetry (esp Western); **puitis** *adj*
poetic
puja worship; **pujaan** *n* something wor-
shipped or idolized; **memuja** *vt* to
worship; **pemuja** *n* worshipper, fan

Pujakesuma Sumatran-born Javanese
← **putra Jawa kelahiran Sumatera**
pujangga *n, lit* poet; ~ *Baru* Malay-
language literary group formed in the
1930s
pujaséra *n* food court, collection of
food stalls ← **pusat jajan serba rasa**
puji praise; ~ *syukur,* ~ *Tuhan Chr*
thank God, Praise the Lord; **pujian** *n*
praise; **memuji** *vt* to praise; **memuji-
muji** *vt* to praise excessively; **terpuji**
adj highly-praised
pukau: memukau *vt* to fascinate; to
drug; **terpukau** *adj* fascinated, engrossed; drugged
pukul strike; *form* hour; ~ *tiga belas* 1
pm; ~ *rata* in general; **pukul-
memukul, berpukul-pukulan** *vi* to hit
each other; **pukulan** *n* strike, beat, hit;
memukul *vt* to hit, beat, strike;
memukuli *vt* to hit repeatedly, batter;
pemukul *n* beater, something used for
hitting; **terpukul** *adj* hit, hard-hit
pul *n* (vehicle) pool
pula *adv* also, too; again; *lagi*~ moreover
pulang *vi* to go home, return; ~ *hari* to
return on the same day, not stay overnight; ~ *kampung* to go home to the
village; ~ *pergi (PP)* there and back,
both ways; ~ *ke rahmat Allah,* ~ *ke
rahmatullah Isl* to die, **berpulang** *vi*
to pass away, die; **memulangkan** *vt*
to give back; to send back, repatriate;
pemulangan *n* return, repatriation;
sepulang *adv* upon arriving home, as
soon as one gets home
pulas *tidur* ~ sleep soundly, sound
asleep
pulau *n* island; ~ *Aspal* Buton; ~
Dewata Bali, Island of the Gods; ~
karang coral island, atoll; ~ *Paskah*
Easter Island; ~ *Seribu* the Thousand
Islands; *antar* ~ between islands, inter-
island; **kepulauan** *n* archipelago,
chain; ~ *Maladewa* the Maldives
pulen *nasi* ~ delicious, well-cooked rice
pulih recovered; **memulihkan** *vt* to restore; **pemulihan** *n* recovery, restoration; ~ *nama baik* rehabilitation
pulpén *n* fountain pen

pulsa *n* unit of credit (for a mobile or cell phone); *hemat* ~ cheap rates

puluh *dua* ~ twenty; *tiga* ~ thirty; *empat* ~ forty; *lima* ~ fifty; **puluhan** *n* dozens; *tahun delapan* ~ the eighties; **sepuluh** *n* ten

pulung: memulung *vt* to scavenge; **pemulung** *n* scavenger

pun emphasizing particle; too, also; even; then

punah *adj* extinct; **kepunahan** *n* extinction

punai *burung* ~ kind of green pigeon

puncak *n* peak, summit, top; ~ *gunung* mountain-top, summit; ~ *kenikmatan* orgasm; ~ *popularitas* peak of popularity; *pimpinan* ~ top-level management; ~ *gunung es* tip of the iceberg; **memuncak** *vi* to culminate, reach a peak

pundak *n* shoulder

pundi *n* piggybank, purse; ~ *amal* charitable fund

punggung *n* back; *tulang* ~ spine; **memunggungi** *vt* to turn your back on

pungkas → **pamungkas**

pungli *n* unofficial charge ← **pungutan liar**

pungut pick up; *anak* ~ adopted child; **pungutan** *n* amount collected, levy; ~ *liar (pungli)* unofficial charge; **memungut** *vt* to pick up, collect; **pemungut** *n* collector; **pemungutan** *n* collection; ~ *suara* vote

puntung ~ *rokok* cigarette butt

punuk, ponok *n* hump (of a camel)

punya have, own; ~ *hajat* hold a feast; *yang* ~ the owner; *orang tidak* ~ the poor, the have-nots; **kepunyaan** *n* possession, belonging; **mempunyai** *vt* to have, own, possess

pup *sl* poo, poop, empty the bowels

pupu: sepupu *n* cousin; *saudara* ~ cousin

pupuk *n* fertilizer; ~ *kandang* manure, dung; ~ *urea* kind of fertilizer

pupus wiped out, disappeared; **memupuskan** *v* to wipe out, destroy

pura *n* Balinese or Hindu temple

pura-pura pretend; **berpura-pura** *vi* to pretend, fake

purba *adj* ancient; *zaman* ~ ancient times; **purbakala** *n* ancient times: *ahli* ~ archeologist

puré purée, mash; *kentang* ~ mashed potatoes

puri *n* palace, castle

purna- *pref* post-, after; **purnabakti** *adj* retirement; **purnajual** *adj* post-sales; **purnawirawan** *n* retired soldier

purnama *bulan* ~ full moon

purnawirawan *n* retired soldier

puruk: terpuruk *adj* hidden, buried, sunk; **keterpurukan** *n* depression, abyss

pus *n, coll* pussycat; **pus-pus-pus** puss-puss-puss, used to call a cat

pusaka *n* heirloom, inheritance

pusar *n* navel, belly button; ~ *kepala* crown; *tali* ~ umbilical cord; **pusaran** *n* vortex; ~ *air* eddy, whirlpool; ~ *angin* whirlwind; **berpusar** *vi* to revolve, whirl

pusara *n* grave; graveyard, cemetery

pusat *n* center; ~ *berat* center of gravity; ~ *kebudayaan* cultural center; ~ *kebugaran* fitness center; ~ *kota* downtown, city center; ~ *perbelanjaan* shopping center, mall; ~ *perhatian* center of attention; *Jakarta* ~ *(Jakpus)* Central Jakarta; *kantor* ~ head office; *pemerintah* ~ central government, national government; ~ *Kesehatan Masyarakat (Puskesmas)* clinic, public health center; **berpusat** *vi* ~ *pada* to focus or center on; **memusatkan** *vt* to focus; ~ *perhatian* to concentrate; **pemusatan** *n* focus, concentration

pusing *adj* dizzy; ~ *kepala* headache; ~ *tujuh keliling* completely confused; **memusingkan** ~ *kepala* puzzling

puskésmas *n* clinic, public health center ← **pusat keséhatan masyarakat**

puso *adj* dried up (of rice fields)

puspa *n, lit* flower

pustaka *n, lit* book; *daftar* ~ list of references; **kepustakaan** *n* bibliography, list of references; literature; **perpustakaan** *n* library; ~ *keliling* mobile library; **pustakawan** *n* librarian

putar turn around, rotate; **putaran** *n*

round, revolution; ~ *kedua* Wimbledon second round of Wimbledon; **berputar** *vi* to rotate, turn; ~ *balik* to turn around, do a U-turn; **memutar** *vt* to wind; to rotate; **memutar-balikkan** *vt* to reverse, distort; **memutari** *vt* to go around, orbit; **pemutaran** *n* screening; ~ *perdana* premiere, opening night (of a film); **perputaran** rotation; **seputar** *adj* around, about

puter *es* ~ homemade ice cream in a cup

putera → **putra**

puteri → **putri**

putih *adj* white; ~ *bersih* clean and white, spotless; ~ *telur* albumen, egg white; *air* ~ drinking water; *merah* ~ red and white; *orang kulit* ~ white person, Westerner; **keputihan** *n* thrush, vaginal itching (white discharge); **memutih** *vi* to fade, become white; **memutihkan** *vt* to whiten, bleach; **mutih** *vi, coll* to only eat white rice, as a form of fasting; **pemutih** *n* bleach; **seputih** *adv* as white as; ~ *kapas lit* as white as cotton, snow-white

puting *n* nipple; ~ *susu* nipple; *(angin)* ~ *beliung* whirlwind, willy-willy

putra, putera *n, pol* son; ~ *mahkota* crown prince; ~*putri* children, sons and daughters; *bumi*~ native or indigenous inhabitant

putri, puteri *n, pol* daughter; ~ *duyung* mermaid; ~ *Indonesia* Miss Indonesia; ~ *malu* a kind of shrub; ~ *salju* kind of biscuit with white icing sugar

putu *kue* ~ steamed pandan cake eaten with coconut and palm sugar

putus broken off; ~ *asa* give up hope; ~ *kuliah* leave or drop out of university or college (prematurely); ~ *sekolah* leave or drop out of school (prematurely); **putusan** *n* judgment, verdict; **keputusan** *n* decision, decree; **memutus** *vt* to break; ~ *hubungan* to break or sever contact; **memutuskan** *vt* to terminate or break; to decide; **pemutusan** *n* termination, breaking-off; ~ *hubungan kerja (PHK)* to lose your job; **terputus** *adj* cut off; **terputus-putus** *vi* to keep cutting out

puyeng *adj* dizzy, confused; with a headache

puyer *n* medicinal powder

puyuh *angin* ~ whirlwind

puyuh *burung* ~ quail; *telur* ~ quail egg

puyung hai → **fuyung hai**

Q

q [ki] q, 17th letter of the alphabet

qari, qori *n, m* **qariah, qoriah** *n, f* reciter of the Koran

Qatar *n* Qatar; *orang* ~ Qatari

qoriah *n, f* reciter of the Koran

QS *abbrev Quran Suci* Holy Koran

Quran *al-*~ the Koran

R

r [ér] r, 18th letter of the alphabet

R. *Radén* Javanese title for male nobility; ~ *Mas (RM)* Javanese title for minor male nobility

RA, RAj *abbrev Radén Ajeng* Javanese title for unmarried female nobility

RA, RAy *abbrev Radén Ayu* Javanese title for married female nobility

raba: rabaan *n* caress, stroke; **meraba** *vt* to feel or grope something; **meraba-raba** *vi* to feel around or grope (in the dark); **peraba** *alat* ~ (sense of) touch; feeler; *indera* ~ sense of touch

rabat *n* rebate, (bulk) discount

rabiés *n* rabies → **sakit anjing gila**

Rabu, Rebo *hari* ~ Wednesday

rabun *adj* blurry; ~ *dekat* long-sighted; ~ *jauh* short-sighted

racik: racikan *n* blend, concoction; prescription; **meracik** *vt* to create a mix of; ~ *obat* to mix up medicine

racun *n* poison (not from animals); ~ *tikus* rat poison; **beracun** *adj* poisonous; *vi* to contain poison; *gas* ~ poison gas; **keracunan** *adj* poisoned; ~ *makanan* food poisoning; **meracuni** *vt* to poison; **peracunan** *n* (deliberate) poisoning

rada *adv, coll* quite, rather

radang *adj* inflamed; ~ *amandel* tonsilitis; ~ *gusi* gingivitis; ~ *mata* conjunctivitis; ~ *otak* meningitis; ~ *paru-paru* pneumonia; **meradang** *vi* to become inflamed; to become angry

Radén *tit, Jav, m* Javanese title for male nobility; ~ *Ajeng (RA, Raj) f* title for unmarried female nobility; ~ *Ayu (RA, Ray) f* title for married female nobility

radio *n* radio; ~ *panggil* pager; *acara* ~ radio program; *penyiar* ~ broadcaster, radio announcer; *penyiaran* ~ broadcast(ing); *pesawat* ~ radio, wireless (set); ~ *Republik Indonesia (RRI)* Indonesian state radio

radioaktif *adj* radioactive; **radioaktivitas** *n* radioactivity

radiografi *n* radiography

radiologi *n* radiology

radiotérapi *n* radiotherapy

radius *n* radius

rafia *tali* ~ plastic twine

raflésia *bunga* ~ Rafflesia flower → **bunga bangkai**

raga *n* body; *bina* ~ body-building; *jiwa* ~ body and soul; *olah*~ sport; **peraga** *n* visual aid; **memeragakan** *vt* to model, show; **peragawati** *n, f* model; **peragawan** *n, m* (male) model

ragam *n* manner, way; kind; **beragam** *adj* various; **keragaman** *n* variety; **seragam** *n* uniform

ragbol *n* long brush or mop with round bristles for cleaning ceilings, toilets etc

ragi *n* yeast

ragos *n, sl* gossip (queen) ← **raja gosip**

ragu doubt, doubtful; **ragu-ragu** *adj* doubtful, unsure; **keraguan, keraguraguan** *n* doubt, uncertainty; **meragukan** *vt* to doubt something

rahang *n* jaw; *tulang* ~ jawbone

rahasia *n* secret, mystery; ~ *negara* state secret; ~ *umum* open secret; *agén* ~ secret agent; *membuka* ~ *vi* to reveal a secret; **kerahasiaan** *n* secrecy; **merahasiakan** *vt* to keep secret

rahib *n, Chr, m* monk; *f* nun

rahim *n* uterus, womb

raib vanished, disappeared

raih: meraih *vt* to reach for; to achieve; **peraih** *n* winner; one who achieves or receives something; ~ *medali perak langsung naik ke atas podium* the silver medalist stepped straight up onto the podium

RAj, RA *abbrev* **Radén Ajeng** Javanese title for unmarried female nobility

raja *n* king; ~ *gosip (ragos)* gossip; ~ *hutan* king of the jungle; ~ *minyak* oil baron, sheik; ~ *sehari* (bride)groom; ~ *singa* syphilis; ~ *Spanyol* the King of Spain; **kerajaan** *n* kingdom, monarchy; ~ *Inggris* the United Kingdom

rajah: rajahan *n* tattoo; **merajah** *vt* to tattoo

rajaléla: merajaléla *vi* to be out of control; to act violently

rajam: merajam *vt* to stone (to death)

rajawali *n* kind of hawk

rajin *adj* diligent, hard-working, industrious; ~ *belajar* study hard; **kerajinan** *n* crafts; ~ *tangan* handicrafts; **pengrajin, perajin** *n* craftsman, artisan; ~ *perak* silversmith

rajungan *n* kind of small edible crab

rajut: rajutan *n* knitting, crochet work; **merajut** *vt* to knit; to crochet

rak *n* shelf; ~ *buku* bookshelf; ~ *piring* dish rack

rakaat *n, Isl* one complete set of prostrations (during daily prayers); *sholat subuh terdiri dari dua* ~ the dawn prayer consists of two *rakaat*

raker *n* working meeting ← **rapat kerja**; **rakerda** *n* regional working meeting ← **rapat kerja daérah**; **rakernas** *n* national working meeting ← **rapat kerja nasional**

rakét *n* racquet, racket; ~ *bulu tangkis* badminton racquet

rakit *n* raft; ~ *penyelamat* life raft; **rakitan** *n* something built or assembled, finished product; **berakit** *vi* to (travel by) raft; **berakit-rakit** *vi* ~ *ke hulu, berenang-renang ke tepian, bersakit-sakit dahulu, bersenangsenang kemudian* after trouble, success will come (*lit.* raft upstream, swim to the bank; suffer a little first then enjoy the fruits of your labors); **merakit** *vt* to assemble; **perakitan** *n* assembly

raksa *air* ~ mercury, quicksilver

raksasa *adj, n* giant

rakus *adj* greedy; **kerakusan** *n* greed

rakyat *n* people; ~ *jelata* common people, proletariat; ~ *miskin (raskin)* the poor or underprivileged; poor people; *Dewan Perwakilan* ~ *(DPR)* House of Representatives, parliament; **kerakyatan** *adj* populist; democratic; **merakyat** *vi* to become popular

ralat *n* correction, errata; **meralat** *vt* to correct a mistake

ram *n* window (frame) → **kusén**

rama → **romo**

Ramadan Muslim fasting month

ramah *adj* friendly; ~ *tamah* informal get-together; **keramahan** *n* friendliness

ramai, ramé *adj* busy, lively; crowded; *orang* ~ the public; **ramai-ramai** *adv* in a group, together; **keramaian** *n* noise, din; lively atmosphere; **meramaikan** *vt* to liven up, enliven

ramal: ramalan *n* prediction, prophecy, forecast; ~ *cuaca* weather forecast; **meramal** *vt* to tell fortunes; **meramalkan** *vt* to predict, foretell; **peramal** *n* fortune-teller, clairvoyant

Ramayana *n* Hindu epic, performed in shadow-puppet plays and other traditional arts

rambah: merambah *vi* ~ *hutan* to clear away the forest, clear the land

rambat: merambat *vi* to spread; *tanaman* ~ vine, climbing plant

rambu *n* sign, signpost; ~ *jalan* traffic sign

rambut *n* hair; ~ *berketombe* dry scalp, dandruff; ~ *cepak* crew cut; ~ *ikal*, ~ *keriting* curly hair; ~ *kribo* Afro; ~ *kusut* messy, uncombed hair; ~ *lurus* straight hair; ~ *palsu* wig; ~ *tipis* fine hair; **rambutan** *n* rambutan, fruit with hairy red skin; **berambut** *adj* hairy; *vi* to have hair; ~ *coklat* dark-haired, *f* brunette; ~ *pirang m* blond *f* blonde

ramé → **ramai**

rames *nasi* ~ rice with a mix of side-dishes

rami *n* hemp, jute

rampai *bunga* ~ bouquet, bunch of flowers

rampas, merampas *vt* to take by force, rob, plunder; **rampasan** *n* booty, plunder, loot; **perampasan** *n* hold-up, robbery

ramping *adj* slender; **merampingkan** *vt* to make slender or slim; *Diah cepat* ~ *badan setelah melahirkan* Diah slimmed down quickly after giving birth

rampok, merampok *vt* to rob, hold up; ~ *bank vt* to rob or hold up a bank; **perampok** *n* robber; **perampokan** *n* robbery

rampung *adj* finished; completed

ramu: ramuan *n* mixture; **meramu** *vt* to gather, collect

rana: merana *vi* to suffer, waste away; to live miserably, in poverty

ranah ~ *Minang* the Minangkabau lands (West Sumatra)

rancang: rancangan *n* plan, design; **merancang** *vt* to plan, design; **perancang** *n* designer, planner; ~ *busana* fashion designer; **perancangan** *n* design, planning

rancap *n* masturbation; **merancap** *vi* to masturbate

rancu *adj* confused; *pengertian itu sedikit* ~ that understanding is a little unclear; **kerancuan** *n* confusion

randa → **janda**

Rangda *n* mythical Balinese witch

rangka *n* skeleton, framework; *dalam* ~ in connection with, in the context of ← **kerangka**

rangkai: rangkaian *n* combination, series; **merangkai** *vt* to bind together, combine

rangkak: merangkak *vi* to crawl; *pada umur 8 bulan, Lastri sudah bisa* ~ Lastri could crawl at 8 months

rangkap multiple; *tiga* ~ three copies, in triplicate; **merangkap** *vi* to hold another position (temporarily)

rangkap → **perangkap**

rangking → **ranking**

rangkul, merangkul *vt* to hug, embrace; to get someone involved; **rangkulan** *n* hug, embrace

rangkum, merangkum *vt* to carry in your arms; **rangkuman** *n* armful

rangkup: rangkupan *n* coverage; **merangkup** *vi* to cup hands together; *vt* to cover, embrace

rangsang: rangsangan *n* stimulation; **merangsang** *vt* to stimulate, excite; **perangsang** *n* stimulant; *obat* ~ aphrodisiac; **perangsangan** *n* stimulation; *fase* ~, *masa* ~ foreplay

ranjang *n* bed; *pisah* ~ separate (of a couple); **seranjang** *adv* in the same bed; *mereka kakak-beradik masih tidur* ~ the brothers still sleep in the same bed

ranjau *n* mine; ~ *darat* land mine; *kapal penyapu* ~ minesweeper

ranjing: keranjingan *adj* addicted to, fanatic

ranking, rangking [réngking] *n* process of ranking marks in class

ransel *n* backpack; *turis* ~ backpacker

ransum *n* ration

rantai *n* chain; ~ *sepeda* bicycle chain; **berantai** *vi* to have a chain; *adj* in a chain or sequence; *pembunuh* ~ chain-killer, mass murderer; *reaksi* ~ chain reaction; **merantai** *vt* to chain up

rantang *n* stacked set of portable food containers

rantau *n* abroad, across the sea; shore; **merantau** *vi* to sail away, seek your fortune, settle overseas; **perantau** *n* settler (in a foreign place); **perantau-an** *n* abroad, in another place

ranting *n* twig; small branch (of parties, banks)

ranum *adj* (very) ripe

rapat *adj* close to; tight; **merapat** *vi* to move closer; *perahu mulai* ~ *pada jeti* the boat began to approach the jetty; **merapatkan** *vt* to bring close to

rapat meeting, meet; ~ *kerja* (raker) working meeting

RAPBD *abbrev Rencana Anggaran Pendapatan dan Belanja Daerah* Regional Income and Expenditure Budget Plan, regional (provincial) budget

RAPBN *abbrev Rencana Anggaran Pendapatan dan Belanja Negara* State Income and Expenditure Budget Plan, national budget

rapél *n* back-pay; *guru SD di kota itu masih menunggu* ~ teachers in that town are still waiting for their outstanding salary

rapi *n* neat, tidy, organized; **kerapian** *n* neatness, tidiness; **merapikan** *vt* to clean or tidy up, neaten; ~ *kamar vi* to clean up a room

rapor, rapot *n* (school) report; *membagi* ~ to hand out reports

rapuh *adj* brittle, weak; **kerapuhan** *n* fragility, brittle state

ras *n* breed; pure-bred; *anjing* ~ pure-bred dog

ras *n* race; ~ *kulit putih* the white or Caucasian race

rasa feel, feeling; sense; taste; ~*nya* it appears, it seems; ~ *benci* hatred; ~ *gelisah* nervousness, unease; ~ *hormat* respect; ~ *kaget* surprise; ~ *kangen* longing; ~ *kantuk* sleepiness; ~ *malu* shame, embarrassment; ~ *minder* feeling of inferiority; ~ *ngilu* pain; ~ *pahit* bitterness, bitter taste; ~ *sakit* pain; ~ *salah* (feeling of) guilt; ~ *syukur* gratitude; ~ *takut* fear; ~ *vanili* vanilla(-flavored); *saya* ~ I think, I feel; ~ *ingin tahu* curiosity; **berasa** *vi* to feel (a physical sensation); *tanganku* ~ *sakit* my hand hurts; **kerasan** *coll* feel at home; **merasa** *vi* to think, feel; **merasakan** *vt* to feel something; **perasa** *n* sensitive person; *alat* ~, *indera* ~ sense of taste; **perasaan** *n* feeling; **serasa** *conj* like; ~ *di alam bebas* as if in the great outdoors; **terasa** *v* to be felt

rasamala *n* a kind of tree

rasbéri *n* raspberry

rasé *n* civet cat

rasi *n* constellation; **serasi** *adj* suited, compatible; **keserasian** *n* compatibility, suitability

rasial *adj* racial; **rasialis** *adj* racist;
  rasialisme *n* racism

rasio *n* ratio

rasional *adj* rational

raskin *abbrev rakyat miskin* the poor or
  underprivileged; poor people

rasuk: merasuk *vt* to enter into, possess;
  kerasukan *adj* possessed

rasul *n* prophet, messenger of God,
  apostle; *~ullah Isl* the Prophet
  (Muhammad)

rata *adj* flat, even, level; **rata-rata** *adv*
  equally; on average; **merata** *vi* to level
  out, become evenly distributed; **pemerataan** *n* levelling out, equal distribution; **meratakan** *vt* to level, flatten

ratap, meratap *vi* to lament, wail;
  ratapan *n* lamentation

rata-rata *adv* equally; on average ← **rata**

ratib: ratiban *n* prayer recitation

ratifikasi *n* ratification; **meratifikasi** *vt*
  to ratify

ratna *n* precious stone

ratu *n* queen; *~ Adil* the Just Ruler, who
  is believed will save Indonesia (Java)
  one day; *~ Beatrix* Queen Beatrix (of
  the Netherlands); *~ gosip (ragos)* gossip (queen); *~ kecantikan* beauty
  queen; *~ lebah* queen bee; *~ sejagad*
  Miss Universe

ratus *n* hundred; *dua ~* two hundred; **ratusan** *n* hundred (denomination); *adj*
  hundreds (of); **beratus-ratus** *adj* hundreds of; **seratus** *adj* one hundred, a
  hundred; *~ perak coll* one hundred
  rupiah

raun: meraun-raun *vi, coll* to go out,
  around

raung: raungan *n* roar; **meraung** *vi* to
  roar

raup: meraup *vt* to scoop up in your
  hands

raut *~ muka* (facial) expression, look on
  one's face; **rautan** *n* (pencil) sharpener; **meraut** *vt* to shape; to sharpen; *~
  pensil* to sharpen a pencil

rawa *n* swamp, marsh

rawan *adj* vulnerable, troubled, unsafe

rawat *~ inap* stay in hospital, be hospitalized; *~ jalan* outpatient; *juru ~*

nurse; **merawat** *vt* to nurse, care for;
  to maintain, look after; **perawat** *n*
  nurse, sister; **perawatan** treatment;
  maintenance, upkeep; *biaya ~* cost of
  treatment, cost of upkeep; **terawat** *adj*
  cared for; *tidak ~* unkempt, neglected;
  banyak bangunan lama yang tidak ~
  many old buildings are left neglected

rawit *cabe ~* small hot red chilli; *kecil-
  kecil cabe ~* small but fiery

rawon *n* black meat soup from East Java

RAy, RA *abbrev Raden Ayu* Javanese
  title for married female nobility

raya *adj* great, greater; *hari ~* holiday,
  feast day; *Indonesia ~* the national anthem; *Inggris ~* Great Britain; *jalan ~*
  highway, main road; *kaya ~* wealthy;
  merayakan *vt* to celebrate; **perayaan**
  n celebration

rayap *n* termite, white ant; *kena ~, dimakan ~* eaten by termites; **merayap**
  vi to crawl, creep

rayon *n* district, precinct, administrative
  unit

rayu: rayuan *n* flattery; *~ gombal* sweet
  talk; **merayu** *vt* to tempt, flatter,
  seduce

razia *n* raid, spot-check

RCTI *abbrev Rajawali Citra Televisi
  Indonesia* RCTI, a privately-owned
  television network

réak → **riak**

réaksi *n* reaction; *~ berantai* chain
  reaction; *~ kimia* chemical reaction;
  beréaksi *v* to react; **réaktor** *n* reactor

réalisasi: meréalisasikan *vt* to realize,
  make happen → **melaksanakan**; **réalistis** *adj* realistic; **réalitas** *n* reality

rebab *n* two-stringed musical instrument

rebah, merebah *vi* to fall down, collapse

rebana *n* tambourine

rébéwés *coll, arch* driving license

Rebo → **Rabu**

réboisasi *n* reforestation; **meréboisasi**
  vi to reforest, replant trees

rebung *n* cooked young bamboo shoot

rebus *vt* boil; *adj* boiled; *mi ~* boiled
  noodles (with soup); **merebus** *vt* to
  boil in water; *~ air* to boil water

rebut, merebut *vt* to snatch, capture; ~ **kembali** *vt* to recapture; **rebutan** *n* something sought after by many people; *vi* fighting for something; **berebut** *vi* to fight for; **berebutan** *vi* to fight each other for; **merebutkan** *vt* to snatch something; **memperebutkan** *vt* to seize, take by force; **perebutan** *n* fight, struggle, grab

récéh, récéhan *uang* ~ small change

red. *abbrev* **redaksi** editor, (ed)

reda, mereda *vi* to subside, abate; **meredakan** *vt* to soothe; to calm something down

redaksi *n* editors, editorial staff; **rédaksional** *adj* editorial; **redaktur** *n* editor

redam *adj* faint, muffled; **meredamkan** *vt* to muffle or stifle; **peredam** *n* device to muffle or reduce noise

redup dim, go out

réferéndum *n* referendum

referénsi *n* reference; *surat* ~ reference (for a job)

réfléksi *n* reflection

réformasi *n* reform (esp after 1998); **réformis** *adj* reformist, pro-reform

regang *adj* tightly stretched, taut; **regangan** *n* strain, tightness; **meregang** *vi* to become tight or taut; **meregangkan** *vt* to tighten, make taut; **peregangan** *n* tightening, straining

régional *adj* regional

régistrasi *n* registration

regu *n* group, team; **beregu** *vi* to be in a team; *adj* in teams

reguk: mereguk *vt* to gulp down, take a shot

régulér *adj* regular → **sedang**

régulasi *n* regulation

réhat *n* break; ~ *kopi* coffee break

rejeki, rezeki, rizki *n* fortune, luck; livelihood, living; ~ *nomplok* windfall; **mengais** ~ *vi* to scrape a living

réka ~*yasa* engineering; **rékaan** *n* fiction, creation; **meréka** *vt* to create, engineer

rekam: rekaman *n* recording; ~ *medis* medical records; ~ *video* video recording; *dapur* ~ recording studio; **merekam** *vi* to record; **perekam** *alat* ~ recording device

rekan *n* colleague, partner, associate; **rekanan** *n* regular service provider

rekat: perekat *n* glue, adhesive

rékayasa *n* engineering; ~ *genetika* genetic engineering; ~ *sosial* social engineering; **merékayasa** *vt* to engineer ← **réka**

rékening *n* (bank) account; ~ *koran* bank statement; ~ *tabungan* savings account

réklamasi *n* reclamation; *tanah* ~ reclaimed land

réklame *n* advertisement, banner

rékoméndasi *n* recommendation; **merékoméndasikan** *vt* to recommend

rékonsiliasi *n* reconciliation

rékonstruksi *n* reconstruction (of an incident); **merékonstruksi** *vt* to reconstruct

rékor *n* record; ~ *dunia* world record

rékréasi *n* recreation, relaxing, fun

rékrut recruit; **merékrut** *vt* to recruit

réktor *n* vice-chancellor, rector; **réktorat** *n* vice-chancellor's office

rél *n* rail; ~ *kereta api* railway line, railroad, train tracks

réla, réd(h)a, ridha, ridho willing; *secara sukarela* ~ voluntarily; **rélawan** *n* volunteer; **kerélaan** *n* willingness, readiness; **merélakan** *vt* to approve, agree to

réláks → **rilék, riléks**

rélasi *n* customer, client

rélatif *adj* relative

rélawan *n* volunteer ← **réla**

rélevan *adj* relevant; **rélevansi** *n* relevance

réli *n* (vehicle) rally; **péréli** *n* rally driver

réligius *adj* religious → **beragama**

rélikui *n* relic

rém *n* brake; ~ *cakram* disc brakes; ~ *kaki* foot brake; ~ *tangan* hand brake; **mengerém** *v* to brake; **pengeréman** *n* braking

remah *n* crumb; ~ *roti* bread crumbs

remaja *n* teen, adolescent, young single person, youth; *masa* ~ youth; puberty; **meremajakan** *vt* to revitalize, refurbish, update; **peremajaan** *n* renewal, revitalization remang: remang-remang *n* shadows, darkness

remas, meremas *vt* to press, squeeze, knead

rématik *n* rheumatism

rembes: rembesan *n* seepage, oozing liquid; merembes *vi* to seep in, leak, ooze

rembuk, rembug: berembuk *vi* to confer, discuss

rembulan *n, lit* moon ← bulan

réméh *adj* small, unimportant, trifling; ~-*temeh* unimportant; meréméhkan *vt* to belittle, treat as unimportant

rémi *n* rummy (card game); *kartu* ~ playing cards

remis *n* small shellfish

rémisi *n* remission (in jail)

rempah *n* spice; rempah-rempah *n* spices

rempak: serempak *adj* simultaneous, in unison

rempéyék *n* péyék *sl* peanut crisp

remuk *adj* crushed, smashed; meremukkan *vt* to crush, smash into pieces

renang swimming; ~ *indah* synchronized swimming, water ballet; *baju* ~, *pakaian* ~ swimming costume, swimsuit; *kolam* ~ swimming pool; berenang *vi* to swim; perenang *n* swimmer

rencana *n* plan, program, draft; ~ *lima tahun (Repelita)* five-year plan (under Suharto); ~ *Undang-Undang (RUU)* draft act; ~ *Anggaran Pembelanjaan dan Biaya Negara (RAPBN)* State Income and Expenditure Budget Plan, national budget; berencana *vi* to plan; *Keluarga* ~ *(KB)* family planning; merencanakan *vt* to plan; perencana *n* planner; perencanaan *n* planning; terencana *adj* planned

réncong *n* Acehnese dagger; *Tanah* ~ Aceh

rénda *n* lace; berénda *adj* lacy, lace; merénda *v* to crochet

rendah *adj* low, humble; ~ *hati* humble; kerendahan *n* lowness; ~ *hati* humility; merendah *vi* to be humble; *sikap* ~ humility; merendahkan *vt* to lower; to humiliate; serendah-rendahnya *adv* as low as possible; terendah *adj* lowest

rendam soak; *mandi* ~ soak in a bathtub; berendam *vi* to soak; merendam *vt* to soak something; terendam *adj* inundated, flooded, soaked

rendang *n* meat cooked in coconut milk

réng *n* lath for roof tiles

réngék: réngékan *n* whine, whimper; meréngék *vi* to whimper, whine

renggang *adj* distant, apart; kerenggangan *n* rift, gulf, distance; merenggangkan *vt* to keep or pull apart, split

renggut: merenggut *vt* to snatch, tug; ~ *nyawa* to take a life, kill

réngking → ranking

rengut, rungut: merengut *vi* to grumble

rénovasi renovation; merénovasi *vt* to renovate

rénta *adj* worn; *tua* ~ worn with age, decrepit

rentak stamp (with one's foot)

rentak: serentak *adj* all at once, simultaneous, at the same time

rentan *adj* susceptible

rentang: rentangan *n* stretch, span; merentang *vi* to span, stretch over; merentangkan *vt* to extend, stretch out

réntét: réntétan *n* string, series; seréntétan *n* a string or series of

renung: renungan *n* reflection, musing, contemplation; merenung *vi* to daydream; merenungi, merenungkan *vt* to think about, reflect on, muse

renyah *adj* crisp, crispy; kerenyahan *n* crispness, crispiness

réog *n* trance dance, most famously in Ponorogo, East Java

réot, réyot *adj* falling apart, in disrepair

Rep. *Republik* Republic

réparasi *n* repair(s); meréparasi *vt* to repair → baik

répatriasi *n* repatriation

Repelita *n, arch* Five-Year Plan (under Suharto) ← Rencana Pembangunan Lima Tahun

réportase *n* reporting

répot very busy; bothered; répot-répot *vi* to go to great trouble; merépotkan *vt* to make someone busy or go to some trouble

répro *n* (art) reproduction ← **réproduksi**

réproduksi *n* reproduction; ~ *seksual* sexual reproduction

républik *n* republic; ~ *Dominika* the Dominican Republic; ~ *Indonesia* the Republic of Indonesia; ~ *Indonesia Serikat (RIS)* United Republic of Indonesia, which existed from 1949-50; ~ *Maluku Selatan (RMS)* Republic of the South Moluccas/South Maluku, a separatist movement; ~ *Rakyat Cina (RRC)*, ~ *Rakyat Tiongkok (RRT)* People's Republic of China

réputasi *n* reputation

reruntuhan, runtuhan *n* ruins ← **runtuh**

resah *adj* restless; **keresahan** *n* restlessness, nervous energy; **meresahkan** *adj* disturbing, worrying

resap: resapan *n* absorption; **meresap** *vi* to be absorbed; to penetrate, seep into

résbang *n* cot, couch

résé *adj, sl* annoying; uncomfortable → **risi**

résénsi, risénsi *n* review; ~ *buku* book review

resép *n* recipe; prescription; **meresépkan** *vt* to write a prescription for a drug

resépsi *n* reception; *meja* ~ reception desk; ~ *perkawinan*, ~ *pernikahan* wedding reception; **resépsionis** *n* receptionist

resérse *n* detective, forensic; ~ *kriminal (reskrim)* crime squad

resés *n* recess (of parliament)

resési *n* recession

resi *n* receipt; baggage check label

résidén *n, arch* Resident, official during Dutch times (lower than a Governor but higher than a *Bupati*); **karésidénan** *n, arch* residency, administrative unit in Dutch times headed by a Resident

résidivis *n* repeat offender

resik *adj* clean; *geladi* ~, *gladi* ~ dress-rehearsal

résimén *n* regiment; ~ *Mahasiswa (Menwa)* student regiment

réskrim crime squad ← **resérse kriminal**

resmi *adj* official, formal; *kunjungan* ~

state visit; *pakaian* ~ formal dress; *secara* ~ officially; **meresmikan** *vt* to formalize, make official; **peresmian** *n* formal opening, inauguration

résolusi *n* resolution

resort *polisi* ~ *(polres)* local police, county police

résort, résor *n* (holiday) resort

réspék *sl* respect → **hormat**

réspon, réspons respond, response; **réspondan** *n* respondent

réstan *pos* ~ post to be kept at a post office for collection by the addressee, *poste réstante*

résto *n* up-market restaurant; **réstoran** *n* restaurant

réstorasi *gerbong* ~, *kereta* ~ restaurant car

réstorasi *n* restoration; **meréstorasi** *vt* to restore

restu *n* blessing; *doa* ~ prayers and blessings; **merestui** *vt* to agree to, give your blessing to

retak *adj* cracked; *tak ada gading yang tak* ~ nobody is perfect (*lit.* there is no ivory that isn't cracked); **retakan, keretakan** *n* crack, fissure; **meretak** *vi* to crack

retas: meretas *vi* to break or split open (of stitches); **peretas** *n* tool used to break or split open

rétina *n* retina

rétorika *n* rhetoric

retrét *n, Chr* retreat, period of religious contemplation

rétribusi *n* fee to use a public facility; *uang* ~ fee paid

rétur, retour *adj* return; *loket* ~ return ticket counter

réuni *n* (school) reunion

réunifikasi *n* reunification

révisi *n* revision; **merévisi** *vt* to revise, rewrite

révitalisasi *n* revitalization, renewal

révolusi *n* revolution; *zaman* ~ the Indonesian Revolution, 1945-49; **révolusionér** *adj* revolutionary

réwél *adj* fussy, troublesome, difficult; **keréwélan** *n* fussiness, choosiness

réyot, réot *adj* falling apart, in disrepair

rezeki, rizki ← **rejeki**

rézim *n* regime

RI *abbrev Republik Indonesia* Republic of Indonesia

ria *adj* merry, joyous, cheerful; *bergembira* ~ to be happy, overjoyed

ria *adj* arrogant, proud

riak *n* ripples of water; **beriak, meriak** *vi* to ripple

riak, réak *n* phlegm

rial *n* (Saudi) rial, unit of currency

riam *n* (river) rapids

riang *adj* cheerful; ~ *gembira* overjoyed, over the moon; **periang** *n* cheerful person

riang: meriang feel unwell, sick

rias ~ *panggung* stage make-up; *kamar* ~ dressing room; *meja* ~ dressing table; *tukang* ~ make-up artist; **riasan** *n* make-up; **merias** *vt* to make up; **perias** *n* make-up artist

riba *n* high interest on a loan, usury

riba, ribaan, haribaan *n* lap

ribu *n* thousand; *sepuluh* ~ ten thousand; **ribuan** *n* thousand (denomination); *adj* thousands (of); **beribu, beribu-ribu** *adj* thousands of; **seribu** *adj* one thousand, a thousand; ~ *maaf* a thousand apologies; *Pulau* ~ the Thousand Islands

ribut noise; noisy; *angin* ~ storm; **keributan** *n* disturbance; loud noise; **meributkan** *vt* to make a fuss about

rica: rica-rica *adj* spicy Menadonese food; *ikan* ~ spicy Menadonese-style fish

ricuh *adj* chaotic, out of control; **kericuhan** *n* chaos

riil *adj* real → **nyata**

rijstafel [réstafel] *n* colonial-style dinner of rice with small trays of side-dishes

rikuh *adj* awkward; **kerikuhan** *n* feeling of awkwardness

rilék, riléks, rélaks relax, relaxed

rilis release (of an album or film); **merilis** *vt* to release, put out

rim *n* ream of paper

rim *n* cream, skim (of milk) → **kepala susu**

rimba *n* jungle, forest; ~ *belantara,* ~

raya deep jungle; ~ *beton* concrete jungle; *tidak tentu ~nya* disappeared, lost without a trace

rimbun *adj* leafy, dense, thick; **kerimbunan** *n* denseness (of foliage)

rimpel *n* pleat

rinci detail; **rincian** *n* details; **merinci** *vt* to specify, detail; **perincian** *n* details, detailed explanation

rindang *adj* leafy, shady

rinding: merinding *vi* to have goose-bumps or an eerie feeling, be spooked

rindu longing; ~ *akan,* ~ *pada* long for, miss; *benci tapi* ~ love-hate relationship; **kerinduan** *n* longing, craving; **merindu** *vi* to feel longing; **merindukan** *vt* to miss, long for

ring *n* (boxing) ring

ringan *adj* light, easy; ~ *tangan* light-fingered; prone to violence; *kredit* ~ easy credit; *luka* ~ slight wound, mild injury; **keringanan** *n* ease, assistance, relief; **meringankan** *vt* to ease, relieve, make easier

ringgit *n* ringgit, Malaysian currency (100 cents)

ringis: meringis *vi* to grimace

ringkas *adj* brief, short, concise; **ringkasan** *n* summary, synopsis; **meringkaskan** *vt* to summarize

ringkik: meringkik *vi* to whinny (of horses)

ringkus: meringkus *vt* to catch (esp by the arm or leg), take into custody

rintang: rintangan *n* obstacle; barricade

rintih moan; **rintihan** *n* moan, groan; **merintih** *vi* to moan or groan

rintik: rintik-rintik *hujan* ~ drizzle, light rain

rintis: merintis *vt* to pioneer; **perintis** *n* pioneer

riol *n* (underground) sewer

RIS *abbrev Republik Indonesia Serikat* United Republic of Indonesia, which existed from 1949-50

risalah, risalat *n* pamphlet, brochure, circular

risau *adj* uneasy, anxious; **kerisauan** *n* worry, anxiety; **merisaukan** *vt* to worry about risénsi → résénsi

risét *n* research; *mengadakan* ~ *vi* to do research; ~ *dan teknologi (ristek)* research and technology

risih, risi, résé feel uncomfortable; **merisihkan** *vt* to disturb, make you feel uncomfortable

risik: berisik *adj* noisy, loud; *vi* to rustle

risiko *n* risk; **berisiko** *adj* risky

riskan *adj* risky

risoles *n* croquette, rissole

risték *n* research and technology ← **risét dan téknologi**

rit *n* full trip (on public transport); *rata-rata angkot ini mengadakan sebelas ~ sehari* in general, this minibus makes eleven full trips a day

ritme *n* rhythm → **irama**

ritus *n* rite, ritual

ritsléting *n* zip, zipper; ~ *celana* fly

riuh *n* noise, uproar; **keriuhan** *n* din, clamor

riwayat *n* story, tale; ~ *hidup* biography; curriculum vitae, CV

RM *abbrev Rumah Makan* restaurant, roadhouse

RM *abbrev Radén Mas* Javanese title for minor male nobility

RMS *abbrev Republik Maluku Selatan* Republic of the South Moluccas/South Maluku, a separatist movement

robah, rubah → **ubah**

robék *adj* torn (of cloth), holey; *tangan* ~ grazed or cut arm; **merobék** *vt* to tear up, shred

roboh, rubuh *vi* collapse, fall down; *pohon* ~ tree that has been blown down; **kerobohan** *n* collapse; **merobohkan** *vt* to knock down, demolish

robot *n* robot

roda *n* wheel; ~ *air* water wheel; ~ *belakang* rear wheel; ~ *gigi* cog; ~ *gila* flywheel; ~ *stir* steering wheel; *kursi* ~ wheelchair; *kendaraan* ~ *dua* two-wheeled vehicle; **beroda** *adj* wheeled; *vi* to have wheels

rodi *kerja* ~ forced labor

rogoh: merogoh *vt* to grope around in, search for inside

roh *n* spirit, ghost; ~ *Kudus* the Holy

Ghost; **rohani** *adj* spiritual, religious; *lagu* ~ gospel or religious song

rok *n* skirt; dress; ~ *dalam* slip, petticoat; ~ *midi* mid-length skirt or dress; ~ *mini* miniskirt; ~ *pensil* straight skirt; ~ *span* (tight) skirt

rokét *n* rocket; **merokét** *vi* to soar to prominence; *namanya* ~ *sejak dia pindah dari Surabaya* she became very famous after she left Surabaya

rokok *n* cigarette; ~ *kretek* clove cigarette; ~ *linting,* ~ *tingwe* hand-rolled cigarette; ~ *putih* non-clove cigarette; *mengisap* ~ *vi* to smoke a cigarette; *uang* ~ tip; **merokok** *v* to smoke; *dilarang* ~ no smoking

rol *n* roll (of film); hair roller

rolade *n* small snack of rolled meat

roltar *n* Swiss roll, jam roll, cake rolled into a cylinder shape with filling

rom, room → **rum**

Roma *n* Rome

roma *bulu* ~ body hair

roman *n* appearance, looks

roman *n* novel; ~ *picisan* cheap novel, dime novel

Romania, Rumania *n* Romania, Rumania; *bahasa* ~, *orang* ~ Romanian, Rumanian

romansa *n* romance; **romántik** *adj* romantic

romantika ~ *hidup* the ups and downs of life

romantis *adj* romantic

Romawi, Rumawi *adj* Roman; *bangsa* ~ the Romans; *huruf* ~ Roman letters, Latin alphabet; *tiga* ~ III; *kekaisaran* ~ *kuno* ancient Rome, the Roman Empire ← **Roma**

rombak: merombak *vi* to pull down, demolish; to reorganize; **perombakan** *n* reorganization

rombéng *adj* tattered, torn; **rombéngan** *n* junk

rombong: rombongan *n* group, party

romo, Romo *n, pron, Cath* (Catholic) priest, Father

rompak: merompak *vt* to commit piracy; **perompak** *n* pirate; **perompakan** *n* piracy

rompal *Jkt* fall out, knocked out (of teeth)

rompéng *adj* chipped

rompi *n* waistcoat, vest

romusa, romusya *n* forced laborer under the Japanese occupation

rona *n* color, shade; **perona** ~ *mata* eyeshadow; ~ *pipi* rouge

ronda patrol; ~ *malam* night watch, night patrol; **meronda** *vi* to do the rounds, keep guard

ronde *n* round (in sport)

rondé *wedang* ~ warm Javanese beverage

rongga *n* cavity, hollow, hole

ronggéng *n, f* traditional dancer hired on festive occasions

rongkong: kerongkongan *n* throat

rongrong: merongrong *vt* to gnaw at, undermine

rongsok *adj* ruined, spoiled, damaged

ronsen → **rontgen**

ronta: meronta, meronta-ronta *vi* to struggle, squirm to get loose

rontak → **berontak**

rontgen [ronsen], ronsen *n* x-ray; *hasil* ~ x-ray (photograph); **dironsen** *v* to be x-rayed

rontok fall out, shed; *gigi* ~ tooth that has fallen out; *musim* ~ autumn, fall; **kerontokan** *n* shedding; ~ *rambut* hair loss

room, rom → **rum**

ros *bunga* ~ rose

rosario *n, Cath* rosary

rosot: merosot *vi* to fall down, descend, plummet; **kemerosotan** *n* descent, deterioration; **pemerosotan** *n* decline; **perosotan** *n* (children's) slide

rotan *n* rattan; *kursi* ~ wicker chair

roti *n* bread, bun; ~ *bakar*, ~ *panggang* toast; ~ *canai* kind of pancake; ~ *gandum* (brown or wholemeal) bread; ~ *jala* kind of Malay bread; ~ *kering* biscuit, cracker; ~ *kismis* currant bun; raisin bread; ~ *sobek* sweet bread which can be torn into sections; ~ *tawar* plain white (sliced) bread; *remah* ~ bread crumbs; *sepotong* ~ a slice of bread; *tempat* ~ bread basket,

bread bin; *toko* ~ bakery; *tukang* ~ baker; bread-seller

royal *adj* extravagant, wasteful (with money)

royalti *n* royalty → **honor**

royan *n* pains after giving birth

royong *gotong* ~ mutual assistance

Rp. *abbrev* rupiah

RRC *abbrev Republik Rakyat Cina* People's Republic of China

RRI *abbrev Radio Republik Indonesia* Indonesian state radio

RRT *abbrev Republik Rakyat Tiongkok* People's Republic of China

RS *abbrev rumah sakit* hospital

RSAB *abbrev Rumah Sakit Anak dan Bunda* Mothers' and Children's Hospital

RSAD *abbrev Rumah Sakit Angkatan Darat* army hospital

RSAL *abbrev Rumah Sakit Angkatan Laut* navy hospital

RSAU *abbrev Rumah Sakit Angkatan Udara* air force hospital

RSB *abbrev Rumah Sakit Bersalin* maternity hospital

RSI *abbrev Rumah Sakit Islam* Islamic hospital

RSJ *abbrev Rumah Sakit Jiwa* mental hospital

RSS *abbrev rumah sangat sederhana* basic housing

RSU *abbrev Rumah Sakit Umum* public hospital

RSUD *abbrev Rumah Sakit Umum Daerah* regional public hospital

RT/RW *abbrev Rukun Tetangga/ Rukun Warga* neighborhood association/citizens' association: smallest administrative unit, comprising one or more neighborhood blocks

ruah *melimpah* ~ to overflow, be in abundance

ruam *n* rash; ~ *popok* nappy rash

ruang *n* space, room; ~ *angkasa* outer space; ~ *kelas* classroom; ~ *keluarga* family room; ~ *kuliah* lecture theater; ~ *makan* dining room; ~ *masuk* lobby; ~ *menyusui* nursing room; ~ *mesin* engine room; ~ *operasi* operating theater; ~ *periksa* consultation room; ~ *tamu* front room, room for receiving guests; living room; ~ *tunggu* waiting room; ~ *hijau terbuka (RHT)* open green space; **ruangan** *n* room; hall; *sedang keluar* ~ not in the office

ruas *n* space between joints; ~ *jari* knucklebone, phalanx; ~ *tulang punggung* vertebrae

ruat → **ruwat**

rubah *n* fox

rubel *n* rouble

rubrik *n* column, rubric

rubuh collapse, fall down → **roboh**

rudal *n* guided missile ← **peluru kendali**

rugi loss, lose out; *ganti* ~ compensation; *untung* ~ gains and losses, pros and cons; **kerugian** *n* loss; damage; **merugi** *vi* to make a loss, lose out; **merugikan** *vt* to hurt, harm, injure

ruh → **roh**

ruilslag [*rélslag*] *n* land swap; **diruilslag** *v* to be swapped, exchanged

rujak *n* fruit salad with spicy sauce; ~ *cingur* fruit salad with beef snout, specialty of Surabaya

ruji *n* (bicycle) spoke; grill

rujuk reconciliation (after separation)

rujuk: rujukan *n* reference; **merujuk** *vi* to refer, use as a source; **perujukan** *n* cross-reference

rukan *n* office with a dwelling upstairs, shophouse ← **rumah kantor**

ruko *n* shophouse ← **rumah toko**

ruku', rukuk *n, Isl* part of a full set of prostrations (*rakaat*), consisting of leaning forward with the hands on the knees

rukun *adj* harmonious; ~ *tetangga (RT)* neighborhood association; ~ *warga (RW)* citizens' association; *hidup* ~ live in harmony

rukun *n* pillar, principle; *lima* ~ *Islam* five pillars of Islam

rum, rhum, rom, room *n* cream

Rum → **Roma**

rumah *n* house; ~ *bertingkat* multi-story house; ~ *bordil* brothel; ~ *gadai* pawnshop; ~ *gadang* traditional Minangkabau house; ~ *hantu* haunted house;

~ *idaman* dream home; ~ *jabatan* official residence; ~ *joglo* traditional Javanese house; ~ *jompo* old person's home, senior citizen's home; ~ *keong* snail's shell; ~ *laba-laba* cobweb; ~ *lanting* traditional house in Kalimantan; ~ *lelang* auction house; ~ *makan* restaurant; ~ *panjang (Dayak)* longhouse; ~ *penyu* (tortoise) shell; ~ *petak* tenement, communal house; ~ *sakit (RS)* hospital; ~ *sakit bersalin (RSB)* maternity hospital; ~ *sakit jiwa (RSJ)* mental hospital, asylum; ~ *Sakit Umum (RSU)* public hospital; ~ *sebelah* next door; ~ *sewa* rented house; ~ *susun (rusun)* (government) flat, apartment, high-rise housing; ~ *tahanan (rutan)* lock-up, detention center; ~ *tinggal* dwelling; ~ *walet* building where swiftlet nests are cultivated; *di* ~ at home; *isi* ~ household, people in a house; *nyonya* ~ hostess, mistress; *perabot* ~ furniture; *tuan* ~ host, master; ~ *tangga* household, family; ~ *sangat sederhana (RSS)* basic housing; ~ *susun sederhana (rusuna)* basic high-rise housing; **berumah tangga** *adj* married; *vi* to have your own family; **perumahtanggaan** *n* household affairs; **merumahkan** *vt* to lay off (from work); **perumahan** *n* housing (complex); **rumah-rumahan** dolls' house; **serumah** *adv* in the same house; *pasangan itu sudah lama tidak tinggal* ~ that couple have not lived together for a long time

Rumania, Romania *n* Rumania, Romania; *bahasa* ~, *orang* ~ Rumanian, Romanian

Rumawi → **Romawi**

rumbai, umbai *n* tassel; **berumbai** *vi* to have tassels; *adj* tasseled

rumbia *n* sago palm; sago palm thatch; *beratap* ~ *vi* to have a thatched roof

rumit *adj* complicated, difficult; complex; **kerumitan** *n* complication; complexity; **merumitkan** *vt* to complicate or make difficult

rumpi: rumpian *n* chat, chatter, gossip; **ngerumpi** *vi, sl* to (get together for a) chat or gossip

rumpun *n* clump, cluster; **serumpun** *adj* related, of one family; *bahasa ~* languages related to Indonesian (such as Malagasy and Tagalog)

rumput *n* grass, lawn; weed; *~ gajah* a type of thick grass; *~ kering* hay; *~ laut* seaweed; *hewan pemakan ~* ruminant

rumus *n* formula; **merumuskan** *vt* to formulate; **perumusan** *n* formulation

runcing *adj* sharp, pointed; *bambu ~* bamboo spear; **meruncing** *vi* to become critical or sharp

runding: berunding *vi* to discuss; **merundingkan** *vt* to discuss something, deliberate over; **perundingan** *n* discussion; *meja ~* discussion table

rundung: dirundung *v ~ malang* to be cursed with or to suffer bad luck

rungut, rengut: merungut *vi* to grumble, complain

runtai: meruntai *vi* to hang loosely → **untai**

runtuh fall down, collapse; **runtuhan, reruntuhan** *n* ruins; **keruntuhan** *n* collapse, fall; **meruntuhkan** *vt* to overthrow, destroy

runtun: beruntun *adj* in a chain; *tabrakan ~* pile-up

runyam be in difficulties, flounder

rupa shape, appearance, look; *~nya* it seems, appears; *Si Cantik dan si Buruk ~* Beauty and the Beast; **rupa-rupa** *adj* all kinds of; **berupa** *adj* in the shape or form of; *vi* to have a shape or form; **merupakan** *vt* to be; to form, constitute; **perupa** *n* sculptor; **rupawan** good-looking (person); **serupa** *adj* similar; **menyerupai** *vt* to resemble, be similar to, look like

rupiah *n* rupiah, Indonesian currency; **merupiahkan** *vt* to convert into rupiah; *kalau dirupiahkan, kira-kira satu milyar* if you convert it to rupiah, it's about one billion

rusa *n* deer; *~ betina* doe; *~ jantan* buck; *sate ~* deer satay

rusak *adj* broken, damaged, destroyed, spoilt; *~ parah* badly damaged; **kerusakan** *n* damage; **merusak** *vt* to

spoil, damage; **merusakkan** *vt* to destroy, break

Rusia *n* Russia; *bahasa ~, orang ~* Russian

rusuh restless, disturbed, riotous; **kerusuhan** *n* riot, disturbance

rusuk *n* flank, side; *tulang ~* rib

rusun *n* (government) flat, apartment, high-rise housing ← **rumah susun**; **rusuna** *n* basic high-rise housing ← **rumah susun sederhana**

rutan *n* lock-up, detention center ← **rumah tahanan**

rute *n* route

rutin *adj* routine; **rutinitas** *n* routineness, boredom

RUU *abbrev Rencana Undang-Undang* draft act

ruwat, ruat purify, exorcise, clean; **ruwatan** *n* purification or exorcism ritual; **meruwat** *vt* to purify or cleanse someone (through such a ritual)

ruwet *adj* complicated; **keruwetan** *n* complexity

RW *abbrev er-we, rintek wuuk euph* "fine hair" meaning dog meat, in North Sulawesi

Rwanda *n* Rwanda; *orang ~* Rwandan

S

s [és] s, 19th letter of the alphabet

S1 *abbrev Stratum Satu* bachelor degree

S2 *abbrev Stratum Dua* Masters degree

S3 *abbrev Stratum Tiga* doctoral degree, Ph.D.

saat *n* moment, time; *~ ini* at this moment; **sesaat** *adv* momentarily, for an instant

saban *adj* every, each; *~ hari* every day

sabana *n* savannah

sabar *adj* patient; *tidak ~* impatient; **bersabar** *vi* to be patient; **kesabaran** *n* patience; *batas ~* limit of one's patience

sabatikal *n* sabbatical, leave of absence

sabda *n, pol* word; *~ Tuhan* the word of God; **bersabda** *vi* to say or speak; *Sri Sultan ~* the Sultan spoke

sabet: menyabet *vt* to snatch or grab; to whip

sabit *n* sickle; *bulan* ~ crescent moon; **menyabit** *vt* to cut with a sickle

sableng *adj, coll, derog* crazy, mad

sablon *n* screen-printed cloth banner; screen-printing; **mensablon** *vt* to screen-print

sabot: menyabot, menyabotase *vt* to sabotage; **penyabot** *n* saboteur; **sabotase** *n* sabotage

Sabtu *hari* ~ Saturday

sabu-sabu → **shabu-shabu**

sabuk *n* belt, sash; ~ *hitam* black belt (in martial arts); ~ *pengaman* safety belt, seat beat

sabun *n* soap; ~ *cair* liquid soap; ~ *colek* cream soap for scrubbing clothes; *opera* ~ soap opera; ~ *cuci baju* washing detergent; ~ *cuci piring* dishwashing liquid; **bersabun** *adj* soapy; **menyabuni** *vt* to soap or lather

sabung ~ *ayam* cock fighting; *ayam* ~ fighting cock

sabut ~ *kelapa* coconut fiber

sadap: sadapan *n* something tapped; **menyadap** *vt* to tap (rubber, telephones); **penyadap** *n* tapper; **penyadapan** *n* tapping

sadaqah, sadaqoh → **sedekah**

sadar conscious, aware; ~ *lingkungan* environmentally aware; ~ *politik* politically aware; *tidak* ~ unconscious; **kesadaran** *n* consciousness, awareness; **menyadari** *vt* to realize, be aware of; *dia tidak* ~ *bahayanya* he did not realize the danger; **menyadarkan** *vt* to make someone realize, raise someone's awareness; *guru berusaha* ~ *murid akan pentingnya belajar* teachers try to make students aware of the importance of studying

sadel *n* saddle (on a bicycle)

sadis *adj* sadistic, cruel

sado *n* two-wheeled horse carriage

sadur, saduran *n* plating, coating; adaptation, rewrite; ~ *emas* gold-plated, gilt; **menyadur** *vt* to gild; to rewrite, adapt

safari *n* safari, tour; *baju* ~ safari suit

safir *batu* ~ sapphire

saga natural red dye obtained from the saga tree; *pohon* ~ tree producing a natural red dye

sagu *n* sago; *tepung* ~ sago flour

sah *adj* legal, legitimate, valid; *anak* ~ legitimate child; *tidak* ~ illegal, illegitimate; **mengesahkan** *vt* to validate, ratify, legitimize, legalize; **disahkan** *v* to be legalized; **pengesahan** *n* validation, legalization

sahabat *n* friend; ~ *karib* close friend; ~ *pena* pen friend, penpal; ~ *sejati* real or true friend; **bersahabat** *adj* to be friends; **persahabatan** *n* friendship; *pertandingan* ~ friendly (match)

sahaja, bersahaja *adj* simple, natural; **kesahajaan** *n* simplicity ← **saja**

saham *n* share; *main* ~ play the share market

sahaya → **saya**

sahid → **syahid**

sahur, saur *n, Isl* meal before dawn during fasting month; **nyahur** *vi, sl* to eat at this hour

sahut, menyahut *vt* to answer, reply, respond

saing compete; **saingan** *n* competitor, the competition; **bersaing** *vi* to compete; **bersaingan** *vi* to compete with each other; *perusahaan layanan HP sekarang saling* ~ *untuk mendapat konsumen* mobile phone providers are now competing against each other to get customers; *harga* ~ competitive price; **menyaingi** *vt* to compete with; **penyaing** *n* competitor (in nature); **persaingan** *n* competition; ~ *ketat* intense competition; **pesaing** *n* competitor; *sekarang di pasar ponsel ada begitu banyak* ~ there are so many competitors in the mobile phone market nowadays

sains *n* science → **ilmu pengetahuan alam, IPA**

sais *n* coachman

saja *adv* **aja** *coll* only, just; exactly; alone; -ever; *itu* ~ just that; *kapan* ~ whenever; *siapa* ~ whoever; *ke mana* ~ *liburnya?* where (which places) are you going to for your holiday?; *kembalikan langsung ke saya* ~ return it directly to me ← **sahaja**

sajadah, sejadah *n, Isl* prayer mat or rug

sajak *n* rhyme; poem

saji serve; *siap* ~ ready to serve, ready to eat; **sajian** *n* dish; offering; **sesajén** *n, Jav* ritual offering; **menyajikan** *vt* to serve, present, offer; **penyajian** *n* presentation

sak *n* sack (of cement)

Saka *Tahun* ~ Balinese calendar

sakaguru → **sokoguru**

sakarin *n* saccharine

sakelar *n* (electric) switch

sakinah *adj, Isl* peaceful, prosperous; *keluarga* ~ happy family

saking *conj, coll* all because of, due to, as a result of; ~ *marahnya* due to his anger

sakit sick, ill; pain, ache; ~ *gigi* toothache; ~ *ginjal* kidney disease; ~ *gondok* mumps; ~ *hati* offended, hurt; upset; ~ *jiwa* mentally disturbed; ~ *kepala* headache; ~ *kepala sebelah* migraine; ~ *keras* gravely ill; ~ *kuning* jaundice; ~ *maag*, ~ *mag* weak stomach, gastric pain; ~ *mens* menstrual pain; ~ *panas* fever, feverish; ~ *parah* gravely ill; ~ *perut* stomach ache, upset stomach; *cuti* ~ sick leave; *rumah* ~ hospital; **sakit-sakitan** *adv* often ill, frequently unwell; **kesakitan** *adj* in pain; **menyakiti** *vt* to hurt, treat badly; **menyakitkan** *adj* painful; **penyakit** *n* disease, illness, complaint; ~ *cacar* smallpox; ~ *campak* measles; ~ *gula* diabetes; ~ *jiwa* mental problem; ~ *gula* diabetes; ~ *kelamin*, ~ *kotor*, ~ *menular seksual (PMS)* sexually transmitted disease (STD), venereal disease; ~ *kusta* leprosy; ~ *menahun* chronic illness; ~ *menular* infectious or contagious disease; ~ *tenggorokan* sore throat; ~ *anjing gila* rabies; ~ *kuku mulut* foot and mouth disease; **pesakitan** *n* accused or convicted party, prisoner

sakral *adj* holy, sacred; **kesakralan** *n* holy or sacred state

sakratulmaut *n* death agony, death throes

saksama → **seksama**

saksi witness; ~ *kunci* key witness; ~ *mata* eyewitness; **bersaksi** *vi* to testify; **kesaksian** *n* evidence, testimony; *memberi* ~ *vi* to give evidence, bear witness; **menyaksikan** *vt* to witness

saksofon *n* saxophone; **saksofonis** *n* saxophonist

sakti *adj* magically or supernaturally powerful; **kesaktian** *n* magic power

saku *n* pocket; *uang* ~ pocket money

sakura *n* (Japanese) cherry blossom; *pohon* ~ cherry tree

Sala → **Solo**

salada → **selada**

salah *adj* wrong, mistaken, faulty; ~ *alamat* wrong address, wrong person; ~ *bantal* have a sore neck from an uncomfortable sleeping position; ~ *cetak* misprint; ~ *faham* misunderstanding; ~ *pilih* make the wrong choice; ~ *sambung* wrong number; ~ *satu* one of; ~ *sendiri* one's own fault; ~ *urat* strained or pulled muscle; *apa* ~*nya* what's wrong; *kalau tidak* ~ if I'm not mistaken; **bersalah** *adj* guilty; *vi* to be guilty; **kesalahan** *n* mistake; **menyalahi** *vt* to blame someone; **menyalahkan, mempersalahkan** *vt* to blame

salai → **salé**

salak *buah* ~ fruit with a hard brown skin like a snake, snakefruit; *kolak biji* ~ a kind of sweet porridge made to break the fast

salam peace; ~ *alaikum Isl* peace be upon you; *wa alaikum* ~ and upon you be peace (the response); ~ *hormat* respectfully yours, yours sincerely; ~ *saya* best wishes, regards; ~ *takzim* respectful greetings; *kirim* ~ say hello, send best wishes to; **salaman** *vi, coll* to say hello, greet; **bersalam-salaman** *vi, pl* to shake hands with others; **menyalami** *vt* to greet

salam *daun* ~ bay leaf

salat → **sholat**

salat → **selada**

salawat → **shalawat**

saldo *n* balance; ~ *terakhir* current balance

salé *pisang* ~ dried banana chips

saléh → **soléh**

salem, salmon *ikan* ~ salmon

salep *n* ointment, cream

salib *n* cross; **menyalib** *vt* to crucify; **penyaliban** *n* crucifixion

salin copy, duplicate; *baju* ~ change of clothes, spare clothes; **salinan** *n* copy; **bersalin** *vi* to give birth; *rumah sakit* ~ maternity hospital; **menyalin** *vt* to copy; **persalinan** *n* childbirth

saling *pron* each other, mutual; ~ *mencintai* *vi* to love each other

salinitas *n* salinity

salip, menyalip *vt* overtake, slip past

salju *n* snow; *main* ~ *vi* to play in the snow; *manusia* ~ snowman; *musim* ~ snow season, winter; *putri* ~ kind of biscuit with white icing sugar; **bersalju** *adj* snowy, snow-covered

salmon, salem *(ikan)* ~ salmon

salon *n* ~ *(kecantikan)* beauty salon, hairdresser's

salto *n* somersault; **bersalto** *vi* to (do a) somersault

salur: saluran *n* channel; ~ *kencing* urinary tract; ~ *pernafasan* windpipe, esophagus; *pipa* ~ pipeline; **menyalurkan** *vt* to channel; **penyaluran** *n* channelling; **tersalurkan** *adj* channelled

salut *vi, coll* to admire, salute

salvo *n* salvo, volley

sama *adj, adv* same, both; ~ *dengan* equals, equal to; ~ *sekali neg* completely; ~ *tingginya* of equal height, the same height (as each other); ~ *rata* equal, level; **menyamaratakan** *v* to treat equally; **sama-sama** you're welcome, think nothing of it (said in response to *terima kasih*); *adv* both, equally; **bersama** *adv* together; jointly; *kepentingan* ~ common interest; **bersamaan** *vi* to coincide, be equal; *adv* at the same time; **kebersamaan** *n* sense of togetherness, solidarity; **menyamai** *vt* to resemble, be like; to equal; **menyamakan** *vt* to equate, consider the same; **persamaan** *n* similari-

ty, likeness, resemblance; equation; **sesama** *adj* fellow, another; ~ *manusia* fellow human being

saman *tari* ~ traditional Acehnese dance

samar *adj* disguised, hidden; **samaran** *n* disguise, alias; *nama* ~ pseudonym, alias; **menyamar** *vi* to be in disguise; **menyamarkan** ~ *diri vi* to disguise yourself; **penyamaran** *n* disguise

sama-sama you're welcome, think nothing of it (said in response to *terima kasih*; *adv* both, equally) ← **sama**

sambal, sambel *n* chilli sauce; ~ *bajak* fried chilli sauce; ~ *terasi* chilli sauce containing shrimp paste; ~ *ulek* fresh(ly ground) chilli sauce

sambar: sambaran *n* strike; ~ *petir* lightning bolt; **menyambar** *vt* to pounce on, strike; *disambar petir* to be struck by lightning

sambel → **sambal**

sambi: menyambi *vi* **nyambi** *coll* to do a side job, work part-time; *Ibu pernah* ~ *sebagai tukang cuci* Mother once worked part-time as a washerwoman

sambil *conj* while, at the same time; ~ *lalu* in passing; ~ *menyelam minum air* to kill two birds with one stone (to drink water while diving); **sambilan** *pekerjaan* ~ part-time job, side-job

sambung connect; *salah* ~ wrong number; **sambung-menyambung** *adj* continuous; **sambungan** *n* connection; ~ *langsung internasional (SLI)* international direct dialling (IDD); ~ *langsung jarak jauh (SLJJ)* long-distance direct dialling; **bersinambung** *adj* continuous; **kesinambungan** *n* continuity; **berkesinambungan** *adj* sustained, continuous; *perkembangan yang* ~ sustainable development; **bersambung** *adj* in parts; to be continued; *cerita* ~ *(cerber)* serial; **menyambung** *vt* to join, continue; **menyambungkan** *vt* to connect to (something else); **penyambung** ~ *lidah* mouthpiece, spokesperson; *Bung Karno dikenal sebagai* ~ *lidah rakyat Indonesia* Sukarno was known as the mouthpiece of the Indonesian people; **tersambung** *adj* connected

sambut welcome; **sambutan** *n* reception, welcome; **bersambut** *gayung* ~ *vi* receive a response; **menyambut** *vt* to welcome or receive; **penyambut** *n* person with task of welcoming; **penyambutan** *n* welcoming, welcome ceremony

samenléven *vi* to live together (outside marriage) → **kumpul kebo**

Samoa *n* Samoa; ~ *Barat* Western Samoa; *bahasa* ~, *orang* ~ Samoan

sampah *n* rubbish, garbage, trash, waste; ~ *basah* organic rubbish; ~ *kering* non-organic rubbish; ~ *radioaktif* radioactive waste; *tempat* ~ rubbish bin, garbage can, trashcan; *tukang* ~ garbage collector, garbage man

sampai *conj* **sampé** *coll* arrive, reach; until; ~ *ajalnya* to die; ~ *dengan* to, until, up to the point of, as far as; ~ *bertemu*, ~ *jumpa*, ~ *nanti* see you later; *kasih tak* ~ love that never was; **kesampaian** *adj* achieved, reached, realized; **menyampaikan** *vt* to deliver, hand over, pass on; **penyampaian** *n* handing over, presentation; **sesampai** *adv* upon arrival, on arriving, as soon as arriving

sampan *n* type of boat, sampan

sampanye *n* champagne

sampar *n* plague, pest

samper: menyamper *vt, sl* to greet, acknowledge, say hello

sampéyan *pron, Jav, pol* you

samping *n* side; *dari* ~ *ke* ~ from side to side; *di* ~ next to, beside(s); **sampingan** *n* side-job, extra work; **bersampingan** *adj* next to each other; **mengesampingkan** *vt* to put aside, put to one side, sideline; **menyampingi** *vt* to escort, accompany, flank

sampo *n* shampoo; ~ *anti-ketombe* anti-dandruff shampoo

sampul *n* cover, folder, envelope; ~ *buku* book cover; ~ *surat* envelope; *gadis* ~ cover girl; *diberi* ~ to be given a protective jacket or wrapped in plastic (for a book); **bersampul** *adj* in an envelope or folder

Samsat *abbrev Sistem Administrasi Manunggal Satu Atap* all-in-one administrative center (for extending licenses, obtaining permits, etc)

samudera, samudra *n* ocean; ~ *Atlantik* Atlantic Ocean; ~ *Hindia*, ~ *Indonesia* Indian Ocean

samun: menyamun *vt* to rob, plunder; **penyamun** *n* robber, bandit

sana *adv* yonder, over there (far from speaker and listener); ~*-sini* here and there; *di* ~ over there (far from both speaker and listener)

sanak ~ *saudara* relatives, family

sanatorium *n* sanatorium (esp for respiratory illnesses)

sanca *ular* ~ python

sandal, sendal *n* sandals (open-toed shoes); ~ *jepit* thongs, flip flops

sandang *n* clothing; ~ *pangan* food and clothing

sandang: menyandang *vt* to bear or have; *Mario sudah* ~ *gelar sarjana kedokteran* Mario already has a medical degree; **penyandang** *n* bearer; ~ *cacat* disabled person

sandar: sandaran *n* support, prop; ~ *kursi* chair back; **bersandar, menyandar** *vi* to lean; **menyandarkan** *vt* to tilt back

sandera *n* hostage; **menyandera** *vt* to take hostage; **penyandera** *n* hostage-taker; **penyanderaan** *n* taking of hostages

sandi *n* code, cipher; ~ *rahasia*, *kata* ~ code, password; *nomor* ~ (secret) code

sanding: bersanding *vi* to stand or sit next to; **bersandingan** *vi* to stand or sit next to each other; **mempersandingkan** *vt* to place next to each other (of the bride and groom at a wedding)

sandiwara *n* drama, play; **bersandiwara** *vi* to pretend

sandung: sandungan *batu* ~ stumbling block; **kesandung** *adj, coll* **tersandung** *adj* to stumble on, trip (up) on

sang *pref, pol* used to denote respect; ~ *guru* respected teacher; ~ *Surya* the Sun; ~ *Merah Putih* the Red and White (Indonesian flag)

sanga → **songo**

sangat *adv* very, extremely; *amat* ~ terribly, extremely

sangga: menyangga *vt* to hold up, support

sanggah: menyanggah *vt* to object to, oppose, protest

sanggama, senggama *n* sexual relations; **bersanggama** *vi* to have sex

sanggar *n* workshop, studio; ~ *senam* (small) fitness center

sanggrah: pesanggrahan *n* resting-place

sanggul *n* bun (worn with women's national costume); **sanggulan** *vi, coll* **bersanggul** *vi* to wear a bun; **disanggul** *v* to have your hair put into a bun

sanggup *v, aux* to be able to, to be capable of; **kesanggupan** *n* ability; **menyanggupi** *vt* to be capable of, prepared to; to promise

sanggurdi *n* stirrup

sangka *v* to guess, suspect; **sangkaan** *n* suspicion; **bersangka** *vi* to suspect or think; ~ *buruk vi* to think the worst; **menyangka** *vt* to suspect, suppose, presume; *tidak* ~ never thought; **prasangka** *n* prejudice; **berprasangka** *vi* to be prejudiced; **tersangka** *n (yang)* ~ suspect; *tak* ~ unexpected

sangkal, menyangkal *vt* to deny; **penyangkalan** *n* denial

sangkar *n* cage

sangkar *n* diagonal; *bujur* ~ square, rectangle

sangkut ~ *paut* connection, link; **bersangkut** *vi* to be concerned; ~ *paut* to have a connection or link; **bersangkutan** *adj* concerned, involved; *yang* ~ *(ybs)* person concerned or involved; **menyangkut** *vi* to involve, concern; *coll* to get caught, snagged; *conj* about; **nyangkut** *vi, coll* to get caught, snagged; **tersangkut** *adj* involved; caught, snagged

sangon: pesangon *n* severance pay

sangrai: menyangrai *vt, Sund* to fry without oil

sangsi, sanksi *n* doubt; **mensangsikan** *vt* **menyangsikan** *coll* to doubt

sanitasi *n* sanitation

sanjung: menyanjung *vt* to flatter; **tersanjung** *adj* flattered

sanksi *n* disciplinary action, sanction

Sansekerta, Sanskerta *bahasa* ~ Sanskrit

santa *tit, f, Chr* Saint; ~ *Ursula* Saint (St) Ursula; **santo** *tit, m, Chr* Saint; ~ *Petrus* St Peter

santai *adj* relaxed, easy-going, informal; **bersantai** *vi* to relax, take it easy

santan *n* coconut milk (used in cooking); **bersantan** *adj* containing coconut milk; *vi* to contain coconut milk

santap, bersantap *vi, pol* to eat, partake of; ~ *pagi* breakfast; **santapan** *n* meal, dish, food

santer *adj* strong, rife; *isu yang* ~ hot topic

santét *n* black magic; *dukun* ~, *tukang* ~ witchdoctor, sorcerer; **disantét** *v* to have spells cast on you, be a victim of black magic; **menyantét** *vt* to cast spells on someone

santo *tit, m, Chr* Saint; ~ *Petrus* St Peter

santri *n* student at a *pesantren* or Islamic school (esp a boarder); strict Muslim; **nyantri, nyantrik** *vi, coll* to study at an Islamic boarding school; **pesantrén** *n* Islamic boarding school

santun *adj* polite, well-mannered; *sopan* ~ good manners; **kesopan-santunan** *n* manners, etiquette; **santunan** *n* benefit, compensation (from insurance)

santung *n* shantung, cloth from China

sanubari *hati* ~ innermost heart

saos → **saus**

sapa greet; *tegur* ~ greeting; **sapaan** *n* greeting; **menyapa** *vt* to greet

sapi *n* cow; ~ *jantan* bull; ~ *muda, anak* ~ calf; ~ *perah* dairy cow; ~ *perahan* something valuable to milk dry; endless source; *susu* ~ cow's milk; *telur mata* ~ fried egg, sunnyside up

sapih, menyapih *vt* to wean

sapta *pref* seven; ~ *Marga* the seven guiding principles of the military

sapu broom; ~ *ijuk* broom made from black sugar-palm fibers; ~ *jagat* 'sweeper' train at Idul Fitri to take passengers who haven't already obtained a ticket to their hometown; ~

kaca windscreen wiper; ~ *lidi* small broom to swat mosquitoes; ~ *tangan* handkerchief, hanky; *tukang* ~ cleaner, sweeper, janitor; **menyapu** *vt* to sweep or wipe; ~ *bersih* to clean thoroughly; to clean-sweep, wipe out, annihilate; *tim Indonesia ~ bersih lawannya dalam Piala Thomas* the Indonesian team wiped out its opponents in the Thomas Cup; **penyapuan** *n* sweeping

saput: menyaput *vt* to cover, veil, shroud; **tersaput** *adj* covered, shrouded; ~ *awan* clouded over

SARA *adj* communal, sectarian; related to ethnicity, religion, race or socioeconomic group; *berbau* ~ potentially sensitive issue ← **suku agama ras antargolongan**

saraf *n* nerve; *dokter* ~ neurologist; *penyakit* ~ nervous disorder; *perang* ~ war of nerves

saran *n* suggestion; ~ *saya* I suggest, my suggestion; **menyarankan** *vt* to suggest

sarana *n* facility, means; ~ *umum* public amenity; *pra*~ infrastructure

sarang *n* nest; ~ *burung* bird's nest; ~ *laba-laba* cobweb, spider's web; ~ *lebah* beehive; ~ *madu* honeycomb; ~ *penyakit* breeding ground for disease; ~ *semut* anthill; **bersarang** *vi* to (make a) nest

sarap: sarapan *n* breakfast; **menyarap** *vi, coll* to eat breakfast

saraséhan *n* meeting, symposium

Saraswati *n, Hind* Hindu goddess of knowledge and the arts

sarat *adj* full of, laden with

sarat → **syarat**

sardén, sardin *ikan* ~ sardine; **sardéncis** *n* (tinned) sardines

Sarékat Islam (SI) an Islamic organization active early in the 20th century → **serikat**

sari *n* essence, extract; flower; ~ *berita* news in brief, headlines; ~ *buah* fruit juice; ~ *bunga* pollen; *inti* ~ essence; *taman* ~ garden

sariawan, seriawan (mouth) ulcer, have an ulcer

saring filter; **saringan** *n* filter, sieve; **menyaring** *vt* to filter (through), screen, select; **penyaringan** *n* filtration, screening

sarjana *n* university graduate; ~ *Ekonomi (SE)* Bachelor of Economics; ~ *Hukum (SH)* Bachelor of Law (LL.B); ~ *muda* undergraduate; ~ *Sastra (SS)* Bachelor of Arts (BA); ~ *Teknik (ST)* Bachelor of Engineering (B.Eng); *pasca* ~ postgraduate

sarung *n* sarong; cover, case; ~ *bantal* pillowcase, pillowslip; ~ *pistol* holster; ~ *tangan* glove; **bersarung** *adj* in a sarong; with a cover

Sasak ethnic group of Lombok; *bahasa* ~, *orang* ~ Sasak

sasak: menyasak *vt* ~ *rambut* to tease hair into a stiff position

sasana *n* center; ~ *krida* youth center; ~ *tinju* boxing stadium

sasando *n* harp-like musical instrument from Timor

sasar: sasaran *n* target; **menyasar** *vi* **kesasar** *coll* to lose your way, (get) lost

sasis *n* chassis

sastra *n* literature; ~ *Indonesia* Indonesian literature; ~ *lisan* oral traditions; *Fakultas* ~ Arts Faculty; **kesusasteraan, kesusastraan** *n* literature; **sastrawan** *n* literary figure

Satal *n, abbrev Sangihe dan Talaud* Sangihe and Talaud, archipelagos in North Sulawesi

sate, satai *n* satay, kebab, roasted pieces of meat on a skewer; ~ *ayam* chicken satay; ~ *kelinci* rabbit satay; ~ *kambing* goat satay; ~ *Padang* satay made from buffalo meat with a spicy sauce; ~ *rusa* deer satay; **disaté** *v* to be made into satay

satelit *kota* ~ satellite, dormitory town

satgas *n* security unit, task force (of a party) ← **satuan tugas**

satpam *n* security guard; *pos* ~ security post ← **satuan pengamanan**

satron: menyatroni *vt* to break into (with intent to rob)

satu *adj* one; ~ *arah* one way; same direction; ~ *dua* one or two; ~ *sama lain* each other; *salah* ~ one of; ~ *per* ~ one by one; **satu-satu** *adv* one by one, individually; ~*nya* the one and only; **satuan** *n* unit; ~ *tugas (satgas)* security unit, task force (of a party); ~ *pengamanan (satpam)* security guard; **bersatu** *vi* to be united; ~ *padu vi* to unite, integrate; **kesatu** *adj, sl* first; **kesatuan** *n* unity; ~ *dan persatuan* national unity and integration; **menyatu** *vi* to become one; **menyatukan, mempersatukan** *vt* to unite various things; **pemersatu** *n* unifying agent, unifier; **persatuan** *n* union, association; ~ *Guru Republik Indonesia (PGRI)* Indonesian Teachers' Association

Saturnus *n* (the planet) Saturn

satwa *n* animal, fauna; ~ *liar* wild animal

saudagar *n, arch* large-scale merchant

saudara *n* family (member); sibling, brother, sister; *pron* you; brother, sister; ~ *angkat* person considered family; ~ *kembar* twin; ~ *laki-laki* brother; ~ *perempuan* sister; ~*saudari* brothers and sisters (to an audience); ~ *sepupu* cousin; ~ *susu*, ~ *susuan* children fed by the same wet-nurse; *hubungan* ~ family (relationship); *perang* ~ civil war; ~ *sebangsa dan setanah air* fellow Indonesians; **bersaudara** *vi* to be related; to have brothers and sisters; ~ *enam* to be one of six (children); **persaudaraan** *n* brotherhood, fraternity; sisterhood; family ties; **saudari** *pron, f* you, sister; *saudara-~* brothers and sisters, fellow Indonesians

sauh *n* anchor; *membongkar* ~ *vi* to weigh anchor; *membuang* ~ *vi* to cast anchor

sauna *n* sauna; small steaming box in a salon

saung *n* open-air restaurant by a fishpond, esp in West Java

saur → **sahur**

saus, saos *n* sauce, gravy; ~ *tomat* tomato sauce

saw. *salallahu alaihi wassalam* peace be upon Him, used after saying the name of the Prophet Muhammad

sawah *n* (irrigated or wet) rice paddy, ricefield

sawan *n* fit, convulsions

sawat → **pesawat**

sawér custom of audience throwing money to performers; custom in western Java of throwing rice, coins or sweets (as part of a wedding ceremony)

sawi *n* bok choy, mustard greens; green leafy vegetable; ~ *putih* Chinese cabbage

sawit *kelapa* ~ oil palm

sawo *n* brown, sweet fruit; sapodilla; ~ *matang* brown-skinned

saya *pron* I, me, my; ~ *pribadi* personally; ~ *sendiri* I (myself); speaking (on telephone); *diri* ~ myself; *kepada* ~ to me; *komputer* ~ my computer

sayang pity, regret; love; *pron* darling; ~*ku* my darling; ~ *sekali* what a pity; *kasih* ~ love; **disayangkan** *adj* regrettable, unfortunate; **kesayangan** *adj* favorite; *anak* ~ favorite, pet; **menyayangi** *vt* to love; **menyayangkan** *vt* to regret; **penyayang** *adj* merciful; **tersayang** *adj* dear, dearest; *yang* ~ *(yts)* beloved; dear (in letters)

sayap *n* wing; ~ *kiri* left-wing; ~ *roda* mudguard, fender; **bersayap** *adj* winged; *vi* to have wings

sayat, menyayat *vt* to slice or cut off; **sayatan** *n* slice; ~ *daging* slice of meat

sayembara *n* contest, competition; ~ *menulis* writing competition

sayu *mata* ~ sloping, slanting or heavy eyes

sayup: sayup-sayup *adv* faintly; ~ *kedengaran* faintly audible

sayur *n* vegetable; ~ *asem* sour vegetable soup; ~ *bening* vegetables (usu spinach and corn) in a clear soup; ~ *hijau* greens, green vegetables; ~ *lodeh* vegetables in coconut milk; ~ *mayur* (all kinds of) vegetables; **sayur-sayuran** *n* vegetables

SBY *abbrev Susilo Bambang Yudhoyono* Indonesia's sixth President

SCTV *abbrev Surya Cipta Televisi SCTV*, a privately-owned television network

SD *abbrev Sekolah Dasar* primary/ elementary school

s/d, s.d., sd. *abbrev sampai dengan* until

SDM *abbrev sumber daya manusia* human resources

Sdr. *abbrev Saudara Mr* (*lit.* Brother); **Sdri** *abbrev Saudari Ms* (*lit.* Sister)

SE *abbrev Sarjana Ekonomi* Bachelor of Economics, BE

se- *pref* one; with; after (having); the same; all; *~potong* a slice; *~sudah* after; *~mobil* in the same car; *~Indonesia* all-Indonesia, across Indonesia

seabrek *adj* lots, many, a large number, numerous ← **abrek**

seadanya *adj* what's there; *makan ~* eat what's there ← **ada**

seakan-akan *conj* as if, as though ← **akan**

seandainya *conj* supposing, if ← **andai**

seantéro *~ dunia* across the entire world ← **antéro**

searah *adj* the same direction ← **arah**

sebab *n* reason, cause; *conj* because; *~nya* the reason is, the reason being; *~ akibat* cause and effect; *oleh ~ itu* therefore, consequently; **menyebabkan** *vt* to cause; **penyebab** *n* cause

sebagai *conj* like, as; **sebagaimana** *conj* in such a way that, in that way; **sebagainya** *dan ~* and so on ← **bagai**

sebagian *n* some, a section of ← **bagian, bagi**

sebahu *adj* shoulder-length ← **bahu**

sebaiknya *adv* preferably, it's best if ← **baik**

sebal *adj* fed up, annoyed, cheesed off; **menyebalkan** *adj* annoying, tiresome

sebaliknya *adv* on the contrary, on the other hand ← **balik**

sebam *adj* blue-gray, clouded

sebanding *adj* comparable, proportionate, in balance ← **banding**

sebar: menyebar *vi* to spread; **menyebarkan** *vt* to spread, distribute; **menyebarluaskan** *vt* to disseminate, spread something; **penyebarluasan** *n* dissemination; **penyebar** *n* carrier,

infectious person; **penyebaran** *n* distribution

sebatang *~kara* alone in the world ← **batang**

sebaya *adj* of the same age ← **baya**

sebelah *prep* next to; *n* half, side; *~ mana* which side, where; *(di) ~ kanan* on the right (side); *rumah ~* next door ← **belah**

sebelas *adj* eleven; **kesebelasan** *n* team (of eleven) ← **belas**

sebelum *prep* before; **sebelumnya** *adj* previously, before, beforehand; *~ itu* before that; *~ Masehi (SM)* BC, before Christ; *~ waktunya* prematurely ← **belum**

sebenarnya *adv* in fact, actually ← **benar**

sebentar *n* **bentar, entar** *coll* a moment, minute, while; *~ lagi* in a few minutes, soon; *tunggu ~* wait a minute

seberang *prep* other side, across; *negeri ~* overseas, foreign country (usu neighboring); **berseberangan** *adj* opposing, in disagreement; **menyeberang** *v* to cross; **menyeberangi** *vt* to cross something; **penyeberangan** *n* crossing; *jembatan ~* footbridge

seberapa *tidak ~* not much, not many; *~ jauh* as far as ← **berapa, apa**

sebetulnya *adv* in fact, actually ← **betul**

sebilah *n* counter for long, narrow objects; *~ tombak* one spear, a spear ← **bilah**

sebisanya, sebisa-bisanya *adv* as well as you can, to the best of your ability ← **bisa**

sebuah *adj* a, one (generic counter); *~ kursi* a chair ← **buah**

sebut mention; *~ saja* take (for instance); **sebutan** *n* mention; **disebut-sebut** *v* to be frequently mentioned; **menyebut** *vt* to mention, name, say; **menyebut-nyebut** *vt* to frequently mention; **tersebut** *adj* mentioned, aforementioned, said

secang *n* red dye from a certain tree, can also be made into a drink

Secapa *abbrev Sekolah Calon Perwira* Officer Training School

secara *adv* in a way; used to form adverbs; ~ *besar-besaran* on a large scale; ~ *curang* dishonestly ← **cara**

secepat *conj* as fast as; ~ *mungkin*, **secepatnya, secepat-cepatnya** *adv* as fast as possible ← **cepat**

secubit *n* pinch; ~ *garam* a pinch of salt ← **cubit**

secuil *n* tiny bit; ~ *pun tidak* not one bit ← **cuil**

secukupnya *adj* sufficient, adequate ← **cukup**

sedak: tersedak *adj* choking; *vi* to choke

sedan *sedu* ~ sobs; **tersedan-sedan** *adj* sobbing

sédan *(mobil)* ~ sedan, saloon

sedang *adj* medium, moderate; *ukuran* ~ medium-sized, M (of clothes)

sedang *aux* while, -ing; ~ *pergi* out, not here; ~ *tidur* sleeping; **sedangkan** *conj* whereas, while

sedap *adj* delicious, tasty; **penyedap** *n* ~ *rasa* flavoring agent, commercial spice powder, usu MSG

sedapatnya *adv* what you can get ← **dapat**

sedari *conj* since, from the time when ← **dari**

sedekah, sadaqah, sadaqoh *n* alms, charity, handout; **bersedekah** *vi* to make a donation; **menyedekahkan** *vt* to donate something to the poor

sedekap: bersedekap *vi* to put your hands on your stomach (as during the daily prayers in Islam) ← **dekap**

sedemikian ~ *rupa sehingga* in such a way that ← **demikian**

sedeng → **sedang**

sederhana *adj* simple, plain; *rumah sangat* ~ *(RSS)* basic housing; **kesederhanaan** *n* simplicity, modesty; **menyederhanakan** *vt* to simplify

sedia ready, prepared; willing; ~*nya* actually, in fact, as a matter of fact (introducing something opposite); **bersedia** *vi* to be prepared or willing; **kesediaan** *n* readiness, willingness;

menyediakan *vt* to prepare, get ready; **persediaan** *n* stock, supply; **tersedia** *adj* available, prepared; **ketersediaan** *n* availability; readiness

sediakala *adj* of old, former; usual

sedih *adj* sad; **bersedih** *vi* to be or feel sad; **kesedihan** *n* sadness, sorrow; **menyedihkan** *adj* depressing, sad

sedikit *adj* a little, a few, a bit; ~*nya* lack, paucity; ~ *banyak* at least, some; ~ *demi* ~ bit by bit, gradually ← **dikit**

sédimén *n* sediment; **sédiméntasi** *n* sedimentation

sedini ~ *mungkin* as early as possible ← **dini**

sedot suck; **sedotan** *n* straw; **menyedot** *vt* to suck (up); **penyedot** *mesin ~ debu* vacuum cleaner

sedu sob; ~ *sedan* sobs; **tersedu-sedu** *vi* to sob, sniffle

seduh: menyeduh *vt* to add hot water (when making a drink)

sedunia *adj* all around the world, global ← **dunia**

seénaknya *adv, neg* just how you like, at will ← **énak**

segala *adj* all, every; ~ *sesuatu* all (kinds of); **segala-galanya** *n* everything, the lot

segan *adj* reluctant, averse; respectful; **keseganan** *n* reluctance, unwillingness; **disegani** *v* to be respected; **menyegani** *vt* to respect

segar *adj* fresh; ~ *bugar* fit and healthy; **kesegaran** *n* freshness; **menyegarkan** *adj* refreshing; **penyegar** *minuman* ~ tonic, energy drink

ségel seal, stamp; **menyégel** *vt* to seal (off), close (a building); **penyégelan** *n* blocking off, seizure

segelintir *n* a small number ← **gelintir**

segenap *adj* each, all ← **genap**

segenggam *n* handful ← **genggam**

segepok *n* a bundle, bunch, wad ← **gepok**

segera *adv* immediately, directly; soon; ~ *dibuka* opening soon; *dengan* ~ express, immediately

segi *n* side, angle; point of view; ~ *delapan* octagon; ~ *empat* square, rectangle; ~ *enam* hexagon; ~ *lima* pentagon; ~ *tiga* triangle; ~ *tujuh* septagon; *dari* ~ from the point of view of; **persegi** *adj* square, rectangular; ~ *empat adj* square; *(empat)* ~ *panjang n* rectangle

segini *adj, coll* like this, as far as this, to this degree ← **ini**

segitu *adj, coll* like that, as far as that, to that degree ← **itu**

ségmén *n* segment

sehabis *conj* after ← **habis**

seharga *adj* of equal value, the same price ← **harga**

sehari *n* one day; ~ *penuh* a full or whole day; **sehari-hari** *adv* every day, daily; **seharian** *adv, coll* all day ← **hari**

seharusnya should ← **harus**

séhat *adj* healthy; ~ *sejahtera* healthy and prosperous; ~ *walafiat* healthy, hale and hearty, in good health; **keséhatan** *n* health; *dinas* ~ health service; **menyéhatkan** *adj* healthy, with curing powers; *vt* to cure

sehati *adj* of one mind ← **hati**

sehelai *n* a strand, thread, page; ~ *kertas* a piece of paper; *beberapa* ~ *rambut tertinggal di atas bantal* several strands of hair were left on the pillow

sehingga *conj* until, to the point that, as far as; so that ← **hingga**

seia ~ *sekata* in complete agreement, unanimous ← **ia**

seibu *adj* having the same mother ← **ibu**

seimbang *adj* balanced, well-proportioned ← **imbang**

séin, sén *lampu* ~ indicator (on a vehicle)

seIndonésia *adj* all-Indonesia, across Indonesia ← **Indonésia**

seiring ~ *dengan* along with, together ← **iring**

seisi ~ *rumah* the whole family, everyone at home ← **isi**

séismik *adj* seismic; **séismograf** *n* seismograph

seizin *adv* with the permission of ← **izin**

sejadah → **sajadah**

sejagad, sejagat *adj* worldwide; *ratu* ~ Miss Universe ← **jagad, jagat**

sejahtera *adj* prosperous; **kesejahteraan** *n* welfare; **menyejahterakan** *vt* to make prosperous, enrich

sejajar *adj* parallel ← **jajar**

sejak, semenjak *conj* since, from the time when

sejalan *adv* in line, in the same direction; ~ *dengan kebijakan partai* in line with party policy ← **jalan**

sejarah *n* history; **bersejarah** *adj* historic, historical; **prasejarah** *adj* prehistoric; *n* ancient history; **sejarahwan** *n* historian

sejati *adj* original, genuine, real ← **jati**

sejauh *conj* how far; ~ *mana* to what point; **sejauh-jauhnya** *adv* as far away as possible ← **jauh**

sejenak *adv* briefly, a moment ← **jenak**

sejengkal *adj* handspan (between thumb and little finger) ← **jengkal**

sejenis *adj* of the same type or species; *pasangan* ~ same-sex couple ← **jenis**

sejoli *dua* ~ a couple ← **joli**

sejuk *adj* cool; **kesejukan** *n* coolness; **menyejukkan** *adj* cooling, refreshing; *vt* to cool; **penyejuk** *n* cooler, cooling agent, coolant; *minuman* ~ cooling drink

sejumlah *adj* a number of, some ← **jumlah**

séka, menyéka *vt* to wipe or rub off

sekadar *adj* just; ~*nya* as necessary ← **kadar**

sekak check! (in chess); **sekakmat** checkmate!

sekali *adv* very; *indah* ~ very beautiful

sekali *adv* once; ~ *waktu* once upon a time; *jangan* ~-*kali* never (do this); **sekali-sekali, sesekali** *adv* every now and then, occasionally; **sekalian** *adv* all together, all at once; *anda* ~ all of you; *coll* at the same time ← **kali**

sekaligus *adv* all at once ← **sekali, kali**

sekalipun *conj* even though ← **sekali, kali**

sekali-sekali *adv* every now and then, occasionally ← **sekali, kali**

sekap: menyekap *vt* to lock up, detain; **penyekapan** *n* detention

sekapur ~ *sirih* foreword, opening words ← **kapur**

sekar n, lit flower; **nyekar** vi, coll to strew flower petals on a grave; to visit a grave

sekarang adv now, at present; ~ ini nowadays; ~ juga immediately

sekarat adj dying

sekat bar, block, partition; **menyekat** vt to partition, block off

Sekatén n folk festival (usu in Java) celebrating the Prophet Muhammad's birthday

sekawan tiga ~ a trio (of friends) ← **kawan**

sekecil adj as small as; masa hal ~ itu menjadi masalah! how come such a small thing is such a big problem? ← **kecil**

sekejap n moment, flash, blink; dalam ~ mata in a moment, in the twinkling of an eye ← **kejap**

sekeliling adj around, surrounding ← **keliling**

sekeluarga adj and family; Anton ~ Anton and family ← **keluarga**

sekelumit adj a very small amount, a bit, a little ← **kelumit**

séken adj, coll second-hand; barang ~ second-hand goods

sekepal adj fistful, handful ← **kepal**

sékering, sékring n fuse

seketika n a second, a moment; dalam ~, pencopet sudah menghilang in an instant, the pickpocket disappeared ← **ketika**

sekian adv so much, this much; ~ banyak so many, so much; ~ dulu that's all for now (used in speeches and letters); **kesekian** adj umpteenth, nth; untuk ~ kali dia tidak hadir for the umpteenth time, he hasn't shown up ← **kian**

sekilas n flash, glance ← **kilas**

sekiranya adv if perhaps ← **kira**

sekitar prep around; adv around; near; **sekitarnya** di ~ around (a place); dan ~ and environs ← **kitar**

sékjén n secretary-general ← **sékretaris jénderal**

Séknég n Minister of the Interior ← **Sékretaris Negara**

sekoci n dinghy; ~ penyelamat lifeboat

sekoci n bobbin (of sewing machine)

sekolah n school; institute of learning; ~ Dasar (SD) primary school, elementary school; ~ favorit, ~ unggulan top or elite school; ~ kejuruan vocational school, technical college; ~ lanjutan secondary school; ~ Lanjutan Tingkat Atas (SLTA) upper secondary school, senior high school; ~ Lanjutan Tingkat Pertama (SLTP) lower secondary school, junior high school; ~ menengah secondary school, high school; ~ menengah atas (SMA) senior high school; ~ menengah pertama (SMP) junior high school; ~ Menengah Umum (SMU) secondary school, high school; ~ negeri state school, government school; ~ perawat nursing school; ~ pertanian agricultural college; ~ Rakyat (SR) arch elementary school in early years of independence; ~ swasta private school, independent school; ~ tinggi college (of higher education); alat-alat ~ school supplies; kepala ~ principal; masuk ~ to go to school; putus ~ drop out from or finish school (prematurely); tamat ~ to graduate from school; uang ~ school fees, tuition; ~ Calon Perwira (Secapa) officer training school; ~ luar biasa (SLB) special school; ujian masuk ~ entrance test; **sekolahan** n, coll school (building); schooling; **bersekolah** vi to go to school; **menyekolahkan** vt to send to school; **persekolahan** n schooling; ~ di rumah home schooling

sekongkol, bersekongkol vi to plot, conspire against; **persekongkolan** n plot, intrigue, conspiracy ← **kongkol**

sekonyong-konyong adv suddenly ← **konyong**

sekop, skop n spade, shovel; spades (in cards)

sekors, sekorsing → **skors, skorsing**

sekoteng, sekoténg n hot drink containing ginger

sékretariat n secretariat; ~~jenderal (setjen) secretariat-general; ~ Negara

(Setneg) Ministry of the Interior; **sékretaris** *n* secretary; *~ daerah (sekda)* regional secretary; *~ jenderal (sekjen)* secretary-general; *~ Negara (Sekneg)* Minister of the Interior

sékring → **sékering**

sekrup *n* screw

séks *n* sex; *~ oral* oral sex; *hubungan ~* sexual relations, sexual intercourse; **séksi** *adj* sexy; **séksolog** *n* sex expert; **séksual** *adj* sexual; *pelecehan ~* sexual harassment; **séksualitas** *n* sexuality

seksama, saksama *adj* careful, thorough, detailed; **keseksamaan** *n* thoroughness, care

séksi *n* section; *kepala ~* head of section

séksi *adj* sexy ← **séks**

sékte *n* sect

séktor *n* sector

sekuat *adj* as strong as; **sekuat-kuatnya** *adv* as strong or hard as possible; *dia berusaha ~ untuk menang* she strove her best to win ← **kuat**

sekujur *~ badan* whole body; *~ badan Iskandar penuh dengan gigitan serangga* Iskandar's whole body was covered in insect bites ← **kujur**

sékulér *n* secular

sekundér *adj* secondary

sekurangnya, sekurang-kurangnya *adv* at least ← **kurang**

sekuriti *n* security → **pengamanan**

sekuritas *n, fin* security, securities

sekuter → **skuter**

sekutu *n* partner, ally; *negara ~* the Allies; allied countries; **bersekutu** *vi* to be allies; **persekutuan** *n* alliance, partnership

sékwilda *n* provincial secretary ← **sékretaris wilayah daérah**

sél *n* cell, cells; *~ induk* stem cells; *~ darah merah* red blood cells; *~ darah putih* white blood cells

sela *n* gap, pause; **menyela** *vt* to interrupt

selada, salada, salat *n* salad; lettuce

selagi *prep* during, as ← **lagi**

selai *n* jelly, jam; *~ jeruk* marmalade; *~ kacang* peanut butter

selain *conj* except, besides, apart from lain

selak: terselak *vi* **keselak** *coll* to choke

selaksa *adj, lit* ten thousand ← **laksa**

selaku *conj* as, in the capacity of ← **laku**

selalu *adv* always ← **lalu**

selam diving; *baju ~* diving suit; *kapal ~* submarine; **menyelam** *vi* to dive; *sambil ~ minum air* to kill two birds with one stone; **menyelami** *vt* to dive into; to study in depth; **penyelam** *n* diver

selama *conj* during, as long as; **selamanya** *adv* always, forever; **selama-lamanya** *adv* forever and ever ← **lama**

selamat safe; congratulations; good luck; *~ belajar* good luck with your studies, happy studying; *~ berbahagia* congratulations (at a wedding); *~ berpuasa* happy fasting; *~ datang* welcome; *~ jalan* goodbye; bon voyage, have a safe trip; *~ Lebaran, ~ Idul Fitri* Happy Idul Fitri, Eid Mubarak; *~ malam* good evening; *~ pagi* good morning; *~ siang* good morning (before midday); good afternoon (after midday); *~ sore* good afternoon; *~ tidur* good night, sleep well; *~ tinggal* goodbye (to someone who is staying); *dengan ~* safely, safe and sound; *juru ~* savior; *memberi ~* *vt* to congratulate; *~ ulang tahun* happy birthday; happy anniversary; *~ menempuh hidup baru* good luck (in your new life, to newlyweds); **selamatan** *n* (thanksgiving) feast; **keselamatan** *n* safety; salvation; *Bala ~* Salvation Army; **menyelamatkan** *vt* to save, rescue; **penyelamatan** *n* rescue (operation)

selambat-lambatnya *adv* at the latest ← **lambat**

selancar *~ angin* windsurfing; *papan ~* surfboard; **berselancar** *vi* to surf, go surfing; **peselancar** *n* surfer ← **lancar**

Sélandia Baru *n* New Zealand; *keju ~* New Zealand cheese; *orang ~* New Zealander

selang *n* interval; *~ sehari* every other day, every second day; *~-seling* alternating; **berselang** *adj* with an interval of; ~*seling* alternating, staggered; **menyelangi** *vt* to interrupt

selang *n* hose

selangit *adj* very high, sky-high ← **langit**

selangkang, selangkangan *n* groin

selanjutnya *adv* then, after that ← **lanjut**

selapan: selapanan *n, Jav* 35-day ceremony (usu for newborn baby)

selaput *n* membrane; ~ *dara* hymen; ~ *lendir* viscous membrane

selaras *adj* harmonious, in harmony; **keselarasan** *n* harmony ← **laras**

Selasa *hari* ~ Tuesday

selasar *n* verandah, balcony; gallery

selasih *n* basil; *biji* ~ sweet drink containing seeds

selat *n* strait; ~ *Bali* the Bali Strait; ~ *Inggris* the English Channel; ~ *Malaka* the Straits of Malacca; ~ *Sunda* the Sunda Straits

selatan *adj* south; *Sumatera* ~ *(Sumsel)* South Sumatra; *daerah* ~ southern region, the south

selawat → **shalawat**

selayaknya *adv* properly, should ← **layak**

selayang ~*pandang* overview ← **layang**

selebaran *n* leaflet, brochure, newsletter

selebihnya *n* the rest or remainder ← **lebih**

sélébriti *n* **séléb** *sl* celebrity; **sélébritis** *n* celebrities, celebrity

selédri *n* celery

séléksi *n* selection; *lolos* ~ to be selected

selémpang *n* sash (over the shoulder)

seléndang, sléndang *n* shawl; sash worn over the shoulder with women's national costume

selenggara: menyelenggarakan *vt* to run, hold, organize; **penyelenggara** *n* organizer; *panitia* ~ organizing committee; **penyelenggaraan** *n* organization; **terselenggara** *adj* held, organized (successfully)

selenting, selentingan *n* gossip

seléo → **keseléo**

selepas *prep, conj* after ← **lepas**

seléra *n* appetite, taste; ~ *tinggi* good taste; expensive tastes; *bukan* ~ *saya* not to my taste; **berseléra** *vi* to have a

taste or appetite for; *adj* tasteful, classy

selesai finished, over; **menyelesaikan** *vt* to finish, end, settle; ~ *masalah* *vt* to overcome a problem; **penyelesaian** *n* solution, settlement

selesma, selésma (to have a) cold

seletuk → **celetuk**

seléwéng: menyeléwéng *vi* to deviate; to have an affair; **penyeléwéngan** *n* affair, deviation

selidik: menyelidiki *vt* to investigate; **penyelidik** *n* investigator, detective; **penyelidikan** *n* investigation

selimut *n* blanket; **berselimutkan** *vi* to have a blanket of; **menyelimuti** *vt* to (cover with a) blanket; **terselimuti** *adj* blanketed in or by; *Gunung Bromo* ~ *awan* Mount Bromo was blanketed in clouds

selinap: menyelinap *vi* to sneak, move quietly

seling *selang* ~, **berselang** ~ alternating; **selingan** *n* change, break; **menyelingi** *vt* to go between, intervene

selingkuh, berselingkuh *vi* to have an affair; **perselingkuhan** *n* affair

selip: menyelip *vi* to slip; **menyelipkan** *vt* to slip an object (into something); **terselip** *adj* fallen or slipped into

selir *n* concubine

selisih *n* difference; ~ *harga* price difference; ~ *kurs* difference in exchange rate; ~ *pendapat* difference of opinion; **berselisih** *vi* to differ in opinion, have a different opinion, quarrel; **perselisihan** *n* dispute, difference of opinion

seliwer: seliweran, berseliweran *vi* to move around, come and go

sélo *n* cello

sélofan *n* cellophane

selok: selokan *n* ditch, trench, drain

seloki *n* small glass for drinking spirits

selonjor sit with legs sticking out in front; **berselonjor** *adj* with outstretched legs

selonong: menyelonong *vi* **nyelonong** *coll* to appear suddenly, turn up (often by accident)

selop *n* slipper

seloroh: berseloroh *vi* to joke

selot *kunci* ~ bolt; **diselot** *v* to be bolted

sélotip *n* sellotape, adhesive or sticky tape

sélsius Celsius; *35 derajat* ~ 35 degrees Celsius

selubung: berselubung *adj* veiled; **menyelubungi** *vt* to veil or cover; **terselubung** *adj* hidden, veiled

seluk ~ *beluk* ins and outs, details

sélulér *telepon* ~ *(ponsel)* mobile phone, handphone, cell phone

selundup: selundupan *barang* ~ contraband, smuggled goods; **menyelundup** *vi* to sneak in illegally, infiltrate; **menyelundupkan** *vt* to smuggle (in); **penyelundup** *n* smuggler

seluruh *adj* entire, whole; ~ *dunia* all over the world; **seluruhnya** *adv* completely; *adj* all; **keseluruhan** *secara* ~ totally, completely; **menyeluruh** *vi* to spread, cover completely; *adj* comprehensive

selusin *n* a dozen; *teh botol* ~ a dozen bottles of tea ← **lusin**

selusup: menyelusup *vi* to penetrate, infiltrate ← **susup**

selusur: menyelusur *vi* to slide; **menyelusuri** *vt* to follow something, go along

semacam *adj* a kind or type of; ~ *itu* like that, of that type ← **macam**

semadi → **semedi**

sémafor *n* semaphore (a system of using flags to send messages)

semai, semaian *n* shoot, seedling; **menyemai, menyemaikan** *vt* to grow seedlings, propagate; **penyemaian** *n* process of growing seedlings; **persemaian** *n* nursery, bed

semak shrub, bush; ~*belukar* scrub; **semak-semak** *n* bush(land), scrub

semakin *adv* even more ← **makin**

semak-semak *n* bush(land), scrub ← **semak**

semaksimal ~ *mungkin* to the maximum ← **maksimal**

semalam *adv* last night; ~ *suntuk* all night long; **semalaman** *adv* all night long ← **malam**

semampai *tinggi* ~ tall and slender

semampunya *adv* as well as you can, to the best of your ability ← **mampu**

semang *induk* ~ house-mother, landlady

semangat *n* spirit, enthusiasm; *kurang* ~ lacking enthusiasm; **bersemangat** *adj* spirited, enthusiastic; **menyemangati** *vt* to enthuse, inspire, give spirit to

semanggi *n* clover leaf; *perempatan* ~ clover-leaf intersection

semangka *n* watermelon

Semar *n* clown character in shadow-puppet plays

semarak *adj* glittering, exciting; shine, glow, bright; **menyemarakkan** *vt* to brighten

semasa *conj* when, during, throughout ← **masa**

semat, menyematkan *vt* to pin, fasten with pins; **penyemat** *n* pin

semata *adj* only, entirely, solely; *anak* ~ *wayang* only child; **semata-mata** *adv* only, entirely, solely ← **mata**

semau ~ *gue* as I please; **semaunya** *adv* at will, as you like ← **mau**

semayam: disemayamkan *v* to be laid out (of a dead body)

sembab, sembam *adj* swollen (of face or body)

sembada capable; **swasembada** *adj* self-sufficient

sembah *n* homage, tribute, respect; **menyembah** *vt* to pay homage to, worship; **mempersembahkan** *vt* to offer (up), present; **persembahan** *n* offering; product or service

sembahyang pray, prayer; ~ *asar* afternoon prayer; ~ *id* mass prayer at Idul Fitri or Idul Adha; ~ *isya* evening prayer; ~ *Jumat* Friday prayers; ~ *lohor* midday prayer; ~ *magrib* sunset prayer; ~ *subuh* dawn prayer; **bersembahyang** *vi* to pray, perform a prayer

sembako *n* nine daily necessities (rice, meat, corn, salt, flour, sugar, eggs, cooking oil, kerosene) ← **sembilan bahan pokok**

sembarang *adj* any, whichever; **sembarangan** *adj* arbitrary, random ← **barang**

sembari *conj* while

sembelih: menyembelih *vt* to slaughter, butcher; **penyembelih** *n* butcher, slaughterer; **penyembelihan** *n* slaughter

sembelit constipation, constipated

sembilan *adj* nine; ~ *belas* nineteen; ~ *puluh* ninety; **kesembilan** *adj* ninth

semboyan *n* motto, slogan; **bersemboyan** *adj* with the motto

sembrono *adj* thoughtless, reckless

sembuh recovered, better; *cepat* ~, *lekas* ~ get well soon; **kesembuhan** *n* recovery; **menyembuhkan** *vt* to cure, heal; **penyembuhan** *n* cure, healing

sembunyi hide, conceal; **sembunyi-sembunyi** *adv* secretly, in secret; **bersembunyi** *vi* to hide (yourself); **menyembunyikan** *vt* to hide or conceal something; **persembunyian** *n* hiding place, hideout; *dalam* ~ in hiding

sembur: semburan *n* spout, fountain; outpouring; ~ *air panas* geyser; **menyembur** *vi* to spurt out; **menyembur-kan** *vt* to spit or spray something out

semburit *n* sodomy, homosexuality

semedi, semédi, semadi: bersemedi *vi* to meditate

semén *n* (wet) cement

semena *adj* balanced; **semena-mena** *(tidak)* ~ arbitrary, without reason, unjust ← **mena**

semenanjung *n* peninsula; ~ *Melayu* Malaya, the Malay Peninsula ← **tanjung**

semenjak, sejak *conj* since

sementara *conj* during, while; *adj* temporary; ~ *itu* in the meantime, meanwhile; *alamat* ~ temporary address; *buat* ~, *untuk* ~ for the time being

semerbak *adj* fragrant

semésta *alam* ~ universe; *Perjuangan* ~ *(Permesta)* 1950s secessionist movement

seméster *n* semester; ~ *ganjil* odd-numbered semester (1, 3, 5 etc); ~ *genap* even-numbered semester (2, 4, 6 etc); ~ *pendek* summer semester

semestinya should have (been) ← **mesti**

semi *musim* ~ spring; **bersemi** *vi* to sprout buds

sémifinal *n* semi-final; **semifinalis** *n* semi-finalist

séminar *n* seminar

seminggu *adj* a week; *tiga kali* ~ three times a week ← **minggu**

semir polish; ~ *rambut* dye to cover gray hairs; hair oil; ~ *sepatu* shoe polish; *tukang* ~ shoeshine boy; **menyemir** *vt* to polish; ~ *rambut* to touch up gray roots, dye to cover gray hairs; to use hair oil

semoga may, hopefully; ~ *sukses* good luck, every success ← **moga**

sempadan *n* border, boundary; ~ *jalan* right of way (ROW)

sempat chance, opportunity; *kalau* ~ when possible; *tidak* ~ not get the chance to; **kesempatan** *n* opportunity; ~ *emas* golden opportunity; ~ *dalam kesempitan* an opportunity in difficult circumstances; **berkesempatan** *vi* to have an opportunity; **menyempatkan** *vt* ~ *diri* to make time to

sempit *adj* narrow; *berpikiran* ~ narrow-minded; *waktunya* ~ *sekali* there isn't much time; **kesempitan** *n* narrowness; **menyempit** *vi* to (become) narrow; **penyempitan** *n* narrowing

sempoa *n* abacus

sempoyong: sempoyongan *adv* staggering

semprit *n* whistle; **menyemprit** *vt* to blow a whistle

semprong *n* chimney; *kue* ~ tubular wafers shaped like brandy snaps

semprot squirt; spurt; *kena* ~ *coll* be shouted at or told off; **semprotan** *n* spray-gun; **menyemprot** *vt* to spray; **menyemprotkan** *vt* to spray with something

sempurna *adj* perfect, complete; **kesempurnaan** *n* perfection; **menyempurnakan** *vt* to perfect, complete; *Ejaan Yang Disempurnakan (EYD)* reformed spelling of 1972

semrawut *adj* haphazard, uncontrolled; **kesemrawutan** *n* chaos

semu *adj* false, apparent

semua *adj* all; *~nya* all, everyone

semula *adj* original; *adv* originally ← **mula**

semur *n* meat or tofu dish with soy sauce

semut *n* ant; *~ api* small, stinging ant; *~ merah* red ant; *~ putih* white ant, termite; *ada gula, ada ~* if you have money, people will come (*lit.* where there's sugar, there are ants); **kesemutan** *vi* to have pins and needles

sén cent

sén, séin *lampu ~* indicator (on a vehicle)

senam *n* gymnastics, aerobics; exercise; *~ hamil* pre-natal exercises; *~ pagi* morning exercise; *baju ~* leotard

senandung hum; **bersenandung** *vi* to hum, sing

senang *adj* happy, content; *v* to like; *~ nonton TV* to like watching TV; **bersenang-senang** *vi* to enjoy yourself, have fun; **kesenangan** *n* amusement, hobby; **menyenangi** *vt* to like, enjoy; **menyenangkan** *adj* pleasing, agreeable

senantiasa *adv* always

senapan *n* rifle; *~ mesin* machine gun

senar *n* (guitar) string, line (on fishing rod etc)

senarai *n, Mal* list

senasib *adj* fellow sufferer ← **nasib**

sénat *n* senate; *~ mahasiswa* student council

senda *~ gurau* joke; **bersenda** *vi ~ gurau* to joke around

sendal, sandal *n* sandals (open-toed shoes); *~ jepit* thongs, flip flops

sendat: tersendat *adj* jammed, blocked

sendawa *n* saltpetre, saltpeter, potassium nitrate; gunpowder; *asam ~* nitric acid

sendawa, serdawa *n* burp, belch; **bersendawa** *vi* to burp, belch

sendi *n* joint; **persendian** *n* joints

sendiri *adv* alone; *pron* self; *salah ~* it's your own fault; *dengan ~nya* automatic, by itself; **sendiri-sendiri** *adv, pl* alone, individually; **sendirian** *adv* alone, single-handedly; **kesendirian** *n* solitude; **menyendiri** *vi* to go off by yourself; **penyendiri** *n* loner; **tersendiri** *adj* its own; apart, separate ← **diri**

séndok *n* spoon; *~ bebek* ceramic spoon for eating Chinese soup dishes; *~ garpu* spoon and fork; *~ makan* (dessert)spoon; *~ nasi* rice scoop; *~ sup* soup spoon; *~ teh* teaspoon

séndratari *n* traditional performing arts, dance and drama ← **seni, drama, tari**

sendu *adj* sad; **kesenduan** *n* sadness

Sénégal *n* Senegal; *orang ~* Senegalese

Senén → **Senin**

senéwen *adj* nervous, neurotic

séng *n* zinc

sengaja *adv* deliberately, on purpose; *tidak ~* unintentionally; **disengaja** *v* to be done deliberately, intentionally or on purpose; **kesengajaan** *n* deliberate or intentional act

sengat sting; **sengatan** *n* sting, bite; **menyengat** *vt* to sting; **penyengat** *n* something which stings, stinging insect

sengau *adj* nasal

senggama → **sanggama**

senggang *adj* free, unoccupied; *waktu ~* free time

sénggol brush, bump; *pasar ~* crowded market; **bersénggolan** *vi, pl* to bump into each other; **menyénggol** *vt* to bump, brush, tweak; **tersénggol** *adj* bumped, brushed

sengir: menyengir *vi* to smile nervously, grimace

sengit *adj* bitter, sharp, violent

sengkéta *n* dispute; *tanah ~* disputed land; **persengkétaan** *n* dispute

sengsara misery; **kesengsaraan** *n* torture, misery, suffering; **menyengsarakan** *vt* to torture, cause suffering

sengsem: kesengsem *adj, coll* engrossed in, absorbed with

seni *n* art; *~ budaya* the arts, art and culture; *~ grafis* graphic design; *~ lukis* painting; *~ pahat* sculpture; *~ peran* drama; *~ rupa* fine art; *~ tari* dance; *~ suara* voice, singing; *~ ukir* sculpture; art of carving; *nilai ~* artistic value; **kesenian** *n* art (form); *~ tradisional* traditional art form; **seniman** *n, m* **seniwati** *n, f* artist

seni *air ~* urine

Senin, Senén *hari* ~ Monday

sénior *n* person in higher class or of higher position ← **kakak kelas**

senja, senjakala *n* twilight, dusk

senjang: kesenjangan *n* gap, divide; ~ *sosial* social imbalance, social divide

senjata *n* weapon; ~ *api* firearm, gun; ~ *berat* heavy weapons; ~ *tajam* sharp weapon or object, blade; *gencatan* ~ ceasefire; *meletakkan* ~ to lay down arms; ~ *makan tuan* to backfire (*lit.* the weapon eats its owner); **bersenjata** *adj* armed; *Angkatan* ~ *Republik Indonesia (ABRI)* Indonesian armed forces; **mempersenjatai** *vt* to arm someone

senonoh *adj* fitting, decent; *tidak* ~ indecent, improper

sénsasi *n* sensation; **sénsasional** *adj* sensational

sénsitif *adj* sensitive

sénsor *n* censor; **kena ~, disénsor** censored; **mensénsor** *vt* to censor, cut out

sénsus *n* census

sentak: sentakan *n* jerk; **menyentak** *vt* to pull, jerk; **tersentak** *adj* pulled, jerked

sénter *n (lampu)* ~ flashlight, torch

sénti *n, coll* centimeter, centimetre; *berapa* ~ how many centimeters, how long ← **séntiméter**

sentil: sentilan *n* flick, nudge; **menyentil** *vt* to flick with your finger (often to rebuke a child)

séntimén *adj* having a bad feeling or grudge against something

séntiméter *n* **sénti** *coll* centimeter, centimetre; ~ *kubik* (cc) cubic centimeter, milliliter (ml); *berapa* ~ how many centimeters, how long

sentosa *adj* safe, peaceful

séntra *n* center, centre; ~ *elektronik* electronics center; **séntral** *adj* central; *n* center; ~ *telepon* telephone exchange; ~ *Organisasi Buruh Seluruh Indonesia (SOBSI)* All-Indonesian Federation of Labor Organisations

sentuh touch; **sentuhan** *n* touch; ~ *eksotis* exotic touch; **bersentuh** *vi* to

touch; **bersentuhan** *adv* touching each other; **menyentuh** *vt* to touch; **tersentuh** *adj* touched

senyap *adj* quiet, still; *sunyi* ~ completely still or quiet; **kesenyapan** *n* silence

senyawa *n* compound; **bersenyawa** *vi* to become a chemical compound; **persenyawaan** *n* chemical compound

senyum smile; *murah* ~ quick to smile, always smiling; **senyuman** *n* smile; **tersenyum** *vi* to smile

seolah-olah *adv, conj* as if ← **olah**

seoptimal ~ *mungkin* to the utmost, as well as possible ← **optimal**

seorang a (person); counter for people; ~ *Arab* an Arab; ~ *diri* alone, single-handedly ← **orang**

sép *n, coll* chief, boss, head of section

sepadan *adj* in keeping or proportion with ← **padan**

sepagi ~ *mungkin* as early as possible ← **pagi**

sepah *n* chew; grounds; ~ *kopi* coffee grounds, dregs; *habis manis,* ~ *dibuang* use something then abandon it (*lit.* throw away after sucking out the sweetness)

sepaham *adj* of the same opinion or belief ← **paham**

sépak kick; ~ *bola* soccer, football; ~ *bola Amerika* gridiron; ~ *bola Australia* Australian rules (football); ~ *takraw* game played with a rattan ball; ~ *terjang* behavior, activity; **menyépak** *vt* to kick (out)

sepakat *vi* to agree; **kesepakatan** *n* agreement; **menyepakati** *vt* to agree to ← **pakat**

sepan → **span**

sepanjang *conj, adj* as long as; ~ *hari* all day long; ~ *hidup* lifelong, all your life; ~ *jalan* the whole way ← **panjang**; ~ *masa* forever

sepantasnya *adv* proper, rightly ← **pantas**

séparatis separatist; **séparatisme** *n* separatism

separo, separuh *n* half; **separuh-separuh** *adj* half and half ← **paruh**

sepasang *n* a pair of ← **pasang**

sepat *ikan* ~ a kind of freshwater fish

sepatbor → **spatbor**

sepatu *n* shoe; ~ *es* ice skates; ~ *hak tinggi* high heels; ~ *katak* fins; ~ *kets*, ~ *olahraga* running or sports shoes, sneakers; ~ *lars*, ~ *bot* boots; ~ *roda* rollerblades, rollerskates; ~ *sandal* sandals; *kembang* ~ hibiscus; *tukang* ~ cobbler (for repairs), shoemaker; **bersepatu** *adj* in shoes

sepatutnya *adv* rightly, properly ← **patut**

sepéda *n* bicycle, (push)bike; ~ *balap* racing bicycle; ~ *gunung* mountain bike; ~ *motor* motor bike; ~ *ontel* old-fashioned bicycle; ~ *statis*, ~ *stasioner* exercise bike; *bel* ~ bicycle bell; *naik* ~ ride a bicycle; go by bicycle; **bersepéda** *vi* to ride a bicycle

sepekan *adj* a week ← **pekan**

sepélé *adj* unimportant, trifling; *hal* ~ trifle, small thing; **menyepélékan** *vt* to make light of, treat lightly

sepengetahuan *adj* with knowledge; ~ *saya* to my knowledge ← **pengetahuan, tahu**

sepeninggal *conj* after someone's death ← **tinggal**

sepenuh ~ *hati* with all one's heart; **sepenuhnya** *adv* fully, completely ← **penuh**

seperangkat *n* set, suite ← **perangkat, angkat**

seperempat *n* one quarter ← **perempat, empat**

seperenam *n* one-sixth ← **perenam, enam**

seperlima *n* one-fifth ← **perlima, lima**

seperlunya *adv* as (much as) necessary ← **perlu**

sepermainan *teman* ~ friend you play or hang out with (from childhood) ← **permainan, main**

seperti *conj* like; ~ *nya* it seems

sepertiga *adj* one-third ← **pertiga, tiga**

sepésér *tidak ada* ~ *pun* to have not even a cent ← **pésér**

sepet *adj* acid-tasting, sour

sepi *adj* quiet, still, lonely; ~ *pengunjung* few visitors or customers;

kesepian *n* loneliness, solitude; **menyepi** *vi* to go away by yourself

sepihak *adj* unilateral ← **pihak**

sepintas ~ *lalu* at first glance ← **pintas**

sepoi: sepoi-sepoi *angin* ~ breeze, zephyr

sepotong *n* a slice ← **potong**

seprei, seprai *n* (bed)sheet

Séptémber *bulan* ~ September

sepuasnya *adv* to your heart's content ← **puas**

sepucuk ~ *surat* a letter ← **pucuk**

sepuh ~ *perak* silver plating; **sepuhan** *n* gilt; **menyepuh** *vt* to plate or gild

sepuh *adj, coll, pol* old, elderly

sepulang *adv* upon arriving home, as soon as one gets home ← **pulang**

sepuluh *n* ten ← **puluh**

sepupu *n* cousin; *saudara* ~ cousin ← **pupu**

sepur *n, coll* railway (line); rail; platform

seputar *adj* around, about ← **putar**

seputih *adv* as white as; ~ *kapas* as white as cotton (*lit*), snow-white ← **putih**

serabi *n* small, soft, crumpet-like cake

serabut *n* fiber, fibre; ~ *kelapa* coconut fiber

seragam *n* uniform ← **ragam**

serah hand over, transfer; ~ *terima* hand over to someone else; **seserahan** *n* gifts brought by the groom to the bride's house; **menyerah** *vi* to surrender, give in, give up; **menyerahkan** *vt* to hand over; **penyerahan** *n* handing over, handover; **terserah** *adj* it depends; up to you

serai, séréh *n* lemon grass, citronella

serak *adj* hoarse

sérak: bersérakan *adj* scattered everywhere

serakah *adj* greedy; **keserakahan** *n* greed, avarice

Séram *pulau* ~ Seram, Ceram

seram *adj* weird, creepy; **menyeramkan** *adj* creepy, frightening

serambi *n* verandah; ~ *Mekah* Aceh, Gateway to Mecca

serampang: serampangan *adv* at random, blindly

serang attack; **serangan** n attack, raid; ~ *fajar* dawn raid; ~ *jantung* heart attack; **menyerang** vt to attack; **penyerang** n attacker; **penyerangan** n attack, aggression; **terserang** adj attacked

serangga n insect, bug

seranjang adv in the same bed; *mereka kakak-beradik masih tidur* ~ the brothers still sleep in the same bed ← **ranjang**

serap absorb; *daya* ~ absorbency; **menyerap** vt to absorb, soak up; **penyerapan** n absorption; **terserap** adj absorbed

serasa conj like; ~ *di alam bebas* as if in the great outdoors ← **rasa**

serasi adj suited, compatible, harmonious; **keserasian** n compatibility, suitability ← **rasi**

serat n fiber, fibre; ~ *nanas* pineapple fiber; **berserat** *makanan* ~ high-fiber food

seratus adj one hundred, a hundred; ~ *perak* coll one hundred rupiah ← **ratus**

Serawak n Sarawak

seraya conj while, during

serba adj all kinds of, various; ~-*serbi* all kinds of; ~ *guna* multi-purpose, all-purpose; ~ *salah* damned if you do, damned if you don't; wrong whatever you do; *toko* ~ *ada (toserba)* department store

serban, sorban n turban

serbét n serviette, table napkin

Sérbia n Serbia; *bahasa* ~ Serbian; *orang* ~ adj Serbian; n Serb

serbu: menyerbu vt to attack (as a group), charge, invade; **penyerbuan** n attack, charge, invasion

serbuk n powder; ~ *besi* iron filings; ~ *bunga* pollen; ~ *gergaji* sawdust

serdadu n, arch soldier; ~ *bayaran*, ~ *sewaan* mercenary

serdawa n burp, belch → **sendawa**

séréal n (breakfast) cereal

séréh, serai n lemon grass, citronella

serem → **seram**

serempak adj simultaneous, in unison

serémpét: menyerémpét vt to scrape, scratch against; **terserémpét** adj scraped, scratched

serendah-rendahnya adv as low as possible ← **rendah**

serentak adj all at once, simultaneous, at the same time

seréntétan n a string or series of ← **réntétan, réntét**

sérep adj reserve, change; *ban* ~ spare tire

sérét, menyérét vt to drag; **tersérét** adj dragged

sergap, menyergap vt to apprehend, ambush, catch; **penyergapan** n ambush, capture

seri *gigi* ~ incisor, eye tooth

seri ~*panggung, sripanggung* prima donna, female star; **berseri** adj beaming, glowing

seri n draw, tie

séri n series; *film* ~ serial, series

seriawan → **sariawan**

seribu adj one thousand, a thousand; *Pulau* ~ the Thousand Islands ← **ribu**

serigala n wolf

serikat, sarékat, syarikat union, united; ~ *buruh* labor union; *Amerika* ~ the United States of America, USA; **perserikatan** n federation; ~ *Bangsa-Bangsa (PBB)* the United Nations (UN)

serikaya → **srikaya**

serimpi n, Jav palace dance

sering adv often, frequently; ~ *sakit* sickly; **keseringan** n frequency; adv too often; **sesering** adv as often as; ~ *mungkin* as often as possible

seringai: menyeringai vi to grimace

sériosa n semi-classical music

sérius adj serious; **kesériusan** n solemnity, seriousness

séro n share; **perséro** adj proprietary limited (Pty Ltd); **perséroan** n company; ~ *terbatas (PT)* proprietary limited (Pty Ltd)

serobot push in front; *main* ~ not queue; **menyerobot** vi to push in front

seroja *(bunga)* ~ kind of lotus

sérong adj on an angle, oblique; *main* ~ to commit adultery, have an affair

seronok adj, neg (of dress) flashy, sexy; improper, inappropriate; *Mal* pleasant, pleasing

serpih, serpihan *n* shred, bit, piece; ~ *kayu* wood chip

sérsan *n* sergeant; ~ *mayor* sergeant-major

serta *conj* (together) with; ~*-merta* automatically, immediately; *ikut* ~, *turut* ~ to take part, participate; **keikutsertaan** *n* participation; **beserta** *conj* along with, and; **menyertai** *vt* to accompany; **menyertakan** *vt* to enclose, send with; enter; **peserta** *n* participant

sértifikat *n* certificate; **bersértifikat** *adj* with papers (of a house)

seru shout, call; *kata* ~ exclamation; *tanda* ~ exclamation mark; **seruan** *n* call, cry, exclamation; **berseru** *vi* to call, cry; ~ *kepada* to call on, appeal; **menyeru** *vi* to call out; **menyerukan** *vt* to call out something

seru *adj* exciting, great

seruduk: menyeruduk *vt* to butt, headbutt

seruling, suling *n* flute

serumah *adv* in the same house; *pasangan itu sudah lama tidak tinggal* ~ that couple have not lived together for a long time ← **rumah**

serumpun *adj* related, of one family; *bahasa* ~ languages related to Indonesian (such as Malagasy and Tagalog) ← **rumpun**

serundéng *n* fried desiccated coconut

seruni *(bunga)* ~ coastal flowering plant

serupa *adj* similar; **menyerupai** *vt* to resemble, be similar to, look like ← **serupa, rupa**

serut: serutan ~ *pensil* pencil shavings; *es* ~ shaved ice; **diserut** *v* to be sharpened

sérvis *n* repairs, service, maintenance; **disérvis** *v* to be serviced

sesajén *n, Jav* ritual offering ← **saji**

sesak *adj* close, dense, crowded; ~ *dada*, ~ *napas* short of breath; asthmatic; *penuh* ~ chock-a-block, chock-full

sesal regret; **menyesal** *v* to regret; **menyesali** *vt* to feel bad about (something personal); **menyesalkan** *vt* to feel bad about, regret (another's action); **penyesalan** *n* repentance, remorse

sesama *adj* fellow, another; ~ *manusia* fellow human being ← **sama**

sesampai *adv* upon arrival, on arriving, as soon as arriving ← **sampai**

sésar *operasi* ~ Cesarian (section); **disésar** *v* to have a Cesarian

sesar *n* fault, fault line

sesat lost; **menyesatkan** *adj* misleading, confusing; **tersesat** *adj* lost

sésé *n, sl* cubic centimeter → **séntiméter**

sesekali *adv* every now and then, occasionally ← **sekali, kali**

seseorang *n* somebody, a certain person ← **seorang, orang**

seserahan *n* gifts brought by the groom to the bride's house ← **serah**

sesering *adv* as often as; ~ *mungkin* as often as possible ← **sering**

sési *n* session

séspan *n* sidecar

sesuai *adj* in accordance with, appropriate; ~ *dengan* in accordance with; **menyesuaikan** *vt* to adapt, bring into line; ~ *diri* to adapt; **penyesuaian** *n* adaptation ← **suai**

sesuap *n* mouthful; ~ *nasi* a mouthful of rice; something to eat ← **suap**

sesuatu *n* something ← **suatu**

sesudah *prep* after; ~ *itu*, **sesudahnya** after that, then ← **sudah**

sesuka *adv* as one likes; ~ *hati* as one likes ← **suka**

sesungguhnya *adv* actually, really ← **sungguh**

setahu *conj* as far as is known; ~ *saya* as far as I know ← **tahu**

sétan, syaitan *n* devil, demon; **persétan** *ejac* go to hell!

setandan ~ *pisang* several hands (of bananas) ← **tandan**

setang ← **stang**

setara *adj* equal, equivalent ← **tara**

setaraf *adj* of the same standard ← **taraf**

setater → **starter**

setasiun, setasion → **stasiun**

seteguk *n* a gulp ← **teguk**

seték graft, cutting; **menyeték** *vt* to make a graft or cutting; to grow from a cutting setél *n* set; **setélan** *n* set, suit

setél, menyétel *vt* to tune, set, adjust; ~ *mesin* mobil to tune an engine; **penyetélan** *n* tuning

setelah *prep* after; ~ *itu* after that, then ← **telah**

setém: menyetém *vt* to tune (a piano)

setempat *adj* local ← **tempat**

setémpel ← **stémpel**

setengah *adj* half; ~ *baya* middle-aged; ~ *jam* half an hour; ~ *matang* medium, half-cooked; soft-boiled (of eggs); ~ *mati adv* half-dead; very hard; jam ~ *dua* half past one; **setengah-setengah** *adv* half-heartedly ← **tengah**

seterika → **setrika**

seteru: berseteru *vi* to be hostile, at odds with; **perseteruan** *n* feud

seterusnya *adv* after that, henceforth ← **terus**

setétés *n* a drop ← **tétés**

setia *adj* faithful; ~ *kawan* solidarity; loyal; **kesetiakawanan** *n* solidarity; **kesetiaan** *n* allegiance, faithfulness; **setiawan** *adj* loyal, faithful

setiap *adj* each, every; ~ *saat* any time ← **tiap**

setiba *adv* on arriving, on arrival ← **tiba**

setidaknya, setidak-tidaknya *adv* at least ← **tidak**

setimbal *adj* equivalent, proportional, even ← **timbal**

setimbun *n* a pile ← **timbun**

setinggi *adj* as high as; **setinggi-tingginya** *adv* as high as possible ← **tinggi**

setingkat *adj* of the same level ← **tingkat**

setip *n, coll* eraser, rubber

setir wheel; handlebars; drive; ~ *kanan* right-hand drive; **menyetir** *vt* to drive

sétjén *n* secretariat-general ← **sékré-tariat-jénderal**

Sétnég *n* State Secretariat, Ministry of the Interior ← **Sékrétariat Negara**

setongkol *n* an ear; ~ *jagung* an ear of corn ← **tongkol**

setop, menyetop *vt* to stop (a vehicle); **setopan** *n, coll* traffic lights

setor: setoran (make a) deposit; *n* minimal amount taxi drivers must earn per day; **menyetor** *vt* to pay in, deposit; **penyetor** *n* depositor

setrap: disetrap *v* to be punished (at school)

setrika, seterika iron; **setrikaan** *n* (clothes for) ironing; **menyetrika** *vt* to iron; *Inggris kita linggis, Amerika kita setrika* we'll smash England and flatten America (mid-1960s anti-Western slogan)

setrip, strip *n* (diagonal) slash; strip; section of a mobile phone battery symbol; *tinggal satu* ~ low battery

setruk → **struk**

setrum *n* current; **kesetrum** *v, coll* to receive an electric shock

setubuh: bersetubuh *vi* to have sex; **menyetubuhi** *vt* to have sex with; **persetubuhan** *n* sexual intercourse ← **tubuh**

setuju agree, agreed; **bersetuju** *vi* to agree; **menyetujui** *vt* to agree to, approve, ratify; **persetujuan** *n* agreement, approval ← **tuju**

seumpamanya *conj* for instance ← **umpama**

seumur *adj* the same age; lifelong; ~ *hidup* for life, lifelong; ~ *jagung* lasting not long, short-lived ← **umur**

seutuhnya *adv* completely ← **utuh**

séwa hire, rent; ~ *VCD* VCD rental; *uang* ~ rent; **séwa-menyéwa** *vi* to hire out goods, provide a rental service; **séwaan** *rumah* ~ rented house; **menyéwa** *vt* to rent, hire; **menyéwakan** *vt* to let (a house), hire out, lease

sewajarnya *adv* naturally ← **wajar**

sewaktu *conj* when; **sewaktu-waktu** *adv* at any moment; every now and then ← **waktu**

sewarna *adj* the same color ← **warna**

sewenang-wenang, sewenang-wenangnya *adv* tyrannically, arbitrarily ← **wenang**

sewindu *adj* eight years ← **windu**

séwot *adj* furious

Séychélles *n* Seychelles; *orang* ~ Seychellois, Seychellese

seyogianya *adv* properly, fittingly ← **yogia**

SH *abbrev Sarjana Hukum* legal graduate, LL.B

shabu-shabu *n, sl* heroin

shalawat, salawat, selawat *n, Isl* prayers, usu recited by a group; ~ *Nabi* prayers concerning the Prophet Muhammad

shio *n* Chinese horoscope, based on year born

sholat, shalat, salat, solat *Isl* (perform) one of the five daily prayers; ~ *asar* afternoon prayer; ~ *id* mass prayer at Idul Fitri or Idul Adha; ~ *isya* evening prayer; ~ *Jumat* Friday prayers; ~ *lohor* midday prayer; ~ *magrib* sunset prayer; ~ *subuh* dawn prayer; *seperangkat* ~ prayer shawls (for women); **disholatkan** *v* to be prayed for, have a prayer performed for you (after death)

SI *abbrev Sarékat Islam* an Islamic organization active early in the 20th century

si *pref* used before the name of a familiar third party; ~ *Anu*, ~ *Polan* so-and-so, whatshisname; ~ *jago merah* fire

sia: sia-sia *adj* pointless, useless; **menyia-nyiakan** *vt* to waste

siaga *adj* alert, on guard, ready; ~ *satu* red alert; **bersiaga** *vi* to be on alert, on guard; **kesiagaan** *n* readiness, preparedness

sial unlucky; **sialan** *ejac* damn! hell!

sialang *n* wild bees' nest

siamang *n* gibbon

sian *adj* cyan

siang *n* day; late morning, early afternoon (usu between 10 am and 3 pm); ~ *bolong* broad daylight; ~ *hari* daytime; ~ *ini* this morning, this afternoon; ~ *malam* day and night; *makan* ~ lunch, dinner; *masih* ~ it's still morning, it's only early afternoon; *tidur* ~ (take or have a) nap, siesta; *jam 11* ~ 11 am; *jam 2* ~ 2 pm; **kesiangan** *adj* late, too late in the day

sianida *n* cyanide

siap ready; ~ *pakai* ready-to-wear; *kurang* ~ under-prepared; ~ *saji* ready to serve, ready to eat; ~ *tempur* ready to fight, ready for action; **bersiap** *vi* to get ready; **bersiap-siap** *vi* to make preparations; **kesiapan** *n* readiness, willingness; **menyiapkan, mempersiapkan** *vt* to prepare something, get something ready; **persiapan** *n* preparations

siapa *interrog, pron* who; ~ *lagi* who else; ~ *namanya* what's their name; ~ *punya* whose is this; ~ *saja* anybody; *barang* ~ whosoever; **siapa-siapa** *pron, neg* nobody; *bukan* ~ nobody

siar *hak* ~ telecast or broadcast rights; **siaran** *n* telecast, broadcast; ~ *langsung* direct telecast; ~ *tunda* delayed telecast; ~ *ulang* re-run, repeat; **menyiarkan** *vt* to telecast, broadcast, disseminate; **penyiar** *n* announcer, (radio) broadcaster; **penyiaran** *n* broadcasting

siar: pesiar *n* trip, cruise; *kapal* ~ cruise ship; pleasure craft

siasat *n, neg* tactics, strategy; **menyiasati** *vt* to delve or pry into something, as a tactic

sia-sia *adj* pointless, useless; **menyia-nyiakan** *vt* to waste

sibak *n* part, parting (in hair); **menyibak** *vt* to part; to reveal

sibuk *adj* busy; engaged (of phones); *nada* ~ busy tone; **kesibukan** *n* activity, fuss, bustle, business; **menyibukkan** *vt* ~ *diri* to keep yourself busy, spend your time

sidak *n* spot inspection ← **inspéksi mendadak**

sidang *n* session, meeting; hearing; ~ *istimewa (SI)* special assembly (of parliament); ~ *kabinet* cabinet meeting; ~ *paripurna* plenary session; ~ *pengadilan* court hearing, court session; ~ *pleno* plenary session, full session; ~ *terbuka* public session; *Balai* ~ Jakarta Convention Centre; **bersidang** *vi* to convene, be in session; **menyidangkan** *vt* to hold a session, convene; to put on trial; **persidangan** *n* meeting, assembly; (extended) court session

sidik ~ *jari* fingerprints; **menyidik** *vt* to investigate; **penyidik** *n* investigator, detective; **penyidikan** *n* investigation ← **selidik**

Siérra Léone *n* Sierra Leone

sifat *n* quality, nature, character; **bersifat** *vi* to have the quality of

sifon *n* chiffon; *kue* ~ chiffon cake

sigap *adj* efficient, ready; **kesigapan** *n* efficiency, readiness

signifikan *adj* significant

sih used as a filler; *saya* ~ *tidak keberatan* I myself have no objection; *kenapa kamu harus lari di dalam rumah* ~ why are you running inside?

sihir *n* spells, witchcraft; *ilmu* ~ black magic; **menyihir** *vt* to perform magic; **penyihir** *n* wizard, witch, sorcerer; **tersihir** *adj* bewitched, under a spell

sikap *n* attitude; ~ *kasar* rudeness; **bersikap** *vi* to display an attitude

sikat brush; ~ *baju*, ~ *pakaian* clothes brush; ~ *gigi* toothbrush; ~ *rambut* hairbrush; ~ *sepatu* shoe brush; **menyikat** *vt* to brush

sikeras *vi* to maintain, stick to, be obstinate ← **keras**

sikon *n, sl* circumstances ← **situasi dan kondisi**

siklon *n* cyclone ← **angin**

siklus *n* cycle; ~ *haid* menstrual cycle; ~ *kehidupan* life cycle

siksa torture; **siksaan** *n* torture, torment; **menyiksa** *vt* to torture; **penyiksaan** *n* torture, (process of) torture; **tersiksa** *adj* tortured

siku *n* elbow; bracket; ~ *segi tiga* right angle; **siku-siku** *sudut* ~ right angle

sikut *n, Jav* elbow; angle

sila *n* principle; *Panca*~ Indonesian state philosophy, based on five principles

sila: bersila *duduk* ~ *vi* to sit cross-legged

sila: silakan, silahkan please (when offering); ~ *duduk* please sit down, please be seated; ~ *masuk* please come in; **mempersilakan** *vt* to invite someone to do something

silam *adj* past, ago; *beberapa tahun* ~ several years ago

silang cross, across; *tanda* ~ cross (X); *teka-teki* ~ *(TTS)* crossword puzzle; **silang-menyilang** *vi* to cross (over, of two lines), criss-cross; **bersilang** *adj* crossed; **menyilang** *silang*-~ *vi* to cross (over, of two lines), criss-cross; **persilangan** *n* crossing

silap delusion; wrong; **kesilapan** *n* mistake, error

silat traditional self-defense; *pencak* ~ Indonesian self-defense

silaturahmi, silaturahim *n* good relations, friendship; **bersilaturahmi** *vi* to maintain good relations, visit or meet friends

silau *adj* blinded, dazzled

silét *n* razor, scalpel; **menyilét** *vt* to cut with a knife, slit

silhuét → **siluét**

silih ~ *berganti* *vi* to take turns, replace

silika *n* silica, SiO_2; **silikon** *n* silicon (Si)

silinder *n* (degree of) astigmatism

silsilah *n* family tree, pedigree (of an animal)

siluét *n* silhouette

siluman *adj* invisible; *pesawat* ~ spy plane

SIM *n* driver's license, driving license; ~ *A* car license; ~ *B1* bus or truck license; ~ *B2* vehicle trailer license; ~ *C* motorcycle license; *membuat* ~ *vi* to get your driver's license ← **Surat Izin Mengemudi**

simak: menyimak *vt* to hear, monitor; *latihan* ~ listening practice

simalakama *buah* ~ a mythical fruit, which if eaten, will cause one parent to die, but if not eaten, will cause the other parent to die; dilemma, Catch-22 situation

simbah *pron, f* reference to an older servant

simbah: bersimbah *vi* to be spattered or wet with; **tersimbah** *adj* spattered, wet

simbol *n* symbol; **bersimbol** *vi* to have a symbol, be symbolized by → **berlambang**; **simbolis** *adj* symbolic

simétris *adj* symmetrical

simfoni *n* symphony

simpan *vt* to keep, put; **simpanan** *n* something kept; *uang* ~ savings, deposit; *wanita* ~ kept woman, lover; **menyimpan** *vt* to keep, save up, store; **penyimpanan** *n* storage; **tersimpan** *adj* kept, stored

simpang cross; ~ *empat* crossroads, intersection; ~ *lima* five-way intersection; ~ *semanggi* clover-leaf intersection; ~ *siur* confusing, disordered; ~ *tiga* T-junction, intersection; **bersimpang** *vi* to branch; **menyimpang** *vi* to deviate; **penyimpangan** *n* aberration, deviation; **persimpangan** *n* intersection

simpansé *n* chimpanzee

simpati *n* sympathy; **bersimpati** *adj* sympathetic; **simpatik** *adj* amiable, likeable; **simpatisan** *n* follower, sympathizer (of a party)

simpel *adj* simple → **sederhana**

simping *n* a kind of flat-shelled mollusc

simplifikasi *n* simplification

simposium *n* symposium

simpuh: bersimpuh *vi* to sit kneeling with feet to one side

simpul *n* knot; **kesimpulan** *n* conclusion; **berkesimpulan** *vi* to make the conclusion; **menyimpulkan** *vt* to conclude or summarize

simsalabim abracadabra

simulasi *n* simulation

sinagoga *n* synagogue

sinambung, bersinambung *adj* continuous; **kesinambungan** *n* continuity; **berkesinambungan** *adj* sustained, continuous; *perkembangan yang* ~ sustainable development ← **sambung**

sinar *n* ray, beam; ~ *matahari* sunbeam; ~-*X* x-ray; **sinaran** *n* ray; radiation; **bersinar** *vi* to shine, gleam; **disinar** *v* to have radiotherapy or chemotherapy; **penyinaran** *n* radiation

sindén, pesindén *n, f* singer accompanying a *gamelan* orchestra

sindikat *n* syndicate; gang

sindir, menyindir *vi* to insinuate, allude; **sindiran** *n* allusion, insinuation

sindrom, sindroma *n* syndrome; *sindroma Down* Down's Syndrome

sinéas *n* cinematographer; **sinétron** *n* local TV comedy or drama; *main* ~ to appear in such a program; **pesinétron** *n* actor or actress in such a program ← **sinéma éléktronik**

singa *n* lion; ~ *betina* lioness; ~ *laut* walrus, sealion; *anak* ~ lion cub; *negeri* ~ Singapore

Singapura *n* **Singapor** *coll* Singapore; *orang* ~ Singaporean

singgah *vi* to drop by, call at, stop over; **menyinggahi** *vt* to stop over in; **persinggahan** *n* stopover

singgasana *n* throne

singgung, menyinggung *vi* to touch on; ~ *perasaan* to offend someone, hurt someone's feelings; **tersinggung** *adj* offended, hurt; *mudah* ~ touchy, over-sensitive

singkap: menyingkap *vt* to open slightly, reveal; **menyingkapkan** *vt* to open something slightly; ~ *rahasia* to reveal a secret; **tersingkap** *adj* revealed

singkat *adj* short, brief, concise; ~*nya* in brief; ~ *kata, secara* ~ in brief, briefly; **singkatan** *n* abbreviation; **menyingkatkan** *vt* to abbreviate, shorten; **mempersingkat** *vt* to shorten

singkir: menyingkir *vi* to step or move aside; **menyingkirkan** *vt* to remove, brush aside; **penyingkiran** *n* exclusion, elimination; **tersingkir** *adj* eliminated, swept aside

singkong *n* cassava; *daun* ~ cassava leaves; *ubi* ~ cassava

singlét *n* singlet, vest, sleeveless undergarment

singsing: menyingsing *vt* to lift, rise; ~ *lengan baju* to roll up your shirt sleeves, get to work; *fajar* ~ daybreak

sini *adv* here; *di* ~ here; *dari* ~ from here; *ke* ~ here ← **ini**

sinis *adj* cynical, sarcastic; *nada* ~ mocking tone

sinolog *n* specialist in Chinese studies, sinologist; **sinologi** *n* Chinese studies, sinology

sinkrétisme *n* syncretism

sinkronisasi *n* synchronization

sinonim *n* synonym

sinopsis *n* synopsis

sinsé, sin shé *n* Chinese doctor, practitioner of Chinese medicine or acupuncture

sintal *adj* well-fed, rounded; shapely

Sinterklas *n* Santa Claus

sintésa *n* synthesis

sintétis *adj* synthetic

sinting *adj* silly, crazy

sinyal *n* signal; **sinyalir, mensinyalir** *vt* to signal, make a sign, point out

sinyo *pron, m* (young) master; *arch* term of address used for Western boys

siomay, sio may *n* fishcakes eaten with peanut sauce, a specialty of Bandung

sip, siip *adj, coll* great, fantastic

sipil *adj* civil; *keadaan darurat ~* civil emergency; *pegawai negeri ~ (PNS)* civil servant

sipir *n* prison warden, jailer

sipit *adj* narrow, slanting (of eyes); *mata ~* slanted eyes (esp of East Asians)

Siprus *n* Cyprus; *orang ~* Cypriot

sipu: tersipu(-sipu) *adj* embarrassed, shy

siput *n* snail; *kulit ~, rumah ~* snail shell

siram *vi* to pour; *kwetiau ~* boiled rice noodles; **siraman** *n* bathing ceremony before a wedding; **menyiram** *vt* to pour, water (plants); **menyirami** *vt* to pour onto; **menyiramkan** *vt* to pour something

sirat: tersirat *adj* implied

siréne *n* siren

siri *n* humiliation in Macassarese culture

sirih *n* betel; *makan ~* chew betel; *sekapur ~* foreword, opening words

sirik *adj* envious, jealous

sirip *n* fin; *sup ~ ikan hiu* shark's fin soup

sirkuit *n* (racing) circuit, race track

sirkulasi *n* circulation

sirkus *n* circus

sirna *adj* vanished, disappeared

sirop *n* syrup, cordial

sirsak *n* soursop, green-skinned fruit with white fleshy interior; *jus ~* soursop juice

sisa *n* rest, remainder, remains; *~ kain* remnants; *~ makanan* leftovers; *~ uang* balance, remaining money;

menyisakan *vt* to leave behind; **tersisa** *adj* leftover

sisi *n* side; *~ buruk* bad side, shortcoming; *~ lain* other side, other hand; *~ miring* hypotenuse

sisih: menyisihkan *vt* to set aside; **penyisihan** *n* elimination; *babak ~* elimination round, qualifying round; **tersisihkan** *adj* eliminated

sisik *n* scale (of fish); **bersisik** *adj* scaly, rough; *vi* to have scales

sisip: sisipan *n* infix; **menyisipkan** *vt* to insert

sisir *n* comb; hand (of bananas); *~ kuda* currycomb; **sesisir** *n ~ pisang* a bunch of bananas; **sisiran** *vi, sl* to comb your hair; **menyisir** *vt* to comb, check thoroughly; **penyisiran** *n* combing, checking

siskamling *n* neighborhood security system ← **sistém keamanan lingkungan**

sistém, sistim *n* system; **sistématis** *adj* systematic; *~ pernapasan* respiratory system; *~ Administrasi Manunggal Satu Atap (Samsat)* all-in-one administrative center (for extending licenses, obtaining permits, etc)

siswa *n* pupil; *~ -siswi* pupils; *Organisasi ~ Intra Sekolah (OSIS)* Student Council (secondary school); **siswi** *n, f* pupil

SIT *abbrev Surat Izin Terbit* publishing permit

sita confiscate, seize; *juru ~* bailiff; *sitaan barang ~* confiscated goods; **menyita** *vt* to confiscate; **penyitaan** *n* confiscation, seizure

Siti Hawa *Chr, Isl* Eve

situ *di ~* there (close to listener); *dari ~* from there; *ke ~* there ← **itu**

situ *n, Sund* lake

situasi *n* situation; *~ dan kondisi (sikon)* circumstances

situs *n* site; *~ internet* website; *~ purbakala* archeological site

siul: siulan *n* whistling; **bersiul** *vi* to whistle

siuman *vi* to recover consciousness, come round

siung *n* clove (of garlic); fang, tusk

SIUPP *abbrev Surat Izin Usaha Penerbitan Pers* press publication permit

siur *simpang* ~ in a mess, higgledy-piggledy

Siwa, Syiwa *n, Hind* Shiva, god of destruction

siwak *n* toothpick

SK *abbrev Surat Keputusan* decree, binding decision

skadron, skuadron *n* squadron

skala *n* scale; **berskala** *vi* to be on a scale; ~ *besar* large-scale

skandal *n* scandal

skéma *n* diagram, sketch

skénario *n* scenario

skétsa *n* sketch

ski ski; ~ *air* water-skiing; **berski** *vi* to ski, go skiing

skop → **sekop**

skor *n* score

skors, sekors: diskors *v* to be suspended (from school or work); **skorsing, sekorsing** *n* suspension

Skotlandia *n* Scotland; *bahasa* ~ Scots; Gaelic; *makanan* ~ Scottish food; *orang* ~ Scot; *wiski* ~ Scotch whisky

skripsi *n* (undergraduate) thesis

skuadron → **skadron**

skuter, sekuter *n* moped, (electric) scooter

slahrum *n, arch* whipped cream

slang → **selang**

slébor *n* mudguard; *adj, sl* at random, at will

sléndro 5-tone scale for *gamelan*

SLI *abbrev Sambungan Langsung Internasional* international direct dialling

SLJJ *abbrev Sambungan Langsung Jarak Jauh* long-distance direct dialling

slof *n* carton of cigarettes

slogan *n* slogan

sloki → **seloki**

Slovakia *n* Slovakia; *Ceko*~ Czechoslovakia; *bahasa* ~, *orang* ~ Slovak

Slovénia *n* Slovenia; *bahasa* ~ Slovenian; *orang* ~ Slovenian, Slovene

SLTA *abbrev Sekolah Lanjutan Tingkat Atas* Senior High School

SLTP *abbrev Sekolah Lanjutan Tingkat Pertama* Junior High School

SM *abbrev sebelum Masehi* before Christ, BC

SMA *abbrev Sekolah Menengah Atas* Senior High School

SMEA *abbrev Sekolah Menengah Ekonomi Atas* Senior High School for Economics

smés *n* smash (in tennis, badminton etc)

SMP *abbrev Sekolah Menengah Pertama* Junior High School

SMU *abbrev Sekolah Menengah Umum* Senior High School

so *EInd* already ← **sudah**

soal *n* question, issue, problem, matter; *conj* on the topic of; ~*nya* the problem is; ~ *kecil* small matter; ~ *ujian* exam question; *kunci* ~ answer key; **memecahkan** ~ *vt* to solve a problem; **mempersoalkan** *vt* to question, discuss; **persoalan** *n* problem, issue, matter

sobat *n* friend, comrade; ~ *karib* close friend; **bersobat** *vi* to be friends

sobék torn (esp of paper); **sobékan** *n* scrap, torn piece; **menyobék** *vt* to tear; **menyobék-nyobék** *vt* to rip up

SOBSI *abbrev Sentral Organisasi Buruh Seluruh Indonesia* All-Indonesian Federation of Labour Organisations

soda ~ *gembira* carbonated drink mixed with milk; ~ *kue* baking soda; *air* ~ soda water; **bersoda** *adj* carbonated; *minuman* ~ carbonated drink

sodét, sudét: sudétan *n* diversion, canal; **menyodét** *vt* to make an incision, cut a connecting channel

sodok: sodokan *n* shot (in billiards); **menyodok** *vt* to poke

sodomi *n* sodomy; **menyodomi** *vt* to sodomize

sodor: menyodori *vt* to hand to, offer; **menyodorkan** *vt* to offer up, put forward

sofa *n* sofa

sofbol *n* softball; *pemain* ~ softballer

soga *n* dark brown natural dye

sogok *uang* ~ bribe; **sogokan** *n* bribe; **menyogok** *vt* to bribe

sohor: kesohor *adj, coll* **tersohor** *adj* famous; **pesohor** *n* famous person, celebrity

sohun, so'un *n* vermicelli noodles

sok *coll* pretend; as if; ~ *tahu* be a know-all

sokbréker *n* shock absorber

sokoguru, sakaguru *n, Jav* pillar, esp central pillar of a traditional house

sokong support; **sokongan** *n* support; **menyokong** *vt* to support, bolster

sol ~ *sepatu* (shoe) sole

solar *n (minyak)* ~ diesel fuel

solat → **sholat**

soldér solder; **menyoldér** *vt* to solder

soléh, saléh *adj* pious, religious; **kesoléhan** *n* piety

solék: bersolék *vi* to put on make-up, dress up

solidaritas *n* solidarity

solis, solois *n* soloist

solusi *n* solution

somah *n, Jav* household, home

Somalia *n* Somalia; *bahasa* ~, *orang* ~ Somali

somasi *n* summons; **disomasi** *v* to be summoned → **panggil**

sombong *adj* arrogant, stuck-up; **kesombongan** *n* arrogance, pride; **menyombongkan** ~ *diri vi* to show off, blow your own trumpet

sompél *adj, Jav* chipped

somprét *ejac, Jkt* dammit!

sonder *conj, coll* without

songkét *n (kain)* ~ woven cloth, often with gold thread

songkok *n* traditional velvet fez, esp in Malay areas

songo, sanga *Wali* ~ *Isl* nine holy men who spread Islam across Java

songsong: menyongsong *vt* to welcome, greet

sono *adv, Jkt, coll* yonder, over there (far from speaker and listener) ← **sana**

sontak *mendadak* ~ suddenly

sontak: tersontak *adj* tugged

sonték → **conték**

sontoloyo *adj, coll* crazy, stupid; *ejac*

not care; *n* someone who looks after ducks, duck-keeper

sop *n* (Western-style) soup; ~ *ayam* chicken broth; ~ *buntut* oxtail soup

sopan *adj* polite, well-mannered; ~ *santun* good manners; **kesopanan** *n* manners, politeness; **kesopan-santunan** *n* manners, etiquette

sopir → **supir**

sopran soprano

sorak cheer, shout; applause; ~ *gembira*, ~ *sorai* shout for joy; *pemandu* ~ cheerleader; **bersorak** *vi* to cheer, shout

soré (late) afternoon, early evening; ~ *hari* late in the day; *nanti* ~ this afternoon, this evening; *selamat* ~ good afternoon; **soré-soré** *adv* late in the day; **kesoréan** *adv* too late

sorga → **surga**

sori *sl* sorry, pardon

sorong, menyorong *vt* to push, propose

sorot *n* beam of light; *lampu* ~ spotlight; **sorotan** *n* focus; **menyoroti** *vt* to light up, illuminate, focus on

sortir, mensortir *vt* to sort, organize

sosial *adj* social; *Menteri* ~ *(Mensos)* Minister of Social Affairs; *visa* ~ *budaya (sosbud)* sociocultural visa; **sosialisasi** *n* socialization; **mensosialisasikan** *vt* to introduce to the public, disseminate

sosialis *n* socialist; **sosialisme** *n* socialism

sosiolinguistik *adj* sociolinguistic; *n* sociolinguistics

sosiolog *n* sociologist; **sosiologi** *n* sociology

sosis *n* sausage

sosok *n* figure; **bersosok** *vi* to have a figure; ~ *tinggi* tall

sospol sociopolitic, social studies and politics ← **sosial politik**

soto *n* clear soup; ~ *ayam* chicken soup; ~ *Bandung* mainly vegetable soup from Bandung; ~ *Betawi* soup with coconut milk, a specialty of Jakarta; ~ *Madura* meat soup from Madura; **disoto** *v* to be made into clear soup; **menyoto** *vt* to make into soup

sotong *ikan* ~ cuttlefish, squid

so'un → **sohun**

sowan *vi, Jav* to pay a call on someone (of higher status)

spagéti *n* spaghetti

span *rok* ~ (tight) skirt

spanduk *n* large banner

Spanyol *n* Spain; *bahasa* ~ Spanish; *orang* ~ Spanish, a Spaniard

spasi *n* space, spacing; ~ *ganda* double spacing

spatbor, spakbor, sepatbor *n* mud-guard, fender

SPBU *abbrev setasiun pompa bensin umum* petrol/fuel/gasoline station

spékuk *n, arch* layer cake ← **lapis legit**

spékulasi *n* speculation; **berspékulasi** *vi* to speculate

spérma *n* sperm

spésial *adj* special; **spésialis** *n* specialist; **spésialisasi** *n* specialization

spidol *n* felt-tip marker or pen, texta; whiteboard marker

spidométer *n* speedometer

spion *n* spy; ~ *Melayu derog* (inept) local agent; *kaca* ~ rearview mirror; **spionase** *n* secret intelligence, espionage

spiral *n* IUD (intra-uterine device)

spiritus *n* spirits, alcohol

spons, spon *n* sponge

sponsor *n* sponsor; **mensponsori** *vt* to sponsor

spontan *adj* spontaneous

sportif *adj* sporting

sprei → **seprei**

SR *abbrev Sekolah Rakyat* People's School, forerunner of SD

Sr. *abbrev Suster* Sister, title for nurses

sreg *adj, coll* comfortable, fitting

Sri ~ *Lanka* Sri Lanka; *orang* ~ *Lanka* Sri Lankan; ~ *Paduka* His Royal Highness, Her Royal Highness; ~ *panggung* prima donna, female star; ~ *Paus* the Pope, Holy Father; ~ *Sultan* the Sultan of Jogjakarta; *Dewi* ~ goddess of rice

srigunting *n* a kind of bird

Srikandi *n* Arjuna's wife in shadow-puppet plays

srikaya, serikaya *n* custard-apple

SS *abbrev Sarjana Sastra* Bachelor of Arts, BA

ssst *excl* sssh!

ST *abbrev Sarjana Teknik* Bachelor of Engineering, BE

stabil *adj* stable

stabilo *n* highlighter, fluorescent marker

stadion *n* (sports) stadium

stadium *n* stage (of an illness); *kanker* ~ *satu* early cancer; *kanker* ~ *tiga* advanced

staf *n* staff, employees

stagén *n* corset-like belt worn with women's national costume

stamina *n* stamina (esp sexual)

standar *adj* standard; *n* standard → **mutu**

stang, setang *n* (on bicycles) bar, handlebar, stand

starter *n* ignition, starter

stasionér *adj* stationary; *sepeda* ~ exercise bike

stasiun, setasion, setasiun *n* ~ *(kereta api)* (railway) station; *kepala* ~ stationmaster; ~ *televisi* television station

statis *adj* static, not moving; *sepeda* ~ exercise bike

statistik *n* statistics; *Biro Pusat* ~ *(BPS)* Central Statistics Office

status *n* (marital) status

stéik *n* steak

stémpel, setémpel *n* official stamp; **distémpel** *v* to be stamped

sténo *n, coll* stenography; **sténografer** *n* stenographer; **sténografi** *n* stenography

stérek *adj, coll, arch* strong, healthy

stéril *adj* sterile; **menstérilkan** *vt* to sterilize; to neuter or spay (an animal); **stérilisasi** *n* sterilization

STh *abbrev Sarjana Teologi* Bachelor of Theology

stiker *n* sticker

stimulasi *n* stimulation

STNK *abbrev Surat Tanda Nomor Kendaraan* motor vehicle license

stok *n* stock → **pasokan**

stoking *n* (women's) stockings

stopkontak *n* power point, electricity socket

stoplés *n* glass jar for storing crackers and other loose food

Stovia *n* medical school in Dutch times, Native Doctors Training School ← **School tot Opleiding van Indische Artsen**

strata *n* level; ~ *satu (S1)* bachelor degree; ~ *dua (S2)* Masters degree; ~ *tiga (S3)* doctoral degree, Ph.D

stratégi *n* strategy; **stratégis** *adj* strategic

stréng *adj* strict, harsh, disciplinarian

strés, setrés stress(ed)

strom, stroom → **setrum**

struk *n* docket, receipt

struktur *n* structure; **struktural** *adj* structural

studi *n* studies; ~ *kelayakan* feasibility study; *melanjutkan ~ ke Australia* to continue your studies in Australia

studio *n* studio

stupa *n* stupa, bell-shaped dome covering a Buddha statue

SU *abbrev Sidang Umum* General Assembly

sua: bersua *vi* to meet

suai: sesuai *adj* in accordance or keeping with; ~ *dengan* in accordance with; **menyesuaikan** *vt* to adapt; ~ *diri dengan* to adapt yourself to; **penyesuaian** *n* adaptation

suak, swak *adj* weak (of batteries)

suaka *n* asylum; protection; ~ *alam* nature reserve; ~ *margasatwa* fauna reserve; bird sanctuary; ~ *politik* political asylum; *mencari ~ vi* to seek asylum; *pencari ~* asylum seeker

suam: suam-suam ~ *kuku* lukewarm

suami *n* husband; ~ *isteri* husband and wife, married couple; **bersuami** *adj, f* married; *vi* to have a husband; **bersuamikan** *vi* to be married to

suap *n* mouthful; bribe; **suapan** *n* bribe; **bersuap-suapan** *vi* to feed each other (in marriage rituals); **menyuap** *vt* to feed by hand; to bribe; **menyuapi** *vt* to feed someone by hand; **menyuapkan** *vt* to feed something by hand, to someone; **sesuap** *n* mouthful; ~ *nasi* a mouthful of rice; something to eat

suar *mercu* ~ lighthouse

suara *n* voice; sound (made by an animal); vote; ~ *bulat* unanimous; ~ *kucing* meow, sound of a cat; ~ *miring* dissenting voice, criticism; ~ *sumbang* discordant or tuneless voice; opposing voice; ~ *terbanyak* majority vote; *kotak* ~ ballot box; *memberi ~ vi* to (cast a) vote; *memungut ~ vi* to collect or get votes; *pengeras* ~ loudspeaker; megaphone; *penghitungan* ~ vote-counting; *pita* ~ vocal chords; *tarik* ~ singing, voice; **bersuara** *vi* to sound, have a voice; **menyuarakan** *vt* to voice

suasana *n* atmosphere; ~ *politik* political situation; **bersuasana** *vi* to have an atmosphere; *Bali masih ~ santai* Bali still has a relaxed atmosphere

suatu *adj* a (certain); ~ *hari* one day; **sesuatu** *n* something

subang *n* stud, earring

subhanahu wa taala (swt) *Isl* the Almighty and Most Praiseworthy, said after saying the name of Allah in speeches; *Allah* ~ God, the Almighty and Most Praiseworthy

subkontraktor *n* sub-contractor

subtropis *adj* sub-tropical

subsidi *n* subsidy; **mensubsidi** *vt* to subsidize

subuh *n* dawn; *sholat* ~ dawn prayer

subur *adj* fertile; **kesuburan** *n* fertility; **menyuburkan** *vt* to fertilize

subvérsi *n* subversion

subyék *n* subject; **subyéktif** *adj* subjective

suci *adj* pure, holy; ~ *hama* sterile; *air* ~ holy water; *kitab* ~ holy book; **kesucian** *n* purity; **menyucikan** *vt* to purify, cleanse

sudah *aux* **udah** *coll* already; indicates past time; ~ *makan garam* experienced, an old salt; **kesudahan** *tidak ber~* endless, infinite; **menyudahi** *vt* to end; **sesudah** *prep* after; ~ *itu*, **sesudahnya** *adv* after that, then ← **sudah**

Sudan *n* Sudan; ~ *Selatan* South Sudan; *orang* ~ Sudanese

sudétan n diversion, canal → sodét
sudi adj willing; ~kah would you be
    willing to; please; tidak ~ unwilling;
    kesudian n readiness, willingness
sudra n, Hind lowest caste, commoners
sudut n corner, angle, perspective, point
    of view; ~ lancip acute angle; ~ pandang
    point of view; ~ tumpul obtuse angle;
    ~ 45 derajat 45 degree angle; menyudut-
    kan vt to push into a corner, deflect
suér sl I swear
sugésti n power of suggestion; sugés-
    tif adj suggestive
suguh: suguhan n something offered
    or presented; menyuguhi vt to offer
    (food), present (a performance)
suhu n temperature; ~ badan body tem-
    perature; ~ kamar room temperature;
    ~ maksimal maximum temperature; ~
    minimal minimum temperature; ~ politik
    political climate, political atmosphere;
    bersuhu vi to have a temperature
suit whistling sound; suitan n whistle;
    bersuit vi to whistle using your fingers
sujud touch your head to the floor dur-
    ing prayer, prostration; bersujud vi to
    prostrate yourself
suka vt to like; adv often; ~ cita happi-
    ness; ~ damai peace-loving; ~ duka
    good and bad times, ups and downs,
    happiness and sadness; ~rela volun-
    tary; ~ menolong helpful; to like help-
    ing out; kurang ~ to not really like;
    kesukaan n hobby; enjoyment;
    menyukai vt to like; sesuka adv as
    one likes; ~ hati as one likes
sukar adj difficult, hard; kesukaran n
    difficulty
sukaréla adj voluntary; secara ~ volun-
    tarily; sukarélawan n volunteer ← réla
sukma n spirit, soul
suksés n success; semoga ~ good luck,
    every success; tim ~ team working to-
    wards the election of a candidate;
    mensukséskan vt to make something
    succeed
suku n tribe; part; ~ bangsa ethnic
    group; ~ bunga interest rate; ~ cadang
    spare part; ~ kata syllable; kesukuan
    adj ethnic, tribal

sukun (buah) ~ breadfruit
sukur coll → syukur
Sulaiman n, Chr, Isl Solomon
sulam: sulaman n embroidery; menyu-
    lam vt to embroider
sulang: bersulang vi to toast, drink to
sulap magic, conjure; bermain ~ vi to
    do magic; sulapan n conjuring,
    magic; tukang ~ magician, conjurer;
    menyulap vt to conjure up; to make
    something vanish or change; penyu-
    lap n magician, conjurer
Sulawési, Sulawesi pulau ~ Sulawesi,
    Celebes; ~ Barat (Sulbar) West Sula-
    wesi; ~ Selatan (Sulsel) South Sula-
    wesi; ~ Tengah (Sulteng) Central
    Sulawesi; ~ Tenggara (Sultra) South-
    east Sulawesi; ~ Utara (Sulut) North
    Sulawesi; Sulbar n West Sulawesi ←
    Sulawési Barat
sulfat n sulfate, sulphate; sulfur n sulfur,
    sulphur → belerang
sulih substitute; ~ suara dubbing;
    menyulih-suarakan vt to dub; pe-
    nyulih n ~ suara dubber; penyulihan
    n ~ suara dubbing
suling, seruling n flute; kecapi suling
    flute and zither, instruments in
    traditional Sundanese music; pemain ~
    flautist; suling kereta api train whistle;
    pesuling n flautist
suling: menyuling vt to distill;
    penyulingan n distillation
sulit adj difficult, complicated, hard; ~
    bicara find it hard to speak; masa ~
    hard times; kesulitan n difficulty,
    trouble; menyulitkan vt to make
    difficult, complicate, cause problems;
    mempersulit vt to make harder, further
    complicate; tersulit adj the hardest,
    most difficult
Sulsel n South Sulawesi ← Sulawési
    Selatan
Sultan n Sultan; Sri ~ the Sultan of
    Jogjakarta; kesultanan n sultanate
Sulteng n Central Sulawesi ← Sulawési
    Tengah
Sultra n Southeast Sulawesi ← Sulawési
    Tenggara
suluh n torch; menyuluh vt to illumi-

nate; to inform; **penyuluh** *n* scout;
education worker; **penyuluhan** *n*
education, explanation, dissemination
of information

sulung *anak ~* eldest (child)

Sulut *n* North Sulawesi ← **Sulawési
Utara**

Sumatera, Sumatra *(pulau) ~* Sumatra;
~ Barat (Sumbar) West Sumatra; *~
Selatan (Sumsel)* South Sumatra; *~
Utara (Sumut)* North Sumatra

sumbang *adj* false, out of tune; *suara ~*
tuneless voice

sumbang contribute; *~ saran* brain-
storm; **sumbangan** *n* contribution,
donation; *~ wajib* fee, compulsory donation; **menyumbang** *vt* to contribute,
make a donation; **menyumbangkan** *vt*
to contribute or donate something

Sumbar *n* West Sumatra ← **Sumatera
Barat**

sumbar, sesumbar *vi* to boast, brag

sumbat plug; cork, stopper; **meyum-
bat** *vt* to plug, stop; **penyumbatan** *n*
blockage; **tersumbat** *adj* blocked;
plugged

sumber *n* source; well; *~ air* (water)
source; *~ alam* natural resource; *~
daya* resource; *~ daya manusia (SDM)*
human resources (HR); *~ daya mineral*
mineral resources; *~ devisa* source of
foreign exchange; *~ minyak* oilwell; *~
terpercaya* reliable source; *nara~*
source (person); **bersumber** *vi* to have
a source; *Sungai Mekong ~ di Cina
Selatan* the Mekong River has its
source in southern China

sumbing *bibir ~* harelip, cleft palate

sumbu *n* fuse; wick (of a candle)

sumbu *n* axle

sumpah curse; oath; *~ dokter* the
Hippocratic oath; *~ jabatan* oath of
office; *~ Palapa* famous oath sworn
by Gajah Mada; *~ palsu* perjury; *~
pocong* oath taken while wrapped in a
shroud; *~ serapah* oaths and curses; *~
setia* pledge of loyalty or allegiance;
di bawah ~ under oath; **bersumpah** *vi*
to swear; **menyumpahi** *vt* to swear at
or curse someone

sumpek *adj* crowded, stuffy

sumpit *n* chopsticks; **sumpitan** *n* blowpipe; **menyumpit** *vt* to shoot at with a
blowpipe

Sumsel *n* South Sumatra ← **Sumatera
Selatan**

sumsum *n* bone marrow; *bubur ~* rice-
flour porridge

sumur *n* well; *~ bor* artesian well; *air ~*
well water

Sumut *n* North Sumatra ← **Sumatera
Utara**

sun peck on the cheek, kiss; *memberi ~*
vi to kiss on the cheek; **disun** *v* to be
kissed on the cheek

sunah *adj, Isl* commendable but not
compulsory; *~ Nabi, ~ Rasul* recommended by the Prophet Muhammad

Sunan *pron, Isl* holy man, title used
before the names of the Nine Holy
Men *(Wali Songo)*

sunat: sunatan *n* circumcision (celebration); **disunat** *v* to be circumcised;
menyunatkan *vt* to have someone circumcised

Sunda *bahasa ~, orang ~* Sundanese

sundul, menyundul *~ bola* *vi* to head
the ball (in soccer); **sundulan** *n* header

sungai *n* river; *anak ~* tributary; *~
Gangga* the Ganges; *~ Mahakam* the
Mahakam (River); *~ mati* dry riverbed;
~ Nil the Nile; *~ di bawah tanah* under-
ground river or stream

sungguh *adj* real, true; **sungguh-
sungguh** *adj* serious; **bersungguh-
sungguh** *vi* to do your best; **kesungguhan** *n* earnestness, sincerity, truth;
sesungguhnya *adv* actually, really;
sungguhpun *conj* although, even
though

sungkan *adj, Jav* reluctant; **kesungkanan** *n* reluctance; aversion

sungkawa *bela~* condolences; *menyampaikan bela~* *vi* to express your condolences or sympathy

sungkem, menyungkem *vt* to request
an elder's blessing by kneeling down
and placing one's forehead on an
elder's lap

sungsang *adj* upside down, reversed;

letak ~ breech position (of a baby in the womb)

suntik *jarum* ~ (injecting) needle; **suntikan** *n* vaccination, injection; needle; **menyuntik** *vt* to inject or vaccinate; **menyuntikkan** *vt* to inject something

sunting: menyunting *vt* to edit; **penyunting** *n* editor; **penyuntingan** *n* editing

sunting: mempersunting *vt* to marry (a woman)

suntuk *adj* late; *semalam* ~ all night long

sunyi *adj* lonely, still, quiet; ~ *senyap* completely still or quiet; **kesunyian** *n* quiet, still

sup *n* (Western-style) soup; ~ *ikan hiu* shark's fin soup

supaya *conj* in order that, so (used before nouns); *agar* ~ in order that

supel *adj* sociable, easy-going, flexible

super *adv, coll* super, very; ~*cepat* high-speed; ~*market* supermarket → **swalayan**

supermi, supermie *n* (brand of) instant noodles ← **mi**

Supersémar *abbrev Surat Perintah Sebelas Maret* Eleventh of March Instruction (enabling Suharto to take over power in 1966)

supir, sopir *n* driver, chauffeur; ~ *tembak* unregistered taxi driver; ~ *truk* truck driver; **menyupir** *v* to drive

suplai *n* supply → **pasokan**

suplemén *n* supplement

suporter *n* supporter

Sura, Surah *n* chapter of the Koran

suram *adj* gloomy, dark; **kesuraman** *n* gloom, darkness

surat *n* letter; certificate, card; ~ *angkutan* bill of lading; ~ *berharga* securities; ~ *cerai* divorce certificate; ~ *cinta* love-letter; ~*é*, ~ *éléktronik* email; ~ *edaran* circular, memo; ~ *gadai* pawn ticket; ~ *ijazah* diploma, certificate; ~ *izin* permit; ~ *jaminan* (letter of) guarantee; ~ *kabar* newspaper; ~ *kaleng* anonymous letter; ~ *kawin*, ~ *nikah* marriage certificate; ~ *kematian* death certificate; ~ *keputusan* decree, bind-

ing decision; ~ *kesaksian* testimonial, recommendation; ~ *keterangan* written statement; ~ *kuasa* letter of authorization, proxy letter; power of attorney; ~ *lahir* birth certificate; ~ *lamaran* (letter of) application; ~ *panggilan* summons; ~ *pembaca* letter to the editor; ~ *pengaduan* letter of complaint; ~ *pengantar* letter of introduction; ~ *perintah* warrant; instruction; ~ *rantai* chain letter; ~ *referensi* (letter of) reference (for a job); ~ *rekomendasi* letter of recommendation; ~ *tercatat* registered mail; ~ *undangan* invitation; ~ *utang* IOU (I owe you); ~ *wasiat* (last) will and testament; ~ *Yasin* chapter of the Koran, recited for the dead; ~ *balik nama* certificate of transfer of ownership; ~ *Izin Mengemudi (SIM)* driving license; ~ *Izin Usaha Penerbitan Pers (SIUPP)* press publication permit; ~ *Perintah Sebelas Maret (Supersemar)* Eleventh of March Instruction (enabling Suharto to take over power in 1966); **surat-menyurat** *vi* to correspond with someone; **menyurati** *vt* to write a letter to

surau *n, Isl* small prayer-house

surga, syurga, sorga *n* heaven, paradise; ~ *dunia* heaven on earth

suri *mati* ~ in a coma

suri *timun* ~ large cucumber, often eaten at fast-breaking

suri *ibu* ~ mother of the king or queen

Suriah *n* Syria; *orang* ~ Syrian

Suriname *n* Surinam; *orang* ~ Surinamese, a Surinamer

suruh order, ask; tell; **suruhan** *n* messenger, errand-boy; **menyuruh** *vt* to command, order; **pesuruh** *n* messenger, errand boy; ~ *kantor* office boy

surup: kesurupan *vi* to be possessed by a spirit or ghost

surut *vi* to recede; *air* ~ low tide; *pasang* ~ rise and fall; **menyurut** *vi* to fall, subside

survéi *n* survey

surya *sang* ~ the Sun; *tabir* ~ sunblock, sunscreen; *tenaga* ~ solar energy

Sus *pron, f* term of address for nurses,

Western women; *arch* term of address for Westernized women ← **suster, zuster, Mrs**

sus *kue* ~ small sweet buns containing rum-flavored cream

susah difficult; trouble, sorrow; ~ *makan* won't eat; **bersusah** ~ *payah* *vi* to work hard; **kesusahan** *n* trouble, difficulty; **menyusahkan** *vt* to bother, make difficult

susastra, susastera → **sastra**

susila *adj* modest, polite; *tuna*~ immoral; *wanita tuna*~ *(WTS)* prostitute; **bersusila** *vi* to have good morals; **kesusilaan** *n* modesty, decency; ethics

suspénsi *n* suspension

suster *n* nurse(maid); *n, Cath* nun

susu *n* milk; *n, sl* breast; ~ *bubuk* powdered milk; ~ *formula* milk formula; ~ *jolong* colostrum; ~ *kacang kedelai* soya milk, soymilk; ~ *kaleng* condensed milk; ~ *kental* condensed milk; ~ *murni,* ~ *segar* fresh milk; ~ *sapi* cow's milk; *air* ~*, air* ~ *ibu (ASI)* breast milk; *kepala* ~ cream; *mandi* ~ milk bath; bathe in milk; *saudara* ~ children fed by the same wet-nurse; ~ *tak berlemak* low-fat milk; **susuan** *saudara* ~ children fed by the same wet-nurse; **menyusu** *vi* to feed, suckle; **menyusui** *vt* to feed; *binatang* ~ mammal

susuk *n* implant

susul: susulan *ujian* ~ make-up exams; **menyusul** *vi* to follow, go after

susun heap, pile; *rumah* ~ *(rusun)* block of flats, apartment block; **susunan** *n* arrangement, organization, system; ~ *kalimat* sentence structure; **menyusun** *vt* to heap or pile; to arrange, organize, compile; **penyusun** *n* compiler, author; **tersusun** *adj* compiled; heaped up, organized

susup: menyusup *vt* to penetrate, infiltrate; **menyusupkan** *vt* to slip something in, infiltrate; **penyusupan** *n* infiltration

susur: menyusur *vt* to skirt; **menyusuri** *vt* to skirt or move along, follow; **penyusuran** *n* tracing

susut to shrink; **menyusut** *vi* to shrink,

become smaller; **menyusutkan** *vt* to reduce; **penyusutan** *n* reduction; *fin* depreciation

Sutan *pron, m, Min* Minangkabau title

sutera, sutra *n* silk

sutradara *n* director; **menyutradarai** *vt* to direct

suvenir *n* souvenir → **cenderamata, oleh-oleh**

swa- *pref* self-; ~*daya* self-sufficient; ~*karsa* one's own initiative; ~*karya* self-motivation; ~*layan* self-serve; supermarket; ~*sembada* self-sufficient

swak → **suak**

swakarsa *n* one's own initiative

swakarya *n* self-motivation

swalayan *n* supermarket

swasembada *adj* self-sufficient

swasta *adj* private; *bank* ~ private bank; **menswastakan** *vt* to privatize

Swaziland *n* Swaziland; *bahasa* ~*, orang* ~ Swazi

Swédia *n* Sweden; *bahasa* ~ Swedish; *orang* ~ Swede

swémpak *n, arch* swimming costume, swimsuit

swiké *n* dish consisting of frogs' legs

Swis *n* Switzerland; *orang* ~ Swiss

switer *n* jumper, pullover, sweater

swt. *abbrev subhanahu wa taala* the Almighty and Most Praiseworthy, said after saying the name of Allah in speeches

syahadat *n, Isl* profession of faith: I believe there is no God but God, and Muhammad is His Prophet

syahbandar *n* harbor master

syahdan *conj, lit* so it happened

syahdu *adj* calm, serene

syahid, sahid *Isl mati* ~ martyr

syahwat *n* lust, desire

syair *n* poem; **penyair** *n* poet

syaitan → **sétan**

syal *n* shawl, scarf

syarat, sarat *n* condition, terms; *dengan* ~ on condition; *memenuhi* ~ *vi* to meet requirements; *tanpa* ~ unconditional; **bersyarat** *adj* conditional; *vi* to have conditions; **persyaratan** *n* (set of) conditions

syariah *hukum* ~ Islamic law

Syiwa → **Siwa**

syok *coll, adj* in shock; *n* shock

syukur, sukur thanks, thanksgiving; thank goodness; *excl, sl* serves you right!; *puji* ~ *Chr* thank God; **syukuran** *n* thanksgiving ceremony; **bersyukur** *adj* grateful; *vi* to be grateful; **mensyukuri** *vt* to be thankful for or appreciate

syur *adj* sexy, hot

syurga → **surga**

syuting *n* shooting (a film or TV program); *lokasi* ~ on location

T

t [té] t, the 20th letter of the alphabet

taat *adj* obedient; religious; **ketaatan** *n* obedience; **menaati** *vt* to obey or follow something

tabah *adj* strong, resolute, brave; **ketabahan** *n* strength of character

tabel *n* table, chart; ~ *periodik* periodic table (of elements)

tabiat *n* character, nature, temperament; **bertabiat** *vi* to be of a character

tabib *n, arch* spiritual healer

tabir *n* curtain, screen; ~ *Besi* the Iron Curtain; ~ *surya* sunscreen, sunblock

tablét *n* tablet, pill

tabligh *n, Isl* rally; ~ *akbar* mass rally

tabrak collide; ~ *lari* hit and run; **tabrakan** *n* collision, accident; ~ *beruntun* pile-up; **bertabrakan** *vi* to run into each other, collide; **menabrak** *vt* to collide with; **menabrakkan** *vt* to ram something into; *Tri* ~ *mobil ayahnya pada tembok rumah* Tri drove his father's car into their fence; **tertabrak** *adj* **ketabrak** *coll* to be hit; ~ *mobil* hit by a car

tabu taboo

tabuh *n* drum; drumstick; **menabuh** *vt* to beat (a drum)

tabulasi: mentabulasi *vt* to tabulate, put into a table format

tabung *n* container, tube; ~ *gas* gas cylinder; ~ *kimia* test-tube; ~ *oksigen* oxygen cylinder, oxygen tank; *bayi* ~ test-tube baby; **tabungan** *n* savings; ~ *pos* postal savings account; *uang* ~ savings; **menabung** *vt* to save or deposit money; **penabung** *n* depositor

tabur scatter, sprinkle; ~ *bunga* to scatter flowers on a grave; **taburan** *n* sprinkling; **bertaburan** *adj* scattered over; **menabur** *vt* to scatter or sprinkle; **penabur** *n* sower

tadarus *n, Isl* communal reading of the Koran, esp during fasting month

tadi *adv* just now; ~*nya* originally, at first; ~ *malam* last night; ~ *pagi* this morning

taékwondo *n* taekwondo

taféta *n* taffeta

tafsir *n, Isl* Koranic interpretation or commentary; **tafsiran** *n* interpretation; **menafsirkan** *vt* to interpret something; **penafsiran** *n* interpretation

tagih, menagih *vt* to ask for payment, bill; **tagihan** *n* amount due, bill

tagih: ketagihan *adj* addicted to

-tah *suff, arch* added to words indicating doubt or wonder; *dia~ orangnya?* is he the one? → **kah**

tahajud *Isl sholat* ~ prayers said at night after sleeping for a period

tahan bear, stop, last; ~ *air* waterproof; ~ *api* fireproof; ~ *banting* tough, durable; ~ *lama* durable, lasting; *tidak* ~ can't bear; **tahanan** *n* prisoner, detainee; custody, detention; ~ *kota* confined to one town or city; ~ *politik (tapol)* political prisoner; ~ *rumah* house arrest; **bertahan** *vi* to hold out; **ketahanan** *n* endurance; **menahan** *vt* to bear, endure; to detain; ~ *diri* to hold yourself back, restrain yourself; ~ *nafas* to hold your breath; **mempertahankan** *vt* to defend or maintain; **penahanan** *n* detention, arrest; **pertahanan** *n* defense; ~ *sipil (hansip)* local security guard; civil defense; *Menteri* ~ Minister for Defense; **tertahan** *adj* held back, prevented; **tertahankan** *tak* ~ unbearable

tahap *n* stage, phase; **bertahap** *adj* in stages

tahayul, takhayul *n* superstition

tahbis: menahbiskan *vt* to consecrate, ordain; **penahbisan** *n* consecration, ordination

tahi *n* shit, feces; ~ *kucing* cat poo; bullshit!; ~ *lalat* mole; ~ *mata* mucus in the eye

tahlil *n, Isl* declaration that there is no God but God *(la ilaha illa'llah)*; **tahlilan** *n* recitation of this and other parts of the Koran

tahta → **takhta**

tahu (tau) *vt* to know; ~*nya* it turned out; ~ *diri* humble, to know your place; ~ *sama* ~ between ourselves, between the two of us; *tidak* ~ *malu* shameless, without shame; **tahu-tahu** *adv* suddenly, unexpectedly; **ketahuan** *vi* to be found out; **mengetahui** *vt* to know something, have knowledge of; **pengetahuan** *n* knowledge; *ilmu* ~ *alam (IPA)* science; **berpengetahuan** *adj* knowledgeable; **sepengetahuan** *adj* with knowledge; ~ *saya* to my knowledge; **setahu** *conj* as far as is known; ~ *saya* as far as I know

tahu *n* tofu; ~ *bacem* tofu steeped in a sweet sauce; ~ *gejrot* a tofu dish from the north coast of Java; ~ *gunting* a dish of tofu cut into strips; ~ *isi* stuffed tofu; ~ *petis* fried tofu with a spicy sauce; ~ *pong* tofu eaten with spicy sauce; ~ *sutera* Japanese tofu; ~ *tempe* tofu and unprocessed soybean cake; *bakso* ~ meatballs and tofu, a specialty of Bandung; *pepes* ~ tofu steamed in banana leaves

tahun *n* year; ~ *ajaran* academic year, school year; ~ *anggaran* financial year; ~ *Baru* New Year; ~ *Baru Cina*, ~ *Baru Imlek* Chinese New Year; ~ *cahaya* light year; ~ *depan* next year; ~ *hijriah* the Islamic calendar; ~ *kabisat* leap year; ~ *Masehi* Christian calendar; ~ *Naga* Year of the Dragon; ~ *Saka*, ~ *Çaka* Balinese calendar; **tahunan** *adj* annual, yearly; *buku* ~ yearbook; *laporan* ~ annual report; **bertahun-tahun** *adv* for years and years; **menahun** *adj* chronic; *penyakit* ~ chronic illness

tahu-tahu *adv* suddenly, unexpectedly ← **tahu**

taipan *n* magnate, wealthy financier

Taiwan *n* Taiwan; *orang* ~ Taiwanese

tajam *adj* sharp; *berotak* ~ to be sharp (-witted); **ketajaman** *n* sharpness; **mempertajam** *vt* to sharpen, exacerbate

taji *n* spur (of a cock)

Tajikistan *n* Tajikistan; *bahasa* ~ Tajik; *orang* ~ Tajikistani (nationality)

tajil *n, Isl* food eaten at sunset to break the fast → **buka puasa**

tajin *n* water in which uncooked rice has been washed

tajuk n crown; editorial; ~ *rencana* editorial; **bertajuk** *vi* to have a topic

tak no, not; ~ *ayal* without a doubt; without delay; ~ *becus* incapable, incompetent; ~ *mengapa* it doesn't matter; ~ *terhingga* endless, infinite; ~ *kan*, ~*kan* will not, won't ← **tidak**

tak *n* stroke; *sepeda motor tiga* ~ a three-stroke motorcycle

tak *pron, Jav* me, I; *sudah* ~ *tulis* I've already written it

takabur *adj* arrogant

takar: takaran *n* measuring container or spoon; **menakar** *vt* to measure

takbir *n, Isl* declaration that God is great *(Allah Akbar)*; **takbiran** *vi* to reiterate that God is great; *malam* ~ eve of Idul Fitri when this statement is chanted

takdir *n* fate, predestination; **menakdirkan** *vt* to determine, to predestine

takhayul, tahayul, takhyul *n* superstition

takhta, tahta *n* throne; ~ *Suci* the Holy See; *naik* ~ ascend to the throne; **bertakhta** *vi* to reign

takjub *adj* astonished; **menakjubkan** *adj* astonishing, amazing

takkan will not, won't ← **tak kan**

takluk *vi* to surrender, give in; ~ *pada* defer to; **menaklukkan** *vt* to defeat, conquer, subdue; **penaklukan** *n* surrender, submission

takraw *n* small rattan ball; *sepak* ~ game in which this ball is kicked without touching the ground

taksi *n* taxi; ~ *argo* metered taxi; ~ *borongan* unmetered taxi; ~ *gelap*, ~ *liar* unregistered taxi

taksir guess; **taksiran** *n* estimate, valuation, appraisal; **menaksir** *vt* to estimate, appraise, value; to like, find someone or something attractive; **naksir** *vt, coll* to like, find someone or something attractive; **penaksiran** *n* evaluation

taktik *n* tactic; **taktis** *adj* tactical

takut *adj* scared, afraid; ~ *mati* scared of dying; ~ *Tuhan* God-fearing; *jangan* ~ don't be afraid; *rasa* ~ fear; **ketakutan** *adj* frightened, terrified, scared; **menakuti** *vt* to scare someone; **menakut-nakuti** *vt* to frighten or intimidate (repeatedly); **menakutkan** *vt, adj* frightening; to frighten or scare; **penakut** *n* coward

takwa *adj* piety; **bertakwa** *vi* pious

takzim *salam* ~ respectful greetings

tala *garpu* ~ tuning fork; **menala** *vt* to tune; **penala** *n* tuning fork; **penalaan** *n* tuning

talak *n, Isl* repudiation; step towards divorce; ~ *pertama* first repudiation; ~ *ketiga*, ~ *terakhir* third and final repudiation, thus effecting a divorce

talang *n* (roof) gutter

talas *n* taro, a kind of edible root

talasémia *n* thalassemia

talenan *n* chopping or cutting board

tali *n* rope, cord, tie; ~ *ari-ari*, ~ *pusar* umbilical cord; ~ *beha* bra strap; ~ *kekang* reins; ~ *keluarga* family ties; ~ *pengaman* safety rope; ~ *pengikat* string; ~ *rafia* plastic twine; ~ *sepatu* shoelace; ~ *tambang* thick rope, tow line; ~ *temali* various kinds of ropes; **pertalian** *n* connection, relationship

talk *n* talc, talcum powder ← **bedak**

tamah *ramah-*~ informal get-together

tamak *adj* greedy; **ketamakan** *n* greed

taman *n* garden, park; ~ *atap* roof garden; ~ *bacaan*, ~ *pustaka* reading room, library; ~ *budaya* cultural center; ~ *hiburan (rakyat, THR)* amusement park, fun park; ~ *kanak-kanak (TK)* kindergarten; ~ *laut* marine park; ~ *margasatwa* fauna park, preserve; ~ *nasional* national park; ~ *safari* safari park; ~ *sari* (royal) gardens; ~ *Ismail Marzuki (TIM)* arts and theater complex in Jakarta; ~ *lalu lintas* traffic school, traffic garden; ~ *Makam Pahlawan (TMP)* heroes' cemetery; ~ *Pendidikan Alquran (TPA, TPQ)* Islamic Study Center; ~ *Mini Indonesia Indah (TMII)* Beautiful Indonesia in Miniature theme park (in Jakarta); **pertamanan** *adj* parks and gardens; *dinas* ~ parks service

tamansari *n* (royal) gardens

tamasya view; spectacle; excursion; **bertamasya** *vi* to travel (for pleasure), go sightseeing

tamat end, finish; ~ *Alquran* to complete reading the Koran aloud (in Arabic); ~ *sekolah* graduate; ~ *usia*, ~ *hidupnya*, ~ *riwayatnya* die; **tamatan** *n* graduate; **menamatkan** *vt* to end, finish, conclude

tambah add; ~ *angin* to pump up a tire; **tambahan** *n* addition, increase; *biaya* ~ extra cost; **bertambah** *vi* to increase; **menambah** *vt* to add to or increase; **menambahi** *vt* to increase something; **menambahkan** *vt* to add something to; **pertambahan** *n* increase

tambak *n* dam, pond; dike, levee, embankment; ~ *udang* shrimp pond, shrimp farm; **menambak** *vt* to dam (up)

tambal *n* patch; ~ *ban* tire repair; **tambalan** *n* patch, darn (on a sock); **bertambal** *adj* patched; *vi* to have a patch; **menambal** *vt* to mend, patch, darn; ~ *jalan* to fill in a pothole

tambang *n* mine; ~ *batu bara* coal mine, colliery; ~ *emas* gold mine; ~ *timah* tin mine; **menambang** *vt* to mine, dig for; **penambang** *n* miner; **pertambangan** *n* mining; *Perusahaan* ~ *dan Minyak dan Gas Bumi Negara (Pertamina)* Pertamina, the former state-owned oil company

tambang *n (tali)* ~ thick rope, tow line; *tarik* ~ tug-of-war

tambat tie up, tether; **tambatan** *n* mooring; bollard; **bertambat** *vi* to moor;

tertambat *adj* tied up, moored; **menambat, menambatkan** *vt* to fasten, tie up

tamborin *n* tambourine

tambun *adj* corpulent, fat

tambur *n* drum

tamburin → **tamborin**

taméng *n* shield; **bertaméng** *vi* to hide behind, use as a shield or pretext

tampak visible, appear; *~nya* it seems, apparently; **menampakkan** *vt* to show, make appear; **penampakan** *n* apparition; visitation

tampal → **tambal**

tampan *adj, m* handsome; **ketampanan** *n* good looks

tampang *n* appearance; *coll* face; *jual ~* to succeed on looks alone; show off

tampar slap, smack; **tamparan** *n* slap; **menampar** *vt* to slap

tampi: menampi *vt* to winnow; **penampi** *n* winnow

tampias → **tempias**

tampik: menampik *vt* to reject, refuse

tampil *vi* to appear; **menampilkan** *vt* to present; **penampilan** *n* performance

tampon *n* tampon

tampung: menampung *vt* to collect, hold; **penampung** *n* container; **penampungan** *n* reception, place that receives something; **tertampung** *adj* contained

tamsil *n* parable

tamtama *n, mil* officer

tamu *n* guest, visitor; *~ agung* VIP guest; *~ negara* state guest; *kamar ~, ruang ~* front room, living room; room for receiving guests; spare room; *~ tak diundang* uninvited guest

tanah *n* earth, ground, land, soil; country; *~ adat* land subject to traditional law; *~ air, ~ tumpah darah* Indonesia, native country, homeland; *~ garapan* crop land, arable land; *~ genting* isthmus; *~ Hijau* Greenland; *~ kapur* limestone country; *~ kosong* unused land; *~ labil* shaky ground, unstable ground; *~ lapang* field; square; *~ leluhur* ancestral home; *~ liat* clay; *~ longsor* landslide; *~ milik* private property, pri-

vately-owned land; *~ negara* state land; *~ rata* level ground; *~ reklamasi* reclaimed land; *~ Rencong* Aceh; *~ seberang* the Malay peninsula; lands outside Java; *~ sengketa* disputed land; *~ Suci* the Holy Land; *~ wakaf* *Isl* land donated to the local Muslim community; *air ~* groundwater; *minyak ~* kerosene

tanak: menanak *vi* *~ nasi* to cook rice

tanam *bercocok ~* to till or work the soil; **tanaman** *n* plant; *~ merambat* vine, climbing plant; *~ perdu* shrub, bush; **menanam** *vt* to plant or grow; to invest; **menanamkan** *vt* to plant or invest something; **penanaman** *~ modal* investment

tancap *layar ~* open-air makeshift cinema; **menancap** *vi* *~ gas* to step on the gas, accelerate

tanda *n* sign, mark, symbol; *~ baca* punctuation mark; *~ bahaya* warning signal, siren; *~ bayar* receipt; *~ bintang* asterisk (*); *~ hidup* sign of life; *~ hormat* salute; *~ masuk* admission ticket; *~ pagar* hash (#); *~ panah* arrow (→); *~ salib* sign of the cross; *~ seru* exclamation mark (!); *~ tanya* question mark (?); *~ tangan* signature; *~ terima* receipt; **menandatangani** *vt* to sign something; **bertanda** *adj* marked; *vi* to have a mark; **menandai** *vt* to mark; **penanda** *~ tangan* signatory; **pertanda** *n* sign, omen, indication

tandan *n* bunch, stem (of bananas)

tandang: bertandang *vi* to (pay a) visit

tandas *n* latrine, open toilet (esp over a river)

tandas *adj* finished, wiped out, desolated; **menandaskan** *vt* to use up; to reiterate

tandem *sepeda ~* tandem bike

tanding *n* match, equal; **bertanding** *vi* to compete, play; **pertandingan** *n* contest, competition, match; *~ persahabatan* friendly (match); **tertandingi** *tidak ~* unbeatable, no contest or comparison

tandu *n* litter; **menandu** *vt* to carry in a litter

tanduk *n* horn; (*seperti telur*) *di ujung* ~ hanging in the balance; **menanduk** *vt* to butt

tandus *adj* infertile, barren

tang *n* pliers, tongs

tangan *n* hand, arm; sleeve; ~ *besi* iron hand, iron fist; ~ *dingin* successful; ~ *kanan* right hand; ~ *kiri* left hand; ~ *manis* right hand; *buah* ~ souvenir; *kaki* ~ accomplice; *kerajinan* ~ handicraft; *panjang* ~ light-fingered; a thief; *sapu* ~ handkerchief; *sarung* ~ gloves; *tanda* ~ signature; *telapak* ~ palm; *tertangkap* ~ caught red-handed; *di bawah* ~ secretly; underhand; *kemeja* ~ *panjang* long-sleeved shirt; **bertangan** *adj* -handed; *vi* to have a hand; ~ *hampa* empty-handed; **menangani** *vt* to handle; **penanganan** *n* handling; **tertangani** *adj* handled, managed

tangga *n* ladder, stair(case); ~ *berjalan* escalator; ~ *nada* musical scale; *rumah* ~ household, family; *sudah jatuh tertimpa* ~ *pula* kicked when you're down and out

tanggal *n* date; ~ *kedaluwarsa* expiry date; ~ *lahir* date of birth; ~ *main* performance date, date of an event; ~ *muda* early in the month; ~ *tua* at the end of the month; **bertanggal** *vi* to have a date; *tak* ~ undated; **penanggalan** *n* calendar, dating; **tertanggal** *adj* dated

tanggal: menanggalkan *vt* to take off or remove; ~ *pakaian* to undress

tanggap: tanggapan *n* response, reaction; **menanggapi** *vt* to respond, reply

tanggap, menanggap *vi* ~ *wayang* to host a shadow-puppet performance

tangguh *adj* strong, powerful

tangguh: menangguhkan *vt* to delay, postpone, put something off; **penangguhan** *n* delay, postponement

tanggul *n* dike, levee, embankment

tanggulang: menanggulangi *vt* to deal or cope with; **penanggulangan** *n* tackling, fight against

tanggung *adj* guaranteed; responsible; ~ *jawab* responsibility; *rasa* ~ *jawab* sense of responsibility; **tanggungan** *n* dependent; responsibility; **bertanggung jawab** *vi* to be responsible, have a responsibility; **mempertanggung-jawabkan** *vt* to account for; **menanggung** *vt* to guarantee, be responsible; ~ *beban* to bear; **pertanggungan** *n* responsibility; insurance

tangis *isak* ~ crying; **tangisan** *n* weeping, crying; **menangis** *vi* to cry; **menangisi** *vt* to cry over, mourn

tangkai *n* stem, stalk; ~ *bunga* flower stem

tangkal: menangkal *vt* to ward off, repel; **penangkal** ~ *petir* lightning rod; **penangkalan** *n* preventative measure

tangkap, menangkap *vt* to catch, capture; **ketangkap** *coll* (to be) caught, arrested; **penangkapan** *n* capture, arrest; **tertangkap** *adj* caught; ~ *basah* caught in the act

tangkas *adj* agile, adroit, deft; **ketangkasan** *n* agility, dexterity; *menguji* ~ to test your skill

tangki *n* tank

tangkis *bulu* ~ badminton; **menangkis** *vt* to defend yourself, fend off, parry

tangkring: nangkring *vi, coll* to sit somewhere high up, perch

tangsi *n* barracks

tani *n* farmer; *Pak* ~ farmer; **petani** *n* farmer; ~ *cengkeh* clove farmer; ~ *plasma (pengembangan lahan dan sumber daya alam)* farmer who supplies a commodity to a factory; **bertani** *vi* to farm, till the soil; **pertanian** *n* agriculture; *sekolah* ~ agricultural college

tanjak: tanjakan *n* rise, ascent, climb; **menanjak** *adj* rising, climbing, steep; *vi* to rise, climb

tanjidor *n* brass band found in Jakarta

tanjung *n* cape; ~ *Harapan* the Cape of Good Hope; ~ *Verde* Cape Verde Islands; **semenanjung** *n* peninsula; ~ *Melayu* the Malay Peninsula

tanpa *prep, conj* without; ~ *syarat* unconditional; ~ *timbal (TT)* unleaded

tantang challenge; **tantangan** *n* challenge; **menantang** *vt* to challenge; *adj* challenging

tante *pron* term of address to a familiar but unrelated woman, esp of mother's generation, in Westernized circles; ~ *genit*, ~ *girang* flirtatious older woman

tanya *v* ask; ~ *jawab* question and answer session; *tanda* ~ question mark (?); *sudah tahu, masih* ~ you already know, so why ask?; **bertanya** *vi* to ask; **bertanya-tanya** *vi* to wonder, ask yourself; **menanya** *vt* to ask; **menanyai** *vt* to question someone; **menanyakan** *vt* to ask about; **mempertanyakan** *vt* to query; **penanya** *n* person who asks a question; **pertanyaan** *n* question; *mengajukan* ~ to ask questions

Tanzania *n* Tanzania; *orang* ~ Tanzanian

taoco → **tauco**

taogé, taugé, togé *n* bean sprouts

tapa: bertapa *vi* to live as an ascetic or hermit, seclude oneself; **pertapa** *n* ascetic, hermit, recluse; **pertapaan** *n* hermitage, retreat

tapai → **tapé**

tapak, telapak ~ *kaki* sole; footprint; ~ *tangan* palm; **menapak** *v* ~ *tilas* to retrace your steps, make a journey again

tapal ~ *batas* border, frontier; ~ *kuda* horseshoe

tapé, tapai *n* fermented rice; *air* ~ fermented rice wine

tapi → **tetapi**

tapir *n* tapir

tapis filter; **tapisan** *n* filtrate, something filtered; **menapis** *vt* to filter; **penapis** *n* filter

taplak ~ *meja* tablecloth

tapol *n* political prisoner ← **tahanan politik**

tar, tart *kue* ~ (birthday) cake

tara *tiada* ~ unequalled, incomparable; **setara** *adj* equal, equivalent

taraf *n* standard, level; ~ *hidup* standard of living; **bertaraf** *adj* of a certain standard; **setaraf** *adj* of the same standard

tarawih, taraweh (to go to) evening prayers at the mosque during Ramadan

targét *n* target; **menargétkan** *vt* to aim for

tari *n* (traditional) dance; ~ *balet* ballet; ~ *barong* a Balinese dance; ~ *cakalele* war dance from Minahasa and Maluku; ~ *jaipong* modern Sundanese dance; ~ *kecak* a Balinese dance, monkey dance; ~ *legong* Balinese trance dance performed by young girls; ~ *lenso* dance with a handkerchief; ~ *perang* war dance; ~ *piring* dance from West Sumatra; ~ *topeng* masked dance; **tari-tarian** *n* traditional dancing; **tarian** *n* (traditional) dance; **menari** *v* to dance, perform a traditional dance; **menari-nari** *vi* to dance about; **penari** *n* dancer

tarif, tarip *n* tariff, fare, rate

tarik pull; ~*-menarik* push and pull; ~ *suara* singing, voice; ~ *tambang* tug-of-war; **menarik** *vt* to pull or draw; *adj* interesting, attractive; ~ *kesimpulan* to conclude, draw a conclusion; ~ *napas* to take a breath, inhale; **narik** *v, coll* to work as a driver of public transport; **tertarik** *adj* attracted, interested; **ketertarikan** *n* interest, attraction

taring *n* tusk; fang; *gigi* ~ fang, incisor, canine tooth

tarip → **tarif**

tarling *n* Cirebonese music featuring guitar and flute ← **gitar suling**

taruh *v* to place, put; **taruhan** bet, wager; **bertaruh** *vi* to bet; **menaruh** *vt* to put (away); ~ *dendam* to bear a grudge; **mempertaruhkan** *vt* to stake, risk, bet; ~ *nyawa* to risk your life

taruna, teruna *n* youth; cadet

tas *n* bag; ~ *belanja* shopping bag; ~ *jinjing* bag carried in the hand; ~ *kerja* work bag; briefcase; ~ *pinggang* bum bag; ~ *punggung* backpack; ~ *tangan* handbag

tasbih, tasbéh *n, Isl* prayer beads

taskin *n* eradication of poverty ← **pengentasan kemiskinan**

tata *n* system, layout; ~ *acara* agenda, program; ~ *bahasa* grammar; ~ *cara* procedure; protocol; ~ *krama* manners; ~ *lingkungan* environment; ~ *negara* civics, state administration; ~ *rambut* hairstyle; ~ *ruang* layout; ~ *surya* the

Solar System; ~ *tertib* rules and regulations; ~ *usaha* administration; **menata** *vt* to arrange, lay out, organize; **penata** *n* ~ *rambut* hair stylist; ~ *rias* make-up artist; **penataan** *n* structuring, system

tatakan *n* mat; ~ *gelas* (drinks) coaster; ~ *piring* placemat

tatanan *n* arrangement, system; ~ *sosial* social structure

tatap look, face; ~ *muka* face-to-face; **tatapan** *n* gaze; **bertatapan** *vi* to look at each other, be face-to-face; **menatap** *vt* to gaze at

tatih: tertatih-tatih *adv* tottering, staggering

tatkala *conj* when, at the time

tato *n* tattoo; **bertato** *adj* tattooed; *vi* to have a tattoo

tau → **tahu**

taubat → **tobat**

tauco, taoco *n* brown sauce made from fermented soybeans

taufik *n* guidance; ~ *dan hidayah* divine guidance, God's guidance

taugé, taogé, togé *n* bean sprouts

tauké *n* Chinese boss or businessman

taulan, tolan *handai* ~ friends

Taurat *n* the Torah, the Old Testament

tau-tau *n* effigies of the dead in Tana Toraja

Tavip *abbrev Tahun Vivere Pericoloso* the Year of Living Dangerously (from a Sukarno speech in 1964)

tawa laugh, laughter; **tawaan** *n* object of fun; **ketawa** *vi, coll* to laugh; ~ *keti-wi* giggle; **mengetawakan** *vt* to laugh at; **tertawa** *vi* to laugh or smile; ~ *lepas* to laugh out loud

tawakal *adj* resigned, trusting

tawan: tawanan *n* prisoner of war (POW), detainee; **menawan** *vt* to detain, take someone prisoner, intern; *adj* attractive, appealing

tawar *adj* bland, plain, tasteless; *air* ~ fresh water; **penawar** *n* antidote

tawar bargain; **tawaran** *n* offer, bid; **tawar-menawar** *vi* bargaining; **menawarkan** *vt* to offer or bid; **penawaran** *n* offer, bid

tawas *n* alum

tawon *n* bee; *minyak* ~ oil used for insect bites

tawur: tawuran gang or street fight, often among schoolboys

tayang ~ *ulang* repeat, re-run; *kejar* ~ continuous shooting (of a TV series); **tayangan** *n* program, telecast; ~ *langsung* live telecast; ~ *tunda* delayed telecast; **menayangkan** *vt* to telecast, show on TV

tayub *n* dance to *gamelan* or traditional song

TBC *abbrev tuberkulosa* tuberculosis

té t, the 20th letter of the alphabet

téater *n* theatre (building), theater; drama group

tebak guess; **tebakan** *n* guess; **tebak-tebakan** *n* guessing game; **menebak** *vt* to guess

tebal *adj* thick; ~ *iman* religious, pious; ~ *muka*, ~ *telinga* thick-skinned; *kertas* ~ card(board); **ketebalan** *n* thickness

tebang *vi* fall, be cut down (of trees); **menebang** *vt* to fell, cut down; **penebang** *n* logger, woodcutter; **penebangan** *n* logging; ~ *liar* illegal logging

tébar: bertébaran *adj* scattered; **menébarkan** *vt* to scatter; to cast (a net); **penébaran** *n* spread, spreading

tebas, menebas *vt* to cut down, clear

tébéng → **nébéng**

tébésé, TBC *n* tuberculosis

tebing *n* cliff, gorge, steep bank; *panjat* ~ rock-climbing, abseiling

tebu *n* sugarcane; *air* ~ sugarcane juice; *ladang* ~ cane fields

tebus: tebusan *n* ransom; **menebus** *vt* to pay a ransom; ~ *dosa* to atone for a sin; **penebus** *n* redeemer; ransom; **penebusan** *n* redemption

tédéng *Jav* ~ *aling-aling* screen, blind; cover-up (of a secret)

teduh *adj* shady; quiet, still; *Lautan* ~ the Pacific Ocean; **berteduh** *vi* to take shelter; **keteduhan** *n* calm, stillness

téga *v, aux* to have the heart to, dare to; ~*nya* how could you have the heart; *mereka* ~ *memotong gaji Yanti sebelum dia diberhentikan* they dared to cut Yanti's wages before her job was terminated

tegak *adj* upright, erect; ~ *lurus* perpendicular, 90-degree angle; **menegakkan** *vt* to erect; to uphold or maintain; **penegakan** *n* upholding or maintenance; ~ *hukum* to uphold the law

tegal: tegalan *n* plain; dry or fallow field

tegang *adj* tense, stressed, strained; **tegangan** *n* tension, pressure; ~ *listrik* voltage; **bersitegang** *vi* to stand fast, persevere; **ketegangan** *n* tension; **menegangkan** *adj* tense, stressful

tegap *adj* strong, upright, sturdy

tegar *adj* stubborn, determined, resolute, unbending; **ketegaran** *n* determination

tegas *adj* clear, distinct; **ketegasan** *n* resolve, determination; **menegaskan** *vt* to clarify, point out, affirm; **mempertegas** *vt* to further clarify, reiterate; **penegasan** *n* affirmation, reiteration

tégel *n, arch* (floor) tile → **ubin**

tegor → **tegur**

teguh *adj* firm, fast, strong, solid; ~ *hati* firm, resolute

teguk gulp, swallow, draft; **tegukan** *n* swallow, gulp; **meneguk** *vt* to gulp or guzzle; **seteguk** *n* a gulp

tegun: tertegun *adj* taken aback

tegur *vi* speak; rebuke; ~ *sapa* say hello; **teguran** *n* warning, rebuke; greeting; **menegur** *vt* to speak to, address; to warn, rebuke, tell off

téh *n* tea; ~ *botol* bottled tea; ~ *hijau* green tea; ~ *kotak* sweet tea in a box-shaped container; ~ *melati* jasmine tea; ~ *pelangsing* slimming tea; ~ *poci* tea made in an earthenware pot, specialty of the Tegal area; ~ *susu* tea with milk; ~ *tarik* Malaysian-style sweet tea with milk; ~ *tawar* black tea with no sugar; *es* ~ *(manis)* (sweet) iced tea; *celup* ~, *kantong* ~ tea-bag

téhnik → **téknik**

teka: teka-teki *n* riddle, puzzle; ~ *silang* (TTS) crossword

tékad, tékat will, determination; **bertékad** *vi* to be determined

tekan press; **tekanan** *n* pressure, stress;

~ *darah* blood pressure; ~ *udara* air pressure; **menekan** *vt* to press; **menekankan** *vt* to stress, emphasize; **tertekan** *adj* stressed, pushed, pressured

teka-teki *n* riddle, puzzle; ~ *silang* (TTS) crossword

téken, menéken *vt* to sign, initial

téknik, téhnik *n* engineering; *adj* technical; ~ *elektro* electrical engineering; ~ *mesin* civil engineering

téknis *adj* technical; *bantuan* ~ technical assistance; **téknisi** *n* technician

téknokrat *n* technocrat

téknologi *n* technology; ~ *tinggi* advanced technology

téko *n* kettle, teapot

tekor be short, not have enough

téks *n* text; subtitle

tékstil *n* textile

tékstur *n* texture

ték-ték *mi* → itinerant wandering noodle seller who taps on his cart

téktonik *n* (plate) techtonics; *adj* techtonic; *gempa* ~ earthquake, tectonic movement; *lempeng* ~ techtonic plate

tekuk ~ *lutut* bend your knee; **bertekuk** *vi* to bend your knees; ~ *lutut* to surrender; **menekuk** *vi* ~ *lutut* to go down on your knees

tekukur *n* a kind of dove

tekun *adj* hard-working; **bertekun** *vi* to work hard, be diligent; **ketekunan** *n* diligence, dedication; **menekuni** *vt* to apply yourself to; *Anto* ~ *ilmu hukum* Anto is studying law

tékwan *n* a kind of fishball soup

telaah study, research; **menelaah** *vt* to analyze

teladan *n* example, model

telaga *n* lake

telah *adv* already; **setelah** *conj* after

telak *menang* ~ win outright

telan *v* to swallow; **menelan** *vt* to swallow something; **tertelan** *vi* accidentally swallowed

telanjang *adj* naked, nude, bare; ~ *bulat* stark-naked; ~ *kaki* barefoot; **bertelanjang** *vi* to be bare; ~ *dada m* bare-chested; *f* topless; **menelanjangi** *vt* to strip or denude

telanjur, terlanjur *adv* too late, already;
  ~ *berangkat* already left ← **lanjur**
telantar, terlantar *adj* neglected, abandoned; **ketelantaran** *n* neglect
telapak, tapak ~ *kaki* sole; footprint; ~
  tangan palm
telat *adv, coll* (too) late; **ketelatan** *n*
  lateness
telatén *adj* patient, persevering; **ketelaténan** *n* patience, perseverance
télé: bertélé-télé *adj* long-winded
teledor *adj* careless; **ketelédoran** *n*
  carelessness
téléfon → **télepon**
télékomunikasi *n* telecommunications;
  warung ~ *(wartel)* small office where
  you can make calls and send faxes
telekung *n* women's prayer shawl
télénovéla *n* Latin American soap opera
telentang *adj* on your back, prone ←
  lentang
télépati *n* telepathy, ESP
télepon, télépon, téléfon telephone; ~
  genggam, ~ *seluler (ponsel)* cell phone,
  mobile phone; ~ *interlokal* long-distance
  call; ~ *bebas pulsa* toll-free number;
  buku petunjuk ~ telephone directory,
  phone book; **menélépon** *vt* to ring
  (up), call, (tele)phone
télér *adj* drunk, intoxicated; exhausted
télér *es* ~ iced fruit drink
téléskop *n* telescope
télévisi, tévé, tivi *n* television, TV;
  menonton ~ to watch TV
telinga *n* ear; *daun* ~ ear; *gendang* ~ ear
  drum; *memasang* ~ to listen carefully;
  masuk ~ *kiri, keluar* ~ *kanan* in one ear
  and out the other (of someone who
  doesn't listen); **bertelinga** *vi* to have
  ears; ~ *tebal* thick-skinned, impervious
  to criticism
teliti *adj* accurate, careful, meticulous;
  ketelitian *n* accuracy, care; **meneliti** *vt*
  to investigate or research; **peneliti** *n*
  researcher; **penelitian** *n* research
Télkom *n* state telephone company;
  Télkomsél *n* state mobile phone
  company
telon *minyak* ~ oil used for babies and
  sprains

telor → **telur**
teluk *n* bay, gulf; ~ *Benggala* the Bay of
  Bengal; ~ *Bone* the Gulf of Bone; ~
  Cendrawasih Cendrawasih Bay; ~ *Iran*
  the (Persian) Gulf; ~ *Jakarta* Jakarta
  Bay
telunjuk *jari* ~ index finger, forefinger,
  pointer
telur, telor *n* egg; ~ *asin* pale blue salted duck's egg; ~ *ayam* egg; ~ *busuk*
  rotten egg; ~ *ceplok* fried egg; ~ *dadar*
  omelet; ~ *ikan* roe (as food), spawn; ~
  kodok spawn; ~ *puyuh* quail egg; *indung* ~ ovary; *kuning* ~ yolk; *putih* ~
  albumen, egg white; ~ *mata sapi* fried
  egg, sunnyside up; ~ *setengah matang*
  soft-boiled egg; *seperti* ~ *di ujung tanduk* hanging in the balance; **bertelur**
  vi to lay an egg
telusur: menelusuri *vt* to follow, go
  along, trace
tém: ngetém *vi, coll* to wait for passengers (of public transport)
téma *n* theme; **bertéma** *vi* to have as a
  theme
temali *tali* ~ various kinds of ropes
teman *n* friend; ~ *kencan* date; ~ *sekamar* room-mate; ~ *sekantor* friend
  from work, colleague; ~ *sekelas* classmate; **berteman** *vi* to be friends; **menemani** *vt* to accompany; **pertemanan**
  n friendship
temaram *adj* dark
tembaga *n* copper; ~ *kuning* brass; ~
  perunggu bronze; ~ *putih* pewter
témbak shoot, fire; ~ *mati* shoot dead;
  execute (by firing squad); *supir* ~ unregistered taxi driver; **témbakan** *n*
  shot, shooting; **menémbak** *vt* to
  shoot; **menémbaki** *vt* to shell; **penémbak** *n* marksman, gunman; ~ *jitu*
  sniper; **petémbak** *n* (target) shooter
  (as athlete); **tertémbak** *adj* shot (accidentally)
tembakau *n* tobacco
tembang *n* (esp Jav traditional) song; ~
  kenangan old songs, golden oldies;
  menembangkan *vt* to sing something
tembikar *n* pottery, crockery, ceramics
témbok *n* (concrete or outer) wall; ~

Berlin the Berlin Wall; ~ *Cina* the Great Wall of China; ~ *Ratapan* the Wailing Wall (in Israel); **menémbok** *vt* to wall up; to cover an area with wax (when making batik); **menemboki** *vt* to wall something up

tembuni *n* placenta

tembus pierce, penetrate; go through; ~ *pandang* see-through; **tembusan** *n* copy; **menembus** *vt* to pierce, stab

téméh *remeh-~* unimportant

temen → **teman**

temenggung → **tumenggung**

tempa *besi ~* wrought iron; **menempa** *vt* to forge

tempat *n* place; ~ *beribadah* place of worship; ~ *duduk* seat; ~ *garam* salt-shaker; ~ *gula* sugar bowl; ~ *istirahat* rest area; ~ *keramat* place sacred to locals; ~ *kerja* workplace; ~ *kos* boarding house, lodgings; ~ *lahir* birthplace, place of birth; ~ *lain* somewhere else; ~ *parkir* car park, parking lot; ~ *perkemahan* camping ground, campsite; ~ *roti* bread basket, bread bin; ~ *sabun* soap dish; ~ *sampah* rubbish bin, garbage can, trash can; ~ *teduh* shade; shelter; ~ *tidur* bed; ~ *tinggal* home, residence; ~ *wudu* tap used for washing before praying; *pada ~nya* in its place, proper; ~ *cuci tangan* washbasin; ~ *kejadian perkara (TKP)* scene of the crime, crime scene; ~ *pemakaman umum (TPU)* public cemetery; ~ *pembuangan akhir (TPA)* tip, rubbish dump; ~ *pemungutan suara (TPS)* polling booth; ~ *penitipan anak* child-minding center, creche; **bertempat** *vi* to take place or happen; ~ *tinggal* to live or reside; **menempati** *vt* to occupy, take a place; **menempatkan** *vt* to place; **setempat** *adj* local

tempayan *n* water jar, pitcher

tempé *n* unrefined soybean curd; ~ *penyet* thin, fried slices of tempe; *bangsa ~* small and insignificant nation

témpél stick to; *meterai ~* adhesive seal; **témpélan** *adj* patch, sticker; **menémpél** *vi* to stick or adhere to; **menémpélkan** *vt* to stick, paste or glue something

tempéléng *vt* to slap, box someone's ears

témperatur *n* (body) temperature

tempias, tampias splash; **menempias** *vi* to splash

témpo *n* time, pace; ~ *dulu*, ~ *doeloe* the olden days, colonial times; ~ *hari* the other day, recently

témporér *adj* temporary → **sementara**

tempuh *jarak ~* range (of weapons); distance covered; **menempuh** *vt* to endure, go through; to take on, take up; ~ *jalan* to go a certain way; ~ *ujian* to do an exam

tempur *vi* fight, combat; *pesawat ~* fighter (plane); **bertempur** *vi* to fight; **pertempuran** *n* battle

tempurung *n* coconut shell; ~ *kepala* skull; ~ *lutut* kneecap, patella; *seperti katak di bawah ~* narrow-minded (*lit.* like a frog under half a coconut shell)

temu find, locate; *titik ~* meeting point, point of agreement; **temuan** *n* find, discovery; **bertemu** *vi* to meet; *sampai ~ lagi* see you later, so long; **ketemu** *v, coll* to meet; **mempertemukan** *vt* to bring together (with a view to marriage); **menemui** *vt* to meet up with, arrange to meet; ~ *ajal* to die; **menemukan** *vt* to discover; **penemu** *n* inventor, discoverer; **penemuan** *n* invention, discovery; **pertemuan** *n* meeting

temulawak *n* kind of root, curcuma

temurun *turun-~* passed down through the generations

tenaga *n* energy, power; ~ *ahli* specialist (staff); ~ *air* hydroelectric power; ~ *atom*, ~ *nuklir* atomic energy, nuclear energy; ~ *bayu* wind power; ~ *dalam* spiritual energy; ~ *gerak*, ~ *kinetis* kinetic energy; ~ *kerja (naker)* manpower, workforce; ~ *Kerja Indonesia (TKI)*, ~ *Kerja Wanita (TKW) f* Indonesian worker abroad, Indonesian migrant worker; ~ *kuda* horsepower; ~ *listrik* electricity; ~ *matahari*, ~ *surya* solar energy; ~ *panas bumi* geothermal energy

tenang *adj* calm, still, quiet; **ketenangan** *n* calm, peace; **menenangkan** *vt* to calm someone (down)

tenar *adj* well-known, popular; **ketena-ran** *n* popularity

ténda *n* tent

tendang kick; **tendangan** *n* kick; ~ *bebas* free kick; ~ *penalti* penalty kick; ~ *penjuru* corner kick; ~ *pertama* kick-off; **menendang** *vt* to kick; **tertendang** *adj* kicked (accidentally)

ténder *n* tender, offer

tengadah face up; **menengadah** *vi* to look up; **menengadahi** *vt* to look up at

tengah middle, in the middle of, half; *adj* central; ~ *hari* midday, noon; ~ *malam* midnight; *di* ~ among; *garis* ~ diameter; *Jawa* ~ *(Jateng)* Central Java; *Kalimantan* ~ *(Kalteng)* Central Kalimantan; *Sulawesi* ~ *(Sulteng)* Central Sulawesi; **tengah-tengah** *prep* middle; **menengah** *adj* intermediate; *kelas* ~ middle class; *sekolah* ~ high school, secondary school; **pertengah-an** *n* middle; *Abad* ~ the Middle Ages; **setengah** *adj* half; ~ *matang* medium, half-cooked; soft-boiled (of eggs); ~ *mati adj* half-dead; *adv* very hard; ~ *tiang* at half-mast; *jam* ~ *dua* half past one; **setengah-setengah** *adv* half-heartedly

tengara *n* sign, signal

ténggang *n* period; ~ *waktu* time frame; *masa* ~ (period of) grace (for an unpaid bill or phone card)

ténggang ~ *rasa* considerate, compassionate

tenggara *adj* southeast; *Asia* ~ Southeast Asia; *Nusa* ~ the Lesser Sunda islands

tenggat *n* deadline, time limit

tenggelam sink, sunken; drown; **menenggelamkan** *vt* to sink or drown something

Ténggér *bahasa* ~, *orang* ~ Tenggerese, a Hindu community of East Java

ténggér: berténggér *vi* to perch, land

tenggiling → **trenggiling**

tenggiri *ikan* ~ mackerel

tenggorok, tenggorokan *n* throat; *sakit tenggorokan* sore throat

tengkar: bertengkar *vi* ~ *(mulut)* to quarrel; **pertengkaran** *n* quarrel

tengkorak *n* skull

Tengku *pron, m* title for Malay nobility

tengkuk *n* nape of the neck

tengkulak *n* agent, broker

tengkurap, tengkurup *adv* on your front or face; *tidur* ~ sleep on your stomach

téngok, menéngok *vt* to look or see; to look in on someone

ténis *n* tennis; *permainan* ~ tennis match; *pemain* ~ tennis player; **peténis** *n* tennis player

ténor *adj, noun* tenor

ténsi *n* blood pressure; ~ *rendah* low blood pressure; ~ *tinggi* high blood pressure

tentang *conj* about, concerning; **berten-tangan** *adj* contradictory, contrary, opposing; **menentang** *vt* to oppose, resist; **penentang** *n* opponent; **per-tentangan** *n* conflict

tentara *n* soldier; ~ *payung* paratroops; ~ *pelajar* youth corps; *masuk* ~ to join the army; ~ *Nasional Indonesia (TNI)* Indonesian Army

ténténg, menénténg *vt* to carry dangling from the hand

tenteram, tentram *adj* peaceful, calm; **ketenteraman** *n* peace

tentu *adj* certain, sure, definite; ~*nya,* ~ *saja* of course; **ketentuan** *n* condition, stipulation; **menentu** *tidak* ~ not fixed, vague; **menentukan** *vt* to decide, determine, stipulate; **penentu** *faktor* ~ deciding factor; **penentuan** *n* setting, fixing, determining; **tertentu** *adj* definite, fixed, certain

tenun ~ *ikat* woven cloth from Nusa Tenggara; *kain* ~ woven cloth; **tenunan** *n* weaving, woven fabric; **bertenun** *vi* **menenun** *vt* to weave

téolog *n, Chr* theologian; **téologi** *n* theology

téori *n* theory; ~ *domino* the domino theory

tepak slap; **menepak** *vt* to slap, clap (someone's shoulder)

tepa slira → **tepo seliro**

tepat *adj* precise, exact; ~*nya* to be precise; ~ *guna* appropriate; effective; **bertepatan** *adj* coinciding with, at the same time as; **ketepatan** *n* precision, accuracy; **menepati** *vi* to fulfill; ~ *janji* to keep a promise

tepergok *adj* caught in the act, caught red-handed ← **pergok**

tepi edge, side; ~ *Barat* the West Bank; ~ *jalan* side of the road; ~ *kota* city outskirts; ~ *laut* seaside; ~ *pantai* seaside; ~ *sungai* river bank; **menepi** *vi* to move to the side, move over

tepis: menepis *vt* ward off, deflect

tépos *adj* thin (of buttocks)

tepo seliro, tepa slira *Jav* to put yourself in another's shoes

tepuk ~ *tangan* clap, applause; **bertepuk tangan** *vi* to applaud, clap; **menepuk** *vt* to pat, slap; ~ *bahu* to clap (someone's shoulder)

tepung *n* flour; ~ *beras* rice flour; ~ *gandum* (wholemeal) flour; wheat flour; ~ *kanji* tapioca flour; ~ *maizena* wheat flour; ~ *sagu* sago flour; ~ *terigu* flour; *gula* ~ icing sugar

ter- *pref* (before adjectives) the most; **terbaik** *adj* the best; **tercantik** *adj* the most beautiful; **tertinggi** *adj* the highest

tér *n* tar

tera *n* official stamp, seal; **tertera** *adj* printed, stamped

terabaikan *vi* to be neglected, ignored ← **abai**

terakhir *adj* last, final, latest ← **akhir**

térakota *adj* terracotta

terali *n* trellis, lattice work

teramat ~ *sangat* extremely ← **amat**

terambung-ambung *adj* to float or bob about ← **ambung**

terancam *adj* threatened; *harimau Jawa* ~ *punah* the Javan tiger is threatened with extinction ← **ancam**

terang *adj* clear; ~ *benderang* bright, dazzling; ~ *bulan* full moon; *terus* ~ direct, frank, straightforward; **terang-terangan** *adj* frank, open; **keterangan** *n* explanation; *kata* ~ adverb; **menerangi** *vt* to illuminate; **menerangkan** *vt* to explain; **penerangan** *n* information; lighting, enlightenment; *Departemen* ~ *(Deppen)* Department of Information; *Menteri* ~ *(Menpen)* Minister for Information

terangkut *adj* transported ← **angkut**

teraniaya *adj* oppressed, tyrannized ← **aniaya**

terantuk-antuk *adj* sleepy; *vi* to be sleepy ← **antuk**

terap: terapan *adj* applied; *linguistik* ~ applied linguistics; **menerapkan** *vt* to apply something; **penerapan** *n* application

térapi *n* therapy; *fisio~* physiotherapy

terapung *adj* drifting, floating ← **apung**

terarah *adj* directed ← **arah**

téras *n* balcony, terrace

terasa *vi* to be felt ← **rasa**

terasi *n* shrimp paste

téraso *n* terrazzo

teratai *(bunga)* ~ lotus

teratasi *adj* can be overcome ← **atas**

teratur *adj* organized, (at) regular (intervals) ← **atur**

terawang: menerawang *vi* to appear (through something translucent)

terawat *adj* cared for; *tidak* ~ unkempt, neglected; *banyak bangunan lama yang tidak* ~ many old buildings are left neglected ← **rawat**

terbabar *adj* spread out; explained ← **babar**

terbaik *adj* the best ← **baik**

terbakar *adj* burnt; *kulit Bapak* ~ *matahari* Father was sunburnt ← **bakar**

terbalik *adj* overturned, upside-down, opposite ← **balik**

terbang *vi* fly; blow away; *kapal* ~, *pesawat* ~ aeroplane, airplane; *lapangan* ~ airfield; *piring* ~ flying saucer; **beterbangan** *vi, pl* to fly about; **menerbangkan** *vt* to fly something; **penerbang** *n* pilot, aviator; **penerbangan** *n* flight; aviation; *perusahaan* ~ airline

terbangun *adj* woken up (of your own accord) ← **bangun**

terbanyak *adj* most; *suara* ~ majority ← **banyak**

terbaring *adj* stretched out, lying down ← **baring**

terbaru *adj* latest, newest ← **baru**

terbata-bata *adv* brokenly, not fluently ← **bata**

terbatas *adj* limited; *perseroan* ~ proprietary limited ← **batas**

terbawa *adj* (accidentally) taken away; ~ *arus* swept away in the current ← **bawa**

terbayang *adj* imagine, conceivable ← **bayang**

terbelakang *adj* backward, neglected; **keterbelakangan** *n* backwardness, neglect ← **belakang**

terbelenggu *adj* in shackles, irons ← **belenggu**

terbelit *adj* twisted, involved; ~ *hutang* debt-ridden ← **belit**

terbenam *adj* set, sunken; *matahari* ~ sunset ← **benam**

terbendung *tak* ~ unstoppable ← **bendung**

terbengkalai *adj* neglected, unfinished ← **bengkalai**

terbentuk *adj* formed, shaped, created ← **bentuk**

terbentur *adj* accidentally bumped; *kepalanya* ~ *di atap* he banged his head on the roof ← **bentur**

terbesar *adj* largest, biggest ← **besar**

terbilang *adj* counted; *tidak* ~ countless; *esa hilang, dua* ~ one lost, two scored (epigraph at military cemeteries) ← **bilang**

terbirit-birit *adv* hurriedly, helter-skelter ← **birit**

terbit *vi* to rise, appear; to be published, come out; *matahari* ~ sunrise; **terbitan** *n* publication, edition; **menerbitkan** *vt* to publish, issue; **penerbit** *n* publisher; ~ *efek* issuer

terbuang *adj* thrown out, wasted ← **buang**

terbuat *adj* made ← **buat**

terbuka *adj* open; *sidang* ~ public session ← **buka**

terbukti *adj* proven ← **bukti**

terbunuh *adj* killed ← **bunuh**

terburu, terburu-buru *adj* in a hurry ← **buru**

tercabik-cabik *adj* torn, to shreds ← **cabik**

tercabut *adj* removed ← **cabut**

tercantum *adj* attached, included, inserted ← **cantum**

tercapai *adj* achieved; *cita-cita tak* ~ unfulfilled dreams ← **capai**

tercatat *adj* registered; noted; *surat* ~ registered mail ← **catat**

tercebur *adj* fallen into water ← **cebur**

tercekik *adj* strangled ← **cekik**

tercela *adj* wrong; *perbuatan yang* ~ misdeed, wrong ← **cela**

tercemar *adj* polluted ← **cemar**

tercemplung *adj* fallen into water ← **cemplung**

tercengang *adj* surprised, astonished ← **cengang**

tercepat *adj* fastest ← **cepat**

tercermin *adj* reflected ← **cermin**

tercinta *adj* dear, beloved; *Hari yang* ~ dear Hari ← **cinta**

tercipta *adj* created ← **cipta**

tercium *adj* smelt; found out ← **cium**

terdaftar *adj* registered, enrolled ← **daftar**

terdakwa *n* the accused ← **dakwa**

terdampar *adj* beached, grounded, washed ashore; *ada ikan paus* ~ *di pantai* a whale was beached on the sands ← **dampar**

terdekat *adj* closest, nearest ← **dekat**

terdengar *adj* audible ← **dengar**

terdiam *vi* to fall silent ← **diam**

terdiri ~ *atas,* ~ *dari* to consist of, be based or founded on ← **diri**

terdorong *adj* pushed, shoved ← **dorong**

terduga *tidak* ~ unexpected ← **duga**

terélakkan *tidak* ~ unavoidable, inevitable ← **élak**

teréliminasi *adj* eliminated ← **éliminasi**

terencana *adj* planned ← **rencana**

terendah *adj* lowest ← **rendah**

terendam *adj* inundated, flooded, soaked ← **rendam**

terengah-engah *adj* gasping, puffing ← **engah**

terganggu *adj* bothered, disrupted, disturbed ← **ganggu**

tergantung *adj* depending (on), it depends ← **gantung**

tergelétak *adj* sprawled ← **gelétak**

tergelimpang *adj* sprawled ← **gelimpang**

tergelincir *adj* skidded, slipped; *pesawat itu* ~ the plane skidded ← **gelincir**

tergelitik *adj* tickled ← **gelitik**

tergesa-gesa *adj* in a hurry or rush ← **gesa**

tergiur *adj* tempted ← **giur**

tergoda *adj* tempted ← **goda**

tergolong *adj* to include, be part of or considered ← **golong**

tergopoh-gopoh *adv* hurriedly, in a rush ← **gopoh**

tergorés *adj* scratched ← **gorés**

tergoyahkan *tak* ~ unshakable ← **goyah**

terguyur *adj* soaked, drenched ← **guyur**

terhadap *conj* regarding, against, with respect to ← **hadap**

terhalang *adj* blocked, prevented; ← **halang**

terhanyut *adj* drifting, floating, washed away ← **hanyut**

terhapus *adj* disappeared; accidentally deleted ← **hapus**

terharu *adj* moved, touched ← **haru**

terhempas *adj* thrown down ← **hempas**

terhingga *tidak* ~ unlimited, boundless ← **hingga**

terhormat *adj* respected; *yang* ~ to, dear ← **hormat**

terhunjam *adj* stuck, inserted ← **hunjam**

teri *ikan* ~ small fish, small fry

teriak scream, yell; **berteriak** *vi* to scream or shout; **meneriaki** *vt* to shout at someone; **meneriakkan** *vt* to shout something

terigu *n* wheat; *tepung* ~ flour

terik *panas* ~ hot and dry, dry heat

terikat *adj* bound ← **ikat**

terima *tanda* ~ receipt; ~ *kasih* thank you; ~ *kos* boarder wanted; **menerima** *vt* to receive, accept; **penerima** *n* recipient; addressee; **penerimaan** *n* receipt; revenue; acceptance

terima kasih thank you, thanks; ~ *banyak* thank you very much; *mengucapkan* ~ to say thank you; **berterima kasih** *vi* to be grateful or thankful

terimplikasi *adj* to be implicated ← **implikasi**

terindah *adj* the most beautiful ← **indah**

terinféksi *adj* infected ← **inféksi**

teringa-inga *adj* dazed and confused ← **inga**

teringat *vi* to be reminded of, come to mind ← **ingat**

terinjak *adj* stepped upon; downtrodden ← **injak**

terinspirasi *adj* inspired (by) ← **inspirasi**

teripang, tripang *n* sea slug, sea cucumber, trepang

terisak, terisak-isak *adj* sobbing ← **isak**

terisolasi, terisolir *adj* isolated ← **isolasi, isolir**

teritis *n* balcony

téritorial *adj* territorial; *perairan* ~ territorial waters

terjadi *vi* to happen, become, occur ← **jadi**

terjaga *adj* alert, on guard ← **jaga**

terjal *adj* very steep, precipitous

terjalin *adj* forged, involved ← **jalin**

terjamin *adj* guaranteed ← **jamin**

terjang kick, thrust; *sepak* ~ action, behavior; **menerjang** *vt* to kick, attack, charge; **penerjangan** *n* attack, charge

terjangkau *adj* affordable; within reach or range ← **jangkau**

terjangkit *adj* infected ← **jangkit**

terjaring *adj* netted, caught ← **jaring**

terjatuh *adj* (accidentally) fallen ← **jatuh**

terjawab *adj* answered ← **jawab**

terjebak *adj* trapped, caught; ~ *macet* caught in traffic ← **jebak**

terjemah: terjemahan *n* translation; **menerjemahkan** *vt* to translate (writing); to interpret (speaking); **penerjemah** *n* translator; ~ *lepas* freelance translator; ~ *tersumpah* sworn translator; **penerjemahan** *n* translation

terjepit *adj* pinched, caught in an uncomfortable situation ← **jepit**

terjerat *adj* snared, trapped, caught ← **jerat**

terjerembab *adj* to fall over, fall forward ← **jerembab**

terjerumus *adj* plunged into ← **jerumus**

terjual *adj* sold; *habis* ~ sold out ← **jual**

terjun dive, fall; go down; ~ *payung* parachuting, sky diving; *air* ~ waterfall; **menerjunkan** *vt* to drop something; **penerjun, peterjun** ~ *(payung)* parachutist, sky diver

terka: terkaan *n* guess; **menerka** *vt* to guess

terkabul *adj* granted ← **kabul**

terkadang *adv* sometimes, occasionally ← **kadang**

terkam: menerkam *vt* to pounce, attack

terkantuk-kantuk *adj* sleepy ← **kantuk**

terkapar *adj* fallen, strewn ← **kapar**

terkebelakang *adj* backward ← **belakang**

terkecuali *tidak* ~, *tanpa* ~ without exception ← **kecuali**

terkejut *adj* surprised ← **kejut**

terkekang *adj* held in, curbed, not free ← **kekang**

terkékéh-kékéh *vi* to laugh ← **kékéh**

terkemuka *adj* prominent ← **ke muka**

terkenal *adj* well-known ← **kenal**

terkendali *adj* controlled ← **kendali**

terkesan *adj* impressed; seemed ← **kesan**

terkesima *adj* amazed, astonished; *vi* to be amazed or astonished ← **kesima**

terketuk *vi* ~ *hati* to have it in your heart ← **ketuk**

terkikis *adj* eaten away, eroded ← **kikis**

terkilir *adj* twisted, sprained ← **kilir**

terkini *adj* the latest ← **kini**

terkira *tak* ~ unsuspected, not thought of ← **kira**

terkirim *adj* sent; *pesan* ~ message sent ← **kirim**

terkontaminasi *adj* contaminated ← **kontaminasi**

terkoyak *adj* torn ← **koyak**

terkuak *adj* to part, open; be revealed, exposed ← **kuak**

terkuat *adj* the strongest ← **kuat**

terkubur *adj* buried in an accident ← **kubur**

terkulai *adj* sprawled, splayed, fallen ← **kulai**

terkuras *adj* drained ← **kuras**

terkurung *adj* locked up ← **kurung**

terkutuk *adj* cursed, accursed ← **kutuk**

terlahir *adj* born ← **lahir**

terlalu *adv* too; **keterlaluan** *n* excess, too much ← **lalu**

terlambat *adj* (too) late, delayed ← **lambat**

terlampau *adj* too, extremely ← **lampau**

terlampir *adj* attached, enclosed ← **lampir**

terlanjur, telanjur *adj* too late, already; ~ *berangkat* already left ← **lanjur**

terlantar ← **telantar**

terlarang *adj* forbidden, banned; *buku* ~ banned book ← **larang**

terlatih *adj* trained ← **latih**

terlebih *adj* especially; ~ *dahulu* first, firstly ← **lebih**

terlémpar *adj* thrown, flung ← **lémpar**

terléna *adj* offguard ← **léna**

terletak *adj* situated, located ← **letak**

terlibat *adj* involved, implicated ← **libat**

terlilit *adj* caught up, twisted ← **lilit**

terlindas *adj* run over ← **lindas**

terlindung *adj* protected, guarded ← **lindung**

terluka *adj* wounded, hurt, injured ← **luka**

terlukis *adj* painted; engraved ← **lukis**

terlupakan *tak* ~ unforgettable ← **lupa**

termakan *adj* eaten, consumed (by accident) ← **makan**

termangu-mangu *adj* confused, dazed; speechless ← **mangu**

termasuk *adj* including ← **masuk**

termasyhur *adj* most famous ← **masyhur**

termenung *adj* lost in thought ← **menung**

términal *n* (bus) terminal, bus station

térmométer *n* thermometer

térmos *n* thermos

termurah *adj* the cheapest ← **murah**

ternak *n* cattle, livestock; *makanan* ~ fodder, cattle feed; **menernakkan** *vt* to breed; **peternak** *n* (cattle) farmer; **peternakan** *n* cattle farm, ranch

ternama *adj* famous, well-known ← **nama**

ternganga *adj* gaping, flabbergasted, wide open ← **nganga**

ternilai *adj tidak* ~ priceless, invaluable ← **nilai**

ternyata *adv* apparently, as it turned out ← **nyata**

terobati *adj* soothed, comforted; treated, cured ← **obat**

terobos break through, pierce; **terobosan** *n* breakthrough; **menerobos** *vt* to break through

terombang-ambing *vi* to bob (up and down), float; to fluctuate ← **ombang-ambing**

teromol *n* drum, canister, box (in an automobile) → **tromol**

terompét *n* trumpet; *pemain* ~ trumpet player, trumpeter

térong, térung, terung *n* eggplant, aubergine; small green eggplant eaten raw with salads; ~ *Belanda* tree tomato, tamarillo

teropong *n* telescope, binoculars

téror *n* terror; **menéror** *vt* to terrorize; **téroris** *n* terrorist; **térorisme** *n* terrorism

terowong: terowongan *n* tunnel, shaft

terpa: terpaan *n* target; **menerpa** *vt* to attack

terpadu *adj* integrated ← **padu**

terpakai *adj* used, in use ← **pakai**

terpaksa *adj* forced; *karena* ~ had to do it, was forced to do it ← **paksa**

terpal *n* tarpaulin

terpana *adj* struck, stunned ← **pana**

terpanas *adj* the hottest ← **panas**

terpancar *adj* emitted, sent, broadcast ← **pancar**

terpancing *adj* hooked, caught up; involved ← **pancing**

terpanggil *adj* called upon, summoned; *dia merasa* ~ *untuk mengabdikan diri di daerah terpencil* he feels called upon to serve in a remote area ← **panggil**

terpanjang *adj* the longest ← **panjang**

terpantul *adj* reflected ← **pantul**

terpatah-patah *adj* broken; *bahasa Inggrisnya masih* ~ her English is still halting ← **patah**

terpaut *adj* fastened, bound; separated ← **paut**

terpejam *adj* closed ← **pejam**

terpelajar *adj* educated ← **ajar**

terpelanting *vi* to fall heavily ← **pelanting**

terpelését *adj* slipped, skidded; tripped ← **pelését**

terpelihara *adj* well cared-for, well-maintained ← **pelihara**

terpelintir *adj* twisted ← **pelintir**

terpencar *adj* dispersed ← **pencar**

terpencét *adj* accidentally pressed ← **pencét**

terpencil *adj* isolated, remote ← **pencil**

terpendam *adj* hidden, concealed ← **pendam**

terpéndék *adj* the shortest ← **péndék**

terpengaruh *adj* affected or influenced ← **pengaruh**

terpental *adj* flung, thrown down ← **pental**

térpentin, térpéntin *n* turpentine, turps

terpenuhi *adj* satisfied, fulfilled ← **penuh**

terperangah *adj* open-mouthed, astonished ← **perangah**

terperangkap *adj* trapped, caught ← **perangkap**

terperanjat *adj* startled, surprised ← **peranjat**

terpercaya *adj* trusted, reliable ← **percaya**

terperosok *adj* fallen, sunk, plunged ← **perosok**

terpesona *adj* enthralled, enchanted ← **pesona**

terpidana *n* the condemned ← **pidana**

terpikat *adj* attracted, enchanted ← **pikat**

terpilih *adj* elected; *n* elected party, winner of an election ← **pilih**

terpimpin *adj* led, guided; *Demokrasi* ~ Guided Democracy (under Sukarno) ← **pimpin**

terpisah *adj* separated ← **pisah**

terpojok, terpojokkan *adj* forced into a corner ← **pojok**

terpotong *adj* cut (off) ← **potong**

terpuji *adj* highly-praised ← **puji**

terpukau *adj* fascinated, engrossed; drugged ← **pukau**

terpukul *adj* hit, hard-hit ← **pukul**

terpuruk *adj* hidden, buried, sunk; **keterpurukan** *n* depression, abyss ← **puruk**

terputus *adj* cut off; **terputus-putus** *vi* to keep cutting out; *sinyal HP saya sering* ~ I keep losing reception on my cell phone ← **putus**

tersalurkan *adj* channelled ← **salur**

tersambung *adj* connected ← **sambung**

tersandung *adj* to stumble on, trip (up) on ← **sandung**

tersangka *n (yang)* ~ suspect; *adj tak* ~ unexpected ← **sangka**

tersangkut *adj* involved; caught, snagged ← **sangkut**

tersanjung *adj* flattered ← **sanjung**

tersaput *adj* covered, shrouded; ~ *awan* clouded over ← **saput**

tersayang *adj* dear, dearest; *yang* ~ *(yts)* dear (in letters) ← **sayang**

tersebut *adj* mentioned, aforementioned, said ← **sebut**

tersedak *adj* choking; *vi* to choke ← **sedak**

tersedan-sedan *adj* sobbing ← **sedan**

tersedia *adj* available, prepared ← **sedia**

tersedu-sedu *vi* to sob, sniffle ← **sedu**

terselak *vi* to choke ← **selak**

terselenggara *adj* held, organized (successfully) ← **selenggara**

terselimuti *adj* blanketed in or by; *Gunung Bromo* ~ *awan* Mount Bromo was blanketed in clouds ← **selimut**

terselip *adj* fallen or slipped into ← **selip**

terselubung *adj* hidden, veiled ← **selubung**

tersendat *adj* jammed, blocked ← **sendat**

tersendiri *adj* its own; apart, separate ← **sendiri, diri**

tersénggol *adj* bumped, brushed ← **sénggol**

tersentak *adj* pulled, jerked ← **sentak**

tersentuh *adj* touched ← **sentuh**

tersenyum *v* to smile ← **senyum**

terserah *adj* it depends; up to you ← **serah**

terserang *adj* attacked ← **serang**

terserap *adj* absorbed ← **serap**

terserémpét *adj* scraped, scratched ← **serémpét**

tersérét *adj* dragged ← **sérét**

tersesat *adj* lost ← **sesat**

tersiksa *adj* tortured ← **siksa**

tersinggung *adj* offended, hurt; *mudah* ~ touchy, over-sensitive ← **singgung**

tersingkap *adj* revealed ← **singkap**

tersingkir, tersingkirkan *adj* eliminated, swept aside ← **singkir**

tersipu, tersipu-sipu *adj* embarrassed, shy ← **sipu**

tersirat *adj* implied ← **sirat**

tersisa *adj* leftover ← **sisa**

tersihir *adj* bewitched, under a spell ← **sihir**

tersimbah *adj* spattered, wet ← **simbah**

tersimpan *adj* kept, stored ← **simpan**

tersisihkan *adj* eliminated ← **sisih**

tersohor *adj* famous ← **sohor**

tersontak *adj* tugged ← **sontak**

tersulit *adj* the hardest, most difficult ← **sulit**

tersumbat *adj* blocked; plugged ← **sumbat**

tersusun *adj* compiled; heaped up, organized ← **susun**

tertabrak *adj* hit; ~ *mobil* hit by a car ← **tabrak**

tertahan *adj* held back, prevented; **tertahankan** *tak* ~ unbearable ← **tahan**

tertambat *adj* tied up, moored ← **tambat**

tertampung *adj* contained ← **tampung**

tertandingi *tidak* ~ unbeatable, no contest or comparison ← **tanding**

tertangani *adj* handled ← **tangan**

tertanggal *adj* dated ← **tanggal**

tertangkap *adj* caught; ~ *basah* caught in the act; ~ *tangan* caught red-handed ← **tangkap**

tertarik *adj* attracted, interested ← **tarik**

tertatih-tatih *adv* tottering, staggering ← **tatih**

tertawa *vi* to laugh; ~ *lepas* to laugh out loud; **menertawakan** *vt* to laugh at ← **tawa**

tertegun *adj* taken aback ← **tegun**

tertekan *adj* stressed, pushed, pressured ← **tekan**

tertelan *adj* accidentally swallowed ← **telan**

tertémbak *adj* shot (accidentally) ← **témbak**

tertendang *adj* kicked (accidentally) ← **tendang**

tertentu *adj* definite, fixed, certain ← **tentu**

tertera *adj* printed, stamped ← **tera**

tertib *adj* orderly, organized, disciplined; *tata* ~ rules and regulations; **ketertiban** *n* discipline, order; ~ *lalu lintas* traffic discipline, highway code; *Dinas Ketenteraman dan* ~ *(Tramtib)* city public order agency; **menertibkan** *vt* to keep order, discipline; **penertiban** *n* reorganization, putting in order, crackdown; ~ *kios-kios penjual bunga berdampak besar pada ekonomi lokal* the reorganization of the flower stalls will affect the local economy greatly

tertidur *adj* fallen asleep ← **tidur**

tertimpa *adj* hit or struck by; to suffer; ~ *musibah* struck by disaster ← **timpa**

tertinggal *adj* left behind; *desa* ~ backward village ← **tinggal**

tertiup *adj* blown ← **tiup**

tertolong *adj* saved, rescued; *tidak* ~ beyond help ← **tolong**

tertuduh *n* the accused ← **tuduh**

tertuju *adj* directed, aimed ← **tuju**

tertukar *adj* changed by accident ← **tukar**

tertulis *adj* written; *ujian* ~ written examination ← **tulis**

tertumpah *adj* spilt ← **tumpah**

tertunda *adj* delayed, postponed ← **tunda**

tertunduk *adj* bowed, submissive ← **tunduk**

tertusuk *adj* pricked, jabbed; ~ *hati* hurt, offended ← **tusuk**

tertutup *adj* closed ← **tutup**

terucap *adj* expressed ← **ucap**

teruji *adj* tested ← **uji**

terulang *adj* repeated ← **ulang**

terumbu *n* reef; ~ *karang* coral reef

teruna ← **taruna**

terung, térung ← **térong**

terungkap *adj* expressed, revealed ← **ungkap**

teruntai *adj* dangling, strung up ← **untai**

terurai *adj* hanging loose ← **urai**

terurus *adj* looked-after, cared for; *tidak* ~ neglected, uncared for ← **urus**

terus *adv* straight on; continuous, constant; ~ *terang* direct, frank, straightforward; **terus-menerus** *adv* constantly, continually; **terus-terusan** *adv* constantly, continuously; **terusan** *n* extension; canal; ~ *Panama* the Panama canal; **meneruskan** *vt* to continue, keep doing something; **penerus** *n* successor; someone who continues another's work; **seterusnya** *adv* after that, henceforth

terutama *adv* especially, particularly ← **utama**

terwakili *adj* represented ← **wakil**

terwujud *adj* realized ← **wujud**

tés *n, coll* test; **dités** *vi* to be tested; **mengetés** *vt* to test; **pengetésan, tésting** *n* testing → **uji**

tésaurus *n* thesaurus

tésis *n* thesis

tésting *n* testing → **uji**

tetangga *n* neighbor; *negara* ~ neighbor, neighboring country; *rukun* ~ *(RT)* neighborhood association; **bertetangga** *vi* to have neighbors

tétanus *n* tetanus

tetap *adj* fixed, definite, constant; *adv* still; *penduduk* ~ permanent resident; **ketetapan** *n* regulation; stipulation; **menetap** *vi* to stay; **menetapkan** *vt* to appoint, fix, stipulate; **penetapan** *n* appointment

tetapi, tapi *conj* but; *akan* ~ however

tetas: menetas *vi* to hatch

téték *n, sl* breast; **menéték** *vi* to suck, feed from the breast

tetek *n* ~*bengek* trivialities, unimportant details

tétés drip, drop; *(obat)* ~ *mata* eye drops; *(obat)* ~ *telinga* ear drops; **tétésan** *n* drip, drop, droplet; **menétés** *vi* to drip; **menétéskan** *vt* to drip something; to release something in drips; **setétés** *n* a drop

tetirah go somewhere for rest or recovery from illness

Tétum, Tétun *bahasa* ~ Tetum, language of East Timor

tetumbuhan → **tumbuh**

Teuku, Teungku *pron, m* Acehnese title

tévé, tivi *n* TV; *nonton* ~ watch TV ← **télévisi**

téwas *vi* to be killed, die; killed in action; **menéwaskan** *vt* to kill someone

Tg *abbrev Tanjung* Point, Cape

tgl *abbrev tanggal* date

th. *abbrev tahun* year

Thai *bahasa* ~, *orang* ~ Thai; *Muang* ~ *arch* Thailand; **Thailand** *n* Thailand

THR *abbrev Taman Hiburan Rakyat* amusement park

THR *abbrev Tunjangan Hari Raya* holiday bonus, paid at Idul Fitri or Christmas

THT *abbrev telinga, hidung, tenggorokan* ear, nose and throat

tiada no; there isn't any, there aren't any; ~ *banding,* ~ *tara* unequalled, incomparable; ~ *lagi* there is no other; no more; ~ *tara* unequalled, incomparable; **ketiadaan** *n* absence, lack; **meniadakan** *vt* to undo or cancel; **peniadaan** *n* cancellation, abolition ← **tidak ada**

tiang *n* pillar, pole, mast; ~ *bendera* flagpole, flagstaff; ~ *kapal* (ship's) mast; ~ *telepon* telephone pole

tiap, setiap *adj* each, every; ~ *saat* any time

tiara *n* tiara

tiarap lie face down (on the floor)

tiba *vi* to arrive or come; **tiba-tiba** *adv* suddenly; **setiba** *adv* on arriving, on arrival

tidak, tak, ndak, nggak, enggak no, not; *conj, coll* or; ~ *apa-apa* it doesn't matter; ~ *beralasan* ungrounded, unfounded, without reason; ~ *bisa* cannot, can't; ~ *boleh* not allowed, forbidden; ~ *dapat* can not, unable; ~ *karuan* very badly, in chaos; ~ *sah* illegal, not recognized; ~ *usah* not necessary; *mau* ~? do you want to or not?; ~ *ada* to not be or exist; isn't, aren't; not

here; **ketidakadaan** *n* absence, lack of; **tidak hadir** absent; **ketidakhadiran** *n* absence; **tidak pasti** uncertain; **ketidakpastian** *n* uncertainty; **tidak-tidak** *adj* undesirable, not right; **setidaknya, setidak-tidaknya** *adv* at least

tidur sleep; asleep; ~ *ayam* nap, snooze, doze; ~ *lelap,* ~ *pulas,* ~ *nyenyak* sleep heavily, sleep well; sound asleep; ~ *miring* sleep on your side; ~ *siang* siesta, nap; ~ *tengkurap,* ~ *tengkurup* sleep on your stomach; *kamar* ~ bedroom; *kurang* ~ not enough sleep; *obat* ~ sleeping tablet; *tempat* ~ bed; **tidur-tiduran, tiduran** *vi* to lie down, rest; **ketiduran** *v* to fall asleep; **meniduri** *vt* to sleep with someone, have sex with someone; **menidurkan** *vt* to put to sleep; **tertidur** *adj* fallen asleep

tifa *n* large drum from Papua

tifus, tipus *n* typhoid (fever); *kena* ~ have or get typhoid (fever)

tiga *adj* three; ~ *belas* thirteen; ~ *hari* three days; prayers held three days after a death; ~ *kali* three times; ~ *perempat* three-quarters, $^3/_4$; ~ *puluh* thirty; ~ *sekawan* a trio (of friends); *kembar* ~ triplets; **bertiga** *adj* in threes; **ketiga** *adj* the third; ~*(tiga)nya* all three; **pertiga** *dua* ~ two-thirds; **sepertiga** *adj* one-third; **pertigaan** *n* T-junction

tik *mesin* ~ typewriter; **ketikan** *n* typing; **mengetik** *vt* to type; **pengetikan** *n* typing

tikai: bertikai *vi* to quarrel or disagree; **pertikaian** *n* quarrel, disagreement

tikam stab; *luka* ~ stab wound; **tikaman** *n* stab; **menikam** *vt* to stab

tikar *n* mat; *gulung* ~ close down, close shop; go bankrupt

tikét *n* (relatively expensive) ticket; ~ *kereta api* (long-distance) train ticket; ~ *pesawat* plane ticket

tikung: tikungan *n* bend, curve; **menikung** *vi* to bend, curve

tikus *n* (small) mouse, (large) rat; ~ *besar* rat; ~ *got* sewer rat; ~ *mondok* a mole-like animal; ~ *tanah* field mouse; *jalan* ~ back road, sidestreet;

lem ~ adhesive tape for trapping rats; **tikusan** *n* (computer) mouse

tilang *n* traffic fine; **ditilang** *v* to be fined; **menilang** *vt* to fine ← **bukti pelanggaran**

tilas *menapak ~, coll napak ~* to retrace your steps, make a journey again

tilawah *n, Isl* recitation of the Koran

tilpon → **télépon**

TIM *abbrev Taman Ismail Marzuki* arts and theater complex in Jakarta

tim *n* team; ~ *gabungan* team (comprising various elements)

tim *nasi* ~ steamed rice; **ditim** *v* to be steamed

timah *n* tin; ~ *campuran* pewter; ~ *hitam* lead; ~ *putih* tin; *tambang* ~ tin mine

timang: **menimang-nimang** *vt* to rock (a child)

timba: **menimba** *vt* to bail out, remove water from

timbal ~ *balik* mutual, reciprocal; **setimbal** *adj* equivalent, proportional, even

timbal, timbel *n* lead; *tanpa* ~ *(TT)* lead-free (fuel)

timbang ~ *rasa* consider another person's feelings; *jembatan* ~ weighbridge; **timbangan** *n* scales; **ketimbang** *conj, coll* compared with; **menimbang** *v* to weigh (up); **mempertimbangkan** *vt* to consider; **pertimbangan** *n* consideration

timbel, timbal *n* lead; *tanpa* ~ *(TT)* lead-free (fuel)

timbrung → **nimbrung**

timbul *vi* emerge; **menimbulkan** *vt* to give rise, bring to the surface

timbun *n* pile, heap; **bertimbun-timbun** *adv* in heaps, piled up; **menimbun** *vt* to pile up, accumulate; to hoard, stockpile; ~ *makanan* to hoard food; **penimbun** *n* hoarder; **penimbunan** *n* stockpiling, hoarding; **setimbun** *n* a pile

timnas *n* national team ← **tim nasional**

Timor *n* ~ *Barat* West Timor; ~ *Leste,* ~ *Lorosae* Timor Lorosae, East Timor; ~ *Timur (Timtim) arch* East Timor; *Laut* ~ the Timor Sea; *pulau* ~ Timor

timpa: **menimpa** *vt* to fall upon, befall; **tertimpa** *adj* hit or struck by; to suffer; ~ *musibah* to be struck by disaster

timpang: **ketimpangan** *n* inequality, imbalance; ~ *sosial* social inequality

timsuis *hubungan* ~ conjugal relations, sex ← **hubungan intim suami isteri**

Timteng *n* the Middle East ← **Timur Tengah**

Timtim *n* East Timor, Timor Leste, Timor Loro Sae ← **East Timor**

timun, mentimun *n* cucumber; *timun laut* sea cucumber, trepang; *timun suri* large cucumber, often eaten at fast-breaking ← **mentimun**

timur *adj* east; ~ *laut* northeast; ~ *Tengah (Timteng)* Middle East; *bintang* ~ morning star; *di* ~ *Jakarta* east of Jakarta; **ketimuran** *adj* Eastern, Oriental

tindak act, deed; ~ *pidana* criminal act; ~ *lanjut* follow-up; **bertindak-lanjut** *vi* to take a step or measure; **menindaklanjuti** *vt* to follow up; **tindakan** *n* action, measure, step; ~ *pencegahan* preventive measure; *mengambil* ~ to act, take action or measures; **bertindak** *vi* to act, take action; **penindakan** *n* upholding, taking of measures, action

tindas: **menindas** *vt* to oppress; **penindasan** *n* oppression

tindih *bertumpang* ~ to overlap

tindik ~ *telinga* pierced ears; **menindik** *vt* to pierce (ears)

tinggal *vi* to live, stay, remain; *rumah* ~, *tempat* ~ dwelling; *selamat* ~ goodbye (to someone who is staying); ~ *dua ribu rupiah* there's only Rp. 2000 left; **ketinggalan** *adj* left behind; ~ *jaman,* ~ *zaman* outdated; ~ *kereta api* to miss a train; **meninggal** *vi* ~ *(dunia)* to die; **meninggalkan** *vt* to leave (behind), abandon; **peninggalan** *n* remains, remnants; **sepeninggal** *conj* after someone's death; **tertinggal** *adj* left behind; *desa* ~ backward village

tinggi *adj* high, tall; ~*nya* height; ~ *semampai* tall and slender; *menjunjung* ~ to respect, hold in great esteem; *pejabat* ~ high-ranking official; *sekolah* ~ college; **ketinggian** *n* altitude, height;

meninggikan *vt* to raise, elevate; **petinggi** *n* high-ranking official; **setinggi** *adj* as high as; **setinggi-tingginya** *adv* as high as possible

tingkah action; ~ *laku* behavior, actions; **bertingkah** *vi* to act, behave

tingkat *n* level, floor, story, grade; ~ *pemula* beginner; **tingkatan** *n* grade, degree, level; **bertingkat** *vi* to have different levels; *rumah* ~ multi-story house; **meningkat** *vi* to rise, increase, improve; **meningkatkan** *vt* to increase or raise the level of something; **peningkatan** *n* rise, increase; **setingkat** *adj* of the same level

tingwé *rokok* ~ roll-your-own cigarette ← **linting déwé**

tinja *n* excrement, feces, sewage

tinjau: tinjauan *n* review; **meninjau** *vt* to observe, view; ~ *kembali* to review; **peninjau** *n* observer; **peninjauan** *n* observation; ~ *kembali* review

tinju *n* boxing; fist; **bertinju** *vi* to box; **petinju** *n* boxer

tinta *n* ink; *habis* ~ out of ink

Tionghoa *adj* Chinese; *orang* ~ Chinese; **Tiongkok** *n* China

tip *n* tip, commission

tipe *n* type, sort

tipék, tipéks *n* correction fluid, white-out, Tipp-Ex; **ditipéks** *v* to white-out, be corrected

tipi *n* tepee

tipi *n, coll* TV

tipis *adj* thin; *kemungkinan* ~ slim chance; *rambut* ~ fine hair; **menipis** *vi* to become thin

tips *n* tip, pointer

tipu trick, cheat; ~ *daya* scam, con; ~ *muslihat* (dirty) trick, deceit; **menipu** *vt* to trick, deceive; **penipu** *n* con man, trickster; **penipuan** *n* deception

tipus, tifus *n* typhoid (fever); *kena* ~ catch or have typhoid (fever)

tirai *n* curtain; ~ *Besi* the Iron Curtain; *negeri* ~ *bambu* China

tirakat *vi* to deny oneself, practice austerity (eg. fast or other ascetic practice)

tiram *n* oyster; *saus* ~ oyster sauce

tiras *n* circulation

tiri *adj* step-; *adik* ~, *kakak* ~ stepbrother or stepsister; *ibu* ~ stepmother

tirta *n, lit* water

tiru, meniru *vt* to copy or imitate; **tiruan** *n* imitation, fake; **peniru** *n* imitator, copycat

tirus *adj* pointed, haggard (of a face)

tisu *n* tissue; ~ *basah* wet towel, wipe; ~ *gulung* toilet roll, toilet paper; ~ *meja* box of tissues; *tempat* ~ tissue box

titah *n* royal order, command

titel *n* title (of a person); **bertitel** *vi* to have the title → **gelar**

titik *n* dot, point; full stop, period; ~ *akhir* end (point); ~ *awal* starting point; ~ *beku* freezing point; ~ *berat* center of gravity; ~ *cahaya* point of light; ~ *cair* melting point; ~ *didih* boiling point; ~ *dua* colon; ~ *jenuh* saturation point; ~ *koma* semicolon; ~ *nol* zero; ~ *temu* meeting point, point of agreement; **menitikberatkan** *vt* to emphasize

titinada *n* musical scale

titip, menitip *vt* to leave in someone's care, entrust; *titip beli gula* please buy some sugar; **titipan** *n* parcel, something sent with another person; **penitipan** *n* care; deposit; *tempat* ~ *anak* child-minding center, creche

titis: titisan *n* reincarnation

titit *n, coll, child* (boy's) penis, little bird

tiup blow; **bertiup** *v* to blow; **meniup** *v* to blow; ~ *lilin* to blow out a candle; **tertiup** *adj* blown

tivi, tévé *n, coll* TV; *nonton* ~ to watch TV ← **télévisi**

TK *abbrev* Taman Kanak-kanak kindergarten, preschool

TKI *abbrev* Tenaga Kerja Indonesia Indonesian worker abroad, migrant worker

TKP *abbrev* tempat kejadian perkara scene of the crime, crime scene

TKW *abbrev, f* Tenaga Kerja Wanita Indonesian female worker abroad, migrant worker

TMII *abbrev* Taman Mini Indonesia Indah Beautiful Indonesia in Miniature theme park (in Jakarta)

TMP *abbrev Taman Makam Pahlawan* heroes' cemetery

Tn. *Tuan m* master, sir (esp for foreigners); Mr (with surname)

TNI *abbrev Tentara Nasional Indonesia* Indonesian National Army

toalét, toilét *n* toilet, washroom

tobat, taubat *n* repentance; **bertobat** *vi* to repent

todong, menodong *vt* to threaten or hold up at knifepoint; **penodong** *n* attacker; **penodongan** *n* knife attack

toga *n* academic gown; judge's robes

togé → **taugé, taogé**

togél *n* illegal small-scale gambling, lottery or bingo game ← **toto gelap**

Togo *n* Togo; *orang ~* Togolese

toh *adv, coll* still, after all

toilét, toalét *n* toilet, washroom

tok knock, sound of knocking

tokcér *adj, coll* work, spring to life, effective

tokék *n* large gray house gecko

toko *n* shop, store; *~ bayi* shop selling baby needs; *~ besi* hardware (store); *~ buku* bookstore, bookshop; *~ mas, ~ emas* jewelery shop; *~ kelontong* shop selling cheap goods; *~ loak* second-hand store; opportunity shop; *~ mebel* furniture store; *~ roti* bakery; *~ serba ada (toserba)* general store; department store; *~ swalayan* supermarket; **pertokoan** *n* shopping center or complex, mall

tokoh *n* figure, character; *~ dunia* world figure; *~ utama* main character

toksin *n* toxin

toksoplasmosis *n* **tokso** *coll* toxoplasmosis, parasitic disease from cats which can affect pregnant women

tol *n* toll; *jalan ~* toll road; *gerbang ~, pintu ~* tollbooth, tollgate

tolak *vt* to refuse, reject; *~ bala* talisman, lucky charm; *~ korupsi* down with corruption; *~ peluru* shot put; **bertolak** *vi* form to depart, leave; **menolak** *vt* to refuse, reject; **penolakan** *n* refusal, rejection

tolan, taulan *handai ~* friends

toléh: menoléh *vi* to look in a different direction, turn your head

toléran *adj* tolerant; **toléransi** *n* tolerance

tolérir: mentolérir *vt* to tolerate

tolol *adj* stupid; **ketololan** *n* stupidity

tolong help; please; *minta ~* to ask for help; please help me; *~ dibuka* please open it; **menolong** *vt* to help or assist; **ketolongan** *adj* **ketulungan** *coll tidak ~* beyond help; **pertolongan** *n* help, assistance, aid; *~ pertama* first aid; **tertolong** *adj* saved, rescued; *tidak ~* beyond help

tom *n, coll* bridle

tomat *n* tomato; *sup ~* tomato soup

tombak *n* spear; *ujung ~* spearhead, striker (in soccer)

tomboi *adj* masculine (of a girl), tomboyish; *n* tomboy

tombok → **nombok**

tombol *n* knob, button; *tekan ~* push the button

ton *n* ton, tonne; **tonase** *n* tonnage

tong *n* drum, barrel, bin; *~ sampah* rubbish bin, garbage bin; *~ kosong nyaring bunyinya* empty vessels make the most sound

Tonga *n* Tonga; *bahasa ~, orang ~* Tongan

tongkang *n* barge

tongkat *n* stick, cane; *~ narsis (tongsis) sl* selfie stick; *pakai ~* use a cane; **bertongkat** *adj* with a stick

tongkol *ikan ~* tuna (fish)

tongkol: setongkol *n* an ear; *~ jagung* an ear of corn

tongkrong → **nongkrong**

tongséng *n* goat and cabbage curry

tongsis *n, sl* selfie stick ← **tongkat narsis**

tonik *n ~ rambut* hair tonic

tonjok: tonjokan *n, coll* punch, blow; **menonjok** *vt* to punch, hit

tonjol: menonjol *vi* to stick out, protrude; *adj* prominent; **menonjolkan** *vt* to show; to make something stick out

tonton: tontonan *n* show, performance; **menonton, nonton** *vi* to go to the cinema; *vt* to watch, look on; **penonton** *n* spectator, audience; *para ~* audience; ladies and gentlemen

top *adj, sl* great, wonderful, top; **ngetop** *vi* to be on top

topan *(angin)* ~ typhoon, hurricane

topang: menopang *vt* to prop up, support; **penopang** *n* prop, support

topas *n (batu)* ~ topaz

topéng *n* mask; ~ *gas* gas mask; ~ *monyet* performance by a trained monkey; *tari* ~ masked dance

topi *n* hat; ~ *caping* conical hat worn by agricultural workers; ~ *pet* cap; *Si* ~ *Merah* Little Red Riding Hood

topik *n* topic

toplés → **stoplés**

topografi *n* topography

Toraja Toraja, ethnic group of central Sulawesi; *bahasa* ~, *orang* ~ Toraja, Torajan

toraks *n* thorax

toréh: toréhan *n* notch, incision; **menoréh** *vt* to scratch, etch

torpédo *n* torpedo; **menorpédo** *vt* to torpedo

torsi *n* torsion

tortor *n* traditional *Batak* dance

tosérba *n* general store; department store ← **toko sérba ada**

total *adj* total; *jumlah* ~ total; *adv* totally, absolutely, completely

toto ~ *gelap (togel)* illegal small-scale gambling, lottery or bingo game

totok *adj* full-blood; *Cina* ~ 100% or overseas Chinese

totok ~ *wajah* facial (therapy)

towél *v, Jkt* touch (someone) lightly

TPA *abbrev tempat pembuangan akhir* tip, rubbish dump

TPA, TPQ *abbrev Tempat Pendidikan Alquran* Islamic Study Center

TPI *abbrev Televisi Pendidikan Indonesia* privately-owned television network

TPQ, TPA *abbrev Tempat Pendidikan Alquran* Islamic Study Center

TPS *abbrev tempat pemungutan suara* polling booth

TPU *abbrev tempat pemakaman umum* public cemetery

tra *EInd, coll* no, not; **trada** to not be or exist; isn't, aren't; not here → **tidak**

tradisi *adj* tradition (not *adat*); ~ *lisan* oral tradition; ~ *tertulis* written tradition; **tradisional, tradisionil** *adj* traditional

trafo, travo *n* transformer, adapter

tragédi *n* tragedy; **tragis** *adj* tragic

trah *n* lineage, descent; *anjing* ~ purebreed dog

traktir, mentraktir *vt* to invite out, shout, treat, pay for another

traktor *n* tractor

tralis → **terali**

trampil *adj* skilled; **ketrampilan** *n* skill

trampolin *n* trampoline

transaksi *n* (bank) transaction; **bertransaksi** *vi* to make a transaction

transfer *n* transfer; **mentransfer** *vt* to transfer or send (money)

transformasi *n* transformation

transformator *n* transformer

transfusi *n* transfusion

transisi *n* transition; *masa* ~ transition (period)

transit (be in) transit

transkrip *n* transcript

transmigran *n* migrant (usu from Java to another island); **transmigrasi** *n* transmigration (from Java to other islands); **transmigran** *n* migrant who has joined the internal transmigration program

transparan *adj* transparent, accountable; **transparansi** *n* accountability, transparency

transportasi *n* transportation; ~ *umum* public transport

trap: ditrap *vi* to be layered (of hair)

trapésium *n* trapezium

trauma *n* trauma; *adj* traumatic

travo → **trafo**

trayék *n* route (of public transport)

trém *n* tram, streetcar, cable car

trén, trénd *n* trend, fashion; **ngetrén** *adj, coll* trendy, fashionable; *vi* to be trendy, fashionable

trenggiling, tenggiling *n* anteater

trenyuh *adj, Jav* affected, moved, touched, sad

tribune *n* [tribun] stand, open area in a stadium or concert hall

Trikora Threefold Command, operation

to liberate West Irian prior to 1963

triliun, trilyun *n* trillion (100 000 000 000)

trilogi *n* trilogy

trilyun → **triliun**

Trinidad dan Tobago *n* Trinidad and Tobago; *orang* ~ Trinidadian, Tobagonian

trio *n* trio

tripang → **teripang**

triplék, tripléks *n* plywood, used for ceilings

tripod *n* tripod

trisula *n* trident

triwulan *n* quarter (of a year); trimester; term (when four terms in a year)

troli *n* trolley

trombon *n* trombone; *pemain* ~ trombonist, trombone player

trombosit *n* platelet (count)

tromol, teromol *n* metal box; drum, canister; **tromol pos** road mail box (RMB)

trompét, terompet *n* trumpet; *pemain* ~ trumpeter

tronton *truk* ~ semi-trailer

tropis *adj* tropical

trotoar *n* pavement, sidewalk

truf *n* cards, trumps; *kartu* ~ trump card

truk *n* truck; ~ *barang* goods truck; ~ *gandeng*, ~ *peti kemas*, ~ *tronton* semi-trailer; ~ *jungkit* dump truck; ~ *sampah* garbage truck

tsb. *tersebut* the aforementioned

tsunami *n* tsunami → **gelombang pasang**

TT *abbrev tanpa timbal* unleaded

tt(d) *abbrev tertanda* signed

ttg *abbrev tentang* about, re

TTS *abbrev teka-teki silang* crossword

tua *adj* old; dark (of colors); ~ *renta* very old, senile; *biru* ~ dark blue; *orang* ~ parents; ~~ *keladi* the older... the more...; **ketua** *n* chair(person); chief; **penuaan** *n* ageing (process)

tuah: bertuah *adj* lucky; *vi* to have magic power

tuak *n* palm wine

tualang: bertualang *vi* to have an adventure; **petualang** *n* adventurer;

petualangan *n* adventure

tuan (Tn) *m, pron* master, sir (esp for foreigners, or on medical documents); Mr (with surname); ~ *besar* the big boss; ~ *rumah* host; ~ *tanah* landowner; **tuan-tuan** *pron* gentlemen

tuang *v* to pour; **menuang, menuangkan** *vt* to pour something

tuan-tuan *pron* gentlemen ← **tuan**

tuas *n* lever

Tubagus *pron, m* title in Banten

tubérkulosa, tubérkulosis *n* tuberculosis

tubi: bertubi-tubi *adv* repeatedly, without stopping, unceasingly

tublés *adj* tubeless (of tires)

tubruk *kopi* ~ ground coffee

tubuh *n* body; **bertubuh** *vi* to have a body; ~ *gemuk* fat; **bersetubuh** *vi* to have sex; **menyetubuhi** *vt* to have sex with; **persetubuhan** *n* sexual intercourse

tuding: tudingan *n* accusation; **menuding** *vt* to accuse, point the finger

tuduh: tuduhan *n* charge, accusation; **menuduh** *vt* to accuse; **tertuduh** *n* the accused

tudung *n* cover; head scarf; ~ *lampu* lampshade; ~ *saji* cover for food on a table

tugas *n* task, duty, function; **menugasi** *vt* to assign someone; **menugaskan** *vt* to give a task; **penugasan** *n* assignment

tugu *n* monument, column

tuh *pron, coll* that; *itu* ~ that one ← **itu**

Tuhan *n, pron* God, Allah; ~ *memberkati* God bless; ~ *Yang Maha Kuasa* Almighty God; **tuhan** *n* god; **bertuhan** *vi* to believe in god; *tidak* ~ atheist; **ketuhanan** *n* divinity, deity; belief in God

tuju: tujuan *n* direction, destination; aim, goal; **bertujuan** *adj* with a purpose of; *vi* to have a purpose; **menuju** *vt* to approach, go towards; **setuju** agree, agreed; **bersetuju** *vi* to agree; **menyetujui** *vt* to agree to, approve, ratify; **persetujuan** *n* agreement, approval; **tertuju** *adj* directed, aimed

tujuh *adj* seven; ~ *belas* seventeen; ~ *bulan* ceremony celebrating the seventh month of pregnancy; ~ *hari* prayers seven days after a death; ~ *keliling* very dizzy; ~ *puluh* seventy

tukam *vi, coll* to visit a house in mourning, pay your respects → **layat**

tukang *n* (unskilled) worker; handyman; *coll* habitual (doer of bad things); ~ *becak* pedicab driver; ~ *besi* blacksmith; ~ *bohong* (habitual) liar; ~ *bubut* fitter; ~ *cat* painter; ~ *cukur* barber; ~ *daging* meat vendor; ~ *emas, ~ mas* goldsmith; ~ *gigi* maker of false teeth; ~ *horden* itinerant curtain-rod seller; ~ *ikan* fishmonger; ~ *jagal* butcher; ~ *jahit* tailor; ~ *jam* watch repairer; ~ *kaca* glazier; ~ *kayu* carpenter; ~ *kebun* gardener; ~ *kebut* speed merchant, speedster; ~ *koran* newspaper boy, newspaper seller; ~ *kredit* (small-scale) creditor; ~ *las* welder; ~ *ledeng* plumber; ~ *listrik* electrician; ~ *loak* second-hand dealer; ~ *mabok* drunk, drunkard; ~ *makan* glutton, pig; ~ *ojek* motorcycle taxi driver; ~ *parkir* parking attendant; ~ *pijat, ~ urut* masseur, masseuse; ~ *pos* postman; ~ *potret* photographer; ~ *pukul* strongman, thug; ~ *rias* make-up artist; ~ *roti* itinerant bread-seller; ~ *sampah* garbage collector, garbage man; ~ *santet* witchdoctor, sorcerer; ~ *sapu* cleaner, sweeper, janitor; ~ *sayur* vegetable seller; ~ *sepatu* cobbler; ~ *semir* shoeshine boy; ~ *sepatu* cobbler (for repairs); shoemaker; ~ *sulap* magician, conjurer; **pertukangan** *n* repairs

tukar *vt* to change, exchange; ~ *cincin* to exchange rings; ~*menukar* barter; ~ *tambah* trade in; **bertukar** *vi* to change; **menukar** *vt* to change; **menukarkan** *vt* to change something; **pertukaran** *n* exchange; ~ *mahasiswa, ~ pelajar* student exchange; ~ *pikiran* exchange of ideas or views; **tertukar** *adj* changed by accident

tukas, menukas *vi* to counter, retort

tukik *n* baby turtle

tukik: menukik *vi* to dive, freefall

tulalit *adj* sound of telephone fault or misconnection; doesn't connect or make sense

tulang *n* bone; ~ *belakang, ~ punggung* spine; ~ *belikat* shoulder blade; ~ *belulang* skin and bones; ~ *ekor* coccyx; ~ *iga, ~ rusuk* rib; ~ *kering* shin, shinbone; ~ *muda* cartilage; ~ *pipi* cheekbone; ~ *rahang* jawbone; ~ *selangka* collarbone, clavicle; *membanting* ~ to work yourself to the bone; *sumsum* ~ bone marrow; *tinggal* ~ *dan kulit* nothing but skin and bones

tular: ketularan *adj* infected, caught something; **menular** *vi* to infect; *adj* contagious, infectious; *penyakit* ~ contagious or infectious disease

tulén *adj* real, pure, genuine

tuli *adj* deaf; *bisu* ~ deaf and dumb, deaf-mute

tulip, tulpen *n* tulip

tulis *v* to write; *batu* ~ slate; *buku* ~ notebook, exercise book; *juru* ~ clerk; *meja* ~ writing table; *papan* ~ blackboard, whiteboard; **tulisan** *n* writing, script; ~ *halus* calligraphy; ~ *jawi* Malay/Indonesian writing in Arabic script; ~ *miring* italics; ~ *tangan* handwriting; **menulis** *vt* to write; **penulis** *n* author, writer; ~ *naskah* script writer; ~ *novel* novelist; **tertulis** *adj* written; *ujian* ~ written examination

tulung: ketulungan *coll tidak* ~ beyond help → **tolong**

tulus *adj* sincere; **ketulusan** ~ *hati* sincerity

tumbang fall, fallen; ~*nya* the fall of; **menumbangkan** *vt* to fell, cause something or someone to fall

tumbén *adj, coll* unusual, never before, rare

tumbuh *v* to grow; **tetumbuhan, tumbuh-tumbuhan** *n* plants; **tumbuhan** *n* a growth; plant; **ditumbuhi** *adj* overgrown with; **menumbuhkan** *vt* to nurture, cultivate; **pertumbuhan** *n* growth, development

tumbuk, menumbuk *vt* to pound (rice), crush, grind

tumenggung, temenggung *pron, n, m, arch* high-ranking official

tumis *vt* to stir-fry, sautée; ~ *sayur* stir-fried vegetables

tumit *n* heel (of foot)

tumor *n* tumor; ~ *ganas* malignant growth or lump; ~ *jinak* benign growth

tumpah spill, spilt; **menumpahkan** *vt* to spill something; ~ *darah* to shed blood; **tertumpah** *adj* spilt

tumpang ~ *tindih* overlap, criss-cross; **bertumpang tindih** *vi* to overlap; **menumpang** *vi* to make use of someone else's facilities; to get a lift or ride; **penumpang** *n* passenger

tumpeng *nasi* ~ rice shaped in a tall cone, made on special occasions

tumplek ~ *bleg adj, Jav* spilt everywhere

tumpu: bertumpu *vi* to rest on

tumpuk heap, pile; **tumpukan** *n* heap, pile; **bertumpuk** *vi* to be in piles; **bertumpuk-tumpuk** *adv* in piles; **menumpuk** *vi* to pile up

tumpul *adj* blunt

tuna- *pref* without; ~*aksara* illiterate; ~*daksa* disabled, physically handicapped; ~*grahita* mentally handicapped; ~*karya* jobless, unemployed; ~*netra* blind; ~*rungu* deaf; ~*susila* immoral; ~*wicara* deaf-mute; ~*wisma* homeless

tunai *n* cash; **menunaikan** *vt* to pay cash; to fulfill; ~ *ibadah puasa* to perform the Ramadan fast

tunakarya jobless, unemployed

tunanétra *adj* blind

tunang: tunangan *n, f* fiancée; *n, m* fiancé; *v, coll* to be engaged; **bertunangan** *v* to be engaged; **pertunangan** *n* engagement

tunarungu deaf

tunas *n* shoot, sprout

tunasusila *adj* immoral

tunawicara deaf-mute

tunawisma homeless

tunda delay; *tayangan* ~ delayed telecast; **menunda** *vt* to delay, put off, postpone; **menundakan** *vt* to delay or postpone something; **tertunda** *adj* delayed, postponed

tunduk *vi* to bow to, submit, obey; ~ *pada pemerintah* to submit to the government; **menunduk** *vi* to bow your head; **menundukkan** *vt* to bow or

lower something; to defeat; **tertunduk** *adj* bowed, submissive

tungau *n* dust mite

tunggak: tunggakan *n* debt; ~*sewa* back rent; **menunggak** *vi* to owe money

tunggal *adj* single, sole; *anak* ~ only child; *bentuk* ~ singular (form); *konser* ~ solo concert; *orang tua* ~ single parent, sole parent; *Bhinneka* ~ *Ika* Unity in Diversity

tunggang: menunggang *vt* to ride; ~ *kuda* to ride a horse

tungging: menungging *adv* **nungging** *coll* tail up, with bottom sticking out

tunggu *v* to wait; ~ *dulu* wait a minute; *ruang* ~ waiting room; **menunggu** *v* to wait for something; **menunggu-nunggu** *vt* to wait a long time for; **menunggui** *vt* to wait by or look after someone

tungku *n* furnace, oven

Tunisia *n* Tunisia; *orang* ~ Tunisian

tunjang: tunjangan *n* allowance, bonus; aid, help; ~ *keluarga* family allowance; ~ *Hari Raya* one month's extra pay, awarded on a religious holiday

tunjuk, menunjuk *vi* to indicate, point out, refer to; **menunjukkan** *vt* to show, point out; ~ *jalan* to give directions; **mempertunjukkan** *vt* to display or perform; **penunjuk** *n* guide, indicator; **penunjukan** *n* appointment; **pertunjukan** *n* show, performance; **petunjuk** *n* instruction, direction; *buku* ~ manual, guide; *buku* ~ *jalan* street directory; *buku* ~ *telepon* telephone directory, *coll* phone book

tuntas *adj* complete, total; **menuntaskan** *vt* to finish off, be done with, do thoroughly

tuntun, menuntun *vt* to guide, prop up

tuntut *vi* claim; **tuntutan** *n* claim, charge; **menuntut** *vt* to claim or demand; **penuntut** *n* claimant, plaintiff, prosecuting party

tupai *n* squirrel

tur *n* tour; *pemimpin* ~ tour leader

turangga *n, lit* horse

turap: menurap *vt* to coat, line, seal, plaster; to dam

turbin *n* turbine

turis *n* tourist; ~ *asing* foreign tourist; ~ *lokal* domestic tourist; ~ *ransel* backpacker

Turki *n* Turkey; *bahasa* ~ Turkish; *orang* ~ Turkish, Turk

Turkménistan *n* Turkmenistan; *bahasa* ~, *orang* ~ Turkmen

turnamén *n* tournament

turun *vi* to descend, fall, come down; ~ *temurun* from generation to generation, hereditary; ~ *drastis* to fall drastically; ~ *gunung* to come down from the mountain; to take action; ~ *harga* to fall in price; ~ *mesin* overhaul; ~ *naik* (to go) up and down; ~ *tangan* to get involved, take action; ~ *ke darat* to go ashore; ~ *ke lapangan* to go out into the field; **keturunan** *n* descendant; *WNI* ~ Indonesian of Chinese descent; **menurun** *vi* to fall, drop, decline; **menurunkan** *vt* to lower or reduce; **penurunan** *n* lowering

turut *vi* to take part, join; ~ *serta* participate, take part; ~ *berduka cita* express your condolences; **berturut-turut** *adj* consecutive, successive; **menurut** *conj* according to; ~ *abjad* alphabetically, in alphabetical order; ~ *pendapat saya* in my opinion; **menuruti** *vt* to follow, obey; **penurut** *adj* obedient, meek

tuslah *n* surcharge; ~ *Lebaran* surcharge on transport at Idul Fitri

tustél *n, arch* camera

tusuk skewer, needle; poke; ~ *gigi* toothpick; ~ *jarum* acupuncture; ~ *konde* hair pin; ~ *sate* satay stick; **tusukan** *n* stab wound; **menusuk** *vt* to stab, prick, pierce; **tertusuk** *adj* pricked, jabbed; ~ *hati* hurt, offended

tuts *n* key, button; ~ *piano* piano keys

tutul *adj* spotted; *macan* ~ leopard

tutup lid, cover; close; closed, shut; ~ *botol* bottle-cap; ~ *kepala* head covering, headscarf; ~ *mata* close one's eyes; ~ *mulut* keep your mouth shut; ~ *panci* saucepan or skillet lid; ~ *usia* die; **menutup** *vt* to close or shut; **menutupi** *vt* to cover (up); **penutup** *n* stopper, lid; end; **penutupan** *n* closing; **tertutup** *adj* closed

tutur speak; **bertutur** *vi* to speak or talk; **menuturkan** *vt* to tell; **penutur** *n* speaker; ~ *asli* native speaker

tuyul *n* spirit in the form of a bald child

TV *abbrev* te-ve, ti-vi, *televisi* television; ~ *parabola* satellite TV

TVRI *abbrev Televisi Republik Indonesia* Indonesian state-owned television

twit *n* tweet (on Twitter); **ngetwit** *vi* to tweet (on Twitter)

U

u u, 21st letter of the alphabet

ua → **wa**

uang *n* money; ~ *belanja* money for shopping, shopping budget; ~ *gedung* payment for building development or to a building fund (at a school); ~ *jajan, ~ saku* pocket money; ~ *jaminan* guarantee, collateral; ~ *kecil, ~ receh(an)* small change; ~ *kembali* change; ~ *kertas* banknote; ~ *kontan, ~ tunai* cash; ~ *kos* board and lodging; ~ *langganan* subscription; ~ *Lebaran* money given to children at Idul Fitri; ~ *logam* coin, small change; ~ *mondok* board; ~ *muka* down payment; ~ *palsu* counterfeit money; ~ *pangkal* payment to secure entrance (at a school); ~ *parkir* parking fee; ~ *pelicin, ~ sogok* bribe; ~ *pesangon* severance payment made on ceasing employment or retiring; ~ *rokok* tip; ~ *sekolah* school fees, tuition; ~ *sewa* rent; ~ *simpanan* savings, deposit; ~ *tabungan* savings; ~ *tebusan* ransom (payment); *mata* ~ currency; *setali tiga* ~ six of one, half a dozen of the other; it's all the same; **keuangan** *n* finance; *Menteri ~ (Menkeu)* Minister of Finance, *UK* Chancellor of the Exchequer

uap *n* steam, vapor; *kapal* ~ steamer, steamship; **menguap** *vi* to evaporate or steam; **penguapan** *n* evaporation

ub. *abbrev untuk beliau* for, on behalf of (in letters)

ubah   change; **berubah** *vi* to change;
mengubah *vt* **merubah** *coll* to change
or alter; **perubahan** *n* change, alteration

uban   *n* (strand of) gray or white hair;
beruban *vi* to have gray hairs

Ubaya   *abbrev Universitas Surabaya*
University of Surabaya

uber, menguber   *vt, coll* to chase, go after

ubi   *n* edible tuber or root; sweet potato,
yam; ~ *jalar* sweet potato; ~ *kayu,* ~
singkong cassava

ubin   *n* (floor) tile

ubrak-abrik, obrak-abrik: mengubrak-
abrik   *vt* to upset, turn upside-down

ubun-ubun   *n* crown, fontanel

ubur-ubur   *n* jellyfish

ucap   say; **ucapan** *n* greetings; ~ *selamat* congratulations; **mengucap, mengucapkan** *vt* to say or express something; ~ *terima kasih* to say thank you;
to thank; **pengucapan** *n* expression;
terucap *adj* expressed

ucek, kucek   *v* rub; **mengucek** *vt* ~
mata to rub your eyes; ~ *pakaian* to
rub clothes together when washing

ucok   *pron, Bat* boy, lad, young man

Uda   *pron, Min, m* older brother

udah → **sudah**

udang   *n* shrimp, prawn; *otak* ~ idiot,
birdbrain; *ada* ~ *di balik batu* there's
something going on here, there's
something behind it

udara   *n* air, atmosphere; ~ *bebas* freedom; *angkatan* ~ air force; *pesawat* ~
aeroplane, airplane; *pos* ~ air mail;
tekanan ~ air pressure, atmospheric
pressure; **berudara** *vi* to have air (of a
certain quality); ~ *panas* hot; **mengudarakan** *vt* to broadcast or air

udel   *n, Jav* belly-button, navel

udik   *n* upstream, upper reaches of a
river; *adj* countrified, unsophisticated;
mudik *vi* to go upstream, back to the
village; ~ *Lebaran* to return to your
hometown at Idul Fitri; *arus* ~ flow of
people going back to the village (usu
at Idul Fitri); *hilir* ~ to go up and down
the river, back and forth → **mudik**

udur, udzur → **uzur**

ufuk   *n* horizon

ugal: ugal-ugalan   *adj* reckless

Uganda   *n* Uganda; *orang* ~ Ugandan

UGD   *abbrev Unit Gawat Darurat* emergency room, emergency ward, casualty

UGM   *abbrev Universitas Gadjah Mada*
Gadjah Mada University, in Yogyakarta

uhu   *n* (sound of an) owl

UI   *abbrev Universitas Indonesia*
University of Indonesia, in Jakarta

UII   *abbrev Universitas Islam Indonesia*
Indonesian Islamic University, in
Yogyakarta

ujang   *pron, Sund* boy, lad, young man

ujar   speak, say; ~*nya* says, said; **berujar**
vi to speak or say

uji   test; ~ *coba* experiment, trial; ~ *kelayakan dan kepatutan* fit and proper
test; **ujian** *n* test, exam(ination); ~
akhir final examination; ~ *her,* ~ *susulan* make-up test or exam; ~ *lisan* oral
test; ~ *masuk* entrance test; ~ *tertulis*
written exam or test; *menempuh* ~ to
sit for or do an exam; *lulus* ~ pass an
exam; ~ *akhir semester* end-of-term
test or exam; ~ *tengah semester* mid-
term test or exam; *tidak lulus* ~ fail an
exam; **menguji** *vt* to examine or test;
penguji *n* examiner; **teruji** *adj* tested

ujung   *n* point, end; ~ *jari* fingertip; ~
dunia ends of the earth; ~ *Pandang*
former name for Makassar; ~ *tombak*
spearhead, striker (in soccer); ~~~*nya*
in the end, finally; *di* ~ *tanduk* hanging
in the balance; **berujung** *vi* to (have
an) end; **penghujung** *n* end; ~ *musim
hujan* end of the rainy season

ukhuwah   *n, Isl* brotherhood, fraternity

UKI   *abbrev Universitas Kristen
Indonesia* Indonesian Christian
University, in Jakarta

ukir, mengukir   *v* to carve or engrave;
ukiran *n* carving

Ukraina   *n* Ukraine; *bahasa* ~, *orang* ~
Ukrainian

Ukrida   *abbrev Universitas Kristen Djaya*
a Christian university in Jakarta

ukulélé   *n* ukulele

ukur   measure; **ukuran** *n* size, measurement; ~ *sedang* medium size; **berukuran** *vi* to have a size, -sized; **mengukur**

vt to measure; **pengukur** *n* measuring device; person who measures; **pengukuran** *n* measuring, measurement

ulah *n* behavior, manners; **berulah** *vi* to behave

ulam *n* raw vegetables (as a side-dish)

ulama *n, Isl* religious leader(s)

ulang repeat; ~ *alik* back and forth, both ways; *pesawat* ~ shuttle; ~ *tahun* birthday, anniversary; *tayangan* ~ rerun, repeat; **ulangan** *n* test; *Kitab* ~ (the book of) Deuteronomy; **berulang** *vi* to happen again, recur; **berulang-ulang** *adv* again and again, repeatedly; **mengulang** *vt* to repeat, do again; **mengulangi** *vt* to repeat something; **terulang** *adj* repeated

ular *n* snake; ~ *beludak* viper; ~ *berbisa* venomous snake; ~ *piton*, ~ *sanca* python; ~ *sendok* cobra; **ular-ularan** *n* toy snake

ulas: ulasan *n* comment, review; **mengulas** *vt* to comment, review, critique

ulat *n* worm, caterpillar; ~ *sutera* silkworm

ulek, uleg *sambal* ~ ground chilli sauce; **mengulek** *vt* to make fresh chilli sauce

uler → **ular**

ulet *adj* diligent, hard-working

uli *n* sticky rice mixed with shredded coconut

ulin *kayu* ~ very hard wood

ulir *n* thread (of a screw), spiral

ulos *n* woven cloth used in Batak ceremonies

ultah *n* birthday, anniversary ← **ulang tahun**

ultimatum *n* ultimatum; **mengultimatum** *vt* to give (someone) an ultimatum

ultrasonografi, USG ultra-sound (screening)

ulu ~ *hati* solar plexus

ulung *adj* excellent, first-rate, superior; **keulungan** *n* superiority

ulur: uluran *n* assistance, help; ~ *tangan* helping hand; **mengulur-ulur** *vt* to spin out, take a long time; **mengulurkan** *vt* to extend something

umat *n* people (of one faith); ~ *Islam* the Muslim community

umbai, rumbai *n* tassel; **berumbai** *vi* to have tassels; *adj* tasseled

umbi *n* tuber; **umbi-umbian** *n* tubers

umbul: umbul-umbul *n* pennants, small flags, banner

Ummi, Umi *pron, f, Isl* Mother

umpama *n* example; ~*nya* for example; **perumpamaan** *n* parable, metaphor; **seumpamanya** *conj* for instance

umpan *n* bait; ~ *balik* feedback (in soccer or football); **pengumpan** *n* feeder, someone who passes; someone who sets a bait

umpat, mengumpat *vi* to curse, swear; **umpatan** *n* oath, swear word

umpat, umpet: umpet-umpetan *n, coll* hide and seek; **mengumpet** *vi* to hide or conceal yourself; **mengumpetkan** *vt* to hide something

umroh, umrah *Isl, n* minor pilgrimage to Mecca

umum *adj* general, public, common; *(pada)* ~*nya* generally, in general; *kepentingan* ~ public or common interest; **mengumumkan** *vt* to announce or declare; **pengumuman** *n* notice, announcement

umur *n* age; ~ *berapa?* how old?; *di bawah* ~ underage; **berumur** *adj* aged; **seumur** *adj* the same age; lifelong; ~ *hidup* for life, lifelong; ~ *jagung* lasting briefly, short-lived

Unair *abbrev Univérsitas Airlangga* Airlangga University (in Surabaya)

Unas *abbrev Universitas Nasional* National University, in Jakarta

undang, mengundang *vt* to invite (formally); **undangan** *n* invitation; formal event

undang: undang-undang *n* law, act; ~ *Dasar* constitution; *Kitab* ~ *Hukum Perdata* civil code; **perundang-undangan** *n* legislation

undi *n* lot; **undian** *n* lottery; **mengundi** *vt* to conduct a draw or lottery

undur, mundur *vi* to reverse, go back; **mengundurkan** *vt* to postpone; **pengunduran** *n* postponement, delay

uneg, unek: uneg-uneg, unek-unek *n* grudges

unggas *n* poultry, bird
unggul *adj* superior; **keunggulan** *n* superiority; **mengungguli** *vt* to surpass, outdo; **mengunggulkan** *vt* to consider superior, seed (in tennis)
unggun *api* ~ (camp) fire
ungkap *v* to express, reveal; **ungkapan** *n* expression; **mengungkap** *vt* to uncover; **mengungkapkan** *vt* to express; **pengungkapan** *n* expression, revelation; **terungkap** *adj* expressed, revealed
ungkit: mengungkit *vt* to lever; to pry; **mengungkit-ungkit** *vt* to drag something up (from the past); **pengungkit** *n* lever
ungsi: mengungsi *vi* to evacuate or flee; **mengungsikan** *vt* to evacuate someone; **pengungsi** *n* refugee, evacuee; **pengungsian** *n* evacuation
ungu *adj* purple; ~ *muda* violet
Unhas *abbrev* *Univérsitas Hasanuddin* Hasanuddin University (in Makassar)
uni *n* union; ~ *Eropa (UE)* European Union (EU); ~ *Soviet (US)* Soviet Union; ~ *Arab Emirat (UAE)* United Arab Emirates (UAE); ~ *(Republik) Sovyet (Sosialis) (URSS)* Union of Soviet Socialist Republics (USSR)
Uni *pron, Min, f* older sister
Unibraw *abbrev Univérsitas Brawijaya* Brawijaya University (in Malang)
unik *adj* unique; **keunikan** *n* unique thing, uniqueness
unilatéral *adj* unilateral
Unisba *abbrev Universitas Islam Bandung* Bandung Islamic University
unit *n* facility, unit; ~ *Gawat Darurat (UGD)* emergency room, casualty ward
univérsal *adj* universal
univérsitas *n* university; ~ *Airlangga (Unair)* Airlangga University (in Surábaya); ~ *Brawijaya (Unibraw)* Brawijaya University (in Malang); ~ *Hasanuddin (Unhas)* Hasanuddin University (in Makassar); ~ *Indonesia (UI)* University of Indonesia, in Jakarta; ~ *Nasional (Unas)* National University, in Jakarta; ~ *Padjadjaran* Pajajaran University (in Bandung); ~

Parahyangan (Unpar) Parahyangan University, in Bandung; ~ *Surabaya (Ubaya)* University of Surabaya; ~ *Tarumanagara (Untar)* Tarumanagara University, in Jakarta; ~ *Terbuka (UT)* Open University; ~ *Udayana (Unud)* Udayana University (in Denpasar); *Gadjah Mada (UGM)* Gajah Mada University, in Yogyakarta; ~ *Islam Bandung (Unisba)* Bandung Islamic University; ~ *Islam Indonesia (UII)* Indonesian Islamic University, in Yogyakarta; ~ *Kristen Djaya (Ukrida)* a Christian university in Jakarta; ~ *Kristen Indonesia (UKI)* Indonesian Christian University, in Jakarta; ~ *Sumatera Utara (USU)* University of North Sumatra, in Medan; ~ *Negeri Sebelas Maret (UNS)* Eleventh of March State University, in Solo
unjuk show; ~ *gigi* show your teeth; ~ *rasa* demonstration; **berunjuk** *vi* ~ *rasa* to demonstrate, hold a demonstration; **mengunjukkan** *vt* to show something; **pengunjuk** *n* ~ *rasa* demonstrator, protester
Unpad *abbrev Univérsitas Padjadjaran* Padjadjaran University (in Bandung)
Unpar *abbrev Universitas Parahyangan* Parahyangan University, in Bandung
UNS *abbrev Universitas Negeri Sebelas Maret* Eleventh of March State University, in Solo
unsur *n* element; ~ *kimia* (chemical) element
unta, onta *n* camel; *burung* ~ ostrich
untai string; counter for string-like objects; **untaian** *n* string, chain; **menguntai** *vt* to string, tie together; **teruntai** *adj* dangling, strung up
Untar *abbrev Universitas Tarumanagara* Tarumanagara University, in Jakarta
untuk *prep* for; **memperuntukkan** *vt* to allocate or assign; **peruntukan** *n* allocation
untung advantage, gain, profit; luck; ~*nya* the good thing was; ~ *rugi* gains and losses, pros and cons; **beruntung** *adj* lucky, fortunate; *vi* to have luck, good fortune; **keberuntungan** *n* good

fortune or luck; **keuntungan** *n* advantage, profit; **menguntungkan** *vt* to benefit (someone); *adj* profitable; **peruntungan** *n* (good) fortune or luck

Unud *abbrev Univérsitas Udayana* Udayana University (in Denpasar)

up. *abbrev untuk perhatian* att., attention (on envelopes and letters)

upaboga *n* cuisine, gastronomy

upacara *n* ceremony; ~ *adat* traditional ceremony; ~ *bendera* flag-raising ceremony; ~ *pelantikan* inauguration (ceremony); ~ *pemakaman* funeral; ~ *pernikahan*, ~ *perkawinan* wedding ceremony; ~ *wisuda* (university) graduation ceremony

upah *n* wage, wages; ~ *harian* daily pay; **mengupah** *vt* to employ, hire, pay someone (to do work)

upas *n* plant toxin

upaya *n* effort; ~ *hukum* legal avenue or remedy; **berupaya** *vi* to make an effort, try; **mengupayakan** *vt* to try, to enable

upeti *n* tribute; bribe

upik *n* nickname for a girl, esp in Sumatra; *buyung* ~ boy and girl, son and daughter

upil *n* snot, bogey, nasal mucus; **mengupil** *vi* to pick your nose

urai: uraian *n* explanation, analysis; **berurai** *vi* to hang down or loose; **menguraikan** *vt* to explain; to untangle; **terurai** *adj* hanging loose

urak: urakan *adj* eccentric; bad-mannered

urang-aring *n* kind of medicinal plant

uranium *n* uranium

Uranus *n* (the planet) Uranus

urap *n* vegetable salad with grated coconut

urat *n* tendon, vein; muscle; ~ *nadi* artery; ~ *saraf* nerve; *salah* ~ strained or pulled muscle

urban *adj* urban; **urbanisasi** *n* urbanization

uréa *pupuk* ~ kind of fertilizer

urgénsi *n* urgency

uri *n* placenta, afterbirth

urolog *n* urologist; **urologi** *n* urology

URSS *abbrev Uni Republik Sovyet Sosialis* Union of Soviet Socialist Republics, USSR

Uruguay *n* Uruguay; *orang* ~ Uruguayan

uruk: menguruk *vt* to fill (with earth); **pengurukan** *n* filling; ~ *laut* land reclamation

urun ~ *rembug* to make a joint decision

urung fail, fall through, not succeed; **mengurungkan** *vt* to abandon

urus *vi* organize, arrange; **urusan** *n* arrangement, dealing, affair; ~ *penting* urgent business; *bukan* ~ *saya* none of my business; **berurusan** *vi* to have dealings with, deal with; **mengurus** *vt* to arrange, organize, manage; **mengurusi** *vt* to take care of, look after; **pengurus** *n* manager, organizer; ~ *besar* board of directors, executive; **kepengurusan** *n* management; **terurus** *adj* looked-after, cared for; *tidak* ~ neglected, uncared for

urut massage, rub; *tukang* ~ masseur; **mengurut** *vt* to massage

urut order in a series; *nomor* ~ number; **urutan** *n* order, sequence; **berurut, berurut-urutan** *adj* successive, consecutive, sequential; **mengurut** *vt* to put in order or sequence

urutan *n* order, sequence ← **urut**

US *abbrev Uni Sovyet* Soviet Union

usah *tidak* ~ not necessary; **usahkan** let alone, not to mention

usaha *n* effort; *dunia* ~ business world; *tata* ~ administration; **berusaha** *vi* to try, make an effort; **mengusahakan** *vt* to try, endeavor to; **pengusaha** *n, m* businessman; *n, f* businesswoman; **perusahaan** *n* company; ~ *negara* state company or enterprise

usahkan let alone, not to mention ← **usah**

usai *adj* over, finished; ~ *perang* after the war, post-war

usang *adj* worn out, old, out-of-date

usap wipe, stroke; **usapan** *n* stroke, caress; **mengusap** *vt* to wipe; to stroke or fondle

USDÉK *abbrev Undang-Undang Dasar 45, Sosialisme ala Indonesia,*

Demokrasi Terpimpin, Ekonomi Terpimpin, Kepribadian Indonesia five principles of Sukarno's government in the 1960s (the 1945 Constitution, Indonesian-style socialism, Guided Democracy, a Guided Economy, and Indonesian identity)

USG *abbrev ultrasonografi* ultra-sound (screening)

usia *n, pol* age; ~ *kehamilan* length of pregnancy; ~ *lanjut* old age; ~ *muda* youth; a young age; ~ *produktif* productive age; ~ *senja* old age, twilight years; *lanjut* ~ *adj* old; **berusia** *vi* (to be) aged; **seusia** *adj* the same age

usik: mengusik *vt* to tease, disturb

usil *adj* annoying, cheeky

Using, Osing *orang* ~ Javanese sub-ethnic group living around Banyu-wangi, East Java

usir, mengusir *vt* to drive away or out, chase away, expel

uskup *n* bishop; ~ *agung* archbishop; **keuskupan** *n* diocese

ustad, ustadz *n, Isl* term of address for a religious leader or teacher

USU *abbrev Universitas Sumatera Utara* University of North Sumatra, in Medan

usul *n* origin; *asal* ~ origin(s), back-ground

usul propose, suggest; motion; *atas* ~ on the suggestion of; **usulan** *n* sug-gestion; **mengusulkan** *vt* to propose or suggest

usung, mengusung *vt* to carry on the shoulders

usus *n* intestine; ~ *besar* large intestine; ~ *buntu* appendix; ~ *halus* small intestine

usut: mengusut *v* to investigate, sort out

UT *abbrev Universitas Terbuka* Open University

utak ~*-atik* fiddle or tinker with; **mengutak-atik** *vt* to fiddle or tinker with → **kutak-katik**

utama *adj* main; **mengutamakan** *vt* to give preference or priority to; **teruta-ma** *adv* especially, particularly

utang, hutang *n* debt; ~ *piutang* debits and credits; *surat* ~ IOU (I owe you);

berutang *vi* to owe; ~ *budi* debt of gratitude

utara *adj* north; *Korea* ~ *(Korut)* North Korea; *Sulawesi* ~ *(Sulut)* North Sulawesi

utara: mengutarakan *vt* to put forward

utas *n* string (of beads); counter for ropes etc; *se*~ *tali* a length of string

utk. *abbrev untuk* for

utopia *n* utopia, paradise, dream world

utuh *adj* whole, complete, untouched; **keutuhan** *n* entirety, state of whole-ness; **seutuhnya** *adv* completely

utus, mengutus *vt* to send or delegate; **utusan** *n* delegate, deputy; mission; **perutusan** *n* delegation

UU *abbrev Undang-Undang* legal statutes

UUD *abbrev Undang-Undang Dasar* constitution

Uzbék *bahasa* ~ Uzbek; **Uzbékistan** *n* Uzbekistan; *orang* ~ Uzbekistani

uzur, udur, udzur *adj* old and infirm

V

v [fé] v, 22nd letter of the alphabet

vagina *n* vagina

vakansi, pakansi vacation, on holiday

vaksin *n* vaccine; **vaksinasi** *n* vaccina-tion; **divaksinasi** *v* to be vaccinated; **memvaksinasi** *vt* to vaccinate

vakum *n* vacuum; **divakum** *v* to be vac-uumed; to give birth with the aid of vacuum extraction; **memvakum** *vt* to vacuum

valas *n* foreign currency ← **valuta asing**

validasi *n* validation; **divalidasi** *v* to be validated; **memvalidasi** *vt* to validate

validitas *n* validity

valuta *n* currency; ~ *asing (valas)* foreign currency

vampir *n* vampire

vanili *n* vanilla; *rasa* ~ vanilla (-flavored)

varia *n* variety; **variasi** *n* accessories (esp vehicle), variation

varisés *n* varicose veins

vas *n* vase

Vatikan Vatican; *Kota* ~ Vatican City

vé [fé] *v*, 22nd letter of the alphabet

végetarian, végetaris *adj* vegetarian

vélbéd, pélbét *n* campbed

vélg, véleg, pélek *n* wheel rim

vélodrom *n* velodrome, cycling track

Vénésia *n* Venice

Vénézuéla *n* Venezuela; *orang* ~ Venezuelan

véntilasi *n* ventilation

Vénus *n* (the planet) Venus

vérba *n* verb

verboden, perboden no entry

vérifikasi *n* verification; **divérifikasi** *v* to be verified; **memvérifikasi** *vt* to verify

vermak → **permak**

vernis → **pernis**

vérsi *n* version

versnéling → **persnéling**

vértikal *adj* vertical; *konflik* ~ conflict between higher and lower social groups

véspa *n* moped, motor scooter

véteran *n* returned serviceman, veteran (esp of 1945-49 Revolution)

vétsin *n* MSG (monosodium glutamate)

viaduk *n* viaduct

vibrasi *n* vibration; **bervibrasi** *vi* to vibrate

vibrator *n* [vibrator] vibrator

vidéo video; *kamera* ~ video camera; **vidéoklip** *n* video clip

Viétnam *n* Vietnam; *bahasa* ~, *orang* ~ Vietnamese

vihara, wihara *n* Buddhist temple or monastery

vila *n* villa, holiday house, summer cottage

virus *n* virus

visa *n* visa; ~ *diplomatik*, ~ *dinas* diplomatic passport; *sosial budaya (sosbud)* sociocultural visa

visi ~ *dan misi* mission statement

visibilitas *n* visibility → **jarak pandang**

Visnu, Vishnu → **Wisnu**

visum ~ *ét répértum* autopsy (official report)

vital *adj* vital; *alat* ~ vital organs; genitals

vitamin *n* vitamin

VJ *abbrev* video jockey

vlék → **flék**

VOC *abbrev Vereinigde Oost-Indische Compagnie* United East India Company, in colonial times

vocer → **voucer**

vokal *adj* vocal, outspoken; *huruf* ~ vowel; **vokalis** *n* vocalist

voli *bola* ~ volleyball; *(bola)* ~ *pantai* beach volleyball; *pemain* ~ volleyball player, volleyballer

volt *n* volt; **voltase** *n* voltage

Volta Hulu → **Burkina Faso**

volume *n* volume, size, bulk

vonis *n* ruling; sentence; ~ *mati* death sentence; **divonis** *v* to be sentenced; **memvonis** *vt* to sentence

voucer, vocer *n* credit voucher (for cell and mobile phones)

vulkanolog *n* vulcanologist, expert on volcanoes; **vulkanologi** *n* vulcanology

W

w [wé] w, 23rd letter of the alphabet

wa, ua *pron* term of address to a parents' older sibling (in some areas)

wa alaikum, walaikum *Isl* ~ *salam* (said in response to *salam alaikum*); ~ *salam warahmatullahi wabarakatuh (Wr Wb)* and upon you be peace and may God bestow His mercy and blessing (in formal situations)

wabah *n* epidemic, plague; ~ *belalang* locust plague; ~ *flu burung* bird flu epidemic; **mewabah** *vi* to spread (uncontrollably)

wacana *n* discourse; speech, lecture

wadah *n* pot, container, place to put something

wadam *n* transvestite ← **wanita adam**

waduh *ejac, Jav* wow! how about that? (exclamation of admiration)

waduk *n* reservoir; dam

waé *adv, Sund, Jav* only, just

wafat *vi, pol* to pass away or die; ~*nya* his/her death; ~ *1970* died 1970

Wagé *n* fourth day of the Javanese week

wagub *n* deputy governor ← **wakil gubernur**

wah *excl* wow! oh! *adj* amazing, outstanding; fantastic, wonderful

wahai *lit* oh, o

wahana *n* vehicle, means; ~ *Lingkungan Hidup Indonesia (Walhi)* Indonesian environmental group

wahid *adj* one, single; *nomor* ~ best, number one

wahyu *n* revelation, vision, inspiration; **mewahyukan** *vt* to reveal something (in a vision)

Waisak, Wésak *n* Buddhist New Year

wajah *n, pol* face; **berwajah** *vi* to have a face; ~ *muram* sour-faced

wajan *n* wok

wajar *adj* natural; **kewajaran** *n* sense, logic; **sewajarnya** *adv* naturally

wajib compulsory; must, obliged; ~ *belajar* compulsory education; ~ *militer (wamil)* military service, draft; ~ *pajak* taxpayer; obligation to pay taxes; *lagu* ~ song learned at school, compulsory song; *nomor pokok* ~ *pajak (NPWP)* tax file number; **berwajib** *adj* responsible, competent; *vi* to have responsibility for; *pihak yang* ~ the authorities; **kewajiban** *n* obligation, duty; **mewajibkan** *vt* to enforce, make obligatory

wajik *n* diamonds (card suit); diamond-shaped cake of sticky rice

waka *n* deputy head, second-in-charge ← **wakil kepala**

wakaf *Isl tanah* ~ land donated or bequeathed to the local Muslim community; **mewakafkan** *vt* to donate land or other items in this way

wakil *n* representative, substitute; *adj* vice; ~ *gubernur (wagub)* deputy governor; ~ *ketua* deputy chair; ~ *presiden (wapres)* vice-president; ~ *rakyat* people's representative (member of parliament); ~ *tunggal* sole agent; **mewakili** *vt* to represent; **mewakilkan** *vt* to delegate, send a proxy; *Bapak* ~ *deputinya untuk menghadiri rapat di Surabaya* the boss sent his representative to attend the meeting in Surabaya; **perwakilan** *n* representation, delegation; *Dewan* ~ *Rakyat (DPR)* parliament, legislative assembly; **terwakili** *adj* represented

waktu *n* time, hours; *conj* when; ~ *luang* spare time; *membuang* ~ to waste time; *pada* ~*nya* in due time, at the right time; *sebelum* ~*nya* prematurely; **pewaktu** *n* timer; **sewaktu** *conj* when; **sewaktu-waktu** *adv* at any moment; every now and then

wakuncar *coll* call on or have a date with your girlfriend ← **wajib kunjungi pacar**

walaah *excl* oh no; come on! you must be joking (in disbelief)

walafiat *sehat* ~ healthy, hale and hearty, in good health

walah: kewalahan *adj* unable to cope, overcome

walaikum, wa alaikum *Isl* ~ *salam* and upon you be peace (said in response to *salam alaikum*); ~ *salam warahmatullahi wabarakatuh (Wr Wb)* and upon you be peace and may God bestow His mercy and blessing (in formal situations)

walau, walaupun *conj* although

walét *burung* ~ swift; *rumah* ~ building where swiftlet nests are cultivated

walhasil *conj* with the result that ← **alhasil**

Walhi *n* Indonesian environmental group ← **Wahana Lingkungan Hidup Indonésia**

wali *n* guardian; saint; ~ *gereja* bishop; ~ *(hakim)* man representing the bride during an Islamic wedding ceremony; ~ *kelas* form or homeroom teacher, tutor; ~ *kota* mayor; ~ *murid* legal guardian of a student; ~ *Songo,* ~ *Sanga Isl* nine holy men who spread Islam across Java; **perwalian** *n* guardianship, representation

wallahualam *Isl* only God knows

wals, walsa *n* waltz

wamil *n* military service, draft ← **wajib militér**

-wan *suf, m* -man, one who does something; *negara*~ statesman; *olahraga*~ sportsman

wana- *pref* forest

wangi fragrant; perfume; *minyak* ~ perfume; **wangi-wangian, wewangian** *n* scents, perfumes; **pewangi** *n* scent, fragrance (in washing detergent)

wangsit *n* divine inspiration or revelation

wanita *n* woman; ~ *karir* career woman; ~ *panggilan* call girl; ~ *penghibur* escort, prostitute; ~ *simpanan* kept woman, lover; ~ *tunasusila (WTS)* prostitute; *kaum* ~ women, the fair sex; *polisi* ~ *(polwan)* policewoman; ~ *idaman lain (WIL)* dream woman, lover

wanti: wanti-wanti *n* reminder, warning; **mewanti-wanti** *vt* to warn

waprés *n* vice-president; *calon* ~ *(cawapres)* vice-presidential candidate ← **wakil présidén**

wara: wara-wiri, wira-wiri *adj* back and forth

waralaba *n* franchise

waras *adj* sane, healthy; **kewarasan** *n* sanity, mental health

warga *n* citizen; **warganegara** *n* citizen, national; ~ *asing (WNA)* foreigner, foreign national; ~ *Indonesia (WNI)* Indonesian citizen; ~ *Indonesia keturunan* Indonesian of Chinese descent; **kewarganegaraan** *n* citizenship; **berkewarganegaraan** *vi* to have citizenship or be a citizen of

waria *n* transvestite ← **wanita pria**

waris *ahli* ~ *m* heir *f* heiress; **warisan** *n* inheritance; **mewarisi** *vt* to inherit; **mewariskan** *vt* to bequeath or leave something

warkat *n* official letter, (bank) document

warkop *n* coffee stall ← **warung kopi**

warna *n* color; ~ *putih* white; ~*-warni* colorful, multicolored; **berwarna** *adj* colored; *vi* to have a color; **mewarnai** *vt* to color (in); **pewarna** *n* dye, stain; **pewarnaan** *n* dyeing, coloring; **se-warna** *adj* of the same colour

warnét *n* internet café ← **warung internét**

warok *n* male leader of East Javanese *reog* performance

warpostél *n* office where you can make calls, and send post and faxes ← **warung pos dan télékomunikasi**

Warsawa *n* Warsaw

warta *n* news; ~ *berita* news (items); **wartawan** *m*; **wartawati** *f* journalist, reporter; ~ *amplop* journalist who accepts bribes; ~ *foto* photojournalist; photographer; ~ *lepas* freelance journalist

warteg *n* small, cheap food stall ← **warung Tegal**

wartél *n* small office where you can make calls and send faxes ← **warung télékomunikasi**

waru *pohon* ~ kind of hibiscus tree

waruga *n* stone sarcophagus, found in North Sulawesi

warung *n* stall, small local shop; ~ *internet (warnet)* internet café; ~ *kopi (warkop)* coffee stall; ~ *nasi* small roadside stall or shop selling rice with side-dishes; ~ *remang-remang* dingy roadside stalls (usu for prostitution); ~ *Tegal (warteg)* small, cheap food stall; ~ *telekomunikasi (wartel)* small office where you can make calls and send faxes; ~ *tenda* small tent selling food; ~ *pos dan telekomunikasi (warpostel)* office where you can make calls, and send post and faxes

waserai *n* (commercial) laundry

wasiat *n* will; *surat* ~ will, testament

wasir *n* hemorrhoids

wasit *n* umpire, referee

waslap *n* washcloth, flannel

waspada *adj* on guard, careful, cautious; **kewaspadaan** *n* caution; **mewaspadai** *vt* to watch out for, guard against

wassalam *Isl* upon you be peace, best regards (in closing letters); ~ *alaikum warahmatullahi wabarakatuh (wr wb)* and upon you be peace, mercy and the blessing of God (used as response to *assalamualaikum wr wb*)

wastafel *n* basin, sink (in bathroom)

waswas *adj* worried, anxious, nervous

watak *n* nature, character; **berwatak** *vi* to have a certain nature; ~ *keras* strict, stern, unyielding

-wati *suf, f* -woman, one who does something; *peraga~* model
wawancara *n* interview; ~ *kerja* job interview; **mewawancarai** *vt* to interview; **pewawancara** *n* interviewer
wawas: wawasan *n* outlook, view, concept; **berwawasan** *vi* to have an outlook; ~ *luas* broad- or open-minded
wayang *n* puppet; ~ *golek* wooden, three-dimensional puppet; ~ *kulit* shadow puppet (performance); ~ *orang* traditional performance with actors; ~ *potehi* puppets of Chinese origin; ~ *purba* shadow puppets performing the ancient Ramayana and Mahabharata stories; *pertunjukan* ~ (shadow) puppet play or performance; *anak semata* ~ only child; **pewayang-an** *n* the world of *wayang*
WC [wé sé] *n* toilet, bathroom, lavatory
wé w, 23rd letter of the alphabet
wedana *n, arch* assistant to the regent (*bupati*), overseeing several sub-districts (*kecamatan*)
wédang *n* warm Javanese beverage; ~ *jahe* warm ginger drink; ~ *kopi* hot coffee; ~ *ronde* warm Javanese beverage
wéker *n* alarm; *(jam)* ~ alarm clock; *memasang* ~ to set the alarm (clock)
wektu ~ *telu Isl* community in Lombok which prays three times a day, not five
wenang: berwenang *adj* competent, in charge; **kewenangan, wewenang** *n* authority; **sewenang-wenang, se-wenang-wenangnya** *adv* tyrannically, arbitrarily
Wésak → **Waisak**
wésel *n* money order; points (on a railroad or railway line); *pos* ~ postal money order
wewangian ← **wangi**
wewenang *n* authority ← **wenang**
WIB *abbrev Waktu Indonesia Barat* Western Indonesian time
wibawa *n* authority, esteem; **berwibawa** *adj* esteemed, respected, of good standing
wicara *n* speech; *ahli* ~ speech therapist; *tuna~* deaf mute

wihara, vihara *n* Buddhist temple or monastery
wijén *n* sesame seed
WIL *n, f* dream woman; lover ← **wanita idaman lain**
wilayah *n* area, territory; *kantor* ~ *(kanwil)* regional office
Wina *n* Vienna
wingko ~ *babat* small coconut slice, a specialty of Semarang
windu *n* eight-year cycle; **sewindu** *adj* eight years
wira-: wiraswasta *n, m* businessman *f* businesswoman; **wirausaha** *n* business
wira: wira-wiri, wara-wiri *adv* back and forth
wiraswasta *n, m* businessman *f* businesswoman
wirausaha *n* business
wirid *n* section of the Koran for study
wisata *n* tourism, travel; ~ *alam* outdoor tourism, nature tourism; ~ *bahari* marine or maritime tourism; *biro* ~ travel agent; *pari~* tourism; **berwisata** *vi* to travel or holiday; **wisatawan** *n* tourist; ~ *mancanegara (wisman)* foreign tourist; ~ *Nusantara (wisnu)* domestic or local tourist
wiski *n* whisky, whiskey; ~ *soda* whisky and soda
wisma *n* house, building; *tuna~* homeless
wisman *n* foreign tourist ← **wisatawan mancanegara**
Wisnu, Visnu *n* Vishnu, Hindu god
wisnu *n* domestic or local tourist ← **wisatawan Nusantara**
wisuda graduate; *upacara* ~ (university) graduation ceremony; **wisudawan** *n, m* graduate; **wisudawati** *n, f* graduate
WIT *abbrev Waktu Indonesia Timur* Eastern Indonesian time
WITA *abbrev Waktu Indonesia Tengah* Central Indonesian time
WNA *abbrev warga negara asing* foreign national
WNI *abbrev warga negara Indonesia* Indonesian national; ~ *keturunan* Indonesian of Chinese descent

wol *n* wool

wong *conj, coll* because; what do you mean?

wortel *n* carrot

wréda, werda *adj* old (of age)

Wr Wb. *warahmatullahi wabarakatuh* may God's blessing and mercy be upon you, used to close speeches

WTS *abbrev, euph wanita tuna susila* immoral woman, prostitute

wudu, wudhu, wudlu *n, Isl* ritual ablutions before praying; *air* ~ water for ablutions before praying; *mengambil* ~ to wash before praying; *tempat* ~ tap used for washing before praying; **berwudu** *vi* to wash before praying

wujud *n* existence; **berwujud** *vi* in the form or shape of; **mewujudkan** *vt* to make something real, realize something; **terwujud** *adj* realized

wulan *catur* ~ trimester, term; ~ *(cawu) ketiga* third term

wushu *n* form of Chinese self-defense

X

X [éks] x, 24th letter of the alphabet; *sinar* ~ X-ray

Y

y [yé] y, 25th letter of the alphabet

ya, iya yes; isn't it (as a reinforcing tag); ~ *sudah* well that's that; *saya boleh datang besok,* ~? I can come tomorrow, can't I?

ya *ejac* oh, O; ~ *Allah* oh God!

yad. *yang akan datang* future

yah yes, well ...

Yah *pron, m* Dad ← **Ayah**

yahud *adj* great, number one

Yahudi *adj* Jewish; *agama* ~ Judaism; *bahasa* ~ Yiddish; *orang* ~ Jewish, Jew

yaitu *conj* namely, that is

yakin *adj* sure, convinced; **keyakinan** *n* belief, conviction, faith; **berkeyakinan**

vi to be convinced; **meyakini** *vt* to believe (in), be convinced; **meyakinkan** *adj* convincing, believable; *vt* to convince someone

yakni *conj* namely

Yaman *n* Yemen; *orang* ~ Yemeni

yang, yg *conj* that, which, who; ~ *bersangkutan (ybs)* person concerned or involved; ~ *biru* the blue one; ~ *lalu (yl)* in the past; ~ *tercinta (ytc)* dearest, beloved; ~ *terhormat (yth)* dear; ~ *tersayang (yts)* dearest, beloved; ~ *akan datang (yad)* in the future; ~ *Maha Esa (YME)* the One and Only, when referring to God

yang, yayang *pron, sl* darl, darling ← **sayang**

Yasin *Isl surat* ~ chapter of the Koran, recited for the dead

yatim *n* orphan, fatherless child; ~ *piatu* orphan; *rumah* ~ orphanage

yayang, yang *pron, sl* darling, darl ← **sayang**

yayasan *n* foundation (not for profit)

ybs *abbrev yang bersangkutan* person concerned or involved

yé y, 25th letter of the alphabet

yél *n* chant, war-cry, shout

Yésus *n, Chr* Jesus; ~ *Kristus* Jesus Christ

yg → **yang**

yl. *yang lalu* in the past

YME *abbrev Yang Maha Esa* the One and Only, when referring to God

yodium *n* iodine; **beryodium** *vi garam* ~ iodized salt

yoga *n* yoga

yoghurt, yogurt *n* yogurt, yoghurt

yogia, yogya: seyogianya *adv* properly, fittingly

yogurt → **yoghurt**

yoni *n* square hole, traditional female symbol; *lingga* ~ obelisk in a square hole, traditional symbol of male and female sexuality

Yordania *n* Jordan; *orang* ~ Jordanian

yoyo *n* yoyo

ytc. *abbrev yang tercinta* dearest

yth. *abbrev yang terhormat* the respected (used when addressing letters)

yts. *abbrev yang tersayang* beloved (used when addressing letters to family or friends)
yu → **hiu**
Yugo, Yugoslavia *n, arch* Yugoslavia; *orang* ~ Yugoslav
yuk → **ayo**
Yunani *n* Greece; *bahasa* ~*, orang* ~ Greek
yunior junior (at work or school)
yuridis *adj* jurisdictive, legal
yute → **rami**

Z

z [zét] last letter of the alphabet
Zaire → **Kongo**
zaitun *n* olive; *minyak* ~ olive oil
zakar *n* penis; *buah* ~ testicles
zakat, jakat *n* alms; ~ *fitrah* alms paid before Idul Fitri; ~ *mal* alms paid according to one's wealth and assets
zalim, dzalim *adj* cruel, hateful; **menzalimi** *vt* to oppress, be cruel to
zaman, jaman *n* age, era, time, period; ~ *dahulu,* ~ *dulu* in the old days, times past; ~ *Batu* Stone Age; ~ *Belanda* the Dutch era; ~ *meleset* the Great Depression; ~ *Revolusi* the Indonesian Revolution, 1945-49; ~ *saya* in my day; *ketinggalan* ~ outdated

Zambia *n* Zambia; *orang* ~ Zambian
zamrud, jamrud *n* emerald; ~ *khatulistiwa* emeralds of the Equator (ie. Indonesia)
zamzam *Isl air* ~ holy water from Mecca
zat, jat *n* element, substance; ~ *air* hydrogen; ~ *arang* carbon; ~ *asam* oxygen; ~ *besi* iron (as a vitamin); ~ *hijau* chlorophyll; ~ *kapur* calcium; ~ *pasir* silicon; ~ *pewarna* dye
zébra *n* zebra
Zéni army engineers
zét z, last letter of the alphabet
ziarah *n* pilgrimage, visit to a holy place or cemetery; **berziarah** *vi* to make a pilgrimage, visit a holy place; **peziarah** *n* pilgrim
zikir, dikir, dzikir *Isl* (recite) additional prayers; **berzikir** *vi, Isl* to say additional prayers
Zimbabwé *n* Zimbabwe; *orang* ~ Zimbabwean
zina, zinah *n* adultery; sex outside marriage; **berzina** *vi* to commit adultery
zirkonium *n* zirconium, (Zr)
zodiak *n* zodiac
zohor → **lohor**
zona, zone *n* zone; ~ *penyangga* buffer zone; ~ *Ekonomi Ekslusif (ZEE)* exclusive economic zone
zuhur → **lohor**
zus → **sus**
zuster → **suster**

ENGLISH–INDONESIAN

A

& co *and Company* cs (cum suis)

A [é] *a, first letter of the alphabet*; **A1** nomor satu, terbaik; **A-OK** *adj* baik; sehat walafiat

a *art* (sebelum huruf mati) satu, suatu, sebuah; per, tiap; ~ *cigarette* sebatang rokok; ~ *dog* seékor anjing; ~ *house* sebuah rumah; ~ *letter* sepucuk surat; ~ *man* seorang lelaki; ~ *month* sebulan (sebelum huruf hidup → **an**)

aback *taken* ~ kagét, terkejut

abacus *n* sempoa

abaft *adj* buritan, di belakang (istilah pelayaran)

abalone *n* abalon, kerang mata tujuh

abandon *vt* mengabaikan, menelantarkan; menghentikan, meninggalkan; *Tom ~ed his wife* Tom meninggalkan isterinya; *n with gay* ~ tanpa beban, secara tidak bertanggung jawab; **abandoned** *adj* terabaikan, telantar

abash: abashed *adj* malu

abate *vi* reda, mereda; *the storm soon ~d* badai segera reda

abattoir *n* [abatuar] pejagalan

abbess *n, Chr, f* kepala biarawati; **abbey** *n* biara; **abbot** *n, m* kepala biarawan

abbreviate *vt* menyingkatkan, meméndékkan; **abbreviation** *n* singkatan, kependékan

ABC *abbrev American Broadcasting Corporation, Australian Broadcasting Corporation* ABC

abc *n* abjad, abc; *has he learned his* ~? apakah dia sudah hafal abc?

abdicate *vi* [abdikét] *vt* léngsér (keprabon), turun takhta; *vi* meninggalkan; ~ *responsibility* meninggalkan, menelantarkan, melepaskan tanggung jawab; **abdication** *n* turun takhta; *the* ~ *of Edward VI shocked the public* saat Raja Edward VI turun takhta, masyarakat kagét

abdomen *n* perut (terutama bagian bawah); **abdominal** *adj* [abdominal]~ *pain* rasa sakit di daérah perut

abduct *vt* menculik; melarikan; **abduction** *n* penculikan; **abductor** *n* penculik

aberration *n* penyimpangan, penyeléwéngan

abet *vt* [abét] *aid and* ~ membantu penjahat, bersekongkol dengan

abhor *vt* membenci; *Mother ~s untidiness* Ibu sangat tidak menyukai kamar yang berantakan; **abhorrent** *adj* menjijikkan

ability *n* [abiliti] kemampuan, kesanggupan, kepandaian, bakat ← **able**

abject ~ *poverty* kemiskinan, kemelaratan

ablaze *adj* menyala, terbakar ← **blaze**

able *adj* [ébel] bisa, mampu, sanggup; *she wasn't* ~ *to come* dia tidak bisa datang (waktu itu); *~-bodied* sehat (secara fisik); **ably** *adv* dengan baik, dengan pandai

ablutions *n, pl* pembersihan; *Isl* wudu

abnormal *adj* tidak normal, tidak biasa; **abnormality** *n* cacat

aboard *adv* di atas kendaraan; *to go* ~ naik kapal

abode *n* rumah, kediaman, tempat tinggal; *my humble* ~ gubuk derita

abolish *vt* menghapus, meniadakan; **abolition** *n* penghapusan, pencabutan

abominable *adj* mengerikan, menjijikkan; *the* ~ *Snowman* yeti; **abomination** *n* tindakan yang jahat

Aboriginal *adj, n* [aborijinal] Aborijin; ~ *Affairs* urusan Aborijin; **aboriginal** *adj* penduduk asli; **Aborigine** *n* [aborijini] orang Aborijin, penduduk asli Australia

abort *vt* menggugurkan; **abortion** *n* pengguguran, aborsi; **abortionist** *n* orang yang memberi jasa menggugurkan kandungan; **abortive** *adj* gagal

abound *vi* berlimpah (ruah)

about *prep* tentang, mengenai, seputar (sebuah topik); sekitar, keliling (sebuah tempat); *adv* kurang lebih, kira-kira (jumlah); ~ *to* segera akan; *Stewart knows all ~ it* Stewart yang tahu tentang itu; *they know their way ~ town* meréka tahu jalan di kota; **about-face** putar balik

above *prep* [abav] (di) atas; lebih daripada; ~ *all* terutama, yang paling penting; ~*board* legal, resmi; *heavens ~!* ya Allah!; ~*mentioned* yang tersebut di atas

abracadabra simsalabim

abrasion *n* luka ringan, gorésan pada kulit; **abrasive** *adj* (bersifat) kasar

abreast *adv* [abrést] bersampingan; *to keep ~ of* mengikuti

abridged *adj* [abrijd] singkat; ~ *dictionary* kamus singkat

abroad *adv* luar negeri, negeri orang; *Liz has gone ~* Liz sudah pergi ke luar negeri

abrupt *adj* tiba-tiba; kasar, kurang sopan; **abruptly** *adv* secara mendadak; dengan kasar

abscess *n* absés

abscond *vi* kabur, melarikan diri

absence *n* ketidakhadiran; **absent** *adj* tidak hadir, mangkir; ~*minded* sering lupa; *vt* tidak hadir; *he ~ed himself from the meeting* dia tidak hadir dalam rapat; **absentee** *n* orang yang tidak hadir; **absenteeism** *n* (hal) ketidakhadiran

absolute *adj* mutlak, total; **absolutely** *adv* secara mutlak, betul

absolve *vt* memaafkan, mengampuni (dosa)

absorb *vt* menyerap; ~*ed in* asyik; ~*ed in thought* termenung; **absorbent** *adj* menyerap; **absorption** *n* penyerapan, serapan, absorpsi

abstain *vi* tidak ikut (memilih dalam pemilihan suara), menjadi nétral; berpantang; ~ *from drinking alcohol* tidak minum alkohol; **abstainer** *n* orang yang tidak melakukan sesuatu; **abstinence** *n* pantang

abstract *adj* abstrak; ~ *art* seni abstrak, aliran abstrak; tidak konkrét; *n* ringkasan

absurd *adj* gila, tidak masuk akal; **absurdity** *n* sesuatu yang tidak masuk akal

abundance *n* kelimpahan; **abundant** *adj* berlimpah (ruah)

abuse *n* [abyus] penganiayaan, penyalahgunaan; kekerasan; *child ~* kekerasan terhadap anak-anak; *vt* [abyuz] menganiaya, menyalahgunakan, memperlakukan dengan kasar; mencabuli; **abusive** *adj* kasar; ~ *language* makian, kata-kata kasar atau jorok

abysmal *adj* sangat jelék; **abyss** *n* jurang

academic *adj* akadémis; ~ *record* hasil rapot atau nilai; ~ *year* tahun ajaran; *n* akadémisi; **academy** *n* akadémi, sekolah tinggi

accelerate *vt* mempercepat; menginjak gas (di mobil); **acceleration** *n* percepatan, akselérasi; **accelerator** *n* (pedal) gas

accent *n* [aksént] logat, aksén, nuansa; **accentuate** *vt* menekankan

accept *vt* [aksépt] menerima; **acceptable** *adj* [akséptabel] layak, dapat diterima; **acceptance** *n* penerimaan; **accepted** *adj* biasa, lumrah; **accepting** *adj* bersifat menerima, terbuka

access *n* aksés; *vt* mendapat, memakai, mengaksés; *internet ~* sambungan internét; **accessibility** *n* [aksésibiliti] aksésibilitas, jangkauan; **accessible** *adj* terjangkau, dekat

accessory: accessories *n, pl* aksésoris, variasi (pada mobil), perlengkapan

accident *n* [aksident] kecelakaan; ~*prone* canggung, sering kecelakaan; *it was an ~* tidak sengaja; **accidental** *adj* kebetulan, tidak disengaja; **accidentally** *adv* secara tidak sengaja, tanpa sengaja

acclaim *n* pujian, tepuk tangan; **acclaimed** *adj* terpuji, tersohor

acclimatize *vi* membiasakan diri dengan iklim baru, menyesuaikan diri

accommodate *vt* menampung, menyesuaikan; **accommodation** *n* penginapan, akomodasi; **accommodating** *adj* menyesuaikan

accompaniment *n* [akampaniment] pengiringan; **accompanist** *n* pengiring (yang memainkan alat musik); **accompany** *vt* menemani, mengantarkan, mengiringi

accomplice *n* [akamplis] kaki tangan, anték

accomplish *vt* [akamplisy] melaksanakan; **accomplished** *adj* ulung; **accomplishment** *n* préstasi

accord *n* kesepakatan, persetujuan; *of its own* ~ dengan sendirinya, secara otomatis; *vt* memberi; **accordance** *in* ~ *with* sesuai dengan; **according** ~ *to* menurut; **accordingly** *adv* oleh karena itu, maka

accordion *n* akordion, harmonika tangan

account *n* rekening (bank); pertanggung jawab; laporan, cerita; *on* ~ *of* karena, lantaran; *of no* ~ tidak penting; *on no* ~ sekali-kali tidak; *vt* ~ *for* mempertanggungjawabkan; **accountable** *adj* bertanggung jawab; **accountability** *n* akuntabilitas, tanggung jawab; **accountancy** *n* akuntansi; **accountant** *n* akuntan

accreditation *n* akréditasi; **accredited** *adj* terakréditasi

accumulate *vi* bertumpuk; *vt* menghimpun; **accumulation** *n* timbunan, akumulasi; **accumulator** *n* aki

accuracy *n* [akurasi] ketelitian, ketepatan; **accurate** *adj* teliti, cermat, tepat

accusation *n* tuduhan; **accusative** *adj* akusatif, penderita; **accuse** *vt* menuduh, menuding; **accused** *the* ~ tertuduh, tergugat; **accusingly** *adv* secara menuduh

accustom *vt* [akastem] ~ *yourself* membiasakan diri; **accustomed** *adj* terbiasa

ace *n* (kartu) as; jago; pukulan awal yang langsung memenangkan poin; *adj, coll* mahir, hebat

acetic *adj* [asétik] ~ *acid* cuka, asam asétat

acetylene *n* [asétilin] gas karbit

ache *n* [ék] sakit, pegal; *head*~ sakit kepala, pusing kepala; *tooth*~ gigi ngilu; *vi* sakit; rindu

achieve *vt* [aciv] mencapai, meraih; **achievement** *n* prestasi; **achiever** *high* ~ orang yang banyak berprestasi

Achilles' heel *n* [akiliz hil] titik lemah

acid *n* [asid] asam; ~ *test* tes litmus; *nitric* ~ asam nitrat; *adj* pahit; **acidic** *adj* asam; tajam; *his* ~ *comments did not help matters* koméntarnya yang tajam tidak menolong; **acidity** *n* [asiditi] keasaman, kadar asam

acknowledge *vt* [aknolej] mengakui; menyebut (sebagai ucapan terima kasih); **acknowledgment** *n* pengakuan; ucapan terima kasih; réferénsi (dalam karangan)

acne *n, pl* [akni] jerawat (terutama yang besar dan sulit sembuh)

acorn *n* [ékorn] biji pohon ék

acoustic [akustik] ~ *guitar* gitar (klasik); **acoustics** *n* keadaan suara atau musik berbunyi di dalam ruangan, akustik

acquaint *vi* berkenalan, tahu; *well-~ed with* tahu banyak tentang; *vt* ~ *yourself* memperkenalkan diri, membiasakan diri; **acquaintance** *n* kenalan; *to make your* ~ *with* memperkenalkan diri kepada, berkenalan dengan

acquire *vt* memperoléh; **acquisition** *n* [akuisisyen] peroléhan, barang yang diperoléh

acquit *vi* membebaskan dari tuduhan, menyatakan tidak bersalah; ~ *yourself well* mulai dengan baik; *Mary was* ~*ted of murder* Mary dinyatakan tidak bersalah dalam kasus pembunuhan; **acquittal** *n* pembebasan

acre *n* [éker] ukuran tanah (0,46 héktar)

acrid ~ *smell* bau hangus, bau tajam

acrobat *n* akrobat, pesenam; **acrobatics** *n* gerakan pesawat di udara yang berliku-liku

acronym *n* akronim

across *prep* (di) seberang, melintang, lintas; mendatar; *two* ~ dua mendatar (dalam teka-teki silang)

acrylic *adj* [akrilik] ~ *paint* cat yang tidak mengandung minyak

act *n* perbuatan; babak, lakon (dalam pertunjukan); undang-undang; *Marriage ~ of 1974* Undang-Undang Perkawinan tahun 1974; *caught in the* ~ tertangkap basah; *in the ~ of* sedang; *vi* berbuat, bertindak; berakting; *~ing* pemangku jabatan; **action** *n* perbuatan, aksi; proses; ~ *film* film laga; *killed in* ~ gugur; *to take* ~ bertindak; **activate** *vt* [aktivét] menghidupkan, menggerakkan; **active** *adj* giat, rajin, sibuk, aktif; hidup (telepon genggam); **activist** *n* aktivis, pegiat; **activity** *n* kegiatan, kesibukan; **actor** *n, m* aktor, pemain (film); **actress** *n, f* aktris, pemain (film); **actual** *adj* **actually** *adv* sebenarnya

actuary *n* aktuaris

acupuncture *n* [akupanktyur] tusuk jarum, akupunktur; **acupuncturist** *n* ahli tusuk jarum

acute *adj* [akyut] parah, akut; ~ *attack* serangan mendadak (penyakit); ~ *angle* sudut lancip

AD *abbrev Anno Domini* M (Maséhi)

adage *n* [adij] pepatah, peribahasa

Adam's apple *n* jakun

adamant *adj* tegas, yakin

adapt *vi* menyesuaikan diri; *vt* menyesuaikan, menyadur; **adaptable** *adj* mudah menyesuaikan diri, supel; **adaptation** *n* penyesuaian; saduran; **adaptor** *n* adaptor

add *vi* menambah; *vt* bertambah, menambahkan

adder *n* semacam ular; ular biludak

addict *n* pecandu; *~ed to heroin* ketagihan shabu-shabu; **addiction** *n* ketagihan, shabu-shabu

addition *n* [adisyen] tambahan, penambahan, jumlah; *in ~* ditambah pula, lagipula; **additional** *adj* tambahan, ékstra; **additive** *n* [aditif] bahan tambahan ← **add**

address *n* alamat, adrés; pidato; *wrong* ~ salah alamat; *vt* mengalamatkan (surat); berpidato di depan; menegur, menyapa; **addressee** *n* si alamat

adequate *adj* [adekuet] cukup, memadai

adhere *vt* [adhir] melekat, léngkét; ~ *to* menganut; **adherent** *n* penganut (agama atau aliran); **adhesion** *n* adhési; **adhesive** *n* [adhisif] lém; *adj* léngkét

adjacent *adj* berdekatan, berdampingan, bersebelahan

adjective *n* kata sifat, adjéktif

adjoin *vt* **adjoining** *adj* berdampingan

adjourn *vt* [ajérn] menunda, menangguhkan, mengundurkan; **adjournment** *n* penundaan, penangguhan, pengunduran

adjudicate *vt* memutuskan, menilai

adjust *vi* menyesuaikan diri; *vt* menyetél, mencocokkan, mengatur, menyesuaikan; **adjustment** *n* penyetélan, pengaturan, penyesuaian

adjutant *n* ajudan

administer *vt* [administer] memerintah, mengelola, mengurus; melaksanakan; memberikan; ~ *justice* mengadili; ~ *medicine* memberi obat; ~ *an oath* mengambil sumpah; **administration** *n* pemerintahan; pemerintah; pelaksanaan, pemberian; **administrative** *adj* pengelolaan, pemerintahan; **administrator** *n* pemerintah, pelaksana, pengurus

admirable *adj* [admirabel] mengagumkan, patut dikagumi ← **admire**

admiral *n* [admiral] laksamana; *vice-~* laksamana muda

admiration *n* [admirésyen] kekaguman; **admire** *vt* mengagumi; **admirer** *n* pengagum

admissible *adj* dapat diterima; **admission** *n* penerimaan, izin masuk; pengakuan; **admit** *vt* menerima, mengizinkan masuk; mengakui; **admittance** *no ~* dilarang masuk

admonish *vt* menegur

ado *n* [adu] kegaduhan; *without further* ~ sekarang juga

adobe *n* [adobi] tanah liat yang digunakan untuk membangun rumah (di AS)

adolescence *n* masa remaja, pubertas; **adolescent** *n* remaja, anak puber

adopt *vt* mengangkat atau memungut anak; mengambil; **adoption** *n* adopsi; penerimaan, pemakaian; **adoptive** *adj* ~ *child* anak angkat, anak pungut

adorable *adj* lucu, menggemaskan, manis, jelita; **adoration** *n* penyembahan, pemujaan; **adore** *vt* menyembah, memuja; sangat mencintai, gila akan

adorn *vt* menghiasi, mendandani; *~ed with roses* dihiasi dengan bunga mawar

adrenaline *n* [adrénalin] adrenalin

adrift *adj* terapung, terkatung-katung ← **drift**

adroit *adj* gesit, cekatan

adulation *n* pemujaan ← **adore**

adult *adj* déwasa; *n* orang déwasa; **adulthood** *n* masa déwasa

adulterate *vt* mencampurkan sesuatu ke dalam, mengganggu

adulterer *n* orang yang berbuat zinah; **adultery** *n* zinah

advance *n* kemajuan; uang muka; *in ~* di muka, terlebih dahulu, sebelumnya; *vi* maju; *vt* memajukan, mempercepat; **advanced** *adj* maju, canggih; **advancement** *n* kemajuan

advantage *n* [advantej] untung, keuntungan; bola (dalam pertandingan ténis); *~ Federer* bola Federer; **advantageous** *adj* [advantéjus] menguntungkan, berguna

advent *n* kedatangan; (masa) advén; *~ calendar* kalender advén; untuk bulan Désémber yang menyambut datangnya Natal; *before the ~ of computers* sebelum munculnya zaman komputer; **adventist** *Seventh-Day ~ Church* Géreja Advént Hari Ketujuh

adventure *n* petualangan; *~ playground* tempat ayunan; **adventurous** *adj* berani, suka berpetualangan

adverb *n* kata keterangan (pada kata kerja)

adversary *n* lawan, musuh; **adverse** *adj* bermusuhan; tidak ramah; *~ weather* cuaca buruk; **adversity** *n* malang, sial

advertise *vt* mengiklankan, memasang iklan; **advertiser** *n* pihak yang memasang iklan; **advertisement** *n* iklan, pariwara, reklame

advice *n* [advais] nasihat, saran; **advisable** *adj* sebaiknya, dianjurkan; **advise** *vt* [advaiz] menasihati; **advisor** *n* penasihat; **advisory** *adj* penasihat

advocate *n* [advokat] orang yang memperjuangkan; pengacara, pembéla; *vt* [advokét] menyeru agar

aerate *vt* [érét] memberi karbon dioksida pada cairan; *~d drink* minuman bersoda

aerial *n* [érial] anténa; *adj* angkasa, udara; *~ acrobatics* jungkir-balik di udara

aerobics *n* [érobiks] senam

aerodrome *n* lapangan terbang, lapangan udara (lanud)

aerogram, aerogramme *n* [érogram] surat yang bisa langsung dilipat kemudian dipos

aeronautical *adj, n* aéronautika, ilmu penerbangan; *~ engineering* téknik penerbangan; **aerospace** *n* bidang angkasa dan penerbangan

aeroplane → **airplane**

aerosol *n* [érosol] kaléng penyemprot

afar *from ~* dari jauh

affable *adj* ramah

affair *n* perkara, hal, soal, urusan; perselingkuhan, cerita cinta

affect *vt* mempengaruhi; **affected** *adj* terpengaruh, kena dampak; berpurapura; **affection** *n* rasa kasih sayang; **affectionate** *adj* memperlihatkan kasih sayang

affiliate: affiliated *adj* berafiliasi dengan; **affiliation** *n* afiliasi, penggabungan

affinity *n* daya tarik, rasa dekat atau pengertian; *Angela has an ~ with cats* kucing merasa dekat dengan Angela

affirm *vt* menguatkan, membenarkan, menegaskan, mengiyakan; **affirmation** *n* pembenaran, penegasan; **affirmative** *n* ya; *adj* yang mempromosikan, setuju

affix *n* (kata) imbuhan; *vt* membubuhi, mencantumkan, menémpélkan

afflict *vt* melanda; *~ed by* terkena, menderita; **affliction** *n* penderitaan

affluence *n* kekayaan; **affluent** *adj* kaya, berada, mampu

afford *vt* mampu (membayar dll) *I can't* ~ *it* saya tidak mampu (membayar atau membeli); **affordable** *adj* terjangkau (harganya)

affront *vt* menghina; *n* penghinaan

Afghan *adj* berasal dari Afganistan; **Afghani** *n* orang Afganistan; **Afghanistan** *n* Afganistan

afloat *adv* hanyut, terapung-apung ← **float**

aforementioned, aforesaid *adj* tersebut (di muka), tadi

afraid *adj* takut; kuatir; ~ *of* takut pada, takut akan; *I'm* ~ *so* sayang sekali, ternyata begitu

afresh *adv* baru, sekali lagi ← **fresh**

Africa *n* Afrika; **African** *adj* berasal dari Afrika; *n* orang Africa

Afrikaans *n* bahasa Afrikaans (yang dipakai di Afrika Selatan); **Afrikaner** *n* orang Afrikaans, orang kulit putih keturunan Belanda di Afrika Selatan

Afro-American *n* orang Amérika berkulit hitam (keturunan Afrika); orang Négro

after *prep, conj, adv* kemudian; *prep* setelah, sesudah; ~ *all* lagipula; meskipun demikian; *to be* ~ mendesak, mengejar; **afternoon** *n* soré, petang; sesudah jam 12 siang sampai dengan matahari terbenam; ~ *tea* makan soré; *good* ~ selamat siang (jam 12–3); selamat soré (jam 3–7); **afterbirth** *n* ari-ari, tembuni; **afterlife** *n* dunia akhirat; **afterpains** *n* royan; **aftershave** *n* pewangi pria (selesai dicukur); **afterthought** *n* pikiran kemudian; **afterwards** *prep* sesudahnya, kemudian

again *adv* (sekali) lagi; ~ *and* ~ berulang kali, berkali-kali; *then* ~ tapi

against *prep* terhadap; berlawanan, bertentangan; ~ *all odds* meskipun kemungkinan sangat kecil

agate *n* [aget] batu akik

age *n* [éj] umur, usia; abad, masa; ~ *limit* batas umur; *of* ~ déwasa, akil balig; sampai umur; *under*~ di bawah umur; *the Middle* ~*s* Abad Pertengahan; *thirty years of* ~ berusia tiga puluh tahun; *vi*

menua, menjadi tua; **aged** *adj* sepuh, tua, lanjut usia; berumur; *n* manusia lanjut usia (manula), orang tua; **ageing** *adj* menua, menjadi tua; ~ *process* (prosés) penuaan

agency *n* [éjensi] agén, perwakilan; *news* ~ kantor berita ← **agent**

agenda *n* [ajénda] agénda, acara; rencana; *on the* ~ direncanakan, masuk agénda

agent *n* agén, wakil; *secret* ~ spion, mata-mata

aggravate *vt* memperparah, mengganggu; *the children* ~*d the situation* anak-anak membuat keadaan lebih sulit lagi

aggregate *n, adj* [agreget] jumlah, total

aggression *n* penyerangan, serangan, agrési; **aggressive** *adj* galak, bersifat menyerang, agrésif; **aggressor** *n* penyerang, agrésor

aggrieve: aggrieved *adj* sakit hati, dirugikan

aggro *n, sl* agrési; *adj* agrésif ← **aggression**

aghast *adj* [agast] tercengang, terperanjat, terhéran-héran

agile *adj* gesit; **agility** *n* [ajiliti] ketangkasan, kecerdasan, kegesitan

agitate *vt* mengganggu, menggun-cangkan, menghasut; **agitation** *n* kekacauan, penghasutan; **agitator** *n* pengacau, penghasut; pengaduk

AGM *abbrev Annual General Meeting* rapat tahunan

ago *adv* (yang) lalu, lampau, silam; *three days* ~ tiga hari yang lalu

agonize *vi* sangat kuatir; tidak bisa mengambil keputusan; **agony** *n* kesakitan, penderitaan; sakratulmaut, azab; ~ *aunt* penasihat hal-hal pribadi (di koran atau majalah); *in* ~ sangat kesakitan

agrarian *adj* berkaitan dengan tanah

agree *vi* setuju, bersepakat; menyetujui, mengiyakan; ~ *to* menyetujui, mengabulkan; ~ *with* setuju dengan, menyetujui; **agreeable** *adj* menyenangkan; siap setuju atau sepakat; **agreement** *n* persetujuan, kesepakatan, perjanjian

agricultural *adj* berkaitan dengan pertanian; ~ *fair* pekan raya; ~ *science* ilmu pertanian; **agriculture** *n* pertanian
agronomics *n* agronomi; **agronomist** *n* ahli ilmu tanah
aground *adv* kandas, terdampar; *the ship ran* ~ kapalnya terdampar
AH *abbrev after hours* r, rmh (rumah)
ah *excl* o!
aha *excl* (untuk menunjukkan rasa puas) aha
ahead *adv* [ahéd] di depan, di muka, terlebih dahulu; *go* ~*!* silahkan; ~ *of time* lebih cepat, lebih awal ← **head**
ahem *excl* [ahém] permisi; suara mendeham
aid *n* bantuan, pertolongan; alat; *first* ~ pertolongan pertama; *hearing* ~ alat bantu dengar; *vt* membantu, menolong
AIDS (Acquired Immune Deficiency Syndrome) *n* AIDS; ~ *epidemic* wabah AIDS; ~ *patient* orang dengan HIV/AIDS (ODHA)
ail *vi* sakit; **ailing** *adj* sering sakit, sakit-sakitan; **ailment** *n* penyakit
aim *n* sasaran, maksud, tujuan; *vi* bertujuan; membidik; *vt* mengacukan, mengarahkan, membidik; **aimless** *adj* tanpa tujuan
ain't *sl* tak, tidak ← **is not**
air *n* udara; angin; ~ *conditioner, sl* **aircon** pendingin ruangan, AC; ~ *crew* awak kabin; ~ *force* angkatan udara; ~ *gun*, ~ *rifle* senapan angin; ~ *hostess arch* pramugari; ~ *mail* pos udara; ~ *pump* *n* pompa angin; ~ *raid* serangan udara; ~*s and graces* sikap sombong; *by* ~ dengan pesawat terbang; *on* ~ mengudara; *vt* menjemur, mengangin-kan; ~ *one's views* mengajukan pendapat; **aircraft** *n* pesawat terbang, kapal terbang; ~ *carrier* kapal induk; **airfield** *n* lapangan terbang; **airer** *n* jemuran; **airily** *adv* dengan énténg; **airline** *n* perusahaan penerbangan, maskapai penerbangan; **airliner** pesawat (terbang) penumpang; **airman** *n* penerbang, pilot; **airplane, aeroplane** *n* pesawat terbang; **airport** *n* bandara, bandar udara; **air raid** *n* serangan

udara; **airship** *n* kapal udara; **airsick** *adj* mabuk (udara); **airtight** *adj* kedap udara; **airway** *n* kerongkongan; **airy** *adj* berangin
aisle *n* [ail] lorong; *to walk down the* ~ menikah
ajar *adj* (pintu) terbuka sedikit
aka *abbrev* *also known as* ← **alias**
à la carte *adj* [alakart] dari ménu
alarm *n* weker; tanda bahaya, alarm; rasa kagét; *vt* membuat kagét, mengagétkan; **alarmed** *adj* kagét
alas *ejac* aduh, wahai
Albania *n* [Albénia] Albania; **Albanian** *n* bahasa Albania, orang Albania; *adj* berasal dari Albania
albatross *n* élang laut
albino *n* bulé
album *n* album; *photo* ~ album foto
albumen *n* (zat) putih telur
alchemy *n, arch* [alkemi] ilmu kimia; **alchemist** *n, arch* ahli kimia
alcohol *n* alkohol, minumam keras; **alcoholic** *n* peminum berat, pemabuk; *adj* beralkohol
ale *n* bir
alert *n* tanda (bahaya); *red* ~ siaga satu; *on the* ~ berjaga-jaga; *vt* memperingatkan; ~ *the authorities* melapor kepada pihak yang berwenang; *adj* siaga, waspada
alfalfa *n* tanaman alfalfa, sejenis tanaman ternak
algae *n* [algi] ganggang; *algal bloom* éncéng gondok
algebra *n* [aljebra] aljabar
Algeria *n* Aljazair; **Algerian** *n* orang Aljazair; *adj* berasal dari Aljazair
alias [élias] alias
alibi *n* [alibai] alibi
alien *n* [élien] makhluk asing, orang asing; makhluk luar angkasa; *illegal* ~ orang yang berada di negeri asing tanpa izin; *adj* asing; **alienate** *vt* mengasingkan, menjauhkan; **alienation** *n* pengasingan, penyingkiran
alight *vt* [alait] turun (dari angkutan umum); hinggap
alight *adj* menyala; bercahaya
align *vt* [alain] menyejajarkan; ~ *one-*

self with bergabung dengan; *Non-~ed Movement* Gerakan Non-Blok; **alignment** *n* kesejajaran

alike *adj* serupa, mirip; *to look ~* mirip; *as ~ as two peas in a pod* seperti pinang dibelah dua ← **like**

alimony *n* pembayaran secara berkala kepada mantan suami/isteri (AS)

alive *adj* (dalam keadaan) hidup ← **live**

alkaline *adj* [alkalain] alkali

all *adj* [ol] semua, seantéro; sekalian, seluruh; sama; *~ alone* sendiri saja, sendirian; *~ but* hampir-hampir; semua kecuali; *~ day* sepanjang hari, sehari-an; *~ over* habis; di mana-mana; *~ right* baiklah; baik; *two ~* dua sama; *~ in ~* sesudah dipertimbangkan matang-matang; *~ of us* kita semua; *~ the time* selalu, terus-menerus; *not at ~* sama sekali tidak; **all-round** *adj* berbakat di lebih dari satu bidang; umum; **all-rounder** *n* olahragawan yang berbakat di lebih dari satu bidang

allegation *n* tuduhan, tudingan; pengakuan, pernyataan; **allege** *v* [aléj] menuduh, menuding; mengaku, menyatakan; **alleged** *adj* [aléjd] yang dikatakan, yang disebut; **allegiance** *n* [alijens] kesetiaan; *the Pledge of ~* janji kesetiaan (pada negara AS)

allegory *n* [alegori] ibarat

allergic *adj* (mempunyai) alérgi; *~ to cheese* ada alérgi keju; **allergy** *n* alérgi

alleviate *vt* meringankan, mengurangi; *the doctor tried to ~ the pain* dokter berusaha mengurangi rasa sakit; **alleviation** *n* pengurangan

alley *n* [ali] lorong, gang; *~ cat* kucing kampung; *blind ~* gang buntu, jalan buntu

alliance *n* [alaiens] perserikatan, persekutuan, gabungan, aliansi; **allied** *adj* serikat, sekutu, gabungan; *the ~ Forces* pihak AS, Inggris dan Rusia (dalam Perang Dunia Kedua) ← **ally**

alligator *n* [aligétor] buaya (bermoncong péndék)

allocate *vt* mengalokasikan, memperuntukkan; **allocation** *n* alokasi, peruntukan

allot *vt* memperuntukkan, menjatahkan; **allotment** *n* jatah, bagian; *vacant ~* tanah atau kapling kosong

allow *vt* [alau] mengizinkan, memperboléhkan, memperkenankan; **allowance** *n* tunjangan, uang harian, uang saku

alloy *n* logam campuran

allude *vi* menyindir, menyinggung; *he ~d to my money* dia menyindir soal uang saya

allure *n* daya pikat; **alluring** *adj* memikat, mempesona

allusion *n* sindiran ← **allude**

alluvial *adj* *~ plain* dataran aluvial; **alluvium** *n* (pasir) endapan

ally [alai] *n* sekutu; *vt* bersekutu; *Spain allied itself with Portugal* Spanyol bersekutu dengan Portugal

alma mater *n* [alma mater] bekas sekolah, sekolah dulu; *Harvard is my ~* saya alumni Harvard

almanac *n, arch* almanak, kalénder, penanggalan

almighty *adj* [olmaiti] maha kuasa; *the ~* (Tuhan) Yang Maha Kuasa

almond *n* [amond] kacang almond, buah badam

almost *adv* [olmost] hampir, nyaris

alms *n, pl* [ams] sedakah

aloft *adv* di atas, ke atas; di udara

alone *adj, adv* sendiri, seorang diri; hanya, saja

along *prep* sepanjang; *adj ~ (with)* bersama (dengan); *all ~* selama ini; sepanjang; **alongside** *adv* di sisi, di tepi

aloof *adj* sombong; menjauh; **aloofness** *n* kedinginan, kesombongan

aloud *adv* [alaud] dengan suara keras, dengan suara nyaring; *to read ~* membaca dengan suara keras

ALP *abbrev Australian Labor Party* Partai Buruh Australia

alpaca *n* [alpaka] sejenis héwan seperti lama

alphabet *n* abjad, aksara, alfabét; *the Latin ~* huruf Romawi; **alphabetical** *adj* **alphabetically** *adv* menurut abjad

alpine *adj* gunung; **Alps** *n, pl the ~* pegunungan Alpen

already *adv* [olrédi] sudah, telah

Alsatian *n* anjing hérder → **German shepherd**

also *adv* [olso] juga, pula, pun

altar *n* [oltar] altar; *going to the* ~ menikah

alter *vi* [olter] berubah; *vt* mengubah; memperbaiki; **alteration** *n* perubahan; perbaikan

altercation *n* pertikaian, pertengkaran

alternate *vi* berselang-seling, menyelang-nyeling; *adj* berselang-seling; **alternating** ~ *current* arus bolak-balik; **alternative** *n* pilihan lain, alternatif; *adj* lain, alternatif; ~ *music* musik alternatif; **alternatively** *adv, conj* kalau tidak, atau

although *conj* [oltho] meskipun, walaupun

altitude *n* ketinggian, tinggi

altogether *adj* [oltugéther] semuanya, secara keseluruhan; *neg* sama sekali

altruistic *adj* tanpa pamrih, ikhlas, dengan tidak mengharapkan imbalan

alum *n* tawas

aluminium, aluminum *n* aluminium; ~ *foil* kertas perak

alumni [alamnai] *n, pl* **alumnus** *s* lulusan universitas tertentu

always *adv* selalu, senantiasa

Alzheimer's disease *n* [altshaimerz] pikun

am *abbrev ante meridiem* pagi, siang (jam 0.00–12.00)

am *vt* adalah (bentuk orang pertama) ← **be**

amalgamate *vt* mempersatukan, menggabungkan, melebur; **amalgamation** *n* penggabungan

amateur *adj, n* [amater] amatir; tidak profésional

amaze *vt* menghérankan, menakjubkan, mengagumkan; **amazed** *adj* héran, terkagum-kagum; **amazement** *n* rasa héran, rasa kagum; **amazing** *adj* menghérankan, menakjubkan, hébat

ambassador *n* duta besar

amber *n* ambar; ~ *light* lampu kuning

ambiance, ambience *n* suasana

ambiguity *n* [ambiguiti] hal yang kurang jelas, ambiguitas; **ambiguous** *adj* ambigu, kurang jelas

ambition *n* ambisi, cita-cita; *blind* ~

ambisi belaka; **ambitious** *adj* berambisi, mempunyai cita-cita tinggi

ambulance *n* ambulans; *to call an* ~ memanggil ambulans

ambush *n* serangan mendadak, penyergapan; *vt* menyerang secara mendadak, menyergap

amen *ejac* amin

amenable *adj* setuju

amend *vt* membetulkan, memperbaiki; *to make* ~*s* meminta maaf, mengganti kerugian; **amendment** *n* pembetulan; amandemén

amenities *n, pl* fasilitas, sarana

America *n* Amérika (Serikat); *Latin* ~ Amérika Latin; *North* ~ Amérika Utara; *the* ~*s* Amérika Utara dan Selatan; **American** *n* orang Amérika; *adj* berasal dari Amérika

Amerindian *n, adj* orang Indian di Amérika

amethyst *n* batu kecubung

amiable *adj* [émiabel] ramah, baik hati

amicable *adj* [amikabel] ramah, baik-baik; **amicably** *adv* secara baik-baik

amid, amidst *prep* di tengah, di antara

ammo → **ammunition**

ammonia *n* amonia

ammunition *n* **ammo** *sl* amunisi

amnesia *n* kehilangan ingatan

amnesty *n* grasi, amnésti, pengampunan

amok, amuck *to run* ~ mengamuk

among [amang], **amongst** *prep* di tengah, di antara

amorous *adj* [ameres] bernafsu, berkaitan dengan cinta

amount *n* [amaunt] jumlah, banyaknya; *vi* berjumlah; ~ *to* menjadi; *he won't ever* ~ *to much* dia tidak akan pernah berhasil

ampere *n* **amp** *sl* ampér

ampersand *n* tanda ampersand [&]

amphetamine *n* [amfétamin] amfétamin, sejenis obat psikotropika

amphibian *n* binatang yang tinggal di dua dunia, seperti katak; **amphibious** *adj* amfibi

ample *adj* banyak, besar, luas; **amplifier** *n* **amp** *sl* pengeras; **amplify** *vt* memperbesar

amplitude *n* amplitudo, luas ayunan

amputate *vt* memotong anggota badan, mengamputasi; **amputation** *n* amputasi; **amputee** *n* orang cacat yang kehilangan anggota badan

amulet *n* jimat

amuse *vt* menghibur; **amused** *adj* terhibur, tertawa; **amusement** *n* hiburan, kesenangan; ~ *park* taman hiburan; *to my* ~ yang menggelikan bagi saya; **amusing** *adj* lucu, menyenangkan

an *art* (sebelum huruf vokal) satu, suatu; per, tiap; ~ *apple* sebuah apel; ~ *egg* sebutir telur; ~ *envelope* sehelai amplop; ~ *owl* seékor burung hantu

anaemia → **anémia**

anaesthesia → **anesthesia**

anal *adj* melalui dubur; ~ *retentive* orang yang banyak menguatirkan hal-hal sepélé; ~ *sex* sodomi ← **anus**

analog, analogue *n* analog

analogy *n* [analoji] analogi, persamaan

analysis *n* analisa, analisis, uraian; *in* ~ sedang menjalankan térapi dengan psikiater; **analyst** *n* peneliti; psikiater; **analyze** *vt* menganalisa, meneliti

anarchy *n* [anarki] anarki

anatomy *n* anatomi, ilmu urai tubuh; **anatomically** *adv* sesuai dengan anatomi

ancestor *n* leluhur, nénék moyang; **ancestral** *adj* berasal dari nénék moyang, turun-temurun; **ancestry** *n* [anséstri] silsilah, nénék moyang

anchor *n* [anker] sauh, jangkar; pembaca berita (di télévisi); *vi* membuang sauh, berlabuh; *vt* memasang; *to weigh* ~ mengangkat sauh; **anchorage** *n* pelabuhan

anchovy *n* [ancovi] sejenis ikan kecil

ancient *adj* [énsyent] kuno, zaman purbakala; ~ *Egypt* Mesir Kuno

& co [and ko] *and company* cs (cum suis)

and *conj* dan, serta, bersama; ~ *so on* dan lain sebagainya

anecdote *n* lelucon, cerita, anekdot

anemia, anaemia *n* [animia] kurang darah, anémia; **anemic, anaemic** *adj* kurang darah

anesthesia, anaesthesia *n* [anesthisya] pembiusan, anéstési; **anesthetic, anaesthetic** *n* obat bius; *general* ~ bius total; *local* ~ bius lokal; **anesthetize, anaesthetize** *vt* [anisthetaiz] membius; **anesthetist, anaesthetist** *n* ahli obat bius

anew *adj* sekali lagi, baru ← **new**

angel *n* [énjel] malaikat; *the* ~ *of death* malaikatul maut; **angelic** *adj* [anjélik] seperti malaikat, tanpa dosa

anger *n* [angger] kemarahan, murka; *vt* membuat marah

angle *n* [anggel] sudut; *acute* ~ sudut lancip; *obtuse* ~ sudut tumpul; *right* ~ tegak lurus; **angular** *adj* bersiku-siku; kaku; *an* ~ *figure* berbadan kurus

angle *vi* memancing; *n* pemancing; **angling** *n* memancing; ~ *rod* joran

Anglican *adj* [Anglikan] geréja Inggris

Anglo- *adj* [angglo] Inggris; ~*centric* hanya melihat dari segi Inggris; ~*Saxon* berdarah Inggris (bukan Wales, Skotlandia atau Irlandia)

Angola *n* Angola; **Angolan** *n* orang Angola; *adj* berasal dari Angola

angry *adj* marah, murka ← **anger**

angular *adj* bersiku-siku; kaku; *an* ~ *figure* berbadan kurus ← **angle**

animal *n* binatang, héwan, satwa; *adj* héwani, biadab

animate *vt* menghidupkan; **animated** *adj* bersemangat, hidup; **animation** *n* semangat; kartun animasi, animé

animosity *n* dendam, permusuhan

aniseed, anise *n* adas

ankle *n* [angkel] pergelangan kaki; **anklet** *n* gelang kaki; kaos kaki péndék

annals *n, pl* babad, sejarah; *the Malay* ~ Sejarah Melayu

annexe, annex *n* pavilyun; *vt* mencaplok, menggabungkan; **annexation** *n* penggabungan, pengambilan alih

annihilate *vt* [anaihilét] membinasakan, membasmi, memusnahkan; **annihilation** *n* pembinasaan, pembasmian, pemusnahan; kemenangan besar

anniversary *n* (hari) ulang tahun, hari jadi, hari peringatan (tidak digunakan untuk makhluk hidup); *golden* ~ hari

ulang tahun ke50; *silver* ~ hari ulang
tahun ke25; *wedding* ~ hari ulang
tahun perkawinan
annotate *vt* membubuhi catatan;
annotation *n* catatan
announce *vt* mengumumkan, memberitahukan; **announcer** *n* penyiar;
announcement *n* pengumuman,
maklumat
annoy *vt* mengganggu, mengusik;
annoyance *n* gangguan; **annoying**
adj mengganggu, menjéngkélkan
annual *n* édisi tahunan; *adj* tahunan; ~
general meeting rapat tahunan;
annually *adv* setiap tahun
annuity *n* tunjangan hari tua (dibayar
setiap tahun)
annul *vt* membatalkan, mencabut; *the
wedding was ~led* perkawinan itu
dinyatakan tidak sah; **annulment** *n*
pembatalan
anomaly *n* [anomali] kelainan, keganjilan, penyimpangan; **anomalous** *adj*
anéh, ganjil
anon. *abbrev* **anonymous** *adj* tanpa
nama, anonim; ~ *letter* surat kaléng;
see you anon sampai bertemu lagi
(tidak tahu kapan)
anorak *n* jas hujan
anorexia *n* ~ *(nervosa)* anoréksia,
penyakit ingin kurus; **anorexic** *adj*
mengidap anoréksia; *n* orang yang
mengidap anoréksia
another *pron, adj* [anather] satu lagi,
yang lain
answer *n* [anser] jawaban, jalan keluar
(dari masalah); *vi* menjawab; *vt* membalas (surat); membuka (pintu); mengangkat (télépon); *~ing machine*
mesin penjawab; ~ *back* membantah,
membéla diri; ~ *for* menjawab atas
nama; ~ *to* bertanggung jawab kepada
ant *n* semut; *flying* ~ laron; *white* ~
rayap; **anteater** *n* sejenis landak;
anthill *n* sarang semut
antagonist *n* lawan; **antagonistic** *adj*
bersikap melawan
Antarctic *adj* berasal dari Antartika; *the*
~ Kutub Selatan; **Antarctica** *n*
Antartika, Kutub Selatan

ante- *pref* pra-, sebelum; **antenatal** *adj*
sebelum melahirkan
anteater *n* sejenis landak ← **ant**
antelope *n* sejenis kijang
antenatal *adj* [antinétel] sebelum
melahirkan
antenna *n* anténa
anterior *n* yang mendahului, bagian
depan
anthem *n* lagu wajib; *national* ~ lagu
kebangsaan
anthill *n* [ant hil] sarang semut ← **ant**
anthology *n* [antholoji] kumpulan,
antologi, bunga rampai
anthrax *n* penyakit antraks
anthropological *adj* berkaitan dengan
antropologi; **anthropologist** *n*
antropolog; **anthropology** *n* [anthro-
poloji] ilmu antropologi
anti- *adj* anti-, anti, bersifat melawan;
~clockwise melawan arah jarum jam;
~Semitic anti-Yahudi; *~social* tidak
suka bergaul, penyendiri; **antibiotics**
n [antibayotiks] antibiotik; **anticlimax**
n [antiklaimaks] kekecéwaan, hasil
yang berbéda dengan harapan; **antidepressant** *n* obat anti deprési; **antidote**
n penawar; **antifreeze** *n* cairan anti-
beku (digunakan dalam mobil dalam
cuaca dingin); **antipathy** *n* antipati,
perasaan tidak suka, perasaan benci;
antiseptic *n* obat anti-kuman
antic *n* tingkah lucu, kelucuan
anticipate *vt* mengantisipasi, menghara-
kan, menanti-nanti; **anticipation** *n*
harapan; *thanking you in* ~ *of your
reply* terima kasih sebelumnya (dalam
surat)
anticlimax *n* kekecéwaan, hasil yang
berbéda dengan harapan
antidepressant *n* obat anti deprési
antidote *n* penawar
antifreeze *n* cairan anti-beku (digunakan
dalam mobil dalam cuaca dingin)
Antigua *n* Antigua; **Antiguan** *n* orang
Antigua; *adj* berasal dari Antigua
antipathy *n* antipati, perasaan tidak
suka, perasaan benci
antique *n* [antik] barang kuno, barang
antik; *adj* kuno, antik; **antiquity** *n*

[antikuiti] (barang dari) zaman purbakala

antiseptic *n* obat anti-kuman; *adj* bersih, stéril

antlers *n, pl* tanduk rusa

antonym *n* lawan kata, antonim

anus *n* [énus] dubur

anvil *n* landasan, paron

anxiety *n* [angzayeti] kecemasan, kegelisahan, kekuatiran; anxious *adj* [angsyes] gelisah, cemas

any *adj* [éni] sesuatu, beberapa, sembarang; *neg* sedikit pun; ~ *one* mana saja; ~ *more* lagi; ~ *color is fine* warna apa saja boléh; *do you have ~ food?* apakah ada makanan?; *no, there isn't ~* tidak ada; anybody, anyone *pron* [éniwan] siapa pun, siapa saja; anyhow *adv* bagaimanapun; anything *pron* apa saja, apa pun; anywhere *adv* [éniwér] di mana saja, ke mana saja

aorta *n* [éorta] (pembuluh darah) aorta

apart *adv* terpisah; ~ *from* selain, kecuali

apartheid *n* [apart hét] aparthéid, kebijakan pemisahan antargolongan di Afrika Selatan dari 1948–94

apartment *n* apartemén, rumah susun; ~ *block* gedung apartemén

apathetic *adj* [apathétik] apatis, acuh tidak acuh; apathy *n* [apethi] apati, sikap acuk tak acuh

ape *n* kera, siamang; *vt* meniru; *the child ~s his elders* anak itu meniru orang tuanya

APEC *abbrev* [épék] *Asia-Pacific Economic Cooperation* APEC, Kerjasama Ekonomi Asia Pasifik

aperitif *n* [apéritif] minuman (beralkohol) sebelum makan

aperture *n* [apertyur] lubang, bukaan

aphrodisiac *n* obat kuat, obat cinta

apiarist *n* pemelihara lebah; apiary *n* peternakan lebah

apologize *vi* minta maaf; ~ *for* minta maaf atas; ~ *to* minta maaf kepada; apology *n* permintaan maaf

apostle *n* [aposel] rasul; apostolic *adj* [apostolik] kerasulan

apostrophe *n* [apostrofi] apostrof [']

appall *vt* [epol] membuat ngeri, mengerikan; appalled *adj* ngeri, héran; appalling *adj* mengerikan, sangat buruk

apparatus *n* perkakas, aparat, alat

apparel *n* busana (di toko)

apparent *adj* [aparént] nyata, jelas, kentara; apparently *adv* tampaknya, ternyata ← appear

apparition *n* [aparisyen] hantu, penampakan ← appear

appeal *n* permohonan, permintaan, seruan; banding; penghimpunan dana; *vi* naik banding

appeal *n* daya tarik; *sex* ~ daya tarik séksual; *vi* menarik minat, menarik perhatian; appealing *adj* menarik, menawan

appear *vi* tampak, muncul, timbul, menghadap; appearance *n* tampang, penampilan; *to keep up ~s* menjaga muka atau nama baik; *to put in or make an ~* tampak, hadir

appease *n* [apiz] menenteramkan, menenangkan; appeasement *n* kebijakan membiarkan kejadian buruk terjadi tanpa ditindak

append *vt* menambahkan, membubuhkan, melampirkan

appendicitis *n* [apéndisaitis] radang usus buntu; appendix *n* lampiran; usus buntu

appetite *n* seléra, nafsu makan; *Sue has lost her ~* Sue tidak ada seléra makan; appetizer *n* makanan pembuka; appetizing *adj* enak, lezat, membangkit seléra

applaud *vi* bertepuk tangan; *vt* memuji; applause *n* tepuk tangan

apple *n* buah apel; ~ *core* bagian tengah apel; *the ~ of (someone's) eye* anak emas

appliance *n* [aplayans] peranti, pesawat, alat

applicable *adj* [aplikabel] berlaku, dapat diterapkan ← apply

applicant *n* [aplikant] pelamar, pemohon; application *n* (surat) lamaran; penerapan, pemakai, aplikasi; kerja keras; ~ *form* formulir (pendaftaran);

apply *vi* [aplai] berlaku; *vt* menerapkan, menggunakan; ~ *oneself* bekerja keras; ~ *to* berlaku untuk; ~ *for a job* melamar untuk pekerjaan

applique *n* [apliké] sejenis sulaman

appoint *vt* menunjuk, menetapkan, mengangkat; **appointed** *adj* yang ditentukan; **appointment** *n* penunjukan; perjanjian, janji; *by* ~ dengan perjanjian; *I have an* ~ *at 7 pm* saya ada perjanjian jam 7 malam

appraisal *n* taksiran, penilaian; **appraise** *vt* menaksir nilai, menilai

appreciate *vt* [aprisyiét] berterima kasih atas, menghargai, menaksir harga, menilai; mengerti; *fin* bertambah nilai; **appreciation** *n* penghargaan; pengertian; taksiran; *fin* aprésiasi; **appreciative** *adj* bersikap menghargai

apprehend *vt* menangkap; **apprehension** *n* rasa gelisah, kekuatiran; **apprehensive** *adj* kuatir, gelisah

apprentice *n* [apréntis] murid; *to be ~d to a welder* magang di béngkél las; **apprenticeship** *n* masa magang

approach *n* pendekatan; *vi* datang; *vt* mendekati, menuju (tempat); menjelang (waktu); **approachable** *adj* ramah, dapat didekati

appropriate *adj* [apropriet] patut, layak, pantas, sesuai

approval *n* [apruval] izin, persetujuan; **approve** *vi* setuju; ~ *of* setuju dengan; *vt* memperkenankan, mengizinkan, menyetujui

approximate *vt* [aproksimét] menaksir, menebak; *adj* [aproksimet] kira-kira, kurang lebih; **approximately** *adv* **approx** *abbrev* kira-kira, kurang lebih

apricot *n* [éprikot] aprikot

April *n* [épril] bulan April; ~ *Fools Day* April Mop

apron *n* celemék

apt *adj* layak, patut; cenderung; *children are ~ to tire easily* anak-anak cenderung cepat capék; **aptitude** *n* kecakapan, bakat

aqua *adj* biru toska

aqualung *n* tangki oksigén buat penyelam

aquamarine *adj* [akuamarin] sejenis warna biru terang

aquarium *n* akuarium, kolam ikan

aquatic *adj* [akuotik] berhubungan dengan air atau laut; ~ *center* kompléks kolam renang

aqueduct *n* jalan air (di atas tanah)

aqueous *adj* [akwius] berair

Arab *n* orang Arab; *adj* berasal dari daérah Arab; *United ~ Emirates (UAE)* Uni Emirat ~ (UEA); **Arabia** *n* [arébia] (daérah) Arab; *Saudi ~* Arab Saudi; **Arabian** *adj* berasal dari Arab; **Arabic** *n* [Arabik] bahasa Arab; ~ *script* huruf Arab

arable *adj* [arebel] dapat ditanami

arbitrary *adj* tanpa aturan, secara acak

arbitration *n* arbitrase, perantaraan

arc *n* garis lengkung

arcade *n* lorong atau gang beratap; ~ *game* mesin permainan di tempat umum

arch *n* [arc] garis lengkung; busur; gerbang; *vi* melengkungkan; ~ *enemy* musuh bebuyutan; **archer** *n* pemanah; **archery** *n* panahan

archaic *adj* [arkéik] kuno, sudah tidak dipakai lagi

archbishop *n* uskup agung

archeological, archaeological *adj* purbakala; **archeologist** *n* ahli purbakala, arkéolog; **archeology** *n* ilmu purbakala, arkéologi

archipelago *n* [arkipélago] kepulauan, pulau gugusan; *the Malay ~* Nusantara

architect *n* [arkitekt] arsiték; *landscape ~* arsiték lanskap; **architecture** *n* arsitéktur; **architectural** *adj* **architecturally** *adv* dari segi arsitéktur

archive *n* [arkaiv] arsip; *the State Archives* kearsipan negara

Arctic *adj* Arktik, Artik, berasal dari kawasan Kutub Utara; *sub-~ temperatures* suhu yang sangat dingin; *the ~ (Circle)* daérah (lingkaran) Arktik

ardent *adj* bersemangat, bergairah; **ardor** *n* semangat, gairah, hasrat

arduous *adj* [ardyuus] sulit, keras; *an ~ journey* perjalanan yang sulit

are *vt, pl* adalah → **be**

area *n* [éria] daérah, wilayah, kawasan; luas

areca *n* [arika] pinang

arena *n* [arina] aréna, médan, gelang-gang; *sports* ~ stadion, gelanggang olahraga

aren't *vt, pl* bukan; tidak ← **are not**

Argentina *n* [Arjentina] Argentina; **Argentine** *n, arch* orang Argentina; *the* ~ Argentina; *adj* berasal dari Argentina; **Argentinian** *n* orang Argentina; *adj* berasal dari Argentina

argue *vi* [argyu] berdebat, bertengkar; *vt* memperdebatkan, membantah; **argument** *n* béda pendapat, perteng-karan; alasan, dalih; **argumentative** *adj* suka bertengkar

arid *adj* gersang, kering; *semi-*~ kering; **aridity** *n* ketidaksuburan, kekeringan

arise *vi* **arose arisen** bangkit, bangun, timbul ← **rise**

aristocracy *n* kaum ningrat; **aristocrat** *n* orang ningrat, bangsawan; **aristo-cratic** *adj* bersifat ningrat atau bang-sawan

arithmetic *n* ilmu berhitung

ark *n* bahtera; *Noah's* ~ bahtera Nabi Nuh

arm *n* lengan, tangan (baju); ~ *in* ~ bergandéngan tangan; *it cost an* ~ *and a leg* sangat mahal; **armchair** *n* kursi sofa, kursi tamu; **armpit** *n* ketiak

arm *vt* mempersenjatai; **armed** *adj* bersenjata; ~ *forces* angkatan bersen-jata; **arms** *n, pl* senjata; *call to* ~ seruan untuk berjuang; *up in* ~ marah sekali, kacau-balau; **armament** *n* persenjataan

armada *n* armada kapal

armadillo *n* trenggiling

armband *n* ikat lengan (sebagai tanda berkabung)

armchair *n* kursi sofa, kursi tamu

Armenia *n* [Arminia] Arménia; **Armenian** *n* bahasa Arménia; orang Arménia; *adj* berasal dari Arménia

armistice *n* [armistis] gencatan senjata

armor, armour *n* baju baja; *~ed car* mobil lapis baja

armpit *n* ketiak

arms *n, pl* senjata; ~ *race* lomba senjata;

call to ~ seruan untuk berjuang; *up in* ~ marah sekali, kacau-balau ← **arm**

army *n* tentara, bala tentara; angkatan darat; *the Salvation* ~ Bala Keselamatan

aroma *n* bau harum, aroma; **aromatic** *adj* berbau harum; **aromatherapy** *n* aromatérapi, pengobatan atau rélak-sasi dengan wewangian

around *prep* [araund] sekeliling, sekitar, seputar; dekat; *adv* kira-kira, sekitar

arouse *vt* merangsang, menimbulkan; **aroused** *adj* terangsang

arrange *vt* [arénj] mengurus, menata, mengatur; mengaransemén (lagu); *~d marriage* penjodohan; **arrangement** *n* penataan, pengaturan, perjanjian; aransemén; **arrangements** *n, pl* persiapan

arrest *n* penahanan, penangkapan; *cardiac* ~ serangan jantung; *under* ~ ditahan; *vt* menahan, menangkap

arrival *n* kedatangan; **arrive** *vi* datang, tiba

arrogance *n* kesombongan, keangkuhan; **arrogant** *adj* sombong, angkuh

arrow *n* (anak) panah; *red* ~ tanda bélok yang mérah (di lampu mérah); **arrow-head** *n* mata panah, ujung panah

arse *n, vulg* pantat, kibul; **arsehole** *n, vulg* lubang pantat; orang jelék

arsenal *n* gudang senjata

arsenic *n* arsenikum, arsenik

arson *n* pembakaran yang disengaja; **arsonist** *n* orang yang dengan sengaja menyebabkan kebakaran

art *n* seni lukis; kesenian; ~ *gallery* galéri kesenian; *abstract* ~ seni abstrak; **arts** *n* kesenian; sastra (juru-san); ~ *and crafts* kerajinan (tangan); **arty** *adj, coll* (sok) artistik

artefact → **artifact**

arterial *adj* [artirial] berkaitan dengan pembuluh nadi atau artéri; ~ *road* jalan artéri; **artery** *n* pembuluh nadi, artéri

artesian well *n* sumur bor, sumur artésis

arthritic *adj* [arthritik] berkaitan dengan radang sendi; **arthritis** *n* [arthraitis] encok, radang sendi

artichoke *n* [articok] sejenis sayur

article *n* barang, benda; pasal, bab (hukum); kata sandang; ~ *of clothing* sepotong baju

articulate *vt* menyuarakan pikiran dengan lancar; *adj* menguasai bahasa, pandai menyuarakan pikiran

artifact, artefact *n* benda atau barang bersejarah, pusaka

artificial *adj* buatan, palsu; ~ *insemination* pembuahan buatan; ~ *respiration* pernafasan buatan

artillery *n* artiléri; *heavy* ~ senjata berat, meriam

artisan *n* perajin, pengrajin, tukang

artist *n* seniman, seniwati; artis (seni peran); **artistic** *adj* artistik, indah; **artistry** *n* seni ← **art**

as *adv, conj* sama, se-; seperti; karena, sebab; sebagai; ~ *for* kalau; ~ *well (~)* juga; ~ *if* seolah-olah; ~ *yet* sampai sekarang; ~ *for me* kalau saya; ~ *from Wednesday* mulai hari Rabu; ~ *big* ~ *a house* sebesar rumah; ~ *soon* ~ *possible (asap)* secepat mungkin, secepat-cepatnya; *Rob can't come* ~ *it's raining* Rob tidak bisa datang karena hujan; *Karin worked* ~ *an assistant* Karin bekerja sebagai asistén

asap. *abbrev as soon as possible* secepat mungkin, secepat-cepatnya

asbestos *n* asbés

ascend *vi* [asénd] naik, mendaki; **ascendancy** *n* keunggulan, kekuasaan; **ascending** *adj* menaik; *in* ~ *order* dari kecil sampai besar; **ascension** *n* kenaikan (ke surga); *Isl* Miraj; **ascent** *n* kenaikan; tanjakan

ascertain *vi* [asertén] memastikan, mengetahui dengan pasti, mengecék

ASEAN *abbrev* [aséan] *Association of South East Asian Nations* ASEAN, Persatuan Negara-Negara Asia Tenggara

ash *n* abu; ~ *Wednesday* Rabu Abu; **ashen** *adj* putih, pucat; **ashtray** *n* asbak

ashamed *adj* malu; ~ *of* malu karena ← **shame**

ashen *adj* putih, pucat ← **ash**

ashore *adj* di darat; *go* ~ naik ke darat ← **shore**

ashtray *n* asbak ← **ash**

Asia *n* [ésya] Asia; *Southeast* ~ Asia Tenggara; **Asian** *n* orang Asia; *adj* berhubungan dengan Asia; ~ *Development Bank (ADB)* Bank Pembangunan Asia

aside *adv* di sebelah; ~ *from* selain dari; *cast* ~ dibuang ← **side**

ASIO *abbrev Australian Security Intelligence Organisation* Organisasi Keamanan Intelijen Australia

ask *v* bertanya, minta, memohon; ~ *after* bertanya mengenai (orang); ~ *around* bertanya-tanya (kepada beberapa orang); ~ *for* meminta; ~ *for trouble* mencari masalah, mengundang masalah; ~ *out* mengajak berkencan; ~*ing rate* harga jual; ~ *a question* bertanya; *a big* ~ tantangan besar

asleep *adj* sedang tidur; *sound* ~ tidur pulas, tidur nyenyak; *to fall* ~ tertidur

asp *n* sejenis ular kecil

asparagus *n* asparagus, aspérse

aspect *n* segi pandangan, sudut pandangan, aspék

asphalt *n* [asyfalt] aspal

aspiration *n* cita-cita, harapan, aspirasi; **aspire** *vi* berharap, bercita-cita; *Stewart* ~*s to be an artist* Stewart bercita-cita menjadi seniman

aspirin *n* aspirin

ass *n* keledai; *sl, US* pantat; orang bodoh

assailant *n* penyerang, penyerbu ← **assault**

assassin *n* pembunuh (tokoh terkenal); **assassinate** *vt* membunuh tokoh terkenal; **assassination** *n* pembunuhan tokoh terkenal

assault *n* serangan, serbuan; *vt* menyerang, menyerbu; *sexually* ~ mencabuli, melécéhkan, memperkosa

assemble *vi* berkumpul, berhimpun, bersidang; *vt* mengumpulkan; merakit; **assembly** *n* perkumpulan, perhimpunan, sidang; perakitan; apél (di sekolah); ~ *line* lini perakitan

assent *n* persetujuan, izin; *to give one's* ~ menyetujui; *vi* ~ *to* memperkenankan, mengizinkan, menyetujui

assert *v* menyatakan dengan tegas;

assertion *n* pernyataan, penegasan; **assertive** *adj* berani

assess *vt* menaksir, menilai; **assessment** *n* taksiran, penilaian; **assessor** *n* penguji, orang yang menilai

asset *n* asét, modal; *fin* aktiva; *he is an ~ to the school* sekolah itu bangga padanya

assiduous *adj* rajin

assign *vt* [asain] menugaskan, menetapkan, memperuntukkan; *~ to* menugaskan; *he was ~ed to the Sydney branch* dia ditugaskan di cabang di Sydney; **assignation** *n* [asignésyen] pertemuan (rahasia); **assignment** *n* [asainment] tugas

assimilate *vi* membaur; *Chinese traders ~d into local village life* pedagang Cina membaur dengan masyarakat désa; **assimilation** *n* pembauran, asimilasi

assist *v* menolong, membantu; *Tomoko ~s me in class* Tomoko membantu saya dengan pelajaran; *~ with* membantu dengan; **assistance** *n* pertolongan, bantuan; *may I be of ~?* bisakah saya bantu?; **assistant** *n* pembantu, asistén

associate *n* [asosiet] kawan, mitra, rekan; *vi* [asosiét] bergaul; *she still ~s with the underworld* dia masih berhubungan dengan kalangan penjahat; *vt* mengaitkan, menghubungkan; *I ~ magnolias with spring* bunga magnolia mengingatkan saya pada musim bunga; **association** *n* gabungan, persatuan, asosiasi

assorted *adj* bermacam jenis, beranéka macam; **assortment** *n* campuran, persediaan yang bermacam jenis

assume *v ~ (that)* menganggap; menjabat; *~ed name* alias, nama samaran; **assumption** *n* asumsi, prasangka

assurance *n* kepastian, jaminan, janji; **assure** *vt* memastikan, menjamin; *~d of* dijamin akan; *self-~d* percaya diri; *they ~d him he would not have to pay tax* mereka menjamin bahwa dia tidak perlu membayar pajak

aster *n* sejenis bunga, bunga aster

asterisk *n* tanda bintang [*]

astern *adv* di bagian belakang kapal, di buritan ← **stern**

asthma *n* (penyakit) asma, sesak dada; **asthmatic** *adj* berpenyakit asma

astigmatism *n* silinder

astonish *vt* menghérankan, menakjubkan; **astonished** *adj* héran; **astonishing** *adj* menakjubkan; **astonishment** *n* kehéranan, rasa héran

astound *vt* **astounding** *adj* mengejutkan, mengherankan

astray *adv* sesat, tersesat; *to lead ~* menyesatkan

astride *adv* mengangkang (naik kuda, sepéda dsb)

astrologer *n* [astrolojer] peramal; **astrology** *n* nasib menurut bintang, astrologi

astronaut *n* astronot

astronomer *n* astronom, ahli bintang; **astronomical** *adj* tinggi selangit; **astronomy** *n* (ilmu) astronomi, ilmu bintang

astute *adj* cerdik, berakal

asylum *n* [asailum] suaka, tempat perlindungan; *~-seeker* pencari suaka; *mental ~* rumah sakit jiwa; *to grant ~* memberi suaka; *political ~* suaka politik

asymmetric, asymmetrical *adj* tidak berimbang, asimétris

at *prep* di; pada; *~ all* sama sekali; pernah (dalam pertanyaan); *~ home* di rumah; betah; *~ last* akhirnya; *~ least* paling tidak; *~ once* sekarang juga; *~ times* kadang-kadang; *~ seven o'clock* pada jam tujuh

ate *vt* [ét] makan (bentuk lampau) → **eat**

atheism *n* [éthiizem] atéisme; **atheist** *n* atéis

Athens *n* Athéna

athlete *n* [athlit] atlét, olahragawan; pelari; **athletic** *adj* [athlétik] kuat, berotot, fit; **athletics** *n* cabang atlétik, lari

Atlantic *n the ~ (Ocean)* Laut Atlantik; *trans-~* di antara Eropa dan Amérika; *the South ~* Laut Atlantik Selatan; *North ~ Treaty Organisation (NATO)* Organisasi Pakta Pertahanan Atlantik Utara

atlas *n* atlas, buku peta; *road* ~ buku peta jalan

ATM *abbrev automated teller machine* ATM (anjungan tunai mandiri)

atmosphere *n* [atmosfir] suasana; hawa, udara; angkasa, atmosfér; *in the* ~ di udara; **atmospheric** *adj* [atmosférik] bersuasana khas; ~ *pressure* tekanan udara

atoll *n* pulau karang, atol

atom *n* atom; ~ *bomb* bom nuklir, bom atom; **atomic** *adj* [atomik] berkaitan dengan atom, nuklir; ~ *energy* tenaga nuklir; ~ *power* station pembangkit listrik tenaga nuklir (PLTN)

atone *vi* ~ *for* bertobat, menebus (dosa); **atonement** *n* penebusan dosa; *the Day of* ~ Hari Penebusan (Dosa)

atrocious *adj* [atrosyus] buruk; kejam, bengis; **atrocity** *n* kekejian, kekejaman, kebengisan

attach *vt* menambat, melekatkan, mengaitkan, melampirkan; **attaché** *n* [atasyé] atase; ~ *case* tas kerja (berkulit keras); **attached** *adj* terlampir; berpasangan; ~ *to* sayang pada; *no strings* ~ tanpa ikatan; **attachment** *n* lampiran; rasa sayang

attack *n* serangan; ~ *on* serangan terhadap; *vt* menyerang; **attacker** *n* penyerang

attain *vt* meraih, mencapai; **attainment** *n* peraihan, pencapaian

attempt *n* usaha, percobaan; *an* ~ *on someone's life* upaya pembunuhan (terhadap seseorang); *vi* berusaha; *vt* mencoba; ~*ed murder* upaya pembunuhan

attend *vi* hadir; *vt* menghadiri; ~ *to* melayani; merawat; **attendance** *n* kehadiran; ~ *roll* daftar absén; **attendant** *n* pelayan; *flight* ~ pramugari, pramugara

attention *n* perhatian; *to pay* ~ mendengar, menyimak; *to draw* ~ *to* menarik perhatian pada; *to pay* ~ *to* memperhatikan, menaruh perhatian; **attentive** *adj* [aténtiv] penuh perhatian

attic *n* loténg

attire *n* busana, pakaian; *suitably* ~*d* berbusana yang pantas

attitude *n* [atityud] sikap, pendirian; *sl* keberanian; ~ *problem* masalah sikap yang buruk

attorney *n* [atérni] pengacara; ~*-General* Jaksa Agung; *power of* ~ surat kuasa

attract *vt* menarik atau memikat (hati); **attraction** *n* daya tarik, daya pikat; atraksi; *tourist* ~ obyék wisata; **attractive** *adj* [atraktiv] menawan

attribute *vt* menghubungkan, mengaitkan; ~ *to* dihubungkan dengan, diakibatkan; *the fire was* ~*d to a short-circuit* kebakaran diperkirakan diakibatkan kortsleting; *n* sifat, ciri, lambang

aubergine *n, UK* [oberjin] térong

auction *n* lélang; ~ *house* rumah lélang; *for* ~ dilélang; *vt* melélang; ~ *off* melélangkan; **auctioneer** *n* juru lélang

audacious *adj* [odésyus] berani sekali; **audacity** *n* [odasiti] keberanian

audible *adj* [odibel] kedengaran, terdengar

audience *n* [odiéns] para penonton, pendengar, tamu, hadirin; *to have an* ~ *with* beraudiénsi dengan

audio- *pref* berkaitan dengan mendengar; ~*visual* pandang dengar

audit *n* [odit] pemeriksaan keuangan; *to do an* ~ mengaudit; *vt* memeriksa keuangan, mengaudit; **auditor** *n* akuntan

audition *n* [odisyen] audisi; *vi* mengikuti audisi; ~ *for* mengikuti audisi untuk

auditorium *n* [oditorium] aula

August *n* bulan Agustus

auld lang syne [old lang zain] lagu yang dinyanyikan pada malam tahun baru

aunt *n* [ant] **aunty, auntie** *sl* bibi, tante; *great-*~ saudara perempuan dari kakék atau nénék

au pair *n* [o pér] gadis yang sedang belajar bahasa sambil bekerja menjaga anak di rumah orang

aura *n* [ora] pancaran, suasana

aural *adj* berkaitan dengan telinga atau mendengar; ~ *skills* kemampuan mendengar atau menyimak

auspice [ospes] *under the ~s of* di bawah pengawasan; **auspicious** *adj* menguntungkan

Aussie *n, adj, sl* (orang) Australia, berasal dari Australia; **Australia** *n* [Ostrélia] Australia; *South ~* Australia Selatan; *Western ~* Australia Barat; **Australian** *n* orang Australia; *adj* berasal dari Australia; *~ Rules (football)* sépak bola Australia

Austria *n* Austria; **Austrian** *n* orang Austria; *adj* berasal dari Austria

authentic *adj* asli, oténtik

author *n* pengarang, penulis

authoritarian *adj* (bersifat) otoritér

authoritative *adj* [otoritativ] berkuasa, berwenang, berotoritas; dapat dipercaya; **authority** *n* otoritas, kekuasaan; yang berwajib, instansi; ahli, pakar; **authorization** *n* kewenangan; **authorize** *vt* mengizinkan

autism *n* [otizem] autisme; **autistic** *adj* autis

auto- [oto] *pref* dengan sendirinya

auto *n, coll* [oto] mobil; *adj* otomotif

autobiographical *adj* [otobayografikal] yang berkaitan dengan pengalaman sendiri; **autobiography** *n* otobiografi

autograph *n* [otograf] tanda tangan; *vt* menandatangani

automatic *adj* [otomatik] otomatis, dengan sendirinya; *~ transmission* matik, otomatik; **automatically** *adv* secara otomatis, dengan sendirinya

automobile *n* [otomobil] mobil, kendaraan

autonomous *n* otonom; **autonomy** *n* otonomi; *regional ~* otonomi daérah (otda)

autopsy *n* otopsi, bedah mayat

autumn *n* [otum] musim gugur, musim rontok

auxiliary *n* [oksiliari] alat pembantu; *adj* bantu, pembantu; *~ verb* kata kerja bantu

Av, Ave *abbrev Avenue* Jl (Jalan)

avail *to no ~* sia-sia

available *adj* [avélabel] ada, tersedia; **availability** *n* ketersediaan

avalanche *n* [avalanc] salju longsor

avarice *n* [avaris] ketamakan; **avaricious** *adj* [avarisyes] tamak

Ave, Av *abbrev Avenue* Jl (jalan)

avenge *vt* membalas dendam (terutama atas kematian); **avenger** *n* orang yang membalas dendam

avenue *n av abbrev* [avenyu] jalan (terutama yang di antara dua dérétan pohon)

average *n, adj, vt* [averej] rata-rata; *on ~* rata-rata

averse *adj* enggan, segan; *not ~ to* tidak keberatan; **aversion** *n* keengganan, ketidak-sukaan; **avert** *vt* menghindari, menjauhkan; *~ one's gaze* menghindari pandangan

aviary *n* [éviari] kandang burung yang besar

aviation *n* [éviésyen] penerbangan; **aviator** *n, arch* penerbang

avid *adj* [avid] gemar sekali; *an ~ reader* orang yang sangat gemar membaca

avocado *n* [avokado] alpukat

avoid *vt* mengelakkan, menghindar dari, menghindari; **avoidable** *adj* dapat dihindari

await *vt* menantikan ← **wait**

awake *vi* **awoke awoken** bangun; *adj* dalam keadaan bangun; **awaken** *vt* bangun; **awakening** *n* kesadaran; awal ← **wake**

award *n* penghargaan, hadiah; *~-winning* telah menerima penghargaan; *vt* memberi penghargaan, menghadiahkan, menganugerahkan

aware *adj* sadar akan, menyadari; *I'm not ~ of* saya tidak tahu; *as far as I am ~* setahu saya; **awareness** *n* kesadaran

away *adj* tidak di sini, tidak ada; *adv* dari tempat itu; asyik, sibuk; *go ~!* pergilah!; *he's ~ today* dia tidak masuk hari ini; *three hours ~* tiga jam dari sini; *to get ~* lolos; pergi berlibur; *to get ~ with* berhasil (melakukan sesuatu yang kurang baik); *Megan kept eating ~* Megan tetap asyik makan

awe *n* [oa] perasaan kagum; **awful** *adj* dahsyat, mengerikan; **awfully** *adv* betul-betul; *I'm ~ tired* saya betul-betul capék

awkward *adj* kikuk, canggung;
awkwardness *n* kecanggungan
awning *n* atap aluminium
ax, axe *n* kapak; *to give someone the ~*
memecat; *to have an ~ to grind* mempunyai alasan pribadi; *vt* memecat
axiom *n* aksioma
axis *n* [aksis] poros, sumbu; *the ~ of*
Evil Poros Kejahatan
axle *n* [aksel] as roda
aye *UK* [ai] ya, setuju
azalea *n* [azélia] sejenis tanaman berbunga
Azerbaijan *n* Azerbaijan; **Azerbaijani** *n*
bahasa Azerbaijan; orang Azerbaijan;
adj berasal dari Azerbaijan; **Azeri** *n*
bahasa Azerbaijan, bahasa Azéri
azure *adj* [azur] biru muda

B

b [bi] *b, second letter of the alphabet*
B & B *abbrev bed and breakfast* losmén,
penginapan murah yang termasuk
sarapan
BA *abbrev Bachelor of Arts* SS (Sarjana
Sastra)
babble *vi* bercelotéh, mengocéh; bicara
tanpa kendali, menyerocos; *n* omong
kosong
babe *n, arch* [béb] bayi; *a ~ in arms*
bayi, orok; *sl* céwék ← **baby**
baboon *n* babon; *sl* orang tolol
baby *n* **babies** *pl* bayi; *adj* anak; *~*
boom masa angka kelahiran sangat
tinggi; *~ carriage* keréta anak; *~ ele-*
phant anak gajah; **babyface** wajah
imut-imut; **babyish** *adj* kekanak-
kanakan, masih seperti bayi; **babysit**
vt **babysat babysat** menjaga anak;
babysitter *n* penjaga anak; **babysitting**
n menjaga anak
baccalaureate *n* [bakaloriat] ijazah
SMA di Perancis dan banyak sekolah
intérnasional
bachelor *n* bujangan, jejaka; *~'s degree*
S1 (Strata Satu); *~ of Arts (BA)*
Sarjana Sastra (SS); *~ of Business*
(BB) Sarjana Bisnis; *~ of Economics*

(BE) Sarjana Ekonomi (SE); *~ of*
Education (B.Ed) Sarjana Pendidikan;
~ of Engineering (B.Eng) Sarjana
Téknik (ST); *~ of Law (LL.B)* Sarjana
Hukum (SH); *~ of Medicine (B.Med)*
Sarjana Kedokteran (SK); *~ of*
Science (BSc) Sastra Sains (SSi); *~*
flat apartemén sederhana (seperti
untuk kaum bujangan)
back *vt* mendapat kembali; *vt* mendukung, mendanai; *~ down vi* akhirnya
menyerah; *~ off vi* mundur; *~ out vi*
tidak jadi, mengundurkan diri; *~ up vi*
bertumpuk, menjadi antréan panjang;
vt membéla; membuat cadangan;
memundurkan; *n* belakang, punggung,
balik; *at the ~ of* di belakang; *behind*
his ~ dari belakang, tidak terus terang;
~s to the wall membelakangi témbok,
dalam keadaan terjebak; *adj, adv* ke
belakang, mundur; *~ garden* kebun di
belakang rumah; *~ seat* jok belakang;
kurang penting; *~ yard* pekarangan di
belakang rumah; *~ and forth* mondar-
mandir, bolak-balik; *~ to front* terbalik; *to get ~ vi* kembali; **backache** *n*
[bak ék] sakit punggung; **backbone** *n*
tulang belakang; **backchat** *n* bantah-
an; **backdate** *vt* memberi tanggal
yang sudah léwat; **backdrop** *n* latar
belakang (di panggung); **backfire** *vi*
senjata makan tuan; **backgammon** *n*
permainan dengan papan dan keping-
keping bulat; **background** *n* latar
belakang; **backing** *n* sokongan,
dukungan; **backlash** *n* serangan balik;
backlog *n* tumpukan kerjaan yang
belum selesai; **backpack** *n* ransel;
backpacker *n* turis ransel; **backroom**
~ boys orang di balik tokoh; **backside**
n, sl pantat; **backstab** *vt* memfitnah,
menikam dari belakang; **backstage** *n*
di balik panggung; **backstreet** *adj*,
sl tidak resmi, léwat pintu belakang;
backstroke *n* gaya punggung; **back-**
track *vt* kembali lewat jalan yang
sama; **backup** *n* dukungan; cadangan;
backward, backwards *adj* mundur;
terkebelakang; *adv* ke belakang,
mundur; **backwater** *n* [bakwoter]

daérah udik, daérah terpencil
bacon *n* irisan daging babi asap; *beef* ~
daging sapi yang diasap seperti *bacon*;
to save one's ~ menyelamatkan orang
bacteria *n, pl* baktéri, kuman
bad *adj* jelék, buruk, kurang baik; parah;
~-mannered tidak sopan; *~-mouth*
mengatai, mengéjék; *~-tempered*
pemarah; ~ *at* lemah, kurang bisa; ~
dream mimpi buruk; ~ *language* kata-
kata jorok, bahasa kasar; ~ *luck* sial; ~
mood sedang marah-marah; *not* ~
lumayan, baik-baik saja; *too* ~ sayang;
to go ~ membusuk, menjadi basi;
badly *adv* dengan buruk, secara jelék;
badness *n* keburukan
badge *n* [baj] lencana, pin
badger *n* sejenis binatang hutan di
Eropa, seperti luak
badly *adv* dengan buruk, secara jelék; ~
hurt luka parah ← **bad**
badminton *n* bulu tangkis; ~ *player*
pebulu tangkis, pemain bulu tangkis
badness *n* keburukan ← **bad**
baffle *vt* [bafel] **baffled** *adj* bingung;
baffling *adj* membingungkan
bag *n* tas, karung; *bum* ~ tas pinggang;
carry~ tas ténténg, kerésék; *hand~* tas
tangan; *old* ~ *sl* nénék-nénék; *plastic* ~
kerésék, plastik; *it's in the* ~ sudah
pasti; *vt, sl* memesan tempat
bagel *n, US* sejenis roti berbentuk lingkaran
baggage *n* [bagej] bagasi, koper, tas; ~
claim pengambilan bagasi; *emotional* ~
beban mental; *left* ~ penitipan tas
baggy *adj* [bagi] kendor, kebesaran,
longgar
bagpipes *n, pl* sejenis alat musik khas
Skotlandia
Bahamas *the* ~ Bahama; **Bahamian** *n*
orang Bahama; *adj* berasal dari
Bahama
Bahrain *n* Bahrain; **Bahraini** *n* orang
Bahrain; *adj* berasal dari Bahrain
bail *n* uang jaminan; *released on* ~
dibébaskan dengan jaminan; *vi*
menimba air dari kapal; *sl* cabut; *vt* ~
out menyelamatkan
bailiff *n* juru sita

bait *n* umpan; *vt* menggoda, mengum-
pani; *to rise to the* ~ terpancing
bake *vi* jemur; *vt* membakar; *~d beans*
kacang dalam kaléng; ~ *a cake* membuat kué; **baker** *n* tukang memasak
roti; *~'s dozen* tiga belas; **bakery** *n*
toko roti; **baking** *n* prosés membakar
(roti, kué); ~ *powder* soda kué
balaclava *n* [balaklava] topi wol yang
menutup kepala dengan lubang untuk
muka
balance *n* keseimbangan; neraca, timbangan; *fin* saldo, sisa; *on* ~ setelah
mempertimbangkan semua; *in the* ~
tidak pasti; *vi* berimbang; *vt* menimbang; ~ *sheet* neraca; **balanced** *adj*
berimbang
balcony *n* balkon, téras, beranda
bald *adj* [bold] botak, gundul, plontos;
~ *eagle* sejenis élang yang merupakan
lambang AS; **balding** *adj* membotak;
baldness *n* kebotakan
bale *n* bungkus atau bal (jerami)
baleful *adj* tidak ramah, tidak senang
ball *n* [bol] bola; *~-bearing* bantalan
peluru, laher; *golf* ~ bola golf; *tennis* ~
bola ténis; *on the* ~ cerdas, sadar; *to
start the* ~ *rolling* memulai; *n* pésta
berdansa; *I had a* ~ saya sangat
menikmatinya; **ballboy, ballgirl** *n*
orang yang mengambilkan bola selama pertandingan tenis; **ballpark** *n, US*
stadion atau tempat bermain bisbol;
ballpoint *n* ~ *(pen)* bolpoin; **ballroom**
n ruangan pésta; ~ *dancing* berdansa;
balls *n, pl, sl* kantung pelir; *to have* ~
berani, punya nyali
ballad *n* balada
ballast *n* pemberat (untuk
keseimbangan)
ballboy *n, m* **ballgirl** *f* orang yang
mengambilkan bola selama pertandingan tenis ← **ball**
ballerina *n, f* pebalét; **ballet** *n* [balé]
balét; ~ *dancer* pebalét; ~ *flats,* ~
shoes sepatu balét; ~ *lessons* lés balét
balloon *n* balon; *hot-air* ~ balon udara;
vi membesar seperti balon
ballot *n* [balet] pemilihan suara,
pengambilan undi; ~ *box* kotak suara

ballpark *n* stadion atau tempat bermain bisbol ← **ball**
ballpoint *n* ~ *(pen)* bolpoin ← **ball**
ballroom *n* ruangan pésta; ~ *dancing* berdansa ← **ball**
balls *n, pl, sl* kantung pelir; *to have* ~ berani, punya nyali ← **ball**
balm *n* obat gosok, balsem
balmy *adj* hangat, lembab (cuaca)
bamboo *n* bambu
ban *n* larangan; ~ *on* larangan terhadap, dilarang; *vt* melarang; ~ *from* melarang (masuk); **banned** *adj* dilarang, terlarang
banana *n* pisang; ~ *boat* perahu panjang berbentuk buah pisang untuk rékréasi; ~ *fritter* pisang goréng; ~ *peel*, ~ *skin* kulit pisang; ~ *republic derog* negara miskin (biasanya di Amérika Latin) yang ékonominya tergantung pada ékspor pisang; ~ *split* sejenis puding terdiri dari pisang dan és krim
band *n* gerombolan, géng, kawanan; grup band; gelang; *vi* ~ *together* bersatu, bekerja sama; **bandstand** *n* panggung orkés atau pemain musik (di taman) ← **band**
bandage *n* [bandej] perban; *vt* memerban, membalut
bandaid *n* pléster, hansaplast
bandanna *n* ikat kepala
bandit *n* bandit, penyamun
bandstand *n* panggung orkés atau pemain musik (di taman) ← **band**
bang *ejac* dor!, suara keras; *vi* berdentang; *vt* membanting; ~ *one's head* kejeduk
banger *n, sl, UK* [banger] sosis; ~*s and mash* sosis dan kentang puré
Bangladesh *n* Bangladésh; **Bangladeshi** *n* orang Bangladésh; *adj* berasal dari Bangladésh
bangle *n* [banggel] gelang (berbentuk lingkaran)
banish *vt* [banisy] membuang; **banishment** *n* pembuangan
bank *n* bank; ~ *account* rékéning bank; ~ *holiday* tanggal mérah; *vi* menjadi nasabah; ~ *on* memercayai, bergan-

tung pada; **banker** *n* bankir; **banking** *n* perbankan; **banknote** *n* uang kertas; **bankrupt** *adj* bangkrut, pailit; **bankruptcy** *n* kepailitan
bank *n* tepi, sisi (sungai); *vi* membélok (pesawat terbang)
banned *adj* dilarang, terlarang ← **ban**
banner *n* spanduk
banquet *n* [bankuet] perjamuan lengkap
banter *n* senda gurau; *vi* bersenda gurau
banyan *n* pohon beringin
baptism *n* permandian; ~ *of fire* awal yang mengerikan; **baptist** *n* pembaptis; *John the* ~ *Cath* Yohanes Pembaptis; *Chr* Yahya; **baptize** *vt* mempermandikan, membaptis
bar *n* palang pintu, batang, halangan, rintangan; tempat minum, kafé; *gold* ~ batang emas; *a* ~ *of chocolate* sebatang coklat; *a* ~ *of soap* sabun; *vt* memalang, menghalangi, merintangi; melarang; **barmaid** *n, f* **barman** *n, m* **bartender** *n* pelayan yang menyediakan minuman di bar atau kafé
barb *n* duri; *sl* kata sindiran; ~*ed wire* kawat berduri
Barbadian *n* [barbédian] orang Barbados; *adj* berasal dari Barbados; **Barbados** *n* Barbados
barbarian *n* [barbérian] barbar, orang biadab; **barbarity** *n* [barbariti] kebengisan, kebiadaban; **barbarous**, **barbaric** *adj* bengis, biadab, kejam
barbecue, barbeque, BBQ *n* [barbekyu] acara memanggang daging di luar rumah; *vt* memanggang daging; *we're having a* ~ kami ada acara memanggang daging
barber *n* tukang cukur
bare *adj* telanjang, polos; hanya; ~*chested* *m* bertelanjang dada; *vt* menelanjangi, memamerkan; **barefoot** *adj* dengan kaki telanjang; **bareheaded** *adj* tanpa tutup kepala; **barely** *adv* hampir tidak
bargain *n* [bargen] pembelian yang murah; ~*hunting* mencari barang yang murah; ~ *basement* obral besar di lantai bawah tosérba; *vi* tawar-menawar, menawar

barge *n* tongkang; *vi* ~ *in*, ~ *one's way through* menyerobot masuk

bark *n* kulit kayu

bark *n* gonggongan anjing; *vi* menggonggong

barley *n* [barli] sejenis séréal yang dipakai untuk membuat bir; ~ *sugar* semacam permén

barmaid *n, f* **barman** *n, m* pelayan di kafé ← **bar**

barmitzvah *n* upacara akil balig bagi anak lelaki Yahudi

barmy *adj, coll* gila

barn *n* gudang (tempat menyimpan jerami, rumput kering dsb); **barnyard** *n* pekarangan di pertanian

baron *n, m* **baroness** *f* baron (gelar bangsawan)

barracks *n* barak, tangsi, asrama

barracuda *n* sejenis ikan

barrage *n* [baraj] aliran yang deras; *a ~ of questions* banyak ditanya secara terus-menerus

barrel *n* tong; laras bedil; *a ~ of laughs* lucu sekali, jenaka

barren *adj* tandus, gersang; tidak subur, mandul

barricade *n* [barikéd] rintangan, barikade; *vt* memblokir, merintangi

barrier *n* palang, penghalang, rintangan

barrister *n* advokat, pengacara (yang tampil di pengadilan)

barrow *n* gerobak

bartender *n* pelayan yang menyediakan minuman di bar atau kafé ← **bar**

barter *n* niaga tukar-menukar barang, barter; *vt* tukar-menukar barang, barter

base *n* markas, dasar; *vi* berdasar, mendasarkan; ~*d on* berdasarkan; **baseball** *n* bisbol; ~ *player* pemain bisbol, pebisbol; **baseballer** *n* pemain bisbol, pebisbol; **baseless** *adj* tanpa dasar; **basement** *n* lantai bawah, bésmen; **basic** *adj* asasi, pokok; sederhana; *the* ~*s* prinsip-prinsip dasar; **basically** *adv* pada dasarnya

bash *n, sl* pukulan; *to have a* ~ coba; *vt* ~ *(up)* memukul, menghajar

bashful *adj* malu, tersipu-sipu

basic *adj* asasi, pokok; sederhana; *the* ~*s* prinsip-prinsip dasar; **basically** *adv* pada dasarnya ← **base**

basil *n* [bazil] selasih

basin *n* baskom, wastafel; lembah, daérah aliran sungai (DAS)

basis *n* **bases** [basiz] dasar; *on a weekly* ~ setiap minggu

bask *vi* berjemur, menikmati; ~ *in the sun* berjemur di bawah sinar matahari

basket *n* keranjang, bakul, baskét; ~*ball* bola baskét; ~ *case* tidak ada harapan

bass *n* [bés] bas

bassoon *n* sejenis alat musik tiup

bastard *n* anak haram, anak yang lahir di luar nikah; *sl* bréngsék, bajingan

bat *n* alat pemukul (dalam olahraga); *vi* memukul bola (dalam krikét, bisbol dsb); **batsman** *n* pemukul bola (dalam krikét); **batter** *n* pemukul bola

bat *n* kelelawar, kamprét, kalong

batch *n* sejumlah; séri (keluaran barang)

bath *n* (bak) mandi; ~ *mat* kését (di kamar mandi); ~ *salts* garam untuk mandi rendam; *a hot* ~ mandi air panas; *to take a* ~, *have a* ~ mandi; **bathe** *vi* [béth] mandi; *vt* memandikan; membasuh; **bather** *n* [béth] orang yang mandi; **bathrobe** *n* [bathrob] kimono; **bathroom** *n* [bathrum] kamar mandi; *may I use your* ~? boléh saya ke WC?; **baths** *n, pl* permandian umum; **bathtub** *n* bak untuk mandi rendam, badkip

batik *n* batik

baton *n* tongkat kecil

batsman *n* pemukul bola (dalam krikét)

battalion *n* batalyon

batter *n* adonan kué; pemukul bola; *vt* memukul-mukul; ~*ed wife* isteri yang sering dipukuli

battery *n* [bateri] baterai; *alkaline* ~ baterai alkali; *car* ~ aki

battle *n* [batel] pertempuran, peperangan; perjuangan; ~*cry* yél; *in* ~ di médan perang; *vi* bertempur, berjuang; *vt* melawan; **battleground** *n* medan peperangan; **battler** *n* [batler] pejuang, orang kecil; **battleship** *n* kapal perang, kapal tempur

batty *adj, coll* gila, pikun
bauxite *n* [boksait] bauksit
bawl *vi* berteriak; menangis keras-keras
bay *n* teluk; *Jakarta ~* Teluk Jakarta; *~ leaf* daun salam
bayonet *n* [béyonét] sangkur, bayonét; *vt* membayonét
bazaar *n* [bezar] pasar kagét, bazar
BBC *abbrev British Broadcasting Corporation* penyiar nasional Inggris
BC *abbrev before Christ* SM (sebelum Maséhi)
BE *abbrev Bachelor of Economics* SE (Sarjana Ekonomi)
be *v* **was been** *vi* ada; *vt* menjadi, adalah, merupakan (setelah kata kerja bantu); *will you still ~ here tomorrow?* apa kamu masih di sini bésok?; **being** *n* makhluk; keadaan
beach *n* pantai, pesisir; *~ volleyball* bola voli pantai; *vt* mendamparkan diri; **beached** *adj* terdampar
beacon *n* rambu
bead *n* manik-manik; tétésan; **beady** *little ~ eyes* bola mata yang kecil dan bulat
beak *n* paruk; *sl* hidung
beaker *n* gelas kimia
beam *n* sinar (cahaya); *vi* bersinar, tersenyum lébar
beam *n* balok
bean *n* buncis, kacang; *~ curd* tahu; *~ sprouts* taogé; *kidney ~* kacang mérah; *string ~* kacang panjang; *full of ~* sangat énérgik; *spill the ~s* menceritakan semua; **beanbag** *n* sejenis bantal besar
bear *n* [bér] beruang; *~ hug* pelukan kuat; *polar ~* beruang putih
bear *vt* [bér] **bore born** memikul, menahan; bersalin, melahirkan; *~ in mind* mengingat; *I can't ~ it* saya tidak tahan lagi; *please ~ with me* tolong ditunggu sebentar; **bearer** *n* pembawa; **bearing** *n* sikap; arah, tujuan, pengaruh
beard *n* [bird] jénggot; **bearded** *adj* berjénggot
bearer *n* [bérer] pembawa ← **bear**
bearing *n* [béring] sikap; arah, tujuan, pengaruh ← **bear**

beast *n* binatang; orang yang bengis; *~ of burden* héwan pekerja; **beastly** *adj* seperti binatang, bengis
beat *n* pukulan; denyut, irama, ritme; *heart ~* denyut jantung; *vt* **beat beaten** memukul; mengalahkan; *~ it* pergi lu; *~ up* memukuli, menghajar; *it ~s me* tidak masuk akal; **beater** *n* alat pengocok atau pengaduk
beautiful *adj* [byutiful] cantik (perempuan); asri (pemandangan), bagus, indah; **beautifully** *adv* dengan indah, dengan sempurna; **beautify** *vt* [byutifai] mempercantik; **beauty** *n* kecantikan, keindahan; wanita cantik; *~ parlor, ~ parlour arch* salon; *~ queen* ratu kecantikan; *~ spot* tempat yang asri; tahi lalat
beaver *n* sejenis berang-berang
became *vt, pf →* **become**
because *conj* [bikoz] (oléh) karena, sebab; *~ of* karena, lantaran
beckon *vt* memberi isyarat datang kepada orang
become *vt* [bikam] **became become** menjadi; **becoming** *adj* cocok, menarik
B.Ed. *abbrev Bachelor of Education* Sarjana Pendidikan
bed *n* tempat tidur, ranjang; *~ and breakfast (B & B)* losmén; *wet the ~* mengompol; *to go to ~* tidur; *to go to ~ with someone* tidur bersama, bersetubuh; *vt, sl* meniduri, tidur bersama; **bedbug** *n* tungau, kutu busuk; **bedpan** *n* pispot; **bedroom** *n* kamar (tidur); **bedsit, bedsitter** *n, UK* kamar kos; **bedspread, bedcover** *n* selimut; **bedtime** *n* jam tidur
Bedouin *n* [béduin] orang Badui (di Timur Tengah)
bedpan *n* pispot ← **bed**
bedroom *n* kamar (tidur) ← **bed**
bedsit, bedsitter *n, UK* kamar kus ← **bed**
bedspread, bedcover *n* selimut ← **bed**
bedtime *n* jam tidur ← **bed**
bee *n* lebah, tawon, kumbang; *spelling ~* lomba mengéja; **beehive** *n* sarang lebah
beech *n* sejenis pohon

beef *n* daging sapi; **beefcake** *n, coll,* *US* lelaki berotot; **beefy** *adj* gemuk, berotot

beehive *n* sarang lebah ← **bee**

been *vt, pf* → **be**

beep *n* bunyi (peringatan); *vi* berbunyi, mengklakson

beer *n* bir; ~ *garden* tempat terbuka untuk minum bir

beeswax *n* lilin; *mind your own* ~ *sl* bukan urusanmu ← **bee**

beetle *n* kumbang

beetroot *n* bit

before *prep* di muka, depan; sebelum; *adv* sebelumnya, pernah; **beforehand** *adj* terlebih dahulu

befriend *n* berteman dengan

beg *v* meminta-minta, mengemis; *vt* memohon; ~ *the question* patut diper-tanyakan; ~ *your pardon* maaf; *I* ~ *to inform you* dengan hormat saya mem-beritahu Anda; **beggar** *n* pengemis

begin *v* [begin] **began begun** mulai; bermula; *vt* memulai; **beginner** *n* pemula; **beginning** *n* awal, permula-an; *from the* ~ sejak awal; *in the* ~ pada mulanya

behalf *on* ~ *of* atas nama, demi

behave *vi* berkelakuan (baik); ~ *your-self* berkelakuan baik, sopan; **behav-ior, behaviour** *n* perilaku, kelakuan

behead *vt* [bihéd] memenggal, meman-cung (kepala)

behind *n* [behaind] belakang; *sl* pantat; *prep* di belakang, ke belakang; *adv* tertinggal, ketinggalan

beige *adj* [béj] coklat muda

being *n* makhluk; keadaan ← **be**

Belarus *n* Bélarus

belated *adj* [belated] terlambat; *happy* ~ *birthday!* selamat ulang tahun (disampaikan sesudah hari ulang tahunnya)

belch *n* sendawa; *vi* bersendawa

Belgian *n* [béljen] orang Bélgia; *adj* berasal dari Bélgia; **Belgium** *n* [béljum] Bélgia

belief *n* [belif] **beliefs** pendapat, keper-cayaan, iman, agama; *beyond* ~ mus-tahil; **believable** *adj* dapat dipercaya,

masuk akal; **believe** *vi* berpendapat; *vt* percaya; *make* ~ berpura-pura, mem-bayangkan; ~ *it or not* percaya atau tidak; *I don't* ~ *it* saya tidak percaya; **believer** *n* orang yang beriman

belittle *vt* meréméhkan

bell *n* bel, lonceng, genta; *to ring a* ~ membunyikan bél; *saved by the* ~ nyaris tidak selamat

belligerent *adj* [belijerent] galak, suka berkelahi

bellow *vi* berteriak; *vt* meneriakkan

belly *n* (bagian bawah) perut; ~*ache* sakit perut; ~ *button* pusar; ~ *dance* tari perut

belong *vi* (merasa) sebagian dari ling-kungan; ~ *to* milik, termasuk kepunya-an; menjadi anggota di; *Patrick feels he doesn't* ~ *here* Patrick tidak betah di sini; **belonging** *n* rasa betah, rasa diterima; **belongings** *n* barang milik

Belorussia *n, arch* Bélarus; **Belorus-sian** *n* orang Bélarus; *adj* berasal dari Bélarus ← **Belarus**

beloved *n* [belaved] *adj* yang dicintai, yang dikasihi, yang disayangi

below *prep, adv* bawah; *prep* di bawah, ke bawah; ~ *the belt* di luar aturan, curang

belt *n* ikat pinggang, sabuk; *seat* ~ sabuk pengaman; *vt, sl* mencambuk; ~ *up!* diam!; **beltway** *n, US* jalan bébas hambatan

bemused *adj* [bemuzd] bingung

bench *n* bangku, tempat duduk; **benchmark** *n* tolak ukur, standar

bend *n* bélokan; *the* ~*s* kram akibat menyelam; *it's driving me round the* ~ itu membuat saya gila; *v* **bent bent** *vi* membélok, melengkung; *vt* mem-bélokkan, membéngkokkan; ~ *down* bungkukkan badan; ~ *your knees* bengkokkan kaki; **bent** *adj* béngkok, tidak lurus; *sl* homoséksual; *hell-*~ *on* nékat

beneath *prep* di bawah; ~ *your dignity* merendahkan, menghinakan

benediction *n* doa, ucapan syukur

beneficial *adj* [bénefisyel] mengun-tungkan, bermanfaat; **benefit** *n* manfaat, untung; *fin* faédah; ~ *concert* konsér amal; *for the* ~ *of* demi; *vt* menguntungkan

benevolence *n* [benévolens] kemurahan hati, kebaikan, perbuatan baik; **benevolent** *adj* baik

BEng *abbrev Bachelor of Engineering* ST (Sarjana Téknik), Ir (Insinyur)

benign *adj* [benain] baik; ~ *tumor* tumor jinak

bent *v, pf →* **bend**; *adj* béngkok, tidak lurus; *sl* homoséksual; *hell-*~ *on* nékat

bequeath *vt* [bekuith] mewariskan; **bequest** *n* warisan

beret *n* [béré] barét, pici; *the Blue* ~*s (UN peacekeepers)* pasukan Barét Biru

Bermuda *n* (pulau) Bermuda; ~ *shorts* sejenis celana péndék

berry *n* béri, buah kecil; *rasp*~ frambozen; *straw*~ strobéri

berth *n* kamar, bilik kapal; tempat tidur

beside *prep* di sisi, di dekat; kecuali, di luar, selain dari; *he was* ~ *himself* dia sudah tidak waras lagi; **besides** *adv* lagipula, ditambah lagi

besiege *vt* [besij] mengepung

best *adj* paling bagus, paling baik, terbaik; ~*seller* laris terjual; ~ *man* pendamping pengantin pria; *all the* ~ suksés ya; *the* ~ *part of* bagian terbesar; *to give it your* ~ *shot* berusaha sebisa-bisanya; *it's (all) for the* ~ lebih baik begitu

bestial *adj* seperti binatang, héwani

bestow *vt* menganugerahi; ~ *upon (someone)* menganugerahi

bet *n* taruhan; *a safe* ~ kemungkinan besar; *v* **bet bet** *vi* bertaruh; *vt* mempertaruhkan; *I* ~ *my bottom dollar* saya yakin

betel *n* [bitel] sirih

betray *vt* mengkhianati; **betrayal** *n* pengkhianatan

betrothed *n* tunangan; *adj* bertunangan

better *adj* lebih baik → **good**; sembuh; ~ *not* lebih baik jangan; *get* ~ pulih; membaik; *your* ~*s* orang di atas, orang tua; *vt* memperbaiki, mengungguli

between *prep* (di) antara, di tengah; ~ *girlfriends* sedang sendiri, tanpa pacar

beverage *n* [béverej] minuman (terutama yang panas)

beware *adj* [bewér] awas, berhati-hati; ~ *of the dog* awas anjing

bewilder *vt* membingungkan; **bewildered** *adj* bingung; **bewildering** *adj* membingungkan; **bewilderment** *n* kebingungan

bewitched *adj* tersihir

beyond *prep* (di) sebelah, lebih (jauh), melampaui, melebihi; ~ *belief* tidak masuk akal, mustahil; ~ *repair* tidak dapat diperbaiki lagi

BH *abbrev business hours* k, ktr (kantor)

Bhutan *n* Bhutan; **Bhutanese** *adj* berasal dari Bhutan

bias *n* [bayas] kecenderungan; **biased** *adj* tidak berimbang

biathlon *n* [bayathlon] dwilomba juang

bib *n* oto, kain alas dada, slaber

Bible *n* [baibel] Alkitab; ~*basher n, coll* orang Kristen yang fanatik; **biblical** *adj* [biblikal] berasal dari Alkitab

bibliography *n* [bibliografi] daftar pustaka

bicycle *n* [baisikel] **bike** *coll* sepéda; ~ *lane,* ~ *path* jalur sepéda; *vi, arch* bersepéda

bid *n* tawaran, usaha; *v* **bid bidden** menawar; ~ *for* mengajukan tawaran untuk; **bidder** *n* orang yang menawar; **bidding** *n* penawaran

bide ~ *your time* menanti, menunggu

biennial *n* [bayénial] acara dua tahun sekali; *adj* terjadi dua tahun sekali

bifocal *n* [baifokal] kacamata bifokal

big *adj* besar, gemuk; raksasa; ~*headed* sombong, égois; ~ *brother* abang, kakak (laki-laki); ~ *shot* tokoh penting, orang besar; ~ *toe* jempol kaki; *think* ~ berpikir pada skala besar; *the* ~ *Apple* New York; ~ *Brother is watching* pemerintah atau dinas rahasia sedang mengintai

bigamist *n* [bigamist] orang dengan lebih dari satu suami atau isteri; **bigamy** *n* hal beristeri atau bersuami dua

bight *n* [bait] teluk

bigwig *n, sl* pejabat tinggi, pentolan

bike *n* sepéda (motor); *vi* naik sepéda;

trail ~ sepéda motor gunung; **biker** *n* penggemar sepéda motor

bikini *n* bikini; *to wear a* ~ berbikini

bilateral *adj* [bailateral] bilateral, dua belah pihak

bile *n* empedu

bilingual *adj* [bailingguel] dwibahasa; **bilingualism** *n* kedwibahasaan, berbahasa lebih dari satu

bill *n* bon, rékéning, nota, surat tagihan; wésel, daftar; uang kertas; rancangan undang-undang (RUU); paruh (pada burung); ~ *of lading* surat angkutan; *vt* menagih; **billboard** *n* baliho

billet *n* penginapan; *to be* ~*ed* dikirim ke penginapan yang berbeda-beda

billiards *n, pl* bilyar; *to play* ~ main bilyar

billion *n* satu milyar (1.000.000.000); **billionaire** *n* milyarder

billy *n, Aus* kaléng yang bisa dipakai untuk memasak di tempat perkémahan

bimbo *n, coll* céwék yang mengutamakan penampilan

bimonthly *adj* [baimanthli] sebulan dua kali

bin *n* tempat sampah, tong; *dust*~, *rubbish* ~ tempat sampah; *vt* membuang

bind *n* [baind] *in a* ~ terkekang; *vt* **bound bound** mengikat, menghubungkan; mewajibkan; *the law is* ~*ing* terikat hukum

bind *vt* [baind] menjilid; **binder** *n* map; **binding** *n* penjilidan

binge *vi, n* [binj] makan atau minum secara berlebihan

bingo *n* [binggo] permainan bingo

binoculars *n, pl* teropong, binokular

biodegradable *adj* [bayodegrédabel] ramah lingkungan

biographer *n* [bayografer] penulis biografi; **biographical** *adj* terkait dengan pengalaman sendiri; **biography** *n* biografi, riwayat hidup

biologist *n* [bayalojist] ahli biologi; **biology** *n* ilmu biologi

biplane *n* [baiplén] pesawat terbang bersayap dua lapis

birch *n* sejenis pohon di Eropa Utara

bird *n* burung; ~ *brain* bodoh; ~ *cage* sangkar burung; ~ *flu* flu burung; ~*'s eye view* pandangan dari atas; ~ *of paradise* burung cenderawasih; *a little* ~ *told me* kabar burung; **birdseed** *n* biji-bijian pakan burung; **birdwatching** *n* mengamati perilaku burung

birth *n* kelahiran; ~ *certificate* akte kelahiran; ~ *control* kontrasépsi, KB (keluarga berencana); ~ *extract* surat (kenal) lahir; ~ *mother* ibu kandung; *home* ~ melahirkan di rumah; *date of* ~ tanggal lahir; *to give* ~ bersalin, melahirkan; **birthday** *n* hari ulang tahun; ~ *cake* kué tar, kué ulang tahun; ~ *party* pésta ulang tahun; **birthmark** *n* tahi lalat; **birthplace** *n* tempat lahir

biscuit *n* [bisket] biskuit, kue kering

bisexual *adj* [baiséksyual] biséks

bishop *n* uskup; menteri (catur)

bison *n, US* sejenis banténg atau kerbau

bistro *n* réstoran

bit *n* sedikit, sepotong; ~ *by* ~ sedikit demi sedikit; *not a* ~ sedikit pun tidak, sama sekali tidak; *vt, pf* → **bite**

bitch *n* anjing betina; perempuan jelék; *vi, sl* mengeluh, mengadu; **bitchy** *adj* suka mengatai orang lain

bite *n* gigitan; *to have a* ~ *(to eat)* makan (sedikit); *vt* **bit bitten** menggigit; ~ *the bullet* menerima kenyataan

bitter *adj* pahit; ~ *gourd* paré, paria; **bitterness** *n* kepahitan, rasa pahit; **bittersweet** *adj* manis tercampur pahit

bitumen *n* aspal, tér

bizarre *adj* [bizar] luar biasa anéh

blab *vt* membocorkan rahasia; **blabber** *vi* berbicara tanpa berpikir lebih dahulu; **blabbermouth** *n* orang yang membocorkan rahasia

black *adj* hitam, gelap; ~ *belt* sabuk hitam; ~ *box* kotak hitam; ~ *eye* mata bengkak (karena bekas pukulan); ~ *market* pasar gelap, tidak resmi; *he's* ~ dia berkulit hitam; ~ *and blue* biru lebam; ~ *and white* hitam putih; *in* ~ *and white* di atas kertas, hitam di atas putih; *in the* ~ sedang menguntungkan; *vi* ~ *out* pingsan; **blackboard** *n* papan tulis; **blacken** *vt* menghitamkan; **blackhead** *adj* [blak héd] komé-

do; **blackish** *adj* kehitam-hitaman;
blacklist *n* daftar hitam; *vt* melarang
orang tertentu; **blackmail** *n* pemerasan; **blackout** *n* mati lampu; **blacksmith** *n* pandai besi; *vt* memeras
bladder *n* kandung kemih; ~ *infection*
inféksi saluran kemih
blade *n* mata pisau; *a* ~ *of grass* sebilah
rumput
blah blah blah omong kosong
blame *n* kesalahan; *vt* menyalahkan,
menyalahi (orang); *nobody's to* ~ tidak
ada yang bersalah; **blameless** *adj*
tidak tercela, sempurna
bland *adj* tawar, tanpa rasa
blank *n* tempat kosong; peluru kosong;
~ *check,* ~ *cheque* cék kosong; *mental*
~ tiba-tiba lupa; *adj* kosong, hampa
blanket *n* selimut; *vt* menyelimuti
blaspheme *vi* [blasfim] menggunakan
kata yang menghina Tuhan atau agama,
memaki, mengumpat; **blasphemous**
adj [blasfemus] yang menghina
Tuhan; **blasphemy** *n* penghinaan terhadap Tuhan, cacian, makian
blast *n* angin kencang, letupan, tiupan;
~*off* peluncuran rokét; *sl it was a* ~
sangat asyik; *ejac* keparat
blatant *adj* terang-terangan; **blatantly**
adv secara terang-terangan
blaze *n* kebakaran; *vi* menyala; ~ *away*
membabi buta; **blazing** *adj* menyala
blazer *n* jas (setengah resmi)
bleach *n* pemutih; *vt* memutihkan
(baju); ~ *one's hair* mengecat rambut
pirang
bleak *adj* [blik] suram, gelap; **bleakly**
adv tanpa harapan
bleat *n* embikan; *vi* mengembik; mengeluh (soal kecil)
bleed *nose*~ mimisan; *v* **bled bled**
berdarah; luntur (tinta pada kertas);
bleeding *adj* berdarah; *sl* sialan
blemish *n* [blémisy] noda, cacat
blend *n* campuran; *vi* berbaur; ~ *in*
berbaur, tidak menonjol; ~ *with*
bercampur dengan, mencampurkan; *vt*
mencampur; **blender** *n* blénder
bless *vt* memberkati; ~ *you Isl* alhamdulillah (sesudah bersin); *God* ~ *you*

Chr Tuhan memberkati; **blessed** *adj*
yang diberkati, dikaruniai; *sl* gila;
blessing *n* pemberkatan; doa restu; *a*
~ *in disguise* ada hikmahnya
blew *v, pf* → **blow**
blind *n* [blaind] hordén, penutup
jendéla, kerai; *vt* menyilaukan,
membutakan; ~*ed* silau; *adj* buta; ~
date kencan buta; ~ *in one eye* buta
sebelah mata; **blindfold** *n* kain
penutup mata; *vt* menutup mata
dengan kain; **blindly** *adv* membabi
buta, tanpa melihat atau berpikir;
blindness *n* kebutaan
blink *n* kedipan mata, kejapan mata; *in
the* ~ *of an eye* sekedip mata, sekejap;
vi mengedip, mengejapkan mata;
blinking *adj* berkedip-kedip; *sl* gila
bliss *n* kebahagiaan; *wedded* ~ perkawinan yang membahagiakan; **blissful**
adj bahagia, berbahagia
blister *n* lécét, lepuh; *vi* menjadi lécét,
melepuhkan
blitz *n* serangan kilat; *The* ~ serangan
udara terhadap kota London oléh
angkatan udara Jérman pada tahun
1940
blizzard *n* badai salju
bloat *vi* membengkak, mengembung;
~*ed* bengkak, kembung
blob *n* gumpal, bongkah; *a* ~ *of glue*
sebongkah lém
bloc *n* blok (negara); *the Eastern* ~ blok
Timur
block *n* balok; blok; ~ *letters* huruf
besar; *vt* merintangi, membatasi,
menghambati; **blocked** *adj* tersumbat,
mampet; **blockade** *n* [blokéd]
blokade, pemblokiran; *vt* memblokir;
blockage *n* [blokej] keadaan tersumbat; **blockbuster** *n, adj* (buku atau
film yang) laku keras; **blockhead** *n*
[blok héd] orang bodoh
blog *n* situs pribadi, buku harian di
internet; *vi* menulis di situs pribadi;
blogger *n* orang yang menulis di situs
pribadi
bloke *n, coll, UK* lelaki
blond *adj, m* **blonde** *f* [blond] (berambut)
pirang

blood *n* [blad] darah; ~ *count* trombosit; ~ *group* golongan darah; ~ *nose* mimisan; ~ *pressure* tekanan darah, ténsi; ~ *relation* saudara kandung, hubungan darah; ~ *sport* kegiatan rékréasi yang membunuh héwan; ~ *test* tés darah, periksa darah; ~ *vessel* pembuluh darah; *bad* ~ rasa benci; *flesh and* ~ darah daging; **bloodstain** *n* bekas darah; **bloodthirsty** *adj* ganas, haus darah; **bloody** *adj* berdarah; *sl* gila, persétan; ~ *hell* persétan

bloom *vi* mekar, berbunga; *in* ~ sedang mekar atau berbunga

blossom *n* bunga; *cherry* ~ sakura; *vi* berbunga, berkembang

blot *n* noda (tinta); *vt* menodai, mencemari; *~ting paper* kertas isap

blouse *n* [blauz] blus

blow *n* pukulan, tamparan; tiupan; *v* **blew blown** *vi* bertiup; *vt* meniup; *~dry vt* mengeringkan rambut dengan pengering rambut; *~dryer n* pengering rambut; ~ *up vi* meledak, meletus; *vt* meniup; ~ *your nose* membuang ingus, bersin; ~ *out a candle* tiup lilin; **blowpipe** *n* sumpitan

blubber *n* lapisan lemak (ikan paus); *vi* menangis dengan keras

bludge *vi, sl* tidak bekerja, bermalas-malas; **bludger** *n* pemalas; *dole-~* orang yang hidup dari tunjangan tunakarya

blue *adj* [blu] biru; *~collar* pekerja berpenghasilan rendah; ~ *blood* bangsawan, darah biru; ~ *film* film porno; *~print* cétakan biru; ~ *ribbon* mutu tertinggi; hadiah pertama; *black and* ~ biru lebam; *to feel* ~ bersedih; *once in a* ~ *moon* jarang sekali; *out of the* ~ tiba-tiba; **bluish** *adj* kebiru-biruan

bluff *n* pura-pura; jurang tebing; *v* berpura-pura, berlagak

blunder *n* [blander] kesalahan besar; *vi* berbuat salah

blunt *adj* tumpul; terus terang, ceplas-ceplos; **bluntly** *adv* secara terus terang

blur *n* kabur; *vi* kabur; *vt* mengaburkan; **blurred, blurry** *adj* kabur, kurang jelas

blurb *n* paragraf mengenai isi buku di sampul belakang

blush *vi* memerah (muka); **blusher** *n* pemérah pipi, perona pipi

bluster *n* omong banyak, bicara dengan keras; *vi* omong banyak

Blvd *abbrev Boulevard* Bulevar, Adimarga, Jalan

BM *abbrev Bachelor of Medicine* SK (Sarjana Kedokteran)

BO *abbrev body odor, body odour* bau badan

boa *n* ~ *constrictor* ular besar di Amérika Selatan

boar *n, m* babi jantan

board *n* papan; karton, kardus; ~ *game* mainan (di atas papan); **boardwalk** *n, US* anjungan di pinggir pantai

board *vt* menaiki; *on* ~ di kapal, di pesawat; bersama; **boarding** naik pesawat; ~ *pass n* pas naik pesawat

board *vi* mondok, kos; ~ *and lodging* kos (termasuk makanan); **boarder** *n* anak kos; **boarding** ~ *house* rumah kos, asrama (sekolah); ~ *kennels* tempat penitipan anjing; ~ *school* sekolah dengan asrama

board *n* déwan; ~ *of governors* déwan pengurus; **boardroom** *n* ruang rapat (untuk déwan pengurus)

boardwalk *n, US* [bordwok] anjungan di pinggir pantai ← **board**

boast *n* bualan; *vi* membual, menyombongkan diri; ~ *that* menyombongkan diri soal; ~ *about his new car* menyebut-nyebut mobil barunya; *vt* membanggakan; **boastful** *adj* sombong, sok hébat

boat *n* kapal, perahu; ~ *people* orang perahu, pengungsi yang datang naik perahu (biasanya orang Viétnam); *all in the same* ~ dalam keadaan yang sama; **boating** *n* rékréasi naik kapal kecil

bob *n* potongan rambut péndék untuk wanita; *vi* membungkuk; turun naik, terapung-apung

bobbin *n* bobin, kumparan, gulungan

bobby *n, sl* Ing polisi; *~socks adj* kaus kaki péndék yang berwarna menyolok

bobsled *n* keréta luncur

bodice *n* [bodis] korsét

body *n* badan, tubuh; jenazah, mayat;

organisasi, himpunan; karoséri (mobil); ~ *language* gerak-gerik; ~ *odor*, ~ *odour (BO)* bau badan; *dead* ~ mayat; ~ *and soul* jiwa raga; **body-builder** *n* binaragawan; **bodybuilding** *n* binaraga; **bodyguard** *n* pengawal pribadi; **bodysurfing** *n* berselancar tanpa papan

Boer *n, arch* [bur] orang keturunan Belanda di Afrika Selatan, orang Afrikaner; ~ *War* Perang Boer

bog *n* rawa, payau; *vi* terhenti (kendaraan)

bohemian *adj* [bohimian] gaya bébas, seperti seniman

boil *n* bisul

boil *vi* mendidih; *vt* merebus; *on the* ~ sedang memanas; **boiled** *adj* rebus; ~ *lolly Aus* ~ *sweet UK* permén; **boiler** *n* kétel (kukus); *old* ~ *sl* perempuan tua yang jelék; **boiling** *adj* mendidih; ~ *hot* sangat panas; ~ *point* titik didih

boisterous *adj* ribut, ramai, riuh

bold *adj* berani; ~ *type* huruf tebal

Bolivia *n* Bolivia; **Bolivian** *n* orang Bolivia; *adj* berasal dari Bolivia

bolster *n* guling, bantal

bolt *n* baut, selot; ~ *of lightning* halilin-tar, petir; *vi* kabur; *vt* mengunci

bomb *n* [bom] bom; ~ *squad* pasukan gegana; *vt* mengebom; **bomber** *n* pesawat pengebom; **bombing** *n* pengeboman

bombard *v* [bombard] mengebom; **bom-bardment** *n* pemboman, pengeboman

bombing *n* pengeboman ← **bomb**

bonanza *n* sumber keberuntungan

bond *n* pengikat; ikatan; kewajiban; obligasi; *vi* menjadi akrab, bersatu

bone *n* tulang; gading; ~ *dry* kering kerontang; *jaw*~ tulang rahang; *skin and* ~ tulang belulang; *adj* gading; **bony** *adj* kurus sekali (sehingga tulang kelihatan)

bonfire *n* api unggun

bonk *v, coll, vi* berhubungan séks; *vt* melakukan hubungan séks dengan

bonnet *n* topi (untuk bayi atau perempuan)

bonus *n, adj* tambahan, bonus

bony *adj* kurus sekali (sehingga tulang kelihatan)

boob *n, sl* susu, téték

book *n* buku, kitab, novel; *vt* memesan; ~~*binding* penjilidan buku; ~*case*, ~ *shelf* rak buku, lemari buku; **booking** *n* pemesanan, buking; *to make a* ~ membuking, membuat buking; **book-keeper** *n* akuntan; **book-keeping** *n* pembukuan; **booklet** buku kecil, buklet; **bookmaker** *n* **bookie** *coll* bandar taruhan; **bookmark** *n* pembatas buku; **bookseller** penjual buku, toko buku; **bookshop** *n* toko buku; **book-worm** *n* [bukwerm] kutu buku

boom *n* ledakan; masa kejayaan ékonomi; *vi* meledak; *ejac* dor!; **booming** *adj* laris

boomerang *n* bumerang

boost *n* dorongan, kemajuan; *vt* menaikkan; **booster** *n* tambahan

boot *n* sepatu (bot), sepatu lars; ~ *camp* latihan militer; *football* ~s sepatu sépak bola; *vt* menghidupkan (komputer); *re*~ menghidupkan (komputer) kembali; ~ *out* mendepak, mengusir; ~ *polish* semir sepatu; **bootlace** *n* tali sepatu (bot)

booth *n* loket, gerai

bootie, bootee *n* kaus kaki atau sepatu bayi

bootlace *n* tali sepatu (bot) ← **boot**

bootleg *adj* bajakan; *vt* membajak, merekam secara ilégal

booty *n* (hasil) rampasan

booze *sl, n* minuman keras; *vi* banyak minum alkohol; **boozer** *n* peminum berat

border *n* tepi, sisi, pinggir; perbatasan, tapal batas; *vt* berbatasan dengan; **bor-derline** *n* batas; *adj* hampir, nyaris

bore *n* orang atau kegiatan yang mem-bosankan; *vt* membosankan, menje-mukan; **boredom** *n* kebosanan, kejenuhan, rasa bosan atau jenuh; **bor-ing** *adj* membosankan, menjemukan

bore *vt* mengebor

bore *vt, pf* → **bear**; **born** *vt, pf* dilahirkan, lahir, terlahir → **bear**; **borne** *vt, pf* [born] → **bear**

borrow *vt* pinjam, meminjam; **borrower** *n* orang yang meminjam

Bosnia *n* Bosnia (dan Herzegovina);

Bosnian, Bosniak *n* orang Bosnia; *adj* berasal dari Bosnia

boss *n* pemimpin, bos; *vt* menyuruh-nyuruh; **bossy** *adj* suka menyuruh

botanic, botanical *adj* [botanik] ~ *gardens* kebun raya; **botanist** *n* ahli tumbuh-tumbuhan, ahli botani; **botany** *n* ahli tumbuh-tumbuhan

both *adj* kedua, kedua(-kedua)nya; *both … and …* baik … maupun …

bother *n* repot, kesusahan; *vi don't* ~ tidak usah; *vt* merepotkan, menyusahkan; mengganggu; *ejac* sialan!; *I can't be* ~*ed* malas

Botswana *n* Botswana; **Botswanan** *n* orang Botswana; *adj* berasal dari Botswana

bottle *n* botol; ~*opener* pembuka botol, kotrék; ~ *green* hijau tua; *to lose your* ~ tiba-tiba kehilangan keberanian; *vt* membotolkan; **bottleneck** *n* léhér botol; jalan yang menyempit sehingga menjadi macet

bottom *n* bawah, pantat, alas; *adj* bawah; *at the* ~ *of* di bawahnya, di tempat (paling) bawah; **bottomless** *adj* tidak berdasar, dalam sekali

bougainvillea *n* [bogénvilia] bugénvil

bough [bau] cabang (pohon)

bought *vt, pf* [bot] → **buy**

boulder *n* [bolder] batu besar

bounce *n* lambungan; semangat; *vi* melambung, memantul; *vt* melambungkan; *the check* ~*d* cék pembayaran tidak diterima oleh bank; **bouncy** *adj* bersifat melambung

bound *vi* melompat, berlari-lari; ~ *for* menuju; *vt, pf* → **bind**

boundary *n* (tapal) batas; **boundless** *adj* tanpa batas; **bounds** *n, pl* batasan; *out of* ~ di luar daérah yang diizinkan

bounty *n* hadiah uang; ~ *hunter* pemburu buronan demi hadiah

bouquet *n* [buké] karangan bunga, buket

bourgeois *adj* [burjua] borjuis

boutique *n* butik

bow [bau] *n* tundukan; haluan; *to take a* ~ membungkukkan badan (sebagai tanda terima kasih); *vi* membungkukkan badan, menunduk; ~ *to* menyerah

kepada; membungkukkan badan kepada; ~ *one's head* menundukkan kepala

bow [bo] *n* busur; penggésék (alat musik); **bow-legged** *adj* [boléged] kaki O

bow [bo] *n* ikatan simpul; ~ *tie* dasi kupu-kupu

bowel *n* [baul] usus; ~ *cancer* kanker usus besar; *small* ~ usus kecil; *to move your* ~*s* membuang air besar

bowl *n* [bol] mangkuk, pinggan; lémparan (bola)

bowl *vi* [bol] melémpar bola; *vt* melémpar; **bowler** *n* pelémpar; **bowling** *n* boling; **bowls** *n* boling (di rumput)

box *n* kotak, dus, peti; ~*office* lokét karcis di téater atau bioskop

box *vi* bertinju; *vt* meninju; ~ *someone's ears* menempéléng orang; **boxer** *n* petinju; ~ *shorts* celana kolor; **boxing** *n* tinju; ~ *Day* tanggal 26 Desember

boy *n* anak lelaki; ~ *band* grup band pria; ~ *scout* pramuka, pandu, penggalang

boycott *n* boikot; *vt* memboikot

boyfriend *n, m* [boifrénd] pacar ← **boy**

boyhood *n, m* masa kanak-kanak ← **boy**

boyish *adj* seperti anak lelaki ← **boy**

bra *n* béha, kutang; *strapless* ~ béha tanpa tali ← **brassiere**

brace *n* penahan; ~ *yourself* mempersiapkan diri; *pl* kawat gigi, béhél

bracelet *n* [bréslét] gelang tangan (berantai)

bracken *n* tumbuhan paku

bracket *n* penyangga; *pl* tanda kurung (); *curly* ~ tanda kurawal {}; *square* ~ tanda kurung besar []

brackish *adj* payau, masin (air)

brag *vi* membual, menyombong

braid *n* képang

brain *n* otak, benak; *sl* orang yang pinter; ~ *damage* kerusakan pada otak; ~ *drain* kuras otak; *pl* akal séhat; otak (makanan); **brainless** *adj* bodoh, tidak berotak; **brainpower** *n* daya pikir; **brainwash** *vt* mencuci otak; **brainwave** *n* idé gemilang; **brainy** *adj* pandai, pintar

brake *n* rém; *emergency* ~ rém darurat; *hand*~ rém tangan; *the* ~*s failed* rémnya blong; *vi* mengerém bran *n* sejenis sereal, kulit gandum

branch *n* cabang; bagian; ~ *office* kantor cabang; *vi* bercabang; ~ *out* memulai usaha baru

brand *n* cap, mérek; *v* mengecap; ~-*new* sama sekali baru; **branded** *adj* bermérek

brandy *n* bréndi; ~ *snap* semacam kué semprong

brass *n* kuningan; ~ *band* band yang memainkan alat-alat tiup kuningan; **brassy** *adj, sl* menyolok, norak

brassiere *n, form* [brasir] béha → **bra**

brat *n* anak nakal, anak manja

brave *adj* berani; **bravely** *adv* dengan berani; **bravery** *n* keberanian

brawl *n* tawuran, pertikaian; *vi* tinju, bergumul

brawn *n* kekuatan; *more* ~ *than brain* lebih banyak otot daripada otak; **brawny** *adj* berotot, tegap

bray *vi* meringkik (binatang)

brazen *adj* terang-terangan

Brazil *n* Brasil; ~ *nut* kacang Brazil; **Brazilian** *n* orang Brasil; *adj* berasal dari Brasil; ~ *wax* pencabutan bulu kemaluan dengan lilin

breach *vt* [bric] melanggar, meléwati batas; *in the* ~ kekecualian

bread *n* [bréd] roti; ~ *bin*, ~ *box* tempat roti; ~ *crumbs* remah-remah roti; *short*~ semacam biskuit; *brown* ~, *wholemeal* ~ roti gandum; ~ *and butter* roti dengan lapisan mentéga; **bread-winner** *n* pencari nafkah

breadth *n* [brédth] lebar

breadwinner *n* [brédwiner] pencari nafkah

break *n* [brék] istirahat, réhat, jeda; patah, putus; *vi* **broke broken** rusak, putus, pecah, patah; *vt* memecahkan, mematahkan; ~ *down vi* gagal, rusak, mogok (kendaraan); *vt* memecahkan menjadi lebih kecil; ~ *in*, ~ *into*, ~ *and enter* memasuki dengan maksud mencuri; ~ *off* mematahkan; memutuskan (hubungan); ~ *up* putus; memulai liburan sekolah; ~ *a promise* ingkar janji; ~ *a record* memecahkan rékor, membuat rékor baru; ~ *an arm* tangan patah; **breakdown** *n* perincian; kega-galan, kerusakan; *nervous* ~ gangguan mental; **breaker** *n* ombak besar; **breakfast** [brékfast] *n, vi* sarapan, makan pagi; **breakthrough** *n* [brék-thru] terobosan; **breakwater** *n* [brék-woter] témbok laut

breast *n* [brést] dada, payudara; *sl* susu, téték; ~ *cancer* kanker payudara; ~ *milk* ASI (air susu ibu); *chicken* ~ ayam dada; **breastfeed** *vt* menyusui; **breaststroke** *n* gaya dada

breath *n* [bréth] nafas, napas; *out of* ~ kehabisan nafas; *short of* ~ sesak nafas; **breathe** *v* [brith] bernafas; ~ *in* menarik nafas; ~ *out* menghembus nafas; **breather** *n* waktu istirahat; **breathless** *adj* [bréthles] tanpa bernafas; **breath-taking** *adj* menakjubkan

breech ~ *birth* kelahiran sungsang; **breeches** *n, pl* celana péndék

breed *n* ras; *v* **bred bred** *vi* berkem-bangbiak; *vt* mengembangbiakkan; mendidik; **breeder** *n* peternak; **breeding** *n* trah, nénék moyang; sopan santun

breeze *n* angin sepoi-sepoi; *vi* ~ *through* melakukan dengan enteng

brethren *n, pl, arch* saudara-saudara ← **brother**

brevity *n* [bréviti] keringkasan; ~ *is the soul of wit* semakin singkat, semakin lucu

brew *n* [bru] minuman panas; *vi a storm is* ~*ing* badai sudah dekat; *vt* membuat minuman (terutama bir); **brewer** *n* [bruer] orang atau perusahaan yang membuat bir; **brewery** *n* [brueri] tempat pembuatan bir

bribe *n* uang sogok, uang suap; *vt* menyogok, menyuap; **bribery** *n* sua-pan, sogokan; ~ *and corruption* KKN (korupsi, kolusi, népotisme)

bric-a-brac *n* loak, pecah-belah

brick *n* batu bata; ~ *kiln* oven pembakar-an keramik; ~ *up* menémbok, meném-boki; **bricklayer** *n* tukang batu

bridal *adj* berkaitan dengan acara pernikahan; **bride** *n* pengantin wanita, mempelai wanita; **bridegroom** *n* pengantin pria; **bridesmaid** *n, f* pengiring pengantin wanita

bridge *n* jembatan; *foot~* jembatan kaki;
  suspension ~ jembatan gantung; *vt*
  menjembatani, mempertemukan
bridge *n* sejenis permainan kartu
bridle *n* [braidel] tali kekang, kendali;
  vt mengekang, mengendalikan;
  membrédel
brief *adj* pendek, ringkas, singkat; *in* ~
  secara singkat, secara ringkas; *vt*
  memberi informasi kepada orang
  secara singkat; *n* celana dalam; **briefcase** *n* tas kerja; **briefing** *n* rapat
  péndék, penyebaran informasi; **briefly**
  adv secara singkat, secara ringkas
brigade *n* [brigéd] regu, pasukan; *fire* ~
  pasukan pemadam kebakaran;
  brigadier *n* brigjén (brigadir-jénderal)
bright *n* [brait] terang, gemilang; cerdik, cemerlang, pandai; *~ly* dengan
  gembira; **brighten** *vi* menjadi terang;
  vt menerangkan; menggembirakan;
  brightly *adv* (secara) terang; **bright-
  ness** *n* kecerahan
brilliant *adj* gemilang, berseri
brim *n* tepi, pinggir (topi); *to the* ~
  hampir penuh
bring *vt* **brought brought** [brot] membawa; ~ *about* menghasilkan, mengakibatkan; ~ *along* membawa serta; ~
  forward memajukan, mempercepat; ~
  on menyebabkan, mendatangkan; ~ *up*
  membesarkan (anak); memuntahkan
  (makanan)
brink *n* sisi, tepi, pinggir
brisk *adj* cepat; segar, dingin
Britain *n* [Briten] Britania *coll* Inggris;
  Great ~ Inggris Raya; **British** *adj*
  orang berkewarganegaraan Inggris/
  Britania; *the* ~ bangsa Inggris; **Briton**
  n [Briton] orang yang berasal dari
  Inggris, Wales, Skotlandia atau
  Irlandia Utara
brittle *adj* rapuh
broad *adj* lébar, luas; *~-minded*
  berwawasan luas; *in* ~ daylight siang
  bolong; **broadband** *n* jalur lébar;
  broadcast *n* siaran; *delayed* ~ siaran
  tunda; *live* ~ siaran langsung; *vi*
  broadcast broadcast bersiaran; *vt*
  menyiarkan; **broadcaster** *n* (stasiun)

penyiar; **broadcasting** *n* penyiaran;
  broaden *vi* melébar, meluas; *vt*
  melébarkan, meluaskan
brocade *n* [brokéd] kain brokat
broccoli *n* brokoli
brochure *n* [brosyur] brosur
broil *v* memanggang
broke *v, pf* → **break**; *adj* rusak; tidak
  mempunyai uang, *sl* bokék; **broken**
  v, pf → **break**; *adj* rusak
broker *n* makelar, calo, perantara,
  pialang
bronchitis *n* [bronkaitis] bronkitis,
  radang cabang tenggorokan
bronze *n* perunggu; *~d* berkulit warna
  perunggu atau gelap
brooch *n* [broc] bros
brood *n* anak-anak; *vi* merenung;
  mengeram; *vt* merenungkan; **brooding**
  adj banyak merenung, cepat marah
brook *n* kali, anak sungai
broom *n* sapu
Bros *abbrev* *brothers* bersaudara
broth *n* kaldu
brothel *n* tempat pelacuran, bordil
brother *n, m* [brather] abang, kakak
  atau adik lelaki; saudara; *~-in-law*
  (adik atau kakak) ipar; **brotherhood** *n*
  persaudaraan
brought *v, pf* [brot] → **bring**
brow *n* [brau] kening, dahi; *eye~* alis
brown *adj* [braun] (warna) coklat; *~-
  skinned* berkulit sawo matang; **brownish** *adj* kecoklat-coklatan
brownies *n, pl* [brauniz] kué coklat;
  Brownies kegiatan kepanduan untuk
  anak perempuan
brownish *adj* kecoklat-coklatan ←
  brown
browse *vi* melihat-lihat (buku); *vt*
  mencari-cari informasi (di internét);
  browser *n* mesin pencari (di internét)
bruise *n* [bruz] memar; *vi* memar; *vt*
  memukul sehingga timbul memar;
  bruised *adj* memar, bengkak
brunch *n* makan pada siang hari,
  sesudah sarapan tapi sebelum makan
  siang ← **breakfast** + **lunch**
Brunei *n* Brunéi; **Bruneian** *n* orang
  Brunéi; *adj* berasal dari Brunéi

brunette *n, f* [brunét] wanita yang berambut coklat

brush *n* sikat, kuas (alat seni); *vi* bergéséran, serémpét; *vt* menyikat; ~ *one's hair* sikat rambut; ~ *one's teeth* sikat gigi, gosok gigi

Brussels *n* [Brasels] Brussel; ~ *sprouts* kubis Brussel

brutal *adj* brutal, bengis, kasar, kejam; **brutality** *n* kebrutalan, kebengisan, kekasaran; **brutally** *adv* dengan kasar, secara brutal; **brute** *n* orang yang brutal atau kasar; **brutish** *adj* seperti orang kasar

BSc *abbrev Bachelor of Science* SSi (Sarjana Sains)

BSE *abbrev bovine spongiform encephalopathy* penyakit sapi gila

BTW *abbrev by the way* ngomong-ngomong

bubble *n* gelembung; ~ *bath* busa mandi; ~ *gum* permén karét; *vi* membual; menggelembung; **bubbly** *adj* bersoda; ceria

buck *n* rusa jantan; *sl* dolar; *to pass the* ~ mengélakkan tanggung jawab

bucket *n* émbér; ~ *down* hujan deras

buckle *n* [bakel] gésper; *vi* ~ *down* bekerja keras; ~ *up* pasang sabuk pengaman

bud *n* kuntum; *vi* berkuntum, bersemi; **budding** *adj* calon, yang diharapkan

Buddha *n* [buda] Budha; **Buddhism** *n* [budizem] agama Budha; **Buddhist** *n* orang Budha; *adj* berkaitan dengan agama Budha

buddy *n, coll* teman, sahabat

budge *vi* bergerak sedikit

budgerigar, budgie *n* [bajerigar] sejenis burung bayan kecil

budget *n* [bajét] anggaran; *vt* menganggarkan; *adj* murah; ~ *airline* pesawat murah

budgie → **budgerigar**

buff *n* penggemar; *film* ~ penggemar film; *in the* ~ telanjang

buffalo *n* kerbau

buffer *n* penyangga; ~ *zone* daérah penyangga

buffet *n* [bafé] bufét, prasmanan; ~ *car* gerbong réstorasi

bug *n* serangga, kumbang, kutu; *coll* penyakit menular; *vt* mengganggu; menyadap

bugger *n* orang yang berhubungan badan dengan binatang; *ejac* sialan; ~ *off* pergi!

buggy *n* keréta atau kendaraan kecil

build *vt* [bild] **built built** mendirikan, membangun, membina; ~ *up vi* bertambah; *vt* membina; **builder** *n* pemborong; **building** *n* gedung, bangunan; ~ *site* proyék

bulb *n* lampu pijar, bola lampu, bohlam; ubi-ubian (tanaman)

Bulgaria *n* [Balgéria] Bulgaria; **Bulgarian** *n* bahasa Bulgaria; *adj* berasal dari Bulgaria

bulge *n* benjolan, tumpukan, tonjolan; *vi* membengkak, menonjol

bulimia *n* [bulimia] penyakit dimana makanan dimuntahkan kembali

bulk *n* tumpukan, timbunan; ~*-billing* disubsidi pemerintah; *to buy in* ~ belanja secara grosir; **bulky** *adj* besar, bertumpuk

bull *n* [bul] sapi jantan; ~*-fighter* mata-dor; ~*-fighting* pertandingan antara manusia dan banteng; ~*'s eye* sasaran; **bullfight** *n* [bulfait] adu sapi (di Spanyol); **bullshit** *n, vulg* tahi kerbau, omong kosong

bulldog *n* sejenis anjing galak

bulldoze *vt* membongkar, meratakan (tanah); **bulldozer** *n* alat berat untuk membongkar tanah, buldoser

bullet *n* [bulet] peluru; ~*-proof* anti-peluru; ~*-train* shinkansén

bulletin *n* [buletin] selebaran, berita kilat; ~ *board* papan untuk meném-pélkan kertas-kertas

bullfight *n* [bulfait] adu sepi (di Spanyol) ← **bull**

bullshit *n, vulg* tahi kerbau, omong kosong ← **bull**

bully *n* [buli] orang yang menakut-nakuti atau mengéjék orang lain; *vt* menakut-nakuti orang lain

bum *n, sl* pantat, kibul; gelandangan; ~ *bag* tas pinggang

bumblebee *n* [bambelbi] lebah, tawon

bump *n* pukulan, tonjokan, sénggolan; *vt* menabrak; **bumpy** *adj* tidak rata, bergelombang

bumper *n* ~ *(bar)* bémper (mobil)

bun *n* sanggul, kondé; roti berbentuk bola, biasanya manis; *Boston* ~ semacam roti berisi kismis dan kayu manis

bunch *n* gugus, segenggam; segerombolan; *a* ~ *of bananas* sesisir pisang; *a* ~ *of fives* kepalan tangan; *a* ~ *of flowers* seikat bunga; *a* ~ *of children* segerombolan anak-anak

bundle *n* [bandel] berkas, paket; *vt* membungkus

bungalow *n* [banggalo] bungalo, vila

bungle *vt* [banggel] mengerjakan dengan serampangan, mengerjakan dengan salah

bunk *n* ranjang yang sempit; ~ *bed* ranjang yang bertingkat

bunker *n* [bangker] ruang bawah tanah, bungker

bunny *n, sl* kelinci; *the Easter* ~ kelinci yang membawa anak-anak telur cokelat pada saat Paskah

buoy *n* [boi] pelampung; *vt* menyemangati; ~*ed by* disemangati; **buoyancy** *n* sifat mengapung; kegembiraan; **buoyant** *adj* terapung; gembira

burden *n* beban; muatan, tanggungan; *vt* membebani, memberatkan; *don't* ~ *friends with your problems* jangan membebani teman-teman dengan masalahmu sendiri

bureau *n* [byuro] kantor, biro; méja tulis; **bureaucracy** *n* birokrasi; **bureaucrat** *n* birokrat; **bureaucratic** *n* birokratis

burger *n* roti isi daging

burglar *n* maling; ~ *alarm* alarm anti maling; *cat* ~ maling yang masuk dari atas bangunan; **burglary** *n* kemalingan; **burgle** *vt* memasuki rumah atau gedung lalu mencuri

burial *n* [bérial] pemakaman; ~ *ground* kuburan → **bury**

Burkina Faso *n* Burkina Faso, *arch* Volta Hulu; **Burkinabe** *n* [burkinabé] orang Burkina Faso; *adj* berasal dari Burkina Faso

burn *n* luka terkena panas, luka bakar; *vi* **burned burnt** menyala, terbakar; *vt* membakar; ~ *down* membakar (gedung); **burner** *n* sumbu; **burnout** *n* kehabisan tenaga

burp *n* sendawa; *vi* bersendawa

burrow *n* [baro] liang (binatang); *vi* menggali liang

bursar *n* pengurus keuangan di sekolah; **bursary** *n* béasiswa

burst *n* **burst burst** letusan, ledakan; semburan; *vi* meletus; menyembur; ~ *into tears* menangis dengan tiba-tiba; ~ *out laughing* tertawa berbahak-bahak; *the river* ~ *its banks* air sungai meluap

bury *vt* [béri] mengubur, menanam

bus *n* bis; ~ *pass* karcis abonemén untuk bis; ~ *shelter*, ~ *stop* halte bis; *articulated* ~ bis témpél; ~ *station*, ~ *terminal* términal bis; *by* ~ naik bis; *to miss the* ~ ketinggalan bis; terlambat

bush *n* [busy] semak belukar; ~ *tucker* makanan dari semak belukar; **Bushman** *n* penduduk asli gurun Kalahari

busily *adv* [bizili] dengan sibuk ← **busy**

business *n* pekerjaan; perkara, urusan; perdagangan, perniagaan; bisnis; perusahaan; ~*-like* profésional; ~ *card* kartu nama; ~ *studies* kajian bisnis; ~ *trip* perjalanan dinas; *monkey* ~ kenakalan; *not your* ~ bukan urusan anda; **businessman** *n, m* pengusaha, wiraswasta; **businesswoman** *n, f* pengusaha, wiraswasta

busk *vi* mengamén; **busker** *n* pengamén, seniman jalan

bust *n* patung kepala dan dada; dada, payudara; **busty** *adj* berpayudara besar

bust *vi, coll* rusak

bustle *n* [basel] kesibukan, keramaian; *vi* bergegas-gegas, buru-buru

busy *adj* [bizi] sibuk; **busybody** *n* orang yang suka ikut campur, raja gosip

but *conj* tetapi, tapi, namun; kecuali

butcher *n* [bucer] jagal, tukang potong, tukang daging, pembantai; toko daging

butler *n, m* kepala pelayan (di rumah)

butt *n* puntung (rokok); sasaran; *the* ~ *of many jokes* sering menjadi korban lelucon

butter *n* mentéga; ~ *up* merayu

call

butterfly *n* [baterflai] kupu-kupu; gaya kupu-kupu

buttock *n* belah pantat; **buttocks** *pl* pantat

button *n* kancing; ~ *up* mengancing; ~*hole* lubang kancing

buy *n* [bai] pembelian; *vt* **bought bought** [bot] membeli; ~ *up* memborong; **buyer** *n* pembeli

buzz *n* dengung, deru; *vi* mendengung, menderu; ~ *off coll* pergi, enyah

by *prep* [bai] oléh, dengan; di sebelah; ~ *yourself* sendiri; ~ *bus* naik bis, dengan bis; ~ *the* ~, ~ *the way (BTW)* ngomong-ngomong; ~ *God* demi Allah; **bystander** *n* orang di jalan, penonton

bye *ejac* [bai] selamat jalan, selamat tinggal; ~~ *child* selamat jalan, selamat tinggal; *n* giliran tidak bertanding; ~ *laws* peraturan kota

BYO *abbrev bring your own* bawa sendiri (minuman beralkohol)

bypass *n* jalan lingkar luar; *heart* ~ bedah jantung

byte *n* bit, bita

C

C *abbrev Celsius* Célsius, sélsius

c [si] *c, third letter of the alphabet*

c *abbrev cent* sén

cab *n* taksi; bagian depan truk; ~ *driver* supir taksi; **cabbie** *n, sl* supir taksi

cabaret *n* [kabaré] hiburan di réstoran

cabbage *n* [kabej] kol, engkol, kubis

cabbie, cabby *n, sl* supir taksi ← **cab**

cabin *n* bagian depan truk; ~ *crew* awak kabin; ~ *luggage* bagasi kabin; *log* ~ pondok (dibuat dari balok kayu)

cabinet *n* kabinét; lemari; ~*maker* tukang kayu, tukang mebel; ~ *reshuffle* perombakan kabinét

cable *n* [kébel] kabel; *arch* kawat, télégram; ~ *car US* trém; ~ *TV* TV kabel; *vt, arch* mengirim télégram

cacao *n* kakao, buah coklat

cackle *vi* [kakel] berkékék; berkoték

(ayam); *n* suara berkékék; suara berkoték

cactus *n* cacti [kaktai] kaktus

CAD *abbrev computer-aided design* désain gambar dengan komputer

caddie, caddy *n* kédi; *tea caddy* tutup téko téh

cadet *n* kadét; semacam pramuka

cadre *n* [kader] kader

Caesarian, Caesarean *to have a ~, by* ~ *section* disésar

café, cafe *n* kafé, tempat minum kopi; **cafeteria** *n* [kafetiria] ruang makan (di gedung)

caffeine *n* [kafin] kaféin

cage *n* sangkar, kurungan; *vt* mengurung

cajole *vi* [kejol] membujuk

cake *n* kué; ~ *mix* adonan kué; ~ *shop* toko kué; *birthday* ~ kué tar; *wedding* ~ kué pengantin; *a* ~ *of soap* (sepotong) sabun

calamity *n* [kalamiti] bencana, malapetaka; **calamitous** *adj* sangat buruk

calcium *n* kalsium, zat kapur

calculate *vt* menghitung-hitung, memperhitungkan, menaksir; **calculating** *adj* memperhitungkan; **calculation** *n* perhitungan, kalkulasi; **calculator** *n* kalkulator

calendar *n* kalénder, almanak; penanggalan; *Islamic* ~ tahun hijriah

calf *n* [kaf] **calves** [kavs] betis

calf *n* [kaf] **calves** [kavs] anak sapi; *vi* **calved calved** beranak (sapi); **calfskin** *n* kulit anak sapi

caliber, calibre *n* [kaliber] kaliber, mutu

calibrate *vt* [kalibrét] mengalibrasi; **calibrated** *adj* dikalibrasi; **calibration** *n* kalibrasi

calico *n* [kaliko] belacu, kain mori; ~ *cat* kucing yang bulunya berwarna putih, hitam dan coklat

caliph *n* [kalif] khalifah

call *n* [kol] panggilan, seruan; percakapan télepon; kunjungan; ~ *box* télepon umum; ~ *waiting* nadaséla; *collect* ~ sambungan télepon yang dibayar oleh pihak penerima; *your* ~ terserah anda; *vi* panggil, memberi nama kepada; menélepon; *we* ~ *her Susie* kami

panggil dia Susi; ~ *at* mampir di; ~
back menélepon kembali; ~ *for* menjemput, mengambil; membutuhkan;
menuntut; ~ *on* berkunjung ke, mengunjungi; ~ *out* berteriak; ~ *upon*
memanggil; menyeru; *vt* memanggil;
menélepon; *~girl* wanita panggilan; ~
center pusat pelayanan melalui télepon; ~ *off* membatalkan; *on* ~ siap
dipanggil; **caller** *n* penélepon; tamu;
calling *n* panggilan (hidup)

calligrapher *n* [kaligrafer] orang yang
bisa membuat tulisan tangan indah;
calligraphy *n* tulisan tangan yang
indah; *Arabic* ~ kaligrafi

callous *n* [kales] kapal (di kaki); *adj*
tidak berperasaan

calm *n* [kam] ketenangan, keteduhan;
dead ~ tidak ada angin sama sekali;
vt menenangkan, menenteramkan; ~
down menjadi tenang; *adj* tenang,
teduh; **calmness** *n* ketenangan

calorie *n* kalori; *low-*~ kalori rendah

calves *n, pl* → **calf**

camaraderie *n* [kamaraderi] semangat
persahabatan

Cambodia *n* Kamboja; **Cambodian** *n*
orang Kamboja; *adj* berasal dari
Kamboja

camcorder *n* kaméra vidéo, alat perekam
gambar bergerak

came *vi, pf* → **come**

camel *n* [kamel] unta; *adj* warna coklat
atau abu-abu muda

camellia *n* [kamilia] sejenis bunga

cameo *n* [kamio] semacam liontin; peran
kecil yang dimainkan orang terkenal

camera *n* kaméra; **cameraman** *n*
kaméraman, kamérawan, juru kaméra

Cameroon *n* Kamérun; *the ~s arch*
Kamérun; **Cameroonian** *n* orang
Kamérun; *adj* berasal dari Kamérun

camisole *n* kemben, kamisol

camouflage *n* [kamuflaj] kamuflase,
penyamaran; *in* ~ memakai baju loréng;
vt menyamar

camp *adj, sl* (pria yang) tampak seperti
wanita

camp *n* perkémahan, kamp; ~ *bed*
vélbéd; *refugee* ~ kamp pengungsian;

vi berkémah; **camper** *n* orang yang
berkémah; **campervan** *n* karavan;
campfire *n* api unggun; **campground,
campsite** *n* tempat perkémahan;
camping *n* kegiatan berkémah

campaign *n* [kampén] kampanye; *vi*
berkampanye; ~ *for* memperjuangkan,
menuntut

camper *n* orang yang berkémah;
campervan *n* karavan ← **camp**

campground, campsite *n* tempat
perkémahan ← **camp**

camphor *n* [kamfer] kamper, kapur
barus

camping *n* kegiatan berkémah ← **camp**

campsite, campground *n* tempat
perkémahan ← **camp**

campus *n* lokasi univérsitas, kampus

can *v, aux* **could/was able, been able**
dapat, bisa; **cannot, can't** tidak bisa,
tidak dapat

can *n* kaléng; ~ *opener* alat pembuka
kaléng; *vt* mengaléngkan; ~ *it! sl* hen-
tikan!; **canned** *adj* (di dalam) kaléng;
~ *tomatoes* tomat kaléng; **cannery** *n*
pengaléngan

Canada *n* Kanada; **Canadian** *n* [kané-
dian] orang Kanada; *adj* berasal dari
Kanada

canal *n* [kanal] terusan; kali; kanal; *the
Suez* ~ Terusan Suez

canapé *n* [kanapé] makanan kecil di
pésta koktail

canary *n* [kanéri] burung kenari; *~
colored* berwarna kuning muda; *the ~
Islands* Kepulauan Kanari

cancel *vt* membatalkan, mencorét,
menghapus; **cancellation** *n*
pembatalan

cancer *n* kanker; *breast* ~ kanker payudara; *lung* ~ kanker paru-paru; *ovarian*
~ kanker rahim; **cancerous** *adj* ganas

candid *adj* terus terang, terbuka ← **candor**

candidacy *n* [kandidesi] pencalonan;
candidate *n* calon, kandidat

candle *n* lilin; **candlelight** *n* [kandel lait]
cahaya lilin; **candlestick** *n* tempat lilin

candor, candour *n* keterbukaan

candy *n* permén; **candyfloss** *n* kembang
gula

cane ~ *toad* katak ladang tebu; *sugar* ~ tebu

cane *n* tongkat; rotan; *vt* mencambuk

canine *n* anjing; *adj* berhubungan dengan anjing; ~ *tooth* gigi taring

cannabis *n* ganja

canned *adj* (di dalam) kaléng; ~ *tomatoes* tomat kaléng ← **can**

cannery *n* pengaléngan ← **can**

cannibal *n* [kanibol] kanibal, pemakan sejenis; **cannibalism** *n* kebiasaan makan sesama manusia; **cannibalistic** *adj* bersifat makan sejenis

cannon *n* meriam, kanon; ~ *ball* peluru meriam; *vi* ~ *into* menabrak, menghantam

cannot, can't *v, aux* tidak bisa, tidak dapat ← **can**

canoe *n* [kanu] kano; **canoeing** *n* mendayung kano; **canoeist** *n* pedayung kano

canopy *n* [kanopi] lapisan atas

can't, cannot *v, aux* tidak bisa, tidak dapat ← **can**

cantaloupe *n* [kantalop] mélon, bléwah

canteen *n* kantin

canvas *n* kanvas; kain terpal

canvass *vi* mencari dukungan untuk calon tertentu; **canvasser** *n* orang yang mencari dukungan; ~ *support* mencari dukungan

canyon *n* ngarai

cap *n* topi pét; tutup (botol); *vi* ~ *off* mengakhiri

capability *n* [képabiliti] kesanggupan, kemampuan; **capable** *adj* bisa, mampu, dapat

capacity *n* [kapasiti] daya tampung, kapasitas, muatan; *in my* ~ *as mayor* selaku walikota

cape *n* tanjung; *the* ~ *of Good Hope* Tanjung Harapan

cape *n* jubah; **caped** *adj* berjubah

capillary *n* pembuluh darah (kecil); ~ *action* daya serap

capital *n* huruf besar; ~ *(city)* ibukota; ~ *punishment* hukuman mati

capital *n* modal; **capitalist** *n* kapitalis; **capitalism** *n* kapitalisme

capitol *n, US* ibukota

capitulate *vi* menyerah (kalah);

Pakistan finally ~d to America's demands Pakistan akhirnya menyerah pada tuntutan Amérika; **capitulation** *n* penyerahan

capsicum *n* [kapsikum] paprika

capsize *vi* terbalik (kapal atau perahu)

capsule *n* kapsul

captain *n* kaptén, nahkoda; kapitan

caption *n* [kapsyen] keterangan di bawah gambar atau foto; **captioned** *adj* dengan keterangan

captivate *n* **captivating** *adj* memesonakan

captive *n* [kaptiv] tawanan; **captivity** *n* [kaptiviti] penawanan, tahanan; *animals in* ~ satwa di kebun binatang; **capture** *n* penangkapan; *vt* menangkap, menawan; ~ *alive* menangkap hidup-hidup; ~ *on film* mengambil foto

car *n* mobil; gerbong; ~-*jacking* perampasan mobil; ~ *accident* kecelakaan mobil; ~ *bomb* bom di dalam mobil; ~ *crash* tabrakan mobil; ~ *ferry* féri (dengan muatan mobil); ~ *hire* séwa mobil; ~ *park* tempat parkir; ~ *wash* cuci mobil; *dining* ~ (gerbong) réstorasi; ~ *boot sale* pasar kagét dengan barang dipajang di bagasi mobil; **car-port** *n* garasi, atap untuk perlindungan mobil; **carsick** *adj* mabuk jalan

caramel *n* gula bakar, permén rasa karamél; *adj* rasa karamél

carat *n* karat

caravan *n* kafilah; karavan

carbohydrate *n* [karbohaidrét] karbohidrat

carbolic ~ *acid* karbol

carbon *n* karbon, zat arang; ~ *dioxide* karbon dioksida; ~ *credits* krédit karbon; ~ *emissions* émisi karbon; ~ *monoxide* karbon monoksida; *carbonated drink* minuman bersoda

carburettor *n* karburator

carcass *n* bangkai (binatang)

carcinogenic *n* [karsinojénik] menyebabkan kanker

card *n* kartu; kardus; ~ *shark* pemain kartu jagoan; ~ *table* méja lipat (untuk permainan kartu); *credit* ~ kartu krédit; *greetings* ~ kartu ucapan; *name* ~, *business* ~ kartu nama; *playing* ~s

kartu rémi; *to play ~s* main kartu
cardamom *n* kapulaga
cardboard *n* karton, kertas tebal
cardiac *adj* [kardiak] berkaitan dengan
jantung; *~ arrest* serangan jantung
cardigan *n* sejenis switer dengan kancing di depan
cardinal *n* kardinal; *adj* utama, pokok
care *n* [kér] pemeliharaan, perawatan; *~
of (c/-)* dengan alamat (d/a); *child ~*
penitipan anak-anak; *in ~* dalam
perawatan; *to take ~* berhati-hati, jaga
diri; *to take ~ of* memelihara, mengurus; *vi* peduli; *~ about* peduli (tentang), memedulikan; *~ for* merawat;
suka pada; *~ to* berminat; *who ~s?*
peduli amat; *I don't ~* saya tidak
peduli; *sl* émang gué pikirin (EGP); *vt*
memedulikan; **carefree** *adj* tanpa
beban, riang; **careful** *adj* hati-hati;
carefully *adv* dengan hati-hati, dengan
teliti, secara seksama; **careless** *adj*
teledor, lalai, ceroboh; **carelessness**
n keteledoran, kelalaian, kecerobohan;
carer *n* perawat, pengasuh; **caretaker**
n penjaga; **caring** *adj* bersifat peduli,
penyayang
career *n* karir; *~ woman* wanita karir
carefree *adj* tanpa beban, riang ← **care**
careful *adj* hati-hati; **carefully** *adv* dengan hati-hati, dengan teliti, secara
seksama ← **care**
careless *adj* teledor, lalai, ceroboh;
carelessness *n* keteledoran, kelalaian, kecerobohan ← **care**
carer *n* perawat, pengasuh ← **care**
caress *n* [kerés] belaian; *vt* membelai
caretaker *n* penjaga ← **care**
cargo *n* muatan (kapal); *~ boat* kapal
barang
Caribbean *adj* berasal dari kawasan
Laut Karibia; *the ~ (Sea)* Laut Karibia
caricature *n* karikatur
caring *adj* bersifat peduli, penyayang
← **care**
carnation *n* anyelir
carnival *n* pésta, pasar malam
carnivore *n* [karnivor] pemakan daging;
carnivorous *adj* [karniveres] yang
makan daging

carol *n* lagu Natal; *vi* bernyanyi,
berkicau
carousel *n* [karosél] korsél, komedi
putar
carp *n* ikan guramé; *Japanese ~* ikan koi
carpenter *n* tukang kayu; **carpentry** *n*
pekerjaan kayu
carpet *n* permadani, karpét
carport *n* garasi, atap untuk perlindungan mobil ← **car**
carriage *n* [karij] keréta; gerbong; *baby
~* keréta anak; *horse and ~* keréta
kuda ← **carry**; **carriageway** *n* jalan
(ke satu arah)
carrier *n* [karier] pembawa (penyakit
dsb); *~ bag* plastik, kerésék; *~ pigeon*
merpati pos; *aircraft ~* kapal induk ←
carry
carrot *n* wortel; inséntif
carry *vt* mengangkat, mengangkut,
membawa; *~ on* meneruskan; *~ out*
menjalankan, melakukan, melaksanakan
carsick *adj* mabuk jalan ← **car**
cart *n* keréta, pedati, gerobak; *horse
and ~* keréta kuda; *vt, coll* membawa
dalam jumlah besar; *he ~ed the rubbish all the way home* dia membawa
sampah itu pulang
cartographer *n* kartografer; **cartography** *n* pembuatan peta, pemetaan,
kartografi
carton *n* dus, kotak; *milk ~* kotak susu
cartoon *n* (film) kartun, animé; komik;
~ character tokoh kartun; **cartoonist** *n*
kartunis
cartridge *n* [kartrij] tinta (untuk printer
komputer), isi pulpén; pelor, peluru
carve *vt* mengukir; memotong daging
dari tulang; **carver** *n* pengukir, tukang
ukir; **carving** *n* ukiran
cascade *n* air terjun; *vi* terjun
case *n* peti, koper; kasus, perkara, hal,
perihal; *in ~* jika, kalau; *pillow ~*
sarung bantal; *in this ~* dalam hal ini
cash *n* uang kontan, uang tunai; *~ card*
kartu ATM, kartu krédit; *~ crop* hasil
pertanian yang akan dijual; *~ flow* arus
kas; *~ register* mesin kasir; *~ and
carry* toko yang membeli barang

bekas; *short of* ~ tidak punya uang banyak; **cashless** *adj* secara krédit, tanpa uang tunai; **cashier** *n* [kasyir] kasir, kassa

cashew *n* kacang médé

cashier *n* [kasyir] kasir, kassa ← **cash**

cashmere *n, adj* [kasymir] wol lembut

casino *n* tempat berjudi, kasino

casket *n* peti mati

cassava *n* [kasava] singkong

casserole *n* [kaserol] masakan yang berkuah, biasanya mengandung daging; ~ *dish* tempat masakan yang terbuat dari kaca

cassette *n* kasét; ~ *player* radio kasét, tép

cassowary *n* burung kasuari

cast *n* lémparan; tuangan; pemain-pemain dalam film atau sandiwara; *plaster* ~ gips; *in a* ~ digips; *vt* **cast cast** melémpar, melontar; menuang-kan; memilih untuk peran; ~ *iron* besi tuang; ~ *off* menyelesaikan rajutan; ~ *on* memulai rajutan; ~ *a vote* memberi suara

castaway *n* orang yang telantar di pulau

caste *n* [kast] kasta

castle *n* [kasel] puri, bénténg, istana; ~*s in the air* mimpi belaka

castor ~ *oil* minyak jarak, kastroli

casual *adj* [kasyuel] santai; ~ *labor* pekerja yang tidak terikat kontrak; ~ *position* kerja sambilan; **casually** *adv* secara santai

casualty *n* [kasyuelti] korban kecelakaan; ~ *ward* Unit Gawat Darurat (UGD)

cat *n* kucing; ~ *nap* tidur sebentar; ~*'s eye* refléktor (di tengah jalan); *alley* ~ kucing kampung; *ginger* ~ kucing kuning; *Persian* ~ kucing angora; **cat-fish** *n* ikan lélé

catalog, catalogue *n* katalog, daftar; *vt* mendokuméntasi

catalyst *n* [katalist] pemicu

catapult *n* katapél; *vi* terlémpar; *vt* melémparkan, meluncurkan

catastrophe *n* [katastrofi] bencana, malapetaka; **catastrophic** *adj* yang berkait dengan bencana

catch *n* tangkapan, hasil; jepitan, géspér; *vt* **caught caught** [kot] menangkap;

terkena, terjangkit (penyakit); ~ *22 situation* buah simalakama; ~ *cold* masuk angin; ~ *up* mengejar; ~ *the bus* naik bis; mengobrol setelah lama tidak bertemu; **catchphrase** *n* [kacfréz] semboyan; **catching** *adj* menular; **catchment** *n* daérah aliran sungai (DAS); **catchy** *adj* mudah diingat

categorize *vt* mengategorikan; **category** *n* kategori, golongan

cater *vi* memberi layanan; menyediakan makanan; ~ *for* melayani; *vt* melayani; **caterer** *n* perusahaan jasa boga; **catering** *n* jasa boga

caterpillar *n* [katerpilar] ulat

catfish *n* ikan lélé ← **cat**

cathedral *n* [kathidral] katédral

Catholic *n* orang Katolik; *adj* Katolik; *Roman* ~ Katolik

cattle *n* [katel] sapi, ternak

Caucasian *n* [kokésyan] orang kulit putih; *adj* berkulit putih; **Caucasus** *n* [kokesus] *the* ~ Kaukasus

caught *vt, pf* [kot] → **catch**

cauldron *n* kétél, kawah

cauliflower *n* [koliflauer] kembang kol

cause *n* [coz] sebab; *vt* menyebabkan, mengakibatkan, menimbulkan; ~ *problems* membuat masalah

caution *n* [kosyen] sikap hati-hati, kewaspadaan; *vt* mengingatkan, memberi peringatan; **cautious** *adj* hati-hati; **cautiously** *adv* dengan hati-hati

cavalry *n* [kavalri] pasukan kuda

cave *n* gua; **cavern** *n* [kavern] gua (besar); **cavernous** *adj* seperti gua besar

caviar *n* telur terubuk (ikan)

cavity *n* [kaviti] rongga, lubang (gigi)

cayman *n* buaya

CB *abbrev Citizens' Band* radio antar penduduk

cc *cubic centimeter* cc (séntiméter kubik)

cc *abbrev carbon copy* cc; salinan

CD *abbrev compact disk* CD

CD *abbrev Corps Diplomatique* kedutaan

cease *vi* [siis] berhenti; *vt* menghenti-kan; ~ *fire* gencatan senjata

cedar *n* sejenis pohon

cede *vt* menyerahkan

ceilidh *n* [kéli] acara kesenian tradisional (di Skotlandia atau Irlandia)

ceiling *n* [siling] langit-langit, plafon; *glass* ~ tingkat paling atas yang tercapai oleh seorang wanita karir karena diskriminasi

celebrant *n marriage* ~ petugas yang berwenang menikahkan orang; **celebrate** *vi* [sélebrét] berpésta; *vt* merayakan; **celebrated** *adj* ternama, masyhur, termasyhur; **celebration** *n* perayaan

celebrity *n* sélébriti

celery *n* sélédri

celestial *adj* surgawi; dari angkasa

celibacy *n* [sélibesi] keadaan sélibat, hidup melajang; **celibate** *adj* sélibat, tidak melakukan hubungan séks

cell *n* sél; bilik penjara; ~ *phone* télepon sélulér (ponsél), télepon genggam; *stem* ~ sél induk

cellar *n* bésmén, ruang bawah tanah

cello *n* [célo] sélo

cellophane *n* [sélofén] kertas kaca, sélofan

Celt *n* [kélt] orang Kélt (penduduk asli daérah Inggris dan barat laut Perancis); **Celtic** *adj* berkaitan dengan orang Kélt dan kebudayaannya

cement *n* semén, beton; perekat; ~ *mixer* mobil pengaduk beton; *vt* menyemén; merekat

cemetery *n* [sémeteri] kuburan, tempat peristirahatan akhir (TPA)

censor *n* sénsor; *vt* mensénsor; **censorship** *n* pensénsoran

census *n* sénsus; ~*taker* petugas pelaksana sénsus

cent *n* sén

centaur *n* [séntor] makhluk dengan torso manusia tapi kaki dan ékor kuda

centenary, centennial *n* peringatan seratus tahun; **centenarian** *n* orang yang berusia seratus tahun

center, centre *n* pusat, bagian tengah; *shopping* ~ pusat perbelanjaan, mal; ~ *of attention* pusat perhatian; ~ *of gravity* titik berat; *vi* berpusat; ~ *on* berpusat pada, fokus pada; **central** *adj* pusat, tengah, pokok; ~ *bank* Bank

Indonésia; bank séntral; ~ *heating* pemanasan pusat; ~ *Jakarta* Jakarta Pusat (Jakpus); ~ *Java* Jawa Tengah (Jateng); ~ *African Republic* Afrika Tengah; ~ *processing unit (CPU)* CPU; **centralize** *vt* memusatkan; **centralized** *adj* terpusat

Centigrade, C *n* Celsius, sélsius

centimeter, centimetre *n* sénti, séntiméter

centipede *n* [sentipid] kaki seribu, lipan

central *adj* pusat, tengah, pokok; ~ *bank* Bank Indonésia; bank séntral; ~ *Jakarta* Jakarta Pusat (Jakpus); ~ *Java* Jawa Tengah (Jateng); ~ *African Republic* Afrika Tengah ← **center**

centralize *vt* memusatkan; **centralized** *adj* terpusat ← **center**

centre → **center**

century *n* abad, seratus tahun; seratus poin (dalam pertandingan krikét)

CEO *abbrev Chief Executive Officer* Diréktur Utama, Présidén Diréktur (Présdir)

ceramic *adj* [séramik] terbuat dari tanah; *n* kerajinan kéramik

cereal *n* [sirial] séréal

cerebral *adj* ~ *palsy* kerusakan pada otak

ceremonial *adj* [séremoni] berkaitan dengan upacara, sérémonial; **ceremony** *n* upacara

certain *adj* [serten] tentu, pasti, yakin; *to make* ~ memastikan; **certainly** *adv* tentu saja; **certainty** *n* kepastian

certificate *n* sértifikat, ijazah, surat; *birth* ~ akte lahir, akte kelahiran; *marriage* ~ akte kawin, akte perkawinan; **certified** *adj* berijazah; ~ *public accountant (CPA)* akuntan publik; **certify** *vt* mengesahkan

cervical *adj* berhubungan dengan léhér atau léhér rahim; **cervix** *n* léhér rahim

Cesarian, Caesarian *n* [Sisérian] disésar; *to have a* ~, *by* ~ *section* disésar

cessation *n* pemberhentian

Ceylon *n, arch* [sailon] Sri Lanka, Sailan; **Ceylonese** *n* orang Sri Lanka; *adj* berasal dari Sri Lanka

cf *compare* dibandingkan

CFC *abbrev chlorofluorocarbon* kloro-flurokarbon

chain *n* rantai; kalung; serangkaian; ~ *saw* gergaji rantai; ~*smoke* merokok terus-menerus; ~ *letter* surat berantai; ~ *reaction* réaksi berantai; ~ *store* toko waralaba; *in* ~*s* dibelenggu; ~ *of events* rangkaian peristiwa; *vt* merantai

chair *n* [cér] kursi; ketua; *the electric* ~ kursi listrik; **chairlift** *n* keréta gantung; **chairman** *n, m* **chairperson** *n* ketua; *vt* mengetuai

chalet *n* [syalé] vila di gunung

chalk *n* [cok] kapur; *like* ~ *and cheese* seperti langit dan bumi (*lit.* seperti kapur dan kéju)

challenge *n* tantangan; *vt* menantang, menuntut (keputusan); **challenger** *n* penantang; **challenging** *adj* menantang

chamber *n* [cémber] kamar; ~ *music* musik untuk sejumlah kecil pemain; ~ *of commerce* kamar dagang; **chambers** *n* ruangan hakim

chameleon *n* [kamilion] bunglon

champagne *n* [syampéin] sampanye; *adj* warna kuning muda

champion *n* [campion] juara; ~*s League* Liga Kampiun; **championship** *n* kejuaraan

chance *n* [cans] kesempatan, kemungkinan, peluang; *by* ~ secara kebetulan; ~ *of doing,* ~ *to do* kesempatan; *half a* ~ kesempatan; *to take a* ~ mengambil risiko

chancellor *n* kanselir; *vice-*~ pembantu rektor; ~ *of the Exchequer UK* Menteri Keuangan

chandelier *n* [candelir] lampu gantung

change *n* [cénj] perubahan; uang kembali; *climate* ~ perubahan iklim; ~ *of clothes* baju salin; *vi* berubah; ~ *hands* berpindah tangan; *vt* ganti; menukar, mengubah; ~ *the subject* mengalih arah percakapan; ~ *your clothes* ganti pakaian; ~ *your mind* berubah pikiran; ~ *trains at Cardiff* turun di Cardiff; **changeable** *adj* [cénjabel] dapat berubah, tidak tetap; **changing** *adj* sedang berubah; ~ *room* kamar ganti baju

channel *n* saluran, selat; *vt* menyalurkan; *the English* ~ Selat Inggris

chant *n* lagu yang dinyanyikan atau diucapkan; *vi* bernyanyi; *vt* menyanyikan (berulang-ulang)

chaos *n* [kéos] kekacauan; **chaotic** *adj* kacau balau

chap *n, sl, m* orang, lelaki

chapel *n* [capel] kapel, geréja kecil; **chaplain** *n* pastor atau pendéta di lingkungan tertentu

chaperone *n* [syaperon] pendamping, pengantar

chaplain *n* [caplen] pendéta atau pastor yang bekerja di sekolah atau lembaga lain

chapter *n* bab, pasal

character *n* [karakter] sifat; peran, tokoh, watak; huruf; **characteristic** *n* ciri; *adj* khas; **characterize** *vt* menjiwai, memerankan; menggambarkan

charade *n* [syerad] adegan, sandiwara

charcoal *n* arang

charge *n* [carj] muatan; ongkos, harga; serangan, serbuan; tuduhan; *in* ~ berkuasa, berwenang; *free of* ~, *no* ~ gratis, cuma-cuma; *reverse* ~*s* sambungan télepon yang dibayar oleh pihak penerima; *vt* menyerang; meminta bayaran, menagih; (me)ngecas, mengisi; menuduh; ~*d with* dituduh melakukan; ~ *a car battery* mengisi aki; **charger** *n* alat pengecas

charisma *n* karisma, pesona; **charismatic** *adj* memesona

charitable *adj* [caritabel] amal, murah hati; **charity** *n* amal

charm *n* pesona; sihir; gantungan gelang; *vt* memesonakan, menarik hati; menyihir; **charming** *adj* jelita, juwita, memesonakan

chart *n* grafik; peta; *vt* memetakan

charter *n* piagam; ~ *flight* penerbangan carter; *vt* mencarter; **chartered** *adj* carteran

chase *n* pengejaran; *in* ~ sedang mengejar; *vt* mengejar

chasm *n* [kazem] ngarai, jurang

chassis *n* [syasi] sasis

chaste *adj* [céist] suci; **chastity** *n*

[castiti] kesucian; ~ *belt* alat anti-perkosaan

chat *n* percakapan; ~ *room* situs obrolan; ~ *show* acara obrolan; *chit-~* obrolan ringan; *vi* mengobrol, bercakap-cakap; ~ *up* merayu; **chatter** *n* celotéhan, obrolan; *vi* bercelotéh, mengobrol; **chatterbox** *n* orang yang sering cerocos; **chatting** *n* kegiatan berkomunikasi lewat internét

chauffeur *n* [syofer] supir, sopir

cheap *adj* murah; *go* ~ diobral; *on the* ~ dengan murah; **cheapen** *vt* menurunkan harga, merendahkan; **cheapskate** *n* orang pelit; **cheaply** *adv* dengan murah

cheat *n* penipu; *vi* curang; ~ *on* memadu, tidak setia kepada; *vt* menipu; **cheating** *n* curang, kecurangan

check *n* motif kotak-kotak; ~ *shirt* keméja bermotif kotak-kotak

check, cheque *n* cék; bon; ~ *account* rékening giro

check *n* pemeriksaan, uji, cék; sekak; ~-*up* pemeriksaan keséhatan; *vi* periksa, cék; ~ *in* melapor (di hotel atau bandara), cék in; ~ *on* mengecék; ~ *out* membayar lalu meninggalkan hotel; ~ *with* tanya kepada; *vt* memeriksa, menguji, mengecék; **checkmate** *ejac* sekakmat; **checkout** *n* kasir, kassa (terutama di swalayan); ~ *chick sl* gadis kasir

cheek *n* pipi; keberanian; *what a* ~ énak saja; **cheeky** *adj* berani, nakal

cheer *n* kegembiraan; sorak; *vi* memberi semangat, bersorak; ~ *up* bergembira; *vt* mendukung; ~ *up* menghibur; **cheerful** *adj* gembira, senang hati; **cheerleader** *n* pemandu sorak; **cheers** salam; ungkapan saat bersulang

cheese *n* kéju; *cottage* ~ kéju putih yang cair; **cheeseburger** *n* burger dengan isi kéju; **cheesecake** *n* kué yang dibuat dari kéju, bukan tepung

cheetah *n* macan tutul

chef *n* [syéf] juru masak

chemical *n* [kémikel] bahan kimia; *adj* kimiawi; ~ *reaction* réaksi kimiawi; **chemist** *n* ahli kimia; apotéker; **chemistry** *n* ilmu kimia; *the* ~ *between the*

two of them was great interaksi di antara meréka berdua sangat baik

chemotherapy *n* [kimotérapi] **chemo** *coll* kémotérapi

cheque → **check**

cherish *vt* [cérisy] menyayangi, menghargai; **cherished** *adj* tersayang

cherry *n* buah céri

chess *n* catur; ~ *piece* buah catur; **chessboard** *n* papan catur

chest *n* dada; peti, kopor; *a* ~ *of drawers* (susunan) laci

chestnut *n* buah berangan

chew *v* mengunyah; ~*ing gum* permén karét

chic *adj* [syik] anggun, bergaya, modis

chick *n* anak ayam; ~ *pea* kacang kuda, kacang arab; *sl* céwék; **chicken** *n* (rasa) ayam; *adj, sl* takut, penakut; ~ *out* batal karena takut; ~ *pox* cacar air

chief *n* **chiefs** kepala (suku), pemimpin; *commander in* ~ panglima tertinggi; *editor-in-*~ pemimpin redaksi; *adj* utama, pokok; **chiefly** *adv* terutama, pertama-tama

child *n* [caild] **children** [cildren] anak, putra; ~ *abuse* penganiayaan terhadap anak; ~ *care* fasilitas penitipan anak; **childbirth** *n* bersalin, melahirkan; **childhood** *n* [caildhud] masa kanak-kanak, masa kecil; **childish** *adj* kekanak-kanakan; **childless** *adj* tanpa anak; **childproof** *adj* tidak bisa digunakan oléh anak-anak

Chile *n* [cili] Cilé; **Chilean** *n* orang Cilé; *adj* berasal dari Cilé

chili → **chilli**

chill *n* udara dingin; *to have a* ~ masuk angin; *vt* menyejukkan, mendinginkan; **chilly** *adj* sejuk, dingin

chilli *n* cabé; ~ *sauce* (saus) sambal

chilly *adj* sejuk, dingin ← **chill**

chimney *n* **chimneys** cerobong asap

chimpanzee *n* **chimp** *coll* simpansé

chin *n* dagu; **chinwag** *n, sl* obrolan

China *n* [caina] (negeri) Tiongkok; *coll* Cina; **china** *n, adj* porselén; **Chinatown** *n* Pecinan; **Chinese** *n* orang Cina, orang Tionghoa; bahasa Cina; *adj* Cina, Tionghoa chink n celah

chip n keping; keripik; hot ~s kentang goréng; fish and ~s ikan dan kentang goréng; vi pecah, sumbing; ~ in menyeletuk; patungan, memberi sumbangan; vt menyumbingkan, mengelupas; chipped adj sumbing, sompél

chipmunk n tupai atau bajing tanah dengan gigi besar

chiropractor n [kairopraktor] ahli pengobat tulang punggung

chisel n [cizel] pahat; vt memahat; chiselled adj terpahat

chit n nota, surat tagihan

chit-chat n obrolan ringan

chivalrous adj [syivelres] bersifat kesatria; chivalry n kekesatriaan

chives n, pl lokio

chlorine n klorin; chlorinated adj berklorin

chloroform n kloroform, obat bius

chlorophyll n zat hijau, hijau daun, klorofil

chock ~-a-block, ~-full penuh sesak

chocolate n, adj coklat; pl kotak berisi coklat (yang masing-masing dibungkus)

choice n pilihan, terpilih ← choose

choir n [kuaier] paduan suara, koor; choirboy n anak lelaki anggota paduan suara di geréja; choral adj [koral] berhubungan dengan koor atau bernyanyi

choke vi terselak; vt mencekik; choked adj terselak; choker n kalung yang ketat

cholera n (penyakit) koléra

cholesterol n kolésterol; high ~ kolésterol tinggi

choose vt chose chosen memilih; choosy adj suka memilih-milih, réwél

chop n potong; stéik yang bertulang; vt memotong, mencincang; chopper n parang; hélikoptér; choppy adj berombak (laut)

chopsticks n, pl sumpit

chopsuey n capcai

choral adj [koral] berhubungan dengan koor atau bernyanyi ← choir

chore n tugas (rumah)

choreographer n [koriografer] pencipta tarian, koréografer; choreography n koréografi

chorus n paduan suara; refréin

chose, chosen v, pf → choose

Christ n [kraist] (Yésus) Kristus; christen vt [krisen] mempermandikan, membaptis; memberi nama; christening n permandian; Christian n orang Kristen atau Katolik; adj Kristiani, Nasrani, Maséhi; ~ name arch nama depan; Christianity n agama Kristén, Katolik dan Orthodoks; Christmas n (hari) Natal; ~ card kartu Natal; ~ Eve malam Natal; ~ tree pohon Natal, pohon terang

chrome n, adj krom; chromium n krom

chronic adj kronis, menahun; chronicle n [kronikel] sejarah

chronological adj [kronolojikel] menurut tanggal; chronology n kronologi, sejarah

chrysanthemum n [krisanthemum] bunga krisan

chubby adj gemuk, berlebihan berat badan

chuck vi, sl ~ in menyerah, putus asa; ~ (out) membuang; ~ up muntah; memuntahkan; vt, sl membuang

chuckle n, vi [cakel] tertawa kecil

chum n, sl kawan, sobat; chummy adj bersahabat

chunk n gumpal, bongkah; chunky adj berisi, berat

church n geréja; to go to ~ pergi ke geréja; churchyard n kuburan dekat geréja

chutney n [catni] jenis sambal dari India

CIA abbrev Central Intelligence Agency Badan Intélijén Pusat (Amérika Serikat)

cicada n [sikéda] sejenis jangkrik

CID abbrev Criminal Investigation Department Bagian Penyelidikan Kriminal

cider n sari buah (terutama apel)

cigar n [sigar] cerutu; ~ case tempat cerutu; cigarette n [sigarét] rokok; ~ lighter korék api; clove ~ (rokok) krétek

cinder n kerak, sisa bara api

Cinderella *n* Cindelaras

cinema *n* [sinema] (gedung) bioskop

cinnamon *n* kayu manis

circle *n* [serkel] lingkaran, bulatan; kawasan, lingkungan; kalangan; ~ *of friends* kelompok kawan; *vi* berputar-putar; *vt* melingkari; mengédari; **circular** *n* [serkyuler] surat édaran; *adj* bulat, bundar; **circulate** *vi* berédar; *vt* mengédarkan, menyebarkan; **circulation** *n* perédaran, sirkulasi

circuit *n* [serket] sirkuit; perédaran; **circuitous** *adj* [serkyuitus] memutar

circular *n* [serkyuler] surat edaran; *adj* bulat, bundar; **circulate** *vi* berédar; mengédarkan, menyebarkan; **circulation** *n* perédaran, sirkulasi ← **circle**

circumcise *vt* menyunat; ~*d* disunat; **circumcision** *n* [sirkumsisyen] sunatan

circumference *n* [serkamferens] keliling, lingkar, bundaran

circumstances *n, pl* keadaan; *under no* ~ jangan sekali-kali

circus *n* sirkus

citadel *n* [sitadél] bénténg

citation *n* [saitésyen] kutipan; **cite** *vt* mengutip, menyebutkan

citizen *n* [sitizen] warga; warganegara; ~*'s band (CB) radio* radio CB; **citizenship** *n* kewarganegaraan

city *n* [siti] kota; ~ *hall* balaikota; *capital* ~ ibukota

civet ~ *cat* musang

civic *adj* berkaitan dengan kepentingan umum atau kewarganegaraan; **civics** *n, pl* PPKn, ilmu kewarganegaraan

civil *adj* sipil; sopan; ~ *law* hukum perdata; ~ *engineering* téknik sipil; ~ *servant* pegawai negeri sipil (PNS); ~ *war* perang saudara; ~ *registry office* kantor catatan sipil; *American* ~ *War* Perang Sipil Amérika; **civilian** *n* orang sipil; **civility** *n* kesopanan; **civilization** *n* [sivilaizésyen] peradaban; **civilized** *adj* beradab

Ck *creek* K. (kali)

claim *n* tuntutan; tagihan; pengakuan; *vi* mengaku; *vt* menuntut; menagih; mengaku; meminta

clam *n* kerang; ~ *chowder* semacam sup kerang; **clammy** *adj* lembab, basah

clamber *vi* memanjat, naik

clamor, clamour *n* keriuhan, keramaian, kegaduhan; **clamorous** *adj* riuh, ramai, gaduh

clamp *n* klém

clan *n* suku bangsa, kaum, marga; **clannish** *adj* hanya bergaul dengan kaum sendiri

clandestine *adj* [klandéstin] gelap, diam-diam, sembunyi-sembunyi, rahasia

clap *n* tepuk; *a* ~ *of thunder* sambaran petir; *vi* bertepuk tangan; *vt* menepuk; **clapper** *n* anak loncéng

claret *n* [klaret] sejenis anggur mérah; *adj* mérah

clarify *vt* [klarifai] menjelaskan, menerangkan; **clarification** *n* [klarifikésyen] penjelasan, penerangan ← **clear**

clarinet *n* klarinét

clarity *n* [klariti] kejernihan ← **clear**

clash *n* béntrokan; pertandingan; *vi* béntrok; *those colors* ~ dua warna itu ramai; ~ *of civilizations* béntrokan peradaban

clasp *n* jepitan, géspér; pelukan; *vt* menjepit, memegang

class *n* mutu, kualitas (tinggi); **classic** *n* sesuatu yang terkenal; *adj* klasik; **classical** ~ *music* musik klasik; **classy** *adj* bermutu

class *n* kelas; pelajaran; golongan; *first* ~ terbaik; *science* ~ kelas IPA; **classification** *n* klasifikasi; **classified** *adj* dirahasiakan; **classify** *vt* menggolongkan; **classmate** *n* teman sekelas; **classroom** *n* ruang kelas

classic *n* sesuatu yang terkenal; *adj* klasik; **classical** ~ *music* musik klasik ← **class**

classification *n* klasifikasi; **classified** *adj* dirahasiakan; **classify** *vt* menggolongkan ← **class**

classmate *n* teman sekelas ← **class**

classroom *n* ruang kelas ← **class**

classy *adj* bermutu ← **class**

clatter *n* gemertak; *vi* bergerak dengan bunyi ramai

clause *n* ayat, klausa; syarat; *sub-~* anak kalimat

claustrophobia *n* rasa takut di tempat tertutup

clavicle *n* [klavikel] tulang selangka

claw *n* cakar, jepit; *vt* mencakar

clay *n* tanah liat

clean *adj* [klin] bersih; *vt* membersihkan; *~-up* pembersihan, pembérésan; *~ one's teeth* gosok gigi, sikat gigi; *to come ~* mengaku; **cleaner** *n* tukang bersih-bersih, tukang sapu; **cleaning** *n* pembersihan; **cleanliness** *n* [klénlines] kebersihan; **cleanse** *vt* membersihkan, mencuci; **cleanser** *n* pembersih

clear *adj* [klir] terang, jernih, jelas; nyaring, nyata; *~ skies* langit biru, cuaca cerah; *to keep ~* menghindari, mengelakkan; *in the ~* bébas; *vi* menjadi terang; *~ of* menyatakan tidak bersalah; *~ off* pergi; *~ up* berkemas-kemas; *vt* membéréskan; membuka lahan; **clearance** *n* izin; *~ sale* obral; **clearing** *n* tanah terbuka di tengah hutan; *fin* kliring; **clearly** *adv* (dengan) jelas

cleavage *n* [klivej] belahan dada; **cleave** *vt* **clove/cleaved cleft/cloven** membelah

clench *vt* menggenggam; *~ed fist* kepalan tangan

clergy *n* [klérji] kaum pastor atau pendéta; **clergyman** *n* pendéta, pastor

clerical *adj* [klérikal] berkaitan dengan pekerjaan kantor, administratif

clerk *n* [klark] juru tulis

clever *adj* [kléver] pandai, cerdas, pintar; **cleverly** *adv* dengan cerdas; **cleverness** *n* kepandaian, kepintaran

cliché *n* klisé

click *n* klik, pencat; *v* klik; *vt* memencat

client *n* [klaient] nasabah, pelanggan, tamu, klién; **clientele** *n, pl* [klaientél] para nasabah, pelanggan, klien

cliff *n* tebing; *~hanger* cerita yang sangat menegangkan; *~top* di atas tebing

climate *n* [klaimet] iklim; *~ change* perubahan iklim

climax *n* [klaimaks] puncak, klimaks, orgasme

climb *n* [klaim] perjalanan naik; *~ down* turun (dari tempat tinggi); *vt* memanjat; menaiki; *~ing plant* tanaman merambat; **climber** *n* pemanjat

cling *vi* **clung clung** melekat, berpegang; *~ to* melekat pada, memegang; *~ wrap* plastik pembungkus makanan

clinic *n* klinik, pusat keséhatan masyarakat (puskésmas)

clink *vi* berbunyi (gelas)

clip *n* jepitan; klip; *vt* menjepit, menggunting, memotong; **clipboard** *n* papan alas; **clippers** *n* gunting; **clipping** *newspaper ~* guntingan koran, kliping

clique *n* [klik] géng, kelompok

clitoris *n* kelentit, klitoris

cloak *n* mantel; **cloakroom** *n* tempat gantung jas dan mantel

clock *n* jam; *~ radio* jam radio; *~ tower* menara jam; *alarm ~* wéker; *like ~work* seperti mesin jam, sangat teratur; *around the ~* 24 jam; *three o'~* jam tiga; *vi ~ in* melapor setelah tiba di kantor; *vt* mencatat waktu; **clockwise** *adv, adj* arah jarum jam

clod *n* gumpal, bungkah

clog *n* kelom, bakiak

clone *n* klon; *vt* mengklon; **cloning** *n* pengklonan; *coll* kloning

close *adj* [klos] dekat, akrab; *~-fisted* pelit, kikir; *~ friend* teman dekat, kawan akrab; *~ quarters* dari dekat; *~ shave* nyaris celaka; *~ up* dari dekat; gambar yang diperbesar; **closely** *adv* dari dekat, dengan teliti; **closeness** *n* kedekatan

close *v* [kloz] *vi* tutup; *vt* menutup; *~ one's eyes* memejamkan mata, menutup mata; *~ the door* menutup pintu; **closed** *adj* tutup; **closing** *adj* terakhir; *~ hours* jam tutup; *~ remarks* kata-kata penutup; *n* penutupan; **closure** *n* [klosyer] penutupan

closely *adv* [klosli] dari dekat, dengan teliti ← **close**

closeness *n* [klosnes] kedekatan ← **close**

closet *n* [klozet] lemari baju; *to come out of the ~* mengaku sebagai orang homoséksual

closing *adj* terakhir; ~ *remarks* kata-kata penutup; ~ *hours* jam tutup; *n* penutupan ← **close**

closure *n* [klosyer] penutupan ← **close**

clot *n* gumpal; *blood* ~ gumpalan darah beku; *vi* bergumpal; ~ *cream* krim kental

cloth *n* kain, bahan; *table*~ taplak méja; **clothe** *vt* memberi baju; **clothes** *n* pakaian, baju; ~ *dryer* mesin pengering baju; ~ *horse* jemuran pakaian; ~ *line* kawat untuk menjemur pakaian; ~ *peg* jepitan baju

cloud *n* [klaud] awan; *vi* menjadi keruh; ~ *over* menjadi mendung, tertutup awan; *on* ~ *nine* sangat bahagia; *vt* memperkeruh; **cloudless** *adj* tidak berawan, cerah; **cloudy** *adj* berawan, mendung

clove *n* céngkéh; ~ *cigarette* rokok kréték

clove, cloven *vt, pf* → **cleave**

clover *n* semanggi; ~-*leaf interchange* simpangan susun semanggi

clown *n* badut, pelawak; *vi* melucu

club *n* perhimpunan, klub, kelab; ~ *sandwich* roti dengan isi daging dan selada; *night*~ kelab malam, diskoték; *golf* ~ stik golf; kelab golf; *vi* ~ *together* bersatu, bekerja sama (untuk membeli sesuatu); *vt* memukul; **clubbing** *n* pergi ke diskoték; clubs; *adj* keriting (jenis kartu)

clue *n* tanda, petunjuk; *I haven't a* ~ saya tidak tahu sama sekali; **clueless** *adj, sl* bodoh, tanpa idé

clumsy *adj* canggung, kikuk; **clumsiness** *n* kecanggungan

clung *vi, pf* → **cling**

cluster *n* gugus, tandan; *vi* berkerumun

clutch *n* genggam; kopling; ~ *bag* tas tangan tanpa pegangan; *vt* menggenggam

cm *centimeter, centimetre* cm (séntiméter)

Co., Coy. *abbrev company* PT, maskapai, perusahaan

coach *n* pelatih; bis pariwisata; keréta kencana; *vt* melatih, membimbing

coagulate *vi* [koagulét] bergumpal, membeku (darah)

coal *n* batu bara; ~ *mine* tambang batu bara; ~ *miner* pekerja tambang batu bara

coalition *n* koalisi

coarse *adj* [kors] kasar

coast *n* pantai, pesisir; **coastal** *adj* berkaitan dengan pantai; **coastguard** *n* [kostgard] penjaga pantai; **coastline** *n* garis pantai

coast *vi* meluncur, jalan bébas (karena gaya berat)

coaster *n* alas gelas

coastguard *n* [kostgard] penjaga pantai ← **coast**

coastline *n* garis pantai ← **coast**

coat *n* mantel, jas; lapisan; kulit atau bulu binatang; ~ *hanger* gantungan baju; *rain*~ jas hujan; ~ *of paint* lapisan cat; ~ *of arms* lambang (kerajaan, kenegaraan dsb); *vt* melapisi

coax *vt* membujuk

cobble [kobel] ~*stone* batu trotoar; **cobbler** *n* tukang réparasi sepatu; toko réparasi sepatu

cobra *n* kobra, ular séndok

cobweb *n* sarang laba-laba

cocaine *n* [kokéin] kokain

coccyx *n* [koksiks] tulang ékor

cock *n* ayam jantan; ~ *fighting* sabung ayam; ~ *a doodle doo!* kukuruyuk!; *vulg* pénis; **cocky** *adj* arogan

cockatoo *n* [kokatu] burung kakatua

cockle *n* sejenis kerang

Cockney *n* [kokni] penduduk asli London

cockpit *n* kokpit

cockroach *n* kecoa

cocktail *n* sejenis minuman keras, koktil

cocky *adj* arogan ← **cock**

cocoa *n* [koko] (biji) coklat

coconut *n* (buah) kelapa; ~ *milk* santan; ~ *palm* pohon kelapa, pohon nyiur; *desiccated* ~ kelapa parut kering

cocoon *n* [kekun] kepompong

COD *abbrev cash on delivery* membayar saat diantarkan

cod *n* sejenis ikan laut; ~-*liver oil* minyak ikan

code *n* sandi, kode; undang-undang, peraturan; ~ *name* nama sandi; *the highway* ~ undang-undang lalu lintas

co-educational ~ *school* sekolah untuk

murid laki-laki dan perempuan

coerce *vt* [koérs] memaksa; **coercion** *n* [koérsyen] paksaan, pemaksaan

coexist *vi* [ko éksist] hidup bersama, hidup berdua; **coexistence** *n* kehidupan bersama

C of E *abbrev Church of England* Geréja Inggris, Anglikan

coffee *n* kopi; ~ *break* réhat kopi; ~ *table* méja (untuk kopi) di ruang tamu; *instant* ~ kopi instan; *white* ~, *milk* ~ kopi susu

coffin *n* peti mati

cog *n* roda gigi

coherence *n* [kohirens] pertalian, perhubungan; **coherent** *adj* jelas; masuk akal

cohesion *n* [kohisyen] kepaduan; **cohesive** *adj* bersatu, berpadu

coil *n* gulungan, gulung; *mosquito* ~ koil anti nyamuk, obat nyamuk; *vi* bergelung; *vt* menggulungkan

coin *n* uang logam, koin

coincide *vi* [koinsaid] bertepatan; ~ *with* bertepatan dengan; **coincidence** *n* [koinsidens] kebetulan; *by* ~ secara kebetulan; **coincidentally** *adv* secara kebetulan

coitus *n* [koitus] senggama; ~ *interruptus* senggama terputus

coke → **cocaine**

colander *n* saringan (untuk mencuci sayur)

cold *n* masuk angin, pilek; rasa dingin; *to feel the* ~ sering kedinginan; *to have a* ~ pilek, flu; *adj* dingin; ~-*blooded* berdarah dingin; ~-*box* kotak pendingin; ~ *comfort* tidak menghibur; ~ *sore* sariawan; *to give the* ~ *shoulder* menghindari, mencuékkan

collaborate *vi* bekerja sama; ~ *with* bekerja sama dengan; **collaboration** *n* kerjasama; **collaborator** *n* orang yang bekerja sama; kolaborator

collapse *n* keruntuhan, kerobohan; *vi* runtuh, ambruk, roboh; pingsan; **collapsible** *adj* [kolapsibel] dapat dibongkar atau dilipat

collar *n* kerah, leher baju; **collarbone** *n* tulang selangka

collateral *n* jaminan; *adj* tambahan; ~ *damage* kerusakan sampingan

colleague *n* [kolig] rekan, koléga, teman kantor

collect *vt* mengumpulkan, memungut; **collection** *n* kumpulan, koléksi; **collective** *n* koperasi, usaha koléktif; *adj* bersama, koléktif; **collector** *n* koléktor

college *n* [kolej] sekolah, kolése; perguruan tinggi, univérsitas; ~ *student* mahasiswa; *to go to* ~ (sudah) kuliah

collide *vi* bertabrakan; ~ *with* menabrak; **collision** *n* [kolisyen] tabrakan; ~ *course* arah yang akan mengakibatkan tabrakan

collie *n* sejenis anjing besar

colloquial *adj* percakapan, sehari-hari; **colloquialism** *n* ucapan sehari-hari

Cologne *n* [kolon] Keulen; **cologne** *n* kolonye

Colombia *n* Kolombia; **Colombian** *n* orang Kolombia; *adj* berasal dari Kolombia

colon *n* titik dua [:]; **semi-**~ *n* titik koma [;]

colon *n* usus besar; **colonoscopy** *n* pemeriksaan usus besar

colonel *n* [kenel] kolonél; *lieutenant-*~ létkol (létnan kolonél)

colonial *adj* kolonial, penjajah; ~ *house* rumah Belanda; **colonization** *n* penjajahan; **colonize** *vt* menjajah, menduduki; **colonist** *n* penduduk baru; **colony** *n* jajahan

color, colour *n* [kaler] warna; *vi* memérah; *vt* mewarnai; ~*blind* buta warna; *with flying* ~*s* dengan gemilang; **colored** *adj* berwarna; *Cape* ~ orang keturunan campuran di Tanjung Harapan; **colorful** *adj* berwarna-warni; **coloring** *n* (zat) pewarna; mewarnai; ~ *competition* lomba mewarnai

colossal *adj* sangat besar, raksasa

colt *n* kuda jantan yang muda

column *n* tiang; barisan; kolom; *fifth* ~ pihak rahasia; **columnist** *n* pengasuh rubrik

coma *n* koma, mati suri; **comatose** *adj* [komatoz] mati suri, di dalam koma, tidak sadar diri

comb *n* [koom] sisir; *vt* menyisir; ~ *one's hair* menyisir rambut, sisiran

combat *n* peperangan, pertempuran; *vt* memerangi, melawan

combination *n* gabungan, kombinasi; ~ *lock* kunci kombinasi; **combine** *vi* bergabung, menyatu; *vt* menggabungkan, mengombinasikan, memadukan; **combined** *adj* terpadu, bersama

come *vi* [kam] **came come** datang, tiba, sampai; ~ *across* menyeberang; tampak; ~ *back* kembali, balik; ~ *by* mendapat; ~ *clean* mengaku; ~ *forward* tampil, maju; ~ *from* berasal dari, datang dari; ~ *home* pulang; ~ *in* masuk; ~ *on!* ayo!; ~ *out* keluar; ~ *through* lewat, menempuh; ~ *round* datang; ~ *under* termasuk; ~ *up* timbul, muncul; naik; *how* ~? kenapa?; ~ *a cropper* kapok; ~ *up to* mendekati, mendatangi, menghampiri; ~ *what may* bagaimanapun; **comeback** *n* kembali; **coming** *n* kedatangan; *the Second* ~ kembalinya Almasih; *adj* mendatang

comedian *n* [komidien] pelawak; **comedy** *n* lawak, komédi; **comic** *n* pelawak; *adj* lucu; **comical** *adj* lucu, kocak

comet *n* bintang berékor, komét

comfort *n* [kamfert] kenyamanan; hikmah, hiburan; *vt* menghibur; **comfortable** *adj* **comfy** *sl* nyaman; **comfortably** *adv* dengan nyaman; mampu, berada

comic *n* pelawak; *adj* lucu; **comical** *adj* lucu, kocak ← **comedy**

coming *n* [kaming] kedatangan; *the Second* ~ kembalinya Almasih; *adj* mendatang ← **come**

comma *n* tanda koma [,]

command *n* perintah; komando; penguasaan; *in* ~ berkuasa, sedang memerintah; *vt* memimpin; **commandant**, **commander** *n* komandan; **commando** *n* komando, prajurit penyerang

commemorate *vt* memperingati, merayakan; **commemoration** *n* peringatan, perayaan; **commemorative** *adj* dalam rangka memperingati

commence *vi* mulai, bermula; *vt* memulai, memulakan; **commencement** *n* awal, permulaan

commend *vt* memuji, merékomendasikan; **commendable** *adj* terpuji; **commendation** *n* penghargaan, pujian

comment *n* koméntar; *no* ~ tidak ada keterangan; *vi* berkoméntar, memberi koméntar; *vt* mengoméntari; **commentary** *n* tafsir; koméntar, ulasan; **commentator** *n* koméntator

commerce *n* perdagangan, perniagaan; *chamber of* ~ kamar dagang (kadin); **commercial** *n* [komérsyal] iklan; *adj* dagang, perniagaan; komérsial

commission *n* pesan; komisi; *vt* memesan, memerintahkan; **commissioner** *n* komisaris

commit *vi* berjanji; ~ *to* berjanji akan; *vt* melakukan, menjalankan; ~ *a crime* melakukan kejahatan, berbuat jahat; **committed** *adj* terikat; sungguh-sungguh; **commitment** *n* janji, tanggung jawab, ikatan

committee *n* [komiti] panitia, komité

commodity *n* barang dagangan, komoditi; *basic* ~ bahan pokok

common *adj* biasa, umum; bersama; rendah; ~ *knowledge* rahasia umum; ~ *sense* akal séhat; *to have something in* ~ memiliki persamaan; **commoner** *n* orang kebanyakan, rakyat biasa; **commonly** *adv* biasanya; **Commonwealth** *n* Persemakmuran

commotion *n* kegemparan, kegaduhan, huru-hara

commune *n* komunitas yang hidup bersama; **community** *n* masyarakat, umat, komunitas

communicate *vi* berkomunikasi; *vt* memberitahu, menghubungi; **communication** *n* komunikasi, perhubungan; **communicative** *adj* komunikatif; **communiqué** *n* komuniké

communion *n, Chr* perjamuan

communiqué *n* komuniké

communism *n* komunisme; **communist** *n* orang komunis; *adj* komunis; *Indonesian* ~ *Party* Partai Komunis Indonesia (PKI)

community *n* masyarakat, umat, komunitas; ~ *service* pelayanan masyarakat ← **commune**

commute *n* perjalanan ulang-alik; *vi* pulang pergi, wira-wiri; ~ *from* ... *to* ... pulang pergi dari ... ke ...; **commuter** *n* pelaju

Comoros *the* ~ Kepulauan Komoro, Kepulauan Comoros

compact *n* tempat bedak; perjanjian; *vt* memadatkan; *adj* kompak, padat; ~ *disc (CD)* CD, disk

companion *n* kawan, teman; *longtime* ~ pasangan hidup; **company** *n* [kampeni] kawan-kawan; perusahaan, maskapai (penerbangan); *to keep someone* ~ menemani orang

comparative *adj* perbandingan, komparatif; **comparatively** *adv* secara rélatif; **compare** *vi* ~ *with* dibandingkan (dengan); *vt* membandingkan; **comparison** *n* perbandingan; *by* ~ sebagai perbandingan

compartment *n* ruang (keréta), bagian

compass *n* [kampas] pedoman, kompas; **compasses** *a pair of* ~ jangka

compassion *n* rasa (belas) kasih, pengertian; **compassionate** *adj* [kompasynenet] mengasihani, berbelas kasih

compatible *n* [kompatibel] cocok, sesuai; ~ *with* cocok dengan

compatriot *n* saudara sebangsa dan setanah air; orang dari negeri yang sama

compel *vt* memaksa; **compelled** *adj* terpaksa; *she felt* ~ *to help him* dia merasa terpaksa membantu orang itu; **compelling** *adj* sangat menarik; **compulsion** *n* paksaan; **compulsive** *adj* terdorong untuk melakukan; ~ *shopper* sangat gemar berbelanja; **compulsory** *adj* paksa, wajib

compensate *vt* mengganti (rugi); **compensation** *n* ganti rugi, kompénsasi

compere *n* pembawa acara; *vi* membawa acara

compete *vi* [kompit] bersaing, bertanding; ~ *against* bersaing melawan; ~

for memperebutkan; ~ *in* ikut serta dalam; ~ *with* bersaing dengan; **competition** *n* [kompetisyen] persaingan; pertandingan; **competitive** *adj* [kompétitif] (suka) bersaing; **competitor** *n* saingan; peserta

competence *n* kemampuan, kompeténsi; ~*based curriculum* kurikulum berbasis kompeténsi; **competent** *adj* mampu, kompetén

competition *n* persaingan; pertandingan; **competitive** *adj* (suka) bersaing; **competitor** *n* saingan ← **compete**

compilation *n* [kompilésyen] antologi, koléksi, susunan, kompilasi, bunga rampai; **compile** *vt* menyusun; **compiler** *n* penyusun

complacent *adj* [komplésent] (mudah) puas, tidak ambisius; **complacency** *n* rasa mudah puas

complain *vi* berkeluh-kesah, mengadu, mengeluh; ~ *about* mengeluh soal, mengadukan; **complaint** *n* pengaduan, keluhan

complement *n* pelengkap; **complementary** *adj* yang melengkapi

complete *adj* lengkap, komplit; *vi* selesai; *vt* menyelesaikan, merampungkan; **completely** *adv* sama sekali; **completion** *n* selesainya, penyelesaian

complex *n* kompléks; *adj* rumit, ruwet; **complexion** *n* [kompléksyen] kulit wajah, kulit muka

compliant *adj* [komplaient] sesuai dengan ← **comply**

complicate *vt* mempersulit; **complicated** *adj* rumit, kompléks, berbelit-belit; **complication** *n* kesulitan; komplikasi (penyakit)

complicit *adj* [komplisit] terlibat; **complicity** *n* keterlibatan

compliment *n* pujian; *a backhanded* ~ pujian yang mengandung unsur kritik; *my* ~*s to X* salam saya untuk X; *to pay a* ~ *to someone* memuji orang; *vt* memuji; **complimentary** *adj* memuji; cuma-cuma, gratis

comply *vi* [komplai] ~ *(with)* mengikuti, memenuhi; **compliant** *adj* [komplaient] sesuai; ~ *with* sesuai dengan

component *n* unsur, komponén, suku
cadang

compose *vt* menyusun, membentuk,
mengarang; menggubah (lagu atau
musik); ~ *yourself* kendalikan diri
sendiri; **composed** *adj* tenang, kalem,
tidak mudah tergoncang; ~ *of* terdiri
dari, terdiri atas; **composer** *n* komponis, penggubah; **composite** *adj* [kom-
posit] majemuk; **composition** *n*
karangan; susunan; **composure** *n*
ketenangan

compost *n* kompos

composure *n* ketenangan ← **compose**

compote *n* buah masak

compound *n* kompléks (perumahan);
gabungan; senyawa; *adj* gabungan; ~
interest bunga berbunga

comprehend *vi* mengerti; *vt* mengerti,
memahami; **comprehensible** *adj*
dapat dipahami; **comprehension** *n*
pengertian, pemahaman; **comprehensive** *adj* [komprehénsiv] lengkap

compress *n* komprés; *vt* memampatkan,
memadatkan; **compressed** *adj* padat

comprise *vi* meliputi, mencakup; *vt* (~
of) terdiri dari, terdiri atas

compromise *n* [kompromaiz] kompromi; *vi* mencari jalan tengah, berkompromi; *vt* mengorbankan

compulsion *n* paksaan; **compulsive** *adj*
terdorong untuk melakukan; ~ *shopper* sangat gemar berbelanja; **compulsory** *adj* paksa, wajib ← **compel**

computation *n* perhitungan, kalkulasi;
computer *n* komputer; ~ *science* ilmu
komputer; **computerization** *n* komputerisasi

comrade *n* [komrad] kawan, teman;
kamerad

con *n* penipuan; **conman** *n* penipu

concave *adj* cekung

conceal *vt* [konsil] menyembunyikan;
concealed *adj* tersembunyi; **concealment** *n* persembunyian

concede *vi* [konsid] mengaku, menerima; **concession** *n* izin, kelonggaran;
konsési; ~ *fare* ongkos (angkutan
umum) yang lebih murah

conceit *n* [konsit] kesombongan,

keangkuhan; **conceited** *adj* sombong,
angkuh

conceive *vi* [konsiv] menjadi hamil; *vt*
mengerti, membayangkan; **concept** *n*
konsép; **conception** *n* pengertian,
konsepsi; pembuahan

concentrate *vi* memusatkan (perhatian),
konsén; ~ *on* memusatkan perhatian
pada; **concentrate** *n* konséntrat, sirop;
concentrated *adj* kental, padat; ter-
pusatkan; **concentration** *n* pemusatan,
konséntrasi; ~ *camp* kamp tahanan

concept *n* konsép; **conception** *n*
pengertian, konsépsi; pembuahan ←
conceive

concern *n* perkara, hal; perhatian;
keprihatinan; perusahaan; *cause for* ~
bermasalah; *vi* berkaitan; membuat
prihatin; **concerned** *adj* prihatin; tersangkut; *to be* ~ *about* memperhatikan, prihatin, memedulikan; *as far as
I'm* ~ kalau saya; *to whom it may* ~
agar diketahui; **concerning** *conj* tentang, mengenai

concert *n* konsér

concession *n* izin, kelonggaran; konsési; ~ *fare* ongkos (angkutan umum)
yang lebih murah ← **concede**

conch *n* kerang besar

conciliation *n* [konsiliésyen] tindakan
mendamaikan; **conciliatory** *adj* bersifat mendamaikan

concise *adj* péndék, ringkas, singkat

conclude *vi* berakhir; membuat kesimpulan, menyimpulkan; *vt* memutuskan;
conclusion *n* kesimpulan; akhir; *in* ~
sebagai kata akhir; **conclusive** *adj*
[konklusif] meyakinkan, menentukan

concourse *n* tempat terbuka

concrete *n* [konkrit] beton; ~ *mixer* truk
pengaduk beton; *vt* mengecor beton;
adj nyata

concubine *n* selir

concur *vi* setuju, sependapat

concussed *adj* gegar otak; **concussion**
n gegar otak

condemn *vt* [kondém] menghukum;
menghakimi, mengutuk; **condemna-
tion** *n* kritikan, hujatan

condensation *n* pengembunan, kondénsasi; **condense** *vi* mengembun, memadat, mengental; menyingkatkan; **condensed** *adj* singkat, kental; ~ *milk* susu kental

condescend *vi* merendahkan diri; **condescending** *adj* sombong; **condescension** *n* sikap sombong

condition *n* keadaan, kondisi; syarat; *vt* memelihara, membiasakan; **conditional** *adj* dengan syarat; ~ *tense* bentuk pengandaian; **conditioner** *n* pelembab (rambut)

condolences *n, pl* bélasungkawa; *our* ~ kami ikut berduka cita, kami ucapkan bélasungkawa

condom *n* kondom

condominium *n* apartemén

condone *vt* tidak menilai sebagai salah, menerima

conducive *adj* kondusif; ~ *to* kondusif untuk

conduct *n* kelakuan, cara; *good* ~ kelakuan baik; *vt* memimpin, melakukan; **conductor** *n* dirigén (musik); kondéktur (angkutan umum); penghantar

cone *n* kerucut; marka jalan; *pine* ~ buah cemara; **conical** *adj* kerucut, mengerucut

confectioner *n* pembuat permén; **confectionery** *n* permén, gula-gula

confederate *adj* sekutu; bersekutu; ~ *Army* Tentara Konfédérasi (wilayah selatan selama Perang Saudara Amerika); **confederation** *n* persekutuan

confer *vi* bermusyawarah, berembuk; *vt* menganugerahkan; **conference** *n* [konferens] konferénsi, konperénsi, permusyawaratan

confess *v* mengaku; **confession** *n* pengakuan

confetti *n* guntingan kertas yang dilémpar saat berpésta, hujan kertas

confidant *n* orang kepercayaan; **confidante** *n, f* [konfidant] orang kepercayaan; **confide** *vi* ~ *in someone* bercerita kepada orang (tentang rahasia); memercayai, membuka rahasia; **confidence** *n* kepercayaan; *in* ~ rahasia; *self*-~ percaya diri (PD); **confi-**

dent *adj* berani, percaya diri; **confidential** *adj* [konfidénsyel] rahasia

confine *vt* membatasi, mengurung; memingit; **confinement** *n* masa persalinan; pingitan

confirm *vt* menegaskan, memastikan; membaptis; **confirmation** *n* kepastian, penegasan, konfirmasi; pembaptisan

confiscate *vt* menyita; **confiscation** *n* penyitaan

conflict *n* perselisihan, pertikaian, percékcokan, konflik; perang; ~ *of interest* konflik kepentingan; *vi* ~ *with* bertentangan dengan; **conflicting** *adj* bertentangan

confluence *n* pertemuan dua sungai

conform *vi* menurut, sesuai dengan; mengikuti orang kebanyakan; ~ *to* mengikuti

confound *vt* menghérankan, membingungkan; menghalangi; **confounded** *adj* bingung; persétan

confront *vt* [konfrant] **confronting** *adj* menghadapi; menentang, melawan; **confrontation** *n* konfrontasi

confuse *vt* membingungkan; **confused** *adj* bingung; **confusing** *adj* membingungkan; **confusion** *n* kebingungan

congeal *vi* [konjil] membeku (darah)

congenital *adj* [kongénital] ~ *disease* penyakit turunan, penyakit bawaan

congested *adj* macet, sesak; **congestion** *n* kesesakan, kemacetan

conglomeration *n* konglomerasi

Congo *n* [konggo] (*the* ~) Kongo; ~ (*formerly Zaire*) Kongo Kinshasa; *the* ~ *Democratic Republic* Kongo Brazzaville; **Congolese** *n* orang Kongo; *adj* berasal dari Kongo

congratulate *vt* mengucapkan selamat kepada; **congratulations** *n, pl* ucapan selamat; *ejac* selamat

congregate *vi* berkumpul; **congregation** *n* jemaah (geréja)

congress *n* kongrés, muktamar; **Congress** *n* Perwakilan Rakyat Amérika (Sénat dan Déwan Perwakilan Rakyat); **congressional** *adj* berhubungan dengan Perwakilan Rakyat Amérika

conical *adj* kerucut, mengerucut ←
cone
conifer *n* jenis pohon cemara
conjunction *n* kata sambung, kata
penghubung; *in ~ with* bersama
conjunctivitis *n* [konjanktivaitis] kon-
junktivitis
conjure *v* [konjer] menyulap, menyikir;
conjurer *n* tukang sulap, penyulap
conman *n* penipu ← **con**
connect *vi* menyambung; *vt* menyambungkan, menghubungkan; **connected**
adj berkaitan; **connection** *n* hubungan,
sambungan, kaitan; konéksi
connive *vi* berkomplot
connoisseur *n* [konesur] penggemar;
ahli, pakar
connotation *n* konotasi
conquer *vt* [konker] mengalahkan,
menaklukkan, merebut; **conqueror** *n*
penakluk; **conquest** *n* penaklukan
conscience *n* [konsyens] hati nurani;
conscientious *adj* [konsyiénsyes]
rajin
conscious *adj* [konsyus] sadar; *~ of*
sadar akan; **consciousness** *n*
kesadaran
conscript *n* wajib militér; **conscription**
n wajib militér
consecrate *vt* menahbiskan; mengabdikan; **consecration** *n* penahbisan
consecutive *adj* [konsékutiv]
berturut-turut
consensus *n* mufakat; **consent** *vi*
setuju; *~ to* menyetujui; *n* izin;
consenting *adj ~ adults* orang déwasa
yang suka sama suka (dalam hal
bersanggama)
consequence *n* akibat, dampak; **con-
sequent** *adj* yang berikut; **consequently** *adv* oléh karena itu, maka
conservation *n* perlindungan, pemeliharaan, konsérvasi; **conservationist** *n*
aktivis lingkungan; **conservative** *adj*
kolot, konsérvatif; *~ Party* Partai
Konsérvatif (di Inggris); **conservato-
ry** *n* sekolah musik; ruang berkaca
(untuk menangkap cahaya matahari);
conserve *n* [konserv] selai; *vt* [kon-
sérv] menghémat

consider *vt* menganggap, mengindahkan; mempertimbangkan; **consider-
able** *adj* cukup banyak; **considerate**
adj [konsideret] ténggang rasa; **consideration** *n* pertimbangan; **consider-
ing** *conj* mengingat
consign *vt* [konsain] menyerahkan;
mengirimkan; **consignment** *n* kiriman
consist *vi ~ of* terdiri atas, terdiri dari
consistent *adj* konsékuén, tetap, konsistén; **consistently** *adv* terus-menerus
consolation *n* hiburan; *~ prize* juara
harapan; **console** *n* méja atau papan
(untuk peralatan); *vt* menghibur
consolidate *vi* menjadi kuat; *vt* memperkuat, mengukuhkan; **consolidated**
adj gabungan; **consolidation** *n*
penguatan, pengukuhan
consonant *n* huruf mati, konsonan
consort *n* kawan; pasangan raja atau
ratu; *vi* bergaul; *~ with* bergaul dengan
conspicuous *adj* [konspikyues]
menonjol, jelas
conspiracy *n* [konspirasi] komplotan,
persekongkolan; **conspirator** *n*
sekongkol, komplot; **conspire** *vi*
bersekongkol, berkomplot; *~ against*
bersekongkol terhadap
constable *n* [kanstabel] polisi
constant *adj* tetap, selalu; **constantly**
adv selalu, terus-menerus
constellation *n* gugus bintang, konstélasi
constipated *adj* **constipation** *n* sembelit
constituency *n* daérah perwakilan
constitute *vt* [konstityut] merupakan;
terdiri dari; **constitution** *n* undang-
undang dasar (UUD), konstitusi;
keadaan tubuh; **constitutional** *adj*
menurut undang-undang dasar
constrain *vt* membatasi; **constrained**
adj terbatas; **constraint** *n* batasan,
kendala, hambatan
construct *vt* membangun, membuat,
membentuk; **construction** *n* bangunan, pembangunan (gedung), konstruksi; *~ site* proyék; **constructive**
adj bersifat membina, berguna
consul *n* konsul, wakil; **consular** *adj*
berhubungan dengan konsul; **con-**

sulate n konsulat; ~-*General* konjén (konsulat-jénderal)

consult vt menanyakan, mencari pendapat dari, berkonsultasi dengan; ~*ing room* n kamar periksa; ~ *a dictionary* memakai kamus; **consultancy** n layanan penasihat; **consultant** n penasihat; **consultation** n perundingan, konsultasi; **consultative** adj [konsaltativ] bersifat memberi nasihat

consume vt memakan, menghabiskan; memakai, menggunakan; **consumer** n pengguna, pemakai, konsumén; **consumption** n pemakaian; *arch* radang paru-paru, TBC

contact n hubungan, kontak; ~ *lenses* lénsa kontak; vt menghubungi, mengontak

contagious adj [kontéjus] menular, menjangkit

contain vt berisi, memuat, mengandung; menampung, menahan; **container** n tempat; ~ *ship* kapal barang; **containment** n pembatasan, penahanan

contaminate vi tercemar; vt mencemari; **contamination** n kontaminasi, pencemaran

contemplate vt merenungkan; **contemplation** n renungan

contemporary n teman seangkatan; adj modérn, kini, kontémporér

contempt n penghinaan; **contemptible** adj [kontémptibel] hina

contend vi berpendapat; bersaing; ~ *with* menghadapi; **contender** n pesaing, peserta, calon juara

content n [kentént] kepuasan; *to your heart's* ~ sepuas-puasnya; **contented** adj puas, senang

content n [kontént] isi, bahan; **contents** n, pl isi, muatan; *table of* ~ daftar isi

contention n anggapan, pendapat; **contentious** adj [konténsyes] kontrovérsial, dapat diperdebatkan ← **contend**

contest n pertandingan, lomba; *beauty* ~ kontés kecantikan; vt bertanding dalam; memperjuangkan; menantang; **contestant** n peserta

context n hubungan, kaitan; kontéks

contiguous adj [kontigyues] bersebelahan, berdampingan

continent n benua; **continental** adj berhubungan dengan benua (Eropa); ~ *breakfast* sarapan ala Eropa

contingency [kontinjensi] ~ *plan* rencana altérnatif; **contingent** n kontingén

continual adj **continually** adv selalu, terus-menerus; **continuation** n terusan, lanjutan, sambungan; **continue** vi terus; vt melanjutkan, meneruskan; *to be* ~d bersambung; **continuity** n [kontinyuiti] kesinambungan; **continuous** adj [kontinyues] terus-menerus; **continuously** adv secara terus-menerus

contour n [kontur] garis bentuk; ~ *map* peta kontur

contraband n, adj barang selundupan

contraceptive n, adj kontrasépsi; ~ *pill* pil KB

contract n kontrak, surat perjanjian; *under* ~ dikontrak; vi mengecil, berkontraksi; vt kena, mengidap (penyakit); memborong; mengontrak; **contraction** n kepéndékan, singkatan; kontraksi; **contractor** n kontraktor, pemborong; **contractual** adj menurut kontrak

contradict vt membantah, menyanggah; **contradiction** n pertentangan, kontradiksi; **contradictory** adj bertentangan, berlawanan

contrary adj [kontrari] berlawanan; sulit patuh; ~ *to* berlawanan dengan; *on the* ~ sebaliknya

contrast n perbédaan, kontras; vi berbéda; *in* ~ *with* berbéda dengan; membandingkan; **contrasting** adj berbéda, berlawanan

contravene vt [kontravin] melanggar; **contravention** n [kontravénsyen] pelanggaran

contribute vi bersumbang; vt menyumbang, memberikan; **contribution** n sumbangan, kontribusi; **contributor** n penyumbang

contrite adj bersikap menyesal

contrive vi berusaha; vt membuat-buat, merékayasa

control *n* kendali, kontrol; *in ~ of* mengendalikan; *vt* mengendalikan, menguasai; *~ tower* menara pengawas

controversial *adj* kontrovérsial; **controversy** *n* isu, kontrovérsi

convalescence *n* [konvalésens] masa pulih; masa istirahat; **convalescent** *n* orang yang sedang pulih dari sakit

convene *vi* [konvin] bersidang, rapat; **convention** *n* seminar, rapat, konvénsi; kebiasaan

convenience *n* kesempatan; kemudahan; *~ store* minimart, toko serba ada (tosérba); *at your ~* sesempat anda; **convenient** *adj* enak; dekat

convent *n* biara (untuk biarawati); *~ school* sekolah gadis Katolik

convention *n* seminar, rapat, konvénsi ← **convene**

convention *n* kebiasaan; **conventional** *adj* biasa

conversant *adj* kenal, berpengalaman; *~ with the regulations* mengetahui peraturan; **conversation** *n* percakapan, pembicaraan; **converse** *vi* berbincang, bercakap-cakap

conversely *adj* sebaliknya

conversion *n* perubahan, penukaran; *~ rate* kurs; **convert** *n* orang yang masuk agama lain; *Isl* mualaf; *vi* masuk agama lain; mengubah; *~ to Hinduism* masuk agama Hindu; **convertible** *n* mobil yang atapnya bisa dibuka, mobil sport; *adj* dapat disesuaikan

convex *adj* cembung

convey *vt* [konvé] membawa, mengangkut; menyampaikan; **conveyance** *n* kendaraan

convict *n* narapidana; *vt* menghukum, menyatakan bersalah; **conviction** *n* vonis bersalah

conviction *n* keyakinan, kepercayaan

convince *vt* meyakinkan; **convinced** *adj* yakin; **convincing** *adj* meyakinkan; **convincingly** *adv* dengan yakin

convoy *n* iring-iringan, konvoi

convulsed *~ with laughter* tertawa berbahak-bahak; **convulsion** *n* kejang-kejang

cook *n* juru masak, koki; *vi* masak; *vt* memasak; **cookbook** *n* buku resép; **cooked** *adj* matang, masak; **cooker** *n* kompor; *rice ~* tempat menanak nasi; **cooking** *n* masakan; **cookery** *n* cara memasak; *~ book* buku masak; **cookie** *n, US* kué kering yang keras

cool *adj* sejuk, dingin; *sl* gaya; *~-headed* (berpikir) tenang; *to lose your ~* menjadi marah; *vt* menyejukkan, mendinginkan; **cooler** *n* (ruang) pendingin

coolie *n* kuli

co-operate, cooperate *vi* bekerja sama; *~ with* bekerja sama dengan; **co-operation** *n* kerja sama; **co-operative** *n* (toko) kopérasi; *adj* réla bekerja sama, koopératif; **co-operatively** *adv* secara bersama

coop *n* kandang ayam

co-ordinate, coordinate *vt* menyelaraskan; **co-ordination** *n* penyelarasan; **co-ordinator** *n* penyelaras, koordinator

cop *n, sl* polisi

cop *vt, coll* terima

cope *vi ~ (with)* mengatasi, hidup dengan (kesulitan)

copper *n* tembaga; *adj* warna tembaga

copra *n* kopra, kelapa kering

copy *n* salinan, kopi; *vt* menyalin, meniru; memfotokopi; *~ down* mencatat, menyalin; **copycat** *n* peniru; **copyright** *n* hak cipta

coral *n* karang; *adj* warna mérah muda

cord *n* tali

cordial *n* sirop

cordial *adj* ramah, sopan

corduroy *n* beledru, korduroi

core *n* inti, hati; *apple ~* bagian tengah apel; *the Earth's ~* inti bumi

corgi *n* sejenis anjing kecil

coriander *n* ketumbar; *~ leaves* daun ketumbar

cork *n* gabus; sumbat; **corkscrew** *n* pembuka botol, kotrék

corn *n* jagung; katimumul; *~ on the cob* (tongkol) jagung; **cornflakes** *n, pl* sejenis séréal; **cornflour** *n* tepung maizéna

corned *~ beef* kornét

corner *n* sudut, penjuru; *to cut* ~s mencari jalan pintas; *vt* memojokkan

cornet *n* semacam terompét

cornflakes *n, pl* sejenis séréal ← **corn**

cornflour *n* tepung maizéna ← **corn**

Cornish *adj* dari Cornwall; ~ *pasty* sejenis pastél besar; **Cornwall** *n* [kornwol] daérah di barat daya Inggris

corny *adj, coll* kuno, sudah basi (lelucon)

coronary ~ *(attack)* serangan jantung

coronation *n* upacara penobatan

coroner *n* petugas pemeriksa mayat

Corp *abbrev Corporation* Perusahaan, Per.

corporal *n* kopral

corporal ~ *punishment* hukuman badani

corporate *adj* [korporet] berkaitan dengan perusahaan; **corporation** *n* perusahaan, perkumpulan, persekutuan, grup

corps *n* [kor] korps; pasukan

corpse *n* [korps] mayat (manusia)

correct *adj* benar, betul; *vt* membetulkan, memperbaiki; memeriksa; **correction** *n* pembetulan, perbaikan, koréksi; **corrective** *adj* bersifat memperbaiki; ~ *services* lembaga kemasyarakatan; **correctly** *adv* dengan benar

correspond *vi* surat-menyurat; sesuai dengan; ~ *to* sesuai dengan; ~ *with* surat-menyurat dengan; **correspondence** *n* surat-menyurat, koréspondénsi; ~ *course* kursus jarak jauh; **correspondent** *n* orang yang menulis surat atau artikel; wartawan

corridor *n* lorong

corrode *vi* berkarat, karatan; **corrosion** *n* karat; **corrosive** *adj* keras; merusak

corrugated *adj* berombak, bergelombang

corrupt *adj* korup, dapat disuap; *vt* menyuap, merusak; **corruption** *n* korupsi, suap

cosmetic *adj* berkaitan dengan kecantikan; ~ *surgery* bedah plastik; **cosmetics** *n, pl* alat-alat kecantikan (seperti lipstik, perona pipi dsb)

cosmic *adj* berasal dari kosmos; **cosmonaut** *n* antariksawan, astronot (dari Uni Soviét); **cosmos** *n* kosmos, jagat raya; **cosmopolitan** *adj* internasional, kosmopolitan

cost *n* harga (barang), ongkos (perjalanan), biaya (jasa); ~ *of living* ongkos hidup; *at all* ~s bagaimanapun juga; *vt* **cost cost** berharga; **costly** *adj* mahal

Costa Rica *n* Kosta Rika; **Costa Rican** *n* orang Kosta Rika; *adj* berasal dari Kosta Rika

costume *n* pakaian, busana, kostum; ~ *jewelry* perhiasan palsu; *swimming* ~ baju renang

cosy, cozy *adj* énak, mungil

cot *n* tempat tidur bayi, vélbéd

Cote d'Ivoire *n* [kot divwar] Pantai Gading → **Ivory Coast**

cottage *n* [kotej] pondok, bungalo; ~ *cheese* kéju putih lembék; ~ *industry* usaha kecil (di rumah)

cotton *n, adj* kapas, katun; ~ *field* kebun kapas; ~ *wool* kapas

couch *n* [kauc] sofa

cougar *n* [kugar] sejenis kucing besar di AS

cough *n, vi* [kof] batuk; ~ *mixture* obat batuk; *whooping* ~ batuk rejan

could *v* [kud] bisa, dapat, mampu; *pf* → **can**

council *n* déwan; pemerintah setempat (seperti kecamatan); ~ *estate UK* apartemén Perumnas; **councillor** *n* anggota déwan

counsel *n* pengacara; nasihat; *vt* menasihati, memberi nasihat; **counselling** *n* konséling; **counsellor** *n* konselor, penasihat

count *n* penghitungan; *to lose* ~ sudah tidak terhitung; *vi* berhitung; ~ *on* mengandalkan; *vt* menghitung; ~ *your blessings* bersyukur; **countdown** *n* penghitungan dari nomor besar sampai nol; **countless** *adj* tak terhitung

count *n, m* gelar bangsawan; **countess** *n, f* gelar bangsawan

countdown *n* penghitungan dari nomor besar sampai nol ← **count**

counter *n* lokét; *vt* melawan, menangkis; ~*attack* serangan balik

counterfeit *adj* [kaunterfét] palsu

counterpart *n* teman, rekan, pasangan

countersign *vt* [kauntersain] ikut menandatangani

countess *n, f* gelar bangsawan ← **count**

countless *adj* tak terhitung ← **count**

country *n* [kantri] negeri, negara; tanah air; ~ *(and Western) music* musik yang berasal dari bagian selatan AS; *in the* ~ di pedesaan, di pedalaman; **countryman** *n* orang setanah air; **countryside** *n* pedesaan, pedalaman

county *n* [kaunti] kabupaten, wilayah tingkat bawah; ~ *court* pengadilan negeri

coup *n* [ku] kudéta

couple *n* [kapel] pasang, pasangan; *a* ~ *of* satu dua

couplet *n* [kaplet] ayat, bait

coupon *n* kupon

courage *n* [karej] keberanian; *Dutch* ~ minuman keras; **courageous** *adj* [karéjus] berani

courgette *n, UK* [kurjét] sejenis timun

courier *n* kurir; ~ *service* jasa pengiriman barang

course *n* [kors] kursus; sajian; jalan, arah; ~*work* bahan pelajaran; *golf* ~ padang golf; *of* ~ tentu saja, memang, pasti; *three-* ~ *meal* santapan dengan tiga tahap; *in due* ~ pada waktunya

court *n* [kort] pengadilan; ~*-martial* pengadilan tentara; *the High* ~ Pengadilan Tinggi

court *n* [kort] jalan buntu; taman; lapangan main; *basketball* ~ lapangan basket

court *n* [kort] istana; *at* ~ di istana; **courtier** *n* anggota istana

court *vi* [kort] berpacaran dengan, mengencani, memacari; **courting** *adj* berpacaran; **courtship** *n* masa cumbuan, masa pacaran

courteous *adj* [kertiyes] sopan; **courtesy** *n* [kertesi] kesopanan, sopan-santun

courtier *n* anggota istana ← **court**

courtship *n* [kortsyip] masa cumbuan, masa pacaran ← **court**

courtyard *n* pekarangan, halaman

cousin *n* [kazen] (saudara) sepupu; *distant* ~ sepupu jauh; *first* ~ saudara sepupu

cove *n* teluk kecil

cover *n* [kaver] tutup, penutup; sampul (buku); sarung (bantal); perlindungan; *vt* menutup; meliputi; ~ *up* menutupi; ~ *your back* melindungi diri sendiri; **coverage** *n* [kaverej] liputan

cow *n* sapi, lembu; ~*'s milk* susu sapi; *dairy* ~ sapi susu; *milk* ~ sapi susu, sapi perah; **cowboy** *n, m* **cowgirl** *f* koboi

coward *n* pengecut, penakut; **cowardice** *n* [kauerdis] rasa takut, ketidakberanian; **cowardly** *adj* penakut, pengecut

cower *vi* [kauer] tunduk

cowrie *n* [kauri] kerang kecil

coyote *n, US* [koyoti] sejenis anjing liar

cozy, cosy *adj* énak, mungil

CPR *abbrev cardiopulmonary resuscitation* pernafasan buatan

CPU *abbrev central processing unit* CPU

crab *n* kepiting, rajingan; **crabby** *adj* marah-marah, réwél

crack *n* retak; bunyi; *sl* kokain; *a* ~*-ing pace* sangat cepat; **cracked** *adj* retak; gila; *vi* retak, pecah dengan bunyi gemeretak; *vt* memecahkan; ~ *up* menjadi gila; **crackdown** *n* razia, penertiban; **cracker** *n* petasan; biskuit kering

cracker *n* sejenis biskuit

cradle *n* [krédel] buaian, ayunan

craft *n* kapal, pesawat

craft *n* kerajinan tangan; ketrampilan; **craftsman** *n* perajin, tukang

crafty *adj* licik

crag *n* tebing

cram *n* keadaan penuh sesak, macet; *vi* belajar mati-matian sebelum ujian; *vt* menjejalkan, memasukkan dengan paksa; ~ *school* bimbingan belajar; ~*med in* penuh sesak

cramp *n* kejang; kram; *don't* ~ *my style* jangan mencoréng citraku, jangan mengganggu gayaku; **cramped** *adj* sempit

cranberry *n* sejenis béri kecil berwarna mérah

crane *n* mobil dérék

crane *n* burung bangau

cranium *n* [kréniem] tengkorak, batok kepala

crank *n* engkol; orang yang anéh; **cranky** *adj* marah-marah, réwél

crap *n, vulg* tahi; barang tidak berguna; *adj* tidak berguna atau bermutu rendah; *vi* bérak; **crappy** *adj* tidak berguna, bermutu rendah

crash *n* tabrakan; ~ *course* kursus kilat; *plane* ~ kecelakaan pesawat; *vi* ambruk, bertabrakan; ~ *into* menubruk; jatuh (pesawat terbang)

crate *n* peti kayu

crater *n* kawah

cravat *n* [kravat] semacam dasi

crave *vt* mengidamkan, merindukan; **craving** *n* idaman; *to have* ~s mengidam; *sl* ngidam

crawl *n (front)* ~ gaya bébas; *back* ~ gaya punggung; *vi* merangkak, merayap

crayfish *n* sejenis udang besar

crayon *n* krayon, kapur tulis lilin

craze *n* trén, kegemaran; **crazy** *adj* gila

creak *vi* [krik] **creaky** *adj* berbunyi karena diinjak

cream *n* krim, kepala susu; ~ *cheese* sejenis kéju untuk membuat kué; *the* ~ *of the crop* yang terbaik; *adj* (warna) krém

crease *n* [kris] lipatan, wiron; *vi* kusut; mengerut; *vt* membuat lipatan; mengerutkan; **creased** *adj* kusut

create *vt* [kriét] menciptakan, membuat; **creation** *n* ciptaan, kréasi; Kejadian; **creative** *adj* kréatif; **creator** *n* pencipta; **creature** *n* [krityur] makhluk

creche *n* [krésy] tempat penitipan anakanak

credible *adj* [krédibel] dapat dipercaya

credit *n* penghargaan; krédit; ~ *card* kartu krédit

creek *n* kali, sungai kecil

creep *n, sl* orang yang menjijikkan atau mengerikan; *vi* **crept crept** merangkak, merayap, menjalar; *it made my flesh* ~ bulu roma saya berdiri; **creepy** *adj* angker, mengerikan; **creeper** *n* tanaman merambat

cremate *vt* membakar mayat, memperabukan; **cremation** *n* krémasi,

pembakaran mayat; **crematorium** *n* krématorium

crepe *n* [krép] sejenis panekuk; kain tipis; ~ *paper* kertas tipis

crept *vi, pt* → **creep**

crescent *n* [krésent] jalan yang melingkar; ~ *(moon)* bulan sabit; *the Red* ~ Sabit Mérah

crest *n* jambul, puncak; lambang keluarga atau lembaga

crevice *n* [krévis] celah

crew *n* awak kapal; regu, kru; ~ *cut* rambut cepak; *cabin* ~ awak kabin

crib *n* tempat tidur bayi

cricket *n* jangkrik, belalang

cricket *n* semacam olahraga seperti kasti, krikét; **cricketer** *n* pemain krikét

crier *arch* [kraier] *town* ~ petugas yang mengumumkan berita di tempat umum

crime *n* kejahatan; *to commit a* ~ melakukan kejahatan, berbuat jahat; **criminal** *n* [kriminal] penjahat; *adj* jahat; pidana

crimson *adj* mérah tua

cringe *vi* [krinj] ngeri, malu

cripple *n* [kripel] timpang, pincang; *vt* melumpuhkan, membuat pincang; **crippled** *adj* lumpuh, pincang, cacat; **crippling** *adj* melumpuhkan, berat

crisis *n* [kraisis] **crises** *pl* krisis

crisp *n* (kripik) kentang; *adj* garing; segar

criterion *n* [kraitirien] **criteria** syarat; patokan, norma

critic *n* [kritik] pemerhati; **critical** *adj* kritis, genting; **criticism** *n* kritik; **criticize** *vt* mengkritik

croak *n* suara kodok; *vi* menguak; *vt* mengatakan dengan suara serak

Croat *n* [kroat] orang Kroasia; *Serbo-*~ *arch* bahasa Serbia dan Kroasia; **Croatia** *n* [kroésya] Kroasia; **Croatian** *n* bahasa Kroasia; *adj* berasal dari Kroasia

crochet *n* [krosyé] rajutan; *v* merajut

crockery *n* tembikar

crocodile *n* buaya; ~ *tears* air mata yang dibuat-buat

crony *n* kawan seperkongkolan, konco

crook *n, sl* penipu, penjahat; **crooked** *adj* [kruked] béngkok

crop *n* panén; *vt* memotong; ~ *up*
timbul; *close-~ped hair* rambut cepak
croquet *n* [kroké] semacam permainan
seperti mini-golf
cross *n* silang; salib; persimpangan,
persilangan; *~-country* lari lintas alam;
~-dresser banci, béncong; *~-eyed*
juling; *~-legged* bersila; *~-section*
potong melintang; *~-stitch* kristik; *vi*
saling léwat; menyeberang; *vt* melin-
tasi, menyeberangi; ~ *off* mencorét,
memberi tanda pada; ~ *out* mencorét;
crossbar *n* mistar; **crossing** *n* penyeberangan, perlintasan; *pedestrian* ~
zébrakros; **crossroads** *n* simpang,
perempatan; **crossword** *n* [kroswerd]
teka-teki silang (TTS)
cross *adj* marah, jéngkél; **crossly** *adv*
dengan marah
crouch *vi* [krauc] berjongkok; *n* posisi
jongkok
crow *n* [kro] burung gagak; *vi* berkokok;
membual; *as the* ~ *flies* jalan lurus
crowbar *n* [krobar] linggis
crowd *n* orang banyak, gerombolan
orang, kerumunan orang; *vi* berkeru-
munan; *vt* mengerumuni; **crowded** *adj*
penuh sesak, ramai
crown *n* mahkota; ubun-ubun; ~ *Prince*
Putra Mahkota; *vt* menobatkan sebagai
raja atau ratu
crucial *adj* [krusyel] utama, pokok;
penting
crucifix *n* salib; **crucifixion** *n* penyaliban; **crucify** *vt* menyalibkan
crude *adj* kasar, mentah; primitif; ~ *oil*
minyak mentah; **crudely** *adv* dengan
kasar
cruel *adj* bengis, kejam; **cruelty** *n*
kebengisan, kekejaman
cruise *n* [kruz] pelayaran pesiar; ~ *ship*
kapal pesiar; ~ *control* kendali otomatis; *vi* menjelajah; *vt* menjelajahi;
cruiser *n* kapal jelajah
crumb *n* [kram] remah; *~s!* ampun!;
crumble *vi* [krambel] merepih,
ambruk, merapuh; *vt* meremukkan;
crumbly *adj* repih
crumpet *n* sejenis roti panggang
crumple *vi* [krampel] rebah; *vt* meng-

gumpalkan; **crumpled** *adj* kusut
crunch *n* saat yang menentukan; *vi*
mengerkah, menimbulkan bunyi
berderak; **crunchy** *adj* garing
crusade *n* perjuangan; perang salib; ~
against melawan; *vi* ~ *for* memperjuangkan; **crusader** *n* orang yang
memperjuangkan sesuatu
crush *n, sl* cinta monyét; *to have a* ~ *on*
cinta monyét pada; *vt* menghancurkan;
menekan
crust *n* kerak, kulit; *the Earth's* ~ kerak
bumi
crustacean *n* [krastésyen] keluarga
kerang-kerangan
crutch *n* **crutches** *pl* kruk
cry *n* [krai] teriak, pekik; tangis; *vi*
berteriak, memekik; menangis; ~ *for*
menangisi; menyerukan; *vt* meneriakkan; **crying** *n* tangisan
cryptic *adj* [kriptik] tidak jelas, samar
crystal *n, adj* hablur, kristal; ~ *clear*
sangat jelas
Ct *Court* jalan buntu
cub *n* anak héwan; ~ *Scout* Siaga
(pramuka setingkat siswa SD); *lion* ~
anak singa
Cuba *n* Kuba; **Cuban** *n* orang Kuba;
adj berasal dari Kuba
cubby-house *n* rumah bermain untuk
anak-anak
cube *n* kubus; **cubic** ~ *meter (cm³)*
meter kubik
cubicle *n* [kyubikel] bilik
cuckoo *n* [kuku] sejenis burung besar;
~ *clock* jam khas Swis
cucumber *n* [kyukamber] timun,
ketimun, mentimun
cuddle *n* [kadel] pelukan; *v* memeluk,
mengemong; **cuddly** *adj* énak
diemong atau dipeluk
cue *n* petunjuk, isyarat; kiu (bilyar); *to*
give a ~ memberi isyarat; *vt* memberi
isyarat, mengisyaratkan; mempersiapkan (kasét)
cuff *n* ujung tangan, mansét; *off the* ~
secara spontan
cuisine *n* [kuisin] santapan, masakan
culminate *vi* memuncak, berakhir; ~ *in*
memuncak pada; **culmination** *n* puncak

culprit *n* pelaku, yang bersalah

cult *n* [kalt] kultus; *personality* ~ kultus individu

cultivate *vt* memelihara, menanam; mengolah; **cultivated** *adj* sopan, beradab, berpendidikan; **cultivation** *n* pemeliharaan, penanaman

cultural *adj* kebudayaan, budaya; ~ *center* pusat kebudayaan; **culture** *n* kebudayaan, budaya; ~ *shock* gegar budaya; **cross-cultural** silang budaya, antarbudaya

cumin *n* [kamin] jintan

cunning *n, adj* cerdik, licik

cup *n* cangkir, cawan; piala; *a* ~ *of tea* secangkir téh; **cupboard** *n* [kaberd] lemari; **cupcake** *n* kué kecil (seperti kué bolu)

cupola *n* [kyupola] kubah

curator *n* [kyurétor] kepala musium, kurator

curb *n, US* (*UK* **kerb**) pinggiran jalan; penahan; *vt* mengekang, membatasi

cure *n* obat, pengobatan; *vt* mengobati (sampai sembuh)

curfew *n* jam malam

curiosity *n* penasaran, keingintahuan; keajaiban; **curious** *adj* penasaran, ingin tahu; anéh

curl *n, vi* keriting; *vt* mengeriting (rambut); ~ *up* melekuk, meringkuk; **curly** *adj* ikal, keriting; *a* ~ *question* pertanyaan yang susah

currant *n* kismis (kecil, berwarna hitam); ~ *bun* roti kismis

currency *n* mata uang; *foreign* ~ mata uang asing

current *n* arus; *alternating* ~ *(AC)* arus bolak-balik; *direct* ~ *(DC)* arus searah; *against the* ~ melawan arus

current *adj* kini; berlaku; ~ *affairs* berita kini; **currently** *adv* kini, sekarang

curricular *adj* berhubungan dengan kurikulum; *extra-*~ ékskul; **curriculum** *n* **curriculums, curricula** *pl* kurikulum; ~ *vitae (CV)* riwayat hidup; *competency-based* ~ kurikulum berbasis kompeténsi

curry *n* kari, gulai

curse *n* kutukan; umpatan, makian; *v* mengutuk; mengumpat, memaki; *Greg* ~*s a lot* Greg sering mengumpat; *the witch* ~*d the princess* penyihir mengutuk permaisyuri

cursive *n* [kersiv] tulisan miring, tulisan bersambung

cursor *n* kursor

curtain *n* [kerten] hordén, gordén, tirai; *the Iron* ~ Tirai Besi, Tabir Besi

curtsey *vi, f* [kertsi] membungkukkan badan di depan anggota kerajaan

curve *n* lengkung; *vi* melengkung, membélok; *vt* membélokkan; **curved** *adj* melengkung; **curvy** *adj* sintal, montok

cushion *n* [kusyen] bantal; *vt* melindungi dengan bantalan

custard *n* sejenis puding

custodian *n* pemegang kunci, pemilik; **custody** *n* tahanan, kurungan; *in* ~ dalam tahanan, sedang ditahan

custom *n* adat, kebiasaan; langganan; **customary** *adj* biasa, lazim

customer *n* tamu, langganan, nasabah (bank)

customs *n* béa cukai, pabéan; ~ *house* kantor, pabéan; ~ *officer* petugas béa cukai

cut *n* cut cut potongan; *final* ~ vérsi terakhir; *price* ~ potongan harga, diskon; *short* ~ jalan pintas; *vt* memotong, menggunting; terpotong, luka; ~ *back* mengurangi; ~ *corners* mencari jalan pintas; ~ *down* menebang; mengurangi; ~ *off* memutuskan; ~ *out* putus; menggunting, mengeluarkan; ~ *your thumb* jempol tersayat; **cutback** *n* pengurangan; **cutter** *n* pisau; **cutting** *n* guntingan, kliping; potongan

cute *adj* lucu; mungil, manis

cuticle *n* [kyutikel] kulit tipis di sekitar kuku

cutlery *n* garpu, séndok, pisau dan sebagainya

cutlet *n* potongan daging

cutter *n* pisau ← **cut**

cutting *n* guntingan, kliping; potongan ← **cut**

cuttlefish *n* [katelfisy] ikan sotong

CV *abbrev curriculum vitae*, riwayat kerja

cyberspace *n* [saiberspés] dunia maya

cycle *n* [saikel] daur, siklus; sepéda; *life* ~ siklus hidup; *vi* bersepéda, naik sepéda; **cycling** *n* bersepéda; **cyclist** *n* pengendara sepéda; *(professional)* ~ pembalap sepéda

cyclone *n* [saiklon] angin topan, siklon

cylinder *n* silinder; *gas* ~ tabung gas; **cylindrical** *adj* berbentuk silinder, bulat panjang

cynic *n* orang yang suka mengéjék; **cynical** *adj* sinis, suka mengéjék; **cynicism** *n* sifat mau mengéjék atau memperolok

cypress *n* [saipres] pohon eru

Cypriot *n* [sipriet] orang Siprus; *adj* berasal dari Siprus; **Cyprus** *n* [saiprus] Siprus

Czech *n* [cék] bahasa Céko, orang Céko; *adj* Céko; **Czechoslovakia** *arch* Czechoslovakia; *the* ~ *Republic* Republik Céko; Céska

D

DA *abbrev District Attorney* jaksa wilayah

dab *vi* mengolés, mencolék; *a* ~ *hand* pandai

dabble *vi* [dabel] mencoba-coba; ~ *in painting* mencoba-coba melukis

dachshund *n* [dakshund] sejenis anjing kecil

Dad *n, sl* Pak; *my* ~ ayahku; **Daddy** *n, sl, child* Papa; ~-*long-legs* sejenis laba-laba

daffodil *n* sejenis bunga kuning

daft *adj* gila, sinting

dagger *n* [dager] keris, badik

dahlia *n* [délia] sejenis tanaman berbunga

daily *n* harian; ~ *(newspaper)* (koran) harian; *adv* tiap hari, setiap hari, sehari-hari

dainty *adj* manis, cantik

dairy *n* [déri] perusahaan susu; *adj* susu; ~ *cow* sapi perah, sapi susu; ~ *products* produk olahan susu

dais *n* [déis] mimbar, panggung kecil, pelaminan

daisy *n* bunga aster; ~ *chain* rangkaian bunga aster

Dalmatian *n* sejenis anjing besar berwarna putih dengan bintik-bintik hitam

dam *n* bendungan; *vt* membendung

damage *n* [damej] kerusakan; rugi, kerugian; *vt* merugikan, merusak; **damages** *n, pl* ganti rugi

dame *n, f* gelar bangsawan

dammit *ejac* persétan!; **damn** *vt* mengutuk; *adj* terkutuk; ~*ing evidence* bukti yang sangat memberatkan; *ejac* persétan; ~ *it, dammit* persétan; **damned** *adj* terkutuk

damp *n* kelembaban, iklim lembab; *adj* lembab; **dampen** *vt* melembabkan, membasahi; ~ *someone's enthusiasm* mengurangi semangat; **dampness** *n* kelembaban

dance *n* tari, tari-tarian; dansa; ~ *floor* lantai dansa; *vi* berdansa, menari; *vt* menari; **dancer** *n* penari; **dancing** *n* tari-tarian, seni tari

dandruff *n* ketombé; *anti-*~ *shampoo* sampo anti ketombé

Dane *n* orang Dénmark; *Great* ~ sejenis anjing besar; **Danish** *n* bahasa Denmark; *adj* berasal dari Denmark; ~ *blue* sejenis kéju putih; ~ *pastry* semacam roti dengan buah

danger *n* [dénjer] bahaya; *in* ~ dalam bahaya; **dangerous** *adj* berbahaya

dangle *vi* [danggel] menjuntai; me-nguntai; *vt* menjuntaikan; **dangling** *adj* terjuntai

Danish *n* bahasa Denmark; *adj* berasal dari Denmark; ~ *pastry* semacam roti dengan buah ← **Dane**

Danube [danyub] *the (River)* ~ sungai Donau

dare *n* [dér] tantangan; *vt* menantang; *adj* berani; *don't you* ~*!* jangan sekali-kali!; *he doesn't* ~ dia tidak berani; *how* ~ *you!* énak saja!; *I* ~ *say* berani saya katakan; **daredevil** *n* pemberani, orang yang berani mati; **daring** *n* keberanian; *adj* berani

dark *n* gelap, kegelapan; ~-*skinned* berkulit gelap; *after* ~ sesudah magrib,

pada waktu malam; *adj* gelap; tua; ~
glasses kacamata hitam; ~ *green* hijau
tua; **darken** *vi* menjadi gelap; *vt* membuat gelap, menggelapkan; **darkness**
n kegelapan; **darkroom** *n* kamar gelap
darling *n* **darl** *coll* sayang, buah hati;
adj tersayang
darn *vt* menambal, menjerumat; *ejac*
sialan; **darned** *adj* sialan; **darning** *n*
kerjaan menambal; ~ *needle* jarum
tisik
dart *n* anak panah; *pl* permainan lémpar
anak panah
dash *n* garis datar [—]; lari cepat; *the*
100 m ~ lomba lari seratus meter; *vi*
berlari
dashboard *n* dasbor, panel peralatan
data *n* [déta] data; **database** *n* bank
data
date *n* korma; ~ *palm* pohon korma
date *n* tanggal; kencan; *due* ~ batas
waktu; tanggal perkiraan kelahiran;
best before ~, *use-by* ~ tanggal
kedaluwarsa; *out of* ~ kolot, kuno; *up*
to ~ modern, mutakhir; *vt* mengencani, memacari; ~ *from* sejak; **dated**
adj tertanggal; ketinggalan jaman,
kuno; **dating** *vi* berkencan; ~ *agency*
biro perjodohan
daughter *n, f* [doter] anak perempuan,
putri; *god-*~ putri anak baptis; *grand*~
cucu; ~*-in-law* menantu
daunt: **daunted** *adj* takut, segan;
daunting *adj* menakutkan, berat;
dauntless *adj* tidak takut, berani
dawdle *vi* berjalan perlahan-lahan sambil membuang waktu
dawn *n* dini hari, fajar; permulaan; *at* ~
waktu fajar menyingsing; *the* ~ *prayer*
sholat subuh; *vi* menyingsing; ~ *upon*
disadari
day *n* hari; siang; ~ *school* sekolah yang
tidak memiliki asrama; ~ *student* pelajar yang tidak tinggal di asrama; *all* ~
sepanjang hari; *one* ~ sekali waktu;
sehari; *the other* ~ baru-baru ini; *twice*
a ~ sehari dua kali; ~ *of Judgment* hari
kiamat; *during the* ~ siang hari; *the* ~
after tomorrow lusa; *the* ~ *before yes-*
terday kemarin dulu; *the good old* ~s

témpo dulu; **daybreak** *n* [débrék]
dini hari, fajar; **daydream** *n* [dédrim]
lamunan, khayalan; *vi* melamun; **day-**
light *n* [délait] siang, sinar matahari; ~
saving kebijakan memajukan jam
selama musim panas; *in broad* ~ siang
bolong; **daytime** *n, adj* siang hari; *in*
the ~ siang hari
daze *n* keadaan pusing; ~*d* linglung,
pusing
dazzle *vt* [dazel] menyilaukan,
memesonakan; **dazzling** *adj* memesonakan, menyilaukan
dead *adj* [déd] → **die**; *adj* mati; sunyi
senyap; ~ *end* jalan buntu; ~ *heat*
seri (dalam perlombaan); **deaden** *vt*
mematikan; **deadline** *n* batas waktu;
deadlock *n* jalan buntu; **deadly** *adj*
mematikan; sungguh-sungguh
deaf *adj* [déf] tuli; ~*-mute* bisu tuli;
stone-~ tuli; *tone-*~ tidak bisa
mendengar nada lagu; **deafen** *vt*
merusak telinga; **deafening** *adj* sangat
keras atau berisik
deal *n* persetujuan; *big* ~ soal yang
penting; *a good* ~, *a great* ~ sebagian
besar; cukup banyak; *it's a* ~ setuju; *vt*
dealt dealt [délt] membagi (kartu); ~
in jual-beli; ~ *with* memperlakukan,
menghadapi, menangani; **dealer** *n*
pedagang; **dealings** *n, pl* urusan,
transaksi
dear *adj, n* yang baik, yang terhormat
(in letters); *my* ~ sayangku; **dearest**
adj tersayang
dear *adj* mahal; **dearest** *adj* paling
mahal; **dearly** *adv* amat
death *n* [déth] kematian; ~ *certificate*
surat kematian; ~ *penalty*, ~ *sentence*
hukuman mati; ~ *rate* angka kematian;
to ~ sangat, sungguh; **deathly** *adj*
seperti kematian
debate *n* perdebatan; *vi* berdebat; *vt*
memperdebatkan; **debatable** *adj* dapat
diperdebatkan; **debater** *n* orang yang
berdebat; **debating** *n* kegiatan berdebat
debit *n* débit; ~ *card* kartu débit; *vt*
mendébitkan, membebankan
debrief *vt* **debriefing** *n* tanya jawab
sepulang dari tugas

debris *n* [debri] reruntuhan, puing
debt *n* [dét] hutang; ~*collector* petugas penagih hutang; *in* ~ berhutang; **debtor** *n* [détor] orang yang berhutang
debut *n* [débyu] penampilan pertama; *vi* tampil untuk pertama kali
decadence *n* kemerosotan, dékadénsi; **decadent** *adj* merosot
decaffeinated [dekafenéted] ~ *coffee (decaf)* kopi tanpa kaféin
decapitate *vt* [dekapitét] memenggal kepala; **decapitation** *n* pemenggalan kepala
decathlete *n* atlet dasalomba; **decathlon** *n* dasalomba
decay *n* kerusakan, kebusukan; *in* ~ dalam keadaan tidak terawat; *tooth* ~ karis; *vi* melapuk, membusuk
deceased *n* [desisd] *the* ~ orang yang meninggal; *adj* telah meninggal, mangkat, wafat; ~ *estate* bangunan dan tanah milik orang yang meninggal
deceit *n* [disit] tipu daya; **deceitful** *adj* penuh tipu daya, bersifat menipu; **deceive** *v* menipu; **deceived** *adj* tertipu; **deceiver** *n* penipu; **deception** *n* penipuan; **deceptive** *adj* [deséptif] bersifat menipu, tidak mudah terbaca
December *n* bulan Désémber
decency *n* [disensi] kesopanan; **decent** *adj* sopan, patut, layak; lumayan; **decently** *adv* dengan sopan
decentralization *n* déséntralisasi; **decentralize** *vt* mendéséntralisasi
deception *n* penipuan; **deceptive** *adj* [deséptif] bersifat menipu, tidak mudah terbaca ← **deceit**
decide *vi* mengambil keputusan; *vt* memutuskan, menentukan, menetapkan; **decider** *n* tahap atau babak yang menentukan; **deciding** *adj* yang menentukan; **decision** *n* [desisyen] keputusan; **decisive** *adj* [desaisif] menentukan
deciduous *adj* [desidyues] berganti daun
decimal *n* persepuluhan, désimal; ~ *point* koma (désimal); *Dewey* ~ *System* sistem klasifikasi Dewey (di perpustakaan)

decision *n* [desisyen] keputusan; **decisive** *adj* [desaisif] menentukan ← **decide**
deck *n* geladak, dék; ~ *chair* kursi pantai, kursi malas; *on* ~ di geladak; ~ *of cards* kartu rémi
declaration *n* pernyataan, pengumuman, maklumat, déklarasi; **declare** *vt* menyatakan, mengumumkan
decline *n* kemunduran, kemerosotan; *vi* mundur, menjadi kurang, merosot; *vt* menolak; *the minister* ~*d to comment* menteri menolak berkoméntar
decode *vt* membaca atau memecahkan sandi
decompose *vi* membusuk; **decomposed** *adj* busuk
décor *n* dékor, hiasan; **decorate** *vt* menghiasi; **decoration** *n* hiasan, perhiasan; tanda kehormatan; **decorative** *adj* hias; **decorator** *n* tukang hias
decorous *adj* [dekorus] sopan (santun); **decorum** *n* kesopanan
decoy *n, adj* umpan, pemikat
decrease *n* pengurangan, penurunan; *vi* berkurang; *vt* mengurangi, menurunkan
decree *n* keputusan, dékrit, penetapan; *vt* memutuskan, menetapkan
dedicate *vt* [dédikét] mempersembahkan, mengabdikan; **dedicated** *adj* setia, rajin; **dedication** *n* pengabdian, persembahan, dédikasi
deduce *vi* mengambil kesimpulan; **deduction** *n* kesimpulan
deduct *vt* memotong, mengurangi; **deduction** *n* potongan, pengurangan
deduction *n* kesimpulan ← **deduce**
deed *n* perbuatan ← **do**
deem *vt* menganggap, menyatakan
deep *adj* dalam; ~*rooted* berurat-berakar; ~*seated* yang mendalam; ~ *freeze* lemari és; *a* ~ *sleep* tidur pulas; **deepen** *vi* mendalam; *vt* memperdalam; **deeply** *adv* dalam; **depth** *n* kedalaman
deer *n* rusa, menjangan
deface *vt* merusak; mengotori, mencorét-morét
defamation *n* **defamatory** *adj* fitnah; **defame** *vt* memfitnah

default *n* [defolt] gagal; lalai membayar; *by* ~ dengan tak hadir; secara otomatis; *vi* gagal; lalai membayar; *Argentina ~ed on its loans* Argentina gagal melunasi pinjaman

defeat *n* [defit] kekalahan; *vt* mengalahkan, menggagalkan; **defeated** *adj* kalah, terkalahkan

defecate *vi* [defékét] buang air besar, bérak

defect *vi* [defékt] durhaka, menyeberang ke pihak lain; *Boris ~ed to America* Boris mencari suaka di Amérika

defect *n* [difékt] cacat, cela, kerusakan; **defective** *adj* rusak, cacat

defend *vt* membéla, mempertahankan; **defendant** *n* tergugat; **defender** *n* pembéla; bék; **defense, defence** *n* pertahanan, pembélaan, perlawanan; **defenseless, defenceless** *adj* tidak dapat melawan, tak berdaya; **defensive** *adj* bersikap bertahan, defénsif

defer *vi* ~ *to* tunduk pada; *vt* menunda, menangguhkan; **deference** *n* sikap tunduk, hormat

defiance *n* [defaiens] pemberontakan; **defiant** *adj* bersifat menentang, bersifat melawan; **defy** *vt* menentang, melawan; ~ *convention* melabrak kebiasaan, menjadi béda; ~ *definition* sulit digambarkan

deficiency *n* [defisyensi] kekurangan; **deficient** *adj* kurang

deficit *n* kekurangan (uang), défisit

defile *vt* mencemarkan, memerkosa

define *vt* menentukan, menetapkan, mengartikan; **defined** *adj* jelas, ditentukan; **definite** *adj* [définit] tertentu, pasti; **definitely** *adv* tentu; **definition** *n* definisi

deflate *vi* kempés; *vt* mengempéskan; **deflated** *adj* kempés; *after his rejection, he suffered from a ~ ego* setelah ditolak, dia menjadi kurang percaya diri; **deflation** *n* déflasi

deflect *vt* menepis, menangkis, membélokkan; **deflection** *n* pembélokan, defléksi

deflower *vt* memerawani; **deflowering** *n* déflorasi

deforestation *n* deforéstasi, penebangan hutan

deformed *adj* **deformity** *n* cacat

defraud *vt* menipu

defrost *vt* ~ *the refrigerator* mematikan kulkas supaya és mencair

defuse *vt* menjinakkan; ~ *a bomb* menjinakkan bom; ~ *a situation* mencari jalan keluar dari situasi yang sulit

defy *vt* menentang, melawan; ~ *convention* melabrak kebiasaan, menjadi béda; ~ *definition* sulit digambarkan

degenerate *vi* [dijénerét] memburuk, merosot; *the discussion ~d into an argument* perbincangan itu lama-lama malah menjadi perseteruan; **degeneration** *n* kemerosotan, degénérasi

degradation *n* penurunan pangkat; pelécéhan; **degrading** *adj* hina, melécéhkan

degree *n* (suhu) derajat; tingkat; gelar sarjana; *Bachelor's* ~ S1; *Master's* ~ S2

dehydrated *adj* [dihaidréted] déhidrasi, kurang minum

deign *vi* [déin] sudi, berkenan; ~ *to speak to the masses* berkenan bicara kepada rakyat

deity *n* [déiti] tuhan, déwa, déwi

dejected *adj* murung, tanpa semangat

delay *n* keterlambatan, penundaan; *without* ~ segera; *vt* menunda, memperlambat, menangguhkan; **delayed** *adj* terlambat; *the flight to Singapore is* ~ penerbangan ke Singapura mengalami keterlambatan

delegate *n* [déleget] wakil, utusan; *vt* [délegét] menyerahkan; mengutus; **delegation** *n* délégasi, perwakilan

delete *vt* menghapus, mencorét; **deletion** *n* penghapusan, pencorétan

deli *n, sl* toko makanan kering (seperti daging asap, kéju) ← **delicatessen**

deliberate *vi* [deliberét] menimbang-nimbang; berembuk; *adj* [deliberet] (dengan) sengaja; **deliberately** *adv* dengan sengaja; **deliberation** *n* pertimbangan, perundingan

delicacy *n* [délikasi] makanan istiméwa; kehalusan; **delicate** *adj* [déliket] halus, mungil; sering sakit; **delicates-**

sen *n* **deli** *sl* toko makanan kering (seperti daging asap, kéju)

delicious *adj* [delisyus] énak, sedap, lezat

delight *n* [delait] kesenangan, kegembiraan; *Turkish* ~ sejenis agar yang ditaburi tepung gula; **delighted** *adj* gembira, bahagia; **delightful** *adj* menyenangkan, membahagiakan

delinquent *n* anak nakal; *adj* nakal

delirious *adj* mengigau, berdemam tinggi; **delirium** *n* keadaan mengigau atau kurang waras

deliver *vt* mengirim, mengantarkan, menghantarkan, memberi; membidani; melahirkan; ~ *a speech* berpidato; **delivery** *n* penyerahan, pengiriman; persalinan; pesan antar; ~ *boy* kurir, pengantar

delta *n* tanah segi tiga di muara

deluded *adj* hidup berkhayal; **delusion** *n* khayal, angan-angan

demand *n* tuntutan, permintaan; *in* ~ laku; *supply and* ~ persediaan dan permintaan; *vt* menuntut, minta; **demanding** *adj* banyak meminta atau menuntut, menantang, berat

dementia *n* [deménsye] pikun

demo *n, sl* démo; *to hold or have a* ~ berdémo, berunjuk rasa

democracy *n* démokrasi, kerakyatan; **democrat** *n* démokrat; **democratic** *adj* démokratis

demolish *vt* membongkar, merobohkan; **demolition** *n* [démolisyen] pembongkaran

demon *n* [dimon] jin, iblis, sétan; **demonic** *adj* jahat, seperti jin

demonstrate *vi* berunjuk rasa; *vt* menunjukkan, memperlihatkan, membuktikan; **demonstration** *n* **demo** *sl* pertunjukan; démonstrasi, démo, unjuk rasa; *to hold or have a* ~ berdémonstrasi, berunjuk rasa; **demonstrator** *n* pengunjuk rasa, pendémo

demoralize *vt* **demoralizing** *adj* merusak semangat

den *n* sarang, liang; ruang santai

dengue [déngi] ~ *fever* demam berdarah

denial *n* [denayal] penyangkalan; *in* ~ tidak mengakui keadaan yang benar;

deny *vt* menyangkal, memungkiri, menolak

denim *n* [dénim] (bahan) jins

Denmark *n* Dénmark

denomination *n* satuan; pecahan, lembaran (uang); aliran (geréja); **denominator** *n* angka sebutan

denounce *vt* mengecam, mengutuk

dense *adj* padat, rapat, lebat; *sl* bodoh; **density** *n* kepadatan

dent *n* péot, péyok; *vi* melekukkan; **dented** *adj* péot, péyok

dental *adj* berhubungan dengan gigi; ~ *floss* pita pembersih gigi, benang pembersih gigi; **dentist** *n* dokter gigi; **dentistry** *n* (ilmu) kedokteran gigi; **denture** *n* [déntyur] gigi palsu

dented *adj* péot, péyok ← **dent**

deny *v* [denai] menyangkal, memungkiri, menolak

deodorant *n* déodoran, pewangi

depart *vi* berangkat, pergi; *vt* ~ *this world* meninggal dunia; **departed** *adj* almarhum, mendiang; **departure** *n* [departyur] keberangkatan

department *n* departemén; bagian; ~ *of Agriculture* Departemén Pertanian; ~ *store* toko serba ada (tosérba); **departmental** *adj* berhubungan dengan departemén

departure *n* [departyur] keberangkatan ← **depart**

depend *vi* bergantung, tergantung; ~ *on* bergantung pada, tergantung pada; *it* ~*s* tergantung; **dependant, dependent** *n* orang tanggungan; **dependency** *n* daérah jajahan; **dependent** *adj* tergantung pada; tanggungan

depict *vt* menggambarkan; **depiction** *n* menggambarkan

deplete *vt* menghabiskan, mengurangi; **depleted** *adj* kurang; **depletion** *n* kehabisan, penipisan

deplorable *adj* tercela, patut disesalkan; **deplore** *vt* menyesali, mengecam

deport *vt* mendéportasi, memulangkan, membuang; **deportation** *n* déportasi, pembuangan

deposit *n* déposito, simpanan; uang muka, uang pangkal; endapan; *term* ~

déposito berjangka; *vt* menaruh, menyimpan

depot *n* [dépo] depot, dépo, gudang

depreciate *vi* [deprisyét] nilai menurun; **depreciation** *n* penurunan nilai, deprésiasi

depress *vt* menekan, menyusahkan hati; **depressed** *adj* déprési, tanpa semangat, murung; **depressing** *adj* menyedihkan; **depression** *n* bagian yang rendah; déprési, jaman melését; kehilangan gairah hidup

deprivation *n* [déprivésyen] kehilangan; *sleep* ~ kurang tidur; **deprive** *vt* [depraiv] mengambil, merampas; ~ *of his right to vote* kehilangan hak memilih; **deprived** *adj* kekurangan

Dept *Department* Dep. (Departemén)

depth *n* kedalaman ← **deep**

deputize *vi* mewakili; **deputy** *n* wakil; ~ *head* wakil kepala (waka)

derail *vi* anjlok, keluar dari rél; *vt* mengeluarkan dari rél; **derailment** *n* kejadian anjlok

derelict *n* orang gila, gémbél, gelandangan; *adj* tertinggal, tidak terpelihara

derivation *n* asal; **derive** *vi* berasal; *that word ~s from the French* kata itu berasal dari bahasa Perancis; *vt* mendapat; *Daniel ~d little income from his work* Daniel tidak mendapat uang banyak dari pekerjaan

derrick *n* kerekan, dérék, menara pengeboran minyak

descend *vi* turun; *~ed from* keturunan; **descendant** *n* keturunan, anak cucu; **descending** *adj* menurun; *in ~ order* dari besar menjadi kecil; **descent** *n* jalan turun; keturunan; *of Chinese ~* keturunan Cina

describe *vt* melukiskan, menggambarkan; **description** *n* penggambaran, déskripsi; **descriptive** *adj* yang menggambarkan, déskriptif

desert *n* [désért] gurun, padang pasir; ~ *island* pulau tak terhuni

desert *vi* [desert] membelot; desérsi; *vt* meninggalkan; **deserted** *adj* sunyi (senyap); **deserter** *n* pembelot; **desertion** *n* desérsi

deserve *vt* berhak mendapat, pantas (menerima); *you ~ it* pantas, sepantasnya; **deservedly** *adv* sepantasnya, seharusnya; **deserving** *adj* patut terima

desiccated *adj* [désikéted] kering; ~ *coconut* kelapa parut kering

design *n* [desain] rancangan, contoh, gambar, désain, bentuk; *by* ~ dengan sengaja; *graphic* ~ désain grafik; *to have ~s on* menginginkan, menaksir; *vt* merancang, mendésain; **designer** *n* perancang, désainer; *fashion* ~ perancang busana; *adj* bermérek

designate *vt* [désignét] menandai, memperuntukkan; **designated** *adj* tertandai, yang ditunjuk

designer *n* perancang, désainer; *fashion* ~ perancang busana; *adj* bermérek ← **design**

desirable *adj* yang diinginkan; **desire** *n* keinginan, nafsu, hasrat; *vt* ingin, menginginkan, mendambakan; **desired** *adj* yang diinginkan; *to leave much to be* ~ kurang memuaskan

desk *n* méja (tulis); bangku (di sekolah); *front* ~ (méja) resépsi; **desktop** *n* atas méja (tulis); ~ *computer* komputer (yang memiliki CPU dan méja sendiri); ~ *publishing* usaha penerbitan kecil

desolate *adj* [désolet] sepi, sunyi; gersang; **desolation** *n* kesunyian, kesepian

despair *n* keputusasaan; *vi* putus asa; ~ *of* putus asa soal; **desperate** *adj* [désperet] gawat, seperti sudah putus asa; **desperation** *n* keputusasaan, kenékatan

despicable *adj* [despikabel] dibenci; **despise** *vt* [despaiz] membenci

despite *conj* meskipun, kendati

despondent *adj* sedih (hati)

despot *n* diktator

dessert *n* [desert] pencuci mulut, puding; ~ *spoon* séndok makan

destabilize *vt* melawan atau menggerogoti kedaulatan; *the group was accused of trying to ~ the government* kelompok itu dituduh makar

destination *n* tujuan, jurusan

destined *adj* [déstind] ditakdirkan;
destiny *n* [déstini] nasib, takdir
destitute *adj* miskin, papa; **destitution**
n kepapaan, kemiskinan
destroy *vt* menghancurkan, memusnahkan, membinasakan; **destroyed**
adj rusak, hancur; **destroyer** *n* (kapal)
perusak; **destruction** *n* kerusakan,
kehancuran, pemusnahan, pembinasaan; **destructive** *adj* [destraktiv]
merusak, membinasakan
detach *vt* melepaskan; **detached** *adj*
obyéktif, bersifat nétral; **detachment**
n obyéktivitas, hati dingin
detail *n* rinci, perincian, seluk-beluk; *in*
~ secara terinci; *vt* merincikan;
detailed *adj* terinci
detain *vt* menahan; *~ed at Her Majesty's*
pleasure dipenjara; **detainee** *n*
tahanan; **detention** *n* penahanan,
penawanan; *in* ~ disetrap
detect *vt* menemukan, mendapatkan,
mendétéksi; **detection** *n* penemuan,
détéksi; **detective** *n* resérse, détéktif;
detector *n* alat détéksi
detention *n* penahanan, penawanan; *in*
~ disetrap; ditahan ← **detain**
deter *vt* [détér] menghalangi; **deterrent**
n pencegah
detergent *n* sabun, obat, détérjén
deteriorate *vi* [detiriorét] memburuk,
merosot; **deterioration** *n* kemerosotan
determination *n* [determinésyen] tékad
bulat; **determine** *vt* menetapkan,
menentukan, memutuskan;
determined *adj* bertékad, bersikeras
deterrent *n* pencegah ← **deter**
detest *vt* membenci
detonate *vt* meledakkan; **detonator** *n*
alat peledak
detour *n* [ditur] jalan yang meléncéng;
to take a ~ meléncéng dari jalan yang
mau ditempuh
detract ~ *from* mengurangi, menurunkan nilai, mengecilkan nilai; **detractor**
n kritik
detrimental *adj* merugikan
deuce *adj* [dyus] jus, skor 40-40
(dalam pertandingan tenis)
devaluation *n* penurunan nilai,

dévaluasi; **devalued** *adj* tidak dihargai
sepantasnya, telah turun nilainya;
didévaluasi
devastate *vt* menghancurkan; **devastat-
ed** *adj* (hati) hancur; **devastating** *adj*
menghancurkan; ~ *looks* sangat rupawan; **devastation** *n* penghancuran
develop *vi* berkembang; ~ *into* menjadi;
vt mengembangkan, membangun,
membina; mencuci (film); **developer**
n pengembang, pemborong; **developing** *adj* berkembang; ~ *country* negara
berkembang; **development** *n* pembangunan, perkembangan; pengembangan, pembinaan
deviate *vi* [diviét] menyimpang,
meléncéng; ~ *from* menyimpang dari;
deviation *n* penyimpangan; jalan
alternatif
device *n* alat; *left to your own* ~*s* telantar,
dibiarkan
devil *n* sétan, iblis; *speak of the* ~ panjang umur (ketika orang yang baru
disebut tiba-tiba muncul); **devilish** *adj*
seperti sétan
devious *adj* [divius] berbelit-belit, culas
devise *vt* memikirkan, merencanakan
devolve *vt* menyerahkan; **devolution** *n*
dévolusi; ~ *to the provinces* otonomi
daérah (otda)
devote *vt* mengabdikan, menyediakan;
devoted *adj* tekun, setia; **devotee** *n*
penggemar; **devotion** *n* ketaatan,
kebaktian, kesetiaan; rasa sayang;
devout *adj* soléh, beriman
devour *vt* melahap
devout *adj* soléh, beriman ← **devote**
dew *n* embun; **dewy** *adj* [dyuwi]
berembun
dexterity *n* ketangkasan; **dextrous** *adj*
tangkas, gesit
diabetes *n* [daiabitis] penyakit gula,
kencing manis; **diabetic** *n* [daiabétik]
penderita kencing manis
diagnose *vt* [daiagnoz] mendiagnosa,
menentukan; **diagnosis** *n* diagnosa
diagonal *n* [daiagonal] garis sudut-
menyudut, diagonal; *adj* sudut-
menyudut, diagonal
diagram *n* [daiagram] denah, bagan

dial *n* [daial] piringan, muka jam; *vt* memencét (nomor télépon)

dialect *n* [daialékt] dialék

dialogue *adj* [daialog] percakapan, dialog

diameter *n* [daiameter] garis tengah, diaméter

diamond *n* [daiamend] berlian, intan; ~ *anniversary* ulang tahun ke60

diaper *n* [daiaper] popok, lampin; *disposable* ~ pampers, popok pakai buang

diarrhoea, diarrhea *n* [daiaria] mencrét, sakit perut, diaré

diary *n* [daiari] buku harian; *to keep a* ~ menulis buku harian

dice *n*, *pl* dadu ← die

dick *n*, *sl* pénis

dictate *vt* mendikté; **dictation** *n* dikté, imla

dictator *n* diktator

dictionary *n* kamus; *abridged* ~ kamus singkat; *bilingual* ~ kamus dwibahasa

did *vt*, *pf* → **do**

didn't *vt*, *pf* tidak → **do**

die *vi* [dai] **died died** mati, meninggal, *pol* wafat; gugur (dalam perang); ~ *away* lama-lama hilang; ~ *out* menjadi punah; padam; *never say* ~ pantang menyerah; *when did he* ~? kapan dia meninggal?; *lots of rats* ~ *from poison* banyak tikus mati diracun; **dying** *vi* sekarat; ~ *to* ingin sekali

die *n*, *s* [dai] **dice** dadu

diesel *n* [disel] minyak solar; mesin disel

diet *n* [daiet] diét; makanan; *on a* ~ (mengikuti) diét; *vi* berdiét, mengikuti diét, membatasi makan; **dietary** *adj* berhubungan dengan pola makan; **dietician** *n* [daietisyen] ahli diét

differ *vi* berbéda; *I beg to* ~ saya berpendapat lain; **difference** *n* béda, perbédaan; **different** *adj* béda, lain, berbéda; **differentiate** *v* membédakan; *he couldn't* ~ *between right and wrong* dia tidak dapat membédakan di antara apa yang benar dan salah; **differentiation** *n* pembédaan

difficult *adj* susah, sulit, sukar; **difficulty** *n* kesulitan, kesusahan

dig *v* **dug dug** menggali; ~ *a hole* menggali lubang; **digger** *n* penggali,

békho; **diggings** *n* penggalian

digest *vt* mencerna; **digestion** *n* pencernaan

digger *n* penggali, békho ← **dig**

diggings *n* penggalian ← **dig**

digit *n* [dijit] angka; jari; **digital** *adj* digital; ~ *camera* kaméra digital

dignified *adj* [dignifaid] bermartabat, mulia; **dignitary** *n* pejabat; **dignity** *n* martabat; *with* ~ secara bermartabat

digress *vi* [daigrés] menyimpang; **digression** *n* penyimpangan

dike *n* pematang, bendung, tanggul

dilapidated *adj* [dilapidéted] telantar, bobrok, buruk

dilate *vi* membesar; **dilated** *adj* membesar; ~ *pupils* pupil mata membesar; ~ *8 cm* pembukaan 8 cm

dilemma *n* pilihan sulit, diléma

diligence *n* [dilijens] kerajinan, ketekunan; **diligent** *adj* rajin, telatén

dilute *vt* meredup; mengéncérkan; *adj* éncér; **diluted** *adj* éncér

dim *vi* meredup; *vt* meredupkan; *adj* redup, suram; *sl* kurang cemerlang otaknya; **dimmer switch** *n* lampu redup; **dimwit** *n* orang bodoh; **dimwitted** *adj* bodoh

dime *n* sepuluh sén (Amérika); *a* ~ *a dozen* banyak, mudah didapat

dimension *n* matra, diménsi; **dimensional** *three-*~ tiga diménsi

diminish *vi* berkurang; *vt* mengurangi; **diminutive** *n* nama kecil; kata pengecil

dimple *n* lesung pipi

dimwit *n* orang bodoh; **dimwitted** *adj* bodoh ← **dim**

din *n* gempar, gaduh, riuh

dine *vt* bersantap (malam); ~ *on fish* makan ikan; ~ *out* makan di réstoran; **diner** *n* rumah makan kecil; **dining** *n*, *adj* santapan; ~ *car* réstorasi, gerbong makan; ~ *room* ruang makan

dinghy *n* [dinggi] sekoci

dingo *n* [dinggo] anjing liar khas Australia

dingy *adj* [dinji] kotor, suram

dining *n* santapan; ~ *car* réstorasi, gerbong makan; ~ *room* ruang makan ← **dine**

dinner *n* makan malam; makan siang; ~
party acara makan malam; *school* ~
makan siang yang tersedia di sekolah

dinosaur *n* [dainosor] dinosaurus

dioxide *n* [daioksaid] dioksida; *carbon*
~ karbon dioksida

dip *n* bagian yang turun; cocolan seperti
saus atau kéju lunak; pencelupan, mandi
sebentar; *vi* turun; *vt* mencelupkan

diphthong *n* [difthong] bunyi rangkap,
diftong

diploma *n* ijazah, diploma

diplomacy *n* diplomasi; **diplomat** *n*
pegawai kedutaan, diplomat; **diplomatic** *adj* diplomatik, berkaitan dengan kedutaan; ~ *immunity* kekebalan
diplomatik

dipper *n* gayung ← **dip**

direct *adj* langsung; serta merta; terus
terang; ~ *current* arus searah; *vt*
memimpin, mengarahkan, memerintahkan, menunjukkan; menyutradarai;
direction *n* arah, petunjuk; **directive** *n*
petunjuk, pedoman, pengarahan;
directly *adv* secara langsung, serta
merta, segera; **director** *n* diréktur,
pemimpin; sutradara; **directorate** *n*
diréktorat

directory *n* buku alamat, buku daftar;
telephone ~ buku petunjuk télépon

dirt *n* kotoran, debu; tanah; ~*-cheap*
murah sekali; ~*-poor* miskin sekali; ~
road jalan tanah; **dirty** *adj* kotor,
dekil; ~ *word* kata jorok

disability *n* cacat; **disable** *vt* [disébel]
mematikan, menonaktifkan; **disabled**
adj cacat; *n* orang cacat

disadvantage *n* rugi, kerugian; *at a* ~
dirugikan, dalam keadaan yang
merugikan; **disadvantaged** *adj*
dirugikan, merugi; **disadvantageous**
adj [disadvantéjus] merugikan

disagree *vi* tidak setuju; *the speaker* ~*s*
with that policy pembicara tidak setuju
dengan kebijakan tersebut; **disagree-
able** *adj* tidak énak, marah-marah;
disagreement *n* percékcokan, perbédaan pendapat

disallow *vt* tidak membenarkan,
menolak

disappear *vi* hilang, lenyap; **disappear-
ance** *n* hilangnya, lenyapnya

disappoint *vt* **disappointing** *adj*
mengecéwakan; **disappointed** *adj*
kecéwa; **disappointment** *n*
kekecéwaan, rasa kecéwa

disapproval *n* [disapruval] sikap tidak
setuju atau tidak suka; **disapprove** *vi*
tidak menyetujui, tidak suka, menolak; *David's mother* ~*d of his girlfriend*
ibunya David tidak suka pacarnya;
disapproving *adj* bersikap tidak suka

disarm *vt* melucuti senjata; **disarmament** *n* perlucutan senjata

disaster *n* musibah, malapetaka, bencana; ~ *area* daérah bencana; *natural* ~
bencana alam; **disastrous** *adj* malang,
celaka

disband *vi* bubar; *vt* membubarkan

disbelief *n* ketidakpercayaan, rasa tidak
percaya; *he shook his head in* ~ dia
menggéléng kepala tidak percaya; **dis-
believe** *vt* tidak percaya

disc → **disk**

discard *vt* membuang; **discarded** *adj*
terbuang

discharge *n* pemecatan, pemberhentian;
pengeluaran, pemulangan; cairan
yang keluar, keputihan; *honorable* ~
pemberhentian dengan hormat; *vt*
memecat, melepaskan; memulangkan
(dari rumah sakit)

disciple *n* [disaipel] murid; *the Twelve*
~*s* dua belas murid Yesus

discipline *n* disiplin, tata tertib, ketertiban; *vt* menghukum, menyetrap;
disciplined *adj* tertib, berdisiplin

disclose *vt* membuka, menyatakan,
menyingkap; **disclosure** *n* pernyataan

disco *n* diskoték, disko

discolored *adj* luntur, berubah warna

discomfort *n* rasa tidak nyaman,
kesusahan

disconcert *vt* [diskonsért] **disconcert-
ing** *adj* membingungkan; **disconcert-
ed** *adj* bingung

disconnect *vt* mencabut, memutuskan;
disconnected *adj* terputus, terputus-
putus

disconsolate *adj* [diskonsolet] putus

asa, tidak dapat terhibur

discontent *n* rasa kurang senang, rasa tidak puas; **discontented** *adj* kurang senang atau puas

discontinue *vt* berhenti membuat, memberhentikan; *the shop ~d that line of bread* toko roti berhenti membuat roti sejenis itu

discord *n* perselisihan, bunyi sumbang; **discordant** *adj* tak selaras, sumbang

discount *n* potongan (harga), diskon, korting; *vt* memotong harga, mendiskon

discourage *vt* [diskarej] tidak menganjurkan; mengecilkan hati; **discouraged** *adj* kecil hati, kehilangan semangat; **discouraging** *adj* mengecilkan hati, tidak memberi semangat

discourse *n* pembicaraan, percakapan, wacana

discover *vt* [diskaver] menemukan, mendapati; **discovery** *n* penemuan

discredit *vt* tidak percaya; mencoréng nama; **discredited** *adj* rusak namanya, tidak dipercaya

discreet *adj* sopan, bijaksana, berhati-hati (dalam keadaan yang sulit); **discretion** *n* [diskrésyen] kebijaksanaan; *at your ~* tergantung anda

discrepancy *n* [diskrépansi] selisih, ketidaksesuaian, perbédaan

discretion *n* [diskrésyen] kebijaksanaan; *at your ~* tergantung anda ← **discreet**

discriminate *vi* membédakan, mendiskriminasikan; *~ against* mendiskriminasikan; *~ between* membédakan; **discrimination** *n* pembédaan, diskriminasi; *racial ~* diskriminasi berdasarkan warna kulit atau ras

discus *n* (lémpar) cakram; *~ throw* lémpar cakram

discuss *vt* [diskas] membicarakan; **discussion** *n* pembicaraan, diskusi

disdain *n* hina, penghinaan; *vt* menghina; **disdainful** *adj* penuh penghinaan

disease *n* penyakit

disembark *vi* mendarat, turun dari kapal; **disembarkation** *n* pendaratan

disengage *vi* lepas, keluar; *vt* melepaskan, membébaskan; **disengage-**

ment *n* pelepasan, pembébasan

disentangle *vt* [disentanggel] menguraikan

disfigured *adj* [disfigurd] cacat

disgrace *n* aib, malu; *in ~* kena aib; *a ~ to one's family* membuat keluarga malu; *vt* mencoréng muka, memalukan; **disgraced** *adj* dipermalukan, kena aib; **disgraceful** *adj* memalukan

disguise *n* [disgaiz] samaran; *in ~* menyamar; *vt* menyembunyikan; *Harry ~d himself as a painter* Harry menyamar sebagai pelukis

disgust *n* rasa muak; *vt* menjijikkan, memuakkan; **disgusted** *adj* muak; **disgusting** *adj* menjijikkan; *that's ~!* idih!

dish *n* piring, pinggan; sajian, hidangan; *satellite ~* parabola; *an Indian ~* makanan India; *to do the ~es* mencuci piring; **dishcloth** *n* lap piring; **dishwasher** *n* mesin pencuci piring; **dishwater** *n* [disywoter] air bekas cuci piring

disheartened *adj* [dishartend] kehilangan semangat; **disheartening** *adj* mengecéwakan

dishonest *adj* [disonest] tidak jujur, suka bohong; **dishonesty** *n* ketidakjujuran

dishonor *n* [disonor] aib, malu; *vt* mempermalukan; **dishonorable** *adj* dengan tidak hormat

dishwasher *n* mesin pencuci piring; **dishwater** *n* air bekas cuci piring ← **dish**

disillusion *vt* mengecéwakan; **disillusioned** *adj* kecéwa, tidak percaya lagi

disinclined *adj* enggan, segan

disinfect *vt* membasmi kuman; **disinfectant** *n* obat pembasmi kuman; **disinfection** *n* pembasmian kuman

disinherit *vt* mencabut hak warisan; **disinherited** *adj* tercabut hak warisannya

disintegrate *vi* hancur, memecah-belah; **disintegration** *n* kehancuran

disinterested *adj* tidak memihak, obyéktif

disjointed *adj* terpotong-potong, terputus-putus

disk, disc *n* cakram; ~ *brakes* rém cakram; ~ *jockey (DJ)* DJ; *compact ~ (CD)* CD; *floppy* ~ diskét

dislike *n* ketidaksukaan; *vt* tidak suka

dislocate *vt* keluar dari tempatnya, tergelincir; **dislocation** *n* dislokasi

dislodge *vt* mengeluarkan, mencabut

disloyal *adj* tidak setia; **disloyalty** *n* ketidaksetiaan

dismal *adj* memelas, menyedihkan

dismantle *vt* [dismantel] membongkar

dismay *n* kecemasan; *vt* mencemaskan; *to her ~, Janette was told to move offices* Janette cemas karena disuruh pindah ruangan; **dismayed** *adj* cemas

dismiss *vt* menolak; membubarkan, memecat; **dismissal** *n* pembubaran, pemecatan; **dismissive** *adj* tidak mau mendengar

dismount *vi* turun (dari kuda)

disobedience *n* ketidakpatuhan; *civil ~* melawan tanpa kekerasan; **disobedient** *adj* tidak patuh, nakal; **disobey** *vt* melawan, tidak mematuhi

disorder *n* kekacauan; penyakit; **disorderly** *adj* kacau

disorganized *adj* berantakan, kacau-balau, tidak teratur

disown *vt* tidak mengakui

disparate *adj* [disparat] tidak sama; **disparity** *n* selisih, ketidaksamaan, perbédaan

dispassionate *adj* tidak berpihak

dispatch, despatch *n* pengiriman; *vt* mengirimkan

dispensary *n* apotik

dispensation *n* kelonggaran, dispénsasi

dispenser *n* alat atau mesin dengan persediaan; *water ~* tempat akua

dispersal *n* berhamburnya; **disperse** *vi* berhamburan; bubar; *vt* menghamburkan, membubarkan

dispirited *adj* kecil hati, tanpa semangat

displace *vt* menggantikan, menggésér; **displaced** *adj* ~ *person* pengungsi

display *n* paméran, pertunjukan; *vt* memperlihatkan, mempertunjukkan, memamérkan; ~ *cabinet* lemari pajang; ~ *case* pajangan; *on ~* dipamérkan

displease *vt* membuat tidak senang atau sakit hati; **displeased** *adj* sakit hati, tidak senang; **displeasing** *adj* tidak menyenangkan; **displeasure** *n* [displésyur] ketidaksenangan

disposable *adj* dapat dibuang; ~ *nappy* pampers, lampin pakai buang; ~ *contact lenses* lénsa kontak pakai buang; **disposal** *n* persediaan; pembuangan; **dispose** ~ *of* membuang; membunuh

disposed *adj* cenderung; **disposition** *n* kepribadian, kecenderungan

dispossess *vt* menyita, mencabut hak milik

disproportionate *adj* [disproporsyionet] tidak sebanding

disprove *vt* [dispruv] membantah, menyangkal; membuktikan salah

dispute *n* perselisihan, percékcokan, pertikaian; *open to ~* dapat diperdébat; *vt* membantah; mempermasalahkan

disqualified *adj* [diskualifaid] dinyatakan tidak berhak atau keluar, dibatalkan; **disqualify** *vt* membatalkan, mengeluarkan

disregard *n* sikap acuh, pengabaian; *vt* tidak mengindahkan, mengabaikan

disrepair *n* keadaan tidak terawat; *to fall into ~* terabaikan, menjadi tidak terawat

disreputable *adj* bernama buruk; **disrepute** *n* nama buruk

disrespect *n* sikap tidak hormat; **disrespectful** *adj* tidak hormat

disrupt *vt* mengganggu; **disruption** *n* gangguan; **disruptive** *adj* (bersifat) mengganggu

dissatisfaction *n* ketidakpuasan, kekecéwaan; **dissatisfied** *adj* kecéwa, tidak puas; **dissatisfy** *vt* [dis satisfai] membuat tidak puas, mengecéwakan

dissect *vt* [daisékt] membedah, membelah; **dissection** *n* pembedahan

dissent *n* ketidaksetujuan, perbédaan pendapat; **dissenter** *n* orang yang berbéda pendapat

dissertation *n* skripsi, disértasi

dissident *n* orang yang melawan kekuasaan

dissimilar *adj* tidak sama, berbéda

dissolve *vi* larut; *aspirin ~s in water* aspirin larut dalam air; *vt* melarutkan

dissuade *vt* meyakinkan agar jangan; *the policeman ~d him from jumping off the bridge* polisi itu berhasil meyakinkan dia agar tidak loncat dari jembatan

distance *n* jarak, kejauhan; *long ~* jarak jauh; *short ~* jarak dekat; *walking ~* jarak yang dapat ditempuh dengan berjalan kaki; *in the ~* dari kejauhan; *to keep a ~* menjaga jarak; **distant** *adj* jauh

distaste *n* [distést] rasa tidak suka; **distasteful** *adj* memuakkan

distill *vt* menyuling; *~ed water* air suling; **distillation** *n* penyulingan, distilasi

distinct *adj* jelas, kentara; berbéda; **distinction** *n* perbedaan; nilai unggul; **distinctive** *adj* tersendiri; **distinctly** *adv* secara jelas

distinguish *v* membédakan; *they couldn't ~ between Japanese and Koreans* mereka tidak bisa membédakan orang Jepang dan orang Korea; **distinguished** *adj* terhormat, ternama

distort *vt* mengubah (bentuk); **distorted** *adj* berubah; diubah; **distortion** *n* distorsi

distract *vt* mengalihkan perhatian; menyesatkan; *don't ~ me from my work* jangan mengganggu saya kalau sedang bekerja; **distracted** *adj* tersesat, bingung; **distraction** *n* selingan; gangguan, kesesatan

distress *n* kesulitan, kesusahan; **distressed** *adj* menderita

distribute *vt* menyebarluaskan, menyiarkan, membagikan, mendistribusikan; **distribution** *n* penyebarluasan, pendistribusian; penyiaran; pembagian; penyaluran, distribusi; **distributor** *n* penyalur, pengécér

district *n, adj* distrik, daérah; *~ attorney* jaksa; *~ court* pengadilan wilayah, pengadilan negeri

distrust *n* rasa curiga; *vt* mencurigai

disturb *vt* mengganggu; **disturbance** *n* kekacauan, kegaduhan, gangguan; **disturbed** *adj* terganggu; **disturbing** *adj* mengganggu, menguatirkan

disunited *adj* tidak bersatu, terceraiberai; **disunity** *n* keadaan tidak bersatu

disused *adj* usang, tidak terpakai lagi

ditch *n* selokan, parit; *vt, sl* membuang, meninggalkan

ditto *adj* sama

divan *n* dipan, ranjang

dive *vi* menyelam, terjun; menukik; *~ bomber* pesawat pengebom; **diver** *n* penyelam; *sky~* penerjun payung; **diving** *n* selam; loncat indah; *~ board* papan loncat; *sky~* terjun payung

diverge *vi* menyimpang; bercabang; **divergence** *n* penyimpangan, perbédaan; **divergent** *adj* menyimpang, berbéda

diverse *adj* berbagai (macam), anéka, pelbagai; **diversion** *n* sesuatu yang mengalihkan perhatian; hiburan; **diversity** *n* keanékaragaman; **divert** *vt* menangkis, mengalihkan perhatian; menghibur

divide *n* jurang, kesenjangan; *v* membagi; *six ~d by two is three* enam dibagi dua sama dengan tiga; **divider** *n* sekat; **dividers** *n, pl* kompas; **division** *n* pembagian; bagian; divisi; **divisive** *adj* bersifat memecah-belahkan

divine *adj* ilahi; *sl* hébat; **divinity** *n* [diviniti] ketuhanan; théologi

diving *n* selam; loncat indah; *~ board* papan loncat; *sky~* terjun payung ← **dive**

division *n* [divisyen] pembagian; bagian; divisi ← **divide**

divorce *n* perceraian; *vi* bercerai; *vt* menceraikan; **divorced** *adj* cerai; *~ man* duda; **divorcée** *n* janda

divulge *vt* membuka rahasia

DIY *abbrev* do it yourself rakit sendiri

dizziness *n* rasa pusing; **dizzy** *adj* pusing (kepala), pening, bingung

DJ *abbrev disc jockey* DJ

Djibouti *n* [jibuti] Djibouti; **Djiboutian** *n* orang Djibouti

do *vt* [du] **did done** [dan] berbuat, bikin; membuat, melakukan, mengerjakan; *~ up* memperbaiki, mempercantik; mengancing (baju); *~ without* jalan tanpa; *~ it yourself (DIY)* rakit sendiri;

~ *your best* kerjakan sebaik-baiknya; *so ~ I* saya juga; *that will ~* sudah cukup; *how are you ~ing?* bagaimana kabarnya?; *how ~ you ~* apa kabar; *what ~ you ~?* bekerja di mana?; **doing** *n* perbuatan; *vt what are you ~?* sedang apa?

docile *adj* jinak, mudah diajar

dock *n* galangan, dok; *vi* berlabuh; **docker** *n* buruh pelabuhan; **dockyard** *n* galangan; **dockland** *n* daérah pelabuhan

docket *n* struk (belanja)

dockland *n* daérah pelabuhan ← **dock**

doctor *n* dokter; doktor (S3); *at the ~'s* di klinik; **doctorate** *n* [doktoret] gelar S3

doctrine *n* [doktren] ajaran, doktrin

document *n* surat, dokumén; *vt* men-dokuméntasi; **documentary** *n* film dokuméntér; **documentation** *n* catatan, dokuméntasi

dodge *vt* mengelakkan, menghindar; **dodgy** *adj, sl* tidak dapat dipercaya atau diandalkan

dodgem ~ *car* bom-bom car

doe *n* [do] rusa betina; *~-eyed* bermata besar

does *vt* [daz] **doesn't** [dazent] → **do**

dog *n* anjing; *~-eared* kertas yang sudutnya terlipat; *~-tired* capék sekali; ~ *paddle* berenang seperti anjing; *in the ~-house* sedang diacuhkan

dog *vt* membuntuti, selalu menjadi masalah; *~ged by bad luck* dirundung malang; **dogged** *adj* [doged] berkeras kepala, nékat

dogma *n* dogma, kepercayaan agama; **dogmatic** *adj* fanatik mengikuti ajaran

doing *n* [duing] perbuatan; *vt what are you ~?* sedang apa? ← **do**

dole *n* tunjangan pengangguran; *on the ~* sedang menganggur

doleful *adj* murung

doll *n* bonéka; *~'s house* rumah bonéka; **dolly** *n, child* bonéka

dollar *n* dolar; *US ~* dolar AS

dolphin *n* [dolfin] lumba-lumba

domain *n* daérah, wilayah

dome *n* kubah; **domed** *adj* berkubah

domestic *adj* dalam negeri, doméstik; ~ *servant* pembantu (rumah tangga, PRT), pramuwisma; **domesticate** *vt* menjinakkan; *cats are ~d animals* kucing itu héwan jinak

dominant *adj* berkuasa, berpengaruh, dominan; **dominance** *n* kekuasaan; **dominate** *vt* menguasai, mendominasi; **domination** *n* penguasaan, dominasi

Dominica *n* Dominika; **Dominican** *n* orang Dominika; ~ *Republic* Republik Dominika

domino *n* gaplé, domino; ~ *effect* éfék domino

donate *vi* bersumbang; *vt* menyumbang-kan; **donation** *n* sumbangan; **donor** *n* pemberi, donor; *blood ~* donor darah

done *v, pf* [dan] *a well-~ steak* stéik yang matang → **do**

donkey *n* [dongki] keledai; *~'s years* lama sekali

donor *n* pemberi, donor; *blood ~* donor darah ← **donate**

donut, doughnut *n* donat

don't *vt* jangan ← **do**

doodle *n* [dudel] corétan, lukisan iseng; *vi* mencorét-corét

doom *n* malapetaka, ajal; **doomed** *adj* bernasib sial; **doomsday** *n* hari kiamat

door *n* [dor] pintu; **doorbell** *n* bél (pintu); **doorman** *n* petugas pembuka pintu; **doormat** *n* kését; **doorstep** *n* ambang pintu; **doorway** *n* pintu; *trap~* pintu di lantai atau langit-langit

dope *n, sl* obat-obatan, obat bius; orang bodoh; ~ *fiend* pecandu obat; *vt* membius; ~ *test* tés darah untuk mengetahui adanya obat-obat terlarang; **dopey** *adj* pusing; tolol; **doping** *n* prakték memakai obat-obat terlarang oleh atlét

dormant *adj* tidur

dormitory *n* **dorm** *sl* asrama; ~ *suburb* daérah perumahan yang cukup jauh dari kota

dosage *n* [dosej] takaran, dosis; **dose** *n* dosis

dossier *n* [dosier] berkas

dot *n* titik, noktah, percik; *polka ~* bercorak bulatan besar; *join the ~s* menyambung titik; *on the* ~ tepat, pas pada waktunya; **dotty** *adj* pikun

double *adj* [dabel] ganda; dobel; *n* kembaran; *vi* berlipat ganda; *vt* melipatgandakan; *~click* klik dua kali; *~cross* mengkhianati; *~decker (bus)* bis tingkat; ~ *agent* mata-mata yang bekerja untuk dua pihak; ~ *bed* tempat tidur untuk dua orang; ~ *Dutch* katakata yang tidak dimengerti; ~ *glazing* kaca dua lapis; *on the* ~ segera; **doubles** *n* ganda; *men's* ~ ganda putra

doubt *n* [daut] ragu, keraguan; *no* ~ sudah pasti; *vt* menyangsikan, meragukan; **doubtful** *adj* sangsi, ragu-ragu; **doubtless** *adj* tidak ragu-ragu, pasti

dough *n* [do] adonan; **doughnut** → **donut**

dove *n* [dav] burung merpati; **dovecote** *n* pagupon

dowdy *adj* berbaju kuno, tidak menarik

down *n* bulu halus (burung); *adv* di bawah, ke bawah; *~hearted adj* kecil hati; tidak berfungsi; *~to-earth* sederhana, bersahaja; ~ *under* di Australia; ~ *and out* melarat, sengsara; *to feel* ~ merasa sedih; **downcast** *adj* murung, sedih; **downfall** *n* jatuhnya; **downpour** *n* hujan lebat; **downright** *adj* [daunrait] terus terang; **downsize** *vt* merampingkan (perusahaan); **downstairs** *adv* di lantai bawah; **downstream** *n* hilir; *adv* ke hilir; **downtown** *adv* di pusat kota, ke pusat kota; **downward, downwards** *adv* ke bawah

Down's syndrome *n* sindroma Down

dowry *n* [dauri] mas kawin, mahar

doze *n* tidur sebentar, tidur ayam

dozen *n* [dazen] lusin; *~s* berpuluh-puluh, puluhan

Dr *Doctor* dr (dokter)

draft *n* rancangan; wajib militér; *bank* ~ wésel; *vt* merancang; memanggil untuk wajib militer; *Ian didn't get ~ed* Ian tidak dipanggil untuk wajib militér

drag *n* gaya tolak; *vt* menyérét, menarik; ~ *on* berlama-lama; ~ *up* mengungkit; *what a ~!* membosankan

dragon *n* naga; **dragonfruit** *n* buah naga

dragonfly *n* capung

drain *n* saluran, parit, got; kali; aliran; *vt* menguras, mengalirkan, mengeringkan; ~ *away* terkuras, mengalir; **drained** *adj* capék, lemas; **drainage** *n* [drénej] saluran, drainase; **drainer, draining board** *n* rak piring

drama *n* seni peran, drama, sandiwara; **dramatic** *adj* mengesankan, dramatis; **dramatically** *adv* secara mengesankan

drank *v, pf* → **drink**

drapes *n, pl* hordén

drastic *adj* drastis, radikal; **drastically** *adv* secara drastis

draught *n* [draft] angin (di dalam bangunan); sejenis bir; ~ *horse* kuda pedati; **draughts** *n, pl* dam; **draughtsman** *n* juru gambar, perancang; **draughty** *adj* berangin

draw *v* **drew drawn** menggambar; **drawing** *n* lukisan, gambar

draw *vt* menarik; ~ *on* menggunakan, memakai; ~ *out* mengulur-ulur; **drawback** *n* kekurangan, sisi buruk; **drawer** *n* laci; *chest of ~s* (lemari) laci; *~ing pin* paku; *~ing room arch* kamar penerima tamu

draw *n* **drew drawn** *vi* seri; *Spain drew two all with Poland* Spanyol seri dengan Polandia 2-2

dread *n* [dréd] ketakutan, rasa takut; *vt* takut akan; *Debbie ~s exams* Debbie takut akan ujian; **dreadful** *adj* menakutkan, dahsyat

dreadlocks *n, pl* [drédloks] rambut gimbal

dream *n* mimpi, impian; *bad* ~ mimpi buruk; *wet* ~ mimpi basah; *vi* mimpi; bermimpi; *vt* mengimpikan; **dreamer** *n* pemimpi; orang yang melamun

dreary *adj* [driri] berawan; suram, redup

dredge *n* kapal keruk; *vt* mengeruk

dregs *n, pl* sisa (minyak, kopi)

drench *vt* membasahi; **drenched** *adj* basah kuyup

dress *n* rok; pakaian, baju, kostum; *vi* berpakaian, mengenakan pakaian; *vt* menghiasi; ~ *pattern* pola pakaian, patron; ~ *rehearsal* gladi resik, gladi bersih; ~ *up* berdandan, berpakaian formal; **dressed** *adj* berpakaian;

dressing *n* perban; saus (untuk salada); ~ *gown* kimono; **dressmaker** *n* tukang jahit; **dressy** *adj* bergaya formal

dresser *n* kabinét, laci

drew *v, pf →* **draw**

dried *v, pf →* **dry**; *adj* kering

drift *n* arus, aliran, arah; *vi* terbawa arus, terhanyut; **drifter** *n* orang tanpa pekerjaan atau rumah tetap, gelandangan; **driftwood** *n* kayu yang terbawa arus

drill *n* bor; latihan; *v* mengebor; melatih

drink *n* **drank drunk** minuman; *v* minum; *vt* meminum; ~*ing water* air putih, air minum; **drinker** *n* peminum; *heavy* ~ peminum berat

drip *n* tétés, tétésan; *vi* menétés; ~*-dry* tidak perlu disetrika

drive *n* **drove driven** [drivven] semangat, dorongan; *vt* menjalankan atau membawa (mobil), mengemudikan, menyupir; mengantarkan; ~ *someone mad*, ~ *someone crazy* membuat gila; **driver** *n* supir, sopir, pengemudi, pengendara (mobil); kusir, sais (kendaraan berkuda); ~*'s license* surat izin mengemudi (SIM); *engine* ~, *train* ~ masinis; **driveway** *n* jalanan masuk halaman untuk mobil; **driving** *adj* mendorong; ~ *lesson* lés mengemudi; ~ *rain* hujan deras

drizzle *n, vi* [drizel] hujan rintik-rintik

droll *adj* lucu, ironis

drone *n* dengung; lebah jantan yang pekerja; *vi* berdengung, mendengung

drool *vi* mengiler, mengeluarkan air liur; *n* air liur

droop *vi* merana, lemas; **droopy** *adj* berjuntai

drop *n* titik, tétés; *cough* ~ permen obat batuk; *vi* jatuh, turun, terjun; ~ *by*, ~ *in* mampir; ~ *out* tidak meneruskan (pelajaran); *vt* menjatuhkan, menurunkan; ~ *a hint* mengingatkan; ~ *a line* mengirim surat; ~ *a subject* berhenti mata pelajaran; **droppings** *n, pl* kotoran binatang

drought *n* [draut] masa kering tanpa hujan

drove *vt, pf →* **drive**

drover *n* gembala

drown *vi* tenggelam; *vt* menenggelamkan; *Andy nearly* ~*ed* Andy nyaris mati tenggelam

drowsy *adj* mengantuk

drudge *n* tugas yang melelahkan

drug *n* obat (bius), obat-obatan, narkoba; ~ *addict* pecandu narkoba; ~ *dealer* bandar narkoba; *to do* ~*s, to take* ~*s* memakai narkoba; *vt* membius; ~*store* toko kecil; apotik

drum *n* gendang, tambur; tong; *ear*~ gendang telinga; *vt* mengetuk; **drummer** *n* penabuh; **drumstick** *n* tongkat pemukul drum; paha ayam

drunk *n* mabuk; *v, pf →* **drink**; **drunkard** *n* peminum, pemabuk

dry *adj* [drai] kering, haus; membosankan; *vi* kering, mengering, berjemur; *vt* menjemur, mengeringkan; ~*-cleaning* binatu, waserai; ~ *season* musim kemarau; **dryer** *n* alat atau mesin pengering; *clothes* ~ mesin pengering baju; *hair* ~ pengering rambut; **dryness** *n* kekeringan

dual *adj* dwi, (rangkap) dua; ~ *purpose* dwifungsi

dub *vt* menyulih-suarakan; **dubbing** *n* sulih suara

dubious *adj* [dyubius] ragu-ragu, meragukan

duchess *n, f* **duke** *m* gelar bangsawan di Inggris

duck *n* itik, bébék; *v* berjongkok (menghindari); **duckling** *n* anak itik

duct *n* saluran, pipa

due *adj* jatuh témpo; perlu, wajib; ~ *date* perkiraan tanggal kelahiran; tanggal harus sudah dikembalikan; ~ *to* karena; *in* ~ *time, in* ~ *course* pada waktunya; *the train is* ~ *at 12* keréta api dijadwalkan masuk jam 12; **dues** *n, pl* béa, cukai

dug *v, pf →* **dig**; **dugout** *n* bungker; ~ *canoe* kano yang terukir dari sepotong kayu

duke *n, m* gelar bangsawan di Inggris

dull *adj* dof; bodoh, dungu

dumb *adj* [dam] bisu; bodoh; ~*bell* halter; **dumbfound** *vt* membuat tercengang; **dumbfounded** *adj* tercengang

dummy *n* manekin, orang-orangan; *n, adj* tiruan; *n, sl* orang bodoh; *n* dot

dump *n (rubbish)* ~ tempat pembuangan sampah, tempat pembuangan akhir (TPA); ~ *truck* truk sampah; *vt* membuang; **dumpster** *n* tong sampah yang besar

dumpling *n* pangsit

dunce *n* orang bodoh; ~*'s cap arch* topi kertas dikenakan pada murid yang menjawab salah

dune *n* bukit pasir

dung *n* tahi, pupuk; ~ *beetle* semacam kumbang tahi; **dunghill** *n* timbunan tahi

dungeon *n* [danjen] sél bawah tanah

dunno *sl* tidak tahu ← **don't know**

dupe *vt* menipu, mengibuli

duplicate *n* [dyupliket] rangkap kedua, salinan, kopi, duplikat; *vt* [dyuplikét] membuat kopi atau rangkap

durability *n* [dyurabiliti] keawétan, daya tahan; **durable** *adj* awét

duration *n* lamanya; *for the* ~ *of* selama

during *conj, prep* selama, sementara

dusk *n* senja

dust *n* abu, debu; *vt* membersihkan, menghilangkan debu; ~ *jacket* sampul buku; **dustbin** *n* tempat sampah; **duster** *n* lap debu, penyapu; **dustman** *n* tukang sampah; **dustpan** *n* sérokan sampah; **dusty** *adj* berdebu

Dutch *n* bahasa Belanda; *adj* berasal dari Belanda; *double*-~ kata-kata yang tidak dimengerti; *the* ~ orang Belanda, bangsa Belanda; *to go* ~ membayar masing-masing; **Dutchman** *n, m* lelaki Belanda; **Dutchwoman** *n, f* [dacwuman] wanita Belanda

dutiful *adj* patuh, menurut; **duty** *n* kewajiban; pekerjaan, tugas; béa; ~ *free* toko bébas béa; *on* ~ sedang bertugas

duvet *n* [duvé] selimut untuk tempat tidur

dwarf *n* [dworf] katai, cébol; *vt* tampak jauh lebih besar daripada; *Yao Ming* ~*s the other players* Yao Ming jauh lebih tinggi daripada pemain lainnya

dwell *vi* berdiam, tinggal; **dweller** *n* penghuni; **dwelling** *n* tempat tinggal

dwindle *vi* [dwindel] berangsur-angsur berkurang, surut, susut

dye *n* [dai] zat pewarna; *natural* ~ zat pewarna alam; *vt* mencelupkan, mengecat (rambut)

dying *vi* sekarat; ~ *to* ingin sekali ← **die**

dyke *n, sl* lésbi, orang lésbian

dynamic *adj* [dainamik] dinamis, hidup

dynamite *n* dinamit, bahan peledak

dynamo *n* dinamo

dynasty *n* keluarga, dinasti

dysentery *n* diséntri

dyslexia *n* disléksia

E

e: **e-book** *n* buku yang dibaca di internét; **e-business** *n* bisnis léwat internét; **e-learning** *n* belajar léwat internét; **e-mail** *n* surat éléktronik, surat é, imél; ~ *address* alamat imél; *vt* mengimél

each *pron* [ic] masing-masing; setiap, tiap-tiap, saban; ~ *other* saling, satu sama lain

eager *adj* ingin sekali, péngén; ~ *beaver* orang yang rajin; **eagerly** *adv* dengan antusias; **eagerness** *n* keinginan yang besar

eagle *n* [igel] burung rajawali, burung elang, burung garuda; ~-*eyed* bermata tajam; *sea* ~ elang laut

ear *n* [ir] telinga, kuping; ~, *nose and throat specialist* dokter telinga, hidung dan tenggorokan (THT); **earache** *n* [irék] sakit telinga; **eardrum** *n* gendang telinga; **earlobe** *n* cuping telinga; **earmark** *vt* memilih secara khusus; **earplug** *n* penyumbat telinga; **earring** *n* anting

earl *n, tit* [érl] gelar bangsawan di Inggris

earlier *adj* [érlier] lebih awal; tadi; *the* ~ *the better* lebih awal lebih baik; **earliest** *adj* paling awal; *at the* ~ paling cepat; **early** *adj* [érli] pagi-pagi, dini; ~ *bird* orang yang bangun pagi atau cepat datang; ~ *next month* awal

bulan depan; *the ~ hours* tengah
malam; *to have an ~ night* tidur cepat
earlobe *n* cuping telinga ← **ear**
earmark *vt* memilih secara khusus ← **ear**
earn *vt* [érn] mendapat gaji, memperoléh; **earner** *n* sumber uang; **earnings**
n, pl pendapatan, gaji, upah
earnest *adj* [érnest] sungguh-sungguh;
in ~ sungguh-sungguh; **earnestly** *adv*
dengan sungguh-sungguh
earnings *n, pl* pendapatan, gaji, upah
← **earn**
earplug *n* penyumbat telinga ← **ear**
earring *n* anting ← **ear**
earth *n* [érth] bumi, dunia; tanah, debu;
on ~ di dunia; *planet ~* Bumi; *down to
~* sederhana, bersahaja; *what on ~
were you thinking?* apa ya pikiranmu
waktu itu?; **earthenware** *n* tembikar;
earthquake *n* gempa bumi; **earthworm** *n* [érthwérm] cacing tanah
ease *n* [iiz] kemudahan, kesenangan; *at
~* tenang, santai; *with ~* dengan
mudah; *vt* mempermudah,
meringankan; **easily** *adv* dengan
mudah; **easy** *adj* mudah, gampang; *~
chair* kursi malas; *~-going* bersikap
santai; *take it ~* tenang
easel *n* kuda-kuda
easily *adv* dengan mudah ← **ease**
east *adj* timur; *the Far ~* Asia; *the
Middle ~* Timur Tengah (Timteng); *~
Timor* Timor Loro Sae; *arch* Timor
Timur (Timtim); **easterly** *~ (wind)*
angin dari arah timur; **eastern** *adj*
(daérah) timur; *~ Europe* Eropa
Timur; **eastward** *adv* ke (arah) timur
Easter *n* Paskah; *~ egg* telur cokelat; *~
Monday* hari Senin sesudah Paskah;
the ~ Bunny kelinci yang membagikan
telur coklat kepada anak-anak
easterly *~ (wind)* angin dari arah timur;
eastern *adj* (daérah) timur; **eastward**
adv ke (arah) timur ← **east**
easy *adj* [izi] mudah, gampang; *~ chair*
kursi malas; *~-going* bersikap santai;
take it ~ tenang ← **ease**
eat *v* ate eaten makan
eaves *n, pl* ujung bawah atap; **eavesdrop** *vt* menguping; **eavesdropper** *n*

orang yang suka menguping
ebb *vi* surut; *~ tide* air surut; *~ and flow*
pasang surut
ebony *n* kayu éboni
e-book *n* buku yang dibaca di internét
← **e**
e-business *n* bisnis léwat internét ← **e**
EC *abbrev European Community*
Masyarakat Eropa (ME)
eccentric *adj* [ékséntrik] anéh, antik
echo *n* [éko] gema, gaung, kumandang;
vi bergema, bergaung, berkumandang;
vt menggemakan
éclair *n* semacam kué berisi krim
eclipse *n* gerhana; *lunar ~* gerhana
bulan; *solar ~* gerhana matahari; *vt*
tidak tertanding, memudarkan; *Hackett
~d his rivals in the 400m* Hackett tidak
tertanding di nomor 400m
ecological *adj* berkaitan dengan ékologi; **ecology** *n* ékologi
economic *adj* berkaitan dengan ékonomi; *~ crisis* krisis ékonomi, krismon
(tahun 1998); **economical** *adj* hémat,
ékonomis; **economics** *n* ilmu ékonomi; **economist** *n* ékonom; **economize**
vi menghémat; *we have to ~ on paper*
kita harus menghémat kertas; **economy** *n* ékonomi, dunia usaha; kehé-
matan; *planned ~* ékonomi berencana
ecosystem *n* ékosistem
ecstasy *n* kegembiraan, kebahagiaan;
ékstasi; *in ~* sangat gembira atau
bahagia; **ecstatic** *adj* sangat gembira
atau bahagia
Ecuador *n* Ekuador; **Ecuadorian** *n* orang
Ekuador; *adj* berasal dari Ekuador
eczema *n* éksema
ed. *editor* red. (redaksi); *edition* édisi,
cétakan
eddy *n* pusaran air
edge *n* [éj] pinggir, sisi, tepi; mata
(pisau); *on ~* tegang; *at the ~ of the
pond* di pinggir kolam; *on the ~ of
their seats* di pinggir kursi; tegang;
edgy *adj* tegang, suka marah
edible *adj* [édibel] dapat dimakan;
edibles *n, pl* makanan
edit *vt* menyunting, mengédit; **edition** *n*
terbitan, keluaran, édisi, cétakan;

editing *n* penyuntingan; **editor** *n* redaktur, penyunting, éditor; *~-in-chief* pemimpin redaksi; **editorial** *n* tajuk rencana; *~ board* déwan redaksi

educate *vt* mendidik; **educated** *adj* berpendidikan; **education** *n* pendidikan; *primary ~* sekolah dasar; *secondary ~* sekolah menengah; *tertiary ~* perguruan tinggi; **educational** *adj* mendidik, édukatif; **educator** *n* pendidik, pengajar, guru

EEC *abbrev, arch European Economic Community* MEE (Masyarakat Ekonomi Eropa)

eel *n* [iel] belut, lindung

eerie *adj* mengerikan; *there was an ~ light in the sky* ada cahaya anéh di langit

effect *n* pengaruh, éfék; akibat, hasil; *to take ~* mulai berlaku; *vt* mengerjakan, mengadakan; *~ a change* mengadakan perubahan, mengubah; **effects** *n, pl* barang-barang, harta milik; **effective** *adj* berhasil, éféktif; **effectiveness** *n* éféktivitas

effeminate *adj* seperti perempuan

efficiency *n* daya guna, éfisiénsi; **efficient** *adj* berdaya guna, tepat guna, éfisién; **efficiently** *adv* secara éfisién

effluent *n* limbah cairan

effort *n* usaha, upaya; *to make an ~* berusaha; **effortless** *adj* dengan mudah

eg *exempli gratia (for example)* mis., (seperti) misalnya

egalitarian *adj* egalitér, percaya bahwa semua orang sederajat

egg *n* telur; *~ cup* tempat telur rebus; *~ white* putih telur; *quail's ~* telur puyuh; *fried ~* telur mata sapi; *hard-boiled ~* telur rebus; *poached ~* telur kukus; *scrambled ~s* telur aduk; **eggplant** *n* térong; **eggshell** *n* kulit telur

ego *n* [igo] égo; **egoism** *n* [igoizem] égoisme; **egoist** *adj* égois; **egotistic, egotistical** *adj* égois, suka mementingkan diri sendiri

Egypt *n* [ijipt] Mesir; *ancient ~* Mesir Kuno; **Egyptian** *n* orang Mesir; *adj* berasal dari Mesir

eiderdown *n* [aiderdaun] sejenis selimut tebal

eight *adj, n* [éit] delapan; **eighteen** *adj, n* delapan belas; **eighteenth** *adj, n* kedelapan belas; *the ~ of January* tanggal delapan belas Januari; **eighth** *adj, n* kedelapan; **eighty** *adj, n* delapan puluh; *pl* **eighties** *the ~* tahun 80an

either *adv* [ither, aither] salah satu; *conj ~ ... or ... ...* atau...; *I don't like ~* dua-duanya saya tidak suka; *on ~ side of the street* kiri-kanan jalan

ejaculate *vi* berseru; **ejaculation** *n* éjakulasi; kata seru

eject *vi* keluar; *vt* mengeluarkan, mengusir

elaborate *vi* [ilaborét] *~ on* menguraikan, menjelaskan secara panjang lébar; membumbui; *reporters often ~ the real story* wartawan sering membumbui cerita yang sebenarnya; *adj* [ilaboret] rumit, panjang lebar, teliti; **elaboration** *n* penjelasan, perincian

elapse *vi* léwat, berlalu

elastic *n* karet; *adj* karet, kenyal, élastis; *~ band* karet (gelang)

elated *adj* bahagia; **elation** *n* kegembiraan

elbow *n* siku; *vt* menyikut; *~ grease* bekerja keras

elder *n* yang lebih tua; sesepuh; *adj* kakak; *~ brother* kakak (laki-laki), abang; *~ sister* kakak (perempuan); **elderly** *adj* sepuh, sudah tua; **eldest** *n* anak sulung; *adj* paling tua, sulung

e-learning *n* belajar léwat internét ← **e**

elect *v* memilih; *~ to* memilih, memutuskan; *~ed president* présidén terpilih; **election** *n* pemilihan; *general ~* pemilihan umum (pemilu); **elective** *n* mata pelajaran pilihan; **elector** *n* pemilih; **electoral** *~ roll* daftar pemilih

electric *adj* listrik; *~ blanket* selimut penghangat; *the ~ chair* kursi listrik; **electrical** *adj* (berkaitan dengan) listrik; *~ engineering* teknik éléktro; **electrician** *n* tukang listrik; **electricity** *n* listrik; **electrocute** *vi* menyetrum; *to get ~d* disetrum, kena setrum

electron *n* éléktron; **electronic** *adj* éléktronik; **electronics** *n, pl* barang éléktronik, éléktronika; **electronically**

adv secara éléktronik; léwat imél

elegance *n* keanggunan; **elegant** *adj* anggun, élok; **elegantly** *adv* dengan anggun

element *n* unsur, bagian, bahan, élemén; *he's in his ~* dia sangat betah; *(periodic) table of ~s* tabel périodik; **elementary** *adj* dasar; *~ school* sekolah dasar (SD)

elephant *n* [élefant] gajah; *white ~* barang tidak berguna

elevate *vt* [élevét] menaikkan, mengangkat; **elevated** *adj* tinggi, agung; **elevation** *n* ketinggian; **elevator** *n* lift

eleven *adj, n* [eléven] sebelas; **eleventh** *adj, n* kesebelas; *at the ~ hour* pada saat terakhir

elf *n* **elves** peri; **elfin** *adj* mungil, seperti peri

elicit *vt* [elisit] memperoléh (arti), mengeluarkan

eligibility *n* [élijibiliti] memenuhi syarat; kepantasan; **eligible** *adj* memenuhi syarat, dapat dipilih

eliminate *vt* [eliminét] menyisihkan, menyingkirkan; **elimination** *n* penyisihan, éliminasi; *~ round* babak penyisihan

elite *the ~* para élit, kaum atas; *adj* élit

ellipse *n* bulat panjang, élips; **elliptical** *adj* bulat panjang; tidak langsung

elope *vi* kawin lari; *she ~d with the gardener* dia kawin lari dengan tukang kebun

eloquence *n* [elokuens] kefasihan, kepandaian bicara; **eloquent** *adj* fasih, pandai bicara; **eloquently** *adv* dengan fasih

El Salvador *n* El Salvador; **Salvadorean** *n* orang El Salvador; *adj* berasal dari El Salvador

else *adv* lain; *anything ~* yang lain; *or ~* jika tidak; *someone ~* orang lain; *what ~* apa lagi; **elsewhere** *adv* [élswér] di lain tempat

elucidate *vt* menjelaskan, menerangkan; **elucidation** *n* penjelasan, keterangan

elude *v* menghindar dari, menghindari, mengelak; **elusive** *adj* [elusiv] sulit dicari

emaciated *adj* [emésiéted] sangat kurus, ceking

e-mail *n* surat éléktronik, surat e, imél; *~ address* alamat imél; *v* mengimél ← **e**

emanate *vi* berasal atau keluar dari; mengeluarkan; *an awful smell ~d from the room* bau busuk berasal dari kamar itu

emancipate *vt* memerdékakan, membébaskan; **emancipation** *n* kemerdékaan, pembébasan; *the ~ of women* penyejajaran perempuan

embalm *vt* membalsem; **embalming** *n* pembalseman

embankment *n* tepi

embargo *n* perbatasan perdagangan

embark *v* naik (kendaraan); *~ on a journey* memulai perjalanan; **embarkation** *n* naiknya, émbarkasi

embarrass *vt* memalukan, mempermalukan; **embarrassed** *adj* malu; **embarrassing** *adj* memalukan; **embarrassment** *n* keadaan yang membuat malu, rasa malu

embassy *n* kedutaan

embellish *vt* menghiasi, membesar-besarkan, membumbui; **embellishment** *n* perhiasan

embers *n, pl* bara

embezzle *vt* [embézel] menggelapkan; **embezzlement** *n* korupsi, penggelapan uang

embittered *adj* dendam, sakit hati

emblem *n* lambang, tanda; *the school ~ was gold with a blue border* lambang sekolah berwarna emas dengan pinggiran biru

embrace *n* pelukan; *vi* berpelukan; *vt* memeluk

embroider *v* menyulam, membordir; membesar-besarkan; **embroidery** *n* sulaman, bordiran

embryo *n* [émbrio] janin; **embryonic** *adj* masih sangat kecil

emerald *n* zamrud; *adj* hijau; *the ~ Isle* Irlandia

emerge *vi* [emérj] timbul, muncul; *~ from* muncul dari; **emergence** *n* timbulnya, munculnya; **emergent** *adj* [emérjent] sedang muncul, naik daun

emergency *n* [emérjénsi] keadaaan
darurat; *adj* darurat; ~ *brake* rém
bahaya; ~ *exit* pintu darurat

emergent *adj* [emérjent] sedang
muncul, naik daun ← **emerge**

emery [émeri] ~ *board* kertas ampelas,
amril

emigrant *n* émigran; **emigrate** *vi* pindah,
berémigrasi; *Glen ~d from Croatia as
a child* Glen datang dari Kroasia waktu
masih kecil; **emigration** *n* émigrasi

emigré *n* [émigré] orang yang tinggal
di pengasingan di luar negeri

eminent *adj* [éminent] ternama, terpan-
dang, unggul; ~ *person* begawan

emission *n* pancaran, buangan, émisi;
vehicle ~s emisi kendaraan; **emit** *vt*
memancarkan, mengeluarkan; *the
engine ~ted a whistling sound* bunyi
siulan berasal dari mesin

emotion *n* perasaan, émosi; **emotional**
adj émosi; **emotive** *adj* yang menimbulkan perasaan; ~ *language* pilihan
kata yang menimbulkan perasaan

empathy *n* tenggang rasa, émpati

emperor *n* kaisar ← **empire**

emphasis *n* [émfasis] tekanan; **emphasize** *v.*menekankan, menitikberatkan;
emphatic *adj* tegas, kuat

empire *n* kekaisaran, kerajaan; grup
perusahaan; *the British* ~ kerajaan
Inggris; **emperor** *n* kaisar; *Roman* ~
Julius Caesar Kaisar Romawi Yulius
Caesar; **empress** *n, f* kaisar wanita

employ *vt* mempekerjakan; menggunakan, memakai; **employed** *adj* mempunyai pekerjaan, bekerja; digunakan;
employee *n* pegawai, buruh, pekerja,
karyawan, karyawati; **employer** *n*
majikan; **employment** *n* pekerjaan

empower *vt* memperdayakan; **empowerment** *n* pemberdayaan; ~ *of women*
pemberdayaan perempuan

empress *n, f* kaisar wanita, ratu ←
empire

emptiness *n* kekosongan, kehampaan;
empty *adj* kosong, hampa; *vt* mengosongkan; *~-handed* dengan tangan
kosong, tanpa hasil; *~-headed* bodoh

emu *n* ému, burung besar khas Australia

emulate *vt* berusaha menyaingi atau
melebihi; *Chad wanted to ~ his
father's success as a footballer* Chad
ingin berhasil sebagai pemain sépak
bola seperti ayahnya

enable *vt* [enébel] memungkinkan;
memasang

enact *vt* menjadikan; ~ *a law* menjadikan undang-undang; **enactment** *n*
pembuatan

enamel *n* glasir, cat halus; émail; *nail* ~
cat kuku, kuték

encephalitis *n* [énséfalaitis] radang otak

enchant *vt* **enchanting** *adj* memesonakan, memikat, menyihir, memukau;
enchanted *adj* tersihir, terpesona,
terpikat; **enchantment** *n* sihir

encircle *vt* [ensérkel] mengepung,
mengelilingi, melingkari

enclave *n* [énklév, onklav] daérah
kantung

enclose *vt* memagari; melampirkan,
menyertakan; **enclosed** *adj* terlampir;
enclosure *n* kandang

encore *ejac* [onkor] lagi! (di pertunjukan); *n* lagu terakhir atas permintaan
penonton

encounter *n* pertemuan; *vt* bertemu atau
berjumpa dengan; *Joni ~ed a tiger on
the road* Joni secara tidak sengaja
bertemu dengan harimau di jalan

encourage *vt* [énkarej] mendorong,
mendukung, memberi semangat,
membesarkan hati; **encouraging** *adj*
menggembirakan; **encouragement** *n*
dorongan, desakan

encumber *vt* membebani; **encumbrance**
n beban

encyclopedia *n* [énsaiklopidia] énsiklopédi; **encyclopedic** *adj* sangat luas;
he has an ~ knowledge of aircraft dia
punya pengetahuan sangat luas tentang pesawat

end *n* akhir, ujung; *loose ~s* urusan
yang belum selesai; *The* ~ tamat; *in
the* ~ akhirnya; *at a loose* ~ bosan,
tanpa kegiatan; *vi* berakhir, tamat; *vt*
menyudahi; mengakhiri; **ending** *n* akhir (cerita); *happy* ~ akhir cerita yang
bahagia; **endless** *adj* tanpa ujung,

tiada hentinya, tidak ada akhirnya, tak terhingga, tidak berkeputusan

endanger vt [endéinjer] membahayakan, mengancam; ~ life membahayakan jiwa; **endangered** adj ~ species binatang yang terancam punah

endear vi ~ yourself membuat dirinya disayangi; **endearing** adj manis, lucu

endeavor, endeavour n [éndévor] usaha; vi berusaha, mencoba; ~ to berusaha untuk, berusaha agar

ending n akhir (cerita); happy ~ akhir cerita yang bahagia ← **end**

endless adj tanpa ujung, tiada hentinya, tidak ada akhirnya, tak terhingga, tidak berkeputusan ← **end**

endorse vt menyokong, mendukung (secara resmi); mengiklankan; **endorsement** n dukungan; iklan

endow vi ~ with memberkati atau menganugerahi dengan; **endowed** adj diberkati, dianugerahi; **endowment** n tunjangan

endurance n daya tahan, stamina; **endure** vt bertahan; menahan, menderita, menempuh

enema n [énema] obat urus-urus, obat pencahar

enemy n [énemi] musuh, seteru; the ~ lawan; arch ~ musuh bebuyutan

energetic adj [énerjétik] énérgik, bersemangat; **energy** n tenaga, usaha; geothermal ~ tenaga panas bumi; hydroelectric ~ tenaga air; nuclear ~ tenaga nuklir; wave ~ tenaga ombak

enforce vt menjalankan, melaksanakan; menegakkan; **enforcement** n penegakan; law ~ penegakan hukum

engage v [engéj] memasang; **engaged** adj bertunangan; the line's ~ nada sibuk; **engagement** n janji; pertunangan; ~ ring cincin tunangan; to have a prior ~ terlanjur janji

engender vt melahirkan, menimbulkan

engine n [énjin] mesin; ~ driver masinis; train ~ lokomotif, lok; **engineer** n insinyur; masinis; vt merékayasa; **engineering** n ilmu téknik, rékayasa; aeronautical ~ téknik dirgantara; chemical ~ téknik kimia; civil ~ téknik

mesin; electrical ~ téknik éléktro; genetic ~ rékayasa génétik

England n [ingland] Inggris; **English** n bahasa Inggris; the ~ orang Inggris, bangsa Inggris; adj berasal dari Inggris; **Englishman** n, m lelaki Inggris; **Englishwoman** n, f [inglisywuman] perempuan Inggris

engrave vt mengukir atau melukis pada batu atau logam; menggoréskan; **engraver** n pengukir, pelukis; **engraving** n étsa

engulf vt membanjiri, melanda; the tsunami ~d the small village tsunami membanjiri désa kecil

enhance vt meningkatkan; memperkaya; **enhanced** adj lebih jelas; diperkaya; **enhancement** n peningkatan, perbaikan

enigma n teka-teki; **enigmatic** adj [énigmatik] mistérius

enjoy vt menikmati; ~ oneself bersenang-senang; **enjoyable** adj menyenangkan; **enjoyment** n kenikmatan, kesenangan

enlarge vt membesarkan, memperbesar, memperluas; **enlargement** n pembesaran

enlighten vt [énlaiten] memperjelas, memberi keterangan; ~ me as to your situation tolong jelaskan keadaan anda; **enlightenment** the ~ Masa Pencerahan

enlist vi mendaftarkan diri; thousands of young men ~ed in the army ribuan pemuda bergabung dengan tentara; **enlistment** n pendaftaran

enormous adj sangat besar; **enormously** adv amat sangat; you've helped ~ kamu sudah sangat menolong; **enormity** n besarnya

enough adv [enaf] cukup, sudah; that's enough! cukup!; I didn't study hard ~ saya kurang rajin belajar

enquire vi bertanya; menyelidiki; ~ about bertanya tentang; ~ into menyelidiki; **enquiry** n pertanyaan; the police are making enquiries polisi sedang mengadakan penyelidikan

enrage vt menimbulkan atau membuat marah; **enraged** adj marah, bérang

enrich *vt* memperkaya; **enrichment** *n* pengayaan; *uranium* ~ pengayaan uranium

enroll, enrol *vi* daftar; ~ *in a German course* daftar untuk kursus bahasa Jérman; *vt* mendaftarkan; **enrolled** *adj* terdaftar; **enrollment** *n* pendaftaran

ensign *n* [ensain] bendéra

ensue *vi* [énsiu] terjadi; *a terrible fight ~d* kemudian terjadi perkelahian yang hébat

en suite *adv* [onsuit] kamar mandi dalam, kamar mandi di kamar tidur utama

ensure *v* memastikan, menjamin; *please ~ you complete the form correctly* memastikan agar formulir dilengkapi dengan benar; **ensured** *adj* terjamin

enter *vi* masuk; *vt* masuk, memasuki, memasukkan; ~ *a competition* ikut lomba atau sayembara; *Vasundara ~ed the room* Vasundara masuk ruangan; *it's easy for thieves to ~ this house* maling dapat memasuki rumah ini dengan mudah; *she ~ed her details into the computer* dia memasukkan data pribadinya ke dalam komputer; **entrance** *n* pintu masuk; ~ *fee* biaya masuk; ~ *test* ujian masuk; *to make an ~* masuk; **entrant** *n* peserta

enterprise *n* perusahaan, usaha; inisiatif; **enterprising** *adj* yang mengambil inisiatif, yang berusaha

entertain *vi* menjamu; *vt* menghibur; **entertainer** *n* artis, penghibur; **entertaining** *adj* menghibur; **entertainment** *n* hiburan

enthusiasm *n* semangat, gairah, antusiasme, gelora; kegemaran, hobi; **enthusiast** *n* penggemar; **enthusiastic** *adj* antusias, bersemangat; **enthusiastically** *adv* dengan semangat, dengan antusias

entice *vt* membujuk; **enticement** *n* tawaran, bujukan

entire *adj* seluruh, seantéro; **entirely** *adv* benar-benar; **entirety** *n* keseluruhan, keutuhan; *in its* ~ secara keseluruhan

entitled *adj* [entaitld] berhak; berjudul

entourage *n* [onturaj] rombongan, para pengiring

entrails *n, pl* isi perut, jeroan

entrance *n* pintu masuk; ~ *fee* biaya masuk; ~ *test* ujian masuk; *to make an* ~ masuk; **entrant** *n* peserta ← **enter**

entrap *vt* menjerat, menangkap; **entrapment** *n* penjeratan, penangkapan

entrepreneur *n* [ontreprenur] pengusaha, wiraswasta; **entrepreneurial** *adj* berjiwa pengusaha, berjiwa pedagang

entrust *vt* memercayakan kepada; *I ~ed him with my house keys* saya titipkan kunci rumah kepadanya

entry *n* jalan masuk, pintu masuk; pembukuan; masukan, kata kepala; *no* ~ dilarang masuk ← **enter**

enunciate *vt* melafalkan, mengucapkan; **enunciation** *n* lafal, pengucapan

envelop *vt* [envélop] menyelubungi, menyampuli; **envelope** *n* [énvelop] amplop, sampul surat

envious *adj* [énvius] iri; **envy** *n* (rasa) iri; *vt* ingin seperti, merindukan, iri pada

environs *in the* ~ sekitar, sekeliling, dekat; **environment** *n* lingkungan; **environmental** *adj* berkaitan dengan lingkungan; **environmentally** *adv* ~ *aware* sadar akan lingkungan; ~ *friendly* ramah lingkungan; **environmentalist** *n* aktivis lingkungan

envoy *n* utusan

envy *n* (rasa) iri; *vt* ingin seperti, merindukan

epic *n* cerita panjang, épik; *adj* hébat, patut dikenang

epicenter *n* titik pusat gempa bumi, épiséntrum

epidemic *n* wabah

epilepsy *n* penyakit ayan, épilépsi, sawan; **epileptic** *n* penderita penyakit ayan; *adj* ~ *fit* serangan ayan

epilogue *n* kata penutup, épilog

episode *n* bagian (waktu), épisode; peristiwa

equal *n* [ikuel] bandingan; *vt* menyamai, menyamakan; *adj* sama, setara; **equality** *n* [ikuoliti] kesamaan; **equalize** *vt* menyamakan; **equally** *adv* sama; ~ *busy* sama sibuknya; **equation** *n* persamaan; *chemical* ~ persamaan kimia

equator *n* katulistiwa; **equatorial** *adj* berhubungan dengan katulistiwa; ~ *Guinea* Guinea Katulistiwa

equestrian *n* atlét penunggang kuda; *adj* berkaitan dengan penunggangan kuda; ~ *event* lomba penunggangan kuda

equilateral *adj* sama sisi; ~ *triangle* segi tiga sama sisi

equilibrium *n* keseimbangan

equine *adj* berkaitan dengan kuda

equinox *n* saat malam dan siang sama panjangnya

equip *vt* melengkapi; *the boat was ~ped with lifejackets* perahu dilengkapi dengan baju pelampung; **equipment** *n* perlengkapan; *play* ~ tempat bermain anak-anak, ayunan

equitable *adj* [ékuitabel] adil; **equitably** *adv* secara adil; **equity** *n* keadilan; *fin* ékuiti

equivalent *n* yang sama atau setara; *adj* sama harga atau nilainya

equivocal *adj* [ékuivokel] ambivalén, tidak berpihak

era *n* [ira] masa, zaman, éra

eradicate *vt* membasmi; **eradication** *n* pembasmian

erase *vt* menghapus; **eraser** *n* penghapus, setip; *board* ~ penghapus papan

erect *vt* mendirikan, membangun; *adj* tegak, tegang; **erection** *n* pembangunan; éréksi

Eritrea *n* Eritréa; **Eritrean** *n* orang Eritréa; *adj* berasal dari Eritréa

erode *vi* aus, terkikis; *vt* mengikis; **erosion** *n* kikisan, érosi

erotic *adj* érotis, merangsang

err *vi* berbuat salah; **error** *n* salah, kesalahan

errand *n* urusan, pesan; *to do ~s* pergi karena ada keperluan (ke bank, pasar dsb)

erratic *adj* tidak menentu, tidak teratur

error *n* salah, kesalahan ← **err**

erupt *vi* meletus; **eruption** *n* letusan, érupsi

escalate *vi* naik, tambah; *the conflict ~d* peperangan menjadi makin seru; *vt* meningkatkan; **escalator** *n* tangga berjalan, éskalator

escape *n* pelarian; *fire* ~ tangga darurat; *a narrow* ~ nyaris tidak lolos; *to make an* ~ melarikan diri, kabur, lolos; *vi* melarikan diri, kabur, lolos; *vt* menghindari; *the bank robbers ~d being sent to jail* para perampok menghindari dihukum penjara; **escapee** *n* buronan

escort *n* pendamping, rombongan; *vt* mendampingi, mengiringi; ~ *agency* jasa wanita penghibur

Eskimo *n* orang Eskimo, orang Inuit, penghuni daérah Artik ← **Inuit**

ESL *abbrev English as a Second Language* bahasa Inggris sebagai bahasa kedua

ESP *abbrev extra-sensory perception* indera keenam

especially *adv* khususnya, terutama ← **special**

Esperanto *n* bahasa Esperanto

espionage *n* [éspionaj] pengintaian, spionase

essay *n* karangan, ésai; *to write an* ~ membuat karangan; **essayist** *n* ésais

essence *n* inti, sari, ésénsi; *vanilla* ~ sari vanili; **essential** *adj* mutlak; ~ *oil* minyak ésénsial

establish *vt* mendirikan, mengadakan; menentukan, menetapkan; membina, membangunkan; *Indonesia finally ~ed relations with Malaysia* akhirnya Indonésia membina hubungan dengan Malaysia; **established** *adj* kokoh; **establishment** *n* pendirian, penentuan, penetapan; pembangunan

estate *n* tanah milik; kebun, perkebunan; ~ *agent* agén properti; *deceased* ~ harta benda orang yang sudah meninggal; *housing* ~ perumahan; *real* ~ propérti

esteem *n* hormat, kehormatan; *held in high* ~ dipandang dengan hormat; **esteemed** *adj* terhormat

estimate *n* [éstimet] taksiran, anggaran, perkiraan; pendapat; *rough* ~ kira-kira; *vt* [éstimét] menaksir, memperkirakan; *~d time of arrival (ETA)* perkiraan waktu kedatangan

Estonia *n* Estonia; **Estonian** *n* bahasa Estonia; *adj* orang Estonia

estranged *adj* [estrénjd] terpisah, menjadi asing; ~ *wife* isteri (yang sudah tidak tinggal bersama)

estuary *n* muara, kuala

ETA *abbrev estimated time of arrival* perkiraan waktu kedatangan

etc *et cetera* [ét sétera] dll (dan lain-lain), dsb (dan sebagainya)

etch *vt* mengetsa; **etching** *n* étsa

eternal *adj* abadi, kekal; **eternally** *adv* untuk selamanya; ~ *grateful* selalu berterima kasih; **eternity** *n* keabadian, kekekalan

ethanol *n* étanol

ethical *adj* étis; ~ *Policy* Politik Etis; **ethic** *n* étos; *work* ~ étos kerja; **ethics** *n, pl* étika

Ethiopia *n* Etiopia; **Ethiopian** *n* orang Etiopia; *adj* berasal dari Etiopia

ethnic *adj* étnis, kesukuan; tradisional; ~ *art* seni tradisional; ~ *group* suku (bangsa), kelompok étnis; ~ *minority* minoritas; **ethnicity** *n* [éthnisiti] kesukuan, asal-usul

etiquette *n* tata cara, sopan santun, étikét

EU *abbrev European Union* UE (Uni Eropa)

eucalyptus *n* [yukaliptus] sejenis pohon kayu putih; ~ *oil* minyak kayu putih

eulogy *n* [yuloji] pujian

euphemism *n* [yufemizem] kata pengganti yang lebih sopan atau lembut; *'pass away' is a* ~ *for 'die'* 'pass away' adalah kata yang lebih sopan daripada 'die'; **euphemistic** *adj* yang memakai kata lebih sopan

Eurasian *n* [yurésyen] orang campuran Asia dan Eropa

euro *n* [yuro] euro

Europe *n* [Yurop] Eropa; *Eastern* ~ Eropa Timur; **European** *n* orang Eropa; *adj* berasal dari Eropa; ~ *Union* Uni Eropa; ~ *Economic Community arch* Masyarakat Ekonomi Eropa

euthanasia *n* [yutanésia] mencabut jiwa karena belas kasihan, eutanasia, mati tenang

evacuate *vi* mengungsi; *vt* mengungsikan; **evacuation** *n* pengungsian, évakuasi; ~ *procedure* latihan darurat;

evacuee *n* pengungsi

evade *vt* mengelakkan, menghindar dari; *Tom ~d the teacher on duty* Tom menghindar dari guru yang sedang bertugas; **evasion** *n* pengelakan; penghindaran; *tax* ~ tidak membayar pajak; **evasive** *adj* mengelak

evaluate *vt* menilai, mengévaluasi; **evaluation** *n* évaluasi, penilaian

evangelical *adj* [ivanjélikel] yang menyebarkan agama Kristen; **evangelist** *n* penyebar agama Kristen

evaporate *vi* menguap; **evaporation** *n* penguapan

evasion *n* pengelakan; penghindaran; *tax* ~ tidak membayar pajak; **evasive** *adj* mengelak ← **evade**

eve *n* [iv] malam (sebelumnya); *Christmas* ~ malam Natal; *New Year's* ~ Malam Tahun Baru; *on the* ~ *of* malam sebelum

Eve *n* Hawa; *Isl* Siti Hawa

even *adj* rata; genap; *to break* ~ tidak merugi; *to get* ~ membalas dendam

even *pun; adv* bahkan; ~ *better* lebih baik lagi; ~ *if* kalaupun; ~ *though* meskipun; *it's so hot,* ~ *the aircon doesn't feel cool* hari ini begitu panas, AC saja tidak terasa dingin

evening *n* sore, petang; malam; ~ *class* kelas malam; ~ *dress* pakaian resmi, pakaian formal; *good* ~ selamat malam; *this* ~ nanti malam; *yesterday* ~ tadi malam, kemarin malam

event *n* peristiwa, kejadian, acara; ~ *organizer (EO)* penyelenggara (acara); *200m freestyle* ~ lomba 200 meter gaya bébas; *in the* ~ *of* seandainya; **eventful** *adj* penuh kejadian; **eventual** *adj* akhir, **eventually** *adv* akhirnya

ever *adv* [éver] pernah; ~ *since* (mulai) sejak; *don't* ~ jangan sekali-kali; *for~ more* untuk selamanya; *have you* ~? pernahkah?; selalu, senantiasa; *thank you* ~ *so much* terima kasih banyak; **evergreen** *adj* yang tetap hijau dan tidak rontok; **everlasting** *adj* kekal, abadi

every *pron* [évri] setiap, tiap; ~ *day* setiap hari, saban hari; ~ *other day*

selang hari; ~ *now and then* sekali-
sekali; **everybody, everyone** *pron*
[évriwan] semua orang, setiap orang;
everyday *adj* sehari-hari; **everything**
pron semua; **everywhere** *pron, adv*
[évriwér] di mana-mana; *you can see
sparrows* ~ *now* burung geréja
sekarang kelihatan di mana-mana
evict *vt* mengusir, menggusurkan;
*the flower sellers were ~d from the
park* para penjual bunga digusur dari
taman; **eviction** *n* pengusiran, penggusuran
evidence *n* bukti; *to give* ~ menjadi
saksi; **evident** *adj* jelas, nyata, terang;
evidently *adv* jelas
evil *n* [ivel] kejahatan; *adj* jahat; *axis of*
~ poros kejahatan; *good versus* ~
kebaikan melawan kejahatan
evolution *n* évolusi; **evolve** *v* berkembang
ewe *n* [yu] domba betina
ex *n, sl* mantan (pasangan)
exacerbate *vt* [égzaserbét] memperparah, membuat lebih buruk
exact *adj* tepat, persis; betul; **exactly**
adv persis; benar sekali; *not* ~ bukan
itu; **exactness** *n* ketelitian
exaggerate *vt* [egzajerét] membesar-
besarkan; **exaggeration** *n* pernyataan
yang berlebihan
examination *n* **exam** *sl* ujian; *mid-
semester* ~ ujian tengah seméster;
examine *vt* [égzamin] menguji,
memeriksa; **examiner** *n* penguji,
pemeriksa
example *n* [égzampel] contoh, teladan;
for ~ (seperti) misalnya, seumpamanya; **exemplary** *adj* (seperti contoh) baik
exasperate *vt* menjéngkélkan, membuat kesal; **exasperated** *adj* jéngkél,
kesal; **exasperation** *n* kejéngkélan,
kekesalan
excavate *vt* menggali; **excavation** *n*
penggalian; **excavator** *n* mesin gali
exceed *vt* melebihi, melampaui; ~
expectations melampaui harapan; ~
the speed limit melebihi batas
kecepatan; **exceedingly** *adv* teramat,

sangat; **excess** *n* kelebihan; **excessive** *adj* berlebihan, melampaui batas
excel *vi* unggul; ~ *at math* pintar belajar
matématika; **excellency** *Your* ~ Yang
Mulia; **excellent** *adj* bagus sekali, hébat
except *prep* kecuali; ~ *for* kecuali; ~
that hanya; *vt* mengecualikan; **except-
ing** *conj* terkecuali; **exception** *n* kekecualian, pengecualian, éksépsi; **excep-
tional** *adj* luar biasa, istiméwa; **excep-
tionally** *adv* luar biasa
excerpt *n* kutipan
excess *n* [égsés] kelebihan; ~ *baggage,
~ luggage* kelebihan bagasi; *in* ~ *of*
lebih dari; **excessive** *adj* berlebihan,
melampaui batas; **excessively** *adv*
amat, sangat
exchange *n* pertukaran, penukaran;
kantor télépon; ~ *rate* kurs; ~ *student*
pertukaran mahasiswa; *foreign* ~
dévisa, mata uang asing; *in* ~ *for* sebagai imbalan; diganti dengan; *vt*
menukar; mengembalikan (ke toko)
exchequer *UK* [ékscéker] *Chancellor of
the* ~ Menteri Keuangan
excise *n* [éksais] cukai
excite *vt* merangsang, membangkitkan;
excited *adj* gembira; **exciting** *adj*
mengasyikkan, menggembirakan;
excitement *n* kegembiraan
exclaim *vi* berseru; **exclamation** *n* seruan; ~ *mark* tanda seru [!]
exclude *vt* mengecualikan; **excluding**
prep tidak termasuk; **exclusion** *n*
pengecualian; **exclusive** *adj* éksklusif,
élit; ~ *to* hanya di; **exclusively** *adv*
secara éksklusif; terus-menerus
excrete *v* mengeluarkan cairan; buang
air; **excretion** *n* hal buang air
excruciating *adj* sangat menyiksa atau
menyakitkan; ~ *pain* rasa sakit yang
menyiksa
excursion *n* kunjungan; *school* ~ kunjungan pelajar
excuse *n* [ékskyus] alasan, dalih; *no* ~
tidak ada alasan; *vt* [ékskyuz]
memaafkan; ~ *me* permisi
execute *vt* [éksekyut] melakukan,
melaksanakan, mengerjakan; menjalankan keputusan; melakukan huku-

man mati; **execution** *n* pelaksanaan (hukuman mati); **executioner** *n* algojo; **executive** *n* pemimpin (harian), éksékutif; *adj* éksékutif

exemplary *adj* (seperti contoh) baik

exempt *adj* bébas; ~ *from tax* bebas pajak; *vt* membébaskan; **exemption** *n* pembébasan, pengecualian

exercise *n* olahraga; latihan, pelajaran; ~ *bike* sepéda stasionér; ~ *book* buku tulis *vi* berlatih; melakukan, menggunakan; ~ *one's rights* menggunakan hak

exert *vt* menggunakan; ~ *influence* menggunakan pengaruh, mendesak; ~ *yourself* membanting tulang; **exertion** *n* usaha keras

exhale *vi* buang napas, tiup, menghembuskan napas

exhaust *n* [ekshost] asap kendaraan; *vt* menyelesaikan sampai tuntas; menguras tenaga; **exhausted** *adj* capék sekali; **exhaustion** *n* kecapékan yang luar biasa

exhibit *n* [éksibit] barang yang dipamérkan; barang bukti; *vt* mempertunjukkan, memperlihatkan; **exhibition** *n* paméran

exhilarate *vt* **exhilirating** *adj* menyegarkan, menggembirakan; **exhilaration** *n* rasa gembira

exhorbitant *adj* sangat mahal

exile *n* buangan, orang yang hidup dalam pengasingan; *in* ~ dalam pengasingan; pembuangan; *vt* membuang; *Sukarno was ~d to Bengkulu* Soekarno dibuang ke Bengkulu

exist *vi* ada; *it doesn't* ~ tidak ada; **existence** *n* keberadaan; **existent** *adj* yang ada; **existing** *adj* yang sudah ada, yang masih ada

exit *n* pintu atau jalan keluar; kepergian; *vt* pergi keluar; *she ~ed the room* dia keluar dari kamar

exodus *n* kepergian, éksodus

exonerate *vt* membébaskan dari hukuman

exorcise *vt* mengusir sétan; **exorcist** *n* pengusir sétan

exotic *adj* éksotik, dari negeri asing

expand *vi* mengembang, memuai; ~ *on* memberi perincian; *vt* memperluas, mengembangkan; **expandable** *adj* dapat diperluas; **expanse** *n* luas; **expansion** *n* perluasan, pengembangan; **expansive** *adj* luas

expatriate *n* **expat** *sl* orang asing, orang yang tinggal di luar negeri, ékspatriat

expect *vt* mengharapkan, menantikan; **expectancy** *n* harapan, pengharapan; *life* ~ harapan hidup; **expectant** *adj* menunggu; ~ *mother* ibu hamil; **expectation** *n* harapan; **expecting** *adj* hamil

expedition *n* perjalanan, ékspédisi

expel *vt* membuang; mengeluarkan; **expulsion** *n* pengeluaran

expend *vt* mengeluarkan, membelanjakan, memakai; ~ *energy* mengeluarkan tenaga; **expendable** *adj* dapat dipakai habis; **expenditure** *n* pengeluaran, pembelanjaan; **expense** *n* belanja, biaya, ongkos; **expensive** *adj* mahal

experience *n* pengalaman; *vt* mengalami; *with* ~ *in the oil industry* yang memiliki pengalaman dalam perminyakan; **experienced** *adj* berpengalaman

experiment *n* percobaan, uji coba; *vi* mengadakan percobaan, menguji coba; **experimental** *adj* bersifat percobaan; **experimentation** *n* percobaan, ékspériméntasi

expert *n* ahli, pakar; *adj* ahli; **expertise** *n* [ékspertiz] keahlian

expire *vi* kedaluwarsa, jatuh tempo; mati; **expiry** ~ *date* tanggal kedaluwarsa

explain *v* menjelaskan, menerangkan, menyatakan; ~ *away* membenarkan, mencari alasan; **explanation** *n* penjelasan; **explanatory** *adj* bersifat menerangkan, menjelaskan

expletive *n* [éksplitif] kata umpatan

explicit *adj* tegas, jelas, éksplisit; ~ *language* kata-kata jorok; **explicitly** *adv* dengan jelas, secara gamblang

explode *vi* meletus, meledak; *vt* meledakkan; **explosion** *n* letusan, ledakan; **explosive** *adj* dapat meledak; **explosives** *n, pl* bahan peledak

exploit *vt* memanfaatkan, mengéksploitasi; **exploitation** *n* éksploitasi
exploration *n* penjelajahan, éksplorasi; **explore** *vi* melihat-lihat di sekitar; *v* menjelajah; *vt* menjelajahi; mengadakan penelitian; *~ possibilities* mempertimbangkan beberapa kemungkinan; **explorer** *n* penjelajah
explosion *n* letusan, ledakan; **explosive** *adj* dapat meledak; **explosives** *n, pl* bahan peledak ← **explode**
expo *n* paméran (besar)
export *n, adj* ékspor; *vt* mengékspor; *~ shoes to Australia* mengékspor sepatu ke Australia; **exporter** *n* pengékspor, éksportir
expose *vt* menyingkapkan, mempertunjukkan, memamérkan, membuka; **exposed** *adj* terbuka, tersingkap; *~ to* kena; **exposure** *n* pembukaan, pencahayaan
express *n* yang cepat, kilat, éksprés; *adj* cepat, kilat; *~ lane* jalur éksprés, jalur cepat (di swalayan); *~ mail* pos kilat khusus; *~ train* keréta api éksprés; *vt* mengucapkan, mengungkapkan, menyatakan, mengutarakan; **expression** *n* ucapan, peribahasa; raut muka; **expressive** *adj* éksprésif, menyatakan perasaan; **expressway** *n* jalan bébas hambatan
expropriate *vt* [ékspropriét] mengambil, merampas; **expropriation** *n* pengambilan, perampasan
expulsion *n* pengeluaran ← **expel**
exquisite *adj* [ékskuisit] sempurna, indah sekali
extend *vi* sampai; *vt* merentangkan, membentangkan; memperluas; memperpanjang; *~ed family* keluarga besar; **extension** *n* perpanjangan; rénovasi; pesawat; *~ lead*, *~ cord* kabel penyambung tambahan; *ask for ~ 213* minta pesawat 213; **extensive** *adj* luas, panjang lébar; **extensively** *adv* secara besar-besaran, secara panjang lébar; **extent** *n* luas cakupan, derajat, tingkat; *to what ~* sejauh mana
extenuating *adj* meringankan
exterior *n* luar

exterminate *vt* membasmi, memusnahkan; **extermination** *n* pembasmian, pemusnahan
external *adj* (di) luar
extinct *adj* punah; **extinction** *n* pemadaman; kepunahan
extinguish *vt* [ékstinguisy] memadamkan; **extinguisher** *n* pemadam api
extol *vt* memuji; *~ the virtues of* memuji keunggulan
extort *vt* memeras; **extortion** *n* pemerasan; **extortionate** *adj* sangat mahal; **extortionist** *n* pemeras, pemalak
extra *adj* ékstra; *~-curricular* ékskul; **extraordinary** *adj* [ékstrodinari] luar biasa, istiméwa
extract *n* sari, ékstrak, petikan; *birth ~* surat kelahiran; *~ of* sari; *vt* mencabut (gigi); mengambil; **extraction** *n* pencabutan; asal; *of Chinese ~* berdarah Cina
extradite *vt* menyerahkan ke negara lain; *they tried to ~ him from Singapore* orang Singapura berusaha menyerahkan dia ke negaranya; **extradition** *n* penyerahan, ékstradisi
extraordinary *adj* [ékstrodinari] luar biasa, istiméwa ← **extra**
extravagance *n* [ékstravagans] keborosan; **extravagant** *adj* boros, berfoya-foya, royal; **extravagantly** *adv* secara boros, secara royal
extreme *adj* terlampau, ékstrém; **extremely** *adv* sangat, teramat; **extremist** *n* fanatik, ékstrémis; **extremities** *n, pl* tangan dan kaki
extricate *vt* mengeluarkan, membébaskan; *~ from* mengeluarkan dari
exuberance *n* semangat, keriangan; **exuberant** *adj* riang gembira, bersemangat
exultant *adj* sangat bergembira
eye *n* [ai] mata; *~-catching* menarik, menonjol; *black ~* lebam biru di mata; *green-~d* bermata hijau; *a roving ~* mata keranjang; *to keep an ~ on* mengawasi, menjaga; *vt* melirik; **eyeball** *n* [aibol] bola mata; **eyebrow** *n* alis; **eyelash** *n* bulu mata; **eyelid** *n* kelopak mata; **eyeliner** *n* pénsil mata; **eyeshadow** *n* perona mata; **eyesight** *n*

[aisait] penglihatan; **eyesore** n yang merusak pemandangan; **eyewitness** n saksi mata

F

fab → **fabulous**

fable n [fébel] dongéng, cerita rakyat; **fabled** adj terkenal, ternama; **fabulous** adj hébat

fabric n kain, bahan

fabricate vt membuat, merékayasa, mengarang; ~ a story mengarang-ngarang; **fabrication** n pembuatan, fabrikasi

fabulous adj **fab** sl hebat, menakjubkan ← **fable**

façade n [fasad] bagian muka gedung; muka, topéng; his glamorous appearance was all a ~ penampilannya yang glamor ternyata hanya topéng belaka

face n muka, paras, wajah; sisi; ~ value harga nominal; pada permukaan; to lose ~ kehilangan muka, malu; ~ to ~ empat mata; Everest's west ~ sisi barat Gunung Everést; vt menghadapi; ~ the music menghadapi hukuman; ~ up to it hadapilah; **facet** n [faset] sudut; **facial** n perawatan muka, perawatan wajah; adj berkaitan dengan muka; ~ expression raut wajah

facilitate vt mempermudah, melaksanakan; **facilitator** n pelaksana, pengurus, pengajar; **facility** n sarana, fasilitas; kemudahan

facsimile n [faksimili] salinan, kopi; ~ machine mesin faks; **fax** n, coll ~ (machine) mesin faks; vt mengefaks, mengirim léwat faks; sl ngefaks

fact n kenyataan, fakta; in ~ sesungguhnya; bahkan; ~-finding mission studi banding; after the ~ sesudahnya, kemudian; the ~s of life pengetahuan tentang réproduksi; **factual** adj berdasarkan kenyataan

faction n fraksi

factor n unsur, faktor, élemén

factory n pabrik

factual adj berdasarkan kenyataan ← **fact**

faculty n daya, kemampuan; fakultas; ~ of Arts Fakultas Sastra; ~ of Engineering Fakultas Téknik; ~ of Medicine Fakultas Kedokteran

fad n trén, mode; wearing plastic shoes was the latest ~ trén terbaru adalah sepatu plastik

fade vi luntur, pudar; mengecil (suara); **faded** adj luntur, pudar, redam

faeces → **feces**

fag n, sl rokok; orang homo; give us a ~ minta rokok

fail v gagal; tidak jadi; jatuh; tidak lulus; ~ing that kalau tidak; ~ to tidak; without ~ pasti; ~ an exam gagal dalam ujian; **failure** n kegagalan, gagalnya; a complete ~ gagal total

faint n pingsan; vi (jatuh) pingsan; adj lemah, kecil; ~-hearted cepat takut; **faintly** adv sedikit

fair adj adil, berimbang; cukup; it was a ~ walk jalannya cukup jauh; **fairly** adv cukup, agak; dengan adil

fair adj berkulit atau berambut terang; the ~ sex kaum wanita

fair n paméran, pekan raya, pasar malam; trade ~ pameran; **fairground** n aréna pekan raya atau pasar malam

fairly adv cukup, agak; dengan adil ← **fair**

fairy n peri; sl béncong; ~ floss kembang gula; ~ godmother ibu peri; ~ lights lampu hias; ~ tale cerita dongéng, cerita rakyat; away with the fairies melamun; tidak waras

faith n iman, kepercayaan; agama; in good ~ dengan itikad baik; the Christian ~ agama Kristen; **faithful** adj beriman, setia; **faithfully** adv dengan setia; yours ~ hormat kami

fake n tipuan; vt menirukan, memalsukan; adj palsu; ~ ID idéntitas palsu; ~ leather kulit imitasi

falcon n burung elang

fall n [fol] kejatuhan, keruntuhan, keguguran; musim gugur, musim rontok; vi **fell fallen** jatuh, runtuh, gugur; ~ apart pecah; ~ for jatuh cinta pada; ~

ill jatuh sakit; ~ *out* berkelahi; ~ *preg-nant* hamil; ~ *through* gagal, tidak jadi; ~ *under* termasuk; ~ *in love* jatuh cinta

fallacious *adj* [falésyus] salah, keliru, sesat, menyesatkan; **fallacy** *n* [falasi] kesalahan, kekeliruan

fallen *vi, pf* → **fall**

fallible *adj* [falibel] dapat bersalah

fallow *adj* tidur, sedang tidak digarap; ~ *field* tanah tidur

falls *n, pl* air terjun ← **waterfall**

false *adj* [fols] palsu; *true or* ~ benar atau salah; **falsehood** *n* bohong, dusta; **falsification** *n* pemalsuan; **falsify** *vt* [folsifai] memalsukan; *the clerk falsified several documents* pegawai itu memalsukan beberapa surat

falter *vi* [folter] bergoyang, terputus-putus; *her voice ~ed on the high note* suaranya goyang di nada tinggi

fame *n* ketenaran, nama harum; **famed** *adj* tenar, kenamaan, termasyhur, ternama, tersohor; **famous** *adj* terkenal, ternama

familiar *adj* dikenal; akrab; ~ *to* dikenal; ~ *with* kenal; **familiarize** *vt* ~ *oneself* membiasakan diri; **familiarization** *n* prosés pengenalan; **family** *n* keluarga; rumah tangga; ~ *name* nama keluarga, marga, nama fam; ~ *planning* keluarga berencana (KB); ~ *tree* silsilah keluarga; ~ *values* nilai kekeluargaan; *single-parent* ~ keluarga dengan orang tua tunggal

famine *n* [famin] kelaparan

famous *adj* terkenal, ternama ← **fame**

fan *n* kipas; *electric* ~ kipas angin; *vt* mengipasi, mengembusi

fan *n* penggemar, fans; *Sarah was a huge* ~ *of the Beach Boys* Sarah dulu penggemar berat Beach Boys; **fanatic** *n* fanatik; **fanatical** *adj* fanatic; **fanaticism** *n* aliran fanatik

fancy *n* khayal, kesukaan, angan-angan; ~ *dress* kostum; *vt* menginginkan; *do you* ~ *a drink?* mau minum?; *adj* rumit, megah

fang *n* taring

fantastic *adj* ajaib, fantastis, tidak masuk akal; **fantasy** *n* fantasi, khayalan

fanzine *n* [fanzin] majalah untuk penggemar

FAQ *abbrev frequently-asked questions* pertanyaan biasa

far *adj* jauh; ~-*sighted* bijaksana; ~ *away* jauh; ~ *from* tidak, bukan; *so* ~ sejauh ini, selama ini; *as* ~ *as* sejauh, sepanjang; *the* ~ *East* Asia Timur dan Tenggara; *as* ~ *as I know* setahu saya

farce *n* lelucon; **farcical** *adj* lucu

fare *n* ongkos perjalanan; makanan; ~*s please!* karcis!; *vi* berjalan, berlangsung; *how did you* ~? bagaimana jadinya?

farewell *n* perpisahan; *ejac* selamat tinggal, selamat jalan

farm *n* pertanian, peternakan; *vi* bercocok tanam, berladang; **farmer** *n* petani; **farming** *n* pertanian

fart *n, coll* bunyi kentut; *vi* kentut, membuang angin

farther, further *adj, adv* lebih jauh; **farthermost, farthest** *adj, adv* terjauh, paling jauh

fascinate *vt* [fasinét] memesonakan, menarik hati; **fascinated** *adj* terpesona; ~ *by*, ~ *with* terpesona oléh; **fascinating** *adj* memesonakan; **fascination** *n* pesona

fascism *n* [fasyisem] fasisme, sayap kanan; **fascist** *adj* fasis, sayap kanan

fashion *n* [fasyen] mode; *in* ~ bergaya, gaya; *out of* ~ sudah tidak laku; *the latest* ~ mode terbaru; cara; *vt* membentuk; **fashionable** *adj* bergaya, gaya; **fashionista** *n, coll* orang yang peduli mode

fast *n* puasa; *vi* berpuasa; ~*ing month* bulan puasa; *to break the* ~ membuka puasa

fast *adj* cepat, laju; ~ *food* makan cepat saji; ~-*track*, ~ *lane* jalur cepat; ~ *train* keréta api cepat

fast *adj* kokoh; tutup; ~ *asleep* tidur pulas, tidur nyenyak; **fasten** *vt* [fasen] mengikatkan, menambatkan; ~ *your seat belts* pasang sabuk pengaman; **fastener** *n* ritsléting; kait

fastidious *adj* réwél, rapi sekali

fat *n* lemak; *adj* gemuk, tambun; ~-*free*

tanpa lemak; **fatten** *vt* ~ *up* membuat gemuk, memberi makanan banyak; **fattening** *adj* membuat gemuk; **fatty** *n, sl* si gendut; *adj* berlemak

fatal *adj* [fétal] mematikan; **fatality** *n* korban jiwa

fate *n* nasib; **fated** *adj* ditakdirkan; **fateful** *adj* yang menentukan nasib

father *n* ayah, bapak; ~ *Christmas* Sinterklas, Santa; *adopted* ~ ayah angkat; *founding* ~*s* bapak-bapak bangsa; *Our* ~ *Chr* Bapa kami; **fatherhood** *n* pengalaman menjadi ayah; **father-in-law** *n* mertua (lelaki); **fatherland** *n* tanah air; **fatherly** *adj* kebapakan

fathom *n* depa, ukuran kedalaman air; *vt* menduga; **fathomless** *adj* dalam sekali; tidak terduga

fatigue [fatig] *army* ~*s* seragam tentara; *n* kelelahan, kecapékan; kerusakan; **fatigued** *adj* capék; *chronic* ~ *syndrome* sindrom kelelahan kronis

fatten ~ *up* membuat gemuk, memberi makanan banyak; **fattening** *adj* membuat gemuk ← **fat**

fatty *n, sl* si gendut; *adj* berlemak ← **fat**

faucet *n* [foset] keran

fault *n* kesalahan, salah; cacat; kelemahan; pemukulan awal yang melését (ténis); *it's my* ~ salah saya; *to find* ~ mencari kesalahan; **faultless** *adj* tanpa kesalahan, tanpa cela, sempurna; **faulty** *adj* cacat, rusak, kurang sempurna

fauna *n* fauna, margasatwa

favor, favour *n* pertolongan; karunia, anugerah; ampun; *in* ~ *of* mendukung; *in our* ~ menguntungkan kita; *to do someone a* ~ menolong orang, memberi bantuan; *v* lebih suka; **favorable** *adj* baik, menguntungkan; **favorite** *n* kesukaan, anak emas, kesayangan; *adj* kesukaan, yang paling disukai, favorit

fawn *adj* cokelat muda

fax *n* ~ *(machine)* mesin faks; *vt* mengefaks, mengirim léwat faks; *sl* ngefaks ← **facsimile**

FBI *abbrev Federal Bureau of Investigation* Biro Nasional Penyelidikan (Amérika Serikat)

fear *n* [fir] ketakutan, rasa takut; *vt* takut akan; ~ *for, in* ~ *of* takut akan; *no* ~ saya tidak takut; ~ *of heights* takut ketinggian; **feared** *adj* menakutkan; **fearful** *adj* takut akan; **fearless** *adj* tidak takut, berani; **fearsome** *adj* [firsem] menakutkan

feasibility *n* [fisibiliti] kemungkinan dilakukan; ~ *study* studi kelayakan; **feasible** *adj* dapat dilakukan, memungkinkan

feast *n* [fist] pésta, perjamuan, perayaan; ~ *of the Sacrifice Isl* Idul Adha; *vi* ~ *on* melahap, makan

feat *n* préstasi, hasil; *no mean* ~ bukan hal yang rémeh

feather *n* [féther] bulu; ~ *duster* kemocéng; **feathered, feathery** *adj* berbulu; **featherweight** *adj* [fétherwéit] kelas bulu

feature *n* ciri (khas); pertunjukan utama; *pl* wajah, paras; *vt* mempertunjukkan, memperlihatkan; *his latest film* ~*s Jackie Chan* film terbarunya dibintangi Jackie Chan

February *n* bulan Fébruari; *in* ~ pada bulan Fébruari; *on the 29th of* ~ pada tanggal 29 Fébruari

feces *n, pl* **faeces** [fisiz] tinja

fed *v, pf* → **feed**; ~ *up with* kesal, bosan, jenuh karena

federal *adj* fédéral, berserikat; **federalism** *n* fédéralisme; **federation** *n* fédérasi, perserikatan

fee *n* upah, gaji, biaya, iuran; *membership* ~ iuran keanggotaan

feeble *adj* lemah

feed *n* pakan, makanan héwan; waktu makan (bayi); *v* **fed fed** memberi makan; ~ *on* makan (dari); **feedback** *n* tanggapan; **feeder** *n* pengumpan, penyalur

feel *v* **felt felt** *vi* berasa; ~ *cold* kedinginan; ~ *free* silahkan; bébas; ~ *small* merasa minder; ~ *like doing* ingin; *n* rasa; *to have a* ~ *for* mempunyai bakat; *vt* merasa; meraba; **feeler** *n* sungut; peraba; **feeling** *n* perasaan; *hurt* ~*s* tersinggung; *to have* ~*s for someone* suka, menyukai

feet *n, pl* → **foot**

feign *vt* [féin] pura-pura; *Megan ~ed illness to miss the party* Megan pura-pura sakit karena tidak mau hadir di pésta

feint *n* [féint] perbuatan atau gerakan pura-pura; *vi* pura-pura bergerak

feline *n* (binatang dari keluarga) kucing; *adj* berkaitan dengan kucing

fell *vt* menebang, memotong (pohon); *vi* → **fall**; **felling** *n* penebangan

fellatio *n* [felésyio] séks oral

fellow *n* lelaki; *adj* sesama; *~ Indonesians* saudara-saudara sebangsa dan setanah air; *~ man* sesama manusia; *~ worker* teman sekerja; **fellowship** *n* persahabatan, persaudaraan, peranggotaan; béasiswa

felt *n* bulu kempa; *~-tip pen* spidol; *v, pf* → **feel**

female *n, adj* perempuan, wanita; betina (animals)

feminine *adj* [féminin] féminin; yang berkaitan dengan kewanitaan; **feminism** *n* féminisme, gerakan menuju persamaan hak perempuan; **feminist** *adj, n* orang féminis

fen *n, UK* rawa, paya

fence *n* pagar; *barbed-wire ~* pagar kawat berduri; *vt* memagari; bermain anggar; **fenced** *adj* berpagar; **fencer** *n* pembuat pagar; pemain anggar; **fencing** *n* anggar

fend *vi ~ off* menepis, menangkis; *~ for yourself* mencari makanan sendiri, menjaga diri sendiri

fender *n* spatbor

fennel *n* adas

feral *adj* liar; *~ pig* babi liar

ferment *vi* meragi, berendam; **fermentation** *n* férméntasi, peragian

fern *n* paku; **ferny** *adj* dengan banyak paku

ferocious *adj* [ferosyes] ganas, buas; **ferocity** *n* keganasan, kebuasan

ferret *n* semacam musang; *vi* mencaricari, menguber

ferry *n* féri; *vt* membawa penumpang bolak-balik, menyeberangkan; **ferryman** *n* pengemudi féri

fertile *adj* [fértail] subur; **fertility** *n*

[fértiliti] kesuburan; *~ symbol* lambang kesuburan; **fertilization** *n* pembuahan; **fertilize** *vt* membuahi; **fertilizer** *n* pupuk

fervent *adj* bersemangat, bernafsu, bergairah; **fervor, fervour** *n* semangat, nafsu, gairah

fester *vi* bernanah, membusuk

festival *n* pésta, perayaan, hari raya, féstival; **festive** *adj* [féstiv] perayaan, pésta; *~ season* masa Natal; **festivity** *n* pésta, perayaan, acara

feta *n* [féta] sejenis kéju putih

fetal, foetal *adj* berkaitan dengan janin; *~ heartbeat* detak jantung janin; **fetus** *n* **foetus** [fitus] janin

fetch *vt* menjemput (orang), mengambilkan; *~ a price* dilélang atau dijual dengan harga; **fetching** *adj* menarik

fete *n* [féit] pekan raya, pasar malam

fetid *adj* berbau busuk

fetus, foetus *n* [fitus] janin

feud *n* [fyuud] permusuhan, perseteruan; *vi* bertengkar, berkelahi; *they ~ed over the inheritance* mereka bertengkar soal warisan

feudal *adj* féodal; **feudalism** *n* féodalisme

fever *n* demam; *dengue ~* demam berdarah; **feverish** *adj* demam, panas

few *adj* sedikit, beberapa; *a ~ friends* beberapa kawan; *there are ~ visitors here* tidak banyak wisatawan di sini

fez *n* péci Turki

fiancé *n, m* [fiansé] tunangan (laki-laki); **fiancée** *n, f* tunangan (perempuan)

fiasco *n* kegagalan, kesalahan besar

fib *n* dusta; *vi* berdusta

fiber, fibre *n* [faiber] serabut, serat; *high-~ foods* makanan berserat tinggi; **fiberglass** *n, adj* kaca serat; **fibrous** *adj* berserabut

fiction *n* fiksi; **fictional** *adj* fiksi; **fictitious** *adj* palsu, tidak benar, fiktif; *a ~ address* alamat palsu

fiddle *n, arch* [fidel] biola; **fiddler** *n* pemain biola

fiddle *vi* [fidel] *~ (around) with* mengutak-atik, memprételi; *vt* mengacaukan; *~ the books* menggelapkan uang; **fiddly** *adj* sulit, rumit

fiddlesticks *ejac* [fidelstiks] omong kosong

fiddly *adj* sulit, rumit ← **fiddle**

fidelity *n* [fidéliti] kesetiaan; kemurnian; *high-~ (hi-fi)* kualitas tinggi (suara)

fidget *n* orang yang tidak bisa duduk diam; *vi* bergerak terus karena gelisah; *~ with* memainkan; **fidgety** *adj* gelisah

field *n* bidang, daérah; padang, médan, ladang; *~ marshal* panglima tertinggi, jénderal besar; *~ trip* kunjungan lapangan; *~ work* prakték, penelitian lapangan; *magnetic ~* médan maknit; *rice~* sawah; *vi* mengambil bola (olahraga); *vt* mengambil, mengembalikan; *~ questions* menjawab pertanyaan

fiend *n* hantu jahat, setan; **fiendish** *adj* jahat

fierce *adj* buas, galak, ganas; **fierceness** *n* keganasan

fiery *adj* [faieri] berapi-api; **fire** *n* api; kebakaran; *~ brigade, ~ department* pasukan pemadam kebakaran; *~ engine* mobil pemadam kebakaran; *~ escape* tangga darurat; *~ extinguisher* alat pemadam kebakaran; *~ station* kantor pasukan pemadam kebakaran; *on ~* sedang terbakar; *wood ~* perapian; *under ~* sedang diserang; *to catch ~* terbakar; *to set ~ to* membakar; *vi* hidup, nyala; *~ up* memberi semangat; *vt* melepaskan tembakan, menembak; *firing squad* regu tembak; **firearm** *n* senjata api; **firefighter, fireman** *n* anggota pasukan pemadam kebakaran; **firefly** *n* kunang-kunang; **fireplace** *n* perapian; **fireproof** *adj* tahan api; **firewall** *n* [faierwol] peranti keamanan; **fireworks** *n* [faierwérks] kembang api, petasan, mercon

fifteen *adj, n* lima belas; **fifteenth** *adj* kelima belas; **fifth** *adj* kelima; *one-~* seperlima; **five** *n, adj* lima; *~-star hotel* hotel bintang lima; *~ ways* simpang lima; **fiver** *n* uang kertas lima pon

fiftieth *adj* kelima puluh; **fifty** *adj, n* lima puluh; *~-~* dibagi dua; **fifties** *n, pl* tahun lima puluhan; umur lima puluhan

fig *n* buah ara; *~ tree* pohon ara; *I don't give a ~* saya sama sekali tidak peduli

fight *n* [fait] pertengkaran; perkelahian; pertempuran, perjuangan; *v* **fought** **fought** *vi* [fot] bertengkar; berkelahi; bertempur, berperang, berjuang; *~ back* membéla diri; *~ for* memperjuangkan; *he ~s with his sister* dia berkelahi dengan adiknya; *vt* melawan; **fighter** *n* pejuang; pesawat tempur; **fighting** *n* pertempuran, perkelahian

figurative *adj* [figurativ] kiasan; **figure** *n* rupa, bentuk; bagan, gambar; angka; harga; *~-skating* main sepatu és; *a good ~* sintal, montok; *vi* menghitung, berpikir; *~ out* mencari solusi, memahami

Fiji *n* Fiji; **Fijian** *n* bahasa Fiji; orang Fiji; *adj* berasal dari Fiji

filch *vt* mengutil, mencuri sedikit demi sedikit

file *n* berkas, arsip, dokuméntasi; *on ~* didokuméntasi; *single ~* antri satu per satu; *vt* menyimpan; *filing cabinet* lemari arsip; *~ a suit against* menuntut, mendaftar di pengadilan

file *n* kikir, amril; *vt* mengikir; **filings** *iron ~* serbuk besi

filigree *n* [filigri] cara menempa logam sehingga menjadi benang halus

filings *iron ~* serbuk besi ← **file**

fill *n* jatah; *vt* mengisi (sampai penuh), menempati, memenuhi; *~ in* mengisi (formulir); *~ out* menjadi gempal atau gemuk; *~ up* mengisi bénsin; *~ someone's shoes* mengganti orang; **filling** *n* tambalan gigi; *~ station* pom bénsin

fillet *n* filét, stéik, potongan daging tanpa tulang

filling *n* tambalan gigi ← **fill**

filly *n* kuda betina yang belum beranak

film *n* film; *~-maker* sinéas; *~ review* risénsi film; *~ star* bintang film; *action ~* film laga; *vi* syuting, mengambil gambar; *vt* merekam, mengambil gambar

film *n* selaput; **filmy** *adj* berselaput

filter *n* saringan, filter; *vt* menyaring, menyéléksi; *~ paper* kertas saring;

filtrate *n* (air) saringan; **filtration** *n* penyaringan

filth *n* kotoran, sampah; **filthy** *adj* kotor sekali, jorok, najis; ~ *language* kata-kata jorok

filtrate *n* (air) saringan; **filtration** *n* penyaringan ← **filter**

fin *n* sirip; *shark's* ~ *soup* sup sirip ikan hiu

final *n* (pertandingan) final; *adj* final, penghabisan, terakhir; **finalist** *n* finalis; **finalize** *vt* memastikan, menentukan; **finally** *adv* akhirnya

finance *n* [fainans] keuangan; *vt* membiayai, mendanai; **financial** *adj* [fainansyel] keuangan; ~ *adviser* penasihat keuangan; ~ *year* tahun anggaran; **financier** *n* pemilik modal

find *n* [faind] (hasil) temuan; *vt* **found** **found** menemukan; menyimpulkan, merasa; ~ *fault* mencari kesalahan; ~ *out* menemukan, dapat informasi; **findings** *n, pl* temuan, hasil penelitian

fine *n* denda, tilang; *vt* mendenda, menilang

fine *adj* bagus, baik; halus; ~ *art* seni lukis; ~ *weather* cuaca baik, cerah; *I'm* ~ saya baik; *that's* ~ *with me* baiklah; **finery** *n* hiasan, perhiasan, keméwahan

finger *n* [fingger] jari; ~ *bowl* tempat cuci tangan, kobokan; ~ *food* makanan kecil; *index* ~ telunjuk; *little* ~ keling-king; *middle* ~ jari tengah; *ring* ~ jari manis; **fingernail** *n* kuku jari; **finger-print** *n* sidik jari; **fingertip** *n* ujung jari; *at your* ~s di ujung jari, mudah diaksés

finish *n* (garis) akhir; penghabisan, penyelesaian; *vi* berhenti, selesai; ~ *off* menghabiskan; ~ *up* menyelesaikan *vt* mengakhiri, menghentikan; menyele-saikan; menghabiskan

Finland *n* Finlandia; **Finn** *n* orang Finlandia; **Finnish** *n* bahasa Finlandia; *adj* berasal dari Finlandia

fire *n* api; kebakaran; ~ *alarm* tanda kebakaran; ~ *brigade*, ~ *department* pasukan pemadam kebakaran; ~ *engine* mobil pemadam kebakaran; ~ *escape* tangga darurat; ~ *extinguisher*

alat pemadam kebakaran; ~ *station* kantor pasukan pemadam kebakaran; *on* ~ sedang terbakar; *wood* ~ perapi-an; *under* ~ sedang diserang; *to catch* ~ terbakar; *to set* ~ *to* membakar; *vi* hidup, nyala; ~ *up* memberi semangat; *vt* melepaskan tembakan, menembak; **firing** ~ *squad* regu tembak; **firearm** *n* senjata api; **firefighter, fireman** *n* ang-gota pasukan pemadam kebakaran; **firefly** *n* kunang-kunang; **fireplace** *n* perapian; **fireproof** *adj* tahan api; **firewall** *n* [faierwol] peranti keamanan; **fireworks** *n, pl* [faierwerks] kem-bang api, petasan, mercon

fire *vt* memecat; **fired** *adj* dipecat ← **fire**

firing [fairing] ~ *squad* regu tembak ← **fire**

firm *n* perusahaan

firm *adj* tetap, pasti, tegas; keras, kuat; **firmly** *adv* dengan tegas

first *adj* pertama; juara; ~*-born* anak sulung, anak pertama; ~*-hand* lang-sung; ~*-rate* terbaik, nomor satu; ~ *aid* pertolongan pertama; ~ *aid kit* pusat pertolongan pertama kecelakaan (PPPK); ~ *cousin* (saudara) sepupu; ~ *floor US* lantai bawah, lantai satu; *UK* lantai dua; ~ *Lady* ibu negara; ~ *name* nama depan; ~ *prize* hadiah utama; *at* ~ pada awalnya, semula; ~ *of all* perta-ma-tama; *to come* ~ menang, menjadi juara; ~ *come*, ~ *served* yang cepat dapat; **firstly** *adv* pertama-tama

fish *n* ikan; ~ *and chips* ikan dan ken-tang goréng; *to drink like a* ~ banyak minum (alkohol); *vi* memancing; ~ *for* mencari; **fishbone** *n* duri ikan; **fisher-man** *n* nelayan; **fisheries** *n, pl* perikanan; **fishing** *n* memancing; ~ *rod* joran; **fishy** *adj* berbau amis atau anyir; mencurigakan

fission *n* pembelahan, fisi; **fissure** *n* celah

fist *n* tinju, kepalan tangan; **fistful** *n* segenggam, sekepal

fit *adj* pas, tepat, layak, patut; fit, séhat; *to have a* ~ serangan ayan; marah sekali; *vi* pas; ~ *in* sesuai, klop; **fitting**

room kamar pas; *vt* menyesuaikan; **fitness** *n* kebugaran, kesehatan; ~ *center* pusat kebugaran, tempat fitnes

five *adj, n* lima; ~-*star hotel* hotel bintang lima; ~ *ways* simpang lima; *a bunch of ~s* sekepal tangan, pukulan; **fiver** *n* uang kertas lima pon

fix *n* masalah; *vt* memperbaiki; menetapkan, memasang; **fixation** *n* obsési; **fixed** *adj* tetap; diperbaiki; ~ *price* harga pas; **fixture** *n* [fikstyur] acara yang diadakan secara teratur; *Ron's Christmas party is a regular ~ here* Ron mengadakan pésta Natal setiap tahun di sini

fizz *n* busa; **fizzle** *vi* [fizel] berbusa, berdesar, mendesis; ~ *out* lama-lama mati; **fizzy** *adj* bersoda; ~ *drinks* minuman bersoda

flab *n* lemak; **flabby** *adj* gemuk, tidak berotot

flag *n* bendéra; ~ *Day US* 14 Juni; *the Indonesian* ~ Sang Mérah Putih; *vi* menjadi capék; ~ *down* memberhentikan kendaraan di pinggir jalan; **flagpole, flagstaff** *n* tiang bendéra

flake *n* serpih, lapis, keping; *vi* hancur; **flaky** adj berlapis-lapis

flamboyant *adj* flamboyan

flame *n* (kobaran) api; *an old* ~ kekasih lama; *eternal* ~ api abadi; **flaming** *adj, sl* gila; **flammable** *adj* [flamabel] dapat terbakar

flamingo *n* [flaminggo] burung flamingo

flammable *adj* [flamabel] dapat terbakar

flank *n* sisi; *vt* mendampingi, mengiringi

flannel *n* kain panas, flanél; waslap

flap *n* tutup, penutup; *in a* ~ dalam kesulitan; *vi* mengepak; *vt* mengepakkan

flapjack *n* semacam panekuk

flare *n* nyala api; *vi* bernyala, menyala; ~ *up* bangkit marahnya

flash *n* kilau; blits; ~ *flood* banjir dadakan; *in a* ~ dalam sekajap mata; *a* ~ *of lightning* halilintar, kilat; *vi* berkilat-kilat; *vt* memperlihatkan secara kilat; **flashback** *n* sorot kembali; **flashcard** *n* kartu (pengingat) untuk menghafalkan kosa kata; **flashlight** *n*

[flasylait] (lampu) sénter; **flashpoint** *n* titik nyala; **flashy** *adj, coll* norak, menyolok

flask *n* botol minuman

flat *n* apartemén; *adj* rata, datar; ~ *out* secepat-cepatnya; ~ *shoes* sepatu hak rendah; ~ *tire* ban kempés; **flatmate** *n* teman serumah (apartemén); **flatten** *vt* meratakan

flatter *vt* membujuk, merayu, menyanjung; **flattery** *n* rayuan gombal, kata-kata manis

flautist *n* **flutist** pemain suling, pesuling ← **flute**

flavor *n* **flavour** rasa, perisa; *vt* membumbui; **flavoring** *n* perisa

flaw *n* **flawed** *adj* cacat, cela; **flawless** *adj* sempurna, tanpa cacat

flax *n* rami; **flaxen** ~-*haired* berambut pirang

flea *n* [fli] kutu (binatang); ~ *market* pasar loak

fled *v, pf* → **flee**

fledgling, fledgeling *n* [flejling] anak burung; *adj* muda, belum berpengalaman

flee *v* **fled fled** *vi* melarikan diri, kabur, minggat; *vt* melarikan diri dari; *many ethnic Chinese had to* ~ *Jakarta in 1998* banyak orang Cina terpaksa melarikan diri dari Jakarta pada tahun 1998

fleet *n* armada (angkatan laut); ~ *of foot*, ~-*footed* cepat; **fleeting** *adj* sepintas lalu, sekejap

flesh *n* daging; ~ *and blood* darah daging

flew *v, pf* → **fly**

flexible *adj* lentur; fléksibel; **flexibility** *n* kelenturan; **flexi-time** *n* jam kerja yang mudah disesuaikan

flick *n* sentilan; *vi* ~ *through* membuka-buka halaman buku; *vt* menyentil; **flicker** *vi* berkedip-kedip

flier → **flyer**

flight *n* [flait] penerbangan; ~ *attendant* pramugari, pramugara; ~ *deck* geladak pesawat terbang; ~ *of stairs* tangga; **flighty** *adj* ringan, tidak bisa diandalkan, mudah terpengaruh

flimsy *adj* lemah, tidak kuat; halus

flinch *vi* beréaksi terhadap sesuatu yang mengagetkan; *Jane didn't even* ~ Jane tidak beréaksi sama sekali

fling *n* lémparan; *sl* perselingkuhan; *highland* ~ tari adat Skotlandia; *vt* **flung flung** melémparkan

flip *n* salto; *vi* membalik; *vt* memutar-balikkan; ~ *side* (sisi) balik; **flip-flops** *n, pl, UK* sandal jepit

flippant *adj* énténg, sembrono

flirt *n* orang genit; *vi* bermain mata; **flirtatious** *adj* genit

flit *vi* melayang, terbang; *flying ants* ~*ted around the light* banyak laron terbang mengelilingi lampu

float *n* pelampung; semacam minuman és; gerobak dalam arak-arakan; *vi* mengapung, terapung; *vt* mengapung-kan; **flotation** ~ *aid* pelampung

flock *n* kawanan, gerombolan, kumpu-lan; *a* ~ *of sheep* segerombolan domba; *vi* datang berbondong-bon-dong, berkumpul, berhimpun; *visitors* ~*ed to the palace* banyak tamu berbondong-bondong datang ke istana

flog *vt* memukuli, mencambuk; *sl* menjual

flood *n* [flad] banjir, air bah; ~ *tide* air rob; *flash* ~ banjir dadakan; ~*s of tears* banyak menangis; *vi* banjir; *vt* mem-banjiri; **flooded** *adj* banjir; **floodgate** *n* pintu air; **floodlight** *n* [fladlait] lampu sorot

floor *n* lantai, tingkat; ~ *cleaner* obat pél, obat pembersih lantai; ~ *plan* denah; *dance* ~ lantai dansa; *first* ~ *US* lantai bawah, lantai satu; *UK* lantai dua

flop *n, sl* kegagalan; *vi* gagal; jatuh, tidak berdiri; *vt* merebahkan badan; **floppy** *adj* tidak tegak, lembut; ~ *disk* diskét

flora *n* flora, tumbuh-tumbuhan; **floral** *adj* berkaitan dengan bunga; **florist** *n* (pemilik) toko bunga; **floristry** *n* seni merangkai bunga

floss *n dental* ~ benang gigi; *vi* mem-bersihkan gigi dengan benang

flotation ~ *aid* pelampung ← **float**

flounder *n* semacam ikan laut; *vi* bersusah-susah

flour *n* tepung (terigu); *corn*~ tepung maizéna; **floury** *adj* cepat hancur, seperti tepung

flourish *n* [flarisy] gerakan yang lincah; *vi* mekar, tumbuh subur; *vt* melambai-lambaikan

flow *n* aliran; ~ *chart* diagram alir; *ebb and* ~ *pasang* surut; *to go with the* ~ mengikuti arus; *vi* mengalir; **flowing** *adj* mengalir

flower *n* bunga, kembang; ~*-seller* penjual bunga; ~ *pot* pot bunga; *vi* berbunga, mekar; berkembang; **flow-ery** *adj* berbunga-bunga, méwah

flown *v, pf* [flon] → **fly**

flu *n* flu, selesma; *bird* ~ flu burung ← **influenza**

fluctuate *vi* naik turun, bergejolak; **fluctuation** *n* naik turunnya, gejolak, fluktuasi

fluency *n* [fluensi] kelancaran, kefasih-an; **fluent** *adj* lancar, fasih; **fluently** *adv* dengan lancar, fasih; *Jonathan speaks Portuguese* ~ Jonathan lancar berbahasa Portugis

fluff *n* bulu (kain), debu; isi yang tidak berarti; **fluffy** *adj* berbulu

fluid *n* cairan; *adj* cair, tidak tentu

fluke *n* kebetulan, untung

flung *vt, pf* → **fling**

flunk *v, coll* gagal dalam ujian; *I know I'll* ~ *my Japanese exam* saya tahu, pasti tidak akan lulus ujian bahasa Jepang

fluorescent *adj* [flurésent] berpijar; ~ *light* lampu néon; ~ *pen* stabilo

flurry *n* kesibukan; hujan salju yang tiba-tiba

flush *n* serangkaian kartu; *vi* memérah (muka); *vt* menyiram, membersihkan; ~ *the toilet* menyiram WC

flute *n* suling; **flutist** → **flautist**

flutter *n* kepakan sayap; *vi* berkibar-kibar; *vt* mengepakkan

fly *n* lalat; **flyswat, flyswatter** *n* [flais-wot] pemukul lalat

fly *v* **flew flown** [flon] *vi* terbang; ber-kibar-kibar; *vt* menerbangkan; mengi-barkan; ~ *ball* bola yang dipukul ting-gi; *frequent* ~*er* orang yang sering naik pesawat; *to let* ~ melepaskan (kendali); ~ *a helicopter* menerbang-kan hélikopter; ~ *a kite* main layang-layang; ~ *into a rage* naik darah; **fly-ing** *adj* ~ *saucer* piring terbang; ~ *visit* kunjungan singkat; **flywheel** *n* [flai-wil] roda gila

fly *n* ritsléting (di celana)

flyer, flier *n* selebaran, brosur

flyover *n* jembatan layang

flyswat, flyswatter *n* [flaiswot] pemukul lalat ← **fly**

flywheel *n* [flaiwil] roda gila ← **fly**

foal *n* anak kuda

foam *n* buih, busa; *bath* ~ sabun cair; *polystyrene* ~ busa; *vi* berbuih, berbusa

focus *n* titik perhatian, pusat perhatian, fokus; *in* ~ jelas; *out of* ~ kabur; *vi* melihat dengan jelas; konséntrasi; ~ *on* memusatkan perhatian pada; *vt* memfokuskan, memusatkan perhatian; **focused** *adj* terarah

fodder *n* makanan ternak

foe *n* musuh

foetid → **fetid**

foetus → **fetus**

fog *n* kabut; ~ *up* berembun; **foggy** *adj* berkabut; *I haven't the foggiest (idea)* saya sama sekali tidak tahu

foil *n* *(aluminium)* ~ kertas pérak; *vt* menggagalkan

fold *n* lipatan; *vi* bangkrut, hancur; *vt* melipat

folder *n* map

folk *n* orang; ~ *tale* cerita rakyat; *my* ~*s* keluarga saya; **folksy** *adj* kampungan

follow *vi* ikut, turut, bergabung; ~ *through* berlanjut; ~ *up* menindak-lanjuti; *as* ~*s* sebagai berikut; *vt* mengikuti, menuruti; **follower** *n* peng-ikut, anggota; **following** *adj, n* yang berikut; para pengikut

fond *adj* suka, gemar; ~ *of* suka akan, menggemari; **fondly** *adv* dengan mesra; **fondness** *n* kesukaan

fondle *vt* [fondel] membelai, mengusap

font *n* jenis huruf (cetakan)

food *n* makanan, pangan; pakan (héwan); ~ *poisoning* keracunan (makanan); ~ *technology* pelajaran memasak; ~ *for thought* bahan untuk dipertimbangkan;

World ~ *Organization* Organisasi Pangan Sedunia

fool *n* orang bodoh; *to make a* ~ *of* memperolok-olokkan; *vi* ~ *around* main-main; berselingkuh; *vt* menipu; **foolhardy** *adj* terlalu berani, tidak aman; **foolish** *adj* bodoh; **foolishly** *adv* secara bodoh; **foolproof** *adj* mudah sekali

foot *n* feet kaki; *athlete's* ~ jamur (di kaki); *on* ~ berjalan kaki; *six* ~ *tall* tinggi badan lebih dari 180 sénti; *hand,* ~ *and mouth disease* penyakit tangan kaki mulut; **footage** *n* rekaman; **foot-ball** *n* sépak bola; ~ *player*, **footballer** *n* pemain sépak bola; **foothill** *n* [fut hil] kaki gunung, bukit; **foothold** *n* [fut hold] pijakan kaki; **footing** *on equal* ~ sederajat; **footnote** *n* catatan kaki; **footpath** *n* jalan setapak, trotoar; **foot-print** *n* tapak kaki; **footstep** *n* derap kaki; **footwear** *n* [futwér] sepatu

for *prep* bagi, untuk; selama; ~ *hours* berjam-jam; ~ *and against* pro dan anti; ~ *my mother* untuk ibuku; ~ *all I know* sepengetahuan saya; *Kelvin was sick* ~ *two days* Kelvin sakit selama dua hari; *conj* karena

forbid *vt* **forbade forbidden** melarang; **forbidden** *adj* terlarang, dilarang

force *n* kekuatan, tenaga, daya; **armed** ~*s* angkatan bersenjata; *by* ~ dengan paksa; *vt* memaksa; **forceful** *adj* tegas

forceps *n, pl* tang

fore *to the* ~ muncul (ke depan)

forecast *n* ramalan; *weather* ~ ramalan cuaca; *vt* meramalkan; **forecaster** *n* peramal, analis

forefather *n* nénék moyang, leluhur

forefinger *n* [forfingger] jari telunjuk

forefront *n* [forfrant] paling depan

forego *vt* **foregone forewent** menolak, meninggalkan; **foregone** [forgon] *a* ~ *conclusion* sudah ditentukan

forehead *n* [forid, forhéd] dahi, kening

foreign *adj* [foren] asing, luar negeri; ~ *exchange*, ~ *currency* mata uang asing, devisa; **foreigner** *n* orang asing

foreman *n* **foremen** mandor

foremost *first and* ~ terutama

forensic *adj* forénsik; ~ *science* ilmu forénsik

foreplay *n* pemanasan

foresee *vt* **foresaw foreseen** meramal, memprédiksi

foreshore *n* daérah di balik pantai

foreskin *n* kulup

forest *n* hutan; ~ *fire* kebakaran hutan; *protected* ~ hutan lindung; *urban* ~ hutan kota; **forestry** *n* kehutanan

forestall *vt* [forstol] mencegah, menghambat

foretell *vt* **foretold foretold** meramalkan

forever, forevermore *adv* untuk selamanya

forewent *vt, pf* → **forego**

foreword *n* [forwérd] prakata

forfeit *vt* [forfet] kehilangan; *as a prisoner, he ~s his right to vote* sebagai tahanan, dia kehilangan hak memberi suara

forgave *vt, pf* → **forgive**

forge *vt* memalsukan; menempa, membuat; ~ *a friendship* berteman; **forger** *n* pemalsu; **forgery** *n* pemalsuan, tiruan

forget *v* **forgot forgotten** *vi* lupa, terlupa; *vt* melupakan; ~ *oneself* lupa diri; **forgetful** *adj* pelupa

forgive *vt* [forgiv] **forgave forgiven** memaafkan, mengampuni; ~ *and forget* memaafkan dan melupakan; **forgiveness** *n* ampun, maaf

forgot, forgotten *v, pf* → **forget**

fork *n* garpu; *knife and* ~ garpu pisau; belokan, pertigaan, cabang; *pitch*~ trisula; *vi* bercabang; **forklift** *n* mesin pengangkat barang

forlorn *adj* memelas

form *n* bentuk, rupa; formulir, blangko; *in fine* ~ dalam keadaan baik; *true to* ~ seperti biasa; *vi* terbentuk; *vt* merupakan, membentuk

formal *adj* formal, resmi; ~ *wear* busana malam, pakaian resmi; **formality** *n* formalitas

format *n* bentuk, format; **formation** *n* pembentukan, formasi ← **form**

former *adj* dahulu, bekas, mantan (orang), lama; **formerly** *adv* dahulu (d/h), sebelumnya

formidable *adj* [formidabel] disegani; berat

formula *n* rumus, formula; *milk* ~ susu bubuk, susu formula; **formulate** *vt* merumuskan, menyusun

fort *n* bénténg; **fortification** *n* bénténg, kubu; **fortify** *vt* memperkuat; **fortress** *n* bénténg

forth *adj* ke depan; *and so* ~ dan seterusnya (dst); *back and* ~ ulang alik

forthcoming *adj* [forthkaming] yang akan datang, mendatang; memberi informasi, terbuka

forthright *adj* [forthrait] terus terang, blak-blakan, ceplas-ceplos

forthwith *adj* serta merta, pada saat ini juga

fortieth *adj* [fortieth] keempat puluh; **forty** *adj, n* empat puluh

fortification *n* bénténg, kubu; **fortify** *vt* memperkuat

fortitude *n* ketabahan, kekuatan

fortnight *n* [fortnait] dua minggu; **fortnightly** *adj, adv* dwimingguan, tiap dua minggu

fortress *n* bénténg ← **fort**

fortuitous *adj* kebetulan

fortunate *adj* beruntung, bernasib baik; **fortunately** *adv* secara beruntung; **fortune** *n* rezeki; harta karun; *to cost a* ~ mahal sekali; *to earn a* ~ mempunyai gaji besar sekali; *to seek your* ~ merantau; ~-*teller* peramal, dukun

forty *adj, n* empat puluh; ~ *winks* tidur sebentar ← **four**

forum *n* wacana, ajang diskusi

forward *adj, adv* ke depan, maju; berani; *from this day* ~ mulai hari ini; *vt* mengirimkan; **forwarding** ~ *agent* agén pengiriman barang, ékspédisi

fossil *n* fosil; ~ *fuel* bahan bakar fosil; **fossilized** *adj* telah menjadi fosil; tidak dapat berubah lagi

foster *vt* memelihara; ~ *child* anak angkat, anak pungut; ~ *mother* ibu angkat

fought *v, pf* [fot] → **fight**

foul *adj* [faul] jorok, kotor, najis, jijik; ~ *play* kejahatan; ~ *weather* cuaca buruk; *vi* melanggar peraturan (olahraga); *vt* mengotori

found *vt* [faund] mendirikan; *~ing fathers* bapak-bapak bangsa; *vt, pf →* **find**; **foundation** *n* yayasan; fondasi, alas; bedak dasar; **founder** *n* pendiri

fountain *n* [faunten] air mancur, pancuran air; *~ pen* pulpén; *~ of knowledge* sumber pengetahuan

four *adj, n* empat; **fourteen** *adj, n* empat belas; **fourteenth** *adj* keempat belas; **fourth** *adj* keempat; *the ~ of July* tanggal empat Juli (hari kemerdékaan AS)

fowl *n* unggas; ayam

fox *n* rubah; *vt* menipu; **foxy** *adj* séksi; licik

foyer *n* ruang masuk

fraction *n* pecahan; *a ~ of a second* sejenak; *a ~ of the cost* jauh lebih murah

fracture *n* [fraktyur] keretakan, patah; *vi* patah, retak; *vt* mematahkan, meretakkan; *Pierre ~d his collarbone* tulang selangka Pierre retak

fragile *adj* [frajail] mudah pecah atau patah

fragment *n* potong, pecahan, keping; **fragmentary** *adj* terpotong-potong

fragrance *n* [frégrans] **fragrant** *adj* harum, wangi

frail *adj* lemah, rapuh; *Grandma is looking very ~* Nénék tampak kurang kuat

frame *n* rangka, kerangka; bingkai, lis (gambar); kusén (pintu); tubuh, badan; *time ~* kerangka waktu; *vt* membingkai; menjebak; **framework** *n* [frémwérk] kerangka, rangka

France *n* Perancis

franchise *n* waralaba

frangipani *n* [franjipani] pohon atau bunga kamboja

frank *adj* terus terang, ceplas-ceplos; **frankly** *adv* terus terang saja

frankfurter *n* semacam sosis

frantic *adj* kalang kabut

fraternal *adj* persaudaraan (terutama yang laki-laki); *~ twins* kembar lelaki dan perempuan; **fraternity** *n* persatuan, persaudaraan; *college ~* perkumpulan mahasiswa laki-laki

fraud *n* penipuan, penipu; **fraudulent** *adj* palsu

fray *vi* mulai robék; **frayed** *adj* compang-camping

freak *n* orang dengan cacat yang luar biasa; *adj* luar biasa, kebetulan; *vi ~ out* panik; freakish, **freaky** *adj* luar biasa, kebetulan

freckle *n* [frekel] bintik-bintik; **freckled** *adj* berbintik-bintik

free *vt* membébaskan, melepaskan; *adj* bébas, merdéka; cuma-cuma, gratis; kosong; *~ from, ~ of* bébas (dari); *~ kick* tendangan bébas; *~ port* pelabuhan bébas; *~ sex* bersanggama di luar ikatan perkawinan; *~ time* waktu senggang; *~ trade* perdagangan bébas; *for ~* gratis, cuma-cuma; *~-range chicken* ayam kampung; **freebie** *n, coll* hadiah; **freedom** *n* kemerdékaan, kebébasan, keleluasaan; *~ fighter* pejuang (kemerdékaan); *~ of choice* kebébasan memilih; *~ of speech* kebébasan bersuara; **freelance** *adj* lepas; *~ journalist* wartawan lepas; **freely** *adv* dengan bébas; **freestyle** *n* gaya bébas; **freeway** *n* jalan bébas hambatan, jalan tol

freeze *v* **froze frozen** *vi* membeku; *vt* membekukan; **freezer** *n* lemari és; **freezing** *adj* membekukan, sangat dingin; *~ point* titik beku; *I'm ~!* saya sangat kedinginan!

freight *n* [frét] muatan, kargo; *~ train* keréta api barang; *vt* mengirim; **freighter** *n* kapal barang, kapal pengangkut

French *n* bahasa Perancis; *adj* berasal dari Perancis; *~ fries* kentang goréng; *~ kiss* mencium dengan lidah; **Frenchman** *n* lelaki Perancis; **Frenchwoman** *n* perempuan Perancis

frequency *n* gelombang, frékuénsi; **frequent** *adj* berulang kali, sering, kerap; *vt* sering mengunjungi; *David ~s nightclubs with his friends* David sering ke kelab malam dengan teman-temannya

fresh *adj* segar; baru; sejuk; *~ graduate* orang yang baru tamat; **freshness** *n* kesegaran; **freshwater** *adj* air tawar

fret *vi* kuatir, resah; *~ about, ~ over* menguatirkan

friar *n* [fraier] biarawan

friction *n* gésékan; ~ *between* perselisihan di antara

Friday *n* hari Jum'at; *Good* ~ Jum'at Agung

fridge *n, coll* kulkas, lemari és ← **refrigerator**

fried *adj* goréng; ~ *egg* telur mata sapi; ~ *noodles* mi goréng; ~ *rice* nasi goréng; *v, pf* → **fry**

friend *n* [frénd] kawan, sahabat, teman; *best* ~ sahabat yang paling dekat (satu orang); *to be* ~*s, make* ~*s* bersahabat, berkawan, berteman; **friendliness** *n* keramahan; **friendly** *adj* ramah, bersahabat; ~ *match* pertandingan persahabatan; *in a* ~ *way* dengan ramah; **friendship** *n* persahabatan

fright *n* [frait] rasa takut; *in* ~ ketakutan; **frighten** *vt* menakut-nakuti, menakutkan; **frightened** *adj* takut, ketakutan; **frightening** *adj* menakutkan; **frightful** *adj* dahsyat, menakutkan; **frightfully** *adv* amat sangat; *I'm* ~ *sorry* seribu maaf

frigid *adj* [frijid] dingin, tidak suka bercinta

frill *n* émbél-émbél; *no* ~*s* sederhana, polos; **frilly** *adj* berjumbai

fringe *n* pinggir; poni

frisbee *n* frisbi

frisk *vt* menggeledah; *the policewoman* ~*ed Nia for stolen goods* polisi wanita menggeledah Nia untuk mencari barang-barang curian

frisky *adj* berlompat-lompat

fritter *n* goréngan, perkedél; *banana* ~ pisang goréng (pisgor); *corn* ~ perkedél jagung

frivolity *n* [frivoliti] hura-hura, foya-foya; **frivolous** *adj* sepélé, sembrono

frizz *vi* mengeriting; **frizzy** *adj* keriting, kribo

fro *adv to and* ~ mondar-mandir, pontang-panting

frock *n, arch* rok

frog *n* kodok, katak; **frogman** *n* penyelam; **frogkick** *n* gaya kodok

from *prep* dari, daripada; ~ *my childhood* sejak kecil

front *n* [frant] bagian muka; hadapan; barisan; *adj* muka; ~ *door* pintu depan, pintu masuk; *in* ~ *of* di depan, di muka; **frontage** *n* [frantej] bagian yang hadap ke depan; **frontier** *n* [frantir] tapal batas, perbatasan

frost *n* embun beku; ~*-bitten* radang dingin; **frostbite** *n* radang dingin; **frosting** *n* lapisan manis di atas kué; **frosty** *adj* dingin, tidak ramah

froth *n* busa, buih; *vi* berbusa, berbuih; **frothy** *adj* berbusa, berbuih

frown *n* [fraun] muka cemberut; *vi* mengernyit dahi; ~ *on,* ~ *upon* tidak setuju dengan, tidak menyukai

froze, frozen *v, pf* → **freeze**

frugal *adj* pelit, menghémat, sederhana, bersahaja; *Bridget is* ~ *with money* Bridget tidak memboroskan uang

fruit *n* [frut] buah, buah-buahan; ~ *juice* jus buah, sari buah; ~ *salad* buah campur; **fruitcake** *n* kué berisi kismis dan buah kering lainnya; **fruiterer** *n* penjual buah; **fruitful** *adj* berbuah; **fruitless** *adj* tidak berguna, percuma, sia-sia, tanpa hasil

frustrate *vt* menghambat, menggagalkan; **frustrated** *adj* kesal; terhambat; **frustrating** *adj* membuat frustrasi, menyebalkan; *it is so* ~ *waiting for that letter* menunggu surat itu sangat menyebalkan; **frustration** *n* frustasi

fry *small* ~ ikan teri; *vi* menjadi panas; *vt* menggoréng; ~ *pan* penggoréngan, kuali; *out of the* ~*ing pan, into the fire* lepas dari mulut harimau, jatuh ke mulut buaya

ft *abbrev* **foot** kaki

fuchsia *n* [fyusya] sejenis bunga; *adj* mérah muda

fuck *n, vulg* persetubuhan; *I don't give a* ~ aku tidak peduli; *vt* mengéntot; ~ *around* mempermainkan; *ejac* ancuk! (untuk menunjukkan rasa marah)

fudge *n* semacam gula-gula

fuel *n* [fyul] bahan bakar; *diesel* ~ solar; *vt* memasok bahan bakar; ~ *discontent* menghasut

fugitive *n* [fyujitiv] buron; *adj* buronan

fulfill *vt* **fulfil** memenuhi; ~ *a promise* menepati janji; **fulfillment** *n* terlaksananya, kepuasan, pemenuhan

full *adj* penuh; kenyang; lengkap; *~ blood* totok; *~grown* akil balig, déwasa; *~on coll* habis-habisan; *~ blast* sekeras-kerasnya (suara); *~ moon* bulan purnama, terang bulan; *~ stop* titik; *I'm ~* saya sudah kenyang; *~ of oneself* sombong, arogan; **fully** *adv* secara penuh

fumble *vi* [fambel] salah tangkap; *vt* meraba-raba

fume *vi* marah; **fumes** *n, pl* asap, uap, émisi

fumigate *v* menyemprot; **fumigation** *n* penyemprotan, fumigasi

fun *n* keasyikan; *adj* asyik; *~ park* taman hiburan; *~ run* lomba lari jarak jauh; *have ~!* selamat menikmati; *to make ~ of* memperolok-olokkan

function *n* fungsi; acara; *Fiona's at a ~ at the Embassy* Fiona sedang menghadiri acara di kedutaan; *vi* berfungsi, berjalan, bekerja; *the pram also ~s as a bed* keréta anak ini juga berfungsi sebagai tempat tidur; **functional** *adj* praktis; **functionary** *n* pejabat, fungsionaris

fund *n* dana; *vt* mendanai

fundamental *n* dasar-dasar; *adj* dasar, asasi; **fundamentalism** *n* fundaméntalisme

funeral *n* (upacara) pemakaman; *~ parlor* pelayanan pemakaman

funfair *n* taman hiburan; pasar malam

fungus *n* fungi [fanggai] jamur, cendawan

funicular *~ railway* keréta gantung

funky *adj, coll* ngetrén, gaya, gaul

funnel *n* corong

funny *adj* lucu, jenaka; anéh; *~ bone* senyar

fur *n* bulu (binatang); **furry** *adj* berbulu

furious *adj* [fyurius] marah sekali, geram, naik pitam; **fury** *n* kemarahan, berang

furnace *n* [fernes] oven, tungku

furnish *vt* melengkapi; **furnished** *adj* dilengkapi dengan mébel; **furniture** *n* mébel, perabot rumah

furry *adj* berbulu ← **fur**

further, farther *adj* lebih jauh, lebih

lanjut; *~ education* pendidikan lanjutan; *vt* melanjutkan; **furthermore** *adv* lagipula; **furthermost** *adj* yang paling jauh

fury *n* kemarahan, bérang

fuse *n* sumbu, sekering; *to have a short ~* cepat marah; *v* melebur, menyatu; **fusion** *n* fusi; santapan yang memadukan dua unsur daérah

fuss *n* répot; kekacauan; *vi* ceréwét; **fussy** *adj* teliti, ceréwét

futile *adj* sia-sia, percuma

future *n in (the) ~* di masa depan; *adj* yang akan datang, mendatang, bakal, calon (orang)

fuzz *n* bulu; **fuzzy** *adj* berbulu

Fwy *abbrev Freeway* jalan bébas hambatan, jalan tol

FYI *abbrev for your information* agar diketahui

G

g *gram* g (gram)

G-string *n* celana dalam tali

gab *gift of the ~* banyak bicara, pandai bicara

gabble *vi* [gabel] bicara terlalu cepat dan kurang jelas

gable *n* [gébel] dinding rumah berbentuk segi tiga di bawah ujung atap

Gabon *n* Gabon; **Gabonese** *n* orang Gabon; *adj* berasal dari Gabon

gad *~ about* jalan-jalan, sering pergi

gadget *n* [gajet] alat, perkakas

Gaelic *n* [gélik] bahasa Skotlandia, bahasa Irlandia

gag *n* ikat mulut; lelucon; *vi* nyaris muntah; *vt* menyumbat mulut

gaiety *n* [géiti] kegirangan, keramaian; **gay** *adj* girang, senang hati, meriah; homoséks

gain *n* untung, keuntungan, laba; *vi* beruntung; *vt* memperoléh, mendapat, mencapai; *~ entrance* dapat masuk; *~ time* mendapat waktu; *~ weight* bertambah berat badan

gait *n* gaya berjalan

gala [gala] ~ *performance* pertunjukan méwah, pertunjukan akbar

galaxy *n* bimasakti

gale *n* angin besar, badai; ~ *force wind* badai

gall *n* [gol] empedu; ~ *bladder* kandung empedu; keberanian; *David had the* ~ *to ask for my phone number* berani-beraninya David minta nomor téléponku; **galling** *adj* pahit

gallant *adj* berani, gagah perkasa; **gallantry** *n* keberanian, kekesatriaan

gallery *n* serambi; ruang paméran, galéri

galley *n* [gali] dapur (di kapal)

galling *adj* pahit

gallon *n* galon (4,54 liter)

gallop *vi* mencongklang, lari congklang, berlari cepat

gallows *n, pl* tiang gantung; *to the* ~ digantung, dihukum mati

galore *adj* sesukanya, banyak; *there were cakes* ~ ada banyak sekali macam kué

galvanized ~ *iron* besi berlapiskan séng

Gambia *n* Gambia; **Gambian** *n* orang Gambia; *adj* berasal dari Gambia

gamble *vi* [gambel] berjudi, bertaruh; ~ *on* menggantungkan harapan pada; *vt* mempertaruhkan; *it's a* ~ ada risiko; **gambler** *n* penjudi; **gambling** *n* judi, perjudian

game *n* permainan, pertandingan; satwa buruan; ~ *show* acara permainan (di télévisi); *board* ~ permainan di atas papan; *the Olympic* ~*s* Pertandingan Olimpiade; *to have a* ~ bermain; *adj* berani; **gaming** ~ *laws* undang-undang perjudian; ~ *machines* mesin judi

gander *n* angsa jantan

gang *n* kawanan, gerombolan, géng; **gangster** *n* préman, penjahat, perampok, garong

gangway *n* tangga naik kapal; jalanan sempit

gaol *n* [jéil] penjara; **gaoler** *n* penjaga penjara

gap *n* lubang, celah, jurang pemisah; ~ *toothed* bergigi celah; ~ *year* tahun sesudah tamat SMA sebelum kuliah; *mind the* ~ hati-hati melangkah

gape *vi* menganga, memandang dengan mulut terbuka; *the children* ~*d at the tourists* anak-anak menganga melihat para wisatawan

garage *n* [garaj] garasi; béngkél; ~ *sale* acara menjual barang bekas di rumah; *his car is parked in the* ~ mobilnya diparkir di garasi; *it needs repairing at the* ~ harus diperbaiki di béngkél

garbage *n* [garbej] sampah; ~ *bin*, ~ *can* tempat sampah, tong sampah; ~ *collectors*, ~ *men* tukang sampah; ~ *truck* truk sampah; *coll* omong kosong

garden *n* kebun, taman; ~ *center* pusat perbelanjaan perlengkapan kebun; ~ *party* pésta taman; *botanic* ~*s* kebun raya; *front* ~ taman di depan rumah; *rock* ~ taman batu; **gardener** *n* tukang kebun; **gardening** *n* berkebun

gardenia *n* kacapiring

gargle *vi* [gargel] berkumur; ~ *with salty water* berkumur pakai air garam

garish *adj* [garisy] norak, ramai, berwarna mencolok

garland *n* karangan bunga

garlic *n* bawang putih; ~ *bread* roti yang diolés dengan mentéga dan bawang putih

garment *n* garmén, pakaian; ~ *factory* pabrik garmén

garnish *n* hiasan; *vt* menghiasi; *lamb* ~*ed with parsley* daging domba dengan hiasan péterséli

garter *n* ikat stoking

gas *n* gas; bénsin; ~ *bill* rékening gas; ~ *chamber* kamar gas; ~ *cooker* kompor gas; ~ *cylinder* tabung gas; ~ *fitter* tukang gas; ~ *meter* alat pengukur pemakaian gas; **gasometer** *n* tangki gas; **gasworks** *n* pabrik gas

gash *n, vt* luka; *she* ~*ed her leg on the wire* kakinya luka kena kawat

gasoline *n* [gasolin] **gas** *sl* bénsin; ~ *station* pom bénsin

gasometer *n* tangki gas ← **gas**

gasp *n* embusan napas; *vi* menarik nafas dengan cepat; *last* ~ mati-matian

gastric *adj* berkaitan dengan perut

gasworks *n* pabrik gas ← **gas**

gate *n* pintu (masuk), gerbang; pintu pagar; *the flight departs from* ~ 3 penerbangan itu berangkat dari Pintu 3; **gatecrash** *v* datang tanpa diundang; **gatecrasher** *n* tamu tak diundang; **gated** *adj* berportal; **gatehouse** *n* rumah jaga monyét; **gatekeeper** *n* penjaga pintu; **gateway** *n* pintu masuk; *Cardiff is the ~ to Wales* Cardiff adalah pintu masuk utama Wales

gather *vi* berkumpul; merasa; *I ~ed they were not happily married* saya merasa perkawinan mereka tidak bahagia; *vt* mengumpulkan, memetik; *~ speed* melaju; **gathering** *n* perkumpulan

GATT *abbrev General Agreement on Tariffs and Trade* Persetujuan Umum tentang Tarif dan Perdagangan

gaudy *adj* norak, mencolok

gauge *n* [géj] ukuran, kadar; *narrow ~ track* rél sempit; *rain ~* alat pengukur curah hujan; *vt* mengukur, menaksir

gaunt *adj* kurus, ceking

gauze *n* kain kasa

gay *n* orang homoséksual; *adj* homoséksual; girang, senang hati, meriah; *~-bashing* pemukulan terhadap orang homoséksual

gaze *n* pandangan; *vi* memandang; *he ~d into his mother's eyes* dia memandang mata ibunya; *vt* menatap, memandangi

gazebo *n* [gazibo] bangunan kecil di taman

gazelle *n* [gazél] semacam rusa

gazette *n* [gazét] surat berita, koran

GB *abbrev Great Britain* Inggris Raya

GBH *abbrev grievous bodily harm* terluka berat (oleh penjahat)

GCSE *abbrev, UK General Certificate of Secondary Education* ijazah SMA

GDP *abbrev Gross Domestic Product* Hasil PBD, Penghasilan Bersih Doméstik

GDR *abbrev, arch German Democratic Republic* Républik Démokratik Jérman, Jérman Timur

gear *n* [gir] peralatan, perkakas, perabot; persnéling, gigi; gir; *sporting ~* perlengkapan olahraga; *second ~* gigi dua

gecko *n* [géko] cicak

gee *ejac* [ji] wah, aduh

geese *n, pl* [gis] → **goose**

gel *n* [jél] gél; *hair ~* gél rambut

gelatine *n* [jélatin] semacam agar-agar; **gelatinous** *adj* seperti agar-agar, léngkét

gem *n* [jém] permata; yang gemilang; **gemstone** *n* batu mulia

gender *n* jenis kelamin; jénder; *~-specific* khusus untuk laki-laki atau perempuan; *~ studies* kajian jénder

gene *n* [jin] gén; **genetic** *adj* génétik; *~ engineering* rékayasa génétik; **genetics** *n, pl* génétika

genealogy *n* [jinialoji] ilmu sejarah keluarga

general *n* jénderal; *adj* umum; *~ election* pemilihan umum (pemilu); *~ knowledge* pengetahuan umum; *~ practitioner (GP)* dokter umum; *Attorney-~* Jaksa Agung; *director-~* diréktur-jénderal (dirjén); *in ~* pada umumnya; *~ Assembly (of the United Nations)* Sidang Umum (Persatuan Bangsa-Bangsa); *~ Certificate of Secondary Education (GCSE)* ijazah SMA; **generalization** *n* pendapat yang terlalu luas, penyamarataan; **generalize** *vi* menyamaratakan; **generally** *adv* biasanya, umumnya; **generic** *adj* umum

generate *vt* menghasilkan, membangkitkan; **generation** *n* angkatan, générasi; pembangkitan; **generator** *n* pembangkit listrik, génsét

generic *adj* umum

generosity *n* kemurahan hati; **generous** *adj* murah hati, dermawan

genesis *n* [jénesis] asal; *Chr* Kejadian

genetic *adj* génétik; *~ engineering* rékayasa génétik; **genetically** *adv* secara génétik; *~ modified* dirékayasa génétik; **genetics** *n, pl* génétika ← **gene**

genial *adj* [jinial] ramah

genie *n* [jini] jin

genital *n* [jénital] kemaluan; *adj* berhubungan dengan kemaluan; **genitalia** *n* [jénitélia] kemaluan

genius *n* [jinius] kecerdasan; jénius, orang berotak cemerlang; *Rob is a ~ with electronics* Rob adalah jénius soal éléktronik

genocide *n* [jénosaid] pembunuhan massal; **genocidal** *adj* yang berkaitan dengan pembunuhan massal

genre *n* [jonre] gaya, aliran

gentile *n* [jéntail] orang non-Yahudi

gentle *adj* [jéntel] (lemah) lembut, halus, jinak; *a ~ breeze* angin sepoi-sepoi; **gentleman** *n* **gentlemen** tuan; orang pria; orang sopan; *ladies and gentlemen* bapak-bapak dan ibu-ibu; **gentlemanly** *adv* sopan; sportif; **gently** *adv* perlahan-lahan, lemah lembut

gents *n* pria (di WC) ← **gentlemen**

genuflect *vi* berlutut; **genuflection** *n* tekuk lutut

genuine *adj* [jényuin] asli, sejati, tulén; ikhlas; **genuinely** *adv* sesungguhnya; dengan ikhlas

geographic, geographical *adj* [jiografik, jiografikal] geografis, berkaitan dengan ilmu bumi; **geography** *n* ilmu bumi, géografi

geological *adj* [jiolojikal] géologis, berkaitan dengan géologi; **geologist** *n* géolog, ahli géologi; **geology** *n* géologi

geometric *adj* [jiométrik] géométris; **geometry** *n* ilmu ukur sudut, géométri

geophysicist *n* [jiofisisist] ahli géofisika; **geophysics** *n* géofisika

Georgia *n* [jorjia] Georgia; **Georgian** *n* bahasa Georgia; orang Georgia; *adj* berasal dari Georgia

geothermal *adj* [jiotérmal] berhubungan dengan panas bumi; *~ energy* tenaga panas bumi; *~ springs* air panas (gunung)

geranium *n* [jerénium] sejenis bunga

geriatric *n* [jériatrik] orang lanjut usia (lansia), manusia lanjut usia (manula); *adj* sangat tua

germ *n* kuman; *~-free* bébas kuman

German *n* bahasa Jérman; orang Jérman; *adj* berasal dari Jérman; *~ measles* campak Jérman, rubéla; *~ shepherd* anjing hérder; **Germanic** *n* berkaitan dengan rumpun Jérman (Skandinavia, Belanda & Austria); **Germany** *n* Jérman; *East ~* Jérman Timur

germinate *vi* berkecambah ← **germ**

gesture *n* [jéstyur] isyarat, gerak-gerik tangan; *v* memberi isyarat

get *vt* **got gotten** mendapat, menerima; mengerti; menjadi; mengurus agar; *~ across* menyampaikan, mengungkapkan; *~ ahead, ~ along, ~ on* maju; berangkat; bergaul; *~ away* pergi; lari, kabur; *~ away with* berhasil; *~ back* (mendapat) kembali; *~ better* sembuh; menjadi lebih baik; *~ by* bertahan; *~ down* turun; *~ lost* menyasar; enyahlah; *~ off* turun; *~ out* pergi, keluar, turun; *~ through* menempuh, meléwati; *~ over* mengatasi; *~ round* meluangkan waktu; *~ together vi* berkumpul; mulai pacaran; *vt* mengumpulkan; *~ up* bangun; *~ a taxi* naik taksi; *~ into trouble* mendapat masalah; *~ well soon* semoga lekas sembuh; *~ one's hair cut* potong rambut; *~ one's own way* menang sendiri; **getaway** *n* pelarian

geyser *n* [giser] air mancur panas

Ghana *n* Gana; **Ghanaian** *n* [ganéan] orang Gana; *adj* berasal dari Gana

ghastly *adj* pucat, mengerikan

gherkin *n* mentimun (yang diasamkan)

ghetto *n* kampung (kelompok étnis tertentu)

ghost *n* hantu; *~ story* cerita hantu; *~ town* kota mati; **ghostly** *adj* seperti hantu

GI *abbrev government issue* tentara Amerika Serikat

giant *n, adj* [jaiant] raksasa

gibbon *n* [gibon] siamang

giblets *n, pl* [jiblets] jeroan burung

giddiness *n* [gidines] rasa pusing; **giddy** *adj* pusing, pening

gift [gift] kado, hadiah, pemberian; bakat; *~ shop* toko kado, toko suvenir; *~ voucher* kupon belanja; *~ wrap* bungkus kado; *free ~* hadiah; **gifted** *adj* berbakat; *Charlie was ~ at playing piano* Charlie berbakat main piano

gig *n* [gig] acara main musik, acara panggung

gigantic *adj* [jaigantik] besar sekali, raksasa

giggle *n* [gigel] kikikan, *v* cekikik; *vi* tertawa terkikik-kikik; *Elina ~d at the film* Elina menonton film sambil tertawa terkikik-kikik gigolo *n, m* [jigolo] pelacur pria

gild *vt* [gild] menyepuh, menyadur dengas emas; menghiasi

gills *n, pl* [gils] insang

gilt *n* [gilt] sepuh ← **gild**

gin *n* [jin] jénéwer, minuman keras; ~ *and tonic (G & T)* gin dan tonik

ginger *n* [jinjer] jahé; adj mérah (rambut); kuning (bulu kucing); ~ *ale* minuman bersoda berasa jahé; **gingerbread** *n* roti keras rasa jahé

gingerly *adv* dengan hati-hati, perlahan-lahan

gipsy → **gypsy**

giraffe *n* [jiraf] jerapah

girl *n* [gerl] anak perempuan, putri, gadis; ~ *Guide*, ~ *Scout* pramuka remaja putri; *little* ~ anak gadis, anak perempuan; *young* ~ gadis, dara; **girlhood** *n* masa gadis, masa kecil; **girlfriend** *n, f* [gerlfrénd] pacar, kekasih; **girlish** *adj* seperti gadis; **girly** *adj, coll* bersifat anak perempuan

gist *n* [jist] intisari, garis besar, pokok cerita

give *vt* [giv] **gave given** memberi; ~ *away* membagikan, memberikan; membuka rahasia; ~ *back* mengembalikan; ~ *birth* bersalin, melahirkan; ~ *in* mengalah; ~ *off* mengeluarkan, menghasilkan; ~ *out* menyebarkan; ~ *up* menyerah, menyerahkan; ~ *way* memberi jalan; ~ *and take* memberi dan menerima; ~ *to charity* beramal; mengamalkan; ~ *your word* berjanji; **giveaway** *n* hadiah; **given** *adj* tertentu; ~ *name* nama depan; **giver** *n* pemberi

glacial *adj* [glésyial] sangat dingin; **glacier** *n* glétser

glad *adj* gembira, senang; **gladden** *vt* menggembirakan, menyenangkan; **gladly** *adv* dengan senang hati; **gladness** *n* kegembiraan

gladiolus *n* gladioli [gladiolai] gladiol

glamorous *adj* **glam** *sl* memesona, menarik, menawan, glamor; **glamor** *n* **glamour** keméwahan, daya tarik, pesona

glance *n* pandangan sekilas, pandangan sekejap; *at first* ~ sekilas; *vi* melirik, memandang sekejap mata; *I* ~*d at him* saya memandang dia sekejap

gland *n* kelenjar; *glandular fever* radang kelenjar

glare *n* cahaya yang menyilaukan; *vt* membelalak, melihat dengan sikap marah; *the teacher* ~*d at the naughty boy* gurunya melihat anak nakal dengan rasa marah; **glaring** *adj* menyolok; ~ *mistake* kesalahan yang menyolok

glass *n* kaca; gelas; *looking*-~ cermin; **glasses** *n* kacamata; *dark* ~ kacamata hitam; **glasshouse** *n* rumah kaca; **glassy** *adj* seperti kaca; **glazier** *n* tukang kaca

glaucoma *n* [glokoma] glaukoma

gleam *n* sinar, cahaya, kilap; *vi* bersinar, bercahaya, mengkilap

glen *n* lembah

glib *adj* fasih, énténg

glide *vi* meluncur; **glider** *n* pesawat peluncur, pesawat layang; *hang*-~ gantole

glimmer *n* cahaya redup; *a* ~ *of hope* ada sedikit harapan

glimpse *n* pandangan sekilas; *vi* melihat sekilas

glisten *vi* [glisen] berkilau-kilauan

glitter *n* kegemilapan; *vi* gemilap

gloat *vi* menyombongkan diri tentang; *Jill* ~*ed about her son's prize* Jill membanggakan diri tentang hadiah anaknya

global *adj* seluruh dunia; ~ *warming* pemanasan bumi; **globalization** *n* globalisasi; **globe** *n* bola dunia; bola lampu, bohlam; **globetrotter** *n* penjelajah dunia

glockenspiel *n* [glokensypil] sejenis xilofon

gloom *n* remang-remang, kesuraman; ~ *and doom* sikap yang pésimis; **gloomy** *adj* suram

glorification *n* pemujaan; **glorify** *vt* memujakan; **glorious** *adj* megah, mulia, agung; **glory** *n* kemuliaan; kemenangan

gloss *n* kilau, kilap; ~ *over* meréméhkan, menyembunyikan; **glossy** *adj* licin, mengkilap

glossary *n* daftar istilah

glossy *adj* licin, mengkilap ← **gloss**

glove *n* [glav] sarung tangan; ~ *box* kotak depan (di mobil); *hand in* ~ bekerja sama

glow *n* sinar, cahaya; *vi* bersinar, berseri; menyala; ~*-worm* ulat yang mengeluarkan cahaya; **glowing** *adj* **glowingly** *adv* sangat memuja

glucose *n* glukosa

glue *n* [glu] lém, perekat; ~*-sniffing* ngelém; *v* mengelém; ~*d to the spot* terpaku di tempat

glum *adj* murung

glut *n* kebanyakan; **glutton** *n* orang rakus; **gluttonous** *adj* rakus

GM *abbrev genetically modified* dirékayasa génétik

GMT *abbrev Greenwich Mean Time* waktu GMT

gnarled *adj* [narld] berbonggol

gnash [nasy] ~ *your teeth* mengertakkan gigi

gnaw *v* [noa] ~ *(at)* menggerogoti

gnome *n* [nom] orang kerdil, katai; *garden* ~ patung kerdil sebagai hiasan taman

GNP *abbrev Gross National Product* Penghasilan Kotor Nasional (PKN)

go *n* giliran; ~*-ahead* izin; ~*-between* perantara, calo; ~*-kart* gokar; *no* ~ tidak bisa; *to have a* ~ berusaha; *vi* **went gone** pergi, berjalan; hilang; ~ *after* mengejar; menyusul; ~ *along* ikut serta; ~ *away* pergi; ~ *back* kembali; ~ *before* mendahului; ~ *by vi* berlalu; *vt* naik; ~ *cheap* diobral; ~ *down* turun; ~ *for* menyukai; menyerang; ~ *in* masuk; ~ *off* meledak; membusuk, menjadi basi; berbunyi; mati, padam; ~ *on* meneruskan; ~ *out* keluar; jalan-jalan; berpacaran; padam, mati; ~ *under* bangkrut; ~ *out with* berpacaran dengan; ~ *through with* menyelesaikan; ~ *through a lot* mengalami banyak kesulitan; ~ *up* naik; ~ *with* pergi bersama; cocok dengan; *how did it* ~? bagaimana?; **going** *vi* ~ *to* mau, akan; naik; ~*-s-on* kejadian

goal *n* gawang, gol; tujuan; *vi (to score a)* ~ mencetak gol; **goalie** *n, sl* **goalkeeper** *n* penjaga gawang, kiper; **goalpost** *n* tiang gawang

goat *n* kambing; ~ *milk* susu kambing

goatee *n* jénggot péndék

gobble *v* makan dengan cepat, melahap

goblet *n* piala

goblin *n* makhluk kecil dalam cerita dongéng

god *n* déwa; **God** *Isl, Chr* Allah, Tuhan; *Chr* Bapa; ~*mother* ibu baptis, ibu permandian; ~ *speed* selamat jalan; ~ *willing Isl* insya Allah; *thank* ~ *Isl* alhamdulillah; *Chr* puji Tuhan; ~ *bless you* Tuhan memberkati; *for* ~*'s sake* demi Tuhan; **goddess** *n, f* déwi; **godparent** *n* [godpérent] orang tua baptis

goggles *n, pl* [gogels] kaca mata renang; kaca mata balap

going *vi* ~ *to* mau, akan; naik; ~*-s-on* kejadian ← **go**

gold *n* emas; ~*-digger* penambang emas; wanita yang mencari suami kaya; ~*-leaf* emas prada; ~ *dust* serbuk emas; ~ *medal* médali emas; ~ *mine* tambang emas; **golden** *adj* terbuat dari emas; berwarna emas; ~ *anniversary* hari ulang tahun perkawinan yang kelimapuluh; ~ *opportunity* kesempatan emas; *silence is* ~ diam itu emas; *the* ~ *years* tahun-tahun paling bahagia; **goldfish** *n* ikan emas

golf *n* golf; ~ *club* kelab golf; stik golf; ~ *course* padang golf; **golfer** *n* pegolf, pemain golf

golliwog *n* bonéka hitam

gone *vi, pf* [gon] ← **go**

gong *n* gong

gonna *v, aux, sl* akan; *she's* ~ *get caught* dia akan tertangkap ← **going to**

goo *n* cairan léngkét, seperti lém

good *adj* baik, bagus; énak; séhat; ~*looking* rupawan, ganteng, sl cakep; ~*natured* baik hati; ~ *at* pandai; ~ *evening* selamat malam; ~ *Friday* Jumat Agung; ~ *lord* astaga; ~ *night* selamat tidur; *for* ~ untuk selamalamanya; *no* ~ tidak ada gunanya, tidak ada baiknya; ~ *for you* séhat; ~ *on you* selamat, syukur; *for your own* ~ demi kebaikan sendiri; *what* ~ *is it?* apa gunanya?; **goodbye** *ejac* selamat tinggal, selamat jalan; **goodness** *n* kebaikan, kebajikan; ~ *me* ampun; *thank* ~ syukur; **goods** *n, pl* barang-barang; ~ *train* keréta api barang; **goodwill** *n* niat baik; **goody** *n* permén; sesuatu yang énak; ~-~ murid yang terlampau baik hingga terkesan menjilat

goose *n* **geese** [gis] angsa; **gooseberry** *n* semacam buah frambus; **goose-pimples** *n, pl* bulu roma berdiri

GOP *abbrev Grand Old Party* Partai Républik (AS)

gorge *n* [gorj] jurang, ngarai; *vi* melahap; *Katherine ~d herself on chocolate* Katherine banyak melahap cokelat

gorgeous *adj* [gorjes] sangat menawan atau menarik, indah

gorilla *n* gorila

gory *adj* berdarah, penuh kekerasan; *I can't watch ~ films* saya tidak bisa menonton film dengan banyak adégan berdarah

gosh *ejac* wah!

gospel *n* injil, ajaran; ~ *music* musik gospel; ~ *(truth)* kebenaran

gossip *n* gosip, isu, gunjingan, buah bibir, kabar burung; raja gosip (ragos); *vi* bergosip; ~ *about* menggosipkan

got, gotten *vi, pf; to have* ~ *to* harus, terpaksa → **get**

Gothic *adj* Gotik

gotta *v, aux, sl* harus; ~ *go* saya harus pergi ← **(have) got to**

gourmet *adj* [gormé] mutu kulinér yang tinggi

gout *n* [gaut] asam urat

govern *v* [gavern] memerintah; *self-~ing* swapraja; **governance** *n* pemerintahan; *good* ~ pemerintahan yang baik; **government** *n* [gaverment] pemerintah, pemerintahan; **governor** *n* gubernur; *sl* bos; ~-*general* gubernur-jénderal; **gubernatorial** *adj* berkaitan dengan gubernur

governess *n, f* [gavernés] guru pribadi yang mengajar di rumah zaman dahulu

government *n* [gaverment] pemerintah, pemerintahan; **governor** *n* gubernur; *sl* bos; ~-*general* gubernur-jénderal ← **govern**

gown *n* gaun; jubah; *dressing* ~ kimono

GP *abbrev General Practitioner* dokter umum

GPA *abbrev grade point average* IP (indéks préstasi)

GPO *abbrev General Post Office* Kantor Pos Besar

grab *n* rampasan; *vt* merampas, menjambret, menyambar, menangkap; *up for ~s* tersedia, tinggal diambil

grace *n* keanggunan; rahmat, anugerah, karunia; *period of* ~ masa ténggang; *to say* ~ *Chr* membaca doa bersyukur sebelum makan; *vt* menyemarakkan; **graceful** *adj* anggun, lemah gemulai; **gracious** *adj* [grésyes] ramah; murah hati; *(good)* ~ astaga

grade *n* tingkat, pangkat, derajat; nilai (rapot); kelas; ~ *school* AS sekolah dasar; *first* ~ kelas satu; *point* ~ *average (GPA)* indéks préstasi (IP); *vt* memberi angka atau nilai; memeriksa, menyortir; **gradual** *adj* **gradually** *adv* lama-kelamaan, berangsur-angsur

graduate *n* [gradyuet] lulusan, tamatan; sarjana; ~ *school* program pascasarjana; *post-~* pascasarjana; *under~* sarjana muda; *vi* [gradyuét] lulus, tamat; wisuda; *Betty's son just ~d from junior high school* anaknya Betty baru lulus SMP; **graduation** *n* tamat sekolah, acara lulus-lulusan; wisuda

graffiti *n* [grafiti] corét-corétan (di témbok)

graft *n* [graft] korupsi, kolusi

graft *n* pencangkokan; *vt* mencangkokkan

grain *n* butir; séréal, biji-bijian; urat kayu; *against the* ~ melawan arus; **grainy** *adj* berserat, tidak mulus; **granular** *n* berupa butiran atau biji-bijian

gram *n* **gramme** gram

grammar *n* tata bahasa, gramatika; ~ *school* sekolah swasta; **grammatical** *adj* menurut tata bahasa, gramatikal; **grammatically** *adv* menurut tata bahasa, secara gramatika

gramophone *n, arch* [gramafon] alat pemutar piringan hitam

gran → **granny**

grand *n* besar, agung; bagus, méwah; ~

piano piano besar; **grandly** *adv* dengan méwah; dengan sombong

grandchild *n* [grandcaild] cucu; **grand-dad** *n, sl* kakék; kék; **granddaughter** *n* [grandoter] cucu (perempuan); **grandfather** *n* kakék; ~ *clock* jam dentang besar; **grandma** *n, sl* nénék; nék; **grandmother** *n* [grandmather] nénék; **grandpa** *n, sl* kakék; kék; **grandparents** *n, pl* kakék nénék; **grandson** *n* [grandsan] cucu (lelaki); **granny** *n* nénék, perempuan tua

grandly *adv* dengan méwah; dengan sombong ← **grand**

grandstand *n* tribun

granite *n, adj* [granit] granit

granny *n* nenek, perempuan tua ← **grandmother**

grant *n* (dana) pemberian, sumbangan, subsidi, béasiswa; *vt* memberi, menganugerahkan; ~ *a prayer,* ~ *a wish* mengabulkan doa, mengizinkan; *taken for* ~*ed* dianggap sudah begitu

granular *n* berupa butiran atau biji-bijian ← **grain**

grape *n* buah anggur; *sour* ~*s* sikap tidak sportif; *adj* (rasa) anggur; **grapefruit** *n* [grépfrut] semacam jeruk kuning yang besar; *pink* ~ jeruk bali; **grapevine** *n* tanaman anggur; *to hear it on the* ~ mendengar kabar burung

graph *n* grafik; **graphic** *adj* grafik, bergambar, jelas; ~ *artist* pelukis grafis; **graphically** *adv* secara grafis, secara gamblang

grapple *vi* [grapel] bergulat; *Shannon is busy grappling with his maths homework* Shannon tengah sibuk bergulat dengan PR matématika

grasp *n* genggaman, pegangan; *vt* memegang, menggenggam, menangkap, mengerti

grass *n* rumput; **grasshopper** *n* belalang; **grassy** *adj* berumput

grate *n* tutup riol, kisi

grate *vi* mengganggu; *his loud voice* ~*d on me* saya terganggu oléh suaranya yang keras; *vt* memarut; **grater** *n* parutan; **grating** *n* riol, kisi; *adj* kasar, mengganggu

grateful *n* berterima kasih; **gratitude** *n* [gratityud] rasa terima kasih, rasa syukur

grater *n* parut ← **grate**

gratis *adj* [gratis] cuma-cuma, gratis

gratitude *n* [gratityud] rasa terima kasih, rasa syukur; *to express one's* ~ mengungkapkan (rasa) terima kasih

gratuitous *adj* [gratyuitus] tidak perlu; **gratuity** *n* persénan

grave *adj* berat, genting, gawat, sérius

grave *n* kuburan, makam; ~ *digger* penggali kubur; **gravestone** *n* batu nisan; **graveyard** *n* kuburan; ~ *shift* jam kerja malam

gravel *n* [gravel] batu kerikil; **gravelly** ~ *voice* suara serak-serak

gravestone *n* batu nisan ← **grave**

graveyard *n* kuburan; ~ *shift* jam kerja malam ← **grave**

gravitate *vi* [gravitét] condong, cenderung; mengendap; *Australia is now gravitating more towards Asia* Australia sekarang cenderung bergabung dengan Asia; **gravitation** *n* gravitasi; kecenderungan; **gravitational** *adj* berkaitan dengan daya tarik bumi; **gravity** *n* daya tarik bumi, gaya berat; kegawatan, kegentingan; *specific* ~ berat jenis

gravy *n* [grévi] saus atau kuah daging

gray *adj* grey (warna) abu-abu, kelabu; suram; ~-*haired* beruban; ~ *area* sesuatu yang kurang jelas (hitam putihnya); ~ *matter* sél-sél otak; *a* ~ *day* hari yang sedih; *a* ~ *hair* uban; **grayhound** *n* anjing pacu; ~ *racing* pacuan anjing; **grayish** *adj* keabu-abuan

graze *n, vi* lécét; *Shane* ~*d his knee* lututnya Shane lécét

graze *vi* makan rumput; **grazier** *n* petani sapi atau domba

grease *n* [gris] gemuk, minyak; ~*proof paper* kertas tahan air; *v* [griz] memberi gemuk, meminyaki; ~ *monkey* montir; *elbow* ~ kerja keras; **greasy** *adj* [grizi] berlemak, berminyak; bermanis mulut

great *adj* [grét] besar, agung, mulia, raya; ~ *Britain* Inggris Raya, Britania Raya; ~ *Dane* sejenis anjing besar;

greatness *n* kebesaran, keagungan, kemuliaan

great-aunt *n* nénék; **great-grandchild** *n* cicit; **great-granddaughter** *n* cicit (perempuan); **great-grandfather** *n* kakék buyut; **great-grandmother** *n* nénék buyut; **great-grandson** *n* cicit (lelaki); *~-uncle* kakék

greatness *n* kebesaran, keagungan, kemuliaan ← **great**

Greece *n* Yunani; *Ancient ~* Yunani Kuno; **Greek** *n* bahasa Yunani; orang Yunani; *adj* berasal dari Yunani

greed *n* kerakusan, ketamakan; **greedy** *adj* rakus, tamak, loba

Greek *n* bahasa Yunani; orang Yunani; *it's all ~ to me* saya tidak mengerti; *adj* berasal dari Yunani ← **Greece**

green *adj* hijau; mentah; baru, muda; ramah lingkungan; *~ finger* kemampuan berkebun atau memelihara tanaman; *~ light* lampu hijau; izin; *~ tea* téh hijau; *dark ~* hijau tua; *light ~* hijau muda; *the ~ room* ruang tunggu sebelum naik ke atas panggung; *~ with envy* sangat iri; **greenback** *n* dolar AS; **green-eyed** *adj* bermata hijau; *the ~ monster* rasa cemburu, kecemburuan; **greengrocer** *n* tukang sayur; toko sayur; **greenhorn** *n* orang yang masih baru, pemula; **greenhouse** *n* rumah kaca; *~ effect* éfék rumah kaca, pemanasan bumi; *~ gas* gas yang ikut memperparah éfék rumah kaca; **greenish** *adj* kehijau-hijauan; **greens** *n, pl* sayuran, sayur-mayur; partai hijau, partai peduli lingkungan

Greenwich Mean Time (GMT) *n* [grénic] waktu GMT

greet *vt* memberi salam, menegur, menyambut; *meet and ~* acara ramah tamah; **greeting** *n* salam, ucapan selamat; *~ card* kartu ucapan; *~ from* salam dari; *season's ~s* Selamat (Hari Natal)

gregarious *adj* [gregérius] ramah, mempunyai banyak kawan

gremlin *n* makhluk kecil yang merusak

Grenada *n* [grenéda] Grenada; **Grenadian** *n* [grenédian] orang

Grenada; *adj* berasal dari Grenada

grenade *n* granat

grew *v, pf* → **grow**

grey → **gray**

grid *n* jaringan; *~ reference* rujukan (kisi); *electricity ~* jaringan listrik

gridiron *n* [gridairon] sépak bola Amérika

grief *n* kesedihan, duka cita; **grieve** *vi* menangisi, meratapi; *Pakistan is still grieving for Benazir Bhutto* negara Pakistan masih menangisi kepergiannya Benazir Bhutto

grievous *adj* berat, menyakitkan; *~ bodily harm (GBH)* terluka berat (oléh penjahat)

grill *n* pemanggangan; kisi-kisi; *vt* memanggang; memeriksa; **griller** *n* pemanggangan (di kompor)

grim *adj* seram

grime *n* kotoran, daki; **grimy** *adj* kotor

grin *n* senyum, seringai; *vt* tersenyum, menyeringai; *he ~ned at his friends* dia tersenyum di depan kawan-kawannya

grind *n* [graind] pengalaman yang susah, kesusahan; *vt* **ground ground** menggerinda, menggiling, mengasah; *~ your teeth* mengertakkan gigi; **grinder** *n* gerinda; **grindstone** *n* batu gerinda, batu pengasah; *keep your nose to the ~* bekerja keras, membanting tulang

grip *n* pegangan, genggaman; *get a ~ on yourself!* kendalikan diri!; *vt* memegang, menggenggam; *to come to ~s with* bergulat dengan, membiasakan diri dengan; **gripping** *adj* menegangkan, mengasyikkan

grisly *adj* berdarah, menjijikkan

gristle *n* [grissel] tulang muda

grit *n* kerikil, pasir; kenekatan; **gritty** *adj* berpasir; dengan unsur nékat

grizzle *v* [grizel] mengadu, réwél, céngéng

grizzled *adj* beruban

grizzly *~ bear* sejenis beruang

groan *n* keluh, erang; *vi* berkeluh, mengeluh, mengerang

grocer *n* penjual bahan makanan; **grocery** *n* toko bahan makanan; **groceries** *n, pl* bahan makanan

grog *n, sl* minuman keras; **groggy** *adj* grogi, pusing

groin *n* selangkangan, lipat paha

groom *n (bride)~* mempelai pria, pengantin pria, calon suami; **groomsman** *n* pendamping mempelai pria

groom *n* pengasuh kuda; *vt* memelihara penampilan, merias; **grooming** *n* penampilan

groove *n* alur; gaya; **groovy** *adj* bergaya

grope *vi ~ for* merogoh; *vt* meraba-raba; *Karin was ~d crossing the street last night* badan Karin diraba-raba saat dia menyeberang jalan tadi malam

gross *n* gros, 12 lusin, 144; *adj* kotor; jorok; sangat gemuk; *~ salary* gaji kotor; *~ national product (GNP)* penghasilan kotor nasional

grotto *n* gua

ground *vt, pf* → **grind**

ground *n* [graund] tanah, bumi; *~ floor* lantai dasar; *below ~* di bawah tanah; *home ~* lapangan sendiri, kandang sendiri; *vt* mendasarkan; melarang (pergi); *well ~ed* beralasan; **groundless** *adj* tidak beralasan; **grounds** *n, pl* pekarangan, taman; alasan; *coffee ~* ampas kopi; *on the ~ of* berdasarkan

group *n* [grup] kelompok, grup; *vt* mengelompokkan; *Stuart ~ed the students according to age* Stuart mengelompokkan murid-murid menurut umur

grow *v* [gro] **grew grown** *vi* tumbuh; bertambah; menjadi; *~ out of* tidak muat lagi; *babies quickly ~ out of their clothes* baju bayi sudah cepat tidak muat lagi; *vt* menanam; *~ up* jadi besar, tumbuh; **grown-up** *adj* déwasa, sudah besar; **growth** *n* pertumbuhan, pertambahan; bénjolan

growl *n* [graul] geram; *vi* menggeram

grown *v, pf* → **grow**

growth *n* pertumbuhan, pertambahan; bénjolan ← **grow**

grub *n* tempayak; *sl* makanan; **grubby** *adj* kotor

grudge *n* dendam; *to bear a ~, have a ~* menaruh dendam; **grudgingly** *adv* dengan segan-segan, ogah-ogahan

gruesome *adj* [grusam] mengerikan, berdarah

gruff *adj* kasar, péndék; **gruffly** *adv* secara péndék

grumble *n* [grambel] keluhan; *vi* bersungut-sungut, menggerutu

grumpy *adj* mengomél, marah-marah

grunt *n* dengkur; *v* mengeluarkan bunyi dengkur

G-string *n* celana dalam tali

guano *n* [guano] pupuk dari kotoran burung

guarantee *n* [garanti] jaminan; *vt* menjamin, menanggung; **guaranteed** *adj* terjamin, dijamin

guard *n* [gard] jaga, pengawal; kondéktur; *~ dog* anjing penjaga; *on ~, to stand ~* menjaga; *v* menjaga, mengawal; **guarded** *adj* terjaga, hati-hati; **guardian** *n* wali, orang tua asuh; penjaga; *~ angel* malaikat pelindung

Guatemala *n* [gwatemala] Guatemala; **Guatemalan** *n* orang Guatemala; *adj* berasal dari Guatemala

guava *n* [gwava] jambu

gubernatorial *adj* berkaitan dengan gubernur ← **governor**

guerilla, guerrilla *n, adj* gerilya, gerilyawan

guess *n* [gés] tebakan, terkaan, sangkaan; *vt* menebak, menerka; *~ what?* coba tebak!; *anyone's ~* siapa tahu; *at a ~* kira-kira

guest *n* [gést] tamu; *~ room* kamar (tidur untuk) tamu; *~ worker* pekerja asing; **guesthouse** *n* losmén, hotél kecil;

guidance *n* [gaidans] pimpinan, tuntunan, bimbingan; **guide** *n* (buku) pemandu, pembimbing; *~ dog* anjing pemandu; *Girl ~, Girl Scout* pramuka remaja putri; *vt* membimbing, memandu; *~d missile* peluru kendali (rudal); **guidebook** *n* buku petunjuk, buku panduan; **guideline** *n* pedoman

guilder *n, arch* [gilder] gulden

guillotine *n* [gilotin] alat pemenggal kepala

guilt *n* [gilt] kesalahan, rasa bersalah; *~ free* tanpa rasa bersalah; **guilty** *adj* bersalah; *he has a ~ conscience* dia merasa bersalah

Guinea *n* [gini] Guinea; *~-Bissau* Guinea-Bissau; *Equatorial ~* Guinea Katulistiwa; **Guinean** *n* orang Guinea; *adj* berasal dari Guinea

guinea *~ fowl* ayam mutiara; *~ pig* marmot; kelinci percobaan

guitar *n* gitar; *bass ~* gitar bas; *electric ~* gitar listrik; **guitarist** *n* pemain gitar

gulf *n* teluk besar; jurang; *the (Persian) ~* kawasan Teluk (Persia)

gull *n (sea)~* burung camar

gullet *n* kerongkongan

gullible *adj* lekas percaya, mudah tertipu

gully *n* jurang

gulp *n* teguk; *v* meneguk, menelan

gum *n* getah; *~ tree* pohon kayu putih; *chewing ~* permén karét; **gumboot** *n* sepatu karét

gum *n* gusi; **gummy** *adj* ompong

gun *n* bedil, senapan, revolver, pistol; *vi ~ down* menémbak; **gunboat** *n* kapal meriam; **gunman** *n* orang bersenjata; **gunpowder** *n* mesiu; **gunrunner** *n* penyelendup senjata, pedagang senjata

gurgle *vi* [gergel] berdeguk, mendeguk

gush *n* pancaran, semburan; *vi* memancar, mengalir dengan deras; memuji-muji secara berlebihan

gust *n* hembusan angin; **gusty** *adj* berangin

gusto *n* cita rasa; semangat, kesukaan

gusty *adj* berangin ← **gust**

gut *n* usus; **guts** *n, pl* nyali, keberanian; *they hate my ~* meréka sangat membenci saya; **gutsy** *adj* berani

gutter *n* parit, selokan

guy *n, sl* [gai] orang, lelaki, cowok; *good ~* orang baik

Guyana *n* [gaiyana] Guyana; *French ~* Guyana Perancis; **Guyanese** *n* orang Guyana; *adj* berasal dari Guyana

guzzle *vt* [gazel] makan dengan rakus; *gas ~r* mobil yang boros bénsin

gym *n* [jim] aula, tempat senam; pusat kebugaran; **gymnasium** *n* aula, tempat senam, gimnasium; **gymnast** *n* pesenam; **gymnastics** *n* senam

gynecologist *n* **gynaecologist** [gainekolojist] ginékolog; **gynecology** *n* ginékologi

gypsum *n* [jipsem] gipsum

gypsy, gipsy *n* [jipsi] nomaden, gipsi; *Sea ~* orang Bajau

H

haberdashery *n, arch* [haberdasyeri] toko peralatan menjahit

habit *n* kebiasaan; *bad ~* kebiasaan buruk; *force of ~* karena biasa; *to kick the ~* berhenti merokok; **habitat** *n* tempat tinggal, lingkungan; **habitual** *adj* biasa, sehari-hari; **habitually** *adv* biasanya

hack *vt* memotong-motong, mencincang; *~ into* memasuki jaringan komputer; *they ~ed their way through the forest* meréka memotong jalan di hutan; **hacker** *n* orang yang memasuki jaringan komputer; **hacksaw** *n* gergaji besi

had *vt, pf* → **have**

hadn't *vt, pf, neg* tidak ada ← **had not**; → **have**

haemorrhage → **hemorrhage**

haemorrhoid → **hemorrhoid**

haggard *adj* kurus, ceking; tidak terawat

haggis *n* [hagis] makanan khas Skotlandia, dibuat dari jeroan domba

haggle *vi* [hagel] tawar-menawar; *the two women ~d over the price of bananas* dua wanita itu tawar-menawar harga pisang

Hague [hég] *the ~* Den Haag

hail *n, vi* hujan és; **hailstone** *n* hujan és

hail *n* salam, hormat; *vi ~ from* berasal dari; *Laura ~s from Melbourne* Laura berasal dari Melbourne; *vt* memberi salam

hair *n* rambut, bulu; *~-raising* mengerikan, menakutkan; *~ gel* gél rambut; *~ pin* tusuk konde; *~ tie* ikat rambut; *black-~ed* berambut hitam; *blonde ~* rambut pirang; *body ~* bulu; *to have ~* berambut; *to brush one's ~* menyikat rambut; *to comb one's* ~ menyisir rambut; *to wash one's* ~ keramas, mencuci rambut; *to have one's* ~ *cut* potong rambut; **hairband** *n* bando; **hairbrush** *n* sikat rambut; **haircut** *n* potong rambut; **hairdo** *n, sl* [hérdu] rias rambut, tata rambut; **hairdresser** *n* penata rambut, potong rambut; **hairdryer** *n* pengering rambut; **hairpiece** *n* rambut palsu; **hairpin** *n* arnal; ~ *bend* bélokan tajam; **hairspray** *n* semprot rambut; **hairstyle** *n* gaya rambut; **hairy** *adj* berbulu

Haiti *n* [héti] Haiti; **Haitian** *n* [hésyen] orang Haiti; *adj* berasal dari Haiti

haj *n* naik haji; *to go on the* ~ naik haji

half *n* [haf] **halves** *adj* setengah, separuh; ~*-baked* setengah matang, tidak masuk akal; ~*-blood* berdarah campuran, peranakan; ~*-hearted* setengah hati; ~*-price* separuh harga; ~*-sister* adik atau kakak tiri; ~*-term* liburan tengah caturwulan; ~ *time* istirahat (dalam pertandingan); ~ *a dozen* setengah lusin; ~ *past three* (jam) setengah empat; *to cut in* ~ membelah, membagi dua; *two and a* ~ dua setengah; **halfway** *adj* setengah jalan; ~ *house* rumah singgah; **halve** *vi* [hav] berkurang menjadi separuh; *vt* membagi dua

hall *n* [hol] aula, balai, ruang; lorong, koridor; *concert* ~ gedung konsér, gedung pertunjukan; ~ *of residence* asrama mahasiswa; **hallmark** *n* cap; **hallway** *n* lorong, koridor

hallo → **hello**

Hallowe'en *n* malam 31 Oktober

hallucinate *vi* berhalusinasi; **hallucination** *n* khayal, halusinasi

hallway *n* lorong, koridor ← **hall**

halo *n* [hélo] lingkaran cahaya di sekitar kepala

halt *n* [holt] pemberhentian; *to come to a* ~ berhenti, terhenti; *vi* berhenti; *vt* memberhentikan; **halting** *adj* terpatah-patah; *she speaks* ~ *French* dia berbahasa Perancis secara terpatah-patah

halter *n* [holter] tali léhér; ~*-neck* baju dengan tali di léhér

halve *v* [hav] membagi dua ← **half**

ham *n* irisan daging babi; ~*-fisted* secara kasar, secara salah;

hamburger *n* burger

hamlet *n* dusun

hammer *n* palu; ~ *and sickle* palu arit; *vt* memalu, memukul

hammock *n* tempat tidur gantung

hamper *n* bakul, keranjang

hamper *vt* menghambat; *the heavy rain* ~*ed their efforts* usaha meréka terhambat oléh hujan deras

hamster *n* marmut

hand *n* tangan; jarum (jam); ~*-in-glove* bekerja sama; ~*-me-down* pakaian lungsuran; ~ *out* membagi-bagikan; ~*s free* tangan bébas; ~*s off* jangan ikut campur, jangan disentuh; ~*s up* angkat tangan; ~ *towel* lap; *old* ~ orang lama, orang berpengalaman; *on* ~ hadir, tersedia; ~ *in* ~ bergandéngan tangan; *on the other* ~ di lain pihak; *to lend a* ~, *to give a* ~ menolong, membantu; *vt* memberi, menyampaikan; ~ *in* menyerahkan; ~ *out* membagikan; ~ *over* menyerahkan; **handbag** *n* tas tangan; **handball** *n* bola tangan; **handbook** *n* buku panduan, pedoman; **handbrake** *n* rém tangan; **handcuff** *n* belenggu, borgol; *vt* memborgol, membelenggu; **handful** *n* segenggam; **handicraft** *n* kerajinan tangan; **handkerchief** *n* sapu tangan; **handle** *n* [handel] pegangan; *vt* menangani, memegang; **handlebar** *n* setang; **handling** *n* penanganan, perlakuan; **handmade** *adj* buatan tangan; **handover** *n* penyerahan; **handset** *n* gagang télépon; **handshake** *n* jabatan tangan; **handwriting** *n* [handraiting] tulisan tangan; **handy** *adj* berguna, praktis; **handyman** *n* tukang

handicap *n* rintangan, cacat; **handicapped** *adj* cacat

handicraft *n* kerajinan tangan ← **hand**

handkerchief *n* sapu tangan ← **hand**

handle *n* [handel] pegangan; *vt* menangani, memegang; **handlebar** *n* setang; **handling** *n* penanganan, perlakuan ← **hand** handmade *adj* buatan tangan ← **hand**

handphone → **phone**

handsome *adj* [handsam] ganteng, tampan

handwriting *n* [handraiting] tulisan tangan ← **hand**

handy *adj* berguna, praktis; **handyman** *n* tukang ← **hand**

hang *v* **hung hung** *vi* bergantung; ~ *around* nongkrong; ~ *back* menunggu; tinggal; ~ *on* menunggu; ~ *out* menonjol; nongkrong; ~ *up* memutuskan sambungan télépon; ~*up* masalah; *to get the* ~ *of* mengerti; *vt* menggantung; **hanger** *n* gantungan; *clothes* ~ gantungan baju; **hang-glider** *n* gantole; **hangman** *n* algojo; **hangout** *n* tempat tongkrongan; **hangover** *n* tidak énak badan setelah banyak minum

hangar *n* hanggar, bangsal

hangman *n* algojo ← **hang**

hangout *n* tempat tongkrongan ← **hang**

hangover *n* tidak énak badan setelah banyak minum ← **hang**

happen *vi* terjadi; *as it* ~*s* kebetulan; **happening** *n* kejadian, peristiwa

happily *adv* dengan senang hati; **happiness** *n* kebahagiaan; **happy** *adj* bahagia, berbahagia, senang; ~*go-lucky* santai; ~ *anniversary*, ~ *birthday* selamat ulang tahun; ~ *hour* jam minuman keras dijual murah; ~ *with* puas dengan

harass *vt* mengganggu, mengusik; **harassment** *n* gangguan; *sexual* ~ pelécéhan séksual

harbor, harbour *n* [harber] pelabuhan; **harbormaster** *n* syahbandar, kepala pelabuhan; *vt* menyembunyikan, menyimpan

hard *adj* keras; susah, sulit; *adv* dengan rajin; ~*hearted* keras hati; ~*working* rajin; ~ *cash* uang tunai; ~ *copy* di atas kertas; ~ *currency* mata uang yang kuat; ~ *labor* kerja paksa; ~ *shoulder* bahu jalan; ~ *up* tidak punya uang banyak; ~ *work* kerja keras; ~ *of hearing* agak tuli; **hardback** *n* buku sampul keras; **harden** *vi* mengeras; *vt* mengeraskan, menguatkan; **hardened** *adj* tegar; **hardship** *n* kesusahan, kekurangan, penderitaan; **hardware** *n*

alat-alat pertukangan; peranti keras; **hardy** *adj* bertahan, awét

hardly *adv* nyaris tidak, hampir tidak; ~ *ever* jarang sekali

hardship *n* kesusahan, kekurangan, penderitaan ← **hard**

hardware *n* alat-alat pertukangan; peranti keras ← **hard**

hardy *adj* bertahan, awét ← **hard**

hare *n* kelinci besar; ~*-brained idea* pikiran gila; **harelip** *n* bibir sumbing

harm *n* bahaya; kerugian, kerusakan, kejahatan; *no* ~ *done* tidak apa-apa; *to come to* ~ celaka; *vt* merusak, mengganggu; **harmful** *adj* membahayakan, merusak, merugikan; **harmless** *adj* tidak jahat

harmonica *n* harmonika

harmonious *adj* selaras, serasi, sepadan, harmonis; **harmony** *n* keselarasan, kerukunan, kecocokan; *in* ~ harmonis, dalam damai

harness *n* tali pengaman, tali keselamatan; pakaian kuda; *vt* memasang; memanfaatkan; ~ *wind energy* memanfaatkan tenaga angin

harp *n* harpa; **harpist** *n* pemain harpa

harsh *adj* kasar, keras hati; tidak ramah; **harshness** *n* kekasaran, kekerasan

harvest *n* (hasil) panén; *vt* memanén, memotong (padi)

has → **have**; **has-been** *n* orang yang ketinggalan zaman, sudah tidak terkenal lagi

hash *n* pagar [#]

hasn't *v, pf, neg* tidak ada ← **has not**; → **has**

hassle *n* [hasel] répot; *vt* mengganggu, mendesak; *he keeps hassling me to lend him money* dia tetap mendesak saya agar meminjamkan uang

haste *n* [hést] perbuatan tergesa-gesa, kegopohan; *more* ~ *less speed* terlalu cepat jadi lambat; **hasten** *vi* [hésen] cepat-cepat; *vt* mempercepat; **hasty** *adj* tergesa-gesa, tergopoh-gopoh

hat *n* topi; *to take your* ~ *off to* mengangkat topi terhadap; *to wear many* ~*s* merangkap

hatch *n* pintu kecil

hatch *vi* menetas; *vt* menetaskan;
  hatchback *n* mobil kodok
hatchet *n* kapak; *to bury the* ~ berdamai
hate *n* kebencian, rasa benci; *vt* membenci; **hateful** *adj* membangkitkan
  benci; **hatred** *n* [hétred] kebencian,
  rasa benci
haughty *adj* [hoti] sombong, angkuh
haul *n* hasil tangkapan; muatan; *long-~*
  flight penerbangan jarak jauh; *vt* menarik, menghéla
haunt *n* tempat yang sering dikunjungi;
  vt menghantui; **haunted** *adj* dihantui;
  ~ *house* rumah hantu; **haunting** *adj*
  menghantui, sering teringat
have *vi, aux* [hav] **had had** sudah; *I* ~
  eaten saya sudah makan; *vt* mempunyai, memiliki; ada; mendapat;
  menyuruh; ~ *it* mengerti; ~ *lunch*
  makan siang; ~ *on* memakai, berpakaian; ~ *to* harus, terpaksa; ~ *a shower*
  mandi; ~ *a tooth out* gigi dicabut (oléh
  dokter); ~ *one's hair cut* potong rambut; *the* ~*s and the* ~*nots* si kaya
  dan si miskin; *Patricia will* ~ *a coffee*
  Patricia memesan kopi
haven n pelabuhan, tempat berlindung
haven't *vi, pf, neg* ← **have not**; → **have**
havoc *n* [havek] kerusakan
hawk *n* burung elang
hawk *vt* berjualan, menjajakan; **hawker**
  n penjaja, pedagang kaki lima; ~ *center*
  pujaséra, tempat pedagang kaki lima
hay *n* rumput kering, jerami; ~ *fever*
  alérgi rumput; ~ *stack* tumpukan
  rumput kering
hazard *n* bahaya, risiko; ~ *lights* lampu
  darurat; *health* ~ membahayakan
  keséhatan; **hazardous** *adj* berbahaya
haze *n* kabut, asap; **hazy** *adj* berkabut;
  tidak jelas
hazel *adj* warna mata yang hijau kecoklatan; **hazelnut** *n* semacam buah kemiri
hazy *adj* berkabut; tidak jelas ← **haze**
he *pron, m* [hi] dia, ia (subyék); **He** *pron*
  Dia, Tuhan; **him** *pron, m* dia, ia (obyék);
  himself *pron* dirinya, sendiri; *by* ~
  sendiri; **his** *pron, m* -nya (kepunyaan)
head *n* [héd] kepala; pemimpin, diréktur, ketua; puncak; ~*dress* hiasan

kepala; ~*first* kepala terlebih dahulu;
langsung; ~*hunter* pengayau; pencari
bakat; ~ *office* kantor pusat; ~ *start*
mulai lebih awal; ~*s or tails* permainan atas atau bawah dengan keping
logam; ~ *teacher* guru kepala; ~ *over*
heels kepala terlebih dahulu; tergila-
gila; *Rp 60.000 a* ~ 60,000 rupiah
per orang; *section* ~ kepala bagian
(kabag); *vt* mengepalai, memimpin;
menyundul (bola); ~ *for* menuju;
headache *n* [hédék] sakit kepala, pusing; **headband** *n* ikat kepala; **headbutt** *n* serudukan; *vt* menyeruduk;
heading *n* judul (karangan); **headland**
n tanjung; **headlights** *n, pl* [hédlaits]
lampu depan (mobil); **headline** *n*
kepala berita; **headlong** *adj* tunggang
langgang; **headmaster** *n, arch, m*
headmistress *f* kepala sekolah; **headquarters** *n* [hédkorters] markas besar;
headscarf *n* kerudung; **headstone**
n batu nisan; **headstrong** *adj* keras
kepala; **headway** *n* kemajuan; **heady**
adj memabukkan, gegabah
heal *vi* menjadi séhat, sembuh; *vt*
menyembuhkan, menyéhatkan; **healer**
n dukun, sinsé; **health** *n* keséhatan; ~
center klinik; *in good* ~ séhat walafiat;
healthy *adj* séhat
heap *n* timbunan, tumpukan, susunan; *v*
menimbun; ~ *praise on* memuji;
heaps *adj, coll* banyak; *adv* jauh,
sangat; *there's* ~ *of cakes left* kué
masih ada banyak
hear *v* **heard heard** [hérd] mendengar;
~ *from* mendapat kabar dari; ~ *of*
mendengar tentang; mengetahui; ~ *out*
mendengarkan sampai selesai; **hearing** *n* (indera) pendengaran; sidang; ~
aid alat bantu dengar
hearse *n* [hérs] mobil atau keréta mayat
heart *n* [hart] jantung; hati, inti; ~*rend-
ing* yang mengiris hati; ~*shaped*
berbentuk hati; ~*throb* idola; ~*warming* menyentuh, menggembirakan; ~
attack serangan jantung; ~ *disease*
sakit jantung; *by* ~ hafal; ~ *of gold*
berhati baik; ~ *of stone* tidak berhati,
tidak mempunyai hati; *change of* ~

perubahan pikiran; *cross my ~*
bersumpah; *to lose ~* putus asa; *to
take ~* mendapat semangat, mengambil hikmah; **heartbeat** *n* denyut jantung; **heartbreak** *n* [hartbrék] **heart-
broken** *adj* patah hati; **heartburn** *n*
panas dalam; **hearten** *vt* membesarkan
hati; **heartily** *adv* sungguh-sungguh,
dengan semangat; **heartless** *adj* tidak
punya perasaan, tidak punya hati;
hearty *adj* sungguh-sungguh, dengan
semangat
heat *n* panas, kepanasan, hangat; bagian
dari balapan; *dry ~* panas terik; *in ~*
musim kawin; *vt* memanaskan, menghangatkan; *~ up* memanas; memanaskan; **heated** *adj* panas; **heater, heating** *n* alat pemanas; **heatstroke** *n* sakit
panas karena kelamaan di bawah sinar
matahari; **heatwave** *n* berhari-hari
cuaca panas
heathen *adj* kafir, penyembah berhala
heating *n* alat pemanas ← **heat**
heatstroke *n* sakit panas karena kelamaan di bawah sinar matahari ← **heat**
heatwave *n* berhari-hari cuaca panas
← **heat**
heave *vt* mengangkat; *~ a sigh of relief*
menarik nafas karena lega
heaven *n* [héven] surga; *to go to ~* masuk
surga; **heavens** *n, pl* langit; *ejac*
masya Allah; *for ~'s sake* demi Allah;
heavenly *adj* sangat menyenangkan
heavily *adv* dengan berat; deras; *it rained
~ just now* tadi hujan deras; **heavy** *adj*
[hévi] berat, berbobot; *~ rain* hujan
lebat; *a ~ smoker* perokok berat
Hebrew *n* [hibru] bahasa Ibrani; *arch*
orang Ibrani
hectare *n* [héktér] héktar
hectic *adj* sibuk, ramai, hiruk-pikuk
hedge *n* pagar hidup; *vi* mengelak dari
memberi jawaban
hedgehog *n* landak
heed *n* perhatian; *to pay ~ to, to take ~
of* mengindahkan
heel *n* tumit; hak; *high ~s* sepatu hak
tinggi; *vi* mengikuti, menuruti
hefty *adj* (berbadan) besar
height *n* [hait] ketinggian; tinggi badan;

puncak; **heighten** *vi* memuncak,
menambah
heir *n* [ér] **heiress** *f* ahli waris; **heirloom**
n harta pusaka
held *vt, pf* → **hold**
helicopter *n* hélikopter, héli; **helipad** *n*
landasan hélikopter; **heliport** *n*
lapangan hélikopter
helium *n* [hilium] hélium
hell *n* neraka; *ejac* persétan, celaka; *~
bent* nekat; *go to ~* masuk neraka; *to ~
with it* persétan; *a ~ of a match* pertandingan yang seru; **hellish** *adj*
seperti neraka
hello, hallo *ejac* halo; apa kabar?
helm *n* kemudi; **helmsman** *n* juru mudi
helmet *n* helm
helmsman *n* juru mudi ← **helm**
help *n* pertolongan, bantuan; *a great ~*
sangat menolong; *v* menolong, membantu; *please ~ yourself* silahkan; *it
can't be ~ed* apa boléh buat; **helpful**
adj suka menolong; berguna; **helpless**
adj tidak berdaya
hem *n* kelim; *vt* mengelim
hemisphere *n* [hémisfir] belahan (bumi);
Southern ~ belahan bumi bagian Selatan;
the left ~ of the brain otak bagian kiri
hemorrhage *n* **haemorrhage** [hémerej]
perdarahan, pendarahan; *vi* berdarah
hemorrhoid *n* **haemorrhoid** [hémeroid]
wasir, ambéien
hemp *n* ganja
hen *n, f* ayam betina; *~ party, ~'s night*
pésta untuk calon pengantin perem-
puan dan kawan-kawan perempuan-
nya; **henhouse** *n* kandang ayam; **hen-
pecked** *adj* dikuasai isteri
hence *adv* maka; dari sini; **henceforth**
adv mulai sekarang
henhouse *n* kandang ayam ← **hen**
henna *n* inai, pacar
hepatitis *n* [hépataitis] hépatitis, radang
hati, sakit kuning
heptagon *n* segi tujuh
her *pron, f* -nya (kepunyaan); dia, ia
(obyék); **hers** *pron, f* miliknya; **herself**
pron dirinya, sendiri; *by ~* sendiri
herald *n* bentara, pelopor; *vt* memberi
tahu, memaklumkan

herb *n* hérba, jamu, bumbu; *pl* ramuan bumbu; **herbal** *adj* terbuat dari hérba atau ramuan jamu; **herbivore** *n* [hér-bivor] pemakan tumbuh-tumbuhan, *lit* lataboga; **herbivorous** *adj* memakan tumbuh-tumbuhan

herd *n* kawanan; *vt* menggembala

here *adv* di sini; *come* ~ (ke) sini; ~ *and there* di sana-sini; ~ *she is* ini dia; *Eileen lives* ~ Eileen tinggal di sini; ~ *is my card* ini kartu nama saya; **here-after** *the* ~ dunia akhirat; **hereby** *adv* dengan ini, bersama ini

hereditary *adj* [heréditeri] turun-temu-run, génétik; **heredity** *n* keturunan

herewith *adv* [hirwith] dengan ini, bersama ini ← **here**

heritage *n* [héritej] warisan, harta pusa-ka; ~ *building* bangunan bersejarah

hermit *n* petapa; **hermitage** *n* [hermitej] pertapaan

hernia *n* burut

hero *n* [hiro] pahlawan; **heroic** *adj* seperti pahlawan, héroik, berani; **heroine** *n, f* [héroin] pahlawan (wani-ta); **heroism** *n* kepahlawanan

heroin *n* [héroin] héroin, putau; ~ *addict* pecandu héroin

heroine *n, f* [héroin] pahlawan (wanita); **heroism** *n* kepahlawanan ← **hero**

heron *n* burung bangau

herring *n* ikan haring

hers *pron, f* miliknya; **herself** *pron* dirinya, sendiri; *by* ~ sendiri ← **her**

hesitancy *n* keraguan; **hesitant** *adj* **hesitate** *vi* ragu-ragu, bimbang; *I* ~ *to leave the baby at home* saya ragu-ragu meninggalkan bayi di rumah; **hesita-tion** *n* keraguan, kebimbangan

heterosexual *n* **hetero** *sl* hétéroséksual, orang yang suka lawan jenis

hexagon *n* segi enam; **hexagonal** *adj* berbentuk segi enam

hey *ejac* hé, oi

heyday *n* zaman emas

hi *ejac, coll* hai

hibernate *vi* **hibernation** *n* tidur selama musim dingin

hibiscus *n* [haibiskus] bunga sepatu

hiccup, hiccough *n* cegukan, sedu; *vi* cegukan, bersedu

hid, hidden *v, pf* → **hide**; **hidden** *adj* terpendam, tersembunyi

hide *n* kulit (binatang)

hide *v* **hid hidden** *vi* bersembunyi, berlindung, mengumpet; *vt* menyem-bunyikan; ~*-and-seek* petak umpet, sembunyi-sembunyian; **hideaway** *n* tempat persembunyian; **hid-ing** *n* persembunyian; *in* ~ bersembu-nyi; ~ *place* tempat sembunyi, tempat berlindung

hideous *adj* [hidius] mengerikan

hideout *n* [haidaut] tempat persembu-nyian ← **hide**

hiding *n* persembunyian; *in* ~ bersem-bunyi; ~ *place* tempat sembunyi, tempat berlindung ← **hide**

hierarchy *n* [haierarki] susunan, hiérarki

hi-fi *n* [hai fai] radio kompo (dengan suara berkualitas tinggi) ← **high fidelity**

high *adj* [hai] tinggi, mulia; mabuk; ~ *class* kelas satu; ~*-handed* angkuh, otoritér; ~*-pitched* nyaring; ~*-rise* ber-tingkat tinggi; ~*-spirited* bersemangat; ~ *chair* kursi tinggi tempat bayi makan; ~ *court* pengadilan tinggi; ~ *heels* (sepatu) hak tinggi; ~ *jump* lon-cat tinggi; ~ *life* cara hidup kaum atas; ~ *noon* tengah hari, jam 12 siang; ~ *school* sekolah menengah (atas); ~ *tide* air pasang; ~ *and low* di mana-mana; *on a* ~ sedang bahagia; *on your* ~ *horse* sombong; *(the)* ~ *street* jalan utama; *the* ~ *seas* laut lepas; **high-brow** cendekiawan; **higher** *adj* lebih tinggi; ~ *education* pendidikan tinggi; **highlands** *n* tanah tinggi, pegunu-ngan; **highlight** *n* puncak; **highlighter** *n* stabilo; **highly** *adj* tinggi; sangat; **highness** Your ~ Yang Mulia; **high-way** *n* jalan raya, jalan besar

hijack *vt* membajak; **hijacker** *n* memba-jak; **hijacking** *n* pembajakan

hike *n* perjalanan kaki; kenaikan (harga, gaji); *vi* berjalan kaki, mendaki gunung; **hiker** *n* pendaki gunung, orang yang gemar berjalan kaki; **hik-ing** *n* mendaki gunung; berjalan kaki

hilarious *adj* [hilérius] lucu sekali, sangat menggelikan; **hilarity** *n* keriangan

hill *n* bukit; **hillside** *n* léréng bukit; **hilltop** *n* puncak bukit; **hilly** *adj* berbukit-bukit

hilt *n* pangkal (pedang), hulu (keris)

him *pron, m* dia, ia (obyék); **himself** *pron* dirinya, sendiri; *by* ~ sendiri

hind [haind] ~ *leg* kaki belakang (binatang)

hinder *vt* merintangi, menyusahkan; **hindrance** *n* rintangan, gangguan

Hindi *n* bahasa Hindi

hindsight *n* [haindsait] peninjauan kembali, melihat ke belakang

Hindu *n* orang Hindu; *adj* Hindu; **Hinduism** *n* agama Hindu

hinge *n* [hinj] éngsél; sendi; *vi* ~ *on* bergantung pada

hint *n* tanda, isyarat, sindiran; *v* mengisyaratkan; *handy* ~ *tips*

hinterland *n* kawasan pedalaman

hip *adj* gaya, gaul, ngetrénd; **hippie** *n* orang berpenampilan urak-urakan, hipi

hip *n* pangkal paha, pinggul; **hipsters** *n* celana dengan pinggang rendah

hippopotamus *n* **hippo** *coll* kuda nil

hipsters *n* celana dengan pinggang rendah

hire *n* séwa; *vt* menyéwa; mempekerjakan; ~ *car* mobil séwaan; ~ *out* menyéwakan; ~ *purchase* séwa beli

his *pron, m* -nya (kepunyaan)

Hispanic *adj* berasal dari negara berbahasa Spanyol

hiss *n* desis; *vi* berdesis, mendesis

historian *n* sejarahwan; **historic** *adj* bersejarah; **historical** *adj* historis, berkaitan dengan sejarah; **history** *n* sejarah, hikayat; *medical* ~ riwayat médis

hit *n* pukulan; *v* **hit hit** memukul, kena, mengenai; ~*and-run* tabrak lari; ~ *out* menyerang; ~ *it off* bergaul dengan baik; **hitman** *n* pembunuh, pemukul

hit *n* (lagu) yang sedang naik daun; *adj* laku, populér

hitch *n* rintangan, halangan, masalah; *vt* menambatkan, mengaitkan

hitchhike *vi* menumpang mobil orang

yang léwat; **hitchhiker** *n* orang yang menumpang mobil yang léwat

hitman *n* pembunuh, pemukul ← **hit**

HIV *abbrev Human Immunodeficiency Virus* virus yang merusak sistem kekebalan tubuh

hive *n* sarang lebah, sialang

hives *n, pl* penyakit gatal-gatal

HM *abbrev Her Majesty, His Majesty* Yang Dipertuan Agung

hoard *n* timbunan; *vt* menimbun, mengumpulkan; **hoarder** *n* penimbun

hoarding *n* balého, iklan besar

hoarse *adj* serak, parau; **hoarsely** *adv* dengan suara serak

hoax *n* [hooks] tipuan, cerita bohong; *vt* menipu; **hoaxer** *n* penipu

hobble *vi* [hobel] berjalan pincang

hobby *n* hobi, kegemaran, kesukaan; ~ *farm* pertanian sebagai tempat peristirahatan; ~-*horse* kuda-kudaan, kuda mainan

hockey *n* hoki; ~ *stick* tongkat hoki; *ice* ~ hoki és

hoe *n* [ho] pacul, cangkul; *vt* memacul, mencangkul

hog *n* babi; orang rakus; *vt* mengambil semua untuk diri sendiri, memonopoli; *don't* ~ *the phone!* jangan terus-menerus memakai télépon

hoist *clothes* ~ jemuran (baju); *vt* menaikkan; ~ *the flag* menaikkan bendéra

hold *n* pegangan, genggaman; palka; *v* **held held** *vi* bertahan; ~ *fast* bersikukuh; ~ *forth* mengutarakan pendapat; berbicara lama; ~ *out* bertahan; ~ *up* (tolerate) tahan; *vt* memegang, menggenggam; bermuatan; ~ *it!* tunggu! berhenti!; ~ *off* menjauhkan, menahan; ~ *up* menodong; ~-*up* *n* perampokan, penodongan; ~ *with* setuju, percaya, ~ *a position* menjabat; ~ *the line please* tunggu sebentar; **holdall** *n* tas besar; **holder** *n* pemegang; tempat; **holding** ~ *company* perséroan induk; **holdings** *n, pl* saham, séro

hole *n* lubang, liang; ~-*in-one* memasukkan bola golf ke dalam lubang dengan sekali pukul saja

holiday *n* hari libur; *~-maker* orang berlibur, pelancong; *religious ~* hari raya; *vi* berlibur; *they are ~ing in Hong Kong this year* tahun ini meréka berlibur ke Hong Kong

holiness *n* kesucian; *His ~* Yang Mulia Sri Paus; **holy** *adj* suci, kudus; *Cath ~ Father* Sri Paus; *~ Ghost, ~ Spirit* Roh Kudus; *~ water* air suci

holistic *adj* secara keseluruhan, secara terpadu

Holland *n, sl* Belanda; *propinsi Holland* di negeri Belanda

hollow *n* rongga, ruang; lembah kecil; *vi ~ out* mengorok, membuat rongga; *adj* hampa, kosong

holly *n* tanaman dengan daun berbentuk tajam dan buah merah, digunakan sebagai hiasan Natal

holocaust *n* [holokost] bencana (pembakaran), pemusnahan; *nuclear ~* bencana akibat perang nuklir; *The ~* pembinasaan orang Yahudi di Eropa selama Perang Dunia Kedua

hologram *n* hologram

holster *n* sarung (senjata)

holy *adj* suci, kudus; *Cath ~ Father* Sri Paus; *~ Ghost, ~ Spirit* Roh Kudus; *~ water* air suci; *the ~ City* Yerusalém

homage *n* [hommej] hormat, sembah; *to pay ~ to* menghormati, menyembah

home *n* rumah; panti jompo; *adj* di rumah, di kandang sendiri; *~ address* alamat rumah; *~ Counties* wilayah di sekitar kota London; *~ economics* pendidikan kesejahteraan keluarga (PKK); *~ ground* kandang sendiri, lapangan sendiri; *~ help* pembantu, pramuwisma; *~ Office* Departemén Dalam Negeri; *~ schooling* persekolahan di rumah; *~ Secretary* Menteri Dalam Negeri; *~ truth* kenyataan yang kurang énak; *at ~* di rumah; betah, mapan; *children's ~* panti asuhan; *~ sweet ~* hujan emas di negeri orang, hujan batu di negeri awak, lebih senang di negeri sendiri; *to go ~* pulang; *to bring ~ to* membuat sadar; *to go ~ to the village* pulang kampung, mudik; *to see someone ~* mengan-

tarkan pulang; **homeland** *n* tanah air; **homeless** *adj* tunawisma; **homely** *adj* sederhana, bersahaja; buruk rupa; **homemade** *adj* buatan sendiri; **homesick** *adj* **homesickness** *n* rindu pada rumah, kampung halaman atau negeri sendiri; **homestead** *n* [homstéd] rumah dan pekarangan, rumah pertanian; **hometown** *n* kampung (halaman); **homeward** *adv* pulang, ke (arah) rumah; *~ bound* dalam perjalanan pulang; **homework** *n* [homwerk] pekerjaan rumah (PR); **homing** *~ pigeon* merpati pos

homeopathy *n* pengobatan altérnatif

homesick *adj* **homesickness** *n* rindu pada rumah, kampung halaman atau negeri sendiri ← **home**

homestead *n* [homstéd] rumah dan pekarangan, rumah pertanian ← **home**

hometown *n* kampung (halaman) ← **home**

homeward *adv* pulang, ke (arah) rumah; *~ bound* dalam perjalanan pulang ← **home**

homework *n* [homwerk] pekerjaan rumah (PR) ← **home**

homicide *n* [homisaid] pembunuhan; **homicidal** *adj* bersifat pembunuh

homing *~ pigeon* merpati pos ← **home**

homo *n, sl* orang homo; **homosexual** *n* orang homoséksual; *adj* homoséksual, suka sesama jenis; sejenis

homonym *n* homonim, kata dengan éjaan yang sama tapi makna yang berbéda

homophone *n* homofon, kata dengan lafal yang sama tapi éjaan yang berbéda

homosexual *n* orang homoseksual; *adj* homoseksual, suka sesama jenis; sejenis

Hon. *abbrev the Honorable* Yang Terhormat

Honduran *n* orang Honduras; *adj* berasal dari Honduras

honest *adj* [onest] jujur; **honestly** *adv* dengan jujur; **honesty** *n* kejujuran; *in all ~* jujur saja

honey *n* [hani] madu; sayang, sayangku; **honeyed** *adj* manis; **honeybee** *n* lebah madu; **honeycomb** *n* [hanikom] sarang madu, sarang lebah; **honeydew** *~ melon* mélon; **honeymoon** *n* bulan madu; *they went to Venice on their ~* meréka berbulan madu ke Venezia; *vi* berbulan madu; **honeymooners** *n, pl* pengantin baru yang berbulan madu; **honeysuckle** *n* sejenis tanaman merambat

Hong Kong *n* Hong Kong; *adj* berasal dari Hong Kong

honk *n* bunyi klakson; *v* mengklakson, membunyikan klakson

honor *n* **honour** hormat, kehormatan; *in ~ of* untuk menghormati; *on my ~* sungguh mati; *vt* menghormati; **honorable** *adj* terhormat; *~ discharge* pemberhentian dengan hormat; *The ~ (Hon.)* Yang Terhormat (Yth.); **honorably** *adv* dengan hormat; **honorary** *adj* kehormatan; *~ member* anggota kehormatan; **honored** *adj* terhormat; **honorific** *n* gelar; *'teacher' is an ~ title in Japan* 'guru' adalah kata gelar di Jepang

Hons *abbrev Honors* cum laude

hood *n* topi (pada baju)

hoodwink *vt* menipu, memperdayakan

hoof *n* **hooves** kuku (binatang)

hook *n* kait, kali; *~ and eye* kancing cantel, kait; *off the ~* lepas, selamat; *to swallow ~, line and sinker* percaya semua dari ceritanya; *vt* mengait; *~ up* memasang, menghubungkan; **hooked** *adj* keranjingan; *~ nose* hidung bengkok

hooker *n, sl* pelacur

hooligan *n* pengacau; penggemar sépak bola yang brutal, bonék

hoop *n* gelindingan, simpai; *hula ~* hulahup

hooray, hurrah, hurray *ejac* horé!; *hip, hip ~* hip hip horé

hoot *n* suara burung hantu; bunyi klakson; suara tertawa; *vi* bersuara (burung hantu); tertawa; *I don't give a ~* saya tidak peduli; **hooter** *n* klakson

hop *n* lompat (pada satu kaki); *vi* melompat-lompat, melonjak-lonjak; *~, step and jump* tidak jauh; *arch* lompat tiga

hope *n* harapan; *vi* berharap; *vt* mengharapkan; *no ~* tidak ada harapan; **hopeful** *adj* penuh harapan; *~ of succeeding* sangat berharap akan suksés; **hopefully** *adv* mudah-mudahan, semoga; **hopeless** *adj* putus asa

hopscotch *n* éngklék

horde *n* [hord] kelompok, kawanan

horizon *n* [horaizon] cakrawala, kaki langit, ufuk, horison; **horizontal** *adj* [horizontel] melintang, horisontal

hormonal *adj* berkaitan dengan hormon; **hormone** *n* hormon; *~ replacement therapy* térapi pengganti hormon

horn *n* tanduk; terompet, klakson; *to sound the ~* mengklakson; **horned** *adj* bertanduk

hornbill *n* burung enggang

hornet *n* penyengat, langau

horny *adj, coll* terangsang (secara séksual)

horoscope *n* horoskop; *your ~* bintang anda

horrible, horrific *adj* mengerikan, dahsyat; **horrified** *adj* ketakutan, ngeri; **horrify** *vt* mengerikan; **horror** *n* kengerian, ketakutan, horor; *~ film* film horor, film hantu; *house of ~s* rumah hantu; *to his ~, he saw his wallet was missing* dia ketakutan begitu tahu dompétnya hilang

horse *n* kuda; *~ around* bermain-main; *~ racing* balapan kuda; *clothes ~* jemuran (baju); *dark ~* kuda hitam; *rocking-~* kuda goyang, kuda mainan; *saw-~* kuda-kuda; *~ and cart* keréta kuda; **horseback** *on ~* berkuda; **horseplay** *n* permainan kasar; **horsepower** *n* daya kuda, tenaga kuda, PK *(paardekracht)*; **horseshoe** *n* [hors syu] ladam, tapal kuda, sepatu kuda

horticultural *adj* berkaitan dengan perkebunan, hortikultural; **horticulture** *n* perkebunan, hortikultura

hose *n* selang; *panty-~* stoking; *vt* menyiram (dengan air dari selang)

hospice *n* [hospis] panti (untuk orang sakit)

hospitable *adj* [hospitabel] ramah

hospital *n* rumah sakit; *mental* ~ rumah sakit jiwa

hospitality *n* keramahtamahan

host *n, m* [hoost] tuan rumah; *vt* menyelenggarakan, menjadi tuan rumah; **hostess** *n, f* nyonya rumah; *arch air* ~ pramugari

hostage *n* [hostej] sandera, tawanan; *to take* ~ menyandera

hostel *n* asrama; *youth* ~ losmen

hostess *n, f* [hoostés] nyonya rumah; *arch air* ~ pramugari ← **host**

hostile *adj* bermusuhan; ~ *towards* tidak ramah kepada, bermusuhan dengan; **hostility** *n* [hostiliti] permusuhan

hot *adj* panas, hangat; pedas; séksi, menggairahkan; ~-*blooded* cepat marah; ~-*cross-bun* roti Paskah; ~ *dog* roti sosis; ~ *plate* tungku; ~ *property* barang laku, barang yang sedang dicari; ~ *spring* sumber air panas; ~ *air balloon* balon udara; ~ *water bottle* botol karét; *in* ~ *water* dalam kesulitan; **hothead** *n* [hot héd] pemarah; **hothouse** *n* [hot haus] rumah kaca; **hotline** *n* sambungan langsung, nomor télépon langsung; **hotshot** *n* jagoan

hotel *n* hotél; *four-star* ~ hotel bintang empat

hothead *n* [hot héd] pemarah ← **hot**

hothouse *n* [hot haus] rumah kaca

hotline *n* sambungan langsung, nomor télépon langsung ← **hot**

hotshot *n* jagoan ← **hot**

hound *n* anjing pemburu; *vt* memburu, mengejar

hour *n* [auer] jam; ~ *hand* jarum péndék; *by the* ~ per jam, setiap jam; *on the* ~ setiap jam (pada pukul 1, 2, 3 dsb); *half-*~, *half an* ~ setengah jam; *quarter of an* ~ seperempat jam; **hourglass** *n* jam pasir; **hourly** *adj* per jam, setiap jam; **hours** *(for)* ~ berjam-jam, lama; *after* ~ *(ah)* setelah jam kerja

house *n* rumah; déwan; ~-*sit* menjaga rumah orang; ~ *arrest* tahanan rumah; ~ *of Representatives* Déwan Perwakilan Rakyat; *on the* ~ gratis;

houseboat *n* rumah perahu; **houseboy** *n, m* pembantu, pelayan rumah; **housecoat** *n* daster; **household** *n* rumah tangga; **housekeeper** *n* kepala pembantu; **housekeeping** *n* pengelolaan (rumah tangga); **housemaid** *n, f* pembantu, pramuwisma; **housemate** *n* teman serumah; **housemother** *n, f* ibu asrama, ibu kos; **housewarming** *n* pésta atau selamatan untuk rumah baru; **housewife** *n, f* ibu rumah tangga; **housework** *n* [hauswerk] pekerjaan rumah; **housing** *n* perumahan; ~ *estate* perumahan

hovel *n* gubuk (derita)

hover *vi* melayang-layang, terbang di tempat; **hovercraft** *n* kapal amfibi

how *adv* bagaimana; betapa; ~ *about* bagaimana kalau; ~ *beautiful* betapa cantiknya; ~ *come? coll* kenapa; ~ *much?*, ~ *many?* berapa banyak?; ~ *are you?* apa kabar?; ~ *do you do?* apa kabar?; ~ *much is it?* berapa (harganya)?; **however** *adv* biarpun, akan tetapi, namun; bagaimanapun

howl *n* gonggong; teriak, tangis; *vi* melolong; menangis (dengan keras); **howler** *n* kesalahan yang sangat lucu

HP *abbrev horsepower* GK (gaya kuda), PK *(paardekracht)*

HQ *abbrev headquarters* mabes (markas besar)

HR *abbrev human resources* SDM (sumber daya manusia)

HRH *abbrev His/Her Royal Highness* Yang Dipertuan Agung

HS *abbrev high school* sekolah menengah (umum, SMU)

hub *n* pusat (kota); **hubcap** *n* dop

huddle *n, vi* berkumpul, berhimpitan

hue *n* [hiu] warna, rona; ~ *and cry* keributan, tampik sorak

hug *n* pelukan; *vi* berpelukan; *vt* memeluk; ~*s and kisses* peluk cium; *bear-*~ memeluk erat

huge *adj* besar sekali

hull *n* lambung kapal

hum *n* senandung; dengung; *vi* bersenandung; mendengung; **hummingbird** *n* semacam burung kolibri

human *n, adj* manusia, orang; ~ *being* manusia, orang; ~ *resources (HR)* sumber daya manusia (SDM); ~ *rights* hak asasi manusia (HAM); **humane** *adj* manusiawi, berperikemanusiaan; **humanitarian** *adj* berperikemanusiaan; ~ *aid* bantuan kemanusiaan; **humanities** *n, pl* ilmu pengetahuan sosial (IPS); **humanity** *n* umat manusia; perikemanusiaan

humble *adj* rendah hati; *vt* merendahkan

humbug *n* penipu; semacam permén

humdrum *adj* membosankan, menjemukan, biasa

humid *adj* lembab; **humidity** *n* [humiditi] kelembaban

humiliate *vt* [humiliét] **humiliating** *adj* menghina, merendahkan; **humiliation** *n* penghinaan

humility *n* [humiliti] kerendahan hati

hummingbird *n* semacam burung kolibri

humorous *adj* lucu, kocak, menggelikan; **humor** *n* **humour** *n* kelucuan; sifat; *sense of* ~ seléra humor

hump *n* punuk (unta), bongkol; ~ *backed whale* ikan paus bongkok

hunch *n* perasaan, firasat, dugaan

hunchback *n, adj* bungkuk

hundred *n* ratusan; *adj* seratus; *pl* beratus-ratus, ratusan; ~ *of rats* ratusan tikus; **hundredth** *n* perseratus; *adj* keseratus

hung *v, pf* → **hang**

Hungarian *n* [hanggérian] bahasa Hongaria; orang Hongaria; *adj* berasal dari Hongaria; **Hungary** *n* Hongaria

hunger *n* [hangger] rasa lapar; ~ *for* rindu akan, merindukan; ~ *strike* mogok makan; **hungry** *adj* lapar

hunt *n* perburuan, buruan; *vi* berburu; *vt* memburu; mencari; **hunter** *n* pemburu; **hunting** *n* pemburuan, perburuan

hurdle *n* gawang; rintangan; *vt* melompati; mengatasi; **hurdles** *n* lari gawang

hurl *vt* melémpar, melémparkan

hurrah, hurray, hooray *ejac* hore!; *hip, hip* ~ hip hip hore

hurricane *n* angin topan

hurried *adj* [harid] terburu-buru, tergopoh-gopoh; **hurriedly** *adv* secara

terburu-buru; **hurry** *n* ketergopohgopohan; *in a* ~ terburu-buru; tergesagesa; *vi* bergegas; *vt* menggegaskan; ~ *up* bergegaslah; *sl* cepatan, ayo cepat

hurt *n* sakit (hati), luka; *vi* sakit; *vt* melukai, menyakiti, mencederai, merusak; **hurtful** *adj* menyakitkan

husband *n* suami; ~ *and wife* suami isteri

hush *n* kesunyian (sejenak), keheningan; *ejac* diam; *vi* ~ *up* menutup-nutupi

husk *n* kulit (biji)

husky *n* (Siberian) ~ *anjing* Eskimo; *adj* serak, parau

hut *n* pondok, gubuk

hutch *n* kandang (kelinci)

HW *abbrev homework* PR (pekerjaan rumah)

Hwy *Highway* Jl Ry (Jalan Raya)

hyacinth *n* [haiasinth] sejenis bunga bakung

hydrangea *n* [haidrénja] sejenis bunga biru, putih atau mérah muda

hydrant *n* [haidrant] hidran

hydraulic *adj* [haidrolik] hidrolik, hidrolis; **hydraulics** *n, pl* hidrolika

hydrocarbon *n* [haidrokarbon] hidrokarbon

hydrochloric [haidroklorik] ~ *acid* asam garam; **hydroelectric** ~ *power* station pembangkit listrik tenaga air; **hydrogen** *n* [haidrojen] hidrogén, zat air; **hydrology** *n* [haidroloji] hidrologi; **hydrophobia** *n* [haidrofobia] takut air

hydrofoil *n* [haidrofoil] hidrofoil

hyena *n* [haiina] sejenis anjing liar

hygiene *n* [haijin] kebersihan; higiene; **hygienic** *adj* bersih; higienis

hymen *n* [haimen] selaput dara

hymn *n* himne, kidung

hyperactive *adj* [haiperaktif] sangat aktif, hiperaktif

hypermarket *n* [haipermarket] swalayan besar

hypertension *n* hiperténsi, darah tinggi

hyphen *n* [haifen] garis tengah [-]

hypnotism *n* [hipnotisem] hipnotisme; **hypnotist** *n* (ahli) hipnotis; **hypnotize** *vt* menghipnosis

hypochondriac *n* [haipokondriak] orang yang selalu merasa dirinya sakit

hypocrite *n* [hipokrit] orang munafik;
  hypocritical *adj* munafik
hypodermic [haipodermik] ~ *syringe*
  jarum suntik
hypotenuse *n* [haipotenyuz] sisi miring
hypothesis *n* [haipothesis] hipotésis
hysteria *n* penyakit histéria; **hysterical**
  adj histéris

I

I *pron* saya, aku; *lit* béta; *coll* gué, gua
IBRA *abbrev, arch Indonesian Bank
  Restructuring Agency* BPPN, Badan
  Penyéhatan Perbankan Nasional
ice *n* és; ~*breaker* kapal penghancur és;
  kegiatan perkenalan; ~*d tea* és téh; ~
  skating bermain sepatu (luncur) és; ~
  skating rink gelanggang és; ~ *Age*
  Zaman Es; ~ *block* és batu; ~ *cube* és
  batu; ~ *hockey* hoki és; ~ *lolly* és lilin;
  ~ *pack* komprés dingin; *vt* ~ *a cake*
  memberi lapisan manis pada kué; **ice
  cream** *n* és krim, és puter; **iceberg** *n*
  gunung és; **Iceland** *n* Eslandia;
  Icelandic *n* bahasa Eslandia; *adj*
  berasal dari Eslandia; **icing** *n* lapisan
  gula di atas kué; sugar tepung gula;
  the ~ *on the cake* penutup yang indah;
  icy *adj* [aisi] dingin sekali, sedingin
  és; *an* ~ *reception* penerimaan yang
  dingin; **icypole** *n* és lilin ← **icy**
icon *n* orang ternama; *Chr* ikon, gambar orang suci
ICT *abbrev Information and Computer
  Technology* Téknologi Informasi (TI)
ICU *abbrev Intensive Care Unit* Unit
  Perawatan Inténsif
icy *adj* [aisi] dingin sekali, sedingin és;
  an ~ *reception* penerimaan yang dingin ← **ice**
icypole *n* és lilin
ID *abbrev identification* idéntitas, jati diri
IDD *abbrev international direct dialing*
  SLI (sambungan langsung internasional)
idea *n* [aidia] idé, gagasan; *good* ~ idé
  yang baik; *to have no* ~ sama sekali

tidak tahu; **ideal** *adj* [aidil] yang
diinginkan atau diidamkan, idéal,
yang terbaik; **ideally** *adv* sebaiknya,
dalam téori
identical *adj* sama, serupa, idéntik
identification *n* pengenalan, idéntifikasi; **identify** *vt* mengenal,
  mengidéntifikasi; **identity** *n* idéntitas,
  jati diri; ~ *card* kartu pengenal, kartu
  tanda penduduk (KTP)
ideology *n* [aidioloji] paham, idéologi
idiom *n* ungkapan, idiom
idiot *n* orang dungu; **idiotic** *adj* dungu,
  idiot
idle *vi* [aidel] menganggur, bermalas-
  malas; jalan tapi belum tarik (mesin);
  adj malas, tidak dipakai
idol *n* idola; berhala; **idolize** *vt*
  mendéwakan, memuji-muji
idyllic *adj* [aidilik] yang didambakan,
  asri
ie *abbrev id est (that is)* yaitu, yakni
if *conj* kalau, jika, seandainya,
  andaikan; apabila, bila; ~ *not* kalau
  tidak; ~ *only* kalau saja; ~ *so* kalau
  begitu
ignite *vi* menyala, membakar; *vt*
  menyalakan; **ignition** *n* starter, kontak; ~ *key* kunci kontak
ignorance *n* ketidaktahuan, kebodohan;
  ignorant *adj* tidak tahu; **ignore** *vt* tidak
  menghiraukan, tidak mengindahkan
iguana *n* iguana, sejenis biawak
ill *adj* sakit; jahat, salah; buruk; ~-
  advised keliru; ~-*fated* (bernasib) sial,
  naas; ~-*gotten* didapat secara tidak
  halal; ~-*mannered* kurang ajar, tidak
  sopan; ~-*suited* tidak cocok; ~-*tem-
  pered* cepat marah; ~-*treat* menganiaya; ~ *at ease* tidak betah; **illness** *n*
  penyakit; *mental* ~ penyakit jiwa
illegal *adj* melanggar hukum, tidak sah,
  ilégal; ~ *immigrant* pendatang gelap,
  imigran gelap; **illegally** *adv* secara ilégal, secara haram
illegible *adj* [iléjibel] tidak terbaca
illegitimate *adj* [ilejitimet] lahir di luar
  nikah; ~ *child* anak yang lahir di luar
  nikah, anak haram
illicit *adj* [ilisit] gelap, tidak sah

illiteracy *n* [iliteresi] kebutahurufan; **illiterate** *adj* [iliteret] buta huruf

illness *n* penyakit; *mental* ~ penyakit jiwa ← **ill**

illogical *adj* tidak logis

illuminate *vt* menerangkan; **illuminated** *adj* bercahaya

illusion *n* ilusi, khayal; *optical* ~ ilusi optik; **illusionist** *n* tukang sulap

illustrate *vt* menggambarkan, melukiskan; **illustration** *n* gambar, lukisan, ilustrasi; **illustrator** *n* pelukis

illustrious *adj* ternama

ILO *abbrev International Labour Organisation* Organisasi Buruh Internasional

image *n* [imej] gambar; **imaginary** *adj* khayal; **imagination** *n* daya cipta, khayal, fantasi; **imagine** *v* membayang; membayangkan; *just* ~ bayangkan saja

imbalance *n* [imbalans] ketidakseimbangan, ketimpangan

imbecile *n* [imbesil] orang berpikiran lemah

IMF *abbrev International Monetary Fund* Dana Monétér Internasional

imitate *vt* [imitét] meniru; **imitation** *n* tiruan, imitasi; ~ *leather* kulit palsu; ~ *rum* rum imitasi; **imitator** *n* peniru

immaculate *adj* [imakulet] rapi sekali, apik; *Chr* suci

immature *adj* [imatyur] belum déwasa, kekanak-kanakan

immediate *adj* [imidiet] langsung; segera; *with* ~ *effect* berlaku segera; **immediately** *adv* dengan segera, serta merta

immense *adj* sangat besar; **immensely** *adv* sangat (besar)

immerse *vt* mencelupkan, membenamkan; **immersed** *adj* ~ *in* terendam dalam; asyik dengan; **immersion** *n* pencelupan

immigrant *n* pendatang, imigran; *illegal* ~ pendatang gelap, imigran gelap; **immigrate** *vi* datang dari daérah lain untuk menetap; *Helen* ~*d from Russia in the 1970s* Helen datang dari Rusia pada tahun 1970an; **immigration** *n* imigrasi

imminent *adj* [iminent] segera

immobile *adj* tidak bisa bergerak

immoral *adj* tuna susila, cabul; **immorality** *n* perbuatan cabul

immortal *adj* kekal, abadi, baka; **immortality** *n* keabadian, kekekalan; **immortalize** *vt* mengabadikan; *the city of Melbourne was* ~*d in that film* kota Melbourne diabadikan dalam film itu

immovable *adj* [imuvabel] tidak bisa dipindahkan

immune *adj* kebal, imun; ~ *system* sistem kekebalan tubuh; ~ *to* sudah kebal (terhadap); **immunity** *n* kekebalan; **immunization** *n* imunisasi, pengebalan

imp *n* sejenis roh jahat; anak nakal

impact *n* pengaruh, dampak; tubrukan; ~ *on* pengaruh pada; *vi* berdampak

impaired *adj* rusak, terganggu; ~ *vision* buta, penglihatan lemah

impartial *adj* [imparsyal] tidak memihak, adil, obyéktif

impassable *adj* [impasabel] tidak dapat dilintasi atau dilalui; **impasse** *n* [impas] jalan buntu, impas

impassive *adj* tanpa perasaan, tenang; **impassively** *adv* tanpa émosi

impatience *n* [impésyens] ketidaksabaran, rasa tidak sabar; **impatient** *adj* tidak sabar; ~ *with* tidak sabar karena; **impatiently** *adv* dengan tidak sabar

impeach *vt* [impic] menuduh, mendakwa, memanggil ke pengadilan; **impeachment** *n* dakwaan, tuduhan; pemanggilan

impede *vt* [impid] menghalangi, merintangi; **impediment** *n* [impédiment] halangan, rintangan

impending *adj* mendatang

impenetrable *adj* [impénetrabel] tidak bisa dimasuki atau dilalui

imperative *n* bentuk perintah; *adj* harus

imperceptible *adj* [imperséptibel] nyaris tidak kelihatan

imperfect *adj* kurang sempurna, tercela

imperial *adj* [impirial] kerajaan, kekaisaran; **imperialism** *n* impérialisme; **imperialist** *n* orang penjajah, imperialis; *adj* impérialis, penjajahan ← **empire**

impersonal *adj* bersikap dingin; tidak mengenai orang tertentu

impersonate *vt* menyamar sebagai; *it's easy for a policeman to ~ a criminal* bagi seorang polisi, mudah menyamar sebagai penjahat; **impersonation** *n* penyamaran

impertinence *n* [impértinens] tindakan kurang ajar; **impertinent** *adj* kurang ajar

imperturbable *adj* tenang

impervious *adj* tahan air; tak terpengaruh

impetuous *adj* [impétyuus] tidak sabar, cepat beréaksi

impetus *n* [impetus] pemicu; dorongan

implant *n* operasi pembesaran; *breast ~* pembesaran payudara; *vt* menanam (ke dalam tubuh)

implement *n* [implemént] perkakas, perabot, alat; *vt* menerapkan, melaksanakan; **implementation** *n* penerapan, impleméntasi

implicate *vt* melibatkan; *an actress was ~d in the death* seorang aktris terlibat dalam pembunuhan itu

implication *n* implikasi, dampak; kesan secara tersirat; *the ~ was that I was incapable* secara tersirat, saya dianggap tidak mampu; **imply** *v* [implai] menyindir, menyiratkan

implicit *adj* secara tersirat, implisit

implode *vi* hancur, runtuh (ke dalam)

implore *vt* memohon; *I ~ you to stop* saya mohon agar anda berhenti

imply *v* [implai] menyindir, menyiratkan

impolite *adj* tidak sopan

import *n* barang impor, pemasukan; *vt* mengimpor, mendatangkan; **imported** *adj* impor, luar; **importer** *n* pengimpor, importir

importance *n* pentingnya; *of ~* penting; **important** *adj* penting; **importantly** *adv* yang penting

imported *adj* impor, luar ← **import**

importer *n* pengimpor, importir ← **import**

impose *vt* membebankan; **imposing** *adj* mengagumkan, mengesankan; *the teacher was an ~ figure* guru itu mengesankan; **imposition** *n* [imposisyen] beban

impossible *adj* mustahil, tidak mungkin; *the ~* yang mustahil, yang tidak mungkin; **impossibility** *n* [imposibiliti] sesuatu yang mustahil

impostor *n* penipu, penyamar, gadungan

impotence *n* lemah syahwat, impoténsi; **impotent** *adj* tidak berkuasa; lemah syahwat, impotén

impoverished *adj* [impoverisyd] miskin

impractical *adj* tidak praktis

impress *vt* memberi kesan, mengesankan; *he tries so hard to ~ others* dia begitu berusaha mencari muka di depan orang lain; **impression** *n* kesan; cétakan; **impressionable** *adj* mudah terpengaruh; **impressionist** *adj* (seni lukis) gaya imprésionis; **impressive** *adj* mengesankan, hébat, dahsyat

imprint *n* cétakan; *vt* mencétak, meninggalkan bekas

imprison *vt* [imprizon] memenjarakan; **imprisonment** *n* hukuman penjara; *five years' ~* hukuman penjara lima tahun

improbable *adj* [improbabel] kemungkinan kecil

impromptu *adj* dadakan, mendadak; *an ~ performance* pertunjukan dadakan

improper *adj* tidak layak, tidak senonoh; **impropriety** *n* [improprayeti] ketidakpantasan

improve *vi* [impruv] menjadi sembuh, membaik; *~ on* memperbaiki; meningkatkan; *vt* memperbaiki; meningkatkan; **improved** *adj* lebih baik; **improvement** *n* perbaikan, peningkatan, kemajuan

improvise *vi* bertindak spontan, tanpa persiapan

impudent *adj* kurang ajar, tidak sopan

impulse *n* kata hati, dorongan hati; *~ purchase* pembelian tanpa banyak berpikir; **impulsive** *adj* menurut kata hati

impure *adj* kotor, cemar, najis, tidak murni, tidak suci; **impurity** *n* noda

in *prep* di (dalam), dalam, pada; *adj, coll* laku, populér; *~-depth* secara mendalam; *~-laws* keluarga suami/ isteri, ipar; *~-service* latihan dalam perusahaan; *~ addition* lagipula; *~ contrast* sebaliknya, di sisi lain; *~ Indo-*

nesian dalam Bahasa Indonésia; ~
Semarang di Semarang; ~ *that* dalam
hal; ~ *spite of* walaupun, meskipun; ~
and out keluar masuk; ~*s and outs*
seluk-beluk; ~ *the pond* di dalam
kolam; *Rhonda's not* ~ Rhonda tidak
ada; Rhonda tidak masuk

inability *n* [inabiliti] ketidakmampuan

inaccessible *adj* [inaksésibel] tidak
dapat diaksés, terpencil; ~ *forest* hutan
terpencil

inaccuracy *n* kesalahan; **inaccurate** *adj*
tidak teliti, tidak tepat; **inaccurately**
adv secara tidak tepat

inactive *adj* [inaktif] tidak aktif, tidak
bergerak

inadequacy *n* [inadekuasi] kekurangan;
inadequate *adj* [inadekuet] kurang,
tidak cukup; *she feels* ~ *as a mother*
sebagai seorang ibu, dia merasakan
dirinya kurang mampu

inadmissible *adj* tidak dapat diterima

inadvertent *adj* lalai, tidak sengaja;
inadvertently *adj* secara tidak sengaja;
she ~ *sent the money to the wrong
bank* secara tidak sengaja dia mengirim
uang ke bank lain

inappropriate *adj* [inapropriet] tidak
pantas

inarticulate *adj* [inartikulet] tidak jelas

inaudible *adj* [inodibel] tidak kedengaran, tidak terdengar

inaugural *adj* [inogyural] perdana;
inaugurate *vt* melantik; membuka,
memulai; *Megawati was* ~*d as President*
Ibu Mégawati dilantik sebagai Présidén;
inauguration *n* pelantikan; pembukaan

inborn *adj* asli, bawaan, naluriah

incalculable *adj* tidak terhitung

incapable *adj* tidak mampu; ~ *of love*
tidak mampu menyayangi

incarnation *n* penjelmaan

incendiary *n* [inséndiari] pembakar; ~
device bom pembakar

incense *n* dupa, kemenyan

incentive *n* [inséntiv] inséntif, dorongan

incessant *adj* tidak berhenti-henti, selalu;
incessantly *adv* secara terus-menerus

incest *n* (perbuatan) sumbang

inch *n* inci

incident *n* [insiden] peristiwa, kejadian,
·insidén; **incidental** *adj* soal kecil;
kebetulan, tidak penting; **incidentally**
adv ngomong-ngomong

incinerate *v* membakar; **incinerator** *n*
tempat pembakaran sampah

incision *n* [insisyen] toréhan, irisan;
incisive *adj* tajam; ~ *commentary*
ulasan tajam; **incisor** *n* gigi seri

incite *vt* menghasut; *the unions* ~*d the
workers to strike* serikat kerja menghasut buruh agar mogok kerja; **incite-
ment** *n* hasutan

inclination *n* [inklinasyen] kecenderungan,
kecondongan; **incline** *n* léréngan,
tanjakan; *vi* ~ *to* cenderung, condong

include *vt* mengandung, meliputi;
including *conj* termasuk; **inclusive**
adj inklusif; sampai dengan

incognito *adj* [inkognito] dengan
menyamar

incoherent *adj* tidak jelas

income *n* [incam] pendapatan, penghasilan, gaji; ~ *tax* pajak penghasilan;
incoming *adj* yang masuk

incomparable *adj* [inkomparabel] tiada
tanding, tiada banding

incompatible *adj* [inkompatibel] tidak
cocok; **incompatibility** *n* ketidakco-
cokan

incompetence *n* [inkompetens] ketidakmampuan; **incompetent** *adj* tidak
mampu

incomplete *adj* [inkomplit] kurang
lengkap, tidak komplét

incomprehensible *adj* [inkomprehénsi-
bel] tidak masuk akal; tidak dapat
dimengerti

inconceivable *adj* [inkonsivabel] tak
terbayangkan

incongruous *adj* [inkonggrues] tidak
sesuai

inconsiderate *adj* [inkonsideret] tidak
memperhatikan (perasaan orang lain)

inconsistent *adj* tidak konsisten

inconsolable *adj* [inkonsolabel] tidak
dapat dihibur

inconvenience *n* [inkonviniens] répot,
gangguan, kesulitan; **inconvenient**
adj merépotkan, mengganggu

incorporate *vt* merangkum, menggabungkan; **incorporated** *adj inc*
abbrev perseroan terbatas
incorrect *adj* tidak benar, salah
increase *n* [inkris] pertambahan,
kenaikan; *vi* tambah, bertambah; *vt*
menambah, menaikkan, meningkatkan; **increasingly** *adv* semakin
incredible *adj* [inkrédibel] luar biasa,
tidak dapat dipercaya, hébat
incredulous *adj* [inkrédulus] kurang
percaya
incriminate *vt* melibatkan, memberatkan; **incriminating** *adj* yang melibatkan, yang memberatkan
incubate *vi* mengeram; **incubation** *n*
penetasan, pengeraman; ~ *period* masa
perkembangan (penyakit); **incubator**
n inkubator
incumbent *n* pemegang jabatan
incur *vt* mendatangkan; ~ *expenses*
memakan biaya
incurable *adj* [inkyurabel] tidak dapat
diobati, tidak dapat disembuhkan
indebted [indéted] ~ *to* berhutang
(budi) kepada
indecency *n* perbuatan cabul; **indecent**
adj tak senonoh, tidak sopan, jorok
indecision *n* [indesisyen] kebimbangan,
kebingungan; **indecisive** [indesaisiv]
adj ragu-ragu, bimbang, tidak bisa
mengambil keputusan
indeed *adj, adv* betul, sebetulnya; *conj*
memang; bahkan; *it is* ~ benar sekali
indefinite *adj* [indéfinet] tidak tentu,
tidak tetap; **indefinitely** *adv* untuk
jangka waktu tidak terbatas
indelible *adj* [indélibel] tidak bisa
dihapus; ~ *pen* spidol dengan tinta
permanén
indent *n* lekuk; *vi* memasukkan ke dalam
(alinéa)
independence *n* kemerdékaan;
kebébasan; ~ *Day* Hari Kemerdékaan;
independent *adj* mandiri, merdéka,
bébas, tidak tergantung; **independent-
ly** *adv* secara mandiri, secara sepihak
indescribable *adj* **indescribably** *adv*
tidak dapat digambarkan
indestructible *adj* [indestraktibel] tidak

dapat dibinasakan atau dimusnahkan
indeterminate *adj* [indetérminet] tidak
jelas
index *n* **indices** daftar, indéks; ~ *finger*
telunjuk
India *n* India; *the Dutch East* ~ *Company* VOC; Kompeni; **Indian** *n* orang
India; orang Indian, orang asli Amérika;
adj berasal dari India; ~ *file* berjalan
satu per satu; ~ *ink* tinta hitam; ~
Ocean Samudera Hindia, Samudera
Indonesia
indicate *vi* memberi isyarat; *vt* menunjukkan; **indication** *n* tanda, petunjuk,
alamat; **indicator** *n* penunjuk; indikator; lampu séin
indict *vt* [indait] mendakwa; *he was
~ed on charges of treason* dia didakwa
sebagai pengkhianat; **indictment** *n*
dakwaan
indie *n, sl* perusahaan rekaman inde-
péndén ← **independent**
Indies *the East* ~ Hindia Belanda; *the
West* ~ Hindia Barat
indifference *n* sikap acuh tak acuh,
sikap masa bodoh; **indifferent** *adj*
acuh tak acuh, masa bodoh
indigenous *adj* [indijenus] asli; ~ *people* penduduk asli
indigestion *n* salah cerna
indignant *adj* [indignant] marah, jengkel
indigo *n* [indigo] nila; *adj* biru tua
indirect *adj* tidak langsung; **indirectly**
adv secara tidak langsung
indiscreet *adj* tidak bijaksana; bocor
mulut
indiscriminate *adj* [indiskriminet] tak
pandang bulu, membabi buta, sembarangan
indispensable *adj* [indispensabel]
perlu, wajib
indisposed *adj* tidak enak badan
indisputable *adj* [indisputabel] tidak
dapat dibantah
indistinct *adj* kurang terang, kurang
jelas, samar-samar
individual *n* [individyuel] pribadi,
orang, oknum; *adj* perseorangan;
individually *adv* masing-masing;
secara individu; **individualism** *n*

[individualizem] individualisme;
individuality *n* kepribadian
indivisible *adj* [indivisibel] tidak dapat
dibagi
Indochina *n* [indocaina] Indocina;
Indochinese *adj* berasal dari Indocina
indolent *adj* malas
Indonesia *n* Indonésia; **Indonesian** *n*
Bahasa Indonésia; orang Indonésia;
adj berasal dari Indonésia; ~ *Embassy*
Kedutaan Besar Republik Indonésia
(KBRI)
indoor *adj* di dalam rumah atau gedung; ~ *cricket* krikét yang dimainkan
di dalam gedung; **indoors** *adv* di
dalam rumah atau gedung
induce *vt* mempercepat, menyebabkan;
membujuk; menginduksi; **inducement**
n dorongan, inséntif, pancingan;
induction *n* induksi (persalinan)
induct *vt* melantik; **induction** *n* pelantikan; induksi
induction *n* induksi ← **induce**
indulge *vi* [indalj] ~ *in* menikmati;
indulgent *adj* terlalu baik, sabar;
indulgence *n* kegemaran
industrial *adj* [indastriel] berkaitan
dengan industri atau pabrik; ~ *action*
pemogokan; ~ *estate* kawasan industri;
industrious *adj* rajin, telatén; **industry**
n industri, perindustrian; kegiatan
inebriated *adj* [inibriéted] mabuk
inedible *adj* [inédibel] tidak dapat
dimakan; *yesterday's cake was*
already ~ kué yang dibuat kemarin
sudah tidak dapat dimakan lagi
inefficiency *n* ketidakéfisiénan;
inefficient *adj* tidak éfisién, tidak
jalan dengan baik
ineligible *adj* [nélijibel] tidak dapat dipilih
inept *adj* tidak cekatan, kurang bisa
inequality *n* [inikuoliti] ketidaksamaan,
kesenjangan
inert *adj* lembam, tidak bergerak; ~ *gas*
gas lembam, gas mulia; **inertia** *n*
kelembaman, inérsia
inevitable *adj* [inévitabel] tidak dapat
diélakkan, mau tidak mau
inexact *adj* kurang tepat
inexcusable *adj* [inékskyusabel] tidak

dapat dimaafkan
inexhaustible *adj* [inexostabel] tidak
habis-habisnya
inexpensive *adj* [inékspénsiv] tidak
mahal, murah
inexperienced *adj* [inékspiriensd]
kurang berpengalaman
inexplicable *adj* [inéksplikabel] tidak
dapat dijelaskan, tidak masuk akal
infallible *adj* [infalibel] sempurna, bisa
diandalkan, tidak pernah salah
infamous *adj* [infemus] punya réputasi
buruk; *the* ~ *Adolf Hitler* Adolf Hitler
yang terkenal jahat itu; **infamy** *n*
nama buruk
infant *n, adj* bayi, balita, anak kecil; *n,*
pl ~ *school* taman kanak-kanak (TK);
infantile *adj* berkaitan dengan bayi;
seperti anak kecil, kekanak-kanakan
infantry *n* infantri
infatuated *adj* [infatuéted] tergila-gila
pada
infect *vt* menulari, menjangkiti; **infection** *n* penyakit, inféksi, ketularan;
infectious *adj* menular; ~ *disease*
penyakit menular
infer *vi* mengambil kesimpulan; **inference**
n [infrens] kesimpulan, dugaan
inferior *adj* [infirior] kurang bagus atau
baik, bermutu rendah; **inferiority** ~
complex perasaan minder
infernal *adj* dari neraka; **inferno** *n*
kebakaran besar, api besar
infertile *adj* mandul, tidak subur;
infertility *n* [infértiliti] kemandulan
infidel *n* [infidél] kafir
infidelity *n* [infidéliti] perselingkuhan;
ketidaksetiaan
infighting *n* pertengkaran di dalam;
there is too much ~ *within the govern-*
ment terlalu banyak pertengkaran di
dalam pemerintah
infiltrate *vt* menyusup, (diam-diam)
memasuki; *the foreign agents* ~ *the*
organization mata-mata asing
menyusup ke dalam organisasi;
infiltration *n* penyusupan, infiltrasi
infinite *adj* [infinit] tak terhitung;
infinitive *n* bentuk dasar kata kerja;
infinity *n* jumlah tak berakhir

infirm *adj* sakit(-sakitan); **infirmary** *n* rumah sakit

infix *n* kata sisipan

inflame *vt* meradangkan; memperparah; **inflammable** *adj* dapat terbakar

inflatable *adj* dapat diisi dengan angin; **inflate** *vi* membesar; *vt* meniup, mengisi; ~ *a balloon* meniup balon, mengisi balon; **inflation** *n* inflasi; ~ *rate* laju inflasi

inflect *vi* mengubah (suara, kata); **inflection** *n* perubahan suara

inflexible *adj* [infléksibel] kaku

inflict *vt* membebankan; memberikan, menimbulkan; ~ *damage* menye-babkan kerusakan, merusak

influence *n* [influens] pengaruh, éfék; *vt* mempengaruhi; **influential** *adj* berpengaruh

influenza *n* **flu** *coll* flu, selesma

influx *n* masukan; gelombang; *there was a huge ~ of refugees from Vietnam* banyak sekali pengungsi dari Vietnam datang

info *n, coll* info, informasi; **inform** *vt* memberitahu, mengabarkan, mengin-formasikan; **informant** *n* sumber, narasumber, pelapor; **informer** *n* pela-por, pengadu; **information** *n* **info** *coll* informasi, keterangan, penerangan; *Department of Information* Departemén Penerangan (Deppen); **informed** *adj* berpengetahuan luas

informal *adj* santai, tidak resmi; ~ *dress* baju santai

informant *n* sumber, narasumber, pela-por; **informer** *n* pelapor, pengadu; **information** *n* informasi, keterangan, penerangan; *Department of* ~ Departemén Penerangan (Deppen); **informed** *adj* berpengetahuan luas ← **inform**

infra ~*-red* infra mérah; **infrastructure** *n* prasarana

infrequent *adj* [infrikuent] jarang

infringe *vt* melanggar, menyalahi; **infringement** *n* pelanggaran

infuriate *vt* [infyuriét] **infuriating** *adj* membuat marah

infusion *blood* ~ tambah darah; seduhan

ingenious *adj* [injinius] sangat pandai (tentang barang)

ingredient *n* [ingridient] bahan (mentah)

inhabit *vt* mendiami, menghuni; **inhab-itant** *n* penduduk, penghuni

inhale *v* menarik nafas, mengisap; **inhaler** *n* isapan, sedotan

inherent *adj* tersirat; berpautan

inherit *vt* mewarisi; **inheritance** *n* warisan

inhuman *adj* tidak manusiawi, bengis, biadab; **inhumane** *adj* tidak berperikemanusiaan

initial *n* huruf pertama, paraf; *vt* téken, memaraf; *adj* pertama, perdana, per-mulaan; **initially** *adv* awalnya; **initiate** *vt* [inisyiét] memulai, memprakarsai; **initiation** *n* (upacara) pengenalan; **ini-tiative** *n* [inisyiativ] prakarsa, inisiatif; **initiator** *n* [inisyiétor] pemrakarsa

inject *vt* menyuntik, menyuntikkan; **injection** *n* suntik, suntikan; injéksi

injure *vi* merugikan, mencederai melukai; **injured** *adj* cedera; **injury** *n* cedera, luka; kerugian; hinaan

injustice *n* [injastis] ketidakadilan

ink *n* tinta; **inky** *adj* berwarna gelap

inlaid *adj* bertatahkan

inland *n* pedalaman; *the ~ Revenue* kantor pajak

inlet *n* teluk kecil

inmate *n* tahanan, narapidana, penghuni

inn *n* penginapan; ~*-keeper* pengurus penginapan

innate *adj* bawaan, naluriah

inner *adj* (di) dalam; batin; ~ *tube* ban dalam

innings *n* babak, giliran, masa memukul (krikét, bisbol)

innocence *n* keadaan tidak bersalah, keadaan tanpa dosa; **innocent** *adj* tidak bersalah, tanpa dosa; **innocently** *adv* secara tidak bersalah, dengan polos

innovate *vi* mencari atau menciptakan yang baru; **innovation** *n* ciptaan baru, inovasi; **innovative** *adj* inovatif, mampu menciptakan yang baru

input *n* masukan; *vt* memasukkan

inquest *n* pemeriksaan, penyelidikan; *coroner's ~* pemeriksaan mayat

inquire, enquire *vi* [inkuair] bertanya;

inquiry *n* pertanyaan; penyelidikan, pemeriksaan; *to make inquiries* minta keterangan; **inquisitive** *adj* [inkuisitif] ingin tahu

inroads *to make* ~ mencapai keberhasilan, maju; *you won't make* ~ *into the market unless you know the national culture* tidak mungkin masuk ke dalam pasar tanpa mengetahui budaya nasional

insane *adj* [inséin] gila, sakit jiwa; **insanity** *n* [insaniti] kegilaan

insanitary *adj* [insanitari] tidak bersih, jorok

insatiable *adj* [insésyabel] tidak dapat dipuaskan

inscribe *v* menulis, memahat, menoréh; **inscription** *n* tulisan, suratan, prasasti

insect *n* serangga; **insecticide** *n* obat pembasmi serangga; ~ *repellent* obat nyamuk

insecure *adj* gelisah, tidak percaya diri; **insecurity** *n* [insekuriti] rasa gelisah atau tidak percaya diri

insemination *n* pembuahan; *artificial* ~ inséminasi buatan

insensitive *adj* [insénsitif] tidak peka, tidak sénsitif; ~ *to* tidak peka terhadap

inseparable *adj* [inséparabel] tidak terpisahkan

insert *n* sisipan; *vt* menyisipkan, menyelipkan, memasukkan; **insertion** *n* [insérsyen] penyisipan

inside *prep, adj* (di) dalam; *adv* ke dalam; *n* (bagian) dalam; ~ *information* informasi dari orang dalam; ~ *out* terbalik; **insider** *n* orang dalam

insight *n* [insait] wawasan, pemahaman

insignificance *n* **insignificant** *adj* tidak berarti, sepélé

insinuate *v* [insinyuét] menyindir; **insinuation** *n* sindiran

insipid *adj* [insipid] tawar; lemah

insist *v* mengotot, bersikeras, bersikukuh; mendesak; **insistence** *n* desakan; **insistent** *adj* mengotot; **insistently** *adv* secara mengotot

insolence *n* sikap tidak sopan atau kurang ajar; **insolent** *adj* tidak sopan, kurang ajar

insoluble *adj* [insolyubel] tidak dapat larut; *an* ~ *problem* masalah yang tidak dapat dipecahkan

insolvent *adj* bangkrut, palit, tidak mampu membayar

insomnia *n* (keadaan) sulit tidur; **insomniac** *n* [insomniak] orang yang sulit tidur

inspect *vt* memeriksa; **inspection** *n* pemeriksaan, inspéksi; **inspector** *n* pemeriksa; inspéktur; ~*-general* inspéktur-jénderal

inspiration *n* [inspirésyen] ilham, inspirasi; **inspirational** *adj* yang mengilhami atau memberi inspirasi; **inspire** *vt* mengilhami, memberi inspirasi; **inspiring** *adj* yang mengilhami atau memberi inspirasi

instability *n* [instabiliti] ketidakstabilan

install, instal *vt* melantik; memasang; **installation** *n* pelantikan; pemasangan; instalasi; **instalment, installment** *n* angsuran; *to pay in* ~*s* mencicil, membayar dengan mengangsur

instance *for* ~ misalnya, seumpamanya; *in this* ~ pada kasus ini

instant *n* saat; ~ *coffee* kopi instan; ~ *noodles* mi instan; **instantaneous** *adj* [instanténius] **instantly** *adv* saat itu juga, serta-merta, dengan segera

instead *conj* [instéd] alih-alih, melainkan, malah; ~ *of* daripada, sebagai pengganti; *we're not going home, we're going shopping* ~ kita tidak pulang, melainkan pergi berbelanja

instinct *n* naluri, insting

institute *n* [instityut] lembaga, institut; **institution** *n* adat (istiadat); lembaga, institusi

instruct *vt* mengajar; memerintahkan, menginstruksikan; **instruction** *n* pengajaran; perintah, instruksi; *pl* petunjuk, buku panduan; **instructor** *n* pengajar, guru, pelatih, instruktor

instrument *n* alat, perkakas, pesawat; *string* ~ alat musik gésék; **instrumental** *adj* tanpa kata; sangat penting

insubordinate *adj* [insabordinet] membangkang; **insubordination** *n* pembangkangan

insufficient *adj* [insafisyent] kurang cukup

insular *adj* berkaitan dengan pulau; berwawasan sempit

insulate *vt* mengisolasikan; **insulation** *n* isolasi; **insulator** *n* isolator

insult *n* cemoohan, hinaan; *vt* menghina, mencemoohkan; *an ~ to* menghina, mencemoohkan

insurance *n* asuransi, pertanggungan; *~ agent* agén asuransi; *~ policy* polis asuransi; **insure** *vt* mengasuransikan; memastikan; **insurer** *n* penanggung asuransi

insurgent *n, adj* pemberontak; **insurgency** *n* pemberontakan

insurrection *n* pemberontakan

intact *adj* utuh

intake *n* masukan, kiriman, asupan

integral *adj* perlu; pokok; **integrate** *vi* bersatu padu; *vt* memadukan; **integrated** *adj* terpadu; **integration** *n* keterpaduan, intégrasi; **integrity** *n* ketulusan hati, kejujuran

intellect *n* akal budi, intélék; **intellectual** *n* cendékiawan; *adj* pandai; *~ property rights (IPR)* hak kekayaan inteléktual (HAKI)

intelligence *n* [intélijens] kecerdasan; perintélan, intélijén; *artificial ~* kecerdasan buatan; **intelligent** *adj* cerdas, pandai

intend *v* berniat, bermaksud; **intended** *n* calon, tunangan; intent, **intention** *n* maksud, niat, kehendak, tujuan; **intentional** *adj* sengaja; **intentionally** *adv* dengan sengaja

intense *adj* hébat, mendalam, kuat, inténs; **intensify** *vi* naik; *vt* meningkatkan; **intensity** *n* inténsitas, kekuatan; **intensive** *adj* inténsif; *~ care unit (ICU)* perawatan inténsif

intent, intention *n* maksud, niat, kehendak, tujuan; **intentional** *adj* sengaja; **intentionally** *adv* dengan sengaja ← **intend**

inter *vt* [intér] menguburkan

interact *vi* bergaul; **interaction** *n* pergaulan, interaksi; **interactive** *adj* [interaktif] interaktif

intercede *vi* [intersid] menjadi perantara, mengetengahi; **intercession** *n* perantaraan

intercept *vt* mencegat; *the security guard ~ed the escaping pickpocket* seorang satpam mencegat copét yang mau kabur

interchange *n* simpang, bélokan; *clover-leaf ~* simpang susun semanggi; **interchangeable** *adj* dapat ditukar

intercom *n* radio antar ruangan

intercontinental *adj* antarbenua

intercourse *n* pergaulan, perhubungan; *(sexual) ~* persetubuhan; *social ~* pergaulan (sosial)

interest *n* kepentingan; perhatian, minat; daya tarik; bunga (uang); *~ rates* suku bunga; *of ~* menarik perhatian; *vt* menarik perhatian; **interested** *adj* tertarik, berminat; *~ in* tertarik pada; **interesting** *adj* menarik (perhatian); **interestingly** *adv* secara menarik

interfaith *adj* antar agama

interfere *vi* [interfir] campur tangan; *~ in, ~ with* mencampuri, mengganggu; **interference** *n* campur tangan, gangguan

interim *n, adj* sementara

interior *n* [intirior] pedalaman, dalamnya; *adj* (bagian) dalam; *~ design* nirmana; *Minister of the ~* Menteri Dalam Negeri (Mendagri)

interject *vi* berseru; menyeletuk, menyisipkan; **interjection** *n* kata seru

interlude *n* selingan, jeda

intermediary *n* perantara; **intermediate** *adj* sedang; tingkat lanjut; *I attend an ~-level Japanese class* saya ikut kursus bahasa Jepang tingkat lanjut

interminable *adj* [intérminabel] lama sekali, tidak berkeputusan

intermission *n* waktu istirahat

intermittent *adj* selang-seling, terkadang-kadang

intern *vt* menawan, menginternir; *n* orang magang; **internee** *n* tawanan; **internment** *n* penawanan, penahanan; *~ camp* kamp tawanan; **internship** *n* masa magang (di rumah sakit)

internal *adj* dalam (negeri)

international *adj* internasional, antar
bangsa
internee *n* tawanan; **internment** *n*
penawanan, penahanan; ~ *camp* kamp
tawanan; **internship** *n* masa magang
(di rumah sakit) ← **intern**
internet *n* internét; ~ *café* warung
internét (warnét); *on the* ~ di internét
interpret *vt* menafsirkan; menerjemahkan
(secara lisan); **interpretation** *n* penafsiran; **interpreter** *n* penerjemah, juru
bahasa; **interpreting** *n* penerjemahan
interrogate *vt* [intérogét] memeriksa,
mengintérogasi, menanyai; **interrogation** *n* pemeriksaan, intérogasi; **inter-
rogator** *n* pemeriksa
interrupt *vi* menyéla, menyeletuk,
memotong pembicaraan; **interruption**
n interupsi, gangguan
intersect *vt* memotong, menyilang;
intersecting *adj* silang-menyilang;
intersection *n* perempatan, simpang;
persilangan
interstate *adj* antar negara bagian; *adv*
ke negara bagian lain; *I'm going* ~ *this
weekend* saya ke negara bagian lain
akhir minggu ini
interval *n* antara, selang, jeda, waktu
istirahat; *at regular* ~*s* pada saat-saat
tertentu
intervene *vi* [intervin] campur tangan;
~ *in* menghalangi; **intervention** *n*
halangan, campur tangan, intervénsi
interview *n* [interviu] wawancara, tanya
jawab, interpiu; *vt* mewawancara,
mewawancarai; **interviewee** *n* orang
yang diwawancarai; **interviewer** *n*
pewawancara
intestine *n* [intéstin] usus, isi perut;
large ~ usus besar; *small* ~ usus kecil
intimacy *n* [intimesi] kemesraan; **intimate** [intimet] *adj* mesra, intim, karib,
akrab; ~ *relations* hubungan intim
intimidate *vt* [intimidét] menakut-
nakuti, mengintimidasi; **intimidation**
n intimidasi
into *prep* ke (dalam); menjadi; menuju;
Amy went ~ *the shop* Amy masuk toko
itu; *David's* ~ *Japanese girls* David
suka gadis-gadis Jepang; *that company*

has gone ~ *debt* perusahaan itu sedang
banyak hutang
intolerable *adj* tidak tertahankan, tidak
dapat dibiarkan; **intolerant** *adj* tidak
tenggang rasa, tidak bertoléransi
intonation *n* intonasi, nada
intoxicant *n* obat atau minuman
perangsang; **intoxicate** *vt* intoxicating
adj memabukkan; **intoxication** *n*
keadaan mabuk
intransitive *adj* [intransitiv] tanpa
pelengkap atau obyék; ~ *verb* kata
kerja tanpa pelengkap
intravenous ~ *drip* infus
intrepid *adj* [intrépid] berani
intricacy *n* [intrikesi] keruwetan; **intri-
cate** *adj* [intriket] berbelit-belit, ruwet
intrigue *n* [intrig] intrik; *vt* membuat
penasaran, menuntut berpikir; *it* ~*s me
how quickly they found us* cepatnya
mereka menemukan kami membuat
saya penasaran
intrinsic *adj* hakiki; **intrinsically** *adv*
secara hakiki
introduce *vt* memperkenalkan; memulai; ~ *oneself* memperkenalkan diri;
introduction *n* perkenalan; (kata)
pengantar; **introductory** *adj* awal
introvert *n* orang yang suka menyendiri
dan tidak bergaul; **introverted** *adj*
suka menyendiri
intrude *vi* mengganggu; ~ *on* mengganggu; **intruder** *n* orang yang memasuki tempat tanpa izin; maling; **intru-
sive** *adj* [intrusiv] yang mengganggu
urusan pribadi
intuition *n* [intyuisyen] intuisi, gerak
hati; **intuitive** *adj* naluriah
Inuit *n* orang Eskimo dari Amérika
Utara, orang Inuit
inundate *vt* membanjiri, menggenangi;
the town was ~*d by refugees* kota itu
dibanjiri para pengungsi; **inundation**
n banjir, air bah
invade *vt* menyerang, menyerbu; **invad-
er** *n* penyerang; **invasion** *n* serangan,
serbuan
invalid *n* [invelid] orang sakit, orang
cacat; *adj* [invalid] tidak berlaku,
tidak sah; **invalidate** *vt* membatalkan

invaluable *adj* tak ternilai

invariably *adv* [invériabli] selalu, senantiasa, setiap kali

invasion *n* serangan, serbuan ← **invade**

invent *vt* menciptakan, menemukan; membuat-buat; **invention** *n* ciptaan; **inventor** *n* pencipta

inventory *n* inventaris

inverse *n* kebalikan; *adj* terbalik; **inversion** *n* pembalikan, invérsi; **invert** *vt* membalikkan; *~ed commas* tanda kutip [" "]

invest *vt* menanamkan (modal), menginvéstasikan; *~ money in* menanamkan dana dalam; **investment** *n* penanaman modal, invéstasi; **investor** *n* penanam modal

investigate *vi* membuat penyelidikan; *vt* menyelidiki; **investigation** *n* penyelidikan; **investigator** *n* penyelidik

investment *n* penanaman modal, invéstasi; **investor** *n* penanam modal ← **invest**

invigilate *vt* menjaga, mengawasi; *Adam will ~ an exam at 3 o'clock* Adam akan mengawasi ujian jam 3 nanti

invincible *adj* [invinsibel] tidak terkalahkan

invisible *adj* [invisibel] tak terlihat, gaib

invitation *n* [invitésyen] undangan, ajakan; *by ~* khusus undangan; **invite** *vt* [invait] mengundang, mengajak; mempersilakan; **invitee** *n* tamu, orang yang diundang; **inviting** *adj* mengundang, menggoda

invoice *n* faktur, surat tagihan

involuntary *adj* tidak sengaja, secara tanpa sadar

involve *vt* melibatkan; **involved** *adj* terlibat, yang bersangkutan; *to be ~ with someone* berpacaran dengan, berhubungan dengan; *to get ~ with* terlibat dalam; **involvement** *n* keterlibatan

invulnerable *adj* kebal

inward *adj* ke dalam; batin

IOC *abbrev International Olympic Committee* Komité Olimpiade Internasional

iodine *n* [aiodin] yodium

IOU *abbrev I owe you* saya berhutang kepada anda

IQ *abbrev intelligence quotient* tingkat kecerdasan

IRA *abbrev Irish Republican Army* Tentara Républik Irlandia

Iran *n* Iran; **Iranian** *n* [irénian] orang Iran; *adj* berasal dari Iran

Iraq *n* Irak; **Iraqi** *adj* orang Irak; *adj* berasal dari Irak

irate *adj* [airét] marah sekali, geram, berang

Ireland *n* Irlandia; *Northern ~* Irlandia Utara; **Irish** *n* [airisy] orang Irlandia; *~ (Gaelic)* bahasa Irlandia; *~ Republican Army (IRA)* Tentara Republik Irlandia; *the ~ Sea* Laut Irlandia; *adj* berasal dari Irlandia; **Irishman** *n* lelaki Irlandia; **Irishwoman** *n* wanita Irlandia

iris *n* bunga iris; selaput pelangi, iris

Irish *n* [airisy] orang Irlandia; *~ (Gaelic)* bahasa Irlandia; *~ Republican Army (IRA)* Tentara Republik Irlandia; *the ~ Sea* Laut Irlandia; *adj* berasal dari Irlandia; **Irishman** *n* lelaki Irlandia; **Irishwoman** *n* wanita Irlandia ← **Ireland**

irk *vt* [érk] membuat jéngkél, menjéngkélkan, mengganggu; *it ~s me* itu membuat saya jéngkél; **irksome** *adj* menjéngkélkan, menyusahkan

iron *n* besi; setrika; *~ filings* serbuk besi; *~ tablets* vitamin penambah zat besi; *cast ~* besi tuang; *the ~ Curtain* Tabir Besi, Tirai Besi; *v* menyetrika; *~ out* menyelesaikan, meluruskan, membuat rata; **ironing** *n* setrikaan; kegiatan menyetrika; *~ board* papan setrika

ironic *adj* [aironik] ironis; **ironically** *adv* secara ironis; **irony** *n* ironi, éjékan

irrational *adj* [irasyonel] tidak masuk akal

irreconcilable *adj* [irékonsiliabel] tidak dapat didamaikan

irredeemable *adj* tidak dapat lagi diterima atau diselamatkan

irregular *adj* tidak teratur, luar biasa;

irregularity *n* ketidakbérésan, kekecualian

irrelevance *n* **irrelevant** *adj* tidak rélevan

irreparable *adj* [iréperabel] tidak dapat diperbaiki

irreplaceable *adj* [ireplésabel] tidak dapat diganti

irrepressible *adj* [ireprésibel] tidak dapat dilawan atau ditahan

irresponsible *adj* [iresponsibel] tidak bertanggung jawab

irreverence *n* [iréverens] **irreverent** *adj* kurang hormat

irrevocable *adj* [irévekebel] tidak dapat diubah atau ditarik lagi

irrigate *vt* [irigét] mengairi; **irrigation** *n* pengairan, irigasi

irritable *adj* [iritabel] cepat marah, marah-marah; **irritant** *n* yang mengganggu; **irritate** *vt* [iritét] **irritating** *adj* mengganggu, membuat jéngkél; **irritation** *n* rasa gatal, iritasi

is *vi* adalah → **be**

Is. *abbrev* island P. (pulau)

Islam *n* agama Islam; **Islamic** *adj* berkaitan dengan Islam; ~ *law* syariah

island *n* [ailand] pulau; *the Andaman ~s* Kepulauan Andaman; **islander** *n* penghuni pulau; **isle** *n* [ail] pulau; *the ~ of Man* Pulau Man; **islet** *n* [ailet] pulau kecil

isolate *vt* mengasingkan, menjauhkan; **isolated** *adj* terpencil; **isolation** *n* pengasingan; *in ~* sendiri

Israel *n* [isrél] Israél; **Israeli** *n* orang Israél; *adj* berasal dari Israél; **Israelite** *n, arch* orang Israél

issue *n* [isyu] masalah, desas-desus, isu; terbitan, édisi; *back ~* édisi lama; *to take ~ with* mempermasalahkan; *vt* menerbitkan; mengeluarkan, memancarkan

isthmus *n* tanah genting; *the ~ of Kra* tanah genting Kra

it *pron* dia, ia (barang); -nya; itu; *who is ~?* siapa?; *~ is (it's) hot* hari ini panas; **its** *pron* -nya (barang); *the clock lost ~ hand* tangan jam hilang; **itself** *pron* sendiri

Italian *n* bahasa Italia; orang Italia; *adj* berasal dari Italia; **Italy** *n* Italia; *Little ~* kampung Italia

italic *n* [italik] tulisan miring; *adj* miring; **italicize** *vt* [italisaiz] membuat (tulisan) miring

Italy *n* Italia; *Little ~* kampung Italia

itch *n, vi* **itchy** *adj* gatal; *vt* menggaruk

item *n* [aitem] barang; pasal, ayat; nomor; **itemize** *vt* membukukan

itinerant *adj* [aitinerant] keliling; *~ trader* pedagang keliling

itinerary *n* [aitinereri] rencana perjalanan

its *pron* -nya (barang); *the clock lost ~ hand* tangan jam hilang

it's → **it**

itself *pron* sendiri ← **it**

IUD *abbrev intra-uterine device* IUD

ivory *n* [aivori] gading; *~ Coast* Pantai Gading; *~ tower* menara gading

ivy *n* tanaman menjalar, tanaman merambat

J

jab *n* tusukan; suntikan; pukulan péndék

jack *n* dongkrak, tuas, kuda-kuda; *~ rabbit* kelinci jantan; *~ up* mendongkrak; *~ of all trades* tukang serba bisa

jackal *n* serigala

jackass *n* orang bodoh

jacket *n* jaket; sampul buku; *potatoes in ~s* kentang yang dibakar dalam kulitnya

jackfruit *n* buah nangka

jackpot *n* hadiah utama

jacks *n, pl* békel

jacuzzi *n* [jakuzi] bak rendam besar dengan pancuran air

jade *n* batu giok

jaded *adj* sayu, lesu; jemu

jagged *adj* [jaged] bergerigi

jaguar *n* sejenis macan di Amérika

jail, gaol *n* penjara; *in ~, to go to ~* dipenjara; *vt* memenjarakan; **jailer** *n* sipir

jalopy *n, US* [jalopi] mobil lama, mobil bekas

jam *n* selai; ~ *jar* tempat selai; *strawberry* ~ selai strobéri; *money for* ~ hasil tanpa kerja keras

jam *vi* berlatihan main musik; ~ *session* latihan bermain musik

jam *n* kemacetan; keadaan macet atau tersumbat; ~*packed* penuh sesak; *traffic* ~ kemacetan lalu lintas; *in a* ~ dalam kesulitan; *vi* macet; *vt* menyumbat, menjepit; **jammed** *adj* macet

Jamaica *n* [jaméka] Jamaika; **Jamaican** *n* orang Jamaika; *adj* berasal dari Jamaika

jamb [jam] *door* ~ kusén pintu

jamboree *n* jamboré

jammed *v, pf* ← **jam**; *adj* macet

janitor *n* [janitor] petugas pembersihan, penjaga

January *n* bulan Januari

Japan *n* Jepang; **Japanese** *n* bahasa Jepang; orang Jepang; *adj* berasal dari Jepang

jar *n* kendi, stoplés, botol, tempat (makanan); *vi* menggelegar; mengganggu; ~ *one's nerves* mengganggu saraf, membuat tidak nyaman; *vt* menggetarkan

jargon *n* bahasa khusus, istilah di bidang tertentu

jasmine *n* [jasmin] bunga melati

jaundice *n* [jondis] kuning

jaunty *adj* periang, bergaya

Java *n* pulau Jawa; *Central* ~ Jawa Tengah (Jateng); *West* ~ Jawa Barat (Jabar); **Javanese** *n* bahasa Jawa; orang Jawa; *adj* berasal dari Jawa Tengah atau Jawa Timur

javelin *n* lembing; ~ *throw* lempar lembing

jaw *n* rahang; **jawbone** *n* tulang rahang

jay *n* semacam burung

jaywalk *vi* menyeberang jalan tanpa melihat rambu lalu lintas; **jaywalker** *n* penyeberang jalan yang sembrono

jazz *n* musik jazz; ~ *up* meramaikan, mendandani, mempercantik; **jazzy** *adj* bergaya, menyolok

jealous *adj* [jélus] cemburu; ~ *of* cem-

buru pada; **jealousy** *n* kecemburuan, rasa cemburu

jeans *n, pl* [jins] celana jins

jeep *n* mobil jip

jeer *n* éjékan, cemoohan; *vi* mengolok-olok, mencemooh; *the opposition team was* ~*ed at* tim lawan diolok-olok

jell *vi* mengeras, membeku, mengental; **jellied** *adj* yang dibekukan; **jelly** *n* agar-agar; jéli; **jelly-baby**, **jelly-bean** *n* semacam gula-gula agar; **jellyfish** *n* ubur-ubur

jeopardize *vt* [jépardaiz] membahayakan; ~ *one's chances* membahayakan masa depan; **jeopardy** *n* bahaya; *in* ~ dalam bahaya

jerk *n* sentakan, renggutan; orang bodoh; *vt* menyentak, merenggut

jerrycan *n* jérigén

jersey *n* [jérsi] switer, baju hangat

jest *n* kelucuan, senda gurau; *in* ~ sedang bercanda; *vi* bersenda gurau; **jester** *n, arch* badut

Jesus *n* [jisus] Yésus, Isa; ~ *Christ* Yésus Kristus

jet *n* semburan air; pancar gas; jét; *vi, sl* terbang; ~ *off* terbang; ~*black* hitam legam; ~ *fighter* pesawat perang jet; ~ *lag* rasa letih akibat perubahan waktu setelah perjalanan udara; **jetset** *n* gaya hidup yang sering terbang ke luar negeri

jetty *n* jéti, dermaga

Jew *n* orang Yahudi; **Jewish** *adj* Yahudi; **Judaism** *n* [judéizem] agama Yahudi

jewel *n* [jul] (batu) permata; **jeweler** *n* **jeweller** tukang emas; ~*'s (shop)* toko emas; **jewelry** *n* **jewellery** perhiasan

Jewish *adj* Yahudi; **Judaism** *n* [judéizem] agama Yahudi ← **Jew**

jiffy *in a* ~ dalam sekejap mata; ~ *bag* paket pos berlapisan empuk

jigger *n* anu, barang kecil

jigsaw *n* gergaji ukir; ~ *puzzle* teka-teki menyusun potongan kayu

jilt *vt* meninggalkan (calon suami atau isteri); **jilted** *adj* ditinggalkan calon suami atau isteri

jingle *n* [jinggel] lagu iklan; *vi* bergemerincing

jinx *n* nasib malang, sial

jitters *to have the* ~ gelisah, kegugupan; **jittery** *adj* gelisah, gugup; *Beryl was* ~ *before her interview* Beryl gugup sebelum diwawancara

jive *n* sejenis musik atau tarian dengan irama cepat; *vi* berdansa diiringi musik tersebut

Jnr *abbrev, US junior* anak dari ayah (dengan nama yang sama); *John Kennedy* ~ John Kennedy, anak dari John Kennedy juga

job *n* pekerjaan, tugas; *~-hunting* mencari pekerjaan; *~-sharing* membagi pekerjaan; ~ *center* pusat mencari kerja; ~ *satisfaction* kepuasan kerja; *good* ~ bagus; *part-time* ~ pekerjaan paruh waktu; ~ *creation scheme* program penciptaan peluang kerja; *~s for the boys* jabatan untuk keluarga; **jobless** *adj* menganggur; *the* ~ kaum penganggur; **jobseeker** *n* pencari kerja

jockey *n* joki; *disc* ~ DJ; *vi* ~ *for a position* (berebut) mencari tempat

jog *n, vi* lari pagi, lari sore; ~ *one's memory* membantu mengingat; **jogger** *n* orang yang lari pagi, pelari; **jogging** *n* [joging] kegiatan lari; ~ *shoes* sepatu olahraga; ~ *track* jalan untuk lari

join *vi* ~ *(in)* bergabung, ikut serta; *may I* ~ *you?* boléh saya ikut?; *vt* masuk; menghubungkan, menggabungkan; ~ *the army* masuk tentara; **joint** *adj* bersama; ~ *venture* usaha patungan; *n, sl* ganja

joiner *n* tukang kayu, tukang kusén

joint *n* sendi, ruas; *adj* bersama; ~ *venture* usaha patungan ← **join**

joke *n* senda gurau, lelucon, guyonan; *beyond a* ~ sudah tidak lucu; *to tell a* ~ bersenda gurau, bercanda; *to play a* ~ *on someone* mempermainkan orang; *vi* ~ *(around)* bersenda gurau, melucu, melawak, bercanda; *only joking* bercanda kok; **joker** *n* pelawak; joker (kartu)

jolly *adj* riang, gembira

jolt *n* goyangan, guncangan; *vt* bergoyang; *the taxi ~ed to a stop* taksi berhenti dengan guncangan

Jordan *n* Yordania; **Jordanian** *n* orang Yordania; *adj* berasal dari Yordania

joss ~ *stick* kemenyan, dupa

jostle *vi* [josel] berdesak-desakkan

jot *vi* ~ *down* mencatat; *~ting pad* bloknot; **jotter** *n* bloknot

journal *n* (buku) harian, majalah, jurnal; **journalism** *n* [jernalizem] kewartawanan, jurnalisme; **journalist** *n* wartawan, jurnalis

journey *n* [jurni] perjalanan; *vi* pergi

jovial *adj* riang, gembira

joy *n* kebahagiaan, kegembiraan; **joyful, joyous** *adj* berbahagia, gembira; **joyfully, joyously** *adv* dengan gembira

joystick *n* stik

JP *abbrev Justice of the Peace* hakim setempat

jubilant *adj* bergembira; **jubilation** *n* kegembiraan

jubilee *n* [jubili] peringatan, hari ulang tahun; *silver* ~ peringatan 25 tahun

Judaism *n* [judéizem] agama Yahudi

judge *n* hakim; *vt* menghakimi, menilai; **judgment** *n* [jajment] keputusan; ~ *Day* Hari Kiamat; **judicial** *adj* [judisyel] berkaitan dengan hakim dan kehakiman; **judiciary** *n* [judisyari] pengadilan, kehakiman; **judicious** *adj* [judisyes] bijaksana

judo *n* judo, yudo

jug *n* tempat untuk saus atau minuman; téko; ~ *ears* caplang; *hot* ~ téko, kétél; *milk* ~ tempat susu

juggle *vi* [jagel] bermain sunglap; bermain sulap; menyunglap, menyulap; **juggler** *n* tukang sunglap; tukang sulap; **juggling** *n* sunglapan; sulapan

juice *n* air (buah), sari buah, jus; *orange* ~ air jeruk; **juicer** *n* blénder; **juicy** *adj* berair banyak

jukebox *n* kotak musik, mesin pemutar lagu

July *n* bulan Juli; *the fourth of* ~ tanggal 4 Juli, hari kemerdékaan Amérika

jumble *n* [jambel] campuran; ~ *sale* pasar barang bekas; *vt* mencampuradukkan

jumbo *adj* (berukuran) besar; ~ *jet* pesawat jét besar

jump *n* lompatan, loncatan; lonjakan; *vi* melompat, meloncat; *vt* melompati; ~ *rope* lompat tali; *high* ~ lompat tinggi; ~ *the queue* menyerobot mau tidak antri; *to make someone* ~ membuat kagét; **jumpy** *adj* gelisah

jumper *n* switer, baju hangat

jumpy *adj* gelisah ← **jump**

junction *n* simpang (jalan), perempatan; *T-*~ simpang tiga

June *n* bulan Juni

jungle *n* [janggel] hutan, rimba (raya); ~ *gym* permainan panjat-memanjat

junior *n* yunior; *adj* yunior, lebih muda, lebih rendah pangkatnya; ~ *school* sekolah dasar; ~ *high school* sekolah menengah pertama (SMP); *her boyfriend is 17 years her* ~ pacarnya lebih muda 17 tahun

junk *n* barang bekas, barang loak, sampah; ~ *food* makanan ringan, makanan siap saji; ~ *mail* iklan

junkie *n, sl* pecandu obat-obatan

jurisdiction *n* yurisdiksi, wilayah kekuasaan; **jurisprudence** *n* ilmu hukum, yurisprudensi; **jury** *n* juri

just *adj, adv* hanya, saja; tepat, persis; ~ *now* baru saja; ~ *a minute* tunggu sebentar

just *adj* adil; **justice** *n* [jastis] keadilan; **justify** *vt* [jastifai] membenarkan

jute *n* rami, goni

juvenile *adj* kekanak-kanakan; muda; *n* pemuda, anak di bawah umur

K

kale *n* sejenis sayur hijau

kaleidoscope *n* [kalaidoskop] kalé-doskop

kangaroo *n* [kanggaru] kanguru, kang-guru

kapok *n* [képok] kapuk

kaput *adj, coll* rusak

karaoke *n* [karaoki] karaoké

karate *n* [karati] karaté

karma *n* karma

kayak *n* dayung; kayak, kano; sampan;

kayaker *n* pedayung; **kayaking** *n* dayung kayak

Kazakh *n* [kazak] bahasa Kazakh; orang Kazakh; **Kazakhstan** *n* Kazakhstan; **Kazakhstani** *n* orang Kazakh; *adj* berasal dari Kazakhstan

kebab *n* kebab

keel ~ *over* terjatuh, oléng

keen *adj* antusias; tajam; ~ *as mustard* sangat antusias; *a* ~ *tennis player* sangat gemar main ténis; *to be* ~ *on* menyukai, menaksir

keep *vt* **kept kept** menyimpan, me-megang, menaruh, memelihara, men-jaga; selalu; ~ *back* menahan; ~ *healthy* menjaga keséhatan; ~ *on* terus melakukan; ~ *off* tidak mengganggu; ~ *out* dilarang masuk; ~ *time* menghi-tung waktu; ~ *up* melanjutkan, mene-ruskan; *for* ~*s* untuk selamanya; ~ *a promise* menepati janji; ~ *a secret* menyimpan rahasia; ~ *at it* menerus-kan; *I* ~ *falling asleep* saya selalu ke-tiduran; **keeper** *n* pemegang, penjaga, kurator; **keeping** *in* ~ *with* sesuai de-ngan, selaras dengan; **keepsake** *n* kenang-kenangan, oléh-oléh

keg *n* tong

kelp *n* sejenis rumput laut

kennel *n* kandang anjing; *pl* tempat penitipan anjing

Kenya *n* Kénia; **Kenyan** *n* orang Kénia; *adj* berasal dari Kénia

kept *vt, pf* → **keep**

kerb *n, UK* **curb** *US* pinggiran jalan, penahan

kernel *n* biji, inti

kerosene *n* [kerosin] minyak tanah; ~ *lamp* lampu petromaks

ketchup *n* saus, kécap; *tomato* ~ AS saus tomat

kettle *n* téko; *electric* ~ alat pemanas air minum; **kettledrum** *n* genderang kecil

key *n* [ki] (anak) kunci; tuts; nada; ~ *card* kartu kunci; ~ *chain* rantai kunci; ~ *ring* gantungan kunci; *major* ~ nada mayor; *piano* ~ tuts (piano); *the* ~ *to success* kunci keberhasilan; *adj* pokok; *vi* ~ *in* memasukkan, mengetik; **keyboard** *n* kibor; papan tuts; **keyhole**

n lubang kunci; **keynote** ~ *speech* pidato pembukaan; **keypad** *n* tuts

kg *abbrev kilogram* kg (kilogram)

khaki *adj* [kaki] warna hijau kecoklat-coklatan; *n* bahan untuk seragam militér

Khmer *n* [kemér] bahasa Kamboja; ~ *Rouge* Khmér Mérah

kibbutz *n* [kibuts] pertanian koléktif di Israél

kick *n* tendangan, sépak; perangsang; *vt* menendang, menyépak; ~ *off* memulai; *alive and ~ing* ternyata masih hidup; *just for* ~s iseng

kid *n* anak kambing; *sl* anak; **kiddie, kiddy, kids** *adj, coll* kanak-kanak

kidnap *vt* menculik; **kidnapper** *n* penculik; **kidnapping** *n* penculikan

kidney *n* [kidni] ginjal; ~*-bean* kacang mérah; ~*-shaped* berbentuk seperti ginjal

kill *v* membunuh; ~ *oneself* membunuh diri; ~ *off* menghancurkan, membinasakan; ~ *time* menghabiskan waktu; **killed** *adj* terbunuh, mati, gugur, téwas; ~ *in action* gugur, téwas; **killer** *n* pembunuh; **killing** *n* pembunuhan; *to make a* ~ mendapat untung besar; **killjoy** *n* orang yang merusak kesenangan orang lain

kiln *n* tempat pembakaran (genténg, keramik)

kilogram, kilo *n* kilogram, kilo

kilometer, kilo *n* kilo, kilométer

kilt *n* rok khas Skotlandia

kilter *out of* ~ tidak sesuai, rusak

kimono *n* [kimono] pakaian khas Jepang, kimono

kin *n* kerabat, kaum, keluarga; *next of* ~ saudara terdekat; **kinship** *n* kekeluargaan

kind *n* [kaind] macam, jenis, ragam; ~ *of* agak; *of a* ~ sejenis; *a* ~ *of fruit* semacam buah

kind *adj* [kaind] baik hati, simpatis; ~*-hearted* baik hati; **kindly** *adv* dengan baik hati; tolong; ~ *inform me* tolong diberitahu; **kindness** *n* kebaikan hati

kindergarten *n* **kinder** *coll* taman kanak-kanak (TK)

kindle *vt* [kindel] menyalakan, mengobarkan; **kindling** *n* ranting-ranting kecil untuk perapian

kindly *adv* [kaindli] dengan baik hati; tolong; ~ *inform me* tolong diberitahu ← **kind**

kindness *n* [kaindness] kebaikan hati ← **kind**

kinetic *adj* [kinétik] kinétika; ~ *energy* tenaga kinétis

king *n* raja; ~*-sized* ukuran paling besar; *the* ~ *of Thailand* Raja Thailand; **kingdom** *n* kerajaan; *the* ~ *of Spain* Kerajaan Spanyol

kingfisher *n* sejenis burung

kink *n* kekusutan; *there's a* ~ *in the hose* selang itu béngkok; **kinky** *adj* anéh

kinship *n* kekeluargaan ← **kin**

kiosk *n* [kiosk] kios, lokét, warung

kipper *n* ikan haring yang diasinkan

Kiribati *n, adj* [kiribas] Kiribati

kiss *n* ciuman, sun, kecupan; *French* ~ mencium dengan lidah; *hugs and* ~*es* peluk cium; *vi* berciuman; (memberi) sun; ~ *on the cheek* cium pipi, sun; memberi sun; *vt* mencium; memberi sun kepada

kit *n* peralatan, perlengkapan; *sewing* ~ perlengkapan menjahit; *sports* ~ seragam olahraga; *tool* ~ alat-alat pertukangan; *first aid* ~ kotak pusat pertolongan pertama; **kitbag** *n* tas perlengkapan

kitchen *n* dapur; ~ *sink* tempat cuci piring; ~ *stove* kompor; **kitchenware** *n* perlengkapan dapur

kite *n* layang-layang; *to fly a* ~ main layang-layang

kitten *n* anak kucing; ~ *heels* (sepatu) hak rendah; **kitty** *n, coll* kucing (kecil); *n* céléngan, dana

kiwi *n* burung kiwi; **kiwifruit** *n* [kiwifrut] (buah) kiwi

kleptomania *n* [kléptoménia] keinginan mengutil barang; **kleptomaniac** *n, adj* pengutil

km *abbrev kilometer* km (kilométer)

knack [nak] *to get the* ~, *to have the* ~ mampu, mengetahui caranya

knead vt [nid] menguli; ~able eraser penghapus yang bentuknya bisa diubah

knee n [ni] lutut, dengkul; ~ deep, ~ high selutut; ~-high socks kaus kaki selutut; ~-jerk reaction langsung ditanggapi (tanpa banyak berpikir); vt menggebuk dengan lutut; **kneecap** n tempurung lutut; **kneepad** n pelindung lutut

kneel vi [nil] **knelt knelt** berlutut

kneepad n pelindung lutut ← **knee**

knew v, pf → **know**

knickers n, sl [nikers] celana dalam; n, arch celana

knife n [naif] knives pisau; pen~ pisau lipat; vt menikam; at ~point ditodong

knight n [nait] kesatria; **knighthood** n [nait hud] gelar bangsawan Inggris

knit v [nit] merajut; ~ a scarf merajut syal; ~ your brow mengernyitkan alis; **knitter** n orang yang merajut; **knitting** n rajutan; ~ needle jarum rajut; **knitwear** n [nitwér] baju rajutan, busana rajutan

knives n, pl [naivs] → **knife**

knob n [nob] tombol, pegangan, kenop; door ~ kenop (pintu); **knobby, knobbly** ~ knees tulang lutut menonjol

knock n [nok] pukulan, ketok; ~-kneed kaki X; a ~ at the door ketukan di pintu; v mengetuk; ~ back menolak; ~ down membongkar; memukul sampai jatuh; ~ out mendorong keluar; memukul sampai pingsan; ~ up sl menghamili; vt memukul; **knockout** n (pukulan) yang sangat hébat

knot n [not] simpul; buku, mata kayu; mil laut; to make or tie a ~ menyimpul; to tie the ~ menikah; vt menyimpulkan; **knotty** adj sulit

know v [no] **knew known** tahu, mengetahui; mengenal; mengerti, memahami; ~-all sok tahu; ~-how pengetahuan, keahlian; ~ about tahu tentang; ~ that tahu bahwa; in the ~ tahu; you never ~ siapa tahu; to get to ~ berkenalan dengan; **knowing** adj pengertian; **knowledge** n [nolej] pengetahuan; to my ~ setahu saya; **knowledgable** adj [nole-

jabel] banyak tahu; **known** adj dikenal; diketahui

knuckle n [nakel] buku jari; ~ down bekerja dengan rajin

KO abbrev knockout pukulan yang sangat hébat

koala n koala

kookaburra n [kukabara] burung khas Australia

Koran the ~ al-Quran; to read the ~ mengaji; **Koranic** adj dari al-Quran; ~ recital pengajian

Korea n [Koria] Koréa (Selatan); **North** ~ Koréa Utara; **Korean** n bahasa Koréa; orang Koréa; adj berasal dari Koréa

kosher adj halal (menurut adat Yahudi); ~ restaurant réstoran yang menganut aturan makan orang Yahudi

Kosovan adj berasal dari Kosovo; **Kosovar** n orang Kosovo; **Kosovo** n Kosovo

kph kilometers per hour kilométer per jam

Kuwait n [kuwét] Kuwait; **Kuwaiti** n orang Kuwait; adj berasal dari Kuwait

Kyrgyz n [kirgiz] bahasa Kirgistan; orang Kirgis; **Kyrgyzstan, Kirgistan** n Kirgistan; adj berasal dari Kirgistan; **Kyrgyzstani, Kirgistani** n orang Kirgistan

L

L abbrev Lane Gg (Gang)

L abbrev liter liter

L-plate n tanda pengendara pelajar

lab n, coll laboratorium; ~ assistant asistén (lab) ← **laboratory**

label n mérek; nama; vi memberi nama, menulis nama pada barang; she ~led the discounted goods with the new price dia memasang harga baru pada barang-barang diskon

labial adj [lébiel] berkaitan dengan bibir

labor, labour n pekerjaan (kasar); prosés persalinan; ~ Day Hari Buruh; ~ force tenaga kerja; ~ Party Partai Buruh; in ~ sedang bersalin; vi beker-

ja; *Stuart ~ed away in the garden*
Stuart bekerja keras di kebun;
laborer, labourer *n* buruh, tukang,
pekerja; **laborious** *adj* berat
laboratory *n* **lab** *coll* laboratorium, lab;
~ assistant asistén (lab)
labour → **labor**
labyrinth *n* [labirinth] susunan yang
simpang siur, labirin
lace *n* renda; **lacy** *adj* berenda
lack *n* kekurangan; *vt* kurang, tidak
memiliki, tidak mempunyai; *new
workers ~ experience* pekerja baru
kurang berpengalaman
lackluster, lacklustre *adj* [laklaster]
kurang semarak, biasa
laconic *adj* [lakonik] péndék (kata)
lacquer *n* [laker] lak, pernis; *v* memberi
pernis; **lacquered** *adj* dipernis
lacrosse *n* [lakros] permainan yang
memakai tongkat dengan keranjangan
kecil dan bola
lactose *n* laktosa; *~-intolerant* intoléran-
si laktosa
lacy *adj* berenda ← **lace**
lad *n* anak lelaki; *when I was a ~* waktu
aku kecil; **laddie** *n, sl* anak lelaki
ladder *n* tangga, jenjang
laddie *n, sl* anak lelaki ← **lad**
laden *adj* dimuat
ladies *n (the) Ladies* WC wanita; *ladies
and gentlemen* bapak-bapak dan
ibu-ibu ← **lady**
ladle *n* [lédel] séndok besar; *vt*
menyéndok
lady *n, f* [lédi] nyonya, wanita; gelar
bangsawan; *~ friend* teman wanita,
pacar; *First ~* ibu negara; *(the) Ladies*
WC wanita; *ladies and gentlemen*
bapak-bapak dan ibu-ibu; **ladybird,
ladybug** *n* kepik; **ladylike** *adj* seperti
wanita yang sopan
lag *n* ketertinggalan, kelambatan; *jet ~*
rasa letih akibat perubahan waktu
setelah perjalanan udara; *vi ~ (behind)*
tertinggal, ketinggalan
lager *n* [lager] sejenis bir
lagoon *n* laguna
laid *vt, pf* → **lay**; *~-back* tenang, santai
lain *vi, pf* → **lie**

lair *n* sarang binatang buas
lake *n* danau, telaga; *~ Toba* Danau
Toba; **lakeside** *adj* di tepi danau
lamb *n* [lam] anak domba, anak biri-biri;
~ chop potongan daging (iga) domba
lame *adj* lumpuh, pincang; lemah; *~
duck* macan ompong; *a ~ excuse*
alasan yang dibuat-buat
lament *n* [lamént] ratapan; *vt* meratapi;
lamentation *n* ratapan, tangisan
laminate *vt* melaminasi, melapis dengan lembaran plastik, laminating;
laminated *adj* dilaminasi, dilaminat-
ing; **lamination, laminating** *n* laminasi, laminating
lamp *n* lampu, pelita; *kerosene ~*
lentéra, lampu pétromaks; **lamplight** *n*
cahaya lampu; **lamppost** *n* tiang
lampu, tiang lentéra; **lampshade** *n*
kap lampu
lance *n* tombak lembing; *vt* menusuk; *~
a boil* menyedot bisul
land *n* tanah, bumi, darat; negeri,
negara; *~ tax* pajak tanah; *by ~* jalan
darat, léwat darat; *on ~* di darat; *on
the ~* di pertanian; *the Holy ~* Tanah
Suci; *vi* mendarat; **landing** *n* pendaratan; tempat beristirahat di tangga;
landlady *n, f* induk semang; **landline**
n pesawat Télkom; **landlocked** *adj*
tidak berbatasan dengan laut; **landlord**
n, m tuan tanah, pemilik rumah; **land-
mark** *n* patokan, petunjuk; peristiwa
penting; **landmine** *n* ranjau (darat);
landowner *n* tuan tanah; **landscape** *n*
pemandangan, lanskap; *~ architect*
arsiték lanskap; **landslide** *n* tanah
longsor
lane *n* gang, lorong; jalur; lajur; *fast ~*
jalur cepat; *slow ~* jalur lambat; *to
change ~s* pindah jalur
language *n* [languej] bahasa; *~ course*
kursus bahasa; *bad ~* kata-kata jorok,
makian; *first ~* bahasa ibu; *foreign ~*
bahasa asing; *second ~* bahasa kedua;
to speak a ~ berbahasa
languish *vi* merana; *his team ~es in
Division 1* timnya tetap saja di Divisi 1
lank *adj* lepék, berminyak (rambut)
lanky *adj* tinggi, jangkung

lantern *n* lentéra; *Chinese* ~ lampion

Lao *n* bahasa Laos; orang Laos; **Laos** *n* Laos; **Laotian** *n* [laosyen] orang Laos; *adj* berasal dari Laos

lap *n* haribaan, pangkuan; putaran; *I swam 40 ~s* saya berenang sampai 40 putaran; **lapdog** *n* anjing piaraan yang kecil; penjilat

lap *vi* meluap; minum dengan lidah; menerima banyak dengan senang hati; *she ~ped up the attention* dia sangat menikmati perhatian; *the cat ~ped up the milk* kucing itu minum susu; **laptop** *n* komputer laptop

Lapland *n, arch* Lapland, Samiland; **Lapp** *n* orang Sami

lapse *n* jatuh; kehilangan; selang; *vi* kambuh, menjadi; habis, berlalu; *a ~ in concentration* kehilangan konséntrasi

laptop *n* komputer laptop ← **lap**

larch *n* sejenis pohon

lard *n* lemak babi

larder *n* tempat menyimpan makanan

large *adj* besar, luas; *~ size* ukuran besar; *at ~* bebas; *~r than life* dibesar-besarkan; **largely** *adv* kebanyakan; *it was ~ my fault* saya yang paling bersalah

lark *n* semacam burung; *sl* iseng

larva *n* larvae jentik-jentik

laryngitis *n* [larinjaitis] radang tenggorokan (sehingga suara hilang); **larynx** *n* [laringks] pangkal tenggorokan

lascivious *adj* [lasivius] merangsang, menggairahkan

laser *n* [léser] (sinar) laser; *~ printer* printer laser; *to have ~ surgery* dilaser

lash *n* cambukan; bulu mata

lass, lassie *n, sl* anak perempuan

lasso *n* jerat; *vt* menjerat

last *vi* tahan, bertahan, berlangsung; awét; *it will ~ a year* setahun lamanya; *adj* terakhir, penghabisan, (yang) lalu; *~ month* bulan lalu; *~ night* semalam; *~ resort* pilihan terakhir; *at ~* akhirnya; **lasting** *adj* awét, abadi; **lastly** *adv* terakhir

latch *n* palang pintu, kunci, gréndel; **latchkey** *n, adj* [lacki] kunci pintu

late *adj, adv* lambat, terlambat; almarhum, mendiang, *f* almarhumah; **late-**

comer *n* pendatang baru; **lately** *adv* belum lama, belakangan ini, baru-baru ini; **lateness** *n* keterlambatan; **later** *adj, adv* nanti; kemudian; **latest** *adj, adv* terakhir, paling akhir; *~ news* berita terkini; *at the ~* paling lambat, selambat-lambatnya

latent *adj* tersembunyi, terpendam

later *adj, adv* nanti; kemudian ← **late**

latest *adj, adv* terakhir, paling akhir; *~ news* berita terkini; *at the ~* paling lambat, selambat-lambatnya ← **late**

latex *n* getah

lathe *n* [léth] mesin bubut

lather *n* buih, busa (sabun); *v* menyabun

Latin *n* [latin] bahasa Latin, bahasa Romawi; *~ America* Amérika Latin; *~ script* huruf Romawi

latitude *n* [latityud] lintang; *southern ~* lintang selatan

latrine *n* [latrin] kakus

latte *n* [laté] (kopi) susu

latter *n, adj* yang kemudian, yang tersebut, yang terakhir; *he took Music and Art; the ~ was more interesting* dia mengambil mata pelajaran Musik dan Seni Lukis; yang terakhir ternyata lebih menarik

lattice *n* [latis] kisi-kisi, ruji-ruji; **latticework** *n* [latiswerk] kisi-kisi

Latvia *n* Latvia; **Latvian** *adj* berasal dari Latvia; *n* bahasa Latvia; orang Latvia

laugh *n, vi* [laf] tertawa, *coll* ketawa; *~ at* menertawakan, menertawai; *a good ~* sangat lucu; **laughable** *adj* [lafabel] menggelikan; tidak masuk akal; **laughter** *n* ketawa, tawa

launch *n* peluncuran; kapal berkas; *book ~* peluncuran buku; *vt* meluncurkan; *~ into* memulai

launder *vt* mencuci; *money ~ing* pencucian uang; **laundromat** *n* tempat cuci pakai mesin otomat; **laundry** *n* cucian, baju kotor; binatu, waserai

lava *n* lahar, lava

lavatory *n* [lavetori] kamar kecil, WC

lavender *adj* ungu muda; *n* semacam bunga harum berwarna ungu

lavish *adj* méwah, berlebihan; *vt* mencurahkan, menghamburkan; *~ atten-*

tion on sangat memperhatikan; **lavish-
ly** *adv* secara méwah, secara besar-
besaran

law *n* hukum, undang-undang; peraturan; *~-abiding* taat hukum; *~ school*
fakultas hukum; *common ~* hukum
adat; *against the ~* melanggar hukum;
~ of the jungle hukum rimba; **lawful**
adj sesuai dengan hukum, sah; **law-
less** *adj* tanpa hukum; **lawmaker** *n*
pembuat undang-undang; **lawsuit** *n*
perkara, dakwaan; *to bring a ~ against*
menuntut; **lawyer** *n* pengacara,
advokat, praktisi hukum

lawn *n* lapangan rumput; *~ bowls* boling
taman; *~ mower* mesin potong
rumput; *~ tennis* ténis

lawsuit *n* perkara, dakwaan; *to bring a ~
against* menuntut ← **law**

lawyer *n* pengacara, advokat, praktisi
hukum ← **law**

lax *adj* lemah, longgar, lalai

laxative *n* [laksativ] obat peluntur,
pencahar

lay *vt* laid laid meletakkan; *~ down*
meletakkan; menetapkan; *~ eggs*
bertelur; *~ off* memberhentikan, mempehakakan; *coll* membiarkan; *~ on*
menyediakan; *~ the table* menyiapkan
méja makan; **layout** *n* tata letak; rancangan, rencana

layer *n* lapis, lapisan; *~ cake* kue lapis
legit

layette *n* seperangkat pakaian untuk bayi

layman *n* orang awam

layout *n* tata letak; rancangan, rencana
← **lay**

laze *vi* bermalas-malas; **lazily** *adv*
secara malas; **laziness** *n* kemalasan;
lazy *adj* malas; *~ river* kolam renang
berbentuk aliran air; *~ susan* baki
makanan yang berputar; **lazybones** *n*
pemalas

lb *abbrev pound* pon

leach *vi* rembes, bocor; *effluent ~ed into
the river* kotoran bocor ke dalam sungai

lead *n* [léd] timbal, timah hitam,
plumbum; *~ pencil* pénsil; *~-free petrol*
bénsin tanpa timbal; **leaden** *adj* terbuat dari timah hitam

lead *v* [lid] **led led** memimpin; *vi*
menuju; *~ to* menuju; *~ the way*
memelopori, merintis; *n* petunjuk; *~
role* peranan utama; *~ singer* vokalis;
~ story berita utama; *to follow someone's ~* mengikuti (petunjuk) orang
lain; **leader** *n* pemimpin; **leadership** *n*
kepemimpinan; **leading** *adj* penting,
utama, terkemuka; *~ question* pertanyaan yang mengharuskan jawaban
tertentu

leaf *n* **leaves** daun; *vi* membuka-buka
(halaman); *~ through a magazine*
membuka-buka halaman majalah;
leafy *adj* rimbun, rindang

leaflet *n* selebaran

leafy *adj* rimbun, rindang ← **leaf**

league *n* [lig] liga, persatuan,
perserikatan; *~ table* klasemén tim;
Premier ~ Liga Inggris

leak *n, vi* bocor, merembes; *vt* membocorkan; **leakage** *n* [likej] bocoran,
rembesan; **leaky** *adj* bocor, rembes

lean *n* kurus; sedikit

lean *vi* **leant leant** [lént] tidak lurus,
condong, bersandar; **leaning** *n*
kecenderungan

leap *n* lompatan; *~ year* tahun kabisat;
vi **leapt leapt** [lépt] melompat; *~ at*
menyambut dengan baik; *vt* melompati;
leapfrog *n* permainan loncat katak

leapt *v, pf* [lépt] → **leap**

learn *v* **learnt/learned learnt/learned**
belajar; mendengar berita; *vt* mempelajari; *~ one's lesson* kapok;
learned *adj* [lérnéd] terpelajar; **learner** *n* pelajar; *~ driver* pengendara pelajar; **learning** *n* pembelajaran

lease *n* séwa; *vt ~ out* menyéwakan;
Denise ~d her holiday flat out Denise
menyéwakan vilanya; **leaseholder** *n*
penyéwa

leash *n* pengikat binatang, tali, rantai;
on a ~ dirantai

least *adj* terkecil, paling sedikit; *at ~*
setidak-tidaknya, sekurang-kurangnya;
it's the ~ I can do hanya itu saja (yang
bisa saya bantu); *not in the ~* tidak
sama sekali; *the ~ of my worries* tidak
usah dirisaukan

leather n [léther] kulit; ~ *jacket* jaket kulit; *fake* ~ kulit imitasi

leave n cuti; *compassionate* ~ cuti karena ada yang meninggal; *long-service* ~ cuti panjang; *maternity* ~ cuti hamil; *paternity* ~ cuti untuk ayah baru; *on* ~ sedang cuti; *to take* ~ pamit, mohon diri; cuti; *vi* **left left** berangkat, pergi, bertolak; *he left for the Philippines* dia sudah berangkat ke Filipina; *vt* membiarkan; meninggalkan; ~ *behind* meninggalkan; *Callum left his cap behind* topi Callum ketinggalan; ~ *out* tidak memasukkan; ~ *me alone* biarkan saya sendiri; jangan ganggu saya

leaves n, pl → **leaf**

Lebanese adj berasal dari Libanon; n orang Libanon; **Lebanon** n Libanon

lecture n kuliah, ceramah, pidato; *vi* memberi teguran; memberi kuliah; *his mother ~d him about his poor marks* dia ditegur oléh ibunya soal nilai rapot yang jélék; *vt* menguliahi; **lecturer** n dosén, léktor; ~ *in economics* dosén ilmu ékonomi

led v, pf → **lead**

ledge n kusén (jendéla); pinggiran

ledger n buku kas

leech n lintah

leek n bawang perai

leer n pandangan yang tidak senonoh; *vi* mengerling, melirik

leeward adj di bawah angin

leeway n waktu tambahan, tempat tambahan

left adj (sebelah) kiri; ~*-click* klik kiri; ~*-handed* kidal; ~ *wing* sayap kiri; ~ *and right* kiri kanan

left adj, v, pf tertinggal → **leave**; ~ *luggage* layanan penitipan bagasi; *there's no cake* ~ sudah tidak ada kué lagi; **leftover** n, adj sisa

leg n kaki; *chicken* ~ paha ayam; *a broken* ~ kakinya patah; *you're pulling my* ~ kamu memperolok-olokkan saya; **leggy** adj berkaki panjang; **legless** adj, coll sangat mabuk; **legroom** n ruang untuk kaki (selama duduk)

legacy n [légasi] warisan, harta pusaka

legal adj sah, legal, menurut undang-undang; hukum; ~ *adviser* penasihat hukum, pengacara; ~ *aid* bantuan hukum; **legalization** n pengesahan, legalisasi; **legalize** vt mengesahkan, memboléhkan, melégalisir (dokumén); **legally** adv secara sah, secara legal

legend n [léjend] legénda; kunci peta; **legendary** adj terkenal

leggings n, pl [légings] stoking tebal, celana ketat ← **leg**

leggy adj berkaki panjang ← **leg**

legible adj [léjibel] dapat dibaca

legion n [lijen] légiun, pasukan; *a* ~ *of* banyak sekali

legislate vi [léjislét] membuat undang-undang; **legislation** n perundang-undangan; **legislative** adj [léjislatif] législatif; **legislator** n pembuat undang-undang; **legislature** n badan pembuat undang-undang

legitimacy n [lejitimasi] hak kekuasaan; **legitimate** adj [lejitimet] sah

legless adj, coll sangat mabuk ← **leg**

legroom n ruang untuk kaki (selama duduk) ← **leg**

legume n kacang-kacangan; *snow peas are* ~*s* kacang kapri termasuk jenis kacang-kacangan

leisure n [lésyer] waktu luang, waktu senggang; ~ *center* pusat rékréasi, gelanggang olahraga; *at your* ~ di waktu senggang; **leisurely** adj dengan santai

lemon n jeruk nipis, limun; adj kuning muda; **lemonade** n air jeruk nipis; Sprite; **lemongrass** n serai

lemur n sejenis binatang seperti monyét di Madagaskar

lend vt **lent lent** meminjamkan; ~ *a (helping) hand* menolong; **lender** n pemberi pinjaman

length n panjang; jarak, lama; *at* ~ panjang lébar; *at arm's* ~ menjaga jarak; **lengthen** vt memperpanjang; **lengthwise** adj menurut panjangnya; **lengthy** adj panjang lebar; panjang, lama; **long** adj panjang; lama; ~*-distance call* télepon interlokal; ~*-haired* berambut panjang; ~*-haired cat* kucing

angora; ~-*playing record (LP)* piringan
hitam; ~-*range* jarak jauh; ~-*sighted*
rabun dekat; ~-*winded* bertélé-télé; ~
jump lompat jauh; *before* ~ tidak lama
kemudian; *so* ~ sampai jumpa, sampai
bertemu; *as* ~ *as* selama; *I won't be* ~
saya tidak akan lama; **longhouse** *n*
rumah panjang ← **long**

leniency *n* sikap lunak, toléransi; **lenient**
adj lunak, toléran

lens *n* lénsa; *contact* ~ lénsa kontak

Lent *n* puasa Maséhi selama 40 hari
sebelum Paskah

lent *vt, pf* → **lend**

lentils *n, pl* kacang léntil

leopard *n* [lépard] macan kumbang

leotard *n* [liotard] baju senam

leper *n* [léper] penderita kusta; **leprosy**
n penyakit kusta

leprechaun *n* [léprekon] makhluk halus
dalam dongéng Irlandia

lesbian *n, adj* lésbi

Lesotho *n* [lesutu] Lesotho

less *adj* kurang, lebih kecil; *no* ~ tidak
kurang; *ten* ~ *six is four* sepuluh
kurang enam sama dengan empat;
lessen *vi* berkurang, mengecil; *vt*
mengurangi, mengecilkan; **lesser** *adj*
lebih kecil; *the* ~ *Sundas* Nusa
Tenggara

lesson *n* pelajaran; lés; *geography* ~
pelajaran ilmu bumi; *piano* ~ lés
piano; *to give* ~*s* memberi lés; *to have*
~*s, to take* ~*s* (mengambil) lés

lest *conj* agar tidak, supaya tidak;
kalau-kalau; ~ *we forget* jangan dilu-
pakan (jasa pahlawan perang)

let *vt* **let let** membiarkan; menyéwakan
(rumah); ~-*down n* kekécewaan; ~
alone apalagi, jangankan; ~ *down*
mengecéwakan; menurunkan; ~ *fly*
melepaskan; ~ *go* melepaskan; ~ *off*
meledakkan; meloloskan; ~ *up* reda,
berhenti; ~ *us, let's* marilah; *to* ~
diséwakan; *to* ~ *someone know* kasih
tahu, memberitahu

lethal *adj* [lithal] mematikan

lethargic *adj* malas, lesu; **lethargy** *n*
[létharji] rasa lesu, rasa letih

let's → **let us**

letter *n* surat; huruf, aksara; ~ *box* kotak
surat; bis surat; *Chinese* ~ huruf Cina;
love ~ surat cinta; *man of* ~*s* sarjana;
Faculty of ~*s* Fakultas Sastra; **letterhead** *n* kop surat; **lettering** *n* tulisan
(tangan)

lettuce *n* [létes] selada

leukemia, leukaemia *n* [lukimia]
kanker darah, leukemia

levee *n* [lévi] tanggul; dermaga

level *adj* [lével] datar, rata; *n* tingkat;
permukaan; ~-*headed* berkepala di-
ngin; *A-*~*s* ujian akhir SMA; *O-*~*s*
ujian setingkat kelas 1 SMA; ~ *crossing* perlintasan keréta api; *spirit* ~
waterpas; *on the* ~ jujur; *vi* ~ *off,* ~ *out*
mendatar; *vt* meratakan

lever *n* pengungkit, tuas, tuil

levy *n* [lévi] pajak, rétribusi; *a* ~ *on
imports* pajak impor; *vt* memungut

lewd *adj* cabul, jorok

lexical *adj* [léksikal] berkaitan dengan
kata; **lexicographer** *n* penyusun
kamus; **lexicon** *n* kosa kata

liability *n* [laiabiliti] tanggungan; **liable**
adj [layabel] tanggung; bertanggung
jawab; ~ *to* cenderung; kena

liaise *vi* [liéz] ~ *with* bekerja sama dengan, menghubungi; **liaison** *n* hubungan; ~ *officer* pegawai hubungan
masyarakat (humas)

liar *n* [laier] pembohong; **lie** *vi* bohong,
berbohong, membohong; ~ *to* membo-
hongi

libel *n* fitnah (secara tertulis)

liberal *adj* murah hati; libéral; **liberate**
vt membébaskan; **liberated** *adj* bébas,
merdéka; dibébaskan, dimerdékakan;
liberation *n* pembébasan; **liberator** *n*
pihak yang membébaskan; **liberty** *n*
kemerdékaan, kebébasan; *at* ~ *to* bébas

Liberia *n* [laibiria] Libéria; **Liberian** *adj*
berasal dari Libéria; *n* orang Libéria

libido *n* [libido] gairah séksual

librarian *n* [laibrérian] pustakawan,
kepala perpustakaan; **library** *n* perpustakaan; *mobile* ~ perpustakaan keliling

libretto *n* lirik opéra

Libya *n* Libia; **Libyan** *adj* berasal dari
Libia; *n* orang Libia

lice *n, pl* kutu → **louse**
license, licence *n* [laisens] izin, ijazah; ~ *plate* pelat polisi; *driving* ~ surat izin mengemudi (SIM); *off–*~ toko minuman keras; **license** *vt* mengizinkan, memboléhkan; **licensed** *adj* boléh menjual minuman beralkohol; **licensee** *n* pihak yang diizinkan
lichen *n* [laiken] sejenis lumut
lick *n* jilatan; *v* menjilat; *vt, coll* mengalahkan dengan telak
lie *n* bohong, kebohongan; ~ *detector test* tés kebohongan; *vi* bohong, berbohong, membohong; ~ *to vt* membohongi
lie *vi* **lay lain** terletak, berada; berbaring; *~–in* bangun siang; ~ *down* merebahkan diri, berbaring, tiduran
Liechtenstein *adj* [likhtenstain] berasal dari Liechtenstein; *n* Liechtenstein; **Liechtensteiner** *n* orang Liechtenstein
lieu [liu] *in* ~ *of* sebagai pengganti
lieutenant *n* [UK léfténant; US luténant] létnan; *~–Colonel* Létkol (Létnan Kolonél)
life *n* **lives** hidup, kehidupan; nyawa; ~ *size* berukuran yang sebenarnya; ~ *cycle* siklus hidup; ~ *expectancy* harapan hidup; ~ *imprisonment* hukuman penjara sepanjang hidup; ~ *insurance* asuransi jiwa; ~ *story* kisah hidup; *for* ~ sepanjang hidup; *to save a* ~ menyelamatkan jiwa; **lifeboat** *n* sekoci (penyelamat); **lifebuoy** *n* [laifboi] pelampung; **lifeguard** *n* [laifgard] penjaga pantai, penjaga kolam renang; **lifejacket** *n* baju pelampung; **lifeless** *adj* tidak hidup lagi, mati; **lifelike** *adj* seperti hidup; **lifelong** *adj* seumur hidup, sepanjang hidup; **lifesaver** *n* penjaga pantai; *sl* yang sangat menolong; **lifestyle** *n* gaya hidup; **lifetime** *n* seumur hidup ← **live**
lift *n* lift, pengangkat barang; *to give someone a* ~ membonchéngkan; memberi semangat; *vt* mengangkat; *to get a* ~ menumpang, *coll* tébéng
light *n* [lait] cahaya, sinar; lampu; *sl* korék api; ~ *bulb* bohlam, bola lampu; ~ *year* tahun cahaya; *in* ~ *of* mengi-

ngat; *to bring to* ~ membukakan; *to come to* ~ terbuka, terkuak; *adj* terang; ringan, énténg; *~–fingered* tangan panjang; *~–headed* pusing; *~–hearted* énténg, menyenangkan; *to make* ~ *of* meréméhkan; *v* **lit lit** *vi* nyala; *vt* menyalakan, memasang (lampu); **lighten** *vi* menjadi terang; *vt* meringankan, menerangkan; ~ *cream* krim pemutih; **lighter** *n* korék api, gerétan; **lighthouse** *n* mercu suar; **lightly** *adv* dengan énténg; **lightning** *n* kilat, halilintar, petir; ~ *rod* penangkal petir
like *adj* sama, serupa, sepadan, setara; *conj* seperti, sama dengan; *~–minded* sependapat; **likelihood** *n* kemungkinan; **likely** *adj, adv* agaknya, kemungkinan; mungkin; **liken** *vi* menyamakan, mengibaratkan; *he ~s himself to Mao* dia mengibaratkan diri sebagai penerus Mao; **likeness** *n* kesamaan, kemiripan; **likewise** *adv* begitu juga, demikian pula
like *vt* suka, menyukai, gemar; *I* ~ *fish* saya suka ikan; **likeable** *adj* ramah, menyenangkan; **liking** *n* kesukaan
likelihood *n* kemungkinan; **likely** *adj* agaknya, kemungkinan ← **like**
liken *vi* menyamakan, mengibaratkan; *he ~s himself to Mao* dia mengibaratkan diri sebagai penerus Mao ← **like**
likeness *n* kesamaan, kemiripan ← **like**
likewise *adv* begitu juga, demikian pula ← **like**
lilac *adj* ungu muda; *n* semacam tanaman yang berbunga ungu
lilo *n* pelampung seperti kasur
lily *n* [lili] teratai; *~–white* tidak berdosa
limb *n* [lim] anggota badan
limbo *in* ~ telantar
lime *n* limau, jeruk (nipis); kapur; ~ *green* hijau lumut; **limestone** *n* batu kapur, gamping
limelight *n* [laimlait] pusat perhatian; sorotan
limestone *n* batu kapur, gamping ← **lime**
limit *n* batas, limit; *city ~s* pinggiran kota; *vt* membatasi; *that's the* ~ itu keterlaluan; **limitation** *n* pembatasan;

limited adj terbatas; Proprietary ~ (Pty Ltd) perseroan terbatas (PT)
limo n, sl limosin, limo; **limousine** n [limosin] limosin
limp vi berjalan pincang; adj lemah
line n garis, gorés; tali; baris, dérét; ~ dancing dansa seperti poco-poco; ~ manager atasan; shipping ~ perusahaan perkapalan; in ~ with sesuai dengan; out of ~ menyimpang; to stand in ~ antri; to toe the ~ mematuhi peraturan; vi ~ up antri; she ~s her dresses with silk dia memberi lapisan sutera pada roknya; vt melapisi; **liner** n pelapis; nappy ~ pelapis popok; panty ~ pembalut; **linesman** n, m **lineswoman** f wasit garis; **lining** n lapisan, furing
linen n kain linan; ~ cupboard lemari sepréi
liner n kapal penumpang yang besar
liner n pelapis; nappy ~ pelapis popok; panty ~ pembalut ← **line**
linesman n, m **lineswoman** f wasit garis ← **line**
linger vi [lingger] tidak mau pergi-pergi
lingerie n [lonjeri] pakaian dalam wanita
linguist n [lingguist] ahli bahasa, munsyi; **linguistics** n ilmu bahasa, ilmu linguistik; applied ~ linguistik terapan
lining n lapisan, furing ← **line**
link n mata rantai, hubungan; diplomatic ~s hubungan diplomatik; golf ~s padang golf; vt menghubungkan, mengaitkan; her name was ~ed with a high-ranking official namanya dikaitkan dengan pejabat tinggi
lino n, coll **linoleum** n [lainolium] linolium
lion n [laion] singa; ~-hearted pemberani; ~'s share bagian terbesar; **lioness** n, f singa betina
lip n bibir; ~-service basa-basi, purapura melakukan; ~ gloss gincu; **lip-liner** n pénsil bibir; **lipread** v **lipread** [lipréd] membaca gerakan bibir; **lipstick** n lipstik
liqueur n [likur] sopi manis, minuman keras yang manis

liquid adj cair; n cairan, zat cair; ~ petroleum gas (LPG) elpiji
liquidate vt menghentikan, membubarkan, melikuidasi; **liquidation** n likuidasi, pembubaran
liquor n [liker] minuman keras
liquorice n [likorisy] permén hitam yang kenyal
Lisbon n Lisboa
lisp n cadel, pelat; vi berbicara cadel
list n daftar; short ~ daftar péndék; vt mendaftar, menyebutkan
listen vi [lisen] mendengarkan, menyimak; ~ to mendengarkan; **listener** n pendengar; ~s para pendengar; **listening** n (pelajaran) menyimak
lit v, pf → **light**
liter, litre n liter; per ~ seliter, per liter
literacy n [literasi] (angka) melék huruf; **literal** adj harfiah; **literally** adv secara harfiah; benar-benar; **literate** adj melék huruf; terpelajar; **literary** adj sastra; **literature** n kesusastraan
Lithuania n [lithuénia] Lituania; **Lithuanian** adj berasal dari Lituania; n orang Lituania
litigate vi [litigét] menuntut (secara hukum); **litigation** n proses pengadilan
litre → **liter**
litter n usungan, tandu
litter n seperindukan (anak binatang)
litter n sampah (di jalan); v membuang sampah sembarangan; **litterbug** n orang yang sering membuang sampah sembarangan
little adj [litel] kecil; sedikit; ~ finger kelingking; n sedikit; tidak banyak; there's ~ hope tidak banyak harapan; have a ~ wine left saya masih ada sedikit anggur; ~ by ~ lambat laun, sedikit demi sedikit; ~ Red Riding Hood Si Topi Mérah
live vt [liv] hidup, tinggal, berdiam; ~ off hidup dari; ~ with hidup dengan; kumpul kebo dengan; ~ a life of menjalani hidup; ~ up to expectations memenuhi harapan; **live** adj [laiv] langsung; hidup; ~ broadcast siaran langsung; ~ music musik hidup; ~ wire kawat yang ada setrum; **livelihood** n

rezeki, nafkah; *to seek a* ~ mencari nafkah, cari makan; **lively** *adj* bersemangat, hidup; **liven** *vi* ~ *up* memeriahkan; **lives** *n, pl* → **life**; **livestock** *n* héwan ternak; **livewire** *n* orang yang penuh semangat; **living** *n* [living] mata pencarian; *to make a* ~ mencari nafkah; ~ *room* kamar keluarga

liver *n* [liver] hati, lévér

lives *n, pl* → **life**

livestock *n* hewan ternak ← **live**

livewire *n* orang yang penuh semangat ← **live**

livid *adj* [livid] pucat; sangat marah

living *n* [living] mata pencarian; *to make a* ~ mencari nafkah; ~ *room* kamar keluarga ← **live**

lizard *n* [lizerd] kadal, biawak, cicak; *lounge* ~ orang yang banyak bermalas-malas

llama *n* [lama] sejenis binatang di Amérika Selatan seperti unta

LLB *abbrev Bachelor of Laws* SH Sarjana Hukum

load *n* muatan, beban; ~*s of coll* banyak; *vi* memuat; *vt* memuat dengan; **loaded** *adj, sl* kaya raya; **loading** *n* pemuatan; ~ *bay* tempat bongkar muat

loaf *n* **loaves** roti; *vi* bermalas-malas; **loafer** *n* pemalas; sejenis sepatu santai

loan *n* pinjaman; ~ *shark* lintah darat; *vt* meminjamkan, meminjami → **lend**

loathe *vi* membenci; **loathsome** *adj* [lothsem] memuakkan

loaves *n, pl* → **loaf**

lob *n* bola yang dipukul tinggi; *vt* memukul tinggi-tinggi

lobby *n* ruang masuk, lobi (hotél); gerakan; *the green* ~ gerakan pro lingkungan; *vt* berusaha memengaruhi, memperjuangkan; **lobbyist** *n* aktivis, pejuang

lobe *ear* ~ cuping

lobster *n* udang karang, udang laut

local *adj* setempat, lokal; ~ *government* pemerintah setempat, kelurahan; *n* orang setempat; **locality** *n* kawasan, tempat; **locally** *adv* setempat; *she lives* ~ dia tinggal dekat; **locate** *vt* mencari; **location** *n* lokasi, tempat;

penempatan; *on* ~ di lokasi

loch *n* [lokh] danau (di Skotlandia)

lock *n* kunci, gembok; pintu air; ~*-up* sél tahanan; *combination* ~ kuncikombinasi; *steering* ~ kunci stir; ~, *stock and barrel* semuanya; *a* ~ *of hair* seikat rambut; *vi* terkunci; *vt* mengunci; **locked** *adj* terkunci; ~ *out* terkunci di luar; **locker** *n* loker; ~ *room* ruang ganti baju (di fasilitas olahraga)

locket *n* liontin (yang dapat dikunci atau dipasang foto kecil) ← **lock**

lockjaw *n* kejang mulut ← **lock**

locksmith *n* tukang kunci ← **lock**

locomotion *n* daya penggerak; **locomotive** *n* [lokomotiv] lokomotif, lok

locust *n* belalang

lodge *n* pondok, pemondokan; *vi* mondok, menginap; ~ *a complaint* mengajukan pengaduan; **lodger** *n* pemondok, anak kos; **lodging** *n* pemondokan; akomodasi

loft *n* loténg; **lofty** *adj* tinggi, mulia

log *n* catatan, buku harian; *ship's* ~ buku harian di kapal; *vt* mencatat; ~ *in*, ~ *on* memasukkan nama atau kata kunci; ~ *off*, ~ *out* keluar dari program; **logbook** *n* buku harian di kapal

log *n* batang kayu, kayu gelondongan; ~ *cabin* pondok (dibuat dari balok kayu); *vt* menebang (pohon); **logging** *n* penebangan; *illegal* ~ penebangan liar, pembalakan liar

logarithm *n* [logarithem] logaritma

logbook *n* buku harian di kapal ← **log**

logic *n* [lojik] logika, akal; **logical** *adj* logis, masuk akal; **logistics** *n, pl* logistik

logistic *adj* [lojistik] logistik; **logistically** *adv* secara logistik; **logistics** *n, pl* logistik

logo *n* logo, lambang

loincloth *n* cawat; **loins** *n, pl* selangkangan

loiter *vi* mondar-mandir, berlama-lama di suatu tempat

lolly *n* permén, gula-gula; **lollypop** *n* permén bulat di tangkai

London *n* [landen] London; **Londoner** *n* orang London

lone *adj* tunggal, sendiri; **loneliness** *n* (rasa) kesepian; **lonely** *adj* sepi, kesepian, sunyi, sendirian; ~ *hearts column* kontak jodoh; **loner** *n* penyendiri

long *adj* panjang; lama; ~-*distance call* télépon interlokal; ~-*haired* berambut panjang; ~-*haired cat* kucing angora; ~-*playing record (LP)* *arch* piringan hitam; ~-*range* jarak jauh; ~-*sighted* rabun dekat; ~-*winded* bertélé-télé; ~ *jump* lompat jauh; ~ *time* (waktu yang) lama; ~ *weekend* libur panjang akhir minggu; *coll* hari kejepit; *before* ~ tidak lama kemudian; *how* ~? berapa lama?; *so* ~ sampai jumpa, sampai bertemu; *as* ~ *as* selama; *I won't be* ~ saya tidak akan lama; **longer** *adj* [longger] lebih panjang; lebih lama; *no* ~ tidak lagi; **longhouse** *n* rumah panjang

long *vi* ~ *for* rindu akan, merindukan, mengidamkan; **longing** *n* hasrat, kerinduan

longitude *n* [longgityud] bujur

loo *n, sl* WC, belakang

look *n* penampilan, gaya; *vi* melihat; tampak; ~ *after* merawat, menjaga; ~ *around* melihat-lihat; ~ *at* melihat; ~ *back* menoléh; ~ *for* mencari; ~ *forward to* menantikan; ~ *into* mencari tahu; ~ *like* mirip; ~ *on* menonton; ~ *out!* awas!; ~ *up* mencari; ~*ing glass* cermin; *she* ~*s beautiful tonight* dia tampak cantik malam ini; **lookout** *n* tempat meninjau; pengintai; **looks** *n, pl* paras, wajah, penampilan

loom *n* perkakas tenun; *vi* terbayang, timbul

loon *n* sejenis burung; *sl* orang gila; **loony** *adj, n* gila ← **lunatic**

loop *n* lingkaran, ikal, putaran; *vt* menyimpulkan; ~ *the* ~ terbang jungkir balik; **loophole** *n* jalan keluar

loose *adj* longgar, kendur, terurai; lepas; ~-*fitting* longgar; ~ *change* uang kecil; ~ *end* hal yang belum bérés; ~ *living* kehidupan bebas; **loosen** *vt* melonggarkan, mengendurkan

loot *n* rampasan, hasil jarahan; *v* merampas, menjarah; **looter** *n* penjarah; **looting** *n* penjarahan

lop *vt* memenggal; ~ *trees* menebang pohon

loquacious *adj* [lokuésyius] berbicara banyak

lord *pron* tuan; *vi* ~ *(it) over* bertindak sombong; **Lord** *n, Chr* Tuhan

lorry *n* truk

lose *v* [luz] **lost lost** *vi* rugi, kalah; *vt* hilang, kehilangan; ~ *face* malu; ~ *weight* mengurangi berat badan; ~ *a match* kalah dalam pertandingan; ~ *count of* sudah tidak terhitung; ~ *your way* tersesat; **loser** *n* yang kalah; **loss** *n* rugi, kerugian, kehilangan; *at a* ~ tidak mengerti; **lost** *adj* hilang; tersesat; téwas; ~ *property* barang-barang hilang; ~ *for words* kehabisan kata-kata

lot *n* undi

lot *a* ~ banyak; *the* ~ semua; *you* ~ *coll* kalian; *not a* ~ tidak begitu; **lots** *n, pl* banyak; *Alex has* ~ *of money* Alex punya banyak uang

lotion *n* salep

lottery *n* loteré, undian ← **lot**

lotus *n* bunga seroja, bunga teratai

loud *adj* berisik, riuh, gempar, bising; *out* ~ dengan suara keras; *this music is too* ~ musik ini berisik sekali; **loudly** *adv* dengan keras; **loudspeaker** *n* pengeras suara

lounge *n* [launj] sofa; ruang istirahat; *vi* ~ *around* bermalas-malas

louse *n* **lice** kutu; **lousy** *adj* [lauzi] jelék

lout *n* orang yang berkelakuan tidak baik; **loutish** *adj* berkelakuan tidak baik, brutal

louver, louvre *n, adj* [luver] jalusi

love *adj* [lav] kosong (dalam permainan tenis); *forty* ~ empat puluh kosong (40-0)

love *n* [lav] cinta, asmara; kasih (sayang); *pron* kekasih, sayang; ~-*hate relationship* benci tapi rindu; ~ *triangle* cinta segitiga; *in* ~ kasmaran; *to make* ~ bercinta; *with* ~ *from* salam hangat; *for the* ~ *of* demi; *to fall in* ~ jatuh cinta; *vt* mencintai, menyayangi; menyukai; *I* ~ *you* aku cinta kamu;

she ~s swimming dia suka sekali berenang; would ~ to ingin, mau; **lovely** adj manis, cantik, asri; bagus, énak; a ~ day hari yang cerah; a ~ trip perjalanan yang menyenangkan; **lover** n kekasih; penggemar; **loving** adj penyayang

low adj [lo] rendah, hina; murah; n titik rendah, nadir; ~-cholesterol kolésterol rendah; ~ profile tidak menonjol; ~ season masa sepi; ~ spirits sedih hati; ~ tide air surut; highs and ~s suka duka; **lower** adj lebih rendah; ~ case huruf kecil; vt menurunkan; **lowland** n tanah rendah; **lowly** adj hina

loyal adj setia, setiakawan; **loyalty** n kesetiaan, kesetiakawanan

lozenge n [lozenj] obat isap

LPG abbrev liquid petroleum gas élpiji

L-plate n, abbrev learner plate tanda pengendara pelajar

Lt abbrev lieutenant Lt (létnan)

Ltd abbrev Limited Terbatas (Tbs); Pty ~ (Proprietary Limited) Perséroan Terbatas (PT)

lubricant n [lubrikant] pelumas; **lubricate** vt meminyaki, melumasi

lucid adj terang, jelas

luck n untung; bad ~ sial; good ~ untung; good ~! semoga; down on your ~ celaka, bernasib sial; to push your ~ mencari untung secara berlebihan; **luckily** adv secara beruntung; kebetulan; **lucky** adj beruntung

lucrative adj [lukratif] menguntungkan; **lucre** filthy ~ duit, uang

luggage n bagasi, barang-barang; ~ tag tanda bagasi; left ~ layanan penitipan bagasi

lukewarm adj [lukworm] suam-suam kuku

lullaby n [lalabai] (kidung) ninabobo

lumbago n [lambégo] sakit pinggang

lumber n kayu; vi berjalan dengan berat; **lumberjack** n penebang kayu

luminary n [luminari] orang terkenal, tokoh; **luminous** adj terang, bercahaya

lump n gumpal, bongkah; benjolan; a ~ in my throat ingin menangis; vt menaruh tanpa banyak berpikir;

menyatukan; like it or ~ it walau tidak suka, harus terima; **lumpy** adj bergumpal, tidak éncér

lunacy n [lunasi] sakit gila; **lunatic** adj gila; n orang gila

lunar adj berkaitan dengan bulan; ~ eclipse gerhana bulan

lunatic adj [lunatik] gila; n orang gila ← lunacy

lunch n, vi makan siang; we ~ed on caviar kami menyantap telur ikan untuk makan siang; **luncheon** n, arch [lancen] makan siang

lung n paru-paru; ~ cancer kanker paru-paru; to shout at the top of your ~s berteriak sekeras-kerasnya

lunge n sergapan, terjangan; vi menyergap

lurch vi bergerak secara mendadak; to leave in the ~ meninggalkan dalam kesulitan

lure n iming-iming, bujukan; vt memancing, mengiming-iming; they tried to ~ him with money mereka coba mengiming-iming dia dengan uang

lurid adj menyolok, berwarna terang; jorok

lurk vi bersembunyi, menunggu diam-diam

luscious adj [lasyes] sangat énak

lush adj lebat, subur

lust n hawa nafsu, berahi; vi ~ after menaksir

luster, lustre n kegemilangan; **lustrous** adj berseri

lusty adj kuat, bersemangat

lute n kecapi

Luxembourg adj berasal dari Luksemburg; n Luksemburg; **Luxembourger** n orang Luksemburg

luxurious adj [laksyurius] méwah, luks; **luxury** n keméwahan

lychee n [laici] buah léci

lymph n [limf] getah bening; ~ node kelenjar getah bening; **lymphatic** ~ cancer kanker getah bening

lyrics n, pl lirik, kata-kata yang dinyanyikan

M

m *abbrev meter* m (méter)

ma'am *pron* Nyonya, Nona ← **madam**

mac, mack *n, coll* jas hujan →
mackintosh

Macau *n* Makau; **Macanese** *n* orang
Makau

macaroni *n* makaroni

macaw *n* sejenis burung béo di Amérika

mace *n* bunga pala

Macedonia *n* [Masedonia] Makedonia;
Former Yugoslav Republic of ~
(FYROM) Makedonia; **Macedonian**
adj berasal dari Makedonia; *n* orang
Makedonia

machete *n* [masyéti] golok

machine *n* [masyin] mesin, alat; *~ gun*
mitraliur, senapan mesin; *washing ~*
mesin cuci; **machinery** *n* mesin-
mesin, alat-alat

macho *adj, coll* [maco] bersifat kelaki-
lakian; *Russell grew a beard and
acted very ~* Russell memelihara jenggot dan bersikap sangat kelaki-lakian

mackerel *n* sejenis ikan air tawar

mackintosh *n* **mac, mack** *coll* jas hujan

mad *adj* gila, tergila-gila; marah; *like ~*
cepat sekali; *~ about cars* tergila-gila
akan mobil; *~ cow disease* penyakit
sapi gila; *as ~ as a hatter* gila betul;
madden *vt* **maddening** *adj* membuat
marah; **madly** *adv* sekuat tenaga,
mabuk; *she ran ~ for the bus* dia
mengejar bis sekuat tenaga; **madman**
n orang gila; **madness** *n* kegilaan,
penyakit gila

Madagascar *n* Madagaskar

madam *pron* **ma'am** *coll* Nyonya; *n, sl*
mami, mucikari; *a little madam* anak
perempuan yang manja

madden *vt* **maddening** *adj* membuat
marah ← **mad**

made *vt, pf* → **make**; *~ in China* buatan
RRC; *~ for each other* saling berjodoh

madly *adv* sekuat tenaga, mabuk; *she
ran ~ for the bus* dia mengejar bis
sekuat tenaga ← **mad**

madman *n* orang gila ← **mad**

madness *n* kegilaan, penyakit gila ←
mad

maestro *n* [maistro] musisi ternama,
maéstro

mafia *n* persekongkolan, mafia

magazine *n* [magazin] **mag** *coll* majalah

magenta *adj* [majénta] mérah tua

maggot *n* belatung

magic *n* [majik] ilmu sihir, ilmu sulap;
~ carpet karpét terbang; *like ~* seperti
disulap; **magical** *adj* berkaitan dengan
sihir; ajaib; **magically** *adv* secara ajaib;
magician *n* [majisyen] penyihir, penyulap

magistrate *n* [majistrét] hakim; *~'s
court* pengadilan negeri

magnate *n* pengusaha, konglomerat;
mining ~ pengusaha pertambangan

magnesium *n* [magnisium] magnésium

magnet *n* magnét, maknit; **magnetic**
adj magnétik; *~ attraction* daya
magnétik

magnificent *adj* [magnifisent] sangat
bagus, méwah

magnify *vt* [magnifai] memperbesar;
~ing glass kaca pembesar

magnitude *n* [magnityud] besar(nya);
kebesaran; *of that ~* sebesar itu

magpie *n* [magpai] burung murai

mahogany *n* [mahogani] pohon
mahoni, kayu mahoni

maid *n* pembantu; gadis; *~'s room*
kamar pembantu; *old ~* perawan tua; *~
of honor* pendamping pengantin wanita; **maiden** *adj* perdana; *~ voyage*
pelayaran perdana; *n* perawan, gadis;
~ name nama gadis

mail *n* pos; surat éléktronik, imél; *vt*
mengepos, mengirim léwat pos; *~
order* pesanan léwat pos; *junk ~* iklan
(yang dikirim ke rumah); *snail ~* pos
biasa (bukan imél); *it's in the ~* sudah
dipos; **mailbox** *n* kotak surat; **mail-
man** *n* tukang pos

maim *vt* memuntungkan, mencederai
sehingga cacat; **maimed** *adj* cacat

main *adj* utama; *~ clause* induk kalimat; *~ road* jalan utama, jalan raya; *~
Street US* jalan utama; *in the ~* umumnya; **mainland** *n* daratan; **mainly** *adv*
terutama

maintain *vt* memelihara, mempertahankan; **maintenance** *n* pemeliharaan

maize *n* [méiz] jagung

majestic *adj* [majéstik] agung; **majesty** *n* keagungan; *Your ~* Baginda, Sri Paduka

major *adj* utama, terbesar; *vi ~ in* mengambil jurusan; *Natalie's ~ing in Indonesian* Natalie mengambil jurusan Bahasa Indonésia; *n* jurusan; mayor; *~-general* mayjén (mayor jénderal); **majority** *n* kebanyakan, mayoritas; *silent ~* kebanyakan orang (yang tidak bersuara); *the ~ of women have two children* kebanyakan perempuan punya dua orang anak

make *n* jenis, macam; *vt* **made made** membuat, membikin, mengadakan; memaksa; *~-believe* khayalan; berkhayal, berpura-pura; *~-up* rias wajah; *~-up artist* perias; *~ breakfast* mempersiapkan sarapan; *~ do* puas; *~ for* menuju; *~ friends* berteman; *~ it* berhasil; *~ love* bercinta; *~ off* lari, kabur; *~ out* mengerti, memahami; *sl* bercumbu; *~ up* merias; mengarang, berdusta; mengganti; *~ way* meminggir, gésér, memberi jalan; *~ fun of* melédék; *~ light of* menganggap énténg; *~ one's bed* merapikan tempat tidur; *~ or break* berhasil atau gagal; *~ up your mind* memutuskan, mengambil keputusan; **makeover** *n* perubahan gaya rambut atau rias; **maker** *n* pembuat, pencipta; **makeshift** *adj* sementara; **making** *n* (proses) pembuatan; *in the ~* dalam prosés (pembuatan)

malady *n* [maladi] penyakit

Malagasy *adj* berasal dari Madagaskar; *n* bahasa Malagasi; orang Malagasi; *~ Republic* Madagaskar

malaria *n* [maléria] malaria; *~ tablets* obat anti malaria

Malawi *n* Malawi; **Malawian** *adj* berasal dari Malawi; *n* orang Malawi

Malay *adj* Melayu; *n* Bahasa Melayu, Bahasa Malaysia; orang Melayu; *the ~ Annals* Sejarah Melayu; **Malaya** *n*, *arch* Semenanjung Melayu; **Malayan** *adj* berasal dari Semenanjung Melayu;

Malaysia *n* Malaysia; *East ~* Sarawak dan Sabah; **Malaysian** *n* orang Malaysia

Maldives [maldivs] *the ~* (Kepulauan) Maladéwa; **Maldivian** *adj* berasal dari Maladéwa; *n* orang Maladéwa

male *adj* lelaki, pria; jantan; *~ dog* anjing jantan; *~ friend* teman lelaki

malfunction *n* kerusakan, kegagalan; *vi* gagal

Mali *n* Mali; **Malian** *adj* berasal dari Mali; *n* orang Mali

malice *n* [malis] kebencian, niat jahat; **malicious** *adj* [malisyes] jahat; dengan sengaja

malign *vt* [malain] memfitnah; *much-~ed* sering difitnah; **malignant** *adj* [malignant] jahat; ganas

mall *n* [mol] mal; *~-crawl* mengunjungi beberapa mal dalam waktu singkat; *~ rat sl* remaja yang sering nongkrong di mal; *shopping ~* pusat perbelanjaan, mal

mallet *n* palu dari kayu

malnourished *adj* [malnarisyd] **malnutrition** *n* [malnyutrisyen] malagizi

malpractice *n* [malpraktis] malpraktek

Malta *n* (pulau) Malta; **Maltese** *adj* berasal dari Malta; *n* orang Malta

mama, mamma *n*, *pron* ibu

mammal *n* mamalia, binatang menyusui

mammoth *adj* [mameth] raksasa; *a ~ task* tugas yang sangat berat

Man *the Isle of ~* Pulau Man; **Manx** *adj* dari Pulau Man; *n, arch* bahasa Pulau Man; *~ cat* kucing yang tidak berékor

man *n* **men** orang laki-laki, pria; suami, pasangan; pacar; *arch* orang, manusia; *~-made* buatan manusia; *men at work* awas ada penggalian; *to a ~* semua; *~ in the street* orang kebanyakan; *~ of the match* pemain terbaik; *vt* mengawaki, bekerja di suatu tempat; **manhood** *n, m* kedéwasaan; kejantanan; **manhunt** *n* pencarian orang, pemburuan orang; **mankind** *n* [mankaind] umat manusia; **manly** *adj* jantan, perkasa; **manned** *adj* diawaki; **manpower** *n* tenaga kerja; *Ministry of ~* Départemén Tenaga Kerja (Depnaker)

manservant *n, m, arch* pelayan, jongos; **manslaughter** *n* [mansloter] pembunuhan yang tidak disengaja; *Robin was convicted of* ~ Robin divonis bersalah telah membunuh orang

manage *vi* bertahan; *vt* mengelola, memimpin; mengurus, menangani; **manageable** *adj* dapat ditangani, dapat diurus; **management** *n* pimpinan, diréksi; pengelolaan, pemerintahan, pengurusan, manajemén; **manager** *n* **managerial** *adj* manajer, pemimpin, pengurus; **managing** ~ *director* diréktur pelaksana

Mandarin *n* bahasa Cina, bahasa Mandarin

mandarin *n* jeruk (keprok)

mandate *n* mandat, amanat; ~ *to govern* amanat rakyat; **mandatory** *adj* wajib, keharusan

mane *n* surai; rambut yang lebat

maneuver, manoeuvre *n* [manuver] latihan perang-perangan; tipu daya; manuver

manganese *n* [mangganiz] manggan

mange *n* [ménj] kudis; **mangy** *adj* kudisan

manger *n* [ménjer] palung

mangle *v* [manggel] merusak, mengacaukan; **mangled** *adj* rusak, kacau; ~ *English* bahasa Inggris yang kacau

mango *n* mangga

mangosteen *n* manggis

mangrove *n* bakau

mangy *adj* kudisan ← **mange**

manhood *n, m* kedewasaan; kejantanan ← **man**

manhunt *n* pencarian orang, pemburuan orang ← **man**

mania *n* [ménia] kegilaan, demam; **maniac** *n* orang gila, penggila; **manic** *adj* [manik] seperti orang gila, kegilagilaan

manicure *n* perawatan tangan, manikur; *to have a* ~ dimanikur

manifest *adj* nyata; *n* manifés; *vt* menampakkan; **manifestation** *n* maniféstasi, perwujudan

manikin, mannequin *n* orang-orangan, manekin

manipulate *vt* memanipulasi; memainkan, mendalangi; **manipulation** *n* manipulasi, perbuatan curang; **manipulative** *adj* suka memanipulasi

mankind *n* [mankaind] umat manusia ← **man**

manly *adj* jantan, perkasa ← **man**

manned *adj* diawaki ← **man**

mannequin → **manikin**

manner *n* cara, jalan; macam; *in a* ~ *of speaking* boléh dikatakan; *pl* sopan santun; **mannered** *adj* *well-*~ sopan, beradat

manpower *n* tenaga kerja; *Ministry of* ~ Départemén Tenaga Kerja (Depnaker) ← **man**

manservant *n, m, arch* pelayan, jongos ← **man**

mansion *n* [mansyen] rumah besar

manslaughter *n* [mansloter] pembunuhan yang tidak disengaja; *Robin was convicted of* ~ Robin divonis bersalah telah membunuh orang ← **man**

mantelpiece *n* [mantelpis] rak di atas perapian

manual *adj* [manyuel] dengan tangan, tidak otomatis; *n* pedoman, buku panduan; ~ *car* mobil manual; ~ *labor* pekerjaan kasar; **manually** *adv* secara manual, tidak otomatis

manufacture *n* [manyufaktyur] pembuatan; *vt* membuat, membikin; **manufacturer** *n* pabrik; **manufacturing** *n* pembuatan, pabrik

manure *n* pupuk (kotoran)

manuscript *n* naskah

Manx *adj* dari Pulau Man; *n, arch* bahasa Pulau Man; ~ *cat* kucing yang tidak berékor ← **Man**

many *adj* [méni] banyak; ~ *thanks* terima kasih banyak; *how* ~? berapa banyak?; *so* ~ begitu banyak; ~ *a time* beberapa kali

Maori *n* orang asli Sélandia Baru; bahasa Maori; *adj* berkaitan dengan orang Maori atau bahasanya

map *n* peta; *vt* memetakan; *road* ~ peta jalan; **mapping** *n* pemetaan

maple *n* [mépel] sejenis pohon; ~ *syrup*

semacam cairan manis dari pohon
tersebut

marathon *n* maraton; ~ *runner* pelari
maraton

marauder *n* [maroder] perampok, perusak

marble *n* [marbel] marmer, pualam;
marbles *pl* keléréng; *to play* ~ main
keléréng; *to lose one's* ~ menjadi gila;
menjadi pikun

March *n* bulan Maret

march *n* perjalanan (militér); mars; *long*
~ gerak jalan; *student* ~ démo mahasiswa; *vi* jalan kaki; ~ *fly* lalat besar

mare *n* kuda betina

margarine *n* [marjarin] mentéga; *low-
cholesterol* ~ mentéga rendah kolésterol; *low-salt* ~ mentéga rendah garam

margin *n* [marjin] (garis) tepi, batas,
pinggiran; *in the* ~ di pinggir halaman;
marginal *adj* tipis; ~ *seat* daérah
pemilihan yang tidak mudah dipré-
diksi hasilnya; **marginalized** *adj*
terpinggirkan

marijuana *n* [marihuana] ganja

marina *n* [marina] dermaga; **marine** *adj*
[marin] berhubungan dengan laut; ~
biology biologi laut; **mariner** *n, arch*
[marener] pelaut; **maritime** *adj* [mari-
taim] berhubungan dengan laut

marinade *n* [marinéd] saus perendam;
marinate *vt* merendam

marital *adj* [maritel] berhubungan dengan perkawinan; ~ *problems* masalah
rumah tangga, masalah perkawinan; ~
status status (perkawinan)

marjoram *n* sejenis daun rempah untuk
memasak

mark *n* tanda, alamat; cap; sasaran;
bekas; nilai; *black* ~ noda hitam; nilai
buruk; *good* ~s nilai (rapot) yang
baik; ~ *of quality* tanda bermutu, tanda
kualitas; *to miss the* ~ melését; *vt*
menandai, mengecap; mencatat, memperhatikan; mengoréksi; ~ *up*
menaikkan harga agar dapat komisi
sendiri; ~ *my words* ingat (kata saya
nanti); **marked** *adj* tertanda, jelas; *a* ~
change perubahan yang nyata; **marker**
n penanda; spidol besar; penilai;
marksman *n* penembak jitu

market *n* pasar, pasaran; ~ *share* pangsa
pasar; *black* ~ pasar gelap; *on the* ~
dijual; *to go to* ~ pergi ke pasar; *vt*
memasarkan; **marketing** *n* pemasaran;
marketplace *n* pasar

marksman *n* penembak jitu ← **mark**

marmalade *n* selai jeruk

maroon *adj* [maron] mérah tua

marooned *adj* tertinggal, terdampar (di
pulau pasir)

marquee *n* ténda (makanan)

marriage *n* [marijj] perkawinan,
pernikahan; ~ *celebrant* orang yang
berwenang mengesahkan pernikahan;
related by ~ berkerabat karena
perkawinan; *to ask for her hand in* ~
meminang; ~ *certificate* surat kawin,
akte pernikahan; **married** *adj* kawin,
nikah; *m* beristri; *f* bersuami; ~ *couple*
pasangan suami isteri; *not* ~ belum nikah;
to get ~ menikah, kawin ← **marry**

marrow *n* sumsum; labu

marry *vi* menikah, kawin; ~ *off*
menikahkan, mengawinkan; *vt* menikahi;
~ *money* menikah dengan orang kaya

Mars *n* planét Mars

marsh *n* rawa; **marshland** *n* daérah
rawa; **marshy** *adj* berawa

marshal *n* marsekal; *field-*~ panglima;
vt memanggil, mengatur

marshmallow *n* penganan manis yang
putih dan empuk

marshy *adj* berawa ← **marsh**

marsupial *n* binatang berkantung; *kan-
garoos are* ~s kangguru itu héwan
berkantung

Martinique *n* [martinik] Martinik;
Martiniquais *adj* [martiniké] berasal
dari Martinik; *n* orang Martinik

martyr *n* [marter] martir; **martyrdom** *n*
mati syahid

marvel *n* keajaiban; marvelous, **marvel-
lous** *adj* ajaib, hebat, mengagumkan

Marxism *n* [markzizem] Marxisme;
Marxist *adj* marxis; *n* orang Marxis

mascara *n* perona mata, maskara

mascot *n* maskot

masculine *adj* [maskulin] laki-laki, lelaki,
jantan; **masculinity** *n* kejantanan

mash *vt* menghancurkan, mengaduk

sampai halus; ~ed potato kentang rebus yang dihaluskan

mask n topéng; masker; vt menyamarkan; she ~s her nervousness by laughing dia tertawa untuk menyamarkan rasa gelisah; masked adj bertopéng, berkedok

mason n tukang batu

masquerade n [maskeréd] pesta bertopéng; vi menyamar; ~ as menyamar sebagai

mass n massa; banyak sekali; misa; ~ media média massa; ~ rally démo, unjuk rasa; pl ~ of banyak sekali; massive adj raksasa, besar sekali

massacre n [masaker] pembunuhan atau pembantaian besar-besaran; vt membunuh secara besar-besaran; indigenous Australians were ~d in the 19th century orang asli Australia dibunuh secara besar-besaran pada abad ke19

massage n [masajj] pijatan; ~ parlor panti pijat; vt memijat, mengurut; masseur m masseuse f [maser] tukang pijat

massive adj raksasa, besar sekali ← mass

mast n tiang (kapal)

mastectomy n opérasi pengangkatan payudara

master n tuan (rumah); ahli, guru; ~ bedroom kamar tidur utama; ~'s (degree) S2, magister; ~ of ceremonies (MC) pembawa acara, émsi; vt menguasai; Kevin quickly ~ed the Chinese language Kevin menguasai bahasa Mandarin dengan cepat; masterly adj ulung; mastermind n [mastermaind] dalang, otak; vt mendalangi; masterpiece n [masterpis] adikarya; mastery n penguasaan, keahlian

masturbate vi beronani; masturbation n onani, masturbasi

mat n tikar; matras; tilam; door ~ kését; prayer ~ Isl sejadah; table ~ alas piring; matting n anyaman jerami, tikar

match n korék api; matchbox n tempat korék api

match n tara, jodoh; pertandingan; vi sesuai, cocok, pas, sepadan; vt menyesuaikan; menyamai, menandingi; matching adj sesuai, cocok, pas, sepadan; matchless adj tiada taranya; matchmaker n mak jomblang

mate n kawan, sahabat; pasangan; pron Bung; vi kawin (binatang)

material n bahan, kain; perkakas, alat; matéri; ~ girl céwék matré; materialism n materialisme; materialistic adj materialistis; materialize vt mewujudkan; failed to ~ tidak terwujud

maternal adj keibuan; dari pihak ibu; ~ grandfather kakék dari pihak ibu; ~ instinct nurani keibuan; maternity adj masa kehamilan; ~ clothes pakaian hamil; ~ leave cuti hamil

mathematician n [mathematisyen] ahli matématika; US mathematics, math UK maths n matématika

matrimony n [matrimoni] perkawinan

matron n [métron] kepala perawat, suster; matronly adj berbadan keibuan; berbadan montok

matter n perkara, hal, perihal; bahan; ~-of-fact terus terang; gray ~ sél-sél otak; what's the ~? ada apa?; as a ~ of fact ngomong-ngomong; sebenarnya; vi berarti, penting; it doesn't ~ tidak apa-apa; no ~ what bagaimanapun juga

matting n anyaman jerami, tikar ← mat

mattress n kasur; matras (olahraga)

mature adj déwasa, tua, matang; ~age student mahasiswa déwasa; maturity n kedéwasaan, kematangan; fin batas waktu

Maundy ~ Thursday Chr hari Kamis Putih

Mauritania n [moriténia] Mauritania; Mauritanian adj berasal dari Mauritania; n orang Mauritania

Mauritius n [morisyes] Mauritius; Mauritian adj berasal dari Mauritius; n orang Mauritius

mausoleum n [mosolium] bangunan kuburan

mauve adj [mov] lembayung muda, mérah tua

maximal adj maksimal, sebanyak-banyaknya; **maximize** *vt* memaksi-malkan, memanfaatkan sebaik mungkin; **maximum** *adj* maksimal; *n* maksimum, sebanyak-banyaknya

May *n* bulan Méi; ~ *Day* Hari Buruh

may *vi, aux* boleh, dapat; *I* ~ *be some time* mungkin saya akan lama; **maybe** [mébi] *adv* mungkin, barangkali, boléh jadi

mayday *ejac* tolong! (perkapalan)

mayonnaise *n* **mayo** *coll* mayonés

mayor *n* [mér] walikota; *the* ~ *of London* walikota London

maze *n* labirin, jalan yang ruwet atau simpang siur; *a* ~ *of streets* banyak jalan yang simpang siur

MBA *abbrev Master of Business Administration* MBA

MD *abbrev medical doctor* dr, dokter

me *pron, obj* saya, aku, daku; *he made* ~ *a cup of tea* dia membuatkan saya secangkir téh

meadow *n* [médo] padang rumput

meager, meagre *adj* [miger] sedikit

meal *n* makanan, santapan; ~ *on wheels* layanan antar makanan ke rumah; *a square* ~ makan yang cukup; *the evening* ~ makan malam; **mealtime** *n* waktu makan

mean *adj* sedang, rata-rata

mean *adj* jahat, membuat sakit hati; kurang, hina; pelit; *Alistair's very* ~ *with money* Alistair pelit soal uang

mean *v* **meant meant** [mént] *vi* berarti, bermaksud; *vt* memaksudkan, menghendaki; **meaning** *n* arti, maksud; **meaningful** *adj* berarti, bermakna

means *n* harta, kekayaan; alat; cara; *of* ~ kaya, berada; *by all* ~ tentu, pasti

meant *v, pf* → **mean**

meantime *in the* ~ sementara itu; **meanwhile** *adv* sementara itu

measles *n, pl* [mizels] penyakit campak; *German* ~ campak Jérman, rubéla

measure *n* [mésyer] ukuran, takaran; besarnya; tindakan; *vt* mengukur; **measurement** *n* ukuran

meat *n* daging; **meatball** *n* bakso, bola daging; **meatloaf** *n* perpaduan daging dan sayur berbentuk roti

Mecca *n* Mekkah; *to go on the pilgrimage to* ~ naik haji

mechanic *n* [mekanik] montir, ahli mesin; **mechanical** *adj* teknik; ~ *engineering* téknik mesin; **mechanics** *n, pl* ilmu mékanika

medal *n* medali, médali; *bronze* ~ medali perunggu; *gold* ~ medali emas; *silver* ~ medali perak; **medalist, medallist** *n* peraih medali; **medallion** *n* liontin

meddle *v* campur tangan; ~ *in* mencampuri, ikut campur dalam; **meddler** *n* orang yang campur tangan

media *n, pl* [midia] pérs, média; perantara, bahan; *electronic* ~ éléktronik média; *mass* ~ média massa; *mixed* ~ média campuran; *print* ~ media cétak; *the* ~ pérs

median [midian] ~ *strip* jalur hijau

mediate *vi* [midiét] menjadi perantara; *vt* menengahi; **mediation** *n* perantaraan; **mediator** *n* perantara

medical *adj* kedokteran, médis; ~ *check-up* pemeriksaan fisik; ~ *school* jurusan kedokteran; **medically** *adv* secara médis; **medicated** *adj* mengandung obat; **medication** *n* obat; *on* ~ menjalani pengobatan; **medicine** *n* [médisin] obat; jurusan kedokteran, ilmu kedokteran; *Harris wants to study* ~ Harris ingin ambil jurusan kedokteran

medieval, mediaeval *adj* [médiivel] dari Abad Pertengahan

mediocre *adj* [midioker] cukupan, tidak istiméwa

meditate *vi* berméditasi, bersemadi; ~ *on* merenungkan; **meditation** *n* médi-tasi, semadi; ~ *class* kelas méditasi

Mediterranean *the* ~ *(Sea)* Laut Tengah; ~ *countries* kawasan Laut Tengah

medium *n* **media** cenayang, dukun, perantara; bahasa; bahan; *adj* sedang; ~ *size* berukuran sedang; *English-*~ *school* sekolah berbahasa Inggris

medley *n* campuran (lagu); ~ *relay* nomor éstafét gaya ganti (renang)

meet *n* perlombaan atlétik atau renang;

v **met met** *vi* bertemu, berjumpa; berkumpul; *Mum happened to ~ Jane on the train* Ibu kebetulan bertemu dengan Jane di keréta api; *vt* menemui; *~ requirements* memenuhi syarat; **meeting** *n* rapat, pertemuan; *~ place* tempat pertemuan

megabyte, MB *n* [mégabait] mégabit

megaphone *n* [mégafon] pengeras suara, mégafon

melancholic *adj* [mélankolik] **melancholy** *n* murung, sayu

mellow *adj* matang, empuk

melodious *adj* merdu; **melody** *n* lagu

melon *n* semangka; *honeydew ~* mélon

melt *vi* meléléh, mencair, melebur; *vt* meléléhkan, meleburkan; **melted** *adj* cair; **melting** *adj ~ point* titik lebur; *~ pot* *n* tempat pertemuan berbagai budaya; **molten** *adj* cair, léléh

member *n* anggota; *~ of Parliament (MP)* anggota Déwan Perwakilan Rakyat (DPR); **membership** *n* keanggotaan; *~ card* kartu keanggotaan

membrane *n* selaput

memento *n* [mémento] kenang-kenangan, cinderamata; **memoir** *n* [mémoar] (buku) kenangan; **memorable** *adj* sulit terlupakan, patut diingat; memorandum, **memo** *n* mémorandum, surat peringatan; **memorial** *adj* peringatan; *~ Day AS* Hari Pahlawan; *n* tanda atau tugu peringatan; **memorize** *vt* menghafalkan; *have you ~d the physics formula?* apakah sudah menghafalkan rumus fisika?; **memory** *n* ingatan, daya ingat, mémori; *computer ~* mémori komputer; *a poor ~* sering lupa

men *n, pl →* **man**; **menswear** *n* busana pria

menace *n* [ménas] ancaman; *vt* mengancam

mend *vi* baik kembali, sembuh; *on the ~* mulai sembuh, sedang pulih; *vt* memperbaiki, membetulkan; menambal; *~ a sock* menambal kaus kaki; *~ your ways* mengubah kebiasaan buruk

menial *adj* [minial] kasar; *~ work* pekerjaan kasar

meningitis *n* [méninjaitis] radang selaput (otak)

menopause *n* [ménopoz] mati haid; **menstrual** *adj* berkaitan dengan datang bulan; *~ cycle* siklus datang bulan; *~ pain* sakit méns; **menstruate** *vi* **menstruation** *n* datang bulan, méns, haid

menswear *n* busana pria ← **men**

mental *adj* [méntel] jiwa; *~ arithmetic* mencongak, berhitung di kepala; *~ hospital* rumah sakit jiwa; **mentality** *n* méntalitas, cara berpikir; **mentally** *adv* di dalam hati; secara batin; *he ~ made a note of the number* dia coba menghafalkan nomor itu

menthol *adj, n* méntol, mint; *~ cigarette* rokok méntol

mention *n* [ménsyen] sebutan; *vt* menyebutkan; *don't ~ it* (terima kasih) kembali, sama-sama

mentor *n* penasihat

menu *n* daftar makanan, ménu; pilihan; *help ~* pilihan bantuan; *on the ~* di ménu

meow → **miaow**

mercantile *adj* perniagaan, perdagangan

mercenary *adj* [mérseneri] demi uang; *n* tentara bayaran

merchandise *n* (barang) dagangan; *you can buy team ~ at the ground* atribut tim bisa dibeli di stadion; **merchant** *n* pedagang, saudagar; *~ bank* bank dagang; *~ navy* kapal dagang

merciful *adj* [mérsifal] murah hati; **merciless** *adj* tanpa belas kasih, tidak mengampuni; **mercy** *n* belas kasih, kemurahan hati; *~ killing* mati tenang

Mercury *n* planét Mérkurius

mercury *n* air raksa

mercy *n* belas kasih, kemurahan hati; *~ killing* mati tenang

mere *adj* [mir] hanya, saja, belaka; *a ~ child* hanya anak-anak, masih anak-anak; **merely** *adv* hanya, belaka

merge *vi* menyatu; *vt* menggabungkan; **merger** *n* pemersatuan, penggabungan

meridian *n* [méridian] garis bujur

meringue *n* [merang] kué terbuat dari putih telur yang dikocok

merit *n* [mérit] jasa; manfaat;
meritorious *adj* berjasa
mermaid *n* putri duyung
merrily *adv* [mérili] dengan gembira;
merriment *n* keramaian; **merry** *adj*
ria; ~ *Christmas* Selamat (Hari) Natal;
~~-go-round* komedi putar
mesh *n* mata jala, lubang
mess *n* kekacauan, keadaan berantakan; *in a* ~ dalam kesulitan, dalam
keadaan; *vt* mengacaukan; ~ *about,* ~
around vi bermain-main; *vt* tidak
memperlakukan dengan jujur; ~ *up*
mengacaukan; **messy** *adj* berantakan,
tidak rapi; ~ *hair* rambut kusut
message *n* [mésej] pesan; **messenger**
n pesuruh, kurir
Messrs *abbrev messieurs* Tuan-Tuan,
dkk
messy *adj* berantakan, tidak rapi ← **mess**
met *v, pf* → **meet**
metal *n* [métal] logam; ~ *detector*
détéktor métal; *heavy* ~ *(music)* musik
métal; **metallic** *adj* dibuat dari logam,
mengkilap; **metalwork** *n* kerajinan besi
metamorphosis *n* métamorfosis
metaphor [métafor] *n* kiasan, ibarat,
perumpamaan; **metaphorical** *adj*
secara kiasan
meteor *n* [mitior] bintang jatuh; **mete-
orologist** *n* ahli cuaca; **meteorology** *n*
[mitioroloji] ilmu cuaca, météorologi
meter, metre *n* méter; **metered** *adj* ~
taxi taksi argo; **metric** *adj* [métrik]
(berdasarkan sistem) métrik
method *n* métode, cara, jalan; **methodi-
cal** *adj* métodis
meths *n, pl, coll* **methylated spirits** *n,
pl* spiritus
metre → **meter**
metric *adj* [métrik] (berdasarkan sistem) métrik
mew *vi* mengéong (anak kucing)
Mexican *adj* berasal dari Méksiko; *n*
orang Méksiko; **Mexico** *n* Méksiko
mezzanine *adj* [mézanin] lantai tengah
(di antara lantai satu dan lantai dua)
mg *abbrev milligram* mg (miligram)
Mgr *abbrev, Cath Monsignor* Mgr, Uskup
MI5 Dinas Intelijén Inggris

miaow, meow *vi* [miau] mengéong
mice *n, pl* → **mouse**
Micronesia *n* [maikronisia] Mikronésia;
Micronesian *adj* berasal dari Mikronésia
microphone *n* [maikrofon] mikrofon,
corong radio
microscope *n* [maikroskop] mikroskop;
microscopic *adj* amat kecil
microwave *n* oven gelombang mikro
midday *n* tengah hari, jam 12 siang
middle *adj* [midel] tengah, menengah; *n*
pertengahan, titik tengah; ~~-aged* setengah baya; ~~-class* kelas menengah;
~ *finger* jari tengah; ~ *name* nama tengah; *the* ~ *Ages* Zaman Pertengahan;
the ~ *East* Timur Tengah; *in the* ~ *of*
tengah, asyik; **middleman** *n* perantara,
tengkulak
midget *n* katai, cebol
midnight *n* [midnait] tengah malam,
jam 12 malam
midriff *n* daérah pinggang
mid-sized *adj* berukuran sedang
midst *n* tengah; *in the* ~ *of* di tengah
midway *adj* di pertengahan jalan, di
tengah jalan
midweek *adj* tengah pekan
midwife *n* bidan
might *vi, aux* [mait] mungkin, boléh jadi
might *n* [mait] kuasa, kekuasaan;
mighty *adj* berkuasa; besar
migraine *n* [maigrén] migrén, sakit
kepala sebelah
migrant *n* [maigrant] pendatang;
migrate *vi* pindah, bermigrasi; *the*
family ~*d to Australia* keluarga itu pindah ke Australia; **migration** *n* migrasi
mike *n, coll* mikrofon, corong radio ←
microphone
mild *adj* [maild] lembut, ringan, énténg;
~ *weather* cuaca yang tidak panas atau
dingin
mile *n* mil; **mileage** *n* jarak tempuh;
milestone *n* batu peringatan; tonggak
bersejarah
militant *adj* militan, berhaluan keras; *n*
orang militan; **military** *adj, n* militér,
ketentaraan; **militia** *n* [milisya] milisi,
wajib militér (wamil)
milk *n* susu; *vt* memerah susu; ~ *bar*

warung (susu); ~ *cow* sapi perah; ~
teeth gigi susu; *cow's* ~ susu sapi;
goat's ~ susu kambing; *powdered* ~
susu bubuk, susu formula; *soy* ~ susu
kedelai; **milkman** *n* tukang susu; **milk-
shake** *n* minuman susu bercampur
(coklat dsb); **milky** *adj* (mengandung)
susu, tidak jernih; *the* ~ *Way* Bimasakti
mill *n* penggilingan, kilang; *vi* bergerak
dalam keramaian; *vt* menggiling;
miller *n* penggiling
millenium *n* [milénium] milénium
milliliter, millilitre, ml *n* mili, mililiter
millimeter, mm *n* mili, miliméter
million *n* juta; **millionaire** *n* jutawan,
milyunér
millipede *n* [milipid] kaki seribu
mimic *n* pemain mimik, peniru; *vt* **mimicked mimicked** meniru
minaret *n* [minarét] menara (mesjid)
mince *n* (daging) cincang; ~ *pie* kué
Natal yang berisi buah cincang; *vt*
mencincang, mengiris
mind *n* [maind] akal (budi), pikiran,
jiwa; *of one* ~ sependapat; *to change
your* ~ berubah pikiran; *to keep in* ~,
to bear in ~ ingat akan, mempertimbangkan; *to lose your* ~ menjadi gila;
vi merasa keberatan; *never* ~ tidak
apa-apa; *do you* ~? apa anda keberatan?; *vt* ingat akan, memperhatikan,
menjaga, mengindahkan; ~ *your own
business* jangan ikut campur; **mind-
less** *adj* tanpa alasan; **mindreader** *n*
orang yang bisa membaca pikiran
orang lain
mine *pron, poss* milikku, saya punya;
he's a relation of ~ dia salah seorang
saudara saya
mine *n* ranjau; **minefield** *n* daérah ranjau
mine *n* tambang; *tin* ~ tambang timah;
miner *n* buruh tambang; **mineral** *n*
[mineral] barang tambang, barang
galian; ~ *water* air dari sumber
gunung, air mineral
mingle *vi* [minggel] campur, bergaul
mini *adj, sl* [mini] kecil, mungil, mini;
miniature *adj* [miniatyur] kecil; *n*
ukuran kecil; *in* ~ berskala kecil,
berukuran kecil; **minibus** *n* mobil

angkot, kol, bus sedang; **minicab** *n,
UK* taksi; **miniskirt** *n* rok mini
minimum *adj, n* minimum, sedikit-
sedikitnya, terendah; ~ *wage* upah
minimum régional
mining *n* [maining] pertambangan
miniskirt *n* rok mini ← **mini**
minister *n* menteri; pendéta; *Foreign* ~
Menteri Luar Negeri (Ménlu); *Prime* ~
Perdana Menteri; ~ *of Agriculture*
Menteri Pertanian (Méntan); ~ *for
Health* Menteri Keséhatan (Ménkés);
~ *of the Interior* Menteri Dalam Negeri
(Méndagri); **ministry** *n* kementerian,
départemén
minor *adj* [mainor] kecil, tidak penting,
sepélé; di bawah umur, belum déwasa;
n anak; **minority** *n* golongan kecil,
minoritas
mint *n* percétakan mata uang; *vt*
menempa uang; ~ *condition* sempurna
mint *n* sejenis kemangi; permén penyegar mulut
minus *vt* [mainus] kurang; tanpa; *six* ~
one is five enam kurang satu sama
dengan lima
minute *adj* [mainyut] kecil sekali
minute *n* [minet] menit; ~ *hand* jarum
panjang; *wait a* ~ tunggu sebentar; *pl*
notulen, laporan
miracle *n* [mirakel] keajaiban, mukjizat;
miraculous *adj* [mirakyulus] ajaib
mirage *n* [miraj] fatamorgana
mirror *n* cermin; *vt* mencerminkan
misadventure *n* kemalangan, nasib
buruk
misbehave *vi* ~ *(oneself)* berkelakuan
buruk; **misbehavior, misbehaviour** *n*
kelakuan buruk
miscalculate *vi* **miscalculation** *n* salah
hitung
miscarriage *n* [miskarej] **miscarry** *vi*
keguguran
miscellaneous *adj* [miselénius] beranéka ragam; lain-lain
mischief *n* [mischef] kenakalan, kejahil-
an; **mischievous** *adj* nakal, jahil
misconception *n* salah paham, salah
pengertian
misconduct *n* kelakuan buruk

misdeed *n* perbuatan jahat

miser *n* [maizer] orang kikir, orang pelit; **miserable** *adj* [mizerabel] sedih, murung; **miserly** *adj* [maizerli] kikir, pelit; **misery** *n* [mizeri] penderitaan, kesusahan

misfortune *n* kecelakaan, kesialan

misgovernment *n* [misgaverment] pemerintahan yang buruk

mishmash *n* campuran

misinformation *n* salah informasi

misinterpret *vt* menyalahtafsirkan; **misinterpretation** *n* kesalahtafsiran, penyalahtafsiran

misjudge *vt* salah sangka, salah menilai

mislay *vt* **mislaid mislaid** salah simpan, salah taruh, kehilangan

mislead *vt* **misled misled**; **misleading** *adj* menipu, menyesatkan

misprint *n* salah cétak

Miss *n, pron* Nona (sebelum nama keluarga); ~ *Jones* Nona Jones

miss *vi* melését; *vt* rindu akan, merindukan; ketinggalan; ~ *the train* ketinggalan keréta api; **missing** *adj* tidak hadir; hilang, kurang; ~ *person* orang hilang

misshapen *adj* salah bentuk, cacat

mission *n* zénding; *Cath* misi; perutusan; ~ *statement* misi dan visi; **missionary** *n* misionaris

mist *n* kabut, halimun

mistake *n* kesalahan; *by* ~ tidak sengaja; *vt* **mistook mistaken** keliru, salah mengerti; *I mistook him for my friend* saya salah kira, dia kawan saya

Mister *pron* Tuan (sebelum nama keluarga); ~ *Brown* Tuan Brown; **mistress** *n* kekasih, gundik; ~ *of the house* nyonya rumah

mistook *vt, pf* → **mistake**

mistreat *vt* memperlakukan secara tidak benar, menganiaya

mistrust *vt* tidak percaya

misty *adj* berkabut ← **mist**

misunderstand *v* **misunderstood misunderstood** salah mengerti, salah paham, salah tangkap; **misunderstanding** *n* kesalahpahaman

misuse *n* penyalahgunaan; *vt* menyalahgunakan

mitt *n* sarung tangan (untuk bisbol, memegang panci panas); **mitten** *n* sarung tangan, kaus tangan

mix *n* campuran; ~*-up* kekeliruan, kesalahfahaman; *vi* campur; ~ *up* keliru; *vt* mencampur, mencampurkan; mencampuradukkan; membingungkan; **mixed** *adj* ~ *marriage* perkawinan campuran; **mixer** *n* alat pengaduk; **mixture** *n* campuran, adonan

ml *abbrev milliliter* mili, mililiter

mm *abbrev millimeter n* mili, miliméter

moan *n* erangan; keluhan; *vi* mengerang, mengeluh; ~ *about* mengeluh

moat *n* parit; *the castle had a large* ~ bénténg itu dikelilingi parit besar

mob *n* orang banyak; *vt* mengerumuni

mobile *adj* dapat bergerak, dapat dipindahkan; *n* mainan gantung; ~ *home* karavan; ~ *library* perpustakaan keliling; ~ *phone* télépon genggam, ponsél; **mobility** *n* [mobiliti] mobilitas; **mobilization** *n* mobilisasi, pengerahan

moccasin *n* [mokasin] sejenis selop terbuat dari kulit lembut

mock *adj* palsu, pura-pura, tiruan; ~ *exam* latihan ujian; *vt* mengéjék; **mockery** *n* penghinaan

MOD *abbrev, UK Ministry of Defence* Departemén Pertahanan

mode *n* cara, jalan

model *adj* contoh; *n* contoh, macam, modél; peragawati, peragawan; ~ *aircraft* modél pesawat terbang; *male* ~ peragawan; *vt* memperagakan

moderate *adj* sedang, moderat; *n* orang moderat; **moderately** *adv* cukup, lumayan; **moderator** *n* moderator, pembawa acara

modern *adj* modérn, baru, kini; ~ *language* bahasa yang masih dipakai kini; *Japanese is a* ~ *language, but Sanskrit is not* bahasa Jepang termasuk bahasa yang masih dipakai, tidak seperti bahasa Sanskerta; **modernize** *vt* memperbarui

modest *adj* sederhana, rendah hati;

sopan; **modesty** *n* kerendahan hati;
kesopanan

modification *n* [modifikésyen] perubahan, modifikasi; **modify** *vi* mengubah;
memodifikasi

module *n* [modyul] satuan, unit; mata
kuliah

moist *adj* basah, lembab; **moisten** *vt*
[moisen] membasahi; **moisture** *n*
embun, kelembaban; **moisturizer** *n*
pelembab

molar *n* gigi geraham

mold, mould *n* cétakan; *vi* membentuk,
mencétak

mold, mould *n* jamur; **moldy, mouldy**
adj berjamur, jamuran, apak

Moldova, Moldavia *n* Moldova;
Moldovan *adj* berasal dari Moldova; *n*
orang Moldova

moldy, mouldy *adj* berjamur, jamuran,
apak ← **mold**

mole *n* sejenis tikus; spion, mata-mata

mole *n* tahi lalat

molecule *n* molekul

molest *vt* mengganggu (secara seksual),
mencampuri; **molester** *n child* ~
pédofil

mollusc *n* kerang-kerangan

Molotov cocktail *n* bom molotov

molt, moult *vi* berganti bulu atau kulit

molten *adj* cair, léléh ← **melt**

Moluccan *adj* [molakan] berasal dari
Maluku; *n* orang Maluku; **Moluccas**
the ~ Maluku

Mom, Mum *pron* Bu, Mak; **mommy,
mummy** *pron* Ibu, Mama, Mami

moment *n* saat; *any* ~ *now* segera; *at the*
~ sekarang; *in a* ~, *just a* ~ sebentar

momma, mommy, mummy *pron* Ibu,
Mama, Mami ← **mom**

Monaco *n* Monako; **Monegasque,
Monacan** *adj* berasal dari Monaco; *n*
orang Monaco

monarch *n* [monark] raja, ratu;
Elizabeth II is the reigning British ~
Ratu Elizabeth II adalah ratu Inggris
sekarang; **monarchy** *n* kerajaan

monastery *n* [monastri] biara

Monday *n* [Mandé] hari Senin; *Easter* ~
hari Senin sesudah Paskah; ~ *to Friday*

hari Senin sampai Jumat

monetary *adj* [manetéri] keuangan,
monetér; ~ *crisis* krisis monéter (krismon); **money** *n* uang; ~*-minded* mata
duitan; ~ *changer* penukar uang asing;
~ *laundering* pencucian uang; ~ *market*
pasar uang; ~ *order* poswésel; *dirty* ~
uang haram; ~ *for jam* digaji setelah
hanya bekerja sedikit; *time is* ~ waktu
itu uang; **moneybox** *n* céléngan

Mongolia *n* [monggolia] Mongolia;
Mongolian *adj* berasal dari Mongolia;
n bahasa Mongolia, orang Mongolia;
Mongoloid *adj, n* bangsa Asia

mongrel *adj, derog* [manggrel] campuran; *n* anjing kampung

monitor *n* pengawas; layar, monitor
(komputer); *vt* mengawasi

monitor *n* ~ *lizard* biawak

monk *n* [mank] biarawan, rahib

monkey *n* [mangki] monyét; ~ *business*
kenakalan; ~ *wrench* kunci Inggris

monologue *n* [monolog] monolog;
Butét is famous for his ~*s* Butet terkenal atas monolog-monolognya

monopolize *vt* memonopoli; **monopoly**
n monopoli

monorail *n* monorél, keréta api rél
tunggal, keréta layang

monotheism *n* kepercayaan pada
keesaan Tuhan

monotone *n* nada tunggal; *the mayor
spoke in a* ~ walikota berbicara secara
monoton; **monotonous** *adj* monoton,
senada

monsoon *n* musim hujan, muson

monster *adj* raksasa; *a* ~ *sale* obral
besar; *n* makhluk besar yang mengerikan; **monstrous** *adj* amat besar, mengerikan

Montenegro *n* Montenégro; **Montenegrin** *adj* berasal dari Montenégro; *n*
orang Montenégro

month *n* [manth] bulan; *a* ~ *of Sundays*
lama sekali; *at the end of the* ~ akhir
bulan; *pl* berbulan-bulan; **monthly**
adj, adv bulanan; *n* majalah bulanan

Montserrat *n* Montserrat; **Montserra-
tian** *adj* berasal dari Montserrat; *n*
orang Montserrat

monument *n* monumén, tanda peringatan, tugu peringatan; **monumental** *adj* sangat besar

mood *n* suasana hati; *in a good* ~ angin sedang baik; *in the* ~ *for* sedang ingin; **moody** *adj* muram, murung

moon *n* bulan, rembulan; *crescent* ~ bulan sabit; *full* ~ terang bulan, bulan purnama; *new* ~ bulan muda; *many* ~*s ago* sudah lama; *over the* ~ sangat bahagia; *once in a blue* ~ jarang sekali; **moonlight** *n* [munlait] sinar bulan; **moonlit** *adj* di bawah sinar rembulan; **moonshine** *n* minuman keras yang dibuat secara gelap

moor *n, UK* tanah tinggi yang berumput

moor *vi* bertambat; *vt* menambatkan

moose *n* rusa besar (di Amerika Utara)

mop *n* pél; *v* mengepél; ~ *the floor* mengepél lantai

mope *vi* bermuram, mengasihani diri sendiri; *stop moping over your problems* jangan bermuram saja memikirkan masalah

moped *n* [mopéd] sepéda motor bébék, Véspa

moral *n* [morel] kesusilaan, étika; moral, moril; ~ *support* dukungan moral; *the* ~ *of the story* pelajarannya, pesannya; **morale** *n* [moral] semangat juang; **morality** *n* moralitas, kesusilaan

morbid *adj* yang banyak memikirkan kematian dan hal buruk

more *adv* lebih, lagi; ~ *than* lebih dari; ~ *and* ~ semakin; ~ *or less* kurang lebih; *one* ~ *glass* satu (gelas) lagi; *the* ~ *the merrier* makin banyak, semakin ramai; **moreover** *adv* [morover] lagipula

morgue *n* [morg] kamar mayat

morning *n* pagi (hari); ~ *paper* koran pagi; *good* ~ selamat pagi (diucapkan sampai jam 12 siang); ~ *sickness* rasa mual pada ibu hamil; *this* ~ tadi pagi; *in the* ~ pagi hari; *besok* pagi; ~, *noon and night* sepanjang hari

Moroccan *adj* berasal dari Maroko; *n* orang Maroko; **Morocco** *n* Maroko

moron *n* orang bodoh; **moronic** *adj* bodoh sekali

morose *adj* murung, muram

morphine *n* [morfin] morfin

morsel *n* sesuap, secuil (makanan)

mortality *n* [mortaliti] kematian; ~ *rate* tingkat kematian

mortar *n* adukan semén dan pasir; mortir; lumpang; ~ *and pestle* alu lumpang; **mortarboard** *n* topi mahasiswa

mortgage *n* [morgej] hipoték; *vt* menggadaikan, menghipotékkan

mortified *adj* sangat malu; **mortify** *vt* membuat malu, menghina

mortuary *n* kamar mayat

mosaic *n* [moséik] mosaik

Moscow *n* [mosko] Moskwa

Moses *n* Nabi Musa

Moslem → **Muslim**

mosque *n* [mosk] mesjid

mosquito *n* [moskito] nyamuk; ~ *net* kelambu; ~ *repellent* obat nyamuk

moss *n* lumut; **mossy** *adj* berlumut

most *adj, adv* paling, maha; ~ *of* kebanyakan; *at (the)* ~ sebanyak-banyaknya, paling-paling; *to make the* ~ *of* benar-benar memanfaatkan; **mostly** *adv* kebanyakan

MOT *abbrev, UK Ministry of Transport* Departemén Perhubungan, Departemén Transportasi

motel *n* hotél transit

moth *n* ngengat; ~*eaten* usang, lusuh, dimakan ngengat; ~*ball* kapur barus

mother *n* [mather] ibu; induk; *pron* Ibu, Mama, Mami; ~*in-law* (ibu) mertua; ~*of-pearl* kulit mutiara; ~*to-be* calon ibu; ~*'s Day* Hari Ibu; ~ *Nature* alam; ~ *ship* kapal induk; ~ *tongue* bahasa ibu; *father and* ~ bapak ibu; **motherhood** *n* keibuan; **motherland** *n* ibu pertiwi; **motherless** *adj* piatu, tidak beribu

motion *n* gerak; mosi, usul; *in* ~ sedang bergerak, sedang jalan; ~ *sickness* mabuk (jalan); **motionless** *adj* tidak bergerak, diam

motivate *vt* **motivating** *adj* memotivasi, menggerakkan hati; **motivated** *adj* bermotivasi; **motivation** *n* dorongan, dukungan, motivasi; **motivational** *adj* memberi motivasi, memberi semangat;

motive *n* [motiv] alasan, dalil, motif
motor *n* motor, mesin; **motorbike** *sl*
sepéda motor; **motorboat** *n* perahu
bermotor; **motorcade** *n* konvoi pejabat; **motorcar** *n, arch* mobil; **motor-**
cycle *n* **motorbike** *sl* sepéda motor;
motorcyclist *n* pengendara sepéda
motor; **motorist** *n* pengendara mobil;
motorway *n, UK* jalan bébas hambatan
mottled *adj* burik
motto *n* semboyan, slogan, moto
mould → **mold**
mount *n* (nama) gunung; ~ *Bromo*
Gunung Bromo; *vt* naik; menaiki,
menaikkan; memasang; ~ *up*
meningkat, menumpuk; **mountain** *n*
[maunten] gunung; **mountaineer** *n*
pendaki gunung; **mountainous** *adj*
[mauntenes] bergunung-gunung;
mountainside *n* léréng gunung, sisi
gunung; **Mounties** *the* ~ polisi berkuda di Kanada
mourn *vt* [morn] berkabung; meratapi,
menangisi; **mourner** *n* orang yang
berkabung; **mournful** *adj* penuh
kesedihan, memilukan; **mournfully**
adv dengan penuh kesedihan; **mourn-**
ing *n* perkabungan; *in* ~ berkabung
mouse *n* **mice** tikus; tetikus (komputer);
~*deer* kancil; **mousehole** *n* lubang
tikus; **mousetrap** *n* perangkap tikus
mousse *n* [mus] sejenis puding; gél
rambut
moustache, mustache *n* [mustasy]
kumis, misai
mouth *n* mulut; muara; ~*watering*
menggiurkan; ~ *organ* harmonika; *big*
~ orang yang tidak dapat menjaga
rahasia; ~*to*~ *resuscitation* pernafasan buatan; *by word of* ~ secara lisan;
mouthful *n* sesuap; **mouthwash** *n*
[mauthwosy] obat kumur; **mouthy** *adj*
bermulut besar
movable *adj* [muvabel] dapat digerak-
kan; **move** *n* perpindahan, gerakan;
on the ~ sedang jalan; *to make a* ~
pulang; berangkat; *vi* bergerak;
berpindah (rumah); ~ *house* pindah
rumah; *vt* menggerakkan, memindahkan; **movement** *n* gerak, gerakan,

pergerakan; **movers** *n, pl* jasa pindah
rumah; **moving** *adj* mengharukan
movie *n, sl* [muvi] film
moving *adj* mengharukan ← **move**
mow *vt* [mo] memotong rumput; ~
down menumbangkan; **mower** *n*
mesin pemotong rumput
Mozambican *adj* berasal dari
Mozambik; *n* orang Mozambik;
Mozambique *n* Mozambik
MP *abbrev Member of Parliament*
anggota DPR
mpg *miles per gallon* mil per galon
mph *miles per hour* mil per jam
Mr *Mister* Tn (Tuan) (harus dipakai
dengan nama keluarga, mis. *Mr*
Brown)
Mrs *Mistress, Missus* Ny (Nyonya)
(harus dipakai dengan nama keluarga,
mis. *Mrs Thatcher*)
MS *abbrev multiple sclerosis* sklérosis
multipel
Ms Ny, Ibu (status perkawinan tidak
disebut, harus dipakai dengan nama
keluarga, mis. *Ms Smith*)
Mt *Mount* G, Gg (gunung)
much *adv, n* banyak; *how* ~ berapa
banyak, berapa harganya; *not* ~ tidak
banyak, tidak begitu; *so* ~ sekian; *very*
~ sangat; *as* ~ *as* sebanyak; ~ *of a*
muchness hampir sama semua; *thank*
you very ~ terima kasih banyak
muck *n* kotoran, sampah, lumpur; *vi* ~
around iseng, membuang waktu
mucus *n* lendir, ingus, dahak
mud *n* lumpur; **muddy** *adj* berlumpur;
mudguard *n* [madgard] spatbor
muddle *n* [madel] kekacauan, kekusutan;
vt mengacaukan
muddy *adj* berlumpur ← **mud**
mudguard *n* [madgard] spatbor ← **mud**
muesli *n* [myusli] séréal
muezzin *n, Isl* [muézin] modin, muazin
muffin *n* sejenis roti panggang; sejenis
kué
muffled *adj* [mafeld] tidak jelas
kedengaran, sayup-sayup; **muffler** *n*
kenalpot; seléndang
mufti *n, UK, arch* pakaian sehari-hari,
pakaian bébas

mug *n* cangkir besar; *vt* menodong, merampok; **mugger** *n* penodong; **mugging** *n* penodongan

muggy *adj* lembab (cuaca)

Muhammad *n, Isl* (Nabi) Muhammad

mulberry *n* murbéi

mule *n* bagal; semacam selop wanita

multi- *pref* lebih dari satu, anéka; **multicolored** *adj* warna-warni, beranéka warna; **multi-level** ~ *marketing (MLM)* pemasaran berpola piramida; **multilateral** *adj* yang melibatkan beberapa pihak; **multimedia** *n, adj* [maltimidia] multimédia; **multinational** ~ *company* perusahaan multinasional

multiple *adj* [maltipel] berlipat ganda; ~ *sclerosis (MS)* sklérosis ganda; ~ *choice test* ujian pilihan ganda; *n* kelipatan; **multiplication** *n* perkalian; **multiply** *vi* berkembang biak; *vt* mengalikan

multitude *n* [maltityud] banyak; *a* ~ *of* banyak

Mum → **Mom**

mumble *vi* [mambel] bergumam, berkomat-kamit; *vt* mengatakan dengan kurang jelas

mummy *n* mumi → **mommy**

mumps *n* penyakit gondok; *to have the* ~ gondokan

munch *v* mengunyah; **munchies** *n, pl, sl* cemilan

municipal *adj* [munisipal] berkaitan dengan kotamadya; **municipality** *n* [munisipaliti] kota, kotapraja, kotamadya

munitions *n, pl* mesiu, munisi

mural *n* lukisan pada témbok atau dinding

murder *n* pembunuhan; *vt* membunuh (orang); **murdered** *adj* terbunuh; **murderer** *n* pembunuh

murky *adj* gelap, suram, keruh

murmur *n* bisikan; *vi* berbisik; *vt* membisikkan

muscle *n* [masel] urat, otot; kekuatan; **muscled** [maseld] **muscly** [masly] **muscular** *adj* berotot

muse *n* ilham, inspirasi; *v* termenung, melamun

museum *n* [musium] musium

mushroom *n* cendawan, jamur

music *n* musik, lagu; *classical* ~ musik klasik; *folk* ~ musik rakyat; *to face the* ~ menghadapi hukuman; **musical** *adj* [musikal] (berbakat) musik; *n* sandiwara dengan banyak lagu; **musician** *n* [musisyen] musikus, pemain musik

Muslim, Moslem *adj* Islam, Muslim; *n* orang Islam

muslin *n* kain kasa

mussel *n* kerang, remis, kepah

must *n* keharusan; *vi, aux* harus, wajib, terpaksa; pasti; *it* ~ *be difficult being a stranger* pasti susah menjadi orang asing

mustache, moustache *n* [mustasy] kumis, misai

mustard *n* mostar

musty *adj* lapuk

mutate *vi* berubah, bermutasi; **mutation** *n* mutasi, perubahan

mute *adj* bisu; *deaf-*~ bisu tuli

mutilate *vt* memotong (anggota badan); **mutilation** *n* mutilasi, pemotongan

mutiny *n* [myutini] pemberontakan (di kapal); *vi* memberontak

mutt *n, coll* anjing (bukan ras)

mutter *vi* bergumam, berkomat-kamit; *vt* menggumam

mutton *n* daging biri-biri, daging domba; ~ *bird* sejenis burung laut

mutual *adj* [myutyual] saling, dari kedua pihak, timbal balik; ~ *friend* saling berteman; ~ *interest* kepentingan bersama; *the feeling's* ~ dia pun merasa begitu

muzzle *n* moncong, mulut; *vt* membrédel, memberangus; *the press is still* ~*d here* pers masih dibrédel di sini

my *pron, poss* [mai] saya, -ku; **myself** *pron* saya sendiri; *adv* sendirian, seorang diri

Myanmar *n* [mianmar] Myanmar

mynah [mainah] ~ *(bird)* burung béo

myopia *n* [maiopia] **myopic** *adj* rabun dekat

myriad *adj* [miriad] beribu-ribu, tidak terbilang

myrtle *n* [mertel] sejenis pohon kemuning

myself *pron* [maisélf] saya sendiri; sendirian, seorang diri

mysterious *adj* gaib, mistérius, penuh mistéri; **mysteriously** *adv* secara mistérius; **mystery** *n* kegaiban, mistéri

mystic *n* mistik; *Isl* tasawuf; **mystical** *adj* **mysticism** *n* mistik, aliran kebatinan; *Javanese* ~ kejawén

mystified *adj* bingung; **mystify** *vt* membingungkan, menakjubkan

myth *n* [mith] isapan jempol, dongéng, mitos; **mythological** *adj* berkaitan dengan mitologi; **mythology** *n* mitologi; *Greek* ~ mitos Yunani

N

nag *vi* ceréwét; *vt* mengoméli; *a ~ging feeling* perasaan yang tak kunjung hilang

nail kuku; ~ *file* kikir kuku, amril; ~ *polish*, ~ *varnish cat* kuku, kutéks; ~ *scissors* gunting kuku; **nailbrush** *n* sikat kuku

nail *n* paku; kuku; *to bite one's ~s* menggigit kuku; *to hit the ~ on the head* benar sekali; *vt* memaku

naïve *adj* [naiv] lugu, naif; **naïvety** *n* [naiveti] keluguan

naked *adj* [néked] telanjang; *the ~ eye* mata telanjang; *stark ~* telanjang bulat

name *n* nama; *vt* menamai, menamakan, memberi nama; *~-dropping* menyebut-nyebut orang ternama; ~ *card* kartu nama; *assumed ~* nama lain, nama samaran; *family ~, last ~* nama keluarga, nama marga; *Christian ~, first ~* nama depan; *middle ~* nama tengah; *a bad ~* nama buruk, réputasi buruk; *to call ~s* mengéjék; *in the ~ of* atas nama; demi; *in the ~ of God, stop it* demi Tuhan, berhenti!; **named** *adj* bernama; **nameless** *adj* tidak bernama, anonim; **namely** *conj* yakni, yaitu; **nameplate** *n* papan nama

Namibia *n* Namibia; **Namibian** *adj* berasal dari Namibia; *n* orang Namibia

nanny *n* penjaga anak, pengasuh anak

nap *n* tidur siang; *to take a ~* tidur sebentar; *vt* tidur sebentar

nape *n* tengkuk

napkin *n* serbét; popok; **nappy** *n, coll* popok; ~ *rash* ruam popok; *disposable ~* pampers, lampin pakai buang; *table ~* serbét

narcotic *n* obat-obatan, narkotika

narrate *vi* [narét] bercerita; *vt* menceritakan; **narrative** *n, adj* [narativ] cerita; **narrator** *n* [narétor] orang yang bercerita

narrow *adj* sempit; *~-minded* picik, berpikiran sempit; ~ *escape* nyaris celaka; *vi* menjadi kecil, menjadi sempit; ~ *down* memusatkan pada; *vt* menyempitkan; **narrowly** *adv* hampir, nyaris; *he ~ missed the selection for the team* dia hampir dipilih masuk tim

NASA *abbrev National Aeronautics and Space Administration* Administrasi Angkasa dan Aéronautika Nasional

nasal *adj* berhubungan dengan hidung, sengau

nastiness *n* kejahatan, keburukan; **nasty** *adj* buruk, jahat; *a ~ cut* luka yang dalam; *a ~ person* orang judes

nation *n* [nésyen] negara, bangsa; **national** *n, adj* [nasyonal] nasional, kebangsaan; ~ *anthem* lagu kebangsaan; ~ *park* taman nasional; ~ *service* wajib militér; **nationalism** *n* nasionalisme; **nationalist** *adj* nasionalis; **nationality** *n* kebangsaan, kewarganegaraan; **nationalize** *vt* menasionalisasi; **nationwide** *adj, adv* di seantéro negara

native *adj* [nétif] asli; ~ *speaker* penutur asli; *to go ~* hidup seperti orang setempat; *n* orang asli, pribumi; *a ~ of New Zealand* orang Sélandia Baru

NATO *abbrev North Atlantic Treaty Organization* NATO, Pakta Pertahanan Atlantik Utara

natural *adj* [natyurel] alami, alamiah; wajar; ~ *gas* gas alam; *n* orang berbakat; *Alf is a ~ at tennis* Alf punya bakat main ténis; **naturalist** *n* pakar alam, pecinta alam; **naturalize** *vt*

menjadikan warganegara; **naturally** *adj, v* tentu, memang; **nature**
n [nétyur] alam (semésta); tabiat,
kepribadian, sifat; ~ *reserve* cagar
alam; *good-~d* berhati baik
naught → **nought**
naughtiness *n* [notines] kenakalan;
naughty *adj* nakal, jahil
Nauru *n* pulau Nauru; **Nauruan** *adj*
berasal dari Nauru; *n* bahasa Nauru;
orang Nauru
nausea *n* [nozia] (rasa) mual, mabuk;
nauseating *adj* [noziéting] memualkan, memabukkan; **nauseous** *adj*
[nosius] mual, mabuk
nautical *adj* [notikel] berkaitan dengan
pelayaran, kelautan; ~ *mile* mil laut
naval *adj* perkapalan, berhubungan
dengan angkatan laut ← **navy**
navel *n* pusar, udel
navigate *vi* [navigét] menjadi navigator,
mengemudikan kapal; melayari; **navi-
gation** *n* pelayaran, navigasi; **navigator** *n* mualim; **navy** *n* [névi] angkatan
laut; ~ *blue* biru tua, biru donker; *merchant* ~ kapal dagang
nb. *nota bene* = *note well* catatan
NCO *abbrev non-commissioned officer*
perwira tanpa jabatan
NE *abbrev northeast* timur laut
near *adj* dekat; ~*-sighted* rabun jauh; *a
~ thing, a ~ miss* hampir saja, nyaris;
the ~ East kawasan pantai timur Laut
Tengah; *vt* menjelang, menuju,
mendekati; *it's ~ing dusk* sudah menjelang senja; *we're ~ing the city* kita
mendekati kota; **nearby** *adv* [nirbai]
dekat; **nearest** *adj* terdekat, paling
dekat; **nearly** *adv* [nirli] hampir, nyaris
neat *adj* apik, rapi, bersih; *sl* hébat, bagus;
~ *handwriting* tulisan rapi; **neatly** *adv*
dengan rapi; **neatness** *n* kerapian
necessarily [nésesérili] *not* ~ tidak
selalu, tidak harus; **necessary** *adj*
[néseséri] perlu; **necessitate** *vt* mengharuskan; **necessity** *n* [nésésiti] kebutuhan, keperluan; *daily necessities*
kebutuhan sehari-hari
neck *n* léhér, tengkuk; ~ *and* ~ sedang
bersaing; *a pain in the* ~ orang yang

menyebalkan; *to break your* ~ léhér
patah; *to stick your* ~ *out* mengambil
risiko; *vi, sl* berciuman; **necklace** *n*
kalung; **neckline** *n* garis léhér; **necktie** *n* dasi
necropolis *n* kuburan
nectarine *n* [néktarin] sejenis buah persik kecil
nee, née [ni, né] nama gadis
need *n* kebutuhan, keperluan; *in* ~ perlu
bantuan; *if* ~ *be* jika perlu; *no* ~ tidak
usah, tidak perlu; *vt* perlu, butuh,
membutuhkan, memerlukan; **needless** ~ *to say* tidak usah dikatakan;
needy *adj, n* miskin, melarat; *the* ~
kaum miskin
needle *n* [nidel] jarum; *darning* ~ jarum
tisik; *knitting* ~ jarum rajut; *vt, sl*
mengéjék, menyindir; **needlepoint,
needlework** *n* semacam sulaman
needless ~ *to say* tidak usah dikatakan
← **need**
needy *adj, n* miskin, melarat; *the* ~
kaum miskin ← **need**
negate *vt* [negét] menyangkal, meniadakan; **negative** *adj* [négativ] négatif,
buruk; **negatively** *adv* secara négatif
negative *n* [négativ] klise
negatively *adv* [négativli] secara négatif
← **negative**
neglect *n* keadaan telantar; *vt* mengabaikan; **neglected** *adj* telantar, tidak terawat, terbengkalai; **neglectful** *adj*
lalai, alpa
negligence *n* [néglijens] kelalaian,
kealpaan, keteledoran; **negligent** *adj*
lalai, alpa; **negligible** *adj* [néglijibel]
sedikit sekali, tidak usah diindahkan
negotiable *adj* [negosyabel] dapat
ditawar; **negotiate** *vi* bermusyawarah,
berunding; *vt* merundingkan; **negotia-
tion** *n* negosiasi, perundingan; **nego-
tiator** *n* juru runding
Negro *adj, n, arch* [nigro] orang hitam
neigh *vi* [néi] meringkik
neighbor, neighbour *n* [nébor] tetangga; **neighborhood** *n* lingkungan
(dekat rumah); **neighboring** *adj* bertetangga, berdekatan; **neighborly** *adj*
selaku tetangga

neither *conj* [nither, naither] kedua-duanya (tidak); ~ ... *nor* bukan ... maupun

neocolonialism *n* [niokolonializem] néokolonialisme; **neocolonialist** *adj* néokolonialis

neon *n* [nion] néon; ~ *light* lampu néon

Nepal *n* Népal; **Nepalese** *adj* berasal dari Népal; **Nepali** *n* bahasa Népal; orang Népal

nephew *n, m* [néfyu] keponakan (lela-ki); *great-*~ anak (lelaki) dari kepo-nakan

nepotism *n* [népotizem] nepotisme

Neptune *n* planet Néptunus

nerve *n* saraf; nyali, keberanian; ~*-rack-ing* menggelisahkan; ~ *gas* gas saraf; *what a* ~*!* énak saja! berani-berani-nya!; *to get on one's* ~*s* mengganggu; *to lose one's* ~ tiba-tiba tidak berani; **nervous** *adj* gelisah, gugup; ~ *system* jaringan saraf

nest *n* sarang; *vi* bersarang; ~ *egg* tabungan, persediaan; **nestle** *vi* [nésel] bersarang

net *adj* bersih, nétto; *n* jala, jaring; *badminton* ~ nét bulu tangkis; *fishing* ~ jala ikan; *mosquito* ~ kelambu; *to surf the* ~ menjelajahi internét; *vt* menjaring; **netball** *n* bola jaring; **network** *n* jaringan; *vi* menjalin hubungan

Netherlands *the* ~ (negeri) Belanda

nettle *n* jelatang; *vt* mengganggu, membuat sakit hati; *stop nettling your brother* jangan mengganggu adikmu

network *n* jaringan; *vi* bergaul, menja-lin hubungan

neurologist *n* [nurolojist] ahli saraf, neurolog; **neurology** *n* ilmu penyakit saraf, neurologi; **neurotic** *adj* berpenyakit saraf, menderita gang-guan jiwa

neuter *adj* bukan maskulin atau féminin; *vt* mengebiri, menstéril; *Belang has been neutered* si Belang sudah distéril

neutral *adj* [nutral] nétral, tidak memihak; ~ *color* warna yang teduh;

neutrality *n* kenétralan; **neutralize** *vt* menétralkan

never *adv* [néver] tidak pernah; ~ *again* tidak pernah lagi; ~ *before* belum pernah; ~ *mind* tidak apa-apa; ~ *say that again* jangan sekali-kali mengata-kan begitu lagi; *well I* ~ astaga

nevertheless *conj* [névertheléssalt] walaupun demikian, namun

new *adj* baru; ~ *Caledonia* kepulauan Kalédonia Baru; ~ *Caledonian* berasal dari Kalédonia Baru; orang Kalédonia Baru; ~ *moon* bulan muda; ~ *Testa-ment* Injil; ~ *Year* tahun baru; ~ *Year's Eve* malam tahun baru; *Chinese* ~ *Year* Imlék; *Happy* ~ *Year* Selamat Tahun Baru; ~ *Zealand* Sélandia Baru; berasal dari Sélandia Baru; ~ *Zea-lander* orang Sélandia Baru; *Papua* ~ *Guinea* Papua Nugini; **newborn** *adj* baru saja lahir; ~ *baby* orok; **newcomer** *n* pendatang baru; **newly** *adv* baru saja, belum lama; ~*-weds* pengantin baru; **news** *n* berita, warta, warta berita; kabar; ~ *anchor* pembaca berita; **newsagency** *n* toko koran; **newsagent** *n* pemilik toko koran; **newsflash** *n* berita terbaru; **newsletter** *n* selébaran; **newspaper** *n* surat kabar, koran; **newsreader** *n* pembaca berita

next *prep* berikut, sebelah, samping; ~ *door* rumah sebelah; ~ *month* bulan depan; ~ *time* lain kali; ~ *of kin* keluar-ga terdekat

NFL *abbrev, US National Football League* Liga Sépak Bola Nasional

NGO *abbrev non-governmental organi-zation* LSM (lembaga swadaya masyarakat)

NHK *abbrev Nihon Housou Kyoukai* NHK, penyiaran nasional Jepang

NHS *abbrev, UK National Health Service* Pelayanan Keséhatan Nasional

nib *n* mata péna

nibble *v* [nibel] mengunggis, menggi-git-gigit; *n* gigitan kecil; *pl* makanan kecil

Nicaragua *n* Nikaragua; **Nicaraguan** *adj* berasal dari Nikaragua; *n* orang Nikaragua nice *adj* énak, sedap; manis, cantik, apik; ~ *food* makanan énak; ~ *weather* cuaca baik; *a* ~ *dress* rok yang cantik; ~ *person* orang baik

nick *n* toréhan; *sl* sél tahanan; *in the* ~ *of time* pas waktunya; *vt, sl* mengutil; *people always* ~ *flowers from my garden* orang selalu ambil bunga dari taman saya

nickel *n* nikel

nickname *n* nama kecil, nama panggilan; *Tony's* ~ *was Plugger* Plugger adalah nama panggilan Tony

nicotine *n* nikotin

niece *n, f* [nis] keponakan (perempuan); *great-*~ anak perempuan dari keponakan

Niger *n* [niger] Niger; **Nigerien** *adj* [nijérien] berasal dari Niger; *n* orang Niger

Nigeria *n* [naijiria] Nigeria; **Nigerian** *adj* berasal dari Nigeria; *n* orang Nigeria

nigger *n, derog* orang hitam

niggle *v* [nigel] mengorék, mengganggu; *Peter had a niggling injury cedera* Peter sering mengganggu

night *n* [nait] malam; ~ *club* kelab malam, kafé; ~ *owl* orang yang suka bangun waktu malam; ~ *school* kursus malam; ~ *shift* jam kerja malam; *at* ~ *pada* waktu malam, malam hari; *good* ~ selamat tidur; *last* ~ tadi malam, semalam; ~ *and day* siang (dan) malam; *all through the* ~ sepanjang malam; *in the dead of* ~ tengah malam; *I want a room for two* ~*s* saya cari kamar untuk dua malam; **nightcap** *n* minumam keras (diminum sebelum tidur); **nightdress, nightgown** *n* **nightie** *f, sl* daster; **nightfall** *n* senja, magrib; **nightingale** *n* bulbul; **nightlife** *n* kehidupan malam; **nightly** *adv* tiap malam; **nightmare** *n* mimpi buruk; **nightwatchman** *n* jaga (malam)

nil *adj* kosong, nol; *the score was three* ~ skornya tiga kosong

nimble *adj* [nimbel] cekatan, tangkas, gesit

nine *n, adj* sembilan; ~ *to five* jam sembilan (pagi) sampai jam lima (sore), jam

kerja; **ninth** *adj* [nainth] kesembilan

nineteen *n, adj* sembilan belas; **nineteenth** *adj* kesembilan belas ← **nine**

nineties *n, pl* (tahun) sembilan puluhan; **ninetieth** *adj* kesembilan puluh; **ninety** *adj, n* sembilan puluh ← **nine**

ninth *adj* [nainth] kesembilan ← **nine**

nip *n* gigitan kecil; *vt* mencubit, menggigit

nipper *n, sl* anak kecil

nipple *n* [nipel] puting, pentil, dot

nirvana *n, Budd* nirwana

nit *n, coll* (telur) kutu

nitrogen *n* [naitrojen] nitrogen

no. *number* no. (nomor)

no tidak; bukan; ~*-nonsense* tidak main-main, sérius; ~*-one* bukan siapa-siapa; *pron* tidak seorang pun; *Grandma has no-one to look after her* tidak ada yang menjaga Nénék; ~ *chance,* ~ *way* tidak mungkin; ~ *smoking* dilarang merokok; *there's* ~ *money* tidak ada uang; *Will you come?/*~*, I can't* Apakah anda mau datang?/Tidak, saya tidak bisa; *he's* ~ *friend of mine* dia bukan kawan saya

nobility *n* [nobiliti] kaum bangsawan, kaum ningrat; **noble** *adj* [nobel] bangsawan, ningrat; **nobleman** *n* bangsawan

nobody, no-one *pron* [nobodi] bukan siapa-siapa; *pron* tidak seorang pun; *Grandma has* ~ *to look after her* tidak ada yang menjaga Nénék

nocturnal *adj* (hidup pada waktu) malam

nod *n* anggukan, tanda setuju; *to get the* ~ mendapat persetujuan; *vi* mengangguk, terangguk-angguk; ~ *off* tertidur, ketiduran; *vt* menganggukkan; *the baby* ~*ded his head* bayi itu menganggukkan kepala

noise *n* [noiz] bunyi, kegaduhan, keributan, suara bising; ~ *pollution* polusi suara; *to make a* ~ berbunyi; **noiseless** *adj* tidak bersuara, tidak berbunyi; **noisy** *adj* gaduh, ribut, berisik, bising; **noisily** *adv* dengan berisik

nomad *n* **nomadic** *adj* [nomadik] pengembara, nomaden

nominal *adj* nominal, hanya atas nama saja; **nominate** *vt* mencalonkan; **nomination** *n* pencalonan, nominasi; **nominative** *adj, n* subyék, nominatif; **nominee** *n* calon

non- *pref* tidak, non-; *~alcoholic* tidak mengandung alkohol; *~aligned* nétral; *~committal* tidak berkoméntar; *~existent* tidak ada; *~fiction* cerita nyata, bukan fiksi; *~party* tidak berpartai; *~profit* nirlaba; *~smoking* tidak merokok; *~stick* tidak léngkét; *~stop* tanpa berhenti; *~violent* tidak menggunakan kekerasan

nonchalant *adj* [nonsyalant] énténg, tanpa beban

none *pron* [nan] seorang pun tidak, sesuatu pun tidak; tidak sama sekali; *there's ~ left* tidak ada sisanya; *~ of the family liked her* semua keluarga tidak suka dia

nonsense *n* omong kosong

noodles *n, pl* mi; *fried ~* mi goréng

nook *n* sudut, pojok

noon *(at) ~* jam duabelas siang; *morning, ~ and night* sepanjang hari

no-one, no one *pron* [nowan] bukan siapa-siapa; *pron* tidak seorang pun; *Grandma has ~ to look after her* tidak ada yang menjaga Nénék

noose *n* jerat

nope *sl* enggak, ndak, tidak; bukan ← **no**

nor *neither ... ~* bukan ... maupun; juga tidak

Nordic *adj* berasal dari daérah Skandinavia (Dénmark, Eslandia, Finlandia, Norwégia, Swédia)

norm *n* norma; **normal** *adj* biasa, lazim, lumrah, umum; normal; **normalcy, normality** *n* keadaan normal; **normalize** *vt* menormalkan, kembali membina; *America has already ~d relations with Vietnam* Amérika sudah menormalkan hubungan dengan Viétnam; **normally** *adv* biasanya, pada umumnya

north *adj* utara; *adv* ke utara; *n* (sebelah) utara; *~ America* Amérika Utara; *~ Korea* Koréa Utara (Korut); *~ Korean* orang Koréa Utara; berasal dari Koréa Utara; *~ Pole* Kutub Utara; *~ Sea* Laut Utara; *to the ~ of* di sebelah utara; **northeast** *adj, n* timur laut; **northerly** *adj* ke arah utara; *n* angin dari arah utara; **northern** *adj* utara; *~ Ireland* Irlandia Utara; *the ~ Hemisphere* belahan bumi bagian utara; *(the) ~ Territory (NT)* Australia Utara; **northerner** *n* orang dari utara; **northwest** *adj, n* barat laut

Norway *n* Norwégia; **Norwegian** *adj* [norwijen] berasal dari Norwégia; *n* bahasa Norwégia; orang Norwégia

nose *n* hidung; *on the ~* bau; *to pick one's ~* mengupil; *to have a blood ~* mimisan; *to look down one's ~ at* memandang rendah; *to stick one's ~ in* ikut campur; **nosebleed** *n* mimisan; **nosedive** *n* terjun bébas; *vi* menukik; **nostril** *n* lubang hidung; **nosy, nosey** *adj* ingin tahu

nostalgia *n* [nostalja] rasa rindu, nostalgia; **nostalgic** *adj* bernuansa nostalgia

not *adv* tidak, tak; belum; bukan; *~ including* tidak termasuk; *~ me* bukan saya; *~ ready* belum siap; *~ yet* belum; *~ at all* sama sekali tidak; *~ my type* bukan seléra saya; *~ only ... but also* tidak hanya ... tapi juga, bukan hanya ... tapi juga

notable *adj* [notabel] istimewa, patut dicatat; *n* orang ternama; **note** *n* catatan, peringatan; nada, not; nota; *vt* mencatat, menulis; memperhatikan; *to take ~ of* memperhatikan; **noted** *adj* masyhur, tersohor, kenamaan

notary *n* notaris

notch *n* takik, torehan; *vt* menakik; *a ~ above* lebih baik dari

note *n* catatan, peringatan; nada, not; nota; *to take ~ of* memperhatikan; *v* mencatat, menulis; memperhatikan; **notebook** *n* buku catatan, buku tulis, notes; *~ (computer)* komputer jinjing; **noted** *adj* masyhur, tersohor, kenamaan; **notepaper** *n* kertas tulis; **noteworthy** *adj* patut diperhatikan

nothing *pron* [nathing] tidak sesuatu pun; *~ like* tidak seperti; *he does ~* dia tidak melakukan apa-apa; *to come to ~* gagal

notice *n* [notis] perhatian; pemberitahuan, pengumuman, maklumat; ~
board papan pengumuman; *at short* ~
dengan mendadak, serta merta; *until
further* ~ untuk sementara; *to take no* ~
tidak menghiraukan; *vt* melihat;
memerhatikan; *to take* ~ *of* mengindahkan, memerhatikan; **noticeable**
adj [notisabel] nyata, tampak, kelihatan

notification *n* [notifikésyen] pemberitahuan, surat panggilan; **notify** *vt*
[notifai] memberitahu; memberitahukan

notion *n* pikiran, idé

notorious *adj* [notorius] mempunyai
nama buruk

notwithstanding *conj* meskipun,
walaupun

nougat *n* [nuga] gula-gula keras terbuat
dari kacang

nought, naught *n, arch* [not] nol,
kosong; tanpa hasil; *to come to* ~ tidak
berhasil

noun *n* [naun] kata benda

nourish *vt* [narisy] memberi gizi, memelihara; **nourishing** *adj* bergizi;
nourishment *n* gizi

novel *adj* baru; *n* buku roman, novél;
novelist *n* pengarang novél; **novelty** *n*
hal baru, barang baru

November *n* bulan Novémber

novice *adj, n* [novis] pemula, orang
baru

now *adv* [nau] sekarang, kini; ~ *that*
sejak; *just* ~ baru saja, tadi; *(every)* ~
and then, ~ *and again* sekali-sekali,
kadang-kadang; *from* ~ *(on)* mulai
sekarang; *conj* nah; **nowadays** *adv*
sekarang (ini)

nowhere *adv, pron* [nowér] tidak di
mana-mana; *to go* ~ tidak ke mana-
mana, tidak bergerak

nuance *n* nuansa

nuclear *adj* nuklir; ~ *energy,* ~ *power*
tenaga nuklir; ~ *family* rumah tangga;
nucleus *n* [nuklius] inti

nude *adj* telanjang, bugil; *in the* ~
telanjang; **nudist** *n* orang yang suka
bertelanjang; **nudity** *n* ketelanjangan

nudge *n* [naj] sentuhan; *vt* menyentuh,
menyinggung

nugget *n* bongkah, gumpal; *chicken* ~
nugét ayam; *gold* ~ gumpal emas

nuisance *n* [nusens] gangguan; orang
pengganggu; *what a* ~ mengganggu saja

null ~ *and void* tidak berlaku

numb *adj* [nam] mati rasa, kesemutan,
kebas

number *n* **no.** *abbrev* nomor; bilangan,
angka; banyaknya; ~ *plate* plat polisi;
lucky ~ angka keberuntungan; *telephone* ~ nomor télepon; *unlucky* ~
angka sial; *a large* ~ banyak; *in great*
~s berbondong-bondong; *vi* berjumlah; *vt* memberi nomor; **numbering** *n*
penomoran; **numeral** *n* angka; *Roman*
~s angka Romawi; **numerous** *adj*
[numerus] banyak sekali

nun *n* biarawati, suster

nuptial *adj* [naptyel] berkaitan dengan
perkawinan; *pl* upacara perkawinan

nurse *n* juru rawat, perawat; *vt* merawat;
menyusui; **nursemaid** *n* pengasuh anak;
nursery *n* kamar anak; toko tanaman;
~ *rhyme* lagu anak-anak; ~ *school*
taman kanak-kanak (TK); **nursing** *adj*
menyusui; merawat; ~ *home* panti
asuhan; ~ *mother* ibu menyusui

nut *n* kacang; mur; *sl* penggemar berat,
penggila; orang gila; *cashew* ~ kacang
médé; *to go* ~s menjadi marah, menjadi gila; *he's a soccer* ~ dia tergila-gila
pada sépak bola; **nutmeg** *n* pala; **nutshell** *n in a* ~ péndéknya, intinya;
nutty *adj* berasa kacang; *sl* gila

nutrient *n* [nutrient] gizi; **nutrition** *n*
[nutrisyen] ilmu gizi; **nutritionist** *n*
ahli gizi; **nutritious** *adj* [nutrisyes]
bergizi

nutshell *n in a* ~ péndéknya, intinya ←
nut

nutty *adj* berasa kacang; *sl* gila ← **nut**

NW *abbrev northwest* barat laut

nylon *n* [nailon] nilon; **nylons** *n, pl*
stoking

nymph *n* [nimf] bidadari, peri;
nymphomaniac *n, f* perempuan yang
gila séks

NZ *abbrev New Zealand* Sélandia Baru

O

o/s *abbrev overseas* LN (luar negeri)

oak *n* pohon ék

oar *n* dayung; **oarsman** *n* pendayung

oasis *n* [oésis] **oases** oase

oath *n* sumpah; umpatan; *under* ~ di bawah sumpah; ~ *of office* sumpah jabatan; *to take an* ~, *to swear an* ~ bersumpah

oatmeal *n* havermut; **oats** *n, pl* sejenis gandum; *to sow your wild* ~ berfoya-foya ketika masih muda

OBE *abbrev, UK Officer (of the Order) of the British Empire* gelar pemberian

obedience *n* [obidiens] ketaatan, kepatuhan; **obedient** *adj* taat, patuh; **obediently** *adv* dengan taat; **obey** *v* [obé] taat, patuh; ~ *the law* mematuhi peraturan yang berlaku

obelisk *n* tugu

obese *adj* [obis] gemuk sekali; **obesity** *n* keadaan sangat gemuk, obésitas; ~ *is a big problem in America* obésitas sekarang menjadi masalah besar di Amérika

obey *v* [obé] taat, patuh; ~ *the law* mematuhi peraturan yang berlaku

obituary *n* berita duka, berita kematian, obituari

object *n* benda, obyék; **objective** *adj* obyéktif, tidak memihak; *n* tujuan; **objectively** *adv* secara obyéktif

object *vi* berkeberatan; ~ *to* berkeberatan; **objection** *n* keberatan

obligation *n* [obligésyen] kewajiban; **obligated** *adj* diharuskan; **obligatory** *adj* [obligatri] wajib; **oblige** *vt* [oblaij] membantu, menolong; **obliged** *adj* diharuskan; tertolong; *visitors are* ~ *to report to security* tamu harus lapor ke sekuriti; **obliging** *adj* bersifat siap menolong

oblivious *adj* [oblivius] tidak sadar, tidak mengindahkan

oblong *adj, n* persegi panjang

obnoxious *adj* [obnoksyes] menjéngkélkan, berkepribadian buruk

oboe *n* obo

obscene *adj* [obsin] cabul, jorok

obscure *adj* tidak terkenal, terpencil; *vt* mengaburkan; **obscurity** *n* [obskuriti] kesunyian, keadaan tidak dikenal

observant *adj* suka memperhatikan; taat; **observation** *n* pengamatan, peninjauan; *under* ~ ditinjau; **observatory** *n* [obsérvatri] obsérvatorium, teropong; **observe** *vt* mengamati, meninjau; menghormati; **observer** *n* pengamat, peninjau

obsessed *adj* berobsési; ~ *with* terobsési; **obsession** *n* obsési; **obsessive** *adj* obsésif; **obsessively** *adv* secara obsésif

obstacle *n* [obstakel] rintangan, hambatan; ~ *race* lari rintangan

obstetrician *n* dokter kandungan; **obstetrics** *n* ilmu kebidanan

obstinate *adj* [obstinet] keras kepala

obstruct *vt* merintangi, menghalangi; **obstructed** *adj* terhalang; **obstruction** *n* rintangan, halangan

obtain *vt* memperoléh, mendapatkan, menerima; *it's hard to* ~ *a permit nowadays* sekarang ini susah mendapat izin

obtrusive *adj* [obtrusiv] menonjol

obtuse *adj* ~ *angle* sudut tumpul

obvious *adj* [obvius] jelas, terang, nyata; *to state the* ~ mengatakan yang sudah diketahui; **obviously** *adv* dengan jelas; tentunya

occasion *n* [okésyen] kesempatan, peluang; peristiwa, acara; *special* ~ acara khusus; **occasional** *adj* **occasionally** *adv* kadang-kadang

Occident *n, arch* [oksident] *the* ~ dunia Barat; **Occidental** *adj* barat, kebaratan

occult *the* ~ dunia gaib

occupancy *n* tingkat penghunian; **occupant** *n* penghuni; **occupation** *n* pekerjaan; pendudukan; **occupational** *adj* terkait dengan pekerjaan; ~ *hazard* risiko pekerjaan; ~ *therapy* térapi okupasi; **occupy** *vt* [okupai] mengisi; menduduki; ~*ing forces* tentara pendudukan

occur *vi* terjadi; ~ *to* terpikir; **occurrence** *n* kejadian, peristiwa

ocean *n* [osyan] samudera, lautan; *the Atlantic* ~ Lautan Atlantik; *the Indian* ~ Samudera Hindia, Samudera Indonesia; *the Pacific* ~ Lautan Teduh; **Oceania** *n* Oséania, kawasan Pasifik

o'clock jam, pukul; *it's six* ~ sekarang jam enam

octagon *n* segi delapan; **octagonal** *adj* bersegi delapan

octane *n* oktan; *high-* ~ oktan tinggi

October *n* bulan Oktober

octopus *n* ikan gurita

OD *abbrev overdose* overdosis

odd *adj* anéh, ganjil; ~ *number* nomor ganjil; ~ *socks* kaus kaki yang tidak sepasang; ~ *one out* barang tanpa pasangan; **oddball** *adj* anéh; *n* orang anéh; **oddity** *n* keanéhan; **oddly** *adv* secara anéh

odds *n, pl* kemungkinan; ~*on* kemungkinan besar; *against the* ~ kemungkinan kecil

odious *adj* menjijikkan, membangkitkan kebencian

odor, odour *n* bau; *body* ~ *(BO)* bau badan

OECD *abbrev Organisation for Economic Cooperation and Development* Organisasi Pembangunan dan Kerjasama Ekonomi

of *prep* [ov] milik; dari, daripada; *a cup* ~ *tea* secangkir téh; *to consist* ~ terdiri dari, terdiri atas

off *prep* jauh; *adj* mati, tidak hidup; basi (makanan); tidak jadi; pergi, berangkat; ~*chance* kemungkinan kecil; ~*key* bersuara sumbang; ~*license* toko minuman keras; ~*limits* tidak boléh; ~*peak* tidak pada jam sibuk; ~ *duty* tidak sedang dinas; ~ *work* tidak masuk kerja; ~ *the record* (dikatakan) secara tidak resmi; ~ *and on* sekali-sekali; *a day* ~ hari libur; *the milk is* ~ susu sudah basi; *turn* ~ *the light* lampu tolong dimatikan; *he's* ~ *to Bangkok* dia mau ke Bangkok; **offbeat** *adj* tidak biasa, antik; **offhand** *adj* begitu saja, énténg; ~ *remark* komentar iseng; *on the* ~ sedang menyerang, agrésif; **offset** *vt* **offset offset** meng-

ganti rugi; **offshoot** *n* cabang; **offshore** *adj* lepas pantai; **offside** *adj* opsét; **offspring** *n* anak, keturunan

offbeat *adj* tidak biasa, antik ← **off**

offence → **offense**

offend *vt* menghina, membuat tersinggung; melanggar hukum; **offender** *n* yang bersalah, yang melakukan; *repeat* ~ residivis; **offense, offence** *n* pelanggaran hukum, kesalahan; serangan (olahraga); **offensive** *adj* menghina, tidak sopan; serangan; ~ *language* kata-kata tidak sopan

offer *n* tawaran, penawaran; *vt* menawarkan, menawari; mempersembahkan; **offering** *n* persembahan, sesajén

offhand *adj* begitu saja, énténg; ~ *remark* komentar iseng ← **off**

office *n* [ofis] kantor, ruangan, tempat kerja; jabatan; ~ *block* gedung perkantoran; ~ *boy m* ~ *girl f* pesuruh; ~ *hours (OH)* jam kerja; ~ *party* acara pésta di kantor; *at the* ~ di kantor; **officer** *n* pegawai, petugas; perwira; *police* ~ polisi; **official** *adj* resmi; *n* pegawai, pejabat

offset *vt* **offset offset** mengganti rugi ← **off**

offshoot *n* cabang ← **off**

offshore *adj* lepas pantai ← **off**

offside *adj* opsét ← **off**

offspring *n* anak, keturunan ← **off**

often *adv* sering; *every so* ~ sekali-sekali; *more* ~ *than not* cukup sering; *once too* ~ terlalu sering

ogre *n* [oger] raksasa; makhluk yang menakutkan

oh *ejac* o!

oil *n* minyak; ~ *colors,* ~ *paint* cat minyak; ~ *lamp* lampu minyak, lampu pétromaks; ~ *palm* kelapa sawit; ~ *rig* pengebor minyak; ~ *slick* tumpahan minyak; ~ *tanker* kapal minyak; ~ *well* menara minyak; *castor* ~ minyak jarak, kastroli; *essential* ~ minyak aromatérapi; *fish* ~ minyak ikan; *olive* ~ minyak zaitun; *vt* meminyaki; **oilfield** *n* ladang minyak; **oilwell** *n* sumur minyak; **oily** *adj* berminyak

ointment *n* salep, balsem

OK, okay [oké] baik, oke, jadi; *vt* menyetujui; *the government ~ed the project* pemerintah menyetujui pembangunan proyék itu

old *adj* tua; sepuh, lanjut usia; lama; bekas, mantan; *~-fashioned* kuno, kolot; *~ maid* perawan tua; *~ money* keluarga yang sudah lama kaya; *~ school* kuno; *~ Testament* Perjanjian Lama, Taurat; *~ people's home* panti jompo; *an ~ house* rumah lama, rumah tua; *any ~ how* sembarangan; *my ~ school* sekolah saya dulu; *twelve years ~* berumur dua belas tahun; *how ~ is he?* berapa umurnya?; **olden ~** *days* masa lalu, témpo dulu, zaman baheula; **older** *adj* lebih tua; *~ brother* kakak (laki-laki), abang; *~ sister* kakak (perempuan); **oldest** *adj* paling tua; *~ child* anak sulung

olive *n* [oliv] (buah) zaitun; *~ branch* dahan pohon zaitun (perlambang perdamaian); *~ green* berwarna hijau pudar; *~ oil* minyak zaitun

Olympiad *n* Olimpiade; **Olympian** *n* atlét yang pernah bertanding di Olimpiade; **Olympic** *adj* Olimpiade; *~ Games* Pertandingan Olimpiade; **Olympics** *the ~* (Pertandingan) Olimpiade

Oman *n* Oman; **Omani** *adj* berasal dari Oman; *n* orang Oman

omelet, omelette *n* telur dadar

omen *n* tanda, pertanda, alamat; **ominous** *adj* [ominus] buruk kelihatannya

omission *n* kelupaan; **omit** *vi* melupakan, menghilangkan; **omitted** *adj* terlupakan, dihilangkan

omnibus *n* kumpulan, antologi; *arch* bis → **bus**

omnipotent *adj* mahakuasa

omnivore *n* **omnivorous** *adj* pemakan segala, omnivora

on *adj* hidup; *~ and off* kadang-kadang; *to switch the light ~* menyalakan lampu; *prep* di (atas), pada; *~ the table* di atas méja; *adv* terus; sedang berjalan, sedang berlangsung; *~ foot* jalan kaki; *~ and ~* terus-menerus; *~ the phone* sedang menélépon; *~ the way*

sedang dalam perjalanan; *from that day ~* mulai hari itu; *conj* tentang, mengenai; *a seminar ~ drugs* seminar tentang narkoba; **oncoming** *adj* [onkaming] yang mendekat; **ongoing** *adj* terus-menerus; **online** *adj* di internét; **onlooker** *n* penonton; **onset** *n* awal, permulaan; **onward** *adv* ke depan, seterusnya; *ever ~* maju tak gentar; **onto** *prep* ke atas; ke; *the letter fell ~ the floor* surat itu jatuh ke lantai

once *adv* [wans] sekali (waktu); dahulu kala; *~ again* sekali lagi; *at ~* pada saat itu juga, segera; *the ~-over* pandangan sekilas; *all at ~* serentak; tiba-tiba; *just this ~* sekali ini saja; *~ and for all* untuk terakhir kali; *~ upon a time* sekali waktu; *I ~ visited Belgium* saya pernah mengunjungi Bélgia

oncoming *adj* [onkaming] yang mendekat ← **on**

one *n, adj* [wan] satu, suatu; seorang; *pron* orang; *n* yang; *~-eyed* bermata satu; berat sebelah; *~-sided* sepihak, berat sebelah; *~ another* satu sama lain; *~ apple* sebuah apel; *~ day* kapan-kapan; suatu hari, sekali waktu; *~ hundred* seratus; *~ million* sejuta; *~ of* salah satu (dari); *~ thousand* seribu; *~-way street* jalan satu arah; *as ~* serentak; *not (even) ~* tidak satu pun; *the ~* yang satu itu; *~ by ~* satu per satu; *a bigger ~* yang lebih besar; *I for ~* menurut pendapat saya; **oneself** *pron* [wansélf] diri sendiri; *to do ~* melakukan sendiri; **only** *adj* tunggal; *~ child* anak tunggal; *one and ~* satu-satunya; *adv* saja, hanya; *if ~* kalau saja; *not ~ ... but also* tidak hanya ... tetapi juga

ongoing *adj* terus-menerus ← **on**

onion *n* [anien] bawang; *spring ~* daun bawang

online *adj* di internét ← **on**

onlooker *n* penonton ← **on**

only *adj* tunggal, satu-satunya; *~ child* anak tunggal; *one and ~* satu-satunya; *adv* saja, hanya; *if ~* kalau saja; *not ~ ... but also* tidak hanya ... tetapi juga ← **one**

onset *n* awal, permulaan ← **on**

onshore *adj* di daratan

onto *prep* ke atas; ke; *the letter fell ~ the floor* surat itu jatuh ke lantai ← **on**

onward *adv* ke depan, seterusnya; mulai, sejak; *ever ~* maju tak gentar; **onwards** *adv* sejak; *from August ~* mulai Agustus ← **on**

onyx *n* [oniks] batu akik

ooze *v* [uz] mengalir, meléléh, melumér; *the wound ~d blood* darah melumér dari luka itu

opal *n* opal, baiduri; *white ~* kalimaya

opaque *adj* [opék] tidak tembus pandang, buram

OPEC *abbrev Organisation of Petroleum-Exporting Countries* Organisasi Negara Penghasil Minyak

open *adj* buka, terbuka; terang-terangan; *~-air* terbuka; *~-door* pintu terbuka, aksés bébas; *~-minded* berpandangan terbuka; *~ house* acara menerima tamu di rumah sepanjang hari; *~ invitation* undangan untuk datang kapan saja; *~ sea* laut lepas; *~ secret* rahasia umum; *~ ticket* tikét pesawat yang tanggalnya dapat diubah; *(out) in the ~* (di alam) terbuka; *vi* buka, terbuka; *vt* membuka; *~ a present* membuka kado; **opener** *n* pembuka; **opening** *adj* pembuka; *~ hours* jam kantor, jam buka; *~ night* malam pertama (pertunjukan); *n* pembukaan; lubang, celah, lowongan; **openly** *adv* secara terbuka, dengan terus terang

opera *n* opera; *~ house* gedung opera

operate *vi* [operét] beroperasi, membedah; *that doctor ~d on her mother* dokter itu membedah ibunya; *vt* mengoperasi; menjalankan (mesin), mengoperasikan; **operating** *adj ~ theater* kamar operasi; **operation** *n* pembedahan, operasi; cara menjalankan; **operational** *adj* operasional; **operator** *n* penjaga mesin, penjaga télepon

opinion *n* [opinion] pendapat; *~ poll* jajak pendapat; *in my ~* menurut pendapat saya; *to have an ~* berpendapat

opium *n* candu

opossum, possum *n* semacam tupai

opponent *n* lawan, oponan

opportunity *n* kesempatan, peluang; *job ~* lowongan kerja; *~ shop* toko loak; *to take an ~* memanfaatkan kesempatan

oppose *vt* menentang, melawan; **opposing** *adj* saling bertentangan; **opposite** *n, adj* [opozet] berlawanan, bertentangan, lawan (kata); *the ~ sex* lawan jenis; *black is the ~ of white* hitam itu lawannya putih; **opposition** *n* perlawanan, oposisi

oppress *vt* menindas, menekan; **oppression** *n* penindasan, tekanan; **oppressive** *adj* bersifat menindas, menekan; menyesakkan napas; **oppressor** *n* penindas

opt *vi ~ for* memilih; *~ out of* memilih tidak; **option** *n* [opsyen] opsi, pilihan; **optional** *adj* bébas (memilih)

optical *adj* optik; *~ illusion* tipu mata; **optician** *n* ahli kaca mata

optimism *n* sikap positif, sikap optimis; **optimist** *n* **optimistic** *adj* optimis

optimize *vt* mengoptimalkan; **optimum** *adj* optimal

optimum *adj* optimal

option *n* [opsyen] opsi, pilihan; **optional** *adj* bébas (memilih) ← **opt**

optometrist *n* dokter mata; ahli kacamata

opulence *n* kekayaan, keméwahan; **opulent** *adj* kaya, méwah

or *conj* atau; *either ... ~* salah satu

oral *adj* lisan, berkaitan dengan mulut; *~ examination* ujian lisan; *~ sex* séks oral

orange *adj* [orenj] oranye, jingga; *n* jeruk; *~-flavored* rasa jeruk; *~ juice* air jeruk, jus jeruk

orangutan *n* orang hutan

orator *n* orator, ahli pidato

orbit *n* orbit, perédaran, garis édar; *vt* mengitari

orchard *n* [orced] kebun buah

orchestra *n* [orkestra] orkés

orchid *n* [orkid] (bunga) anggrék

ordeal *n* cobaan atau pengalaman berat

order *n* urutan; peraturan; perintah; pesanan, pemesanan; *in ~* teratur; bérés;

in ~ to supaya; *on his ~s* atas perintahnya;
out of ~ rusak; *vt* memerintahkan,
menyuruh, mengatur, memesan;
orderly *adj* rapi, tertib; *n* juru rawat
ordinary *adj* [ordineri] biasa, lazim
ore *n* bijih; *gold ~* bijih emas; *iron ~*
bijih besi
oregano *n* [orégano] semacam rempah
organ *n* orgel, organ; **organist** *n*
pemain orgel
organ *n* bagian badan; **organic** *adj*
organik; **organism** *n* makhluk
organization *n* organisasi, persatuan;
penyusunan, pengaturan; **organize** *vt*
menyusun, mengatur, mengurus;
organized *adj* teratur, siap; **organizer**
n pengurus
orgasm *n* [orgazem] orgasme, puncak
(nafsu)
Orient *n* [oriént] *the ~* kawasan Timur;
oriental *adj* timur, ketimuran
orientate *vt* [oriéntét] menentukan arah,
mencari arah; **orientation** *n* oriéntasi,
pencarian jalan
orienteer *n* [oriyéntir] atlét lintas alam;
orienteering *n* olahraga lintas alam
origin *n* [orijin] asal, asal-usul; **original**
adj orisinil, asli, semula; **originality** *n*
keaslian; **originally** *adv* pada asalnya,
semula; **originate** *vt* berasal dari;
memulai; *that sport ~d in France*
olahraga itu berasal dari Perancis
ornament *n* hiasan; **ornamental** *adj*
hiasan, hias
orphan *n* [orfan] anak yatim piatu;
orphanage *n* [orfanej] rumah yatim
piatu; **orphaned** *adj* yatim piatu
orthodontist *n* dokter gigi
orthodox *adj* ortodoks, biasa; *Russian*
~ geréja Rusia (ortodoks)
ostentatious *adj* [ostentésyus] suka
pamér
ostracize *vt* [ostrasaiz] mengasingkan,
mengucilkan; *she was ~d by her friends*
dia dikucilkan kawan-kawannya
ostrich *n* burung unta; *~ egg* telur
burung unta
other *pron, adj* [ather] lain, berlainan;
every ~ day selang sehari; *the ~ day*
kemarin, belum lama ini; *the ~ one*

yang satu lagi; *the ~ woman* orang
ketiga; *pl* orang lainnya, yang lain;
otherwise *conj* kalau tidak, bila tidak;
Sanjay needs to sleep now, ~ he won't
wake up on time kalau Sanjay tidak
tidur sekarang, dia takkan bangun
pada waktunya
otter *n* berang-berang
ouch *excl* [auc] aduh, sakit
ought *aux, v* [out] seharusnya, semestinya, sebaiknya; *you ~ to report the*
burglary sebaiknya pencurian
dilaporkan
ounce *n* [auns] ons
our *pron* kita, kami; **ours** *pron* milik
kita, milik kami; **ourselves** *pron* kita
sendiri, kami sendiri; *we enjoyed ~*
kami menikmati
oust *vt* mengusir, menggésér; *the old*
President was ~ed from power
Présidén lama diusir dari kekuasaan
out *prep* (di) luar; *adj* di luar, tidak ada;
tidak berlaku lagi; mati; *vt* mengumumkan sebagai homoséks; *~-of-date*
ketinggalan zaman, kolot; *~-of-the-*
way jauh, terpencil; *~-of-work* menganggur; *~ and ~* betul-betul, sungguh-sungguh; *the lights are ~* mati
lampu; **outback** *n* pedalaman
(Australia); **outbreak** *n* [autbrék] pe-
cahnya, meletusnya (perang); ter-
jangkitnya (penyakit); **outbuilding** *n*
[autbilding] bangunan tambahan,
bangunan luar; **outburst** *n* letusan,
ledakan; **outcast** *n* orang buangan;
outcome *n* [autkam] hasil, keputusan;
outdated *adj* [autdéted] ketinggalan
zaman, kuno; **outdo** *vt* [autdu] mengungguli, melebihi; **outdoor** *adj* **out-**
doors *prep* (di) luar (rumah); **outer**
adj bagian luar; *~ space* angkasa luar;
outfit *n* busana; perlengkapan; **out-**
going *adj* ramah; **outing** *n* jalan-jalan,
kunjungan (pulang pergi); **outlandish**
adj aneh; **outlaw** *n* (orang) buronan;
outlet *n* jalan keluar, saluran pembuangan; toko, cabang; **outline** *n* garis
besar; **outlive** *vt* hidup lebih lama
dari; *my aunt ~d my uncle* bibi saya
ternyata hidup lebih lama daripada

paman; **outlook** *n* wawasan; masa depan; *the ~ is not good* masa depannya kelam; **outlying** *adj* jauh, terpencil; **outpatient** *n* [autpésyent] rawat jalan; **outpost** *n* pos yang terpencil; **output** *n* hasil, produksi; keluaran; **outrageous** *adj* [autréjus] keterlaluan; **outrigger** *n* balas; **outright** *adj* [autrait] langsung, terus terang, tulus; **outset** *n from the ~* sejak awal; **outside** *n, prep* (di) luar, ke luar, bagian luar; **outsider** *n* orang luar; **outskirts** *n, pl* pinggir, daérah pinggiran; **outspoken** *adj* blak-blakan, terang-terangan; **outstanding** *adj* luar biasa; *~ debts* hutang yang belum dilunasi; **outstretched** *adj* terentang; *an ~ hand* tangan yang diulurkan; **outward** *adj* berpenampilan; *adv* keluar; **outwit** *vt* menipu, memperdayakan

oval *adj* lonjong, oval; *n* (lapangan) bulat panjang

ovary *n* [overi] indung telur

ovation *n* sambutan tepuk tangan; *standing ~* sambutan tepuk tangan sambil berdiri

oven *n* [aven] oven, kompor, tungku; **ovenware** *n* piring untuk membakar makanan di oven

over *prep* selesai, rampung; *prep* di atas; melalui; tentang, mengenai; lebih daripada; *all ~* seluruh; selesai semua; *~ and ~* berulang kali; *~ there* di sebelah sana, di seberang; *~ the road* di seberang jalan; **overact** *vi* bertindak secara berlebihan; **overall** *adj* secara keseluruhan; **overalls** *n, pl* [overolz] pakaian montir; **overarm** *adv* (melémpar) dengan tangan dari atas; **overbearing** *adj* sombong; **overboard** *adj* ke dalam air (dari atas kapal); **overcast** *adj* mendung, berawan; **overcharge** *v* meminta bayaran terlalu tinggi; *she ~d me for the wool* saya diminta bayar lebih dari harga wol yang sebenarnya; **overcoat** *n* mantel; **overcome** *adj* [overkam] **overcame overcome** kewalahan; *vt* mengalahkan, mengatasi; **overcrowded** *adj* penuh sesak; **overdo** *vt* [overdu] **over-**

did overdone melakukan secara berlebihan; **overdose** *n* overdosis, OD; *vi* OD; *~ on sleeping tablets* OD minum obat tidur; **overdue** *adj* kedaluwarsa, terlambat; **overeat** *vi* [overit] **overate overeaten** terlalu banyak makan; **overflow** *vi* banjir; *n* tumpahan, banjir; **overgrown** *adj* penuh tetumbuhan; **overhaul** *n, vt* menurunkan mesin untuk diperiksa; **overhead** *adj* di atas (kepala); *n* ongkos eksploitasi; **overhear** *vt* [overhir] **overheard overheard** menguping; terdengar; **overkill** *n* tindakan yang berlebihan; **overlap** *vt, n* bertumpang tindih; **overload** *vt* kebanyakan (muatan); **overlook** *vt* melupakan; **overnight** *adv, prep* [overnait] bermalam, menginap, semalaman; **overpass** *n* jembatan penyeberangan; **overpower** *vt* [overpauer] menguasai; **overrate** *vt* menilai terlalu tinggi; **overrated** *adj* tidak sebagus rekomendasinya, dinilai terlalu tinggi; **overreact** *vi* [over riakt] beréaksi secara berlebihan; **overripe** *adj* busuk, kematangan; **overseas** *adv, adj* (di) luar negeri; **oversee** *vt* **oversaw overseen** mengawasi; **overseer** *n* mandor, pengawas; **overshadow** *vt* membayangi; *the youngest child was ~ed by his brothers' achievements* anak bungsu dibayang-bayangi préstasi kedua abangnya; **oversight** *n* [oversait] kelupaan; **oversleep** *vi* **overslept overslept** bangun kesiangan; **overtake** *vt* **overtook overtaken** menyalip; **overtime** *n* (kerja) lembur; **overthrow** *vt* [overthro] **overthrew overthrown** menjatuhkan, meruntuhkan; **overview** *n* [overvyu] selayang pandang; **overweight** *n* [overwéit] kelebihan berat (badan); **overwhelm** *vt* [overwélm] membanjiri, membuat kewalahan; **overwhelmed** *adj* kewalahan; **overwhelming** *adj* besar sekali

oviduct *n* saluran indung telur

ovum *n* telur

owe *vt* [o] berhutang kepada, berhutang sebesar; *she ~s me over a thousand* *dollars* dia berhutang kepada saya sebesar seribu dolar lebih; **owing** ~ *to* berkat, sebab, karena

owl *n* [aul] burung hantu

own *adj* [oun] sendiri; *my* ~ *house* rumahku sendiri

own *vt* memiliki, mempunyai; ~ *up* mengaku; **owner** *n* pemilik; **ownership** *n* kepemilikan, hak milik

ox *n* **oxen** sapi, lembu; **oxtail** *n* ~ *soup* sop buntut

oxide *n* [oksaid] oksida; **oxidize** *v* [oksidaiz] mengoksidasi; **oxygen** *n* [oksijen] oksigén; ~ *mask* masker oksigén

oxtail ~ *soup* sop buntut ← **ox**

oxygen *n* [oksijen] oksigén; ~ *mask* masker oksigén

oyster *n* tiram; ~ *sauce* saus tiram

oz *abbrev* ounce ons

ozone *n, pl* ozon; ~ *layer* lapisan ozon; ~ *therapy* térapi ozon

P

p *page, pp (pages)* halaman

pa *per annum* per tahun, setahun

PA *abbrev personal assistant* asistén pribadi (aspri)

Pa *pron, sl* Pak, Yah

pace *n* langkah; kecepatan; *snail's* ~ sangat lambat; *to keep* ~ *with* sama cepat; *vi* melangkah; mengukur kegiatan; **pacemaker** *n* alat pacu jantung

Pacific [pasifik] ~ *Ocean* Lautan Teduh, Samudera Pasifik; **pacifier** *n* [pasifaier] dot; **pacifist** *n* [pasifist] orang yang anti kekerasan; **pacify** *vt* mendamaikan, menenteramkan, menenangkan

pack *n* bungkusan, pak; ~ *horse* kuda beban; *ice* ~ komprés dingin; *vt* membungkus, mengepak, menyusun; ~ *up* berkemas-kemas; ~ *one's suitcase* mengepak koper; **package** *n* [pakej] bungkus; bingkisan, pakét; ~ *deal*, ~ *holiday*, ~ *tour* pakét; **packaging** *n* pengemasan; **packed** *adj* penuh

(sesak); ~ *lunch* bekal; **packer** *n* pembungkus; **packet** *n* pakét, pak, bungkus; **packing** *n* pengepakan, pengemasan

pact *n* pakta, perjanjian

pad *n* bantalan; *sanitary* ~ pembalut (wanita); *writing* ~ bloknot; *vi* ~ *out* mengisi

paddle *n* [padel] kayuh; *v* mengayuh; ~ *steamer* kapal kincir

paddock *n* [padek] ladang rumput

paddy *n* ~ *(field)* sawah

padlock *n* gembok; *vt* mengunci, menggembok

paediatrician → **pediatrician**

paedophile → **pedophile**

pagan *adj* [pégan] *n* penyembah berhala

page *n* halaman, lembar; ~ *four* halaman empat; *how many* ~*s?* berapa lembar?; *vt* memanggil; **pager** *n* radio panggil

pageant *n* [pajent] lomba; arak-arakan; *beauty* ~ lomba kecantikan

pager *n* radio panggil ← **page**

pagoda *n* kuil

paid *v, pf* → **pay**

pail *n* émbér

pain *n* rasa sakit, rasa nyeri; *in* ~ kesakitan; ~ *in the neck* orang yang menyebalkan; **painful** *adj* sakit, pedih; **painkiller** *n* obat anti nyeri; **painless** *adj* tanpa rasa sakit; **painstaking** *adj* teliti, cermat

paint *n* cat; *oil* ~ cat minyak; *wet* ~ cat basah; *vi* melukis; *vt* mengecat; **paintbox** *n* kotak cat air; **paintbrush** *n* sikat; **painter** *n* tukang cat; pelukis; **painting** *n* lukisan; seni lukis; *Dot likes* ~ *in her spare time* Dot suka melukis pada waktu senggang; **paintwork** *n* pengecatan

pair *n* pasang, rangkap; pasangan; ~ *of glasses* kacamata; *a* ~ *of shoes* (sepasang) sepatu; ~ *of trousers* celana; *vi* ~ *off* berpasang-pasangan

pajamas ← **pyjamas**

Pakistan *n* Pakistan; **Pakistani** *adj* berasal dari Pakistan; *n* orang Pakistan

pal *n, sl* kawan, sobat

palace *n* [pales] istana, puri
palatable *adj* dapat dimakan, énak; **palate** *n* [palet] langit-langit
pale *adj* pucat, lemah; ~ *green* hijau muda; *to turn* ~ menjadi pucat
Palestine *n* [Palestain] Palestina; **Palestinian** *adj* [Palestinian] berasal dari Palestina; *n* orang Palestina; ~ *Liberation Front (PLO)* Front Pembébasan Palestina
paling *n* [péling] tiang (pagar)
pall-bearer *n* pengusung jenazah
palm *n* [pam] telapak tangan; ~*reading* membaca garis tangan
palm *n* [pam] palem; ~ *oil* minyak kelapa sawit; ~ *sugar* gula arén; *coconut* ~ pohon kelapa, nyiur
palsy *n* [polzi] kelumpuhan; *cerebral* ~ kelumpuhan akibat penyakit otak
pamper *vt* memanjakan; **pampered** *adj* manja, kolokan
pamphlet *n* brosur, selebaran, pamflet
pan *n* panci, wajan, kuali; **pancake** *n* panekuk
Panama *n* Panama; **Panamanian** *adj* [panaménian] berasal dari Panama; *n* orang Panama
panda *n* panda
pane *n* daun kaca (jendéla)
panel *n* panél; sehelai papan; ~ *beating* ketok; **panelist** *n* anggota panél
panic *n* panik, ketakutan; *vi* panik; *don't* ~ jangan panik
panorama *n* pemandangan
pansy *n* sejenis bunga
pant *vi* terengah-engah
panther *n* macan kumbang
pantomime *n* pertunjukan sandiwara
pantry *n* [pantri] gudang (dapur), lemari untuk menyimpan makanan kering
pants *n, pl* celana; *hot* ~ celana ketat; **pantsuit** *n* wérkpak, baju kerja
panty ~ *hose* stoking; ~ *liner* pembalut (tipis); **panties** *n, pl* celana dalam wanita
papa *pron* pak, ayah
papal *adj* [pépal] berkaitan dengan Sri Paus
papaya *n* pepaya, pawpaw
paper *n* kertas; koran, surat kabar;

makalah; *pl* surat-surat, dokumén; ~ *clip* jepitan kertas; ~ *money* uang kertas; ~ *round* pekerjaan mengantar koran; ~ *weight* penindih kertas; **paperback** *n* buku bersampul tipis; **paperboy** *n* tukang koran, loper koran; **paperwork** *n* [péperwerk] pekerjaan tulis-menulis
paprika *n* semacam rempah dari paprika
Papua *n* Irian (Jaya); ~ *New Guinea (PNG)* Papua Nugini; ~ *New Guinean* berasal dari Papua Nugini; orang Papua Nugini; *Free ~ Organisation* Organisasi Papua Merdéka (OPM); **Papuan** *n* orang Papua
par *n* derajat, tingkat; *below* ~ lebih rendah, kurang baik; *on a ~ with* sederajat, sama dengan; *this tournament is on a ~ with Wimbledon* pertandingan ini sederajat kejuaraan Wimbledon
parachute *n* payung, parasut; *vi* terjun payung; **parachuting** *n* terjun payung; **parachutist** *n* penerjun payung
parade *n* [paréid] pawai, arak-arakan; jalan; *vi* berpawai, berbaris; *vt* memamérkan
paradise *n* surga; ~ *on earth* surga duniawi
paraffin *n* parafin, malam
paragraph *n* paragraf, alinéa; *read the third ~ carefully* baca alinéa ketiga dengan teliti
Paraguay *n* Paraguay; **Paraguayan** *adj* berasal dari Paraguay; *n* orang Paraguay
parakeet *n* parkit, burung bayan
parallel *adj* sejajar, paralél; *n* garis lintang; *without* ~ tanpa tanding, tanpa tara; *the 23rd* ~ garis lintang 23 derajat
paralysis *n* [paralisis] layuh, kelumpuhan; **paralyze** *vt* [paralaiz] melumpuhkan; **paralyzed** *adj* lumpuh
paramedic *n* tenaga médis, tenaga bantu dokter
paramilitary *adj* ~ *force* laskar, milisi
paramount *adj* [paramaunt] terpenting, paling penting; *education is ~ to improving living standards* bidang pen-

didikan yang paling penting dalam
usaha meningkatkan tarif kehidupan

paranoia *n* rasa takut karena dibenci,
kecurigaan yang luar biasa; **paranoid**
adj takut sekali, curiga luar biasa
(sakit jiwa)

paranormal *adj, n* [paranormel] dukun,
paranormal

paraphrase *vt* [parafréiz] menguraikan
dengan kata-kata sendiri, memfrasa-
kan

paraplegic *n* [paraplijik] orang yang
separuh badannya lumpuh, orang
cacat

parasite *n* [parasait] parasit, benalu

parasol *n* payung (hias)

paratrooper *n* pasukan payung

parcel *n* bingkisan, pakét; parsél;
Monica sent a ~ from Norway Monica
mengirim pakét dari Norwégia

pardon *n* ampun, maaf; grasi; *vt*
mengampuni, memaafkan; *~ me*
maaf

parent *n* [pérent] orang tua; *pl* ibu bapak,
ayah bunda; *~-teacher evening* pertemuan orang tua dari murid (dengan
guru); *~ company* perusahaan induk;
single ~, sole ~ orang tua tunggal; *~
teacher association* persatuan orang tua
murid; **parental** *adj* orang tua; **parent-
hood** *n* [pérent hud] masa orang tua,
pengalaman menjadi orang tua

parentheses *n, pl* [parénthesiz] *in ~*
dalam kurung

Paris *n* [paris] Paris; **Parisian** *adj* berasal
dari kota Paris; *n* warga Paris

parish *n* paroki

Parisian *adj* [parizian] berasal dari kota
Paris; *n* warga Paris ← **Paris**

park *n* taman; *~ bench* bangku; *amusement ~, theme ~* taman hiburan; *car ~*
tempat parkir; *safari ~* taman safari;
~s and gardens service dinas pertamanan; *vi* parkir; *vt* memarkirkan
mobil; **parking** *n ~ lot* tempat parkir;
~ attendant tukang parkir; *~ meter*
méter parkir; *~ ticket* tilang, bukti
pelanggaran; *no ~* dilarang parkir;
valet ~ layanan mobil diparkirkan;
parkway *n* jalan raya dengan jalur

hijau di tengah

parka *n* jas hujan

parliament *n* [parlemén] Déwan Perwakilan Rakyat (DPR), parlemén;
parliamentary *adj* berhubungan dengan déwan perwakilan rakyat; *~ sitting* sidang DPR

parlor, parlour *n, arch* kamar tamu,
kamar duduk

parody *n* parodi, plésétan; *vt* memaro-
dikan, memelésétkan

parrot *n* burung nuri, burung béo; *to
repeat ~-fashion* membéo; *vt* membéo

parsley *n* [parsli] péterséli

parsnip *n* semacam wortel

parson *n* pendéta

part *n* bagian, potong; peranan; belahan;
~-time paruh waktu, kerja sambilan; *in
~* sebagian; *side ~* belahan samping; *~
of speech* bagian bahasa; *a bit ~* peranan kecil; *on my ~* dari pihak saya; *to
play a ~* memainkan peranan, berperan; *to take ~ (in)* ikut serta, mengambil bagian; *vi* membelah; berpisah;
bercerai; *~ with* melepaskan; *vt* membagi, memisahkan; **partial** *adj* sebagian; memihak; *~ to* suka, menggemari; *Stewart was very ~ to cake*
Stewart sangat suka makan kué; **par-
tially** *adv* separuh; **parting** *n* perpisahan; belahan (rambut); **partition** *n*
sekat, dinding pemisah; pembagian;
partly *adv* sebagian

participant *n* peserta; **participate** *vi*
ikut serta, mengambil bagian; *~ in* ikut
serta dalam; **participation** *n* keikutsertaan, partisipasi

particle *n* butir; unsur; partikel; kata
sandang; **particular** *adj* istiméwa, spésial, khusus; *in ~* khususnya, terutama;
very ~ berpilih-pilih; *n, pl* keterangan,
data; *the policewoman took down my
~s* data pribadi saya dicatat oléh polwan; **particularly** *adv* terutama,
khususnya

parting *n* perpisahan; belahan (rambut)
← **part**

partition *n* sekat, dinding pemisah;
pembagian ← **part**

partly *adv* sebagian ← **part**

partner *n* pasangan, mitra; **partnership** *n* persekutuan
partridge *n* sejenis burung puyuh
party *n* pésta, perayaan; partai, kelompok, pihak; rombongan; ~ *animal* orang yang suka berpésta; ~ *line* sambungan télépon bersama; *third* ~ pihak ketiga; *to follow the* ~ *line* mengikuti garis partai; *vi* berpésta, berfoya-foya
pashmina *n* [pasymina] syal wol tipis
pass *n* surat izin masuk, pas jalan; jalan kecil; *boarding* ~ pas naik pesawat; *press* ~ kartu pérs; *v* lulus ujian; léwat, berlalu; *vt* melalui, meléwati; mengesahkan; ~*er-by* orang léwat, orang di jalan; ~ *away* meninggal dunia, berpulang; ~ *for* dipandang sebagai, mirip; ~ *on* meninggal dunia; meneruskan; ~ *out* pingsan; ~ *sentence* menjatuhkan hukuman; ~ *sentence on* menghakimi; ~ *time* iseng, mengisi waktu; ~ *up* meléwatkan; ~ *urine*, ~ *water* buang air kecil; *don't* ~ *up this amazing opportunity* jangan léwatkan kesempatan emas ini; ~ *wind* kentut; *to come to* ~ terjadi; **passable** *adj* dapat dilalui, dapat diléwati; dapat diterima, boléh juga; **passage** *n* [pasej] jalan lintas, jalan tembus, lorong, terusan; bagian dari tulisan; pelayaran; **passenger** *n* [pasenjer] penumpang; **passing** *in* ~ sepintas lalu
passion *n* [pasyen] hawa nafsu, gairah; *a* ~ *for* kegilaan akan; **passionate** *adj* [pasyenet] bernafsu, bergairah, bersemangat; **passionately** *adv* sungguh-sungguh
passionfruit *n* [pasyenfrut] buah markisa
passive *adj* [pasiv] pasif, terdiam; ~ *form* bentuk pasif; ~ *smoker* orang yang terpengaruh oléh asap rokok orang lain
Passover *n* perayaan Yahudi
passport *n* paspor; ~ *photo* pasfoto
password *n* [paswérd] kata sandi
past *adj* lalu, léwat, lampau, silam; ~ *tense* bentuk lampau; *n* masa lalu; *in the* ~ dahulu (kala); *adv* léwat; *five* ~ *eight* jam delapan léwat lima menit;

prep léwat; *I walked* ~ *his house* saya léwat di depan rumahnya
paste *n* [pést] adonan, pasta; lém, perekat; *tomato* ~ pasta tomat; *tooth*~ pasta gigi, *coll* odol; *vt* témpél, menémpélkan
pastel *n* warna pastél; kapur berwarna
pastille *n* [pastil] permén
pastime *n* pengisi waktu
pastor *n* pastor, pendéta
pastry *n* [péstri] kué
pasture *n* padang rumput
pat *n* tepukan; *vt* menepuk, mengelus; ~ *a cat* mengelus kucing
patch *n* tambal, témpélan; *vt* menambal; **patched** *adj* bertambal; **patchwork** *n* penjahitan kain perca; campur aduk; **patchy** *adj* tidak konsistén
paté *n* [paté] semacam selai terbuat dari daging atau ikan
patent *n* [pétent] patén; *vt* mematénkan
paternal *adj* [patérnal] kebapakan; dari pihak bapak; ~ *grandmother* nénék dari pihak bapak; **paternity** *n* hal menjadi ayah; ~ *leave* cuti untuk ayah baru
path *n* jalan (tapak), lorong
pathetic *adj* [pathétik] menyedihkan, memelas; *a* ~ *excuse* alasan lemah
patience *n* [pésyens] kesabaran; solitér; *to lose* ~ kehilangan kesabaran; **patient** *adj* sabar; *n* pasién; **patiently** *adv* dengan sabar
patio *n* téras
patriarchal *adj* [pétriarkal] bersifat patriarki (ayah sebagai kepala keluarga); **patriarchy** *n* patriarki
patriot *n* [pétriot] patriot, pecinta tanah air; **patriotic** *adj* cinta tanah air; **patriotism** *n* patriotisme, kecintaan kepada tanah air
patrol *n* patroli, ronda; ~ *car* mobil polisi; *vi* berpatroli, meronda; ~ *the streets* berpatroli di jalan
patron *n* [pétron] pengasuh, pelindung; ~ *saint Cath* orang suci yang dijadikan pelindung; ~ *of the arts* pengasuh; **patronize** *vt* berlangganan; memperlakukan sebagai sesuatu yang rendah; *the mayor's wife only* ~*s expensive boutiques* ibu walikota hanya berbe-

lanja di butik-butik mahal
pattern *n* pola, corak; patron, contoh;
batik ~ corak batik; *dress* ~ patron
rok
patty *n* perkedél; *beef* ~ perkedél daging;
~ *cake* kué mangkuk
pauper *n* [pouper] orang miskin, orang
papa
pause *n* [pouz] jeda, waktu istirahat; *vi*
berhenti sebentar; *vt* menghentikan
sementara
pave *vi* mengaspal, memberi lapisan
beton atau konblok; ~ *the way* merintis jalan; **pavement** *n* trotoar
pavilion *n* [pavilion] anjungan; ténda
besar; bangunan dekat taman atau
lapangan
paw *n* kaki binatang; *cat's* ~ diperalat
pawn *n* gadai; pion; *vt* menggadaikan;
he ~ed his wife's diamond ring dia
menggadaikan cincin berlian milik
isterinya; **pawnbroker** *n* penggadai;
pegadaian; **pawnshop** *n* rumah gadai,
pegadaian
pay *n* pembayaran; gaji, upah; *vt* **paid**
paid membayar; ~ *attention* memperhatikan; ~ *back* mengganti, membayar
kembali; membalas dendam; ~ *for*
membayar; membayarkan; *Grandma*
will ~ *for my trip* Nénék akan membayarkan ongkos perjalananku; ~ *off*
berhasil; *his hard work paid off in the*
exams oléh karena belajar dengan
rajin, hasil ujiannya bagus; melunasi;
Mum was able to ~ *off the mortgage*
for the house quickly Ibu berhasil
cepat melunasi cicilan rumah; ~ *rise*
kenaikan gaji; ~ *TV* TV kabel; ~ *a*
visit berkunjung; mengunjungi; ~ *your*
respects melayat; **payable** *adj* dapat
dibayarkan, untuk dibayarkan; **payday**
n (hari) gajian; **payee** *n* [péyi] orang
yang dibayar; **payment** *n* pembayaran;
payoff *n* imbalan; **payphone** *n* [péi-
fon] telepon umum; **payslip** *n* slip
gaji
PC *abbrev personal computer* komputer
PC *abbrev police constable* polisi
PC *abbrev politically correct* tidak
mengandung unsur SARA

PDA *abbrev Personal Digital Assistant*
PDA, Pembantu Digital Pribadi
Pde *Parade* Jl (Jalan)
PE *abbrev Physical Education* (mata
pelajaran) Olahraga; ~ *teacher* guru
olahraga
pea *n* kacang polong; *like two* ~*s in a*
pod seperti pinang dibelah dua
peace *n* perdamaian; ~ *Corps* organisasi
AS yang mengirim sukarélawan ke
luar negeri; ~ *talks* perundingan perdamaian; ~ *of mind* ketentraman hati;
rest in ~ *(RIP)* beristirahat dengan tenang; **peaceful** *adj* damai, tenteram,
tenang; **peacefully** *adv* secara damai,
dengan tenang; **peacekeepers** *n, pl*
pasukan pendamai; **peacetime** *n* masa
tidak berperang, masa perdamaian
peach *adj* warna kuning kemérahan,
warna persik; *n* buah persik
peacock *n, m* **peahen** *n, f* burung merak
peak *n, adj* puncak; ~ *hour* jam-jam
sibuk (di jalan); ~ *season* musim
ramai; *vi* memuncak; *inflation has* ~*ed*
at 11% inflasi memuncak pada 11%
peanut *n* kacang tanah; ~ *butter* selai
kacang, pindakas; ~ *sauce* bumbu
kacang
pear *n* [pér] buah pir
pearl *n* mutiara; *black* ~ mutiara hitam;
~ *of wisdom* kata mutiara
peasant *n* [pézent] petani; **peasantry** *n*
kaum tani
peat *n* tanah gemuk (dipakai sebagai
bahan bakar)
pebble *n* [pébel] batu kerikil; ~ *beach*
pantai batu
pecan *n* semacam kemiri
peck *v* mematuk; *the chickens* ~*ed at*
the ground ayam-ayam mematuk tanah
peculiar *adj* [pekyulier] anéh, ganjil; ~
to khas; **peculiarity** *n* keganjilan,
keanéhan
pedal *n* [pédel] injakan kaki, pedal; *v*
mengayuh (sepéda)
peddle *vt* [pédel] menjajakan, mengédarkan; ~ *drugs* mengédarkan narkoba;
peddler *n* penjaja, pengédar; **pedlar** *n*
penjaja, pedagang
pedestrian *n* [pedéstrien] pejalan kaki;

~ *crossing* penyeberangan jalan;
zébrakros; ~ *mall* daérah khusus pejalan kaki; ~ *overpass* jembatan penyeberangan

pediatrician, paediatrician *n* [pidia-
trisyen] dokter anak-anak

pedicab *n* [pedikab] bécak; ~ *driver*
tukang bécak

pedicure *n* pedikur, perawatan kaki

pedigree *n* [pédigri] trah; silsilah

pedlar *n* penjaja, pedagang ← **peddle**

pedophile, paedophile *n* pédofil

pee *vi, sl* kencing, pipis; *n* air seni, air
kencing; *to have a* ~ kencing

peek *vi* mengintip, menéngok sejenak;
peekaboo cilukba

peel *n* kulit (buah); *vt* mengelupas; *his
sunburn is ~ing* kulit yang hitam kena
matahari sudah terkelupas; *vt* menguliti, mengupas; **peeler** *n* alat pengupas;
peelings *n, pl* kulit buah yang sudah
dikelupas

peep *vi* mengintip, mengintai; menéngok; *~ing Tom* orang yang mengintip;
n not a ~ diam, tidak bersuara; **peep-
hole** *n* lubang pengintai

peer *n* kawan sebaya (sesama rekan
kerja, pelajar dsb); bangsawan, orang
bergelar; ~ *pressure* tekanan dari
teman-teman sekolah

peer *vi* melihat dengan susah

peg *n* pasak; sangkutan; patokan; *vt*
mematok, memasak; ~ *doll* bonéka pasak;
~ *leg* kaki kayu, kaki palsu; *clothes* ~
jepitan (baju); *tent* ~ pasak ténda

Pekinese *n* [pikiniz] anjing Péking

pellet *n* pil, pélét

pelican *n* [pélikan] burung pélikan,
burung undan

pelt *vt* melémparkan, menghujani; *the
children ~ed stones at the train* anak-
anak melémparkan batu ke arah keréta
api; ~ *down* hujan deras; *n* kulit bulu

pelvic *adj* daérah panggul; **pelvis** *n*
panggul, tulang pinggul

pen *n* péna, kalam; bolpoin, pulpén; ~
name nama samaran; **penfriend** *n*
sahabat péna; **penknife** *n* [pén naif]
pisau lipat; **penpal** *n* sahabat péna

pen *n* kandang; *pig* ~ kandang babi

penal *adj* [pinal] berkaitan dengan
hukuman atau hukum pidana; ~ *code*
kitab undang-undang hukum pidana; ~
colony koloni kaum buangan; **penal-
ize** *vt* [pinalaiz] menghukum; **penalty**
n [pénalti] denda, hukuman, pénalti; ~
shootout adu pénalti

pencil *n* pénsil; ~ *case* tempat pénsil; ~
sharpener rautan pénsil; *color* ~ pénsil
warna

pendant *n* liontin

pending *adj* belum diputuskan, pénding;
prep menunggu

pendulum *n* bandul

penetrate *vt* tembus, menerobos,
menembus; **penetrating** *adj* tajam,
menusuk; **penetration** *n* penerobosan,
penembusan, pénétrasi

penfriend *n* sahabat péna ← **pen**

penguin *n* pinguin

penicillin *n* pénisilin

peninsula *n* [peninsula] semenanjung;
the Malay ~ Semenanjung Melayu

penis *n* [pinis] pénis, zakar; ~ *sheath*
kotéka

penitentiary *n, US* [péniténsyeri] penjara, lembaga pemasyarakatan (LP)

penknife *n* [pén naif] pisau lipat ← **pen**

pennant *n* panji, umbul-umbul

penniless *adj* tak memiliki sepésér pun,
papa; **penny** *n* **pence** *pl* sén Inggris

penpal *n* sahabat pena ← **pen**

pension *n* [pénsyen] pénsiun; *vt* ~ *off*
memensiunkan; **pensioner** *n* orang
pénsiunan

Pentagon *n, US* Departemén Pertahanan
AS

pentagon *n* segi lima

pentathlete *n* atlét pancalomba; **pentathlon** *n* pancalomba

penthouse *n* [pént haus] apartemén
(méwah)

pent-up *adj* tertahan, terpendam; *she
releases all her* ~ *feelings through
sport* dia melampiaskan semua émosi
terpendam melalui olahraga

people *n, pl* [pipel] orang, bangsa,
rakyat, kaum; ~ *say* kata orang; *the
~'s Republic of China (PRC)* Républik
Rakyat Cina (RRC)

pep *n* semangat; ~ *talk* percakapan guna memberi semangat

pepper *n* merica, lada; paprika; *red* ~ paprika mérah; *salt and* ~ garam merica; beruban (rambut); **peppermint** *adj* méntol; *n* permén

per *prep* setiap, tiap, per; ~ *annum* tahunan, per tahun; ~ *capita* per orang; ~ *cent, percent* persén; *two dollars* ~ *person* satu orang dua dolar

perceive *vi* [persiv] menafsirkan; **perceptive** *adj* [perséptiv] cepat mengerti, suka memerhatikan; **perception** *n* persépsi, tanggapan

percent *adj* persén; *one hundred* ~ *fruit juice* seratus persén sari buah; **percentage** *n* perséntase

perception *n* persépsi, tanggapan ← **perceive**

perch *n* tempat berténgger di sangkar burung; sejenis ikan; *vi* berténgger

percolate *vt* menyaring, menapis; **percolator** *n* penyaring kopi

percussion *n* pérkusi

perennial *adj, n* [perénial] tahunan, selalu, kekal

perfect *adj* [pérfekt] sempurna; *vt* [perfékt] menyempurnakan; **perfection** *n* kesempurnaan; **perfectionist** *n* orang yang mementingkan kesempurnaan; **perfectly** *adv* dengan sempurna

perforate *vt* melubangi; **perforation** *n* lubang

perform *vi* beraksi; *vt* melakukan, menyelenggarakan, memainkan (peran); ~ *the pilgrimage to Mecca* menunaikan ibadah haji; **performance** *n* pertunjukan; **performer** *n* pemain, pemeran; **performing** ~ *arts* seni peran, musik dan tari (séndratari)

perfume *n* wewangian, minyak wangi, parfum; wangi; **perfumed** *adj* wangi

perhaps *adv* mungkin, barangkali

peril *n* [péril] bahaya; *in* ~ dalam bahaya; **perilous** *adj* [périlus] berbahaya

perimeter *n* [perimeter] batas pinggir; garis keliling

period *n* [piried] zaman, masa, kala, waktu; titik; *coll* datang bulan, haid; ~ *pain* nyeri haid; *Jurassic* ~ période

Jura; **periodic** *adj* berkala, périodik; **periodical** *n* terbitan berkala, majalah

peripheral *adj* [periferal] **periphery** *n* tepi, pinggir

periscope *n* périskop

perish *vi* hilang, téwas; molor (karét); **perishable** *n* [périsyabel] makanan yang dapat menjadi busuk

perjury *n* [pérjeri] sumpah palsu; *the official was charged with* ~ pegawai itu dituduh telah membuat sumpah palsu

perk *n, sl* untung, sisi baik; *vi* ~ *up* berdiri, menjadi bersemangat; *the dog's ears* ~*ed up at the sound of his master's footsteps* telinga anjing berdiri begitu terdengar derap kaki tuannya

perm *n, coll* keriting rambut; **permanent** *adj* tetap, permanén; ~ *residence (PR)* izin tinggal tetap; ~ *resident* penghuni tetap; ~ *wave (perm)* keriting rambut; **permanently** *adv* secara tetap, untuk selamanya; **permed** *adj* [pérmd] dikeriting

permeate *v* [pérmiét] meresap

permed *adj* [pérmd] dikeriting ← **perm**

permissible *adj* [pérmisibel] boléh, diizinkan; **permission** *n* [pérmisyen] izin; *to ask for* ~ minta izin; **permissive** *adj* [pérmisiv] serba boléh; **permit** *n* surat izin; *vt* mengizinkan, memperboléh

perpendicular *adj, n* [pérpendikuler] tegak lurus

perpetual *adj* [pérpétyual] terus-menerus, abadi; ~ *fund* dana abadi

perplex *vt* membingungkan; **perplexed** *adj* bingung

persecute *vt* [pérsekyut] menyiksa, mengejar-ngejar, membédakan; **persecution** *n* penyiksaan, penganiayaan; *religious* ~ *cannot be tolerated* penganiayaan karena agama tidak bisa diterima

perseverance *n* [persevirens] ketekunan, kegigihan; **persevere** *vi* [pérsevir] bertekun, gigih

Persia *n, arch* Pérsia, Iran; **Persian** *adj* berasal dari Pérsia; *n, arch* orang Pérsia; ~ *cat* kucing angora

persimmon *n* buah kesemak
persist *vi* tetap (melakukan), bertekun, bertahan; **persistence** *n* ketekunan; **persistent** *adj* gigih, tekun; **persistently** *adv* secara terus-menerus
person *n* people [pipel] orang, pribadi; *in* ~ sendiri; **personal** *adj* pribadi; perorangan; ~ *assistant* asistén pribadi (aspri); ~ *column* kontak jodoh; ~ *computer (PC)* komputer, PC; **personality** *n* [pérsonaliti] kepribadian; tokoh, sélébriti; ~ *cult* kultus individu; **personalize** *vt* menyesuaikan untuk orang tertentu; **personally** *adv* secara perorangan; secara pribadi; ~, *I dislike it* secara pribadi, saya tidak suka; **personnel** *n* [pérsonél] personalia, para karyawan; ~ *department* bagian personalia
perspective *n* [pérspéktiv] sudut, perspéktif
perspiration *n* [pérspirésyen] keringat, peluh; **perspire** *vt* [pérspair] berkeringat
persuade *vt* [pérsuéd] meyakinkan; *Patrick ~d him that he should study medicine* Patrick meyakinkan dia bahwa sebaiknya dia mengambil ilmu kedokteran; **persuasion** *n* [pérsuésyen] keyakinan, persuasi; **persuasive** *adj* [pérsuésiv] meyakinkan
Peru *n* Péru; **Peruvian** *adj* [peruvian] berasal dari Péru; *n* orang Péru
perverse *adj* menyimpang; **pervert** *n* orang yang mengidap kelainan séksual; orang yang suka mengintip
pessimism *n* [pésimizem] sikap tidak banyak berharap, sikap pésimis; **pessimist** *n* orang pésimis; **pessimistic** *adj* pésimis, bersangka buruk
pest *n* hama; gangguan; *Adrian's little sister is a* ~ adiknya Adrian banyak mengganggu; **pester** *vt* mengganggu, mengusik; *she ~s her mother for sweets* dia berulang kali minta permén kepada ibunya
pesticide *n* [péstisaid] péstisida, obat pembasmi serangga
pestle *n* [pésel] alu; *mortar and* ~ alu lumpang

pet *adj* kesayangan; *n* héwan peliharaan; ~ *hate* hal yang paling tidak disukai; ~ *shop* toko héwan; *teacher's* ~ murid kesayangan; *v* mengelus; bercumbu; **petting** *n* cumbuan; *heavy* ~ bercinta, indehoi
petal *n* [pétel] daun bunga
petite *adj* [petit] (berukuran) kecil, mungil
petition *n* [petisyen] permohonan, petisi; *vt* memohon; *the activists ~ed the government to release their leader* para aktivis memohon agar pemerintah membébaskan pemimpinnya
petrified *adj* [pétrifaid] membatu, sangat ketakutan
petrochemical *n, adj* [pétrokémikel] pétrokimia; **petrol** *n* bénsin; *~-head sl* penggemar balap mobil; *~-sniffing sl* ngelém; ~ *station* pompa bénsin, SPBU; *unleaded* ~ bénsin tanpa timbal (TT); **petroleum** *n* [petrolium] minyak bumi olahan
petticoat *n* rok dalam
petting *n* cumbuan; *heavy* ~ bercinta, indehoi ← **pet**
petty *adj* kecil, réméh, sepélé; ~ *cash* uang kecil, uang récéh
petunia *n* semacam bunga
pew *n* bangku geréja
pewter *n* [pyuter] campuran timah
phantom *n* [fantom] hantu, momok
pharaoh *n* [féro] firaun
pharmacist *n* [farmasist] apotéker; **pharmaceutical** *n* [farmasutikel] farmasi, kefarmasian; **pharmacy** *n* apoték, apotik
phase *n* [féiz] tahap, masa, fase; *vi* ~ *out* menghapus secara bertahap
Ph.D. *abbrev Doctor of Philosophy* S3 (Strata Tiga)
pheasant *n* [fézant] burung kuau, burung pegar
phenomenal *adj* luar biasa, istiméwa, menakjubkan; **phenomenon** *n* **phenomena** *pl* fenoména
phew *excl* [fyu] aduh
philanthropist *n* [filantropist] dermawan; **philanthropy** *n* cinta kepada sesama manusia

philatelist *n* filatelis, pengumpul perangko; **philately** *n* filateli, koléksi perangko

Philippines [filipins] *the* ~ Filipina

philosopher *n* [filosofer] filsuf, ahli filsafat; **philosophical** *adj* berfilsafat, filosofis; **philosophy** *n* (ilmu) filsafat

phlegm *n* [flém] dahak

phobia *n* penyakit ketakutan, fobi; *Johnny has a ~ about spiders* Johnny sangat takut pada laba-laba

phone *n, coll* télepon; ~ *book* daftar nomor télepon; ~ *box* télepon umum; ~ *bill* tagihan télepon; ~ *call* panggilan, percakapan; ~ *card* kartu télepon; ~ *number* nomor télepon; ~ *tap* sadapan télepon; *on the* ~ sedang télepon, bertélepon; *vi* ~ *in* memberitahu lewat télepon; *vt* menélepon ← **telephone**

phonetic *adj* fonétik, sesuai dengan abjad

phoney, phony *adj* [foni] palsu

phosphorus *n* fosfor

photo *n, sl* foto; ~ *album* album foto; **photocopy** *n* fotokopi; ~ *machine* mesin fotokopi; *vt* memfotokopi; **photograph** *n* foto, potrét, gambar; *vt* memotrét; **photographer** *n* tukang foto, tukang potrét, fotografer; **photography** *n* potrét-memotrét, fotografi

photosynthesis *n* fotosintésa

phrase *n* [fréz] frase, kelompok kata; **phrasebook** *n* buku ungkapan bahasa asing

physical *adj* (secara) fisik; jasmani; ~ *education (PE)* (pelajaran) olahraga; ~ *sciences* ilmu-ilmu éksakta

physician *n* [fizisyen] dokter

physicist *n* [fizisist] fisikawan; **physics** *n* ilmu fisika

physiotherapist *n* ahli fisiotérapi; **physiotherapy** *n* fisiotérapi

pianist *n* [pienist] pemain piano; **piano** *n* piano; ~ *key* tuts piano

piccolo *n* [pikelo] pikolo, semacam suling kecil

pick *n* pilihan; *first* ~ pilihan pertama; *v* memilih; ~ *on* mengganggu, mengusik; ~ *up* mengambil; menjemput; *vt* mencungkil; memetik; ~ *flowers* memetik bunga; ~ *your nose* mengupil; **pickpocket** *n* copét, pencopét; **pickup** *n* pikap; **picky** *adj* memilih-milih

pick *n* beliung

picket *n* tiang pancang; ~ *fence* pagar kayu; ~ *line* barisan depan pemogok

pickle *n* [pikel] acar; *vt* mengasinkan; *in a* ~ dalam kesulitan

pickpocket *n* copét, pencopét ← **pick**

pickup *n* pikap ← **pick**

picky *adj* memilih-milih ← **pick**

picnic *n* piknik; ~ *ground* tempat piknik; *vi* berpiknik; *they ~ked by the river* meréka berpiknik di tepi sungai; **picnicker** *n* orang yang berpiknik

pictorial *adj* bergambar; **picture** *vt* membayangkan; melukiskan; *n* gambar, lukisan; *in the* ~ sudah tahu; *pl, coll the* ~ bioskop; **picturesque** *adj* [piktyurésk] asri

piddle *n, coll* [pidel] air kencing; *vi* kencing

pidgin *n* bahasa pasaran

pie *n* pai; sejenis kué; ~ *chart* grafik lingkaran; *as easy as* ~ gampang, mudah

piece *n* [pis] potong, keping, bagian; ~ *together* menyusun; *a ~ of cake* sepotong kué; *coll* tugas yang mudah; *a ~ of music* sebuah lagu; *vt* ~ *together* menyusun

pier *n* [pir] jéti, dermaga, pelabuhan

pierce *v* [pirs] menembus, menindik, menusuk; **pierced** *adj* ~ *ears* telinga yang ditindik

pig *n* babi; orang yang bengis atau jorok; ~*-headed* keras kepala; ~*s might fly* mustahil; **piggyback** *adv* di punggung, naik kuda-kudaan; **piggybank** *n* [pigibank] céléngan; **piglet** *n* anak babi; **pigsty** *n* [pigstai] kandang babi; *sl* kamar yang berantakan; **pigtail** *n* képang dua

pigeon *n* [pijen] burung merpati, burung dara; **pigeonhole** *n* kotak pribadi

piggyback *adv* [pigibak] digéndong

piggybank *n* [pigibank] céléngan ← **pig**

piglet *n* anak babi ← **pig**

pigment *n* pigmen, zat warna

pigsty *n* [pigstai] kandang babi; *sl* kamar yang berantakan ← **pig**

pigtail *n* képang dua ← **pig**

pilchard *n* sejenis ikan kecil

pile *n* timbunan; *vi* bertumpuk; *vt* menimbun; *~-up* tabrakan beruntun

piles *n, pl* ambéien, wasir

pilgrim *n* peziarah; *Isl* haji; **pilgrimage** *n* [pilgrimej] ziarah, peziarah; *Isl the lesser ~* umroh; *to make a ~* berziarah; *Isl to go on the ~ to Mecca* naik haji

pill *n* pil, obat; *the (contraceptive) ~* pil KB; **pillbox** *n* tempat obat

pillar *n* [piler] tiang, soko guru; *~ box UK* bis surat

pillion *adv to ride ~* memboncéng (sepéda motor)

pillow *n* [pilo] bantal; *~ case, ~ slip* sarung bantal

pilot *adj* percontohan; *~ project* proyék percontohan; *n* pilot, penerbang, pandu; contoh; *vt* memandu; *the big ship was ~ed into the bay* kapal besar dipandu masuk teluk

pimp *n* mucikari

pimple *n* [pimpel] jerawat; **pimply** *adj* berjerawat, jerawatan

PIN *abbrev Personal Identification Number* PIN

pin *n* peniti; jarum tumpul; *~-stripe* garis-garis halus; *~-up girl* gadis pujaan; *safety ~* peniti cantél; *~s and needles* kesemutan; *vt* menyematkan; **pincushion** *n* bantalan jarum; **pinpoint** *n* menentukan; *adj* tepat, akurat

pinafore *n* [pinafor] sejenis rok anak

pinball *n* pacinko

pincers *n, pl* sepit

pinch *n* cubitan; sedikit; *a ~ of salt* sedikit garam; *to feel the ~* merasa tertekan; *take it with a ~ of salt* jangan percaya; *vi* sempit, terjepit; *vt* mencubit; *coll* mengutil, mencuri; *these shoes ~* sepatu ini terlalu sempit

pine *n ~ (tree)* pohon pinus; **pinecone** *n* buah cemara

pineapple *n* [painapel] nanas

pingpong *n* tenis méja, pingpong

pink *adj* mérah muda, mérah jambu, pink; *in the ~* sedang dalam keadaan séhat

pinky *n, coll* jari kelingking

pinnacle *n* [pinakel] puncak, titik tertinggi

pinpoint *n* menentukan; *adj* tepat, akurat

pint *n* [paint] ukuran cairan sebesar seperdelapan galon (0,568 liter); *~-sized* kecil sekali; *to have a ~* minum bir

pioneer *n* [payonir] perintis, pelopor; *vt* memelopori

pious *adj* [payus] soléh, saléh

pipe *n* pipa; *~ dream* impian belaka; *vt* menyalurkan; *~ up* menyeletuk, ikut berbicara; *~ down!* diam!; **pipeline** *n* saluran pipa; *in the ~* sedang dikembangkan; **piper** *n* pemain alat tiup

piracy *n* [pairasi] pembajakan; **pirate** *n* [pairat] bajak laut, pembajak; *adj* bajakan; **pirated** *adj* bajakan; *~ CD* CD bajakan

piss *n, vulg* air kencing; *coll* minuman keras; *vi* kencing; *~ off!* pergi lu!; **pissed** *adj, coll* mabuk; kesal; *~ off* kesal

pistol *n* pistol

piston *n* silinder penggerak

pit *n* lubang, terowongan dalam tambang; biji (buah); *the ~s* (keadaan) yang terburuk; *the ~ of your stomach* ulu hati; *vt* memperadukan; *this contest ~s brawn against brain* lomba ini memperadukan otak dengan otot; **pitted** *adj* tanpa biji

pitch *n* pola titinada; lémparan (bisbol); usaha; lapangan, landasan (sépak bola); *~-dark, ~ black* gelap gulita; *to make a ~ for* berusaha; *vt ~ in* ikut membantu; *vt* melémparkan; mendirikan; *~ a tent* mendirikan ténda; **pitcher** *n* pelémpar; kendi, tempat air

pitchfork *n* trisula

pith *n* intisari

pitiful *adj* [pitiful] memelas, menyedihkan; **pitiless** *adj* kejam, bengis; **pity** *n* belas kasihan; *vt* mengasihani; *what a ~* sayang (sekali); *to have ~ on, to take ~ on* mengasihani; *I ~ the woman* saya prihatin dengan perempuan itu

pivot *n* [pivet] poros, pasak, sumbu; *vi* berputar; **pivotal** *adj* sangat penting

pixel *n* piksel

pixie *n* [piksi] peri, makhluk halus

PJs *abbrev pyjamas coll* [pijéz] piyama, baju tidur

Pl *abbrev Place* jalan buntu; gedung

placard *n* plakat

place *n* tempat; kedudukan; ~ *card* kartu nama tempat duduk; ~ *mat* tatakan piring; *first* ~ pemenang, juara; *my* ~ rumah (saya); ~ *of worship* rumah ibadah; *in* ~ *of* sebagai pengganti; *to change* ~*s* tukar tempat; *to take* ~ terjadi, berlangsung; *vt* menempatkan, meletakkan; **placement** *n* penempatan

placenta *n* [plasénta] ari-ari, tembuni

plagiarize *vt* [pléjeraiz] menjiplak, menconték; **plagiarism** [pléjerizem] *n* plagiat

plague *n* [plég] penyakit sampar, wabah; *vt* sangat mengganggu; *Dan was ~d by bad luck* Dan dirundungi nasib malang

plain *adj* polos; sederhana, bersahaja; nyata; ~*-spoken* ceplas-ceplos, terus terang; ~ *sailing* lancar; ~ *clothes police* polisi reserse; ~ *to see* jelas sekali; *n* médan, dataran; **plainly** *adv* terus terang

plaintiff *n* penggugat

plaintive *adj* [plaintiv] sedih, sayu; **plaintively** *adv* dengan sedih; *"Can I come too?" she asked* ~ 'Boleh aku ikut?' dia tanya dengan sedih

plait *n* [plat] képang; *in* ~*s*, *in a* ~ diképang; *vt* mengépang

plan *n* rencana, rancangan, bagan, dénah; **planned** *adj* ~ *economy* ékonomi terencana, ékonomi séntral; *five-year* ~ rencana lima tahun (Repelita); *according to* ~ sesuai dengan rencana; *vi* berencana; *vt* merancang, merencanakan; **planner** *n* perencana; *daily* ~ buku agénda; *town* ~ planolog; **planning** *n* perencanaan; *family* ~ keluarga berencana

plane *n*, *sl* pesawat terbang ← **airplane, aeroplane**

planet *n* planét; ~ *Earth* Bumi

plank *n* papan

planner *n* perencana; *daily* ~ buku agénda; *town* ~ planolog; **planning** *n*

perencanaan; *family* ~ keluarga berencana ← **plan**

plant *n* tetumbuhan, tanaman; pabrik; *pot* ~ tanaman di pot; *vt* menanam, menanamkan; **plantation** *n* perkebunan; *tea* ~ kebun téh; **planter** *n* penanam; pemilik (pengusaha) perkebunan

plaque *n* plak (di gigi)

plaque *n* papan, logam piagam

plaster *n* kapur, gips, pléster; ~ *cast* gips; *in* ~ digips; *sticking* ~ pléster; *vt* mengapur; *coll* memasang secara sembarangan

plastic *adj*, *n* plastik; ~ *bag* kerésék, kantong plastik; ~ *surgery* bedah plastik; ~ *wrap* plastic pembungkus makanan

plate *n* piring; pelat; ~ *glass* sehelai kaca jendéla; *dinner* ~ piring makan; *number* ~ pelat polisi; *vt* menyepuh, melapis

plateau *n* [plato] dataran tinggi; *the Dieng* ~ dataran tinggi Diéng

platform *n* péron; panggung; ~ *heels* hak tinggi yang tebal

platinum *n* [platinum] platina, emas putih; ~ *blonde* pirang sekali; *to go* ~ menjual jutaan keping (album musik)

platoon *n* [platun] peleton

platter *n* piring besar

platypus *n* [platipus] sejenis binatang khas Australia

plausible *adj* [plozibel] dapat diterima, masuk akal

play *vi* main, bermain; *vt* memainkan; ~*ing cards* kartu rémi; ~ *along* berpura-pura kerjasama; ~ *around* berfoya-foya; ~ *back* memutar kembali; ~ *down* mengecilkan; ~ *equipment* tempat bermain anak-anak, ayunan; ~ *tag* main kejar-kejaran; ~ *truant* membolos dari sekolah; ~ *up* membesar-besarkan; menjadi nakal; ~ *a part* memainkan peran; ~ *a trick on* mempermainkan; **playboy** *n* lelaki yang suka mempermainkan perempuan; seorang Arjuna; **player** *n* pemain; **playful** *adj* jenaka; **playground** *n* sarana bermain anak-anak; **playgroup** *n* kelompok bermain (KB); **playmate** *n* teman sepermainan;

playpen *n* boks (bayi); **plaything** *n* mainan; **playtime** *n* waktu bermain

play *n* pertunjukan, sandiwara; permainan; **playwright** *n* [plérait] pengarang drama

plaza *n* alun-alun

plea *n* permohonan, permintaan; pembélaan, dalih; **plead** *vi* memohon; *vt* mengaku; ~ *guilty* mengaku bersalah

pleasant *adj* [plézant] menyenangkan, énak, nyaman, nikmat; sopan; **pleasantry** *n* basa-basi; **please** tolong; silahkan; coba; ~ *try* cobalah; ~ *help me* tolong bantu saya; ~ *sit down* silahkan duduk; *vt* menyenangkan; ~ *yourself* terserah; **pleased** *adj* senang, puas; **pleasure** *n* [plézyur] kesukaan, kenikmatan; *for* ~ sebagai hiburan

pledge *n* [pléj] janji, ikrar; ~ *of allegiance* janji setia; *vi* berjanji, berikrar; *vt* menjanjikan; *the businessman* ~*d a sum to the hospital* pengusaha itu menjanjikan akan mengirim uang untuk rumah sakit

plenary *adj* pléno; ~ *session* sidang pléno

plenty *adj* banyak, cukup; ~ *of* cukup banyak; *of* ~ makmur; *n* kemakmuran

pliers *n, pl* [players] tang

plight *n* [plait] keadaan buruk

plot *n* sebidang tanah

plot *n* alur cerita

plot komplotan; *vi* berkomplot, bersekongkol; *vt* merencanakan; **plotter** *n* anggota komplotan

plow, plough *n* [plau] bajak; *vi* membajak

pluck *vt* memetik, mencabut; ~ *flowers* memetik bunga; ~ *up the courage* memberanikan diri

pluck *n* keberanian, nyali; **plucky** *adj* berani

plug *n* sumbat; stéker, stopkontak; *vt* menyumbat

plum *n* buah prem

plumber *n* [plamer] tukang lédeng; **plumbing** *n* lédeng

plump *adj* tambun, subur

plunder *n* hasil rampasan, hasil jarahan; *vt* merampas, menjarah

plunge *n, vi* [planj] terjun, cemplung, menukik; *to take the* ~ terjun, mencemplungkan diri

plural *adj* jamak, pluralis; ~ *society* masyarakat yang hétérogén

plus [plas] *n* nilai plus; *vt* plus, ditambah; *two* ~ *two is four* dua tambah dua sama dengan empat

plywood *n* [plaiwud] kayu olahan

pm *abbrev post meridiem* siang, sore, malam (jam 12.00–24.00)

PM *abbrev Prime Minister* PM (Perdana Menteri)

PMS *abbrev pre-menstrual syndrome* sindrom pra ménstruasi

pneumatic *adj* [nyumatik] berisi udara, berisi angin; ~ *tire* ban pompa

pneumonia *n* [nyumonia] radang paru-paru

PNG *abbrev Papua New Guinea* PNG (Papua Nugini)

PO *abbrev Post Office* kantor pos; ~ *Box 4120* Kotak Pos 4120

poach *v* memburu tanpa izin; **poacher** *n* pemburu liar

poach *vt* mengukus; ~*ed eggs* telur kukus

poacher *n* pemburu liar ← **poach**

pocket *n* saku, kantong, kocék; ~ *money* uang saku, uang jajan; *air* ~ kantong udara; *vt* mengantungi; **pocketknife** *n* [poketnaif] pisau lipat

pod *n* kelopak, polong

podiatrist *n* [podayatrist] ahli penyakit kaki

poem *n* [poem] syair, pantun; **poet** *n* penyair; **poetic** *adj* [poétik] puitis; **poetry** *n* [poetri] puisi

point *n* titik, noktah; tanjung; ~*-blank* langsung, terus terang; *compass* ~ mata angin; *no* ~ tidak ada gunanya; ~ *of view* (sudut) pandangan, pendapat; *beside the* ~ tidak penting; *three* ~ *eight (3.8)* tiga koma delapan (3,8); *to the* ~ tepat, pendek; *that's not the* ~ bukan itu; *vt* menunjuk, menunjukkan; ~ *out* menunjukkan; ~ *a gun at* mengacukan senjata ke arah; **pointed** *adj* runcing, tajam; sengaja; **pointer** *n* (jari) penunjuk; **pointless** *adj* tiada gunanya

poison *adj* beracun; *n* racun; bisa; *food* ~*ing* keracunan makanan; *rat* ~ racun tikus; *vt* meracuni; **poisonous** *adj* beracun, berbisa; ~ *snake* ular berbisa
poke *vt* menyodok, menusuk
Poland *n* Polandia; **Pole** *n* orang Polandia; **Polish** *adj* berasal dari Polandia; *n* bahasa Polandia
polar *adj* berhubungan dengan kutub; ~ *bear* beruang kutub; ~ *ice cap* kutub és; **polarity** *n* [polariti] polaritas; **pole** *n* kutub; *the North* ~ Kutub Utara; *the South* ~ Kutub Selatan
pole *n* tiang; ~ *position* posisi terdepan (di awal balapan); ~ *vault* loncat galah
Pole *n* orang Polandia; **Polish** *adj* berasal dari Polandia; *n* bahasa Polandia
police *n* [polis] polisi; ~ *car* mobil polisi; ~ *force* angkatan polisi; Polri; ~ *officer* polisi; ~ *station* kantor polisi, pos polisi; **policeman** *n, m* polisi; **policewoman** *n, f* [poliswumen] polisi wanita (polwan)
policy *n* [polisi] kebijaksanaan; *insurance* ~ polis (asuransi)
polio *n* penyakit lumpuh layuh, penyakit polio
Polish *adj* berasal dari Polandia; *n* bahasa Polandia ← **Pole**
polish *n* pelitur, semir; *nail* ~ kuték, cat kuku; *shoe* ~ semir sepatu; *vt* menggosok, menyemir; ~ *off* menghabiskan; ~ *one's skills* meningkatkan kemampuan; **polished** *adj* mengkilap; halus, profésional
polite *adj* sopan (santun); **politely** *adv* dengan sopan, secara sopan; **politeness** *n* kesopanan, kesopan-santunan
political *adj* [politikal] politik; ~ *asylum* suaka politik; ~ *party* partai politik (parpol); ~ *science* ilmu politik; **politically** *adv* secara politik; ~ *correct* tidak mengandung unsur SARA; **politician** *n* [politisyen] politikus, politisi; **politics** *n* [ilmu] politik; *Martin studies* ~ Martin belajar ilmu politik
polka ~ *dot* berbintik-bintik
poll *n* pemberian suara; *opinion* ~ jajak pendapat; *the* ~*s* tempat pemungutan suara (TPS)

pollen *n* tepung sari; ~ *count* tingkat tepung sari di udara
pollute *vt* mencemarkan; **polluted** *adj* tercemar; **pollution** *n* pencemaran, kecemaran, polusi; *air* ~ polusi udara
polo *n* polo; ~ *neck,* ~ *shirt* kaus berkerah; *water* ~ polo air
polyclinic *n* poliklinik
polygamy *n* poligami, beristeri lebih dari satu
Polynesia *n* Polinésia; *French* ~ Polinésia Perancis; **Polynesian** *adj* berasal dari Polinésia; *n* orang Polinésia
polyp *n* polip
polystyrene *n, adj* [polistairin] busa
polytechnic *n* politéknik, SMAK (sekolah kejuruan)
pomelo *n* jeruk bali
pompous *adj* [pompes] sombong, angkuh
poncho *n* ponco, mantel besar
pond *n* kolam; *fish* ~ kolam ikan
ponder *vt* memikirkan, menimbang, merenungkan; ~ *the meaning of life* merenungkan makna hidup
pong *n, coll, UK* bau busuk
pony *n* kuda kerdil, kuda poni; **ponytail** *n* ékor kuda
poo, pooh *n, sl* tahi; *vi* bérak; **poohpooh** *vt* meréméhkan; *his suggestion was* ~*ed by the others* sarannya diréméhkan oléh yang lain
poodle *n* anjing pudel
pool *n* kolam (renang); genangan; bilyar; pul; *swimming* ~ kolam renang; *vt* menggabungkan, menyatukan; ~ *resources* menggabungkan, memakai bersama
poor *adj* miskin, papa; hina, malang; ~ *you!* kasihan; *the* ~ kaum miskin, orang papa; *a* ~ *excuse* alasan yang lemah; *in* ~ *health* kurang séhat
pop *n* ~ *(music)* lagu pop, musik populér ← **popular**
pop *vi* meletup; ~*gun* pistol mainan; ~ *in,* ~ *over,* ~ *round* mampir; ~ *out* keluar sebentar; ~ *up* muncul; ~ *the question* meminang, melamar
Pope *the* ~ Sri Paus; ~ *Benedict XVI* Paus Bénédiktus XVI

poppy *n* bunga opium, bunga madat

popular *adj* populér, laku; **popularity** *n* [populariti] popularitas; **popularize** *vt* memopulérkan; **populate** *vt* mendiami, menghuni; **population** *n* (jumlah) penduduk, populasi; **populous** *adj* [populus] banyak penduduk, padat penduduk

porcelain *adj, n* porselén, keramik

porch *n* serambi, beranda, téras

porcupine *n* [porkyupain] landak

pore *n* pori; **porous** *adj* [porus] berpori

pork *n* daging babi

pornographic *adj* **porno** *coll* jorok, cabul, pornografis; **pornography** *n* **porn** *n* pornografi

porous *adj* [porus] berpori ← **pore**

porpoise *n* [porpus] lumba-lumba

porridge *n* [porij] bubur

port *adj* kiri (di kapal); *n* pelabuhan; lubang, colokan; anggur port; *free* ~ pelabuhan bébas; ~ *of call* pelabuhan persinggahan, pelabuhan transit

port *n* anggur port; ~ *wine* (berwarna) anggur port

portable *adj* dapat dibawa ke manamana, jinjing

porter *n* kuli

portfolio *n* tas, map, sampul; koléksi

porthole *n* [port hol] tingkapan kapal

portion *n* porsi, bagian

portrait *n* [portret] potrét, lukisan, gambar; **portray** *vt* melukiskan, menggambarkan; **portrayal** *n* cara memerankan, pelukisan; lukisan

Portugal *n* Portugal; **Portuguese** *adj* [Portugis] berasal dari Portugal; *n* bahasa Portugal; orang Portugal

pose *n* [poz] gaya, lagak; *to strike a* ~ bergaya; *vi* bergaya

posh *adj, sl* méwah, berkelas tinggi

position *n* [posisyen] letak, kedudukan, pangkat, jabatan; keadaan; *vt* memosisikan

positive *adj, n* [positiv] positif, pasti, tentu

possess *vt* memiliki, mempunyai; **possessed** *adj* yang dimiliki; kesurupan, kerasukan; **possession** *n* [posésyen] kepunyaan, (harta) milik; **possessive**

adj [posésiv] ingin memiliki, posésif; *n* kata kepunyaan

possibility *n* [posibiliti] kemungkinan; *a slight* ~ kemungkinan kecil; **possible** *adj* [posibel] mungkin; **possibly** *adv* barangkali, mungkin

possum, opossum *n* semacam binatang malam seperti tupai; *to play* ~ pura-pura tidur

post *suf* sesudah, pasca; ~*graduate* pascasarjana; ~*mortem* otopsi; ~*war* pascaperang

post *n* pos; jabatan; layanan pos; ~ *office* kantor pos; *vt* mengeposkan; menémpélkan; **postage** *n* [postej] perangko, ongkos kirim; ~ *stamp* perangko; **postal** *adj* berkaitan dengan pos; ~ *address* alamat pos; **postcard** *n* kartu pos; **postcode** *n* kode pos; **poster** *n* plakat, gambar; **postman** *n* tukang pos; **postmark** *n* cap pos; **postmaster** *n* kepala kantor pos

post *n* tiang; *lamp*~ tiang lampu

posterior *adj* [postirior] belakang; *n* pantat

postman *n* tukang pos ← **post**

postmark *n* cap pos ← **post**

postmaster *n* kepala kantor pos ← **post**

postpone *vt* menunda, mengundurkan; *Olivia* ~*d her wedding* Olivia menunda hari pernikahannya

postscript, PS tambahan tulisan

posture *n* [postyur] sikap badan, postur

pot *n* pot, periuk, tempat bunga, tempat tanaman; *sl* ganja; ~ *belly* gendut; ~ *luck* bisa baik, bisa tidak; seadanya; ~ *scourer* penggosok panci; *coffee* ~ tempat kopi; *tea*~ téko, poci; **pothole** *n* [pot hol] lubang di jalan; **potpourri** *n* [potpuri, popuri] bunga rampai; **potter** *n* perajin tembikar; **pottery** *n* tembikar, pecah belah, keramik

potassium *n* kalium, potasium

potato *n* [potéto] kentang; *(hot)* ~ *chips* kentang goréng; ~ *chips,* ~ *crisps* kripik kentang; *baked* ~ kentang bakar; *mashed* ~ kentang puré

potent *adj* kuat, manjur, mujarab; **potential** *adj* [poténsyel] mungkin, berpeluang, calon; *n* kemungkinan,

kekuatan, tenaga; **potentially** *adv*
dapat, mampu; ~ *dangerous* dapat
membahayakan, bisa berbahaya
pothole *n* [pot hol] lubang di jalan ←
pot
potion *n* ramuan
potpourri *n* [potpuri, popuri] bunga
rampai ← **pot**
potter *n* perajin tembikar; **pottery** *n*
tembikar, pecah belah, keramik ← **pot**
potty *n* klosét anak-anak
pouch *n* kantong
poultry *n* [poltri] unggas
pounce *vt* menerkam; *the cat ~d on the
rat* kucing itu menerkam tikus
pound *n* pon; tempat penerimaan
barang yang hilang; ~ *sterling* pon
stérling, pon Inggris; *vt* menumbuk;
memukul-mukul; ~ *on* memukuli
pour *vi* hujan besar; mengalir; ~ *with
rain* hujan lebat; ~ *out your heart*
mencurahkan hati (curhat); *vt* menuangkan, mencurahkan; menyiram
pout *n* bibir mencibir; *vi* mencibir
poverty *n* [poverti] kemiskinan; *below
the ~ line* di bawah garis kemiskinan
POW *abbrev prisoner-of-war* tawanan
perang
powder *n* [pauder] bubuk, serbuk,
puyer; bedak; *~ed milk* susu bubuk;
talcum ~ bedak; *vt* membedaki; **pow-
dery** *adj* seperti bubuk
power *n* kekuasaan, kekuatan, daya,
tenaga; *~-hungry* haus akan
kekuasaan; *~-sharing* membagi
kekuasaan; ~ *cut* mati lampu,
pemadaman lampu; ~ *line* saluran
listrik; ~ *station* pembangkit listrik; ~
steering setir daya; *in ~* berkuasa;
powerful *adj* berkuasa, kuat; **powerless** *adj* tak berkuasa, tak berdaya
PR *abbrev public relations* hubungan
masyarakan (humas)
practical *n* praktis, berguna; ~ *lesson*
prakték; **practically** *adv* hampir-hampir, benar-benar; **practice** *n* prakték,
kebiasaan, adat; latihan; *doctor's ~*
prakték dokter; *piano ~* latihan piano;
to put into ~ mempraktékkan; *vi*
berlatih; *vt* mempraktékkan, melatih;

practicing *adj* taat, aktif; ~ *Muslim*
orang Islam yang taat; **practise** *vi, UK*
berlatih; *vt* mempraktékkan, melatih;
practitioner *n* praktisi; *medical ~* dokter
Prague *n* [prag] Praha
prairie *n, US* kawasan padang rumput,
sabana
praise *n* [préiz] pujian; *vt* memuji; ~
the Lord puji Tuhan
pram *n* keréta bayi, keréta anak-anak ←
perambulator
prank *n* gurauan, permainan; **prankster**
n orang yang suka bergurau
prawn *n* udang; ~ *cracker* krupuk udang
pray *vi* berdoa, sholat, bersembahyang;
~ *for* mendoakan; **prayer** *n* [préir] doa,
sembahyang; ~ *beads Isl* tasbih; *Cath*
rosario; ~ *book* buku kumpulan doa; ~
mat sejadah; *Friday ~s Isl* sholat
Jumat; *the sunset ~* sholat magrib,
sembahyang magrib
pre- *pref* [pri] pra-, sebelum; *~menstru-
al syndrome (PMT)* sindrom pra ménstruasi; *~school* taman kanak-kanak
(TK); *~war* sebelum perang
preach *vi* berkhotbah; *vt* mengajari;
preacher *n* pemuka agama; *Isl* khotib,
dai
precarious *adj* [prekérius] berbahaya
precaution *n* tindakan pencegahan; **pre-
cautionary** *adj* kalau-kalau, pencegahan
precede *vt* [presid] mendahului; **precedence** *n* [présedens] prioritas; **precedent** *n* présedén; **preceding** *adj* yang
sebelumnya
precinct *n* [prisinkt] daérah
precious *adj* [présyus] berharga, mahal;
mulia; ~ *metal* logam mulia; ~ *stone*
batu mulia; *semi-~ stone* batu setengah mulia
precipice *n* [présipis] ngarai, tebing
tinggi
precipitate *n* endapan; *vt* mempercepat,
memicu; **precipitation** *n* hujan, salju
precise *adj* tepat, saksama; **precisely**
adv dengan tepat, tepat sekali; **precision** *n* [presisyen] kesaksamaan,
ketelitian
predator *n* [prédater] pemangsa,
pemakan héwan lain

predicate *n* sebutan (kalimat), prédikat

predict *vt* meramalkan; **predictable** *adj* [prediktabel] dapat ditebak; **prediction** *n* ramalan

preface *n* [préfas] pendahuluan, kata pengantar, prakata; *vt* mengawali, memulai

prefect *n* wali murid, jabatan siswa

prefer *vt* [prifér] lebih suka, memilih; **preferably** *adv* [préferabli] lebih baik; **preference** *n* [préferens] kecenderungan, pilihan; *in ~ to* daripada; **preferential** *adj* [préferénsyal] istiméwa, diutamakan

prefix *n* awalan

pregnancy *n* (masa) kehamilan; *~ test* tés kehamilan; **pregnant** *adj* hamil, mengandung; *heavily ~* hamil tua; *seven months ~* hamil tujuh bulan

prehistoric *adj* prasejarah

prejudice *n* [préjudis] prasangka; **prejudiced** *adj* berprasangka; *~ against people from the south* berprasangka buruk terhadap orang dari selatan

preliminary *adj* [primineri] pendahuluan, persiapan, awal

premarital *adj* pranikah; *~ sex* (hubungan) séks pranikah

premature *adj* prématur, sebelum waktunya, pradini; **prematurely** *adv* secara prématur, sebelum waktunya

premier *adj* utama, terbaik; *~ League* Liga Inggris; *n* pemimpin, perdana menteri, kepala negara bagian

premiere *n* [prémiér] pemutaran perdana, pertunjukan perdana

premises *n* tempat; *on the ~* di tempat (tersebut)

premonition *n* [premonisyen] firasat

preoccupied *adj* [priokupaid] asyik memikirkan, termenung; **preoccupation** *n* keasyikan

prepaid *adj* prabayar; **prepay** *vt* **prepaid prepaid** membayar di muka

preparation *n* [préparésyen] persiapan; **preparatory** *adj* (dalam rangka) persiapan; *prep school UK* sekolah dasar swasta; **prepare** *vi* bersiap-siap; *vt* menyiapkan, mempersiapkan; **prepared** *adj* siap, bersedia

prepay *vt* **prepaid prepaid** membayar di muka

preposition *n* [préposisyen] kata depan

prerequisite *n* [prirékuisit] prasyarat, syarat

preschool *n* [priskul] taman kanak-kanak (TK)

prescribe *vt* menetapkan; memberikan resép; **prescription** *n* resép; *~ drug* obat resép

presence *n* [prézens] hadirat, hadapan; kehadiran; *~ of mind* kesadaran, kecepatan berpikir; **present** *adj* [prézent] sekarang, kini; hadir; *~ tense* (kata kerja) masa kini; *at ~* sekarang ini; **presently** *adv* segera

present *n* [prézent] hadiah, kado, pemberian; *vt* [prezént] menyajikan, mempersembahkan; *the principal ~ed the winner with the prize* kepala sekolah yang memberi hadiah kepada pemenang; **presentation** *n* [présentésyen] penyajian, préséntasi; **presenter** *n* pembawa acara, pembaca berita

presentation *n* [présentésyen] penyajian, préséntasi ← **present**

presenter *n* pembawa acara, pembaca berita ← **present**

presently *adv* segera ← **present**

preservation *n* [préservésyen] pelindungan, présérvasi; **preservative** *n* [présérvativ] pengawét; *no ~s* tanpa pengawét; **preserve** *n* [présérv] cagar; selai; *nature ~* cagar alam; *vt* mengawétkan, melindungi, memelihara

preside *vi* [prezaid] *~ over* mengetuai; **presidency** *n* [présidénsi] masa jabatan présidén; **president** *n* présidén; ketua; *~ of the United States* Présidén Amérika Serikat; **presidential** *adj* [prézidéntyal] untuk présidén

press *n* percétakan; pérs; alat penekan; *~ agency* kantor berita; *~ clipping* guntingan koran; *~ conference* jumpa pérs; *~ gallery* ruang wartawan; *~ pass* kartu pérs; *in ~* sedang dicétak; *vt* menekan, menindih, mendesak; menyetrika; *~stud* kancing pencét; *~ on* maju, menekan; **pressed** *adj* tertekan; *~ for time* terburu-buru;

pressing *adj* mendesak; **pressure** *n* [présyur] tekanan; *blood* ~ ténsi, tekanan darah; *under* ~ sedang ditekan; *vt* menekan, memaksa; **pressurize** *vt* menekan, memaksa

prestige *n* [préstij] géngsi; **prestigious** *adj* bergéngsi

presumably *adv* kiranya, agaknya; **presume** *vt* menganggap; mengira; **presumption** *n* anggapan; **presumptuous** *adj* lancang, sombong

pretend *vi* berpura-pura, berdalih; **pretense** *n* dalih, kepura-puraan; **pretentious** *adj* [preténsyes] berprétensi, mengada-ada

pretext *n* dalih

pretty *adj* [priti] manis, cantik, molék; *adv* cukup; *it's* ~ *hot* hari ini cuaca cukup panas

pretzel *n* cemilan kering yang asin

prevail *vi* [prevél] menang, bertahan; **prevalent** *adj* [prévalent] umum, berlaku, lazim

prevent *vt* [prevént] mencegah, menghalangi, menangkis; *the guard ~ed him from leaving* satpam itu menghadang dia agar tidak keluar; **preventative, preventive** *adj* [prevéntativ, prevéntiv] pencegahan; **prevention** *n* pencegahan

preview *n* préviu; prapertunjukan; *vi* memberi risénsi tentang acara yang akan datang

previous *adj* [privius] yang dahulu, yang sebelumnya; **previously** *adv* sebelumnya

prey *n* [pré] mangsa; *bird of* ~ burung pemburu; *vi* ~ *on* memburu

price *n* harga; ~ *list* daftar harga; ~ *war* perang harga; **priceless** *adj* tidak ternilai

prick *n* tusukan; *vt* menusuk; **prickly** *adj* [prikeli] tajam, berduri, menusuk

pride *n* kesombongan, kebanggaan, harga diri; ~ *yourself on* bangga pada

priest *n, Cath* [prist] pastor; *Hind* pedanda

primary *adj* pertama, terpenting, dasar; ~ *colors* warna dasar; ~ *school UK* sekolah dasar (SD); **prime** *adj* per-

dana, utama; ~ *minister (PM)* Perdana Menteri (PM); ~ *number* bilangan pokok; *in your* ~ pada masa keemasan

primitive *adj* [primitiv] sederhana, primitif

primrose *n* semacam bunga berwarna kuning muda

prince *n, m* pangeran; *crown* ~ putera mahkota; **princess** *n, f* putri, permaisuri

principal *adj* utama; *n* kepala sekolah; uang pokok; **principality** *n* negara di bawah kekuasaan pangeran

principle *n* [prinsipel] asas, prinsip; *in* ~ pada prinsipnya, pada dasarnya; *on* ~ karena keyakinan

print *n* tapak (kaki); gambar, réproduksi; tulisan, ketikan; ~ *media* media cétak; *fine* ~ tulisan kecil; *in* ~ masih dicétak; *out of* ~ sudah tidak dicétak lagi; *vt* mencetak; menulis dengan huruf cétak; ~*ing press* mesin cétak; **printer** *n* printer, pencétak; ~*s* percétakan; **printout** *n* hasil cétak

prior *adj* [praior] terlebih dahulu; **prioritize** *vt* mengutamakan; **priority** *n* prioritas

prism *n* [prizem] prisma

prison *n* [prizon] penjara, lembaga pemasyarakatan (LP); *in* ~ dipenjara; **prisoner** *n* orang yang dipenjara, terpidana

privacy *n* kebébasan pribadi; **private** *adj* [praivet] pribadi; swasta; milik sendiri; ~ *life* kehidupan pribadi; ~ *sector* (perusahaan) swasta; ~ *school* sekolah swasta; *in* ~ tidak di depan umum; *n* tamtama, prajurit biasa; *pl, sl* kemaluan; **privately** *adv* secara pribadi; **privatization** *n* swastanisasi; **privatize** *vt* menswastakan

privilege *n* [privilej] hak istiméwa; **privileged** *adj* punya hak istiméwa; berada, mampu

prize *n* hadiah; *consolation* ~ hadiah hiburan, juara harapan; *first* ~ hadiah pertama, juara; *vt* menilai tinggi

pro *adj* pro, setuju dengan; ~*-abortion* setuju dengan aborsi; *adj, n* (olahragawan) profésional

probable *adj* **probably** *adv* kemungki-nan besar, mungkin

probe *n* pemeriksaan, penelitian; pesawat penjelajah; *v* menyelidiki

problem *n* masalah, soal; ~ *child* anak bermasalah; *no ~!* tidak masalah; *to solve a* ~ memecahkan masalah

procedure *n* [prosidyur] prosédur, tata cara; **proceed** *vi* maju, jalan; ~ *with* meneruskan; **proceedings** *n, pl* cara kerja, acara kerja; **proceeds** *n, pl* hasil dari jualan; penghasilan; **process** *n* cara, prosés; *in the* ~ *of* sedang; *vt* memprosés, mengolah; **processed** *adj* ~ *meat* daging olahan; **procession** *n* arak-arakan, prosési; **processor** *n* alat pengolah, alat pem-rosés; *word* ~ semacam mesin tik éléktronik

proclaim *v* menyatakan, memprokla-masikan, mengumumkan; **proclama-tion** *n* proklamasi, pengumuman; ~ *of independence* proklamasi kemerdékaan

prodigious *adj* [prodijus] sangat banyak; **prodigy** *n* [prodiji] anak ajaib; *Mozart was a musical* ~ Mozart adalah anak yang sangat berbakat dalam bidang musik

produce *n* [prodyus] hasil; *vt* [predyus] menghasilkan; **producer** *n* [pre-dyuser] produsén; **product** *n* hasil, produk; **production** *n* produksi, per-tunjukan; **productive** *adj* produktif, subur; **productively** *adv* secara pro-duktif; *use your time* ~ gunakan waktu secara produktif; **productivity** *n* pro-duktivitas, daya hasil

profess *vi* mengaku; *vt* menyatakan; *he ~ed to know all about cars* dia mengaku tahu banyak tentang mobil; **profession** *n* [profésyen] profési, pekerjaan; pernyataan; **professional** *adj* profésional; **professionally** *adv* secara profésional; dalam rangka pekerjaan

professor *n* guru besar; ~ *of Asian Languages* Guru Besar Bahasa-bahasa Asia

profile *n* profil; *high* ~ posisi menonjol; *low* ~ posisi tidak menonjol; *that famous author keeps a very low* ~ pe-ngarang terkenal itu jarang muncul di depan umum

profit *n* untung, keuntungan, laba; ~ *and loss* laba rugi; *non-*~ nirlaba; *vi* beruntung, memperoléh keuntungan; ~ *from* memperoléh keuntungan dari; **profitable** *adj* menguntungkan

profound *adj* dalam, mendalam

program, programme *n* acara, pro-gram; *computer* ~ program komputer; *TV* ~ acara télévisi; *on the* ~ di daftar acara; *vt* memprogram; **programmer** *n* pembuat program (komputer)

progress *n* [progres] kemajuan; *in* ~ sedang berlangsung; *vi* [progrés] maju; **progressive** *adj* berpikiran maju, progrésif; **progressively** *adv* sedikit demi sedikit, secara berangsur

prohibit *vt* [prohibit] melarang; **pro-hibited** *adj* dilarang, terlarang; **prohibition** *n* [prohibisyen] larangan

project *n* [projekt] proyék; *vt* [projékt] memproyéksikan; *the company ~ed sales of up to $4,000* perusahaan itu memproyéksikan penjualan sebesar $4.000; **projection** *n* proyéksi; **projector** *n* proyéktor

prolific *adj* [prolifik] subur, banyak hasil

prolog, prologue *n* prolog, pendahuluan

prolong *vt* memperpanjang

promenade *n* jalan di tepi pantai; *vi* berjalan di depan umum; *the model ~s down the catwalk* peragawati itu ber-jalan di atas panggung

prominent *adj* terkemuka, menonjol; **prominently** *adv* secara terbuka

promise *n* [promis] janji; *to break a* ~ mengingkari janji; *to keep a* ~ menepati janji; *vi* berjanji; *vt* menjan-jikan; **promising** *adj* menjanjikan

promote *vt* memajukan, menaikkan pangkat, mempromosikan; **promoter** *n* penyelenggara, promotor; **promo-tion** *n* kenaikan pangkat, kenaikan jabatan; promosi; *Johnny received a* ~ *at work* Johnny kenaikan pangkat di kantor prompt *adj* cepat; *n* bisikan; *vt* membisiki; mendorong; **promptly** *adv* dengan cepat, dengan segera

prone *adj* cenderung; tengkurap; ~ *to* cenderung

prong *n* gigi garpu; cabang tanduk

pronoun *n* kata ganti

pronounce *vt* melafalkan; menyatakan; **pronunciation** *n* lafal

proof *n* bukti; ~*read* mengoréksi naskah; **prove** *vt* [pruv] membuktikan; **proven** *adj* ternyata, terbukti

prop *n* penopang, sangga; alat-alat yang diperlukan di panggung; *vi* ~ *up* menyangga, menopang; *she lay in the front seat and ~ped up her feet on the dashboard* dia tidur di jok depan seraya menopangkan kaki di atas dasbor

propaganda *n* propaganda

propagate *vt* [propagét] mengembangbiakkan; menyebarkan

propel *vt* mendorong, menggerakkan; **propeller** *n* baling-baling

proper *adj* benar, betul, patut, layak; **properly** *adv* benar-benar, dengan betul

property *n* kepunyaan, (harta) milik; sifat; properti; ~ *agent* agén properti; *personal* ~ milik pribadi

prophecy *n* [profesi] ramalan; **prophet** *n* nabi, rasul; *the* ~ *(Muhammad)* Nabi Mohammad (s.a.w.); *the* ~*s* Rasul-Rasul

proportion *n* perbandingan, proporsi; **proportional** *adj* proporsional, sebanding; **proportionate** *adj* [proporsyenét] yang sebanding

proposal *n* usul; lamaran; **propose** *v* mengusulkan; *vi* meminang; *Ben* ~*d at a moonlight dinner* Ben melamar dia saat makan malam di bawah cahaya rembulan; **proposition** *n* usul, rencana

proprietary [proprayetri] ~ *limited (Pty Ltd)* perséro, perséroan terbatas (PT); **proprietor** *n* [proprayetor] pemilik

prose *n* prosa

prosecute *vt* menuntut; **prosecution** *n* pihak penuntut; **prosecutor** *n* jaksa, penuntut; *public* ~ jaksa umum

prospect *n* kemungkinan, harapan; *this*

student has excellent ~*s* banyak yang bisa diharapkan dari pelajar ini; **prospective** *adj* calon, bakal

prospectus *n* buku promosi, iklan

prosper *vi* berhasil, menjadi makmur; **prosperity** *n* [prospériti] kemakmuran; **prosperous** *adj* [prosperus] makmur

prostate *n* (kelenjar) prostat; ~ *cancer* kanker prostat; *enlargement of the* ~ pembesaran (kelenjar) prostat

prostitute *n* [prostitut] pelacur, pekerja séks komersial (PSK); *f* wanita tunasusila (WTS); **prostitution** *n* pelacuran, prostitusi

protect *vt* melindungi; ~ *from* melindungi dari; **protected** *adj* terlindung; **protection** *n* perlindungan; **protective** *adj* [protéktif] bersifat melindungi; pencegah; **protector** *n* pelindung

protein *n* [protin] protéin

protest *n* [protest] protés, pembangkangan, unjuk rasa; *vi* [protést] berunjuk rasa; *vt* memprotés, melawan, membangkang; **Protestant** *adj* Kristen; *n* orang Kristen; **protester** *n* pemrotés, pengunjuk rasa

protocol *n* protokol; *to follow* ~ menurut protokol

protractor *n* busur derajat

protrude *vi* menjorok, menonjol keluar; *the tennis racket* ~*d from the cupboard* raket itu menonjol keluar lemari; **protruding** *adj* yang menonjol

proud *adj* bangga; angkuh, sombong; ~ *of her son* bangga akan anaknya; *to do someone* ~ membanggakan orang; **proudly** *adv* dengan bangga

prove *vt* [pruv] membuktikan; **proven** *adj* ternyata, terbukti ← **proof**

proverb *n* peribahasa

provide *vt* menyediakan, membekali, melengkapi; ~ *for* mengurus, memelihara; **provided, providing** ~ *(that)* asal, asalkan; **provider** *n* pemberi nafkah; pemberi jasa; **provision** *n* [provisyen] persediaan; ketetapan; **provisional** *adj* sementara

province *n* propinsi; **provincial** *adj* berhubungan dengan provinsi; picik, kampungan

provision *n* [provisyen] persediaan;
ketetapan; *pl* bekal; **provisional** *adj*
sementara ← **provide**
provocation *n* provokasi, hasutan,
pancingan; **provocative** *adj* provoka-
tif, menghasut, memancing;
provoke *vt* menghasut, memancing
proxy *n* wakil, kuasa; ~ *letter* surat kuasa
prudent *adj* bijaksana, hati-hati
prune *n* buah prem kering
pry *vi* ikut campur; ~ *into* mencampuri;
~ *open* mencongkel
PS *abbrev postscript* catatan tambahan
pada akhir surat
PS *abbrev primary school* SD (sekolah
dasar)
psalm *n* [sam] mazmur
pseudonym *n* [siudonim] nama samaran
psychiatric *adj* [saikiatrik] berhubungan dengan penyakit jiwa; ~ *hospital*
rumah sakit jiwa; **psychiatrist** *n*
[saikayetrist] psikiater, ahli jiwa; **psy-
chiatry** *n* ilmu penyakit jiwa, psikiatri
psychic *adj, n* [saikik] mempunyai
indera keenam, cenayang
psychological *adj* [saikolojikal] kejiwaan; **psychologist** *n* psikolog, ahli
ilmu jiwa; **psychology** *n* ilmu jiwa,
psikologi
PTO *abbrev please turn over* di halaman
berikut
Pty Ltd, Pte *Proprietary Limited* PT
(Perseroan Terbatas), CV, NV
pub *n* tempat minum-minum, pub; **publican** *n* pemilik pub
puberty *n* masa puber, pubertas; **pubic**
adj ~ *hair* bulu yang tumbuh di sekitar
kemaluan
public *n* orang banyak, umum; ~ *administration* tata usaha negara; ~ *health*
keséhatan masyarakat; ~ *holiday* tanggal mérah; ~ *opinion* pendapat umum;
~ *relations (PR)* hubungan masyarakat
(humas); ~ *servant* pegawai negeri; ~
speaking berpidato di depan umum; ~
telephone télépon umum; ~ *toilet* WC
umum; ~ *transport* angkutan umum; *in*
~ di depan umum; *the* ~ orang umum
publican *n* pemilik pub
publication *n* terbitan, keluaran; pengu-

muman; **publicity** *n* [pablisiti] hubungan masyarakat (humas); publisitas;
~ *stunt* kegiatan untuk membuat berita; **publicize** *vt* mengumumkan,
memasarkan; **publish** *vt* menerbitkan,
mengeluarkan, mengumumkan; **publisher** *n* penerbit
pudding *n* puding, pencuci mulut, podéng
puddle *n* [padel] genangan
Puerto Rican *adj* [porto rikan] berasal
dari Puerto Rico; *n* orang Puerto Rico;
Puerto Rico *n* Puerto Rico
puff *n* embusan; isapan; tiupan; kepulan; *vi* terengah-engah; mengepul;
meniup; **puffy** *adj* bengkak
puffin *n* sejenis burung laut
pug *n* sejenis anjing kecil
puke *vi, sl* muntah
pull *n* tarikan, daya tarik; *v* [pul] menarik; ~ *back* menarik ke samping;
mundur; ~ *down* menarik ke bawah;
membongkar, merobohkan; ~ *out*
batal; mencabut; ~ *over* minggir,
menepi; ~ *strings* mengatur, menggunakan konéksi; ~ *through* sembuh;
meléwati; ~ *together* bekerja sama; ~
up berhenti (kendaraan); ~ *a muscle*
keseléo; **pulley** *n* [puli] katrol;
pullover *n* switer, baju hangat
pulp *n* bubur; daging buah; ampas; ~ *fiction* fiksi murahan; *wood* ~ bubur kayu
pulpit *n* [pulpit] mimbar
pulsate *vi* berdenyut; **pulse** *n* nadi
puma *n* sejenis kucing besar di Amérika
pumice *n* [pamis] batu apung
pump *n* pompa; *vt* memompa
pumpkin *n* labu
punch *n* pukulan, tonjokan; *vt* menghantam, meninju, menonjok; ~*up*
perkelahian
punch *n* minuman campuran
punctual *adj* tepat waktu; **punctuality** *n*
sikap selalu tepat waktu
punctuation *n* [pangktyuésyen]
pemberian tanda-tanda baca; ~ *mark*
tanda baca
puncture *n* [pangktyur] lubang kecil,
kempés; *I had a* ~ ban mobil saya
kempés
punish *vt* [panisy] menghukum; **punish-**

ment *n* hukuman; *capital* ~ hukuman mati; *corporal* ~ hukum badaniah

punk *n* kaum muda yang memakai baju robék, perhiasan logam serta rambutnya dicat

pup *n* anak anjing, anak binatang; *seal* ~ anak anjing laut

pupil *n* murid

pupil *n* anak mata, pupil

puppet *n* bonéka; wayang; ~ *government* pemerintahan bonéka; *shadow* ~ wayang kulit; **puppeteer** *n* dalang

puppy *n* [papi] anak anjing; ~ *love* cinta monyét

purchase *n* [perces] pembelian, pembelanjaan; *vt* membeli

pure *adj* murni, bersih; **purification** *n* pembersihan, penyaringan; **purify** *vt* [pyurifai] membersihkan, menyaring, memurnikan; **purity** *n* [pyuriti] kemurnian

purple *adj* [perpel] ungu, lembayung; ~ *patch* keberhasilan secara mendadak; **purplish** *adj* keungu-unguan

purpose *n* maksud, niat, tujuan; *on* ~ dengan sengaja; **purposeful** *adj* dengan maksud tertenu; **purposely** *adv* dengan sengaja

purr *n* dengkur (kucing); *vi* mendengkur

purse *n* dompét

purser *n* penata usaha di kapal atau pesawat terbang

pursue *vt* mengejar, mengikuti, memburu; **pursuit** *n* pengejaran, pencarian; *in* ~ *of* sedang mengejar, sedang memburu

purveyor *n* [pervéyer] pemasok

pus *n* [pas] nanah

push *n* [pusy] dorongan; *v* mendorong; ~*bike* sepéda; ~ *around* menyuruhnyuruh; ~ *button* tombol; ~ *drugs* mengédarkan obat-obatan; ~ *in* menyerobot, mendorong masuk; ~ *off* pergi; ~ *on* meneruskan; ~ *one's luck* mencari untung secara berlebihan; **pusher** *n* keréta anak; *sl* bandar narkoba; **pushover** *n* sesuatu yang mudah; **pushy** *adj* suka memaksa kehendak, lancang

puss, pussycat *n, sl* [pus, pusikat]

kucing; *Puss in Boots* Sepatu Ajaib

put *vt* **put put** [put] meletakkan, menaruh, menyimpan; menempatkan; ~*down* hinaan; ~ *across* menyampaikan; ~ *aside* mengesampingkan; ~ *away* menyimpan; ~ *back* mengembalikan, meletakkan kembali; ~ *down* memadamkan; meréméhkan; menyuntik mati binatang; ~ *forward* mengemukakan; ~ *on* mengenakan (baju); ~ *on weight* menjadi lebih gemuk; ~ *off* menunda, mengundurkan; ~ *out* mengeluarkan; tersinggung; ~ *up* memasang; menginap; ~ *up with* tahan; ~ *upon* membebankan; ~ *a child to bed* menidurkan anak

put *shot* ~ tolak peluru

putrid *adj* [pyutrid] busuk

puzzle *n* [pazel] mainan, teka-teki; *crossword* ~ teka-teki silang (TTS); *jigsaw* ~ teka-teki menyusun; **puzzled** *adj* [pazeld] bingung; **puzzling** *adj* membingungkan

pygmy *n* [pigmi] orang kerdil; *adj* kerdil

pyjamas, pajamas *n, pl* piyama, baju tidur

pylon *n* [pailon] menara listrik, tiang listrik yang besar

pyramid *n* piramida

pyre *n* [pair] tumpukan kayu untuk upacara pembakaran mayat

python *n* [paithon] ular sanca, piton

Q

Q&A *abbrev* question and answer tanya jawab

Qatar *n* [katar] Qatar; **Qatari** *adj* berasal dari Qatar; *n* orang Qatar

QC *abbrev* Queen's Counsel pengacara kerajaan

quack *n* suara bébék; *sl* dukun, tukang obat; *vi* membébék

quad, quadrangle *n* [kuodranggel] (lapangan) segi empat

quadratic *adj* kuadrat; ~ *equation* persamaan kuadrat

quadrilateral *adj, n* segi empat

quadruped *n* [kuodrupéd] binatang berkaki empat

quadruple *v* [kuodrupel] berlipat empat; *population density has ~d* kepadatan penduduk telah naik berlipat empat

quadruplets *n, pl* [kuodruplet] **quads** *coll* kembar empat

quail *n* burung puyuh; *~'s egg* telur puyuh

quaint *adj* kuno, anéh; *what a ~ idea in this day and age!* idé yang kuno kalau sekarang

quake *n* gempa; *vi* gemetar; *Alex sat in the examination hall, quaking with fear* Alex duduk gemetar karena takut di ruang ujian

qualification *n* kualifikasi, ijazah; **qualified** *adj* berkualifikasi, berhak, berijazah; **qualify** *vi* memenuhi syarat, lolos; *Ian qualified for the Olympics* Ian lolos séléksi Olimpiade; *vt* memberi perincian, mengubah; *he qualified his statement on budget spending* dia memberi perincian pernyataannya soal pembelanjaan anggaran

qualitative *adj* [kuolitatif] kualitatif, menurut mutu; **quality** *n* mutu, kualitas; sifat; *good ~* kualitas baik, mutu baik; *high-~* berkualitas tinggi

qualm *n* [kuam] *no ~s* tidak merasa cemas atau ragu

quantity *n* [kuontiti] banyaknya, kuantitas; *~ control* pengendalian mutu; *the sheer ~ of cars causes problems* jumlah mobil saja menjadi masalah

quarantine *n* [kuorantin] karantina; *in ~* dikarantina; *vt* mengarantina

quarrel *n* [kuorel] pertengkaran, percékcokan; *vi* bertengkar, ribut; *they ~led over which cake to buy* meréka bertengkar soal pilihan kué yang mau dibeli

quarry *n* [kuori] tambang, penggalian batu

quart *n* [kuort] ukuran cairan (944 ml)

quarter *n* [kuorter] perempat; kampung, daérah; *three ~s* (³/₄) tiga perempat; *a ~ past one* jam satu léwat seperempat; *a ~ to five* jam lima kurang seperempat; *pl* tempat tinggal; *at close ~s,*

from close ~s dari dekat; **quarterly** *adv* tiap tiga bulan; *n* majalah triwulan

quartet *n* [kuortét] empat sekawan, kwartét

quartz *n* kuarsa

quasi- *pref* [kuazi] pura-pura, tidak benar

quay *n* [ki] dermaga; *there were many seagulls on the ~* banyak burung camar di dermaga

queasy *adj* [kuizi] mual, muak

queen *n* [kuin] ratu; *~ bee* ratu lebah; *the ~ Mother* Ibu Suri; *the ~ of England* Ratu Inggris

queer *adj* anéh; *adj, n, sl* homoséksual

quell *vt* memadamkan, mengatasi; *~ a riot* mengamankan kerusuhan

query *n* [kuiri] pertanyaan; *vt* menanyakan, meragukan; *she queried the decision to leave* dia meragukan keputusan pergi

quest *n* [kuést] pencarian; *in ~ of* mencari

question *n* [kuéstion] pertanyaan; masalah, soal; *~ mark* tanda tanya [?]; *exam ~s* soal-soal ujian; *without ~* tentu saja, niscaya; *~ and answer (Q&A)* tanya jawab; *a ~ of money* soal uang; *out of the ~* tidak mungkin; *to beg the ~* menerima tanpa bukti; *to call into ~* mempertanyakan; *vi* bertanya; *vt* menanyai, menanyakan; meragukan; mempersoalkan; **questionable** *adj* [kuéstionabel] patut dipertanyakan, dapat diragukan; **questioning** *n* pemeriksaan; *the witness was taken in for ~ by the police* saksinya dibawa ke kantor polisi untuk diperiksa; **questionnaire** *n* [kuéstionér] angkét

queue *n* [kyu] antré, antréan; *to jump the ~* menyerobot (masuk); *vi* antri, berantri

quiche *n* [kisy] semacam pai yang dibuat dari telur kocok

quick *adj* [kuik] cepat; *~-witted* cepat berpikir; *~ smart* sekarang juga; **quicksand** *n* pasir hanyut; **quicksilver** *n* air raksa; **quicken** *vi* menjadi lebih cepat; *his heart rate ~ed* detak jantungnya menjadi lebih cepat

quid *n, sl* [kuid] pon sterling

quiet *adj* [kuayet] teduh, tenang; *be ~!*

diam!; *on the* ~ diam-diam; *n*
keteduhan, ketenangan; **quieten** *vi*
menjadi tenang; *vt* menenangkan,
meredakan; **quietly** *adv* dengan
tenang, tanpa suara; **quietness** *n*
keteduhan, kesunyian
quiff *n* jambul
quilt *n* [kuilt] selimut tebal; *vi* membuat
selimut tebal (dari kain perca)
quinine *n* [kuinin] kina
quintuplets *n, pl* kembar lima
quip *n* [kuip] sindiran, éjékan; *vi*
menyindir, mengejek, melucu
quirk *n* kebiasaan yang lucu; **quirky** *adj*
lucu, mempunyai kebiasaan yang anéh
quit *vi* [kuit] **quit quit** putus asa, berhenti, menyerah; *vt* meninggalkan,
menghentikan; *Ralph* ~ *his job* Ralph
berhenti bekerja
quite *adv* [kuait] cukup sama, rada,
lumayan; ~ *difficult* cukup sulit; *not* ~
tidak begitu
quiver *n, v* [kuiver] gemetar; *the cat's
whiskers ~ed* kumis kucing itu gemetar
quiz *n* [kuiz] kuis, ulangan singkat, tanya
jawab; *vt* menanyai; *his mother ~zed
him on where he had been* ibunya
menanyai dia soal ke mana dia pergi
quota *n* [kuota] jatah, kuota; *to exceed
~s* melebihi kuota
quotation *n* [kuotésyen] kutipan;
penawaran; ~ *marks* tanda kutip; *can
you give me a* ~ *for the paint job?*
berapa perkiraan biaya pekerjaan
pengecatan?; **quote** *vt* mengutip,
menyebut, mencatat; *n* kutipan
quotient *n* [kuosyent] hasil bagi;
emotional ~ *(EQ)* tingkat kecerdasan
emosional; *intelligence* ~ *(IQ)* tingkat
kecerdasan

R

R *abbrev rand* mata uang Afrika Selatan
R. *abbrev river* S. (sungai)
rabbi *n* [rabai] pendéta Yahudi
rabbit *n* kelinci; ~ *warren* sarang kelinci; *vi* ~ *on* mencerocos

rabble *n* [rabel] rakyat jelata
rabies *n* [rébis] penyakit anjing gila,
rabiés
raccoon *n* sejenis musang, rakun
race *n* (suku) bangsa, ras; ~ *relations*
hubungan antar suku bangsa; ~ *riots*
kerusuhan étnis; *the human* ~ umat
manusia; **racial** *adj* rasial, berhubungan dengan suku bangsa; **racism** *n*
[résizem] rasisme, pembédaan rasial;
racist *adj* rasis; *n* orang yang membenci suku bangsa lain
race *n* lomba, balap, pacuan; *vi* berlomba; *vt* membalap; **racecourse** *n*
pacuan kuda; **racehorse** *n* kuda
pacu, kuda balap; **racetrack** *n* sirkuit;
pacuan kuda; **racing** *n* balapan; ~ *car*
mobil balap; ~ *driver* pembalap
racial *adj* rasial, berhubungan dengan
suku bangsa; **racism** *n* [résizem]
rasisme, pembédaan rasial; **racist** *adj*
rasis; *n* orang yang membenci suku
bangsa lain ← **race**
racing *n* balapan; ~ *car* mobil balap; ~
driver pembalap ← **race**
rack *n* rak; *luggage* ~ tempat barang; *off
the* ~ écéran
racket, racquet *n* rakét; *badminton* ~
rakét bulu tangkis; *tennis* ~ rakét ténis
radar *n* [rédar] radar
radial ~ *tire* ban radial
radiant *adj* [rédient] bersinar; berseri-seri;
radiate *vt* memancarkan; **radiation** *n*
radiasi, penyinaran; **radiator** *n* [rédiétor]
radiator; alat pemanas
radical *adj* [radikel] radikal, ékstrém; *n*
orang radikal
radio *n* [rédio] radio; ~ *announcer*
penyiar; ~ *program* acara radio; ~ *station* stasiun radio; ~-*controlled* di-
kendalikan radio
radioactive *adj* [rédioaktif] radioaktif;
radiology *n* [rédioloji] radiologi
radiotherapy *n* [rédiothérapi] radiotérapi
radish *n* [radisy] lobak
radius *n* [rédius] jari-jari, radius; *a* ~ *of
1 kilometer* dalam jarak 1 kilométer
RAF *abbrev Royal Air Force* Angkatan
Udara Kerajaan Inggris
raffle *n* [rafel] undian; *vt* mengundi; *his*

school is raffling a car sekolahnya mengadakan undian berhadiah mobil

raft *n* rakit; *white water ~ing* arung jeram

rafter *n* kuda-kuda

rag *n* lap, kain perca; *~ doll* bonéka dari kain perca; *in ~s* compang-camping; *the ~ trade* industri busana; *from ~s to riches* orang miskin yang menjadi kaya raya; **ragged** *adj* [raged] compang-camping, robék-robék

rage *n* kemarahan, geram; *all the ~* sangat digemari; *in a ~* marah-marah; *vt* mengamuk, marah-marah; *sl* berpésta; **raging** *adj* bergelora

ragged *adj* [raged] compang-camping, robék-robék ← **rag**

raging *adj* bergelora ← **rage**

raid *n* razia, serangan, penggerébékan; *dawn ~* serangan fajar; *to launch a ~ on* menyerang, menyerbu; *vt* merazia; menyerang, menyerbu; **raider** *n* perompak

rail *n* rél; *by ~* dengan keréta api; *off the ~s* tergelincir; **railing** *n* susuran; **railroad, railway** *n* jalan keréta api; *railway station* stasiun keréta api; *railway yards* langsiran

rain *n, vi* hujan; *driving ~, heavy ~* hujan deras; *light ~* gerimis; *to be ~ed out* batal karena hujan; *to get caught in the ~* kehujanan; **rainbow** *n* pelangi, bianglala; **raincheck** *n to take a ~ on* menerima undangan untuk lain waktu; **raincoat** *n* jas hujan; **raindrop** *n* tétésan hujan; **rainfall** *n* curah hujan; **rainforest** *n* hutan tropis; **rainwater** *n* [rénwoter] air hujan; **rainy** *adj* banyak hujan; *~ season* musim hujan; *to save for a ~ day* menabung untuk masa depan

raise *n* kenaikan; *vt* mengangkat, menaikkan, meninggikan, meningkatkan; menimbulkan; *~ a child* membesarkan (anak); *~ money* mengumpulkan dana

raisin *n* kismis

rake *n* penggaruk; *v* menggaruk, menyapu

rally *n* réli; pertemuan; *~ driver* peréli;

vi berkumpul, berhimpun; *~ around* mendukung, memberi dukungan

ram *n* biri-biri jantan; *vt* membenturkan

ramble *n* [rambel] pengembaraan; *vi* berjalan kaki, mengembara; berbicara bertélé-télé

ramification *n* [ramifikésyen] dampak

ramp *n* jalur mendaki, jalur yang melandai

rampant *adj* merajaléla; *an effect of the crisis was ~ inflation* satu dampak akibat krisis adalah inflasi yang naik secara tidak terkendali

ran *v, pf →* **run**

ranch *n* peternakan, pertanian

rancid *adj* anyir

rancor, rancour *n* dendam, benci

rand, R *n* rand, mata uang Afrika Selatan

random *at ~* secara sembarangan, membabi buta; **randomly** *adv* secara acak

rang *v, pf →* **ring**

range *n* [rénj] jajaran, barisan; kisaran, jangkauan; lapangan, tempat; *~ hood* penangkap asap dapur; *mountain ~* pegunungan; *rifle ~* lapangan témbak; *vi* berkisar; *prices ~ between cheap and expensive* harga berkisar dari murah hingga mahal; **ranger** *n* penjaga hutan; **rangy** *adj* [rénji] tinggi (badan)

rank *n* pangkat, derajat; pangkalan; *taxi ~* pangkalan taksi; *~ and file* militér bawahan; rakyat jelata; *vi* menduduki; *Henin ~s no.1 in the world* Henin menduduki peringkat pertama di dunia; *vt* mengatur, menyusun; menggolongkan; **ranking** *n* urutan

ransack *vt* menggeledah; *the burglars ~ed the house* maling menggeledah rumah

ransom *n* (uang) tebusan, penebusan; *to hold someone to ~* menyandera

rap *n* musik rap; ketukan; *to take the ~* menerima hukuman; *vi* mengetuk; *~ on the door* mengetuk pintu

rape *n* perkosaan, pemerkosaan; *vt* memerkosa, menggagahi; **rapist** *n* pemerkosa

rapid *adj* [rapid] cepat, lekas; *mass ~*

transit (MRT) angkutan umum massal
dan cepat; **rapids** *n, pl* jeram; **rapidly**
adv dengan cepat

rapist *n* pemerkosa ← **rape**

rapt *adj, coll* suka sekali

rare *adj* mentah; jarang; *~, medium or
well done?* mentah, setengah matang
atau matang?; **rarely** *adv* jarang

rascal *n* bangsat

rash *n* gatal-gatal; *nappy* ~ ruam popok

raspberry *n* rasbéri, *arch* frambozen

rat *n* tikus (besar); *~ poison* racun tikus;
~ race kehidupan kota yang amat
sibuk; *to smell a ~* menjadi curiga

rate *n* tarif, perbandingan, angka;
kecepatan; *birth ~* angka kelahiran; *exchange ~* kurs; *interest ~* suku bunga;
at any ~ bagaimanapun; *vt* menilai; *to
~ a mention* disebut; **rated** *adj* dinilai,
dianggap; **rating** *n* penilaian

rather *adv* agak, rada, cukup; melainkan;
~ than daripada; *I'd ~* saya lebih suka

ratification *n* [ratifikésyen] ratifikasi,
pengesahan; **ratify** *vt* [ratifai] mengesahkan, meratifikasi

rating *n* penilaian ← **rate**

ratio *n* [résyio] perbandingan

ration *n* rangsum, jatah; *vt* merangsum;
petrol is ~ed bénsin dijatah; **rationing**
n penjatahan

rational *adj* rasional, masuk akal

rationale *n* [rasional] alasan

rattan *n* rotan; *~ chair* kursi rotan

rattle *n* [ratel] mainan bayi yang berbunyi; *vi* gemertak; *~ on* mencerocos;
vt, coll membuat bingung

ravage *vt* [ravej] membinasakan,
merusakkan

rave *n ~ (party)* pésta dansa; *vi* meraban;
sl sangat memuji; *raving mad* sangat
gila

raven *n* burung gagak; *~-haired* berambut hitam

ravenous *adj* [ravenus] sangat lapar

ravine *n* [ravin] jurang

ravishing *adj* menggairahkan, sangat
menarik

raw *adj* mentah; kasar; *~ materials* bahan
mentah; *~ meat* daging mentah; *~ silk*
sutera kasar

ray *n* sinar; *a ~ of hope* seberkas harapan

ray *n* ikan pari

raze *vt* membongkar, menghancurkan
sampai rata; *the authorities ~d the
shacks under the bridge* pemerintah
membongkar gubuk-gubuk di kolong
jembatan

razor *n* pisau cukur

RC *abbrev Roman Catholic* Katolik

Rd *abbrev Road* Jl (Jalan), Jl Ry (Jalan
Raya)

RE *abbrev Religious Education* pendidikan agama

re *conj* [ri] soal, perihal

re- *pref* kembali, ulang

reach *n* [ric] jangkauan; *within ~* terjangkau; *vt* sampai, tiba, mencapai;
menghubungi; *Sandra has already
~ed the advanced class* Sandra sudah
sampai kelas lanjut

react *vi* [riakt] beréaksi; menanggapi;
reaction *n* tanggapan, réaksi; **reac-
tionary** *adj* konsérvatif; *n* orang konsérvatif; **reactive** *adj* réaktif; **reactor**
n réaktor

read *vi* [rid] **read read** [réd] membaca;
~ aloud membaca dengan suara keras;
~ to membacakan; *~ the Koran, ~
Arabic* mengaji; *~ between the lines*
mengerti pesan yang tersirat; *~ up on*
mempelajari; *~ someone's mind* membaca pikiran orang; *a good ~* buku
yang menarik untuk dibaca; **reader** *n*
pembaca; buku bacaan; **reading** *n*
membaca; bacaan; *he doesn't like ~*
dia tidak suka membaca

readily *adv* [rédili] laku, laris, cepat;
ready *adj* siap, sedia; selesai, sudah; *~
to use* siap pakai

reading *n* [riding] membaca; bacaan; *~
room* ruang baca ← **read**

real *adj* [riil] nyata, betul, sejati; *adv*
sangat, benar-benar; *~-life story* kisah
sejati; *~ estate* properti; **reality** *n* [rial-
iti] kenyataan, réalitas; **realization**
n kesadaran; perwujudan; **realize** *vi*
sadar; *vt* mewujudkan, melaksanakan;
*the young man finally ~d his dream of
becoming a singer* pemuda itu akhirnya
mewujudkan cita-citanya menjadi

penyanyi; **realistic** *adj* [rialistik] realistis; **realistically** *adv* secara réalistis; **really** *adv* sangat, benar-benar; betulkah

realm *n* [rélm] dunia; kerajaan

ream *n* [rim] rim; ~s banyak sekali

reap *vt* [rip] menuai, memungut; **reaper** *n* penuai; *grim* ~ malaikat maut

rear *adj, n* [rir] (bagian) belakang; pantat; ~ *view mirror* kaca spion; *at the* ~ di belakang; *vt* membesarkan; *that couple has* ~*ed over ten children* pasangan itu telah membesarkan lebih dari sepuluh anak

reason *n* [rizen] sebab, alasan; akal (budi); *it stands to* ~ sudah tentu, mémang; *within* ~ yang pantas, yang masuk akal; *without* ~*, no* ~ tanpa sebab; *vi* berunding; **reasonable** *adj* [rizenabel] masuk akal; **reasonably** *adv* cukup

reassure *vt* [riasyur] menenteramkan hati, menenangkan

rebate *n* potongan harga

rebel *n* [rébel] pemberontak; *vi* [rebél] memberontak; *the farmers* ~*led against the new agrarian laws* para petani memberontak karena peraturan pertanahan yang baru; **rebellion** *n* pemberontakan; **rebellious** *adj* bersifat melawan

rebuke *n* teguran; *vi* menegur, memberi teguran

recalcitrant *adj* keras kepala, kurang ajar

recall *n* [rikol] ingatan; pemanggilan kembali; *v* ingat; *vt* memanggil kembali, menarik kembali; *the 2004 model was* ~*ed to the factory* tipe tahun 2004 ditarik kembali oléh pabrik

recapitulate *vi* [rikapityulét] **recap** *coll* mengambil kesimpulan, melihat kembali pokok-pokok utama

recapture *n* [rikaptyur] perebutan kembali; *vt* merebut kembali

recede *vi* surut, menyusut, mundur; *receding hairline* mulai botak

receipt *n* [risit] kuitansi, tanda terima, struk; penerimaan; *on* ~ *of* setelah menerima; **receive** *vt* menerima, mendapat, memperoléh; menyambut;

receiver *n* (pesawat) penerima; gagang télépon; **reception** *n* resépsi; penyambutan; tangkapan

recent *adj* baru; **recently** *adv* baru-baru ini

reception *n* [resépsyen] resépsi; penyambutan; tangkapan; **receptionist** *n* resépsionis; **receptive** *adj* [reséptiv] terbuka ← **receive**

recess *n* [risés] istirahat; *in* ~ sedang istirahat, tidak bersidang

recession *n* resési

recharge *vt* mengecas, mengisi ulang

recipe *n* [résipi] resép

reciprocal *adj* [resiprokal] saling, timbal balik; **reciprocate** *v* membalas

recital *n* pertunjukan, konsér; **recite** *v* membaca dari luar kepala, mendéklamasikan; ~ *from the Koran* mengaji

reckless *adj* nékat, ugal-ugalan, berani; **recklessly** *adv* ugal-ugalan, secara nékat

reckon *vt* menghitung; *sl* pikir; ~ *with* berurusan dengan; **reckoning** *n* perhitungan

reclaim *vt* memperoléh kembali; menguruk pantai; **reclamation** *n* pengurukan pantai, réklamasi

recline *vi* menyandar, tiduran; *reclining chair* kursi pantai

recognition *n* [rékognisyen] pengenalan; penghargaan; **recognizable** *adj* [rékognaizabel] dapat dikenal; **recognize** *vt* mengenal, mengenali; mengakui, menghargai

recollect *v* ingat akan, mengingat; **recollection** *n* ingatan; *to the best of my* ~ seingat saya

recommend *vt* menganjurkan; memuji; merékomendasi; **recommendation** *n* rékomendasi, saran

reconcile *vi* berdamai

reconciliation *n* [rékonsilésyen] rékonsiliasi, perdamaian

reconsider *v* [rikonsider] mempertimbangkan kembali

record *n* [rékord] catatan; daftar; rékor; piringan hitam; dokumén; ~ *player* gramofon; *off the* ~ tidak boléh disiarkan; *to break a* ~ memecahkan rékor; *pl* arsip; *vt* [rekord] mencatat,

mendaftar, merekam; **recording** *n*
rekaman; ~ *artist* penyanyi, artis
recorder *n* semacam suling; alat perekam
recording *n* rekaman; ~ *artist* penyanyi,
artis ← **record**
recount *n* penghitungan ulang; *vi*
menghitung ulang; *vt* menceritakan
kembali
recover *vi* [rikaver] sembuh, pulih; *vt*
menemukan kembali, menyelamatkan;
Ian ~ed the camera he left on the train
Ian mendapatkan kembali kaméra
yang ketinggalan di keréta api;
recovery *n* [rikaveri] kesembuhan;
penemuan kembali
recreate *vt* [rikriét] menciptakan ulang;
recreation *n* [rékriésyen] **recreational**
adj hiburan, rékréasi
recruit *n* [rekrut] pegawai baru, orang
baru; *vt* merékrut; **recruitment** *n*
penerimaan pegawai baru, perekrutan
rectangle *n* [rektanggel] **rectangular**
adj empat persegi panjang
rectify *vt* [rektifai] membetulkan,
meralat
rector *n* réktor
rectum *n* dubur
recur *vi* (terjadi) kembali, terulang;
recurrence *n* [rekarens] terjadinya
kembali
recycle *v* [risaikel] didaur ulang; **recycled** *adj* daur ulang; **recycling** *n* daur
ulang
red *adj* mérah; ~ *alert* siaga satu; ~
bean kacang mérah; ~ *card* kartu
mérah; ~ *Cross* Palang Mérah; ~ *hair*
rambut mérah; ~ *herring* sesuatu yang
menyesatkan; ~ *light* lampu mérah; ~
meat daging mérah; ~ *pepper* paprika
mérah; ~ *tape* birokrasi; ~ *wine* anggur
mérah; *in the* ~ berhutang; ~*letter day*
hari penting, tanggal mérah; ~*light
district* daérah lampu mérah; *caught*
~*handed* tertangkap basah; **redden**
vi memérah; **reddish** *adj* keméráh-
mérahan; **redhead** *n* [rédhéd] orang
yang berambut mérah
redecorate *v* menata kembali, menghias
kembali
redeem *vi* menebus; ~ *a voucher*

memakai vocer belanja; **redemption** *n*
penyelamatan; penebusan
redhead *n* [rédhéd] orang yang berambut mérah ← **red**
redirect *vi* meneruskan; *the post office
~ed Rebecca's mail to her brother
when she was away* kantor pos
meneruskan surat ke alamat adiknya
selama Rebecca pergi
redo *vt* [ridu] **redid redone** membuat
kembali, melakukan kembali; *he had
to ~ his painting* dia terpaksa membuat
kembali lukisannya
reduce *vt* mengurangi, memperkecil; ~
speed mengurangi kecepatan; **reduction** *n* potongan, pengurangan, penurunan, réduksi
redwood *n, US* sejenis pohon tinggi
reef *n* (batu) karang; *coral* ~ terumbu
karang
reek *n* bau; *vi* ~ *of* berbau
re-elect *vt* [ri elékt] memilih kembali;
re-elected *adj* terpilih kembali; **re-
election** *n* pilihan kembali
ref. *reference* rujukan
refer *vi* mengacu; ~ *to* mengacu pada;
menyebut, menunjukkan; mengenai; *vt*
merujuk, mengarahkan; **referee** *n*
wasit; **reference** *n* surat keterangan,
réferénsi; **referral** *n* (surat) rujukan
refill *n* isi ulang; pengisian kembali
refine *vt* menghaluskan, memperhalus,
menyaring; **refined** *adj* halus; **refinery**
n kilang
reflect *vi* membayang; merenung; ~ *on*
merenungkan; *vt* mencerminkan,
memantulkan; **reflection** *n* bayangan;
renungan; **reflective** *adj* [refléktiv]
memantulkan sinar; termenung;
reflector *n* refléktor, pemantul cahaya
reflex *adj, n* [rifléks] réfléks
reforestation *n* réboisasi
reform *n* perubahan, réformasi; ~ *process* prosés réformasi; *vt* mengubah;
menyusun kembali; ~ *school* sekolah
untuk anak-anak nakal; **reformation** *n*
penyusunan kembali; **reformed** *adj*
sudah berubah
refrain *n* bagian ulangan; refréin; *vi* ~
from tidak, jangan (melakukan)

refresh *vt* **refreshing** *adj* menyegarkan; **refreshed** *adj* segar kembali; **refresher** ~ *course* kursus penyegaran; **refreshments** *n, pl* minuman, makanan

refrigerate *vt* [refrijerét] mendinginkan; **refrigeration** *n* pendinginan; **refrigerator** *n* lemari és, kulkas

refuel *vi* mengisi bensin; *the plane ~s at Colombo* pesawat mengisi avtur di Colombo

refuge *n* [réfyuj] tempat suaka, perlindungan; *to take* ~ berlindung; **refugee** *n* pengungsi

refund *n* pembayaran kembali; *vt* mengembalikan uang

refusal *n* penolakan; **refuse** *n* [réfyus] sampah; *v* [refyuz] menolak

regain *vi* mendapat kembali; ~ *consciousness* siuman; *Chris ~ed his world boxing title* Chris meraih kembali gelar tinju dunia

regard *n* hormat; *as ~s, in ~ to, with ~ to* sehubungan dengan, mengenai; *my ~s* salam saya; *vt* menganggap; **regarding** *conj* mengenai, tentang; **regardless** *conj* ~ *(of)* tanpa menghiraukan; *the band played on* ~ para pemain musik tetap bermain

regency *n* kabupatén; **regent** *n* bupati

regenerate *vi* [rijénerét] hidup kembali, tumbuh kembali; *vt* menghidupkan kembali

reggae *n* [régé] sejenis musik dari Hindia Barat

regiment *n* [réjiment] résimén

region *n* [rijen] daérah, wilayah; **regional** *adj* daérah; ~ *government* pemerintah daérah (pémda)

register *n* [réjister] daftar; *vi* daftar; *vt* mendaftarkan; mencatat; **registered** *adj* tercatat, terdaftar; ~ *mail* pos tercatat; **registrar** *n* pendaftar, pencatat; panitera; **registration** *n* pendaftaran, pencatatan; *vehicle* ~ surat tanda nomor kendaraan (STNK); **registry** *n* (kantor) pendaftaran; ~ *office* kantor catatan sipil

regret *n* rasa sesal; *v* menyesal; *we ~ the incident* peristiwa itu kami sesalkan

regular *adj* [réguler] biasa; teratur;

tetap; sedang; *a ~ soda* soda ukuran sedang; *at ~ intervals* secara teratur; *n* pelanggan; **regularly** *adv* secara teratur

regulate *vt* [régulét] mengatur; **regulation** *n* aturan, peraturan

rehabilitate *vt* [rihabilitét] meréhabilitasi; **rehabilitation** *n* réhabilitasi; *in ~* sedang menjalani réhabilitasi

rehearsal *n* [rihérsal] latihan; *dress ~* gladi bersih, gladi resik; **rehearse** *vi* berlatih; *vt* melatih

reign *n* [réin] pemerintahan, masa bertakhta; ~ *of terror* masa pemerintahan yang mengerikan; *vi* memerintah, bertakhta

reimburse *vt* [riimburs] membayar kembali, mengganti uang; *his office ~d him for all expenses* kantornya mengganti uang yang telah dia keluarkan; **reimbursement** *n* penggantian uang

reindeer *n* [reindir] *pl* **reindeer** rusa kutub

reinforce *vt* [riinfors] memperkuat, memperkokoh; **reinforcement** *n* penguatan, pengokohan; *pl* pasukan tambahan

reins *n, pl* kekang, tali kuda

reject *n* [rijékt] barang yang ditolak, apkiran; *vt* [rejékt] menolak; **rejection** *n* penolakan

rejoice *vi* bergembira, bersyukur; ~ *in* mensyukuri

rejoin *vi* membalas, menjawab; *vt* bergabung kembali dengan; *South Africa has ~ed the UN* Afrika Selatan telah bergabung kembali dengan PBB

relapse *n* kambuh, sakit lagi

relate *vi* berkaitan; *vt* menceritakan; mengaitkan, menghubungkan; ~ *to* memahami, bersimpati; **related** *adj* bersanak saudara; berkaitan, berhubungan; **relation** *n* saudara, keluarga; hubungan; *in ~ to* mengenai, tentang; **relationship** *n* hubungan; *in a ~* pacaran; **relative** *adj* rélatif; *n* saudara, keluarga; **relatively** *adv* secara rélatif

relax *vi* bersantai-santai, riléks; *vt* mengendurkan; **relaxation** *n* rélaksasi; **relaxing** *adj* santai relay *n* (lari) éstafét; *vt* menyampaikan, meneruskan

release *n* pembébasan; rilis, keluaran; *vt* melepaskan, membébaskan, memerdékakan; merelis

relegate *vt* [rélegét] membuang; menurunkan; *his favorite team was ~d to Division 1* tim kesayangannya didégradasi ke Divisi 1

relent *vi* mengalah, menyerah; **relentless** *adj* terus-menerus

relevance *n* hubungan, sangkut paut, rélevansi; *of ~* rélevan; **relevant** *adj* bersangkut paut, rélevan

reliability *n* [rilayabiliti] keadaan yang dapat dipercaya; **reliable** *adj* [rilayabel] andal, tepercaya; **reliance** *n* ketergantungan; **reliant** *adj* tergantung; *~ on* tergantung pada; *self-~* mandiri; **rely** *vi* [relai] *~ on* percaya pada, tergantung pada; *you can ~ on me* kamu bisa percaya pada saya, kamu bisa mengandalkan saya

relic *n* [rélik] (barang) peninggalan; *that house is a ~ of the Dutch era* rumah itu peninggalan jaman Belanda

relief *n* [rilif] bantuan, pertolongan, sumbangan; rasa lega; *what a ~* syukur; *Isl* alhamdulillah; *in ~* timbul; **relieve** *vt* membantu, menolong; *~ yourself* buang air; **relieved** *adj* lega, plong

religion *n* [rilijen] agama; **religious** *adj* beragama, soléh, réligius; **religiously** *adv* dengan rajin

relinquish *vt* menyerahkan, meninggalkan, melepaskan; *Dave did not want to ~ his work car* Dave tidak mau menyerahkan mobil kantor

relish *n* [rélisy] acar, bumbu; *n* cita rasa, nikmat; *with ~* dengan antusias; *vi* menikmati; *Harris ~ed his opportunity to study abroad* Harris menikmati kesempatan belajar di luar negeri

relocate *v* pindah; *next year we will ~ to new premises* tahun depan kami akan pindah ke tempat baru; **relocation** *n* perpindahan, rélokasi

reluctance *n* keengganan; **reluctant** *adj* enggan; *they were ~ to leave* meréka

enggan pergi; **reluctantly** *adv* dengan enggan

rely *vi* [relai] *~ on* percaya pada, tergantung pada, tergantung pada; *you can ~ on me* kamu bisa percaya pada saya, kamu bisa mengandalkan saya

remain *vi* tinggal, tetap; *pl* sisa, peninggalan; *Portuguese ~* peninggalan Portugis; **remainder** *n* sisa; **remaining** *adj* tersisa

remake *n* pembuatan kembali, pembuatan ulang; *a ~ of 'Grease'* vérsi baru film *Grease*; *vt* **remade remade** membuat kembali, membuat ulang

remand *vt* mengirim kembali; *on ~* menunggu sidang pengadilan; *the suspect was ~ed in custody* tersangka kembali ditahan

remark *n* koméntar; catatan; *opening ~s* kata-kata pembuka; *vi* berkoméntar; berkata; *~ on* mengoméntari; **remarkable** *adj* pantas diperhatikan, luar biasa; **remarkably** *adv* secara luar biasa; *you're looking ~ well* anda tampak sangat séhat

remarry *vi* menikah lagi; *vt* menikah

remedial *adj* [remidial] yang berhubungan dengan perbaikan; *~ English* pelajaran tambahan bahasa Inggris (di sekolah); **remedy** *n* [rémédi] obat, penawar; *home ~* obat tradisional; *vt* memperbaiki

remember *vi* ingat, mengingat; *vt* menyampaikan salam; *~ me to* salam saya untuk; **remembrance** *n* kenangan; *~ Day UK* Hari Pahlawan (tgl 11 November); *in ~ of* mengenang

remind *vt* [remaind] mengingatkan; *please ~ me* tolong ingatkan saya; *this shirt ~s me of him* baju ini mengingatkan saya padanya; **reminder** *n* surat peringatan

reminisce *vi* [réminis] bernostalgia; *~ about* mengenang; **reminiscence** *n* kenangan

remix *n* campuran ulang; *vt* mencampur

remnant *n* sisa, bekas; *pl* kain perca

remote *adj, n* terpencil; jarak jauh; *~ control* rémot

removable *adj* [remuvabel] dapat diambil, dapat dipindahkan; **removal** *n* pemindahan; **removalists** *n, pl* layanan ékspédisi; **remove** *vt* memindahkan; menjauhkan; *cousin once ~d* anak sepupu; **remover** *n* penghilang; *stain* ~ penghilang noda; *nail polish* ~ bahan penghilang kuték

render *vt* membuat; *the new law ~s this regulation null and void* akibat undang-undang baru, peraturan ini sudah tidak berlaku lagi

rendezvous *n* [rondévu] (tempat) pertemuan; *vi* bertemu

renew *vt* memperbarui, memperpanjang; ~ *a passport* memperpanjang paspor; **renewable** *adj* dapat diperbarui; ~ *energy* énérgi yang bisa diperbaharui; **renewal** *n* pembaruan, pembaharuan; *urban* ~ pembaharuan kota

renovate *v* merénovasi; *vt* merénovasi, memperbaiki; *we're renovating at the moment* kami sedang merénovasi rumah; **renovation** *n* perbaikan, rénovasi

renowned *adj* [renaund] masyhur, kenamaan, tersohor

rent *n* (uang) séwa; *to pay the* ~ membayar uang séwa; *vt* menyéwa, mengontrak; ~ *out* menyéwakan, mengontrakkan; ~ *a house* mengontrak rumah; **rental** *adj* séwaan; ~ *car* mobil séwaan; *DVD* ~ réntal DVD

reorganization, reorganisation *n* pengaturan kembali, penyusunan ulang; **reorganize** *vt* mengatur kembali, mengatur ulang

Rep. *abbrev Republic* Rep. (Républik)

repaid *vt, pf* → **repay**

reparations *n, pl* (uang) pampasan; ganti rugi; *the losing side had to pay ~ to their conqueror* pihak yang kalah diwajibkan membayar ganti rugi ke pihak pemenang; **repair** n perbaikan, réparasi; *shoe ~s* réparasi sepatu; *vt* memperbaiki, meréparasi

repatriate *v* [ripatriét] memulangkan ke negaranya; **repatriation** *n* pemulangan

repay *vt* **repaid repaid** membayar kembali, mengganti; *how can I ever ~ you?* bagaimana saya bisa membalas kebaikan anda?; **repayment** *n* angsuran, cicilan

repeal *vt* [repil] membatalkan, mencabut

repeat *n* [repit] pengulangan, tindakan yang diulang-ulang; tayangan ulang; ~ *offender* résidivis, bromocorah; *vi* berulang; *vt* mengulangi; **repeatedly** *adv* [repitedli] berulang kali; **repetition** *n* [répetisyen] perulangan; **repetitive** *adj* [repétitiv] berulang-ulang; **repetitively** *adv* secara berulang-ulang

repel *vt* menolak; **repellent** *n* obat (nyamuk, serangga)

repent *vi* bertobat, insaf; *vt* menyesali; **repentance** *n* tobat; **repentant** *adj* insaf

rephrase *vt* [rifréz] menyusun kembali (kalimat), mengatakan dengan kata lain

replace *vt* mengganti, menggantikan; **replacement** *n* ganti, pengganti; pergantian

replay *n* tayangan ulang (pertandingan olahraga); *vt* memutarkan kembali

replica *n* [réplika] tiruan

reply *n* [replai] jawaban, sahutan, balasan; *right of* ~ hak menjawab; *vi* menjawab, menyahut, membalas; ~ *to* menjawab kepada, membalas kepada; ~ *with* membalas dengan, menukas

report *n* laporan, pemberitaan; *financial* ~ laporan keuangan; *school* ~ rapot; *vi* melapor; *you must* ~ *to the embassy* anda harus melapor di kedutaan besar; *vt* melaporkan, memberitakan; **reporter** *n* wartawan; **reporting** *n* réportase

represent *vt* mewakili; menggambarkan, melambangkan; **representation** *n* perwakilan; gambaran; **representative** *adj* [réprezéntativ] terwakili; *n* wakil, utusan

repressive *adj* [représiv] bersifat menekan, menindas

reprimand *n* [réprimand] teguran; *vt* menegur; *the naughty schoolboys were ~ed by the principal* murid-murid nakal ditegur oléh kepala sekolah

reprint *n* cétak ulang; *vt* mencétak ulang

reproduce *vi* mempunyai keturunan,

berkembang biak; *vt* meniru; **reproduction** *n* réproduksi, perkembang-
biakan; **reproductive** *adj* berkaitan
dengan réproduksi manusia
reptile *n* binatang melata
republic *n* républik; *the ~ of Indonesia*
Républik Indonesia (RI); *the People's
~ of China (PRC)* Républik Rakyat
Cina (RRC); *Union of Soviet Socialist
~s (USSR)* Uni Soviét (US); **republican** *adj* berkaitan dengan républik,
républikan; pro-républik; *n* pendukung
républik; **Republican** *~ Party* Partai
Républik
repulsive *adj* [repalsiv] menjijikkan
reputable *adj* [répyutabel] mempunyai
nama baik; **reputation** *n* [répyutésyen]
nama baik, réputasi; **repute** *ill ~* nama
buruk
request *n* [rekuést] permohonan, permintaan; *by ~* atas permintaan; *vt*
memohon, minta; *~ a song* kirim lagu
require *vt* [rekuair] memerlukan;
requirement *n* syarat; *pl* kebutuhan
rescue *n* [réskyu] penyelamatan; *search
and ~ (SAR)* (usaha) penyelamatan; *to
come to someone's ~* menyelamatkan
orang; *vt* menolong, menyelamatkan;
the lifeguard ~d the drowning tourist
penjaga pantai menyelamatkan wisatawan yang tenggelam; **rescuer** *n*
penyelamat
research *n* [riserc] penelitian, risét; *~
and development (R & D)* penelitian
dan pengembangan (litbang); *to do ~*
mengadakan penelitian; *vt* [resérc]
meneliti, merisét; **researcher** *n*
peneliti
resemblance *n* [rezémblens] kemiripan; **resemble** *vt* [rezémbel] menyerupai, mirip; *Andrew ~s his father*
Andrew mirip ayahnya
resent *vt* benci, marah, cemburu;
Joshua did not ~ his new stepmother
Joshua tidak benci ibu tirinya; **resentful** *adj* marah, cemburu; **resentment** *n*
rasa marah, dendam
reservation *n* résérvasi, pesanan, buking; keraguan; *Terri had ~s about
whether the program would succeed*

Terri ragua kan keberhasilan program
itu; **reserve** *n* cadangan, persediaan;
nature ~ cagar alam; *vt* memesan,
menyediakan; **reserved** *adj* pendiam;
telah dipesan
reservoir *n* [résérvwar] waduk
reshuffle *n* [risyafel] perombakan;
cabinet ~ perombakan kabinét; *vt*
merombak
reside *vi* berdiam; *the Ambassador ~s
in the city center* Duta Besar berdiam
di pusat kota; **residence** *n* kediaman;
permanent ~ (PR) hak tinggal secara
tetap; **residency** *n, arch* karésidénan;
resident *n* penduduk, penghuni; *arch*
résidén; **residential** *adj* berkaitan
dengan perumahan; *~ address* alamat
rumah
resign *vi* [rizain] mundur, mengundurkan diri, berhenti bekerja; **resigned**
adj [rezaind] pasrah; **resignation**
n [rézignésyen] pengunduran diri;
kepasrahan; *to hand in one's ~* mengundurkan diri
resin *n* [rézin] damar
resist *vt* [rezist] melawan, menahan
(diri); *I can't ~ chocolate* saya tidak
bisa menahan diri kalau makan cokelat; **resistance** *n* perlawanan, pertahanan
resit *vt* resat resat menempuh kembali
(ujian), hér; *When can they ~ their
exam?* Kapan meréka bisa ikut ujian
hér?
resolution *n* keputusan, résolusi;
resolve *vi* memutuskan, bermaksud;
*the Security Council ~d to assist
Myanmar* Déwan Keamanan memutuskan agar membantu Myanmar
resonance *n* gema, gaung
resort *n* tempat beristirahat, résor
resource *n* [resors] sumber daya;
human ~s (HR) personalia, sumber
daya manusia (SDM); *natural ~* sumber daya alam; **resourceful** *adj* cerdas, banyak akal
respect *n* hormat; hal; *in that ~* mengenai, berhubungan dengan hal itu; *with
~ to* dalam hal itu; *to pay your ~s*
melayat; memberi hormat; *vt* meng-

hormati; **respectable** *adj* [respékta-bel] baik-baik, terhormat; **respectful** *adj* (penuh) hormat; **respectfully** *adv* yours ~ hormat kami
respective *adj* **respectively** *adv* [respéktivli] masing-masing; *Karin and Josie visited their ~ fathers today* Karin dan Josie mengunjungi ayahnya masing-masing hari ini
respiration *n* pernapasan, pernafasan; *artificial* ~ pernapasan buatan; **respire** *vi* bernapas
respond *vt* membalas, menjawab; *~ to* menanggapi; **respondent** *n* orang yang menjawab; **response** *n* tanggapan, jawaban, réspons; *in ~ to* sebagai tanggapan atas; **responsive** *adj* [responsiv] mau mendengarkan, menanggapi
responsibility *n* [responsibiliti] tanggung jawab; **responsible** *adj* [responsibel] bertanggung jawab; *~ for* bertanggung jawab atas; *~ to* bertanggung jawab kepada; **responsibly** *adv* secara bertanggung jawab
rest *n* (waktu) istirahat; sisa; *~ area* tempat istirahat; *vi* berhenti, beristirahat, mengaso; tinggal; *~ in peace (RIP)* beristirahat dengan tenang; *~ on* berdasarkan, bersandarkan; *vt* menyandarkan, meletakkan; **restless** *adj* resah, gelisah; **restroom** *n* toilét, WC
restaurant *n* réstoran, rumah makan; *~ car* gerbong réstorasi; **restaurateur, restauranteur** *n* [réstronter] pemilik réstoran
restless *adj* resah, gelisah ← **rest**
restoration *n* perbaikan, pemugaran; pengembalian; **restore** *vt* memperbaiki, mengembalikan, memugar
restrain *vt* menahan; **restraint** *n* penahan
restrict *vt* membatasi; **restricted** *adj* terbatas; **restriction** *n* pembatasan
restroom *n* toilét, WC ← **rest**
restructure *vt* menyusun kembali; **restructuring** *n* penyusunan kembali
result *n* akibat, hasil; *vi ~ in* mengakibatkan, menyebabkan; **resultant** *adj* hasil, akibat
resumé, resume *n* [rézumé] riwayat hidup, ikhtisar

resume *v* [rezyum] mulai lagi, meneruskan; *we ~ broadcasting at 5 am* kami mulai menyiar kembali pada pukul 5 pagi; **resumption** *n* penerusan
resurrect *vt* menghidupkan kembali; **resurrection** *n* kebangkitan
resuscitate *vt* [risasitét] menghidupkan kembali, memberi pernapasan buatan; **resuscitation** *n* [risasitésyen] *artificial* ~ pernapasan buatan
ret. *abbrev retired* pénsiunan, purnawirawan
retail *adj* [ritél] éceran, ritél; *n* perdagangan éceran; *recommended ~ price (RRP)* harga éceran yang disarankan; *vi* berharga éceran; *these jeans ~ for $98* harga éceran celana jins ini $98; **retailer** *n* pengécér, pedagang éceran
retain *vt* menyimpan, menahan, tetap; **retainer** *n* alat penahan (gigi); **retention** *n* daya tahan, daya ingat
retarded *adj, derog* tunagrahita, terkebelakang
retch *vi* [ric] muntah
retention *n* daya tahan, daya ingat
retire *vi* pénsiun; *Klinsmann has ~d* Klinsmann telah menggantung sepatu; **retired** *adj* ret. *abbrev* pénsiunan; *~ general* Jénderal (Purnawirawan); **retiree** *n* orang pénsiunan; **retirement** *n* masa pénsiun
retort *n* jawaban pedas; *v* menjawab dengan ketus
retract *vt* mencabut, menarik kembali; *~ a statement* menarik kembali pernyataan; **retraction** *n* pencabutan
retrain *vt* melatih kembali, melatih ulang
retreat *n* [retrit] penarikan (diri); retrét; *vi* mundur, menarik diri
retrenched *adj* dipéhakakan, diPHK-kan, diberhentikan; **retrenchment** *n* pemutusan hubungan kerja (PHK)
retrieval *n* [retrival] pengambilan kembali; **retrieve** *vt* mengambil, mendapat kembali
retrospective *n* paméran karya sepanjang masa, rétrospéktif; **retrospectively** *adv* secara rétrospéktif, sesudah wafat
return *n* kembali, pemulangan, perjalanan pulang; *~ address* alamat pe-

ngirim; ~ *ticket* karcis pulang pergi, tiket pulang pergi; ~ *to sender* dikembalikan kepada pengirim; *in* ~ *for* sebagai pengganti; *many happy ~s* selamat (ulang tahun); *on my* ~ sekembali saya; *vi* pulang, kembali; *vt* mengembalikan, membalas; ~ *a good deed* membalas budi

reunification *n* [riunifikésyen] penyatuan kembali, réunifikasi

reunion *n* [riunien] réuni; **reunite** *vi* bertemu kembali

reuse *vt* [riyuz] memakai kembali, memakai ulang

Rev. *abbrev Reverend* pendéta, Pdt.

reveal *vt* [revil] membuka, menyingkapkan; menyatakan; **revelation** *n* [révelésyen] wahyu

revenge *n* [revénj] (rasa) dendam, pembalasan; *to take* ~ membalas dendam

revenue *n* [révenyu] penghasilan, pendapatan

reverence *n* [révrens] hormat, takzim; **reverend** *n, Chr, abbrev* **Rev.** pendéta; ~ *Mother* Suster Kepala

reversal *n* pembalikan; **reverse** *adj* terbalik; *n* sisi balik; *in* ~ gigi mundur; *vi* mundur, memundurkan kendaraan; *vt* membalikkan

review *n* [revyu] tinjauan; résénsi; majalah; *vt* meninjau kembali; menilai; **reviewer** *n* penulis résénsi

revise *vi* membaca ulang, belajar untuk ujian; *vt* memperbaiki, memeriksa ulang, merévisi; **revision** *n* perbaikan, periksa ulang, révisi

revival *n* kebangkitan; **revive** *vi* bangun kembali; *vt* menghidupkan lagi

revoke *vt* mencabut, membatalkan

revolt *n* pemberontakan; *vi* memberontak; **revolting** *adj* menjijikkan, jorok

revolution *n* révolusi; perédaran; **revolutionary** *adj* révolusi, révolusionér; **revolve** *vi* berputar, berkisar; *revolving door* pintu putar

revolver *n* pistol, senjata laras péndék

reward *n* [reword] hadiah, imbalan, ganjaran; *vt* mengganjar; menghadiahi; **rewarding** *adj* menguntungkan, berguna, memuaskan; *being a teacher is very* ~ pekerjaan seorang guru sangat memuaskan

rewind *vt* memutar balik

rheumatism *n* [rumatizem] encok, rematik, sengal

rhino *sl* **rhinoceros** *n* [rainoseres] **rhino** *sl* badak; *one-horned* ~ badak bercula satu

rhododendron *n* [rododéndron] sejenis bunga mérah

rhombus *n* [rombus] belah ketupat

rhubarb *n* [rubarb] sejenis sayur

rhyme *n* [raim] sajak; *nursery* ~ lagu anak-anak; *vi* bersajak; **rhythm** *n* [rithem] irama, ritme; **rhythmic** *adj* [rithmik] berirama; ~ *gymnastics* senam irama

rib *n* tulang rusuk, iga; *spare ~s* iga panggang; **ribbed** *adj* bergerigi

ribbon *n* pita; *blue* ~ mutu terbaik

rice *n* padi; beras; nasi; ~ *cake* lontong; ~ *cracker* kerupuk; ~ *field* sawah; ladang; ~ *straw* jerami, mérang; *brown* ~ nasi mérah; *fried* ~ nasi goréng; *husked* ~ beras

rich *adj* kaya, subur; ~ *kid* anak kaya, anak gedongan; ~ *in protein* kaya akan protéin; **riches** *n, pl* kekayaan

rickety *adj* goyah, tidak stabil

rickshaw *n* bécak

rid *vt* membersihkan, membébaskan; *to get* ~ *of* menyingkirkan, menghilangkan; *we need to* ~ *the bedroom of mosquitoes* kita harus membersihkan kamar supaya tidak ada nyamuk; **riddance** *good* ~ syukur (sudah dibuang)

ridden *v, pf* → **ride**

riddle *n* [ridel] teka-teki

ride *n* perjalanan: *to go for a* ~ jalan-jalan (naik kendaraan); *vi* ~ *on* mengendarai, naik; ~ *on a donkey* naik keledai; *vt* **rode ridden** mengendarai, naik; ~ *a horse* naik kuda; ~ *a motorbike* mengendarai sepéda motor; **rider** *n* penunggang; pengendara; **riding** *n* naik kuda; *she goes* ~ *on the weekend* dia naik kuda pada akhir minggu

ridge *n* punggung gunung, punggung bukit

ridicule *n* [ridikyul] éjékan, olok-olok; *vt* menertawakan, mengéjék, memperolok; **ridiculous** *adj* menggelikan

riding *n* naik kuda; *she goes ~ on the weekend* dia naik kuda pada akhir minggu ← **ride**

rifle *n* [raifel] senapan, bedil; *~ range* lapangan témbak; *air ~* senapan angin

rift *n* celah; keretakan

rig *n* perlengkapan; *big ~* truk besar; *oil ~* alat pengebor minyak, alat pengeboran minyak; *vt* melakukan dengan curang; *~ged election* pemilu yang tidak jujur dan adil; **rigging** *n* perlengkapan, tali-temali

right *adj, adv* [rait] (sebelah) kanan; *~ angle* sudut siku-siku, tegak lurus; *~ wing* sayap kanan; *on the ~* di sebelah kanan

right *adv* betul, benar; patut, layak; *~ away* segera; *~ now* sekarang juga; *all ~* baiklah; *n* hak; *by ~s* sebetulnya, sebenarnya; *human ~s* hak azasi manusia (HAM); *~ of way* hak jalan terlebih dahulu; **righteous** *adj* [raices] adil; **rightly** *adv* dengan benar, sepantasnya, selayaknya

rigid *adj* [rijid] tegar, kaku

rigorous *adj* teliti; keras; *a ~ inspection* pemeriksaan yang teliti

rim *n* tepi (roda, piring); *wheel ~* vélg; *the Pacific ~* negara-negara di pinggiran Lautan Pasifik

rind *n* [raind] kulit (buah, kéju)

ring *n* cincin; lingkaran; jaringan; gelanggang; dering; *~ finger* jari manis; *~ road* jalan lingkar; *boxing ~* ring; *wedding ~* cincin kawin; *vi* **rang rung** berdering; *vt, coll ~ (up)* télepon, menélepon; *coll* ngebél; *~ back* télepon kembali; *~ the bell* membunyikan bél, memukul loncéng; **ringleader** *n* dalang, biang keladi; **ringtone** *n* nada dering; **ringworm** *n* kurap

rink *ice (skating) ~* gelanggang és; *roller-skating ~* gelanggang sepatu roda

rinse *n* bilasan; *blue-~* (rambut) dicét agak kebiru-biruan; *vt* membilas

riot *n* [raiot] kerusuhan; kegaduhan; *vi* rusuh, memberontak; *tailors ~ed across the city* tukang jahit memberontak di seantéro kota; **rioter** *n* perusuh, pemberontak

RIP *abbrev rest in peace* beristirahat dengan tenang

rip *n* robékan; *vi* robék; *vt* merobék; *~ off* merobék sampai putus; menipu

ripe *adj* masak, matang; *the time is ~* sudah waktunya; **ripen** *vi* menjadi matang

ripple *n* [ripel] riak

rise *n* kenaikan; *pay ~* kenaikan gaji; *vi* **rose risen** [rizen] bangkit, terbit, berdiri; *an early ~r* orang yang bangun pagi-pagi; *the sun ~s at 5.30* matahari terbit pada jam 5.30

risk *n* risiko; *vt* mengambil risiko; *high-~* berisiko tinggi; *don't ~ losing your job by taking lots of sick leave* jangan mengambil risiko dipecat karena sering cuti sakit; **risky** *adj* berisiko

rissole *n* perkedél daging

rite *n* upacara, tata cara; **ritual** *n* [rityual] upacara (agama)

rival *n* saingan, lawan; *vt* menyaingi; **rivalry** *n* persaingan

river *n* [river] sungai, kali; *~ bank* tepi sungai; *~ bed* dasar sungai; *~ mouth* muara; *the ~ Thames* Sungai Thames; **riverside** *adj* di pinggir sungai

rivet *n* [rivet] paku sumbat, rivet; *vt* memaku, memancangkan (dengan paku sumbat)

RM *abbrev Malaysian ringgit* ringgit

road *n* jalan (raya); *~ accident* kecelakaan lalu lintas; *~ map* peta perjalanan; *~ rage* marah-marah sambil mengendarakan mobil; *~ sign* rambu jalan; *~ show* tur keliling; *~ test* uji coba (mobil); *on the ~* di jalan; *to hit the ~* jalan, berangkat; **roadhouse** *n* rumah makan di pinggir kota; **roadside** *adj* pinggir jalan; **roadwork** *n* [rodwerk] perbaikan jalan; **roadworthy** *adj* [rodwerthi] layak jalan

roam *vi* berkelana, mengembara; *vt* menjelajahi; *dogs ~ed the streets* banyak anjing melalu-lalang di jalan

roar *n* aum; deru; *vi* mengaum; menderu

roast *adj* panggang; *~ beef* sapi pang-

gang; ~ *chicken* ayam bakar; *n* daging
panggang; *vt* memanggang, membakar

rob *vt* merampok, merampas; *I was
~bed of my purse* dompét saya diram-
pas; **robber** *n* perampok; **robbery** *n*
perampokan; *armed* ~ perampokan
bersenjata

robe *n* jubah

robin *n* sejenis burung kecil dengan
bulu dada berwarna mérah

robot *n* robot; **robotic** *adj* secara otomatis,
seperti robot; *n, pl* ilmu robot

robust *adj* kuat, kokoh

rock *n* batu, cadas; *~climbing* panjat
tebing; ~ *music* musik *rock*; ~ *solid*
kokoh, tidak tergoyahkan; *vt* mengayunkan; menggoncang; *~ing chair*
kursi goyang; *~ing horse* kuda goyang,
kuda-kudaan; **rocky** *adj* berbatu-batu

rocket *n* rokét; *vi* merokét

rocky *adj* berbatu-batu ← **rock**

rod *n* batang; *lightning* ~ penangkal petir

rode *v, pf* → **ride**

rodent *n* binatang pengerat

rodeo *n* pertunjukan ketrampilan
menangani kuda dan hewan ternak

rogue *n* [roug] bangsat, bajingan; ~ *element* oknum

role *n* peran, peranan; ~ *model* teladan,
contoh; ~ *play, to play a* ~ memainkan
peran

roll *n* gulung, gulungan; roti bulat; daftar; *~ing pin* gilingan adonan; *~~up*
rokok linting; ~ *call* apél; *toilet* ~ tisu
gulung; *vi* berguling, berputar; ~ *over*
berguling, tengkurap; *vt* menggulung,
menggulingkan, menggelindingkan;
roller *n* ombak besar; alat penggulung
rambut; ~ *blades,* ~ *skates* sepatu
roda; *hair* ~ alat penggulung rambut;
rollercoaster *n* keréta luncur

Roma, Romany *n, adj* kaum gipsi; *n*
bahasa gipsi

Roman *adj* Romawi; *n* orang Romawi;
~ *Catholic* Katolik (Roma); ~ *numeral*
angka Romawi; *the* ~ *Empire*
Kekaisaran Romawi

romance *n* cerita cinta; **romantic** *adj*
romantis; *n* orang yang romantis;
romantically *adv* (secara) romantis

Romania, Rumania *n* Romania;
Romanian *adj* berasal dari Romania;
n orang Romania; bahasa Romania

romantic *adj* romantis; *n* orang yang
romantis ← **romance**

Rome *n* Roma; *all roads lead to* ~
banyak jalan ke Roma; terdapat berbagai cara melakukan sesuatu

roof *n* atap; *~top* di atap; ~ *rack*
kerangka untuk bagasi di atap mobil;
under one ~ serumah; *to raise the* ~
menjadi marah sekali

room *n* ruang, ruangan; kamar; ~ *service*
layanan kamar; *dining* ~ ruang makan;
single ~ kamar untuk satu orang; *vi*
kos, mondok; **roommate** *n* teman
sekamar; **roomy** *adj* lapang

rooster *n* ayam jago

root *n* akar; *to take* ~ berakar; *vi* berakar;
~ed to the spot terpaku di tempat

rope *n* tali; ~ *ladder* tangga tali; *jump* ~
lompat tali; *to know the* ~s tahu tata
caranya

rosary *n, Isl* tasbih; *Cath* rosario

rose *n* bunga mawar, bunga ros; *vi, pf*
→ **rise**; **rosebud** *n* kuncup bunga
mawar; **rosy** *adj* berwarna mérah;
menyenangkan

rosemary *n* sejenis rempah

roster *n* daftar nama

rosy *adj* berwarna mérah; menyenangkan ← **rose**

rot *n* kebusukan; *vi* membusuk; *vt*
membusukkan, membuat busuk; *sugar
~s your teeth* gula membuat gigi
busuk; **rotten** *adj* busuk

rotate *vi* berputar, berkisar; *vt* memutarkan; **rotation** *n* perputaran, per-
kisaran

rote *~~learning* hapalan; *to learn by* ~
menghafalkan

rotten *adj* busuk ← **rot**

rotunda *n* gazébo, bangunan bundar di
taman

rouble, ruble *n* rubel, mata uang Rusia

rouge *n* [ruj] perona pipi

rough *adj* [raf] kasar; mentah; ~ *draft*
naskah pertama; *to sleep* ~ tidur di
jalan; **roughly** *adv* kurang lebih, kira-
kira; secara kasar

round *adj* [raund] bulat, bundar; di sekitar; ~ *here* di sekitar daérah ini; ~ *table* méja bundar; ~ *trip* perjalanan pulang pergi (PP); ~ *the world* keliling dunia; *all year* ~ sepanjang tahun; *n* giliran, putaran, ronde; *to do the* ~*s* berkeliling, meronda; *vt* mengelilingi; ~ *off* membulatkan; **roundabout** *adj* keliling; *n* bundaran; komidi putar; **rounders** *n, pl* kasti

route *n* [rut] trayék, jalur, rute

routine *adj* biasa, sehari-hari, rutin; *n* kebiasaan sehari-hari; **routinely** *adv* secara rutin

row *n* [rau] pertengkaran; keributan; *vi* bertengkar; **rowdy** *adj* berisik

row *n* [ro] baris, jajar, déretan; *in a* ~ berturut-turut; berdérétan

row *vi* [ro] berkayuh; *v* mendayung, mengayuh; **rowboat** *n* perahu dayung; **rower** *n* pendayung, pengayuh; **rowing** *n* (olahraga) mendayung; ~ *machine* mesin dayung

rowdy *adj* [raudi] berisik ← **row**

royal *adj* kerajaan; *n* anggota kerajaan; *Her* ~ *Highness (HRH)* Yang Mulia (YM); **royalist** *n* pendukung kerajaan; **royalty** *n* keluarga raja; honorarium, honor

RRP *abbrev recommended retail price* harga écéran

RSA *abbrev Republic of South Africa* Afsél (Republik Afrika Selatan)

RSPCA *abbrev Royal Society for the Prevention of Cruelty to Animals* Persatuan Melawan Kekerasan terhadap Héwan

RSVP *abbrev répondez s'il vous plaît* minta dikonfirmasi

Rt Hon. *Right Honorable* Yang Terhormat (Yth.)

rub *vt* menggosok, menggosok-gosok; ~ *out* menghapus; ~ *off onto* ikut terpengaruh; ~ *one's eyes* mengucek mata; ~ *shoulders with* bergaul (dengan orang terkenal); **rubber** *n* karét; penghapus, *arch* setip; ~-*stamp* mengizinkan begitu saja; ~ *band* karét gelang

rubella *n* [rubéla] campak Jérman, rubéla

rubbish *n* sampah; omong kosong; ~ *collectors* tukang sampah; ~ *dump* tempat pembuangan akhir (TPA); *adj, sl* jélék; *we played* ~ *today* kami bermain dengan jélék hari ini; *vt, sl* mengéjék, memperolok

rubble *n* [rabel] puing-puing, reruntuhan

ruble, rouble *n* rubel, mata uang Rusia

ruby *n* batu mirah; ~ *anniversary* ulang tahun perkawinan yang ke40

rucksack *n* ransel

rudder *n* kemudi; **rudderless** *adj* tanpa kemudi, tidak terkendali

rude *adj* kasar, tidak sopan; **rudely** *adv* dengan kasar, secara tidak sopan; **rudeness** *n* ketidaksopanan

rug *n* permadani

rugby *n* [ragbi] semacam sépak bola dengan bola lonjong

ruin *n* reruntuhan, puing-puing; *in* ~*s* jadi puing; *vt* meruntuhkan, merobohkan, merusak; *my dress is* ~*ed!* rok saya rusak

rule *vi* ~ *a line* membuat garis, menggaris; **ruler** n penggaris

rule *n* aturan, peraturan; pemerintahan; *to break a* ~ melanggar peraturan; *vi* ~ *out* mengesampingkan; *as a* ~ biasanya; *vt* memerintah; **ruler** *n* kepala pemerintah; **ruling** *adj* yang sedang berkuasa; *n* putusan

rum *n* room

Rumania → **Romania**

rumble *n* [rambel] gemuruh, deruman; *vi* bergemuruh, menderum; berderu

ruminant *n* pemamah biak, pemakan rumput

rummy *n* rémi

rumor, rumour *n* kabar angin, kabar burung, desas-desus

rump *n* pantat; ~ *steak* stéik daging pantat

run *n* perjalanan, latihan berlari, perlombaan; ~-*down* lesu; tidak terpelihara; ~-*in* pertengkaran; *fun* ~ lomba lari untuk amal; *on the* ~ sedang melarikan diri; *in the long* ~ lambat laun, lama-lama, dalam jangka panjang; *to go for a* ~ lari pagi, joging; *vi* **ran run** lari; berlangsung; mengalir; ~

amuck, ~ *amok* mengamuk; ~ *away* kabur, melarikan diri; ~ *into* bertemu (secara tidak sengaja); ~ *out of* kehabisan; *vt* memimpin; menjalankan, melaksanakan, menyelenggarakan; ~ *over* melindas; ~ *through* melatih, mengadakan gladi resik; **runaway** *n* pelarian; **runner** *n* pelari; pesuruh, pengantar; loper; ~*up* juara kedua; **running** *n* lari; ~ *mate* pasangan (calon pejabat); *in the* ~ berpeluang; *Ian loves* ~ Ian suka sekali lari; **runny** *adj* cair, berair; ~ *nose* pilek; **runway** *n* landasan terbang

rung *vi, pf* → **ring**

runner *n* pelari; pesuruh, pengantar; loper; ~*up* juara kedua ← **run**

running *n* lari; ~ *mate* pasangan (calon pejabat); *in the* ~ berpeluang; *Ian loves* ~ Ian suka sekali lari ← **run**

runny *adj* cair, berair; ~ *nose* pilek ← **run**

runt *n* anak binatang yang paling kecil sekelahiran

runway *n* landasan terbang ← **run**

rural *adj* pedésaan, pedalaman

rush *n* ketergesa-gesaan; ~ *hour* jam padat; ~ *job* pekerjaan kilat; *vi* terburu-buru; *vt* menyerbu

rusk *n* biskuit bayi (saat gigi tumbuh)

Russia *n* Rusia; *White* ~ *arch* Belarus; **Russian** *adj* berasal dari Rusia; *n* bahasa Rusia; orang Rusia; ~ *roulette* permainan dengan pistol

rust *n* karat; *vi* berkarat; **rustproof** *adj* anti karat; **rusty** *adj* berkarat, karatan; sudah lama tidak melalukan (ketrampilan); *I can play the piano, but I'm a bit* ~ saya bisa main piano, tapi sudah lama tidak melakukannya

rustle *n, vi* [rasel] gersak, gersik, gemersik; *vt* menggersik

rustproof *adj* anti karat ← **rust**

rusty *adj* berkarat, karatan; sudah lama tidak melalukan (ketrampilan); *I can play the piano, but I'm a bit* ~ saya bisa main piano, tapi sudah lama tidak melakukannya ← **rust**

rut *n* bekas roda, lubang di jalan; *in a* ~ tertahan di keadaan yang membosankan

ruthless *adj* [ruthles] keji, kejam, tanpa belas kasihan

Rwanda *n* Rwanda; **Rwandan** *adj* berasal dari Rwanda; *n* orang Rwanda

rye *n* [rai] gandum hitam; ~ *bread* roti hitam

S

SA *abbrev South Africa* Afrika Selatan

sabbatical *n* cuti tanpa gaji (untuk guru)

sabotage *n* [sabotaj] sabotase; *vt* menyabotase; **saboteur** *n* [saboter] penyabot

sachet *n* [sasyé] kemasan (kecil), sasé (berisi saus, sampo dll)

sack *n* karung, goni; *to hit the* ~ tidur; *to get the* ~ dipéhakakan, diPHKkan, dipecat; *vi* dipéhakakan, diPHKkan, dipecat

sacred *adj* [sékred] suci, kudus

sacrifice *n* [sakrifais] korban, pengorbanan; *Isl* kurban, qurban; *to make a* ~ berkurban; *vt* mengorbankan

sad *adj* susah, sedih; ~ *to say* sayangnya; **sadden** *vt* menyedihkan, membuat sedih; *it* ~*ed me to see him cry* pengalaman melihat dia menangis itu sangat menyedihkan; **sadly** *adv* dengan sedih; **sadness** *n* kesedihan

saddle *n* [sadel] pelana, sadel, tempat duduk; *v* ~ *up* memasang pelana; **saddlebag** *n* tas pelana, tas sepéda; *coll* lemak berlebihan di pinggul

sadistic *adj* sadis

sadly *adv* dengan sedih ← **sad**

sadness *n* kesedihan ← **sad**

safari *n* wisata melihat atau memburu binatang liar (terutama di Afrika); ~ *park* taman safari; *on* ~ sedang mengikuti wisata tersebut

safe *adj* selamat; aman, dapat dipercaya; ~*keeping* penyimpanan yang aman; ~ *bet* pasti, tentu; ~ *sex* senggama yang menggunakan kondom; ~ *and sound* selamat; ~ *as houses* aman sekali; *n* brankas; ~*deposit box* kotak tempat menyimpan barang berharga di bank; **safeguard** *vt* melindungi; ~ *against* menjaga; **safely** *adv* dengan selamat; **safety** *n* keselamatan; keamanan; ~ *belt* sabuk pengaman; ~ *goggles* kacamata pelindung; ~ *net* jaringan pengaman; ~ *pin* peniti cantél; ~ *vest* baju pelampung

saffron *n* kunyit, kuning

sag *vi* turun, mengendur, terkulai; *my old cat's stomach is beginning to ~* perutnya kucing tua saya itu mulai turun; **saggy** *adj* kendor, longgar

saga *n* [saga] hikayat, cerita yang panjang; *it's quite a ~* ceritanya berbelit-belit

saggy *adj* kendor, longgar ← **sag**

sago *n* [ségo] sagu; ~ *pudding* puding sagu

said *v, pf* [séd] → **say**

sail *n* layar; *vi* berlayar; *vt* melayarkan; mengarungi (laut); **sailboat** *n* perahu layar; **sailcloth** *n* kain layar; **sailing** *n* berlayar; ~ *ship* kapal layar; *plain ~* mudah, tidak ada halangan; *to go ~* berlayar; **sailor** *n* pelaut, anak buah kapal (ABK)

saint (St) *n, Chr, m* santo; *f* santa; orang suci, orang kudus; ~ *Peter* Santo Pétrus; **saintly** *adj* seperti orang suci

sake *for God's ~* demi Allah; *for goodness's ~* masya Allah; *for your own ~* untuk (kebaikan) diri sendiri

salad *n* selada; ~ *dressing* bumbu selada; *fruit ~* buah campur

salami *n* [salami] semacam sosis masak besar yang diiris

salary *n* [salari] gaji; ~ *increase* kenaikan gaji

sale *n* obral; penjualan; *for ~* dijual; *on ~* diobral, didiskon; **sales** *n* penjualan; ~ *assistant* pelayan toko, pramuniaga; ~ *representative*, ~ *rep* pedagang, agén; ~ *tax* pajak pertambahan nilai (PPN); **salesgirl, saleswoman** *n, f* **salesman** *m* **salesperson** *n* agén; pramuniaga, pelayan toko

saline *adj* [sélain] asin, mengandung garam; *n* salin, larutan garam

saliva *n* [selaiva] air liur

sallow *adj* pucat, kekuning-kuningan (wajah)

salmon *n* [samen] ikan salmon; *adj* mérah muda kekuningan

salon *n* salon kecantikan

salt *n* [solt] garam; ~ *cellar*, ~ *shaker* tempat garam; ~ *and pepper* garam merica; **salted** *adj* yang diasinkan; **saltpeter, saltpetre** *n* [soltpiter] sendawa; **salty** *adj* asin; ~ *fish* ikan asin

salute *n* pemberian hormat; *vi* memberi hormat; *vt* memberi hormat kepada

salvage *vt* [salvej] menyelamatkan (barang); **salvaged** *adj* selamat, terselamatkan

salvation *n* keselamatan; ~ *Army* Bala Keselamatan

same *adj* sama; serupa; *all the ~, just the ~* walaupun begitu; *adv* sama, seperti itu

sample *n* [sampel] contoh; *vt* coba (barang dagangan); *would you like to ~ this cake?* silahkan coba kué ini; **sampler** *n* semacam sulaman

sanction *n* [sangsyen] persetujuan; sanksi; *economic ~s* sanksi ékonomi; *vt* menyetujui; memberi sanksi; *this government does not ~ violence* pemerintah ini tidak setuju dengan menggunakan kekerasan

sanctuary *n* suaka; *wildlife ~* suaka alam; *to seek ~* mencari suaka

sand *n* pasir; ~ *dune* bukit pasir; **sandbag** *n* karung pasir; **sandbox, sandpit** *n* tempat pasir (untuk anak-anak); **sandcastle** *n* [sandkasel] bénténg (pasir); **sander** *n* mesin penggosok; **sandpaper** *n* kertas gosok, ampelas; *vt* mengampelas; **sandstone** *n* batu pasir; **sandy** *adj* mengandung pasir

sandal *n* [sandel] sepatu sandal

sandalwood *n* kayu cendana

sandbag *n* karung pasir ← **sand**

sandbox *n* tempat pasir (untuk anak-anak) ← **sand**

sandcastle *n* [sandkasel] bénténg (pasir) ← **sand**

sander *n* mesin penggosok ← **sand**

sandpaper *n* kertas gosok, ampelas; *vt*

mengampelas ← **sand**

sandpit *n* tempat pasir (untuk anak-anak) ← **sand**

sandstone *n* batu pasir ← **sand**

sandwich *n* [sandwij] roti lapis

sandy *adj* mengandung pasir ← **sand**

sane *adj* waras, berakal séhat; **sanity** *n* [saniti] keséhatan mental

sang *v, pf* → **sing**

sanitary *adj* bersih, sanitér; ~ *pad*, ~ *napkin*, ~ *towel* pembalut (wanita); **sanitation** *n* kebersihan

sanity *n* [saniti] keséhatan mental ← **sane**

sank *v, pf* → **sink**

Sanskrit *n* bahasa Sansekerta

Santa *n* ~ *(Claus)* Sinterklas, Santa

sap *n* getah; *vt* melemahkan; *the heat ~s your energy* cuaca panas membuat badan orang lemah

sapling *n* anak pohon

sapphire *n* [safair] batu nilam, batu safir

sarcasm *n* [sarkazem] sarkasme, sindiran tajam; **sarcastic** *adj* sarkastis, menyindir

sardine *n* [sardin] ikan sardén

sarong *n* sarung

sash *n* ikat pinggang; selémpang, seléndang

sassy *adj, sl* lancang, berani

sat *v, pf* → **sit**

Satan *n* [séten] sétan, iblis; **satanic** *adj* [satanik] berkaitan dengan sétan

satay *n* saté; *chicken* ~ saté ayam

satchel *n* tas sekolah, tas buku

satellite *n* [satelait] satelit; bulan; ~ *city* kota satelit; ~ *dish* parabola

satire *n* sindiran; **satirical** adj [satirikal] bersifat menyindir; **satirize** *vt* [satiraiz] menyindirkan

satisfaction *n* kepuasan; **satisfactorily** *adv* cukup, secara memuaskan; **satisfactory** *adj* memuaskan, cukup; **satisfy** *vt* [satisfai] memuaskan; memenuhi; **satisfied** *adj* puas; ~ *with* puas dengan

saturated *adj* penuh, jenuh; ~ *fat* lemak jenuh; **saturation** *n* kejenuhan; ~ *point* titik jenuh

Saturday *adj, n* [saterdé] hari Sabtu; ~

night malam Minggu

sauce *n* kuah, saus; *chilli* ~ sambal; *soy* ~ kécap; *tomato* ~ saus tomat

saucepan *n* panci; ~ *lid* tutup panci

saucer *n* piring cawan; *flying* ~ piring terbang

Saudi Arabia *n* Arab Saudi; **Saudi, Saudi Arabian** *adj* berasal dari Arab Saudi; *n* orang Arab Saudi

sauna *n* [sona] sauna

saunter *vi* berjalan-jalan (perlahan-lahan); *the gang ~ed across the playground* gang itu berjalan di lapangan main dengan sikap arogan

sausage *n* [sosej] sosis; ~ *roll* sejenis roti sosis

savage *adj* [savej] buas, liar, ganas; *n* orang biadab

savanna, savannah *n* sabana, padang rumput

save *n* penyelamatan, tangkapan; *prep* kecuali; *all the boys* ~ *Rhys* semua anak laki-laki kecuali Rhys; *vt* menyelamatkan; menghémat; menyimpan; ~ *money* menghemat uang; menabung uang; ~ *up* menabung; ~ *a file* menyimpan file; ~ *a life* menyelamatkan jiwa; **savings** *n, pl* (uang) tabungan, simpanan

Savior, Saviour *n, Chr* Juru Selamat

savory, savoury *adj* tidak manis (asin, tawar); *n* makanan kecil

saw *n* gergaji; *vt* menggergaji; ~ *-horse* kuda-kuda; **sawdust** *n* serbuk kayu

saw *vt, pf* → **see**

saxophone *n* **sax** *coll* saksofon; **saxophonist** *n* [saksafonist] pemain saksofon

say *vt* **said said** [séd] kata, berkata; mengatakan; *the final* ~ kata terakhir, hak memutuskan; *never* ~ *die* jangan putus asa; *to have a* ~ ikut bersuara; *could you* ~ *that again please?* boléh diulang sekali lagi?; **saying** *n* pepatah, peribahasa

SC *abbrev secondary college* SMU (sekolah menengah)

scab *n* keropéng, darah kering (bekas luka)

scabies *n* kudis; *to have* ~ kudisan

scaffold, scaffolding *n* tangga-tangga, perancah

scald *n, vt* [skold] luka kena air panas; *~ing hot* panas sekali

scale *n* skala, ukuran; *~ model* miniatur; *large-~* secara besar-besaran; **scales** *n, pl* timbangan, neraca

scale *n* sisik, kulit; **scaly** *adj* bersisik

scallop *n* semacam kerang laut dalam, simping

scalp *n* kulit kepala; *vt* menguliti (kepala); **scalper** *n* calo, tukang catut

scalpel *n* pisau bedah

scalper *n* calo, tukang catut ← **scalp**

scam *n* tipu daya, penipuan; *the offer of a free motorbike was a ~* tawaran sepéda motor gratis itu ternyata penipuan

scan *n* peninjauan; *vt* meninjau; pindai, memindai; **scanner** *n* pemindai, scanner

scandal *n* skandal, keonaran; **scandalous** *adj* memalukan

Scandinavia *n* [Skandinévia] Skandinavia; Norwégia, Swédia, Finlandia, Dénmark dan Eslandia; **Scandinavian** *adj* berasal dari Skandinavia; *n* orang Skandinavia

scanner *n* pemindai, scanner ← **scan**

scapegoat *n* kambing hitam; *vt* mengambing-hitamkan

scar *n* bekas (luka); *vt* membekas, menggoresi; **scarred** *adj* terluka

scarce *adj* [skérs] jarang; kurang; **scarcely** *adv* hampir tidak, nyaris

scare *n* [skér] peristiwa yang menakutkan; *vi* menjadi takut; *vt* menakut-nakuti, menakutkan; *~ away* mengusir; **scarecrow** *n* orang-orangan untuk mengusir burung di ladang; **scared** *adj* takut; *~ of* takut (pada); **scary** *adj* [skéri] menakutkan

scarf *n* **scarves** syal; *head ~* kerudung

scarlet *adj* mérah tua

scary *adj* [skéri] menakutkan, menyeramkan ← **scare**

scatter *vi* tersebar; *vt* menaburkan, menyebarkan

scavenge *vt* [skavenj] memulung; *~ for food* memulung mencari makanan; **scavenger** *n* pemulung

scenario *n* [senario] skénario

scene *n* [siin] pemandangan; adegan; *behind the ~s* di balik layar; *change of ~* ganti suasana; *not my ~* bukan seléra saya; *~ of the crime* tempat kejadian perkara (TKP); *to make a ~* membuat héboh; **scenery** *n* pemandangan alam; **scenic** *adj* asri, penuh pemandangan

scent *n* [sént] (minyak) wangi, harum, bau; **scented** *adj* wangi

scepter, sceptre *n* [sépter] tongkat lambang kekuasaan

sceptic, sceptical → **skeptic, skeptical**

schedule *n* [skédyul] jadwal, program, daftar acara; *behind ~* terlambat; *on ~* sesuai dengan perencanaan; *vt* merencanakan, mengatur, menjadwalkan

scheme *n* [skim] rencana; bagan, skéma, rancangan; *color ~* susunan warna; *vi* merékayasa; *she was always scheming to inherit Grandma's money* dari dulu dia selalu merékayasa tipu daya agar mewarisi uang Nénék

schizophrenia *n* [skitsofrénia] skizofrénia

scholar *n* [skolar] pelajar; orang terpelajar; **scholarship** *n* béasiswa; pengetahuan; **school** *n* [skul] sekolah; aliran; *~ holidays* liburan sekolah; *~ leaver* tamatan sekolah; *~ uniform* seragam sekolah; *~ year* tahun ajaran; *at ~* di sekolah; *elementary ~, primary ~* sekolah dasar; *~ of thought* aliran; *junior high ~* sekolah menengah pertama (SMP); *medical ~* fakultas kedokteran; *night ~* kursus malam; *secondary ~* sekolah menengah; **schoolbook** *n* buku pelajaran; **schoolboy** *n, m*; **schoolgirl** *f* murid, pelajar, siswa; *f* siswi; **schoolhouse** *n* gedung sekolah; **schooling** *n* pendidikan, studi; **schoolmate** *n* teman sekolah; **schoolmaster** *n, m, arch* guru; **scholarly** *adj* ilmiah

science *n* [sains] ilmu (pengetahuan alam, IPA); sains; *~ fiction* fiksi ilmiah; *political ~* ilmu politik; **scientific** *adj* [saientifik] ilmiah, keilmuan; **scientist** *n* ilmuwan

scissors *n, pl* [sizers] *pair of ~* gunting

scold *vt* menegur, menghardik; *his*

mother ~ed him for arriving late dia ditegur ibunya karena datang terlambat; **scolding** *n* hardikan, teguran

scone *n* [skon] sejenis roti kecil

scoop *n* séndok, ciduk, gayung; *two ~s of ice cream* dua séndok és krim; *vt* menyéndok, menciduk, menyekop; *Glen ~ed up the ball and ran towards the goal* Glen mengambil bola lalu lari menuju gawang

scooter *n* otopet, skuter

scope *n* ruang lingkup, jangkauan; bidang, lapangan; *beyond the ~ of this report* tidak terliput dalam laporan ini

scorch *vt* membakar (tidak sengaja); *~ed earth policy* kebijakan pembumihangusan; *I ~ed my shirt collar with the iron* kerah blus saya kena panas dari setrikaan; **scorcher** *n* hari yang cuacanya panas sekali; **scorching** *adj* panas terik

score *n* skor, angka, nilai; *on that ~* tentang hal itu; *to settle a ~* membalas dendam; *v* mencétak gol, angka atau poin; memperoléh nilai; **scoreboard** *n* papan angka; **scoreline** *n* skor akhir; **scorer** *n* pencétak gol; penghitung skor

scorn *n* cemoohan, caci-maki; *vt* mencemoohkan, mencaci-maki; **scornful** *adj* mencemoohkan, menghinakan; *many people are still ~ of Chinese medicine* banyak orang masih mencemoohkan obat Cina

scorpion *n* kalajengking

Scot *n* orang Skotlandia; **scotch** *n* wiski Skotlandia; **Scotland** *n* Skotlandia; **Scottish, Scots** *adj* berasal dari Skotlandia

scoundrel *n* bangsat

scour *vt* menggosok; menjelajahi; *Liz ~ed the shops in town for a red dress* Liz mencari rok mérah ke semua toko di kota; **scourer** *pot ~* penggosok panci

scout *n* pandu, pramuka; pengintai; *cub ~* Siaga; *girl ~* pandu puteri; **scouting** kepanduan, kepramukaan

scowl *n* pandangan marah; *vi* (melihat dengan) cemberut

scrabble *vi* meraba-raba, merogoh

scramble *n* perebutan; *vi* berebut; memanjat; *the shoppers ~d to get into the sale* para pembelanja berebut masuk ke dalam toko obral; *vt* mengacak; mengocok; *~d eggs* telur kocok (goreng); *~ a code* mengacak sandi

scrap *adj* bekas; *~ metal* besi tua; *~ paper* kertas bekas; *n* sisa, carik; *sl* perkelahian; **scrapbook** *n* buku témpél, album

scrape *n* gorésan; *vi* bergéséran; *~ through* berhasil dengan susah payah; *vt* menggorés, menggésékkan; *Jeremy fell and ~d his knee* lutut Jeremy tergorés saat dia jatuh

scratch *n* gorésan; *vt* menggorés, menggaruk, mencorét; *don't ~ your mosquito bites* gigitan nyamuk jangan digaruk; *from ~* dari nol, dari awal; *up to ~* memenuhi syarat; bermutu baik

scrawl *n* tulisan cakar ayam; *vt* menulis dengan tidak jelas; *the doctor ~ed a prescription* dokter menulis résep dengan tulisan tangan yang tidak jelas

scrawny *adj* kurus

scream *n* jeritan; *what a ~* lucu sekali; *vi* berteriak; *v* menjerit

screech *n* ciutan; jeritan; *vi* menciutciut; *v* menjerit

screen *n* tabir; layar putih; *~ saver* gambar bergerak di layar komputer saat tidak dipakai; *the silver ~* layar lébar; *the small ~* layar télévisi; *vt* menyaring; memutarkan (film); **screening** *n* pemutaran film; **screenplay** *n* skénario

screw *n* sekrup; *vt* menyekrup; *vulg* bersetubuh; *~ up* mengacau; mengacaukan; **screwdriver** *n* obéng

scribble *n* tulisan cakar ayam; *v* mencorét-corét; *Dad ~d a note* Bapak membuat catatan dengan tulisan tangan jélék

script *n* tulisan; naskah; *Latin ~* huruf Romawi; **script writer** *n* penulis skénario

scroll *n* surat gulungan; gorésan berlekuk; *vi* menggulung, naik

scrotum *n* kantong buah pelir, skrotum

scrub *n* semak, belukar

scrub *n* sabun cair yang mengandung butiran; *coll* mandi, pencucian; *those dirty clothes will need a* ~ baju kotor itu harus digosok; *vt* menggosok

scruffy *adj* berpenampilan tidak rapi

scuba ~ *diving* selam dengan tangki udara

scuffle *n* [skafel] perkelahian; *there was a* ~ *among journalists as the minister left* para wartawan berkelahi saat menteri keluar; *vi* berkelahi, berebutan

sculpt *v* memahat patung, mematung; **sculptor** *n* perupa, pematung, pemahat patung; **sculpture** *n* (seni) patung

scum *n* buih kotoran (di atas cairan); *sl* sampah

scythe *n* [saith] sabit besar

SE *abbrev south east* tenggara; **SEA** *abbrev South East Asia* Asia Tenggara

sea *n* laut; *at* ~ di laut; bingung; ~ *breeze* angin laut; *by* ~ dengan kapal laut; ~ *captain* nakhoda kapal laut; ~ *change* perubahan besar; ~ *cow* duyung; ~ *cucumber* teripang, timun laut; ~ *floor* dasar laut; ~ *front* tepi laut, pinggir laut; ~ *green* biru toska; ~ *level* permukaan laut; ~ *urchin* bulu babi; *out to* ~ di laut lepas; *the Java* ~ Laut Jawa; **seaboard** *n* daérah pesisir; **seafarer** *n* pelaut; **seafood** *n* makanan laut; **seagull** *n* burung camar; **seahorse** *n* kuda laut; **sealion** *n* [silayon] singa laut; **seaman** *n* pelaut, kelasi; **seaplane** *n* pesawat terbang air; **seashell** *n* kerang (laut); **seashore** *n* pantai laut; **seasick** *adj* **seasickness** *n* mabuk laut; **seaside** *n* tepi laut; **seaweed** *n* ganggang laut, rumput laut

seal *n* anjing laut

seal *n* méterai, cap; *vt* menutup; *~ed road* jalan beraspal

sealion *n* [silayon] singa laut ← **sea**

seam *n* kelim, pelipit; *bursting at the ~s* penuh sesak; **seamstress** *n, arch* penjahit wanita

seaman *n* pelaut, kelasi ← **sea**

seamstress *n, arch* penjahit wanita ← **seam**

seance *n* [séans] pertemuan untuk mencoba menghubungi arwah orang

seaplane *n* pesawat terbang air ← **sea**

search *n* [sérc] pencarian, penggeledahan; ~ *engine* mesin pencari; ~ *party* rombongan pencari; ~ *warrant* surat kuasa untuk menggeledah; ~ *and rescue (SAR)* regu penyelamat; *vi* ~ *(for)* mencari; *vt* memeriksa, menggeledah; **searcher** *n* pencari; **searchlight** *n* [sérclait] lampu sorot

seashell *n* kerang (laut) ← **sea**

seashore *n* pantai laut ← **sea**

seasick *adj* **seasickness** *n* mabuk laut ← **sea**

seaside *n* tepi laut ← **sea**

season *vt* [sizen] membumbui; **seasoning** *n* bumbu

season *n* [sizen] musim; ~ *ticket* karcis terusan; ~*'s greetings* selamat (Natal); *off* ~ masa sepi; *peak* ~ masa ramai; *the dry* ~ musim kemarau; *the wet* ~ musim hujan; **seasonal** *adj* musiman

seasoning *n* bumbu ← **season**

seat *n* tempat duduk, bangku, kursi; *car* ~ jok; **seatbelt** *n* sabuk pengaman; **seated** *adj* sedang duduk

seaweed *n* ganggang laut, rumput laut ← **sea**

secede *vi* [sesid] memisahkan diri (negara); *Slovenia was the first state to* ~ *from Yugoslavia* Slovénia adalah negara pertama untuk memisahkan diri dari Yugoslavia; **secession** *n* [sesésyen] pemisahan diri

seclude *vt* memingit; **secluded** *adj* sepi; **seclusion** *n* pingitan; *nuns live in* ~ biarawati dipingit

second *n* [sékond] detik; *just a* ~ sebentar

second *adj* [sékond] kedua; ~*-hand* bekas; ~*-rate* bermutu rendah; ~ *class* kelas dua; ~ *cousin* saudara sebuyut; ~ *gear* gigi dua; ~ *hand* jarum detik; ~ *name* nama tengah; ~ *nature* otomatis, naluriah; *every* ~ *day* selang sehari, dua hari sekali; *the* ~ *of October* tanggal dua Oktober; **secondary** *adj* sekundér; ~ *school* sekolah menengah; **secondly** *adv* yang kedua

secrecy *n* [sikresi] kerahasiaan; **secret** *adj, n* [sikret] rahasia; *in* ~ secara

diam-diam; *keep it a* ~ rahasiakanlah;
secretive *adj* [sikretiv] tidak terus
terang; **secretly** *adv* [sikretli] secara
diam-diam, mencuri-curi
secretariat *n* [sékretériet] sékretariat,
kepaniteraan; **secretary** *n* sékretaris,
panitera; ~ *General* Sékretaris-
Jénderal, Sékjén; ~ *of State US*
Menteri Luar Negeri
secrete *v* [sekrit] mengeluarkan;
menyembunyikan; **secretion** *n*
pengeluaran
secretive *adj* [sikretiv] tidak terus
terang ← **secret**
secretly *adv* [sikretli] secara diam-
diam, mencuri-curi ← **secret**
sect *n* sékte, aliran; *sectarian* ~ *violence*
kekerasan berbau SARA
section *n* séksi, bagian, belahan; ~ *head*
kepala bagian; **sector** *n* séktor, bidang
secular *adj* [sékuler] sékulér
secure *adj* [sekyur] kukuh; aman; *vt*
mengukuhkan; memperoléh; **security**
n keamanan; ~ *guard* satuan keamanan
(satpam), sekuriti; ~ *police* polisi rahasia; *UN* ~ *Council* Déwan Keamanan
PBB; **securities** *n, pl* surat-surat
berharga
sedate *vi* [sedét] membius, menenangkan dengan obat penenang;
sedated *adj* [sedéted] dibius; **seda-
tive** *n* [sédatif] obat penenang
sediment *n* sédimén, endapan; **sedi-
mentary** ~ *rock* batu endapan; **sedimentation** *n* pengendapan, sédiméntasi
sedition *n* [sedisyen] **seditious** *adj* makar
seduce *vt* menggoda, merayu; **seduc-
tion** *n* penggodaan, godaan; **seductive**
adj menggodakan
see *v* **saw seen** melihat; mengunjungi;
~*through* tembus pandang, transparan; ~ *Paris* berkunjung ke Paris; ~
red menjadi marah; ~ *to* mengurus; *I* ~
saya mengerti; ~ *someone off,* ~
someone out mengantarkan; ~ *a lot of*
sering bertemu dengan
seed *n* biji, benih; *sunflower* ~*s* kuaci;
~*less grapes* anggur tanpa biji;
seedling *n* bibit
seek *vt* **sought sought** [sot] mencari;

hide and ~ petak umpet; **seeker** *n*
pencari
seem *vi* nampak; ternyata, kelihatannya;
rupanya, rasanya; *so it* ~*s* begitulah
seen *v, pf* → **see**
seep *vi* merembes, bocor; *the water* ~*ed
through the wall* air merembes melalui
témbok
seesaw *n* papan jungkat-jungkit; *vi*
naik turun secara tidak stabil
segment *n* bagian, golongan, pangsa,
ségmén
segregate *vt* memisahkan (golongan);
segregation *n* pemisahan; *racial* ~
pemisahan berdasarkan suku bangsa
seismic *adj* [saizmik] yang berkaitan
dengan gempa bumi; **seismograph** *n*
[saizmograf] séismograf
seize *vt* [siz] menangkap; menyita; *the
police* ~*d the stolen goods* polisi
menyita barang curian; **seizure** *n*
[sizyur] serangan (penyakit);
penyitaan
seldom *adv* jarang
select *adj* [selékt] terpilih, pilihan; *a* ~
few beberapa saja yang terpilih; *vt*
memilih, menyaring; **selection** *n* pilihan, pemilihan, séléksi; **selective** *adj*
bersifat memilih-milih
self *pron* **selves** sendiri, pribadi; ~
assured percaya diri; ~*centred* égois;
~*confidence* percaya diri (PD);
~*control* pengawasan diri sendiri; ~
conscious sadar akan dirinya, canggung; ~*defense* béla diri; ~*educated*
otodidak; ~*employed* swausaha; ~
esteem rasa percaya diri; ~*government*
otonomi, swapraja; ~*interest* kepentingan diri sendiri; ~*portrait* potrét
diri; ~*reliant* mandiri; ~*respect* harga
diri; ~*service* swalayan; ~*sufficient*
berdikari, mandiri; **selfish** *adj* égois,
suka mementingkan diri sendiri; **selfie**
n, sl foto diri yang diambil sendiri
sell *vi* **sold sold** terjual, laku; ~ *out*
habis terjual; ~ *like hot cakes* laku
(seperti pisang goreng); *vt* menjual,
berjualan; ~ *off* menjual habis, mengobral; **seller** *n* penjual
semaphore *n* sémafor

semen *n* [simen] air mani

semester *n* seméster, paruh tahun; *summer* ~ seméster péndék

semi- *pref* tengah, separuh; *~circle* setengah lingkaran; *~colon* titik koma [;]; *~detached* sebagian bersambung, bersampingan (rumah); *~trailer* truk gandéng

Semitic [Semitik] *anti-~* anti Yahudi

senate *n* [sénet] sénat; **senator** *n* anggota sénat, sénator

send *vt* **sent sent** mengirim, mengirimkan, mengirimi; *~ back* mengembalikan, mengirim kembali; *~ for* memanggil, minta datang; *~ off n* upacara pemberangkatan; *~ off vt* mengantarkan; *~ on* meneruskan; *~ away for, ~ out for* memesan; *~ my love* kirim salam; **sender** *n* pengirim

Senegal *n* Sénégal; **Senegalese** *adj* berasal dari Sénégal; *n* orang Sénégal

senile *adj* pikun

senior *adj* [sinior] lebih tua, tertua, sénior; *n* orang yang lebih tua; *~ high school* sekolah menengah atas (SMA); **seniority** *n* sénioritas, kedudukan yang lebih tinggi

sensation *n* kegemparan, sénsasi; rasa; **sensational** *adj* menggemparkan, sénsasional

sense *n* indera; perasaan; arti, pengertian; *common ~* akal séhat; *~ of humor* seléra humor; *the five ~s* pancaindera; *to make ~* masuk akal; *vt* merasakan; **senseless** *adj* tanpa arti, tidak masuk akal; *~ violence* kekerasan tanpa alasan; **sensible** *adj* waras, berpikiran séhat, berakal séhat; **sensitive** *adj* peka, sénsitif; *~ to light* peka terhadap cahaya; **sensual** *adj* yang berkaitan dengan hawa nafsu

sent *v, pf* → **send**

sentence *n* keputusan, hukuman; *death ~* hukuman mati; *to pass ~* menghukum; *vt* menghukum; *~ to 20 years imprisonment* dihukum 20 tahun penjara

sentence *n* kalimat

sentiment *n* perasaan, séntimén; **sentimental** *adj* séntiméntil

sentinel *n* [séntinel] pengawal, prajurit penjaga

sentry *n* [séntri] penjaga; *~ box* gardu jaga, rumah monyét

separate *adj* [séperet] terpisah; *vi* [séperét] berpisah; pisah ranjang; *vt* memisahkan; **separated** *adj* pisah, terpisah; *Alison and Charles are now ~* Alison dan Charles sudah pisah; **separately** *adv* secara terpisah; **separation** *n* pemisahan; **separatism** *n* séparatisme; **separatist** *adj* séparatis; *Fretilin was always a ~ organization* sejak dulu, Fretilin adalah organisasi séparatis

sepia *adj* [sipia] (warna) coklat

September *n* bulan Séptémber

septic *adj* busuk, terinféksi; *~ tank* tangki séptik

sequel *n* [sikuel] lanjutan, sambungan; *the ~ to 'Star Wars' was 'The Empire Strikes Back'* film *Star Wars* dilanjutkan dengan *The Empire Strikes Back*

sequence *n* [sikuens] urutan, rangkaian

sequin *n* [sikuin] manik-manik bulat berlubang satu

Serb *n* orang Sérbia; **Serbia** *n* Sérbia; **Serbian** *adj* berasal dari Sérbia; *n* bahasa Sérbia; **Serbo-Croat** *n, arch* bahasa Sérbia-Kroasia

sergeant *n* [sarjent] sérsan

serial *n* [siriel] séri; film séri; cerita bersambung (cerber); *~ killer* pembunuh berantai; *~ number* nomor séri, nomor urutan; **series** *n* séri, rangkaian

serious *adj* sungguh-sungguh, sérius; **seriously** *adv* sungguh-sungguh; berat; *to take ~* menganggap penting

sermon *n* khotbah, ceramah

serpent *n* ular, naga

serrated *adj* bergerigi; *~ knife* pisau bergerigi

servant *n* pembantu, pelayan, pramuwisma, babu; *civil ~, public ~* pegawai negeri, pegawai negeri sipil (PNS); **serve** *vi* mengabdi; *vt* melayani; menghidangkan; *this branch ~s the southern area* cabang ini melayani daérah selatan; *Justine ~d*

fish at the party Justine menghidangkan ikan di pésta; **service** *n*
pelayanan; pemeliharaan; kebaktian;
masa bakti, jasa; sérvis; *~ charge*
pajak pendapatan daérah; *~ station*
pompa bénsin; *dinner* ~ seperangkat
piring; *vt* memperbaiki (mobil); **serviceman** *n* tentara, anggota angkatan
bersenjata; **serving** *n* porsi
serviette *n* [sérviét] serbét
serving *n* porsi ← **serve**
sesame *n* [sésami] wijén
session *n* [sésyen] sidang, sési; *in* ~
bersidang
set *adj* sudah ditentukan; siap; *~-up*
susunan; *~ price* harga pas; *n* sepasang, seperangkat, perlengkapan;
pesawat (radio/télévisi); kelompok; *vi*
set set mengental, membeku; terbenam (matahari); *~ off, ~ out* berangkat;
vt menaruh; memasang, menyetel;
menetapkan; *~ (down)* meletakkan; *~
aside* menyisihkan; **setback** *n* kemunduran, halangan; **setting** *n* penyetélan;
lingkungan, latar belakang
settle *vi* [sétel] berdiam; *~ down* menjadi tenang; berumah tangga; *~ for*
bersedia menerima; *~ in* menempati; *~
on* memilih; *vt* menyelesaikan,
menenangkan; mengatur, mengurus;
settled *adj* mapan, betah; **settlement**
n perkampungan; penyelesaian; **settler** *n* pendatang, penghuni
seven *adj, n* [séven] tujuh; **seventeen**
adj, n tujuh belas; **seventeenth** *adj*
ketujuh belas; **seventh** *adj* ketujuh;
seventy *adj, n* tujuh puluh; *the seven-
ties* tahun 70an
sever *vt* memutuskan, memotong; *vt ~
ties with* memutuskan hubungan dengan
several *adj* [séveral] beberapa
severe *adj* [sévir] keras, ketat, parah;
stréng (guru); **severely** *adv* dengan
keras
sew *v* [so] **sewed sewn** menjahit;
sewing *n* jahitan; menjahit; *~ machine*
mesin jahit; *I enjoy ~* saya suka menjahit
sewage *n* [suej] tinja; **sewer** *n* selokan,
saluran air kotor; **sewerage** *n* [suerej]
penyaluran tinja

sewn *v, pf* [son] → **sew**
sex *n* jenis kelamin; (hubungan) séks,
persetubuhan, sanggama; *~ appeal*
daya tarik séksual; *~ education* pendidikan séks; *~ life* kehidupan séks; *to
have* ~ bersetubuh, bersanggama; **sexual** *adj* séksual; *~ harassment* pelécéhan séksual; *~ intercourse, ~ relations*
hubungan badan; **sexually** *adv* secara
séksual; *~ transmitted disease (STD)*
penyakit menular séksual (PMT); **sexuality** *n* séksualitas; **sexy** *adj* séksi
Seychelles *n* [séisyéls] Kepulauan
Seychelles; **Seychellois** *adj* [séisyé-
lwa] berasal dari Seychelles; *n* orang
Seychelles
shabby *adj* lusuh, jélék
shack *n* gubuk, pondok
shackles *n, pl* [syakels] belenggu
shade *vt* mewarnai; *n* naungan, tempat
teduh; kréi; warna; *in the ~* di tempat
teduh; *pl, sl* kacamata hitam; **shading**
n pewarnaan; **shady** *adj* teduh; tidak
légal, curang
shadow *n* [syado] bayangan; *vt* membayangi; membuntuti; **shadowy** *adj*
remang-remang
shady *adj* teduh; tidak légal, curang ←
shade
shaft *n* lubang, terowongan; batang;
mine ~ lubang tambang
shaggy *adj* tidak rata, kasar (rambut,
bulu)
shake *n* goncangan, géléngan (kepala);
jabat tangan; *vi* **shook shaken**
gemetar, bergoyang, berguncang; *vt*
mengguncang, mengocok; *~ hands*
berjabatan tangan; *~ off* melepaskan
diri dari; *~ a leg* ayo cepat; *~ one's leg*
menggéléng kepala; **shaky** *adj*
goyang, goyah, kurang kuat
shake *n* minuman bercampuran susu
(coklat/biskuit/es)
shall *vi, aux* akan; *I ~ be there* saya
akan datang; *~ not (shan't)* takkan,
tidak akan
shallot *n* daun bawang
shallow *adj* dangkal; *the ~s* tempat
dangkal
sham *adj, n* pura-pura; *vi* berpura-pura

shambles n [syambels] kekacauan; *in a* ~ kacau-balau

shame n malu; *what a* ~ sayang sekali; *vt* membuat malu; **shameful** *adj* memalukan; **shameless** *adj* tanpa malu

shampoo n [syampu] sampo; *anti-dandruff* ~ sampo anti ketombé; *vi* berkeramas; *vt* mencuci rambut

shamrock n sejenis semanggi, lambang negara Irlandia

shan't *vi, aux* takkan, tidak akan → **shall**

shanty n gubuk, pondok; ~ *town* daérah kumuh

shape n bentuk; *in good* ~ séhat; langsing; *in the* ~ *of* berbentuk; *vt* membentuk; ~ *up* menjadi; **shapeless** *adj* tanpa bentuk; **shapely** *adj* sintal, montok

share n bagian, andil, saham; *the lion's* ~ bagian paling besar; *vi* berbagi; *vt* membagi; ~ *a room* sekamar; **sharecropper** *n* petani bagi hasil; **shareholder** *n* pemegang saham

shark n ikan hiu; *loan* ~ lintah darat; ~*'s fin soup* sup sirip ikan hiu, sup hisit

sharp *adj* tajam, runcing; cerdik; *C* ~ Cis; *F* ~ Fis; *ten o'clock* ~ jam sepuluh tepat; **sharpen** *vt* meruncingkan, mengasah, meraut; **sharpener** *n* raut pensil; **sharply** *adv* dengan tajam; **sharpness** *n* ketajaman

shave *vi* bercukur; *vt* mencukur; mengiris; ~ *one's legs* mencukur bulu kaki; ~*n head* gundul; *n* cukur; *a close* ~ nyaris celaka; *to have a* ~ bercukur; **shaving** *n* serutan; ~ *cream*, ~ *foam* sabun cukur; **shaver** *n* alat cukur (listrik)

shawl n syal, seléndang

she *pron, f* [syi] dia; *form* beliau; ~*'s*, ~ *is* dia (adalah); ~*'s my friend* dia temanku

shear *vt* [syir] mencukur (domba), memotong; **shearer** *n* pencukur domba; **shears** *n, pl* gunting besar; *pinking* ~ gunting bergerigi

sheath n [syith] sarung; pelapah; *penis* ~ kotéka

shed n gudang

shed *vt* rontok; ~ *blood* menumpahkan

darah; ~ *leaves* merontokkan daun; ~ *light* memberi keterangan; ~ *tears* mencucurkan air mata

sheep n **sheep** domba, biri-biri; *a flock of* ~ sekawanan domba; **sheepdog** *n* anjing gembala; **sheepish** *adj* malu; **sheepskin** *n* kulit domba

sheer *adj* tipis; curam; belaka; ~ *joy* kebahagiaan besar; ~ *stockings* stoking tipis

sheet n helai, lembar; seprai; ~ *lightning* kilat; *a* ~ *of paper* sehelai kertas

shelf n **shelves** papan, rak; ~*-life* masa berlaku; *book*~ rak buku

shell n kulit, kerang; *coconut* ~ tempurung kelapa; *vt* mengupas; ~ *out coll* membelanjakan, mengeluarkan (uang); **shellfish** *n* kerang-kerangan

shell n bom kecil, peledak; ~ *shock* trauma (karena perang); **shelling, shellfire** *n* penémbakan atau peledakan (dalam perang)

shellfish n kerang-kerangan ← **shell**

shelter n tempat berlindung, tempat teduh; *animal* ~ karantina; *bus* ~ halte bis; *vi* berlindung, bernaung; *vt* melindungi; ~ *a criminal* melindungi penjahat

shepherd n [shéperd] gembala; *German* ~ anjing hérder; *vt* menggiring

sherbet n serbat

sheriff n, *US* [syérif] kepala polisi daérah

sherry n semacam anggur

shield n [syild] perisai, taméng, pelindung; *vt* melindungi

shift n perubahan, pergéséran; jam kerja; *night* ~ jam kerja malam; *vi* berpindah tempat, beralih; *vt* mengubah, menggeser; **shifty** *adj* licik, tidak dapat dipercaya

shilling n, *arch* mata uang Inggris

shin, shinbone n tulang kering

shine n cahaya, sinar; *vi* **shone shone** [syon] bercahaya, bersinar; *vt* memancarkan; *the sun's shining* matahari bersinar; ~ *shoes* menggosok sepatu; **shiny** *adj* berkilap, mengkilap

shingles n, *pl* [syinggels] penyakit ruam syaraf

shiny *adj* berkilap, mengkilap ← **shine**

ship *vt* mengirim (lewat kapal); *n* kapal, perahu; *~'s log* buku harian di kapal; **shipment** *n* kiriman; pengiriman; **shipowner** *n* pemilik kapal; **shipping** *n* perkapalan, pengiriman dengan kapal; *~ agent* perwakilan ékspédisi, ékspéditur; *~ line* perusahaan perkapalan; **shipwreck** *n* [syiprék] peristiwa kapal karam; **shipyard** *n* galangan kapal

shire *n* daérah administratif; *UK, arch* kabupatén

shirt *n* baju, kaus; keméja, hém; *longsleeved ~* baju tangan panjang; *polo ~* kaus berkerah; *T-~* kaus oblong; *I wear this ~ to work* saya pakai keméja ini ke kantor

shit *vulg, adj* jélék; *n* tahi, kotoran; *in the ~* bermasalah; *I don't give a ~* émang gué pikirin; *v* bérak; *~ oneself* ketakutan; mengompol; **shitty** *adj* jélék

shiver *n* [syiver] getaran; *vi* menggigil, gemetar

shock *n* guncangan; kejutan; *~ absorber* sokbréker; *electric ~* kena setrum; *in ~* sedang syok; **shocking** *adj* mengejutkan

shoe *n* [syu] sepatu; *~ polish* semir sepatu; *~ shop, ~ store* toko sepatu; *horse~* ladam, tapal kuda; *running ~s, sports ~* sepatu olahraga; *vt* **shod shod** *~ a horse* meladami kuda; **shoelace** *n* tali sepatu; **shoemaker** *n* tukang sepatu; **shoeshine** *~ boy* penggosok sepatu; **shoestring** *n, arch* tali sepatu; *on a ~* dengan uang sedikit

shone *v, pf* [syon] → **shine**

shook *v, pf* → **shake**

shoot *n* tunas, pucuk

shoot *v* **shot shot** menémbak; merekam; *~ by* léwat dengan cepat; *~ up* tumbuh dengan cepat; *~ a film* membuat film; *~ a goal* mencétak gol; **shooting** *n* penémbakan; menémbak (olahraga); syuting, pengambilan gambar; *~ star* bintang jatuh

shop *n* toko; *~ assistant* pramuniaga, pelayan toko; *~ window* étalase; *to talk ~* membicarakan soal pekerjaan; *vi*

berbelanja; *~ around* melihat-lihat; *~ for* berbelanja mencari; **shopkeeper** *n* pemilik toko; **shoplift** *v* mengutil atau mencuri dari toko; **shopper** *n* orang yang berbelanja, pembeli; **shopping** *n* hasil belanja, belanjaan; *~ center, ~ mall* (pusat) pertokoan, mal

shore *n* pantai, tepi; *off ~* lepas pantai; *on ~* di darat; **shoreline** *n* garis pantai

shorn *vt, pf* → **shear**

short *adj* péndék, ringkas, singkat; kurang; kekurangan; *~-changed* dapat uang kembali yang kurang; *~-haul* jarak péndék; *~-lived* tidak berlangsung lama; *~-sighted* rabun jauh; *~-tempered* cepat marah; *~-term* jangka péndék; *~ circuit* kortsléting; *~ cut* jalan pintas, jalan tikus; *~ film* film péndék; *~ list* daftar péndék; *~ story* cerita péndék (cerpén); *~ wave* gelombang péndék; *caught ~* tidak mempunyai uang yang cukup; kebelet; *for ~* singkatannya, nama péndéknya; *in ~* singkatnya, péndék kata; *~ of breath* terengah-engah; *~ of money* tidak mempunyai uang yang cukup; *at ~ notice* secara mendadak; *to cut ~* memperpéndék, memotong; *n* film péndék; **shortage** *n* [shortej] kekurangan; **shorten** *vt* meméndékkan, memperpéndék; **shortcoming** *n* [syortkaming] kekurangan, kelemahan; **shortfall** *n* [syortfol] kekurangan; **shorthand** *n* tulisan sténo; **shortly** *adv* tidak lama lagi; secara ketus; **shorts** *n, pl* celana péndék, kolor

shot *n* tembakan; suntikan; *~ glass* seloki; *~ put* (tolak) peluru; *~ tower* menara mésiu; *big ~* pembesar; *vt, pf* → **shoot**; **shotgun** *n* senapan berburu

should *vi, aux* [syud] seharusnya, sebaiknya, semestinya; **shouldn't** *~ not* seharusnya tidak, seharusnya jangan

shoulder *n* [syolder] bahu, pundak; *hard ~* bahu jalan; *~ blade* tulang belikat; *~-length hair* rambut sebatas bahu; *~ to ~* bahu-membahu; *to give someone the cold ~* mengucilkan; *vt* memikul, menanggung

shout *n* [syaut] teriakan; *vi* berteriak, bersorak; *vt* meneriakkan; ~ *down* teriak supaya orang lain tidak kedengaran; *the audience ~ed down the MC* para penonton teriak supaya suara pembawa acara tidak kedengaran; ~ *at the top of your lungs* berteriak sekeras-kerasnya

shout *n* [syaut] giliran membayar; *it's my* ~ giliran saya membayar; *vt* traktir, membayarkan; *can I* ~ *you a drink?* boléh kubelikan minuman?

shove *n* [shav] dorongan; *v* mendorong dengan kasar; ~ *off derog* pergi

shovel *n* [shavel] sekop; *vt* menyekop

show *n* [sho] pertunjukan, tontonan; acara di televisi; paméran; ~*-off* orang yang berlagak; *no* ~ tidak jadi, tidak datang; *run the* ~ berkuasa, memerintah; *vt* memperlihatkan, mempertunjukkan; menunjukkan, menampakkan; membuktikan; ~ *off* beraksi; berlagak, sok; memamérkan; ~ *up* muncul; mempermalukan; *it* ~*s* memang tampak begitu, sudah jelas; ~ *one's face* hadir (karena basa-basi); ~ *someone in* membawa orang masuk; ~ *someone out* mengantarkan orang (keluar); **showbusiness** *n* **showbiz** *sl* dunia hiburan; **showcase** *n* lemari kaca untuk paméran; contoh yang baik; **showdown** *n* [shodaun] bentrokan; **showroom** *n* ruang paméran, ruang pajangan

shower *n* [syauer] pancuran (mandi); hujan sebentar; ~ *cap* tutup kepala; *baby* ~ perayaan kelahiran anak; *vi* mandi (di pancuran); *vt* menghujani, menaburi

shown *vt, pf* → **show**

showroom *n* ruang paméran, ruang pajangan ← **show**

shrank *v, pf* → **shrink**

shrapnel *n* serpihan dari bahan peledak

shred *n* carik, sobékan; *vt* mencarik, memarut, menghancurkan; **shredder** *n* mesin penghancur dokumén

shrewd *adj* cerdik, lihai

shriek *n* [syrik] jeritan, pekikan; *v* menjerit, memekik

shrill *adj* nyaring, melengking

shrimp *n* udang

shrine *n* kuil, tempat keramat

shrink *vi* **shrank shrunk** susut; *vt* menyusutkan; ~ *back* mundur, segan; **shrunken** *adj* berkerut, menyusut

shrink *n, coll* psikiater, dokter jiwa

shrivel [syrivel] *vi* ~ *(up)* keriput, layu; *after a week, the flowers ~led up and died* bunga jadi layu sesudah seminggu

shroud *n* kain kapan; *vt* menyelimuti, menyaput; ~*ed in mystery* disaput misteri

shrub *n* tanaman kecil; **shrubbery** *n* semak, belukar

shrug *n* angkat bahu; *vi* mengangkat bahu; *to* ~ *off* menganggap énténg

shrunk *v, pf* → **shrink**; **shrunken** *adj* berkerut, menyusut

shudder *n* gigil, getar; *vi* menggigil, gemetaran

shuffle *vi* [shafel] menyérét kaki; *vt* mengocok; ~ *cards* mengocok kartu

shun *vt* menghindarkan, mengélakkan

shush, ssh *ejac* [syusy] hus, sst

shut *vi* **shut shut** tutup; *vt* menutup; ~ *down* mematikan; tutup, gulung tikar; ~ *in* mengurung, memingit; ~ *up* tutup mulut, diam; menutup; ~ *one's eyes* memejamkan mata, menutup mata; **shutter** *n* daun penutup jendéla

shuttle *adj* [syatel] ulang-alik; ~ *bus* bis ulang-alik; *n* kendaraan ulang-alik; puntalan, kumparan; *space* ~ pesawat ulang-alik

shuttlecock *n* kok

shy *adj* [syai] malu, pemalu; **shyly** *adv* kemalu-maluan; **shyness** *n* rasa malu

Siam *n, arch* [sayam] Thailand, Muang Thai; **Siamese** *adj* [sayamiz] ~ *cat* kucing Siam; ~ *twin* kembar Siam

sibling *n* saudara (kandung); *John has three ~s* John bersaudara empat

sick *adj* sakit; ~ *bay* kamar untuk orang sakit; ~ *leave* cuti sakit; ~ *of* bosan, jenuh, jemu; *I feel* ~ saya tidak énak badan; *to be* ~ muntah; **sickening** *adj* memualkan, menjijikkan; **sickly** *adj* sering sakit, sakit-sakitan; **sickness** *n* sakit, penyakit

sickle *n* [sikel] sabit; *hammer and ~* palu arit

sickly *adj* sering sakit, sakit-sakitan ← sick

sickness *n* sakit, penyakit ← sick

side *n* sisi, segi; samping; tepi, pinggir; pihak; *~ dish* lauk-pauk; *~ effect* éfék samping; *~ street* jalan kecil; *both ~s* kedua belah pihak; *~ by ~* bersebelahan; *on the ~* diam-diam, sampingan; *to take ~s* berpihak, memihak; *by the ~ of the house* di samping rumah, di sebelah rumah; *by the ~ of the road* di pinggir jalan; sideboard *n* laci besar yang panjang; sideburns *n* bréwokan, cambang; sidecar *n* séspan; sideline *vt* mengesampingkan, menyingkirkan; sidelong *adj* dari samping; *~ glance* lirikan; sidetrack *v* meléncéng; menggelincirkan; *to get ~ed* meléncéng dari tujuan; sidewalk *n* [saidwok] trotoar; sideways *adv* miring, ke samping

siege *n* [sij] pengepungan

Sierra Leone *n* [siéra léon] Siérra Léone; Sierra Leonean *adj* berasal dari Siérra Léone; *n* orang Siérra Léone

siesta *n* [siésta] tidur siang

sieve *n* [siv] ayakan, saringan; *vt* menyaring, mengayak

sift *vt* mengayak; menyaring

sigh *n* [sai] keluh, nafas panjang; *a ~ of relief* bernafas lega; *vi* menarik nafas panjang; mendesah

sight *n* [sait] pemandangan; penglihatan; *in ~* kelihatan; *at first ~* pada pandangan pertama; *to see the ~s* mengunjungi obyék wisata; sighted *adj* terlihat; *n* orang yang bisa melihat; *long-~* rabun dekat; sighting *n* kelihatan, terlihat; sightseeing *n* [saitsiing] wisata, tamasya; sightseer *n* [saitsier] wisatawan, turis

sign *n* [sain] tanda, pertanda, isyarat; rambu; plang; papan; *~ language* bahasa isyarat; *star ~* bintang; *vi* tékén, memberi paraf; berkomunikasi léwat bahasa isyarat; *~ off* mengakhiri, menutup; *~ on, ~ up* mendaftar; *~ over* membalik nama; *vt* menandatangani;

signal *n* [signal] tanda, isyarat; *vi* memberi tanda; *vt* mengisyaratkan; signature *n* [signatyur] tanda tangan; signpost *n* [sainpost] rambu

significance *n* [signifikans] arti, makna; significant *adj* [signifikant] berarti, penting; significantly *adv* cukup; signify *vt* [signifai] berarti, bermakna, menandakan

signpost *n* [sainpost] rambu ← sign

silence *n* [sailens] keheningan; *~ is golden* diam itu emas; *to observe a minute's ~* mengheningkan cipta; *vt* mendiamkan; silent *adj* diam; *~ letter* huruf yang tidak diucapkan; *a ~ person* orang pendiam

silhouette *n* [siluét] bayangan hitam

silicon *n* [silikon] silikon

silk *adj, n* sutera; silkworm *n* [silkwerm] ulat sutera; silky *adj* terbuat dari sutera; *~-smooth* sehalus sutera

silliness *n* kelucuan; kebodohan; silly *adj* bodoh, tolol; lucu

silo *n* gudang (terigu, jagung dsb)

silver *adj, n* pérak; *~ anniversary* ulang tahun perkawinan pérak; *~ screen* layar pérak; *~ tongue* pandai berbicara; silverfish *n* gegat; silversmith *n* pandai pérak, perajin pérak; silverware *n* séndok garpu; barang-barang pérak

SIM *~ card* kartu SIM

similar *adj* [similer] serupa, mirip; similarity *n* keserupaan, kemiripan; similarly *adv* demikian pula, juga, dengan cara yang sama

simmer *vi* sedikit mendidih; *~ down coll* reda; tenanglah!

simple *adj* [simpel] sederhana, bersahaja; bodoh; *George led a ~ life* George hidup sederhana; simplicity *n* [simplisiti] kesederhanaan; simplify *vt* [simplifai] menyederhanakan; simply *adv* dengan sederhana; hanya; benar-benar, sungguh-sungguh

simulation *n* simulasi

simultaneous *adj* [simulténius] serentak, serempak; *~ equation* persamaan berganda

sin *n* dosa; *to commit a ~* berdosa; *to*

live in ~ hidup bersama tanpa menikah; *vi* berdosa; ~ *against* berdosa pada; **sinful** *adj* penuh dosa; **sinner** *n* orang yang berdosa

since *conj* sejak, sedari; sebab, karena; ~ *you've been gone, things have changed* sejak kamu pergi, keadaan sudah berubah; ~ *you're here now, you can do the dishes* mumpung kamu sedang di sini, tolong cuci piring

sincere *adj* [sinsir] tulus (hati), ikhlas; bersungguh-sungguh; **sincerely** [sin-sirli] *yours* ~ salam hormat; **sincerity** [sinsériti] ketulusan, keikhlasan

sinful *adj* penuh dosa ← **sin**

sing *vi* **sang sung** bernyanyi, menyanyi; *vt* menyanyikan; ~-*a-long*, ~-*song* menyanyi bersama; **singer** *n* [singer] penyanyi; *backing* ~ penyanyi latar; **singing** *n* [singing] nyanyian; *Peter enjoys* ~ *at church* Peter suka bernyanyi di geréja; **song** *n* nyanyian, lagu; **songwriter** *n* pencipta lagu

Singapore *n* Singapura; **Singaporean** *adj* [singaporian] berasal dari Singapura; *n* orang Singapura

singer *n* penyanyi

single *adj* [singgel] tunggal, sendiri, satu; lajang, *m* bujangan; lagu; ~-*handed* sendirian; ~ *bed* tempat tidur untuk satu orang; ~ *file* antri satu per satu; ~ *parent* orang tua tunggal; ~ *ticket* karcis sekali jalan; *women's* ~*s* pertandingan tunggal putri; *every* ~ *time* setiap kali; *vi* ~ *out* memilih satu; **singular** *adj, n* [singguler] bentuk tunggal

singlet *n* singlét

singular *adj, n* [singguler] bentuk tunggal ← **single**

sinister *adj* [sinister] angker, seram

sink *n* tempat cuci (piring); *vi* **sank sunk** tenggelam, mengendap; ~ *in* meresap, masuk ke dalam hati; ~*ing feeling* perasaan tertekan; ~ *or swim* berjuang sendiri; *vt* menenggelamkan; *that ship was sunk during the war* kapal itu ditenggelamkan waktu perang

sinner *n* orang yang berdosa ← **sin**

sinus *adj* berkaitan dengan lubang antara hidung dan mulut; **sinusitis** *n* [sainusaitus] radang hidung, sinusitis

sip *n* isapan; *v* mengisap, meminum sedikit

sir *pron, m* tuan

siren *n* siréne

sirloin *n* [sérloin] daging pinggang

sister *n* saudara perempuan, adik atau kakak perempuan; kepala perawat, suster; ~ *city* kota kembar; ~-*in-law* kakak/adik ipar (yang perempuan); *half*-~ kakak/adik tiri (yang perempuan)

sit *vi* **sat sat** duduk; bersidang; ~ *cross-legged* duduk bersila; ~ *down* (pergi) duduk; ~ *nicely*, ~ *properly* duduk dengan manis; ~ *through* duduk sampai selesai; ~ *on the fence* tidak memihak, nétral; *vt* menempuh; ~ *an exam* menempuh ujian; **sitting** *adj* ~ *duck* sasaran empuk; ~ *room* kamar duduk; *n* sidang

sitcom *n* film séri komédi, sinétron ← **situation comedy**

site *n* lokasi, situs, tempat; *archeological* ~ situs purbakala; *web*~ situs (di) internet

sitting *adj* ~ *room* kamar duduk; *n* sidang ← **sit**

situated *adj* [sityuéted] terletak; **situation** *n* keadaan, situasi; ~ *comedy (sitcom)* film séri komédi, sinétron

six *adj, n* enam; ~-*pack* kotak berisi enam botol minuman; ~ *of one, half a dozen of the other* setali tiga uang, sama saja; *at* ~*es and sevens* kacau balau; **sixteen** *adj, n* enam belas; **sixteenth** *adj* keenam belas; **sixth** *adj* keenam; ~ *sense* indera keenam; **sixtieth** *adj* [sikstieth] keenam puluh; **sixty** *adj, n* enam puluh; *the nineteen-sixties (1960s)* tahun enam puluhan

size *n* ukuran, nomor; besarnya; *one* ~ *fits all* satu ukuran; *vi* ~ *up* menaksir, menilai

sizzle *n* *sausage* ~ acara panggang sosis; *vi* mendesis; **sizzler** *n* hari yang sangat panas; **sizzling** *adj* sangat panas; *this pie is* ~ *hot* pai ini masih panas sekali

skate *n* sepatu luncur, sepatu és; *ice*-~ sepatu és; *roller*-~ sepatu roda; *vi* meluncur, bermain sepatu luncur atau sepatu roda; **skateboard** *n* papan luncur; **skater** *n* pemain sepatu luncur; pemain papan luncur; **skateboarding** *n* bermain papan luncur; **skating** *n* bermain sepatu luncur; ~ *rink* gelanggang sepatu roda; *ice-*~ *rink* gelanggang és; ~ *on thin ice* mengambil risiko

skeleton *n* [skéleton] kerangka; ~ *key* kunci induk

skeptical, sceptical *adj* ragu-ragu, kurang percaya, sképtis; *I am very ~ about his schemes* saya sangat meragukan rencananya

sketch *n* skétsa; gambar; *v* membuat skétsa; menggambar; **sketchbook** *n* buku skétsa; **sketchy** *adj* kurang jelas

skewer *n* [skyuer] tusuk daging, tusuk saté; *vt* menusuk

ski *n* (sepatu) ski; *vi* main ski; **skier** *n* [skier] pemain ski; **skiing** *n* [skiing] main ski

skid *n* bekas gelincir; ~ *row* daérah kumuh; *on the ~s* sedang kesulitan; *vi* gelincir, tergelincir, selip

skier *n* [skier] pemain ski ← **ski**

skiing *n* [skiing] main ski ← **ski**

skill *n* keterampilan, keahlian; ~*ed craftsman* perajin; ~*ed at* mahir, trampil; **skillful, skilful** *adj* terampil

skim *vt* melintas secara pintas; ~ *milk* susu tanpa kepala susu; ~ *reading* membaca secara pintas

skimpy *adj* kecil, sedikit; *that tank top's a bit ~* baju tali spagéti itu agak terbuka

skin *n* kulit; ~ *cancer* kanker kulit; *thick-*~*ed* berkulit badak; *white ~* kulit putih; *vt* menguliti; **skinhead** *n* [skinhéd] préman gundul

skinny *adj* [skini] kurus, ceking

skip *vi* melompat-lompat; ~*ping rope* tali lompat; *hop, ~ and jump* sangat dekat; *vt* meléwati; meloncati; *Claire ~ped chapter 6* Claire tidak membaca bab 6

skipper *n* nakhoda; kaptén

skirt *n* rok; *mini-* rok mini

skive *v, coll, UK* bolos; *Sarah ~d English class* Sarah bolos pelajaran bahasa Inggris

skivvy *n* kaos tangan panjang berkerah gulung

skull *n* tengkorak, batok kepala; ~ *and crossbones* bendéra bajak laut; **skullcap** *n, Isl* kopiah

skunk *n* sigung; orang yang kurang ajar

sky *n* [skai] langit, angkasa, udara; ~ *high* selangit, setinggi langit; ~ *blue* biru muda; **skydiver** *n* penerjun payung; **skydiving** *n* terjun payung; **skylight** *n* [skailait] jendéla langit; **skyline** *n* kaki langit; **skyscraper** *n* pencakar langit; **skywriter** *n* [skairaiter] pesawat yang meninggalkan tulisan asap

slab *n* papan, potong

slack *adj* kendur, lesu; tidak rajin; **slacken** *vi* mengendur, berkurang; *the pace of development has ~ed* laju pembangunan telah melambat

slacks *n, pl* celana panjang (perempuan)

slain *vt, pf →* **slay**

slam *n* gerdam; *Grand ~* empat pertandingan tenis yang besar (Australia, Perancis dan AS Terbuka, dan Wimbledon); *vt* membanting, menggerdam, menutup dengan keras

slander *n* fitnah (secara lisan); *vt* memfitnah; *Nicholas was accused of ~* Nicholas dituduh telah memfitnah orang

slang *n* **slangy** *adj* bahasa percakapan, bahasa gaul

slant *n* kemiringan, sudut, pandangan; ~*-eyed* bermata sipit

slap *n* tampar, tamparan; *a ~ in the face* muka ditampar; penolakan; *a ~ on the wrist* teguran; *vt* menampar; **slapdash** *adj* sembrono, asal jadi

slash *n* garis miring (/); *vt* memotong, menyayat; ~ *one's wrists* memotong urat nadi

slate *n* batu tulis; *to have a clean ~* tidak bersalah, punya lembaran yang putih bersih

slaughter *n* [sloter] pembantaian; penyembelihan; *vt* membantai; memotong, menyembelih

Slav *n* orang Slavia; Slavic [slavik] ~ *language* bahasa Slavia; **Slavonic** *adj* [slavonik] berasal dari daérah orang Slavia (Eropa Timur)

slave *n* budak; **slavery** *n* perbudakan

Slavonic *adj* [slavonik] berasal dari daérah orang Slavia (Eropa Timur) ← **Slav**

slay *vt* **slew slain** membunuh; *St George slew the dragon* Santo George membunuh naga itu

sleazy *adj* [slizi] jorok, tidak senonoh, tidak sopan

sled, sledge *n* keréta luncur

sledgehammer *n* palu besar

sleek *adj* licin, mengkilap

sleep *vi* **slept slept** tidur; *~ around* meniduri banyak orang; *~ in* bangun siang; *~ together, ~ with* tidur bersama; bersetubuh; *~ well* selamat tidur; *my foot's gone to ~* kaki saya kesemutan; **sleeper** *n* orang yang tidur; gerbong kabin; balok rél keréta api; **sleeping** *~ bag* kantong tidur; *~ tablet* obat tidur; **sleepless** *adj* tanpa tidur; **sleepover** *n* acara tidur ramai-ramai bagi anak-anak; **sleepwalk** *vi* mimpi jalan; **sleepy** *adj* mengantuk; sepi

sleet *n* hujan bercampur és dan salju

sleeve *n* lengan baju; sisipan kertas di CD; **sleeveless** *adj* tanpa lengan

sleigh *n* [slé] keréta luncur; *Santa travels in a ~* Sinterklaas jalan naik keréta luncur

slender *adj* ramping, langsing

slept *vi, pf* → **sleep**

slew *vt, pf* → **slay**

slice *n* irisan, sayatan, potongan; *a ~ of cake* sepotong kué; *vt* mengiris, menyayat; *~d bread* roti yang telah dipotong

slick *adj* licin, cekatan; *n* tumpahan, lapisan; *oil ~* tumpahan minyak

slide *n* perosotan; *vi* **slid slid** meluncur; tergelincir; *~ down* merosot; *vt* mendorong; *sliding door* pintu gésér; *sliding window* jendéla gésér

slight *adj* [slait] sedikit; mungil; **slightly** *adv* sedikit

slim *adj* ramping, langsing, lampai; *a ~ chance* tidak banyak harapan; *vi ~*

down menjadi (lebih) langsing; *~ming tea* téh pelangsing; **slimline** *adj* berbentuk mulus, ramping

slime *n* kotoran, lumpur, lumut; **slimy** *adj* berlumpur, kotor

sling *n* kain géndongan; *his broken arm was in a ~* tangannya yang patah digéndong; *Singapore ~* sejenis koktail; **slingshot** *n* ketapél

slip *n* kesalahan; longsor; rok dalam; *~ of the tongue* lidah keseléo; *vi* tergelincir; terlupa; *~ away* diam-diam pergi; *~ in* menyelinap masuk; *~ up* keliru, berbuat salah; *vt* menyelipkan; *it ~ped my mind* saya terlupa akan hal itu; **slippery** *adj* licin

slipper *n* selop; sandal

slippery *adj* licin ← **slip**

slit *n* celah, belah; *vt* membelah; *~ your wrists* memotong urat nadi; *~ your throat* menggorok

slither *vi* melata, merayap (ular)

slob *n* orang yang sembrono; *Fred is a terrible ~; his kitchen is full of dirty dishes* Fred itu sembrono sekali, dapurnya penuh piring kotor

slogan *n* semboyan, slogan

slope *n* léréng; *vi* melandai; **sloping** *adj* miring

sloppy *adj* tidak rapi; *coll* céngéng

slosh *vi* tumpah; terkocok-kocok (air)

slot *n* celah, lubang (kunci); tempat; *~ machine* mesin otomatis; mesin judi; *vi ~ in* masuk (dengan pas)

Slovak *n* bahasa Slovakia; orang Slovakia; **Slovakia** *n* Slovakia

Slovene *n* [slovin] orang Slovénia; **Slovenia** *n* Slovénia; **Slovenian** *adj* berasal dari Slovénia; *n* bahasa Slovénia

slovenly *adj* [slavenli] jorok, tidak rapi

slow *adj* perlahan-lahan, pelan-pelan; lambat, lamban; lama; *~ food* makanan bermutu tinggi; *~ lane* jalur lambat; *~ motion* (slo-mo) gerak pelan; *that clock is ~* jam itu terlambat; *vi ~ down* mengurangi kecepatan; *vt* melambatkan, memperlambat; **slowly** *adv* pelan-pelan

sludge *n* lumpur

slug *n* semacam siput; **sluggish** *adj* [slagisy] malas; **sluggishly** *adv* dengan malas

sluice *n* [slus] pintu air

slum *n* daérah kumuh; *vi, coll ~ it* menginap di sembarang tempat

slumber *n, vi* tidur

slump *n* kemerosotan; *vi* merosot; terjatuh, rebah; *Trevor ~ed on his desk when the exam finished* Trevor rebah di atas méja ketika ujian selesai

sly *adj* cerdik; *on the ~* diam-diam, sembunyi-sembunyi; **slyly** *adv* dengan cerdik

smack *n* tampar, tamparan, tempéléng; *sl* héroin; *vt* menampar, menempéléng

small *adj* kecil; *~-minded* berpikiran sempit; *~-time* kelas teri; *~ change* uang kecil, uang récéh; *~ child* anak kecil; *~ fry* ikan teri; *~ talk* basa-basi, obrolan ringan; *too ~* kekecilan; *~ is beautiful* kecil itu indah; *a ~ fortune* uang banyak sekali; *the ~ hours* dini hari; *the ~ screen* layar télévisi; *to feel ~* merasa malu; merasa minder; *it's a ~ world* dunia ini kecil; **smallholder** *n* petani yang mengerjakan ladang kecil; **smallpox** *n* cacar

smart *adj* cerdas, pintar; cantik, tampan; cepat; *~ arse vulg* orang sok pinter; *~ card* kartu pintar; *quick ~* sekarang juga; *vi* pedih, sakit; **smartly** *adv* dengan cepat; dengan gaya; *Sinead always dresses ~* Sinead selalu berpakaian gaya

smash *n* tabrakan, kecelakaan (mobil); smés; *~ hit* laku keras; *vi* hancur, pecah; *vt* memecahkan, menghancurkan; *~ a record* memecahkan rékor

smear *n* coréngan; *vt* mencoréng; *~ campaign* usaha mencoréng nama orang

smell *n* bau; *delicious ~* harum; *sense of ~* indera penciuman; *vi* bau; *~ of* berbau; *~ sweet* wangi; *vt* mencium; *to ~ a rat* menjadi curiga; **smelly** *adj* berbau (tidak sedap)

smile *n* senyum, senyuman; *vi* tersenyum

smith *n* pandai besi; **smithy** *n* tempat pandai besi

smog *n* asbut (asap kabut); **smoggy** *adj* [smogi] berasap

smock *n* baju kerja, baju luar, baju pelindung

smoke *n* asap; *sl* rokok; *~-free* dilarang merokok; *no ~ without fire* ada asap ada api; *to have a ~* merokok; *vi* berasap; merokok; *vt* merokok; mengasapi; **smoker** *n* perokok; **smoking** *n* merokok; *no ~* dilarang merokok; *you should stop ~* sebaiknya berhenti merokok; **smoky** *adj* berasap

smolder, smoulder *vi* membara

smooth *adj* licin; lancar; *~-talking* pandai berbicara; *~ as silk* licin sekali; *vt* melicinkan, meluruskan; **smoothly** *adv* dengan lancar; *proceedings went ahead ~* acara berjalan dengan lancar

smorgasbord *n* sajian prasmanan

smoulder → smolder

smudge *n* coréngan, noda tinta di kertas; *vi* mencoréng

smug *adj* sombong, bangga sendiri; **smugly** *adv* [smagli] dengan sombong

smuggle *vt* [smagel] menyelundupkan; *~ in* menyelundupkan masuk; **smuggler** *n* penyelundup; **smuggling** *n* penyelundupan

snack *n* makanan kecil, camilan; *~ bar* warung, tempat menjual makanan kecil; *vi* mengemil; *~ on* mengemil; *Jonathan ~s on nuts* Jonathan suka mengemil kacang

snag *n* masalah kecil, masalah sepéle; *coll* sosis; *vi* menyangkut; *vt* menyangkutkan

snail *n* kéong, siput; *~ shell* rumah siput, rumah kéong; *~'s pace* sangat lama, sangat lambat

snake *n* ular; *poisonous ~* ular berbisa; *~s and ladders* permainan ular dan tangga; *~ in the grass* orang yang berpura-pura menjadi teman

snap *n* bunyi yang keras; *cold ~* cuaca yang tiba-tiba dingin; *vt* mematahkan; kehilangan kesabaran; *~ at* membentak; *~ up* cepat membeli; *~ your fingers* mengertak jari; **snappily** *adv* dengan nada marah; **snappy** *adj* dengan cepat, lekas; *make it ~!* cepatan!; **snapshot** *n* potrét, foto

snarl *n* gertak; *v* menggeram; membentak

snatch *in* ~*es* sepotong-sepotong; *vt* menjambrét, merampas; **snatcher** *bag* ~ jambrét

sneak *n* [snik] orang yang melaporkan kawan; *vi* menyelinap; ~ *off* pergi secara diam-diam, kabur; ~ *out* diam-diam keluar; ~*ing suspicion* semakin curiga; ~ *preview* pertunjukan terlebih dahulu yang terbatas; ~ *up on* diam-diam mendekati; **sneakers** *n* sepatu kéts, sepatu olahraga; **sneaky** *adj* tidak terus terang

sneer *n* mimik wajah yang menyeringai; *vi* menyeringai; ~ *at* menertawakan; memandang rendah

sneeze *n, vi* bersin; *not to be* ~*d at* lumayan, tidak sepéle

snicker → **snigger**

sniff *n* hirupan; *v* mencium, menciumcium; ~ *at* merémehkan; ~ *out* mencari; ~*er dog* anjing pencium

sniffle *n* [snifel] pilek; *vi* tersedu-sedu

snigger, snicker *n, vi* tertawa dengan nada menyindir

snip *n* potongan kecil, guntingan; *to have the* ~ *coll* disunat; *vt* menggunting; **snippet** *n* secuil; *a* ~ *of information* sedikit informasi

sniper *n* penembak jitu

snippet *n* secuil; *a* ~ *of information* sedikit informasi ← **snip**

snivel *vi, derog* [snivel] tersedu-sedu; céngéng

snob *n* orang sombong; *there are lots of* ~*s at private schools* banyak orang sombong di sekolah swasta; **snobbish, snobby** *adj* sombong

snooker *n* semacam permainan bilyar

snoop *n* orang yang diam-diam ingin mencari tahu; *vi* mencari-cari informasi tanpa izin

snooze *n, sl* tidur sebentar

snore *vi* mendengkur; *sl* mengorok; **snorer** *n* orang yang mendengkur

snorkel *n* snorkel; *vi* snorkeling; ~ *and fins* snorkel dan fin

snot *n* ingus; *dried* ~ upil; **snotty** *adj* beringus; *coll* sombong

snout *n* moncong

snow *n* salju; ~*-white, as white as* ~ seputih salju, seputih kapas; ~ *line* garis salju; ~ *White* Putri Salju; *vi* hujan salju; **snowball** *n* [snobol] bola salju; **snowcapped** *adj* tertutup salju (gunung); *vi* berkembang menjadi besar; **snowdrift** *n* timbunan salju; **snowfall** *n* [snofol] curah salju; **snowflake** *n* kepingan salju; **snowman** *n* bonéka salju; **snowshoe** *n* [snosyu] alas untuk sepatu kalau menginjak salju; **snowstorm** *n* badai salju; **snowy** *adj* bersalju; putih; ~*-haired* berambut putih

Snr *abbrev, US* **senior** yang tua; *John F. Kennedy* ~ John F. Kennedy yang tua (bukan John F. Kennedy yang muda)

snub *n* penghinaan; ~ *nose* hidung pésék; *vt* mencuékkan, menghina, menolak tegur sapa; *Meg* ~*bed me at university* Meg mencuékkan saya waktu kuliah

snuck *v, pf* → **sneak**

snug *adj* hangat, nyaman; pas; **snugly** *adv* [snagli] dengan pas; **snuggle** *vi* (tidur) meringkuk; *the baby* ~*d up against its mother* anak bayi meringkuk didekap ibunya

so *adv* begitu; sangat; demikian; ~*called* apa yang dinamakan; ~*-*~ biasa saja; ~*-and-*~ (si) anu; ~ *much*, ~ *many* begitu banyak; ~ *are we* kami juga; *and* ~ *on, and* ~ *forth* dan sebagainya (dsb); *I think* ~ saya kira begitu; *conj* jadi, maka, oleh sebab itu; ~ *that* supaya; sehingga; ~ *what* terus?; *sl* emang gue pikirin (EGP)

soak *vi* rendam; ~ *into* meresap ke dalam; ~ *through* tembus; *vt* merendam; ~*ing wet*, **soaked** *adj* basah kuyup

soap *n* sabun; ~ *opera* opéra sabun; ~ *powder* sabun cuci baju; *liquid* ~ sabun cair; **soapdish** *n* tempat sabun; **soapsuds** *n* busa; **soapy** *adj* bersabun, berbusa

soar *vi* membubung tinggi, melonjak; *the eagle* ~*ed over the mountain* burung élang terbang tinggi di atas gunung

sob *n* sedu, isak; *vi* tersedu-sedu, terisak-isak; **sobbing** *n* sedu, isak
sober *adj* tidak mabuk; waras; sérius
soccer *n* sépak bola; ~ *field* lapangan
sépak bola; ~ *player* pemain (sépak)
bola; *vt* menendang dari tanah
social *adj* [sosyal] sosial, kemasyarakatan; ramah; ~ *conscience* kepedulian sosial; ~ *life* pergaulan; ~ *media*
média sosial (médsos); ~ *security*
jaminan sosial, tunjangan pemerintah;
~ *studies,* ~ *science* ilmu pengetahuan
sosial (IPS); ~ *welfare* kesejahteraan
sosial; ~ *worker* pekerja sosial; **socialite** *n* [sosyalait] sosialita; **socialize** *vi*
bergaul
socialism *n* [sosyalizem] sosialisme;
socialist *n* sosialis; *Union of Soviet* ~
Republics (USSR) Républik Sosialis
Uni Soviet (URSS)
socialite *n* [sosyalait] sosialita ←
social
socialize *vi* bergaul ← **social**
society *n* [sosayeti] masyarakat;
perkumpulan, perhimpunan; *high* ~
kalangan atas; **sociologist** *n* sosiolog;
sociology *n* sosiologi, ilmu
masyarakat
sock *n* kaus kaki; *odd* ~s kaus kaki
yang tidak sepasang; *to pull your* ~s *up*
memperbaiki préstasi
socket *n* lubang, rongga; stopkontak
soda ~ *water* air soda; *baking* ~ soda
kué; *whiskey and* ~ wiski soda
sodium *n* sodium, natrium; ~ *bicarbon-
ate* soda kué
sodomize *vt* menyodomi; **sodomy** *n*
semburit, sodomi
sofa *n* dipan, sofa, kursi empuk
soft *adj* lunak, lembék, lembut; ~-*boiled
egg* telur setengah matang; ~-*spoken*
bersuara lembut; ~ *drink* minuman
ringan, minuman tanpa alkohol; ~ *on*
lemah, lunak; ~ *option* pilihan yang
mudah; ~ *spot* titik lemah, kelemahan;
~ *toy* bonéka; **softball** *n* sofbal; **soften**
vi [sofen] melunak, melembut; *vt*
melunakkan, melembutkan; **softener**
n [sofener] pelembut; **softly** *adv* [soft-
li] dengan lembut; ; **softness** *n*

kelembutan, sifat lembut; **software** *n*
peranti lunak
soggy *adj* berair, basah; *this cake's
gone all* ~ kué ini jadi basah
soil *n* tanah; *vt* mengotori; **soiled** *adj*
kotor
solar *adj* [soler] berhubungan dengan
matahari; ~ *eclipse* gerhana matahari;
~ *energy,* ~ *power* tenaga surya, tenaga matahari; ~ *system* tata surya
sold *v, pf* → **sell**; *adj* terjual; ~ *out*
habis terjual (tiket, barang, tapi bukan
makanan)
solder *v* patri, mematri; ~*ing iron* patri
soldér
soldier *n* [soljer] tentara, prajurit,
laskar, serdadu; ~ *of* fortune tentara
bayaran; *vi* ~ *on* bertahan, tetap jalan
sole *adj* satu-satunya, tunggal; ~ *parent*
orang tua tunggal; **solely** *adv* semata-
mata, hanya; **solitary** *adj* sendiri; sepi;
~ *confinement* dikurung tersendiri
sole *n* telapak kaki, alas sepatu
sole *n* ikan lidah
solemn *adj* [solem] khidmat, sérius;
solemnly *adv* dengan sérius; *I do* ~
declare saya menyatakan secara sungguh-sungguh; **solemnize** *vt* mengesahkan; *the marriage was* ~*d in the
registry office* perkawinan itu disahkan
di kantor catatan sipil
solicitor *n* [solisiter] pengacara, ahli
hukum
solid *adj* padat; kuat, kokoh; *rock* ~
sangat kuat; *n* zat padat; *pl* makanan
padat; **solidarity** *n* solidaritas, kesetiakawanan; **solidify** *vi* mengeras, membeku
solitaire *n* [solitér] permainan solitér
solitary *adj* sendiri; sepi; ~ *confinement*
dikurung tersendiri ← **sole**
solo *adj, adv* sendiri, solo; ~ *concert*
konsér tunggal; **soloist** *n* solois,
penyanyi atau pemain tunggal
Solomon ~ *Islander* [solomon ailander]
orang dari Kepulauan Solomon; ~
Islands Kepulauan Solomon
solstice *n* [solstis] titik balik matahari;
summer ~ titik balik matahari musim
panas

soluble *adj* [solyubel] dapat larut atau dilarutkan, mudah larut; **solution** *n* larutan, solusi; **solvent** *n* pelarut

solution *n* cara pemecahan, cara penyelesaian, solusi; **solve** *vt* memecahkan; menyelesaikan; *~ a problem* memecahkan masalah; *~ a mystery* mencari jawaban teka-teki, membongkar misteri

solvent *n* pelarut

Somalia *n* Somalia; **Somali** *adj* berasal dari Somalia; *n* orang Somalia

some *adj* [sam] beberapa, sebagian; kurang lebih; salah satu; sedikit; *~ time*, *~ day* kapan-kapan; **somebody** *pron* seseorang, ada orang; **somehow** *adv* bagaimanapun juga; **someone** *pron* [samwan] seseorang, ada orang; **something** *pron* sesuatu; *~ like that* semacam itu; **sometimes** *adv* kadang-kadang; **somewhat** *adv* [samwot] agak, sedikit; **somewhere** *adv* [samwér] entah di mana

somersault *n* [samersolt] jungkir balik, salto; *vi* berjungkir balik, bersalti

something *pron* [samthing] sesuatu ← **some**

sometimes *adv* [samtaimz] kadang-kadang ← **some**

somewhat *adv* [samwot] agak, sedikit ← **some**

somewhere *adv* [samwér] entah di mana ← **some**

son *n* [san] anak (lelaki), putera; *pron* nak, bung; *~-in-law* menantu; *~-of-a-bitch vulg* bangsat; *god~* anak baptis; *grand~* cucu

song *n* nyanyian, lagu; **songwriter** *n* [songraiter] pencipta lagu

soon *adv* segera, lekas; *as ~ as* begitu; *as ~ as possible (asap)* secepat mungkin, secepat-cepatnya; **sooner** *adv* lebih cepat; *~ or later* lambat laun, lama-lama; *no ~ than* begitu; *the ~, the better* makin cepat makin baik

soothe *vt* **soothing** *adj* menghibur, menenangkan; *~ music* lagu yang menghibur

sophisticated *adj* [sofistikéted] canggih, pintar, berpengalaman; **sophistication** *n* kecanggihan, pengalaman duniawi

soppy *adj* séntimentil

soprano *n* sopran

sorcerer *n* penyihir; **sorcery** *n* ilmu sihir

sore *adj* sakit, pedih; *a ~ point* masalah; *a ~ throat* sakit tenggorokan; *sl* marah; *n* luka kecil; **sorely** *adv* sangat; *~ missed* sangat dirindukan

sorrow *n* kesedihan, duka cita; **sorrowful** *adj* sedih; **sorry** *adj* menyesal; maaf; *~ about* menyesal soal; *I'm ~* maaf, maafkan saya; *you'll be ~* kamu akan menyesal; *to feel ~ for* mengasihani

sort *n* macam, jenis; *~ of ... ya*, *tapi ...*; *what ~ of food do you like?* suka makanan seperti apa?; *vt* menyortir, memilih, memilah-milah; *~ out, to get something ~ed* mengurus, mengatur

SOS *abbrev* save our souls tolong, selamatkan jiwa kami

souffle *n* [suflé] semacam panekuk

sought *vt, pf →* **seek**

soul *n* sukma, roh, nyawa, jiwa, semangat; *~-searching* introspéksi; *~ (music)* musik khas orang hitam; *a good ~* orang baik; *body and ~* jiwa raga

sound *n* bunyi, suara; *~ barrier* témbok suara; *~ effect* éfék suara; *vi* berbunyi, kedengaran; *~ like, ~ as if* kedengarannya; **soundless** *adj* **soundlessly** *adv* tanpa suara; **soundproof** *adj* kedap suara; **soundtrack** *n* musik dari film

sound *adj* séhat, kuat; *~ asleep* tidur nyenyak, tidur pulas; *a ~ decision* keputusan yang bijak; **soundly** *adv* sungguh-sungguh; nyenyak, pulas

soundproof *adj* kedap suara ← **sound**

soundtrack *n* musik dari film ← **sound**

soup *n* [sup] sop, sup; *~ kitchen* dapur umum; *chicken ~* soto ayam; *clear ~* soto; *fish ~* gulai ikan; *ox-tail ~* sop buntut

sour *adj* [saur] asam, kecut; basi; *~ grapes*, *~puss* orang yang céngéng karena tidak dapat sesuatu; *~ milk* susu basi; *~ sweet and ~* asam manis

source *n* [sors] sumber, mata air; narasumber

south *adj, n* [sauth] selatan; *~ Africa* Afrika Selatan (Afsél); *~ America*

Amérika Selatan; ~ *Pole* Kutub Selatan; *the* ~ daérah selatan; *the Deep* ~ kawasan selatan AS; **southbound** *adj* [sauthbaund] menuju selatan; **southeast** *adj, n* [sauth ist] tenggara; **southern** *adj* [sathern] sebelah selatan; ~ *Cross* Bintang Pari; *the* ~ *hemisphere* belahan bumi bagian selatan; **southpaw** *n* orang kidal; **southwest** *adj* [sauthwést] barat laut

souvenir *n* [suvenir] oléh-oléh, kenang-kenangan, cenderamata; ~ *shop* toko cenderamata

sovereign *adj* [soveren] berdaulat; *n* raja, ratu; **sovereignty** *n* kedaulatan

sow *vt* [so] menaburkan; **sower** *n* penabur

soy ~ *milk* susu kedelai; ~ *sauce* kécap asin; *sweet* ~ sauce kécap manis; **soya** ~ *bean* kacang kedelai

spa *n* pemandian air panas

space *n* ruang, tempat; spasi, jarak; angkasa; ~ *probe* pesawat penyelidik; *outer* ~ angkasa luar; *parking* ~ tempat parkir; *up in* ~ di angkasa; **spacecraft, spaceship** *n* kapal angkasa; **spaceman** *n, m* angkasawan, astronot; **spacious** *adj* [spésyus] luas, lapang

spade *n* sekop; *the ace of* ~*s as* sekop

spaghetti *n* [spagéti] spagéti

Spain *n* Spanyol; **Spaniard** *n* [spanyard] orang Spanyol; **Spanish** *adj* [spanisy] berasal dari Spanyol; *n* bahasa Spanyol

spam *n* imél sampah

span *n* jangka; masa; rentang; *vt* merentang

Spaniard *n* [spanyard] orang Spanyol; **Spanish** *adj* [spanisy] berasal dari Spanyol; *n* bahasa Spanyol ← **Spain**

spaniel *n* [spanyel] sejenis anjing, anjing spaniel

spanner *n* kunci

spare *adj* [spér] cadangan; ~ *part* suku cadang, onderdil; ~ *ribs* iga panggang; ~ *room* ruang tamu; ~ *time* waktu luang; ~ *tire* ban sérep; *n* cadangan; *vi* menyisakan; ~ *time* meluangkan waktu; **sparingly** *adv* [spéringli] dengan irit, dengan hémat

spark *n* (percikan) api; ~ *plug* busi;

sparkle *n* kilau; *vi* berkilau-kilauan, bergemerlapan; **sparkler** *n* mercon; **sparkling** *adj* kilau, gemerlap; bersoda; ~ *wine* anggur bersoda

sparrow *n* [sparo] burung geréja

spasm *n* [spazem] kejang-kejang; **spastic** *adj* kejang; *n* orang yang mengalami kejang-kejang

spat *n* pertengkaran, pertikaian; *lovers'* ~ pertikaian di antara sepasang kekasih; *v, pf* → **spit**

spawn *n* telur ikan; menimbulkan, menghasilkan; *his invention* ~*ed a number of copycat products* penemuan dia menyebabkan munculnya beberapa produk tiruan

spay *vt* mensteriIkan (binatang betina); *Kuro has already been* ~*ed* si Kuro sudah disterilkan

speak *vi* [spik] **spoke spoken** berbicara, berkata; ~ *about,* ~ *on* membicarakan; ~ *for* berbicara atas nama; ~*ing of ...* kalau bicara soal ...; ~ *Japanese* berbahasa Jepang; ~ *out* menegaskan, ikut bersuara; ~ *to* menegur; ~ *up* berbicara dengan suara keras; ~ *well of* memuji; *so to* ~ boléh dikatakan; ~ *of the devil* panjang umur (dikatakan saat orang yang baru dibicarakan muncul); *can I please* ~ *to Darcy?* bisa bicara dengan Darcy?; **speaker** *n* pembicara, penutur; Ketua Déwan; *native* ~ penutur asli; **speaking** *n* berpidato; saya sendiri (saat menjawab télepon); *public* ~ berpidato di depan umum; **speech** *n* pidato; cara bicara; ~ *writer* penulis pidato; **speechless** *adj* terdiam, kehabisan kata-kata

spear *n* [spir] tombak, lembing; *vt* menombak; ~ *fish* menombak ikan, menikam ikan

special *adj* [spésyal] istiméwa, khusus, spésial; ~ *needs* kebutuhan khusus; ~ *school* sekolah luar biasa (SLB); **specialist** *n* spésialis, ahli; **specially** *adv* khususnya; **specialty, speciality** *n* bidang khusus

species *n* [spisyis] jenis, macam

specific *adj* khusus, tertentu, spésifik;

specifically *adv* khususnya, secara spésifik; **specification** *n* spésifikasi
specimen *n* [spésimen] contoh
specs *n, coll* kacamata; **spectacle** *n* [spéktakel] tontonan; **spectacles** *n, pl* kacamata; **spectacular** *adj* hébat, spéktakulér; **spectator** *n* penonton; ~ *sport* olahraga yang ditonton
speculation *n, fin* [spékyulésyen] spékulasi
sped *vi, pf* → **speed**
speech *n* pidato; cara bicara; ~ *impediment* cadel; ~ *therapy* térapi bicara; ~ *writer* penulis pidato; **speechless** *adj* terdiam, kehabisan kata-kata ← **speak**
speed *n* laju, kecepatan; *top* ~ secepat-cepatnya; *vi* **sped sped** mengebut; ~ *up* mempercepat; ~ *limit* batas kecepatan, kecepatan maksimum; ~ *trap* polisi tidur; *ten-*~ *bike* sepéda sepuluh gigi kecepatan; **speedboat** *n* perahu motor cepat; **speeding** *n* mengebut, léwat batas kecepatan; **speedometer** *n* [spidométer] spidométer; **speedy** *adj* lekas, cepat
spell *n* pesona, sihir; masa; *a dry* ~ masa kering; *to cast a* ~ menyihir; *to be under the* ~ *of* diperdaya, disihir
spell *vi* **spelt spelt** mengéja; **spelling** *n* éjaan; ~ *bee* lomba mengéja
spend *vt* **spent spent** membelanjakan, memakai, menghabiskan; ~ *money* menghabiskan uang; ~ *time* menghabiskan waktu; **spendthrift** *n* pemboros
sperm *n* spérma, air mani
spew *n, v, sl* muntah
sphere *n* [sfir] bulatan, bola; bidang; **spherical** *adj* [sférikal] bulat, berbentuk bola
spice *n* bumbu, rempah-rempah; *the* ~ *Islands* Nusantara; *vt* ~ *(up)* membumbui; **spicy** *adj* pedas
spider *n* laba-laba; ~ *web* rumah laba-laba, jaring laba-laba
spike *n* paku; *n, pl* sepatu lari; **spiky** *adj* berduri, tajam; ~ *hair* rambut gaya landak
spill *vi* **spilt spilt** tumpah; *vt* menumpahkan; ~ *the beans* menceritakan; **spillage** *n* tumpahan

spin *vi* **spun spun** berputar-putar; ~ *out* melama-lamakan; *vt* memutarkan; memintal; *n* putaran, kisaran; ~*-off* produk yang terkait; ~ *doctor coll* penasihat politisi; ~ *dryer* mesin pengering baju; **spinner** *n* pemintal; **spinning** *n* memintal; ~ *wheel* mesin pintal
spinach *n* [spinec] bayam
spinal *adj* berkaitan dengan tulang punggung; ~ *block* suntikan obat bius ke dalam sumsum tulang punggung; ~ *cord* urat saraf tulang belakang; **spine** *n* tulang punggung; ~*-chilling* mengerikan; **spineless** *adj* tak bertulang; lemah
spinner *n* pemintal ← **spin**
spinning *n* memintal; ~ *wheel* mesin pintal ← **spin**
spinster *n, f* perawan tua
spiral *adj* [spairal] spiral; *vi* bergerak naik atau turun; *the plane* ~*led downwards* pesawat menukik
spire *n* puncak menara (geréja)
spirit *n* [spirit] semangat; roh, hantu; **spirits** *n, pl* minuman keras; *(methylated)* ~ spiritus; *in high* ~*s* bergembira; **spirited** *adj* bersemangat; **spiritedly** *adv* dengan semangat; **spiritual** *adj* batin, rohani; keagamaan; *n* lagu rohani; **spirituality** *n* kejiwaan, hal keagamaan
spit *n* air ludah; *vi* **spat spat** meludah; ~ *out* meludahi, melepéh; ~ *up* meludahkan; ~*-ting image of* persis sama dengan (orang)
spite *n* dendam, dengki; *in* ~ *of* kendati, walaupun; *vt* membuat sakit hati, menyakitkan hati; **spiteful** *adj* pendendam; **spitefully** *adv* secara dengki
splash *n* bunyi ceburan atau cemplungan; *vi* bepercikan; ~ *out* memanjakan diri; *vt* memercikkan
spleen *n* limpa
splendid *adj* bagus sekali; **splendor, splendour** *n* kemegahan
splinter *n* serpihan; ~ *group* kelompok yang memisahkan diri; *vi* memecah, menyerpih

split *adj* retak, sobék; ~ *ends* ujung rambut yang bercabang; ~ *second* sekejap; *n* belahan, retakan; *banana* ~ puding yang terdiri dari és krim dan pisang dibelah dua; *vi* **split split** retak, membelah; ~ *up* pisah, berpisah; *~ting headache* sakit kepala yang parah; *vt* membagi

spoil *vi* busuk, basi, rusak; *vt* memanjakan; merusak; **spoiled, spoilt** *adj* manja, kolokan; ~ *brat derog* anak manja; **spoilsport** *n* orang yang merusak suasana

spoke *n* ruji, jari-jari roda

spoke, spoken *vi, pf* → **speak**; *spoken for* sudah milik orang lain; **spokesman** *n, m* **spokeswoman** *f* **spokesperson** juru bicara (jubir)

sponge *n* [spanj] spons, bunga karang; ~ *bag* kantong perlengkapan mandi; ~ *cake* semacam kué; *vi* ~ *off coll* menampung; **spongy** *adj* [spanji] empuk

sponsor *n* sponsor; *vt* mendukung, mensponsori; **sponsorship** *n* dukungan

spontaneous *adj* [sponténius] spontan; **spontaneously** *adv* secara spontan

spoof *n* parodi

spooky *adj* angker, ngeri

spool ~ *of thread* kumparan, segeléndong benang

spoon *n* séndok; *~-feed* menyuapi; *dessert* ~ séndok makan; *plastic* ~ séndok plastik; *table~* séndok besar; *tea~* séndok téh; *wooden* ~ séndok kayu; *vt* menyéndok; **spoonful** *n* seséndok; *a* ~ *of honey* seséndok madu

spore *n* spora

sport *n* olahraga; orang yang sportif; *Adi is good at* ~ Adi pandai berolahraga; *don't be a bad* ~ jangan bersikap tidak sportif; **sporting** *adj* berhubungan dengan olahraga; sportif; **sports** *adj* olahraga; ~ *car* mobil sport; ~ *day* pésta olahraga; **sportsman** *n, m* **sportsmen** olahragawan; **sportsmanship** *n* sportivitas; **sportsperson** olahragawan; **sportswear** *n* baju olahraga; **sportswoman** *n, f* **sports-**

women olahragawati; **sporty** *adj* suka berolahraga

spot *n* titik, noda; *sl* jerawat; ~ *check* sidak (inspéksi mendadak); ~ *on* tepat; *on the* ~ di tempat, di situ juga; *vi* kena noda; *vt* melihat; **spotless** *adj* bersih tanpa noda; **spotlight** *n* lampu sorot; **spotty** *adj* berjerawat, jerawatan

spouse *n* pasangan; suami, isteri

spout *n* bibir, corot; *vi* memancar

sprain *n, vt* salah urat, keseléo; *I ~ed my ankle* pergelangan kaki saya keseléo

sprang *vi, pf* → **spring**

spray *n* percikan, semprotan; *vt* menyemprot, memerciki; **spraying** *n* penyemprotan

spread *n* [spréd] penyebaran; sajian; mentéga, selai; *vi* **spread spread** menyebar; ~ *out* bersebar; *the bird flu* ~ *overseas* flu burung menyebar ke luar negeri; *vt* mengolési; menyiarkan, menyebarkan, membentangkan; *Jim* ~ *out the map on the table* Jim membentangkan peta di atas méja

spree *n* pesta; *shopping* ~ acara berbelanja

spring *n* musim semi, musim bunga; sumber (air), mata air; pér, pegas; ~ *bed* kasur pegas; ~ *chicken* masih muda; ~ *cleaning* pembersihan (pada musim semi); ~ *onion* daun bawang; ~ *tide* pasang purnama; *hot* ~ sumber air panas, mata air panas; *vi* **sprang sprung** melompat, meloncat; **springboard** *n* papan loncat; **springtime** *n* musim semi

springbok *n* sejenis rusa di Afrika Selatan

sprinkle *vt* [springkel] menaburkan, membubuhi; **sprinkles** *n, pl chocolate* ~ méses; **sprinkler** *n* alat penyiram

sprint *n* lari cepat (jarak péndék); *vi* berlari dengan cepat; **sprinter** *n* pelari cepat

sprout *n* tunas; *bean ~s* taugé; *brussel ~s* kubis Brussel; *vi* bertunas, tumbuh

sprung *vi, pf* → **spring**

spud *n, sl* kentang

spun *v, pf* → **spin**

spur *n* pacu, taji; *on the ~ of the moment* tanpa berpikir terlebih dahulu, secara mendadak; *vi ~ on* mendorong, memacu, menyemangati; *he was ~red on by the thought of all that money* dia menjadi semangat karena ingat semua uang itu

spurt *n* semburan; *vi* berlari atau bekerja dengan cepat; menyembur; *vt* menyemburkan

spy *n* [spai] mata-mata, spion; *vi ~ on* memata-matai, mengintip; *vt* melihat; **spyglass** *n* teropong, kéker

Sq *abbrev square* alun-alun

squabble *n* [skuobel] pertengkaran kecil; *vi* bertengkar; *~ over* bertengkar soal

squad *n* [skuod] regu, pasukan; *~ car* mobil polisi

squadron *n* skadron, skuadron

square *adj* [skuér] persegi; *~ brackets* tanda kurung besar ([]); *55 ~ meters* 55 meter persegi; *n* persegi empat; alun-alun, médan; hasil perkalian; *~ dance* tarian rakyat Amérika; *~ meal* makan yang cukup; *~ root* akar dua; *town ~* alun-alun; *vt* mengkuadratkan

squash *n* semacam labu

squash *n* olahraga squash

squash *n* [skuosy] posisi yang sempit atau penuh sesak; *vi* masuk dengan paksa; *vt* memasukkan dengan paksa; **squashed** *adj* terpencét, kehilangan bentuk

squat *vi* [skuot] jongkok, berjongkok

squeak *n* [skuik] ciutan; cicit; *a narrow ~* nyaris celaka; *vi* menciut-ciut; mencicit; **squeaky** *adj* menciut-ciut; *~ clean* bersih sekali, tak bernoda

squeeze *vt* memeras; memeluk; *~ in* nyaris tidak masuk; *a tight ~* sempit

squid *n* cumi-cumi

squint *n* mata juling; *vi* melihat dengan susah

squirrel *n* tupai, bajing

squirt *vt* menyemprot, menyemprotkan; *Gran ~ed the cat with water* Nénék menyemprot kucing dengan air

Sri Lanka *n* Sri Lanka; **Sri Lankan** *adj* berasal dari Sri Lanka; *n* orang Sri Lanka

St *abbrev Saint* Santo, Santa

St *abbrev street* Jl (jalan)

stab *n* tikam, tikaman; *~ wound* luka tikam; *to have a ~ at* mencoba; *vt* menikam; *~ someone in the back* menikam dari belakang; **stabbing** *n* penikaman

stability *n* [stabiliti] kemantapan, stabilitas; **stabilize** *vi* [stébilaiz] menjadi stabil; *vt* menstabilkan; **stable** *adj* [stébel] mantap, stabil

stable *n* [stébel] kandang kuda, istal

stack *n* susunan, tumpukan; *~s of, a ~ of coll* banyak sekali

stadium *n* stadion, gelanggang, aréna

staff *n* staf, para karyawan, para pegawai; para guru atau pengajar; tongkat; *~ room* ruang guru; *editorial ~* (staf) redaksi

stag *n* rusa jantan; *~ night* pésta bujang

stage *n* tahap; panggung, pentas; tahap; *~ fright* demam panggung; *~ show* pertunjukan; *in ~s* secara bertahap; *on ~* di pentas, di panggung; *on the ~* menjadi pemain di panggung; *vt* mengadakan, menyelenggarakan

stagger *vi* tertatih-tatih; *vt* mengadakan secara bertahap

stagnant *adj* **stagnate** *vi* tidak bergerak atau berkembang; *~ water* air yang tidak bergerak

stain *n* noda; *~ remover* cairan pembersih; *vt* menodai, mencemarkan; **stained** *adj* ternoda; *~ glass* kaca patri; **stainless** *~ steel* baja anti karat

stair *n* anak tangga; **stairs** *pl* tangga; *down~* turun tangga; *up~* naik tangga; **staircase, stairway** *n* tangga; **stairwell** *n* ruangan tempat tangga

stake *n* pancang; taruhan; bagian; *at ~* yang dipertaruhkan; *vi ~ out* mematok, memancang

stalactite *n* stalaktit

stalagmite *n* stalagmit

stale *adj* keras (roti); basi, pengap, apak; membosankan; *~ bread* roti yang sudah keras; **stalemate** *n* mutu; jalan buntu

stalk *n* [stok] tangkai; *vt* mengikuti, mengejar, membuntuti; *the actress was ~ed by a crazed fan* aktris itu dibuntuti oléh penggemar gila; **stalker** *n* orang yang mengikuti atau mengejar

stall *n* [stol] warung, kedai, kios; kandang; *vi* mogok, tidak langsung hidup; *the car ~ed on top of the bridge* mobil mogok di atas jembatan

stallion *n* kuda jantan

stamina *n* daya tahan; *Kate didn't have the ~ to run a marathon* daya tahan Kate tidak cukup untuk lari maraton

stammer *n* kegagapan; *vi* menggagap

stamp *n* perangko; méterai, ségel, tera, cap; *~ album* album perangko; *~ collector* filatelis, pengumpul perangko; *~ed addressed envelope (sae)* amplop berperangko dengan tulisan alamat sendiri; *vi* mengentakkan kaki; *vt* membubuhi perangko, memberi méterai, mengecap; *~ out* memadamkan; membasmi, memberantas; *~ your foot* mengentakkan kaki; **stampede** *n* penyerbuan (gajah); perebutan; *vi* lari berebutan

stand *n* tribune; pendirian, sikap; kios, gerai; *to take a ~, to make a ~* bertahan; *vi* **stood stood** berdiri; tahan; *~-by* siap siaga; *~ by* membéla, menunggu; *~ down* mundur, mengundurkan diri; *~ for* berarti, melambangkan; *~ out* menonjol; *~ up* bangun, bangkit, berdiri; *~-up comic* pelawak solo; *~ in line* antri; **standing** *adj* tetap; *n* martabat, réputasi; **standout** *adj* luar biasa, menonjol; **standpoint** *n* pendirian, sudut

standard *adj* baku, standar, tolok, biasa; *~ procedure* prosédur tetap, prosédur standar; *n* patokan, ukuran, norma, standar; **standardize** *vt* membakukan; **standardized** *adj* baku, biasa

standing *adj* tetap; *n* martabat, réputasi ← **stand**

standpoint *n* pendirian, sudut ← **stand**

stank *vi, pf* → **stink**

staple *vt* [stépel] menjeprét (kertas); **stapler** *n* jeprétan

staple *adj* [stépel] pokok; *~ food* makanan pokok, sembako (sembilan makanan pokok); *rice is the ~ food in*

Asia nasi adalah makanan pokok di Asia; *n* makanan atau bahan pokok

star *n* bintang; *~ sign* bintang; *guest ~* bintang tamu; *shooting ~* bintang jatuh; *to see ~s* pusing, nenar; *the ~s and the Stripes* bendéra AS; *vi* menjadi bintang; *~ in* membintangi; *Rowan Atkinson ~s in 'Mr Bean'* Rowan Atkinson membintangi film *Mr Bean*; **starfish** *n* bintang laut

starboard *adj, n* [starbed] sebelah kanan kapal

starch *n* kanji; sari pati; *rich in ~* kaya akan sari pati

stare *n* pandangan, tatapan; *vi* memelototkan mata; *~ at* memandang, menatap; *what are you staring at?* apa lihat-lihat?

starfish *n* bintang laut ← **star**

starfruit *n* [starfrut] belimbing

stark *adj* jelas, kentara; *~ naked* telanjang bulat

starlight *n* [starlait] cahaya bintang; **starlit** *adj* tampak di bawah cahaya bulan

starling *n* burung jalak

start *n* awal, permulaan; *from the ~* sejak awal; *to give a ~* kagét; *to make a ~* mulai; *vi* mulai, berangkat; *vt* memulai; menghidupkan mesin; *~ a family* memiliki momongan; **starter** *n* starter; makanan pembuka

startle *vt* [startel] mengejutkan, mengagétkan; **startled** *adj* kagét, terkejut; **startling** *adj* mengejutkan, mengagétkan

starvation *n* kelaparan; **starve** *vi* (mati) kelaparan; *vt* membuat kelaparan; **starving** *adj* sangat lapar, kelaparan

state *adj* kenegaraan; *~ Department* Departemén Luar Negeri (Amérika Serikat); *~ funeral* upacara pemakaman kenegaraan; *the (United) ~s* Amérika (Serikat); *n* negara (bagian); keadaan, suasana; *~-of-the-art* canggih, terbaru; *the ~ of California* negara bagian California; *vt* menyatakan, menyebutkan, memaparkan; **stateless** *adj* tanpa kewarganegaraan; **statement** *n* pernyataan, pengumuman;

bank ~ rékening koran; **statesman** *n* negarawan

station *n* stasiun, pos; pangkalan; ~ *master* kepala stasiun; *fire* ~ kantor pasukan pemadaman kebakaran; *police* ~ kantor polisi; *television* ~ stasiun télévisi

stationary *adj* tetap, tidak bergerak

stationery *n* alat tulis

statistical *adj* secara statistik, dalam angka; **statistician** *n* [statistisyen] ahli statistik; **statistics** *n, pl* statistik, angka

statue *n* [statyu] patung

status *n* keadaan, kedudukan, status; pangkat, derajat; ~ *quo* keadaan tetap; *marital* ~ status

stay *n* (masa) tinggal; *vi* tinggal, menginap; bertahan; ~ *away* menghindar; ~ *behind* tidak ikut, tetap tinggal; ~ *in* tinggal di (untuk sementara), menginap di; ~ *over* menginap; ~ *overnight* menginap, bermalam; ~ *up* tidak tidur, begadang; ~ *for dinner* tinggal supaya ikut makan malam

STD *abbrev sexually transmitted disease* PMS (penyakit menular séksual)

STD *abbrev subscriber trunk dialing* SLJJ (sambungan langsung jarak jauh)

steadfast *adj* [stédfast] tetap, teguh; **steadily** *adv* secara tetap, terus-menerus; **steady** *adj* [stédi] tetap, terus-menerus, teguh, mantap; *to go* ~ pacaran; *vi* menenangkan, memegang; ~ *on!* tenang!

steak *n* [sték] stéik; ~ *sauce* saus stéik; *do you like your* ~ *rare, medium or well-done?* dagingnya mau mentah, setengah matang atau matang?

steal *v* [stil] **stole stolen** mencuri; ~ *into* menyelinap

stealthy *adj* [stélthi] mencuri-curi, diam-diam

steam *vi* [stim] beruap; *vt* mengukus; *n* uap; ~ *engine* (keréta api) mesin uap; *to let off* ~ melampiaskan rasa marah; **steamboat** *n* kapal uap; jenis masakan yang direbus di tempat; **steamer** *n* kapal uap; **steamroller** *n* penggiling jalan; **steamy** *adj* beruap, panas, lembab; ~ *scene* adegan panas

steel *n* baja; *stainless* ~ baja anti tidak berkarat; **steelworks** *n* pabrik baja

steep *adj* curam, terjal; *sl* mahal; **steeply** *adv* dengan curam; *prices rose* ~ harga melonjak naik

steeple *n* [stipel] menara geréja

steeplechase *n* [stipelcés] lari halang rintang

steer *vt* mengemudikan; **steering** *n* ~ *committee* panitia; ~ *wheel* roda stir; *power* ~ stir daya

stem *n* batang, tangkai; ~ *cell* sél induk; *vi* ~ *from* berasal dari, bersumber pada

stench *n* bau busuk

stencil *n* sténsil

stenographer *n* [sténografer] juru sténo; **stenography** *n* [sténografi] sténo

step *n* langkah, jejak; anak tangga; tahap; *in* ~ sejalan; ~ *by* ~ selangkah demi selangkah; *out of* ~ tidak sejalan, salah langkah; *watch your* ~ hati-hati melangkah; *pl* tangga; **stepladder** *n* tangga; *vi* melangkah; ~ *aside* minggir; mundur; ~ *down* meletakkan jabatan, mengundurkan diri; ~ *on* menginjak; ~*ping stone* batu loncatan; ~ *on it* ayo cepat; ~ *this way* silahkan (kemari); **step-** *pref* tiri; **stepbrother** *n, m* [stepbrather] kakak/adik tiri yang laki-laki; **stepdaughter** *n, f* [stépdoter] anak tiri yang perempuan; **stepfather** *n, m* bapak tiri, ayah tiri; **stepmother** *n, f* ibu tiri; **stepsister** *n, f* kakak/adik tiri yang perempuan; **stepson** *n, m* anak tiri yang laki-laki

stepladder *n* tangga ← **step**

stereo *n* [stério] peralatan pemutaran musik; *in* ~ dari kiri dan kanan (suara), stéréo

stereotype *n* [stériotaip] stéréotip, klisé; **stereotypical** *adj* [stériotipikal] tipikal; *Donna was your* ~ *empty-headed celebrity* Donna adalah sélébriti tipikal yang berkepala kosong

sterile *adj* [stérail] stéril, sucihama; mandul; **sterilize** *vt* menyucihamakan, mensterilkan; *Mother* ~*d baby's bottle* Ibu mensterilkan botol bayinya; **sterilized** *adj* stéril

sterling *pound* ~ pon Inggris (£)

stern *adj* keras, tidak senyum; *n* buritan (kapal); **sternly** *adv* dengan keras

stethoscope *n* stétoskop

stew *n* rebusan; *vt* merebus

steward *n* pramugara; **stewardess** *n, arch* pramugari

stick *n* tongkat, batang; *walking ~* tongkat; *in the ~s* daérah udik

stick *vi* **stuck stuck** melekat; *~ out* menonjol; *~ at it* bertekun, bertahan; *vt* melekatkan; *coll* meletakkan, memasukkan, menaruh; *~ at* tetap (melakukan); *~ by* setia pada; *~ together* bergabung; *~ it out* bertahan; *~ your things in your bag* taruh barang-barang di tas; **sticker** *n* stiker, témpélan; **sticky** *adj* léngkét, lekat; *coll* susah; *~ situation* keadaan yang sulit; *~ tape* sélotip, isolasi

stiff *adj* keras, kaku; pegal; *that's a bit ~* itu sedikit keterlaluan; *to have a ~ neck* salah bantal; *to keep a ~ upper lip* tidak menangis

stiletto *n* sepatu berhak tinggi dan meruncing

still *adv* masih, tetap; *conj* bahkan, tetapi; *sl* toh; *he might be stupid, but he's ~ my friend* mungkin dia bodoh, tapi dia tetap teman saya; *it's not much money. ~ it's better than nothing* uangnya sedikit, tapi masih mendingan daripada tidak ada

still *adj* tenang, teduh, sepi; *~ life* lukisan benda mati; *stay ~* jangan bergerak; **stillborn** *adj* lahir mati; **stillness** *n* keteduhan, ketenangan

stimulate *vt* [stimyulét] **stimulating** *adj* mendorong, merangsang; **stimulation** *n* [stimyulésyen] rangsangan, stimulasi

sting *n* sengatan; *v* **stung stung** menyengat; **stingray** *n* [sting ré] ikan pari

stingy *adj* [stinji] kikir, pelit

stink *n* bau (busuk); *vi* **stank stunk** berbau (busuk)

stipulate *v* mensyaratkan, menetapkan; *he ~d that all students must study three science subjects* dia menetapkan agár semua murid mengambil tiga mata pelajaran IPA; **stipulation** *n*

ketentuan, syarat

stir *n* [ster] keributan, kekacauan; *to cause a ~* membuat onar; *vi* bergerak; *vt* mengaduk; *~ (up)* mengacaukan; *~ fry* oséng-oséng; **stirring** *adj* yang memberi semangat

stirrup *n* pemijak kaki, sanggurdi

stitch *n* jahitan; *cross-~* kristik; *a ~ in time saves nine* pencegahan lebih baik dari pengobatan; *my wound required eight ~es* luka saya terpaksa dijahit; *vt* menjahit

stock *n* héwan ternak; *~ cube* kaldu

stock *n* persediaan; *~ exchange* bursa éfék; *~ market* pasar saham; *out of ~* persediaan habis; *vt* menjual; *~ up on* menimbun; **stockbroker** *n* pedagang saham; **stockpile** *n* persediaan, penimbunan; *vt* menimbun

stocking *n* stoking

stockpile *n* persediaan, penimbunan; *vt* menimbun ← **stock**

stocky *adj* berbadan péndék gemuk

stole, stolen *v, pf* → **steal**

stomach *n* [stamek] perut, lambung; *~ ache* sakit perut

stone *n* batu; biji (buah); ukuran timbang (14 pon); *~-deaf* tuli, pekak batu; *~ Age* Zaman Batu; *gall~* batu empedu; *a ~'s throw* dekat sekali; *vt* merajam; **stoned** *adj, coll* mabuk

stood *vi, pf* → **stand**; *Michelle was ~ up by the boy she liked* pemuda yang disukai Michelle tidak jadi datang pada saat dijanjikan

stool *n* bangku, dingklik

stool *n* tinja, kotoran

stoop *vi* membungkuk, merendahkan diri

stop *n* perhentian, akhir; *bus ~* halte (bis); *full ~* titik; *vi* berhenti; *~ over* singgah; *vt* menahan, menghentikan; *~ work* mogok kerja; **stopover** *n* tempat persinggahan; **stopper** *n* penyumbat, tutup; **stopwatch** *n* [stopwoc] penghitung detik

storage *n* penyimpanan; gudang; *in ~* di gudang; **store** *n* toko; persediaan, perbekalan, gudang; *vt* menyimpan; **storeroom** *n* gudang storey → **story**

stork *n* (burung) bangau; *to have a visit from the* ~ kelahiran bayi

storm *n* angin badai; *vi* datang dengan sikap marah-marah; *the angry customer ~ed out of the shop* tamu meninggalkan toko dengan sikap sangat marah; **stormy** *adj* (berangin) ribut

story, storey *n* lantai, tingkat; *two-~ house* rumah berlantai dua

story *n* cerita, riwayat, kisah, dongéng; *fairy* ~ dongéng; *to tell stories* berdongéng; berdusta, berbohong; *to cut a long* ~ *short* péndék kata; **storybook** *n* buku cerita; **storyteller** *n* orang yang mendongéng

stout *adj* gemuk, tambun; *~-hearted* berani

stove *n* kompor; *electric* ~ kompor listrik; *gas* ~ kompor gas

stowaway *n* [stowewé] penumpang gelap (di kapal)

straddle *vt* [stradel] mengangkang

straight *adj* [strét] lurus, terus; *sl* héteroséksual; *adv* langsung; jujur, terus terang; ~ *ahead* terus, lurus; ~ *away* langsung, segera; *to think* ~ berpikir dengan jelas; **straighten** *vt* meluruskan; ~ *hair* meluruskan rambut; **straightforward** *adj* terus terang

strain *n* ketegangan; *vi* bersusah payah; mengejan; *vt* menyaring; memaksakan; ~ *a muscle* salah urat, keséléo; **strained** *adj* tegang; **strainer** *n* saringan

strait *n* selat; *the Sunda* ~ Selat Sunda; *the ~s of Malacca* Selat Malaka

strand *n a* ~ *of hair* sehelai rambut; **stranded** *adj* terdampar

strange *adj* [strénj] anéh, ganjil, asing; **stranger** *n* orang asing, orang luar; **strangely** *adv* secara anéh, yang anéh

strangle *vt* [stranggel] mencekik

strap *n* tali; cambuk; *to get the* ~ dicambuk; **strapless** *adj* tanpa tali baju; **strappy** *adj* bertali

strategic *adj* [stratijik] stratégis; **strategy** *n* [strateji] stratégi, siasat

straw *n* sedotan; jerami, mérang; ~ *hat* topi jerami; *the last* ~ sesuatu yang

tidak lagi bisa diterima

strawberry *n* strobéri, arbéi; ~ *juice* jus strobéri

stray *adj* yang tersesat; tidak bertuan (binatang); ~ *bullet* peluru nyasar; ~ *cat* kucing jalanan; *n* binatang yang tidak bertuan; *vi* sesat, menyasar

streak *n* [strik] garis, corét, coréng; *a* ~ *of* sedikit; *blonde ~s in her hair* rambutnya bergaris pirang; *vt* mencoréng

stream *n* sungai, kali; aliran; *vi* mengalir; *vt* mengalirkan; **streamer** *n* pita hiasan; **streamline** *vt* merampingkan; **streamlined** *adj* ramping, éfisién

street *n* jalan; ~ *children* anak-anak jalanan; ~ *light* lampu penerang jalan; ~ *sweeper* penyapu jalan; ~*s ahead* jauh ke depan; *one-way* ~ jalan satu arah; **streetcar** *n* trém

strength *n* kekuatan, tenaga, kekuasaan; **strengthen** *vt* memperkuat, memperkokoh; **strong** *adj* kuat, kokoh; keras (minuman); ~*-arm* tangan besi; ~ *tea* teh kental

strenuous *adj* [strényuus] berat, melelahkan; kuat

stress *n* tekanan; ketegangan, strés; *to cope with* ~ mengatasi strés; *vi* ~ *(out)* menjadi tegang atau strés; *vt* menekan, mementingkan, menitikberatkan; **stressed** *adj* strés; **stressful** *adj* menegangkan

stretch *n* bagian, ruas (jalan); jangkauan; *adj* lentur; *vi* terentang; *vt* menegangkan; merentangkan; *to* ~ *your arms* meregangkan tangan, mengulur-ulurkan tangan; *to* ~ *your legs* meregangkan kaki, mengulur-ulurkan kaki; jalan kaki

stretcher *n* usungan

strict *adj* keras; stréng (guru); *Rebecca is a* ~ *Catholic* Rebecca itu orang Katolik yang taat; **strictly** *adv* dengan ketat, hanya

strike *n* pukulan; pemogokan, mogok kerja; serangan; *on* ~ mogok; *vt* **struck struck** memukul; menyerang; *vi* mogok; ~ *down* menjatuhkan; ~ *off* mencorét; ~ *up* memulai; **striker** *n* pemogok; (sépak bola) pemain depan, ujung tombak; **striking** *adj* mengesankan, menyolok

string *n* tali; senar (raket, alat musik); untaian; ~ *instrument* alat musik gésék; *vt* **strung strung** ~ *along* menipu; ~ *out* memperpanjang; ~ *up* memasang, menggantung

strip *n* garis, jalur; *vi* ~ *(off)* membuka baju; *vt* menghilangkan, membersihkan; **stripper** *n* penari telanjang, penari striptis; **striptease** *n* tari telanjang, striptis

stripe *n* garis, belang; **striped, stripy** *adj* bergaris, belang

striptease *n* tari telanjang, striptis ← **strip**

stripy *adj* bergaris, belang ← **stripe**

strive *vi* **striven strove** berusaha; ~ *for* menuntut, mengejar

stroke *n* pukulan; gaya (renang); serangan otak; *a* ~ *of luck* untung; *on the* ~ *of five* tepat pukul lima; *vt* mengelus, mengusap

stroll *n* jalan kaki yang santai; *vi* berjalan kaki; **stroller** *n* keréta dorong anak

strong *adj* kuat, kokoh; keras (minuman); ~-*arm* tangan besi; ~ *tea* téh kental; *be* ~ tabahlah; **strongly** *adv* dengan kuat, secara keras, sangat

strove *vi, pf* → **strive**

struck *v, pf* → **strike**

structural *adj* struktural, mendasar; **structure** *n* bangunan, susunan, struktur; *vt* menyusun

struggle *n* [stragel] perjuangan; *Indonesian Democratic Party of* ~ Partai Démokrasi Indonesia (Perjuangan) (PDIP); *vi* berjuang; ~ *against* berjuang terhadap, berjuang melawan

strung *vt, pf* → **string**

stubborn *adj* keras kepala; **stubbornness** *n* sifat keras kepala, kenékatan

stuck *adj* terjebak, terjepit; ~-*up* congkak, sombong; ~ *on* suka, menaksir; ~ *in traffic* terjebak macét; *to get* ~ terjebak; *v, pf* → **stick**

stud *n* kancing; subang, anting; *Scott has a* ~ *in his left ear* Scott pakai anting di kuping kiri

stud *n* tempat pembiakan kuda; *coll* pejantan

student *n* pelajar, murid, mahasiswa; ~ *council* majelis pelajar, OSIS; ~ *teacher* calon guru; **studies** *n, pl* [stadiz] pelajaran, penelitian ← **study**

studio *n* studio; sanggar; *recording* ~ dapur rekaman

studious *adj* [styudius] rajin belajar; **studiously** *adv* dengan rajin; **study** *n, v* [stadi] belajar; *vt* mempelajari, mengkaji; *n* pelajaran, studi; penelitian, risét; ruang belajar; *pl* kajian; *Asian* ~ kajian Asia

stuff *n* bahan; barang-barang; *vt* mengisi; ~ *this* persétan dengan ini; **stuffed** *adj* terisi; ~ *animal* bonéka; *get* ~ *vulg* persétan dengan kau; **stuffing** *n* isi, pengisi; busa; **stuffy** *adj* pengap; membosankan

stumble *vi* [stambel] tersandung; ~ *across* menemukan; **stumbling block** batu sandungan, halangan

stump *n* puntung; bekas pohon; tiang (krikét); *vt* membingungkan, membuat bingung; **stumped** *adj* bingung, habis pikiran

stun *vt* membuat tertegun atau pingsan; mengagétkan; **stunned** *adj* tertegun, kagét; **stunning** *adj* memesonakan, cantik sekali

stung *v, pf* → **sting**

stunk *vi, pf* → **stink**

stunt *n* perbuatan yang luar biasa; pertunjukan, akrobatik; *publicity* ~ kegiatan untuk membuat berita; **stuntman** *n* pemeran pengganti

stunt *vt* menghalangi, memperlambat; *smoking* ~*s your growth* merokok mengganggu pertumbuhan orang; **stunted** *adj* kerdil, terhalang

stuntman *n* pemeran pengganti ← **stunt**

stupid *adj* bodoh, dungu; **stupidly** *adv* secara bodoh, dengan bodohnya; **stupidity** *n* [stupiditi] kebodohan, kedunguan

sturdy *adj* kokoh

stutter *n* bicara menggagap; *v* menggagap, berbicara dengan gagap

sty n [stai] kandang babi

sty, stye n bintitan

style n [stail] gaya, cara; *not my* ~ bukan seléra saya; vt merias, mengatur, memberi pengarahan gaya; ~ *yourself on* meniru; **stylish** adj bergaya; **stylishly** adv dengan bergaya

stylus n alat tajam untuk menulis di layar (plastik atau kaca)

sub- *pref* (di) bawah; *~clause* anak kalimat

subconscious adj, n [sabkonsyes] bawah sadar; **subconsciously** adv di bawah sadar

subcontinent n [sabkontinent] anak benua; *the (Indian)* ~ Asia Selatan

subcontract vt mengontrakkan kepada orang lain; **subcontractor** n pemborong bawahan

subculture n [sabkaltyur] cabang kebudayaan, aliran; *teen* ~ budaya remaja

subdistrict n kecamatan, wilayah; ~ *head* camat

subdivide vt membagi; **subdivision** n [sabdivisyen] pembagian, pengkaplingan

subdue vt [sabdyu] menaklukkan; mengendalikan; **subdued** adj tertunduk

subject n [sabjekt] soal, topik, subyék; mata pelajaran; *school* ~ mata pelajaran; *university* ~ mata kuliah; *on the* ~ *of* tentang; *to change the* ~ mengalihkan arah percakapan; vt [sabjékt] menaklukkan, menundukkan; ~ *to* kena, menjadi sasaran; **subjective** adj [sabjéktivli] subyéktif, berat sebelah; **subjectively** adv [sabjéktivli] secara subyéktif

subjugate vt [sabjegét] menaklukkan, menundukkan; **subjugation** n penaklukan, penundukan

submarine adj [sabmarin] di bawah (permukaan) laut; n kapal selam

submerge vi menyelam; vt merendamkan; **submerged** adj di bawah permukaan air

submission n [sabmisyen] penyerahan, pengajuan; ketundukan; **submissive** adj [sabmisiv] bersifat menyerah, bersikap tunduk; **submit** vi menyerah;

~ *to* tunduk; mematuhi; vt menyerahkan, menyampaikan; ~ *an assignment* menyerahkan tugas

subordinate adj, n [sabordinet] bawahan

subscribe vi ~ *(to)* berlangganan; menganut; ~ *to a magazine* berlangganan majalah; ~ *to a theory* percaya; **subscriber** n pelanggan; **subscription** n [sabskriptsyen] langganan

subsequent adj [sabsekuent] berikut; *I attended the first class, but not* ~ *sessions* saya hadir di kelas pertama, tapi tidak di kelas-kelas berikutnya; **subsequently** adv kemudian, setelah itu

subside vi surut, turun, reda; *the snow has* ~*d* hujan salju sudah reda

subsidize vt mensubsidi, memberi subsidi kepada; **subsidy** n tunjangan, subsidi

subsistence ~ *agriculture* pertanian untuk bertahan hidup

substance n zat; bahan; isi pokok; hakikat; *of* ~ berbobot; **substantial** adj (cukup) besar, banyak, berbobot; *he donated a* ~ *amount to his party* dia menyumbangkan cukup banyak pada partai politik

substitute adj, n [sabstityut] ganti, pengganti; wakil; vt mengganti; **substitution** n penggantian

subtitler n [sabtaiteler] pemberi téks (pada film berbahasa asing); **subtitles** n, pl téks

subtle adj [satel] halus, tidak kentara; *a* ~ *hint* sindiran halus

subtract vt ~ *two from four* empat dikurangi dua; **subtraction** n mengurangi

subtropical adj subtropis

suburb n [sabérb] daérah perumahan, daérah perkotaan; *Kebayoran is a* ~ *of Jakarta* Kebayoran adalah daérah perumahan di Jakarta; **suburban** adj [sebérben] di daérah perumahan atau perkotaan; **suburbia** n daérah perumahan

subversive adj subvérsif, melawan tata sosial; n orang yang makar

subway n keréta api bawah tanah; terowongan penyeberangan

subzero *adj* di bawah nol derajat sélsius

succeed *vi* [saksid] berhasil, menjadi suksés; *vt* mengganti; *King George VI was ~ed by Queen Elizabeth II* Raja George VI diganti Ratu Elizabeth II; **success** *n* keberhasilan, suksés; *wishing you every ~* semoga suksés; **successful** *adj* berhasil, suksés; **successfully** *adv* dengan suksés, berhasil; **succession** *n* [saksésyen] penggantian, penerusan; *in ~* berturut-turut; **successively** *adv* [saksésivli] secara berturut-turut; **successor** *n* pengganti

such *adj* seperti itu, sedemikian; sungguh; *adv* demikian, begini, begitu; *~ a surprise* begitu mengejutkan; *pron* demikian, begitu; *~ as* seperti misalnya, sebagaimana; *~ that* sehingga; *as ~* sebagai; *no ~ thing* tidak ada

suck *vt* mengisap, mengemut; *~ up to coll* menjilat; **suckle** *vi* [sakel] **suckling** *adj* menyusui

sucrose *n* sukrosa

Sudan *n* Sudan; **Sudanese** *adj* berasal dari Sudan; *n* orang Sudan

sudden *adj* tiba-tiba, mendadak; *~ death* gol pertama mengakhiri pertandingan; *all of a ~* tiba-tiba, tahu-tahu; **suddenly** *adv* tiba-tiba, secara mendadak

suds *n, pl* busa

sue *vt* menggugat, menuntut; *the doctor was ~d for malpractice* dokter itu digugat malaprakték

suede *n* [suéd] kulit halus

suffer *v* menderita; *~ from* mengidap; **sufferer** *n* penderita, pasién; **suffering** *n* penderitaan

sufficient *adj* [safisyent] cukup; **sufficiently** *adv* (dengan) cukup

suffix *n* akhiran

suffocate *vi* mati lemas; *vt* mencekik; **suffocating** *adj* lembab, panas

sugar *n* [syuger] gula; *~ cane* tebu; *~ palm* arén; *brown ~* gula arén; *castor ~* gula; *icing ~* tepung gula; **sugary** *adj* manis, mengandung gula

suggest *vt* [sejést] menyarankan, mengusulkan, menganjurkan; **suggestion** *n* saran, usul, anjuran; **suggestive** *adj* [sejéstiv] sugésti

suicidal *adj* [suisaidel] bertékad membunuh diri; **suicide** *n* [suisaid] bunuh diri; *to commit ~* bunuh diri

suit *n* [sut] setélan (pakaian); rupa (kartu); *birthday ~* telanjang; *to follow ~* mengikuti; *vi* cocok; berpadanan, sepadan; *vt* cocok dengan, sesuai dengan; *~ yourself* sesukamu; **suitability** *n* [sutabiliti] kecocokan; **suitable** *adj* [sutabel] patut, layak, cocok; **suitcase** *n* koper

suite *n* [swit] setélan; sedérétan (kamar); rangkaian (musik)

suitor *n* calon (suami); *the mayor's daughter had a lot of ~s* anak walikota didekati banyak pemuda

sulfate, sulphate *n* [salfét] sulfat; **sulfide** *n* sulfida; **sulfur** *n* belérang; **sulfuric** *~ acid* asam sulfat, asam belérang

sulk *vi* **sulky** *adj* mendongkol, merajuk

sullen *adj* cemberut, murung

sulphur → **sulfur**

sultan *n* [saltan] sultan; **sultanate** *n* [saltanét] kesulatanan

sultana *n* kismis

sultanate *n* [saltanét] kesulatanan ← **sultan**

sum *n* jumlah; perjumlahan; *~ total* total, jumlah total; *a ~ of* sejumlah; *the ~ of* jumlah, total; *to do ~s* menjumlahkan; *vi ~ up* menyimpulkan, mengambil kesimpulan; **summing-up** *n* kesimpulan, ringkasan

Sumatra *n* (pulau) Sumatera; *North ~* Sumatera Utara (Sumut); *South ~* Sumatera Selatan (Sumsel); *West ~* Sumatera Barat (Sumbar); **Sumatran** *adj* berasal dari Sumatera; *n* orang Sumatera

summarize *vt* meringkas; **summary** *n* ringkasan, ikhtisar

summer *n* musim panas; *~ camp* kegiatan untuk anak-anak selama liburan musim panas; *~ holidays* liburan musim panas; *~ school* seméster péndék; *Indian ~* cuaca panas pada musim gugur; **summertime** *n* musim panas

summing-up *n* kesimpulan, ringkasan ← **sum**

summit *n* (pertemuan) puncak; *G8* ~ pertemuan puncak G8; *Australia's highest* ~ *is Mt Kosciuszko* puncak tertinggi di Australia adalah Gunung Kosciuszko

summon *vt* memanggil; **summons** *n* (surat) panggilan

sumo *n* sumo; ~ *wrestler* pesumo

sun *n* matahari; *~-baked* terjemur, kering; *~-dried* kering; ~ *lamp* alat penyinar; *in the* ~ di bawah sinar matahari; *vi* ~ *yourself* berjemur; **sunbathe** *vi* [sanbéth] berjemur; **sunbeam** *n* sinar matahari; **sunblock** *n* tabir surya; **sunburn** *n* terbakar sinar matahari; **sundial** *n* [sandail] jam matahari; **sundown** *n* matahari terbenam, matahari tenggelam, magrib; **sunflower** *n* bunga matahari; ~ *seeds* biji bunga matahari; **sunglasses** *n, pl* kacamata hitam; **sunlight** *n* [sanlait] cahaya matahari; **sunlit** *adj* tampak di bawah cahaya matahari; **sunny** *adj* cerah; riang; **sunrise** *n* matahari terbit; **sunroof** *n* jendéla atap; **sunscreen** *n* tabir surya; **sunset** *n* matahari terbenam, matahari tenggelam, magrib; ~ *prayer* (sholat) magrib; **sunshade** *n* pelindung dari sinar matahari; **sunshine** *n* sinar matahari, cahaya matahari; **sunstroke** *n* kelengar matahari; **suntan** *n* kulit berwarna coklat karena kena sinar matahari

sundae *n* [sandé] és krim dengan sirop

Sundanese *adj* [sundaniz] berasal dari daérah Jawa Barat atau Banten; ~ *restaurant* rumah makan Sunda; *n* bahasa Sunda; orang Sunda

Sunday *n* hari Minggu; ~ *school* sekolah hari Minggu (ajaran Kristen) ← **sun**

sundial *n* [sandail] jam matahari ← **sun**

sundown *n* matahari terbenam, matahari tenggelam, magrib ← **sun**

sunflower *n* bunga matahari; ~ *seeds* biji bunga matahari ← **sun**

sung *v, pf* → **sing**

sunglasses *n, pl* kacamata hitam ← **sun**

sunk *adj* tenggelam; *v, pf* → **sink**; **sunken** *adj* cekung; tenggelam; ~ *treasure* harta karun di dasar laut

sunlight *n* [sanlait] cahaya matahari ← **sun**

sunlit *adj* tampak di bawah cahaya matahari ← **sun**

sunny *adj* cerah; riang ← **sun**

sunrise *n* matahari terbit ← **sun**

sunroof *n* jendéla atap ← **sun**

sunscreen *n* tabir surya ← **sun**

sunset *n* matahari terbenam, matahari tenggelam, magrib; ~ *prayer* (sholat) magrib ← **sun**

sunshade *n* pelindung dari sinar matahari ← **sun**

sunshine *n* sinar matahari, cahaya matahari ← **sun**

sunstroke *n* kelengar matahari ← **sun**

suntan *n* kulit berwarna coklat karena kena sinar matahari ← **sun**

super *adj* luar biasa, hébat

superannuation *n* uang pénsiun, dana pénsiun

superb *adj* bagus sekali, istiméwa; **superbly** *adv* secara luar biasa

superficial *adj* [superfisyel] dangkal, énténg

superfluous *adj* [supérfluus] berlebihan, tidak perlu

superintendent *n* pengawas, pemimpin, kepala instansi

superior *adj* [supirior] ulung, unggul, tinggi; sombong; *Mother* ~ suster kepala; *n* atasan; **superiority** *n* keunggulan

supermarket *n* (toko) swalayan

supernatural *adj* [supernatyurel] gaib; *the* ~ dunia gaib

superpower *n* [superpauer] negara adidaya

superstar *n* mégabintang

superstition *n* [superstisyen] takhayul; **superstitious** *adj* [superstisyes] sering percaya takhayul

supervise *vt* mengawasi; **supervision** *n* [supervisyen] pengawasan; **supervisor** *n* [supervaizer] pengawas

supper *n* makan malam; *to have* ~ makan malam

supple *adj* [sapel] lentur, gemulai

supplement *n* [saplement] tambahan, pelengkap, suplemén; **supplement** *vt* melengkapi; **supplementary** *adj* tambahan, pelengkap

supplier *n* [saplayer] pemasok; **supply** *n* pasokan, persediaan, suplai; ~ *teacher* guru pengawas; ~ *and demand* persediaan dan permintaan; *vt* memasok, menyediakan

support *n* dukungan, sokongan, bantuan; *vt* mendukung, membantu; **supporter** *n* pendukung; **supportive** *adj* [suportiv] bersifat mendukung, pendukung

suppose *vt* mengandaikan, menganggap, mengira; ~*d to* seharusnya; katanya; **supposing** *conj* andaikata, seandainya

suppress *vt* menekan, menindas; **suppression** *n* [suprésyen] penekanan, penindasan

supremacy *n* [suprémasi] keunggulan; **supreme** *adj* [suprim] unggul, teratas; ~ *command* komando tertinggi, pimpinan tertinggi; ~ *Court* Mahkamah Agung

surcharge *n* biaya tambahan, tunjangan

sure *adj* [syur] tentu, pasti; yakin; ~ *enough* ternyata benar; ~ *thing* tentu saja, pasti; *for* ~ pasti; *a* ~ *thing* kepastian; *are you* ~? yakin?; **surely** *adv* tentu, tentu saja, pasti

surf *n* buih ombak; *vi* berselancar; ~ *the Web* menjelajahi internét; **surfboard** *n* papan selancar; **surfer** *n* peselancar; **surfing** *n* (main) selancar, berselancar; menjelajahi internét; *wind-*~ selancar angin

surface *n* [sérfes] muka, permukaan; dangkal; ~ *mail* pos biasa; *vi* naik ke permukaan, muncul

surfboard *n* papan selancar ← **surf**

surfer *n* peselancar ← **surf**; **surfing** *n* (main) selancar, berselancar; menjelajahi internét; *wind-*~ selancar angin ← **surf**

surgeon *n* [serjen] ahli bedah; *plastic* ~ ahli bedah plastik; **surgery** *n* pembedahan, operasi; tempat prakték dokter;

surgical *adj* berkaitan dengan bedah; ~ *mask* masker

Surinam *n* Surinam; **Surinamer** *n* orang Surinam; **Surinamese** *adj* berasal dari Surinam

surname *n* nama keluarga, nama marga

surpass *vt* melebihi, mengungguli

surplus *adj, n* kelebihan, sisa, surplus; *a* ~ *of watermelons* kelebihan semangka

surprise *n* kejutan; *vi* membuat kejutan; *vt* mengejutkan; **surprised** *adj* terkejut; **surprising** *adj* mengejutkan

surrender *n* penyerahan; *vi* menyerah; *vt* menyerahkan

surround *vt* mengelilingi, mengepung; **surrounding** *adj* yang di sekitar; **surroundings** *n* daérah sekitar, lingkungan

surveillance *n* [sérvélens] pengawasan, peninjauan; *under* ~ sedang diamati, di bawah pengawasan; **survey** *n* [survé] angkét; penelitian; peninjauan; *vt* meneliti, meninjau; **surveyor** *n* juru ukur tanah

survival *n* [servaivel] kelangsungan hidup; **survive** *vi* bertahan (hidup), tetap hidup, selamat; *vt* tahan terhadap, berhasil meléwati masa sulit; *Paul* ~*d getting lost on the mountain* Paul bertahan hidup saat tersesat di gunung; **survivor** *n* orang yang selamat

suspect *n* [saspekt] tersangka; *vt* [saspékt] menyangka; **suspicion** *n* [sespisyen] kecurigaan; **suspicious** *adj* [sespisyes] curiga, mencurigakan; **suss** *adj, sl* mencurigakan, tidak dapat dipercaya

suspend *v* menggantung; menangguhkan, menunda; **suspenders** *n, pl* tali selempang; **suspense** *n* ketegangan; **suspension** *n* penskorsan; suspénsi; ~ *bridge* jembatan gantung

suspicion *n* [sespisyen] kecurigaan; **suspicious** *adj* curiga, mencurigakan ← **suspect**; **suss** *adj, sl* mencurigakan, tidak dapat dipercaya

sustain *vt* mempertahankan; **sustainable** *adj* [susténabel] berkelanjutan, dapat dipertahankan; ~ *development* pembangunan berkelanjutan

SUV *abbrev sports utility vehicle* mobil jip

SW *abbrev south west* barat daya

swaddle *vt* [swodel] membedong

swagger *n* cara berjalan yang angkuh; *vi* berjalan dengan berlaga

swallow *v* [swolo] menelan; ~ *by accident* tertelan

swallow *n* [swolo] burung layang-layang

swam *v, pf* → **swim**

swamp *n* [swomp] paya, rawa; *vt* membanjiri; **swampy** *adj* berawa

swan *n* [swon] angsa, soang; ~ *song* karya terakhir

swap, swop *n* pertukaran; *vi* bertukar; *vt* menukar; ~ *card* kartu koléksi yang bisa ditukar-menukar; ~ *meet* acara tukar-menukar barang tertentu

swarm *n* [sworm] sekawanan; *a* ~ *of bees* sekawanan lebah; *vi* berkerumun

swat *vt* [swot] memukul (serangga); *fly* ~ alat pemukul lalat

sway *n* goyangan; kekuasaan; *to hold* ~ berpengaruh, berkuasa; *vi* bergoyang; *vt* menggoncangkan; mempengaruhi

swear *vi* [suér] **swore sworn** bersumpah; mengumpat; ~ *at* mengumpati; ~ *by* sangat mengandalkan; ~ *word* kata jorok; ~ *an oath* bersumpah

sweat *n* [swét] keringat, peluh; *vi* berkeringat; **sweatband** *n* gelang penyerap keringat; **sweater** *n* switer; **sweatshirt** *n* semacam baju hangat; **sweatshop** *n* pabrik dengan upah rendah; **sweaty** *adj* berkeringat, keringatan

Swede *n* [swid] orang Swédia; **Sweden** *n* Swédia; **Swedish** *adj* berasal dari Swédia; *n* bahasa Swédia

swede *n* [swid] sejenis ubi

sweep *v* **swept swept** menyapu; *chimney* ~ tukang pembersih cerobong; *clean* ~ sapu bersih; **sweeping** *adj* besar, meyakinkan; ~ *changes* perubahan besar

sweep, sweepstakes *n* taruhan, undian

sweet *adj* manis; *n* permén; ~ *corn* jagung (manis); ~ *potato* ubi jalar; ~ *talk* kata-kata manis, rayuan gombal;

~ *tooth* penggemar makanan manis; ~ *and sour* asam manis; *to be* ~ *on* suka, sayang (pada orang); **sweeten** *vt* memaniskan, membuat manis; **sweetener** *artificial* ~ pemanis buatan; **sweetheart** *n* [swithart] kekasih; *pron, coll* sayang; **sweetie** *pron, coll* sayang

swell *adj, sl* hébat; *n* gelombang; *vi* membesar; ~ *up* bengkak; *vt* menambah besar, membengkakkan; **swelling** *n* pembengkakan; **swollen** *adj* bengkak, kembung

swept *v, pf* → **sweep**

swift *adj* cepat, lancar, deras

swim *v* **swam swum** berenang, mandi; *sink or* ~ berjuang sendiri; *to go for a* ~, *to have a* ~ (pergi) berenang; mandi di laut; **swimmer** *n* perenang; **swimming** *n* renang; ~ *pool* kolam renang; ~ *trunks* baju renang (untuk laki-laki); *synchronized* ~ renang indah; **swimsuit, swimwear** *n* baju renang

swindle *n* [swindel] penipuan; *vt* menipu

swine *n* swine babi; *sl* orang jahat

swing *n* ayunan; pergéséran; *vi* **swung swung** bergoyang, berayun; *vt* menggoyangkan, mengayun

swipe *vt* menggésék; memukul; mencuri; ~ *card* kartu gésék

Swiss *adj* berasal dari Swis; ~ *army knife* pisau lipat; *n* orang Swis; **Switzerland** *n* (negeri) Swis

switch *n* sakelar, penghubung; pertukaran; *vi* tukar, bertukar; ~ *off* mematikan; ~ *on* menghidupkan, memasang; *vt* menukar, menukarkan; **switchboard** *n* séntral télépon

Switzerland *n* (negeri) Swis

swollen *adj* bengkak, kembung ← **swell**

swoop *vi* ~ *(on)* menyambar; *one fell* ~ dalam sekali kejadian

swop → **swap**

sword *n* [sord] pedang

swore, sworn *v, pf* → **swear**

swot *n, coll* orang yang rajin sekali belajar

swum *v, pf* → **swim**

swung *v, pf* → **swing**
syllable *n* [silabel] suku kata
syllabus *n* [silabus] rencana pelajaran,
daftar pelajaran
symbol *n* [simbol] lambang, simbol;
symbolic *adj* simbolis, melambangkan; **symbolically** *adv* secara
simbolis; **symbolize** *vt* melambangkan
symmetrical *adj* [simétrikal] simétris,
setimbal; **symmetry** *n* [simetri]
simétri
sympathetic *adj* [simpathétik] mau
mengerti, perhatian, bersimpati; ~ *to*
mengerti; **sympathize** *vi* [simpathaiz]
bersimpati, menyatakan simpati; *I* ~
with working mothers saya bersimpati
dengan ibu bekerja; **sympathy** *n* [sim-
pathi] simpati
symphony *n* [simfoni] simfoni
symptom *n* [simptom] gejala
synagogue *n* [sinagog] sinagoga, tempat ibadah orang Yahudi
synchronize *vt* [sinkronaiz] menyesuaikan, menyelaraskan; **synchronized** *adj* [sinkronaizd] ~ *swimming*
renang indah
syncretic *adj* [sinkrétik] sinkrétis,
bersifat menyatukan
syndicate *n* [sindikat] sindikat, kongsi
syndrome *n* sindrom, sindroma; *Down's*
~ sindroma Down
synonym *n* [sinonim] padanan, sinonim; **synonymous** [sinonimus] ~ *with*
berarti sama dengan
synopsis *n* [sinopsis] ringkasan, ikhtisar, sinopsis
synthesis *n* [sinthesis] sintésa
synthetic *adj* sintétis; ~ *rubber* karét
sintétis, karét buatan
Syria *n* [siria] Suriah; **Syrian** *adj*
berasal dari Suriah; *n* orang
Suriah
syringe *n* [sirinj] alat suntik, suntikan
syrup *n* [sirep] sirop; **syrupy** *adj* terlalu
manis
system *n* [sistem] sistem, susunan,
jaringan; **systematic** *adj* sistématis; **systematically** *adv* secara
sistématis

T

T ~*bone steak* sejenis stéik; ~*junction*
pertigaan, simpang tiga; ~*shirt* kaus
(oblong)
ta *UK, sl* makasih
tab *n* labél; *to keep* ~s *on* mengawasi
tabby *n* ~ *(cat)* kucing belang
table *n* [tébel] méja; daftar, tabél; ~
napkin serbét; ~ *manners* sopan santun
saat makan; ~ *mat* tatakan piring; ~
tennis ténis méja, pingpong; ~ *of contents* daftar isi; *billiards* ~ méja bilyar;
tablecloth *n* [tébelkloth] taplak méja;
tablespoon *n* [tébelspun] séndok
besar
tablet *n* pil, tablét
tabloid *n* koran, tabloid
taboo *adj* tabu; *n* pantangan
tack *n* paku; *thumb* ~ paku; *as sharp as
a* ~ berotak tajam; *vt* memaku,
memasang (dengan paku)
tackle *n* [takel] serangan, tékel; rangkulan; perkakas, perabot; *vt* mengganjal
kaki; menghadapi, menanggulangi; ~
poverty menanggulangi kemiskinan
tacky *adj, coll* norak; *a* ~ *invitation* surat
undangan yang norak
tact *n* kebijaksanaan, sikap diplomatis;
tactful *adj* bijaksana, diplomatis;
tactfully *adv* dengan bijaksana, secara
diplomatis; **tactless** *adj* membuat
sakit hati, tidak bijaksana; **tactlessly**
adv tanpa berpikir, secara menyakitkan
tactic *n* taktik, siasat, kiat; **tactical** *adj*
taktis
tactless *adj* membuat sakit hati, tidak
bijaksana; **tactlessly** *adv* tanpa
berpikir, secara menyakitkan ← **tact**
tadpole *n* kecebong
taffeta *adj, n* taféta
tag *n* labél, mérek, nama, kartu; *luggage* ~ tanda bagasi; *vt* memberi
tanda; ~ *along* membuntuti, ikut; *to
play* ~ main kejar-kejaran
tail *n* ékor, buntut; bagian belakang; ~
end bagian akhir, buntut; ~ *wind* angin
buritan; *heads or* ~s permainan atas
atau bawah (dengan uang logam); *vt*

membuntuti, mengikuti secara diam-
diam; **tailback** *n* antréan mobil (di
jalan); **tailgate** *vt* mengikuti mobil terlalu dekat; **taillight** *n* [tél lait] lampu
belakang (kendaraan); **tailspin** *n*
tukikan; *in a* ~ menukik

tailor *n* tukang jahit, modist; ~-*made*
buatan tukang jahit; dibuat khusus;
tailored *adj* sesuai, dibuat khusus;
tailor *vt* menyesuaikan

tailspin *n* tukikan; *in a* ~ menukik

taint *vt* mencemarkan; **tainted** *adj*
tercemar, ternoda

Taiwan *n* Taiwan; *made in* ~ buatan
Taiwan; **Taiwanese** *adj* berasal dari
Taiwan; *n* orang Taiwan

Tajik *n* bahasa Tajik; orang Tajik;
Tajikistan *n* Tajikistan; **Tajikistani** *adj*
berasal dari Tajikistan; *n* orang
Tajikistan

take *vt* **took taken** mengambil, membawa (pergi); menganggap; menangkap, menerima; makan (waktu),
memerlukan; ~ *after* mirip; ~ *apart*
membongkar; ~ *for* mengira, menyangka; ~ *back* mengembalikan;
menarik (kembali); ~ *down* mencatat;
~ *ill* jatuh sakit; ~ *in* mengerti; ~ *it*
tahan, menerima; ~ *off* lepas landas;
berangkat; membuka; ~ *on* menerima,
menanggung; ~ *out* mengambil;
mengajak (pergi); ~ *over* mengambil
alih; ~ *part* ikut serta, ambil bagian; ~
place berlangsung, terjadi; ~ *to* suka;
~ *up* mulai mempelajari, menerima; ~
the bus naik bis; *do you* ~ *tea or coffee?* ingin minum téh atau kopi? **takeaway** *adj, n* dibungkus, bawa pulang;
takeoff *n* lepas landas; **takeover** *n*
pengambilan alih; **takings** *n, pl* pendapatan selama masa tertentu

talc *n* bedak; **talcum** ~ *powder* bedak

tale *n* cerita, dongéng; *fairy-*~ (kisah)
dongéng; *to tell* ~s melapor; membohong

talent *n* [talent] bakat; ~ *scout* pencari
bakat; **talented** *adj* berbakat

talk *n* [tok] percakapan, pembicaraan,
ceramah; *n, pl* perundingan; *small* ~
basa-basi, obrolan ringan; ~ *of the*

town buah bibir; *to give a* ~ berceramah, berpidato, memberi préséntasi;
vi berbicara, berunding, bertutur; ~
about berbicara soal, membicarakan;
~ *of* membicarakan; ~ *over* membicarakan, membahas; **talkative** *adj*
[tokatif] ceréwét, banyak omong; **talk-
back** ~ *radio* acara kontak pendengar;
talking ~-*to* teguran; *of* ngomong-
ngomong; ~ *point* topik pembicaraan,
isu; ~ *round* membujuk, meyakinkan;
talkshow *n* acara diskusi

tall *adj* [tol] tinggi, jangkung; ~ *story*
cerita yang sulit dipercaya; *a* ~ *order*
permintaan yang berat; *six feet* ~ tinggi badan 180 sénti(méter)

tally *n* jumlah, perhitungan; *vi* cocok; *vt*
~ *(up)* menjumlahkan

talon *n* [talon] cakar (burung)

tamarind *n* [tamarind] asam jawa

tambourine *n* [tamburin] rebana

tame *adj* jinak; *vt* menjinakkan; **tamer**
n elephant ~ pawang gajah

Tamil *adj* [tamil] berasal dari kebudayaan Tamil atau Keling; *n* bahasa Tamil;
orang Keling, orang Tamil

tamper *vi* ~ *with* merusakkan, mengubah

tampon *n* tampon

tan *adj* coklat muda; *n* kulit berwarna
coklat; *vi* bermandi matahari; menya-
mak (kulit); *coll* mencambuk; **tanner**
n penyamak

tandem ~ *(bike)* sepéda untuk dua
orang; *in* ~ *(with)* bersama, berdua

tang *n* rasa, bau; **tangy** *adj* berasa kecut

tangerine *n* [tanjerin] jeruk garut, jeruk
keprok

tangle *n* [tanggel] kekusutan, kekacauan; **tangled** *adj* kusut, kacau

tango *n* [tanggo] (dansa) tango; *vi*
berdansa tango; *it takes two to* ~
kegiatan yang melibatkan dua orang

tank *n* tangki; panser; ~ *top* kaus tanpa
lengan, kaus tali spagéti; **tanker** *n*
kapal tangki

tanner *n* penyamak ← **tan**

tantrum *n* marah (seperti anak-anak);
the child threw a ~ *when the wrong
cake was delivered* anak itu marah
sekali saat pesanan kué yang salah tiba

Tanzania *n* Tanzania; **Tanzanian** *adj* berasal dari Tanzania; *n* orang Tanzania

tap *n* keran; ketukan; *~ dance* dansa tép; *~ water* air keran, air PAM; *on ~* tersedia; *phone ~* sadapan télépon; *vi* mengetuk; *vt* menyadap; *~ a rubber tree* menyadap pohon karét; *~ a telephone conversation* menyadap percakapan télépon; *~ on the door* mengetuk pintu; **tapper** *n* penyadap

tape *n* pita; pléster; kasét; *~ measure* méteran; *~ recorder, ~ deck* mesin pemutar kasét, tép; *~ recording* rekaman (suara); *masking ~* lakban; *red ~* urusan birokrasi; *sticky ~* isolasi, sélotip; *v* memakai sélotip; membalut; merekam; **tapeworm** *n* cacing pita

taper *vi* meruncing

tapestry *n* [tapestri] sulaman, permadani hiasan dinding, tenunan

tapeworm *n* cacing pita ← **tape**

tapioca *n* tepung ubi kayu, tapioka

tapir *n* cipan, tenuk

tapper *n* penyadap ← **tap**

tar *n* tér; aspal

tarantula *n* sejenis laba-laba besar

tardy *adj, US* terlambat, telat

target *n* sasaran, tujuan, targét; *vt* mengincar, menargétkan; *this ad is ~ing young mothers* iklan ini ditujukan untuk ibu-ibu muda

tariff *n* tarif, ongkos

tarnish *vi* menjadi buram atau hitam (logam); *vt* mencemarkan

taro *n* [taro] talas

tarot [taro] *~ cards* kartu meramal

tarpaulin *n* [tarpolin] terpal

tart *adj* asam, kecut; *n* kué kecil yang bulat; *coll* perempuan murahan; **tarty** *adj, coll* norak

tartan *n* corak kotak-kotak khas Skotlandia

tartar *n* karang gigi

task *n* tugas, pekerjaan; *~ force* satuan tugas (satgas); *a hard ~* tugas yang berat; *to complete a ~* mengerjakan tugas; menyelesaikan tugas; *to entrust a ~ to* menugaskan

tassels *n, pl* rumbai, jumbai

taste *n* [tést] (cita) rasa; cicipan; nuansa; seléra; *an acquired ~* tidak disukai kebanyakan orang; *in good ~* berseléra tinggi; *a ~ of cinnamon* rasa kayu manis; nuansa kayu manis; *vi* terasa; *~ of* berasa; *vt* mengecap, merasai; **tasteful** *adj* berseléra (baik); **tasteless** *adj* tidak berseléra, norak; **tasty** *adj* énak, sedap; *~ cheese* semacam kéju

tata *UK, coll* da

tattered *adj* sobék-sobék, compang-camping; **tatters** *n, pl in ~s* sobék-sobék, compang-camping; **tatty** *adj* dalam keadaan tidak terpelihara

tattoo *n* tato, rajah; *vt* merajah, menato

tatty *adj* dalam keadaan tidak terpelihara

taught *v, pf →* **teach**

tavern *n* [tavern] tempat minum, hotél yang merangkap sebagai bar

tax *n* pajak, béa; *~-free* bébas pajak; *~ advisor* penasihat pajak; *~ evasion* penghindaran pajak; *income ~* pajak pendapatan; *goods and services ~ (GST)* pajak pelayanan dan barang (PPB); *vt* mengenakan pajak atau béa; membuat kuatir, membuat lelah; **taxable** *adj* [taksabel] yang wajib dikenakan pajak; **taxation** *n* [taksésyen] pajak, perpajakan; **taxing** *adj* menguatirkan, melelahkan; **taxpayer** *n* pembayar pajak

taxi, taxicab *n* taksi; *~ driver* supir taksi; *~ rank* pangkalan taksi; *metered ~* taksi argo; *to order a ~* memesan taksi

taxing *adj* menguatirkan, melelahkan

taxpayer *n* pembayar pajak ← **tax**

TB *abbrev tuberculosis* TBC, radang paru-paru

tbsp *abbrev tablespoon* séndok besar

tea *n* [ti] téh; makan soré; *coll* makan malam; *~ bag* celup téh, kantong téh; *~ break* réhat kopi; *~ cosy* tutup téko; *~ leaves* daun téh; *~ party* acara minum téh bersama; *~ plantation* kebun téh; *~ towel* lap piring; *afternoon ~* makan soré; *strong ~* téh kental; *sweet ~* téh manis; **teacup** *n* cangkir téh, cawan téh; **teapot** *n* poci, téko; **tearooms** *n,* *pl* [tirumz] réstoran kecil tempat minum téh; **teaspoon** *n* séndok téh; **teaspoonful** *n* seséndok téh

teach *v* [tic] **taught taught** [tot] mengajar; **teacher** *n* guru, pengajar; ~*'s pet* murid kesayangan; *science* ~ guru IPA; **teaching** *n* ajaran, pengajaran; ~ *and learning* hal belajar-mengajar; **teachings** *n, pl* ajaran

teacup *n* [tikap] cangkir téh, cawan téh ← **tea**

teak *n* [tik] (kayu) jati

team *n* [tim] regu, tim; ~ *player* anggota tim yang mengutamakan timnya; ~ *spirit* semangat tim; *vi* ~ *up with* bekerja sama dengan; **teammate** *n* kawan (seregu); **teamwork** *n* [timwerk] kerjasama sekelompok

teapot *n* [tipot] poci, téko ← **tea**

tear *n* [tér] sobékan, robékan; *vi* **tore torn** robék, sobék, terkoyak; *vt* menyobék, merobék, mengoyak

tear *n* [tir] air mata; ~ *gas* gas air mata; *in* ~*s* menangis; **teardrop** *n* setétés air mata; **tearful, teary** *adj* (cenderung) menangis

tearooms *n, pl* [tirumz] réstoran kecil tempat minum téh ← **tea**

teary *adj* [tiri] (cenderung) menangis ← **tear**

tease *vt* [tiz] mengganggu, melédék, mengusik; ~ *hair* menyasak rambut; **tease** *n* orang yang suka melédék; penggoda; **teaser** *n* teka-teki; **teasing** *n* usikan, lédékan

teaspoon *n* [tispun] séndok téh; **teaspoonful** *n* seséndok téh ← **tea**

technical *adj* [téknikel] téknis; ~ *college,* ~ *school* SMAK, sekolah kejuruan; ~ *support* bantuan téknis; **technician** *n* téknisi; **technicality** *n* alasan téknis

technique *n* [téknik] cara, téknik

techno *adj* [tékno] ~ *(music)* musik tékno

technological *adj* [téknolojikel] berhubungan dengan téknologi; **technology** *n* téknologi; *science and* ~ ilmu pengetahuan dan téknologi (ipték)

teddy *n* ~ *(bear)* bonéka beruang

tedious *adj* [tidius] membosankan, menjemukan

tee-shirt → **T-shirt**

teen *n* remaja, anak baru gedé (ABG); **teenage** *adj* remaja, umur belasan tahun; ~ *son* anak (lelaki) yang sudah remaja; **teenager** *n* (anak) remaja; **teens** *n, pl* umur belasan tahun

teeth *n, pl* ← **tooth**; **teethe** *vi* tumbuh gigi; *Adi is teething* gigi Adi sedang tumbuh

teetotaler *n* orang yang tidak minum alkohol

tel. *abbrev telephone* tlp (télepon)

telecast *n* [télekast] tayangan (langsung); *vt* menayangkan, menyiarkan; *the Olympics will be* ~ *on this channel* pertandingan Olimpiade akan ditayangkan di saluran ini

telecommunications *n, pl* télekomunikasi

telegram *n, arch* télegram, surat kawat; **telegraph** *n, arch* télegraf; ~ *pole* tiang listrik

telemarketing *n* pemasaran léwat télepon

telepathic *adj* berhubungan dengan télepati; **telepathy** *n* télepati

telephone *n* (pesawat) télepon, télefon; ~ *book* buku petunjuk télepon; ~ *box, public* ~ télepon umum; ~ *number* nomor télepon; ~ *pole* tiang listrik; *v* menélepon

telescope *n* teropong (bintang), téléskop

televise *vt* [télevaiz] menyiarkan léwat télévisi, menayangkan; **television (TV)** *n* **telly** *coll* télévisi (tévé, tivi); *television station* stasiun télévisi, saluran télévisi; *on (the)* ~ di télévisi

tell *vi* **told told** bercerita; *vt* menceritakan, memberitahukan; menyuruh, memerintahkan; ~ *off* menegur, memarahi; ~ *on* melapor, mengadukan; ~ *stories* berdongeng; berdusta, berbohong; ~ *tales* melapor, membuka rahasia; ~ *someone to* menyuruh; ~ *the truth* mengatakan dengan jujur; *I can* ~ saya tahu, saya bisa membédakan; **telltale** *n* orang yang membuka rahasia; ~ *sign* tanda jelas

teller *n* kasir (di bank)

telltale *n* orang yang membuka rahasia; *~ sign* tanda jelas ← **tell**

telly *coll* télévisi (tévé, tivi) ← **television**

temper *n* sifat, watak; *bad--ed* pemarah; *to lose your ~* menjadi marah, kehilangan kesabaran; **temperament** *n* tabiat, perangai; **temperamental** *adj* émosional

temperate *adj* sedang; *~ zone* daérah beriklim sedang

temperature *n* suhu; *Rifki has a ~* badan Rifki panas

temple *n* [témpel] pelipis

temple *n* [témpel] candi, kuil; *Hind* pura, kuil; *the Borobudur ~* Candi Borobudur

temporary *adj* **temporarily** *adv* untuk sementara

tempt *vt* menggoda; **tempted** *adj* tergoda; **tempting** *adj* menggoda, menggodakan; **temptation** *n* godaan

ten *adj, n* sepuluh; *tenpin bowling* boling; **tenth** *adj* kesepuluh; *the ~ of April* tanggal sepuluh April

tenant *n* [ténant] penyéwa

tend *vi ~ to* cenderung; **tendency** *n* kecenderungan

tend *vt* merawat, memelihara; *~ a vegetable garden* berkebun, memelihara kebun sayur

tender *n* penawaran, pelélangan; *legal ~* alat pembayar yang sah

tender *adj* (berhati) lembut; lunak, halus; kurang matang; *a ~ age* masih sangat muda; **tenderizer** *meat ~* alat pemukul untuk melunakkan daging; **tenderly** *adv* dengan lembut; **tenderness** *n* kelembutan (hati)

tendon *n* urat

tennis *n* ténis; *~ ball* bola ténis; *~ club* klub ténis; *~ court* lapangan ténis; *~ match* pertandingan ténis; *~ player* peténis, pemain ténis

tenpin *~ bowling* boling ← **ten**

tense *n* masa; *past ~* bentuk lampau; *present ~* (kata kerja) masa kini

tense *adj* tegang; *vi ~ (up)* menjadi tegang; **tension** *n* ketegangan, tega-

ngan; *high ~ wires* saluran udara tegangan ékstra tinggi (SUTET)

tent *n* kémah, ténda; *~ peg* patok

tenth *adj* kesepuluh; *the ~ of April* tanggal sepuluh April ← **ten**

tepid *adj* [tépid] suam-suam kuku

term *n* istilah; **terminology** *n* [términoloji] peristilahan

term *n* jangka waktu, triwulan, caturwulan (cawu); *~ deposit* déposito (berjangka); *in ~s of* mengenai, dari segi; **terms** *n, pl* syarat-syarat; hubungan; *on good ~* berhubungan baik; *to come to ~s with* menerima, mencapai kesepakatan

terminal *n* términal, pangkalan; *adj* penghabisan, terakhir; *~ cancer* kanker stadium lanjut; **terminally** *adv* secara fatal; *~ ill* sekarat; **terminate** *vi* berakhir; *vt* mengakhiri; *~ someone's services* memberhentikan, memecat; **termination** *n* pemutusan; pengguguran, aborsi; **terminus** *n* términal, tujuan terakhir

terminology *n* [términoloji] peristilahan

termite *n* rayap, anai-anai; *to have ~s* kena rayap

terrace *n* téras

terrapin *n* [térapin] kura-kura

terrible *adj* [téribel] mengerikan, menakutkan, buruk sekali; *I feel ~* saya merasa bersalah; saya pusing; **terribly** *adv* amat sangat

terrier *n* [térier] jenis anjing

terrific *adj* [terifik] hébat; **terrified** *adj* sangat ketakutan; *~ of* takut pada; **terrify** *vt* [terifai] menakutkan, membuat ngeri; **terrifying** *adj* menakutkan, mengerikan

territorial *adj* [téritorial] berhubungan dengan daérah; *~ waters* perairan; **territory** *n* daérah, wilayah; *Northern ~* Australia Utara

terror *n* rasa takut, téror; **terrorism** *n* [térorizem] térorisme; **terrorist** *n* téroris; **terrorize** *vt* méneror; *her mother was ~d by late-night phone calls* ibunya ditéror malam-malam oléh penélepon gelap

tertiary *adj* [térsyeri] ketiga; *~ educa-*

tion pendidikan di perguruan tinggi; ~ *Period* Jaman Tersiér

test *n* ujian, pemeriksaan, tés; percobaan, uji coba; *vt* memeriksa, menguji; mengujicoba; ~ *case* batu ujian; ~ *drive* uji coba mengendarakan mobil; ~ *tube* tabung réaksi; **tester** *n* penguji; contoh; **testing** *n* pengujian, percobaan, tésting

testament *Old* ~ Perjanjian Lama; *last will and* ~ surat wasiat

testicle *n* [téstikel] buah pelir; **testicular** *adj* ~ *cancer* kanker buah pelir

testify *vi* [téstifai] bersaksi; **testimonial** *n* surat kesaksian; tanda penghargaan; **testimony** *n* kesaksian

testing *n* pengujian, percobaan, tésting ← **test**

text *n* naskah, téks; ~ *message* pesan singkat, SMS; *vt* mengirimi orang pesan singkat; *he ~ed me to say thank you* dia mengucapkan terima kasih léwat SMS; **textbook** *n* buku pelajaran

texta *n* spidol

textiles *n, pl* tékstil, barang tenunan

texture *n* tékstur

Thai *adj* [tai] berasal dari Thailand; ~ *silk* sutera Thai; *n* bahasa Thai; orang Thailand; **Thailand** *n* Thailand; *arch* Muang Thai

than *conj* daripada, dari; *bigger* ~ lebih besar daripada

thank *vt* mengucapkan terima kasih; ~ *you* ucapan terima kasih; ~ *God Isl* alhamdulillah; *Chr* puji Tuhan; ~ *goodness* syukur; ~ *you* terima kasih; ~ *you for* terima kasih atas; **thankful** *adj* berterima kasih; **thankfully** *adv* untung; **thanks** *coll* terima kasih, makasih; ~ *to* berkat; ~ *very much* terima kasih banyak; **Thanksgiving** *n* hari pernyataan terima kasih (di Amérika Utara)

that *pron* **those** itu; ~*'s all* sekian; ~*'s* ~ habis perkara; *adv* begitu; ~ *much* begitu besar; ~ *way* begitu; ke arah sana

that *conj* bahwa; yang; supaya; *Bill said* ~ *he was coming* Bill mengatakan bahwa dia akan datang; *the house* ~ *Jack built* rumah yang dibangun Jack

thatch *n* jerami, rumbia; ~*ed cottage* rumah beratap jerami

thaw *n* [tho] cair; *vi* mencair, menjadi cair; *vt* melunakkan (sesuatu yang beku)

the *art* itu, -nya; *the more, the ...-er* semakin banyak, semakin ...

theater, theatre *n* (gedung) téater; ~*goer* orang yang sering nonton pertunjukan téater; *movie* ~ (gedung) bioskop

thee *pron, arch* engkau, kamu

theft *n* pencurian; **thief** *n* [thif] **thieves** pencuri, maling; **thieve** *vt* mencuri

their *pron, pl* [thér] **theirs** meréka (punya), milik meréka; **them** *pron, obj, pl* meréka; **themselves** *pron, pl* meréka sendiri

theme *n* [thim] téma, pokok; ~ *park* taman hiburan; ~ *song* lagu wajib, lagunya; **thematic** *adj* bertéma

themselves *pron, pl* meréka sendiri ← **them**

then *adv* pada waktu itu; *conj* sesudah itu, kemudian, lalu; maka; *n* waktu itu; *now and* ~ sekali-sekali

theology *n* [thioloji] téologi

theoretical *adj* [thiorétikel] téoritis, menurut téori; **theory** *n* téori

therapeutic *adj* [thérapyutik] bersifat menyembuhkan atau mengobatkan; **therapist** *n* ahli; psikolog ← **psychotherapist**; **therapy** *n* térapi; *speech* ~ térapi wicara

there *adv* [thér] (di) situ; (di) sana; ~ *and back* pulang pergi; *ejac* nah; *n* sana; itu; ~ *is (there's)*, ~ *are* ada; *over* ~ di sana; *here and* ~ di sana-sini; ~ *you are* silahkan, itu dia; **thereabouts** *adv* [thérabautz] kira-kira, kurang lebih; **thereby** *adv* [thérbai] dengan (cara) demikian; **therefore** *conj* [thérfor] maka, oleh sebab itu

thermal *adj* berkaitan dengan panas

thermometer *n* térmométer

thermos *n* [thérmes] térmos

thermostat *n* alat pengatur panas, térmostat

thesaurus *n* [tesorus] tésaurus, semacam kamus

these *pron, pl* [thiz] ini ← **this**

thesis *n* **theses** [thisis] skripsi, disértasi, tésis; dalil

they *pron, pl* [thé] meréka; ~ *are (they're)* meréka (adalah); ~ *have (they've)* meréka punya; meréka telah; ~ *say* kata orang; ~ *will (they'll)* meréka akan

thick *adj* gemuk; tebal; kental; *coll* bodoh; ~*skinned* berkulit badak; *(as)* ~ *as thieves* sangat akrab; *in the* ~ *of* ditengah-tengah; *through* ~ *and thin* dalam suka dan duka; **thicken** *vi* mengental; **thickness** *n* ketebalan, kekentalan

thief *n* [thif] **thieves** pencuri, maling; *(as)* **thick as thieves** sangat akrab; **thieve** *vt* [thiv] mencuri

thigh *n* [thai] paha

thimble *n* [thimbel] bidal, sarung jari

thin *adj* kurus; tipis, halus; éncér; *through thick and* ~ dalam suka dan duka; **thinner** *adj* lebih kurus, lebih tipis; *n* bahan pengéncér, téner

thine *pron, arch, poss* kepunyaan engkau

thing *n* barang, benda, alat; *my* ~*s* barang-barang saya; *poor* ~ kasihan; *how are* ~*s?* apa kabar?; *just the* ~ inilah dia; *the* ~ *is* soalnya; **thingy** *n, sl* [thingi] anu, apa namanya, itunya

think *vi* **thought thought** [thot] pikir, berpikir; berpendapat; ~*-tank* lembaga pemikir; ~ *about* memikirkan; ~ *again* berpikir sekali lagi; ~ *back* ingat; ~ *over* menimbang, mempertimbangkan; ~ *up* mengarang, menciptakan; ~*ing of you* saya ingat pada anda; *to have a good* ~ berpikir baik-baik; **thinker** *n* pemikir; **thought** *n* [thot] pikiran, idé; *vi, pf →* **think**; *in my* ~*s* dalam doa saya; **thoughtful** *adj* [thotful] penuh perhatian; **thoughtless** *adj* [thotles] tidak ingat; lalai

thinner *adj* lebih kurus, lebih tipis; *n* bahan pengéncér, téner ← **thin**

third *adj, n* ketiga; pertiga; ~ *degree* penyiksaan; pemeriksaan yang melelahkan; ~ *party* pihak ketiga; ~ *person* orang ketiga (²/₃); ~ *world* dunia ketiga; *two-*~*s* dua pertiga; **thirdly** *adv, conj* (yang) ketiga; **three** *adj, n* tiga;

~*-dimensional* tiga diménsi; ~ *quarters* tiga perempat (³/₄); **threesome** *n* kelompok tiga orang

thirst *n* kehausan, dahaga; *vi* ~ *for* haus akan; **thirsty** *adj* haus

thirteen *adj, n* tiga belas; **thirteenth** *adj* ketiga belas; *Friday the* ~ Jumat tanggal tiga belas (dianggap angker)

thirtieth *adj* ketiga puluh; **thirties** *n, pl* tiga puluhan; **thirty** *adj, n* tiga puluh

this *pron* **these** ini; ~ *evening* nanti malam; malam ini; ~ *morning* tadi pagi; pagi ini; *good morning,* ~ *is Fred* selamat pagi, ini Fred

thong *n* celana dalam berbentuk tali; **thongs** *n, pl* sandal jepit

thorax *n* dada, toraks

thorn *n* duri; **thorny** *adj* berduri; sulit

thorough *adj* [thoro] teliti, cermat; **thoroughly** *adv* dengan teliti

thoroughbred *n* [thorobréd] kuda trah

thoroughfare *n* [thorofér] jalan

those *pron, pl* itu ← **that**; ~ *who* meréka yang, barangsiapa yang

thou *pron, arch* [thau] kamu, engkau

though *adv* [tho] bagaimanapun, tapi; *conj* sungguhpun, meskipun, biarpun; *even* ~ walaupun

thought *n* [thot] pikiran, idé; *food for* ~ bahan pikiran; *in my* ~*s* dalam doa saya; *v, pf →* **think**; **thoughtful** *adj* [thotful] penuh perhatian; **thoughtfully** *adv* [thotfuli] dengan penuh perhatian; **thoughtless** *adj* [thotles] tidak ingat; lalai; **thoughtlessly** *adv* [thotlesli] tanpa berpikir

thousand *adj, n* [thausend] ribu; *one* ~, *a* ~ seribu; *hundreds and* ~*s* méses; *the* ~ *Islands* Pulau Seribu

thrash *vi* menggelepar-gelepar; *vt* mencambuk; **thrashing** *n* dicambuk

thread *n* [thréd] benang; urutan; *vt* ~ *a needle* memasang benang

threat *n* [thrét] ancaman; **threaten** *vt* mengancam; **threatened** *adj* terancam

three *adj, n* tiga; ~*-dimensional* tiga diménsi; ~ *quarters* tiga perempat (³/₄); **threesome** *n* [thrisem] kelompok tiga orang

thresher *n* mesin pengirik

threshold *n* ambang, batas

threw *vt, pf* → **throw**

thrift *n* penghématan; **thrifty** *adj* hémat, irit

thrill *n* getaran (jiwa); sénsasi; *~s and spills* suasana seru; *vt* menggetarkan; **thrilled** *adj* berdebar hati; **thriller** *n* film atau buku yang menyeramkan; **thrilling** *adj* menggetarkan

thrive *vi* tumbuh dengan subur, berkembang dengan cepat

throat *n* tenggorokan, kerongkongan; *sore ~* sakit tenggorokan; *ear, nose and ~ specialist* dokter THT (telinga, hidung dan tenggorokan); *at each other's ~* selalu berkelahi; **throaty** *adj* parau

throb *n* debar, denyut; denyutan; *heart ~ idola*; *vi* berdebar, berdenyut-denyut

throne *n* takhta, singgasana

through *adj* [thru] selesai; *adv* terus; *prep* melalui, meléwati, oléh, karéna, terus; *~ and ~* benar-benar; *no ~ road* jalan buntu; *to go ~ a lot* mengalami banyak kesulitan, banyak menderita; **throughout** *prep* [thru aut] di mana-mana; sepanjang

throw *vt* **threw thrown** *vt* membuang, melémparkan; *~ on* memakai baju (dengan tergesa-gesa); *~ out, ~ away* membuang (sampah); *~ up* muntah; *~ a party* mengadakan pesta; *n* lémparan; *a stone's ~* sangat dekat; **throwaway** *adj* tidak berarti; **throwback** *adj* warisan ciri-ciri dari leluhur

thrush *n* keputihan; sejenis burung murai

thrust *n* daya dorong; serangan; tusukan; *vt* mendorongkan; menyerang; menusuk

thud *n* gedebuk; *vi* bergedebuk

thug *n* préman

thumb *n* [tham] jempol, ibu jari; *~ tack* paku payung; *~s-up* tanda setuju; *vt ~ (through)* membaca sepintas lalu (buku); *~ a lift, ~ a ride* menumpang di mobil yang léwat; **thumbnail** *n* [thamnél] kuku jempol; *~ sketch* gambar sederhana; **thumbprint** *n* [thamprint] cap jempol

thump *n* gebukan; bunyi gedebuk; *vi* berdebar (hati, jantung); *vt* menggebuk

thunder *n* gemuruh, geluduk; **thunderbolt, thunderclap** *n* petir; **thundercloud** *n* awan hujan; **thunderstorm** *n* gemuruh dan petir; **thunderstruck** *adj* seperti disambar petir, terhéran-héran

Thursday *adj, n* (hari) Kamis; *Maundy ~* Kamis Putih

thus *conj, arch* maka; *~ far* selama ini; sampai sekarang, hingga kini

thy *pron, poss, arch* [thai] -mu, kepunyaan engkau

thyme *n* [taim] sejenis rempah

thyroid *~ gland* kelenjar gondok

tiara *n* [tiara] mahkota kecil, tiara

Tibet *n* Tibét; **Tibetan** *adj* berasal dari Tibét; orang Tibét

tick *n* tanda √; detik; kutu (binatang); *vi* berdetik; *~ off* mencorét satu per satu; menegur, memarahi

ticket *n* karcis, tikét; *plane ~* tikét pesawat; *train ~* karcis keréta api; *~ collector* kondéktur; *~ office* lokét; *speeding ~* tilang; **ticketholder** *n* pemilik karcis (langganan)

tickle *vt* [tikel] menggelitik; *~d pink* senang sekali; **ticklish** *adj* geli; **tickly** *adj* menggelikan

tidal *adj* berhubungan dengan air pasang dan surut; *~ wave* gelombang pasang; **tide** *high ~, ~'s in* air pasang; *low ~, ~'s out* air surut; *spring ~* air pasang purnama; *to turn the ~* mengubah arus

tidily *adv* [taidili] dengan rapi; **tidy** *adj* apik, rapi; *n* tempat menyimpan barang; *vt* merapikan; *~ up* merapikan, memberés-berés

tidings *n* berita, kabar, salam

tidy *adj* apik, rapi; *n* tempat menyimpan barang; *vt* merapikan; *~ up* merapikan, memberés-berés

tie *n* tali, ikat; dasi; pertalian; seri; *~ dyed* jumputan; *~in* hubungan; *~ pin* tusuk dasi, jepitan dasi; *hair ~* ikat rambut; *~s of friendship* tali persahabatan; *vt* mengikat; *~ in* bersambung, menyambung; *~ a knot* membuat simpul; ~ *the knot* menikah

tier *n* [tir] tingkat, lapisan

tiger *n* harimau, macan

tight *adj* [tait] erat, tegang, ketat; *coll* sukar, sulit; ~*fisted* pelit; ~*lipped* terdiam; ~ *pants* celana ketat; ~ *squeeze* keadaan terjepit; *adv* rapat, kuat; *sit* ~ duduk tanpa bergerak; *sleep* ~ tidur pulas; **tighten** *vt* [taiten] mengeratkan, mengetatkan; **tightly** *adv* [taitli] dengan ketat; **tightrope** *n* [taitrop] tali akrobat; **tights** *n* [taits] stoking tebal

tile *n* ubin, tégel; genténg; *floor* ~ ubin; *roof* ~ genténg; *vt* memasang ubin, genténg; **tiler** *n* tukang pasang ubin

till *conj, coll* sampai, sehingga

till *n* laci uang

till *vt* bercocok tanam

tiller *n* pasak kemudi

tilt *n* kemiringan; *full* ~ secepat-cepatnya; *vi* miring; *vt* memiringkan

timber *n* kayu (bahan bangunan)

time *n* waktu, masa; kali; ~ *bomb* waktu; ~*consuming* memakan waktu; ~ *limit* batas waktu; ~ *off* waktu cuti, istirahat; ~ *out* istirahat (olahraga); ~ *zone* zona waktu, wilayah waktu; *any* ~ kapan saja; *in* ~ sebelum waktunya; *it's* ~ sudah waktunya; *on* ~ tepat waktu; *next* ~ lain kali; *some* ~ kapan-kapan; *that* ~ waktu itu; ~ *is money* waktu itu uang; ~ *after* ~ berkali-kali; *a good* ~ pengalaman yang menyenangkan; *all the* ~ selalu, senantiasa; sejak semula; *all this* ~ selama ini; *at a* ~ sekaligus; *in no* ~ dengan cepat; *just in* ~ pas waktunya; *to have* ~ sempat, ada waktu; *to pass* ~ iseng, mengisi waktu; *to serve* ~ dipenjara; *to take* ~ memakan waktu; *for the* ~ being untuk sementara; *what* ~ *is it?* pukul berapa?; *vt* mencatat waktu; **timekeeper** *n* pencatat waktu; **times** kali; *two* ~ *three equals six* dua kali tiga sama dengan enam; ~ *table* perkalian; **timeless** *adj* tidak kenal waktu, abadi; **timeline** *n* garis waktu; **timely** *adj* pada waktunya; **timepiece** *n* [taimpis] jam; **timer** *n* jam (pasir), pencatat waktu; **timesaving** *adj* menghemat

waktu; **timetable** *n* [taimtébel] jadwal

timid *adj* [timid] malu-malu, takut-takut

Timor *n* pulau Timor; ~ *Gap* Celah Timor; *East* ~ Timor Lorosaé, *arch* Timor Timur, Timtim; *West* ~ Timor Barat; **Timorese** *adj* berasal dari Timor; *n* orang Timor

tin *n* timah; kaléng; ~ *opener* pembuka kaléng; *vt* mengaléngkan; **tinfoil** *n* kertas pérak

tinker *n* tukang patri; *vi* ~ *with* mengutak-atik, main-main

tinsel *n* kertas ermas

tint *n* warna; *vt* memberi warna

tiny *adj* [taini] kecil sekali, mungil

tip *n* ujung; uang rokok, tip; saran, tips; tempat pembuangan akhir (TPA); ~*off* informasi rahasia; *on the* ~ *of my tongue* di ujung lidah; *vt* memberi tip; menumpahkan; memutar-balikkan; *no* ~*ping* dilarang memberi tip

tipsy *adj* sedikit mabuk

tiptoe *vi* [tipto] jalan berjinjit; *on* ~ berjinjit, berjingkat

tire, tyre *n* [tair] ban; *spare* ~ ban sérep

tire *vi* [tair] menjadi lelah; ~ *of* bosan, jenuh; *vt* melelahkan; **tired** *adj* lelah, capék, letih; **tireless** *adj* tidak tahu lelah; **tiresome** *adj* [tairsem] membosankan, mengganggu; **tiring** *adj* melelahkan

tissue *n* tisu; jaringan; ~ *paper* kertas tisu

tit ~ *for* tat balas dendam, balas-membalas

title *n* [taitel] gelar; judul; **titleholder** *n* [taitelholder] pemegang gelar, juara bertahan

T-junction *n* pertigaan, simpang tiga

to *prep* [tu] ke, kepada; untuk; lawan; ~ *and fro* bolak-balik; *five (minutes)* ~ *three* jam tiga kurang lima (menit); *from ... ~ ...* dari ... sampai ...; sejak ... sampai ...; *give this* ~ *him* berikan ini kepadanya; **toward** [tuwod] **towards** *prep* ke (arah); kepada, akan, untuk, terhadap; menjelang, menuju

toad *n* katak, kodok; **toadstool** *n* cendawan, jamur payung

toast *n* sulangan; *vi* bersulang; ~ *of the town* dipuji semua orang

toast *n* roti bakar; *as warm as* ~ hangat, énak; *vt* memanggang; **toasted** *adj* bakar, panggang; **toaster** *n* alat pemanggang roti; **toasty** *adj, sl* hangat, énak; *it was warm and* ~ *in bed on the cold winter's morning* tempat tidur masih hangat dan énak pada pagi yang dingin itu

tobacco *n* tembakau; **tobacconist** *n* toko tembakau

toboggan *n* kereta peluncur; *vi* main keréta peluncur

today *adv, n* [tudé] hari ini; (masa) kini

toddler *n* (anak) batita (bawah tiga tahun)

toe *n* [to] jari kaki; ujung (kaus kaki); ~ *hold* tumpuan kaki; *baby* ~ kelingking kaki; *big* ~ jempol kaki; *from head to* ~, *from top to* ~ di seluruh badan; *vt* ~ *the line* mematuhi, menurut; **toenail** *n* kuku jari kaki

toffee *n* semacam gula-gula

tofu *n* tahu; ~ *burger* burger tahu (makanan végétarian)

toga *n* jubah

together *adv* [tugéther] bersama, bersama-sama; ~ *with* bersama dengan; **togetherness** *n* [tugéthernes] rasa kebersamaaan

Togo *n* Togo; **Togolese** *adj* berasal dari Togo; *n* orang Togo

togs *n, pl, coll* baju; baju renang

toil *n* kerja keras; *vi* bekerja keras, membanting tulang; ~ *at* mengerjakan

toilet *n* kamar kecil, WC; klosét; ~ *paper*, ~ *roll* tisu gulung; ~ *training* anak kecil belajar menggunakan WC; ~ *water* wewangian; air klosét; *men's* ~ WC pria; *women's* ~ WC wanita; *to flush the* ~ menyiram WC; **toiletries** *n, pl* perlengkapan mandi, alat-alat kecantikan

token *n* tanda (penghargaan), tanda masuk; ~ *gesture* basa-basi; *by the same* ~ sama, begitu pula

told *v, pf* → **tell**

tolerance *n* toléransi, kesabaran; **tolerant** *adj* tenggang rasa, toléran, sabar; **tolerate** *vt* sabar menghadapi, tahan, menerima

toll *n* tol, béa; jumlah korban; bunyi loncéng; ~ *bridge* jembatan tol; ~ *road* jalan tol; *death* ~ jumlah korban jiwa; *road* ~ korban kecelakaan; **tollgate** *n* pintu tol, gerbang tol

tomato *n* **tomatoes** tomat; ~ *sauce* saus tomat; ~ *soup* sup tomat

tomb *n* [tum] kuburan, makam; **tombstone** *n* [tumston] batu nisan

tomboy *n* gadis yang bersifat laki-laki

tombstone *n* [tumston] batu nisan ← **tomb**

tomcat *n* kucing jantan

tomorrow *adv, n* [tumoro] bésok, ésok (hari); masa depan; *the day after* ~ lusa

ton *n, arch* [tan] ton; *a* ~ *of* banyak; **tonne** *n* [ton] ton (1,000 kg)

tone *n* bunyi, nada; warna, rona; ~ *deaf* pekak nada; *ring* ~ nada dering; *to set the* ~ beri contoh yang baik; *vi* ~ *down* mengurangi (sifat); **toner** *n* penyegar

Tonga *n* Tonga; **Tongan** *adj* berasal dari Tonga; *n* bahasa Tonga; orang Tonga

tongs *n, pl* jepitan, tang

tongue *n* [tang] lidah; bahasa; ~*-tied* kehabisan kata, membisu; ~*-in-cheek* secara bercanda; ~ *twister* ucapan ketangkasan lidah; *mother* ~ bahasa ibu; *to hold your* ~ tutup mulut, diam

tonic *n* obat kuat; ~ *water* air tonik; *gin and* ~ gin tonik

tonight *adv, n* [tunait] malam ini, nanti malam

tonsillitis *n* radang amandel; **tonsils** *n, pl* amandel

too *adv* terlalu, terlampau; sekali; juga; ~ *bad!* sayang sekali; ~ *fast* terlalu cepat; ~ *late* terlambat; ~ *much* keterlaluan, kebanyakan

took *vt, pf* → **take**

tool *n* alat, perkakas; **tools** *n, pl* peralatan; *gardening* ~ peralatan kebun; **toolbox** *n* tempat peralatan; **toolset** *n* seperangkat alat-alat pertukangan; **toolshed** *n* gudang

toot *n* [tut] tét, bunyi klakson; *v* membunyikan klakson, mengklakson

tooth *n* **teeth** gigi; *false teeth* gigi palsu; *to have a sweet* ~ suka

makanan manis; **toothache** *n* [tuthék]
sakit gigi; **toothbrush** *n* sikat gigi;
toothless *adj* ompong; **toothpaste** *n*
pasta gigi; **toothpick** *n* tusuk gigi
top *adj* atas; teratas, terbaik, tertinggi;
~*-heavy* berat di atas; ~ *brass* perwira
tinggi; ~ *hat* topi tinggi; ~ *secret* sangat rahasia; ~ *speed* kecepatan tertinggi, secepat-cepatnya; ~ *ten* sepuluh terbaik; *on* ~ di atas; *n* puncak,
(bagian) atas, ujung; tutup; gasing;
over the ~ keterlaluan; *from* ~ *to bottom* dari atas sampai ke bawah; *vt*
melebihi; **topknot** *n* [topnot] kuncir;
topless *adj* dengan dada terbuka; **topping** *n* saus, lapisan atas; **topsoil** *n*
lapisan atas tanah
topaz *n* ratna cempaka
topic *n* topik, isu; **topical** *adj* hangat
topknot *n* [topnot] kuncir ← **top**
topless *adj* dengan dada terbuka ← **top**
topping *n* saus, lapisan atas ← **top**
topple *vi* [topel] tumbang; *vt* menjatuhkan
topsoil *n* lapisan atas tanah ← **top**
topsy-turvy *adj, adv* kacau-balau,
tunggang langgang
torch *n* obor, suluh; sénter; ~ *song* lagu
cinta; *vt* membakar; **torchlight** *n*
[torclait] sinar sénter, cahaya sénter
tore *v, pf* → **tear**
torment *n* siksaan, kesengsaraan; *vt*
menyiksa, menyengsarakan
torn *v, pf* → **tear**
tornado *n* angin topan
torpedo *n* [torpido] torpédo; *vt* menorpédo, menenggelamkan; *the ship was
~ed by the enemy* kapal itu ditenggelamkan pihak musuh
torrent *n* aliran air yang deras, semburan; **torrential** *adj* [torénsyel] lebat,
deras
torso *n* batang tubuh
tortoise *n* [tortes] kura-kura; ~*-shell*
(corak seperti) kulit kura-kura; ~*-shell
cat* kucing tiga warna
torture *n* siksaan; *vt* menyiksa
Tory *n, adj, UK* Partai Konsérvatif
toss *n* lémparan; *to win the* ~ memenangkan undian (olahraga); *vi* tidur

gelisah; ~ *and turn* mengguling kiri
kanan; *vt* melémparkan, melontarkan,
melambungkan; mengundi
tot *coll (tiny)* ~ anak kecil, balita, bayi
total *adj* [totel] sama sekali, seluruh; *n*
jumlah, total; **totalitarian** *adj* [total-
itérien] totalitér; **totally** *adv* sama
sekali, secara total; *I was* ~ *confused*
saya bingung sekali
touch *n* [tac] sentuhan, nuansa; ~
football semacam rugby tanpa kontak
fisik; *finishing* ~ sentuhan terakhir; *in*
~ berhubungan; tahu; *a* ~ *of* sedikit; *to
get in* ~ menghubungi; *to lose* ~ kehilangan hubungan; kehilangan kemampuan; *vi* bersentuhan; *vt* menyentuh,
menyinggung, mengenai; ~*-type*
mengetik tanpa melihat papan tuts; ~*-
and-go* hampir-hampir; ~ *up* memperbaiki; menggerayangi; ~ *wood* semoga
berlanjut; *Isl* insya Allah; **touched** *adj*
[tacd] terharu; *she was* ~ *by Beryl's
gift* dia terharu menerima kado dari
Beryl; **touching** *adj* [tacing] bersentuhan; mengharukan; **touchy** *adj*
[taci] cepat marah
tough *adj* [taf] kasar; liat, alot, awét; ~
guy orang kuat; ~ *luck* sayang sekali;
~ *meat* daging yang liat; **toughen** *vt*
menguatkan, memperkuat; ~ *up*
menjadi lebih kuat; memperkuat
tour *n* [tur] tamasya, tur, perjalanan,
pelayaran; ~ *guide* pemandu wisata; *vt*
mengikuti tur ke, menjelajahi; mengadakan tur; **tourism** *n* [turizem] wisata, pariwisata, turisme; **tourist** *n*
[turist] wisatawan, turis; ~ *brochure*
brosur pariwisata; *domestic* ~ wisnu
(wisatawan nusantara); *foreign* ~
wisman (wisatawan mancanegara);
touristy *adj* [turisti] terlalu kental
nuansa pariwisatanya, sudah tidak asli
lagi
tournament *n* [turnament] kejuaraan,
pertandingan, turnamén
tout *n* [taut] calo; *vt* menjual dengan
harga tinggi
tow *vt* [to] menarik, mendérék; ~*-truck*
mobil dérék
toward [tuwod] **towards** *prep* ke (arah);

kepada, akan, untuk, terhadap; menjelang, menuju; *Nelson walked ~ the gate* Nelson jalan menuju gerbang

towel *n* [taul] handuk; *~ rack* rak handuk; *hand ~* lap; *paper ~* tisu; *v ~ down* mengelap badan (sesudah berolahraga); *to throw in the ~* putus asa, berhenti

tower *n* [tauer] menara; *vi ~ over* menjulang tinggi di atas

town *n* [taun] kota; *~ center* pusat kota; *~ hall* balai kota; *~ planner* planolog; *~ planning* planologi; *~ square* alun-alun; *country ~* kota kecil di pedalaman; *in ~* sedang di kota; *out of ~* keluar kota; *to go into ~* pergi ke kota; **township** *n* [taunsyip] kota

toxic *adj* beracun; **toxin** *n* racun, toksin

toy *n* mainan; *~ boy m* pacar yang lebih muda; *~ car* mobil-mobilan; *~ shop, ~ store* toko mainan; *soft ~* bonéka; *vi ~ with* memainkan; menimbang-nimbang secara tidak sérius

trace *n* bekas, jejak; *to vanish without a ~* hilang tanpa jejak; *vt* merunut, mengikuti jejak, memetakan; meniru (di atas kertas); *tracing paper* kertas kalkir

track *n* jejak, tapak jalan; *~ event* olahraga lari; *~ pants* celana (panjang) olahraga; *~ record* pengalaman, sejarah, riwayat; *athletics ~* lintasan lari; *~ and field* olahraga lari, lompat dan lémpar; *on the right ~* di jalan yang benar; *to lose ~ of* kehilangan, kelupaan; *vt* mengikuti jejak; *~ down* mencari, menemukan; **tracker** *n* alat atau orang yang mengikuti jejak; **tracksuit** *n* baju olahraga

tractor *n* traktor

trade *n* niaga, perniagaan, perdagangan; *~ fair* paméran (perdagangan); *~ secret* rahasia (yang hanya dikenal di lingkungan tertentu); *~ union* serikat kerja, serikat buruh; *the rag ~* industri busana; *vi* berdagang, berbisnis; bertukar; tukar-menukar; *~ in* tukar tambah; memperdagangkan; *~ places* bertukaran tempat; *vt* menukar; *~ in* tukar tambah; **trademark** *n* mérek

dagang; **trader** *n* pedagang; **tradesman** *n* tukang

tradition *n* [tradisyen] adat (istiadat), tradisi; **traditional** *adj* menurut adat, tradisional; *~ dance* tari adat; **traditionally** *adv* menurut adat, sesuai dengan adat

traffic *n* lalu lintas; perédaran, perdagangan; *~ island* batu pemisah jalan; *~ jam* kemacetan lalu lintas; *~ light* lampu mérah, lampu lalu lintas; *Jav* bangjo; *vt* mengédarkan; **trafficker** *n* pengédar narkoba; **trafficking** *n* pengédaran; *people ~* perdagangan manusia

tragedy *n* [trajedi] cerita sedih; kecelakaan; **tragic** *adj* tragis, menyedihkan; **tragically** *adv* [trajikeli] secara tragis

trail *n* tapak jalan, bekas, jejak; *~ bike* (sepéda) motor gunung; *vt* mengikuti jejak; **trailblazer** *n* pelopor, perintis; **trailer** *n* kendaraan gandéngan; iklan untuk film baru

train *n* keréta api; *by ~* dengan keréta api, naik keréta api; *~-spotting* kegiatan mengamati keréta api yang léwat; *~ set* seperangkat keréta api mainan; *express ~* keréta api éksprés; *~ of thought* jalan pikiran

train *vi* berlatih; *vt* melatih; **trainee** *adj* calon; *n* orang yang ikut latihan, orang yang magang; **trained** *adj* terlatih; berpendidikan, berijazah; **trainer** *n* pelatih; *pl, UK* sepatu olahraga; **training** *n* latihan, pelatihan, pendidikan; *education and ~* pendidikan dan pelatihan (diklat)

traitor *n* pengkhianat

trajectory *n* jalan peluru

tram *n* trém; *~ stop* halte trém; **tram-lines** *n, pl* rél trém; garis samping di lapangan bulu tangkis atau ténis; **tramway** *n* jalur trém

tramp *n* gelandangan, orang gila; *vi* mendaki gunung, berjalan kaki di alam bébas

trample *vt* [trampel] menginjak-injak; *several people were ~d to death in the crowd* beberapa orang mati terinjak-injak di keramaian

trampoline *n* trampolin

tramway *n* jalur trém ← **tram**

trance *n* [trans] kerasukan, keadaan tidak sadar diri

tranquil *adj* tenang, teduh; **tranquility** *n* [trankuiliti] ketenangan; **tranquilizer** *n* [trankuilaizer] obat penenang

trans- *pref* lintas, melalui

transaction *n* [tranzaksyen] transaksi

transatlantic *adj* lintas Lautan Atlantik; ~ *accent* logat Amérika

transcribe *vt* menyalin; **transcription** *n* [transkripsyen] salinan, transkrip

transfer *n* pemindahan, mutasi; transfer; *bank* ~ kiriman uang, transfer uang; *vi* pindah; *vt* memindahkan; mengirim (uang)

transform *vi* berubah bentuk; *vt* merubah; **transformation** *n* perubahan bentuk, transformasi; **transformer** *n* travo

transfusion *n* transfusi; *blood* ~ transfusi darah

transit *in* ~ dalam perjalanan; ~ *lounge* ruang tunggu; **transition** *n* peralihan, transisi

transitive *adj* [tranzitiv] transitif, mempunyai obyék

translate *vt* menerjemahkan (secara tertulis); **translation** *n* terjemahan, penerjemahan; *lost in* ~ hilang arti aslinya; **translator** *n* penerjemah

translucent *adj* [tranzlusent] tembus cahaya

transmigration *n* [tranzmaigrésyen] transmigrasi

transmission *n* [tranzmisyen] pengiriman, penyiaran, penyebaran, transmisi; **transmit** *vt* mengirimkan, menyiarkan, memancarkan; **transmitter** *n* pemancar

transparency *overhead* ~ *(OHT)* transparensi; **transparent** *adj* bening, tembus cahaya

transplant *n* cangkok, pencangkokan; *vt* mencangkokkan

transport *n* angkutan, pengangkutan, transportasi; *public* ~ angkutan umum; *vt* mengangkut, membawa; **transportation** *n* [tranzportésyen] transportasi

transsexual *n* [trans séksuel] orang

yang telah menjalani opérasi ganti kelamin

transvestite *n* béncong, banci

trap *n* perangkap, jerat, jebakan; *mouse*~ perangkap tikus; *vt* memerangkap, menjerat, menjebak; **trapdoor** *n* pintu di lantai atau plafon

trapeze *n* rékstok gantung

trash *n* sampah; ~ *can* tempat sampah; *trailer* ~ orang miskin yang tinggal di karavan; *white* ~ orang kulit putih yang miskin; *vt, coll* merusak, menghancurkan; **trashy** *adj* murahan

trauma *n* [troma] pengalaman buruk, trauma; **traumatic** *adj* [tromatik] traumatis; **traumatize** *vt* meninggalkan kesan buruk akibat trauma

travel *vi* [travel] jalan, berjalan, bepergian; ~ *agent,* ~ *agency* biro perjalanan; ~ *guide* buku panduan wisata; **travels** *n, pl* perjalanan-perjalanan; **traveler** *n* orang yang sedang dalam perjalanan, musafir; ~*'s checks* cék perjalanan

trawl *vi* menjaring, memukat; ~ *for fish* menjaring ikan; **trawler** *n* kapal pukat

tray *n* dulang; baki

treacherous *adj* [trécerus] bersifat pengkhianat; sangat berbahaya; **treachery** *n* [tréceri] pengkhianatan

treacle *n, UK* [trikel] sirop gula

tread *n* [tréd] alas sepatu, telapak (ban); *v* **trod trodden** menginjak, memijak; **treadle** *n* [trédel] pédal, tempat injakan kaki; **treadmill** *n* [trédmil] mesin latihan jalan atau lari

treason *n* [trizon] pengkhianatan

treasure *n* [trésyur] barang berharga tinggi; ~ *hunt* pencarian harta karun atau hadiah; ~ *trove, buried* ~ harta karun; *vt* menghargai

treasurer *n* [trésyurer] bendahara; Menteri Keuangan; **treasury** *n* perbendaharaan; Departemén Keuangan

treat *n* [trit] sesuatu yang menyenangkan; *my* ~ saya yang traktir; *vt* mengobati; memperlakukan; **treatment** *n* pengobatan, perawatan; perlakuan

treaty *n* [triti] pakta, perjanjian

tree *n* pohon; *~-lined* dipagari pohon; *~ house* rumah di pohon, rumah mainan; *~ line* garis pohon; *~ surgeon* ahli pangkas pohon; **treetops** *n, pl* puncak pohon

trek *n* perjalanan (yang jauh dan melelahkan); *vi* berjalan jauh, mendaki gunung; *vt* meléwati jarak yang jauh

trellis *n* terali, jari-jari

tremble *n* [trémbel] gemetar, getaran; *vi* bergetar, gemetar; *Jon ~d in fear* Jon gemetar ketakutan

tremendous *adj* [treméndus] hébat, dahsyat

tremor *n* gemetaran; *(earth) ~* gempa bumi

trench *n* parit; *~ coat* jas hujan (tentara)

trend *n* mode, gaya, trén; kecenderungan; *~-setter* pelopor gaya; *the latest ~* trén terbaru; **trendy** *adj* gaya, bergaya, modis

trepidation *n* [trépidésyen] rasa segan, ragu-ragu bercampur takut

trespass *vi* masuk tempat tanpa izin; *no ~ing* dilarang masuk; **trespasser** *n* orang yang masuk tanpa izin

trestle *n* [trésel] kuda-kuda; *~ bridge* jembatan dari batang-batang besi atau kayu

trial *n* [trail] sidang pengadilan, prosés; percobaan; *~ period* masa percobaan; *~ run* percobaan; *on ~* sedang diadili; *~ and error* mencoba-coba; *vt* menguji ← **try**

triangle *n* [trayanggel] segi tiga; kerincing; *love ~* cinta segi tiga; *right-angled ~* segi tiga siku-siku; **triangular** *adj* [trayangguler] berbentuk segi tiga

triathlete *n* atlét triatlon; **triathlon** [trayathlon] triatlon

tribal *adj* suku (bangsa), kesukuan; **tribe** *n* suku (bangsa)

tribunal *n* [traibunal] déwan pengadilan

tributary *n* [tributeri] anak sungai; *this river is a ~ of the Mississippi* sungai ini adalah anak sungai Mississippi

tribute *n* penghargaan; upeti; *~ to* penghargaan kepada

trick *n* tipu daya; permainan; cara, téknik; *the ~ is* caranya; *to play a ~ on* mempermainkan; *vt* menipu; **tricked** *adj* tertipu; **trickster** *n* penipu; **tricky** *adj* sulit, rumit

trickle *n* tétésan, kucuran; *vi* menétés, berlinang, mengucur sedikit; *tears ~d down her cheeks* air mata menétés di pipi

tricycle *n* [traisikel], *coll* trike sepéda roda tiga

trident *n* trisula

trier *n* [trayer] orang yang selalu berusaha; **try** *n* usaha, percobaan; *~-hard* orang yang terlalu ingin diterima oleh kalangan tertentu; *vi* coba, berusaha; *vt* mencoba; *~ on* coba memakai baju; *~ out* ikut séléksi; **tryout** *n* séléksi, percobaan ← **try**

trigger *n* [triger] pelatuk, picu, pemicu; *~-happy* terlalu cepat bertindak; *vt ~ (off)* memicu, menyebabkan; *the earthquake ~ed a volcanic eruption* gempa bumi itu mengakibatkan gunung api meletus

trigonometry *n* [trigonometri] ilmu ukur segi tiga, trigonométri

trike *n, coll* sepéda roda tiga ← **tricycle**

trillion *adj, n* trilyun (1 000 000 000 000)

trilogy *n* [trileji] seri tiga serangkai, trilogi; *have you read the 'Lord of the Rings'?* apakah sudah baca buki trilogi *Lord of the Rings*?

trim *adj* langsing, rapi; *n* potong sedikit; garis hiasan; *vt* menggunting; menghiasi; *~ a Christmas tree* menghiasi pohon Natal

trimester *n* masa tiga bulan, triwulan; *morning sickness is common in the first ~ of pregnancy* rasa mual banyak terjadi selama tiga bulan pertama kehamilan

trinket *n* (barang) perhiasan kecil dan murah; *the market stall sold ~s and souvenirs* barang perhiasan dan cenderamata dijual di kedai di pasar itu

trip *n* perjalanan; *business ~* perjalanan dinas; *vi* tersandung; *vt* menjebloskan

tripe *n* babat; *sl* omong kosong

triple *adj* [tripel] lipat tiga; *~ jump* lompat ganda; *n* rangkap tiga; *vi* berkembang tiga kali lipat; melipattigakan;

triplet *n* kembar tiga

tripod *n* [traipod] (tumpuan) kaki tiga, tripod

trishaw *n* bécak

triumph *n* [trayemf] kemenangan, keberhasilan; *vi* menang, berhasil; *good will* ~ *over evil* kebaikan akan mengalahkan kejahatan; **triumphant** *adj* [trayamfent] dengan jaya

trivial *adj* [triviel] sepélé, tidak berarti

trod, trodden *v, pf* → **tread**

Trojan ~ *horse* kuda Troya

troll *n* jin, makhluk di dongéng Skandinavia

trolley *n* keréta dorong, troli; ~ *bus* bis listrik; *shopping* ~ keréta, troli

trombone *n* trombon; **trombonist** *n* pemain trombon

troop *n* pasukan; *vi* jalan ramai-ramai; **trooper** *n* polisi

trophy *n* [trofi] piala

tropic *the* ~*s* daérah khatulistiwa, daérah tropis; ~ *of Cancer* garis balik utara; ~ *of Capricorn* garis balik selatan; **tropical** *adj* tropis

trot *n* lari derap, lari kecil; *vi* berderap, menderap

trouble *n* [trabel] kesusahan, kesulitan; gangguan; kerusakan; répot; *kidney* ~ sakit ginjal; *to ask for* ~ mencari garagara, mengundang masalah; *to take the* ~ *to* bersusah-payah; *vt* membuat kuatir; menyusahkan; *it* ~*s me* saya kuatir karena itu; **troubled** *adj* [trabeld] susah hati; **troublemaker** *n* [trabelméker] pengacau; **troubleshoot** *vt* [trabelsyut] mencari dan memecahkan kesulitan; **troublesome** *adj* [trabelsam] menyusahkan

trough *n* [trof] palung; titik rendah

troupe *n* [trup] rombongan (pemain); **trouper** *n* anggota rombongan, pemain

trousers *n, pl* [trauzerz] celana panjang; *short* ~, *shorts* celana péndék

trousseau *n* [truso] pakaian dan perlengkapan lain milik pengantin wanita

trout *n* [traut] sejenis ikan air tawar

truant *vt* membolos (sekolah); *to play* ~ membolos sekolah

truce *n* gencatan senjata

truck *n* truk; *dump* ~ truk sampah; ~ *driver*, **trucker** *n* supir truk

true *adj* [tru] benar, betul, sungguh; ~ *blue* setia, tulus; setia; ~*(-life) story* kisah nyata; *to come* ~ terwujud, jadi kenyataan; ~ *to his word* setia pada janjinya; **truly** *adv* sesungguhnya, sungguh-sungguh; *yours* ~ salam hormat

trump ~ *card* kartu truf; *n, pl* permainan kartu truf

trumpet *n* trompét; ~ *player*, *trumpeter* pemain trompét

trunk *n* belalai; batang (tubuh); *arch* koper; ~ *call* sambungan langsung jarak jauh (SLJJ); *swimming* ~*s* baju renang

trust *n* kepercayaan; *in* ~ sebagai titipan; *v* percaya akan, mempercayai; **trustee** *n* wakil, wali; **trusting** *adj* percaya; **trustworthy** *adj* andal, terpercaya; **trusty** *adj* setia

truth *n* [truth] kebenaran; *in* ~ sebenarnya; *some* ~ ada benarnya; *to tell the* ~ mengatakan dengan jujur; **truthful** *adj* jujur; **truthfully** *adv* secara jujur

try *n* usaha, percobaan; ~*-hard* orang yang terlalu ingin diterima oleh kalangan tertentu; *vi* coba, berusaha; *vt* mencoba; ~ *on* coba memakai baju; ~ *out* ikut séléksi; **tryout** *n* séléksi, percobaan

T-shirt *n* kaus (oblong) ← **T**

tsar *n, m, arch* [zar] kaisar Rusia; **tsarina** *f* [zarina] isteri kaisar Rusia

tsp *abbrev teaspoon* séndok téh

tub *n* bak mandi

tuba *n* tuba

tubby *adj* gendut, tambun

tube *n* tabung; pipa, pembuluh, saluran; *inner* ~ ban dalam; *test* ~ tabung réaksi; *the* ~ *sl* keréta api bawah tanah di London; **tubeless** *adj* ~ *tire* ban cublés

tuber *n* akar umbi, ubi

tuberculosis *n* radang paru-paru, tébésé, TBC

tuck *n* lipatan; *tummy* ~ bedah untuk melangsingkan perut; *vt* melipat, menyimpan, memasukkan; ~ *in vi, coll* memulai makan; *vt* memasukkan baju ke dalam celana

Tuesday *adj, n* [tyusdé] (hari) Selasa

tug *n* sentakan, tarikan; *vt* menarik, menyentak; ~*of-love* rebutan hak asuh anak; ~*of-war* tarik tambang; **tugboat** *n* kapal penarik

tuition *n* [tuwisyen] pengajaran; uang belajar, uang kuliah

tulip *n* bunga tulip, tulpen

tumble *n, v* [tambel] jatuh terguling-guling; ~ *dryer* mesin pengering pakaian

tumbler *n* [tambler] gelas minum

tummy *n, coll, child* perut; ~ *button* pusar; ~ *upset* sakit perut

tumor, tumour *n* benjolan, tumbuhan, tumor; *benign* ~ tumor jinak; *malignant* ~ tumor ganas

tuna *n* ikan tongkol; ~ *(fish)* sandwich roti tuna

tune *n* bunyi, lagu; melodi; *in* ~ selaras; *out of* ~ tidak selaras; *to call the* ~ berkuasa, memerintah; *vt* menyetél; menala, menyetém; ~ *in* ikut mendengar; ~ *out* berhenti mendengar; ~ *up* menyetél (mesin), memperbaiki; ~ *a piano* menyetém piano; **tuneful** *adj* merdu; **tunefully** *adv* dengan merdu; **tuning** ~ *fork* garpu tala, penala

tunic *n* semacam baju atas

Tunisia *n* Tunisia; **Tunisian** *adj* berasal dari Tunisia; *n* orang Tunisia

tunnel *n* terowongan; *vi* menggali terowongan atau lubang

turban *n* serban

turbine *n* [terbain] turbin

turbulence *n* pergolakan; cuaca buruk; **turbulent** *adj* bergolak

turf *n* (tanah) berumput

Turk *n* [terk] orang Turki; *young* ~ pemuda, orang muda yang bersemangat; **Turkey** *n* [terki] Turki; **Turkish** *adj* [terkisy] berasal dari Turki; ~ *delight* sejenis agar-agar; *n* bahasa Turki; orang Turki

turkey *n* [terki] kalkun; *roast* ~ kalkun panggang

Turkish *adj* [terkisy] berasal dari Turki;

~ *delight* sejenis agar-agar; *n* bahasa Turki; orang Turki ← **Turkey**

Turkmen *adj* [terkmen] berasal dari Turkmenistan; *n* bahasa Turkmen; orang Turkmenistan; **Turkmenistan** *n* Turkmenistan

turmeric *n* [termerik] kunyit, kuning

turn *n* putaran; giliran; bélok; *to take* ~*s* berantri, bergiliran; *a good* ~ perbuatan baik; ~ *of the century* pergantian abad; *vi* berputar, membélok, menoléh; ~ *around* berputar; ~ *heads* membuat pusing, menarik perhatian; ~ *out* ternyata; ~ *up* muncul; menemukan; ~ *the tide* mengubah arus; ~ *your stomach* memuakkan; *vt* memutar, membalikkan; ~ *away* menolak; ~ *down* menolak; mengecilkan; ~ *into* berubah menjadi; ~ *off* mematikan; ~ *on* menghidupkan; ~ *over* membalikkan; menyerahkan; **turncoat** *n* pembelot, pengkhianat; **turning** *n* bélokan (jalan); ~ *point* saat yang menentukan; **turnoff** *n* pintu keluar (jalan tol); **turnout** *n* [ternaut] jumlah hadirin; **turnover** *n* penjualan, omzét; pergantian; **turnstile** *n* pagar putar

turnip *n* lobak cina

turnoff *n* pintu keluar (jalan tol), bélokan ← **turn**

turnout *n* [ternaut] jumlah hadirin ← **turn**

turnover *n* penjualan, omzét; pergantian ← **turn**

turnstile *n* pagar putar ← **turn**

turpentine *n* [terpentain] **turps** *coll* térpentin

turquoise *adj* [terkoiz] biru toska; *n* (batu) pirus

turtle *n* [tertel] kura-kura, penyu; ~*neck* berléhér tinggi; **turtledove** *n* [terteldav] perkutut

tusk *n* gading

tutor *n* guru pribadi; wali kelas; *vt* memberi lés privat kepada; **tutorial** *n* [tutoriel] kelas diskusi

Tuvalu *n* Tuvalu; **Tuvaluan** *adj* berasal dari Tuvalu; *n* bahasa Tuvalu; orang Tuvalu

tux *n, coll* **tuxedo** *n* [taksido] setelan pakaian malam pria

TV *abbrev television* tévé, tivi, TV
(télévisi); ~ *guide* daftar acara TV
tweed *n* semacam tenunan wol
tweet *n* kicauan burung; *v* berkicau
tweet *n* twit; *vi* ngetwit
twelfth *adj* [twélth] kedua belas; **twelve**
adj, *n* [twélv] dua belas; *the ~ Apos-
tles Chr* Duabelas Rasul
twentieth *adj* [twéntieth] kedua puluh;
twenties *n*, *pl* (tahun) dua puluhan;
the Roaring ~ tahun 1920an; **twenty**
adj, *n* dua puluh; *~~ vision* penglihatan normal
twice *adv* dua kali; *~ the*, *~ as much*
dua kali lipat; *to think ~* berpikir baik-
baik ← **two**
twig *n* ranting
twilight *adj*, *n* [twailait] senjakala
twin *n* kembar; pasangan; *~ bedroom*
kamar dengan dua tempat tidur; *~ city*
kota kembar; *~ sister* saudara kembar;
fraternal ~s kembar dampit; *identical
~s* kembar idéntik; *Siamese ~s* kembar Siam
twine *n* benang ikat
twinkle *n* [twingkel] kelip; *vi* berkedip-
kedip, berbinar-binar; *in the twinkling
of an eye* dalam sekejap mata
twist *n* tikungan; pelintir; putaran; *a ~
in the tale* alur cerita yang tak terduga;
vi terpelintir, putar; *vt* memelintir,
memutar, memintal, menganyam;
twisted *adj* terpelintir; sinting; *bitter
and ~* penuh dendam; **twister** *n* angin
puyuh
twit *n*, *coll* orang bodoh
twitter *n* kicauan; *vi* berkicau
two *adj*, *n* [tu] dua; *~-dimensional* dua
diménsi; *~-edged* bermata dua; *~-
faced* munafik; *~-legged* berkaki dua;
~-timer orang dengan lebih dari satu
pacar; *~-tone* berwarna dua; *~-way*
dua arah; *the ~ of us* kami berdua;
twice *adv* dua kali; *to think ~* berpikir
baik-baik
tycoon *n* [taikun] hartawan, taipan
type *n* [taip] macam, jenis, bentuk, tipe;
golongan; *a ~ of* sejenis, semacam; *not
my ~* bukan seléra saya; **typecast** *vt*
typecast typecast menetapkan

sebagai tipe tertentu
type *n* [taip] huruf cétak; *bold ~* huruf
tebal; *v* mengetik; *to touch-~* mengetik
tanpa melihat; **typing** *n* bahan untuk
diketik; *~ school* sekolah mengetik;
typist *n* juru ketik; **typewriter** *n* mesin
tik; **typical** *adj* biasa, lumrah, tipikal;
typically *adv* biasanya; **typo** *n* [taipo]
kesalahan cétak
typhoid *n* [taifoid] *~ (fever)* tifus, tipus
typhoon *n* [taifun] (angin) topan
typical *adj* [tipikel] biasa, lumrah,
tipikal; **typically** *adv* biasanya ← **type**
typist *n* [taipist] juru ketik ← **type**
typo *n* [taipo] kesalahan cétak ← **type**
tyrannical *adj* [tiranikel] kejam; **tyran-
ny** *n* [tirani] kekejaman, tirani; **tyrant**
n [tairant] orang yang kejam
tyre → **tire**

U

U-turn *n* [yu térn] putar balik; *no ~*
dilarang putar balik
UAE *abbrev United Arab Emirates* UEA
(Uni Emirat Arab)
ubiquitous *adj* [yubikuitus] (ada) di
mana-mana
udder *n* ambing
UEFA *n*, *abbrev* [yuéfa] *Union of
European Football Associations*
Persatuan Asosiasi Sépak Bola Eropa;
~ Cup Piala Eropa
UFO *abbrev unidentified flying object*
piring terbang
Uganda *n* [yuganda] Uganda; **Ugandan**
adj berasal dari Uganda; *n* orang
Uganda
ugh *ejac* [ag, ah] ih, idih
ugliness *n* [aglines] penampilan yang
buruk; **ugly** *adj* buruk (rupa), jélék; *~
duckling* orang yang pada awalnya
bernasib jélék tapi lama-lama berhasil
juga; *~ as sin* sangat jélék
UHF *abbrev ultra-high frequency* UHF
UK *abbrev United Kingdom* Kerajaan
Inggris
Ukraine *n* [yukrén] Ukraina; **Ukrainian**

adj berasal dari Ukraina; *n* bahasa Ukraina; orang Ukraina

ukulele *n* [yukelélé] gitar kecil, ukulélé

ulcer *n* [alser] bisul, borok; *mouth ~* sariawan; *peptic ~* borok usus

ulterior *adj* [altirier] *~ motive* alasan terselubung

ultimate *adj* [altimet] terakhir, penghabisan, mutakhir; paling (méwah); pokok; *the ~ in aerospace technology* yang mutakhir dalam téknologi dirgantara; **ultimately** *adv* pada akhirnya

ultimatum *n* [altimétem] ultimatum; *to give an ~* mengultimatum, memberi ultimatum

ultra- *pref* [altra] teramat sangat; **ultramarine** *adj, n* [altramarin] biru laut; **ultrasound** *adj, n* USG; **ultraviolet** *adj* [altravayolet] *~ rays* sinar UV

um *interj* anu, er

umbilical *~ cord* tali ari-ari, tali pusar

umbrella *n* payung; *~ stand* tempat payung

umpire *n* wasit; *vi* menjadi wasit; *vt* mewasiti

umpteen, umpteenth *adj* kesekian; *I've told you, for the ~ time!* saya sudah bilang untuk kesekian kali

UN *abbrev United Nations* PBB (Persatuan Bangsa-Bangsa)

un- *pref* tidak, tak

unable *adj* [anébel] tidak mampu, tidak dapat, tidak bisa ← **able**

unabridged [anabrijd] *~ dictionary* kamus lengkap ← **abridged**

unacceptable *adj* [anakséptabel] tidak dapat diterima ← **acceptable**

unaccompanied *adj* [anakampanid] sendiri, solo, tidak ditemani ← **accompanied**

unaffected *adj* [anafékted] tidak terpengaruh ← **affect**

unaided *adj* [anéded] tanpa bantuan ← **aid**

unanimous *adj* [yunanimus] **unanimously** *adv* dengan suara bulat, secara aklamasi

unappetizing *adj* [anapetaizing] (tampak) tidak énak, tidak membangkitkan

seléra ← **appetizing**

unappreciated *adj* [anaprisyiéted] tidak dihargai ← **appreciate**

unapproachable *adj* [anaprocabel] tidak dapat didekati, tidak ramah ← **approachable**

unarmed *adj* [anarmd] tidak bersenjata ← **armed**

unashamed *adj* [anasyémd] tanpa merasa malu; **unashamedly** *adv* [anasyémedli] dengan tidak merasa malu, tanpa merasa malu; *he ~ asked for even more money* tanpa merasa malu, dia minta uang lebih banyak lagi ← **ashamed**

unassuming *adj* [anasyuming] sederhana, bersahaja; *Tim was a very ~ type of person* Tim itu orangnya sederhana sekali

unattached *adj* [anatacd] sendiri, belum kawin; tidak terikat ← **attached**

unattended *adj* [anaténded] tanpa pengawasan; *the ticket counter was ~* tidak ada orang jaga di loket karcis ← **attend**

unauthorized *adj* [anothoraizd] tanpa wewenang, tidak sah; *Lea wrote an ~ biography of the artist* Lea menulis biografi pelukis itu secara tidak resmi ← **authorize**

unavailable *adj* [anavélabel] tidak tersedia, habis terjual; **unavailability** *n* keadaan tidak tersedia ← **available**

unavoidable *adj* [anavoidabel] tidak dapat dihindarkan, tidak dapat diélakkan ← **avoidable**

unaware *adj* [anawér] tidak sadar; *~ of* tidak menyadari; **unawares** *adv* tiba-tiba; secara tak terduga; *the soldiers were taken ~* prajurit-prajurit itu disergap ← **aware**

unbalanced *adj* [anbalansd] tidak waras ← **balanced**

unbearable *adj* [anbérabel] tak tertahankan ← **bear**

unbeatable *adj* [anbitabel] tak terkalahkan, tidak dapat dikalahkan; **unbeaten** *adj* belum pernah dikalahkan ← **beat** unbecoming *adj* [anbekaming] tidak pantas ← **becoming**

unbeknownst *adj* [anbenonst] tanpa diketahui; ~ *to me* tanpa sepengetahuan saya ← **know**

unbelievable *adj* [anbelivabel] tidak dapat dipercaya, bukan main, luar biasa; **unbeliever** *n* kafir, orang yang tidak beriman; **unbelieving** *adj* tidak percaya ← **believe**

unbiased *adj* [anbayesd] tidak memihak, berimbang; *an ~ opinion* pendapat berimbang ← **biased**

unbleached *adj* [anblicd] tidak diputihkan ← **bleach**

unblock *vt* membersihkan (sumbatan) ← **block**

unbolt *vt* membuka (kunci selot) ← **bolt**

unborn *adj* belum lahir; ~ *baby,* ~ *child* janin ← **born**

unbreakable *adj* [anbrékabel] anti pecah, tahan banting; **unbroken** *adj* tidak terputus-putus, terus-menerus ← **break**

uncalled [angkold] ~ *for* tidak beralasan, tanpa alasan ← **call**

uncanny *adj* anéh, gaib, luar biasa; *an ~ resemblance* kemiripan yang luar biasa

uncaring *adj* [ankéring] tidak peduli ← **caring**

unceasing *adj* [ansising] tidak berkeputusan, selalu, senantiasa ← **cease**

uncensored *adj* [ansénserd] tidak disénsor ← **censor**

uncertain *adj* [ansérten] tidak yakin; **uncertainty** *n* keadaan tidak menentu ← **certain**

unchain *vt* melepaskan ← **chain**

uncivilized *adj* [ansivilaizd] biadab ← **civilized**

uncle *n* [angkel] paman, om; ~ *Sam* Paman Sam, Abang Sam (Amérika Serikat); *great-*~ kakék

unclean *adj* tidak bersih, kotor; *many cultures consider women to be ~ after childbirth* menurut budaya-budaya tertentu, orang perempuan dianggap tidak bersih setelah melahirkan ← **clean**

unclear *adj* kurang jelas; *it's ~ what he wants* tidak jelas apa yang diinginkannya ← **clear**

uncomfortable *adj* [ankamftabel] tidak énak, kurang nyaman; **uncomfortably** *adv* dengan tidak nyaman ← **comfortable**

uncommon *adj* tidak biasa, luar biasa; **uncommonly** *adv* secara luar biasa ← **common**

unconditional *adj* [ankondisyenel] mutlak, tidak bersyarat ← **conditional**

unconfirmed *adj* belum dipastikan kebenarannya; ~ *report* isu, desas-desus ← **confirm**

unconscious *adj* [ankonsyus] pingsan, tidak sadar; *three casualties are still ~* tiga orang korban masih belum sadar; **unconsciously** *adv* tanpa disadari; *he ~ felt in his pocket for a cigarette* tanpa sadar dia merogoh kantong mencari rokok ← **conscious**

unconstitutional *adj* [ankonstityusyenel] tidak berdasarkan undang-undang dasar, inkonstitusional ← **constitutional**

uncontrollable *adj* [ankontrolabel] tidak terkendali ← **control**

unconventional *adj* [ankonvénsyenel] tidak biasa, di luar kebiasaaan ← **conventional**

uncooked *adj* tidak dimasak, mentah; ~ *vegetables can carry bacteria* sayur-mayur yang tidak dimasak dapat mengandung baktéri ← **cooked**

uncooperative *adj* tidak mau membantu, tidak mau bekerja sama, tidak koopératif; *when questioned, the witness was rather ~* saat diperiksa, saksi itu tidak mau membantu ← **cooperative**

uncoordinated *adj* [anko ordinéted] canggung, tanpa koordinasi ← **coordinate**

uncover *adj* [ankaver] membuka ← **cover**

undated *adj* [andéted] tak bertanggal ← **dated**

undecided *adj* [andesaided] ragu-ragu, bimbang ← **decide**

undefeated *adj* [andefited] tak pernah terkalahkan ← **defeated**

undemocratic *adj* tidak démokratis, tidak menurut démokrasi ← **democratic**

under *conj* menurut; *prep* (di) bawah; ~ *oath* di bawah sumpah; ~ *repair* sedang diperbaiki; ~ *there* di bawah sana, di kolong; ~ *the bed* di kolong tempat tidur; ~ *the bridge* di kolong jembatan; ~ *the table* di kolong méja; *children* ~ *5* anak di bawah 5 tahun; **underage** *adj* di bawah umur; **underclothes** *n, pl* pakaian dalam; **undercoat** *n* lapisan dasar (cat); **undercover** *adj* [anderkaver] rahasia, menyamar; **underdog** *n* pihak yang lemah; **underdone** *adj* [anderdan] masih mentah; **underestimate** *vt* meréméhkan; **underfed** *adj* kurang mendapat makanan; **undergo** *vt* **underwent undergone** menempuh, mengalami; **undergraduate** *adj, n* [andergradyuet] sarjana muda; **underground** *adj* [andergraund] (di) bawah tanah; *n the* ~ keréta api bawah tanah (di London); **undergrowth** *n* [andergroth] semak-semak; di bawah pepohonan; **underline** *vt* menggarisbawahi; **undermine** *vt* merusak, merongrong; **underneath** *adv, prep* [andernith] (di) bawah, di kolong; **undernourished** *adj* [andernarisyd] kurang gizi; **underpaid** *adj* dibayar tidak selayaknya; **underpants** *n, pl* celana dalam; **underpass** *n* terowongan (di bawah jalan); **underprivileged** *adj, n* [anderprivilejd] kurang mampu, prasejahtera; **underscore** *n* tanda _; *vt* menggarisbawahi; **undersecretary** *n* menteri muda; **undersigned** [andersaind] *the* ~ yang tertanda tangan (ytt); **undertake** *vt* **undertook undertaken** menjalankan, melakukan; *Simon undertook a dangerous assignment* Simon menjalankan tugas yang membahayakan dirinya; **undertaker** *n* pengurus jenazah; **undertaking** *n* usaha; **undertow** *n* [anderto] arus bawah; **underwater** *adj* [anderwoter] (di) dalam air; **underway** *adv* sedang berlangsung; *the Olympics are now* ~ pertandingan Olimpiade kini sudah dimulai; **under-**

wear *n* [anderwér] pakaian dalam; **underweight** *adj* [anderwét] memiliki berat badan yang kurang; **underworld** *n* [anderwerld] dunia bawah tanah, dunia penjahat

understand *vi* **understood understood** mengerti, paham; *vt* memahami; **understanding** *adj* pengertian; *n* pengertian, pemahaman; *to come to an* ~ mencapai persetujuan; **understandable** *adj* [anderstandabel] dapat dimengerti, dapat dimaklumi; **understandably** *adv* [anderstandabli] maklum; ~, *she did not want to meet her ex-husband again* maklum, dia tidak ingin bertemu lagi dengan mantan suaminya

undertake *vt* **undertook undertaken** menjalankan, melakukan; *Simon undertook a dangerous assignment* Simon menjalankan tugas yang membahayakan dirinya; **undertaking** *n* usaha

undertaker *n* pengurus jenazah

undertaking *n* usaha ← **undertake**

undertook *vt, pf* → **undertake**

undertow *n* [anderto] arus bawah ← **under**

underwater *adj* [anderwoter] (di) dalam air ← **under**

underway *adv* sedang berlangsung; *the Olympics are now* ~ pertandingan Olimpiade kini sudah dimulai ← **under**

underwear *n* [anderwér] **undies** *pl, coll* pakaian dalam ← **under**

underweight *adj* [anderwét] memiliki berat badan yang kurang ← **under**

underwent *vt, pf* → **undergo**

underworld *n* [anderwerld] dunia bawah tanah, dunia penjahat ← **under**

undesirable *adj* [andisairabel] tidak dikehendaki, tidak diinginkan ← **desirable**

undid *vt, pf* → **undo**

undies *n, pl, coll* celana dalam ← **underwear**

undiluted *adj* tidak diéncérkan; *don't drink from that bottle, it's* ~ *cordial!* jangan minum dari botol itu, isinya sirop yang belum diéncérkan! ← **diluted**

undivided *adj* bulat, seratus persén; *the magician had the children's ~ attention* perhatian anak-anak sudah seratus persén pada pesulap

undo *vt* [andu] **undid undone** membuka (kembali); *~ your laces* buka tali sepatu ← **do**

undoubtedly [andautedli] tentu saja, tidak diragukan lagi ← **doubt**

undress *vi* melepas pakaian ← **dress**

undying [andaying] *adj* kekal, abadi; *~ love* cinta abadi ← **die**

unearth *vt* [anérth] menggali; menemukan; *Stuart ~ed an old clock in the junk shop* Stuart menemukan jam lama di toko loak

uneasy *adj* [anizi] gelisah

uneducated *adj* [anédyukéted] tidak berpendidikan ← **educated**

unemployed *adj, n* [anemploid] pengangguran; **unemployment** *n* pengangguran ← **employed**

unenthusiastic *adj* [anenthuziastik] kurang antusias, tidak bersemangat; *the students were generally ~ about their exam results* para pelajar rata-rata tidak bersemangat akibat hasil ujiannya ← **enthusiastic**

unequal *adj* [anikwel] tidak sama, tidak sederajat, tidak seimbang; **unequaled, unequalled** *adj* tidak ada bandingnya, tiada tara ← **equal**

UNESCO *abbrev* [yunésko] *United Nations Educational, Scientific and Cultural Organization* UNESCO, Organisasi Persatuan Bangsa-Bangsa untuk Budaya, Ilmu Pengetahuan dan Pendidikan

unethical *adj* tidak étis, tidak menurut étika; *the ~ treatment of animals* perlakuan yang tidak étis terhadap héwan ← **ethical**

uneven *adj* [aniven] tidak rata, bergelombang; tidak konsistén, tidak seimbang; *the village road was very ~* jalan désa itu tidak rata ← **even**

unexpected *adj* [anekspéktéd] tidak terduga; **unexpectedly** *adv* tiba-tiba ← **expect**

unexplained *adj* [aneksplénd] mis-térius, tidak diterangkan ← **explain**

unfair *adj* tidak adil, tidak jujur; **unfairness** *n* ketidakadilan, ketidakjujuran; **unfairly** *adv* secara tidak adil ← **fair**

unfaithful *adj* tidak setia, durhaka; menyeléwéng ← **faithful**

unfamiliar *adj* tidak biasa, tidak kenal, tidak lumrah; *the neighborhood was completely ~* daérah itu sama sekali tidak dia kenal ← **familiar**

unfasten *vt* [anfasen] membuka (kancing, kait); *you may ~ your seat belts* silahkan buka kembali sabuk pengaman ← **fasten**

unfinished *adj* tidak terselesaikan, belum selesai; *Beethoven's ~ symphony* simfoni karya Beethoven yang tidak diselesaikannya ← **finish**

unfit *adj* tidak séhat; tidak patut, tidak pantas ← **fit**

unfold *vi* terurai, terjadi; *events ~ed so quickly* semua terjadi begitu cepat; *vt* menguraikan, membuka (lipatan) ← **fold**

unforgettable *adj* [anforgétabel] tak terlupakan; *an ~ evening* malam yang tak terlupakan ← **forget**

unforgivable *adj* [anforgivabel] tidak dapat dimaafkan; **unforgiving** *adj* (bersifat) tidak memaafkan ← **forgive**

unfortunate *adj* [anfortyunet] malang, sial; **unfortunately** *adv* sayang ← **fortunate**

unfounded *adj* [anfaunded] tidak beralasan, tidak berdasar; *the allegations were ~* tuduhan itu tidak berdasar

unfriendly *adj* tidak ramah, bersikap dingin; *those girls are always ~ towards new students* gadis-gadis itu tidak pernah bersikap ramah kepada murid baru

unfurnished *adj* tidak dilengkapi dengan mébel ← **furnished**

ungracious *adj* [angrésyus] tidak sopan, tidak sportif; *the losing team was ~ in defeat and blamed the referee* tim yang kalah tidak sportif karena menyalahi wasit ← **gracious**

ungrammatical *adj* [angramatikel]

tidak menurut tata bahasa, bukan bahasa yang baik dan benar ← **grammatical**

ungrateful *adj* [angrétful] tidak tahu berterima kasih ← **grateful**

unhappiness *n* [anhapines] kesedihan, rasa tidak bahagia; **unhappily** *adv* [anhapili] dengan tidak senang, dengan sedih; **unhappy** *adj* tidak bahagia, sedih; malang ← **happy**

unhealthy *adj* [anhélthi] tidak séhat; *she has an ~ diet of ice cream and chips* makanannya tidak séhat, terdiri dari és krim dan kripik kentang ← **healthy**

unhelpful *adj* tidak menolong ← **helpful**

unhurt *adj* tidak luka, tidak terluka ← **hurt**

unhygienic *adj* [anhaijinik] tidak higénis; *having a dog in the house is very ~* anjing di dalam rumah itu tidak higénis ← **hygienic**

UNICEF *abbrev* [yuniséf] *United Nations International Children's Fund* UNICEF, Organisasi Persatuan Bangsa-Bangsa untuk Anak-anak, Organisasi Anak Sedunia

unicorn *n* pégasus

unidentified *adj* [anaidéntifaid] tidak dikenal, belum diidéntifikasi; *~ body* mayat belum dikenal; *~ flying object (UFO)* piring terbang ← **identify**

unification *n* [yunifikésyen] pemersatuan, unifikasi; **unify** *vt* [yunifai] menyatukan, mempersatukan

uniform *adj, n* [yuniform] (pakaian) seragam; *school ~* seragam (sekolah)

unify *vt* [yunifai] menyatukan, mempersatukan

unilateral *adj* [yunilaterel] sepihak; *~ declaration* pernyataan sepihak

unimportant *adj* tidak penting ← **important**

uninhabitable *adj* [aninhabitabel] tidak dapat dihuni; **uninhabited** *adj* tidak dihuni ← **inhabit**

unintelligible *adj* [anintélijibel] tidak dapat dimengerti; *his speech was ~* pidatonya tidak dapat dimengerti;

unintelligibly *adv* [anintélijibeli] dengan cara yang tidak dapat dimengerti ← **intelligible**

uninterested *adj* tidak tertarik, tidak berminat; *the baby was ~ in the television program* bayi itu tidak tertarik pada télévisi

uninterrupted *adj* [aninterupted] tidak terputus; *~ coverage of the US Open* tayangan AS Terbuka yang tidak terputus ← **interrupt**

uninvited *adj* [aninvaited] tak diundang ← **invite**

union *n* [yunien] persatuan, serikat, uni; *~ Jack* bendéra (Kerajaan) Inggris; *Soviet ~* Uni Soviét; *trade ~* serikat kerja; **unionist** *n* [yunionist] anggota serikat kerja

unique *adj* [unik] tunggal, unik, tiada duanya; *a ~ opportunity* peluang yang tiada duanya; **uniqueness** *n* keunikan

unisex *adj* [yuniséks] untuk pria maupun wanita; *~ hairdresser* potong rambut untuk pria dan wanita

unison [yunison] *in ~* serentak, bersama

unit *n* [yunit] unit, satuan; rumah kecil yang satu kapling dengan rumah lain; *Mum wants to move to a ~ nearer town* Ibu mau pindah ke rumah kecil dekat kota

unite *vi* [yunait] bersatu, menyatu; *vt* menyatukan, mempersatukan; **united** *adj* bersatu, serikat; *(the) ~ Nations (UN)* Persatuan Bangsa-Bangsa (PBB); *(the) ~ Arab Emirates (UAE)* Uni Emirat Arab; *the ~ Kingdom (UK)* Kerajaan Inggris; *the ~ States (US), the ~ States of America (USA)* Amérika Serikat (AS); **unity** *n* kesatuan; *~ in diversity* bhinnéka tunggal ika

universal *adj* [yunivérsel] umum, univérsal; **universally** *adv* [yunivérseli] secara luas, secara univérsal; **universe** *n* alam semésta

university *n* [yunivérsiti] **uni** *coll* univérsitas; *~ student* mahasiswa; *to go to ~* kuliah

unjust *adj* tidak adil ← **just**

unkind *adj* [ankaind] kejam, bengis; **unkindly** *adv* [ankaindli] dengan kejam; tanpa perasaan; *"You've got fat!" she said* ~ "Kamu jadi gemuk!" katanya tanpa perasaan ← **kind**

unknowingly *adv* [an noingli] tanpa mengetahui; **unknown** *adj* tidak ketahuan, tidak dikenal ← **knowing**

unlace *vt* membuka tali (sepatu) ← **lace**

unlawful *adj* tidak sah, terlarang; **unlawfully** *adv* secara tidak sah ← **lawful**

unleaded ~ *petrol* bénsin tanpa timbal (TT)

unless *conj* (kecuali) kalau; ~ *I finish my work, I'm not going to the party* kalau tidak menyelesaikan tugas, saya tidak akan ikut ke pésta

unlike *adj* tidak seperti, tidak sama; ~ *me, Colin enjoys golf* tidak seperti saya, Colin suka main golf ← **like**

unlikely *adj* tidak dapat dipercaya; *an ~ story* cerita yang tidak dapat dipercaya; *adv* kemungkinan kecil; *it's ~ he will attend* hanya ada kemungkinan kecil dia akan hadir ← **likely**

unlimited *adj* [anlimited] tak terhingga, tak terbatas ← **limited**

unlisted ~ *number* nomor télepon rahasia, nomor pribadi ← **list**

unload *vi* bongkar; *vt* membongkar (muatan), mencurahkan; **unloaded** *adj* kosong (senjata) ← **load**

unlock *vt* membuka (kunci, gembok) ← **lock**

unlucky *adj* celaka, sial, malang; **unluckily** *adv* sialnya ← **lucky**

unmade *adj* tidak diselesaikan, tidak dirapikan; ~ *bed* tempat tidur yang belum dirapikan; ~ *road* jalan yang belum diaspal ← **made, make**

unmarried *adj* [anmarid] belum kawin, tidak kawin, lajang ← **married**

unmask *vt* membuka kedok, membuka topéng; *the criminal was ~ed* penjahat itu diketahui idéntitasnya ← **mask**

unmentionable *adj* [anménsyenabel] tidak dapat disebut ← **mention**

unmetered *an* ~ *taxi* taksi borongan ← **metered**

unmistakable *adj* [anmistékabel] **unmistakably** *adv* tidak dapat diragukan, jelas ← **mistake**

unmoved *adj* [anmuvd] tidak terpengaruh, tidak berubah; *the President was ~ by pleas for clemency* Présidén tidak terpengaruh oléh permintaan grasi ← **move**

unnamed *adj* [an némd] tidak dikenal, anonim ← **named**

unnatural *adj* [an natyurel] tidak wajar; **unnaturally** *adv* secara tidak wajar ← **natural**

unnecessary *adj* [an néseseri] tidak perlu, tidak usah; **unnecessarily** *adv* secara tidak perlu; *the waiter was ~ attentive* pelayan itu menunggui kami terus, padahal tidak perlu ← **necessary**

UNO *abbrev United Nations Organisation* Persatuan Bangsa-Bangsa (PBB)

unofficial *adj* tidak resmi; *our ~ national* anthem lagu kebangsaan kita yang tidak resmi; **unofficially** *adv* secara tidak resmi; ~, *he's going to be the new co-ordinator* secara tidak resmi, dia telah terpilih menjadi koordinator baru ← **official**

unopened *adj* tidak terbuka, belum dibuka; *the can was* ~ kaléng itu masih belum dibuka ← **open**

unpack *vt* membongkar (tas, koper) ← **pack**

unpaid *adj* tidak dibayar, belum dibayar ← **pay, paid**

unpleasant *adj* [anplézent] kurang menyenangkan, tidak énak; **unpleasantly** *adv* secara tidak énak atau menyenangkan; *the policeman smiled* ~ polisi itu menyengir ← **pleasant**

unplug *vt* mencabut ← **plug**

unpopular *adj* tidak populér, tidak disukai; *she was the most ~ prime minister ever* dia perdana menteri yang paling tidak disukai sepanjang masa; **unpopularity** *n* rasa ketidaksukaan

unprecedented *adj* [anprésedénted] belum pernah terjadi ← **precedent**

unpredictable *adj* [anprediktabel] **unpredictably** *adv* tidak dapat diramalkan ← **predict**

unprepared *adj* [anprepérd] tidak siap,

belum siap; tidak disiapkan, belum disiapkan; *Katherine was ~ for the difficulty of the exam* Katherine tidak siap menjawab soal-soal ujian yang sulit itu ← **prepared**

unprintable *adj* [anprintabel] tidak patut ditulis (kata jorok) ← **print**

unprofessional *adj* [anprofesyenel] tidak profésional; **unprofessionally** *adv* secara tidak profésional; *the lawyer behaved completely ~* pengacara itu sama sekali tidak profésional ← **professional**

unprofitable *adj* [anprofitabel] tidak menguntungkan; **unprofitably** *adv* secara tidak menguntungkan ← **profitable**

unprotected *adj* tidak dilindungi; *~ sex* hubungan séks tanpa alat kontrasépsi ← **protect**

unpublished *adj* belum diterbit, tidak diterbit ← **published**

unqualified *adj* [ankuolifaid] tidak berijazah, tidak memiliki kualifikasi ← **qualified**

unquestioning *adj* tidak bertanya, tidak diragukan; *~ faith* kepercayaan yang tidak diragukan; **unquestioningly** *adv* tanpa bertanya ← **questioning**

unreal *adj* [riil] tidak nyata; **unrealistic** *adj* tidak réalistis ← **real**

unreasonable *adj* [anriznabel] tidak masuk akal; **unreasonably** *adv* secara tidak masuk akal, secara berlebihan ← **reasonable**

unrelenting *adj* tak henti-hentinya; *the ~ heat* sinar matahari yang tak henti-hentinya ← **relent**

unreliable *adj* [anrelayabel] tidak dapat dipercayai, tidak dapat diandalkan; *don't ask Greg to do it, he's too ~* jangan minta agar Greg melakukannya, karena dia tidak bisa diandalkan ← **reliable**

unrest *n* kerusuhan

unripe *adj* mentah, kurang matang ← **ripe**

unroll *vi* buka, bergulung; *vt* membuka gulungan ← **roll**

unsafe *adj* tidak aman, berbahaya ← **safe**

unsalted *adj* tanpa garam ← **salted**

unsatisfactory *adj* [ansatisfaktori] tidak memuaskan ← **satisfactory**

unscrew *vt* membuka sekrup, melepaskan sekrup; *the thieves entered by ~ing the window* maling itu masuk dengan membuka sekrup jendéla ← **screw**

unsealed [ansild] *~ road* jalan tanah ← **sealed**

unseeded *adj* [ansided] bukan unggulan; *two ~ players made it to the semifinals* dua pemain yang bukan unggulan berhasil sampai di sémifinal ← **seed**

unseen *adj* tidak terlihat, tidak kelihatan ← **seen**

unselfish *adj* tidak égois, tidak mementingkan diri sendiri ← **selfish**

unshaven *adj* tidak bercukur ← **shaven**

unskilled *adj* [anskild] tidak terampil, tidak mahir; *~ labor* tenaga buruh ← **skilled**

unsolved *adj* [ansolvd] belum terbongkar; *~ case* kasus yang belum terbongkar ← **solve**

unspeakable *adj* [anspikabel] tidak terkatakan; sangat buruk; **unspeakably** *adv* amat sangat ← **speak**

unspoilt *adj* tidak ternoda, belum tersentuh; *the island is still an ~ tourist destination* pulau itu masih asli ← **spoilt**

unstable *adj* [anstébel] goyah, tidak stabil; mudah tergoncang ← **stable**

unsteady *adj* [anstédi] tidak tegak, goyah; **unsteadily** *adv* dengan goyah ← **steady**

unstoppable *adj* [anstopabel] tidak bisa dihentikan; *the army's advance was ~* majunya tentara itu tidak bisa dihentikan ← **stop**

unsubscribe *vi* menarik diri sebagai pelanggan (di milis) ← **subscribe**

unsuccessful *adj* [ansaksésful] tidak berhasil, tidak lulus, gagal; **unsuccessfully** *adv* dengan tidak berhasil, gagal; *Melanie ~ tried to swim across the English Channel* Melanie gagal berenang menyeberangi Selat Inggris ← **successful**

unsuitable *adj* [ansutabel] tidak cocok ← **suitable**

unsuited *adj* [ansuted] tidak cocok; *they were ~ to each other* meréka tidak cocok ← **suit**

unsure *adj* [ansyur] tidak yakin, tidak pasti; *Helen was ~ about her plans* Helen tidak yakin soal rencana di masa depan ← **sure**

unsuspecting *adj* tidak curiga ← **suspect**

unsweetened *adj* [answitend] tanpa gula, tanpa pemanis ← **sweeten**

untapped *adj* [antapd] belum dimanfaatkan; *the sun is a great source of ~ energy* surya merupakan sumber énérgi yang belum dimanfaatkan ← **tap**

unthinkable *adj* [anthinkabel] tak terpikirkan, tak terbayangkan; **unthinking** *adj* tidak berpikir, membabi-buta; **unthinkingly** *adv* tanpa berpikir, tanpa ingat; *she ~ ordered meat for her vegetarian friend* tanpa ingat, dia memesan daging untuk temannya yang végétarian ← **think**

untidy *adj* [antaidi] tidak rapi, tidak teratur, jorok; **untidily** *adv* [antaidili] secara jorok ← **tidy**

untie *vt* [antai] membuka (tali), menguraikan ← **tie**

until *conj* sampai; *prep* hingga, sampai (dengan); *~ death do us part* sampai mati (memisahkan kita)

untimely *~ death* meninggal sebelum waktunya ← **timely**

untouchable *n* [antacabel] paria, orang tanpa kasta, orang hina (di India); **untouched** *adj* tak tersentuh; *Solveig left the fried banana ~* Solveig tidak makan pisang goréng itu ← **touch**

untrained *adj* tidak terlatih, tanpa pendidikan ← **train**

untranslatable *adj* [antranslétabel] tidak dapat diterjemahkan ← **translate**

untreated *adj* tidak diobati ← **treat**

untrue *adj* [antru] tidak benar; **untruth** *n* [antruth] bohong, dusta; **untruthful** *adj* tidak benar, bohong; **untruthfully** *adv* dengan tidak benar; *"Of course I*

can swim," he said ~ "Tentu saja aku bisa berenang," dia berbohong ← **true, truth**

unusual *adj* [anyusyuel] tidak biasa, tidak lazim; **unusually** *adv* luar biasa, tidak seperti biasa ← **usual**

unveil *vt* [anvél] membuka (selubung), memperkenalkan; *Toyota ~ed their latest model* Toyota memperkenalkan modél mobil terbarunya ← **veil**

unverified *adj* [anvérifaid] belum diteliti kebenarannya; *~ report* laporan yang belum diteliti kebenarannya ← **verify**

unwanted *adj* [anwonted] tidak diinginkan; *~ pregnancy* kehamilan (yang) tidak diinginkan ← **wanted**

unwelcome *adj* [anwélkem] tidak dikehendaki, tidak disambut; *the rat was an ~ guest at the party* tentunya tikus itu tamu yang tidak dikehendaki di pésta ← **welcome**

unwell *adj* tidak énak badan ← **well**

unwilling *adj* **unwillingly** *adv* tidak mau, segan, malas; *we were unwilling to say goodbye* kami tidak ingin berpisahan ← **willing**

unwind *vi* [anwaind] **unwound unwound** beristirahat, melepaskan lelah; *Karin likes to ~ by listening to music* Karin suka melepaskan lelah sambil mendengarkan musik; *vt* melepaskan ← **wind**

unwise *adj* tidak bijaksana, bodoh; *an ~ choice* pilihan yang tidak bijaksana ← **wise**

unwitting *adj* dengan tidak sengaja, tanpa disadari; **unwittingly** *adv* tanpa sadar; *he ~ gave the stranger his address* tanpa sadar dia memberi alamatnya kepada orang asing itu ← **wit**

unwound *v, pf* → **unwind**

unwrap *vt* [anrap] membuka (bungkus); *~ a present* membuka kado

unwritten *adj* [anriten] tak tertulis, tidak dituliskan; *~ rule* peraturan tak tertulis ← **written**

unzip *vt* membuka ritsléting ← **zip**

up *adj* habis; bangun; naik; *~ north* di kawasan utara; *what's ~?* apa kabar?

ada apa?; ~ *all night* semalam tidak tidur; ~ *at dawn* dinihari sudah bangun; *time is* ~ waktu sudah habis; *adv* ke atas; naik; ~ *and down* naik turun; mondar-mandir; ~*s and downs* suka (dan) duka; *prep* (di) atas; ke atas; ~*-to-date* modern, terbaru, mutakhir; ~*-to-the-minute* terkini; ~ *against* menghadapi; ~ *front* di muka; ~ *to* sampai; sedang; ~ *to you* terserah (anda); *to go* ~ *to* mendatangi, menghampiri; ~ *to no good* sedang berbuat jahat; *what are you* ~ *to?* sedang apa?; **upbringing** *n* asuhan, didikan; **upcoming** *adj* [apkaming] yang mendatang; **update** *n* laporan terbaru; *vt* memperbarui; ~ *on* mengabari orang tentang; **upfront** *adj* [apfrant] terus terang, jujur; **upgrade** *n* penataran; *vt* menaikkan kelas; **uphill** *adj* [aphil] sulit, berat; *adv* ke atas (bukit), menanjak; **uphold** *vt* [aphold] **upheld upheld** menegakkan; ~ *the law* menegakkan hukum; **upkeep** *n* perawatan, pemeliharaan; **upload** *n* pindahan dari peranti keras ke komputer; *vt* memindahkan dari peranti keras ke komputer; **upmarket** *adj* méwah, untuk kelas menengah ke atas; **upon** *prep* [apon] (di) atas; *once* ~ *a time* sekali waktu; **upper** *adj* (tingkat) atas; tinggi; ~ *case* huruf besar; ~ *class*, ~ *crust* golongan atas; *to keep a stiff* ~ *lip* tidak menangis; **upright** *adj* [aprait] tegak (lurus); jujur; **uprising** *n* [apraizing] pemberontakan; **uproar** *n* kegaduhan, keributan; **uproot** *vt* menumbangkan, mencabut dari tanah; **upset** *adj* tersinggung; tidak tenang; terbalik; terganggu; ~ *stomach* sakit perut; *n* gangguan; *vt* membuat tersinggung, mengganggu, merusak; **upsetting** *adj* membingungkan, menguatirkan; **upside** ~ *down* terbalik; **upstairs** *adj* di (lantai) atas; *adv* ke (lantai) atas; *n* lantai atas; **upstream** *adv* ke hulu; **uptake** *quick on the* ~ cepat mengerti; **uptown** *adv* ke kota bagian atas; *n* daérah perumahan, bukan di tengah kota; **upturn** *n* per-

baikan, kemajuan; **upturned** *adj* terbalik; menengadah; **upward** *adj* [apwerd] naik; *adv* (menuju) ke atas; **upwardly** *adv* ~ *mobile* menuju tingkat sosial yang lebih tinggi

upholster *vt* melapisi (mébel) dengan kain; **upholsterer** *n* tukang pelapis mébel; **upholstery** *n* kain pelapis atau bantal di kursi, sofa dll

upkeep *n* perawatan, pemeliharaan ← **up**

upload *n* pindahan dari peranti keras ke komputer; *vt* memindahkan dari peranti keras ke komputer ← **up**

upmarket *adj* méwah, untuk kelas menengah ke atas ← **up**

upon *prep* [apon] (di) atas; *once* ~ *a time* sekali waktu ← **up**

upper *adj* (tingkat) atas; tinggi; ~ *case* huruf besar; ~ *class*, ~ *crust* golongan atas; *to keep a stiff* ~ *lip* tidak menangis ← **up**

upright *adj* [aprait] tegak (lurus); jujur ← **up**

uprising *n* [apraizing] pemberontakan ← **up**

uproar *n* kegaduhan, keributan ← **up**

uproot *vt* menumbangkan, mencabut dari tanah ← **up**

upset *adj* tersinggung; tidak tenang; terbalik; terganggu; ~ *stomach* sakit perut; *n* gangguan; *vt* membuat tersinggung, mengganggu, merusak; **upsetting** *adj* membingungkan, menguatirkan

upside ~ *down* terbalik ← **up**

upstairs *adj* di (lantai) atas; *adv* ke (lantai) atas; *n* lantai atas ← **up**

upstream *adv* ke hulu ← **up**

uptake *quick on the* ~ cepat mengerti ← **up**

uptown *adv* ke kota bagian atas; *n* daérah perumahan, bukan di tengah kota ← **up**

upturn *n* perbaikan, kemajuan; **upturned** *adj* terbalik; menengadah ← **up**

upward *adj* [apwerd] naik; *adv* (menuju) ke atas; **upwardly** *adj* ~ *mobile* menuju tingkat sosial yang lebih tinggi ← **up**

uranium *n* [yurénium] uranium
urban *adj* [érben] perkotaan; *~ renewal* peremajaan kota; *~ sprawl* pertumbuhan (liar) perkotaan; **urbanization** *n* urbanisasi, prosés orang pindah ke kota
urchin [ércin] *sea ~* bulu babi
urethra *n* [yurithra] saluran kencing, saluran kemih
urge *n* [érj] dorongan; *vt* mendorong, mendesak; **urgency** *n* [érjensi] urgénsi, keadaan yang mendesak; **urgent** *adj* [érjent] mendesak, penting, genting
urinal *n* [yurinal] tempat kencing (laki-laki); **urinary** *adj* [yurinari] berkaitan dengan air kencing; *~ tract* saluran kemih; **urinate** *v* [yurinét] kencing, buang air kecil; **urine** *n* air kencing, air seni
urn *n* [érn] jambangan; perabuan; cérék
Uruguay *n* [yuruguai] Uruguay; **Uruguayan** *adj* berasal dari Uruguay; *n* orang Uruguay
us *pron, obj* kita (termasuk lawan bicara); kami
US *abbrev United States* AS (Amérika Serikat); **USAF** *abbrev United States Air Force* Angkatan Udara Amérika Serikat
usage *n* [yusej] pemakaian, penggunaan; **use** *n* [yus] pemakaian, penggunaan; *in ~* masih dipakai, masih dipergunakan; *of ~* berguna, bermanfaat; *directions for ~* cara pemakaian; *what's the ~?* apa gunanya? *it's (of) no ~* tidak ada gunanya, percuma, sia-sia; *to make ~ of* memanfaatkan; *vt* [yuz] memakai, menggunakan; *~ someone* memperalat, memperdaya, memanfaatkan; *~ up* menghabiskan; *I could ~ coll* saya inginkan; **used** *adj* bekas (pakai); *~ car* mobil bekas; *~ to* terbiasa; dulu; *I'm ~ to children* saya biasa bergaul dengan anak-anak; *Jane ~ to work in Nigeria* dulu Jane bekerja di Nigeria; **useful** *adj* [yusfel] berguna, bermanfaat; **useless** *adj* tidak berguna, sia-sia; tidak dapat dipakai; **user** *n* [yuzer] pemakai, pengguna; *(drug) ~* pecandu (obat); *~-friendly* mudah dipakai

USG *abbrev ultrasonogram* USG
usher *n* penjaga pintu (di téater atau bioskop), penerima tamu; *vt* mengantarkan, memandu
USSR *abbrev Union of Soviet Socialist Republics* Républik Sosialis Uni Soviét
usual *adj* [yusyual] biasa, lazim, lumrah; *as ~* seperti biasa; *the ~* yang biasa; **usually** *adv* biasanya
usurer *n, arch* [yuserer] lintah darat; **usury** *n* riba
utensil *n* [yuténsil] alat (masak); *kitchen ~s* alat-alat dapur
uterus *n* [yuterus] rahim, kandungan, peranakan
utility *n* [yutiliti] keperluan; *sport ~ vehicle (SUV)* mobil jip; *n, pl* keperluan (air, listrik, gas); **utilize** *vt* mempergunakan
utmost *adj* yang sepenuhnya; *n* sepenuhnya; *to the ~, to do your ~* berusaha sekeras mungkin
utopia *n* [yutopia] negeri khayalan; **utopian** *adj* bersifat khayalan, tidak praktis
utter *vt* mengucapkan, memanjatkan (doa)
utter *adj* **utterly** *adv* sama sekali; *an utter mess* sama sekali kacau-balau
U-turn *n* [yu térn] putar balik; *no ~* dilarang putar balik
UV *abbrev ultraviolet* ultraviolét
Uzbek *n* [uzbék] bahasa Uzbék; orang Uzbék; **Uzbekistan** *n* Uzbékistan; **Uzbekistani** *adj* berasal dari Uzbékistan; *n* orang Uzbékistan

V

V-necked *adj* léhér berbentuk huruf V (baju)
vacancy *n* lowongan; ada kamar; *no ~* penuh; **vacant** *adj* kosong
vacate *vt* mengosongkan; *you must ~ your room before midday* harus meninggalkan kamar sebelum jam 12 siang

vacation *n, US* [vakésyen] liburan; *on ~*
sedang libur; *summer ~* liburan musim
panas

vaccinate *vt* [vaksinét] memvaksinasi,
menyuntik; **vaccination** *n* vaksinasi,
pencacaran; **vaccine** *n* vaksin, benih
cacar

vacuum *n* [vakyum] kedap udara,
vakum; *~ cleaner* pengisap debu,
penyedot lantai; *~ flask* térmos; *vt*
mengisap debu, menyedot lantai

vagina *n* [vejaina] vagina, liang peranakan; **vaginal** *~ discharge* keputihan

vague *adj* [vég] tidak jelas, samar-
samar; **vaguely** *adv* [végli] secara
tidak jelas; *I asked him about his
father, but he only replied ~* saya
tanyakan ayahnya, tapi dia hanya
menjawab secara tidak jelas

vain *adj* bangga pada penampilan
sendiri; *(in) ~* sia-sia, percuma

valance *n* [valans] tirai péndék atau
rénda di bawah tempat tidur

valedictory [valediktori] *~ dinner*
makan malam sebagai acara
perpisahan

Valentine [valentain] *~'s Day* Hari
Kasih Sayang, Hari Valéntin (tanggal
14 Fébruari); *~'s (Day) card* kartu
(ucapan) Valéntin

valet *n, m* [valé] pelayan pria; *~ parking*
pelayanan parkir

valiant *adj* [valient] berani; **valiantly**
adv dengan berani; *they fought ~ but
still lost* meréka berjuang dengan
berani namun tetap kalah

valid *adj* [valid] berlaku, sah; *~ passport* paspor yang berlaku; *~ reason*
alasan yang kuat; **validate** *vt* mengesahkan, memvalidasi; **validation** *n*
pengesahan, validasi; **validity** *n*
[validiti] masa berlaku; kebenaran

valley *n* [vali] lembah

valor, valour *n* keberanian

valuable *adj* [valyuabel] berharga;
mahal; *n, pl* barang-barang berharga;
valuation *n* penilaian; **value** *vt* [valyu]
menghargai, menilai; *n* nilai; *good ~*
harga baik; *of ~* berharga; *pl* norma,
nilai; **valued** *adj* dihargai, dinilai

valve *n* [valv] klep, katup, pentil; *heart
~* katup jantung

vampire *n* [vampair] vampir, drakula,
pengisap darah; *~ bat* sejenis kelelawar

van *n* mobil bagasi; gerbong; *goods ~*
mobil barang; *luggage ~* gerbong
bagasi

vandal *n* perusak, orang iseng yang
merusak sarana umum; **vandalism** *n*
[vandelizem] kerusakan akibat orang
iseng; **vandalize** *vt* merusak sarana
umum; *the phone box near the bank
has been ~d* télepon umum dekat
bank sudah dirusak

vanilla *n* panili, vanili; *~ ice-cream* és
krim (rasa) vanili; *~ essence* sari vanili

vanish *vi* [vanisy] hilang, menghilang,
lenyap; *~ing cream* krim untuk
menyamarkan noda

vanity *n* [vaniti] kebanggaan pada
penampilan sendiri; *~ set* wastafel
yang dilengkapi cermin dan lemari ←
vain

vanquish *vt, arch* [vankuisy] mengalahkan

vantage [vantej] *~ point* tempat peninjauan

Vanuatu *n* Vanuatu; *ni-~* orang Vanuatu

vapor, vapour *n* uap; **vaporize** *vi*
menguap; **vaporizer** *n* alat penguap

variable *adj* [vériabel] berubah-ubah,
tidak tetap; *n* variabel; **variation** *n*
perubahan, variasi; **vary** *vi* [véri]
berubah-ubah, berbéda-béda; *vt* mengubah

varicose [varikos] *~ veins* varisés

varied *adj* [vérid] berbagai, berbéda-
béda; **variety** *n* [varayeti] macam; keanékaragaman; *~ show* acara dengan
berbagai adegan atau pertunjukan; *a ~
of reasons* berbagai alasan; **various**
adj [vérius] berjenis-jenis, bermacam-
macam; *~ things* berbagai hal; **vary** *vi*
[véri] berubah-ubah, berbeda-beda; *vt*
mengubah

varnish *n* pérnis; *nail ~* cat kuku

vary *vi* [véri] berubah-ubah, berbéda-
béda; *vt* mengubah

vase *n* vas, jambangan

vasectomy *n* vaséktomi

vaseline *n* vaselin

vast *adj* luas, besar sekali; *Australia is a ~ continent* Australia adalah benua yang luas; **vastly** *adv* sangat, amat; **vastness** *n* keluasan

VAT *abbrev value added tax* PPN (pajak pertambahan nilai)

vat *n* tong

Vatican *the ~* kediaman Sri Paus di Roma; *~ City* Kota Vatikan

vaudeville *n* [vodevil] acara dengan berbagai adegan atau pertunjukan

vault *n* [volt] ruang bawah tanah; *she was buried in the family ~* dia dimakamkan di makam keluarga di ruang bawah tanah

vault *n* kuda-kuda loncat; *~ing horse* kuda-kuda pelana; *pole ~* loncat galah; *vt* meloncat (dengan galah)

VCR *abbrev video cassette recorder* alat perekam kasét vidéo

VD *abbrev venereal disease* penyakit menular séksual (PMS)

veal *n* [vil] daging anak sapi

vegan *n* orang yang tidak makan atau memakai produk dari héwan

vegetable *adj* [véjtebel] nabati; *~ fat* lemak nabati; *~ oil* minyak sayur; *n* sayur; *pl* sayur-sayuran, sayur-mayur; **vegetarian** *n* [véjetérien] orang yang hanya makan sayur, orang végétarian; **vegetation** *n* [véjetésyen] tetumbuh-an, tumbuh-tumbuhan

vehement *adj* [viement] berapi-api, penuh semangat, dengan (suara) keras; **vehemently** *adv* dengan berapi-api, dengan semangat; *Rebecca ~ denied taking the keys* dengan sema-ngat Rebecca membantah telah mengambil kunci

vehicle *n* [viekel] kendaraan, wahana; *motor ~* kendaraan bermotor

veil *n* [vél] kerudung, kudungan; jilbab; tudung; selubung; *to take the ~ Chr* menjadi biarawati; *to wear the ~* berjilbab, berkerudung; *vt* menye-lubungi; **veiled** *adj* terselubung; berjilbab, berkerudung; *~ threat* anca-man yang tersirat

vein *n* [vén] urat, pembuluh balik, véna

velocity *n* kecepatan, laju

velvet *adj, n* beledru, beludru; **velvety** *adj* seperti beledru

vendetta *n* dendam (secara turun-temu-run)

vending *~ machine* otomat; **vendor** *n* penjaja, penjual; *street ~* pedagang kaki lima

veneer *n* lapisan (tipis); *brick ~* memberi lapisan batu bata pada rumah kayu

venerate *vt* memuliakan

venereal [veniriel] *~ disease (VD)* penyakit menular seksual (PMS)

Venetian *adj* [venisyen] berasal dari Vénésia; *~ blind* kréi; **Venice** *n* Vénésia

Venezuela *n* Vénezuéla; **Venezuelan** *adj* berasal dari Vénezuéla; *n* orang Vénezuéla

vengeance *n* [vénjens] balas dendam ← **avenge**

Venice *n* [vénis] Vénésia

venison *n* [vénison] daging rusa

venom *n* [vénem] bisa; **venomous** *adj* [vénemus] berbisa; *~ remark* koméntar yang sinis; *~ snake* ular berbisa

vent *n* lubang angin; *vt* melampiaskan; *John ~ed his rage on the mechanic* John melampiaskan amarahnya pada montir; **ventilation** *n* véntilasi, perédaran udara, sirkulasi udara

ventricle *n* [véntrikel] kamar (jantung)

ventriloquist *n* [véntrilokuist] ahli bicara perut

venture *n* usaha; *joint ~* usaha patungan; *v* mengambil risiko, memberanikan diri

venue *n* [vényu] tempat acara berlang-sung

Venus *n* planét Vénus

veranda, verandah *n* beranda

verb *n* kata kerja; **verbal** *adj* lisan

verdict *n* putusan

verge *n* pinggir; jalur hijau; *on the ~ of* di ambang; *vt ~ on* menjelang, mendekati, hampir; *~ on ridiculous* hampir konyol

verification *n* vérifikasi, pembuktian; **verify** *vt* [vérifai] membuktikan, mem-benarkan; *the news has yet to be veri-fied* berita itu masih belum dibenarkan

vermicelli *n* [vérmicéli] ~ *noodles* bihun, soun

versatile *adj* [vérsatail] berbakat dalam berbagai hal; serba guna

verse *n* [vérs] ayat; sajak, syair; pantun; bagian (dari sajak); *chapter and* ~ kitab dan ayat; hafal; ~ *from the* Koran ayat suci dari Alquran

version *n* [vérsyen] vérsi

versus (vs) *conj* lawan, melawan

vertebra *n* vertebrae [vértebré] tulang belakang, tulang punggung; **vertebrate** *n* binatang bertulang belakang

vertical *adj* tegak lurus, vértikal; **vertically** *adv* secara vértikal, tegak lurus

vertigo *n* [vértigo] rasa takut pada ketinggian

very *adv* [véri] amat, sangat, sekali; *adj* benar, betul; *that* ~ *woman* perempuan itu juga

vessel *n* perahu, kapal; bejana; *blood* ~ pembuluh darah; *empty* ~*s make the most sound tong* kosong nyaring bunyinya

vest *n* rompi; singlét; *safety* ~ baju pelampung

vet *n, coll* dokter héwan (drh) ← **veterinarian**

vet *n, coll* véteran; *Vietnam* ~ véteran dari perang Viétnam; **veteran** *adj* [vétran] kawakan; *n* vetéran; ~ *car* mobil kuno

veterinarian *n* [véterinérian] dokter héwan; **veterinary** ~ *surgeon* dokter héwan

veto *n* (hak) veto; *vt* memvéto

VHF *abbrev very high frequency* VHF

via *prep* [vaya] léwat, via; melalui; *to Melbourne* ~ *Sydney* ke Melbourne léwat Sydney

viable *adj* [vayabel] dapat hidup terus; **viability** *n* [vayabiliti] kelangsungan (hidup)

viaduct *n* [vayadakt] viaduk; jembatan

vial *n* [vail] botol kecil

vibe *n, coll* perasaan, kesan; **vibrant** *adj* [vaibrent] berwarna terang; bersemangat; **vibrate** *vi* [vaibrét] bergetar; **vibration** *n* [vaibrésyen] getaran, vibrasi; **vibrator** *n* [vaibréter] alat penggetar, vibrator

vicar *n, Chr* [viker] pendéta; **vicarage** *n* [vikerej] rumah pendéta

vice *n* sifat buruk atau jahat; ~ *squad* polisi kesusilaan

vice- *pref* wakil, muda; ~*consul* konsul muda; ~*president* wakil présidén; ~*principal* wakil kepala sekolah

vice ~ *versa* sebaliknya

vicinity *n* [visiniti] sekitar, dekat; *in the* ~ di sekitar

vicious *adj* [visyes] kejam, jahat; ~ *circle* lingkaran sétan; ~ *dog* anjing galak; **viciously** *adv* [visyesli] dengan kejam, dengan jahat, dengan garang

victim *n* korban; *to fall* ~ *to* menjadi korban; **victimize** *vt* menjadikan korban, menyerang secara terus-menerus

victor *n* pemenang; **victorious** *adj* [viktorius] jaya, yang menang; **victory** *n* [viktori] kemenangan

video [vidio] alat perekam kasét vidéo; ~*conference* konperénsi jarak jauh; ~ *game* mainan vidéo; ~ *cassette recorder (VCR)* alat perekam kasét vidéo; **videotape** *n* kasét vidéo; *vt* merekam pada kasét vidéo

vie [vai] *vi* ~ *for* bersaingan

Vietnam *n* Viétnam; *South* ~ Viétnam Selatan; **Vietnamese** *adj* berasal dari Viétnam; *n* bahasa Viétnam; orang Viétnam

view *n* [vyu] pemandangan; pandangan, pendapat; *in* ~ kelihatan, tampak; *on* ~ dipertontonkan; *scenic* ~ pemandangan yang asri; *in my* ~ menurut saya; *in* ~ *of* mengingat; *point of* ~ sudut pandangan; *with a* ~ *to* dengan maksud; *vt* melihat, meninjau; **viewer** *n* [vyuer] pemirsa; **viewfinder** *n* [vyufainder] lubang kecil untuk mengukur ruang di kamera; **viewpoint** *n* [vyupoint] sudut pandangan

vigil *n* [vijil] berjaga; *to keep a* ~ berjaga; **vigilant** *adj* waspada, berjaga-jaga

vigor, vigour *n* [viger] tenaga, kekuatan; **vigorous** *adj* kuat, bersemangat

vile *adj* jorok, menjijikkan; buruk; keji, hina; ~ *taste* rasa yang menjijikkan

villa *n* vila
village *n* [vilej] désa, kampung, dusun;
~ *chief* lurah, kepala désa; ~ *green*
alun-alun; *my* ~ kampung (halaman);
villager *n* orang désa
villain *n* [vilen] penjahat, orang jahat,
bangsat; **villainous** *adj* jahat
vine *n* tanaman anggur; tanaman merambat; **vineyard** *n* [vinyerd] kebun
anggur
vinegar *n* [vineger] cuka
vineyard *n* [vinyerd] kebun anggur ←
vine
vintage *adj* [vintej] tulén; ~ *car* mobil
lama, mobil kuno; *n* kuno; tahun
(anggur); *a 1934* ~ anggur hasil panén
tahun 1934
vinyl *n* [vainel] plastik tebal
viola *n* biola alto
violate *vt* [vayolét] melanggar; **violation** *n* [vayolésyen] pelanggaran
violence *n* [vayolens] kekerasan;
domestic ~ kekerasan di dalam rumah
tangga (KDRT); **violent** *adj* kasar;
suka memukul; keras, hébat; **violently**
adv [vayolentli] dengan kekerasan,
dengan keras
violet *adj* [vayolet] ungu muda; *n* sejenis bunga berwarna ungu; *shrinking* ~
pemalu
violin *n* [vayolin] biola; **violinist** *n*
pemain biola
VIP *abbrev very important person* orang
yang sangat penting
viper *n* ular biludak, ular berbisa
viral *adj* [vairal] ~ *infection* inféksi akibat virus; **virus** *n* [vairus] virus; *the*
AIDS ~ (virus) AIDS
virgin *n* [vérjin] perawan, gadis; ~
Islander orang dari Kepulauan Virgin;
~ *Islands* Kepulauan Virgin; ~ *Mary*
Perawan Suci; **virginity** *n* [vérjiniti]
kegadisan, keperawanan
virtual *adj* [vértyuel] nyaris; maya; ~
reality dunia maya; **virtually** *adv* nyaris
virtue *n* [vértyu] kebaikan, kebajikan;
by ~ *of* berdasarkan, atas dasar; **virtu-
ous** *adj* [vértyues] berbudi luhur
virus *n* [vairus] virus; *the AIDS* ~
(virus) AIDS

visa *n* [viza] visa; ~ *application* aplikasi
untuk visa; *business* ~ visa bisnis;
tourist ~ visa wisata
visibility *n* [vizibiliti] jarak pandang; ~
was only 20 meters jarak pandang
hanya 20 méter; **visible** *adj* [vizibel]
kelihatan, tampak; **vision** *n* [visyen]
penglihatan; visi; **visionary** *adj*
[visyeneri] bisa melihat ke masa
depan; *n* orang yang memiliki visi
visit *n* [vizit] kunjungan; *vi* berkunjung;
vt mengunjungi; *~ing hours* jam
besuk; **visitation** *n* penampakan; **visitor** *n* [visiter] tamu, pengunjung; *~s
book* buku tamu
visor *n* kaca penutup (di helm); *sun* ~
pelindung (terik matahari)
visual *adj* [visyuel] berkaitan dengan
mata atau penglihatan; ~ *arts* seni
rupa; **visualize** *vt* membayangkan
vital *adj* penting sekali; **vitally** *adv*
sangat, amat; ~ *important* sangat
penting
vitamin *n* vitamin
vivacious *adj* [vivésyes] bersemangat,
periang, gembira
vivid *adj* [vivid] hidup, jelas, terang;
vividly *adv* dengan jelas, secara hidup
viz. yaitu, yakni
VJ *abbrev video jockey* VJ
V-necked *adj* léhér berbentuk huruf V
(baju)
VOA *abbrev Voice of America* VOA,
siaran radio Suara Amérika
vocabulary *n* **vocab** *coll* [vokabuleri]
kosa kata
vocal *adj* bersuara; lantang; berkaitan
dengan suara; ~ *cords* pita suara; *n*
pembawaan lagu; *pl* pembawaan lagu;
vocalist *n* penyanyi, vokalis
vocation *n* panggilan, pekerjaan; **vocational** *adj* kejuruan; ~ *education* pendidikan kejuruan
vogue [vog] *in* ~ sedang digemari
voice *n* [vois] suara; *~over* pembacaan
(dalam iklan); ~ *box* pangkal tenggorokan; ~ *mail* kotak suara; *in a loud*
~ dengan suara keras; *to lose one's* ~
kehabisan suara; *to raise one's* ~
bicara dengan suara lebih keras; *vt*

menyuarakan, mengatakan; ~ *one's*
concerns menyuarakan rasa prihatin
void *adj* tidak berlaku lagi; *null and* ~
tidak berlaku; *n* kekosongan, kehampaan
volatile *adj* [volatail] tidak stabil,
mudah menguap
volcanic *adj* [volkanik] berkaitan dengan gunung api; ~ *ash* abu gunung
berapi; **volcano** *n* [volkéno] **volcanoes** gunung api, gunung berapi;
vulcanologist *n* [valkanolojist] vulkanolog; ahli gunung api, ahli vulkanologi; **vulcanology** *n* ilmu gunung
api, vulkanologi
volley *n* pukulan bola saat belum mulai
jatuh; **volleyball** *n* bola voli; **volleyballer** *n* pemain (bola) voli
volt *n* volt; **voltage** *n* [voltej] tegangan
listrik, voltase
volume *n* [volyum] isi, muatan, volume;
jilid; *to speak ~s* banyak bicara; *to
turn down the* ~ mengecilkan suara
voluntary *adj* [volentri] sukaréla; **voluntarily** *adv* [volentarili] secara sukaréla; **volunteer** *adj* sukarélawan; *vi*
menjadi sukarélawan; *vt* menawarkan
(jasa)
vomit *n* muntah; *v* muntah; ~ *up*
memuntahkan
voodoo *n* guna-guna; ~ *doll* bonéka
yang ditusuki peniti dengan harapan
seseorang akan menderita
vote *n* (pemungutan) suara; hak memilih; ~ *of no confidence* mosi tidak percaya; *v* memberikan suara; memilih;
~ *against*, ~ *out* tidak memilih; ~ *for*, ~
in memilih; *vt* memutuskan; *the people ~d him out of office* rakyat tidak
memberi suara kepadanya, sehingga
dia tidak terpilih lagi; **voter** *n* pemilih;
voting *n* pemungutan suara
vouch [vauc] *vi* ~ *for* menjamin
voucher *n* [vaucer] vocer, bon
vow *n* janji; *marriage ~s* janji kawin; *Isl*
ijab kabul; *to take a* ~, *to swear a* ~
mengangkat sumpah; *vi* bersumpah;
Jan ~ed to quit smoking Jan bersumpah akan berhenti merokok
vowel *n* [vaul] huruf hidup, vokal

vox pop *n, sl* opini umum, wawancara
dengan rakyat
voyage *n* [voyej] pelayaran, perjalanan
léwat laut; **voyager** *n* [voyajer] orang
yang berlayar, orang yang jalan
VP *abbrev, US Vice-President* Wakil
Présidén (Waprés)
vulcanologist *n* [valkanolojist] vulkanolog; ahli gunung api, ahli vulkanologi; **vulcanology** *n* ilmu gunung
api, vulkanologi ← **volcano**
vulgar *adj* [valger] kasar; tidak sopan;
jorok
vulnerable *adj* [valnerabel] mudah diserang, rentan
vulture *n* [vultyur] burung nasar

W

wacky *adj, coll* nyentrik
wad *n* [wod] gumpal; *a* ~ *of gum* permén karét
waddle *n* [wodel] cara berjalan terséok-
séok (seperti bébék), cara berjalan
tergoyang-goyang; *vi* berjalan terséok-
séok
wade *vi* berjalan dalam air; *vt* mengarungi; ~ *a stream* mengarungi kali,
mengarungi sungai; **waders** *n, pl*
setélan celana plastik yang menyatu
dengan sepatu
wafer *n* biskuit tipis; ~*thin* tipis sekali
waffle *n* [wofel] wafel; ~ *iron* cétakan
kué wafel
waffle *n* omong kosong; *vi* [wofel] ~
(on) cerocos, berbicara tanpa tujuan
wag *vi* mengibas, mengibas-ibas; *vt*
mengibaskan
wage *n* upah; *vi* mengadakan; ~ *war*
berperang
wager *n* taruhan; *vi* bertaruh
wagon *n* [wagon] gerbong, keréta; *station* ~ mobil barang berpenumpang
waif *n* [wéf] anak terlantar; orang yang
kurus kerémpéng
wail *n* ratapan; *vi* meratap
waist *n* pinggang; ~*high* sepinggang,
setinggi pinggang; *low-~ed* berping-

gang rendah; **waistband** *n* karét pinggang; **waistcoat** *n* rompi; **waistline** *n*
ukuran pinggang
wait *n* masa menunggu; penantian; *~-list*
memasukkan sebagai cadangan; *vi*
menunggu, menanti; *~ for* menunggui,
menantikan; *~ on* melayani; *~ a
minute* tunggu sebentar; *~ and see*
lihat dulu; *I can't ~* saya sudah tidak
sabar; **waiting** *adj* penantian; *~ list*
daftar cadangan; *~ room* ruang tunggu; **waiter** *n, m* pelayan; **waitress** *f*
pelayan
wake *n* air alur kapal; selamatan sesudah upacara pemakaman; *vi* **woke
woken** bangun; *~ up* bangun; *vt* membangunkan; *~ up* membangunkan;
waken *vi* bangun; *vt* membangkitkan;
*Sean was woken by the sound of the
wind* Sean terbangun oléh suara angin
Wales *n* [wéls] Wales; *the Prince of ~*
Pangeran Wales; Pangeran Charles;
Welsh *adj* berasal dari Wales; *n*
bangsa Wales; bahasa Wales; *~ rarebit*
semacam roti panggang
walk *n* [wok] jalan-jalan, jarak yang
dijalani; *the ~* jalan cepat; *five minutes' ~ away* jaraknya lima menit jalan
kaki; *to go for a ~* jalan-jalan; *vi* jalan
(kaki), berjalan (kaki); *~ away, ~ out*
meninggalkan tempat; *~ away with*
memenangkan; *~ the dog* membawa
anjing jalan; *~ someone home* berjalan kaki mengantarkan orang sampai
di rumahnya; **walkabout** *on ~, to go ~*
mengembara, merantau; **walker** *n*
pejalan kaki; **walkie-talkie** *n* woki-
toki, HT; **walking** *adj* berjalan; *~ stick*
tongkat; **walkout** *n* aksi mogok; **walk-
over** *n* kemenangan mudah, w.o.,
menang telak
wall [wol] *n* témbok, dinding; *~-to-~
carpet* karpét yang menutupi seluruh
lantai; *outer ~* témbok; *the Great ~ (of
China)* Témbok Cina; *vi ~ up* menutup
dengan témbok, menémbok; **wallpaper** *n* [wolpéper] kertas dinding; *vt*
melapisi dinding dengan kertas; *they
~ed the front room* meréka pasang kertas dinding di kamar depan

wallet *n* [wolet] dompét; *I've lost my ~!*
dompét saya hilang
wallop *n, coll* [wolop] pukulan keras; *vt*
melabrak
wallow *vi* [wolo] berkubang; *~ in self-
pity* mengasihani diri sendiri
wallpaper *n* [wolpéper] kertas dinding;
vt melapisi dinding dengan kertas;
they ~ed the front room meréka pasang
kertas dinding di kamar depan
walnut *n* [wolnat] sejenis kenari
walrus *n* [wolras] singa laut
waltz *n* [woltz] vals; *vi* berdansa vals; *~
into* jalan dengan enteng
wan *adj* [won] pucat, lesu; pudar
wand *n* [wond] tongkat sihir
wander *n* jalan-jalan; *vi* mengembara,
berkelana, berputar-putar; melayang;
~ off pergi ke tempat lain; *her thoughts
~ed* pikirannya melayang
wane *on the ~* sedang berkurang
want *n* [wont] keinginan; keperluan; *for
~ of* karena tidak ada; *n, pl* kebutuhan,
keperluan; kekurangan *vi* ingin,
menginginkan, menghendaki; membutuhkan, memerlukan; *~ out* tidak mau
bergabung; *what do you ~?* mau apa?
apa yang diinginkan?; **wanted** *adj*
dicari; **wanting** *adj* kurang
war *n* [wor] perang; *~-torn* hancur akibat perang; *~ correspondent* wartawan
perang; *~ crimes* kejahatan perang; *~
cry* yél, seruan perang; *~ games* latihan
perang; *to wage ~ on* berperang
melawan, memerangi; *World ~ II*
Perang Dunia Kedua; *the First World ~*
Perang Dunia Pertama; **warfare** *n*
[worfér] peperangan, pertempuran,
perjuangan; *guerrilla ~* perang gerilya;
warlike *adj* [worlaik] suka berperang;
warring *adj* sedang berperang; **warrior** *n* [worier] pejuang, prajurit, kesatria; **warship** *n* [worsyip] kapal
perang; **wartime** *n* [wortaim] masa
perang
ward *n* [word] bangsal, ruang; wilayah;
casualty (~) unit gawat darurat
(UGD)
warden *n* [worden] pengawas, penjaga;
sipir, juru kunci

wardrobe *n* [wordrob] lemari baju, lemari pakaian; koléksi busana

ware *n* [wér] barang jualan; **warehouse** *n* [wérhaus] gudang

warfare *n* [worfér] peperangan, pertempuran, perjuangan; *guerrilla* ~ perang gerilya ← **war**

warlike *adj* [worlaik] suka berperang ← **war**

warm *adj* [worm] hangat, panas; ~ *weather* cuaca hangat; *a* ~ *welcome* sambutan yang hangat; *vt* memanaskan, menghangatkan; ~-*up* pemanasan; ~ *to* menjadi tertarik atau bersemangat; ~ *up* menjadi panas; menghangatkan (makanan); memanaskan (badan); **warmly** *adv* [wormli] dengan hangat; **warmth** *n* [wormth] panas, kehangatan

warn *vt* [worn] memperingatkan; **warning** *n* peringatan; ~ *sign* tanda peringatan, gejala

warp *n* [worp] *time* ~ percepatan waktu (ke masa lain); *v* membengkokkan, melengkungkan; **warped** *adj* melengkung; kacau

warrant *n* [worant] surat kuasa; *the police had a* ~ *to search the house* polisi membawa surat kuasa untuk menggeledah rumah

warranty *n* [woranti] jaminan, garansi; *under* ~ masih digaransi

warren [woren] *rabbit* ~ sarang kelinci, lubang kelinci

warring *adj* sedang berperang ← **war**

warrior *n* [worier] pejuang, prajurit, kesatria ← **war**

Warsaw *n* [worso] Warsawa

warship *n* [worsyip] kapal perang ← **war**

wart *n* [wort] kutil

wartime *n* [wortaim] masa perang ← **war**

wary *adj* [wéri] hati-hati, waspada; ~ *of* waspada terhadap

was *vi, pf* [woz] → **be**

wash *n* [wosy] cucian; mandi; *car* ~ cuci mobil; *to have a* ~ mandi; *vi* mandi; *vt* mencuci, membasuh; memandikan (orang); ~ *clothes* mencuci pakaian; ~ *dishes* mencuci piring; ~ *up vi* terhanyut; *vt* mencuci piring; ~*ed up* habis,

selesai; ~ *your hair* keramas, mencuci rambut; ~ *your hands* mencuci tangan; **washbasin** *n* [wosybésin] tempat cuci muka, wastafel; **washcloth** *n* [wosykloth] lap; **washer** *n* [wosyer] cincin karét, gelang karét; **washing** *n* [wosying] cucian; ~-*up* cuci piring; ~ *machine* mesin cuci; ~ *powder*, ~ *detergent* sabun cuci baju; *dirty* ~ baju kotor; *to do the* ~ cuci baju, mencuci pakaian; **washout** *n* [wosyaut] pertandingan ditunda atau dibatalkan karena hujan; kegagalan; **washroom** *n* [wosyrum] kamar kecil, WC

WASP *abbrev White Anglo-Saxon Protestant* orang putih keturunan Inggris, beragama Kristen

wasp *n* [wosp] tawon

waste *n* [wést] sampah; keborosan; ~ *paper* kertas bekas; *a* ~ *of time* membuang waktu; *vt* memboroskan; membuang; *don't* ~ *water* hémat air; *no time to* ~ tidak ada waktu; **wasteful** *adj* boros; **wastepaper** ~ *basket* tempat sampah

watch *n* [woc] jam tangan; jaga; *fob* ~ arloji rantai; *by my* ~ menurut jam saya

watch *v* [woc] menonton; menjaga; ~ *out* hati-hati, waspada; ~ *over* menjaga, melindungi; ~ *out!* awas! hati-hati!; **watchdog** *n* [wocdog] (anjing) penjaga; **watchful** *adj* [wocful] waspada; **watchman** *n* [wocman] jaga, penjaga

water *n* [woter] air; ~-*resistant* tahan air; ~ *bed* kasur air; ~ *buffalo* kerbau; ~ *heater* alat pemanas air; ~ *level* permukaan air; ~ *lily* (bunga) teratai; ~ *polo* polo air; ~ *pump* pompa air; ~ *supply* pengadaan air, persediaan air; ~ *table* permukaan air di bawah tanah; ~ *wheel* kincir air; ~ *wings* pelampung; *reticulated* ~ air lédéng; *in hot* ~ dalam kesulitan; ~ *under the bridge* nasi sudah menjadi bubur; *pl* perairan; *to break your* ~ pecah air ketuban; *vi* berliur; *vt* menyirami, mengairi; **watercolors** *n, pl* [woterkalers] cat air; **waterfall** *n* [woterfol] air terjun; **waterfront** *n* [woterfrant] tepi laut, tepi sungai, tepi danau; **watering** [wotering] ~ *can* cérék; **watermark** *n* [wotermark] cap air; **watermelon** *n* [wotermélon] semangka; **waterproof** *adj* [woterpruf] kedap air; **watershed** *n* [wotersyéd] daérah aliran sungai (DAS); **waterski** *n* [woterski] ski air; *vi* bermain ski air; **watertight** *adj* [wotertait] kedap air, rapat; **waterway** *n* [woterwé] jalan air; **watery** *adj* [woteri] berair

wave *n* ombak, gelombang; lambaian tangan; *permanent* ~ (perm) keriting rambut; *sound* ~ gelombang suara; *vi* berkibar; *vt* melambaikan; ~ *at* melambaikan tangan kepada; **wavelength** *n* panjang gelombang; **wavy** *adj* [wévi] bergelombang, berombak; ~ *hair* rambut berombak

wax *n* lilin; malam (untuk batik); **waxen** *adj* terbuat dari lilin

way *n* jalan; arah; cara; ~ *in* (jalan) masuk; ~ *out* (jalan) keluar; *one* ~ *(street)* (jalan) satu arah; *that* ~ ke (arah) sana; *a long* ~ jauh; *all the* ~ sepanjang jalan; *by the* ~ ngomong-ngomong; *on the* ~ di perjalanan, sedang dalam perjalanan; *to give* ~ memberi jalan; *to get your (own)* ~, *to have your (own)* ~ menang sendiri

we *pron, pl* kami; kita; ~ *want your support* kami menginginkan dukungan anda; ~ *must all help each other* kita harus saling menolong

weak *adj* [wik] lemah; ~ *tea* téh éncér; **weaken** *vi* [wiken] menjadi lemah; *vt* melemahkan; **weakness** *n* kelemahan; *to have a* ~ *for* suka, gemar akan; *Colin has a* ~ *for ice-cream* Colin suka és krim

wealth *adj* [wélth] kekayaan; **wealthy** *adj* [wélthi] kaya

wean *vt* menyapih; *she* ~*ed Chris at six months* Chris disapih pada umur enam bulan

weapon *n* [wépen] senjata; ~ *of mass destruction* senjata pembunuh massal

wear *n* [wér] pakaian; perlengkapan; *evening* ~ busana malam; ~ *and tear* kondisi yang menurun akibat pemakai-

an; *vt* **wore worn** memakai; ~ *away* menjadi aus, tersusut; ~ *out* menjadi usang; menjadi capék; ~ *the veil* berjilbab, berkerudung

weary *adj* [wiri] letih, capék

weasel *n* [wizel] semacam musang

weather *n* [wéther] cuaca; ~ *forecast* prakiraan cuaca; *bad* ~ cuaca buruk; *fine* ~, *good* ~ cuaca baik; *under the* ~ kurang séhat; *vt* bertahan melawan; ~ *the storm* bertahan selama badai, menempuh masa sulit

weave *vi* [wiv] **wove woven** bertenun; *vt* menenun; **weaver** *n* [wiver] penenun, tukang tenun; ~ *bird* burung manyar; **weaving** *n* [wiving] tenunan

web *n* jaringan; rumah laba-laba; ~ *page* halaman, laman; **website** *n* situs (di) internét

wed *vi* nikah, kawin; *vt* nikah dengan, kawin dengan; **wedding** *n* (acara) perkawinan, pernikahan; ~ *cake* kué pengantin; ~ *dress* gaun pengantin; ~ *ring* cincin kawin

wedge *n* [wéj] ganjalan; *vt* mengganjal

Wednesday *adj, n* [wénsdé] (hari) Rabu

weed *n* tanaman liar; gulma; *vt* mencabut tanaman liar; menyiangi; **weedkiller** *n* obat pembasmi tanaman liar; **weedy** *adj* kurus dan kecil

week *n* minggu; **weekday** *n* hari kerja; **weekend** *n* akhir minggu, akhir pekan; *long* ~ libur tiga hari, libur empat hari; *for* ~*s* berminggu-minggu; **weekly** *adj, adv* tiap minggu; mingguan; *n* (majalah) mingguan

weep *v* **wept wept** menangis; **weepy** *adj* cenderung menangis, céngéng

weigh *vi* [wé] memiliki berat badan; *she* ~*s 55 kilos* berat badannya 55 kilo; *vt* menimbang; ~ *anchor* membongkar sauh; ~ *down* membebani; **weight** *n* [wéit] berat, bobot; pemberat; *to lose* ~ mengurangi berat badan; *to put on* ~ menambah berat badan; **weightlifter** *n* [wéitlifter] atlét angkat besi; **weightlifting** *n* [wéitlifting] angkat besi

weird *adj* [wird] anéh, ganjil

welcome *n* [wélkem] sambutan; selamat datang; *vt* (mengucapkan) selamat datang; **welcoming** *adj* [wélkeming] ramah

weld *v* mengelas; **welder** *n* tukang las; **welding** *n* pengelasan

welfare *n* [wélfér] kesejahteraan; ~ *state* negara kesejahteraan; *on* ~ menerima tunjangan sosial dari pemerintah

well *adv* baik; séhat; ~-*behaved* berkelakuan baik; ~*bred* tahu adat, sopan; ~*built* kokoh; ~*dressed* berpakaian rapi; ~*known* ternama, terkenal; ~*loved* tercinta; ~*meaning* bermaksud baik, berniat baik; ~*off* kaya, berada; ~*preserved* awét muda; ~*read* berpengetahuan luas; ~*to-do* kaya, berada, mampu; *as* ~ (begitu) juga, demikian juga; *get* ~ *soon* (semoga) lekas sembuh

well *n* (sumber) mata air, sumur

wellingtons *n, pl* sepatu karét

Welsh *adj* berasal dari Wales; *n* bangsa Wales; bahasa Wales; ~ *rarebit* semacam roti panggang ← **Wales**

went *vi, pf* → **go**

wept *v, pf* → **weep**

west *adj, n* barat; ~ *Germany arch* Jérman Barat; ~ *Irian arch* Irian Barat; ~ *Java* Jawa Barat (Jabar); ~ *Kalimantan* Kalimantan Barat (Kalbar); ~ *Papua* Papua; ~ *Sulawesi* Sulawési Barat (Sulbar); ~ *Sumatra* Sumatera Barat (Sumbar); *south-*~ barat laut; *the* ~ (negeri-negeri) Barat; *the* ~ *Indies* Hindia Barat; **western** *adj* barat; ~ *Australia (WA)* Australia Barat; **westerner** *n* orang Barat; **westernized** *adj* kebarat-baratan

wet *adj* basah, berair; ~ *nurse* ibu susu; *the* ~ *(season)* musim hujan; *vt* **wet wet** membasahi; ~ *oneself* mengompol

whack *n* [wak] pukulan hébat; *vt* memukul dengan kasar

whale *n* [wél] ikan paus; **whaling** *n* pemburuan ikan paus

wharf *n* [worf] **wharves** dermaga

what *adj* [wot] apa; alangkah; ~ *a nice view* alangkah indahnya pemandangan ini; *interrog* [wot] apa; ~ *about*

bagaimana dengan, bagaimana kalau; ~ *for* untuk apa, mengapa; ~*'s your name?* siapa nama anda?; *so* ~ *sl* émang gué pikirin; **whatever** *adj* [wotéver] apa saja, apa pun; **whatsisname** *n* [wotzisném] si anu; **whatsoever** *adj* [wotsoéver] apa saja, apa pun

wheat *n* [wit] gandum

wheel *n* [wil] roda; *steering* ~ roda setir; *water* ~ kincir air; **wheelbarrow** *n* [wilbaro] keréta dorong, gerobak; **wheelchair** *n* kursi roda

wheeze *vi* [wiz] mendesah, bernafas dengan susah

when *conj* [wén] ketika; bila, kalau; *interrog* kapan; *ring me* ~ *you arrive* télepon kalau sudah tiba; *I rang* ~ *I arrived* saya télepon saat tiba; **whenever** *adv, conj* [wénéver] kapan saja

where *adv, conj, pron* [wér] di mana; *interrog* di mana; **whereabouts** *interrog* [wérabauts] tempat berada, di mana; *n* tempat, lokasi; **wherever** *adv, conj* [wéréver] di mana saja, di mana pun

whereas *conj* [wéraz] sedangkan, padahal

wherever *adv, conj* [wéréver] di mana saja, di mana pun ← **where**

whether *conj* [wéther] apakah; *he doesn't know* ~ *it's Monday or Tuesday* dia tidak tahu apakah hari ini Senin atau Selasa

which *conj, pron* [wic] mana; **whichever** *pron* [wicéver] mana saja

while, whilst *conj* [wail] selama; saat, ketika; sedangkan; *n* waktu; *for a* ~ untuk sementara; *in a* ~ nanti; *once in a* ~ sekali-sekali

whine *n* [wain] réngékan; *vi* meréngék

whinge *n* [winj] keluhan; *vi* mengeluh, berkeluh-kesah; ~ *about* mengeluh soal

whinny *n* [wini] ringkikan; *vi* meringkik; *the horse whinnied* kuda itu meringkik

whip *n* [wip] cambuk, cemeti; *vt* mencambuk, mencemeti; ~*ped cream* krim kocok

whir *n* [wér] deru, desing; *vi* menderu, mendesing

whirl *vi* [wérl] berputar, berpusar; *n* pusaran; **whirlpool** *n* [wérlpul] pusaran air; **whirlwind** *adj* [wérlwind] sangat cepat, kilat; *n* angin puyuh, angin beliung

whisk *n* [wisk] alat kocok

whisker *n* [wisker] kumis; *by a* ~ nyaris (tidak berhasil); **whiskers** *n, pl* cambang, beréwok

whiskey, whisky *n* wiski; ~ *and soda* wiski soda

whisper *n* [wisper] bisikan; *vi* berbisik; *vt* membisikkan

whistle *n* [wisel] peluit; *wolf* ~ suitan; *to blow the* ~ *on* melaporkan (orang jahat); *vi* bersiul

white *adj* [wait] (berkulit) putih; ~*-out* tipéks; ~ *ant* rayap; ~ *bread* roti tawar; ~ *elephant* barang tidak berguna; ~ *goods* barang éléktronik (yang besar); ~ *lie* dusta; ~ *Pages* buku petunjuk télepon; ~ *Russia arch* Bélarus; ~ *trash* orang kulit putih yang miskin; ~ *wine* anggur putih; *egg* ~ putih telur; ~*-collar worker* orang kantoran; ~ *water rafting* arung jeram; *black and* ~ hitam putih; *n* (orang kulit) putih; **whiten** *vt* [waiten] memutihkan; **whitewash** *n* [waitwosy] kapur; *vt* mengapur; **whitish** *adj* [waitisy] keputih-putihan

WHO *abbrev World Health Organization* Organisasi Keséhatan Dunia

who *conj* [hu] yang; *interrog, pron* siapa; ~*'s there?* siapa itu?; *this is the girl* ~ *has stolen my heart* inilah gadis yang telah merenggut hatiku; **whoever** *pron* [huéver] barang siapa; **whom** *pron, obj* [hum] siapa; *to* ~ *it may concern* agar diketahui; **whose** *conj* yang; *pron, poss* [huz] milik siapa; ~ *coat is that?* Mantel siapa itu?; *the friend* ~ *car I bought* teman yang mobilnya saya beli

whole *adj* [hol] seantéro, seluruh, semua; lengkap, utuh; *n* semua, keseluruhan; *the* ~ *day* sepanjang hari; **wholehearted** *adj* [holharted] sepenuh hati; **wholeheartedly** *adv* [holhartedli] dengan sepenuh hati; **wholemeal** *adj*

[holmil] tepung terigu yang masih mengandung biji-biji; **wholesale** *adj* [holsél] grosir, rabat; **wholly** *adv* [holi] sama sekali

whom *pron, obj* [hum] siapa; *to* ~ *it may concern* agar diketahui ← **who**

whoopee *ejac* [wupi] horé

whooping [huping] ~ *cough* batuk rejan

whoops *ejac* [wups] aduh

whopper *n, sl* [woper] sesuatu yang sangat besar

whore *n, derog* [hor] pelacur

whose *conj* yang; *pron, poss* [huz] milik siapa; ~ *coat is that?* siapa itu?; *the friend* ~ *car I bought* teman yang mobilnya saya beli ← **who**

why *conj, interrog* [wai] mengapa; ~ *is that?* mengapa begitu?; *ejac* nah; *he didn't know* ~ *it failed* dia tidak tahu mengapa gagal

WI *abbrev West Indies* Hindia Barat

wicked *adj* [wiked] jahat; **wickedly** *adv* [wikedli] dengan jahat; **wickedness** *n* [wikednes] kejahatan

wicker *adj* anyaman; ~ *chair* kursi (anyaman) rotan

wide *adj* lébar, longgar, luas; *adv* jauh, lébar; ~*-eyed* mata terbelalak; ~*-ranging* luas; ~ *awake* sudah bangun (dan tidak mengantuk lagi); ~ *open* terbuka lébar; **widely** *adv* secara luas; **widen** *vi* menjadi lébar; *vt* melébarkan, memperluas; **widespread** *adj* [waidspréd] tersebar luas; **width** *n* lébar(nya)

widow *n, f* [wido] janda (mati); **widower** *n, m* duda (mati)

width *n* lébar(nya) ← **wide**

wife *n* **wives** isteri; *coll* bini; *second* ~ isteri kedua; isteri muda; *husband and* ~ suami isteri

wig *n* rambut palsu, wig

wiggle *vi* [wigel] bergeliat, bergoyang; *vt* menggoyangkan

wild *adj* [waild] liar, ganas, buas; gila; ~ *about* tergila-gila akan; ~ *animal* binatang buas; **wilderness** *n* [wildernes] hutan (belantara), gurun; **wildfire** *n* [waildfair] kebakaran hutan; **wildflower** *n* [waildflauer] bunga liar; **wildlife** *n* [waildlaif] margasatwa,

fauna; ~ *sanctuary* cagar alam; **wildly**
adv [waildli] secara liar, dengan liar
will *n* kehendak, kemauan; wasiat; *at* ~
sesuka hati; *political* ~ kemauan politik; *of your own free* ~ dengan
sukaréla; *where there's a* ~*, there's a*
way kalau ada kemauan, ada jalan; *vi*
would would [wud] akan, mau, pasti,
hendak; ~ *not (won't)* tidak akan,
takkan; **willful, wilful** *adj* disengaja;
willing *adj* réla, bersedia, sudi; *God* ~
insya Allah; **willingly** *adv* dengan
senang hati; **willingness** *n* kesediaan;
willpower *n* [wilpauer] kehendak
willow *n* sejenis pohon
win *vi* **won won** [wan] menang; *vt*
memenangkan; memperoléh, mendap-
at; ~ *someone's heart* memikat hati; *n*
kemenangan; **winner** *n* pemenang;
winnings *n* hasil kemenangan
winch *n* dérék, katrol, kérékan
wind *n* [waind] bélok, bélokan, belitan;
vi **wound wound** memutar, menggulung; *vt* membelit, membalutkan; ~ *up*
berakhir; mengakhiri; *coll* melédék; ~
a clock memutar jam; **winding** *adj*
[wainding] berliku-liku, berputar-
putar
wind *n* [wind] (mata) angin; ~ *power*
tenaga bayu, tenaga angin; *north* ~
angin dari utara; *to break* ~*, pass* ~
kentut; **windbreak** *n* [windbrék] penahan angin; **windbreaker** *n* [wind-
bréker] jakét ringan; **windcheater** *n*
[windciter] sejenis switer yang terbuat
dari katun; **windmill** *n* kincir angin;
windpipe *n* batang tenggorokan;
windscreen, windshield *n* [wind-
syild] kaca depan mobil; ~ *wiper* kipas
kaca mobil; **windsurfer** *n* peselancar
angin; **windsurfing** *n* selancar angin;
to go ~ berselancar angin; **windward**
adj di atas angin, arah dari mana
angin bertiup; *the* ~ *Islands* Kepulauan
Windward; **windy** *adj* banyak angin,
berangin
winding *adj* [wainding] berliku-liku,
berputar-putar ← **wind**
windmill *n* kincir angin ← **wind**
window *n* [windo] jendéla; ~ *box pot*

kembang di jendéla; ~ *frame* kusén
jendéla; *shop* ~ étalase; ~*-shopping*
cuci mata; **windowpane** *n* kaca jendéla
windpipe *n* batang tenggorokan ←
wind
windscreen, windshield *n* [windsyild]
kaca depan mobil; ~ *wiper* sapu kaca
mobil, kipas kaca mobil ← **wind**
windsurfer *n* peselancar angin; **windsurfing** *n* selancar angin; *to go* ~
berselancar angin
windward *adj* di atas angin, arah dari
mana angin bertiup; *the* ~ *Islands*
Kepulauan Windward ← **wind**
windy *adj* banyak angin, berangin ←
wind
windy *adj* [waindi] berliku-liku, berputar-putar ← **wind**
wine *n* (minuman) anggur; *white* ~ anggur putih; ~ *bar* tempat minum anggur; ~ *list* daftar minuman; **wineglass**
n gelas anggur; **winery** *n* [waineri]
kilang anggur, tempat pembuatan
anggur
wing *n* sayap; sisi (panggung); *left-*~
bersayap kiri; *in the* ~*s* sudah siap; *on*
the ~ sedang terbang; *under some-*
one's ~ dilindungi, dibantu; **wingspan**
n panjang sayap pesawat terbang
wink *n* kedip, kedipan; *forty* ~*s* tidur
siang, tidur sebentar; *Dini didn't sleep*
a ~ Dini sama sekali tidak tidur; *vi*
kedip, berkedip
winner *n* pemenang; **winnings** *n* hasil
kemenangan ← **win**
winnow *n* [wino] penampi; *vt* menampi
winter *adj, n* musim dingin; *in* ~ pada
musim dingin; *the* ~ *Olympics* Olimpiade Musim Dingin; **wintertime** *n*
musim dingin; **wintry** *adj* seperti
musim dingin
wipe *n* tisu basah; sapuan; *vt* menyapu,
menyeka, menghapus; ~ *out* menyapu
bersih; menghapuskan; ~ *the board*
menghapus papan; **wiper** *(windscreen)*
~ kipas kaca depan mobil
wire *n* [wair] kawat; *arch* télégram,
surat kawat; ~ *cutters* tang potong
kawat; ~ *netting* kawat kasa; **wireless**
n, arch radio; ~ *operator* markonis;

wiring *n* penggelaran kabel listrik;
wiry *adj* [wairi] bersifat seperti kawat
wisdom *n* kearifan, kebijaksanaan; ~
teeth gigi geraham bungsu; **wise** *adj*
arif, bijaksana; ~ *guy* orang yang sok
tahu; *none the ~r* masih belum tahu
juga; **wisecrack** *n* lelucon; **wisely** *adv*
dengan arif
wish *n* keinginan; *best ~es* salam; *vi*
ingin; *vt* ~ *for* menginginkan; mengharapkan; **wishbone** *n* tulang garpu;
wishful ~ *thinking* mengkhayal
wit *n* kejenakaan; orang jenaka; **wits** *n,
pl* akal (budi); *at your ~'s end* kehilangan akal; **witty** *adj* jenaka, lucu,
bersifat menyindir
witch *n, f* penyihir, tukang sihir; *~-hunt*
pemfitnahan atau pemburuan orang;
witchcraft *n* ilmu sihir; **witchdoctor**
n dukun
with *prep* dengan, bersama, serta;
pakai; ~ *that* maka; *tea ~ milk* téh
pakai susu; **withdraw** *vi* withdrew
withdrawn mundur, mengundurkan
diri; *vt* menarik, mencabut; ~ *money*
menarik uang, mengambil uang; **withdrawal** *n* pengunduran; penarikan
(uang); **withdrawn** *adj* pendiam, suka
menyendiri; **withhold** *vt* **withheld**
withheld menahan, menyembunyikan;
within *adv, prep* (di) dalam; ~ *a week*
dalam waktu seminggu; ~ *this room* di
dalam kamar ini; **without** *prep* tanpa,
dengan tidak; **withstand** *v* **withstood**
withstood *v* tahan; menahan, melawan
wither *vi* layu, kurus
withhold *vt* **withheld withheld** menahan, menyembunyikan ← **with**
within *adv, prep* (di) dalam; ~ *a week*
dalam waktu seminggu; ~ *this room* di
dalam kamar ini ← **with**
without *prep* tanpa, dengan tidak ← **with**
withstand *vt* **withstood withstood** *vt*
tahan; menahan, melawan ← **with**
witness *n* saksi; *to bear* ~ bersaksi; *vt*
menyaksikan
witty *adj* jenaka, lucu, bersifat
menyindir ← **wit**
wives *n, pl* → **wife**
wizard *n, m* [wizerd] penyihir, tukang

sihir; **wizardry** *n* [wizardri] ilmu sihir
wobble *n* [wobel] goyang, goyangan; *vi*
goyang, goyah; **wobbly** *adj* goyang
wok *n* penggoréngan, kuali
woke, woken *v, pf* → **wake**
wolf *n* [wulf] serigala; ~ *whistle* suitan;
to cry ~ pura-pura memberitakan bahaya
woman *n* [wumen] **women** [wimen]
perempuan, wanita; ~ *doctor* dokter wanita; *women's rights* hak-hak
perempuan; *women's toilet* WC wanita; **womanizer** *n* [wumanaizer] lelaki
buaya darat
womb *n* [wum] kandungan, rahim, peranakan; *in the* ~ di dalam kandungan
wombat *n* sejenis binatang khas Australia
won *v, pf* [wan] → **win**
wonder *n* [wander] keajaiban; ~ *drug*
obat manjur; *no* ~ tidak menghérankan, pantas; *vi* berpikir, berpikir-pikir;
wonderful *adj* [wanderful] ajaib,
menghérankan; **wonderfully** *adv*
[wanderfeli] secara ajaib, luar biasa
won't *vi, aux* takkan → **will**
wood *n* kayu; hutan; ~ *carving* ukiran
kayu; ~ *pulp* bubur kayu; *touch* ~
semoga terkabul; *Isl* insya Allah;
woodcut *n* (lukisan dari) ukiran kayu;
woodcutter *n* penebang kayu; **wood-
en** *adj* terbuat dari kayu; **woodland** *n*
daérah hutan; **woodpecker** *n* burung
pelatuk; **woods** *n, pl* hutan; **woodwind** ~ *instrument* alat musik tiup
yang terbuat dari kayu; **woodwork** *n*
[wudwérk] prakarya, pelajaran memotong dan mengolah kayu
wool *n* wol, bulu domba; **woolen,
woollen** *adj* terbuat dari wol; **woolly**
adj terbuat dari wol, berbulu; tidak
jelas
word *n* [wérd] kata; ~ *search* teka-teki
mencari kata; ~ *for* ~ kata demi kata; ~
of mouth secara lisan; *lost for ~s*
kehilangan kata; *in a* ~ secara singkat;
in other ~s dalam perkataan lain; *not a*
~ tidak sepatah kata pun; *~s of a song*
lirik lagu; *to eat your ~s* menarik kembali apa yang diucapkan; *to give your*
~ berjanji; *what's the Indonesian ~?*
apa Bahasa Indonesianya?; **wording** *n*

[wérding] cara mengungkapkan, cara bertutur (spoken); **wordy** adj [wérdi] panjang lébar

wore v, pf → **wear**

work n [wérk] pekerjaan, karya, kerja; kantor, tempat kerja; ~ experience magang; at ~ sedang bekerja; di kantor; hard ~ kerja keras; out of ~ tidak bekerja, menganggur; vi bekerja, berjalan, jalan; ~ at, ~ on mengerjakan; ~ hard bekerja keras; ~ off mengurangi; ~ out menyusun, memecahkan; berolahraga; ~ up menimbulkan; meningkatkan; that old camera still ~s kaméra lama itu masih jalan; **workaholic** n [wérkaholik] orang yang gila bekerja; **workbook** n [wérkbuk] buku tulis; **worker** n [wérker] pekerja, buruh; **workforce** n [wérkfors] tenaga kerja; **working** adj, n [wérking] bekerja; ~ class kaum buruh, rakyat jelata; ~ holiday bekerja sambil berlibur; ~ woman karyawati; **workload** n [wérklod] beban kerja; **workman** n [wérkman] pekerja, tukang; **workmanship** n [wérkmansyip] hasil kerja; **workout** n [wérkaut] latihan; **workplace** n [wérkplés] tempat kerja; **works** n, pl [wérks] pabrik; mesin; Department of Public ~ Departemen Pekerjaan Umum (PU); **worksheet** n [wérksyit] kertas tugas belajar; **workshop** n [wérksyop] béngkél; **workstation** n [wérkstésyen] méja kerja

world n [wérld] dunia, alam; planét; ~ class berkelas dunia; ~-famous terkenal di seluruh dunia; ~ Cup Piala Dunia; ~ record rékor dunia; ~ Food Organization Organisasi Pangan Sedunia; ~ War II (WWII) Perang Dunia Kedua; to go around the ~ mengelilingi dunia; it's a small ~ dunia ini kecil; **worldly** adj [wérldli] duniawi; berpengalaman; **worldwide** adj [wérldwaid] yang meliputi seluruh dunia

worm n [wérm] cacing, ulat; how the ~ turns betapa keadaan sudah berubah; vt memberi obat cacing kepada; ~ing tablets obat cacing

worn v, pf → **wear**

worry n [wari] kekhawatiran, beban pikiran, urusan, kesusahan; vi khawatir, merasa cemas; ~ about mencemaskan; don't ~ jangan khawatir; no worries tidak masalah

worse adj, adv [wérs] lebih buruk, lebih jélék ← **bad**; **worsen** vi [wérsen] menjadi lebih buruk

worship n [wérsyip] ibadah, pujaan, pemujaan; v memuja, menyembah; place of ~ rumah ibadah; **worshipper** n [wérsyiper] pemuja

worst adj, adv [wérst] paling buruk, paling jélék, terburuk; at ~ paling buruk ← **bad**

worth adj [wérth] bernilai, bermanfaat, berharga; setimpal; n nilai, harga, guna; ~ your while berguna, bermanfaat; it was ~ it ada manfaatnya, ada hikmahnya; not ~ mentioning tidak pantas disebutkan; **worthless** adj [wérthles] tidak berguna; **worthwhile** adj [wérthwail] berguna, bermanfaat, setimpal; **worthy** adj [wérthi] layak; berguna; ~ of layak menerima

would vi, aux, pf [wud] akan → **will**; ~ be gadungan; calon, bakal; **wouldn't** vi, aux, neg [wudent] tidak akan, takkan

wound n [wund] luka; stab ~ luka tikam; vt melukai; **wounded** adj terluka; n korban (luka)

wound v, pf [waund] → **wind**

wove, woven vt, pf → **weave**

wow ejac [wau] wah

wrangle n [ranggel] pertengkaran, percekcokan; vi bertengkar

wrap n [rap] semacam roti isi yang digulung; cling ~ plastik pembungkus makanan; vt membungkus; ~ped in asyik dengan; ~ping paper kertas bungkus, kertas kado; **wrapper** n bungkus, pembungkus, kertas

wrath n [roth] murka

wreath n [rith] karangan (bunga); olive ~ karangan daun zaitun

wreck n [rék] rongsokan kapal karam; a nervous ~ gila ketakutan; vt merusak, menghancurkan; **wreckage** n [rékej]

rongsokan, rosokan; **wrecked** *adj*
[rékt] karam, tenggelam; **wrecker** *n*
[réker] perusak; tukang bongkar
wren *n* [rén] semacam burung kecil
wrench *n* [rénc] *(monkey)* ~ kunci
Inggris; renggutan; *vt* merenggut;
keseléo, terkilir; ~ *your ankle*
pergelangan kaki keseléo
wrestle *n* [résel] pergumulan, pergulatan; *vi* bergumul, bergulat; **wrestler** *n*
[résler] pegulat; **wrestling** *n* [résling]
gulat
wretched *adj* [réced] celaka, sial, buruk
wriggle *n, vi* [rigel] geliat-geliut
wring *vt* **wrung wrought** *vt* memeras;
~ *someone's hand* berjabat tangan
dengan keras; ~ *someone's neck*
mencekik; **wringer** *n, arch* [ringer]
alat pemeras baju basah
wrinkle *n* [ringkel] (garis) keriput,
kerut; ~ *one's forehead* mengernyit;
wrinkly *adj* [ringkeli] berkeriput
wrist *n* [rist] pergelangan tangan;
wristwatch *n* [ristwoc] jam tangan
write *v* **wrote written** [rait] menulis,
mengarang; ~ *down* mencatat,
menuliskan; ~ *off* mencorét, menghapuskan; menghancurkan (mobil); ~ *to*
menyurati; ~ *a letter* menulis surat; ~
an essay membuat karangan; **writer** *n*
[raiter] penulis, pengarang; **writing** *n*
[raiting] tulisan, karangan; ~ *desk*
méja tulis; ~ *materials* alat tulis; ~ *pad*
bloknot; ~ *paper* kertas tulis, kertas
surat; *in* ~ secara tertulis; **written** *adj*
[riten] tertulis
wrong *adj* [rong] salah, keliru; *n*
kesalahan, dosa; *what's* ~? ada apa?;
wrongfully *adv* [rongfuli] secara
salah; *Adam was* ~ *accused* Adam
dituduh, padahal dia bukan pelakunya
wrote *v, pf* [rot] → **write**
wrought *vt, pf* [rort] → **wring**; ~ *iron*
besi tempa
wrung *vt, pf* [rang] → **wring**
WWI *abbrev* World War One PD I
(Perang Dunia Pertama)
WWII *abbrev* World War Two PD II, PD
ke2 (Perang Dunia Kedua)

X

xenophobia *n* [zénofobia] **xenophobic**
adj kebencian atau ketakutan pada
orang asing
X-ray *n* [éksré] rontgen, sinar X; *vt*
merontgen, menyinar
xylophone *n* [zailofon] xilofon

Y

yacht *n* [yot] kapal layar, kapal pesiar;
yachting *n* [yoting] berlayar; **yachts-
man** *n, m* [yotsman] **yachtswoman** *f*
[yotswuman] awak kapal layar
yam *n* ubi rambat
yank *n* renggutan, sentakan; *vt*
merenggut, menyentak
Yank, Yankee *n, coll* orang Amérika
(Serikat, terutama dari bagian utara)
yap *vi* menyalak (anak anjing); **yappy**
adj, coll berisik, banyak menyalak
yard *n* ukuran panjang sebesar 0,9144
m; *back* ~ halaman belakang; *railway*
~*s* langsiran; **yardstick** *n* ukuran
yarn *n* benang (rajutan); *coll* cerita
yawn *n, vi* menguap; terbuka lébar
ye *pron, arch* [yi] engkau
yea *arch* [yé] ya
yeah *sl* [yéa] ya, iya ← **yes**
year *n* [yir] tahun; ~*round* sepanjang
tahun; *donkey's* ~*s* lama sekali; *financial* ~ tahun buku; *last* ~ tahun lalu;
next ~ tahun depan; *school* ~ tahun
ajaran; *for* ~*s,* ~ *after.* ~ bertahun-
tahun; *Chinese New* ~ (Tahun Baru)
Imlék; *New* ~*'s Eve* Malam Tahun
Baru; **yearbook** *n* [yirbuk] buku tahunan; **yearly** *adj* [yirli] tahunan
yearn *vi* [yérn] sangat ingin; rindu; ~
for merindukan; **yearning** *n* [yérning]
kerinduan, hasrat
yeast *n* [yist] ragi
yell *n* pekik, pekikan; *v* memekik; ~ *at*
meneriaki
yellow *adj* [yélo] kuning; *sl* takut; ~
card kartu kuning; ~ *Pages* buku

(télepon) kuning; **yellowish** *adj*
kekuning-kuningan

yelp *n* salak; *vi* menyalak

Yemen *n* [yémen] Yémen; **Yemeni** *adj*
berasal dari Yémen; *n* orang Yémen

yen *n* yén (mata uang Jepang)

yep *sl* ya ← **yes**

yes ya; benar, betul; **yeah, yep** *coll* ya,
iya

yesterday *adv, n* kemarin; ~ *evening*
tadi malam, kemarin malam; ~ *morning* kemarin pagi; *the day before* ~
kemarin dulu

yet *adv* masih (belum); *I haven't started*
~ saya masih belum mulai; *as* ~ sampai sekarang, sehingga kini; *not* ~
belum; *conj* namun

Yiddish *n* bahasa Yahudi (dari Eropa
Timur)

yield *n* [yild] hasil, produksi; *vi* ~ *(to)*
mengalah (pada); *vt* menghasilkan; *his
efforts* ~*ed great rewards* usahanya
membawa banyak hasil

yippee *ejac* horé!

YMCA *abbrev Young Men's Christian
Association* Asosiasi Pemuda Kristen

yodel *vi* bernyanyi yodel; *n* lagu yodel;
yodeler, yodeller *n* penyanyi yodel

yoga *n* yoga

yogurt, yoghurt *n* yogurt

yoke *n* kuk, pasang; beban, penindasan;
vt memasang kuk; *the farmer* ~*d the
oxen to the plough* petani itu
memasang sapi pada bajak

yolk *n* [yok] kuning telur

yonder *adv* di sana, di sebelah sana

you *pron* [yu] kamu, engkau; *form*
Anda; *pl* kalian; ~ *all* kalian, anda
sekalian; *you'd* anda akan ← **you
would**; **you'll** anda akan ← **you will**;
your *pron* -mu, kamu punya, milik
anda, kepunyaan anda; **you're** kamu
adalah ← **you are**; **yours** *pron* milik-
mu, milik anda; ~ *truly,* ~ *sincerely,* ~
faithfully hormat kami; **yourself** *pron*
yourselves engkau sendiri, kamu
sendiri, Anda sendiri; *do it* ~ *(DIY)*
kerjakan sendiri

young *adj* [yang] muda; ~ *boy* anak
lelaki; ~ *girl* anak gadis; ~ *man* pemu-

da; ~ *people* remaja, kaum pemuda;
coll anak baru gedé (ABG); ~ *woman*
pemudi; ~ *and old* semua orang, tua
dan muda; ~ *at heart* berjiwa muda;
when (I was) ~ waktu muda; *n* anak
(binatang); **younger** *adj* [yangga]
lebih muda; **youngster** *n* [yangster]
yang muda

your *pron* -mu, kamu punya, milik
anda, kepunyaan anda; **you're** kamu
adalah ← **you are**; **yours** *pron* milik-
mu, milik anda; ~ *truly,* ~ *sincerely,* ~
faithfully hormat kami; **yourself** *pron*
yourselves engkau sendiri, kamu
sendiri, Anda sendiri; *do it* ~ *(DIY)*
kerjakan sendiri ← **you**

youth *n* [yuth] masa muda; kaum
muda; ~ *center* gelanggang remaja; ~
hostel losmén; *in my* ~ waktu masih
muda; **youthful** *adj* [yuthful] muda,
belia

yowl *n* [yaul] méong, raung; *vi*
meméong, meraung

yoyo *n* yoyo

Yugoslav *n, arch* orang Yugo, orang
Yugoslavia; **Yugoslavia** *n* Yugoslavia

Yule ~ *log* kayu yang dibakar saat
Natal; **Yuletide** *n* masa Natal

yum *ejac* sedap, énak; **yummy** *adj*
énak, sedap; *ejac* énak, nyam-nyam

yuppie *n, sl* orang muda yang ambisius,
terutama dalam soal uang; *that restaurant is full of* ~*s every Friday night* réstoran itu penuh dengan orang muda
setiap malam Sabtu

YWCA *abbrev Young Women's Christian
Association* Asosiasi Pemudi Kristen

Z

Zaire *n, arch* Kongo; **Zairean** *adj* [zairi-
an] berasal dari Kongo; *n* orang
Kongo

Zambia *n* Zambia; **Zambian** *adj* berasal
dari Zambia; *n* orang Zambia

zany *adj* jenaka, lucu

zap *vt* membunuh, menghancurkan; *he
*~*ped the spaceman and moved to the*

next level of the game dia membunuh angkasawan kemudian naik ke tingkat berikutnya permainan

zeal *n* [zil] semangat; **zealous** *adj* [zélus] bersemangat, giat

zebra *n* kuda zébra, kuda belang; ~ *cross*, ~ *crossing* tempat penyeberangan, zébrakros

zenith *n* [zénith] puncak, titik tertinggi

zephyr *n* [zéfir] angin sepoi-sepoi

zero *adj, n* [ziro] nol, kosong; ~ *emissions* émisi nol

zest *n* semangat, gairah, animo

zigzag *adj, vi* berkelok-kelok, berliku-liku

Zimbabwe *n* [zimbabwé] Zimbabwe; **Zimbabwean** *adj* berasal dari Zimbabwé; *n* orang Zimbabwé

zinc *n* séng; ~ *cream* tabir surya kental

zip ~ *code US* kode pos

zipper, zip *n* ritsléting, kancing tarik; ~ *up* menutup ritsléting

zit *n, sl* jerawat

zither *n* semacam kecapi

zodiac *n* [zodiak] bintang, zodiak

zone *n* zona, daérah; *war* ~ daérah perang

zoo *n, coll* kebun binatang (bonbin); ~ *keeper* petugas kebun binatang; **zoological** [zuolojikel] ~ *gardens* kebun binatang; **zoologist** *n* zoolog, ahli ilmu héwan; **zoology** *n* zoologi, ilmu héwan

zoom *vi* meningkat, meluncur; ~ *in* memfokuskan lebih dekat pada

zucchini *n* [zukini] sejenis labu